WE ARE AS GODS and might as well get good at it.
So far remotely done power and glory —
as via government, big business, formal
education, church — have succeeded to the
point where gross defects obscure actual gains.
In response to this dilemma and to these gains, a realm
of intimate, personal power is developing —
the power of individuals to conduct their own education,
find their own inspiration, shape their own environment, and
share the adventure with whoever is interested.
Tools that aid this process are
sought and promoted by the
Whole Earth Catalog.
—Stewart Brand, 1968

THE MILLENNIUM
WHOLE EARTH
CATALOG

ACCESS TO TOOLS AND IDEAS FOR THE TWENTY-FIRST CENTURY

What it is, is up to us. *—Howard Rheingold, 1994*

HarperSanFrancisco
A Division of HarperCollinsPublishers

THE MILLENNIUM WHOLE EARTH CATALOG

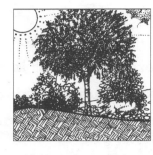

Harper San Francisco and Point Foundation, in association with Global ReLeaf, will plant two trees for every one tree used in the manufacture of this book.

THE MILLENNIUM WHOLE EARTH CATALOG: *Access to Tools and Ideas for the Twenty-first Century.* Copyright © 1994 by Point Foundation. All rights reserved. Printed in the United States of America. No part of this book may be used or reproduced in any manner whatsoever without written permission except in the case of brief quotations embodied in critical articles and reviews. For information address HarperCollins Publishers, 10 East 53rd Street, New York, NY 10022.

The Millennium Whole Earth Catalog and *Whole Earth Catalog* are trademarks of Point Foundation.

FIRST EDITION

Library of Congress Cataloging-in-Publication Data

The Millennium Whole Earth Catalog: access to tools and ideas for the 21st century
Howard Rheingold, ed. — 1st ed.
p. cm.
Includes index.
ISBN 0–06–251141–6 (cloth). — ISBN 0–06–251059–2 (pbk.)

1. Manufacturers — Catalogs. 2. Handicraft — Equipment and supplies — Catalogs. 3. Appropriate technology — Catalogs.
I. Rheingold, Howard.
TS199.M54   1994
380. 1'029'6 — dc20   94–1125
CIP

94 95 96 97 98 JOHN 10 9 8 7 6 5 4 3 2 1

This edition is printed on acid-free paper (100% recycled fiber, 15% post-consumer waste) that meets the American National Standards Institute Z39.48 Standard.

Health

Sex

Family

Taming Technology

Communications

Political Tools

Livelihood

Gate Five Road

Nomadics

Learning

FRANK'S REAL PA

JIM WOODRING
©1994

THE Millennium Whole Earth Catalog is an evaluation and access tool. Our reviewers introduce books, magazines, tools, software, video- and audiotapes, organizations, services, and wild ideas you might not have known about.

We're here to point, not to sell. We have no financial obligation to any of the suppliers listed. Our obligation is accuracy for the reader.

We only review stuff we think is great. Why waste your time with anything else?

An item is listed in the *Catalog* if it is deemed:
- Useful as a tool.
- Relevant to independent education.
- High-quality or low-cost.
- Easily available — preferably by mail order.

The listings are continually revised and updated according to the experience and suggestions of *Whole Earth Catalog* users and staff. The latest news and access can be found in our award-winning magazine, *Whole Earth Review*. (A subscription information card is bound in — see inside back cover.)

You are invited to submit comments, ideas, articles, reviews, photographs, and suggestions. We pay for what we print. For details, see page 384.

• *The Last Whole Earth Catalog* (1971) presented Gurney Norman's "Divine Right's Trip," a serial novel that occupied a corner of each right-hand page. *The Next Whole Earth Catalog* (1980) featured Anne Herbert's similarly situated "Rising Sun Newsletter." *MWEC* is proud to proffer "Frank's Real Pa," a whimsical, mystical, sinister, wordless narrative by Jim Woodring.

• Computer "morphing" technology makes possible the transformation of any image into any other image. We've added some animation to *MWEC* via "flip morphs" in the outside margins of the pages.

• No mere arrows or pointing hands, our cross-reference pointers convey the Whole Earth jump-into-it attitude. "Frank," Jim Woodring's quasi-feline Everyman, jumps into a pool of possibilities to direct you to related material. For example, a page listing Internet-available health care resources will point you to the page where you can learn how to use the Internet.

• JD Smith goes way back with Whole Earth. You'll see his short-short stories here and there throughout *MWEC*. JD's sources are real, his ear is true, and his language is wryly funny.

• Senior editor James Donnelly draws inimitable cartoons during meetings. The more painful or tedious the meeting, the more surreal the byproduct.

Several of these little gems of high weirdness are sprinkled in appropriate places.

Libraries

You probably don't have to buy that book! Most libraries can get just about any book, if you're willing to wait for the interlibrary loan system to perform its elaborate rituals.

And don't forget your local bookstore. You can support diversity and your local economy, and probably save postage and handling charges, by ordering through them.

How to Order from Suppliers Listed in This Catalog

Consider these points of mail-order etiquette essential; they'll make the transaction much more pleasant for you and the supplier. This advice is distilled from the requests of many of the firms listed and from our own experience.

1. **Do not order anything from us at the *Whole Earth Catalog*!** (Except our own publications, of course. See card after p. 384.)

2. **Don't order from excerpts of catalogs we review.** Send for their brochure or catalog, and order from that.

3. **Include payment with your order.** Use a money order or a personal check; cash or stamps won't do. You may be able to do charge-card orders — ask first. Don't send personal checks or US money orders overseas.

4. **Be clear on the supplier's sales-tax policy.** Many (but not all) mail-order companies now charge your state's sales tax, even if they are in another state. Check the catalog or contact the supplier to avoid complications and delay.

5. **Use International Money Orders (IMOs) to send money abroad.** You get them at the post office. To send money to the US *from* abroad, use IMOs or a bank draft in US dollars.

6. **Expect prices to rise.** The prices shown in this *Catalog* are accurate as of mid-1994. Most firms will write back if you don't send enough money; some will bill you for the extra amount.

7. **Expect higher prices if you live outside the continental US.** It's best to write for the overseas price before ordering. Enclose an International Reply Coupon (available at your post office). Be sure to ask about the price difference between sea mail (slower and prone to theft) and air mail (quick and expensive). We recommend air for most items.

8. **Write legibly.** Print in block letters, or type. Use printed address labels if you have them. That way, if your scribble can't be read, at least they'll know where it came from.

9. **Write what you want on the envelope.** "Mail order" or "catalog request" or "subscription order" will help prevent the loss of your order.

10. **Be patient.** It'll take at least two weeks for your goods to arrive. Four to six weeks is normal, especially if you've paid with a personal check. Don't worry too much unless it has taken more than two months. Keep a record of the date of purchase and a photocopy of your check, so if your order is lost, you can give specific details. Include your full name and address (and zip) and order number, if any, every time you write.

11. **Be considerate.** Don't send for catalogs just to keep your mailbox full. Small companies may be swamped by frivolous requests; large ones may respond with big minimum orders if harassed by dilettantes. If you ask for free information, send a stamped, self-addressed envelope (SASE).

How to Order from Real Goods

Many of the books and tools reviewed in this *Catalog* may be ordered from Real Goods Trading Corporation, in Ukiah, California. Real Goods (reviewed on p. 119) is the oldest and largest US supplier of products for energy independence — solar, wind, and hydro power.

Real Goods has established a department to fill orders from *MWEC* readers. This arrangement is for the convenience of readers who prefer to deal with a single source, rather than dealing with multiple publishers and manufacturers. Whole Earth and Real Goods have no operational or financial involvement.

Not all products in this book are available through Real Goods. Questions about order placement should be directed to them. For a list of available products and prices, use the tear-out card inside the back cover, or write to
Real Goods
Dept. MWEC
966 Mazzoni Street
Ukiah, CA 95482-3471

Or call 800/762-7325 (in the US) or 707/468-9214, extension 2000 (from abroad).

Real Goods publishes its own catalogs several times a year, as well as the *Real Goods News*. Feel free to request a complimentary copy.

THE MILLENNIUM Whole Earth Catalog IS HERE

Todd Tibbetts

Civilization and Its Contents

A THEORY OF CIVILIZATION is inherent in the *Whole Earth Catalog*. It came with our first customers, back in 1968 — the communes and "intentional communities." I described them at the time as bands of adventurous malcontents who were setting out to reinvent civilization, trying to get it right this time. Their communes failed (so did Israel's, so did China's), but their process turned out to have surprising value and robustness. The terms you heard then were "back to basics" and "grass roots" and, later, "empowerment." There was a perpetual argument, often fruitful, between advocates of "consensus" and of "do your own thing."

The personal-computer revolution was a direct result of that value system. It was initiated and carried to fruition by youthful longhairs, on purpose, with striking consistency between what was intended and what was accomplished. The impulse was to decentralize society — to undermine the high priests and air-conditioned mainframes of information technology and hand their power to absolutely everybody. There were a few inspirers but no leaders and no books to follow. Only years later did the movement-defining battle cry emerge — FAST, CHEAP, AND OUT OF CONTROL. (It came from roboticist Rodney Brooks, in the same niche of MIT where the original computer hackers had taken root thirty years before.)

One of Whole Earth's editors, Kevin Kelly, has written a superlative book on the subject — *Out of Control: The Rise of Neo-biological Civilization* (see p. 238 for the review). The discovery was made simultaneously, in a whole array of sciences and arts, that truly adaptive systems grow from the bottom up, not from the top down.

BY STEWART BRAND
WHOLE EARTH EDITOR 1968-1984

So *The Millennium Whole Earth Catalog* is what? It is a handing of the tools of a whole civilization to its citizens. The lineage of this service goes back to the *Encyclopédie* (1751–1776) of Denis Diderot, whose thirty-five volumes constituted a "tremendous storehouse of fact and propaganda that swept Europe and taught it what 'reason,' 'rights,' 'authority,' 'government,' 'liberty,' 'equality,' and related social principles are or should be. The work was subversive in its tendency, not in its advocacy: it took for granted toleration, the march of mind exemplified by science, and the good of the whole people. . . . The eleven volumes of plates were in themselves a revolutionary force, for they made public what had previously been kept secret by the guilds, and they supported the philosophe doctrine that the dissemination of knowledge was the high road to emancipation" (*The Columbia History of the World*, 1972). Diderot's *Encyclopédie* was the leading tool of the Enlightenment.

When Jon McIntire, Whole Earth's then director, conceived *The Millennium Whole Earth Catalog* and made the publishing deal with Harper San Francisco, the intent was to surpass everything Whole Earth had done previously. Editor-in-chief Howard Rheingold and present director John Sumser pushed through the prodigious effort required, and you see the result.

Here are the tools to make your life go better. And to make the world go better. That they're the same tools is our theory of civilization.

Two material possessions have survived the three decades since I left my parents' home. One is the original edition of Parker's Big Red fountain pen, given to me by my father, who had received it from his father. The other persistent artifact in my life is the Witter Bynner translation of the *Tao te Ching*. Something at the core of these eighty-one short, almost doggerel-like verses touched me at age sixteen, and still touches me. The older I got, the more recognizably useful the book became.

When I started out on my life's journey, I thought this little book was a mystical tract that would lead eventually to a noetic revelation. Thirty years later, it's easier to recognize it as good, sound, immensely practical, astonishingly enduring advice about the way water flows, people act, history happens, universes evolve. It's a guidebook to anywhere, anytime.

Translating Chinese verse is an art that by its nature leaves room for many different interpretations. Something emerges from between the lines when you read different translations of the same simple verses, something that no single translation captures. —HLR

The *Tao Te Ching* is the oldest guide to whole systems that people still know how to read.

Liang K'ai (fl. mid-thirteenth century): Li Po Chanting a Poem.— *The Way of Life*

The Way of Life According to Lao Tzu
Witter Bynner, Translator.
Perigee Books, 1986; 112 pp.
ISBN 0-399-51298-5
$5.95 ($7.95 postpaid) from Putnam Publishing Group/Order Dept., PO Box 506, East Rutherford, NJ 07073; 800/631-8571

Reflections on the Tao Te Ching
David K. Reynolds. 1993;
81 pp. ISBN 0-688-12258-2
$15 ($16.50 postpaid) from William Morrow and Co./Wilmore Warehouse, 39 Plymouth Street, Fairfield, NJ 07004

Lao-Tzu: Te-Tao Ching
(A New Translation Based on the Recently Discovered Ma-wang-tui Texts)
Robert G. Henricks, Translator.
Ballantine Books, 1992; 283 pp.
ISBN 0-345-37099-6
$10 ($12 postpaid) from Random House/Order Dept., 400 Hahn Road, Westminster, MD 21157; 800/733-3000

Tao Te Ching (three translations)

Witter Bynner: I love this little book. It's a nice size, a bit larger than the palm of my hand. The newer printings retain the original misty Taoist brush-paintings as illustrations. Bynner was a poet, and a man of an earlier part of this century. Some might find him a bit flowery. It is said, however, that the original Chinese verses do adhere to a simple rhyme. Bynner had a twinkle in his eye, as did Lao Tzu, without any doubt.

Robert G. Henricks: This is the scholar's edition, complete with Chinese ideograms and detailed translator's notes. It is probably the most accurate translation in the scholarly sense, based on recently discovered texts that date back further than other versions of Lao Tzu. It's a good touchstone to verify the nuances of the other translations. Where the other editions might fall short in strict interpretation of the text, even the freest versions can capture something of the living spirit of the book — the part that continues to pluck resonant chords in people two and a half millennia later.

David K. Reynolds: This book thunderstruck me so hard that I pulled it out the next morning and reread the whole thing just to make sure I wasn't in a weird mood the first time. Then I got out my other translations and started comparing my favorite verses. This one is a radical departure from orthodox translations and will infuriate purists; the author does say in the subtitle that this is "A New Way of Reading the Classic Book of Wisdom." In the strict sense, this is a "reading," not a straightforward translation. My first impression was surprise at how such absolutely spare prose could remain so rich in meaning. The translator/interpreter has an action-oriented, no-frills, no-mysticism, here-and-now approach. I like this clean, clear, mind-blade koan-with-an-answer interpretation as a contrast and complement to the misty plum blossoms of Bynner's poems and Henricks's lucid but not always sparkling prose. —HLR

Verse Number Ten

Witter Bynner
Can you hold the door of your tent
Wide to the firmament?
Can you, with the simple stature
Of a child, breathing nature,
Become, notwithstanding,
A man?
Can you continue befriending
With no prejudice, no ban?
Can you, mating with heaven,
Serve as the female part?
Can your learned head take leaven
From the wisdom of your heart?
If you can bear issue and nourish its growing,
If you can guide without claim or strife,
If you can stay in the lead of men without their knowing,
You are at the core of life.

Verse Number Ten

Robert G. Henricks
In nourishing the soul and embracing the One
— can you do it without letting them leave?
In concentrating your breath and making it soft
— can you make it like that of a child?
In cultivating and cleaning your profound mirror — can you do it so that it has no blemish?
In loving the people and giving life to the state
— can you do it without using knowledge?
In opening and closing the gates of Heaven —
can you play the part of the female?
In understanding all within the four reaches —
can you do it without using knowledge?

Give birth to them and nourish them.
Give birth to them but don't try to own them;
Help them to grow but don't rule them.

Verse Number Ten

David K. Reynolds
Can you focus totally on the task at hand?
Can you see and hear and touch your surroundings with an open mind?
Can you disregard your own convenience?
Can you feel and act naturally without obsessing with oughts and shoulds?
Whatever change occurs without flying away can you sit on the eggs of Reality?
Can you see clearly enough to know when nonaction is action?
Just offering, however accepted.
Just growing vast while growing small.
Just doing Reality's work.
Recognized or not.

Verse Number Thirty-Three

Witter Bynner
Knowledge studies others,
Wisdom is self-known;
Muscle masters brothers,
Self-mastery is bone;
Content need never borrow,
Ambition wanders blind:
Vitality cleaves to the marrow
Leaving death behind.

Verse Number Thirty-Three

Robert G. Henricks
To understand others is to be knowledgeable;
To understand yourself is to be wise.
To conquer others is to have strength;
To conquer yourself is to be strong.
To know when you have enough is to be rich.
To go forward with strength is to have ambition.
To not lose your place is to last long.
To die but not be forgotten — that's true long life.

Verse Number Thirty-Three

David K. Reynolds
Study others to become skillful.
Study yourself to become wise.
What else is there to study?
Act on others to have influence.
Act on yourself to have strength.
Expressing your needs is one thing.
Working to achieve them is quite another.
Don't be distracted from your purpose.
Don't lose yourself in rumination.

HUMAN MINDS are large enough to contain something that has been expanding at the speed of light for 15 billion years. —HLR

The Mind's Sky

How many categories of being exist? What are the ultimate constituents of the universe? Ever since Descartes published his Meditations on First Philosophy *in 1641, one paradigmatic answer to those questions has been "Two." According to Descartes, everything is either mind (mental) or matter (physical). Of course, having settled upon a metaphysical dualism, Descartes is immediately faced with the problem of how his two categories can ever communicate.*

Timothy Ferris, professor of astronomy and journalism at UC Berkeley, is also struck by the inherent duality of the universe. Rather than attempting to resolve the communication riddle by focusing on features found in either mind or matter, he focuses on their means of communication — information. By studying what we now know about these intangible concepts — how we currently are trying to converse with extraterrestrial intelligences, why a simple, self-replicating network of interstellar probes makes more sense, what current work in cognitive science tells us about the brain and the programs that it runs, how the body "talks" to the brain, the use of the information metaphor to understand complex biological systems from rain forests to mutations of single genes — he believes we can develop a theory that explains how we can live on the inside (in our minds) and yet understand the outside (everything from our bodies to the galaxies).
—Howard Levine

•

I envision our relationship to the universe as symmetrical, hourglass-shaped. On one side is the outer realm, inhabited by galaxies, stars, the plants and animals, and our fellow human beings. Most of us (the solipsists aside) believe that this outer world exists, though we appreciate that our direct perceptions of it are limited and skewed. On the other side is the inner realm of the mind, where each of us is destined to live and die; here resides all we can ever know. Through the neck of the glass flow the sense data by which we perceive the outer realm, and (flowing the opposite way) the models and concepts we apply to nature, and the alterations and abridgments we impose on her. We tip this imaginary hourglass from time to time. In the nineteenth century, when classical physics ruled, we tended to think of the sand as flowing almost entirely from the outer to the inner realm, from an objectively real world to our passively recording minds. In the twentieth century, the concept of observer-dependent phenomena in quantum physics has shifted our attention to the ways our observations influence how we perceive nature. But so long as there are thinking beings in the universe, neither bulb of the hourglass will ever be empty.

•

We are confronted, then, not with *the* universe, which remains an eternal riddle, but with whatever model of the universe we can build within the mind. Every thinking creature in the universe shares this predicament; for all, the ultimate subject of inquiry is not the outer universe but the nature of its dance with the mind. In search for signs of extraterrestrial intelligence, our aim is to better understand the dance by learning how others dance. We hope to widen our perspective, to broaden the base of our perceptions and analysis, to improve the little universes of mind and make them answer more smartly to the vast whole. And what is the emblem of a sound mind, if not conformance between the inner model and the outer reality? What we seek among the stars is sanity.

Amateur Radio Astronomy

Radio astronomy studies the radio waves our sun, far-off galaxies, pulsars, and other exotic phenomena generate within our universe.

The field was born about sixty years ago, when Karl Guthe Jansky, an employee of Bell Labs, was given the task of finding the origin of some unusual static on some of the newer shortwave communication channels and cables used for transatlantic communication.

Jansky did not locate a specific source — but he did determine that the interference peaked in intensity every twenty-four hours, and that the static was more distinct during the daylight hours. After reading Jansky's paper, another Bell Lab engineer attributed the noise to stars.

In 1937, a Wheaton, IL ham-radio operator by the name of Grote Reber read Jansky's paper and became fascinated with the phenomenon. He constructed a 31½-foot parabolic dish antenna in his backyard and began the task of building various receivers at different frequencies. When he finally perfected his electronics, Reber plotted a radio intensity map of radio sources within the galaxy.

There have been many other investigations since Jansky and Reber, but Reber's work has been the most inspiring.

The Society of Amateur Radio Astronomers

(SARA) does radio astronomy research and educates anyone interested in learning how to observe the extraterrestrial radio spectrum.

The members are involved in solar, galactic, planetary, supernova and gamma ray-burst research. The operating receiving frequencies vary: 27 KHz, 144 MHz, 400 MHz, 1420 MHz and higher — in fact, anywhere there is a clear band of frequencies free of manmade noise. SARA meets yearly at the National Radio Astronomy Observatory in Green Bank, WV.

One of the most popular and easiest objects to observe is the planet Jupiter; it emits a static sound like waves crashing on the beach. This phenomenon is generated by extremely powerful electrical disturbances in the planet's atmosphere. These Jupiter noise storms start when one or two of the planet's moons approach the planet's powerful magnetic field. Solar radio flares are easy to observe and at times may be correlated with visual sightings.

SARA has developed a simple radio telescope for solar and Jupiter observations. Observers with computers may use an Analog to Digital (A/D) converter in place of the chart recorder. A Jupiter Loop antenna can be used with the associated antenna preamplifier.

For information about The Society of Amateur Radio Astronomers, contact: Membership Services, 247 N. Linden Street, Massapequa, NY 11758.
—Jeffrey M. Lichtman

The Mind's Sky
(Human Intelligence in a Cosmic Context) Timothy Ferris. Bantam Books, 1992; 281 pp. ISBN 0-553-37133-9 $13.95 ($16.45 postpaid) from Bantam, Doubleday, Dell/Fulfillment Dept., 2451 S. Wolf Road, Des Plaines, IL 60018; 800/223-6834

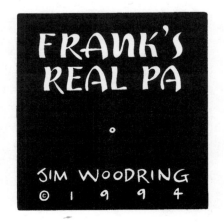

FRANK'S REAL PA
JIM WOODRING ©1994

The Amateur Astronomer

The Whole Earth reviewing crew has always taken delight in certain books that have become "classics," surviving tax laws and bookstore chains' policies that magnify the already deadly effects of fad. This 1957 book immediately established itself as one of the best places to commence an education in astronomy. Unlike most other beginners' books, which either skimp on the science or bury the reader in esoteric math, this one delivers the basics without demanding special prerequisite knowledge.

This new edition is actually a new book — after all, the first edition appeared before space exploration started — so it's respectably up-to-date. The best features of the original have been retained: lucid explanations of difficult concepts, and a very encouraging voice. The author knows that many important discoveries in astronomy have been made by amateurs. He invites and equips you to join their ranks. —J. Baldwin

•

To determine the velocity, height, and orbit of a meteor, three types of data must be provided: the point of appearance of the meteor, the point of disappearance, and the duration. Clearly it is necessary for the same meteor to be observed by two watchers at least twenty miles apart (more if possible), and all serious meteor observers work as members of teams.

No instruments are needed for meteor recording, but the observer has to have a

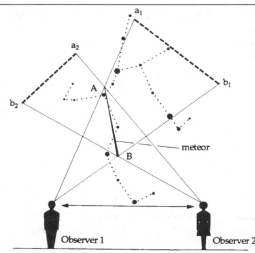

Measuring the true altitude of a meteor. The path of the meteor is given by the line **AB**. Observer A sees it apparently moving from a^1 to b^1: observer 2, from a^2 to b^2. This gives all the information needed for working out the altitude of the meteor above the ground.

really good knowledge of the constellations, as otherwise he will be unable to plot the track. The track should be plotted on a star map, but it is unwise to look down as soon as the meteor has vanished and try to remember where it went, because errors are bound to creep in. The solution is to check the path by holding up a rod or stick along the track which the meteor has followed, giving you the chance to take stock of the background and ensure that no mistake has been made. When you are satisfied, draw in the path on your chart and note the exact positions of the beginning and end of the track, and then write down: time of start, duration, duration of luminous trail, brightness (compared with a known star or stars), colour (if any), and any special features.

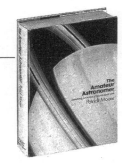

The Amateur Astronomer
Patrick Moore. 1990; 337 pp.
ISBN 0-393-02864-X
$35 postpaid from W. W. Norton & Co.
Order Dept., 800 Keystone Industrial Park,
Scranton, PA 18512; 800/233-4830

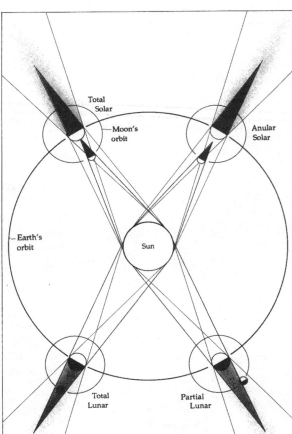

The geometry of solar and lunar eclipses.

How and Why to Make a User-Friendly Sidewalk Telescope

This expensive book will save you money in the long run. The author is a sidewalk astronomer and parts-scrounger par excellence. The body of your 'scope might be plywood instead of aluminum, but it will resolve the moons of Jupiter just as nicely as the high-priced version. —HLR

•

To start making your telescope mirror, use 2 pieces of glass — one for the mirror blank and the other (not necessarily as large) for the tool. You need some carborundum or alundum for abrasive, to generate your mirror curve by grinding one glass against the other with water and abrasive in between (even screened sand can be used). Generate the curve with coarse abrasive — 60 grit will do. It will take several pounds for a big mirror. Much smaller amounts of finer grits, say 100, 220, 400, and 1000, will be needed to smooth the curve before polishing. For the polishing

lap, use some rosin, perhaps a pound or two for a large mirror, plus about a tablespoon of turpentine per pound of rosin — or use prepared pitch. For the polishing agent use 1 or 2 tablespoons of cerium oxide. Rouge is slower, but gives a smoother

How and Why to Make a User-Friendly Sidewalk Telescope
John L. Dobson. 1991; 165 pp.
ISBN 0-913399-63-9
$39.95 ($44.95 postpaid) from Everything in the Universe, 185 John Street, Oakland, CA 94611; 510/547-6523

finish. Kits with appropriate glass, grit, etc., are advertised in some astronomical periodicals and available over-the-counter in telescope shops (true specialty stores, not sidelines of department or camera stores).

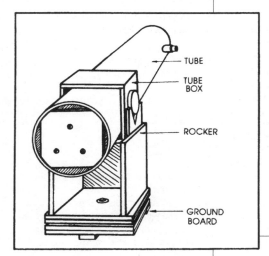

TUBE
TUBE BOX
ROCKER
GROUND BOARD

OTHER GREAT RESOURCES:

Sky Phenomena (A Guide to Naked-Eye Observation of the Stars). Norman Davidson. 1993. Lindisfarne Press.

Discover Space astronomy software; IBM-PC, Tandy and 100% compatible computers. Brøderbund Software, Inc., PO Box 12947, San Rafael, CA 94913-2947; 800/521-6263.

Orion Telescope Center Discount Catalog for Amateur Astronomers. Free from Orion Telescope Center, PO Box 1158, Santa Cruz, CA 95061; 800/447-1001 (800/443-1001 in California).

Astronomical Society of the Pacific. 390 Ashton Avenue, San Francisco, CA 94112; 415/337-2126.

94

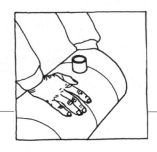

95

96

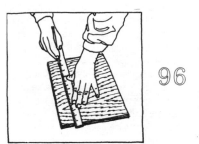

also see
Redshift, p. 363

The North Sea coast of Europe.

The Home Planet

Here are 150 awesome color photographs of Earth from space (most previously unpublished), chosen from NASA and Soviet archives. The comments, from the world's astronauts and cosmonauts, are translated into the nine languages in which this book has been simultaneously published. Editor Kevin W. Kelley has done us a great service by seeing this difficult international enterprise through to such a beautiful result. Most readers come away with a new feeling of what it means to say "our Earth." —JB

The Home Planet
Kevin W. Kelley. 1991; 256 pp.
ISBN 0-201-55095-4
$22.07 ($24.57 postpaid) from Addison-Wesley Publishing Co./Order Dept., 1 Jacob Way, Reading, MA 01867; 800/447-2226

Satellite Surveillance

As a user and critic of many books on technology, I run into one common problem: The writers of the books often forget that their readers don't know what they know. As a consequence, they neglect to explain essential basics. Harold Hough's book avoids this error. It gives you virtual short courses in optics, photography, and several other disciplines necessary to grasp modern satellite "look-down" technology. You learn what satellites can and cannot do, how their diverse capacities can be integrated to reveal military and industrial information, and how satellites are on the leading edge of exploration on earth (not just in space). Satellite surveillance is one of the fastest-growing businesses in America precisely because it helps other businesses grow. Whatever your business, from geology to insurance to intelligence, Hough's book suggests how you can cash in on this technology — and how you can protect yourself from its prying eyes.

—E. G. Ross

Satellite Surveillance
Harold Hough. 1991; 196 pp.
ISBN 1-55950-077-8
$21.95 ($25.95 postpaid) from Loompanics Unlimited, PO Box 1197, Port Townsend, WA 98368

●
There are four factors that make satellite imagery ideal for agriculture.

1. Satellite images cover large tracts of ground. This makes such imagery ideal for government agriculture agents to monitor districts or for farmers to obtain a profile of their whole farm. Therefore, large trends can be monitored with ease. For instance, a plant parasite or disease can be tracked as it moves, giving farmers an opportunity to isolate and attack it before it progresses.

2. Each type of plant has its own reflective pattern. Therefore, two different types of crops that appear to be the same from an aerial picture would look drastically different from a multispectral scanner.

3. Plants change their reflective patterns as they mature. In many cases, these patterns have been studied and analysts can tell how far the plant has progressed and if illness or stress has retarded growth. Based on this information, analysts can tell when a crop is ready for harvesting and the potential yield. Farmers can even tell if they will harvest before their neighbors and, therefore, receive higher prices.

4. Satellite images also identify the condition of the ground. An analyst can look over a large area and tell if the fields are too dry or muddy for planting. By carefully monitoring ground condition, farmers can choose their planting time and the right crops.

EOSAT Satellite Images

In 1984, the U.S. Congress decided to turn the Landsat program over to the private sector. The still-functioning Landsat 4 and 5 satellites, and the huge archive of data accumulated since 1972, have been transferred to the Earth Observation Satellite Company (EOSAT).

Prices range from $50 for a black-and-white photo on paper with 80-meter ground resolution (image size 7.3 inches on an edge, showing approximately 115 square miles), up to $3,300 for a computer-compatible tape of a scene from the Thematic Mapper (TM) on Landsat 5. TM scenes have a ground resolution of 30 meters. The primary sensor has seven spectral filters. This fine spectral discrimination makes it possible to identify different plant species or types of rock by detecting subtle differences in the color of the sunlight they reflect, even when they're not identifiable by shape or texture. —Robert Horvitz

EOSAT Satellite Images
Information from Earth Observation Satellite Company, 4300 Forbes Boulevard, Lanham, MD 20706; 800/344-9933.

OTHER GREAT RESOURCES

Below from Above. Georg Gerster. 1985. Abbeville Press.

The World from Above. Hans Reich. 1966. Hill & Wang. OUT OF PRINT.

Space Focus: Images from the New Frontier. Catalog from Focus, Inc., 4030 Pike Lane, Suite C, Concord, CA 94520. 800/829-2602.

Los Angeles.

Gaia and Biosphere

"This is the assembly of life that took [3.9] billion years to evolve. It has eaten storms — folded them into genes — and created the world that has created us. It holds the world steady." —E. O. Wilson, The Diversity of Life

SOME DISCOVERIES of science have far-reaching technological consequences — the quantum theory produced the A-bomb. The Gaia theory has few technological byproducts, but enormous impacts on human behavior, thoughts, spirit, compassion, and mythology. Twentieth-century science slowly assembled observations into a still-emerging Gaian vision: life as a geological force; plate tectonics; the varied, nonsupportive atmospheres of other planets; stromatalites; images of the little blue planet from satellite photos; aerobic bacteria that took a pollutant (oxygen) and created a livable planet for other species; DDT as it looped through the biosphere. An underground of scientists that had long been ignored suddenly could not be ignored: Vernadsky in the Soviet Union, Lynn Margulis in the United States, James Lovelock in England.

The Gaia theory ended the search for God in outer space. The home planet is now glorious and full of divinity. The Earth holds the same feelings that have characterized outer-space religions: paying homage to awesome patterns. Worshiping is once again "worth-shaping." Gaian stories provide new metaphor that can move the collective mind of humans. If the twenty-first century is to display more compassion than the bleak, destructive twentieth, it will, in part, come from the scientific unifying picture provided by Gaian thought. —Peter Warshall

Microcosmos

A unique book. Nowhere else can one find the microbial history of the planets or a deeper sense of our dependence on the invisible creatures that trap light from the sun, manufacture Earthfood, and regenerate the oxygen for the metabolism of life. Humans appear as a somewhat silly cell conglomerate of latecomers. The importance of symbiosis, cohabitation, cooperative behavior, and mutualism balances out the old views in which competition and predators seemed to govern the patterns of evolution. The prose delights as the facts enlighten. —PW

●

The oxygen holocaust was a worldwide pollution crisis that occurred about 2,000 million years ago. Before this time there was almost no oxygen in the earth's atmosphere. The earth's original biosphere was as different from ours as that of an alien planet. But purple and green photosynthetic microbes, frantic for hydrogen, discovered the ultimate resource, water, and its use led to the ultimate toxic waste, oxygen. Our precious oxygen was originally a gaseous poison dumped into the atmosphere. The appearance of oxygen-using photosynthesis and the resulting oxygen-rich environment tested the ingenuity of microbes, especially those producing oxygen and those nonmobile microorganisms unable to escape the newly abundant and reactive gas by means of motion. The mi-

Two billion years ago: Early Proterozoic Aeon: Hazardous oxygen accumulates in atmosphere as result of bacterial photosynthesis.

Microcosmos
(Four Billion Years of Microbial Evolution)
Lynn Margulis & Dorion Sagan. 1986; 301 pp. ISBN 0-671-74798-3
$10 ($13 postpaid) from Simon & Schuster/ Order Dept., 200 Old Tappan Road, Old Tappan, NJ 07675; 800/223-2336

crobes that stayed around responded by inventing various intercellular devices and scavengers to detoxify — and eventually exploit — the dangerous pollutant.

●

Mitochondria were once bacteria that became symbiotically holed up inside larger bacterial cells. In damp Proterozoic soil or in a microbial mat with grass-green and blue-green bacteria bubbling maddening amounts of polluting oxygen from their every surface, forcing all around them to evade it or evolve, a type of oxygen-breathing bacterium arose. It was probably a fierce predator, perhaps resembling modern predatory bacteria such as *Bdellovibrio* and *Daptobacter*.

The Ages of Gaia

James Lovelock has upgraded his notion of Earth as living organism from hypothesis (testable speculation) to theory (persuasive explanation). One might have expected him to modify its radical nature at this stage. He did not. Instead, in this book he extends its ramifications, arguing convincingly that Earth's personality — its oceans' character, the ingenious delivery of its water as rain over dry land, its transparent, blue-air skin, and perhaps the very mold of the land itself — are all caused by life. In Lovelock's biography of Gaia, life is not a fragile weakling, but a hardy, indomitable force that awakens Gaia herself. This is science writing at its best, and the boldest earth-science book in decades. —Kevin Kelly

●

At the risk of having my membership card of the Friends of the Earth withdrawn, I say that only by pollution do we survive. We animals pollute the air with carbon dioxide, and the vegetation pollutes it with oxygen. The pollution of one is the meat of the other.

●

The name of the living planet, Gaia, is not a synonym for the biosphere. The biosphere is defined as that part of the Earth where living things normally exist. Still less is Gaia the same as the biota, which is simply the collection of all individual living organisms. The biota and the biosphere taken together form part but not all of Gaia. Just as the

Photomicrograph of cyanobacteria. These are the organisms that first used the energy of sunlight to produce organic materials and oxygen. They have been, both in the free state and as endosymbionts, the primary producers from the beginning of the Archean until now.

shell is part of a snail, so the rocks, the air, and the oceans are part of Gaia. Gaia, as we shall see, has continuity with the past back to the origins of life, and extends into the future as long as life persists. Gaia, as a total planetary being, has properties that are not necessarily discernible by just knowing individual species or populations of organisms living together.

The Ages of Gaia
(A Biography of Our Living Earth)
James Lovelock. Bantam Books, 1988; 252 pp. ISBN 0-553-34816-7
$10.95 ($13.45 postpaid) from Bantam, Doubleday, Dell/Fulfillment Dept., 2451 S. Wolf Road, Des Plaines, IL 60018; 800/223-6834

Time-Life Planet Earth Series

There's no book out there on the natural history of the biosphere: the oxygen cycle, the carbon cycle, the sheltering layers of atmosphere, the blips in Gaian physiology from volcanoes and continental plate movements or the buffering action of glaciers. Pieces can be found in various great books like Microcosmos and Life as a Geological Force. The most dramatic and jump-start summaries are the beautifully illustrated Time-Life Series, especially The Atmosphere. —PW

Planet Earth Series
18 volumes;
$13.99 ($17.64 postpaid) each from Time-Life Inc./Customer Service, 1450 E. Parham Road, Richmond, VA 23280; 800/621-7026
Time-Life is phasing out the series. Two book-search companies that carry many of their titles are: Book Search International (615/298-3804) and the Strand Bookstore, 212/473-1452.

Life as a Geological Force

Even many rocks were once alive. Even the hardest rocks can succumb to life's persistence. Even the shifting of continents may be influenced by life's microcosmos. If you think of rock as lifeless and immortal, read this. —PW

Life as a Geological Force
(Dynamics of the Earth)
Peter Westbroek. 1991; 240 pp.
ISBN 0-393-02932-8
$9.95 postpaid from W. W. Norton & Co./Order Dept., 800 Keystone Industrial Park, Scranton, PA 18512; 800/233-4830

OTHER GREAT RESOURCES

For biospheric microbial intense interest:
Early Life. Lynn Margulis. 1982, Jones & Bartlett Publishers.
Symbiosis in Cell Evolution. Lynn Margulis. 1992, W. H. Freeman & Co.

Biospheric views were first spoken by Soviet scientists. This is the elegant classic: **Traces of Bygone Biospheres.** Audrey Lapo. 1988, Biosphere Press.

The Coevolution of Climate and Life

Ah, weather. In one lifetime, we get so little feel for its true extremes — little ice ages, greenhouse effects, El Niño. These are but the passing children of biospheric evolution — or rather, a co-evolution in which life itself helps steer the fickle unknown forces of climate.

This tome analyzes the speculations of "new primitive" scientists trying to understand the sun god's spots or the heavens' and oceans' affinity for dancing carbon molecules. It covers four billion years and focuses on the I'm-going-to-scare-you issues of aerosols, nuclear winter, overheating, acid rains and droughts. It is, at times, tainted by a humorless, clawing "humanism" and a college-sophomore attitude toward topics it cannot fully comprehend (history, Marxism, capitalism, the Gaia hypothesis). But there is no other book so readable and complete. You leave it linked — by each breath, each eddy current created by your waving arm, each belch of your automobile — to the huge involvement of the atmosphere, planet spin, and life. — PW

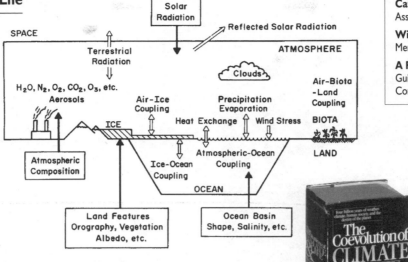

The climatic system of the earth consists of many interacting subsystems: the atmosphere, the oceans, the cryosphere (ice and snow), the biosphere (biota and their environment plus humans and their activities), the bottoms of the oceans, and some of the solid material below land and oceans. The interacting components of these subsystems are called the internal climate system, whereas those forces that drive the climate system, but are not an internal part of that system, are known as external forcing or boundary conditions.

The Coevolution of Climate and Life

Stephen H. Schneider and Randi Londer.
Sierra Club Books, 1984; 576 pp.
ISBN 0-87156-349-5
$25 ($28 postpaid) from Sierra Club Store
Orders, 730 Polk Street, San Francisco, CA
94109; 415/923-5500

Online Resources

If you have an Internet connection, you can download up-to-the-minute weather satellite photos, and display them on your computer screen with appropriate software.

FTP site:

Africa, Australia, Europe, World (Stanford Univ.; Palo Alto, CA)

wilbur.stanford.edu@/pub/weathergifs/

Australia, World, Special Events (James Cook Univ.; Townsville, AU)

marlin.jcu.edu.au@/JCUMetSat/

California, United States, Pacific, World (WEST; Menlo Park, CA)

ftp.netsys.com@/pub/images/

World, Geostationary Meteorological Satellite (NASA Ames; Moffit Field, CA)

explorer.arc.nasa.gov@/pub/Weather/gms

The Ascent of Mind

Why did hominid brains quadruple in size in such a relatively short period of time? What events would have triggered the evolutionary leap that led to culture, civilization, technology — after eons of relatively slow evolutionary progress from amoebas to apes? Calvin thinks that recurrent ice ages, particularly during the extremely recent past — the last 11,000 years — bootstrapped us to where we find ourselves today.

Ominously, Calvin points out that the debate over whether or not greenhouse gases are contributing to a potentially disastrous warming trend might be misplaced: global climate is a complex and often chaotic phenomenon; whether human activities are causing a warming or a cooling trend, it might be more important to consider the possibility that we are triggering an unpredictable instability in the Earth's climate patterns, with enormous consequences to billions of people. —HLR

•

To say the ice ages shaped human consciousness is usually meant in a metaphorical way (those consciousness-raising *awareness* connotations of the word). It's another way of saying that our outlook on the world is changeable in ways that were surely "useful" in our hunter-gatherer days: changes, perhaps, in our aggressiveness, our risk-taking to exploit fleeting opportunities, our tendency to promote the interests of our immediate small group (and frequent inability to think beyond that), in our competitive attitudes toward other omnivores (such as bears), and in our predatory attitudes toward herd animals (back before horses became "pets").

We can only understand the evolution of consciousness, I suspect, by understanding the details: the details of how animal plan-

ning-ahead is carried out, the details of how really precise judgments and movements are crafted, the details of the developmental programs that shape the neural machinery, the details of the regulatory genes that influence those developmental programs. And, of course, how the gene repertoires are prompted during life: selection must choose among the available variants in the developmental programs, those "plays" that make adults out of fetuses. Those modified programs in turn have to be crafted out of new gene combinations, and remembered by the genes that survive.

•

Flips are the foremost reason why I worry about the rapid warming of today: we have no information about what modes lie ahead, how our climate might jump. The Earth on its own has never explored the region into which we're heading, at least not in a comparable way, and we have no idea what strange chattering is likely to develop on the way there. Judging from the history of the last Ice Age, Europe is particularly prone to mode-switching — but then the North Atlantic is far better studied via ocean-bottom cores than oceans elsewhere, and it has the wormfree Greenland ice sheets to provide a second glimpse of its history. The Pacific Ocean might well have such mode-switching too, perhaps an exaggerated version of El Niño-to-La Niña cycling.

If climate change happens gradually over a century's time, we can imagine coping — but if it keeps flipping back and forth, we'll be like a country fighting a war on two fronts, frantically shuttling troops back and forth and generally disrupting civilization at the same time. Except we'll be trying to build new dams and pipelines, grow new forests, build new cities — a century's tasks compressed into a decade, all while com-

batting famines and the political instability that goes with them. And then the climate flips again (probably without warning), and everything has to shift to another front, such mammoth tasks being repeated elsewhere — if we are able to muster the efforts required (a 99 percent decrease in population might be more likely).

About the only way out of the Dryas-style threats to humanity that I can see is if we become considerably more conversant with boom-time reproductive physiology and psychology. And considerably smarter through the use of computers, coming to understand the coupling between the ocean currents and the regional climates well enough to simulate them. Occasionally there is a bonus from predictive simulations: Sometimes you also learn how to give the system a little push in a desired direction. Even in simple systems, such as when pushing a child on a playground swing, there is a right time and place to apply an effective push.

EVENTS DURING HUMAN EVOLUTION

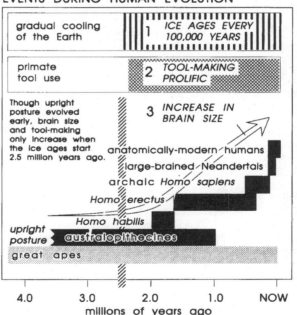

The Ascent of Mind

The U.S. edition is out of print. Softcover copies may be ordered from University Book Store, 4326 University Way N.E., Seattle, WA 98105 USA for $5.98 (and tax if WA resident; shipping free in USA). 206/634-3400; fax 206/634-0810

MAPS can provide the most concise statement of the minutiae of places, be they watersheds, or transmission networks, or what we'll find on the way from here to there. Good maps may also give you the big picture in which trends and generalities may be discerned. We'd be lost without 'em. —Don Ryan

Raven Maps and Images

These smart cookies turned information-rich US government maps into captivatingly lifelike shaded-relief wall maps. Because the maps are made from the Geological Survey's negatives, all the minutiae of the originals are preserved. The addition of intelligent and subtly applied color enhances, never obscures. Raven produces similar maps of selected national parks.

Among their other publications:

Two products derived from the USGS's gorgeous computer-generated terrain base: Landforms and Drainage, looking as though modeled in cool gray clay by some giant Michelangelo. Natural features are named in fine, almost invisible type. The United States is based on the same model, with satisfyingly realistic altitude tints and enough place names and boundaries to settle arguments but not to obscure the beautiful view.

One World. The most velvety-blue ocean you've ever seen in print laps against the shores of altitude-tinted continents. Three 120°-apart views of global Earth. Physical features, including cities, are unobtrusively named.

A series of oblique views, computer-plotted from digital terrain information. Again, the use of color and the design are the arresting attributes. Looking at their view over the Rockies, the High Plains, and the Intermountain West, I found myself smelling distant pinyon

Landforms and Drainage of the 48 States.

Raven Maps and Images:
Catalog free. 34 N. Central Avenue, Medford, OR 97501; 800/237-0798.

smoke and feeling cool, high-altitude breezes.

All these maps are the kind you want to fall face-down into. (They suggest you buy them in their optional laminated versions to protect against greasy faceprints.) Raven is the most intelligently creative bunch in map publishing I know. —DR

Map Use

If I had to limit myself to one book about map making and map use, this would be it. The illustrations show cartographic concepts very well. The author does an excellent job, reminding the reader that the map is not the territory, and that maps can be used to abuse as well as to enlighten. —Ron Hendricks

This astoundingly comprehensive book gets better with each new edition; its "Map Analyses" section can serve you well as a clear and thorough introduction to Geographic Information Systems. —DR

Map Use
(Reading, Analysis, Interpretation)
Phillip C. Muehrcke & Juliana O. Muehrcke. 1978, 1992; 631 pp.
ISBN 0-9602978-3-9
$30 ($33 postpaid)
from JP Publications, PO Box 44173, Madison, WI 53744-4173; 608/231-2373

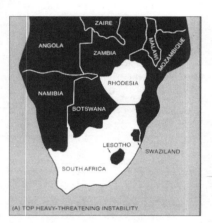

Ordinarily a map or any picture with so much black at the top would be considered poor design, because it seems top-heavy, unbalanced. On this map from *Time* magazine, however, the intent was to show that South Africa was being hemmed in by black-ruled countries, and the map's design helps to convey that impression. South

Africa looks as though it is being threatened, overcome by ominous forces. If we simply interchange the black and white colors, a totally different mood is created. The design slips into visual balance, and the feeling of menace disappears.

•

Simplicity, too, can be seen as a liability as well as an asset. Simplification of the environment through mapping is nothing but an illusion which appeals to our limited information-processing ability. By using maps, we avoid confronting reality in its overwhelming and confusing natural state. But the environment remains unchanged. It is just our view of it that lacks detail and complexity. If we are able to understand map information at a glance, it is only because the map is such a crude model of our surroundings. Yet it is the environment, not the map, which we want to understand.

Goode's World Atlas

Per buck, this atlas has the most and the best — 368 pages of locational maps (from continent right down to city), landforms, climate, weather, vegetation, soil, population, agriculture, trade, language, resources, ocean floor — including a fine pronouncing index. When something in the newspaper puzzles you, check here. —SB

There are some new atlases on the market that promise (through digital technology) vast improvements in locational accuracy. Beware: on maps of this scale the difference between 95% spot-on and 98% is close to imperceptible, and it remains to be seen if digitalization will make any improvement in the cost (hence frequency) of revisions. Goode's remains far superior to its nearest competition in coverage, design, and readability. —DR

Goode's World Atlas:
Edward B. Espenshade, Jr., Editor. 1990; 268 pp.
ISBN 0-528-83128-3.
$29.95 ($37.95 postpaid) from Rand McNally Map & Travel Store, 150 S. Wacker Drive, Chicago, IL 60606; 312/332-2009; call 800/234-0679 for the store nearest you.

Access to The United States Geological Survey

The U.S. Geological Survey produces and distributes information on a wide variety of earth-science specialities such as geology, hydrology, cartography, geography, and remote sensing, as well as land use and energy, mineral, and water resources. It is the government's primary civil mapping agency.

I have found the Geological Survey to be a very user-friendly organization; in most cases your first contact will be able to answer all your questions. Until the last couple of years, USGS public information offices and over-the-counter map sales existed in most big cities. Lamentably, the federal government closed most of these offices as a cost-cutting measure. The major public interface with the Geological Survey is now by telephone, which I consider to be a gross misapplication of thrift. The result is like a library with closed stacks. The phone connection will get you a fairly workable telephone tree: "For map information, press 1; for digital information, press 2; for airphoto information . . ." and you can eventually talk to a live information specialist.

Ask if one of the remaining Earth Science Information Centers is near you. If you don't know what you're looking for, start by requesting these free publications:

Catalog of Maps
— All the kinds of maps the Survey produces or distributes are described, illustrated, and accessed. This is in a poster format, attractively designed and illustrated. If you want to display yours on a bulletin board, get two copies so that you can see both the back and front.

Catalog of Cartographic Data
— Things you didn't know you could get, like software for cartographic computer programs, advance prints of topographic maps in progess, land use (culture) and land cover (nature) maps for much of the US, access to the National High Altitude Photography Program — the USA from 40,000 feet. —DR

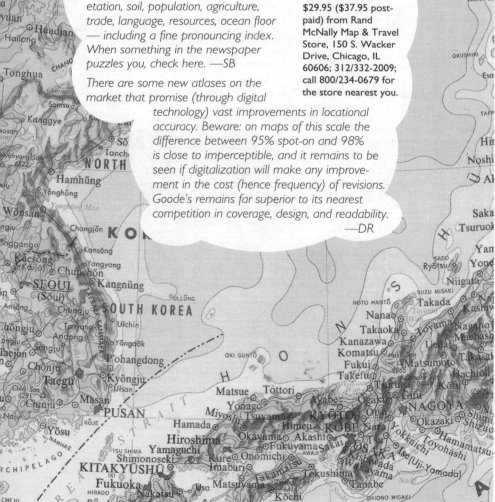

The Earth — From Space

Over 20,000 natural-color NOAA satellite images, chosen for virtually cloudless skies, digitally merged into a seamless mosaic of perpetual summer. Vegetation types show distinctly so it's possible, for example, to compare Amazonian rain forest with that of the Congo basin. Most remarkable thing I learned: the vastness of the Sahara. You may count on seeing more uses of this imagery, including a globe, from collaborators Tom Van Sant and Lloyd Van Warren. —DR

The Earth — From Space (A Satellite View of the World): Tom Van Sant & The Geosphere Project. 24" x 36". Plain paper $15 ($19.50 postpaid); laminated $20 ($24.50 postpaid). Spaceshots, Inc., 526 S. Francisca Avenue, Redondo Beach, CA 90277; 800/272-2779.

DeLorme Atlases

With their large format they look like road atlases, but if you're in a hurry to get to granma's house upstate they won't be much help. If you're like me you'll have long since turned off onto that fine red line that wanders off over hills you've never been behind, to that town you never knew existed. These are serious maps, with the features you'd expect to find on a topographic map — great for field-trip planning. In studying the areas I know well I've yet to find even the smallest track ignored on the page. Each atlas includes a large gazetteer listing bike routes, fishing piers, wilderness areas, and more. —DR

DeLorme Atlas and Gazetteer: AK, $19.95; ME, NH, VT, $12.95; CA (South/Central), CA, (North), FL, MI, MN, NY, OH, PA, TN, VA, WA, WI $14.95 each (add $3 for p & h) from DeLorme Mapping Co, PO Box 298, Freeport, ME 04032; 800/227-1656, x5500.

Alaska

Map Link

*Suppose you're setting off on a trip to the mountains of Mexico and want a map for the region you're going to. You know that there are 1:250,000-scale topographic maps available, but you can't find any locally. Just imagine how useful it would be to be able to pick up the phone and order the map you need with only the coordinates of the town you're visiting, no catalog number or other information necessary. Map Link offers such a service, as well as an impressive **World Map Directory** that accesses maps from all around the world; short but detailed comments on each series display a true love for the subject. They seem to carry the largest-scale and most informative maps available for both towns and regions. —Jonathan Evelegh*

The World Map Directory: Aaron Maizlish & William Tefft. 1992; 335 pp. $29.95 postpaid from Map Link, 25 E. Mason Street, Santa Barbara, CA 93101; 805/965-4402.

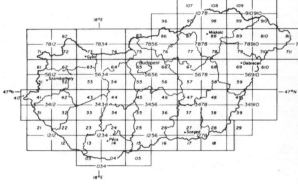

Hungary topographics series
1:1000,000 and 1:200,000

National Geographic World Political Map

Like it or not, this is how the Earth has been subdivided. From Burkina Faso to Tasmania, each political bloc is displayed in full color on heavy paper. A best buy. —Peter Warshall

National Geographic World Political Map: 75" x 49 1/2"; $12.95 ($17.70 postpaid) from National Geographic Society, 1145 17th Street NW, Washington, DC 20036; 800/638-4077.

**Left: Section shown 1/2 lifesize.
Full map size 48" x 68".**

Catalog of Maps and Catalog of Cartographic Data: Free from USGS Earth Science Information Center, 507 National Center, Reston, VA 22092; 800/USA-MAPS.

Globes

For George F. Cram or Replogle globes in many sizes and price ranges.

Globes:
$35–$150 for desk models; $100–$5,000 for floor models. Rand McNally Map & Travel Store, 150 S. Wacker Drive, Chicago, IL 60606; 312/332-2009; call 800/234-0679 for the store nearest you.

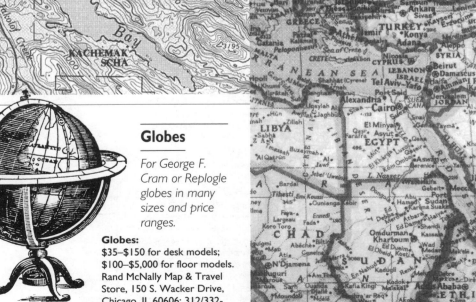

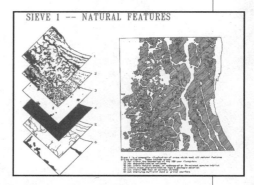

Geographic Information Systems

GIS (please: call it by its acronym) is a computer system that assembles, stores, manipulates, and displays geographically referenced information. The product is a digital map whose elements (points, lines, and areas) are windows into its database. Maximum usefulness is achieved by relating several elements. For instance, emergency response to the disastrous Midwest floods of 1993 was aided by GISs that calculated phone numbers within a certain contour line — seemingly unrelated data that sped the evacuation of flood zones and accomplished in minutes what would have taken hours of poring over telephone books and topo sheets.

GIS's roots predate the digital revolution by at least a century. Dr. John Snow's famous visual correlation of cholera deaths and polluted wells in 1854 London was an early landmark, and the work of Ian McHarg, popularized in his 1969 *Design With Nature* was pre-acronymic GIS. It wasn't until the advent of accessible computers that GIS could grow into the industry it is today.

Don't go out and buy a GIS — yet. The systems can be expensive, learning curves long, and formats not necessarily mutually compatible. Many public jurisdictions and groups with an interest in the land base, e.g., planning departments, forestry services, Audubon chapters (especially where policy battles are being fought) need interns and volunteers to help with data acquisition and digitization. Learn GIS while you work for your favorite cause. —Don Ryan

GIS World

To enter geographic information systems through **GIS World** *is to dive into the deep end. But don't worry, there are plenty of lifeguards and coaches to help the novice. One reason is that GIS is a rapidly growing industry; students and might-be students are needed to fill the job vacancies of the near future. For another thing, GIS feeds on information and cross-fertilization from within and without the industry; ad hoc partnerships and collaborations abound. A high rate of citizen input is desirable, if not essential, especially in matters of public policy such as environmental planning. The GIS industry encourages this, and* **GIS World** *keeps track.*

GIS World *also offers a sister periodical,* **Business Geographics,** *and many more specialized books from their mailorder bookstore. —Don Ryan*

GIS World: $72/year (12 issues).
Business Geographics: Free to qualified individuals. GIS World Inc.: 155 E. Boardwalk Drive, Suite 250, Fort Collins, CO 80525. Phone: 303/223-4848; fax: 303/223-5700.

mulate criteria based on its own values. We felt good about the design. But when I visited a highly favored site, I found one of the most idyllic landscapes in the Eastern United States — the kind of place I would fight to preserve. What troubles me still is that no one ever paid to add aesthetics into that early GIS, even though it would have been technically feasible.

During the years, I have used GIS to help make decisions with great impacts on people's lives, and the memory of that first experience always reminded me that GIS and its practitioners have limits. I doubt GIS will turn us all into "drive-by" developers, but we should question what GIS is doing to us and to society at large.
—Jerome E. Dobson

• My first GIS work taught me a lesson in environmental ethics. We developed an approach for siting noxious facilities, intending to resolve conflicts by enabling each interest group to for-

See "GIS as a
Political Tool" (p. 293).

OGR

International GIS Sourcebook. 1994, GIS World Inc. *A yearbook of biblical proportions that accesses companies (hundreds), educational programs (more than two hundred institutions worldwide), and over three hundred GIS-related software products.*

GIS Applications in Natural Resources. Michael Heit & Art Shortreid, Editors. 1991, GIS World Inc. *The best sixty-three papers from Forestry Canada's "GIS 1987 to 1991" symposium series.*

Simple Computer Imaging and Mapping. Micha Pazner, Nancy Thies & Roberto Chavez. 1993, Think Space, Inc., London, Ontario, Canada. *Low-cost desktop image processing techniques for creating digital spatial and pictorial databases, atlases, and wall maps.*

Profiting from a Geographic Information System. Gilbert H. Castle, Editor. 1993, GIS World Inc. *Increase revenues, reduce costs, enhance customer relations, and improve profitability through GIS.*

U.S. Geological Survey

If you're just curious about the breadth of GIS or are an educator of any stripe who wants to open the world of geographic information systems to a potential practitioner, "Geographic Information Systems" is a very detailed and colorfully illustrated brochure that unfolds into an attractive poster. If you want to put it on the wall for display, get two so you can display both information-packed sides at once.
—Don Ryan

•

If you could relate information about the rainfall of your State ormation from many different sources, in many different forms, can help with such analyses. The primary requirement for the source data is that the locations for the variables are known. Location may be annotated by x, y, and z coordinates of longitude, latitude, and elevation, or by such systems as ZIP Codes or highway mile markers. Any variable that can be located spatially can be fed into a GIS.

Several computer data bases that can be directly entered into a GIS are being produced by Federal agencies and private firms. Different kinds of data in map form can be entered into a GIS. A GIS can also

convert existing digital information, which may not yet be in map form, into forms it can recognize and use. For example, digital satellite images can be analyzed to produce a map-like layer of digital information about vegetative cover. Likewise, census or hydrologic tabular data can be converted to map-like form, serving as layers of thematic information in a GIS.

Geographic Information Systems: Free. USGS Earth Science Information Center, 507 National Center, Reston, VA 22092; 800/USA-MAPS

ARC/INFO

ARC/INFO and PC ARC/INFO have established themselves as the industry-standard GISs.

The MS/DOS version, PC ARC/INFO, requires an IBM-compatible 80286 or faster processor with a minimum of 40 megabytes of hard-disk storage and 80287 or 80387 numerical co-processor. A high-resolution color graphic display is highly recommended. The newly emerging PC standard includes a dedicated graphics coprocessor and screen resolution of 768 x 1024 pixels or better. There is no Macintosh version available.

PC ARC/INFO comes in modules — PC Starter Kit, PC ArcEdit, ArcPlot, PC Overlay, PC Data Conversion, and PC Network. The fully installed program occupies about 29 megabytes of hard-disk storage.

The ARC system stores geographical feature locations as a set of coordinates and as relationships between connected or adjacent features. The relationships used to represent the connectivity of contiguous features are referred to as topology. The geographic features are digitally stored in computer files as layers

or "coverages." Typical coverages assembled for a USGS standard 7.5-minute quadrangle (1:24,000 scale) might include elevation, soil types, vegetation types, hydrography, or roads and ownership boundaries.

After learning the ARC/INFO software system, input of graphic and feature attributes is the largest task associated with building a GIS. Maps may be digitized or scanned into computer files and then imported into ARC coverages. Standard graphical output is to a plotter or to a Postscript- or Laserjet-compatible laser printer. Some dot-matrix printers are supported at lower graphic resolutions.
—Eric and Steve Beckwitt

ARC/INFO: Information from Environmental Systems Research Institute/ Marketing Dept., 380 New York Street, Redlands, CA 92373; 909/793-2853

SIEVE 1 -- NATURAL FEATURES

Lake County (IL) Landfill Site Screening, by Robert Lindquist. This series of maps illustrates the site screening process employed by the Lake County Joint Action Solid Waste Planning Committee to delimit areas of suitability for a new landfill.

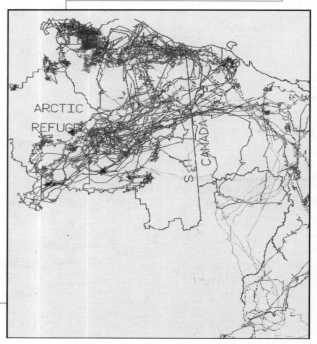

Cro-Magnon hunters drew pictures of the animals they hunted, with tallies and track lines thought to depict migration routes. These records followed the two-element structure of modern geographic information systems: a graphic file linked to an attribute data base. At right is a modern example showing caribou migration in Alaska.

Whatever Happened to Natural History?

"The secondhandedness of the learned world is the secret of its mediocrity."
—Alfred North Whitehead

Molecular biology, experimental biology, and simulation modeling sucked science indoors, stashing natural history in a dusty glass display case. "Real" scientists pooh-poohed outdoor observational biology as "without controls." Physics envy battered naturalists and ecologists who just wanted to know the style and scatter of bluebird nesting sites. Darwin was "real" only in the form of ahistorical mathematical models. The essence of naturalist work — first-hand amazing, detailed patience and attentiveness — lost favor. Audubon's singular observation that rattlesnakes climb bushes and engorge fledgling birds was dismissed as a whimsical fable.

Plate tectonics, biospherics, ecological chemistry, and the twentieth-century Great Holocaust of Diversity have revived the job description: natural historian. Field observation and taxonomy, occupations forever museumed, have returned with passion. There is a desperate need for taxonomists who can identify life's bounty. Will thousands of beetles die nameless? Will evolutionarily significant and ecologically keystone creatures die off because they remained unrecognized?

As the century closes, it's time for a democracy of citizen-naturalists who can feed a growing, global library of intimate earth knowledge. Beware! An environmentalist is not a naturalist. Could be a city lawyer or a philosopher, but a naturalist listens first to woods and streams.
—Peter Warshall

(Thanks to Tony Burgess, Linda Leigh, Elinor Michel, Melissa Savage, Robert Scarborough, and Arthur Okamura)

The Naturalist's Journal

*Anything goes: poems, pasted feathers, pressed plants, sketches, rigorous worksheets. Joseph Grinnell's method divides the journal into two sections: one for notes as the day progresses, one arranged to record events in the species' lives as you observe them. Among scientist-naturalists, this record-keeping is increasingly on Powerbooks and other field computers. (Beware the crash!) In any case, computers just liberate the written journal. Read **Faith in the Seed** by Thoreau or volumes two and three (1850 through April 1852) of his **Journals** (p. 16), if you don't think you know what to write. —PW*

See the last four items listed in the Naturalist's Field Kit (below left) if you don't think you know what to write on or with. —JD

A Basic Field Kit for the Naturalist

Each group of organisms requires its own field kit. You may want to add to your outdoor fieldplay by collecting samples of plants or keeping an indoor cage for more info (such as what butterfly came from that chrysalis). You'll find friends in the community of budding naturalists, discovering more technical equipment, microscopes, satellite photos, museum collections, latinate vocabulary, and rigorous protocols in which to immerse your "naturalist self."

The tools of the citizen-naturalist change with the speed you move. The car naturalist scribbles the odometer reading when a new species, a stupefying geological formation, or a roadkill appears. The backyard naturalist lovingly notes when dogwood blossoms unfold or the robin arrives. The hiker-naturalist throws down the backpack to record the number of nesting holes of the red-cockaded woodpecker. The permanent-camp or safari naturalist sets up for a week or a year to soak up as much as possible. —PW

OGRs

Audubon Society Nature Shops. Contact your local Audubon Society chapter.

Ward's Natural Science Catalogs: Earth Science, $10 postpaid; Biology, $15 postpaid, PO Box 92912, Rochester, NY 14692-9012; 800/962-2660; 716/359-2502.

Carolina Biological Supply Catalog: $17.95 postpaid. PO Box 187, Gladstone, OR 97027; 800/334-5551; 503/656-1641.

Natural History Book Service Ltd. Ecology and environment catalogs free. 2–3 Wills Road, Totnes, Devon TQ9 5XN, UK; 011-44-0803-865-913; email: nhbs@gn.apc.org

Take these along:

A belt to hook "holsters" or canteens; a small backpack or fanny pack.

A hat and a bandanna.

Ziploc ® bags of at least two sizes or 4-mil plastic "soil sample" bags.

A Swiss Army knife and/or a Leatherman pocket tool.

Bungee cord(s) or parachute cord to attach the elk skull to the backpack.

A library of field guides to floras/faunas. More for the car library, backyard and safari camp; fewer for hiking.

A hand lens — or invert your binoculars; they'll act as a hand lens.

A 6", transparent ruler with metric conversion.

"Rite in the Rain" paper products — I ache for a waterproof notebook with unlined paper. Rite in the Rain has the best and most various of every other paper type.*

Polypaper Plastic Paper — unaffected by salt- or freshwater; no rot, mildew, tearing. Rolls or folds. Great in the Alaskan sub-sub-cold.*

Sheet holders for loose-paper storage and protection.*

"Sharpie" or other waterproof marking pen (black: colors fade).

* Available from **Forestry Suppliers, Inc.:** PO Box 8397, Jackson, MS 39284; 800/647-5368.

Naturalist Camera

If you can carry only one lightweight camera and can't carry five different lenses, the Pentax 105R zoom lens is not cheap but is wonderfully multi-purpose. You can photograph at 18 inches (to get the flowers and fruits and fungi) and at about 3 feet (to get small patches of ecosystems) and zoom from 38 to 105 mm. You can add a date to the photo, photograph fast (automatic settings), or modify the automatic light setting. It's not waterproof, there's no wideangle, the speed is not super fast nor the camera super sturdy. Just high-quality photos at many dimensions from one machine.

To be a naturalist,

To be a naturalist, in the broadest sense, is simply to give everyday reality its due. Birds before broadsides. Percepts before concepts. We are inclusive, not exclusive. The explorer-hunter naturalist lineage is long: Isaak Walton, Humboldt, Darwin, Bates, Wallace, Lewis and Clark, Audubon . . . their Pleistocene instincts at home in civilized prose. Even though Melville called his whale a fish, the greatest fictional work of natural history in America is undoubtedly *Moby Dick*. Naturalist-poets include Walt Whitman, Emily Dickinson, Robert Frost, Robinson Jeffers, and Gary Snyder. The naturalist-philosophers sport Emerson, Thoreau, Leopold, and a host of contemporaries. It's a great eccentric tradition of wild walks, wild intellect, and a tactile love of accuracy.
—Peter Warshall

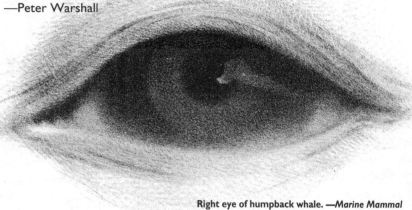

Right eye of humpback whale. —*Marine Mammal*

A Natural History of Sex

Courtship and mating keep the lineage alive. Here's a fun modern bestiary of beasts that change sex, eat their husbands in the act of love, prefer to clone than to mate with males, practice transvestism . . . —PW

•

Female moorhens fight among themselves, especially if one female approaches a courting pair. These fights are reminiscent of rooster fights, where the individuals lean back and rake at each other with their clawed feet. Again, heavy females win most fights. But what are they fighting for? If they form pairs, there is a male for every female. The hens fight for fat males. The fatter the male, the better the job he can do at nest initiation and incubation.

A Natural History of Sex
Adrian Forsyth
1986; 192 pp.
ISBN 09631591-8-6
$10.95 ($14.95 post-paid) from Chapters Bookstore, 2031 Shelburne Road, Shelburne, VT 05482

•

The cleaner wrasse gets its food at traditional spots known as cleaning stations. Other reef fish visit these stations, and the wrasse removes and eats their external parasites, such as copepods. Each station is lorded over by a dominant male that excludes other males and dominates about half a dozen females. He also mates each female once daily.

MANIACAL NATURALIST BOOK LIST

On Nature. Get this book back in print! The finest crafters of nature and anti-nature (can that be?) prose. Wonderful biblio. Daniel Halpern. 1986, North Point Press.

A Species of Eternity. Out of print! The field guide to the origins of American maniacal naturalists. If in print, it would have been the page's feature. Joseph Kastner. 1977, Alfred A. Knopf.

The Insect World of J. Henri Fabre. 1991, Beacon Press.

The Journal of Henry David Thoreau (Bradford Torrey & Francis H. Allen, Eds. 1906, Dover), **The Natural History Essays** (1989, Gibbs Smith), **The Maine Woods** (1988, Penguin), and **Faith in a Seed** (Bradley P. Dean, Editor. 1993, Island Press). Thoreau's naturalist intensity

is awesome. Here is inspiration.

Darwin on Earthworms. The maniacal naturalist himself, setting the standard. 1976, Bookworm Publishing Co.

Refuge. The moral dialogue of the Great Salt Lake and cancer. The most moving contemporary "unnatural history." Terry Tempest Williams. 1991, Vintage Books, Random House.

Travels in Alaska and **My First Summer in the Sierra** (both John Muir. 1993, Penguin Books). The craggy prose of John Muir, mountain wildman and canny converter of America to landscape love.

Curious Naturalists. How gulls and bees and sand wasps and jays reveal their world views. Community aesthetics and cognitive maps by this century's most perspicacious. Niko Tinbergen. 1984, University of Massachusetts Press.

Natural History

The latest news in both cultural- and natural-history happenings. Weird and wonderful nature stories with an intelligence that separates it from the commercialized "eco-media." Includes some of the best scientist-naturalist prose writers. An equal value to kids and adults. —PW and George Putz

Natural History Magazine
Alan P. Ternes, Editor. $28/year (12 issues) from PO Box 3030, Harlan, IA 51593-2091

The Norton Book of Nature Writing

The call of nature. The endless dialog between richness and repulsion. Spinoza says: "Nature abhors a vacuum." Tennessee Williams answers: "A vacuum is a hell of a lot better than some of the stuff that nature replaces it with." An encyclopedic sampler from 1720 to right now of Anglo-European writers. —PW

•

I was curious to know what sort of reception a second male might expect from a recently fertilized female. The result of my enquiry was shocking. The Mantis, in many cases, is never sated with conjugal

raptures and banquets. After a rest that varies in length, whether the eggs be laid or not, a second male is accepted and then devoured like the first. A third succeeds him, performs his function in life, is eaten and disappears. A fourth undergoes a like fate. In the course of two weeks I thus see one and the same Mantis use up seven males. She takes them all to her bosom and makes them all pay for the nuptial ecstasy with their lives.

•

By understanding the dependability of place, we can anchor ourselves as trees.

One night, Jonas Ole Sademaki, a Maasai

elder, and I sit around the fire telling stories. Sparks enter the ebony sky and find their places among stars.

"My people worship trees," he says. "It was the tree that gave birth to the Maasai. Grasses are also trustworthy. When a boy is beaten for an inappropriate act, the boy falls to the ground and clutches a handful of grass. His elder takes this gesture as a sign of humility. The child remembers where the source of his power lies."

As I walk back to my tent, I stop and look up at the southern cross. These are new constellations for me. I kneel in the grasses and hold tight.

The Norton Book of Nature Writing
Robert Finch & John Elder, Editors. 1990; 921 pp. ISBN 0-393-02799-6
$29.95 postpaid from W. W. Norton & Co./Order Dept., 800 Keystone Industrial Park, Scranton, PA 18512; 800/233-4830

The Artist-Naturalist

Start with an odd-sized piece of paper, anything but 8 ½ by 11. Give up the "death grip" of writing and try the "wand grip" to loosen up. Use soft pencils. Start with something that moves you. Drawing reveals. From bestiaries to Audubon to Roger Tory Peterson: eye/hand inseparability. For landscape, cut out a rectangle that is the same proportions as your paper. Use the remaining window to scan the landscape. Find the inevitable boundaries where nature turns to art.

After living outdoor classes with a good teacher, *The Art of Field Sketching* is the best intro — fine biblio of published field sketchbooks (though neglecting Audubon and Agassiz Fuertes). New stuff, such as how to use a Questar for bird sketching, you will need to learn from living naturalists. —PW

J. J. Audubon

Illustration from **The Art of Field Sketching**, by Clare W. Leslie: 1993, Peregrine Smith; ISBN 0-87905-555-3. $14.95 ($16.95 postpaid) from Gibbs Smith, Publisher, PO Box 667, Layton, UT 84041; 801/544-9800.

Outdoor Sounds

The amount and weight of equipment you employ to record nature depends on whether you are hiking, traveling by car, or setting up a long-term safari camp. Big rigs take time to set up; by the time you're in place, the dawn song may be over or the whales may have left the nearshore.

Are you recording for memory — taking an aural snapshot for the scrapbook? If so, any high-quality cassette tape recorder with built-in microphone is enough.

Are you trying to open yourself to sounds that happen so fast, in such complex rhythms and musical tapestries that you need time to reflect again and again? In this case, you will want special filters — like camera lenses — to pick up and magnify the mystery. The practice of unveiling sound can be straightforward: hydrophones in the ocean to listen to orcas, in the Grand Canyon rapids to contemplate turbulence; parabolic dishes or shotgun microphones to single out particular frogs or birds.

Headphones can be annoyingly democratic, giving equal weight to wind gush, water warbles, and fire crackles that may overwhelm birdsong or cricket chorus. The quest requires the auditory equivalent of unbiased vision — letting your ear deconstruct sound textures, moving your body and mic into the right spot, and taking into account the wind and water and cable length between the sound and the recording deck. To give other humans the soulful sound of a seal colony, or pigeons foraging among the taxis, is an art like any other.

A decade ago, 30-pound, $7,000 Nagras and short-duration, reel-to-reel recordings were the ideal. Now, the system of choice is 3" by 2" DATs (digital audio tapes), which record uninterrupted for two hours with a quality far superior to CDs. The technological distance between professional and amateur has shrunk. DATs are for the professional recorder, the naturalist/archival recorder, and the fun recorder. Only one hitch: American recording companies have actively suppressed DATs. The technology produces a sound quality almost equal to the master recording and would prevent "intermediate" technologies like mini-CDs and DCCs from momentarily swamping the market with typical planned obsolescence. Nevertheless, the DAT system is the best for outdoor recording. —Mickey Houlihan

Photo thanks to Mickey Houlihan.

• **Wind Over the Earth** is a one-stop shop for outdoor recording. They can help you choose off-the-shelf studio equipment, wind screens, and other gear, or custom-design a system for you. I recommend them for information on the following:

• Sound Trackers.

• DAT decks (less than $1,000). Dinon DTR-80P is the best for the price, followed by Sony TCD7. Some old-time bird recorders like the Sony TCD cassette series.

• Stereo Microphone. Audio-Technica AT 822. Runs off AA batteries. Unless you set up for a long time, this microphone substitutes for two or more microphones. The very expensive "top-of-the-line" (over $1200) models include the Sennheiser MKH40 and the Schoeps CMC6 + MK41.

There are in-betweens.

• Shotgun microphones. These mikes cancel out surrounding sound. They do not give you more sound or signal from the direction they are pointing. If you want a single sound, as you would in studying some forms of birdsong, they are useful. For car and safari-camp-style travel.

• Headphones. The Sony MDR-7506 fold-up headset lets you hear through the rumbling and white noise of wind and water (or traffic).

Wind Over the Earth: 1980 8th Street, Suite F, Boulder, CO 80302. Fax: 303/443-9824.

• Hydrophones. Hydrophone element #41759 from Edmund Scientific ($23.95). Hydrophone #8103 ($1,500) from Bruel and Kjaer Instruments. If you use a cable in freshwater streams, make sure it's the appropriate length so the hydrophone doesn't bounce between rocks and bottom.

Edmund Scientific Co: 101 E. Gloucester Pike, Barrington, NJ 08007; 609/547-8880.

Bruel and Kjaer: 721 Elkhoff Street, Orange, CA 92668; 508/481-7000.

• Parabolic Dishes and Pressure Zone Method. Sony PBR 230 or Don Gibson Parabolas — both from Geleco Electronics.

Remember that dishes are hard to protect from wind. A Pressure Zone Method sound gatherer (looks like a pyramid) may be preferable. One can be bought at Radio Shack or through Crown International.

Geleco Electronics: Thorncliffe Park Drive #2, Toronto, Ontario, Canada M4H 1H2; 416/421-5631.

Crown International: 1718 W. Mishawaka Road/PO Box 1000, Elkhart, IN 46515; 800/535-6289.

OTHER GREAT RESOURCES

Illusion in Art and Nature: R. L. Gregory & E. H. Gombrich. 1973, Charles Scribner's Sons.

Adaptive Coloration in Animals: H. B. Cott. 1940, Oxford University Press.

Mimicry in Plants and Animals: Wolfgang Wickler. 1968, McGraw-Hill.

Scientific Illustration: Z.T. Jastrzebski. 1985, Prentice-Hall.

Art Pac: The backpack for water colorists: lots of waterproof compartments for sketchbooks, paints and gear. Herbarium Supply, 3483 Edison Way, Menlo Park, CA 94025; 800/348-2338.

A water strider depends on the forces of surface tension to support its weight.

> "Natural history . . . is ecology expressed in the details of biology."
> —E. O. Wilson, *The Diversity of Life*

End of the twentieth century. Ecology theory flounders, ecology work flourishes, and ecopolitics ignores the science when it doesn't please the powers that be. From a naturalist's eye, small understandings undid grandiose mental structures. Ecochemistry was the greatest subversive. Gone are the days of rabbits and bobcats. Instead, please welcome chemical messengers like the odor trails of ants or chemical defenses like the tannins in oak leaves or chemical signals like the perfume of the female cockroach or chemical metabolisms like the microbial detox centers in many insect guts that render pesticides harmless. From flower scents to transforming tadpoles, the participation of atoms cannot be ignored. Species may just be gorgeous containers for the rearrangement of molecules. (Now only available in techno-read: *Introduction to Ecological Biochemistry*).

Ecologists are in search of new words and harmonies:

• Herbivory is out. Instead, the naturalist asks: does the animal clip, skeletonize, perforate, roll, spin, mine, rasp, or suck the leaf? Does it tunnel, strip or suck the bark? Does it sip nectar, eat pollen, or munch the flower's receptacle? Can ecologists really judge the availability of resources from the organism's point of view?

• "Balances of nature" and "equilibrium" are out. Instead, disturbances, erratic catastrophes, and pastiche habitats are the everyday happenings of ecology. Ecologists are looking for patterns in this world of chaotic events (some of them caused by ourselves). Some ecologists now believe the earth has no harmonies (see *Discordant Harmonies*, below). Others seek harmonies equivalent to the polyrhythms of African drumming or the vibrational overtones of Indian raga in the layerings of natural time.

• Tooth 'n' claw competition in a non-equilibrium world has lost favor. What do the rabbits and foxes do when the ecosystem tilts? Replacing old macho competition, long-term success may now come from teaming up. So, mutualisms are "in" as they provide for some stability: the inseparable termite-microbe or ubiquitous plant-fungi "organism."

• The teleconnection of global weather patterns as overriding shapers of ecosystems is "in." El Niño events, starting in the South Pacific, determine fire events in Yellowstone or the breeding of petrels off the coast of California. Just as the biochemical mediators of nature are invisible, so the weather patterns of the planet have been invisible — until satellite photos.

The new naturalist dwells in the invisibles of chemistry and planetary weather as well as the visibles. But no readable book exists on the new ecology. We are left with the Discover Channel and technical papers. So much for books. —PW

Feeding Strategy • Camouflage and Mimicry

Two beautifully illustrated intros to who-eats-who and how: the still visible parts of the eco-web. —PW

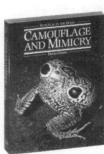

A frog approaches a bombardier beetle. The beetle squirts a hot spray of unpleasant liquid into the frog's face. The gasping frog sits back and the beetle escapes.
— Camouflage and Mimicry

Feeding Strategy
Jennifer Owen. University of Chicago Press, 1982; 160 pp. ISBN 0-226-64186-4
$12.50 ($15.50 postpaid)

Camouflage and Mimicry
Denis Owen. University of Chicago Press, 1982; 160 pp. ISBN 0-226-64188-0
$12.50 ($15.50 postpaid)

Both from Chicago Distribution Center, 11030 S. Langley Avenue, Chicago, IL. 60628; 800/621-2736

On Size and Life • Chemical Communication

These crossover books connect lay readers and scientists and multiple disciplines. Beautifully illustrated, with clear prose. Hints of futuristic naturalist-ecologist job descriptions. —PW

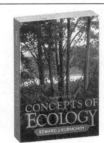

On Size and Life
Thomas McMahon & James Bonner. Scientific American Library, 1983; 255 pp. ISBN 0-7167-5000-7

Chemical Communication
(The Language of Pheromones) William C. Agosta. Scientific American Library, 04/1992; 192 pp. ISBN 0-7167-5036-8
Each $32.95 ($35.95 postpaid) from W. H. Freeman and Company, 4419 W. 1980 S., Salt Lake City, UT 84104; 800/488-5233

Concepts of Ecology

This is the ecology of the 1970s, clearly illustrated and told. —PW

•
In 1904 the sac fungus *Endothia parasitica* was accidently introduced into the US, being first discovered in the Bronx Zoo. In its native China *Endothia parasitica* is a parasite on the bark of the oriental chestnut and is kept in check by a variety of natural factors. In the United States, however, the majestic, towering American chestnut (*Cata-nea dentata*) proved no match for the fungus.

By 1950 about 3.6 million hectares of American chestnut trees were dead or dying. Except for adventitious shoots from the roots, the American chestnut was virtually extinct.

•
Ecology's roots extend to the origins of

Concepts of Ecology
Edward J. Kormondy. 1984; 288 pp. ISBN 0-13-166702-5
$37.80 ($40.80 postpaid) from Prentice-Hall Press/Order Processing Center, PO Box 11071, Des Moines, IA 50336-1071; 800/947-7700

humanity. Our ancestors had to have been students of their environment, else our species would have been extinguished.

WHAT PATTERN LASTS? (OTHER GREAT RESOURCES)

The deep search for patterns in natural history has taxed human cleverness. We now compare old photos to new to see if anything really has changed, or measure tree rings for fire stories. The best stuff has yet to come: long-term research on the same spot of Earth. Here are some of the excruciating techno-boring prose probes for patterns. That's all there is.

The Ecological Web (H. G. Andrewartha & L. C. Birch. University of Chicago Press, 1986). Natural history marries scientific method without losing its richness. Required reading for maniacal naturalists.

Biogeochemistry of a Forested Ecosystem (G. E. Likens. Springer-Verlag, 1991) and **Pattern and Process in a Forested Ecosystem** (F. H. Bormann & G. E. Likens. Springer-Verlag, 1991) . Two classics of invisible biogeochemistry and the vaporous past.

The Pattern of Animal Communities (Charles S. Elton, 1966. John Wiley & Sons; *Out of Print*). One of the few with a longer-term perspective of patchiness and populations. Elton is this century's great eco-thinker. His very readable classics are *Animal Ecology* and *The Ecology of Invasions by Animals and Plants*.

The Changing Mile (James Rodney Hastings & Raymond M. Turner. University of Arizona Press, 1965), **Second View** (Mark Klett, Ellen Manchester, Joann Verburg, Gordon Bushaw, & Rick Dingus. University of New Mexico Press. 1984), **Stopping Time** (Peter Goin. University of New Mexico Press, 1992). The three best books on retaking old photos from the same spot and comparing what happened (if anything).

Lake Sediments and Environmental History (Elizabeth Haworth & John Lund. University of Minnesota Press, 1984). A complex technique.

If you want to know a lake's history, try pollen samplings in the bottom layers or tracking erosion through the layers themselves.

Packrat Middens (Julio Betancourt, Thomas Van Devender & Paul Martin, Editors. University of Arizona Press, 1990). Packrats hoard whatever's nearby. They urinate on their nests, which fossilize into shiny elliptoids. The fossil middens show what grew in the local watershed. The only book on these midden detectives.

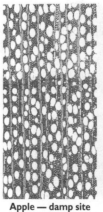

Apple — damp site   **Apple — dry site**

Tree Rings (Fritz Schweingruber. Kluwer Academic Pulblications, 1989). The only book.

Introduction to Ecological Biochemistry. J. B. Harborne. Academic Press, 1988.

Discordant Harmonies: A New Ecology for the Twenty-First Century. Daniel B. Botkin. Oxford University Press, 1992.

The Wealth of Nature. Donald Worster. Oxford University Press, 1993.

Forest Primeval. Chris Maser, 1994. Sierra Club Books.

Art and Physics

Science helps us understand how the world works. Art helps us interpret what reality means. So goes the common wisdom.

Leonard Shlain makes the bold case that art has always been a powerful if unacknowledged driving force behind science, rather than sideline commentary. He juxtaposes examples from the history of science, and a pattern seems to emerge: specific artists' visionary breakthroughs prepared everybody, including scientists, for the changes in thinking that scientists would introduce.

It is one thing to point out an intriguing but inconsequential relationship between artistic and scientific evolution, and quite another thing to insist that the process of art is integral to the progress of science — and furthermore, that both ways of seeing the world are not only complementary but hardwired into human brains. Dr. Shlain directs attention to the idea that there is no such thing as a primacy of art or physics: each discipline is half of a pair.

Is the world as we see it, or as we think it is? This issue was the crux of a two-thousand-year competition of ideas. Physics won. Philosophers and artists haven't gone away since Newton swept the field, but most people today agree that a cure for cancer or a doomsday weapon is more significant than a symphony or a sculpture.

Science has provided an overabundance of new ways of thinking. We all need to learn new ways to see, feel, and find meaning. —HLR

•

In the latter half of the nineteenth century, while scientists fidgeted uneasily at their inability to explain puzzling features of space, time, and light, Impressionist and post-Impressionist artists alike incorporated into their art eccentric images that challenged long-held notions about these same three

Art and Physics
Leonard Shlain.
Quill Books,
1991; 480 pp.
ISBN 0-688-123058
$12 ($13.50 postpaid) from
William Morrow /Wilmore Warehouse,
39 Plymouth Street, Fairfield, NJ 07004

elements. The twentieth century opened with Einstein's brilliant 1905 solution to one of physics' unsolved problems and, simultaneously, introduced three artists who would thrust modern art through a transformative barrier.

Early in their respective careers, Henri Matisse, Pablo Picasso, and Marcel Duchamp assaulted the art world with works that both announced and represented three radical movements: Fauvism, Cubism, and Futurism. (Although Duchamp, a French-

PRESENT
5 MILES PER HOUR

93,000 MILES PER SECOND

140,000 MILES PER SECOND

186,000 MILES PER SECOND
LIGHTSPEED

As one approaches the speed of light, the present expands until it encompasses both past and future. At lightspeed, time ceases to exist because it contains all change.

man, was not involved in the founding of Italian Futurism, his 1910 *Nude Descending a Staircase* is probably the most universally recognized image of this movement.) Fauvist painters were singing the praises of light in the form of color just as Einstein was

enthroning light as the quintessence of the universe. Cubism presented a new way to visualize space, which was the first creative alternative to Euclid's views in more than twenty-two hundred years. Einstein also proposed an alternative concept of space. Futurism declared war on the traditional modes used to represent time. By dilating the present into the past and the future, Futurist painters captured an idea that paralleled Einstein's lightspeed. It was an extraordinary coincidence that these three different art movements, each focusing on a separate element of the special theory of relativity, erupted synchronistically with Einstein's radical publication. In a strange way, it is as if the art world with forethought decided to fracture the trinity of space, time, and light to better understand each element in isolation. Within a few years clustered around 1905, an explosion of the eye accompanied a hyperinflation of the mind.

Doing Physics

This unusual book introduces "the moves, the rituals, the incantations" physicists invoke as they go about conceptualizing Nature. The lucid-but-loaded writing makes quite complex ideas accessible to the mathless reader. That reader had better be ready to work hard, though; the presentation presses the limit of what can be done with hard science candy-coated for popular consumption. The rewards are a better understanding of how physics is done, and insights that are readily adapted to "doing" other, not-necessarily-scientific disciplines. —JB

•

My plot is straightforward: to describe four dominant ways physicists conceive of the world, and to describe how they get at that world and find out about it. In this enterprise: (1) there is a division of labor; (2) things are made up of other things; (3) everything that is not forbidden will happen; (4) whatever happens, happens on a stage; and (5) we find out about the world by poking at it.

•

Now in the Big Bang cosmology, the universe might be taken to be an expanding gas of matter and field and energy and spacetime. As such, it is slowly cooling down (for that is what expanding gases do). And the various discontinuous transformations are analogized to well known behaviors such as freezing. So the Big Bang history is analogized to the corresponding behavior of well known substances, such as an ordinary gas or liquid or magnet. Hence, we have here what might be called an *analogy of substance*. For physicists, the world is always like something we already know quite well, something material and everyday. The macrocosm as we might conceive of it is a mirror of some quite mundane microcosm we already know, or perhaps the analogy goes the other way around.

Finally, physicists account for the appearance of something from nothing by employing models of *discontinuous* transformations as their pictures of Nature's dynamics. These models naturally allow for qualitative transformation without the need to provide, at least manifestly, a continuous con-

Doing Physics
(How Physicists Take Hold of the World)
Martin H. Krieger. 1992; 168 pp.
ISBN 0-253-33123-4
$9.95 ($11.95 postpaid) from Indiana University Press, 601 N. Morton Street, Bloomington, IN 47404; 800/842-6796

nection between something and nothing (and hence the especial attractiveness of transformations that are spontaneous as well). So when physicists take Nothing to be a relatively greater arbitrariness and symmetry, then Something need be just what is in accord with an orderliness that is sufficiently more restricted than and so incommensurable with Nothing's symmetry. And in this manner something arises from nothing.

Einstein for Duckhunters

Albert Menasco and I labored together on a job that chopped Abraham Lincoln's wife's family farm into a subdivision. Al was seventeen, a graduate student at MIT, working on mathematically mutating a basketball into a doughnut without piercing the skin, and on a set of formulae that would predict the motion of an ice cube dropped into a hot skillet. I was twenty-four, fresh out of the Pike County jail, Magnolia, Mississippi, trying to get back into graduate school so I could capitalize on having nearly memorized Yeats' vortical vision.

I was the chainsaw operator, hacking a road right-of-way through old-growth hardwoods that Mary Todd had climbed as a little girl. Al piled the slash in clearings, to be burned in the fall.

During our first lunch together, I asked Albert what he thought about while he was dragging brush, and he said that he'd spent the morning determining that all the humans on the planet

would fit in a cubic-mile box, which, when dropped into a Pacific trench, would have less than a millimeter's impact on sea level. Cheery stuff.

In an effort to change the subject, I asked about his family background. Al's father was an Italian immigrant, a student of Tesla's electromagnetic theories, who worked through the 1940s as a technician in the Princeton laboratories during Einstein's tenure there. He named his first son after Einstein.

I confessed my ignorance of the theory of relativity, figuring Al must have a handle on some of it. A duck flew by, headed for Walden Pond, and Albert launched into a grand synthesis between hunting ducks and applying Einstein's theories, some of which I can remember:

Einstein believed that the measurements of length, time, motion, and mass are not absolute, but depend on the relative velocity of the observer. If a

hunter is standing in a duck blind trying to kill a duck that is flying past, the hunter must lead the duck, shoot in front of it, so the shotgun pellets and the duck arrive at the same place at the same time. If the hunter is moving faster than the duck, from the back of a jeep, for instance, the hunter must shoot behind the duck.

A single shotgun pellet sitting on a duck's head will probably not kill the duck. But grant the pellet a little velocity relative to the duck's head, and the pellet picks up energy, and, in some sense, mass, so that, at enough velocity, the pellet-duck collision is fatal.

Not everything is relative in Einstein's duck blind. The speed of light remains constant independent of the motion of the observer. If a duck is flying toward us at half the speed of light with a flashlight taped to its beak, the light from the flashlight is still going about 186,282 miles per second. If the duck is flying away from us and shines the beam back, the light is traveling 186,282 miles per second. Energy somehow equals

mass times the speed of light squared.

Late that fall, after I had taught Al about motorcycles and drugs, the first snows fell, and we torched the brush piles. Half of them were sitting on an ancient peat bog. The fires burned down into underground seams that smoldered for years, leaving much of the Todd estate useless for human housing. —JD Smith

Universal Patterns • The Surface Plane

The Golden Mean. Fibonacci Numbers. Dynamic Rectangles. Spirals. Do you know what they are? Did you once but can't remember? There is plenty of reason to be interested — much of the natural world and a significant portion of classic architecture is proportioned according to these principles. They're even involved in the Fullerenes ("Buckyballs") and fivefold symmetry investigations that have received so much attention lately. The authors make the abstractions remarkably easy to comprehend by relating them to nature and art.

A companion book, **The Surface Plane,** *brings a similar accessibility to fractals and related phenomena.*

Two more books are on the way: **Structure in Space** *will take up Golden Solids and other spatial constructions.* **Malleable Space** *will attend to topological matters. I expect they will be equally lucid and well produced. —J. Baldwin*

Mathematical Snapshots

The most graphically insightful math book in print. Most math feeds proof; this lovely stuff feeds understanding, and is no less rigorous. If someone were going to see only one mathematics book in their lifetime, this would be the best. —SB

•

To determine the centroid of a stick, we place it horizontally on the edges of our palms and then we bring our hands closer together; finally they meet in the center of gravity. The stick never loses its equilibrium because when the centroid, which is initially between the palms, approaches one of them, the pressure on the nearer palm becomes many times greater than the pressure on the other palm; its product by the coefficient of friction must finally surpass the analogous product for the other palm; when this happens, the relative movement of the first palm ceases and the relative movement of the other one starts. This play continues alternately until both palms meet; the centroid is always between them and it is there at the final stage. The trick is done automatically without any conscious effort.

Mathematical Snapshots
Hugo Steinhaus. 1969; 311 pp.
ISBN 0-19-503267-5
$8.95 ($10.95 postpaid) from Oxford University Press/ Order Dept., 2001 Evans Road, Cary, NC 27513; 800/451-7556

Pi in the Sky

This ride through mathematics and philosophy asks the Big Questions. If our knowledge of the world (especially beyond our senses) is built on mathematical foundations, what holds up the foundations? Is mathematics since Gödel, Chaitin, et al. a set of self-referential squiggles, a useful but limited human invention, or a mystical link to the universe's real stuff? Barrow handles heavy subjects with a light touch; some of his trip's most enjoyable parts are its side roads: the history of counting; geometry and ritual; Marxist mathematics; theoreticians as strange as their theories. The book is intellectually exhilarating. It requires no math. —Michael K. Stone

•

One of the oddities about the origins of numbers and of counting is how little we find out about such things in the very places we would expect to learn most about them. No course of mathematics would ever consider the question. No history book delves into such matters. The origins of the Western world, the beginnings of civilization, or of culture and anatomy, of star-gazing and agriculture, or architecture and art, of all these things we find volume upon volume of evidence, speculation, and detail. But of the origin of counting there is next to nothing. We are going to take a look at the collection of facts.

•

Gödel was a strange man and seems to have become quite mentally deranged near

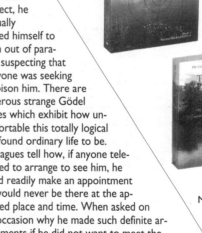

Pi in the Sky
(Counting, Thinking, and Being)
John D. Barrow. 1993; 317 pp.
ISBN 0-316-08259-7
$14.95 ($17.45 postpaid) from Little, Brown and Co./Order Dept., 200 West Street, Waltham, MA 02154; 800/343-9204

The art of finger reckoning: the finger-counting scheme of the Venerable Bede, drawn a thousand years after Bede by Jacob Leupold and published in Germany in 1727.

the end of his life. In effect, he gradually starved himself to death out of paranoia, suspecting that everyone was seeking to poison him. There are numerous strange Gödel stories which exhibit how uncomfortable this totally logical man found ordinary life to be. Colleagues tell how, if anyone telephoned to arrange to see him, he would readily make an appointment but would never be there at the appointed place and time. When asked on one occasion why he made such definite arrangements if he did not want to meet the people concerned, he replied that his procedure was the only one that guaranteed that he would not meet his visitor.

•

More than anything else, mathematics impresses upon us that the deepest ideas are hallmarked by the manner in which an assumption too mundane for anyone to question results in a conclusion so paradoxical that no one can believe it. And out of this growth it has shed the chrysalis of earthly application to emerge as something entirely different: more beautiful, more extensive, less encumbered than ever it was in its youth. In such a form it becomes the closest we have to a 'secret of the Universe'. Yet it is a secret with two sides. It is at once both the key which unlocks for us the unknown structure of the Universe, and the hidden kernel of reality that the Universe guards most impenetrably.

In *Skater,* **the outer dimensions of the painting consist of a Golden Rectangle. The horizontal and vertical lines in the armature connect Golden Cuts of the sides. Diagonals play an important role in defining shapes in space.**

Universal Patterns
(The Golden Relationship: Art, Math and Nature Book 1)
1983, 1992; 298 pp.
ISBN 0-9614504-4-4

The Surface Plane
(Book 2)
1992; 293 pp.
ISBN 0-9614504-2-8
Martha Boles & Rochelle Newman. Each $32.95 ($37.95 postpaid) from Pythagorean Press, PO Box 162, Bradford, MA 01835-0162
Book 3: *Structure In Space* due late 1994;
Book 4: *Malleable Space* due Summer 1995.

Fractals

Graphically presenting the concepts of chaos and self-similarity, "Fractals: An Animated Discussion" provides an excellent whole-brain introduction to the science of complex dynamical systems. Threaded on comments by Benoît Mandelbrot and Edward Lorenz, more than half the video consists of high-quality computer-generated animations of the Mandelbrot set, Julia sets, the "infinitely frayed boundaries" of the Cantor set, strange attractors, and other beasts from the land of mathematical complexity.

Our perceptual world is much more fractal than it is Euclidean. Look at anything long enough and it falls apart. Now, thanks to the processing power emerging from rapidly evolving computer systems, we can simulate fractal worlds that begin to approximate the textured and corrugated landscapes of "nature."

Animated fractal imagery is beautiful and truly hypnotic. With luck, our capacity to model fractal dimensions will also generate tools for "seeing" and understanding the vast scales at which we affect materiality. (It's about seven-

Fractals
(An Animated Discussion with Edward Lorenz and Benoit B. Mandelbrot)
63–minute video; $59.95 ($63.95 postpaid) from W. H. Freeman and Co., 4419 W. 1980 S., Salt Lake City, UT 84104; 800/488-5233

teen orders of magnitude from the atoms nanoengineers manipulate to the Earth's ozone layer.)

Some of the mathematics presented here is nontrivial, and anyone who wants to "understand" fractals has some serious thinking ahead. But even the most math-phobic will gain a visceral understanding of the field from this video. Even the music is based on

a simple fractal recursion. Whichever side of C. P. Snow's great divide you hail from, watch this, at least once — with the sound off, the color up, and your favorite molecules flexing those neural receptors.

Eye candy with radical depth and consequence. —BC Crandall

(NB: The same folks sell interactive Macintosh software, "The Beauty of Fractals Lab.")

Complexity • Complexity

Two simultaneous books, by esteemed science journalists, with identical titles, suggests that something is up. Indeed it is. The "sciences of complexity," particularly as they are focused, blended, and broadcast through the Santa Fe Institute, are an implosive frontier of science these years, and the questions and research are surprisingly accessible to lay understanding. Even two books don't cover all that's cooking, but they offer an intriguing sampler.

Mitchell Waldrop's book comes at the subject through the experience of a few of the main investigators at the Santa Fe Institute — notably economist Brian Arthur, theoretical biologist Stuart Kauffman, computer adaptivist John Holland, artificial-life creator Chris Langton — noting how the stimulation of their ideas on each other leads to the emergent understanding of emergent properties. The process is almost an example of itself. Of the two books, I prefer this one.

Complexity
(Life on the Edge of Chaos)
Roger Lewin. 1992; 256 pp.
ISBN 0-02-570485-0 $22 postpaid from Macmillan Publishing Co., 100 Front Street, Riverside, NJ 08075; 800/257-5755

Complexity
(The Emerging Science at the Edge of Order and Chaos)
M. Mitchell Waldrop. Touchstone Books, 1992; 380 pp. ISBN 0-671-87234-6 $12 ($15 postpaid) from Simon & Schuster/ Order Dept., 200 Old Tappan Road, Old Tappan, NJ 07675; 800/223-2336

Roger Lewin's focus is on evolution and complexity — "complex adaptive systems" — and maybe the evolution of complexity. He branches out from Santa Fe Institute to include discussions with field biologist Edward O. Wilson, Gaia theorist James Lovelock, and consciousness philosopher Daniel Dennett.

Computers have made formerly theoretical sciences into experimental sciences (model your idea and see if it runs), and new comfort with non-linear, chaotic systems means that the models and the real world are growing ever closer together. And formerly divergent disciplines are converging. Both are good news. —SB

●

Increasing returns, lock-in, unpredictability, tiny events that have immense historical consequences — "These properties of increasing-returns economics shocked me at first," says [Brian] Arthur. "But when I recognized that each property had a counterpart in the nonlinear physics I was reading, I got very excited. Instead of being shocked, I became fascinated." Economists had actually been talking about such things for generations, he learned. But their efforts had always been isolated and scattered. He felt as though he were recognizing for the first time that all these problems were the same problem. "I found myself walking into Aladdin's cave," he says, "picking up one treasure after another."

By the autumn, everything had fallen into place. On November 5, 1979, he poured it all out. At the top of one page of his notebook he wrote the words

"Economics Old and New," and under them listed two columns [see box below].

And so it went, for three pages. . . . In Arthur's new economics, the economic world would be part of the human world. It would always be the same, but it would never be the same. It would be fluid, ever-changing, and alive.

●

"I set the thing going, and left it to run overnight," Tom [Ray] said, recalling what obviously had been a tense but exquisite moment in his life. "I didn't sleep much." Tom had already glimpsed fragments of life in Tierra during the debugging process. He knew that something was going to happen, something interesting. But he had no way of predicting just how interesting it would be. "All hell broke loose," was how he described what had occurred overnight in his virtual world. "From the original ancestor, parasites very quickly evolved, then creatures that were immune to the parasites," said Tom. "Some of the descendants were smaller than the ancestral organism, some were bigger. There were hyperparasites, social creatures. I saw arms races, cheaters, there was —" Wait a minute, I interrupted, you have to explain these creatures to me. When Tom described himself as a naturalist of a virtual world, he meant it: the digital organisms were as real to him as the ant butterflies had been. —*Roger Lewin*

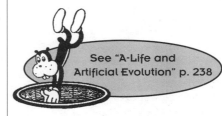

See "A-Life and Artificial Evolution" p. 238

Old Economics	New Economics
• Decreasing returns	• Much use of increasing returns
• Based on 19th-century physics (equilibrium, stability, deterministic dynamics)	• Based on biology (structure, pattern, self-organization, life cycle)
• People identical	• Focus on individual life; people separate and different
• If only there were no externalities and all had equal abilities, we'd reach Nirvana	• Externalities and differences become driving force. No Nirvana. System constantly unfolding.
• Elements are quantities and prices	• Elements are patterns and possibilities
• No real dynamics in the sense that everything is at equilibrium	• Economy is constantly on the edge of time. It rushes forward, structures constantly coalescing, decaying, changing.

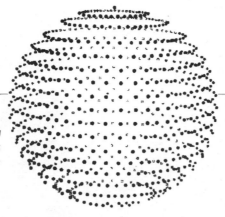

A New Era in Computation

Until recently, computer design rested on a small idea: "All things can be expressed as sequential events." You could approximate anything with a computer if you could slice it thinly enough and put it back together fast enough. For truly complex problems, you would need a faster sequential computer.

Parallel computing acknowledges that reality is not linear. Everything is not quantifiable. By linking many microprocessors for simultaneous operation, this technique enables computers to move beyond numbers. Conventional wisdom says that the radical decentralization of computing power is a natural and permanent path. Predictions of home-based virtual reality, integrated media, and spaceless electronic offices all assume that end users will control the processing. The book's final essay questions parallel computing and technology predictions as a group, pointing out the junkyard of grand prophecies and self-serving forecasts; at the same time, the essay offers intelligent and pragmatic technology forecasts that in themselves are worth the book's price. —John Sumser

A New Era in Computation
N. Metropolis & Gian-Carlo Rota, Editors. 1993; 241 pp. ISBN 0-262-63154-7 $13.95 ($16.95 postpaid) from The MIT Press/Order Dept., 55 Hayward Street, Cambridge, MA 02142; 800/356-0343

•

Complex adaptive systems are so intricate that there is little hope of a coherent theory without the controlled experiments that a massively parallel computer makes possible. At the same time, in an era this complex, experiments unguided by an appropriate theoretical framework usually amount to little more than "watching the pot boil." Sustained progress outside the guidelines of a theory is as unlikely as attempting modern experimental physics outside the framework of theoretical physics. After all, no system currently under investigation in physics is as complex as a full-fledged complex adaptive system. We need experiments to inform theory, but without theory all is lost.

•

New techniques are invariably applied first to older, well-understood problems. But the real future of the methodology lies in applications where traditional methods have not been successful at all: phenomena for which no fundamental partial differential equations have been discovered, only patchwork descriptions. Many of these exist in disciplines now considered soft sciences. I have in mind large-scale economic models, sociological schemes, molecular cell dynamics, and the like.

The fact that one can take the origin of motion either at the inmost center or at the very top of the sphere leads one to think that there may be some great mystery hidden in these true and wonderful results, a mystery related to the creation of the universe (which is said to be spherical in shape), and related also to the seat of the first cause [*prima causa*].

In these systems complexity is usually both emergent and Byzantine. This means that organized extended structures evolve and dominate a system, and the structures themselves are so complex that, when first seen, they produce a sense of beauty followed by a deep feeling of unease. One instinctively realizes that the analytic tools that worked so well in the past are going to be of little use. We will call such large nonlinear systems with emergent and Byzantine behavior *monster systems*. The typical future applications for lattice gas/cellular automation formalisms and machines will be in the search for workable models of important systems for which no such models are currently known.

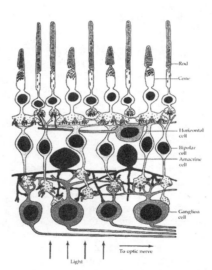

Comparison between the organization of biological and silicon retinae.

Above, diagram showing a close-up of a tiny region on the retina that illustrates several prominent cell types. Below, diagram of the silicon retina showing the resistive network similar in its function to the array of horizontal cells in the retina: a single pixel element is illustrated in the circular window.

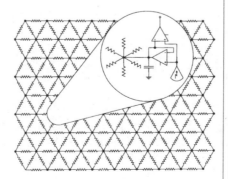

OTHER GREAT RESOURCES

Computerization & Controversy: Value Conflicts & Social Choices. Charles Dunlop & Rob Kling, Editors. 1991, Academic Press.

Global Network

Are computers appropriate technology? The computer industry savages the environment to make a product that can see the world only as numbers. Computers use rare elements, involve toxic chemicals, and consume energy.

On the other hand, computers are powerful tools in the hands of ecologists, activists, scientists, and planners. Meaningful scientific progress on environmental problems requires the modeling and monitoring capacity of the world's ever-growing computing power.

Do the benefits of computer technology outweigh the costs? Worldwatch Institute is particularly well positioned to approach this key question with the necessary nonpartisanship. Their scholarship, science, and journalism have won them an impeccable reputation, and the Institute's reports on global environmental crises qualify them as skeptics regarding technologies that others embrace enthusiastically.

Author John Young weighs the ecological benefits of modeling and monitoring against the environmental degradation caused by computer manufacturing. He looks at the numbers of tons of paper and pollutants, examines the ways computers have become essential to sustainable economies in developing countries, and shows the possibility of a path to "global thinking." Computers alone won't solve our problems. But we might have reached the point where our problems are too complex, too global, too pressing to tackle them without computers. —John Sumser

•

The capacity of the computer to help us bridge the critical gap between information and knowledge is illustrated by the recent history of climate science. Scientists have theorized since 1896 that emissions of carbon dioxide from the burning of fossil fuels could warm the global atmosphere. Their concerns grew in the fifties, sixties and seventies, as increasing atmospheric concentrations of carbon dioxide and other gases were documented. It was not until the early 1980s, however—when computers sufficiently powerful for modeling the complex behavior of the atmosphere became available— that they were able to test their theories. Supercomputers at such centers as the Geophysical Fluid Dynamics Laboratory in Princeton, New Jersey, and the Goddard Institute of Space Studies in New York, have been programmed to simulate the effects of increased greenhouse gas concentrations on the global climate. In minutes, they perform calculations that would take an unaided scientist a lifetime or more.

•

The most intriguing fact about computers is that they vastly increase our ability to control. In this, they have so far followed the pattern of all human history, as each new technology has been turned by its users to the control of nature or other people, rather than of their own increasingly unsustainable behavior.

Global Network
(Computers in a Sustainable Society)
John Young, 1993; 57 pp.
ISBN 1-878071-17-3
$5 postpaid from Worldwatch Institute, 1776 Massachusetts Avenue NW, Washington, DC 20036-1904

Mirror Worlds

Imagine that you have the power to fly above a city, to swoop down every street and alley, in and out of windows, through the doorways of every public building. Imagine having access to all the information pertaining to, or hidden within, those physical structures, the ability to scan the blueprints for those buildings you pass by, and the power to peek at the financial accounts of those businesses you see and to monitor traffic flow and energy and resource use. "Mirror Worlds" are online, updatable, 3-D geographic information systems that will provide instantaneous, accurate images of cities, bureaucracies — any complex system that can be graphed or pictured.

The first real Mirror World probably will be in Singapore, where the government is converting all its databases into GIS and installing a complete fiber optic communication system. A Singapore Mirror World raises questions about the dark side of such a technology, questions that I wish the author had explored in depth. Imagine what a secret police could do with a Mirror World where the city watches the citizens. Realtime models could become invaluable tools for managing the complexities of twenty-first century metropolises. Or they could be nightmares. Best we think about them now. —George P. Mokray

•

You can use the Mirror World's archival propensities to discover the history or background of anything that concerns you. What has the zoning board been doing lately? How did the school board membership get to be this way, what is the history of a particular piece of pending legislation — what was the whole city like, this time last year? Last decade? Merely run the thing backwards through time, using your history key and the time-travel-velocity knob. You can restore this whole dense, multi-layered image-world to any point in its past. You're not guaranteed to get the *whole* picture in every detail; some details may have been forgotten. By and large, though, you can explore the past in the same way you explore the present, and make some attempt to figure out how we got here.

Mirror Worlds
(or The Day Software Put the Universe in a Shoebox)
David Gelernter, 1992; 236 pp. ISBN 0-19-507906-X
$12.95 ($14.95 postpaid) from Oxford University Press/Order Dept., 2001 Evans Road, Cary, NC 27513; 800/451-7556

The Interpretation of Cultures

Around a hundred thousand years ago, something blasted our branch of primates out of some very old behavior patterns and moved us irrevocably into something radically different. Instead of just passing along genetic traits, we began passing along alphabets, astronomical observations, tool-making lore, rules for behaving in the presence of your wife's uncle: Culture. What is culture? How did it originate? What holds it together?

Anthropology has been a grail quest for the deepest generalities that connect every member of our species, despite the particularities of Islam or suburbia, tribes or corporations. By analyzing many different examples of human behavior, social scientists sought to understand these general principles through a process of induction; ethnography, the real-world basis for the symbolic calisthenics of anthropologists, was the raw data. That was the conventional wisdom before Geertz.

Clifford Geertz insists that ethnographers engage in "thick description," more akin to literature than chemical analysis; that there is no universality, but that the truth about human nature is deeply connected with our adaptability, our capacity for becoming that which our culture tells us we can become. —HLR

•

The "control mechanism" view of culture begins with the assumption that human thought is basically both social and public — that its natural habitat is the house yard, the marketplace, and the town square. Thinking consists not of "happenings in the head" (though happening there and elsewhere are necessary for it to occur) but of a traffic in what have been called, by G. H. Mead and others, significant symbols — words for the most part but also gestures, drawings, musical sounds, mechanical devices like clocks, or natural objects like jewels — anything, in fact, that is disengaged from its mere actuality and used to impose meaning upon experience. From the point of view of any particular individual, such symbols are largely given. He finds them already current in the community when he is born, and they remain, with some additions, subtractions, and particular alterations he may or may not have had a hand in, in circulation after he dies. While he lives he uses them, or some of them, sometimes deliberately and with care, most often spontaneously and with ease, but always with the same end in view: to put a construction upon the events through which he lives, to orient himself within "the ongoing course of experienced things," to adopt a vivid phrase of John Dewey's.

Man is so in need of such symbolic sources of illumination to find his bearings in the world because the nonsymbolic sort that are constitutionally ingrained in his body cast so diffused a light. The behavior patterns of lower animals are, at least to a much greater extent, given to them with their physical structure; genetic sources of information order their actions with much narrower ranges of

The Interpretation of Cultures
Clifford Geertz. Basic Books Inc., 1977; 480 pp. ISBN 0-465-09719-7
$15 ($17.75 postpaid) from HarperCollins Publishers/Direct Mail, PO Box 588, Dunmore, PA 18512; 800/331-3761

variation, the narrower and more thoroughgoing the lower the animal. For man, what are innately given are extremely general response capacities, which, although they make possible far greater plasticity, complexity, and, on the scattered occasions when everything works as it should, effectiveness of behavior, leave it much less precisely regulated. This, then, is the second face of our argument: Undirected by cultural patterns — organized systems of significant symbols — man's behavior would be virtually ungovernable, a mere chaos of pointless acts and exploding emotions, his experience virtually shapeless. Culture, the accumulated totality of such patterns, is not just an ornament of human existence but — the principal basis of its specificity — an essential condition for it.

Local Knowledge

The cracks between worldviews, the elements of worldviews, the parallel universes of worldviews, and the institution-warping power of worldviews seem to be Geertz territory.

Local Knowledge is a spearhead, driven deep into the contemporary controversy over the meaning of meaning by an anthropologist who thinks about matters anthropologists never thought about before. Most importantly for the nonspecialist, Clifford Geertz knows how to write a spellbinding sentence about the most esoteric topic. —HLR

•

To see ourselves as others see us can be eye-opening. To see others as sharing a nature with ourselves is the merest decency. But it is from the far more difficult achievement of seeing ourselves amongst others, as a local example of the forms human life has locally taken, a case among cases, a world among worlds, that the largeness of mind, without which objectivity is self-congratulation and tolerance a sham, comes. If interpretive anthropology has any general office in the world it is to keep reteaching this fugitive truth.

•

We like to think that the reality principle is good for us, except perhaps when it finally kills us. But a serious effort to define ourselves by locating ourselves among different others — others neither distanced as Martians, discredited as Primitives, nor disarmed as universal Everypersons, bent like us on sex and survival — involves quite genuine perils, not the least of which are intellectual entropy and moral paralysis. The double perception that ours is but one voice among many and that, as it is the only one we have, we must needs speak with it, is very difficult to maintain. What has been well called the long conversation of man-

Local Knowledge
(Further Essays in Interpretive Anthropology)
Clifford Geertz. Basic Books Inc., 1985; 256 pp. ISBN 0-465-04162-0
$15 ($17.75 postpaid) from HarperCollins Publishers/Direct Mail, PO Box 588, Dunmore, PA 18512; 800/331-3761

kind may be growing so cacophonous that ordered thought of any sort, much less the turning of local forms of legal sensibility into reciprocal commentaries, mutually deepening, may become impossible. But however that may be, there is, so it seems to me, no choice. The primary question, for any cultural institution anywhere, now that nobody is leaving anybody alone and isn't ever going to, is not whether everything is going to come seamlessly together or whether, contrariwise, we are all going to persist sequestered in our separate prejudices. It is whether human beings are going to continue to be able, in Java or Connecticut, through law, anthropology, or anything else, to imagine principled lives they can practically lead.

Always Coming Home

What better way to spark your thinking about the complex whole systems we call cultures than to invent one of your own? The visionary novelist Ursula Le Guin provides the model here.

Always Coming Home is an "archaeology of the future" about a people living in California's Napa Valley sometime after the traumatic destruction of our society. What sets this novel apart from other futurist or fantasy writing is its loving devotion to the concrete particulars of Kesh culture. The main story takes only about a fifth of the book. The remainder invites us to immerse ourselves in Kesh poems, stories, wordplay, computer archives, rhymed insults, oral histories, ceremonies, instructions for dying. There are more than a hundred drawings by Margaret Chodos of Kesh scenes and artifacts; an audiotape of Kesh music (by Oregon composer Todd Barton) is available by mail order.

The book shows the way a whole grows from many parts; it embodies the possibility of appreciating the pattern without losing sight of the pieces. It points to the clues by which cultures reveal themselves and sets me to asking what pieces I would offer an archaeologist bent on building a picture of the culture in which I live.
—Michael K. Stone

•
A VAUNTING
From the town of Tachas Touchas.

The musicians of Tachas Touchas
make flutes of the rivers, make drums of the hills.
The stars come out to listen to them.
People open the doors of the Four Houses,
they open the windows of the rainbow,

Always Coming Home
Ursula K. Le Guin. Bantam Books/Spectra, 1985; 562 pp.
ISBN 0-553-26280-7
$5.99 ($8.49 postpaid) from Bantam, Doubleday, Dell/Fulfillment Dept., 2451 South Wolf Road, Des Plaines, IL 60018; 800/223-6834

Music and Poetry of the Kesh
Todd Barton (music) & Ursula K. Le Guin (lyrics)
$12 postpaid from Valley Productions, PO Box 3220, Ashland, OR 97520

to listen to the musicians of Tachas Touchas.

A RESPONSE
From the town of Madidinou.

The musicians of Tachas Touchas
make flutes of their noses, make drums of their buttocks.
The fleas run away from them.
People shut the doors in Madidinou,
they shut the windows in Sinshan,
when they hear the musicians of Tachas Touchas coming.

•
SAYINGS

If there was only one of anything, it would be the end of the world.

Judgment is poverty.

If you don't teach machines and horses to do what you want in their way they'll teach you to do what they want in your way.

Owning is owing, having is hoarding.

Like and different are quickening words, brooding and hatching. Better and worse are eggsucking words, they leave only the shell.

Anthropology — Its Demise

Anthropology started with colonialism. The conquerors said: "These people are weird. Better to know them in order to control them." Anthro was a more compassionate tool than genocide but it carried, and continues to carry, the karma of conquest (see Cultural Survival, pp. 72-73).

Twenty-first-century anthropology turns its tools on itself. De-program yourself from your own culture. See the weirdness of your own household or workplace or — most important — what mental and economic attachments push your culture into military or intellectual conquest. If you're a Christian, argue why the Hopi religion is preferable. If you're an American, argue for the benefits of living in Ethiopia. Not so easy.

Anthropology remains a crucial study, but not as an isolated discipline. Anthros need to do something else after they study anthropology. In the United States, anthros should be required to serve in public office — just to see if their insights about power and culture really make any sense. All anthros need to speak a non-Indo-European language and to study novels.

Anthropology still provides certain mental tools that can free you from cultural pain and suffering (see *The Savage Mind*, page 38). These "attachments" include kinship (the need to do some dastardly, counterproductive deed because of biological or fictive family), taboos (the need to avoid certain words, ideas, or deeds even if they would restore kindness or peace or justice), rites of passage (the need to understand and celebrate birth, adulthood, death), and "non-everyday experience" (a.k.a. the "exotic" or strange, be it music, psychedelics, art, clothes, or customs). —PW

American Ways

The fish is said to be the last one to recognize the water. **American Ways** *charts US cultural waters to prepare international students for the strangeness they will encounter there. It's an eye-opener. The biggest surprises are the assumptions and practices we take so much for granted that we have stopped noticing them. See also DeToqueville's* **Democracy In America,** *p. 29.* —Michael K. Stone

•

Many Americans do not display the same degree of respect for their parents that people in more traditional or family-oriented societies commonly display. They have the conception that it was a sort of historical or biological accident that put them in the hands of particular parents, that the parents fulfilled their responsibilities to the children when the children were young, and now that the children have reached the "age of independence" the close child-parent tie is loosened, if not broken.

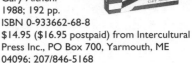

American Ways
(A Guide for Foreigners to the United States)
Gary Althen.
1988; 192 pp.
ISBN 0-933662-68-8
$14.95 ($16.95 postpaid) from Intercultural Press Inc., PO Box 700, Yarmouth, ME 04096; 207/846-5168

•

When they are in a situation where physical contact is unavoidable, Americans will typically try to draw in their shoulders and arms so as to minimize the amount of space they occupy. They will tolerate contact on the outsides of their arms when their arms are hanging straight down from their shoulders, but contacts with other parts of the body make them extremely anxious. When they are in a tightly crowded situation, such as a full elevator ("lift") or bus, they will generally stop talking or will talk only in very low voices. Their discomfort is easy to see.

Kinship

Just do it. Learn the symbols from The Manual for Kinship Analysis *(rather archaic, but the only simple kinship manual) and chart your own kin or a friend's. Remember to include "fictive" kinship in another color. Fictive kin are those aunts and uncles or cousins or bros that are not blood-related. Remarkable discussions result. Your aunt's former husband married a divorced aunt from the other side of the family? The first gay in the family was in 1940! He had a stable household for thirty years!*

We can only remember three generations, Aborigines know seven. I'm a street kid with no biological family but, dude, I got brothers.

Kinship and Marriage *will show you that no kinship chart is isolated from the exchange of humans by marriage, children, or economics. It remains a stunning survey of the planet's complex exchanges despite a rather naive attachment to structured households. After you've made your chart, figure out your own exchanges: who got the kittens from whom? How did inheritance change the kinship relations? Did the dope or homemade jam get passed around? Who sends Christmas cards to whom, and why or why not?*

The Nuer *is the classic of kin and cattle exchanges in the ecology of the planet's largest inland swamp.* As I Lay Dying *is anthropology challenged by the more human insights of a great novelist. The lines between fact and fiction are human-drawn. Good stories make for good kinship. No good scholarly books on American kinship exist. Try your library for* Uncertain Terms.

For deeper self-probing, go to The Source; *read* The Tape-Recorded Interview *and tape members of the kin chart who surprised you.* —PW

•

White ox good is my mother
And we the people of my sister,
The people of Nyariau Bul.
As my black-rumped white ox,
When I went to court the winsome lassie,
I am not a man whom girls refuse.
We court girls by stealth in the night,
I and Kwejok
Nyadeang. —*The Nuer*

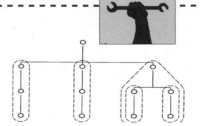

Three lines begin in the second generation and a fourth line has arisen in the third. If the oldest female ancestor shown were forgotten, then there would be at least three lineages.

It is tempting to think that many peoples have kept lineage organization intact by substituting mythical ancestors for forgotten ancestors. That is, many peoples do relate their oldest known ancestor (the lineage founder) to a mythical being who is ancestral to other lineage founders.

—*The Manual for Kinship Analysis*

Manual For Kinship Analysis. Ernest Schusky. 1965, 1983; 104 pp. ISBN 0-8191-3493-7 $14.50 ($17.50 postpaid) from University Press of America, 4720 Boston Way, Lanham, MD 20706; 800/462-6420

Kinship and Marriage: An Anthropological Perspective. Robin Fox. 1967, 1984, Cambridge University Press.

The Nuer. (A Description of the Modes of Livelihood and Political Institutions of a Nilotic People). Edward S. Evans-Pritchard. 1940; ISBN 0-19-500322-5 $15.95 ($17.95 postpaid) from Oxford University Press/Order Dept., 2001 Evans Road, Cary, NC 27513; 800/451-7556

As I Lay Dying. William Faulkner. 1991, Random House, Inc.

Uncertain Terms: Negotiating Gender in American Culture. Faye Ginsburg & Anna Tsing, Editors. 1992, Beacon Press.

Rites of Passage

When is an embryo human? At conception? At three months? At birth? After it is named or has functional sexual organs? America is a lost tribe on the subject. When is a child an adult? (No war for the boys; few or no children for the girls.) After the first menstruation ceremony on a full moon?

Commercials want everyone to always look between twenty-five and thirty. America has no generally accepted rite of passage. Rites of Passage *is the classic about a time when it seemed to all make sense.* Generations *is an attempt to understand*

Sound and Sentiment

A saxophone player goes to New Guinea and writes about his emotions (a taboo subject of anthros), music, and birdsong. The best music-in-culture book. Full of weeping doves reminding families of their love for each other. —PW

Sound and Sentiment
(Birds, Weeping, Poetics and Song in Kaluli Expression) Steven Feld. 1990; 312 pp. ISBN 0-8122-1299-1 $19.95 ($22.45 postpaid) from University of Pennsylvania Press, PO Box 4836, Hampden Sta., Baltimore, MD 21211-4836; 800/445-9880

the passage between adults and children in the history of the United States.

Celebrations *asks: in the twenty-first century, will every individual be a tribe?* —PW

Rites of Passage. Arnold Van Gennep. Monika B. Vizedon & Gabrielle L. Caffee, translators. 1961, University of Chicago Press.

Generations: The History of America's Future, 1584-2069. William Strauss & Neil Howe. 1992, William Morrow and Co.

Celebrations: Studies in Festivity and Ritual. Victor Turner, Editor. 1982, Smithsonian Institution Press (Out of Print).

Taboos

How many Americans share their IRS forms (Here, see mine!)? How many corporations open their pollutant control data to the public? How many men walk down the street holding hands? Taboos are rampant. They are dangerous. They help define the "purity" of one people vs. another. You don't hear the president say to the ambassador from Israel: "Hey, bro', take five." Spotting taboos is a mental exercise. To break taboos is to become David Bowie, or an asshole. In Pigs for the Ancestors, *taboos serve an ecological function.* —PW

Pigs for the Ancestors: Ritual in the Ecology of a New Guinea People. Roy Rappaport. 1984, Yale University Press.

Purity and Danger: An Analysis of Concepts of Pollution and Taboo. Mary Douglas. 1966, 1970, Praeger Publishers (Out of Print).

Language, Thought and Reality: Selected Writings of Benjamin Lee Whorf. John B. Carroll, Editor. 1956, MIT Press.

The Source

Simply the best genealogy book to get if you buy only one. It goes into great detail about where to look, and even where not to look. For instance, it tells you not to count on finding military records from 1912 to 1959, because a disastrous fire burned 80 percent of them in 1973. For additional books, software and indices, start with the free Ancestry Catalog. —Bob Mitchell

•

In family plots, it is frequently possible to determine family relationships from the relative positions of the graves. Usually the dominant couple or parents are in the center with a large stone while children have smaller stones. Positioning of graves can also indicate national origins. Scandinavians seem to position plots with the father in the lower right-hand corner, the mother next to him, with children and spouses placed in order of death clockwise around a large stone bearing the family name.

The Source
(A Guidebook of American Genealogy)
Arlene H. Eakle & Johni Cerny, Editors. 1984; 786 pp. ISBN 0-916489-00-0 $39.95 ($43.95 postpaid)

Ancestry Catalog (free)
Both from Ancestry, PO Box 476, Salt Lake City, UT 84110; 800/531-1790

The Tape-Recorded Interview

Some of your local history is in records, but a lot more of it is in minds. Here's how to ensure it's in both. When you're an old geezer, wouldn't you like to be asked what really happened back in 1993? —SB

The Tape-Recorded Interview
(A Manual for Field Workers in Folklore and Oral History)
Edward D. Ives. University of Tennessee Press, 1980; 144 pp. ISBN 0-87049-291-8 $6.95 ($9.95 postpaid) from Chicago Distribution Center, 11030 S. Langley Avenue, Chicago, IL 60628; 800/621-2736

Shango is the Yoruba god of thunder. He is virile and hardy, violent and just. He punishes liars, thieves, and lawbreakers.

NDIVIDUALS DREAM; cultures create mythologies. From Zeus to Satan to Wonder Woman, the characters who emerge from different cultures in different epochs are clues to the nature of human beings and the functioning of human civilizations. —HLR

The Way of the Animal Powers

This formidable work of art and scholarship concerns the myths of the first peoples — the hunter-gatherers of our ancestry and of today. Their images, their beliefs, are deeply sophisticated and as troubling and inspiring as the reader will let them be. The medium, arch-mythologist Joseph Campbell, is welcoming you to a long night's journey. Maps abound, along with some of the best reproductions yet of mythic creatures both famous and heretofore little known. —SB

●

The male initiation rites of the Ona were conducted in a special lodge of the men's society, the *kloketen*, from which women were excluded; and associated with the mystifications of this institution were a number of such Hallowe'en spooks as we see here. These apparitions would appear from time to time, ranging through the bush of areas about the men's house, and any woman or child seeing one or more of them was to suppose that they were the inhabitants of the *kloketen* with whom the men held converse

in their meetings. An important moment in the initiations of a boy took place when he was compelled to get up and wrestle with one of these characters, who would let the youngster put him down, after which the masquerade was uncovered, and the boy turned into a man. There was a legend of the *kloketen* having been originally of the women, but taken and kept from them by the men.

The Way of the Animal Powers
(Historical Atlas of World Mythology series, Volume 1)
Joseph Campbell.
HarperReference, 1988
Part 1: Mythologies of the Primitive Hunters & Gatherers. 140 pp. ISBN 0-06-096348-4
Part 2: Mythologies of the Great Hunt. 176 pp. ISBN 0-06-096349-2

Each $24.95 ($27.70 postpaid) from HarperCollins Publishers/Direct Mail, PO Box 588, Dunmore, PA 18512; 800/331-3761

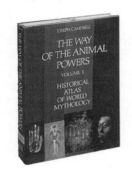

Tangaroa generating gods and men. Wooden image from a temple on Rurutu Island of the Austral Group.

Mythologies

Mythology is a young science; these volumes constitute dispatches from its creative frontier. Essays by nearly one hundred leading scholars elucidate shifting emphases, hypotheses arising from new data, reinterpretations of familiar stories. Plenty of rich, primary material is included, some — Mongolian, Turkish, Vietnamese — largely unknown to Western readers.

Read Joseph Campbell for his quest for universal archetypes. As a counterpoint, read these intellectual heirs of Claude Lévi-Strauss and Georges Dumézil for their careful attention to the specific mythic systems that undergird and animate the beliefs, institutions, and social dynamics of particular times and places (including, of course, our own). —Michael K. Stone

●

To "live" myths thus implies a truly "religious" experience, for it is distinct from the

ordinary experience of daily life. This experience is "religious" because it is a reenactment of fabulous, exalting, meaningful events; one is present once again at the creative works of the Supernatural Beings. Mythical events are not commemorated; they are repeated, reiterated. The characters in myth are brought forth and made present; one becomes their contemporary. One no longer lives in chronological time but in primordial Time, the Time when the event *took place for the first time*. This is why we can speak of the "strong time" of myth: it is the prodigious, "sacred" Time, when something *new*, something *strong*, and something *meaningful* was made fully manifest. To relive that time, to reintegrate it as often as possible, to be present once again at the spectacle of divine works, to rediscover the Supernatural Beings and relearn their lesson of creation — such is the desire that can be read implicitly in all ritual repetitions of myths. In sum, myths reveal that the world, man, and life have a supernatural origin and history, and that this history is meaningful, precious, and exemplary.

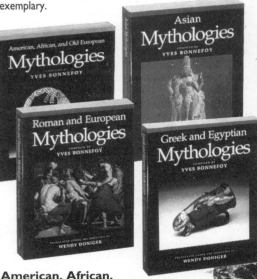

American, African, and Old European Mythologies
274 pp. ISBN 0-226-06457-3
Roman and European Mythologies
319 pp. ISBN 0-226-06455-7
Asian Mythologies
376 pp. ISBN 0-226-06456-5
Greek and Egyptian Mythologies
272 pp. ISBN 0-226-06454-9
Yves Bonnefoy & Wendy Doniger. University of Chicago Press, 1991, 1993; Asian Mythologies $27 ($30 postpaid); all others $25 ($28 postpaid) from Chicago Distribution Center, 11030 S. Langley Avenue, Chicago, IL 60628; 800/621-2736

The Hero with a Thousand Faces

According to Joseph Campbell, there is only one story in the world, retold in many guises. Whether it is cloaked in Finnish or Polynesian language or imagery, the plot of the monomyth is always and everywhere the same: A hero is drawn away from the path of normal life (sometimes by a friendly gnome or mysterious stranger), falls into a quest, travels to the other world, suffers an ordeal, gains a prize, and returns with the prize to the world of his origins. Hopping from Bantu stories to Inuit mythology, Campbell strips away the masks and shows the Hero to be a cultural code: the universal algorithm for transcending mundane consciousness and plugging into the main starry dynamo of Mind. —HLR

●

The hero, therefore, is the man or woman who has been able to battle past his personal and local historical limitations to the generally valid, normal human forms. Such a one's visions, ideas, and inspirations come pristine from the primary springs of human life and thought. Hence they are eloquent, not of the present, disintegrating society and psyche, but of the unquenched source through which society is reborn. The hero has died as a modern man; but as eternal

The Hero with a Thousand Faces
Joseph Campbell. Princeton University Press, 1990; 439 pp. ISBN 0-691-01784-0 $12.95 ($15.95 postpaid) from California/Princeton Fulfillment Services, 1445 Lower Ferry Road, Ewing, NJ 08618; 800/777-4726

man — perfected, unspecific, universal man — he has been reborn. His second solemn task and deed therefore (as Toynbee declares and as all the mythologies of mankind indicate) is to return then to us, transfigured, and teach the lesson he has learned of life renewed.

●

This is an example of one of the ways in which the adventure can begin. A blunder — apparently the merest chance — reveals an unsuspected world, and the individual is drawn into a relationship with forces that are not rightly understood. As Freud has shown, blunders are not the merest chance. They are the result of suppressed desires and conflicts. They are ripples on the surface of life, produced by unsus-

pected springs. And these may be very deep — as deep as the soul itself. The blunder may amount to the opening of a destiny. Thus it happens, in this fairy tale, that the disappearance of the ball is the first sign of something coming for the princess, the frog is the second, and the unconsidered promise is the third.

As a preliminary manifestation of the powers that are breaking into play, the frog, coming up as it were by miracle, can be termed the "herald"; the crisis of his appearance is the "call to adventure." The herald's summons may be to live, as in the present instance, or, at a later moment of the biography, to die. It may sound the call to some high historical undertaking. Or it may mark the dawn of religious illumination. As apprehended by the mystic, it marks what has been termed "the awakening of the self." In the case of the princess of the fairy tale, it signified no more than the coming of adolescence. But whether small or great, and no matter what the stage or grade of life, the call rings up the curtain, always, on a mystery of transfiguration — a rite, or moment, of spiritual passage, which, when complete, amounts to a dying and a birth. The familiar life horizon has been outgrown; the old concepts, ideals, and emotional patterns no longer fit; the time for the passing of a threshold is at hand.

Here are the tools we prefer for developing your own mental map of the economic ecosystem. They range across the political spectrum, deliberately chosen for their ability to make you reconsider your own conventional wisdom (whatever that is). Economics, to be effective, should help us cope not just with how to allocate resources, but how to live right. These books do. For what to do about money in your own life, see the Livelihood section, beginning on page 305. —Art Kleiner

Economic Principals

*David Warsh is like a great sportswriter who somehow ended up on the business pages. (Early on, he compares Milton Keynes to Babe Ruth.) This collection of his **Boston Globe** columns and book reviews is the most wide-ranging, readable, insightful introduction to the economic landscape in print. It covers the views of economists from Marxists to rabid free-marketeers, plus the gossip they've provoked and the broader context of their lives. Occasionally, Warsh permits himself to slip into jargon, but you come away with a feel for this profession, dominated by a few men who talk mainly to each other and who "scramble for the attention of politicians." He has a knack for describing the pivotal, destiny-changing economic moments of our time — like the 1958 dinner party where Robert Coase convinced the University of Chicago economics department (including Milton Friedman) that anything markets could do government could do better. "The intellectual underpinnings of everything from accident law to takeover regulation to the structuring of environmental pollution requirements have been rethought in the last 30 years as a result of the conversions that took place that night."* —Art Kleiner

●
There is some reason to think that a study by Paul Asquith, David W. Mullins Jr., and Eric D. Wolff did what the indictment of Michael Milken earlier didn't — put the junk bond market into a nosedive, causing several billion dollars in value to evaporate from the surface of the $180 billion market in a few days of trading last week — merely by persuasively suggesting that the real rate of default on junk bonds was as much as 10 or 15 times higher than previously had been thought. . . . Asquith & Co. stumbled onto a fascinating wrinkle — that the junk-bond market was growing so explosively that, for all intents and purposes, ordinary calculations of the default rate amounted to a kind of pyramid scheme, in which the new money coming into the game was enough to disguise the effect of old money leaving.

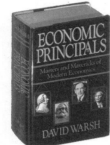

Economic Principals
David Warsh. Free Press, 1993; 244 pp.
ISBN 0-02-933996-0
$29.95 ($32.90 postpaid) from Macmillan Publishing Co., 100 Front Street Riverside, NJ 08075; 800/257-5755

The Next Economy

Economic civilization is going around a corner the like of which it's never seen before. Customers and citizens and adaptive businesses are leading the way. Governments and major corporations are following: Where we come out is better. The now-waning Mass Economy amassed fabulous wealth. The emerging Information Economy may not be so opulent, but it presents greater opportunity for wholeness and happiness. —SB

*Now more than ten years old, this is still the most personable guide to the postindustrial era, and what it might mean to ordinary humans. It goes well with Peter Drucker's **Post-Capitalist Society**. Paul Hawken's newest book carries the ecological mandate to corporations: see page 68.* —AK

●
In an informative economy, we change from an affluent to an *influent* society. If you are affluent, goods and services flow toward you; if you are influent, the information contained within goods flows into you. An affluent society may possess an opulent and abundant amount of goods, but that does not mean it will be able to utilize, appreciate, and maintain them. An influent society will have less, but its relationship to what it has will be more involved and concerned; people will take care of what they have, and what they have will mean more to them. In other words, an affluent society amasses goods, while an influent society processes the information within goods.

The Next Economy
Paul Hawken. Ballantine Books, 1983; 242 pp. ISBN 0-345-31392-5
$4.95 ($6.95 postpaid) from Random House/Order Dept., 400 Hahn Road, Westminster, MD 21157; 800/733-3000

Economics in One Lesson

This 1946 freemarket manifesto was the forerunner of the whole generation of hardheaded, sensible, acerbic, reasonable books that explain why economic idealism — particularly the government-supported kind, including rent control and tariffs — so often leads to tyranny and waste. Hazlitt bases his arguments on an understanding of how systems work, which must have been rare indeed in 1946. At first glance Hazlitt's view, while it would leave free enterprise unshackled, leaves no room for an activist to find a way to make economic life fairer and more sustainable. But even the most determined activist can't afford to ignore the arguments made here.
—AK
[Suggested by Harry Henderson]

●
Each one of us, in brief, has a multiple economic personality. Each one of us is producer, taxpayer, consumer. The policies he advocates depend upon the particular aspect under which he thinks of himself at the moment. For he is sometimes Dr. Jekyll and sometimes Mr. Hyde. As a producer he wants inflation (thinking chiefly of his own services or product); as a consumer he wants price ceilings (thinking chiefly of what he has to pay for the products of others). As a consumer he may advocate or acquiesce in subsidies; as a taxpayer he will resent paying them. Each person is likely to think that he can so manage the political forces that he can benefit from the subsidy more than he loses from the tax, or benefit from a rise for his own product (while his raw material costs are legally held down) and at the same time benefit as a consumer from price control. But the overwhelming majority will be deceiving themselves. For not only must there be at least as much loss as gain from this political manipulation of prices; there must be a great deal *more* loss than gain, because price-fixing discourages and disrupts employment and production.

Economics in One Lesson
Henry Hazlitt. Crown Publishing Group, 1946, 1979; 218 pp. ISBN 0-517-54823-2
$7.95 ($9.95 postpaid) from Random House/Order Dept., 400 Hahn Road, Westminster, MD 21157; 800/733-3000

Small Is Beautiful • Paradigms in Progress • For the Common Good

For twenty years, the debate between economists and environmentalists has been stuck on the same question. Is it better for society to strive for a global-scale, perpetual-growth mass economy, based on ever-larger institutions that make a growing number of people rich? Or is it better to strive for a sustainable economy, full of human-scale interdependent organizations that help people fulfill themselves? The argument has never been more relevant: the economic and corporate ferment of the last few years suggests that all conventional wisdom is void. The time has never been better to set out to design an enterprise (or a society, or a world) that gets better without getting bigger. If that's your aim, these will be valuable and inspiring theoretical tools.

*Small Is Beautiful, published in 1973, is the classic of "Buddhist economics" — a still-eloquent statement of moral principles and practical wisdom for any economic arena. (Instead of corporate taxes, the author suggests that local governments should own 50 percent of the stock of large corporations.) Stewart Brand compared this book to Thomas Paine's **Common Sense**: "Schumacher is fighting a similar oppression, only this time we colonized ourselves."*

*Schumacher was a mentor to self-taught economic gadfly Hazel Henderson. There's a great deal in **Paradigms in Progress** about efforts to "green" the economy, but the most interesting work she describes is taking place in the developing world —* grassroots alternative institutions for raising capital, lending money, and buying supplies.

*Economist Herman Daly and theologian John Cobb spell out the boundaries of the battle in **For the Common Good**. On one side is "chrematistics": the science of maximizing short-term wealth. On the other, "oikonomia": economics as maintaining a household. The ideals will be familiar; **For the Common Good** translates them into understandings of such phenomena as the Gross National Product (a devastating mis-read of how well a society is doing) and tax policies (abolish corporate taxes, the authors say, but build in disincentives to accumulating great individual wealth).* —Art Kleiner
[Suggested by, respectively, Stewart Brand, J. Baldwin, and Stephanie Mills.]

●
[The modern economist] is used to measuring the "standard of living" by the amount of annual consumption, assuming all the time that a man who consumes more is "better off" than a man who consumes less. A Buddhist economist would consider this approach excessively irrational: since consumption is merely a means to human well-being, the aim should be to obtain the maximum of well-being with the minimum of consumption.

●
From an economic point of view, the central concept of wisdom is permanence. We must study the economics of permanence. Nothing makes economic sense unless its continuance for a long time can be projected without running into absurdities. There can be "growth" towards a limited objective, but there cannot be unlimited, generalised growth. —*Small is Beautiful*

The Work of Nations • The End of Equality

The rich keep getting richer. The poor keep getting poorer. Just about every public service imaginable, from schools to parks to roads to airports, is deteriorating. Manufacturing is, seemingly, in utter disarray. American democracy is stagnant, apathetic, and unresponsive to the needs of the people.

What the hell is going on here?

Robert Reich's lucid and compelling study of the global economy and America's place in it gives us an answer. The enterprises that employ most of us have become transnational webs. Knowledge, creativity, and problem-solving have grown more valuable, while the desire and ability to simply work hard and make lots of product can be found almost anywhere in the world. Deep class divisions have developed among those with different roles in this, the new world order. Our inability to see this new world comes from what Reich calls "vestigial thought," a view of American industry, the Ameri-

can workforce, and the social contract between them that ossified in the late 1950s. Here are some whacks on the head to get the mind moving again. —Robert Rossney

Since this book's publication, Robert Reich's book has gained a counterpoint volume: Mickey Kaus's **The End of Equality**. *Kaus believes that we can't (and maybe shouldn't) compensate for inequities in wealth, but we can produce "social egalitarianism" instead — a minimum threshold of support for human dignity, encouraging such things as schools and marriages that cut across class lines. Together, these beltway-ish books define the terrain of economic change, particularly for the labor force, and how to deal with it.* —Art Kleiner

•

The central political fact confronting America's rich, after all, is that they live in a democracy. One man, one vote. Reich's symbol-analysts may be tempted to think

they're better because they have more brain-skills or because they can afford a Lexus. That those sentiments are also arguments against democracy doesn't necessarily make them unappealing to everyone. But the arguments against democracy are not about to prevail. The affluent are going to have to learn to live comfortably with people who may not use the same parks and schools as they do, but who, given the right set of circumstances, might outvote them.

Once the underclass is gone and the bottom class is the working class, the rich and the working poor will have lost their common enemy. Who knows how Americans will react as the income gap between the skilled and unskilled widens—as it comes to be perceived, not just as a difference in income or skills, but increasingly as a difference in "merit" (the Fairness Trap) or even inherited ability (the Hernstein Nightmare)? When the reality of these trends begins to sink in, American society will be subject to terrific strains. Only a strong civic culture will be able to contain the potential insecurities, prejudices, and outright animosities.

The End of Equality
Mickey Kaus. 1993; 304 pp.
ISBN 0-465-09816-9
$12 ($14.75 postpaid) from HarperCollins
Publishers/Direct Mail, PO Box 588,
Dunmore, PA 18512; 800/331-3761

The Work of Nations
Robert B. Reich. 1992; ISBN 0-679-73615-8
$12 ($14 postpaid) from Random House/
Order Dept., 400 Hahn Road, Westminster,
MD 21157; 800/733-3000

Flip to Complexity (page 21).

See also Fernand Braudel's
Capitalism and Material Life (p. 28).

Peter Drucker's
Post-Capitalist Society
is on page 317.

For the Common Good
Herman E. Daly & John B. Cobb, Jr. 1991;
496 pp. ISBN 0-8070-4703-1
$16 ($19.75 postpaid) from Beacon Press,
25 Beacon Street, Boston, MA 02108;
617/742-2110

•

As Third World debt is put behind us, the global playing field can be buttressed by placing an ethical floor under it, one composed of an extended girder work of agreements and protocols on toxic chemicals, worker and consumer protection, environmental standards, and eventually leveling some of the really serious differentials in wages (measured not in GNP terms, but in purchasing power parity equivalents [PPPs]). These differentials in exploiting human labor, just like excessive differentials in consumer and worker safety and environmental protection, are what drives the excessive, unhealthy migrations of populations across borders looking for work and companies looking for short-term market advantage. These massive migrations further fuel the globalization processes and the 24-hour-day financial casino, where money is divorced from real wealth and becomes mere blips of information on thousands of trading screens, where time windows of opportunity to exploit differentials in currencies and interest rates are collapsing to mere nanoseconds.

Much of this ethical girder work of treaties, agreements, and protocols to raise the ethical floor to level the global playing field is already in place, through the United Nations special agencies and such treaties as that in Montreal in 1987 on chlorofluorocarbons and the Law of the Sea, which has been waiting for the United States to ratify

Paradigms In Progress
(Life Beyond Economics)
Hazel Henderson. 1992; 293 pp.
ISBN 0-941705-21-8
$16.95 ($20.45 postpaid) from Knowledge
Systems Inc., 7777 W. Morris Street,
Indianapolis, IN 46231; 800/999-8517

Small is Beautiful
E. F. Schumacher. 1973; 352 pp.
ISBN 0-06-091630-3
$10 ($12.75 postpaid) from HarperCollins
Publishers/Direct Mail, PO Box 588,
Dunmore, PA 18512; 800/331-3761

it after a decade of delaying tactics. Only when this ethical girder work is in place, can ethically aware, responsible companies live up to their moral codes without fear of unfair competition by others willing to cut corners and exploit people and the environment for short-term gain.
—*Paradigms in Progress*

•

The profoundly dehumanizing character of so much work is a function of the inherent drive of the system toward productivity through specialization. There seems to be an inherent tension between humanly satisfying work and the quantity of production per worker. Economic theory has focused on satisfying the human being qua consumer, its *Homo economicus*, and it has viewed the human being as worker only in terms of wages and productivity. But when *Homo economicus* is viewed as person-in-community, satisfaction derived from work is of equal importance with satisfaction derived from consumption. The one-sided approach that has dominated consideration of the aims of the economy must end.
—*For the Common Good*

Toward a History of Needs

Ivan Illich's work, scholarly, iconoclastic, and vicious to sacred cows, always asks two questions: In the social structures that we take for granted in civilized society, what have we lost? And what burdens have we placed on each other? **Toward a History of Needs**, *by revealing the waste and inequity of industrial society, paints a picture of an alternative world: an unprofessionalized, slow, classless world in which people choose poverty because they see how much their needs are self-defeating.* —Art Kleiner

The penetrating mind and needle of Ivan Ilich meets further bloated

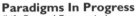

Toward a History of Needs
Ivan Illich. 1978; 160 pp.
ISBN 0-930588-26-6
$8.95 ($10 postpaid) from Heyday Books,
PO Box 9145, Berkeley, CA 94709;
510/549-3564

institutions of the world money made — all commodities and services which bulldoze culture flat. The enemies he identifies are everywhere, handy for your personal, local flanking moves.
—SB

•

Beyond a certain threshold, the multiplication of commodities induces impotence, the incapacity to grow food, to sing, or to build. The toil and pleasure of the human condition become a faddish privilege restricted to some of the rich. When Kennedy launched the Alliance for Progress, Acatzingo, like most Mexican villages of its size, had four groups of musicians who played for a drink and served the population of eight hundred. Today, records and radios, hooked up to loudspeakers, drown out local talent.

After the Fact

The way historians work is as fascinating as the past they recapture. Using what the authors term "the apprentice approach," this book analyzes fourteen incidents from America's past to illustrate the wide range of demands facing historians. There are no footnotes, the prose is readable, and the incidents included are intriguing. This isn't a names-and-dates history text like those we encountered in high school, but something better — a historical work meant for nonacademic adults. —Katherine Kindscher-Waters

●

For better or worse, historians inescapably leave an imprint as they go about their connections between subjects that had not seemed related before, shifting and rearranging evidence until it assumes a coherent pattern. The past is not history; only the raw material of it.

●

In evaluating pictorial evidence, historians must establish the historical context of a

After the Fact
(The Art of Historical Detection)
James W. Davidson & Mark H. Lytle. 1982, 1993; 398 pp. ISBN 0-07-015609-3
$27.50 ($32 postpaid) from McGraw-Hill Publishing Co., Blue Ridge Summit, PA 17214; 800/262-4729

painting just as they would establish the context of any document. They must be sensitive to the artistic conventions that shape or even distort a painting's subject matter. And they must be prepared to acknowledge that some paintings provide more information about their creator than about the subject being portrayed. When visual clues are combined with other printed source materials, whether they be the pedestrian trading inventories of blue glass beads or the literary fantasies of novelists, pictorial evidence can vivify historical narrative and deepen our understanding of American culture.

Robert Oppenheimer, on the reaction of scientists watching the detonation of the first atomic bomb in New Mexico: "A few people laughed, a few people cried, most people were silent. There floated through my mind a line from the *Bhagavad-Gita* in which Krishna is trying to persuade the Prince that he should do his duty: 'I am become death, the shatterer of worlds.' I think we all had this feeling, more or less." The photograph is of an atomic blast detonated at Bikini Island in July 1946.

Inventing the Middle Ages

History is more than a mirror; as Norman Cantor shows here, it is a hall of mirrors. Its images, which can transform our understanding of the present, themselves reflect the perspectives and preoccupations (and often the prejudices) of the historians who produced them. In this masterful portrayal of the lives and work of the major twentieth-century medievalists, current visions of the Middle Ages emerge from a melange of methods and motivations in which painstaking scholarship and brilliant insights are mixed liberally with personal quirkiness, ego collisions, xenophobia, quests for happier worlds.

Cantor does for historians what James Watson's Double Helix *did for scientists — brings them alive in all their human complexity. The book is also a great read, passionate, learned, humorous, gossipy. Cantor illuminates (and makes me care about) the Middle Ages while giving tools and context vital for reading any history. —Michael K. Stone*

●

What Curtius wants is affirmation of continuity and homogeneity of ideas in the Middle Ages and in European culture in general because without this affirmation of structural consistency over time, the way is open for the radicals of left and right to corrupt with treacherous ideas and devastate Western civilization. . . .

We must give up the temptations of intellectual innovation. Curtius is arguing in favor of the preservation of a continuous literary culture that will protect humanity from what happened in Germany in the

1930s. The railroad track to Auschwitz starts where formalism ends.

●

Britain hadn't recovered psychologically before the sixties, possibly the eighties, perhaps never, from those miserable photos of February 1942, showing slim, diminished, embarrassed British officers in their little khaki shorts surrendering Singapore to exultant, masterful Japanese generals, or those heart-stopping photos of smiling young British bomber crews about to leave for their near-suicidal night missions over Germany in 1943 and 1944 and the loss of 59,000 air crews, the cream of a generation, at least half of them secondary school and college graduates. . . .

This was the sad ambience, the bitter, depleted world in which Lewis and Tolkien wrote. They had, however, a more positive response to these conditions and events than the postimperial stoicism, cultural despair, and resigned Christian pessimism that were the common response of their British contemporaries. They were not prepared imaginatively and intellectually to withdraw and accept defeat. Out of the medieval Norse, Celtic, and Grail legends, they conjured fantasies of revenge and recovery, an ethos of return and triumph. As Chaucer said in *Troilus and Criseyde*, they aimed "to make dreams truth and fables histories."

●

Strayer taught graduate students in the Haskins manner by intimidation and by concentration on narrow research study of administrative records. He spent two years (1951-53) doing nothing else in his seminar but reading medieval tax rolls, first of England, then of France. When I proposed that I do a report on the Thomist idea of kingship, he told me I should consider transferring to the philosophy department. "Sure, that is part of medieval history," he said, glowering through his inevitable cigar, "but the philosophers will never study tax rolls. If we historians don't do it, nobody will, so we have to do it." There was a logic in this, after a fashion. . . .

Strayer never turned on the overhead lights in his office during a seminar. The seminar met for three hours at 2:00 P.M. The office was a long, narrow room with only one window. By 4:00 P.M. in winter it was so dark that it was impossible to read one's notes. One day I had the gall to ask Strayer why he didn't turn on the lights. "So you dummies will not be able to bore us by reading your verbose notes and will have to speak succinctly from memory." A good lesson.

Civilization and Capitalism, 15th–18th Century

For the general reader seeking the origins of today's market economy, these volumes provide the best possible introduction.

Gibbon was the greatest historian of the eighteenth century, Macaulay of the nineteenth, and Braudel of the twentieth. Gibbon and Macaulay wrote narrative history about kings and emperors; Braudel (1902-85) wrote analytic history about driving forces, long

trends, and the material culture of everyday life.

Braudel combined a deep knowledge of both history and geography to become the first economic historian to understand (for example) the importance of changes over the centuries in the weather, the incidence of disease, and the flow of trade. The silting of harbors, the harvest cycles, and reduction in travel times meant far more to

him than results on the battlefields or in the marriage beds of royalty.

Reading Braudel is like traveling in a helicopter with the ability to swoop down for a close look at some amazing piece of the historical landscape, and to soar up into the sky to see the complex patterns of ordinary life. No historian has ever made such convincing and telling use of generalization backed up by an uncanny ability to spot details in support. —Napier Collyns

Civilization and Capitalism, 15th-18th Century
Fernand Braudel. Sian Reynolds, Translator.

Volume 1: **The Structures of Everyday Life.** 1981; 623 pp. ISBN 0-520-08114-5

Volume 2: **The Wheels of Commerce.** 1982; 670 pp. ISBN 0-520-08115-3

Volume 3: **The Perspective of the World.** 1984; 699 pp. ISBN 0-520-08116-1

Each $25.50 postpaid from California/ Princeton Fulfillment Services, 1445 Lower Ferry Road, Ewing, NJ 08618; 800/777-4726

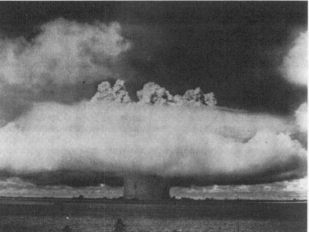

A brickworks in the English countryside. The smoke pouring from chimneys like these was already being accused of polluting the air in the eighteenth century. —*The Perspective...*

Inventing the Middle Ages
(The Lives, Works, and Ideas of the Great Medievalists of the 20th Century)
Norman F. Cantor. Quill Books, 1991; 477 pp. ISBN 0-688-09406-6
$28 ($29.50 postpaid) from William Morrow and Co./Wilmore Warehouse, 39 Plymouth Street, Fairfield, NJ 07004

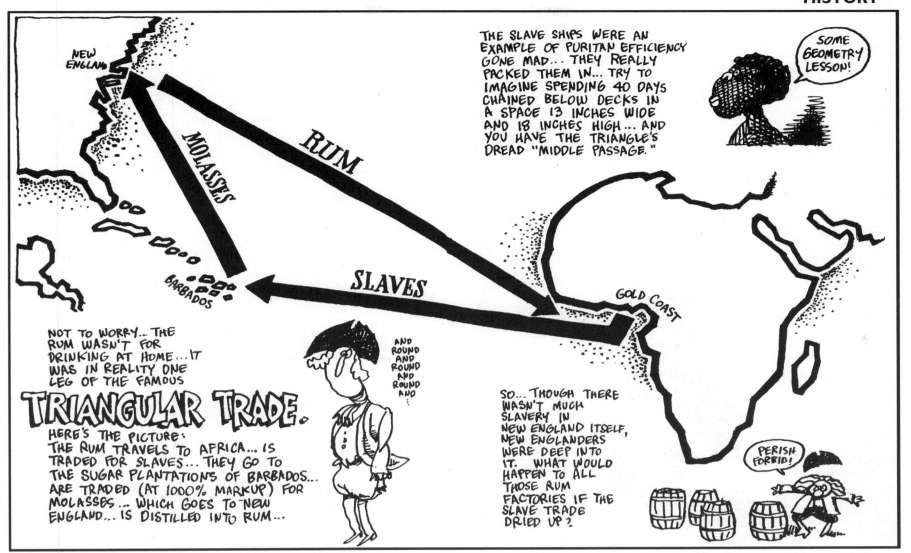

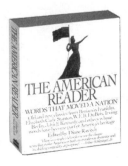

The American Reader • The Cartoon History of the United States

The Reader is a fat collection of (mostly short) documents of American history. Editor Diane Ravitch gives us a remarkably well-done and even-handed collection, including the famous "lost verse" of "This Land is Your Land," which denounces the concept of private property; Newton Minnow's "vast wasteland" speech; "Casey at the Bat"; W. E. B. DuBois's essay on "the talented tenth." It's amazing how often you find what you're looking for. In terms of long extracts of major documents, there are certainly weightier books, but this one has a remarkable collection of good stuff, and will actually get read. I use it all the time teaching history.

The irreverent Cartoon History, written from a pro–downtrodden masses p.o.v., manages to pack a ton of info into its entertaining cartoons. If it were up to me, every high school history student would get one of these in addition to her textbook.
—*Mark McDonough*

•
But where, say some, is the king of America? I'll tell you, friend, he reigns above, and doth not make havoc of mankind like the Royal Brute of Great Britain. Yet that we may not appear to be defective even in earthly honors, let a day be solemnly set apart for proclaiming the charter; let it be brought forth placed on the divine law, the Word of God; let a crown be placed thereon, by which the world may know, that so far as we approve of monarchy, that in America THE LAW IS KING. For as

in absolute governments the king is law, so in free countries the law *ought* to BE king, and there ought to be no other. But lest any ill use should afterwards arise, let the crown at the conclusion of the ceremony be demolished, and scattered among the people whose right it is. . . .

O ye that love mankind! Ye that dare oppose not only the tyranny but the tyrant, stand forth! Every spot of the old world is overrun with oppression. Freedom hath been hunted round the globe. Asia and Africa have long expelled her. Europe regards her like a stranger, and England hath given her warning to depart. O receive the fugitive, and prepare in time an asylum for mankind. —Tom Paine, *Common Sense*, from *The American Reader*

OTHER GREAT RESOURCES

A History of Private Life. Phillipe Aries, et al.; Five volumes. 1987-1991, Harvard University Press.

Practicing History: Selected Essays. Barbara W. Tuchman, 1959, Ballantine Books.

The Shorter Science and **Civilization in China.** Two volumes. Joseph Needham and Colin A. Ronin. 1978, Cambridge University Press.

Eyewitness to History. John Carey, Editor. 1988, Avon Books.

Democracy in America. Alexis De Tocqueville; Bradley Phillips, Editor. Two volumes. 1990, Random House.

A Green History of the World: The Environment and the Collapse of Great Civilizations. Clive Ponting. 1991, Penguin Books.

The Cartoon History of the United States
Larry Gonick. HarperPerennial, 1991; 392 pp. ISBN 0-06-273098-3
$13 ($15.75 postpaid)

The American Reader
(Words That Moved A Nation)
Diane Ravitch, Editor. HarperPerennial, 1990; 383 pp. ISBN 0-06-272016-3
$12.95 ($15.70 postpaid)

Both from HarperCollins Publishers/Direct Mail, PO Box 588, Dunmore, PA 18512; 800/331-3761

The I Ching Workbook

R. L. Wing is a contemporary interpreter of the I Ching *with a long-standing and surprisingly large, surprisingly eclectic following. I know people who have worn out their copies of the* I Ching Workbook *and have had to get a new one.*

The nature of the oracle within this ancient Chinese book of mental maps is both a personal and a disembodied one; when you use the I Ching *for a while, you begin to notice the focuses and blind spots of your own reality filters. And you begin to develop a relationship with the entity that seems to emerge from the pattern of images and poems the book reveals in response to your questions. Whether or not you are a believer in the oracular powers of this process, or whether it is a good guide for art or love or business, as many claim, it is easy to understand that relationship one has with the oracle.*

Wing knows the American way to say things. "The little fox dipped its tail in the icy water" is poetic and there is an image there if you dig for it; but sometimes it helps to hone in on the place of maintaining concentration on a task for a long time without making even the most minor mistake — like a young fox crossing a frozen creek. The American flavor of the Wing Ching, as aficionados call it, has not changed the nature and purpose of the hexagrams. They are tools. Try them. —HLR

●

This hexagram represents the deep, inexhaustible, divinely centered source of nourishment and meaning for humanity. Although people may journey from spiritual discipline to political discipline, explore various philosophies and scholarly pursuits, alter their awareness in myriad ways — they must always return to THE SOURCE of their true nature for fulfillment. The original Chinese text depicts this hexagram as *The Well*. It states: "The town may be changed, but the well cannot be changed. It cannot be increased or decreased." THE SOURCE contains and is born of the collective truth of humanity. It receives from the individual's experience and gives to the individual's nature. Penetrating THE SOURCE of humanity can be seen as the major theme in Chinese philosophy. Confucius, China's great philosopher, said, "If you set your mind on humanity, you will be free from evil." The text of the hexagram points out that if *The Well* is not penetrated fully, there will be misfortune.

THE SOURCE particularly refers to and governs the social and political systems of mankind. These organizations must be centered and planned around the predispositions of human nature. Such organic ordering then rings true in the hearts and minds of the people, as their needs and prejudices are met. It requires an exceptional personality to organize others in this

Drawing on the Right Side of the Brain

This is about drawing as a mind-expanding exercise, as a means of exercising your ability to see the world in new ways.

We all learn a symbolic language in childhood, connecting the pictures in our heads with the representations we make on paper. Unfortunately, few children are taught how to develop that language, and our culture discourages all but the obviously talented from exercising visual communication skills. Most people feel they "can't draw," and thus tend to shy away from using the eye-hand connection to nudge their consciousness into innovation.

Teacher Betty Edwards has found that the adroit use of certain tricks, most notably drawing familiar objects upside down, can help people learn to switch their modes of perception at will. Browsing the illustrations is an education in itself. —HLR

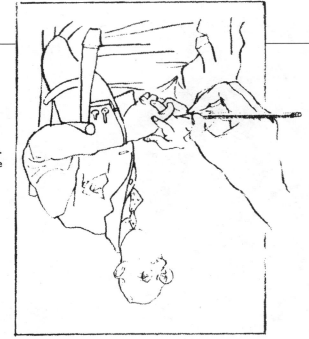

Inverted drawing. Forcing the cognitive shift from the dominant left-hemisphere mode to the subdominant right-hemisphere mode.

Ken Darnell
February 5, 1974

Having completed the course, Ken produced this drawing about a year later.

Drawing on the Right Side of the Brain
Betty Edwards. J. P. Tarcher Inc., 1989; 288 pp.
ISBN 0-87477-513-2
$13.95 ($15.95 postpaid) from Putnam Publishing Group/Attn: Order Dept., PO Box 506, E. Rutherford, NJ 07073; 800/631-8571

The I Ching Workbook
R. L. Wing. Doubleday & Co., 1979; 180 pp.
ISBN 0-385-12838-X
$17.00 ($19.50 postpaid) from Bantam, Doubleday, Dell/Fulfillment Dept., 2451 S. Wolf Road, Des Plaines, IL 60018; 800/223-6834

way. If you are such a leader, be certain that you penetrate the true feeling of your fellow man. Without this forethought and sense of humanity in a leader, good government is impossible, and misfortune results. Social disorder and evil reign because the leader is not the right man to execute the "plan." The right man can be recognized by his ability to inspire those whom he leads. He encourages them in their individual pursuits and promotes cooperation.

OTHER GREAT RESOURCES:

I Ching aficionados have religious arguments over which translation is best. Here are the other two translations I find useful, each in its way:

The I Ching or Book of Changes (translated from Chinese into German by Richard Wilhelm, into English by Cary F. Baynes, 1990, Princeton University Press).

The Portable Dragon: The Western Man's Guide to the I Ching (translated by R.G.H. Siu, 1990, The MIT Press).

Another book that stretches your thinking muscles:

How to Solve It (Gyorgy Polya, 1973, Princeton University Press).

Spare Ching

(heard in Havre, Montana)

"Throwing the Ching is like jerking the handle on a cosmic slot machine, like reading chicken gizzards, like following an eighteen-wheeler through the fog. Depends on how you use it. In all the years I've been flipping coins and fumbling through hexagrams, I've only once seen the Ching be right, exactly, on.

"About ten years back, I woke up one morning in my old stepvan underneath a railroad bridge east of Cut Bank, the coldest spot in the lower forty-eight. Leave a sixpack outside on the Fourth of July in that town, it'll freeze overnight. I was real low on smoke, out of money, too grubby to get a job. Red

Inspiration

Make your own icons by importing graphics

Analytical, hierarchically structured thinking

Visual thinking

Choose from a palette of icons

You can see ideas structured as outlines

You can see ideas and projects structured as maps

Shuttle between right and left brain modes

Inspiration: Visually oriented thought processor

Let the computer structure the information

Stimulate the flow of ideas

Brainstorming mode lets you enter ideas as fast as they occur, then easily drag them into position and link them later.

Put items into bins

Put bins into bins

Inspiration: Version 4.0; MacPlus, System 6.0.4 and above, 1MB RAM. $295 from Inspiration Software, Inc., 2920 SW Dolph Court, Suite 3, Portland, OR 97219; 503/245-9011

More

+ Thinking Tools:
  + **Software That Helps You Think.**
    + Outliners
      + **Outline, externalize, and extend older mental tools**
        + Magic Number Seven:
          - We can only hold 7-10 chunks of info in short-term memory.
        + Hierarchies of Abstractions
          - We can make small chunks into larger chunks that have meaning at a higher level.
  + **What computer outlines can do well**
    + Information Hiding
      - Thinking about complexity means being able to focus on key features, landmarks, backbone, by selectively ignoring or hiding details.
      - An outliner enables you to change your point of view on the same information quickly and in different ways: to fly over the forest, or get up close and examine the trees.
    + Structural flexiblity
      - If you can shuffle pieces of the outline around by pointing and dragging, it's easier to experiment with the way the pieces of a project fit together.
    + Cloning and hoisting
      - Outline elements can coexist in different parts of the same outline.
      - Any element can be elevated to the top level, to zoom in on it and its subcategories.
  + **Brainstorming**
    + Throw out a bunch of ideas in any sort of order:
    - Helps get things flowing at the beginning.
      - Start anywhere.
    - Later, experiment with different ordering.
    - Watch clumps and categories emerge.
    - Outline for brainstorming a project transforms smoothly into a means of managing the project— keeping track of drafts, notes, to-do lists, references, pointers to other parts of the headline.
  + **I used two outliners to organize the *Catalog***
    - *Inspiration* helped me visualize.
    - *More 3.0* helped me keep track.
        —HLR

More: Version 3.1; MacPlus, System 6.0 and above, 1MB RAM. $395 from Symantec Corporation/ Customer Service, 175 W. Broadway, Eugene, OR 97401; 800/441-7234

PC-Outline

PC-Outline is a full-featured, inexpensive outliner for IBM-compatibles. The program itself is charmingly old-fashioned — I don't think it's been updated since '88 or so. All text mode; no mouse support. It is quite powerful, though: besides the hierarchical outline structure and functions for rearranging things, it also supports choices of numbering style, hanging indents, search-and-replace, conditional and hard page breaks, printer formatting (underline, boldface, etc.), windowing (up to nine outlines open at once), sorting, key redefinition, and other stuff. Quick to learn, though some of the keystrokes are quirky.
—Josh Gordon

PC-Outline: Version 3.36; IBM PC and compatible. $89.95 from Brown Bag Software, 2155 S. Bascom Avenue, Suite 105, Campbell, CA 95008; 408/559-4545

Dog wine was ruining my eyes. So I pulled out my three bronze Chinese bus tokens, the kind with a square hole in the middle, and threw the Ching on the question of what I should do next.

"The hexagram came up with a broken line at the bottom and solid lines all the way up from there, Kou, Coming to Meet, talking about how the strong and the weak, the good and the evil, are part of the same thing and are going to meet and join. The first line said that bronze was going to be real important.

"I took it all to mean that it was time to get out of Cut Bank, so I put twenty bucks worth of gas on my brother's Chevron card and headed south. Fifteen miles below Darby, going up the Bitterroot, I came around a long righthand corner and damn near rear-ended a big white Cadillac, stopped in my lane. A couple of senior citizens were waving me down with a Pendleton blanket.

"The folks were from California, headed north out of Jackpot, Nevada, on their way to Glacier Park, when the wife spotted a patch of Indian paintbrush, had the old man pull a U-turn to go back for a bouquet. The car died right there by the flowers, wouldn't turn over.

"When I squoze under that big old cruiser, I found that Mr. Goodwrench, down in Anaheim, had used an impact tool on the starter mounting bolts and had royally screwed the threads. The starter wasn't making contact with the flywheel housing. It was just hanging there on the studs, by gravity, which wasn't quite good enough, considering the negative return path for the battery current depended on something being hard and fast between the starter motor and the engine block.

"Right then I remembered the Ching, Coming to Meet, and the importance of

bronze, so I went back to the stepvan, got my Ching coins and a little ballpeen hammer, and drove the bronze tokens in as shims between the block and the starter motor. The solenoid still threw the starter gear far enough, the Caddy started five times in a row, the old couple were tickled shitless, and the dude laid a hundred silver dollars on me that he had won in Jackpot.

"I told him they should stop in Missoula at a GM dealership and get things fixed right. Last time I saw my Ching coins, they were headed north on Highway 93. Been throwing the Ching with silver dollars ever since."
—JD Smith

Two Series: World Spirituality • The Classics of Western Spirituality

The last decade has seen the ongoing publication of two exciting series of books from religious publishers. Both are notable for their ecumenical sweep and for their emphasis on spiritual depth. And both have issued affordable paperback editions, thus making them easy to acquire. Because of their range, it is unlikely that all volumes will be of equal interest to every reader. No matter: each book stands well on its own. Libraries, however, will want to carry these series as full sets.

Crossroad's series, **World Spirituality,** brings together more than five hundred scholars spanning the world's religions and spiritual paths. The history of each culture's religious quest is examined and presented in an engaging fashion. Each volume focuses on a different tradition and/or span of time (such as **Jewish Spirituality: From the Bible to the Middle Ages, Taoist Spirituality,** or **Islamic Spirituality: Foundations**), and special emphasis is placed on the relations of the religions to the individual's inner experience.

Paulist Press's series, **The Classics of Western Spirituality,** takes a different tack. It presents fresh translations of writings by the greatest thinkers and teachers of Western religion (Jewish, Christian, Islamic, and Native American). Each volume is a different classic or selection of short writings and letters from the likes of Origen, Ibn Al Arabi, Catherine of Siena, Abraham Isaac Kook, and Philo of Alexandria.

Extensive introductions and commentary help draw out the implications of the classics, making them newly relevant for modern readers. —JK

•

And in this he showed me something small, no bigger than a hazelnut, lying in the palm of my hand, as it seemed to me, and it was as round as a ball. I looked at it with the eye of my understanding and thought: What can this be? I was amazed that it could last, for I thought that because of its littleness it would suddenly have fallen into nothing. And I was answered in my understanding: It lasts and always will, because God loves it; and thus everything has being through the love of God.

In this little thing I saw three properties. The first is that God made it, the second is that God loves it, the third is that God preserves it. —Julian of Norwich: *Showings* (*Classics*)

•

A man asked God for a son. A hermaphrodite was born to him. He said: "O God, I asked You for a son, but You have given me a hermaphrodite." He heard a voice: "I know how to give, but you do not know how to ask!" Whoever does not know how to ask will acquire nothing but regret. Whoever worships God because he desires heaven is a slave of his own desire. Whoever worships Him out of a fear of hell is a slave of hell, for anyone who is afraid of anything is a slave of that thing. By the same token, whoever puts his hope in anything is a slave of that thing. Your true reality is that which is within your breast. A man is where his heart is! —Sharafuddin Maneri: *The Hundred Letters* (*Classics*)

SPIRITUALITY — meaning the lived experience of inner growth and unfolding "spirit" concealed beneath all the dogmas and institutions of religions — is slippery stuff. It doesn't make the evening news and it isn't much help in furthering assorted ideological agendas. Its gifts are subtle and rarely "cutting edge." In fact, the best tool for spiritual exploration may simply be to shut up, close your eyes, and sit quietly and observantly for a short stretch every morning.

However, the mind likes something to chew on between bouts of quiet, and the following items are good for digesting the basics of a spiritual life. Faced with choosing a mere handful of items out of an infinity of traditions and approaches, we tilted in two directions: toward engaging overviews, and classic texts. —Jay Kinney

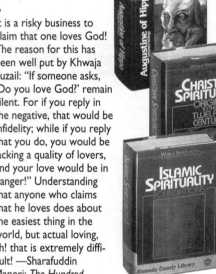

•

It is a risky business to claim that one loves God! The reason for this has been well put by Khwaja Fuzail: "If someone asks, 'Do you love God?' remain silent. For if you reply in the negative, that would be infidelity; while if you reply that you do, you would be lacking a quality of lovers, and your love would be in danger!" Understanding that anyone who claims that he loves does about the easiest thing in the world, but actual loving, ah! that is extremely difficult! —Sharafuddin Maneri: *The Hundred Letters* (*Classics*)

•

The monastic tradition of spiritual fatherhood/motherhood is the phenomenon in early Christianity that most closely resembles the phenomenon of spiritual master and disciple in the other great spiritual traditions. The "abba" of early Christian monasticism played a role quite similar to that of the Hindu guru, Zen master, or Sufi sheik. The desert fathers/mothers stand out as the preeminent spiritual guides of the early Christian era. These desert fathers/mothers were the first Christian monks and nuns who from the fourth to the sixth century peopled the deserts and wilderness regions of Egypt, Palestine, and Syria. Though the origins of Christian monastic life are complex, certainly one of the strongest factors was the simple fact that people were drawn to the desert to find an "elder," an accomplished ascetic and spiritual teacher capable of leading other persons to a greater experience of God. —*Christian Spirituality I: Origins to the Twelfth Century* (*World Spirituality*)

World Spirituality
(An Encyclopedic History of the Religious Quest)
Ewert Cousins, General Editor.
Crossroad Publishing Co.,
12 volumes; $49.50 average price from Publisher Resources/
Crossroad, PO Box 7001,
La Vergne, TN 37086-7001;
800/937-5557

The Classics of Western Spirituality
Richard J. Payne, Editor-in-Chief.
78 volumes; $18-$25 each from
Paulist Press, 997 MacArthur Boulevard, Mahwahm, NJ 07430;
201/825-7300

The Sufis

Sufism represents a substantial path of mystical inquiry, most commonly seen as the nondogmatic inner heart of Islam. Idries Shah recasts Sufism in terms of Western psychology, asserts its importance as a largely unacknowledged influence on world history, and shares numerous anecdotes and intriguing factoids. Many scholars look askance at this book's claims and its lack of substantiating footnotes, and they have a point. But several dozen books along in further reading, **The Sufis** remains unsurpassed for providing both the big picture and the motivation for further study. —JK

•

The process by means of which a foreign word or phrase becomes adopted into another language is well established in literature and custom. There are numerous examples and the system has even been named, being catalogued in dictionaries as Hobson-Jobson. The interminable religious chant in India *Ya Hasan Ya Hussein* (O Hasan! O Hussein!) is accepted in English under the sound Hobson-Jobson, an attempt by British soldiers to reproduce the chant. The standard Indian dictionary of Anglo-Indian terms, containing many examples of the process, is actually called Hobson-Jobson. In West Africa the Arabic word *el-ghaita* (a bagpipe) has been anglicized into "alligator." Nearer home, all Londoners are familiar with the name of a certain tavern, the "Elephant and Castle," originally named the *Infanta de Castile*.

Joseph Campbell and the Power of Myth • The Mahabharata

Every time we're tempted to tout books as the unsurpassed medium for conveying ideas, something comes along to remind us that spoken words and facial gestures preceded print and will probably outlast it. These two videotape sets are happy reminders that the small and large screens are as capable of affecting our higher emotions as anything on the surrounding pages.

The PBS series where Bill Moyers interviewed scholar Joseph Campbell was vastly popular, and with good reason. Campbell made myths and their meanings come alive for a modern audience too often separated from its own past and assaulted by a hit-and-run pop culture devoid of true inspiration. These shows age well precisely because they touch on the timeless themes of human experience that are always with us. —JK

•

The Mahabharata is Peter Brook's film adaptation of the great epic of India. It focuses on the struggle between two clans of heroes, the virtuous Pandavas and the arrogant Kauravas, reflecting the constant seesaw between the forces of order and disorder in the universe. One of its main themes is how an individual should behave in times of disorder. Brook's film features a su-

perb international cast and a tight sense of drama (though the first hour or so, which attempts to depict the heroes' mythological origins, is weaker than the rest). Both sensitive and dynamic, it manages to avoid the cheap sensationalizing that comes out of most attempts to dramatize great works of literature. —Richard Smoley

The Power of Myth
6-tape set, 6 hours
Joseph Campbell.
$124.95 ($131.90 postpaid) from Mystic Fire Video, PO Box 2249, Livonia, MI 48150; 800/292-9001

The Mahabharata
3-tape set, 6 hours
$99 ($106.95 postpaid) from Pacific Spirit, 1334 Pacific Avenue, Forest Grove, OR 97116; 800/634-9057

The Electric Mystic's Guide to the Internet

Michael Strangelove operates a number of electronic publishing projects, including **Contents** and **Review-L**, which discuss current publications in religious studies.

He describes his 5,735-line file, **The Electric Mystic's Guide to the Internet, Vol. 1,** as "A Complete Directory of Networked Electronic Documents, Online Conferences, Serials, Software, and Archives Relevant to Religious Studies."

Most of what I've learned about spirituality on the Internet started with checking out sources he lists. Many discussions of spirituality and religion are going on today on the Internet. Anyone with access to the Internet can join these discussions.

The **EMG** is available by "anonymous ftp" from Strangelove in Ottawa from the node panda1.uottowa.ca in the directory /pub/religion/. [See p. 264 for discussion of ftping on Internet.] —Bruce Schuman

The Gnostic Gospels • The Gnostic Scriptures

*Elaine Pagels' **Gnostic Gospels** was the first book to make the early Christian Gnostics come alive for modern readers, and it remains unsurpassed as a readable introduction to these heretics' ideas and scriptures. The Gnostics valued mystical experience above doctrinal fidelity, fashioned alternate creation myths and gospels that the early Roman church did their best to stamp out, and raised the feminine figure of Sophia (Wisdom) to a stature nearly equal with Christ's. The 1945 discovery, at Nag Hammadi, Egypt, of a cache of Gnostic scriptures dating from 350-400 A.D. has given us a far more solid glimpse of Gnostic myths than previously available, and Dr. Pagels excels at puzzling out their implications for our present understanding of Christianity.*

As for the Gnostic scriptures themselves, several translations have been made, ranging from the careful scholarship of the team headed by Dr. James Robinson to more pop renderings of the Gospel of Thomas, the most famous of the Gnostic texts. Bentley Layton's translation and annotation of the Gnostic scriptures (which includes not only the Nag Hammadi texts, but related ones from other sources as well) has my vote as the single best volume for the lay reader. Layton's lucid translations are supplemented with very helpful introductions, background details, explanatory annotations, and maps. Layton is of no less scholarly standing than other translators, but he has brought the material to life far better than most. —JK

•

The controversy over resurrection, then, proved critical in shaping the Christian movement into an institutional religion. All Christians agreed in principle that only Christ himself — or God — can be the ultimate source of spiritual authority. But the immediate question, of course, was the practical one: Who, in the present, administers that authority?

Valentinus and his followers answered: Whoever comes into direct, personal contact with the "living One." They argued that only one's own experience offers the ultimate criterion of truth, taking precedence over all secondhand testimony and all tradition — even gnostic tradition! They celebrated every form of creative invention as evidence that a person has become spiritually alive. On this theory, the structure of authority can never be fixed into an institutional framework — it must remain spontaneous, charismatic, and open.
— *The Gnostic Gospels*

•

The disciples tell Jesus what he resembles.

Jesus said to his disciples, "Compare me to something and tell me what I resemble."

Simon Peter said to him, "A just angel is what you resemble."

Matthew said to him, "An intelligent philosopher is what you resemble."

Thomas said to him, "Teacher, my mouth utterly will not let me say what you resemble."

Jesus said, "I am not your (sing.) teacher, for you have drunk and become intoxicated from the bubbling wellspring that I have personally measured out." And he took him, withdrew, and said three sayings to him.

Now, when Thomas came to his companions they asked him, "What did Jesus say to you?"

Thomas said to them, "If I say to you (plur.) one of the sayings that he said to me, you will take stones and stone me, and fire will come out of the stones and burn you up."
—*The Gnostic Scriptures*

The Gnostic Gospels
Elaine Pagels. 1989; 182 pp.
ISBN 0-679-72453-2
$9 ($11 postpaid) from Random House/ Order Dept., 400 Hahn Road, Westminster, MD 21157; 800/733-3000

The Gnostic Scriptures
(A New Translation with Annotations)
Bentley Layton. Doubleday & Co., 1987;
ISBN 0-385-17447-0
$35 ($37.50 postpaid) from Bantam, Doubleday, Dell/Fulfillment Dept., 2451 S. Wolf Road, Des Plaines, IL 60018; 800/223-6834

The Thirteen-Petalled Rose

Seekers groping for a spiritual path sometimes feel the need to return to their roots. Those seeking an introduction to the deeper dimensions of Judaism might want to read this work by Rabbi Adin Steinsaltz.

Steinsaltz, a noted Talmudic scholar, is coming from an Orthodox perspective, which at times may seem stringent to those accustomed to more modern perspectives on Judaism. Steinsaltz's vision is based on the Kabbalah, the esoteric tradition that forms the innermost core of Judaism. The Kabbalah teaches that in addition to the material realm we live in, other, unseen worlds resonate with this one, and are subtly affected by our thoughts and actions here. Living in accordance with Torah, the Law that underpins Jewish life and activity (Steinsaltz says), brings greater harmony between the visible and invisible realms. —Richard Smoley

•

A basic idea underlying Jewish life is that there are no special frameworks for holiness. A man's relation to God is not set apart on a higher plane, not relegated to some special corner of time and place with all the rest of life taking place somewhere else. The Jewish attitude is that life in all its aspects, in its totality, must somehow or other be bound up with holiness. This attitude is expressed in part through conscious action: that is, through the utterance of prescribed prayers and blessings and following prescribed forms of conduct; and, in part, by adhering to a number of prohibitions.

Man generally passes through the world aware that it is full of possible colors and meanings; and he tries to make his own connection with all its many possibilities. What he may be less aware of is the fact that there are worlds upon worlds, besides the one he knows, dependent on his actions. In Judaism man is conceived, in all the power of his body and soul, as the central agent, the chief actor on a cosmic stage; he functions, or performs, as a prime mover of worlds, being made in the image of the Creator. Everything he does constitutes an act of creation, both in his own life and in other worlds hidden from his sight. Every single particle of his body and every nuance of his thought and feeling are connected with forces of all kinds in the cosmos, forces without number; so that the more conscious he is of this order of things, the more significantly does he function as a Jewish person.

The Thirteen-Petalled Rose
Adin Steinsaltz. Basic Books, 1985;
181 pp. ISBN 0-465-08561-X
$12 ($14.75 postpaid) from HarperCollins Publishers/Direct Mail, PO Box 588, Dunmore, PA 18512; 800/331-3761

Quite recently, a Middle Eastern friend of mine presented an astonished barrow-pushing scrap collector with a shilling in a London street. The man had been repeating, with fervor, in that plaintive tone of the hawker, "Any old iron?" The way in which he drew out the sounds was for my friend indistinguishable from the mendicant dervish cry of *O Imam Reza!* which shouting dervishes repeat hundreds of times a day as a pious invocation, heard by all in some areas.

•

The false teacher will pay great attention to appearance, and will know how to make the Seeker think that he is a great man, that he understands him, that he has great secrets to reveal. The Sufi has secrets, but he must make them develop within the disciple. Sufism is something which happens to a person, not something which is given to him. The false teacher will keep his followers around him all the time, will not tell them that they are being given a training which must end as soon as possible, so that they may taste their development themselves and carry on as fulfilled people.

Rumi calls upon the scholastic, the theologian, and the follower of the false teacher: "When will you cease to worship and to love the pitcher? When will you begin to look for the water?" Externals are the things which people usually judge by. "Know the difference between the color of the wine and the color of the glass."

The Sufis
Idries Shah. Doubleday & Co., 1964, 1971;
451 pp. ISBN 0-385-07966-4
$9.95 ($12.45 postpaid) from Bantam, Doubleday, Dell/Fulfillment Dept., 2451 S. Wolf Road, Des Plaines, IL 60018; 800/223-6834

The Islanders. Sufic illustrative calligraphy, in the hand of "Mohamed, Son of Shafig, 1291," of the Mevlevi ("Dancing") Dervishes. The image of a ship with people standing in it is apparent.

The Miracle of Mindfulness

Any authentic spiritual teaching, no matter what name it goes by, will bring up the question of attention and awareness. And few traditions have as perfected a repertoire of methods for refining the attention as Buddhism. Thich Nhat Hanh, a Vietnamese Buddhist monk and peace activist, provides an excellent introduction to this central topic of the spiritual path in this simple, eloquent book.

"Mindfulness," as Nhat Hanh calls it, is partly a matter of formal meditation practice — for example, sitting quietly and focusing the attention on the breath (a meditation that is said to go back to the Buddha himself). But it is much more. Mindfulness, he stresses, is something that can and should be practiced in every moment of our lives.

The Miracle of Mindfulness offers clear, simple suggestions for heightening the meditative quality in daily life. Supplementing the book is a selection of Buddhist sutras that provide a traditional context for the practices so evocatively described here.
—Richard Smoley

●

When your mind is liberated your heart floods with compassion: compassion for yourself, for having undergone countless sufferings because you were not yet able to relieve yourself of false views, hatred, ignorance, and anger; and compassion for others because they do not yet see and so are still imprisoned by false views, hatred, and ignorance and continue to create suffering for themselves and for others. Now you look at yourself and at others with the eyes of compassion, like a saint who hears the cry of every creature in the universe and whose voice is the voice of every person who has seen reality in perfect wholeness. As a Buddhist Sutra hears the voice of the Bodhisattva of compassion:

The wondrous voice, the voice of the one
  who attends to the cries of the world
The noble voice, the voice of the rising
  tide surpassing all the sounds of the
  world
Let our mind be attuned to that voice.

Put aside all doubt and meditate on the
  pure and holy nature of the regarder
  of the cries of the world
Because that is our reliance in situations
  of pain, distress, calamity, death.

Perfect in all merits, beholding all sentient
  beings with compassionate eyes, making
  the ocean of blessings limitless,
Before this one, we should incline.

The Miracle of Mindfulness
(A Manual on Meditation)
Thich Nhat Hanh. 1976, 1992; 160 pp.
ISBN 0-8070-1201-7
$10 ($13.75 postpaid) from Beacon Press,
25 Beacon Street, Boston, MA 02108;
617/742-2110

Voices of the First Day

Australian Aboriginal culture is about everything in the imaginal realm and everything in the natural environment. Dreams and springs, states of consciousness and natural cycles, spirituality and survival lore are inextricably connected with one another. If you harbor even the slightest suspicion that Aboriginal culture is "primitive" because these people reject agriculture, architecture, writing, clothing, and animal domestication, this book will awaken you.

Author Robert Lawlor has compiled the best of what the Aboriginals have let outsiders know about their ecological and shamanic practices, origin myths and kinship rituals, social and spiritual practices. The illustrations are spectacular; more than 150 color and duotone illustrations include some of the earliest photographs of Aboriginal people, shown here for the first time.

A portion of the proceeds from sales of Voices of the First Day will go to Denooch Aboriginal Healing Centre and South Australian Earth Sanctuaries. The Healing Center assists Aborigines in using tribal healing methods to cure alcohol, drug, and tobacco addiction. Earth Sanctuaries provide a home for Australian endangered species.
—HLR

●

All creatures — from stars to humans to insects — share in the consciousness of the

Voices of the First Day
(Awakening in the Aboriginal Dreamtime)
Robert Lawlor. 1991; 412 pp.
ISBN 0-89281-355-5
$24.95 ($26.95 postpaid) from Inner Traditions International c/o American International Distribution Corp., 64 Depot Rd., Colchester, VT 05446; 800/445-6638

primary creative force, and each, in its own way, mirrors a form of that consciousness. In this sense the Dreamtime stories perpetuate a unified world view. This unity compelled the Aborigines to respect and adore the earth as if it were a book imprinted with the mystery of the original creation. The goal of life was to preserve the earth, as much as possible, in its initial purity. The subjugation and domestication of plants and animals and all other manipulation and exploitation of the natural world — the basis of Western civilization and "progress" — were antithetical to the sense of a common consciousness and origin shared by every creature and equally with the creators. To exploit this integrated world was to do the same to oneself.

Every land formation and creature, by its very shape and behavior, implied a hidden meaning; the form of a thing was itself an imprint of the metaphysical or ancestral consciousness that created it, as well as the universal energies that brought about its material manifestation. These aspects of the Dreamtime creation myth imply a world in which the metaphysical and physical are held in symbolic integration. One cannot consider the visible and invisible worlds separately. The Aboriginal languages that emerged from this world view are rich in a metaphoric flow integrating physical, psychological, and spiritual levels of experience.

The Mimi spirit with a serpent symbolizes the power of Eros in association with the primal forces of the earth.

OTHER GREAT RESOURCES

Hua Hu Ching (The Unknown Teachings of Lao Tzu.) Brian B. Walker. 1994, HarperSanFrancisco.

See also
Meditation,
p. 368.

Dzogchen

Dzogchen, the "Great Perfection," has always been one of the most elusive teachings of Tibetan Buddhism.

Dzogchen, which bears some resemblance to Zen, teaches that the "self-perfected" state of mind, without the interference of categories or concepts, is the mind's natural state. This makes it difficult to talk about in words, but Namkhai Norbu, a Tibetan Dzogchen master now living in Italy, conveys something of its flavor in this concise, intelligent book. He emphasizes that Dzogchen is not a sect or religion, "but a state of knowledge that masters have transmitted beyond any limits of sect." Once the teacher has familiarized the student with this state of knowledge, it's up to the student to maintain it with his or her own practice. —Richard Smoley

●

When a master teaches Dzogchen, he or she is trying to transmit a state of knowledge. The aim of the master is to awaken the student, opening that individual's consciousness to the primordial state. The master will not say: 'Follow my rules and obey my precepts!', but will say: 'Open your inner eye and observe yourself. Stop seeking an external lamp to enlighten you from outside, but light your own inner lamp. Thus the teachings will come to live in you, and you in the teachings.'

●

Garab Dorje, the first Dzogchen master, after teaching for the whole of his life, left behind, for all the Dzogchen practitioners of the future, a small testament three verses long. The verses read:

Introduce the state directly.
Don't remain in doubt.
Continue in the profound knowledge
  of self-liberation.

'Introducing the state directly' refers to the transmission by the master, who, in various ways, introduces and brings the disciple to understand the condition of 'what is', the individual's primordial state. This is the Base. 'Not remaining in doubt' means that one must have a precise knowledge of this state, finding the state of the presence of contemplation which is one and the same in all the thousands of possible experiences. This is the Path. 'Continue in the profound knowledge of self-liberation' is the Fruit. What it means is that the complete and unchangeable knowledge of self-liberation is totally integrated with one's daily life, and that in all circumstances one continues in that state. All the hundreds and hundreds of original texts of Dzogchen can be considered to be an explanation of these three verses of Garab Dorje. But the teachings are not just a book or a tradition, they are a living state of knowledge.

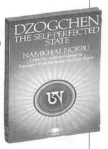

Dzogchen
(The Self-Perfected State)
Namkhai Norbu & Adriano Clemente. Penguin Books, 1990; 96 pp.
ISBN 0-14-019167-4
$7.95 ($9.95 postpaid) from Penguin USA/Cash Sales, 120 Woodbine Street, Bergenfield, NJ 07621; 800/253-6476

ᗡXXIII

REPRESENTATION CONTAINING THE SUM TOTAL OF THE CABALA FOR INSERTION
IN VOL. II, BOOK IV, CONCERNING CABALA OF THE HEBREWS

HORIZON OF ETERNITY
Sephiroth First

Highest Crown

SEPHIROTHIC SYSTEM OF TEN DIVINE NAMES

**The Sephirothic Tree Of
The Later Qabbalists**

The Secret Teachings of All Ages

This volume, first published in 1928, is the grandest compendium ever gathered of esoteric lore, mythology, and historical anecdotes. Originally titled An Encyclopedic Outline of Masonic, Hermetic, Qabbalistic and Rosicrucian Symbolical Philosophy, it is filled to the brim with ancient woodcuts, gloriously old-fashioned paintings of bewigged sages and bearded mages, and column after column of tiny type detailing the meaning of it all. In short, this is the kind of book one dreams of finding on the dusty top shelf of a mysterious occult bookshop, loaded with, well, the secret teachings of all ages.

The late Manly P. Hall's vast knowledge of matters arcane was legendary, and this tome will go down in history as his quirky masterwork. It captivated me over twenty years ago when I first picked it up, and provided my first entry into the lesser-known byways of Western spiritual and esoteric traditions. I still consult it from time to time.
—Jay Kinney

Celestial Virgin with Sun God in her arms.

The Secret Teachings of All Ages
(An Encyclopedic Outline of Masonic, Hermetic, Qabbalistic and Rosicrucian Symbolical Philosophy)
Manly P. Hall. J. Augustus Knapp, Illustrator.
1989; 245 pp. ISBN 0-89314-540-8
$29.95 ($33.45 postpaid) from Philosophical Research Society, 3910 Los Feliz Blvd., Los Angeles, CA 90027; 800/548-4062 (in California: 213/663-2167)

Dreaming the Dark

The "how" of dreaming the dark is simple, interesting, and valuable. During her ten years in a coven, and through her work as a therapist and political activist, Starhawk developed an organic sense of group and individual psychodynamics. She stresses our mortal need for community, offer-

ing what others might term a systems theory or family therapy approach to social change. Starhawk relates her understanding in the good instruction she provides on fostering the life and work of any group, sharing her experiences in therapy, in the craft, and in jail for her protest, with unstinting self-honesty. Persons of all genders, reli-

gions, and politics interested in healing self or planet would do well to avail themselves of this extraordinary text.
—Stephanie Mills
[Suggested by Evy Gershon]

Dreaming the Dark
(Magic, Sex, and Politics)
Starhawk. 1982, 1989; 280 pp.
ISBN 0-8070-1025-1 $12.95 ($16.70 postpaid) from Beacon Press, 25 Beacon Street, Boston, MA 02108; 617/742-2110

• We must demand that our politics serve our sexuality. Too often, we have asked sexuality to serve politics instead. Ironically, the same movements that have criticized sexual repression and bourgeois morality have themselves too often tried to mold their sexual feeling to serve the current political theory. This tradition includes nineteenth century revolutionary asceticism, the New Left's demand that women practice free love (meaning sex without involvement), the fear of lesbianism in the early women's movement, and the mandatory separatist line taken by some in the later women's movement. Too many generations have asked: What do my politics tell me I should feel? The better question is: What do I, at my root, at my core, desire?

In Search of the Miraculous: Fragments of an Unknown Teaching

No discussion of modern spirituality would be complete without a glimpse of G.I. Gurdjieff, the mysterious Greco-Armenian master who informed the Western world early in this century that the mental state we go around in every day is literally a "waking sleep."

In Search of the Miraculous, by Gurdjieff's student P.D. Ouspensky, gives a lucid account of Gurdjieff's unique, provocative style of spiritual instruction and his view of "waking up" as well as a grand and unique view of the cosmos and humanity's part in it. The ideas here range from the inspiring to the perplexing, but practically every page has the power to jolt one from the slumber of daily life.
—Richard Smoley

• G. began the next talk as follows:

"Man's possibilities are very great. You cannot conceive even a shadow of what man is capable of attaining. But nothing can be attained in sleep. In the consciousness of a sleeping man his illusions, his 'dreams' are mixed with reality. He lives in a subjective world and he can never escape from it. And this is the reason why he can never make

use of all the powers he possesses and why he always lives in only a small part of himself.

"It has been said before that self-study and self-observation, if rightly conducted, bring man to the realization of the fact that something is wrong with his machine and with his functions in their ordinary state. A man realizes that it is precisely because he is asleep that he lives and works in a small part of himself. It is precisely for this reason that the vast majority of his possibilities remain unrealized, the vast majority of his powers are left unused. A man feels that he does not get out of life all that it can give him, that he fails to do so owing to definite functional defects in his machine, in his receiving apparatus. The idea of self-study acquires in his eyes a new meaning. He feels that possibly it may not even be worth while studying himself as he is now. He sees every function as it is now and as it could be or ought to be. Self-observation brings man to the realization of the necessity for self-change. And in observing himself a man notices that self-observation itself brings about certain changes in his inner processes. He begins to understand that self-observation is an instrument of self-change, a means of awakening. By observing himself he throws, as it were, a ray of light onto his

In Search of the Miraculous
(Fragments of an Unknown Teaching)
P. D. Ouspensky. Harcourt Brace Jovanovich, 1965; ISBN 0-15-644508-5
$8.95 ($12.45 postpaid) from Harcourt Brace Trade Dept., 6277 Sea Harbor Drive, Orlando, FL 32887-4300; 800/543-1918

inner processes which have hitherto worked in complete darkness. And under the influence of this light the processes themselves begin to change. There are a great many chemical processes that can take place only in the absence of light. Exactly in the same way many psychic processes can take place only in the dark. Even a feeble light of consciousness is enough to change completely the character of a process, while it makes many of them altogether impossible."

BACK in 1967, the insights of Buckminster Fuller initiated the *Whole Earth Catalog.* —Stewart Brand

*"To make the world work
For 100% of humanity
In the shortest possible time
Through spontaneous cooperation
Without ecological offense
Or the disadvantage of anyone."*
—Buckminster Fuller

This sounds like a recent call to action, but Fuller dedicated his life to this goal in 1927, appointing himself as Guinea Pig B (for Bucky, as everyone called him). He developed and demonstrated "comprehensive anticipatory design science," a way of thinking that facilitates the just distribution of the world's resources necessary for a sustainable society. His famous geodesic dome is but one of many examples of his more-with-less (he called it "ephemeralization") philosophy at work. The best domes use only one-fiftieth of the material in a conventional structure of similar utility, and are unusually energy-efficient. His eleven-passenger Dymaxion™ car could top 120 miles per hour, and got 30 mpg — in 1934!

Bucky's everything-is-connected-to-everything vision and detailed language can make his writing and lecturing hard to follow at first. I'd start with a book about him — **Buckminster Fuller** *— or the video* **"World of Buckminster Fuller."** *Then tackle any of his books, gradually working toward the comprehensive* **Synergetics** *and* **Synergetics 2**. *For total aural immersion, there is* **Everything I Know**, *a seven-volume set (six cassettes per volume) of his lectures. These, all of Fuller's books (the out-of-print ones are Xerox copies), and a host of other artifacts — including a new version of the useful* **Dymaxion™ Air-Ocean Map** *— are available from the Buckminster Fuller Institute's catalog. A supporting membership brings you the* **Trimtab Bulletin**, *which reports ongoing Fuller-inspired work. There is now a Fuller BBS called* **FIX** *(Fuller Information Exchange). A Fuller exhibit will appear at the Smithsonian in 1995.*

Fuller said that he was working fifty years ahead to develop the necessary tools and insights to get us through this difficult time. Here they are. —JB

Buckminster Fuller Institute
Institute membership $20/year domestic, $25/year international; Dymaxion Artifacts Catalog and sample issue of Trimtab Bulletin free from Buckminster Fuller Institute, 1743 S. La Cienega Blvd, Los Angeles, CA 90035; 310/837-7710

●

Physics has found no solids! So to keep on teaching our children the word solid immediately is to drive home a way of thinking that is going to be neither reliable nor useful.

There are no surfaces, there are no solids, there are no straight lines, there are no planes.

●

I'm sure none of you know what you're doing with your supper. All you know is you've loaded it in, and you're not saying, "I'm going to send some of it off to this gland and some to that, and tomorrow morning I'm going to grow some hair." I'll simply assert all of you are almost completely automated and always have been. And you talk about automation as though it was something new and rather scary.

●

A human being is what I call a pattern integrity.

I'm going to take a piece of manila rope, and then I'm going to splice into it a piece of cotton rope. I splice into the other end of the cotton rope a piece of nylon rope. I'm going to make the very simplest knot I know, which is to go around 360 degrees in

this plane and 360 degrees in that plane.

I'm not going to pull it tight. There's the knot.

The rope has not done this, I have done it to the rope. At any rate, I can slide it along . . . and now it's on the nylon — suddenly, it's off the end. We say: "The knot was a pattern integrity." It wasn't manila, it wasn't

Buckminster Fuller with his Dymaxion car and "Fly's Eye" dome.

cotton, it wasn't nylon.

Cotton, nylon, and manila — any one of them is good to let us know its shape, what its pattern was; but it wasn't that: it had an integrity of its own. —*Buckminster Fuller*

Composing a Life

Author Mary Catherine Bateson, daughter of anthropologist Margaret Mead and biologist/anthropologist/philosopher Gregory Bateson, combines the best of both and adds her own considerable experience and wisdom. I listen carefully to everything she says. —SB

This is a warm, inspiring, brilliant book. In it, Mary Catherine Bateson explores a new design for the composition of a life that is about ambiguity, discontinuity, metaphor, wholeness — that is a continuous act of creation.

We learn from Bateson and four of her friends that the discontinuity that defines women's lives doesn't hinder achievement, but rather provides a source of light, strength, and creativity. A life that meanders, attending to the changing demands of children and husbands and work, offers a joy that comes from inclusion and process; the limited scope of single-minded purpose cannot offer this sort of joy.

The book's form speaks to this joy; the simple act of talking to a friend over a cup of coffee at the kitchen table leads to connections and metaphors elegant and profound: "We see achievement as purposeful and monolithic, like the sculpting of a massive tree trunk that has first to be brought from the forest and then shaped by long labor to assert the artist's vision, rather than something crafted from odds and ends, like a patchwork quilt, and lovingly used to warm different nights and bodies."

Composing a Life
(Life as a Work in Progress)
Mary Catherine Bateson. Plume Books, 1989; 241 pp. ISBN 0-452-26505-3
$10 ($12 postpaid) from Penguin USA/ Consumer Sales, 120 Woodbine Street, Bergenfield, NJ 07621; 800/253-6476

In the everchanging working world of the late twentieth century, to be mutable and flexible, as a woman is, is to be made of stronger fiber — an imperative when working toward a particular career goal is no guarantee of stability because there is no stability. A life lived this way is also rich with risk — and endless, delightful possibility. —Lisa Winer

●

In this society, we habitually underestimate the impulse in men, women, and even children to care for one another and their need to be taken care of. In a multiplicity of forms, caretaking is part of the composition of almost every life. Because we have so elaborated the caretaking professions, we may not notice the amount of caretaking done by an artist with apprentices or by a chief of engineering or a college president; we fail to notice the aridity of these jobs when they do not involve care for others. A. A. Milne, in the nursery rhyme, understood the impulse of a three year old,

"James James Morrison Morrison," to take care of his mother, but we are largely blind to caretaking by children and often miss the mutual caretaking of men in mines and foxholes. When Johnnetta walks in the morning, she is taking care of herself by dealing with the stress that goes with her job and taking care of her students by giving them a useful model. She is also caring for an idea, the idea of young black women striding out into their lives, limber and free. Coming to New York to care for a hospitalized son could be seen as a distraction from her professional commitment, but in fact it provides a symbolic refocusing of the other kinds of care, a style of response and commitment learned over a lifetime. Being a mommy is part of being a good president.

●

It is now time to explore the creative potential of interrupted and conflicted lives, where energies are not narrowly focused or permanently pointed toward a single ambition. These are not lives without commitment, but rather lives in which commitments are continually refocused and redefined. We must invest time and passion in specific goals and yet at the same time acknowledge that these are mutable. The circumstances of women's lives now and in the past provide examples for new ways of thinking about the lives of both men and women. What are the possible transfers of learning when life is a collage of different tasks? How does creativity flourish on distraction? What insights arise from the experience of multiplicity and ambiguity? And at what point does desperate improvisation become significant achievement? These are important questions in a world in which we are increasingly strangers and sojourners. The knight errant, who finds his challenges along the way, may be a better model for our times than the knight who is questing for the grail.

I and Thou

*You can read **I and Thou** in two hours and not get over it for the rest of your life. Buber tells you how you stand, either in a dialogical relationship with the Creative Force or in a position of "havingness" where you are a thing bounded by other things. —Ken Kesey*

A discovery more prime than Einstein's Relativity is Buber's distinction between the "experience" of I-It and the "relation" of I-You. It can cure the twin pathologies of Transcendent God and Controllable Nature. In "I-You" is the possibility of love that does not possess, as well as the realest perception of learning, which is coevolution. Martin Buber's original German torrent is well served by the translation and prologue by Walter Kaufmann. —SB

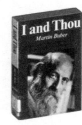

I and Thou
Martin Buber. Charles Scribner's Sons, 1984; 137 pp. ISBN 0-684-18254-8
$5.95 postpaid from Macmillan Publishing Co., 100 Front Street, Riverside, NJ 08075; 800/257-5755

The center of the universe, the most compelling force in human existence, is the possibility of relationship. Buber is a spiritual magnet who pulls your wandering, compulsively ignoring at-tention back to that central fact, even though so many other forces drive us to think of the world as a constellation of things, rather than a plenum of beings. —HLR

•

The You encounters me by grace—it cannot be found by seeking. But that I speak the basic word to it is a deed of my whole being, is my essential deed.

The You encounters me. But I enter into a direct relationship to it. Thus the relationship is election and electing passive and active at once: An action of the whole being must approach passivity, for it does away with all partial actions and thus with any sense of action, which always depends on limited exertions.

The basic word I-You can be spoken only with one's whole being. The concentration and fusion into a whole being can never be accomplished by me, can never be accomplished without me. I require a You to become; becoming I, I say You.

All actual life is encounter.

•

Whoever says You does not have something for his object. For wherever there is something, there is also another something; every It borders on other Its; It is only by virtue of bordering on others. But where You is said there is no something. You has no borders.

Whoever says You does not have something; he has nothing. But he stands in relation.

•

The life of a human being does not exist merely in the sphere of goal-directed verbs. It does not consist merely of activities that have something for their object.

I perceive something. I feel something. I imagine something. I want something. I sense something. I think something. The life of a human being does not consist merely of all this and its like.

All this and its like is the basis of the realm of It.

But the realm of You has another basis.

Miss Manners' Guide to the Turn-of-the-Millennium

Judith Martin, who winks at us from behind her mock-Victorian persona of Miss Manners, is a shrewd social philosopher who uses her readers' questions as a launching pad for essays on a thousand aspects of modern human relationships. She peers through her lorgnette at everything from bridal showers to sexual harassment, pulls apart ceremonies and rituals to expose the underlying attitudes and symbolism, explains old rules of behavior, and provides new rules when the old ones won't do. Yes, she'll tell you which fork to use (and ask you to stop worrying so much about it, too), but she'd much rather be dishing out advice on how to cope with an increasingly rude world without resorting to rudeness oneself. Ms. Martin knows it isn't enough to be polite if you can't defend yourself against those who take advantage of your politeness; and so she offers techniques for dealing with nosy questions, for keeping your job out of your personal life (and vice versa), even for insulting someone when necessary, all with impeccable manners. In her hands, etiquette is no longer a ladder for social climbers or a bludgeon for snobs; it's a tool for transforming ourselves and our society into something nobler, by bringing the ideals of mutual respect, dignity, and equality back into our everyday lives through the way we treat each other. And Ms. Martin is one of the wittiest writers of our time; this may be the only etiquette book you'll ever stay up all night to read.

*This book is the third fat volume of letters and essays collected from Martin's syndicated column. Less well known but well worth seeking out is her slim **Common Courtesy** (Atheneum Books). Ms. Martin here sets aside her Miss Manners mask (but not, fortunately, her brilliant wit) and gives us a mind-opening essay on the role of etiquette in a democratic society. —Scott Marley*

•

Dear Miss Manners:

Occasionally, my husband's best friend drops by (no notice) with his young girlfriend, who repeatedly announces that she's hungry. What is the proper response in order to avoid feeding her?

Gentle Reader:

There is no reason on earth that you should make a connection between a visitor's problem of being hungry and the possibility of your providing a solution. A polite response to this rude announcement would be, "Well, then, I won't keep you. You'll be wanting to get home to dinner. So nice to have seen you."

•

Dear Miss Manners:

What is the correct response when your pregnant friends insist on showing you the photographs from their sonograms? This has happened to me three times, and I somehow feel that saying, "Oh, how cute" is inappropriate. Any suggestions?

Gentle Reader:

None better than "Oh, how cute." Miss Manners presents her compliments to you.

Miss Manners' Guide to the Turn-of-the-Millennium
Judith Martin. 1989; 742 pp.
ISBN 0-671-72228-X
$15.95 ($18.95 postpaid) from Simon & Schuster/Order Dept., 200 Old Tappan Road, Old Tappan, NJ 07675; 800/223-2336

Tales of the Dervishes

"It is a fundamental mistake of man's to think that he is alive, when he has merely fallen asleep in life's waiting room" is the way Idries Shah, contemporary Sufi anthologist, describes the Sufi project: helping people awaken from the illusions of everyday life. Along with attention exercises, physical exercises, and a whole mystic toolkit of self-observation techniques, Sufis use the world's most well-known consciousness-altering tool — stories. The "teaching stories" of the Dervishes and other Sufis resemble simple children's fables, but like well-aimed stones tossed into the pond of consensus trance, their effects ripple out into the minds and lives of those who read them. Attention is the supreme instrument. These stories teach by pointing. —HLR

•

There was once a hard-working and generous farmer who had several idle and greedy sons. On his deathbed he told them that they would find his treasure if they were to dig in a certain field. As soon as the old man was dead, the sons hurried to the fields, which they dug up from one end to the other, and with increasing desperation and concentration when they did not find the gold in the place indicated.

But they found no gold at all. Realizing that in his generosity their father must have given the gold away during his lifetime, they abandoned the search. Finally, it occurred to them that, since the land had been prepared, they might as well now sow a crop. They planted wheat, which produced an abundant yield. They sold this crop and prospered that year.

After the harvest was in, the sons thought again about the bare possibility that they might have missed the buried gold, so they again dug up their fields, with the same result.

After several years they became accustomed to labour, and to the cycle of the seasons, something which they had not understood before. Now they understood the reason for their father's method of training them, and they became honest and contented farmers. Ultimately they found themselves possessed of sufficient wealth no longer to wonder about the hidden hoard.

Thus it is with the teaching of the understanding of human destiny and the meaning of life. The teacher, faced with impatience, confusion and covetousness on the part of the students, must direct them to an activity which is known by him to be constructive and beneficial to them, but whose true function and aim is often hidden from them by their own rawness.

Tales of the Dervishes
(Teaching Stories of the Sufi Masters over the Past Thousand Years)
Idries Shah. Arkana, 1993; 219 pp.
ISBN 0-14-019358-8
$10 ($12 postpaid) from Penguin USA/ Cash Sales, 120 Woodbine Street, Bergenfield, NJ 07621; 800/253-6476

BATESON, KUHN, LÉVI-STRAUSS: three builders of mental models, perceivers of patterns in nature, in science, in human behavior. —HLR

Steps to an Ecology of Mind • Mind and Nature

Gregory Bateson is responsible for a number of formal discoveries, most notably the "Double Bind" theory of schizophrenia. As an anthropologist, he did pioneer work in New Guinea and (with Margaret Mead) in Bali. He participated in the Macy Foundation meetings that founded the science of cybernetics, but kept a healthy distance from computers. He wandered thornily in and out of various disciplines — biology, ethnology, linguistics, epistemology, psychotherapy — and left each of them altered with his passage.

Steps to an Ecology of Mind chronicles that journey. It is a collection of all his major papers, 1935-1971. In recommending the book I've learned to suggest that it be read backwards. Read the broad analyses of mind and ecology at the end of the book and then work back to see where the premises come from.

Bateson has informed everything I've attempted since I read Steps in 1972. Through him I became convinced that much more of whole systems could be understood than I had thought, and that much more existed wholesomely beyond understanding than I thought — that mysticism, mood, ignorance and paradox could be rigorous, for instance, and that the most potent tool for grasping these essences — these influence nets — is cybernetics.

Mind and Nature: A Necessary Unity addresses the hidden, though unoccult, dynamics of life — the misapprehension of which threatens to unhorse our civilization. Bateson doesn't have all the answers, he just has better questions — elegant, mature, embarrassing questions that tweak the quick of things. — SB

●

When you narrow down your epistemology and act on the premise "what interests me is me, or my organization, or my species," you chop off consideration of other loops of the loop structure. You decide that you want to get rid of the by-products of human life and that Lake Erie will be a good place to put them. You forget that the eco-mental system called Lake Erie is part of your wider eco-mental system — and that if Lake Erie is driven insane, its insanity is incorporated in the larger system of *your* thought and experience.

●

Mere purposive rationality unaided by such phenomena as art, religion, dream, and the like, is necessarily pathogenic and destructive of life; its virulence springs specifically from the circumstance that life depends upon interlocking *circuits* of contingency, while consciousness can only see such short arcs as human purpose may direct.

●

In no system which shows mental characteristics can any part have unilateral control

Steps to an Ecology of Mind
Gregory Bateson. Ballantine Books, 1972; 541 pp. ISBN 0-345-33291-1 $5.95 ($7.95 postpaid) from Random House/Order Dept., 400 Hahn Road, Westminster, MD 21157; 800/733-3000

Mind and Nature
(A Necessary Unity)
Gregory Bateson. Bantam Books, 1979; 272 pp. ISBN 0-553-34575-3 $11.50 ($14 postpaid) from Bantam, Doubleday, Dell/Fulfillment Dept., 2451 S. Wolf Road, Des Plaines, IL 60018; 800/223-6834

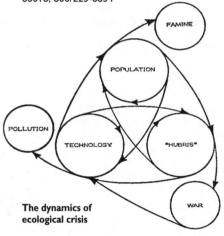

The dynamics of ecological crisis

over the whole. In other words, the mental characteristics of the system are immanent, not in some part, but in the system as a whole. —*Steps to an Ecology of Mind*

●

I do not believe that the original purpose of the rain dance was to make "it" rain. I suspect that that is a degenerate misunderstanding of a much more profound religious need: to affirm membership in what we may call the *ecological tautology*, the eternal verities of life and environment. There's always a tendency — almost a need — to vulgarize religion, to turn it into entertainment or politics or magic or "power."

●

It seems to puzzle psychologists that the exploring tendencies of a rat cannot be simply extinguished by having the rat encounter boxes containing small electric shocks.

A little empathy will show that from the rat's point of view, it is not desirable that he learn the general lesson. His experience of a shock upon putting his nose into a box indicates to him that he did *well* to put his nose into that box in order to gain the information that it contained a shock. In fact, the "purpose" of exploration is, not to discover whether exploration is a good thing, but to discover information about the explored. The larger case is of a totally different nature from that of the particular. —*Mind and Nature*

The Structure of Scientific Revolutions

Paradigms are group mental models. And science is a collective narrative.

Like "left-brained/right-brained" dichotomizing, the application of the notion of "paradigm shifts" to everything from spiritual revelations to advertising campaigns has diluted Kuhn's meaning. But technical terms sometimes diffuse rapidly into the vernacular precisely because something new or newly discovered needs a name.

Kuhn's core idea offers us a mental model of science as a culture, a community of discourse in which research is structured according to what is already widely agreed to be known about the world. The paradigm is the container within which acceptable discourse is defined. The cracks in paradigms are the routes to the next one.

This book should be required reading for scientists-in-training, before they are infected with the old belief that they are participating in an objective quest for absolute truth. It's also a good way to understand how the world is like a story. —HLR

●

Aristotle's *Physica*, Ptolemy's *Almagest*, Newton's *Principia* and *Opticks*, Franklin's *Electricity*, Lavoisier's *Chemistry*, and Lyell's

The Structure of Scientific Revolutions
Thomas S. Kuhn. University of Chicago Press, 1970; 210 pp. ISBN 0-226-45804-0 $9.95 ($12.95 postpaid) from Chicago Distribution Center, 11030 S. Langley Avenue, Chicago, IL 60628; 800/621-2736

Geology — these and many other works served for a time implicitly to define the legitimate problems and methods of a research field for succeeding generations of practitioners. They were able to do so because they shared two essential characteristics. Their achievement was sufficiently unprecedented to attract an enduring group of adherents away from competing modes of scientific activity. Simultaneously, it was sufficiently open-ended to leave all sorts of problems for the redefined group of practitioners to resolve. Achievements that share these two characteristics I shall henceforth refer to as 'paradigms,' a term that relates closely to 'normal science.'

The Savage Mind

Claude Lévi-Strauss is the most famous — I mean, all the anthropologists recommend — He's so — I mean, so what if he's French — The most profound — Sartre couldn't — structural anthropology was what — Primitive doesn't mean — I mean, they knew what they were doing — So when — It looks crazy to us of course — They were just abstracting in a different — But you can analyze it once you — So you see, ritual is the — If you never — The Indians always — I mean, what makes you think you're so logical? —SB

●

The real question is not whether the touch of a woodpecker's beak does in fact cure toothache. It is rather whether there is a point of view from which a woodpecker's beak and a man's tooth can be seen as "going together" (the use of this congruity for therapeutic purposes being only one of its possible uses), and whether some initial order can be introduced into the universe by means of the grouping. Classifying, as opposed to not classifying, has a value of its own, whatever form the classification may take.

●

A native thinker makes the penetrating comment that "All sacred things must have their place." It could even be said that being in their place is what makes them sacred for if

The Savage Mind
Claude Lévi-Strauss. University of Chicago Press, 1968; 290 pp. ISBN 0-226-47484-4 $13.95 ($16.95 postpaid) from Chicago Distribution Center, 11030 S. Langley Avenue, Chicago, IL 60628; 800/621-2736

they were taken out of their place, even in thought, the entire order of the universe would be destroyed. Sacred objects therefore contribute to the maintenance of order in the universe by occupying the places allocated to them.

The opposite of totemism: Naturalized Man. Sketch by Le Brun.

If you read only two books from this Catalog, make them *The Diversity of Life* and *A Sand County Almanac* (p. 65). —PW

In communities there are little players and big players, and the biggest players of all are the keystone species. As the name implies, the removal of a keystone species causes a substantial part of the community to change drastically.

The Diversity of Life

This is the story of life resurgent, the forces of creation and destruction shaping and reshaping all living creatures. Diversity is simply the best introduction, in elegant prose, to every aspect of the ecology of living creatures — "ecology" defined as the story of Earth's grand stage, with a delightful theatre company of millions and millions of wonderful superstars.

In Greek, "ecology" is oikos ("house or dwelling place") + logos (primarily "word, thought, or place"). To early Greeks, logos was the moving and regulating principle in all nature, as well as that part of human nature able to recognize this ordering energy at work. **The Diversity of Life** *is classic ecology, speaking and thinking about the natural governance of our home, the planetary household.* —PW

•

Life was impoverished in five major events, and to lesser degree here and there around the world in countless other episodes. After each downturn it recovered to at least the original level of diversity. How long did it take for evolution to restore the losses after the first-order spasms? The number of families of animals living in the sea is as reliable a measure as we have been able to obtain from the existing fossil evidence. In general, five million years were enough for only a strong start. A complete recovery from each of the five major extinctions required tens of millions of years. In particular the Ordovician dip needed 25 million years, the Devonian 30 million years, the Permian and Triassic (combined because they were so close together in time) 100 million years, and the Cretaceous 20 million years. These figures should give pause to anyone who believes that what *Homo sapiens* destroys, Nature will redeem. Maybe so, but not within any length of time that has meaning for contemporary humanity.

•

Imagine yourself on a journey upward from the center of the earth, taken at the pace of a leisurely walk. For the first twelve weeks you travel through furnace-hot rock and magma devoid of life. Three minutes to the surface, five hundred meters to go, you encounter the first organisms, bacteria feeding on nutrients that have filtered into the deep water-bearing strata. You breach the surface and for ten seconds glimpse a dazzling burst of life, tens of thousands of new species of microorganisms, plants, and animals within horizontal line of sight. Half a minute later almost all are gone. Two hours later only the faintest traces remain, consisting largely of people in airliners who are filled in turn with colon bacteria.

In the realm of physical measurement, evolutionary biology is far behind the rest of the natural sciences. Certain numbers are crucial to our ordinary understanding of the universe. What is the mean diameter of the earth? It is 12,742 kilometers (7,913 miles). How many stars are there in the Milky Way, an ordinary spiral galaxy? Approximately 10^{11}, 100 billion. How many genes are there in a small virus? There are 10 (in øX174 phage). What is the mass of an electron? It is 9.1×10^{-28} grams. And how many species of organisms are there on earth? We don't know, not even to the nearest order of magnitude. The number could be close to 10 million or as high as 100 million. Large numbers of species continue to turn up every year. And of those already discovered, over 99 percent are known only by a scientific name, a handful of specimens in a museum, and a few scraps of anatomical description in scientific journals.

•

From prehistory to the present time, the mindless horsemen of the environmental apocalypse have been overkill, habitat destruction, introduction of animals such as rats and goats, and diseases carried by these exotic animals. In prehistory the paramount agents were overkill and exotic animals. In recent centuries, and to an accelerating degree during our generation, habitat destruction is foremost among the lethal forces, followed by the invasion of exotic animals.

The Diversity of Life
Edward O. Wilson. 1992; 424 pp. ISBN 0-674-21298-3
$29.95 ($32.95 postpaid) from Harvard University Press/Customer Service, 79 Garden Street, Cambridge, MA 02138; 617/495-2600

See also Biomes (pp. 53, 63); **Preserving Plant Knowledge** (p.104); **Ecoactivism** (pp. 109-110); **Endangered Species** (pp. 45, 52).

See also Biomes (pp. 53, 63); Preserving Plant Knowledge (p.104); Ecoactivism (pp. 109-110); Endangered Species (pp. 45, 52).

OTHER GREAT RESOURCES

Global Biodiversity, by the World Conservation Monitoring Centre. The most important reference volume. Need info, need help, need perspective? Ask the librarian for Global Biodiversity. By the save-our-genetic-heritage heavies: International Union for the Conservation of Nature, World Wildlife Fund, and the United Nations Environmental Program.

On the Brink of Extinction (Conserving the Diversity of Life): Edward Wolf. Worldwatch Paper 78. This is the pamphlet to hand to the barbarians who dismiss other lifeforms as minor characters in their opera. The best short intro.

Keeping the Options Alive (The Scientific Basis for Conserving Biodiversit): Walter Reid and Kenton Miller. World Resources Institute. The rational arguments, well spoken. Is biodiversity important? Is there really a holocaust? What are the best policy tools to build a planetary refuge?

Biodiversity, edited by E. O. Wilson. A collection of papers by a well-known cast of characters: E.O. Wilson, Paul Ehrlich, Peter Raven, Michael Soule, Norman Myers, Dan Jantzen, Lester Brown, James Lovelock, David Ehrenfeld . . . need more be said?

Economics and Biodiversity, by J. McNeely. 1988, International Union for the Conservation of Nature. By far the most accessible and sensible understanding of how to calculate the "value" of maintaining nonhuman environments.

Five Kingdoms

If the world of science wasn't so fuzzy and prejudiced, Lynn Margulis and James Lovelock would share a Nobel Prize. Here is just one of Margulis's many contributions to science: the first book clearly spelling out the Five Kingdoms of living things (Plants, Animals, Fungi, Monera, Protists). Not surprisingly (especially to Lynn), the loriciferans were found one year after publication of Five Kingdoms *and are now recognized as a new phylum! This is the best field guide to life on the planet.* —PW

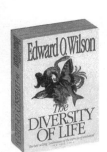

(Above) A phylogeny of life on Earth based on the Whittaker five-kingdom system and the symbiotic theory of the origin of eukaryotic cells.

Five Kingdoms
(An Illustrated Guide to the Phyla of Life on Earth)
Lynn Margulis & Karlene V. Schwartz. 1987; 338 pp.
ISBN 0-7167-1912-6
$27.95 ($31.95 postpaid) from W.H. Freeman and Co., 4419 W. 1980 S., Salt Lake City, UT 84104; 800/488-5233

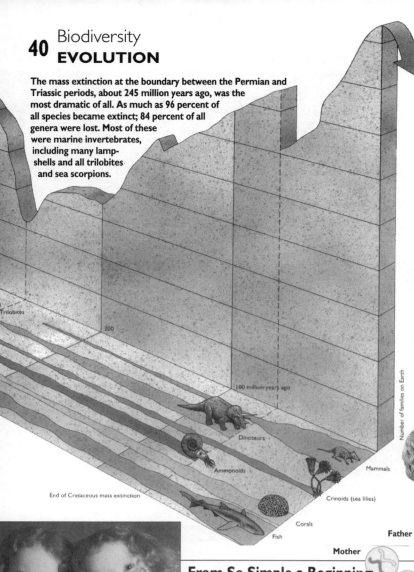

The mass extinction at the boundary between the Permian and Triassic periods, about 245 million years ago, was the most dramatic of all. As much as 96 percent of all species became extinct; 84 percent of all genera were lost. Most of these were marine invertebrates, including many lamp-shells and all trilobites and sea scorpions.

Gibbon Baboon Orangutan Chimpanzee Gorilla Human Frank

Twentieth-Century News

"Guided by no vision, bound to no distant purpose, evolution composes itself word by word to address the requirements of only one or two generations at a time." —E. O. Wilson, *The Diversity of Life*

Evolution is not a system but a description of life's 3.9-billion-year history on the planet Earth; the process that creates biodiversity. The twentieth century added stunning discoveries to Darwin's legacy.

• Raymond Dart found the Taung skull in South Africa, forever changing human history. We are now all Africans by lineage. A few details have evolved in new directions but, in evolutionary essence, we are all African primates.

• Watson and Crick described DNA. Humankind finally put its fingers on the "gene," the genetic blueprints, and a new technique to study phylogeny. In the next century, devolution will take off. Biotechnologists have already

started dismantling DNA to redo the evolutionary mix (p. 234).

• The red-in-tooth-and-claw boys confronted symbiosis. The evolutionary tree just does not always branch; sometimes the branches touch and join. Lynn Margulis says it best: Natural selection is an editor; symbiosis a major author.

• Finally, Raven and Ehrlich found that the arms race in nature had incredibly intricate feedback loops, and that it could evolve into a symbiosis. They called the process "coevolution." Co-evolution stories rapidly became the new evolutionary Just So stories.

Interdependence of critters now has historical coloring — symbiotic and strategic.
—Peter Warshall

(Left): The Taung child — an intermediate between ape and human.

From So Simple a Beginning

Effusively illustrated and well spoken, with the latest news: evolution of the cell, jumping genes, who needs sex?, the origins of life, plate tectonics and mass extinctions. For the newcomer and the oldcomer trying to catch up. —PW

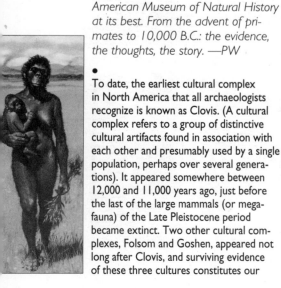

Identical twins result from a single fertilized egg. But early in its development the resulting embryo splits into two.

•

The advent of more complex eukaryote cells, such as the first protozoans about 1.5 billion years ago, signalled a major turning point in evolution. Membranes that had formerly been confined to the boundary of simple prokaryotic cells developed inside the cell and enabled its contents to be organized into compartments. Thus cellular functions, such as DNA information processing, protein synthesis and ATP production, became increasingly sophisticated. This, in turn, meant that the cells of an organism had the potential to differentiate and so evolve highly specialized roles.

Father
Mother
Sperm
Eggs
Fertilized egg
Fertilized egg splits into two
Two genetically identical embryos

From So Simple a Beginning
Philip Whitfield. 1993; 220 pp.
ISBN 0-02-627115-X
$40 postpaid from Macmillan
Publishing Co., 100 Front Street,
Riverside, NJ 08075-7500; 800/257-5755

Stephen Jay Gould: Evolution's Babe Ruth

A beacon of scientific-essay style for years. He finds illustrations of evolutionary themes absolutely everywhere — in comics (the infantilization of Mickey Mouse's face), in batting averages (the extremes narrow with time), in Alfred Kinsey (his landmark sex research followed landmark wasp research). The reader acquires an evolutionary eye constantly rewarded because one theory fits all. —SB

Of his more recent home runs, I like Wonderful Life: The Burgess Shale and the Nature of History. *Eight Little Piggies* *is the most recent collection of essays on natural history with a strong evolution focus. Also* Bully for Brontosaurus, Hen's Teeth and Horse's Toes, The Panda's Thumb, *and* The Flamingo's Smile. *—PW*

Books by Stephen Jay Gould:
Wonderful Life (The Burgess Shale and the Nature of History): 1989; 347 pp. ISBN 0-393-30700-X; $10.95

Eight Little Piggies: 1993; 479 pp. ISBN 0-393-03139-2; $10.95

Bully for Brontosaurus: 1991; 544 pp. ISBN 0-393-30857-X; $11.95

Hen's Teeth and Horse's Toes: 1983; 416 pp. ISBN 0-393-31103-1; $10.95

The Panda's Thumb: 1980; 352 pp. ISBN 0-393-30819-7; $9.95

The Flamingo's Smile: 1985; 480 pp. ISBN 0-393-30375-6; $10.95

All prices postpaid from W.W. Norton & Co./Order Dept., 800 Keystone Industrial Park, Scranton, PA 18512; 800/233-4830.

Richly adorned child burials excavated in Grotte des Enfants at Balzi Rossi, Italy. Their elaborate adornments in the form of clusters of perforated shells are among the earliest examples of what may be hereditary status symbols.

Other Great Fossils

A New Look at the Dinosaurs:
Alan Charig. 1979, 1983, Facts on File.

A Field Guide to Prehistoric Life:
David Lambert, et al. 1985, Facts On File.

Fossils and the History of Life:
George Simpson. Scientific American Library, 1983, W.H. Freeman and Company.

The First Humans

Luxuriously illustrated with expert vignettes on the hominoids, this is the American Museum of Natural History at its best. From the advent of primates to 10,000 B.C.: the evidence, the thoughts, the story. —PW

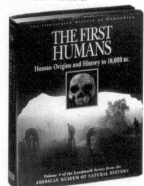

•

To date, the earliest cultural complex in North America that all archaeologists recognize is known as Clovis. (A cultural complex refers to a group of distinctive cultural artifacts found in association with each other and presumably used by a single population, perhaps over several generations). It appeared somewhere between 12,000 and 11,000 years ago, just before the last of the large mammals (or megafauna) of the Late Pleistocene period became extinct. Two other cultural complexes, Folsom and Goshen, appeared not long after Clovis, and surviving evidence of these three cultures constitutes our

knowledge of the early North American Paleoindian hunters.

The First Humans
Göran Burenhult, editor.
HarperSanFrancisco, 1993; 239 pp.
ISBN 0-06-250265-4
$40 ($42.75 postpaid). HarperCollins
Publishers/Direct Mail, PO Box 588,
Dunmore, PA 18512; 800/331-3761

Darwin

While Freud and Marx have been drastically revised, Darwin has been gorgeously elaborated. **Darwin and the Beagle** *is the adventure story: how a Chilean earthquake and a stop at the Galapagos crystallized a new vision of planet process. Darwin wrote enormously. To get a feel for his work, see* **The Darwin Reader** *(Mark Ridley, Ed. 1987, W. W. Norton) and* **The Collected Papers of Charles Darwin** *(Paul Barrett, Ed. 1977, Phoenix Books). —PW*

•

The Galapagos . . . were infinitely strange, unlike any other islands in the world. No one who went there ever forgot them. For the *Beagle* this was just another port of call in a very long voyage, but for Darwin it was much more than that, for it was here, in the most unexpected way — just as a man might have a sudden inspiration while he is travelling in a car or a train — that he be-

gan to form a coherent view of the evolution of life on this planet. To put it into his own words: 'Here, both in space and time, we seem to be brought somewhat near to that great fact — that mystery of mysteries — the first appearance of new beings on this earth.' —*Darwin and the Beagle*

Darwin and the Beagle: Alan Moorehead. Penguin Books, 1969; 224 pp. ISBN 0-14-00327-0. $14.95 ($16.95 postpaid). Penguin USA/Consumer Sales, 120 Woodbine Street, Bergenfield, NJ 07621; 800/253-6476.

Giant tortoises of the Galapagos.

Keeping Up with Science

Nobody can keep up with all the information unleashed by science. The two less technical weeklies are **Science News** *and* **The New Scientist.** **Science News** *is Gringo hot-item journalism with articles like "The Top Scientific Discoveries of 1993."* **The New Scientist** *is our John Bull favorite, scanned by Whole Earth techies and bios for more thoughtful and, at times, difficult-to-read, news. If you're committed and patient,* **The New Scientist** *is probably the bestest for the latest.*

For those willing to read just 10 to 20 percent of a magazine and mind-boggle at the rest, **Nature** *and* **Science** *cover weekly advances in technical language with supplementary essays on science and policy.* **Nature** *(being British) tends to treat certain American concerns with a proper wry wit.* **Science** *struggles more ambiguously with American confusion over the relation of science, religion, economics, technology, and value judgments.* **Science** *is perhaps the heaviest hitter. To be published on its glossy pages brings envy and awe to sci-groupies.*

For broader reviews of academic science as well as the state of theory vs. data, **American Scientist** *and* **Scientific American** *compete for public attention.* **American Scientist** *is a more thorough and strictly science bimonthly with an extensive review of new science books.* **Scientific American** *tries to be hipper ("Is there a genetic basis to gays?") and more relevant to current thought-trends ("Does enviro deterioration increase violence?") and science/policy/ business complexes; it includes select book reviews by the great Philip Morrison as well as amateur do-it-yourself projects. I remain a lover of* **Natural History** *(page 16), but it doesn't cover the physical (vs. life) sciences. —Peter Warshall*

—Greg Becker, *New Scientist*

Science News: Patrick Young, Editor. $44.50/year (51 issues). 1719 N Street NW, Washington, DC 20036; 202/785-2255.

The New Scientist: Alun Anderson, Editor. $140/year (51 issues). New Scientist Subscriptions, PO Box 272, Haywards Heath, West Sussex RH17 3FS, UK; credit card orders 011 44 0622 72155.

Nature: John Maddox, Editor. $135/year (51 issues). PO Box 1733, Riverton, NJ 08077; 800/524-0384.

Science: Daniel Koshland, Editor. $92/year (51 issues). 1333 H Street NW, Washington, DC 20005; 800/347-6969.

American Scientist: Rosalind Reed, Editor. $28/year (6 issues). PO Box 13975, Research Triangle Park, NC 27709-3975; 919/549-0097.

Scientific American: Jonathan Piel, Editor. $34.97/year (12 issues). Box 3187, Harlan, IA 51539; 800/333-1199.

Garden of Microbial Delights

This book makes a long-needed introduction:

Folks, meet the silent majority of life on Earth, the true Gaian citizens: microbes.

Microbes, meet some folks interested in your unrecognized influence and reign.

Fascinating, easy to read, deeply thorough, practical as a field guide, and written by a budding world-class science writer, Dorion Sagan, and his mother, the co-originator of the Gaian Theory, Lynn Margulis. —Kevin Kelly

●

Microbes are, and have been for millions of years, the dominant (most abundant) form of life in the biosphere. Much of the oxygen animals breathe and plants employ in their photosynthetic metabolism originates as a waste gas of plankton — microbes floating in the seas. There would be no agriculture were it not for the widespread presence and fertilizing effects of blue-green and other forms of nitrogen-fixing bacteria. Our forest industry, with its products in the form of furniture, shelter, paper, and so forth, owes its productivity to the continuous growth and chemical activity of microscopic fungi known as mycorrhizae. These fungi break down phosphorus and other nutrient supplies locked up in the rocks and soil into forms usable by the trees' root systems. It is unlikely forests could even grow without such fungi, and fungal symbioses (such as those involved in mycorrhizae) probably were crucial to the formation of the first forests.

●

Microbes makes strange pets. Unlike dogs, cats, fish, or birds, it is impossible to keep a single protoctist or bacterium. Microbes are community organisms with more intricate biological connections to other organisms than animals or plants. Thriving microbes create environments that are attractive to the reproduction of other microbes. Only in rare cases, and then with the specialized and complex techniques of microbiology, can purebred populations or clones, starting from a single cell, be grown.

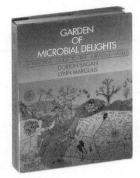

Garden of Microbial Delights
(A Practical Guide to the Subvisible World) Dorion Sagan & Lynn Margulis. 1988; 240 pp. ISBN 0-8403-8529-3 $36.95 ($40.95 postpaid) from Kendall/ Hunt Publishing Company, 4050 Westmark Drive, PO Box 1840, Dubuque, IA 52004-1840; 800/228-0810

These plates from original drawings in a work by 19th-century German naturalist Ernst Haeckel show various slime mold types.

Viruses

A difficult subject to write about. The study of viruses requires an understanding of the edge between life and crystalline chemistry. Sober stories of virulent viruses like HIV or the too-accommodating virus that Australians tried to use to eliminate a plague of exotic hares. —PW

●

The human mind has always been fascinated with the concepts of largest and smallest. For mathematicians, these are infinity and zero; for physicists, the ever-expanding universe and subatomic particles. Biologists have a special feeling for whales and redwood trees, each of which has a grandeur all its own. At the other pole are the smallest of all living things, the viruses. Viruses populate the world between the living and the nonliving, the molecules that can duplicate themselves and the ones that cannot.

●

Rabbit populations infected with this less virulent virus began to show herd immunity

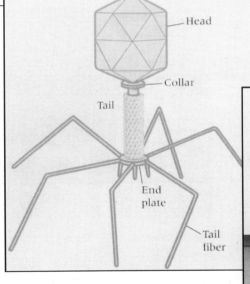

— Head

— Collar

Tail

End
plate

Tail
fiber

Diagram of bacteriophage T4; T4 attached to a bacterium and injecting its DNA.

DNA — Protein coat

Sheath

Plasma membrane

Core

— a phenomenon in which infection of a rabbit already immunized by previous exposure to a virus neutralizes that virus and lowers its probability of transmission to other animals, even if they are not immune. This accelerated the loss of the virulent strain, and the rabbit population resurged.

Viruses
Arnold Levine. Scientific American Library, 1991; ISBN 0-7167-5031-7 $32.95 ($35.95 postpaid) from W. H. Freeman and Co., 4419 W. 1980 S., Salt Lake City, UT 84104; 800/488-5233

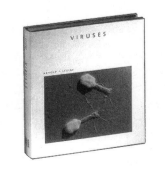

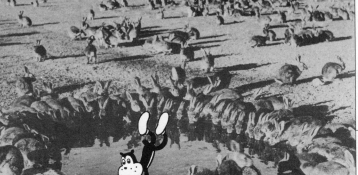

European wild rabbits around an Australian water hole at dusk.

MUSHROOMS, a kingdom unto themselves. Sixty-nine thousand species with thousands to be discovered. They are more closely related to us humans than plants, perhaps separating off from a common ancestor a mere billion or so years ago. Many mushrooms are carnivores with an underground, threadlike lasso that tracks and hogties nematodes (roundworms), dejuices and transforms them to gourmet mushroom flesh.

The fieldkit is easy: a hard container, a roll of wax paper, Fungi Perfecti's spore-print file booklet (to keep it all together and compare spore prints of related 'shrooms), a hori hori (a knife for cutting, digging and sawing), and a waterproof notepad and pen. A tree guide (since many mushrooms have favorite trees) will help sharpen your hunting skills. This is the one natural history profession that snubs plastic bags.

As with all natural history, a real-live fun-guy guru serves best. Call or join the North American Mycological Association; 313/971-2552) to find the nearest group. To grow and cook mushrooms, see page 169. If you think human history was somehow immune from mushrooms, read *In Advance of the Fungi* (E. C. Large. 1940, 1962, Dover Publications). —Peter Warshall

Lepiota procera, tall and delicious.

All That the Rain Promises, and More . . .

The best guide for the beginner. The most compassionate and fun. Only Western mushrooms (two hundred species). I'd buy it no matter where I lived in North America. Only one pound. —PW

All That the Rain Promises, and More...
David Arora. 1991; 256 pp.
ISBN 0-89815-388-3
$15.95 ($18.95 postpaid) from Ten Speed Press, PO Box 7123, Berkeley, CA 94707; 800/841-2665

•

Parasol (*Lepiota procera*)
Other names: *Macrolepiota procera*

Key features:
1. Medium-sized to large: mature cap at least 3" broad.
2. Cap at first smooth and brown but soon breaking up to form shaggy scales on a pale background.
3. Flesh *not* staining orange or red when cut and rubbed.
4. Spores white.

Other features: Drumstick-shaped (with an oval cap) when young.
Where: Alone or in groups on ground in open woods and old pastures, along roads, etc.
Edibility: One of the best! The large, thin caps can be fried or broiled whole, or sliced up.

Down on the Knee Natural History: Lichens, Ferns and Moss

Two-hundred-and-forty million years ago they canopied the earth. Tree ferns and tree horsetails buzzing with yard-long dragonflies and crawling with six-inch roaches. Now, we burn them as coal and I ponder their leaves — hardly ever eaten, clipped, or curled by beast. There are ten-thousand ferns on the planet and about twenty-thousand mosses, liverworts and hornworts. Guides to these cryptogams (organisms with hidden sex organs) are just now ripening and bursting onto the naturalist scene. Here are some we could find. —PW

Peterson Field Guides to Ferns (Boughton Cobb. 1963; Houghton Mifflin). A delicately illustrated and complete guide to the Eastern "ferns" (true ferns, water ferns, succulent ferns, horsetails, clubmosses, spikemosses and quillworts). We badly need a guide of this caliber for the West.

Introduction to Bryology (W. B. Schofield. 1985; McGraw-Hill Publishing Co). Tech intro. Also the *How to Know* series (*How to Know the True Slime Molds*, Marie L. Farr. 1981; William. C. Brown Publishers. *How to Know the Freshwater Algae*, G. W. Prescott. 1978; William. C. Brown Publishers. *How to Know the Lichens*, Mason E. Hale. 1979; William C. Brown Publishers) for slime molds, lichens, and freshwater algae.

For peat's sake. Human's most useful moss and, when dry, what a lovely place to lie down. Books to start: *Focus on Peatland and Peat Mosses* (Howard Crum and Sandra Planisek. 1992; University of Michigan Press) *Field Guide to the Peat Mosses of Boreal North America* (Cyrus B. McQueen. 1990; University Press of New England) and *Peat and Water* (C. H. Fuchsman. 1986; Routledge, Chapman and Hall).

American Bryological and Lichenological Society. Join it, read their journal *Evansia* (American Bryological and Lychenological Society. Biology Department, University of Nebraska , Omaha, NE 68182-0400). The scientific elves of ecology. Best info on rare and threatened species.

Symbiosis (Vernon Ahmadjian and Surindar Paracer. 1986; University Press of New England). How fungi and algae interweave into an inseparable duo called lichen. How cooperation can beat competition.

The Elfin World of Mosses and Liverworts of Michigan's Upper Peninsula and Isle Royale (Janice M. Glime and Marshall L. Strong. 1993; Isle Royale Natural History Assn). The model moss book arranged by habitats (bogs, fens, cedar swamps, tree bases, tree trunks, shaded rocks). Especially for the Great Lakes area, but useful throughout boreal North America.

Mushrooms Demystified

The Encyclopedia Britannica of fungal adoration. Two thousand species. Great introduction for naturalists wanting to know more than if it will kiss the palate or kill the bod. You're bordering on losing perspective when you buy this, the best mid-level to advanced book. —PW

Mushrooms Demystified
David Arora. 1990; 1020 pp.
ISBN 0-89815-169-4
$29.95 ($32.45 postpaid) from Ten Speed Press, PO Box 7123, Berkeley, CA 94707; 800/841-2665

•
AMANITA. Learning to recognize this genus should be an overriding priority for all mushroom hunters, since Amanitas are responsible for 90% of mushroom-induced fatalities. The outstanding attributes of any *Amanita* — what makes even a rotten *Amanita* not just another rotten mushroom, but a rotten *AMANITA* (and therefore worthy of your attention and respect) — are the white spores, pallid gills, and presence of a universal veil...

Most Amanitas — including the most dangerous ones — are also furnished with a partial veil which, upon breaking, often forms a skirtlike ring (annulus) near the top of the stalk. At one time those species without a partial veil were placed in a separate genus, *Amanitopsis*. A feature emphasized by most mushroom books is that the gills in *Amanita* are free. This is *not* necessarily the case, however, and this feature is not stressed here.

Audubon Field Guide to North American Mushrooms (Gary H. Lincoff. 1981; Alfred A. Knopf, Inc.) 762 photos. 703 species, some not in *Mushrooms Demystified*. Since no one book will make you happy, this is back-up and pinch hitter.

The Mushroom Hunter's Field Guide (Alexander H. Smith and Nancy Weber. 1980; University of Michigan Press). Updated version of a classic. Lovely photos of 282 North American species. As a beginner, I used it more to confirm a mushroom I had identified with another guide.

Fun-gal, Fun-guy Foraging

The more field guides you thumb, the better you get. No one guide is ever enough when it comes to fungi. —PW

A Field Guide to Southern Mushrooms (Nancy S. Weber and Alexander H. Smith. 1985; University of Michigan Press). A beautiful guide including 241 species. If you live in or between Pennsylvania and Texas, you're part of this fungal definition of the South.

The New Savory Wild Mushroom (Margaret McKenny, Daniel E. Stuntz and Joseph F. Ammirati. 1962, 1987; University of Washington Press). No better way to start if you're from the Oregonian Provinces, stretching from mid-California to the Alaskan coast.

Mushrooms and Truffles of the Southwest (Jack S. States. 1990; University of Arizona Press). The crucial book for the southwest. Includes over 150 species.

Plantwatching

Deceptive title for a fascinating book. Wilkins is outstanding at explaining and photographing the mechanics of how plants survive and thrive, and at integrating the big picture with what causes this on the cellular level. The color photos of seeds germinating in petri dishes and the diagram of the Krebs cycle won't scare or bore a non-scientist away. This is a first-rate piece of public relations for the ingenuity and resilience of the plant kingdom. —Richard Nilsen

Plantwatching
(How Plants Remember, Tell Time, Form
Relationships and More)
Malcolm Wilkins. 1988; 224 pp.
ISBN 0-8160-1736-0
$29.95 ($31.45 postpaid) from
Facts On File, 460 Park Avenue South
New York, NY 10016; 800/322-8755
●

Plants grow and develop in highly organized ways. They generate enormous forces, which can destroy roads, buildings and pavements; they constantly sense their environmental conditions of light, temperature and gravity; they measure time; some of them can count, some have a memory and some have a sense of touch; they feed, respire and absorb nutrients in a selective way from the soil; they recognize one another when brought into physical contact, and in many cases they move about. They also have systems to combat infection, while many are able to enter into mutually advantageous relationships with one another and with certain kinds of bacteria and fungi. In addition, they have the remarkable property of being able to regenerate themselves from their smallest components — single cells — even though these cells may be taken from a highly specialized organ such as a root or petal.

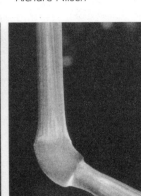

As long as a grass or cereal stem remains upright, there will be no growth at all at swollen leaf sheath bases or nodes (figure I). However, if the stem is knocked over the cells on the lower side of the node will start to grow, producing the familiar "elbow bend" (figure 2) that will return the upper stem and ear to the normal upright position and allow the ear to ripen.

Fig I   Fig 2

OTHER GREAT RESOURCES FOR MANIACAL FLORAPHILES

How To Identify Plants: H. D. Harrington and L. W. Durrell. 1957; Swallow Press. Intro to how botanists sort plants into taxons.

Insects and Flowers: The Biology of a Partnership: Friedrich G. Barth. 1990; Princeton University Press. Once started, cooperation can beat competition to hell. Beautifully illustrated.

The Life of Plants: E. J. Corner. University of Chicago Press, 1981. When you graduate from *Plantwatching*, read this book! A meditation as much as a scientific treatise.

Carnivorous Plants of the United States and Canada: John Blair, Donald E. Schnell. 1976; John F. Blair, Publisher. Another great plant book by an academic groupie of meat-loving floral delights.

Flowering Plants of the World

Ultimately, the pleasures of diversity require intimacy with the design of plants. There are about 250,000 species of flowering plants lumped into 200 families (most of them tropical). **Flowering Plants** *gently moves through the 200 families with a minimum of taxonomic lingo. Until scratch-and-sniff guides are available, it is the most beautiful intro to the 120 million blossoming of the Earth's most familiar plants. —PW*

Flowering Plants of the World
Vernon H. Heywood. 1993; 336 pp.
ISBN 0-19-521037-9
$45.00 ($47.50 postpaid) from Oxford
University Press/Order Dept., 2001 Evans
Road, Cary, NC 27513; 800/451-7556

●
NYMPHAEACEAE

Water Lilies

Number of genera: 9

Number of species:
over 90

Distribution: cosmopolitan, in fresh-water habitats

Economic uses: ornamental aquatics, eg water lilies, lotus, Queen Victoria water lily; some yield edible seeds and rhizomes.

The Nymphaeaceae is a family of water plants including the water lilies, the sacred lotus (*Nelumbo*) and the spectacular Queen Victoria water lily (*Victoria amazonica*).

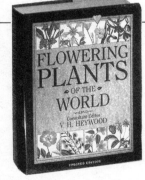
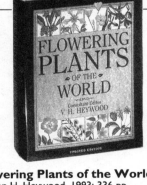

The Biology of Plants

Peter Raven is the Godfather of American botany; this is his sequoian text. Though the prose tastes of leaf-litter, the information sparkles like a virgin tropical jungle at dawn. Everything you want to know and more, beautifully illustrated. —PW

The Biology of Plants
Peter H. Raven, Ray F. Evert, et al.
1992; 791 pp. ISBN 0-87901-532-2
$59.95 ($62.90 postpaid) from Worth
Publishers, 33 Irving Place, New York, NY
10003; 212/475-6000

●
Comparing life on land with that on the sea, we find that only 16 percent of animal species and perhaps 4.5 percent of the species of photosynthesizing organisms (plants and algae) are marine, even though the sea occupies about 71 percent of the earth's surface. The relative scarcity of marine species appears to be a reflection of the much less sharply defined habitants in the sea. Yet, more major groups are found in the sea than on land, probably because they evolved there. Only a few have been able to send successful colonists onto the land, but several of these — notably the insects and the flowering plants — have attained truly spectacular levels of diversity.

Hugo de Vries, shown standing next to *Amorphophallus titanum*, a member of the same family as the calla lily. The plant, a native of the Sumatran jungles, has one of the most massive inflorescences, or flower clusters, of any of the angiosperms. This picture was taken in the arboretum of the Agricultural College at Wageningen, Holland, in 1932.

Oaks of California

Every region should fall in love with its special plants, its totem, or (as ecologists put it) its indicator species. Maybe that's an orchid, a lousewort, a dogwood, a saguaro; in California, it's the oaks.

Oaks tells the story: to be an oak, to live the oak-life; the oak tree as food and shelter, as grove and community keystone species; the oak in scary trouble; the manual for oak preservation and restoration; where to find the remnant and relict sacred groves. Millennial druids: bless the California Oak Association, then start up your own guide to your own plant ally, friend and gateway to local natural history. —Peter Warshall

●

Despite a growing mantle of protection, California's oaks remain at risk. The vast majority of the state's oak woodlands and savannas are found on private property; many of these oak communities are located in suburban and semi-rural areas destined to be transformed by land development. Since the 1940s, California has lost more than a million acres of woodland as a result of range clearing and agricultural conversion. Projections indicate that population growth — and the inevitable suburbanization that accompanies it — may claim another quarter million oak-covered acres by the year 2010.

Early botanists traveled to rural areas to find new oaks.

Oaks of California
Bruce M. Pavlik. 1992; 184 pp.
ISBN 0-9628505-1-9
$21.95 postpaid. Cachuma Press, PO Box 560, Los Olivos, CA 93441; 805/688-0413

Sacred Trees

"Tree" means steadfast, firm, solid in its Indo-European root. It grows words like truce, truth, and tryst (a place where one waits trustingly). **Sacred Trees** *is the gateway to an arboretum of religious and experiential anecdotes. It focuses on the Big Three — the Judeo-Christian, Islamic, and Buddhist texts. But a wind speaks in the rustling of the leaves, a wind that may heal our commodity-obsessed, uncontemplative, ungrateful clearcutting of the planet's grandest flora.* —PW

●

Many early Christian teachers often preached near sacred trees. They erected altars by the most venerated trees and placed crucifixes and images of the Virgin

The Chapel Oak of Allonville.

Sacred Trees
Nathaniel Altman. Sierra Club Books, 1994; 288 pp. ISBN 0-87156-470-X
$16 ($19 postpaid). Sierra Club Store Orders, 730 Polk Street, San Francisco, CA 94109; 800/935-1056

Mary near trees where people used to worship tree and forest spirits. A unique example of such a tree shrine that actually became a church is the oak of Allonville-Bellefosse, perhaps the most famous living tree in France today. Estimated to be over a thousand years old, and with a trunk measuring some forty-five feet in circumference, the Allonville Oak has been a Roman Catholic church since 1696, when it was consecrated to the Virgin Mary by a local priest.

●

It is difficult to place a monetary value on the many vital services that trees provide. However, the California Department of Forestry and Fire Protection calculates that a single tree that lives for fifty years will contribute service worth nearly $200,000 (in 1994 dollars) to the community during its lifetime. This includes providing oxygen ($31,250), recycling water and regulating humidity ($37,000), controlling air pollution ($62,500), producing protein ($2,500), providing shelter for wildlife ($31,250), and controlling land erosion and fertilizing the soil ($31,250).

Knowing Your Trees

This encyclopedia of trees in America has descriptions, illustrations and photos — of leaves, seed pods, bark — and the natural range of each type of tree. Lovingly presented, it's been in print for fifty years. —Lloyd Kahn [Suggested by Roger Reid]

●

Shagbark Hickory is a distinctly American tree. Only one hickory species exists beyond our continent, and this in eastern China.

Regardless of season, Shagbark Hickory is a rugged, picturesque tree with a strong, frequently divided trunk. Heights of 120 to 140 feet are attained, with trunk diameters of twenty to thirty inches.

Drooping catkins of staminate flowers.

Knowing Your Trees
G. H. Collingwood & Warren D. Brush. 1984; 392 pp.
ISBN 0-685-54100-2
$9.50 postpaid. American Forests, PO Box 2000, Washington, DC 20013; 800/368-5748

OTHER GREAT TREES

Peterson publishes separate guides for Western and Eastern trees. Keep one in your glove compartment or backpack. For bare-tree and dry-leaf ID, the **Winter Tree Finder** *is great fun.* —PW

A Field Guide to Eastern Trees:
George A. Petrides & Janet Wehr. 1988; $14.95 ($17.45 postpaid).

A Field Guide to Western Trees:
George A. & Olivia Petrides. 1992; 308 pp.
$15.95 ($18.45 postpaid).

Both from Houghton Mifflin Co./Mail Order Dept., Wayside Road, Burlington, MA 01803; 800/225-3362

Winter Tree Finder:
May T. & Tom Watts. 1970;
$2.50 postpaid. Nature Study Guild, PO Box 10489, Rochester, NY 14610-0489; 716/482-6090

Bark

Obsessive natural history is always delightful. Bark will permanently alter your view of trees. Bark for canoes, cloth, cork; tannins for leather; cinnamon and other flavorings; bark poisons, bark medicines, hallucinogenic bark. Beautifully photographed. Written by the gentle Prances with a scholarly and obvious loving attachment to trees. —PW

●

People everywhere have sought to improve the aesthetic quality of their lives by the use of color and bark has proved a useful source. Many natural vegetable dyes are obtained from the bark of trees. Settlers in North America, a heavily forested area, discovered a wealth of dyes in the barks of trees. From Native Americans they learned to produce a brown dye from butternut

Bark
(The Formation, Characteristics, and Uses of Bark Around the World)
Ghillean Prance, Anne E. Prance & Kjell B. Sandved. 1993; 174 pp.
ISBN 0-88192-262-5
$49.95 ($52.95 postpaid). Timber Press/Order Dept., 9999 SW Wilshire, Portland, OR 97225; 800/327-5680

(*Juglans cinera*) or white walnut bark. This dye became popular in homespun wool and was also used later for the uniforms of the Confederate army.

An Ojibway Lodge. The top half of the lodge is covered with birch bark; the walls are covered with elm bark.

Blue Spruce (*Picea pungens*).

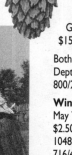

The Gardener's Guide to Plant Conservation

The plants most devastated by collection from the wild are bulbs, insectivorous plants, terrestrial orchids, cacti, and such famous native wildflowers as goldenseal and wintergreen and fringed-ear gentian. One solution to overcollecting is garden propagation. Here's where you can make a difference and cultivate beauty. This is the history, the how and the who book for floral compassion. —PW

●

Trillium is one of our best-loved woodland wildflowers. Consisting of about 40 species distributed throughout North America and eastern Asia, this genus has been a garden favorite for decades. Many species have beautiful large leaves, and some can reach a height of two feet. A wide selection of *Trillium* is offered in catalogs and from roadside wildflower stands. The vast majority of these plants are wild-collected.

Propagation of *Trillium* has been hindered by the length of time required. In general, horticulturists find that four to seven years are needed for a seed-grown plant to reach flowering size. The time span, as well as the expense involved, has kept the market in wild-collected plants active.

The Gardener's Guide to Plant Conservation
Nina T. Marshall. 1993; 187 pp.
ISBN 0-89164-139-4
$12.95 ($15.95 postpaid). World Wildlife Fund, PO Box 4866, Hampden Station, Baltimore, MD 21211; 410/516-6951

Trillium undulatum.

●

T. cernuum (nodding trillium; sugar berry; smiling wake-robin)
Eastern North America. Wild-collected in the United States. Propagation from seed and division is possible but slow. Delaware: Imperiled. Illinois: protected and listed as Endangered. Indiana: T. cernuum var. macranthum is protected and listed as Endangered. Ohio: Presumed Extirpated. South Dakota: Rare. West Virginia: Critically Imperiled.

See also Traffic (p. 52);
Saving Biomes (p. 63);
Restoring Plant
Communities (p. 90);
Plant Knowledge (p. 102).

See also Traffic (p. 52); Saving Biomes (p. 63); Restoring Plant Communities (p. 90); Plant Knowledge (p. 102).

LEAFY RESOURCES

Center for Plant Conservation: Missouri Botanical Gardens, PO Box 299, St. Louis, MO 63166; 314/577-9450. The guardian and archive of rare and endangered plants. They save seeds and cuttings, keep track of which botanical gardens or arboreta have which plants, they maintain a rare plants database, and they supply speakers, brochures, slide shows, directories. The source, in short.

New England Wildflower Society: Garden-in-the-Woods, Framingham, MA 01701; 617/877-7630. The model bioregional society. Only propagated plants, great seeds, and catalogs.

North Carolina Botanical Garden: Box 3375 Totten Center, U. of NC, Chapel Hill, NC 27514. Propagated seeds for Southeastern plants.

Theodore Payne Foundation: 0459 Tuxford Street, Sun Valley, CA 91352. California-native seed access.

Hortus Northwest: PO Box 955, Canby, OR 97013. Pacific Northwest. No disclaimer about wild vs. propagated.

National Wildflower Research Center: Membership $25/year; handbook $15.95 postpaid. 2600 FM 973 North, Austin, TX 78725; 512/929-3600. Their *Wildflower Handbook* is the most comprehensive list of concerned groups. Oddly, the research center does not distinguish between wild-collectors and propagators.

Conservation Monitoring Centre: The Herbarium, Royal Botanic Gardens, Kew, Richmond, Surrey TW9 3AB, England. Best planetary information.

Gardening by Mail (A Source Book): Barbara Barton. 1994, Houghton Mifflin.

Harmful Non-Indigenous Species in the United States

About 2,000 non-indigenous plants now dwell in the United States. In 1991, the control of the top "most wanted" cost taxpayers a mere $91 million. The melaleuca tree is rapidly altering the Florida Everglades. African lovegrasses threaten to change the Sonoran desert into one more pasture of bovine imperialism. The spread of kudzu, purple loosestrife, and water hyacinth leave even the most casual lover of North America wondering whether the continent's integrity is gone forever.

The silent war includes importing insects to fight the imported plants, and using paraquat, fire and cutting to manage competitors with natives. There is no good book on invasives, except this Congressional report — a mix of great facts and policy wonkage. —PW

●

By the mid-21st Century, biological invasions become one of the most prominent ecological issues on Earth. . . . A few small isolated ecosystems have escaped the hand of (humans) and in turn [non-indigenous species]. . . . One place looks like the next and no one cares . . . The homogeneity may not be aesthetically or practically displeasing, but inherently it diminishes the capacity of the biotic world to respond to changing environments such as those imposed by global warming . . . The Australian melaleuca tree continues its invasive spread and increases from occupying half a million acres in the late 1980s to more that 90 percent of the Everglades conservation areas.

Harmful Non-Indigenous Species in the United States
Office of Technology Assessment. 1993; 391 pp.
Stock # 052-003-01347-9
$21 postpaid from Superintendent of Documents/New Orders, PO Box 371954, Pittsburgh, PA 15250-7954; 202/783-3238

Purple Loosestrife (*Lythrum salicaria*) 1985[1]

Salt Cedar (*Tamarix pendantra* and *T. gallica*) 1965[5]

Kudzu (*Pueraria lobata*) 1990[8]

Some High-Impact Non-Indigenous Species.

Last Stand of the Red Spruce

Not by timber cutting, not by collection. Death by acid rain. The complexity of spruce forest ecology is not underestimated, but the stress of industrial emissions, returning in lovely storms, clouds this forest's future. Best book of survival 'midst noxious rains.
—PW
[Suggested by Fred Schauffler]

●

When Henry David Thoreau scanned Vermont from the top of Mt. Greylock, the air was still clean. By 1974, however, the clouds and fogs that enveloped the mountaintops of the northern Green Mountains for up to 2,000 hours per year had become full of poisonous chemicals. Cloud and fog moisture, averaging pH 3.7 during the growing season, is consistently more acidic than acid rain or snow, and it contains higher concentrations of cadmium, copper, zinc, and lead. The turbulent eddies of air and greater wind speeds found at high elevations cause this polluted moisture to be intercepted by the evergreen foliage.

●

In the early 1950s, when man-made pollution caused the precipitation in the Northeast to become unnaturally acidic, the young sugar maples, yellow birches, and American beeches at Hubbard Brook abruptly halted their accelerating rates of growth. As the air pollution worsened over the next ten years, the trend of growth of the trees

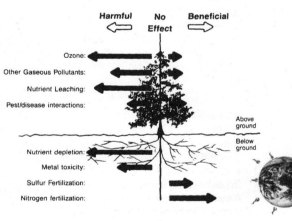

Potential effects of air pollutants (acid deposition, ozone, and other gases) on forest growth.

reversed and sharply declined. The hearty, relatively younger red spruces continued to exhibit strong growth until 1960, when they began to succumb. Moreover, the trees most vulnerable to air pollution injury, the high-elevation red spruces, suffered the severest decline of all.

Last Stand of the Red Spruce
Robert A. Mello. Natural Resources Defense Council, 1987; 199 pp.
ISBN 0-933280-37-8
$14.95 ($19.20 postpaid). Island Press, Box 7, Covelo, CA 95428; 800/828-1302

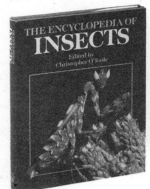

The Encyclopedia of Insects • A Field Guide to the Insects

With these two books, you enter the lovely sci-fi space of the many-legged and multiple-eyed critters that creep and crawl and fly elegantly with their skeletons on the outside of their bodies.
—Peter Warshall

•

If arthropods are the success story of the planet, then pride of place among them must go the the insects. While nearly a million species have been described, several million more await discovery. About 7,000 new insect species are described every year, but this figure is probably exceeded by the

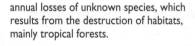

annual losses of unknown species, which results from the destruction of habitats, mainly tropical forests.

•

The success and great diversity of insects depend on a number of key features, including: adaptations to prevent or withstand desiccation; fast, maneuverable flight, which may be sustained for long periods; a usually short life cycle which includes metamorphosis, a high reproductive rate, and the capacity to survive unfavorable seasons; and cooperation between individuals of the social termites, ants, wasps and bees.
—Encyclopedia

The Encyclopedia of Insects
Christopher O'Toole, Editor. 1986;
160 pp. ISBN 0-8160-1358-6
$27.95 ($29.45 postpaid) from
Facts On File, 460 Park Avenue S.,
New York, NY 10016; 800/322-8755

A Field Guide to the Insects of America North of Mexico
Donald Borror & Richard White.
1974; 404 pp.
ISBN 0-395-18523-8
$14.45 ($15.50 postpaid) from
Houghton Mifflin Co./Mail Order
Dept., Wayside Road, Burlington,
MA 01803; 800/225-3362

OTHER GREAT RESOURCES

Backyard BUGwatching: Sonoran Arthropod Studies, Inc., PO Box 5624, Tucson, AZ 85703; 602/883-3945. The best, most fun, and most informative magazine on North American insect, spider and scorpion events. Great ideas and stories to encourage respect and even love for our fine arthropod friends and enemies.

The Food Insects Newsletter: University of Wisconsin, Department of Entomology, 1630 Linden Drive, Madison, WI 93706. Unique. Why it's harder to find chocolate-covered ants, and which big-bottomed species are gourmet. Thumbs up to pupae puffs and a guide to the best restaurants. Love it and eat it. —PW

Let Flutter-bys Be Butterflies

Humans' most beloved insect (when it's flying; yuk to tomato caterpillars). Inspiration of poets and Zen masters. Start with The Butterfly Book *— the simplest entry to species, butterfly watching, butterfly gardens, butterfly zoos, and butterfly life history. As you become further entranced, you'll want* Audubon's Field Guide to North American Butterflies *and* Handbook for Butterfly Watchers. The Brown Company *(800/556-7670) sells butterfly feeders.*
—PW

Handbook for Butterfly Watchers: Robert M. Pyle. 1992; 288 pp. $11.95 ($14.45 postpaid). Houghton Mifflin Co./Mail Order Dept., Wayside Road, Burlington, MA 01803; 800/225-3362.

The Butterfly Book: Donald and Lillian Stokes. 1991; 95 pp. $10.95 ($13.45 postpaid). Little, Brown and Co./Order Dept., 200 West Street, Waltham, MA 02154; 800/343-9204.

The Audubon Society Field Guide to North American Butterflies: Robert M. Pyle. Alfred A. Knopf, Inc., 1981; 864 pp. $17.95 ($19.95 postpaid). Random House/Order Dept., 400 Hahn Road, Westminster, MD 21157; 800/733-3000.

The Xerces Society

The best conservation group for insects on the planet. Beautifully informative magazine called Wings with news and book reviews. How many humans have this large a heart — to extend compassion to the threatened and endangered creepy crawlies as well as the dragonflies and Monarchs of the sky?!

Wings
(Xerces Society Magazine)
Membership $25/year (3 issues). 10 SW Ash Street, Portland, OR 97204; 503/222-2788

The Ants

I believe this is the deepest book of knowledge ever printed. In 732 exquisite pages, it contains almost all that is known about ants. It will feed your mind for a lifetime. The biology of ants is about the history of societies and institutions, and about the future of cities and computers. —Kevin Kelly

Almost all that is known about ants. There's no mention of anteaters or how the ecology of ants structures savannas (or, more recently, Biosphere 2). Lovely old-fashioned science of the organism, bordering on ant worship. —PW

•

Pharaoh's ants (*Monomorium pharaonis*) are worldwide household pests. Their vast, multi-queened colonies thrive in wall spaces and detritus. In hospitals they often visit soiled bandages and track pathogenic microbes onto clean dressings and food. A notorious colony occupied the entire Biological Laboratories of Harvard University during the 1960s and 1970s. An extermination campaign was finally undertaken when workers were discovered carrying radioactive chemicals from culture dishes into the surrounding walls. (The incident was made

The greatest size variation of nestmates ever recorded in ants occurs in the Asian marauder ant *Pheidologeton diversus*. The minor worker depicted in this electron micrograph has a head width exactly $1/10$ that of the major on which it sits, and a dry weight only about $1/500$ that of the larger ant.

the basis of the melodramatic scientific novel *Spirals*, by William Patrick, Houghton Mifflin, Boston, 1983.)

Ants are resistant to hard radiation. Colonies exposed to intense cesium-based irradiation in a French forest suffered no evident decline or change in behavior during 11 months, even when some of the surrounding plants were dying or losing their leaves. At least some ant species are also highly resistant to industrial pollution. Near a nitrogen plant in Poland, populations of *Myrmica ruginodis* and *Lasius niger* remained robust after other invertebrates became scarce. They actually reduced the concentration of the nitrate, apparently by stimulation of microorganisms that bind the pollutant.

•

African habitats are often visited by driver ants (*Dorylus* spp.), single colonies of which occasionally contain more than 20 million workers. And the driver ant case is far from the ultimate. A "supercolony" of the

Spiders and Their Kin

The most informative, accurate, entertaining, and useful guide to spiders ever written. —PW

Hairy Mygalomorphs (Theraphosidae) are commonly called tarantulas in the US.

Spiders and Their Kin
Herbert W. Levi & Lorna R. Levi.
Western Publishing Co. 1969; 160 pp.
ISBN 0-307-24021-5
$4.95 ($8.95 postpaid) from Donovan Distributing, 732 Clinton St., Waukesha, WI 53186; 414/633-2431

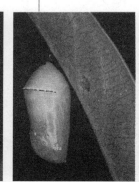

Life stages of the monarch butterfly, from egg to adult. *—The Butterfly Book*

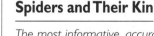

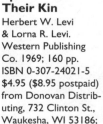

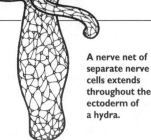

A nerve net of separate nerve cells extends throughout the ectoderm of a hydra.

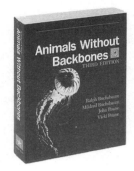

Animals Without Backbones

Spineless wonders account for 97 per-cent of all animals. —Peter Warshall

•

We are all aware of the difference between these two groups of animals when we indulge in fish and lobster dinners. In the fish, the exterior is relatively soft and inviting, but the interior presents numerous hard bones. In the lobster, on the contrary, the exterior consists of a formidable hard covering, but within this covering is a soft edible interior. A similar situation exists in the oyster, lying soft and defenseless within its hard outer shell. Lobsters and oysters are but samples of the tremendous array of animals that lack internal bones and that are, from their lack of the vertebral column in particular, called *invertebrates*.

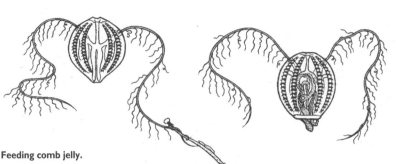

Feeding comb jelly.

The Ants

Bert Hölldobler & Edward O. Wilson. Belknap Press, 1990; 736 pp. ISBN 0-674-04075-9 $70 ($73 postpaid) from Harvard University Press/Customer Service, 79 Garden Street, Cambridge, MA 02138; 617/495-2600

ant *Formica yessensis* on the Ishikari Coast of Hokkaido was reported to be composed of 306 million workers and 1,080,000 queens living in 45,000 interconnected nests across a territory of 2.7 square kilometers.

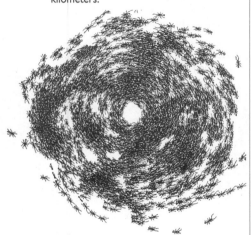

A circular mill of the army ant *Labidus praedator*. This group was cut off from the rest of their colony by rain. The workers were so strongly attracted to each other that none developed enough centrifugal direction to lead the others out of the mill. After a day and a half, all were dead.

Animals Without Backbones

Ralph Buchsbaum, Mildred Buchsbaum, John Pearse, & Vicki Pearse. University of Chicago Press, 1987; 572 pp. ISBN 0-226-07874-4 $19 ($22 postpaid) from Chicago Distribution Center, 11030 S. Langley Avenue, Chicago, IL 60628; 800/621-2736

Philidium larva.

The Encyclopedia of Land Invertebrate Behaviour

*A cheering team for insects, spiders, snails, slugs, worms, and relatives. Looking and listening, courting, mating, raising young, hunting, eating, and fighting — the **Just-So Stories** of lifestyles you never thought possible. —PW*

•

The maternal solicitude of earwigs has been known for many years, and all the species studied so far (only about a dozen out of 1000 or so) exhibit parental care. In the ovoviviparous *Hemimerus talpoides*, which lives on African pouched rats, the degree of assistance may merely extend to the female's efforts to free her emerging offspring from their 'birth membranes'.

The best-known species, *Forficula auricularia*, from Europe, exhibits complex maternal care, extended over a long period and repeated several times through successive broods. The female digs a nest. . . . She exploits the rapidly warming stone as an incubator by placing her eggs against it when it starts to warm up, then taking them down below when the stone becomes too hot later in the day. Sometimes a male helps with the digging, and is allowed to remain with the female until she is ready to lay her eggs. At this point, her tolerance evaporates and she ejects him forcibly from the nest, spurring him on with her mandibles and tail forceps; females of various species may actually kill (and sometimes eat) the male at this time.

Ants of the genus Pseudomyrmex are tenants in the swollen bases in the swollen bases of the stipular thorns on acacias, the plant providing them with all of their food. In return, the ants keep the foliage free of herbivorous animals.

The Audubon Guide to North American Seashore Creatures

A way to get your feet wet, splash through the American seashore's book of life. Squeeze the living sponge, poke the anemone, uncover the flatworms, get dazzled by nudibranchs. Watch out! (sea urchin). —PW

•

Daisy Brittle Star (*Ophiophois aculeata*) Class: *Stelleroidea*

Description: Disk diameter 3/4" (19 mm), arm length 3 5/8" (92 mm). Long-armed. Red, orange, pink, yellow, white, blue, green, tan, brown, gray, and black, in infinite variety of spots, lines, bands, and mottlings. Central disk scalloped, a lobe protruding between adjacent arms, covered with fine, blunt spines and roundish plates. Plates on top of arms surrounded by row of small scales; joints with 5-6 bluntly-tapered spines in vertical rows on side of arm.

Habitat: Under rocks in tidepools, among kelp holdfasts; from low-tide line to water 5435' (1657 m) deep.

Range: Arctic to Cape Cod; Bering Sea to S. California.

Comments: These elegant brittle stars are an exotic sight in a tidepool, scrambling into hiding when one exposes them by lifting away their rock.

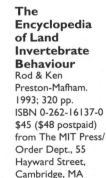

The Audubon Society Field Guide to North American Seashore Creatures

Norman A. Meinkoth. Alfred A. Knopf, Inc., 1981; 799 pp. ISBN 0-394-51993-0 $18 ($20 postpaid) from Random House/Order Dept., 400 Hahn Road, Westminster, MD 21157; 800/733-3000

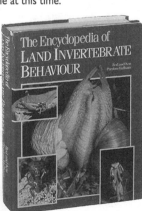

The Encyclopedia of Land Invertebrate Behaviour

Rod & Ken Preston-Mafham. 1993; 320 pp. ISBN 0-262-16137-0 $45 ($48 postpaid) from The MIT Press/Order Dept., 55 Hayward Street, Cambridge, MA 02142; 800/356-0343

Fish: An Enthusiast's Guide

For every fish-lover's bookshelf. We don't provide a fieldkit because author Peter Moyle does it so well. Guidance on snorkeling and diving, fish watching in reefs or streams, a great bibliography on field guides, the best public aquaria, as well as every aspect of ecology and conservation. Simply, the prize catch. —Peter Warshall

•

I have spent a great deal of time under water, watching fish. The observations I make are carefully recorded on special forms and converted into data. The data are analyzed, summarized, and eventually turned into one of the arcane documents known as a scientific paper. The publications enable me to call myself a fish ecologist but they do not convey how enjoyable the underwater excursions are. They also do not allow me to record the myriad of other experiences I have had, such as watching how light and water together create lovely, shifting pat-

terns on a lake or stream bottom, how a larval mayfly scurries across a stone in fast water, or how a lamprey moves a large rock to excavate a nest. I call myself an ecologist, but my motivations and even my methods are nearly the same as those whose work is the foundation of ecology, the natural historians.

•

Angel shark. Hagfish. Sarcastic fringehead. Warmouth. Whitefish. Grayling. Cardinal tetra. Wobbegong. Peacock flounder. Hogchoker. Zebrafish. There are over 21,000 species of fish, with new species being described on a regular basis.

Fish
(An Enthusiast's Guide)
Peter M. Moyle. University of California Press, 1993; 272 pp. ISBN 0-520-07977-9
$25 ($28 postpaid) from California/ Princeton Fulfillment Services, 1445 Lower Ferry Road, Ewing, NJ 08618; 800/777-4726

The largest fish (18 m long) and one of the smallest fishes (12 mm long when mature).

A tooth of *Carcharodon megalodon*, actual size.

Gobies (family Gobiidae) are among the most common fishes in the world, but most are small and many occupy unusual habitats. *Top:* Yellowfin goby, showing the typical goby suction disk created by the fusion of the two pelvic fins. *Bottom:* Mudskippers, which regularly emerge from the water in tropical mangrove areas to feed on land.

A Field Guide to Freshwater Fishes

This is the best overall identification guide. The oceans may be big, but fish love has generated so many local guides that reviewing one is supremely minnowesque. For a complete list, see Fish: An Enthusiast's Guide. —PW

A Field Guide to Freshwater Fishes
(North America North of Mexico)
Lawrence Page & Brooks Burr.
1991; 432 pp. ISBN 0-395-53933-1
$16.95 ($18.95 postpaid) from Houghton Mifflin Co./Mail Order Dept., Wayside Road, Burlington, MA 01803; 800/225-3362

Shovelnose

Pallid and Shovelnose Sturgeons — underside of head.

Pallid

Gyotaku – Japanese Fish Printing

A lovely way to keep fish in your naturalist's notebook. This is the start-up leaflet. —PW

Gyotaku
(Japanese Fish Printing)
Christopher M. Dewees.
1981; 8 pp. Leaflet #2548
$1.50 postpaid. ANR Publications, University of California, 6701 San Pablo Avenue, Oakland, CA 94608-1239; 510/642-2431

The print is carefully removed from the fish.

The Book of Sharks
• Sharks: An Introduction for the Amateur Naturalist

It's simply boring how many pages of shark books are gory photos and scare stories of the Shark Attack. I say this as a former resident of the White Shark Triangle and a savior of one abalone fisherman on the Farallon Islands. The world still needs a book with the right sense of proportion. Until then, The Book of Sharks is the most beautiful intro, along with Sharks. —PW

The reconstructed jaws of *Carcharodon megalodon* in the Hall of Fossil Fishes at the American Museum of Natural History in New York.

The Book of Sharks
Richard Ellis.
Alfred A. Knopf Inc., 1989;
256 pp. ISBN 0-679-72210-6
$24.95 ($26.95 postpaid). Random House/Order Dept., 400 Hahn Road, Westminster, MD 21157; 800/733-3000

Sharks
(An Introduction for the Amateur Naturalist)
Sanford A. Moss. 1984; ISBN 0-13-808304-5
$10.95 ($13.95 postpaid). Prentice Hall/ Order Processing Center, PO Box 11071, Des Moines, IA 50336-1071; 800/947-7700

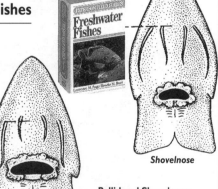

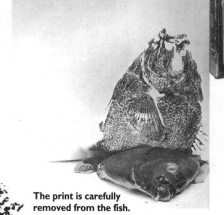

1.

2.

3.

4.

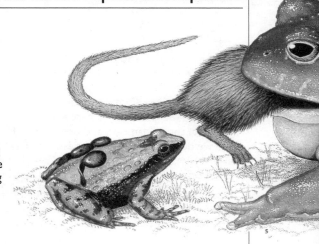

You can solve mysteries. Reptilian and amphibian fieldwork has just begun. Take frogs. Little is known about the timing of the chorusing of most frogs or how loud the croaks or how long the songs, or what climate inspires the song. Nor is much known about the dates of egg laying, egg hatching, time from egg to froglet to frog, longevity, pond hopping, where they brumate (hide for winter) or when they emerge, their diseases, parasites, or exact predators, and, long term, what's behind population booms or busts (with frogs disappearing all over the planet, where is the toad and frog Internet!). Next to no work on frog personalities; individual marking and tape recording will put you at the slimy edge of the knowledge.

Here's a minimal amphibian fieldkit: broadcasting lantern, good headlamp, unbleached muslin bags, plastic containers, a seine, hip boots for cold water. For long-term studies, tattoo ink (MS 222) and a fine hypodermic. For sound recording equipment, see p. 17. —Peter Warshall

The Encyclopedia of Reptiles and Amphibians
• Field Guides to Western and Eastern Reptiles and Amphibians

With these books, you're ready to go outdoors. The Encyclopedia *provides the Big Picture; the* Peterson Field Guides, *the local knowledge. —PW*

•

Parthenogenesis, or "virgin birth," occurs in many invertebrates, such as flies and earthworms, as well as in some species of vertebrates, including fish, amphibians, and lizards. All-female populations, producing viable offspring from eggs unfertilized by males, have been found among rock lizards, geckos and whiptails and racerunners. —*Encyclopedia*

Horned Lizards

The horned lizard (a.k.a. horny toad) is the totem animal of the North American deserts. Easterners think of rattlesnakes, but for the desert resident, love of these warty discoid ant-eaters who wobble about the sands like retired cowboys grows with each summer rain. Wade Sherbrooke is the human voice of the horned lizard. This is not just a most complete and photographically beautiful booklet, but also a model of how biologists should write and research and educate and advocate for their critter of choice. –PW

•

One remarkable feat of Texas, coast, and regal horned lizards is their ability, when provoked, to shoot narrow streams of blood from their eyes. . . . in Mexico people regard them as sacred toads because,

according to folklore, when they cry they weep tears of blood. . . . If a dog gets the spray in its mouth or nostrils it shakes its head and salivates excessively, giving every evidence of distaste.

Horned Lizards
Wade C. Sherbrooke.
1981; 48 pp. ISBN 0-911408-59-2
$4.95 ($8.45 postpaid). Southwest Parks & Monuments Assn., PO Box 2173, Globe, AZ 85502; 602/425-8184

The Encyclopedia of Reptiles and Amphibians
Tim Halliday & Kraig Adler, Editors.
1986; 160 pp. ISBN 0-8160-1359-4
$27.95 ($29.45 postpaid) from Facts On File, 460 Park Avenue South, New York, NY 10016; 800/322-8755

A Field Guide to Western Reptiles and Amphibians
Robert C. Stebbins. 1985; 432 pp.
ISBN 0-395-38253-X

A Field Guide to Reptiles and Amphibians of Eastern and Central North America
Roger Connant & Joseph Collins.
1991; 608 pp. ISBN 0-395-58389-6
Each $16.95 postpaid from Houghton Mifflin Co./Mail Order Dept., Wayside Road, Burlington, MA 01803; 800/225-3362

(Top of page) Jumping sequence: (1) Forelimbs elevate and aim the forepart of the frog; ankles lift the hind limbs off the ground. (2) Take-off: hind limbs swing open from the hip joint; upper and lower legs extend, propelling the frog forward and upward; ankles and hind feet roll off the ground. (3) The flight path follows a curve of approximately 45°; the eyes are shut and withdrawn downward into the mouth cavity. (4) Landing: forelimbs break the fall, and the chest hits the ground, followed by the rest of the underside; the hind limbs flex and press against the body, ready to leap forward again. —*Encyclopedia*

Chelonian Love

Turtles and tortoises are my personal animal allies, my totemic friends, so to speak. The most beautiful book of chelonian love is The Sea Turtle: So Excellent a Fishe. Decline of the Sea Turtles *is the millennial text for these creatures, who have seen about 300,000 millennia. Read both, then join the Center for Marine Conservation (see p. 88). —PW*

•

The big pied slate-and-orange airplane roared down the tree-walled river. Water spouted from under the hull and blotted the view through the portholes. Just opposite the camp we hit planing speed and rose to the surface of the river, the ports cleared, and I could see Larry Ogren, a student from the University of Florida and my staunch assistant in the Tortuguero turtle work. He was waving from the dock, and Leo Martinez, our Creole *mayordomo*, was with him. They were staying behind to gather little turtles for the last trip out. It was going to be hectic there at the turtle camp for a while, with the new peak-season masses of hatchlings coming. The fishing was in one of its poor spells, and the pump was wearing out. Each night the hatchlings were coming up out of the sand in flurries of hurried, paddlefooted little creatures the size of a silver dollar, all in a sweat to be off to wherever little turtles go. —*The Sea Turtle*

Decline of the Sea Turtles
National Research Council. 1990;
259 pp. ISBN 0-309-04247-X
$17.95 ($21.95 postpaid). National Academy Press, PO Box 285, Washington, DC 20055; 800/624-6242

The Sea Turtle
(So Excellent a Fishe)
Archie Carr. 1986; 292 pp.
ISBN 0-292-77595-4
$14.95 ($16.95 postpaid). University of Texas Press, PO Box 7819, Austin, TX 78713-7819; 800/252-3206

Protecting the Herps

Desert Tortoise Council. PO Box 1738, Palm Desert, CA 92261; 619/341-8449. The desert guardians of Xerobates agassizii, a species hammered by cattle hooves, development, off-road vehicles, pet capturers, and lung diseases. Help!

New York Turtle and Tortoise Council. 63 Amsterdam Avenue/Ste. 365, New York, NY 10023; 212/459-4803. The chelonian Red Cross — for habitat conservation, pet care, rehab, propagation. Not just New York. Get the Turtle Help Network for local know-how.

Horned Lizard Conservation Society. Membership $10/year. PO Box 122, Austin, TX 78767; 512/288-4802. See the review of Horned Lizards; *fall in love, then join up.*

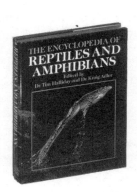

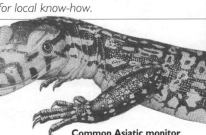
Common Asiatic monitor

Climbing Salamanders

Arboreal   Clouded   Black

Millennial Birds

THIS CENTURY BEGAN WITH BIRD LOVERS FIGHTING HUNTERS to save egrets. Audubon Society started by stopping the egret massacre for egret plumes for ladies' hats. Egrets taught humans to discipline their vanity and cherish living beauty over commodity value. During World War I, pigeons delivered messages between generals on how to fight the war. Their homing abilities taught humans that some animal powers were stronger than their technical inventions. Bird navigation is still mysterious.

By the 1950s, birds began to warn humans that DDT created invisible dangers. Birds died first so Rachel Carson could warn us of a new type of affliction: industrial toxic disease. We saved the pelican and the peregrine as we saved our own health. As the century ends, the spring silence of wood warblers preaches the planetary interdependence of rain forests and New England pines, of the Yanamono and denizens of Maine. The spotted owl asks: What are we doing? Pulling out the resource rug from under our own feet? Save me and you may save your children. Can we ethically absorb the diminuendo of the wood warbler and the hoot and howl of the owls?

Birding is such a soaring outdoor activity that whole catalogs now nest only avian access. Sport-birders know more than roosts on this page. They have opened our intelligence to the prophesies inherent in avian vagrants. The naturalist birder is not only a lister. Equally intriguing are nest materials and their locations; the participation of adults or helpers in nest building, incubation, and feeding; the local diet; the yearly number of eggs, fledglings, and broods; song dialects; flight paths; and the seasonal timing of singing or molt. Each year is unique. Every backyard naturalist can discover something important for the greater ornithophile community. —Peter Warshall

The Birder's Handbook • A Guide to Bird Behavior

*For the naturalist birder, **The Birder's Handbook** is essential. It is the launching pad to the details of bird life, the equivalent of a **Whole Earth Catalog** for North American birds. Stokes' **A Guide to Bird Behavior** will guide your eyes from identification to gestures and song. Along with binoculars (preferably 8 X 40 or 7 X 35) and a spotting scope (or, if you can afford it, the revelatory Questar), the calm magic and seduction of these graceful beauties (even the little brown jobbies) can only increase. To learn songs, listen and find the bird. For help, try your most local bird tapes. Buy a feeder for backyard birding and learn the dos and don'ts of addicting birds to seed-and-nectar welfare programs. The **Brooks Bird Club** (707 Warwood Avenue, Wheeling, WV 26003) has great suggestions for backyard bird sanctuaries. —PW*

The Birder's Handbook
Paul R. Ehrlich, David S. Dobkin & Darryl Wheye. Fireside Books, 1988; 785 pp.
ISBN 0-671-65989-8
$17 postpaid from Simon & Schuster/Order Dept., 200 Old Tappan Road, Old Tappan, NJ 07675; 800/223-2336

A Guide to Bird Behavior
Donald & Lillian Stokes. 1985, 1989; Volume I, ISBN 0-316-81725-2; Volume II, ISBN 0-316-81729-5; Volume III, ISBN 0-316-81717-1
Each $12.95 ($15.45 postpaid) from Little, Brown and Co./Order Dept., 200 West Street, Waltham, MA 02154; 800/343-9204

Examples of nests. Center: woodpecker. Outer, clockwise from upper left: Killdeer, Red-shouldered Hawk, vireo, finch, kingfisher, oriole, Cliff Swallow. —*The Birder's Handbook*

Birds Teach

*Ultimately, globally and locally, birds teach. Second, birders teach. They teach each other about birds. The best human access to birding is the local Audubon shop and local birding clubs. There you can buy the best guide: the National Geographic **Field Guide to the Birds of North America** and the accompanying **Guide to Bird Sounds**. Pick up the Peterson Guides to Eastern and Western Birds, as some pages (especially for the East) have better paintings, more straightforward comparisons, and less rarities clutter. The gourmet guide for maniacal birders is **Advanced Birding** and **Hawks**. Peterson also provides tapes and two written guides on birdsong. The discussion of guides is never ending and is a symptom of how healthy the birding scene has become. —PW*

Field Guide to the Birds of North America
Shirley Scott, Editor. 1983; 464 pp.
ISBN 0-87044-507-3
Field guide: $21 ($25.75 postpaid); audio-cassette Guide to Bird Sounds: $22.50 ($25.50 postpaid); book & cassette set $43.50 ($51.25 postpaid)
All from National Geographic Society, 1145 17th Street NW, Washington, DC 20036; 800/638-4077

A Field Guide to Eastern Birds
Roger Tory Peterson. 1984; 384 pp.
ISBN 0-395-36164-8
$16.95 ($19.45 postpaid)

A Field Guide to Western Birds
Roger Tory Peterson. 1990; 432 pp.
ISBN 0-395-51424-X
Each $16.95 ($19.45 postpaid)

A Field Guide to Advanced Birding
Kenn Kaufman. 1990; 297 pp.
ISBN 0-395-53376-7
$14.95 ($17.45 postpaid)

A Field Guide to Hawks
William Clark. 1987; 198 pp.
ISBN 0-395-44112-9
$13.95 ($16.45 postpaid)
All from Houghton Mifflin Co./Mail Order Dept., Wayside Road, Burlington, MA 01803; 800/225-3362

Loving Birds in This House Called Earth

One bird species in nine is currently threatened with extinction. Here's an overview of organizations concerned with birds and their protection. If your heart is with another bird, start your own foundation. —PW

International Council for Bird Preservation: 202/778-9563. ICBP publishes the "red book" on threatened birds and international bird conservation. Totally global, leading the flight path of practical saviors with skillful means.

*International Crane Foundation: 608/356-9462. See **So Cranes May Dance** on page 52 and then join the flock.*

Ducks Unlimited: See page 77.

Wildfowl Trust of North America: 410/827-6694.

Canvasback Society: 216/443-2340. A single-species love affair.

Online Resources

National Birding Hotline Cooperative

NBHC is a computer network and national cooperative that bulletins all the rare-bird hotlines throughout North America. The avante garde in the new democracy of naturalists. Scientists listen in and wonder, whose data is it? Birders transcribe hotline and sighting information from all over the globe. Contributions welcome.

National Birding Hotline Cooperative: listserv@arizml.ccit.arizona.edu. Then type: subscribe.bird and your full name. Information from Chuck Williamson at cwilliamson@pimacc.pima.edu or Rob Scott at rs18@cornell.edu.

North American Loon Fund: 603/528-4711. Builds nests, stops pollutant havoc, educates, and listens to the haunting songs.

North American Bluebird Society: 301/384-2798. True bluebird naturalists. Builds bluebird trails with nesting boxes, networks info, restores beauty.

Purple Martin Conservation Association: 814/734-4420. A glistening bird almost completely dependent on human-built birdhouses.

World Bird Sanctuary: 314/938-6193. They love their birds of prey (owls, hawks, eagles, falcons). Hands-on internships for rehabilitation and propagation.

Peregrine Fund: 208/362-3716. Great teachers, conservationists and hackers of birds of prey. Operates World Center for Birds of Prey.

The Trumpeter Swan Society (612/476-4663); Prairie Grouse Technical Council (317 W. Prospect, Ft. Collins, CO 80526); International Osprey Foundation (813/472-5218). Education and scientific groups.

Birding Events For Naturalist Birders

The Christmas Count: (40,000 birders in North America). Call your local Audubon Society. The count is now used to discuss weather patterns and global change. "Easter" counts are growing too.

Breeding Bird Census and Winter Population Studies: Contact American Birds c/o National Audubon Society at 212/979-3000. Everyday is Christmas for our avian compatriots. This group monitors their health.

The Nest Record Program: Contact Cornell Lab. of Ornithology at 607/254-2446. Find a nest, add to the database.

The Encyclopedia of Mammals

Considering how close we all are (milk and hair and scents and jawbone and a tendency to herd), I yearn for some out-of-print books at one-third the price. Nevertheless, the photos and drawings, the condensed vignettes of each family and every species (4,070), the wow! and why? (for various extinctions), all slowly erode the them-mammals and us-humans psycho-barriers. To broaden our instinctual parental caring to a more militant mammalian patriotism, this is a worthy long-term investment. —PW

•

The smallest mammal, Kitti's hog-nosed bat, weighs 1.5g (0.05 oz), the Blue whale weighs 100 million times as much; the wolf may journey through 1,000sq km (400sq mi), the Naked mole rat never leaves one burrow; the Virginia opossum gives birth to litters of up to 27, the orangutan to only one; the elephant, like man, may live three score years and ten, while the male Brown antechinus never sees a second season and dies before the birth of the first and only litter he has fathered.

•

Mammals are unique among animals with backbones in the potency and social importance of their smells. This quality also stems from their skin, wherein both sebaceous and sweat glands become adapted to produce complicated odors with which mammals communicate. The sites of scent glands vary between species: capybaras have them aloft their snout, Mule deer have them on the lower leg, elephants have them behind the eyes and hyraxes have them in the middle of their back. It is very common for scent glands to be concentrated in the ano-genital region (urine and feces also serve as socially important odors); the perfume glands of civets lie in a pocket between the anus and genitals and

The non-breeding gray meerkat male is caring for his three-week-old siblings while their mother is away foraging.

for centuries their greasy secretions have been scooped out to make the base of expensive perfumes. Glands around the genitals of Musk deer are a similarly unwholesome starting point of other odors greatly prized by some people. Most carnivores have scent-secreting anal sacs, whose function is largely unknown, although in the case of the skunk it is clear enough. . . .

The mammary glands are unique to mammals and characterize all

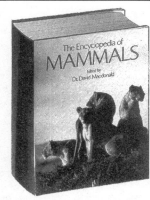

The Encyclopedia of Mammals
David W. Macdonald, Editor. 1984; 960 pp.
ISBN 0-87196-871-1
$69.95 ($73.45 postpaid) from Facts On File, 460 Park Avenue South, New York, NY 10016; 800/322-8755

members of the class. The glands, which are similar to sweat glands, should not be confused with the mammillae or teats which are merely a means of delivering the milk and are absent in the platypus and echidnas. Only the glands of females produce milk. Numbers of teats vary from two in, for example, primates and the Marsupial mole, to 19 in the Pale-bellied mouse opossum.

Saving Mammals

If you love a hairy cousin — prairie dogs or Mexican wolves — and there's no human voice for their chitter-chatter and barks, then start a group of your own!

Save the Manatee Club: 407/539-0990.

Friends of the Sea Otter: 408/373-2747

Beaver Defenders: 609/697-3541.

Bats

*Out of crevices, caves, tree cavities and eaves, or unfurling from tropical trees where they hang like brown papayas, come the bats. Nine-hundred and fifty species of the only mammal to truly take flight. Squeaking inaudibly, navigating by echoes, specializing in nectar, blood, insects, fruit, or fish, the "butterfly-mice" (as Aztecs named them) are finally getting the PR and sympathy they deserve. The toll gate to the chiropteran world view is Bat Conservation International; the best intro, America's **Neighborhood Bats**. For the activist, Bat Conservation also offers **Why Save Bats, Bats, Pesticides and Politics**, and **Batman** (a book), as well as instructions for building bat houses. —PW*

Bat Conservation International: Membership $25/year. PO Box 162603, Austin, TX 78716; 512/327-9721.

America's Neighborhood Bats Merlin D. Tuttle. University of Texas Press, 1988; 104 pp. ISBN 0-292-70406-2. $10.95 ($14.70 postpaid) from Bat Conservation International.

Committee for the Preservation of the Tule Elk: PO Box 3696, San Diego, CA 92103.

Great Bear Foundation: 406/721-3009. Grizzlies.

Mountain Lion Foundation: 906/442-2666.

Project Wolf U.S.A.: 206/283-1957. Timber wolf. Fights aerial killings.

Wild Canid Survival and Research Center: 314/938-5900. Mexican and red wolf.

Sinapu: 303/492-5024. Western wolves.

Greater Ecosystem Alliance: 206/671-9950. Lynx and grizzlies.

Jane Goodall Institute for Wildlife Research, Education, and Conservation: 602/325-1211; 800/999-CHIMP.

Digit Fund: 303/790-2349. Mountain gorilla conservation.

Elephant Interest Group: 313/540-3947.

Rhino Rescue U.S.A.: 212/293-5305.

Friends of the Australian Koala Foundation: 212/779-0700.

International Snow Leopard Trust: 206/632-2421.

Cetaceans

The World's Whales is the best intro to all seventy-six known whales, porpoises and dolphins, with fine photos and high-integrity info. The Whale Watcher's Handbook is the field guide of choice for all North American cetaceans. For "fun," the heartbreaking A Whale for the Killing, by Farley Mowatt (the mammalian patriot scribe of Never Cry Wolf) and, yes, Moby Dick (though Melville insisted it be a fish) will complete your entrance into the echolocating, sounding world of mystery mammals. —PW

Cetacean Society International: 202/793-8400. The global group working against outlaw whalers and for driftnet management, whale sanctuaries and pollution control.

Save the Whales: 202/337-2332. The PR firm for cetaceans. Opposes commercial whaling and monitors the International Whaling Commission.

Sea Shepherd: 310/394-3198. The vigilantes of the open seas, placing their lives between whaler and whale. See page 109.

•

Some time between 70 million and 50 million years ago, after the last of the dinosaurs had died and mammals had inherited the land, one or more groups of mammals waded back into the water, presumably to feed on the abundant plant and animal forms there. These pig-sized, four-legged,

Profile characteristics of the Humpback, Bryde's, and Sperm Whales: blowing, surfacing, and diving. —*Handbook*

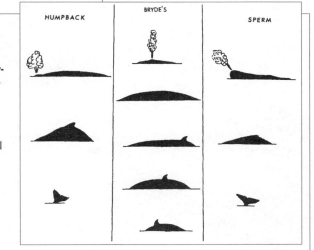

warm-blooded, placental creatures adapted quickly to their new habitat and soon gave rise to a new branch in the evolutionary tree — the order Cetacea, which today includes all of the world's whales, dolphins and porpoises.

•

It is, perhaps, this sense of parental care, of responsibility, almost, together with their apparent intelligence, curiosity, and inoffensiveness that has always drawn us to the whales. Awed by their size, dismayed by the prospect of ever understanding their way of life in a formidable habitat, we nonetheless are fascinated by these animals, with which we feel such an unlikely kinship. The great rise in popularity of whale watching in Hawaii, California and New England bears eloquent witness to our desire to see and know that whales. For all that, we know lamentably little about them.
—*The World's Whales*

The World's Whales: Stanley M. Minasian, Kenneth C. Balcomb, III & Larry Foster. Smithsonian Institution Press, 1984; 224 pp. ISBN 0-89599-014-8. $35 postpaid from TAB Books Inc./Dept. 900, Blue Ridge Summit, PA 17294; 800/782-4612.

The Whale Watcher's Handbook: David K. Bulloch. 1993; 114 pp. ISBN 1-55821-232-9. $13.95 ($16.45 postpaid) from Lyons & Burford Publishers, 31 W. 21st Street, New York, NY 10010; 212/620-9580.

A Whale for the Killing: Farley Mowat. Bantam Books, 1984; 224 pp. ISBN 0-553-26752-3. $3.99 ($6.49 postpaid) from Bantam, Doubleday, Dell/Fulfillment Dept., 2451 S. Wolf Road, Des Plaines, IL 60018; 800/223-6834.

THE TWENTIETH CENTURY will be known for its brutal cruelty to nonhuman critters and ethnic minorities. A century of scattered holocausts. In the twenty-first, it's time to find your animal or plant friend, ally or totem — the creature that moves you. It's time to dedicate your life, if necessary, to keeping your ally from going extinct. Every critter I have tried to save has offered me a journey unknown. Trying to save the Mt. Graham red squirrel I wound up in the Vatican, whose astronomers had insisted that their telescope be put in the center of the squirrel's critical habitat in Arizona. Trying to save the southernmost run of steelhead I wound up in Malibu, or at least its creek. Away from narrowly driven greed and prejudices, compassion is expanding toward ethnic minorities and women and, hopefully, eventually to chimps, rhinos, flycatchers, and butterflies, and bugs. Saving endangered species takes commitment and teaches patience with human sins. The potential reward: flight of the peregrine or dance of the crane endlessly extending into future time. —Peter Warshall

The Last Panda

George Schaller's most soulful work, written in journal style with many asides about a creature who evolved only two to three million years ago (about the same time as humans). Each threatened species has unique problems; Schaller wanders through the panda's: it's a specialist "bear" needing bamboo; its poached market price is high, and climbing; its breeding difficulties keep it a rare commodity; bureaucratic muddling contributes, and so does chronic shortage of habitat. Here, conservation biology confronts an evil that grinds against hope and shatters the planet's diversity. Written with hope. —PW

The Last Panda
George B. Schaller. University of Chicago Press, 1993; 352 pp. ISBN 0-226-73628-8 $24.95 ($27.95 postpaid). Chicago Distribution Center, 11030 S. Langley Avenue, Chicago, IL 60628; 800/621-2736

Staff from the Wolong Reserve transport the body of a female panda found in a poacher's snare.

●
Television shows and magazine articles have given the impression that field biologists lead an exciting life as they wallow with whales and associate with amiable apes. All but forgotten is the fact that many creatures are solitary and rarely seen, and that self-imposed isolation means lack of conveniences, bewildering cultures, and penance in dust, heat, snow, or rain. Most people would find little romance in field work. One night, withdrawn in my sleeping bag, I mused to myself that a field biologist's greatest danger lies not in encountering fierce animals or treacherous terrain but in finding comfort and being seduced by it. But there was no danger of that in this ice-bound, soot-blackened tent, I thought, as I contentedly drifted into sleep.

●
Pandas generally have to spend more than twelve hours a day eating but, because food is so abundant, they need not travel far. . . . Bears have remained opportunistic and adaptable, geared to a boom-or-bust economy, evolving a life-style that has enabled them to settle and thrive in many different habitats. The panda has become a specialist, it has chosen security over uncertainty. But by so doing it has lost its need to explore, to be observant, to try something new; it has tied itself to a fate without a horizon. Both bear and panda are triumphs of evolution, but in this age of environmental destruction, it is the adaptable species that has a better chance of survival.

So Cranes May Dance

When the habitat goes, it's the thirteenth hour: time for captive breeding. One hopes it's a limbo period in which green boddhisattvas can find enough habitat and a safe migratory route for a return to the "wild." This is a story of patience and sadness, persistence on the brink of extirpation. Cranes become spiritual sidekicks for the long haul of survival. —PW

●
A year later, the one thing that everyone feared happened. On Thursday, September 9, 1965, Hurricane Betsy slammed into Louisiana. All the cranes were moved inside and survived. But three days later, when they were back in their pens, a helicopter surveying the damage lingered over the enclosures. Josephine repeatedly threw herself against the fence. By the time the zookeepers got to her, Josephine was bloodied but still standing. The next morning she was dead. The continued

existence of the Louisiana flock, genetically speaking, depended on her offspring: Tony, Angus, Peewee, and Pepper.

●
Horwich designed a crane costume to transform him into a "mother crane." He didn't look much like a crane when he wore it, but more important, he didn't look like a human. A sheet covered his head and body. Over his face was a dark screen that hid his features but permitted him to see where he was going, more or less. On one arm he glued some feathers so he could brood

his little "offspring" with his "wing." On the other arm he wore the head puppet. Under the costume he carried a tape recorder to play crane calls. The chicks became quickly enamored of their bizarre mother.

So Cranes May Dance
(A Rescue from the Brink of Extinction) Barbara Katz. 1993; 279 pp. ISBN 1-55652-171-5 $19.95 postpaid. Chicago Review Press/ Independent Publishers Group, 814 N. Franklin Street, Chicago, IL 60610; 312/337-0747

Birds in Jeopardy • Vanishing Fishes Of North America

Extremely well-written summaries of North American hopes and tragedies. How migrating birds and fish need international cooperation. How intimacy helps provide the cure. If you delight in birds or fish, choose your commitment. —PW

Birds in Jeopardy
Paul Ehrlich, David Dobkin & Darryl Wheye. 1992; 259 pp. ISBN 0-8047-1981-0 $17.95 ($20.95 postpaid) from Stanford University Press, Stanford, CA 94305-2235; 415/723-9434

Vanishing Fishes of North America
R. Dana Ono, James D. Williams & Anne Wagner. Stone Wall Press, 1983. Out of Print.

For information on Endangered Plants, turn back to page 45.

Action Box

Defenders of Wildlife: 1244 19th Street NW, Washington, DC 20036. 202/659-9510. Join 73,000 members in this custom-designed organization dedicated to keepin' them alive. Good info, great lobbying. Be it wolves in Yellowstone or marine mammals strangling in plastic, DOW is there.

Traffic: Quarterly free from World Wildlife Fund, 1250 24th Street NW, Suite 500, Washington, DC 20037; 202/293-4800. The citizen border guards preventing the smuggling of endangered wildlife. They create major ripples of hope in the animal kingdom.

The Captive Breeding Specialist Group: 12101 Johnny Cake Ridge Road, Apple Valley, MN 55124. A truly planetary group from 60 nations concerned with captive breeding of species on the edge on extinction, especially at the last locale of habitat. Another great program associated with the International Union for the Conservation of Nature (p. 63). Quarterly mag for contributing.

IUCN Publications: 219c Huntingdon Road, Cambridge CB3 0DL, UK. (Many also available from Island Press.) The best, updated place to find a long list of the totemic animals that need help and may change your life.

Endangered Species Update: $21/year (10 issues). School of Natural Resources, University of Michigan, Ann Arbor, MI 48109; 313/763-3243. The latest law-and-ethics news.

Books of the Big Outside: Catalog free from Ned Ludd Books, PO Box 85190, Tucson, AZ 85754; 602/628-9610. The most complete catalog of wildlife protection. Books on wolves, bears, jag-uars, red-cockaded woodpeckers, sea turtles, gorillas, and on and on. For the heartbreakers and latest hopes.

UNESCO Biosphere Map

By scanning similar colors on this map you begin to fathom why eucalyptus does so well in California; why "Mediterranean" regions can look to each other for advice on wine, sunlit art, fire, grasses, mellowness, and erosion management. This is the most important map for a sustainable planet.

Biomes are the largest living communities recognized by ecologists: savannas, tundras, deciduous or evergreen forests. Biomes are the grand context with which all human actions must harmonize. Biomes are the meditative means to compare ourselves with our closest Gaian cousins. Biomes are the ethical vehicle for preserving pieces of the planet for our children and grandchildren.

Consider the tropical dry forests: of Mexico, of the Gran Chaco of South America, of the miombo woodlands of Africa, of the Mahandian forests of India or the north coast of Australia. They deserve the same attention as tropical rainforests, but we might miss them without this map. This free map!

No excuses. Tack it up; contemplate, absorb, and dream. —PW

UNESCO Biosphere Map: No charge for small numbers of copies. The MAB Secretariat (Publications), Division of Ecological Sciences, UNESCO, I Rue Miollis, 75732 Paris Cedex 15, France. Telephone: 33-1-45-68-4088; fax: 33-1-40-65-9897.

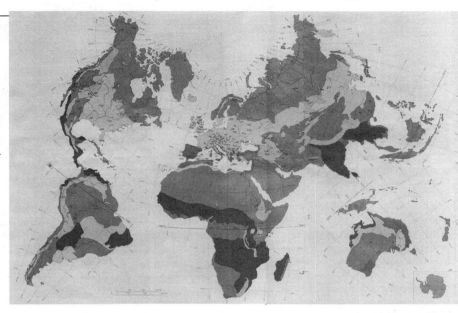

The Living Planet

In the Attenborough style of a long anecdote and a short but pithy conclusion, **The Living Planet** *introduces the larger biological communities (biomes or biogeographical regions): tundras, jungles, grasslands, oceans, deserts, sweet water, etc. A breezy book with gripping color photographs that will entice the reader into more appreciation of how this little spinning sphere got to have so much happening.*
—PW

•

So the wounds inflicted on the land by volcanoes eventually heal. Although volcanoes

The Living Planet
David Attenborough.
1986; 320 pp. ISBN 0-316-05749-5
$17.95 postpaid from Little, Brown and Co./Order Dept., 200 West Street, Waltham, MA 02154; 800/343-9204

may seem, on the short scale by which man experiences time, the most terrifyingly destructive aspect of the natural world, in the longer view they are the great creators.

This Land is Your Land

Best activist directory for biome protection. Lists US government resources, what you can do to help, conservation and environmental organizations, and further reading, and highlights major bioregional issues. —PW

•

By August 1991 the Bush strategy was revealed as a cynical plot to take away 30 percent of the nation's wetlands by redefining them as land that could be used for farming and other purposes. The Bush "revisions" would exempt wet meadows, bogs, floodplains, Alaska moist tundra, and other temporarily flooded wetlands.

Immediate reactions from federal scientists indicated that under the new definition almost half of the Everglades might be lost. At the same time conservationists nationwide mobilized in their opposition to perhaps the largest weakening of a regulation in environmenal history.

This Land Is Your Land
Jon Naar & Alex J. Naar.
1993; 400 pp. ISBN 0-06-096882-6
$15 ($17.75 postpaid) from HarperCollins Publishers/Direct Mail, PO Box 588, Dunmore, PA 18512; 800/331-3761

OTHER GREAT RESOURCES

Biogeographical Processes: Ian Simons (George, Allen, and Unwin). Overview of the Big Picture biology.

Global Climate Map: Forestry Suppliers. Huge size (55" x 33"), tiny details. This is the best summary of "climatograms" and the planet's major global climate influences, greenhouse and ozone impacts, and variability of weather of the world's major cities.

Vegetation of the Earth and Ecological Systems of the Geobiosphere: H. Walter. 1985, Springer-Verlag New York.

Ecosystems of the World

This is the most Whole Earth of any series of books in this catalog. The Encyclopedia Brittanica of biome thought. To know the biomes similar to where you live, find the pertinent volume in your underused library. You won't want to buy them as they cost from $150 to $300. Twenty-nine volumes cover every major biome (including all kinds of marine ecosystems and inland aquatic ecosystems) plus managed grasslands, field-crop ecosystems, tree-crop ecosystems, green-house ecosystems, bioindustrial ecosystems, and managed aquatic ecosystems. All the biome volumes are readable, *with clear photographs and great info: climate, soils, microbes, plants, animals, common parasites, energy flows, human-impacts. Since "ecosystem management" is the new buzzword of the Beltway, use these books as the cavalry for truth. —PW*

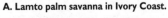

Ecosystems of the World
29 volumes.
Information from Elsevier Science Publishing Co., 655 6th Avenue, New York, NY 10010; 212/989-5800

Between-site, year-to-year and long-term variability in physiognomic structure of tropical African savannas. Views of four areas which have been sites of intensive ecological studies during the past decades.

A. Lamto palm savanna in Ivory Coast.

B. Shortgrass savanna of the Serengeti Plains, Tanzania, with a *kopje* in the background.

C. Sahelian savanna of Fété-Olé, Senegal, at the end of the rains in a "normal" year, September 1969.

D. The same site in September, during the 1972 drought.

The Times Atlas and Encyclopaedia of the Sea

A pure joy to behold. A comprehensive understanding of the ocean as we learn more about the limits of the once-boundless seas. Well-written, graphically pleasing, and logically organized, it includes ship-borne commerce, shoreline development, pollution sources, military strategy, sea law, as well as natural history. —David Burnor

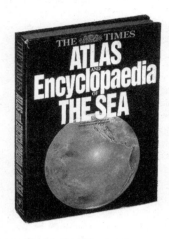

The Times Atlas and Encyclopaedia of the Sea
Alastair Couper. 1989; 272 pp.
ISBN 0-06-016287-2
$65 ($67.75 postpaid) from HarperCollins Publishers/Direct Mail, PO Box 588, Dunmore, PA 18512; 800/331-3761

•

Traditionally, most states have claimed a territorial sea of 3 nm and the exercise of their sovereign jurisdiction over this zone was limited only by the obligation to allow innocent passage for foreign shipping. The outer limit of the territorial also marked the limit of the coastal state's exclusive fishing rights. In recent years, however, two trends have been noticeable. First, there has been a very marked increase in the breadth of territorial sea claimed and the majority of states now claim 12 nm or more; some states claim 200 nm. In contrast to this, the pressure to make excessively large, comprehensive territorial sea claims has to some extent been reduced by the appearance of new jurisdictional zones. The 'exclusive fighting zone' (EFZ) was introduced in the 1960s. More recently, the 'exclusive economic zone' (EEZ) concept has been developed and is now incorporated in the new Convention.

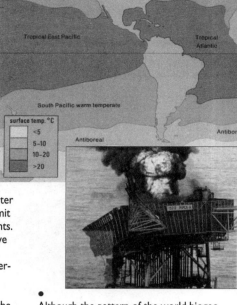

Marine biogeographic areas

surface temp. °C
<5
5–10
10–20
>20

The burning wreck of the Piper Alpha oil platform in the North Sea after a massive explosion, July 1988.

•

Although the pattern of the world biogeographic regions is not as clear cut as that of the vegetation belts on land, it may be readily related to temperature. Cold water populations are found in the Arctic and Southern Ocean, south of the Antarctic Convergence, where surface temperatures lie between 5°C and a little below 0°C. Species diversity is low. Warm water populations are located where the surface temperatures remain above 18-20°C. There is high species diversity and rapid degeneration, although the total biomass may be low. In a few areas, such as the Sargasso Sea, fertility is very low. In between are the temperate populations located between the 5°C and 18°C mean annual isotherms, commonly distinguished into a cool, or boreal, group and a warm temperate group. In these areas productivity is markedly seasonal, and, as in the tropical Indo-Pacific and the eastern Pacific, there is a broad distinction between Western and Eastern provinces separated by the deep ocean.

Global Marine Biological Diversity

Just as the atmosphere binds citizens all over the globe, so does the ocean. This is the crucial handbook for activists and naturalists on the state of the oceans. Comprehensive coverage of the ocean's importance to humans and threats to its living creatures (trawling and siltation, alien species and over-fishing). The starting text for a global biodiversity strategy.
—Peter Warshall

•

Species diversity is probably best viewed as one among a number of useful criteria. All things being equal, it is probably better to conserve an area with 500 species than one with 300, assuming that the 500 include the 300. But all things are seldom equal- what if the 300 (or at least some of them) are *not* among the 500? The smaller assemblage might contain species that people find more important to conserve for some reason such as economic importance, ecological importance, evolutionary significance or endangerment. For example, an area that harbors the only remaining coelacanth species, the last surviving one of its subclass of fishes, might merit special priority even if the area is less diverse than adjacent ones. Or, an area with lower diversity might be better at providing ecological services important to people.

•

The Sian Ka'an Biosphere Reserve is located on the Caribbean coast of the

Global Marine Biological Diversity
(A Strategy for Building Conservation into Decision Making)
Elliott A. Norse, Editor. Center for Marine Conservation, 1993; 383 pp.
ISBN 1-55963-256-9
$27.50 ($31.25 postpaid) from Island Press, Box 7, Covelo, CA 95428; 800/828-1302

Yucatán peninsula. Its objectives are varied: conserving nearshore marine resources associated with the Mexican-Belize Barrier Reef, sustaining the ways of life of local Mayan peoples, and protecting lowland dry tropical forest of the coastal zone. The biosphere reserve management structure gives the local community management authority and paves the way for a strong commitment to stewardship.

Sian Ka'an provides one of the best examples of small-scale marine conservation. A lucrative spiny lobster (Panulirus spp.) fishery is based in Punta Allen, in the heart of the coastal reserve. The locally managed fishing cooperative limits access to the fishery and negative impacts on the marine environment, while keeping profit margins high.

North American bluefin tuna. This **powerful, warm-blooded,** long-distance migrator's population has fallen to a few percent of pristine levels because of overfishing. Existing international organizations seem powerless to stop their decline.

Steller's sea cow. European hunters drove this gigantic seaweed-grazing mammal to extinction 27 years after its discovery in the North Pacific Ocean. Loss of genes, species, and ecosystems is a rapidly worsening problem in the sea, as on land.

The Sea Around Us

Along with Moby Dick, still the salty classic. —PW

•

The greatest depth at which the giant squid lives is not definitely known, but there is one instructive piece of evidence about the depth to which sperm whales descend, presumably in search of the squids. In April 1932, the cable repair ship All America was investigating an apparent break in the submarine cable between Balboa in the Canal Zone and Esmeraldas, Ecuador. The cable was brought to the surface off the coast of Colombia. Entangled in it was a dead 45-foot male sperm whale. The submarine cable was twisted around the lower jaw and was wrapped around one flipper, the body, and the caudal flukes. The cable was raised from a depth of 540 fathoms, or 3240 feet.

See also:
Coasts and Beaches: (p. 88)
Center for Marine Conservation: (p. 88)
Eco-Activism: (p. 109)
Earthwatch: (p. 339)
Coast Alliance: (p. 88)

The Sea Around Us
Rachel L. Carson. 1991; 278 pp.
ISBN 0-19-506997-8
$9.95 ($11.95 postpaid) from Oxford University Press/Order Dept., 2001 Evans Road, Cary, NC 27513; 800/451-7556

PROTECTING OUR OCEANS

Abandoned Seas: Reversing the Decline of the Oceans
by Peter Weber (Worldwatch Paper 116). Best enviro summary in fifty pages.

Sea of Slaughter by Farley Mowat. The holocaust of the northern Atlantic seaboard ecosystem (polar and seabirds, whales and seals). A beachfront assault on greed.

Oceanic Society Expeditions (800/326-7491). Best oceanic eco-tourism.

Coral Reefs & Islands

One of the best combos of coffee table luxury and fine information. From cowfish to gumbo limbos, atolls to barrier reefs, from the Tuamotu Archipelago to Suakin, William Gray balances pop prose and technical detail. If you've skin-dived once, you'll scuba up to this fine work of natural history.
— Peter Warshall

●

The majority of the world's coral reefs are confined to tropical latitudes. Warm and cold ocean currents play a further role in defining reef distribution, as does the presence of suitable reef foundation. Fresh-water flowing from the mouths of rivers, such as the Amazon and Fly, severely inhibit the growth of reefs.

●

Deep within the island a buried lens of rainwater has been accumulating, becoming less brackish as the island gains height above the sea. With shelter, fertilizer and a source of water that can be tapped by large root systems, the island's interior is ready for trees. Flocks of fruit-eating birds, such as white-eyes, blown out to sea and too weak to fly back to the mainland, void the seeds of fig and mulberry trees in their droppings. Each seed lands on the ground with an additional supply of fertilizer, and in time an open parkland with scattered trees and bushes

Reef-building corals flourish at the crest of the Indian Ocean

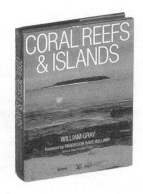

Coral Reefs & Islands
(The Natural History of a Threatened Paradise)
William Gray. David & Charles Publishers, 1993; 192 pp. ISBN 0-7153-0077-6
$29.95 ($31.70 postpaid) from Sterling Publishing Co., 387 Park Avenue S., New York, NY 10016; 800/367-9692

develops. Eventually this mixed wood dominates the central region of the island, leaving only isolated clearings of grasses and herbs.

●

Coral reefs also began to provide the raw materials for various industries. Sea cucumbers were harvested in huge quantities during the 1800s, and exported from the tropical Indo-Pacific as dried and smoked *beche-de-mer*. In the Far East, the shrivelled, black bodies of the sea cucumbers are still regarded as a delicacy. Pearl oysters, green

snails and trochus shells also began to be harvested from the reef waters and they continue to supply a trade in jewellery and fashion accessories made from mother-of-pearl. Turtle canneries were established at nesting sites, such as Heron Island on the Great Barrier Reef. . . . Without doubt,

nuclear testing must rank as the single most devastating form of environmental impact to have been unleashed on coral islands and reefs. Only in 1992 did France declare its intention to end its nuclear programme in French Polynesia.

Underwater Naturalist

Love the coast? Join the American Littoral Society and pull in their bulletin, **Underwater Naturalist.** *Love to fish? Join "Tag-a-Fish," a catch-and-release program in which you tag the fish with markers provided by the Littoral Society. Since most fish migration is out-of-sight, another angler, catching the same fish, also catches a megabyte of information.*

Underwater Naturalist sports tagging reports plus book reviews and articles like "The Dance of the Luminescent Tubeworms" or "Swimming with Snails" or "The Fisheries Management Act and the Mid-Atlantic Fisheries." The tidal society of the informed heart.
—PW

American Littoral Society
Membership $25/year (includes 4 issues of *Underwater Naturalist*). Sandy Hook, Highlands, NJ 07732; 908/291-0055.

Alewives and mussels peaked in 1908 at about 70 million pounds, then fell rather irregularly, to a low of about one million pounds in 1991, a drop of about 88 percent.

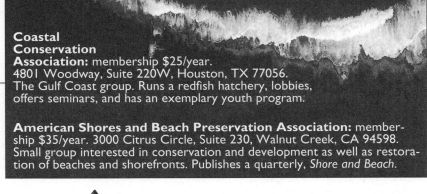

Alewives, mussels

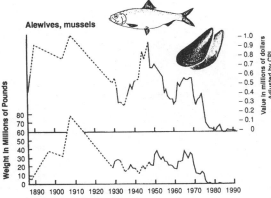

Coastal Conservation Association: membership $25/year. 4801 Woodway, Suite 220W, Houston, TX 77056. The Gulf Coast group. Runs a redfish hatchery, lobbies, offers seminars, and has an exemplary youth program.

American Shores and Beach Preservation Association: membership $35/year. 3000 Citrus Circle, Suite 230, Walnut Creek, CA 94598. Small group interested in conservation and development as well as restoration of beaches and shorefronts. Publishes a quarterly, *Shore and Beach*.

CELEBRATING THE EDGE OF THE SEA

Rachel Carson still holds the prize conch for delicacy and precision among seaside scribes. Besides her **Edge of the Sea,** *here are a few more celebrators of littoral literacy:*

Beautiful Swimmers: William W. Warner. 1994, Little, Brown and Co.
The Seaside Reader: Dery W. Bennett. 1992, Lyons & Burford Publishers.
Waves and Beaches: Willard Bascom. 1980, Doubleday & Co. Out of Print.
Under the Sea Wind: Rachel L. Carson. 1992, Plume-Truman Talley Books.
The Log from the Sea of Cortez: John Steinbeck & Edward Ricketts. 1977, Penguin Books.
The Outermost House: Henry Beston. 1992, Owl Books, Henry Holt & Co.

"The shore has a dual nature, changing with the swing of the tides, belonging now to the land, now to the sea. On the ebb tide it knows the harsh extremes of the land world, being exposed to heat and cold, to wind, to rain and drying sun. On the flood tide it is a water world, returning briefly to the relative stability of the open sea."
—Rachel Carson

The Edge of the Sea: Rachel L. Carson. 1979, Houghton Mifflin Co.

Sea Challengers

A coral reef of written riches, including plastic underwater guides, diving and snorkling guides, and almost every major book of reef and marine life. Some of the best publications are their own.
—PW

Sea Challengers
Catalog free. 4 Somerset Rise, Monterey, CA 93940-4112; 408/373-6306.

Natural History of the Antarctic Peninsula

For those who have never turned their globe upside down.
—Peter Warshall

•

Antarctica is a continent of superlatives. It is the coldest, the driest, the windiest, the iciest, and (with its ice cap) averages as the highest in altitude of all the major land masses of our world. It is the continent with the longest nights, the longest days, the least amount of soil, the greatest amount of fresh water (all locked up as ice), and it is surrounded by the stormiest ocean on earth — the Southern Ocean.

Antarctica is also a continent of contrasts. While having 90 percent of the earth's ice and snow it is also the driest continent in terms of relative humidity and annual precipitation — less than 15 centimeters (6 inches) of rain equivalent a year. Antarctica has a rich history of exploration and discovery by adventurers representing an array of nations, yet it presents a showcase of international cooperation where, by treaty, national territorial claims are held in abeyance. This is the most remote and environmentally hostile of all the continents, but its polar position and relative isolation from man's despoilations make it the most valuable window we have to events going on in our outer atmosphere and the far reaches of space. Because its ice and snow are locked in perpetuity, the depths of the Antarctic ice sheet (which averages about 2,160 meters deep) have deposited in their accumulated layers a record of the earth's atmospheric composition that reaches back tens of thousands of years. So this — the most remote and unfriendly continent — is, scientifically speaking, our most valuable.

The young now have half of their fluffy down gone. The juvenile plumage underneath is like the adult's, but with a white chin. It's a sleek coat compared to the down. They look like clipped French poodles with blobs of fluff here and there. Often the down on top of the head stays a while — looks like a wig.

Natural History of the Antarctic Peninsula
Sanford Moss. 1990; 208 pp.
ISBN 0-231-06269-9
$18 ($21 postpaid). Columbia University Press/Order Dept., 136 S. Broadway, Irvington, NY 10533; 914/591-9111

LITERARY EXTREMISTS

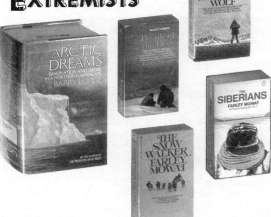

Arctic Dreams: Barry H. Lopez. 1989; 244 pp. ISBN 0-553-34664-4 $11.00 ($13.50 postpaid).
Never Cry Wolf: Farley Mowat. 1983; 176 pp. ISBN 0-553-26624-1 $4.99 ($7.49 postpaid).
The People of the Deer: Farley Mowat. 1984; 304 pp. ISBN 0-7704-2254-3 $5.99 ($8.49 postpaid).
The Siberians: Farley Mowat. 1984; 360 pp. ISBN 0-553-24896-0 $3.95 ($6.45 postpaid).
The Snow Walker: Farley Mowat. 1984; 224 pp. ISBN 0-7704-2209-8 $4.99 ($7.49 postpaid).
All from Bantam, Doubleday, Dell/Fulfillment Dept., 2451 S. Wolf Road, Des Plaines, IL 60018; 800/223-6834

To my surprise, there is no natural history of the extreme Arctic iceflows, the tundra, the taiga, and the boreal forest. But there are great writers in love with permafrost and stories. First, there is Arctic Dreams: lyric, philosophical reflections on the far north, a history of human visions and Barry Lopez's personal quest for the essences of life in this frozen, beautiful land. A bit further south, there are the jovial adventures of Farley Mowat: Never Cry Wolf, People of the Deer, The Siberians, and The Snow Walker. —PW

liberal sprinkling of the cysts of nematode worms. The lungs also were very active even after death. I counted and removed 17 nematode worms, most of them over six inches in length. In the liver there were tapeworm cysts of two species, some of them the size of a tennis ball. The intestines yielded one adult tapeworm of great length and antiquity, and even in the heart muscles I found 6 tapeworm cysts. Of minor parasites, there were 190 warble-fly larvae under the hide and about 75 bott-fly larvae cozily ensconced within the throat and nasal passages. —*People of the Deer*

•

The spring silence is broken by pistol reports of cracking on the river, and then the sound of breaking branches and the whining pop of a falling tree as the careening blocks of ice gouge the riverbanks. A related but far eerier phenomenon occurs in the coastal ice. Suddenly in the middle of winter and without warning a huge piece of sea ice surges hundreds of feet inland, like something alive. The Eskimo call it *ivu.* The silent arrival of caribou in an otherwise empty landscape is another example. The long wait at a seal hole for prey to surface. Waiting for a lead to close. The Eskimo have a word for this kind of long waiting, preparing for a sudden event: *quinuitug.* Deep patience. —*Arctic Dreams*

•

It is a witless misapprehension to think of reindeer solely in terms of Santa Claus and his Disneyland team. Soviet archaeologists believe these Asian caribou were first domesticated about four thousand years ago, and throughout that stretch of time they have been the veritable staff of life to Northern people from Norway to Bering Strait. In all Northern regions of the Soviet Union, but particularly in Siberia, they play an increasingly vital role in human affairs. The arctic and subarctic taiga and tundra are not notably good food-producing regions, but they can produce one thing in abundance — first-rate protein in the form of reindeer meat. In 1968 there were four hundred thousand domestic reindeer in the USSR. —*The Siberians*

Land Above the Trees

As you go very north or very south, the trees pygmify, the soil is made shallow by permafrost, and the flowers floresce. It happens when you go above the timber line as well. This is the alpine natural history — a guide written like talk at a lunchtime stop on the trail and sketched like the best of naturalist notebooks. Ann Zwinger at her most informative and charming. —PW

•

One cannot cross a boulder field and not be aware that lichens are the supreme plants here, for only they can grow on these wind-abraded bare rock surfaces. Light and dark gray, dark brown and black, red-orange, apple green and chartreuse, some encrust the surface so tightly that they cannot be pried off with a knife. They survive in an environment that no green-leafed plant can endure. All they need is a sufficient supply of moisture at some time during the year; often this comes from the half-inch of air immediately above the rock surface that is just warm enough to melt a grain of snow. They carry on photosynthesis at any temperature above 32 degrees F., remaining dormant for long periods and resuming normal growth when thawed or wetted.

Land Above the Trees
(A Guide to American Alpine Tundra)
Ann H. Zwinger & Beatrice E. Willard. 1972; 487 pp. ISBN 0-8165-1110-1 $17.95 ($19.95 postpaid). University of Arizona Press, 1230 N. Park Avenue #102, Tucson, AZ 85719; 602/621-1441

•

Fortunately for their peace of mind few Northerners have any idea of the menageries of other unpleasant beasts that exist under the skin of the deer. Parasites are so numerous, I conclude from my own studies, that there comes a time in the life of every deer, if it survives the other perils, when it is so overloaded with parasites that it simply dies of outright starvation though it spends all day eating. All other things being equal, I doubt if a deer can expect to live more than a dozen years before it is so riddled with worms and cysts that death must inevitably ensue. For the record, and for the enlightenment of any reader who may someday be offered a prime roast of caribou, here is a list of the actual parasites I took from one old buck.

In the bony muscles there was a concentration of tapeworm cysts that averaged two per cubic inch of meat. No part of the muscle tissues was free of these abhorrent things, and in addition to them, there was a

Beyond treelimit, trees are so stunted that they are no longer trees but shrubs. They are called *krummholz,* a descriptive German word which means "elfin timber" or "crooked wood." They look as if they had been cultivated by overly ambitious bonsai gardeners. Krummholz growth habit is shrubby and dense, becoming more prostrate, more twisted and contorted, with altitude. Treetops are flat or flagged or both; trunks are gnarled. Basal branches form impenetrable masses of long intertwined serpentines, impossible to walk through.

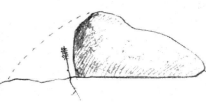

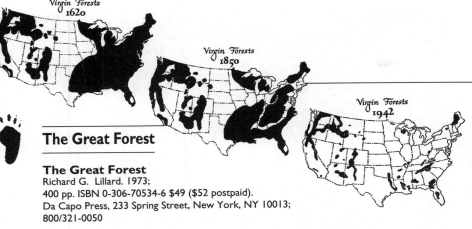

Virgin Forests 1620

Virgin Forests 1850

Virgin Forests 1942

The Great Forest

The Great Forest
Richard G. Lillard. 1973;
400 pp. ISBN 0-306-70534-6 $49 ($52 postpaid).
Da Capo Press, 233 Spring Street, New York, NY 10013;
800/321-0050

In 1947 Richard Lillard wrote our nation's first history of virgin forests, its love of wood (the log cabin complex), and the ever-recurring dialog debating sustainable and maximum use. Now with less than 5 percent of the nation's virgin forest remaining, we still hear Babbittical sophistries about "leaving" half. To set your roots in the mycorrhiza of ligneous history, read this product, printed on, oh yes, temperate-forest tree flesh.
—Peter Warshall

•

For them the trip meant severing age long ties with kingcraft, feudalism, and caste. Sensational in their eyes were the unquestioned rights to hunt game animals and to enjoy unlimited warmth from fuel free for the taking. Many had shivered around faggot fires and suffered for disobeying the harsh poaching laws that went back to William the Conqueror. Many had lived on cereals only. In America they could help themselves to wild turkeys big enough to fill the bellies of sixteen hungry workers at one meal.

The deep soil, rich in the humus of leaves, lay a world apart from the cold thin land of Scottish lairds or the enclosed estates of Irish overlords.

Never before had Christians walked in so leafy and well-provided a paradise as this "Eden newly sprung from the ocean." Heaven and earth had never "agreed better to frame a place for man's habitation." Though the forest together with the fat soil sustaining it had at first glance no recorded past, no hallowed antiquity, it promised a glorious future.

"The most vital material for successful prosecution of the war" is lumber, said Colonel F. G. Sherrill. During the World War the colonel was chief of the Materials and Equipment Section of the U. S. Corps of Army Engineers. He was the hugest buyer of lumber in the world's history. Ton for ton, the armed forces were using more wood than steel, requiring three trees to equip and maintain each man in the army, two for every man in the other services.

Wood went into a thousand articles, into emergency barracks and docks, hangers, airbase control towers, PT boats, Liberty ships, landing boats, life rafts, flagstaffs, latrines, stretchers, crutches, chapels, prefabricated bridges, trucks, trailers, foot lockers for soldiers' clothing, pontoons, cots, wood-cored rubber heels, and tent pegs. Plywood went into many of these and into cargo planes, trainers, gliders, and the famous British bomber, the Mosquito. The biggest single wartime demand on lumber was for specially designed crates and boxes to pack each of the 700,000 different kinds of items needed in a big-scale invasion. Tank crates were the size of a small house.

—Secrets of the Old Growth Forest

coastal temperate rainforests

Coastal temperate rainforests grow along the Pacific rim in Chile, Tasmania, New Zealand, China, Japan, and North America. Some trees are so alike that the wood of Chilean alerce and California redwood was switched in the market and no one noticed. These are forests of fog drip, twig droplets, and tremendous downpours.

Usual rainforests have greenleafers outcompeting needleleafs. But not the Pacific Northwest. Usual rainforests have rain in the warm growing season, but not the Pacific Northwest. Because of the winter-wet/summer-dry seasonal pulse, wintertime leafless oaks cannot compete. For 6,000 years, winter-growth and a mellow coast have grown the cathedral forests.

The most exquisite intro is Secrets of the Old Growth Forest *by David Kelly and Gary Braasch (Peregrine Smith Books, 1988; $29.95). For serious conservation biology try* Ancient Forests of the Pacific Northwest *by Elliott Norse (Island Press, 1990; $19.95).*

A very focused and effective group is Ancient Forests International (PO Box 1850, Redway, CA 95560; 707/923-3015), which has helped save hundreds of thousands of acres of temperate rainforest in Chile by linking Chilean and American scientists, conservationists, and networks with Tasmanian old-growth protectors. —PW

OTHER GREAT FOREST RESOURCES

The Sierra Club Naturalist's Guide Series: 1978-1991, Sierra Club Books. The best intro bioregional guides.

Old Growth in the East (A Survey): Mary Bird Davis. 1993, Cenozoic Society.

The Southern Forest (A Chronicle): Laurence C. Walker. 1991, University of Texas Press. The only history of the southern deciduous hardwood and long-leaf pine forests.

The Big Thicket (An Ecological Reevaluation): Pete Gunter. 1993, University of North Texas Press. The conservation story of Texas' most famous forest.

Audubon Nature Guides: Eastern and Western Forests

The path-starter books for North America. Quick sketches of our forests and a field guide-like lope through the main plants and animals. —PW

•

Black Bear   Ursus americanus

Habitat: In the West, forests and wooded mountains seldom higher than 7,000 feet.

Comments: This uniquely American bear, although primarily nocturnal, may be seen at any time, day or night, ranging in a home area of 8-10 square miles, sometimes as many as 15. It is solitary except briefly during mating season and when congregating to feed at dumps. Its walk is clumsy, but in its bonding trot it attains surprising speed, with bursts up to 30 mph. A powerful swimmer, it also climbs trees, either for protection or food. Though classified as a carnivore, most of its diet consists of vegetation, including twigs, buds, leaves, nuts, roots, various fruit, corn, berries, and newly sprouted plants. In spring, the bear peels off tree bark to get at the inner, or cambium, layer; it tears apart rotting logs for grubs, beetles, crickets, and ants. Small to medium-size mammals or other vertebrates are also eaten. A good fisherman, the Black Bear often wades in streams or lakes, snagging fish with its jaws or pinning them with a paw. It rips open bee trees to feast on honey, honeycomb, bees, and larvae. In the fall, the bear puts on a good supply of fat, then holes up for the winter in a sheltered place, such as a cave, crevice, hollow tree or log, or the roots of a fallen tree.

WESTERN FORESTS

EASTERN FORESTS

Western Forests
Stephen Whitney.
Alfred A. Knopf, Inc., 1984;
670 pp. ISBN 0-394-73127-1

Eastern Forests
Ann Sutton & Myron Sutton.
Alfred A. Knopf, Inc., 1985;
638 pp. ISBN 0-394-73126-3

Both $14.95 ($16.95) postpaid from Random House/ Order Dept., 400 Hahn Road, Westminster, MD 21157; 800/733-3000

Black bear cub sitting in a Red Spruce tree, Great Smoky Mountains National Park, Tennessee
—*Eastern Forests*

From the Forest to the Sea

A unique book on wood come loose: how logs floating and sinking in streams, rivers, estuaries, and the open sea supply living webs with much-needed food; how the shape and size and bulk of trunks and branches and twigs diversifies and stabilizes creeks and sand spits, rivers and dunes. If you haven't seriously contemplated life as a dance of organic carbon molecules circulating the lands and the seas, From the Forest to the Sea *is the watershed showstopper.* —PW

•

The forests, which through the millennia, have fed the ocean energy in the form of driftwood, especially large driftwood, are rapidly disappearing. Without large driftwood, the ocean — from its shallowest estuary to the deepest part of its floor — is

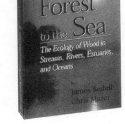

From the Forest to the Sea
The Ecology of Wood in Streams, Rivers, Estuaries, and Oceans

James Sedell
Chris Maser

From the Forest to the Sea
James Sedell & Chris Maser. 1994;
200 pp. ISBN 1-884015-17-4
$55 ($60.95 postpaid). St. Lucie Press,
100 E. Linton Blvd. # 403B, Delray Beach,
FL 33483; 407/274-9906, fax 407/274-9927

being starved of a vital source of energy, terrestrially based carbon.

As our studies progressed, other questions came to the fore: What does it mean to starve the ocean? What exactly is driftwood? Most people associate driftwood with the ocean itself, but where does it really come from? What effect does logging, especially of old-growth forests, have on driftwood? What does driftwood do? Is it important? Can the growing absence of driftwood be part of the problem of declining runs of wild salmon? What role does driftwood play in the life cycle of pelagic tuna?

•

Tunas even time their migration to the Continental Shelf for spawning to coincide with the onset of monsoon rains. In turn, the resulting floods carrying new driftwood to the sea commence as the young tunas are hatching from their eggs. In the eastern Pacific, for example, it is very likely that the association of juvenile yellowfins with large driftwood is important in determining recruitment success. Skipjack, on the other hand, which spawn only infrequently in the eastern Pacific, also have strong tendency to associate with large driftwood. In addition, the association of some species with old driftwood with barnacles and algae may indicate a degree of habitat specificity in the association.

•

If tunas did not accompany floating driftwood but instead swam randomly to find food, it is quite possible they would find themselves in waters poorer in food than the ones they had left. In many cases the transition from rich to poorer areas is abrupt, making it quite possible that tunas will enter one of the poorer areas during random swimming.

Sakuddei shaman (right) with his brothers.

The Last Rain Forests: A World Conservation Atlas

If you own one book on rain forests, this is it. Equal attention is given to all rain forests from Thailand to Cameroon, Madagascar to Amazonia. The Last Rain Forests *harbors an introductory atlas, a good ecological overview, an understanding of native peoples and the World Bank. In a rather sober tone, it tries to combine reason and hope for a compassionate future. If you want a sympathetic narrative in addition to a photographic atlas,* In the Rain Forest *by Catherine Caulfield (University of Chicago Press, 11030 S. Langley Avenue, Chicago, IL 60628; 800/621-2736) remains the best written scientific journalism and clear-headed reporting.*
—Peter Warshall

●

Rain forest covers no more than 8.5 million square kilometres (3.3 million square miles) or six percent of the earth's land surface. This is just over half of what was not long ago a forested area of about 14 million square kilometres (5.5 million square miles). In 1980, the rate of deforestation of rain and monsoon forest was around 71,000 square kilometres (27,000 square miles) a year, about 0.6 percent of the remaining area, according to the Food and Agriculture Organization (FAO). But environmentalist Norman Myers has recently completed a study for Friends of the Earth (FOE) in which he estimates the current rate of loss to be a staggering 142,000 square kilometres (54,000 square miles) a year.

●

Deep inside the forest, agriculturalists are clearing areas too small to show on the maps, and logging companies are exploiting the forest over thousands of square kilometres. By the time the first of such damage becomes apparent much of the whole of the forest may be degraded. But the rain forest does have the potential to recover, given enough time to do so. Even in Kalimantan and Sabah, where in 1982-83 drought followed by massive fires destroyed more than 40,000 square kilometres (15,500 square miles of rain forest), reports are now emerging of extensive regrowth in the affected areas.

The vitality and robustness of the rain forests nonetheless permit no complacency. In Southeast Asia, the rain forests cleared for shifting cultivation are often left fallow for too little time for the soil to replenish itself. The unrelenting pressure of logging, relogging, clearing and burning that is taking place in much of Amazonia, West Africa and Asia is pushing the rain forests into a downward spiral of degradation from which there is little chance of recovery.

People of the Tropical Rain Forest

Callously called "temporary economic dislocations," the development of rainforests has destroyed entire lives. What price progress? And what is progress? **People** *is a combo of engaging photos and detailed text. An excellent overview of what is, with just a little of how it could be.* —PW

●

The few remaining Amazonian, Bornean, or African natives who walk softly through the forest and receive from it all their life's necessities and return to it all they have produced are a vanishing minority among today's rain-forest people. Many more forest folk participate in markets—local, national, or international. They fell large trees with chainsaws; they plant crops that originated on the other side of the globe; their dreams reflect the lives of people who

An Iban tribesman sharpens his chainsaw. Like the badges that travelers collect, his tattoos testify to his many journeys, most of them probably to logging camps.

never saw a rain forest; and they worship gods who only walked in deserts.

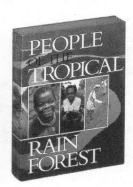

People of the Tropical Rain Forest
Julie Denslow & Christine Padoch, Editors. University of California Press, 1988; 240 pp. ISBN 0-520-06351-1
$27.50 ($30.50 postpaid) from California/ Princeton Fulfillment Services, 1445 Lower Ferry Road, Ewing, NJ 08618; 800/777-4726

Amazonia

The concern is overwhelming. The size of the United States, Amazonia is losing 20 hectares of rainforest per minute, with 8,000 fires per dry season, besides the gold/ oil/coca leaf/land rush. Concern started in 1955 with the publication of **Tristes Tropiques,** *still the most important book on who we are and how we view ourselves; Lévi-Strauss is humbly taught by tropical rainforest folk.* **At Play in the Fields of the Lord** *added the first American cry in the wilderness. Then a thunder-*

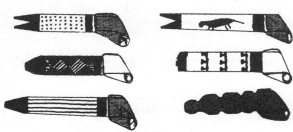

Fig 33. Emblazoned penis sheaths
—*Tristes Tropiques*

storm of books including **Voices From the Amazon** *and* **Rainforests: A Guide to Research at Tourist Facilities and Selected Tropical Forest Sites in Central and South America.**—PW

●

The parcelled-up eagle was unceremoniously dumped by the side of a stream, where it seemed doomed to die rapidly of hunger or be eaten by ants. The Tupi kept eagles and fed them on monkeys, so as to be able to pluck their feathers periodically. It was not surprising, then, that it should have survived among a group of Tupi-Kawahib, nor that the eagle, which they looked upon as their most precious posses-

sion, should have been brought as a present, if the natives had really decided (as I began to suspect and indeed subsequently confirmed) to leave their village for good and join the civilized world. However, that only made it more difficult to understand why they should have abandoned the eagle to its pitiable fate. Yet the whole history of colonization in South America and elsewhere must take into account this kind of radical renunciation of traditional values, when, during the break-up of a way of life, the loss of certain elements lead to the immediate depreciation of all the rest. —*Tristes Tropiques*

Voices from the Amazon: Binka Le Breton. Kumarian Press, 1993.

Tristes Tropiques: Claude Levi-Strauss. Penguin Books, 1955, 1992.

At Play in the Fields of the Lord: Peter Matthiessen. Peter Smith Publisher, Inc., 1992.

Rainforests: A Guide to Research and Tourist Facilities at Selected Tropical Forest Sites in Central and South America. James L. Castner. Feline Press, 1990.

The Forest People

The most unadvertised of rainforests. This book is a classic and beautiful description of the Pygmies of the Congo. No book on rainforest peoples anywhere is so moving. —PW

●

One night in particular will always live for me, because that night I think I learned just how far away we civilized human beings have drifted from reality. The moon was full, so the dancing had gone on for longer than usual. Just before going to sleep I was standing outside my hut when I heard a curious noise from the nearby children's *bopi.* This surprised me, because at nighttime the Pygmies generally never set foot outside the main camp. I wandered over to see what it was.

There, in the tiny clearing, splashed with silver, was the sophisticated Kenge, clad in bark cloth, adorned with leaves, with a flower stuck in his hair. He was all alone, dancing around and singing softly to himself as he gazed up at the treetops.

Now Kenge was the biggest flirt for miles, so, after watching a while, I came into the clearing and asked, jokingly, why he was dancing alone. He stopped, turned slowly around and looked at me as though I was the biggest fool he had ever seen; and he was plainly surprised by my stupidity.

"But I'm not dancing alone," he said. "I am dancing with the forest, dancing with the moon." Then, with the utmost unconcern, he ignored me and continued his dance of love and life.

The Forest People
Colin M. Turnbull. 1988; 295 pp. ISBN 0-8446-6334-4
$18.50 ($19.98 postpaid) from Peter Smith Publisher, 6 Lexington Avenue, Magnolia, MA 01930; 508/525-3562

In the Shipstern Reserve in Belize butterflies are being used to provide funds for conservation. The main objective of the Reserve is to show that the sustainable use of forest resources can provide enough income to support the area. Initially, marketing of captive-bred butterfly pupae, including Thoas swallowtail (Papilio thoas) will provide the money for further work.

The Last Rain Forests
(A World Conservation Atlas) Mark Collins, Editor. 1990; 200 pp. ISBN 0-19-520836-6 $35 ($37 postpaid) from Oxford University Press/Order Dept., 2001 Evans Road, Cary, NC 27513; 800/451-7556

To Grow Is to Turn Green

GROWING IS GENERATING, generating green grass. There is a singular Indo-European word-root for *grow-green-grass*. Llanos, cerrados, prairies, pampas, pustzas, savanna cover 30 to 40 percent of the planet's surface. Overgrazing, agricultural development, overburning, and introduced exotic grasses have caused these grassland biomes to collapse. Bovine imperialism — replacing zebras with zebu and bison with herefords — has stampeded native communities into commodities. Where are the bustards, the black-footed ferrets, the European bison, the steppe marmot, and the Eurasian meadow viper (a non-venomous mouse catcher)? Gone with the grasses.

Grasslands and Tundra (Time-Life Editors. Time-Life, Inc., 1985) is a preliminary sketch of the planet's grasslands. It can lead you to out-of-print sources. But, the book of planetary grassland love awaits an author (which explains a lot about human alienation from bread and butter). Best library access is through the Elsevier Ecosystems of the World series (p. 53). —Peter Warshall

California Grasslands
Intermountain Grasslands
Desert Grasslands
Shortgrass Prairie
Mixed Prairie
Tallgrass Prairie

Grasslands

In the United States, there are about twenty-five grassland types that cover about 17 percent of the nation. Most now sport soybeans, corn, and wheat: our grassland soils contain more natural nutrition than almost any other humanized biome on the planet. The bluestem, bluestem/sacahuista and bluestem/grama grasslands are severly endangered. Dust bowls haunt.

For an overview of the continent's grasslands — California, intermountain, desert, tallgrass, mixed, shortgrass, and Eastern — get Audubon's **Grasslands**. —PW

Grasslands
Lauren Brown. Alfred A. Knopf Inc., 1985; 606 pp. ISBN 0-394-73121-2 $16.95 ($18.95 postpaid) from Random House/Order Dept., 400 Hahn Road, Westminster, MD 21157; 800/733-3000

●

Some grasslands seem to vacillate between being grasslands and being forests, The agent that tips the balance in these cases is fire. Most trees are killed or weakened by fire, but grasses have adapted to survive it and may even grow better after a conflagration. Fire removes litter (dead plant material), which would otherwise shade the soil and keep it from warming up in the early spring. Furthermore it releases the nutrients that are locked up in the litter. The grasses thus begin to grow earlier in the season, and they reach greater heights.

●

Lack of interest in grasslands has been reflected in the national parks and monuments that have been created which are mainly those that include unusual landscapes. Thus, as this book goes to press — and we hope that it will soon be inaccurate — there is not one national park dedicated exclusively to the preservation of grassland.

Why preserve grasslands? Because they are one of the most extensive, productive ecosystems in the United States. Why have they not been preserved? Because they were too productive, and were quickly transformed to croplands; and because, in their vastness, they were considered the quintessence of monotony and were taken for granted.

Conservation and Development in the Rain Forest

There is much healthy skepticism about the world's power brokers (the World, Asian, African and Inter-American Banks, the International Tropical Timber Organization, and even the United Nations Development Program) that call for sustainable rainforests and cultures and provoke tense politics, full of murder and mayhem. How to switch the forest products market from high volumes of low-value timber to low volumes of high-value timber; how to maximize extraction of renewables like rubber or nuts; how to prevent cattle and agricultural colonists from burning and stonewalling forest recovery; how to return fair profits to indigenous peoples; and how to control the cheaters and robbers even when rules are in place — this is the battleground.

There's no one successful strategy or group. Multinational boycotts and preferential purchasing definitely help. Debt-for-nature swaps slow destruction and allow for thought and caring and restructuring of local citizen's livelihoods. Ethical reform of the power brokers is a long shot but could be immensely effective. Here are a few citizens' groups. —PW

Amazonia (from Rainforest Action Network, below). The best citizens' guide to almost every organization in every nation trying to get a grip on Amazonia chaos. Great advocacy book and film list.

Rainforest Action Network: 800/989-7246. This group defined activism. Boycotts of Mitsubishi, muckraking newsletter, letter-writing, lobbying. Good guys (natives) vs. bad guys (World Bank, the big corporations). RAN is the big push from *slightly* offstage.

Chico Mendes Fund: 202/797-6800. Seventy-five percent of all donations goes to training and organizing rubber tappers in the rainforest, 25 percent to people in developing countries whose lives are endangered by their work on behalf of the environment.

Rainforest Foundation: 212/582-6513. Works directly for the Kayapo people and reserve in Brazil: health, resource management, land tenure, education.

Woodworkers Alliance for Rainforest Protection: PO Box 133, Coos Bay, OR 97420. This wonderful small group understands that we create the market for tropical hardwoods and offers information and alternatives so that we can buy ethically and sustainably.

Rainforest Alliance: 212/677-1900. A sober group with such serious projects as the Smart Wood project with timber certification and a medicinal plant project; fellowships and education.

Vanishing Rainforests Education Kit with video: 410/516-6951. Good place for teachers of grades two to six to start.

*See also
Cultural Survival
(pp. 72-73) and
Saving Biomes
(p. 63).*

Beyond Beef

One can always argue with Rifkin. But there is no better book on the global cow and its devastating impact on human health and the planet's ecosystems. From pasture to packing house, the message is clear: beef has become a liability. To reduce hormones and pesticides, to re-allocate water from cows to fishes, to eat healthier, to return grasslands, move beyond beef. Maybe to buffalo or reasonable stocking rates. —PW

●

The medical establishment have begun to suggest that a diet rich in animal fat and cholesterol increases the risk of the "diseases of affluence" — heart disease, cancer, and diabetes. . . . Choice-grade beef has 15 to 19 percent more fat content than select-grade beef and is responsible for a significant amount of the saturated fat and cholesterol in the American and western European diets.

●

Red meats, especially beef, have been associated with maleness and male qualities while the "bloodless" white meats have been associated with femaleness and feminine qualities. During the Victorian era and in the early years of the twentieth century, health journals "often suggested a reduction in [red] meat intake for pregnant and lactating women, putting the emphasis instead on delicate, light dishes like chicken, fish or eggs. The prescribed dishes not only mirrored the women's own delicate 'feminine' condition but avoided any of the stimulation of those qualities of red-bloodedness that seemed inappropriate to those fulfilling the nurturing role."

OGRs

Where the Sky Began: John Madson. Houghton Mifflin, 1982, Out of Print. The midwest, bioregional classic.

Dust Bowl: The Southern Plains in the 1930's: Donald Worster. Oxford University Press, 1982. The 1930s revenge of a destroyed ecosystem.

How Grasses Grow: R. H. M. Langer. Baltimore University Press, 1979, Out of Print.

Planet Earth Series: Time-Life, Inc., 1985.

Beyond Beef
(The Rise and Fall of the Cattle Culture) Jeremy Rifkin. Plume Books, 1993; 368 pp. ISBN 0-452-26952-0 $11 ($13 postpaid) from Penguin USA/Consumer Sales, 120 Woodbine Street, Bergenfield, NJ 07621; 800/253-6476

Arid areas as defined in this book

Estimate of area that may be desert in 30-40 years

Tropic of Cancer

Equator

Tropic of Capricorn

Deserts • Arid Lands

From the great sea sands of the Sahara to the foggy coastal plains of Peru, from the broken rock of the cold Gobi to the searing salt flats of the Danakil, **Deserts** *explores the physical lands and their peoples with highly specific maps. For humans and resources, it is scorching and accurate.* **Arid Lands** *includes the wildlife and plants, better biology, a greater expanse of life, but with a more naive optimism about greening the desert. Start the trek here into the sere and the sunset.* —Peter Warshall

•

For some scientists, intensive grazing is a further contributor to land degradation. This view holds that grazing animals could severely and permanently damage the vegetation of the desert edge. It has led to calls for the reduction of animal numbers to a

point known as the "carrying capacity" of the land. However, for most pastoral peoples, stock means survival. These people are well aware that in good years they can maintain numbers well above any official "carrying capacity", and return to these numbers after bad years. Much of the degradation perceived by early scientists as being caused by grazers was in fact caused by drought. After one drought, pastoralists can seldom build stock numbers up to levels that can damage pastures before the next drought intrudes. The ecosystems of the desert edge are adapted to drought, and can recover remarkably quickly.

There is a growing number of people who dismiss the concept of desertification. The danger this raises is that the very real problems of managing dry lands will be overlooked, especially the perennial problem of drought and the looming threat of climate change. — *Deserts*

Villagers clearing wind-blown Sahara sand from a house in Mauritania, West Africa. Moving dunes are most problematic around desert margins. In these regions, overgrazing, wood cutting and intensive agriculture can remove the scant natural vegetation that helps to contain drifting sand. —*Deserts*

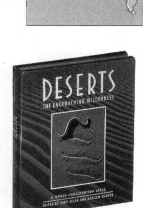

Deserts
(The Encroaching Wilderness)
Tony Allan & Andrew Warren, Editors.
1993; 176 pp. ISBN 0-19-520941-9
$35 ($37 postpaid) from
Oxford University Press/Order Dept.,
2001 Evans Road, Cary, NC 27513;
800/451-7556

Arid Lands
(Planet Earth Series)
Jake Page. 1984; 176 pp.
ISBN 0-8094-4512-3
$12.99 ($16.42 postpaid) from
Time-Life, Inc., 777 Duke Street,
Alexandria, VA 22314; 800/621-7026

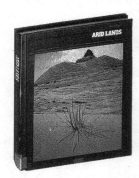

An Australian frog creates a moist world of its own for protection from the desert's aridity. The frog lies dormant in its burrow most of the year, sheathed in a layer of skin that retains body moisture, and reemerges only during infrequent rains. —*Arid Lands*

Guide to North American Deserts

"Motionless and silent, it evokes in us an elusive hint of something unknown, unknowable, about to be revealed." (Ed Abbey). Four deserts: Chihuahuan, Sonoran, Mojave, and Great Basin. The tortoise battles the cow and reintroduced pets. The cottonwood battles the tamarisk. First learn the desert's beauty, then coyote and scorpion tactics. —PW

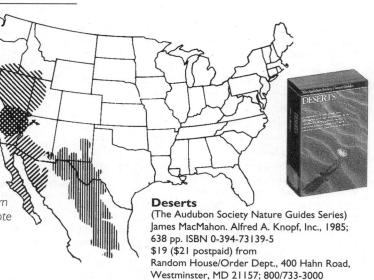

Deserts
(The Audubon Society Nature Guides Series)
James MacMahon. Alfred A. Knopf, Inc., 1985;
638 pp. ISBN 0-394-73139-5
$19 ($21 postpaid) from
Random House/Order Dept., 400 Hahn Road,
Westminster, MD 21157; 800/733-3000

OTHER GREAT ARID LAND RESOURCES

Gathering the Desert: Gary P. Nabhan. 1985; 209 pp. ISBN 0-8165-1014-8, $17.95 ($20.45 postpaid) from University of Arizona Press, 1230 N. Park Avenue #102, Tucson, AZ 85719; 602/621-1441.

Spreading Deserts: The Hand of Man: (Worldwatch Paper #13). Erik Eckholm and Lester R. Brown. 1977, Worldwatch Institute.

Center for the Study of Deserts and Oceans: PO Box 249, Lukeville, AZ 85341. Bilingual group protecting the Gulf of California and Sonoran Desert. Crucial borderlinks conservation effort.

Desert Protective Council: Membership $25/ year. PO Box 2312 Valley Center, CA 92082. Guardians of the Mojave, its culture and nature, Joshua trees, dry lakes, sand dunes, historic sites. A grand coalition.

Defenders of besieged desertlanders:

Horned Lizard Conservation Society: Membership $25/year. PO Box 122, Austin, TX 78767; 512/288-4802.

Desert Bighorn Council: PO Box 5431, Riverside, CA 92517.

Desert Tortoise Council: Membership $12/year. PO Box 1738, Palm Desert, CA 92261.

Desert Fishes Council: Membership $15/ year. PO Box 337, Bishop, CA 93515.

Food from Dryland Gardens

The Whole Earth encyclopedia on and for the millions of village and home gardeners in dry places. Puts the small acts of earth-turning into the global context of good food, high productivity, water-stingy irrigation, famine prevention. Saltburn to neem seed medicine, people-focused. UNICEF rightly sponsored this book, as nutrient for sustainable villages. —PW

Food from Dryland Gardens
(An Ecological, Nutritional, and Social Approach to Small-Scale Household Food Production)
David A. Cleveland & Daniela Soleri. 1991; 387 pp.
ISBN 0-9627997-0-X
$25 ($25 postpaid) from Center for People, Food and Environment, 344 S. Third Avenue, Tucson, AZ 85701

•

Safe Homemade Pesticides

NEEM SEED EXTRACT. Use: spray to repel insects or slow their feeding; kills pests when they eat it. Recipe: Seeds of fruits fallen from the tree are cleaned, dried, and stored in a dry, ventilated place. When needed, seed hulls are removed, and seeds are finely ground and hung in cloth sack in a container of water, using between 25-50 gm seed/liter of water (3-7 oz seed/gal of water). The ground seeds are soaked overnight in the water before using. This mixture should be made fresh for each use as it can lose its effectiveness over time and with exposure to sunlight.

Wetlands in Danger

Wetlands in Danger
(A World Conservation Atlas)
Patrick Dugan, Editor. 1993; 187 pp.
ISBN 0-19-520942-7
$35 ($37 postpaid) from Oxford University
Press/Order Dept., 2001 Evans Road,
Cary, NC 27513; 800/451-7556

*The finest world conservation atlas in
this catalog. Patrick Dugan has assembled the ecology and maps and
thoughtfulness in one place. A true
guide to planetary healing. The inner
delta of the Niger, the Banc d'Arguin
(the largest tidal flats on Earth), lakes
like Baikal and Tanganyika, marshes
like the Everglades, peatlands of the
north, swamp forests of the Amazon
and Indonesia all receive proper
concern. —Peter Warshall*

●

Since 1957, at least 100 hydroelectric dams,
including seven major dams, have been proposed for the Mekong and its tributaries. In
addition to generating electricity, the proposed dams would help to exploit the estimated 39,000 square kilometres (15,000
square miles) of potential agricultural land
in the delta by providing controlled irrigation water.

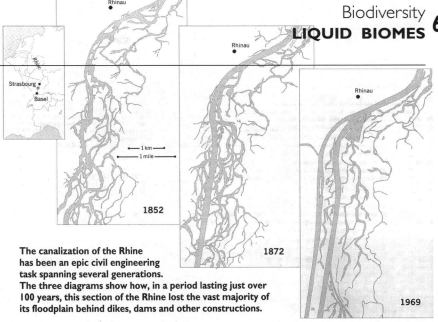

**The canalization of the Rhine
has been an epic civil engineering
task spanning several generations.
The three diagrams show how, in a period lasting just over
100 years, this section of the Rhine lost the vast majority of
its floodplain behind dikes, dams and other constructions.**

So far, just over a dozen dams have been
finished and several others are under construction. While these have helped increase
agricultural production, negative effects are
beginning to be felt. Beneficial flooding during the monsoon season has been reduced.
Freshwater inflow to the coastal ecosystems, including the mangrove forests, has
decreased, and salinity patterns and levels
have been altered.

World Rivers Review

*With clear-lake depth and tsunami
vigilance, the best global newsletter on
every aspect of water politics. News of
Narmada peasants in India practicing
nonviolent rebellion against a series of
dams, the Havasupai fight to prevent
uranium pollution of the Grand Canyon, the battle between Mexico and
the U.S. over borderline canal seepage
— news you don't find anywhere else.
As a waterflow lover, the International
Rivers Network is my favorite
organization. —PW*

●

In an effort to expand the protection a national park in Austria might offer, Friends
of the Earth International has joined with
Czech, Hungarian, and Austrian environmentalists calling for the designation of an
International Park along the Danube between Vienna, Austria, and Gyor, Hungary,
thus preventing the construction of dams
at Hainburg, Gabcikovo, and Nagymaros.
A resolution calling for the International
Park was delivered to the Hungarian Prime
Minister in September.

World Rivers Review
$35/year (4 issues). International Rivers
Network, 1847 Berkeley Way, Berkeley,
CA 94703; 510/848-1155

Wetlands

*According to Delaware Native Ameri-
cans, North America emerged from
the sea as a turtle's back. Down the
shell, in intricate designs, water flowed
toward the seas. Each immigrant to
Turtle Island found special words to fit
their regional wetland: cienaga, bog,
wallow, oxbow, run or kill.*

*This is the best of the Audubon guides
by one of America's best botanists and
ecologists. Immerse yourself in inland
water fun and compassion. —PW*

●

Wetlands evoke powerful emotions. To
some they are dark, mysterious, forbidding
places, to be avoided at all costs. . . . Perhaps one of the most memorable descriptions of a wetland occurs in Sir Arthur
Conan Doyle's "The Hound of the
Baskervilles," in which he describes the
Great Grimpen Mire, where the villain
meets his horrible fate:

Rank weeds and lush, slimy water plants
send an odour of decay and a heavy mias-
matic vapor into our faces, while a false
step plunged us more than once thigh-deep
into the dark, quivering mire, which shook
for yards in soft undulations around our
feet.

This is surely a masterful description of
a bog, one of North America's most fascinating wetlands.

Wetlands
(The Audubon Society Nature Guides Series)
William A. Niering. Alfred A. Knopf, Inc., 1985; 638 pp.
ISBN 0-394-73147-6
$19 ($21 postpaid) from Random House/Order Dept., 400
Hahn Road, Westminster, MD 21157; 800/733-3000

IUCN Wetlands Programme Newsletter

*Earth is a water planet; this is the
clarion call of wetland healers. Lots of
good news and some sad. Access to
international meetings, new books,
and projects by local communities
everywhere. —PW*

●

The Laguna de Terminos on Mexico's Caribbean coast covers approximately 1,800
km^2 of open water, and 2,500 km^2 of
swamps, marshes and small lagoons. There
are three dominant mangrove species and
the total mangrove coverage is 780 km^2.
The Laguna de Terminos and the associated
coastal waters of Campeche Sound, support 40% of Mexico's fisheries, with an estimated annual value of US$150 million.

**IUCN Wetlands
Programme Newsletter**
$20/year (2 issues). Rue Mauverney 28,
CH-1196 GLAND, Switzerland

●

The key steps which must be taken to save our peatlands of European Conservation importance are as follows:

A realistic Government budget of £850,000 needs to be assigned annually if Peatland Conservation targets are to be achieved.

A fen survey must be undertaken to assess the status of this habitat in Ireland, and to identify
fens of European Conservation Importance.

Overgrazing funded by the EC is a serious threat to the surviving blanket bogs such as
the Owenduff, Co. Mayo. Special provisions should be made to farmers so that a
reduction in livestock density on peatlands is not detrimental to their livelihood.

Field Surveys of all peatlands of
archaeological importance are
required urgently.

OTHER AQUATIC RESOURCES

Everglades, River of Grass: Marjory
Stoneham Douglas. The classic. See p. 85.

Wetlands: William J. Mitsch & James G.
Gosselink. 1993, Van Nostrand Reinhold. Best
technical intro.

Pond and Brook: Michael J. Caduto. 1985,
1990, University Press of New England.

Himalayan woman (in tree) lops off new growth for animal feed (near the ground the trees have already been picked clean). The practice is common throughout the region. Many trees die from continual lopping; erosion and environmental deterioration result.

MOUNTAINS, CANYONS, ISLANDS, CAVES — all great Earth media for creative innovation. Creatures become isolated and evolve in bohemian ways. Mountains surrounded by impassable "seas" of desert are called "sky islands" (e.g., Mt. Graham in Arizona). —Peter Warshall

Mountains and Man

The twenty-year-old classic on the billion-year-old ranges. Mythology, geology, land use. —PW

•
The Japanese view mountains as symbols of strength and of the eternal. The use of stones to represent mountains is an ancient art form practiced in both Chinese and Japanese gardens. The culmination of this is what the Japanese call *Ishiyama*: a natural stone about 15 cm (6 in.) high is placed vertically on a small base. This simple piece of nature sculpture, a mountain landscape in miniature, is kept inside the house on a shelf or table, and often has great value and meaning to its owner. Japan has several holy mountains, of which Fujiyama is by far the most famous; it is still climbed annually by thousands as a sacred pilgrimage (over 25,000 per day climb the mountain during the summer).

•
Some mountains are created by the extrusion of volcanic material; others result from the deformation of pre-existing rocks into folded or faulted structures. Mountainous relief can also be created by processes receiving their motive power from the sun and expressed through erosion, but this is generally a secondary process: mountains are fundamentally features of construction produced by energies originating inside the earth. The major mountain types, classified according to mode of origin, are volcanic; faulted; folded; and combinations of these.

Mountains and Man
Larry W. Price. University of California Press, 1981; 496 pp. ISBN 0-520-05886-0 $20 ($23 postpaid) from California/ Princeton Fulfillment Services, 1445 Lower Ferry Road, Ewing, NJ 08618; 800/777-4726

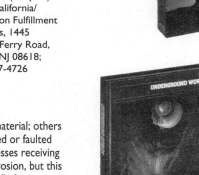

OTHER MOUNTAINOUS RESOURCES

Sky Island Alliance: 1639 E. First, Tucson, AZ 85719. The only group trying to preserve one of the planet's unique mountain-island archipelagos—the sky islands from the Colorado Plateau to the Sierra Madre.

Utah Wilderness Coalition: PO Box 11446, Salt Lake City, UT 84147. Forty-two constituent groups dream up totally reasonable citizens' proposals to save the desert wilds, issue a solid newsletter (*Giving Land a Voice*), and will lobby and educate the BLM until the dams preventing canyonland love finally burst.

Oceanic Islands

Japan, Philippines, New Guinea, the Caribbean, Madagascar, New Zealand, Galapagos, Hawaii, a dozen great archipelagos are the planet's oceanic jewels. Hawaii: The Islands of Life tells the story of one archipelago. Luscious photos with a delightful text on the environmental history of the Hawaiian chain. Behind mass tourism, the lava flow of mass extinction. But still: the beauty, the beauty. Islands (H. W. Menard. 1986; Scientific American Library, W.H. Freeman and Co.) explains how islands originate (plate tectonics and coral). See also Madagascar (Alison Jolly, et al. 1984; Pergamon Press). —PW

•
Most recently emerged of the main islands is Hawai'i, often called the Big Island. Shaped by five volcanoes, it shows the huge creative force of volcanism. Mauna Loa, still active, rises more than twenty-nine thousand feet from the ocean floor, thirteen thousand, six hundred seventy-seven feet from sea level to summit. It is ten thousand cubic miles in bulk, meaning it is the biggest single volcanic structure on earth — a hundred times bigger than Shasta or Fujiyama, indeed the biggest such feature in the solar system anywhere between the sun and the planet Mars.

The Hawaiian chain exists in the most profound oceanic isolation on the face of the globe, more than two thousand miles from the closest continental land mass.

Hawaii: The Islands of Life
Gavan Daws. 1988; 156 pp. ISBN 0-943823-01-3 $24.95 ($27.95 postpaid). Book Lines Hawaii, PO Box 2170, Pearl City, HI 96782-9170; 808/676-0116

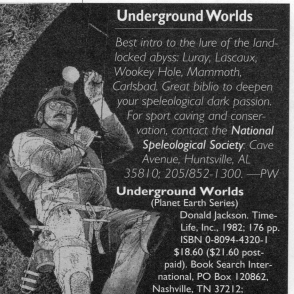

Underground Worlds

*Best intro to the lure of the landlocked abyss: Luray, Lascaux, Wookey Hole, Mammoth, Carlsbad. Great biblio to deepen your speleological dark passion. For sport caving and conservation, contact the **National Speleological Society**: Cave Avenue, Huntsville, AL 35810; 205/852-1300. —PW*

Underground Worlds
(Planet Earth Series) Donald Jackson. Time-Life, Inc., 1982; 176 pp. ISBN 0-8094-4320-1 $18.60 ($21.60 postpaid). Book Search International, PO Box 120862, Nashville, TN 37212; 615/298-3804

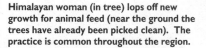

The sun rises over Molokai, unveiling Hawaii's islands of life.

Wilderness at the Edge

*While many mountains of the world have bards, canyon-writers specialize in the Grand. No argument, but the lesser wonders need a voice. There is no good book on the Cañon de Cobre (Mexico), whose volume of empty space surpasses the Grand's. **Wilderness at the Edge** understands canyons and plateaus, desert rivers and world-class landscapes better than any*

BIOME-SAVING ORGANIZATIONS

IUCN
(The World Conservation Union)

IUCN

This organization is the global shadow government for biodiversity and natural national heritage. IUCN has added to its goals the appropriate and equitable human use of natural resources. Membership includes 62 nations, 95 government agencies, about 500 national non-governmental organizations (NGOs), 47 international NGOs, and 34 non-voting affiliates; IUCN represents more than 115 countries.

IUCN's Species Survival Commission and "specialist groups" are almost a United Nations of Flora and Fauna Solidarity. Their regional offices attempt to bring village life together with conservation priorities and respect from regional and national governments. Their educational materials have already begun to alter the shape of national politics in dozens of countries.

They work on two levels: highly general "save the earth" policy wonking and very specific projects (local educational pamphlets, manuals of planetary survival such as the Red Data Books, and a host of great reports). Like all NGOs, IUCN treads the line between pleasing power (so you can do any work at all) and changing it. My favorites include booklets on economics and biodiversity, and illegal trafficking. The IUCN Bulletin is always thoughtful. —Peter Warshall

International Union for the Conservation of Nature: Membership $48/year from IUCN, World Headquarters: Rue Mauverney 28, CH-1196 Gland, Switzerland; North American Headquarters: 1400 16th Street NW, Washington, DC 20036; 202/797-5454.

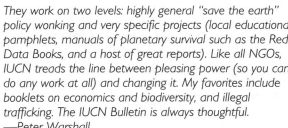

LightHawk

Wanted: Certified pilots in love with the Earth. My favorite group working in the United States, Mexico and Central America. Volunteer pilots who, for the price of the gasoline, will survey the extent of clearcutting in Oregon or Chihuahua, or the condition of mangrove swamps, and map out remaining islands of native forest. The hawk's-eye view has completely turned around officials who cannot see the forests (or lack of them) from the trees. Any flight required by serious environmental groups is their expertise. One of the best returns on your green investment.

LightHawk: Membership $35/year. PO Box 8163, Santa Fe, NM 87504; 505/982-9656.

World Wildlife Fund

WWF

*With over a million members, WWF are top international brass that work in boardrooms as surely as in tropical beef and banana belts. They are strong on debt-for-nature swaps (Madagascar, Mexico) and a bit weak on follow-through (e.g., the national parks of Senegal). They sell stuffed pandas and save biomes; float slick brochures on virgin paper and rescue endangered species; have wonderfully pompous ceremonies and curb illegal trade in rare species and train anti-poaching teams. In the balance, there's a lot more good intentions and activism than hype. Compassion diplomatically moves planetary destroyers to be a bit greener and, when effective, their moves make big waves. WWF underwrites **Traffic**.* —PW

World Wildlife Fund: Membership $15/year. PO Box 4866, Hampden Station, Baltimore, MD 21211; 410/516-6951.

Wildlife Conservation International

Working on the Tibetan plateau, with elephants and rhinos, and, of course, in tropical rainforests, WCI's scientific skills are the best. They are subtle and smart with few illusions. Graduate students and professionals cannot find better jobs. Dr. David Western, in Kenya, is typical: balancing rhinos, Masai cattle-watering holes, targeted aid, eco-tourism, and the conservation of Amboseli Park. WCI is administered by the Bronx Zoo (a.k.a. New York Zoological Society). —PW

Wildlife Conservation International: Membership $25/year. New York Zoological Society, 185th Street & South Boulevard, Bldg. A, New York, NY 10460; 212/220-5155.

Conservation International

*The beauty of CI is its joint projects between local people and partner organizations in the North. Working in twenty-one nations, mostly the megadiversity hot-spots, they forge new ideas and strategies every week. CI initiated many of the debt-for-nature swaps; see their pamphlet, **The Debt-for-Nature Exchange: A Tool for International Conservation**. They are also now working to help nations get patents or at least royalties on potential medicinal uses of native plants; see The Shaman's Apprentice Program (p. 104).* —PW

Conservation International: Membership $35/year. 1015 18th Street NW #1000, Washington, DC 20036; 202/429-5660.

For a good time, see also:
Endangered Plants (p. 45),
Endangered Animals (p. 52),
Nature Conservancy (p. 77),
and EcoActivism (p. 109).

Sky island — a mountain surrounded by a sea of desert. —*The Sagebrush Ocean*

Sky Islands

*The archipelagos of sky islands have yet to receive their due. Africa has a few that are beautifully illustrated and described in **Island Africa** (Jonathan Kingdon. Princeton Univ. Press, 1990). Steve Trimble's **The Sagebrush Ocean** is the best natural history of the Great Basin sky island complex. The southwest Madrean and the Venezuelan archipelagos await their human translators.* —PW

The Sagebrush Ocean
(A Natural History of the Great Basin)
Stephen Trimble. 1989; 248 pp.
ISBN 0-87417-222-5
$21.95 ($24.45 postpaid) from University of Nevada Press, Mail Stop 166, Reno, NV 89557; 702/784-6573

Peekaboo Canyon is part of the thousand-mile-long labyrinth of canyons cut into the stone floor of the Escalante River basin. This haunting slot canyon was left out of the BLM's 1986 draft wilderness recommendation for the Scorpion unit, but public concern may have persuaded the agency to relent.

other intro. Focused on the "Grand Staircase," from the Grand Canyon's bottom to the 7,000-foot staircase of plateaus that ascend to the top of Bryce, this is the blazing dream of hikers and desert lovers. —PW

Wilderness at the Edge
Utah Wilderness Coalition. 1993; 400 pp. ISBN 0-87905-367-4
$23 postpaid. PO Box 11446, Salt Lake City, UT 84147

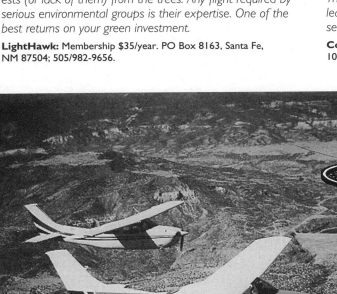

LightHawk volunteers over clearcuts.

Blind salamander. —*Wilderness at the Edge*

Flood basin of the Souf Oasis in Algeria. The palm trees are planted on the bottom of a flood basin so their roots can reach the underground water beneath the dunes. Fences of palm fronds protect the craters from the sandy wind. The palm tree farmer often lives within the crater. Beneath the sand one can find not only water, but also a layer of gypsum that can be used as building material.

—The World From Above

Doctor Sustainability

Sustainability is a word like *democracy, freedom,* or *equality* — a frame for hope, a little preacher sitting on your shoulder or, under attack, a rallying cry for rebellion. Paul Hawken uses "restorative economy" — a better directional signal, but it's two words.

Sustainability is an embryo, slowly developing toward a desired way of living. Its soft bones need robust ideals, humane models, libertarian ideologies, and skillful means to knit the body planetic. Sustainability umbrellas actions that:

• are environmentally friendly;

• provide an equitable return for goods and services;

• direct national budgets and corporate capital to promote environmentally friendly, equitable production;

• educate and cajole politicians and civilians, labor and management toward long-term thinking.

The compass of sustainable practices points to:

• *Waste not, want not.* Use less of the Earth's materials; re-use them again and again. Find a productive use for everything in the landfill, for all chemicals in all excretions, for all acid-dusts in all smokes, and for all lumber from all demolished homes. Dr. Sustainability prescribes the consumption of less, the abolishment of built-in obsolescence, and drastically reduced packaging. All prescriptions celebrate high efficiency, product longevity, and improved environmental quality ("cradle to cradle"). Amory Lovins is the hero, his light show illuminating how "negawatts," not megawatts, are the path to de-consumption in a comfortable future.

• *Respect the sun.* "Production" recently meant output per hours of labor. Now, it's a focus on glorious photosynthesis, the green machine that captures the solar photon flux and converts it into sugars and proteins, our sustenance. Humans hoard 40 percent of the sun's energy. We alter the solar filters of the biosphere as if the sunstream will never rebel and the green machine can never go bust. We mine the earth for sun-substitutes as if there is no end. The Reverend Sustainability preaches that the "primary production" of green plants comes first. It has a higher value than either industrial production or human re-production: food.

See also Walden (p. 109) and The Practice of the Wild (p. 124).

• *Respect unconditionally the network of living creatures of which we are a part.* This is real difficult. In a basically urban world, the earth is buried under asphalt, money dictates behavior, and giant pandas are exotic TV superstars. Hard to make Nature's web a simple part of our living. The truly exceptional, like Lynn Margulis, have tried to widen the boundaries of self. We are not "one self," but colonies of cells living in what we arbitrarily delineate as "our body." We are all fragile cell conglomerates, subject to hostile viral and toxic takeovers as well as to love. To be sustainable, every action must compassionately consider the "existence" value or worth of places and pieces of life with sublime value but no assignable price.

Now add the hopes of modern history. America continues the dreams of the French Revolution: *Equality, Liberty, Solidarity.* We have witnessed huge mistakes. Liberty, in isolation, fostered earth-killing exploitation. Equality, in isolation, became the ideology of the Soviet bloc — with drastic reductions in liberty. Solidarity, in isolation, was totally abused by the Nazis. Despite these holocaustic lessons, a global civilian solidarity remains the glue of hope. A sustainable planet calls for a tightly networked citizenry to challenge the despoilers, ethnic cleansing in all its forms, and short-term greed that cheats the majority out of their future.

The Millennium Whole Earth Catalog inaugurates "sustainability" as a domain because the market economy has worked for only a fraction of humankind, and for only small pieces of the planet. If market economies fail to incorporate the impoverished and the planet's flora and fauna, they can collapse like any other dysfunctional human institution. With market collapse, our fragile democratic institutions can equally bite the dust.

Sustainability is a kind of dough. The market economy is a directed set of hands. As you make your bread, so you eat. —Peter Warshall

---

If the World Were a Village
BY DONELLA H. MEADOWS

If the world were a village of 1,000 people, it would include:

584 Asians
124 Africans
95 East and West Europeans
84 Latin Americans
55 Soviets (including for the moment Lithuanians, Latvians, Estonians, and other national groups)
52 North Americans
6 Australians and New Zealanders

The people of the village have considerable difficulty in communicating:
165 people speak Mandarin
86 English
83 Hindu/Urdu
64 Spanish
58 Russian
37 Arabic

That list accounts for the mother tongues of only half the villagers. The other half speak (in descending order of frequency) Bengali, Portuguese, Indonesian, Japanese, German, French, and 200 other languages.

In this village of 1,000 there are:
329 Christians (among them 187 Catholics, 84 Protestants, 31 Orthodox)
178 Moslems

167 "non-religious"
132 Hindus
60 Buddhists
45 atheists
3 Jews
86 all other religions

One-third (330) of the 1,000 people in the world village are children and only 60 are over the age of 65. Half the children are immunized against preventable infectious diseases such as measles and polio.

Just under half of the married women in the village have access to and use modern contraceptives.

The first year 28 babies are born. That year 10 people die, 3 of them for lack of food, 1 from cancer, 2 of the deaths are of babies born within the year. One person of the 1,000 is infected with the HIV virus; that person most likely has not yet developed a full-blown case of AIDS.

With the 28 births and 10 deaths, the population of the village in the second year is 1,018.

In this 1,000-person community, 200 people receive 75 percent of the income; another 200 receive only 2 percent of the income.

Only 70 people of the 1,000 own an automobile (although some of the 70 own more than one automobile).

About one-third have access to clean, safe drinking water.

Of the 670 adults in the village, half are illiterate.

The village has six acres of land per person, 6,000 acres in all, of which
700 acres are cropland
1,400 acres pasture
1,900 acres woodland
2,000 acres desert, tundra, pavement and other wasteland

The woodland is declining rapidly; the wasteland is increasing. The other land categories are roughly stable.

The village allocates 83 percent of its fertilizer to 40 percent of its cropland — that owned by the richest and best-fed 270 people. Excess fertilizer running off this land causes pollution in lakes and wells. The remaining 60 percent of the land, with its 17 percent of the fertilizer, produces 28 percent of the food grains and feeds for 73 percent of the people. The average grain yield on that land is one-third the harvest achieved by the richer villagers.

In the village of 1,000 people, there are:
5 soldiers
7 teachers
1 doctor
3 refugees driven from home by war or drought

The village has a total budget each year, public and private, of over $3 million — $3,000 per person if it is distributed evenly (which, we have already seen, it isn't).

Of the total $3 million:
$181,000 goes to weapons and warfare
$159,000 for education
$132,000 for health care

The village has buried beneath it enough explosive power in nuclear weapons to blow itself to smithereens many times over. These weapons are under the control of just 100 of the people. The other 900 people are watching them with deep anxiety, wondering whether they can learn to get along together; and if they do, whether they might set off the weapons anyway through inattention or technical bungling; and, if they ever decide to dismantle the weapons, where in the world village they would dispose of the radioactive materials of which the weapons are made.

Value Earth Poster: $7 postpaid from Value Earth c/o David Copeland, 707 White Horse Pike, C-2, Absecon, NJ 08201; 609/641-2400 (fax 609/272-1571)

OTHER GREAT RESOURCES

The Arrogance of Humanism: David Ehrenfeld. 1975, Oxford University Press. A biologist dissects "humanism" and its arrogant insistence that we can reduce the human condition to problems and solutions.

Ecology, Community and Lifestyle (Outline of an Ecosophy): Arne Naess. 1990, Cambridge University Press. "Deep ecology" — meaning: Taking it to heart and changing how we live.

The World From Above: Hanns Reich. 1966, Hill and Wang. Out of Print; check your library. Exquisite bird's-perspective photographs compel fresh visions of the planet, and of humans' place on it.

A Sand County Almanac

*The most important book on ethics ever written on American soil — honest, clear, graceful, superbly crafted. It begins: "There are some who can live without wild things, and some who cannot. These essays are the delights and dilemmas of one who cannot." For Leopold, like Thoreau, human nature and nature's nature are inseparable natures and anything worth saying must be born from both. So the **Almanac** exposes, reflects on, and strays into "values" that humans might cherish; but it never strays too far from wildness, that teacher of many minds. In short, this is the bible of "oikos-logos" — the governing principle of our communal home — "ecology."*
—Peter Warshall

•

A deep chesty bawl echoes from rimrock to rimrock, rolls down the mountain, and fades into the far blackness of the night. It is an outburst of wild defiant sorrow, and of contempt for all the adversities of the world.

Every living thing (and perhaps many a dead one as well) pays heed to that call. To the deer it is a reminder of the way of all flesh, to the pine a forecast of midnight scuffles and of blood upon the snow, to the coyote a promise of gleanings to come, to the cowman a threat of red ink at the bank, to the hunter a challenge of fang against bullet. Yet behind these obvious and immediate hopes and fears there lies a deeper meaning, known only to the mountain itself. Only the mountain has lived long enough to listen objectively to the howl of a wolf. . .

We all strive for safety, prosperity, comfort, long life, and dullness. The deer strives with his supple legs, the cowman with trap and poison, the statesman with pen, the most of us with machines, votes, and dol-

lars, but it all comes to the same thing: peace in our time. A measure of success in this is all well enough, and perhaps is a requisite to objective thinking, but too much safety seems to yield only danger in the long run. Perhaps this is behind Thoreau's dictum: In wildness is the salvation of the world. Perhaps this is the hidden meaning in the howl of the wolf, long known among mountains, but seldom perceived among men.

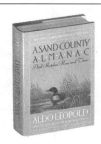

A Sand County Almanac
(And Sketches Here and There)
Aldo Leopold. 1989; 256 pp.
ISBN 0-19-505928-X
$8.95 ($10.95 postpaid) from Oxford University Press/Order Dept., 2001 Evans Road, Cary, NC 27513; 800/451-7556

The Sacred

This book was prepared for use by young Native Americans, and largely put together by Native Americans. It's a spiritual field guide for North America. —SB

It's the durable, robust bridge between modern Euro-American citizenry and the strength, beauty, wisdom, and vitality of North America's long-term residents. Here are the teachings of Turtle Island, teachings aimed at bringing our world back into balance, if (oh if) we would quietly pay attention.
—PW

•

To us a clown is somebody sacred, funny, powerful, ridiculous, holy, shameful, visionary. He is all this and then some more. Fooling around, a clown is really performing a spiritual ceremony. He has a power. It comes from the thunderbeings, not the animals or the earth. In our Indian belief, a clown has more power than the

The beggar dance of the Seneca, Cattaraugus Reservation, New York

atom bomb. This power could blow off the dome of the Capital. I have told you that once I worked as a rodeo clown. This was almost like doing spiritual work. Being a clown, for me, came close to being a medicine man. It was in the same nature.
—Lame Deer

•

Most Native Americans share the following six concepts:

1. A belief in or knowledge of unseen powers, or what some people call The Great Mystery.

2. Knowledge that all things in the universe are dependent on each other.

3. Personal worship reinforces the bond between the individual, the community, and the great powers. Worship is a personal commitment to the sources of life.

4. Sacred traditions and persons knowledgeable in sacred traditions are responsible for teaching *morals* and *ethics*.

5. Most communities and tribes have trained practitioners

The Sacred
(Ways of Knowledge, Sources of Life)
Peggy V. Beck, Anna Lee Walters & Nia Francisco. 1992; 368 pp.
ISBN 0-912586-24-9
$19.95 ($23.70 postpaid) from Navajo Community College Press, Tsaile, AZ 96556; 602/724-3311

who have been given names such as medicine men, priests, shamans, caciques, and other names. These individuals also have titles given them by *The People* which differ from tribe to tribe. These individuals are responsible for specialized, perhaps secret knowledge. They help pass knowledge and sacred practices from generation to generation, storing what they know in their memories.

6. A belief that humor is a necessary part of the sacred. And a belief that human beings are often weak — we are not gods — and our weakness leads us to do foolish things; therefore clowns and similar figures are needed to show us how we act and why.

Ishmael

My working hypothesis is that this book is actually a theological work, possibly a new book of the Bible. (A third testament is about due now anyway.) For some reason it has been superficially structured as a novel. It is a comprehensive and devastating analysis of "civilized" man framed as a Socratic dialog between a man and a gorilla.

*After humans go extinct, civilizations that follow us will (I hope) have books with chapters about us. I have the eerie feeling that **Ishmael** might be an excerpt from a book like that.*
—Jim Britell

•

"The law you're looking for has been obeyed invariably in the living community for three billion years." He nodded to the world outside. "And this is *how things came to be this way*. If this law had not been obeyed from the beginning and in each generation thereafter, the seas would be lifeless deserts and the land would still be dust blowing in the wind. All the countless forms of life that you see here came into being following this law, and following this law, man too came into being. And only once in all the history of this planet has any

Ishmael
Daniel Quinn. Bantam Books, 1992; 262 pp.
ISBN 0-553-56166-9
$5.99 ($8.49 postpaid) from Bantam, Doubleday, Dell/Fulfillment Dept., 2451 S. Wolf Road, Des Plaines, IL 60018; 800/223-6834

species tried to live in defiance of this law — and it wasn't an entire species, it was only one people, those I've named Takers. Ten thousand years ago, this one people said, 'No more. Man was not meant to be bound by this law,' and they began to live in a way that flouts the law at every point. Every single thing that is prohibited under the law they incorporated into their civilization as a *fundamental policy*. And now, after five hundred generations, they are about to pay the penalty that any other species would pay for living contrary to this law."

Ishmael turned over a hand. "That should be guide enough for you."

The Universe Is a Green Dragon

The most hypnotic translation of the cosmic creation story; advocacy of "cosmic allurement" as the basis of love. Science, poetics, and ethics stirred up in a delectable singular soup.
—PW

•

Thomas: I call the universe a green dragon to remind us that we will never be able to capture the universe with language.

Youth: How can you be certain of that?

Thomas: Because the universe is a singularity! To speak, you need to compare things. Thus we say that the house is white, not brown. Or that the man is hostile, not kind. Or that it happened in the nineteenth century, not before. But there is only one universe. We cannot compare the universe with anything. We cannot say the universe.

•

Thomas: The great mystery is that we are interested in anything whatsoever. Think of your friends, how you first met them, how interesting they appeared to you. Why should anyone in the whole world interest us at all? Why don't we experience everyone as utter, unendurable bores? Why isn't the cosmos made that way? Why don't we suffer intolerable boredom with every person, forest, symphony, and seashore in existence? The great surprise is the discovery

The Universe is a Green Dragon
(A Cosmic Creation Story)
Brian Swimme. 1984; 173 pp.
ISBN 0-939680-14-9
$9.95 ($13.45 postpaid) from Bear & Co./Mail Order, PO Box 2860, Santa Fe, NM 87504; 800/932-3277

that something or someone *is* interesting. Love begins there. Love begins when we discover interest. To be interested is to fall in love. To become fascinated is to step into a wild love affair on any level of life.

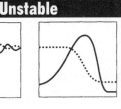
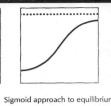

Stable		Unstable	
carrying capacity / population & physical economy / time			
Continuous growth	Sigmoid approach to equilibrium	Overshoot and oscillation	Overshoot and collapse

The central question is: Which of these behavior modes is likely to be the result as the human population and economy approach their carrying capacity? —*Beyond the Limits*

Beyond the Limits • The Global Citizen

Here are two of the many sides of an American rarity. **Beyond the Limits** *is the most direct approach to an understanding of how systems modeling yields both optimistic and pessimistic scenarios of the world's future.* **Global Citizen** *is a collection of Donella Meadows' bright, clear, spade-into-the-spring-earth essays.*

Meadows is an exquisite number-cruncher. Never will an exponential curve seem so natural. Our conclusions are a stark but never impossible set of choices. —PW

•

I was flattered to be asked in 1985 to prepare a paper for the Interaction Council about the state of the world's resources and environment. There was just one problem. "Be sure not to go over two pages," I was told. "They never read anything over two pages."

Two pages on the state of the planet? Well, I did the best I could. Here's what I came up with — the world's shortest report on the state of resources and the environment (the numbers have been updated to 1990).

Every day on this planet 35,000 people die of starvation, 26,000 of them children. This human toll is the equivalent to 100 fully loaded 747-jets crashing every day. It is the same number of deaths every three days as were caused by the Hiroshima atomic bomb explosion. And each day, because of population growth, there are 220,000 more mouths to feed.

Yet enough food is *already* raised each year to feed not only the current human population of 5.2 billion, but also the population of 6.1 billion expected by the year 2000. . . .

For the first time in history over 50 percent of the human race is literate. Seven full-time television channels and 31,000 simultaneous telephone circuits now link 109 nations through 14 satellites in earth-synchronous orbit. —*The Global Citizen*

•

Sustainable limits to throughput:

• For a *renewable resource* — soil, water, forest, fish — the sustainable rate of use can be no greater than the rate of regeneration. (Thus, for example, fish are harvested sustainably when they are caught at a rate that can be replaced by the remaining fish population.)

• For a *nonrenewable resource* — fossil fuel, high-grade mineral ore, fossil ground-water — the sustainable rate of use can be no greater than the rate at which a renew-able resource, used sustainably, can be substituted for it. (For example, an oil deposit would be used sustainably if part of the profits from it were systematically invested in solar collectors or in tree planting, so that when the oil is gone, an equivalent stream of renewable energy is still available.

• For a *pollutant* the sustainable rate of emission can be no greater than the rate at which that pollutant can be recycled, absorbed, or rendered harmless by the environment. (For example, sewage can be put into a stream or lake sustainably at the rate at which the natural ecosystem in the water can absorb its nutrients.)
—*Beyond the Limits*

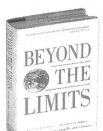

Beyond the Limits
Donella H. Meadows, Dennis L. Meadows & Jorgen Randers. 1992; 300 pp. l SBN 0-930031-55-5 $19.95 ($22.95 postpaid) from Chelsea Green Publishing Co., 52 N. Labombard Road, Lebanon, NH 03766; 800/639-4099

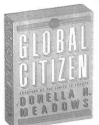

The Global Citizen
(Working Toward A Sustainable World)
Donella H. Meadows. 1991; 300 pp. ISBN 1-55963-058-2 $14.95 ($18.70 postpaid). Island Press, Box 7, Covelo, CA 95428; 800/828-1302

Ecological Imperialism

History has been restructured once again, this time by ecology and biology. Crosby is the rooster at dawn. He argues that European weeds, diseases, domestic animals, and the winds allowed "Neo-Europes" to replace indigenous human ecology. North America fell to the invasive flora as surely as to cannons and muskets. —PW

•

There is an old American folksong of the frontier in which a certain Sweet Betsy from Pike County, Missouri, crosses the mountains, presumably the Rockies or Sierras, "with her lover, Ike, with two yoke of oxen, a large yellow dog, a tall shanghai rooster, and one spotted hog." Betsy was heir to a very old tradition of mixed farming, and whereas it must be pointed out that her oxen were castrated and the other animals without mates, Betsy's party was not the only one to cross the mountains; wagon trains had bulls and cows, plus hens and dogs and pigs of genders opposite to those of her animals. (Betsy herself had the foresight to bring Ike.) Rapid propagation of the colonizing species would be the rule on the far side of the mountains. Betsy came not as an individual immigrant but as part of a grunting, lowing, neighing, crowing, chirping, snarling, buzzing, self-replicating and world-altering avalanche.

Keeping Track of the Vital Signs

Well, here's the best of the global statistics. I skim the new editions each year: **Vital Signs** *from Worldwatch,* **World Development Report** *from the World Bank, and* **World Resources** *by the World Resources Institute and the United Nations.*

The meaning of it all? When the World Bank explores Third World GDP, it never includes the "informal" economy. For instance, the unreported economics of the Muslim Brotherhoods of the Sahel probably did more to alleviate famine than USAID. Ever wonder why non-Muslims die first? No one includes American, Mexican, Colombian or Thai farmer income from marijuana, poppies, or coca. Yet the difference may mark the threshold between hunger and a healthy family.

The ever-optimistic World Resources Institute carefully catalogs planetary "protected areas" or "national parks." But most parks are "paper parks." Half the protected areas I've surveyed in West Africa are filled with woodcutters, hunters, farmers, and villages. One UN "Biosphere Reserve" in Mali is so battered that it would take millions to move villages, replenish now extinct species, and protect it from the guns of the army and from rich cityfolk.

Anyway, **WR** *(the most enviro),* **WDR** *(the most complex and financial), and* **Vital Signs** *(the easiest to read) are more useful for the thoughts they provoke than for their coffee-house arguments or General Assembly policy-wonking.* —PW

•

In poor countries:

• Diarrheal diseases that result from contaminated water kill about 2 million children and cause about 900 million episodes of illness each year.

• Indoor air pollution from burning wood, charcoal, and dung endangers the health of 400 million to 700 million people.

• Dust and soot in city air cause between 300,000 and 700,000 premature deaths a year.

• Soil erosion can cause annual economic losses ranging from 0.5 to 1.5 percent of GNP.

• A quarter of all irrigated land suffers from salinization.

• Tropical forests—the primary source of livelihood for about 140 million people — are being lost at a rate of 0.9 percent annually. —*World Development Report*

Vital Signs 1993 (The Trends That Are Shaping Our Future): Lester R. Brown, Hal Kane, & Ed Ayres. 1993; 150 pp. ISBN 0-393-31024-8. $10.95 postpaid. W.W. Norton & Co./Order Dept., 800 Keystone Industrial Park, Scranton, PA 18512; 800/233-4830.

World Development Report: World Bank Staff. 1992; 304 pp. ISBN 0-19-520876-5. $19.95 ($21.95 postpaid). Oxford University Press/Order Dept., 2001 Evans Road, Cary, NC 27513; 800/451-7556.

World Resources '92-'93: World Resources Institute Staff. 1992; 385 pp. ISBN 0-19-506231-0. $19.95 ($21.95 postpaid). Oxford University Press/ Order Dept., 2001 Evans Road, Cary, NC 27513; 800/451-7556.

The Global Ecology Handbook

Come and get it! Environmental awareness — the all-cotton bedspread, the Robert Redford video, the most-important-oil-slick-photo coffee table book special, the all-Green toothbrush.

Had enuff enviro hype? The **Handbook** *is the only field guide to saving the planet that the Whole Earth staff uses continually (or even tolerates). Great chapters on human foresight and abilities, population, food, agriculture, biodiversity, tropical forests, oceans, coasts, fresh water, energy, nonfuel minerals, atmosphere, toxics, solid waste, global security, and citizen actions. Best biblio, videos, movies, organizations, and teaching aids.* —PW

The Global Ecology Handbook
(What You Can Do About the Environmental Crisis) 1990; 500 pp. ISBN 0-8070-8501-4 $18 ($21.75 postpaid) from Beacon Press, 25 Beacon Street, Boston, MA 02108; 617/742-2110

Ecological Imperialism
Alfred W. Crosby. 1986; 368 pp. ISBN 0-521-45690-8 $11.95 ($13.95 postpaid). Cambridge University Press, 110 Midland Avenue, Port Chester, NY 10573; 800/872-7423 (outside NY) 800/227-0247 (NY only)

Population Management Needs the Most Human Touch

While reviewing an overpopulated box of human population growth books, I found it easiest to scan the index. Only books that indexed "religion," "culture," "Catholic," "abortion," "contraceptive," "family," "household," "the demographic transition," or "medical missionaries" survived my reject box. Here are some field notes:

• No book will dare discuss how irresponsible modern medicine has been — sentimentally saving all kids under five and then abandoning them to fend for themselves. These medical missionaries are, in part, responsible for soil depletion and adult hunger (too many kids subdividing the farm), urban blight (no room on the farm), and the romantic rise of revolving-door revolutions (nothing else looks so good as an AK-47). No book deals with the astronomical rise in "global teenagers" nor the provincial ethics of doctors who separate out prenatal and natal care from the total life of a human being.

• Only *The Population Explosion* clearly argues against the cornucopians, who claim that only when women get rich will they stop having babies. The Ehrlichs show that access to contraceptives is as important as income.

• No book addresses "family" or "household" in any reasonable manner. Yet it is within the family, even a single mom with one kid, that most reproductive decisions are made. (Many groups listed on this page issue good technical booklets.)

• No book tackles the religious dilemma: When does an embryo, an infant, or even a child have a soul? This moment dictates the form of family management: abstinence, contraception, abortion, infanticide, delayed marriage, adoption, sterilization, or sending pre-reproductive sons to war.

Where is the compassionate, well-written, solid history book — written in Sangerese? —Peter Warshall

GAPED CONDOM

To check on the State of the World, see Worldwatch Institute (p. 304)

Planned Parenthood

The valorous legacy of Margaret Sanger. **Planned Parenthood** *is the umbilical heart of family planning, networking from the neighborhood to the whole Earth. Their clinics make them front-line. When states or the Feds abandon poor women,* **Planned Parenthood** *tries their best to fill in for wimpy and inadequate public care. Their nonprofit affiliate is the Alan Guttmacher Institute. Their mission is to protect the reproductive rights of individuals and families, everywhere, especially the young and poor. Great info on unintended pregnancies, freedom to terminate unwanted pregnancies, and the preservation of mom's and baby's health. The first-stop in passionate and compassionate population management.* —PW

Alan Guttmacher Institute: 111 5th Avenue, New York, NY 10003; 212/254-5656.

Planned Parenthood: 810 7th Avenue, New York, NY 10019; 212/541-7800.

OTHER GREAT RESOURCES

Woman of Valor (Margaret Sanger and the Birth Control Movement): Ellen Chesler. Simon and Schuster, 1992.

The Contraceptive Handbook (A Guide To Safe and Effective Choices): Winikoff, et al. 1992, Consumer Reports Books.

A History of Contraception (From Antiquity to the Present Day): Angus McLaren. 1992, Blackwell Publishers.

Population Politics: V. D. Abernathy. 1993, Plenum Publishing Corp. The most scholarly dissection of immigration, foreign aid, causes of fertility and poverty. Sincere academic writing.

Living Within Limits: Garrett Hardin. 1993, Oxford University Press. The no-nonsense generalist fights the Cornucopian School on the white horse of logic.

The Population Institute: 107 2nd Street NE, Washington, DC 20002; 202/544-3300.

Getting Involved

Zero Population Growth. *1400 16th Street NW, Suite 320, Washington, DC 20036; 202/332-2200. Grassroots volunteer programs and great educational materials, including family planning, local-growth issues, enviro impacts, and in-school population study. About 40,000 members. Fact sheets and the ZPG Reporter.*

Sierra Club International Population Program. *202/675-6692. 408 C Street, Washington, DC 20002; Grassroots local committees, heavy legislative lobbying; pushing for 100 percent global access to birth control, influencing doctors to consider family planning.*

Childless By Choice. *PO Box 695, Leavenworth, WA 98826; 509/763-2112. Practical and humorous tips for the childless lifestyle.*

Catholics for a Free Choice. *1436 U Street NW, Suite 301, Washington, DC 20009; 202/986-6093.*

Voters for Choice. *604 Connecticut Avenue NW, 2nd Floor, Washington, DC 20008; 202/588-5200.*

Population Action International. *1120 19th Street NW, Suite 550, Washington DC 20036; 202/659-1833. The biggest budget population group advocating universal access to family planning services, including contraceptive availability.*

The best pop policy wonks on the global scale.

National Abortion Rights Action League. *1101 14th Street NW, 5th floor, Washington, DC 20005; 202/408-4600.*

Population Reference Bureau. *1875 Connecticut Avenue NW, Suite 520, Washington, DC 20009-5728; 800/877-9881. Best source of videos and a great publication list. Super-slick; beltway money.*

How Dense Can We Get?

The Population Explosion is advocacy science at its best : connecting any issue you can think of (and a few more) with the simple fact that, as a species, we've gone beyond the limits. Elephants in the Volkswagen zooms in on the United States with lots of thoughtful comparisons: When is a nation overcrowded? Can you reduce family size by noncoercive measures? Is China the way of the future? What ever happened to "Give me your tired, your hungry, your poor…"? Don't we have an obligation to accept immigrants? How does overcrowding affect citizen happiness and welfare? Most of these essays have a grip on complexity —no pop/demagoguery/demography. A few are fatuous. —PW

•

India's first family planning effort, in 1952, relied heavily on the rhythm method, whose high failure rate is well known. Indeed, the old joke says, "What do you call users of the rhythm method?" The answer is "parents." India's next major foray into family planning was with the vasectomy campaigns of the 1960s, but this campaign was hampered by the fact that many men who were

sterilized had already fathered several children, and some had wives who were already past menopause. Furthermore, there were claims that men were being wrongly coerced into sterilizations by recruiters who (like the person undergoing the vasectomy) were rewarded with a transistor radio or similar premium. The IUD has been available in India since 1961, and abortion was legalized in 1971, but the pill is still not widely distributed. In various areas of India there have been experiments in paying women not to have babies by depositing money in a pension-type account for them each month or year they delay or avoid a pregnancy. Such schemes have been generally successful, but they have had neither the funding nor the local government backing necessary to make them widespread.

Elephants in the Volkswagen
Lindsey Grant. 1992; 272 pp.
ISBN 0-7167-2268-2
$13.95 ($17.45 postpaid) from W. H. Freeman and Co., 4419 W. 1980 S., Salt Lake City, UT 84104; 800/488-5233

The Population Explosion
Paul R. Ehrlich & Anne H. Ehrlich. Touchstone Books, 1991; 320 pp.
ISBN 0-671-73294-3
$11 postpaid from Simon & Schuster/Order Dept., 200 Old Tappan Road, Old Tappan, NJ 07675; 800/223-2336

The Ecology of Commerce

Markets, left to themselves, can become amoral and impersonal, advertising prices without values, boasting eternal life, singing extravagant claims that markets are "good" in and of themselves. This thoughtless market is an addiction, hooking humans into a nightmare circle of production/consumption. All other market impacts are dismissed as "externalities" and "temporary economic dislocations."

Paul Hawken, in a tone remarkably calm and with a firmness remarkably gentle, provides the foundations for the only possible hope: managing commerce to benefit human welfare and to restore the biological productivity of the Earth. The Ecology of Commerce is the most important contemplative book on sustainability in the Catalog. Almost all the other books start from his percepts and must search for the skillful means to accomplish Paul's ideals. —Peter Warshall

●

Globalization makes it easier to shift money rapidly around the globe, leveling out interest rates, introducing competition between an AA-rated bond in New Delhi and an instrument of like quality in London or Mexico. Money can seek its "highest and best" return instantaneously from around the globe, and it has round-the-clock liquidity. Money thus acts as a self-propelled force, ostensibly in the hands of institutions and fiduciaries but, practically speaking, in the control of a programmed calculus that constantly reevaluates where it can find the greatest return, in the form of currencies, interest, or equity, or a combination of the three.

By making the entire world economic system exchangeable on a moment's notice, we have in essence set up a new standard against which all economic activity is measured. We have created a common global value system that is measured in monetary terms alone, one that has little or nothing to do with the search for a sustainable future that will support human civilization. What should the world earn on its money? Seven percent? Five percent? Nine percent? The World Bank uses a discount rate of ten percent, which means that when evaluating any project, one dollar's worth of environmental value fifty years out in time is given an equivalent value of 1 cent today.

●

This book proposes three approaches, all guided by the example of nature. The first is to obey the waste-equals-food principle and entirely eliminate waste from our industrial production. This not only saves resources outright, but it rearranges our relationship to resources from a linear to a cyclical one, greatly enhancing our ability to lead prosperous lives while reducing environmental degradation.

The second principle is to change from an economy based on carbon to one based on hydrogen and sunshine. This is primarily achieved by reversing the historical incentives

The Ecology of Commerce
(A Declaration of Sustainability)
Paul Hawken. HarperBusiness, 1993;
250 pp. ISBN 0-088730-655-1
$23 ($25.75 postpaid) from HarperCollins Publishers/Direct Mail, PO Box 588, Dunmore, PA 18512; 800/331-3761

surrounding the production and consumption of energy, away from the cheapest combustion towards the most enduring production.

Third, we must create systems of feedback and accountability that support and strengthen restorative behavior, whether they are in resource utilities, green fees on agricultural chemicals, or reliance on local production and distribution. Conversely, we have to look at how our present economic system consistently rewards short-term exploitation while penalizing long-term restoration, and then eliminate the ill-placed incentives that allow small sectors of the population to benefit at the expense of the whole.

A restorative economy is not going to lead a life of dulling comfort and convenience. We have to recognize that we've reached a watershed in the economy, a point at which "growth" and profitability will be increasingly derived from the abatement of environmental degradation, the furthering of ecological restoration, and the mimicking of natural systems of production and consumption.

How Much Is Enough?

To population control and taming technology we must add a third urgent necessity: consumption control. While this book is a bit shrill, it is also the only book that compares the use of materials and energy in the North and the South and asks: Is there enough for all of us to live like Americans? Are we promoting two-car and two-thousand-square-foot home dreams that will wreck the planet? How do we relearn to truly value the materials of material wealth? —PW

●

Meat Consumption per Capita,
Selected Countries, 1990

Country	Meat * (kilograms)
United States	112
France	91
Argentina	82
Soviet Union	70
Brazil	47
Japan	41
Mexico	40
China	24
Turkey	16
Philippines	16
Egypt	14
India	2

* Beef, veal, pork, lamb, mutton, goat and poultry in carcass weight equivalents. Poultry figures are for 1989.

●

Germans alone throw away 5 million household appliances year, and Americans toss 7.5 million television sets. Only one fourth of the 280 million tires Americans throw out each year are recycled or retreaded.

Where disposability and planned obsolescence fail to accelerate the trip from cash register to junk heap, fashion sometimes succeeds. Oscar Wilde once asked, "What is fashion? . . . It is usually a form of ugliness so intolerable that we have to alter it every six months."

How Much Is Enough?
(The Consumer Society and the Future of the Earth)
Alan Durning. Worldwatch Environmental Alert Series, 1992; 200 pp.
ISBN 0-393-30891-X
$8.95 postpaid from W.W. Norton & Co./ Order Dept., 800 Keystone Industrial Park, Scranton, PA 18512; 800/233-4830

See Boycott Quarterly, p. 303.

Mortgaging the Earth

It's time to let go of our favorite platitude: Think globally, act locally. It constricts necessary action, especially moral reform of the globalists. Do it all! Act globally, think locally. Act locally and globally. Think globally and locally. Mortgaging the Earth tells this new-style success story: Networking warriors join Brazilian peasants to other global helpers, strategizing in a dozen planetary locales to save a rainforest and provide for sustainable jobs.

Bruce Rich is the most intelligent and persuasive voice for a new global civil society — where civilians actually have a say in the financial structuring of their lives. His critique of the World Bank needs to be force-fed to all globalists and assigned as required reading in all government and educational institutions concerned with the future of the planet. It's hard to plow through the first chapter of World Bank stupidity and disasters — the story borders on being Kafkaesque. But, continue and you find a clear and most moral analysis of the World Bank's history

and, even better, of sustainable compassionate finance. — PW

●

The World Bank lends about $24 billion a year to more than a hundred countries to support economic development projects and programs, the total cost of which is over $70 billion annually. It manages a portfolio of outstanding loans totaling $140 billion, financing development schemes totaling over a third of a trillion dollars. The World Bank operates on a larger scale than any of the other so-called public international financial institutions.

●

The report noted that the Bank had refused to lend to the democratically elected Goulart government in Brazil in the early 1960s, but following the 1964 military coup (which installed a twenty-year military dictatorship), lending rose from zero to average $73 million a year for the rest of the 1960s and reached levels of nearly half a billion dollars a year by the mid-1970s. Chile under the democratically elected regime of Allende received no Bank loans but following the Pinochet coup in 1973 the country suddenly became creditworthy, despite a worsening economic situation. Indonesia under Sukarno — an autocrat, but at least a civilian — received no World Bank loans; Sukarno was overthrown by an extraordinarily bloody military uprising in 1965, which included the mass murder of more than half a million alleged communists, many of whom in fact were ethnic

Chinese. The Bank approved its first loans to Indonesia in late 1968, and McNamara made increased lending to General Suharto's regime a priority in the 1970s, reaching levels of $600 to $700 million annually by the end of the decade. The report noted that "fifteen of the world's most repressive governments will receive $2.9 billion in World Bank loans in fiscal 1979," about a third of the Bank's entire proposed new loan commitments for that year. President Carter and Congress had cut off all U.S. aid for four of the fifteen — Argentina, Chile, Uruguay, and Ethiopia — for flagrant human rights violations.

Mortgaging the Earth
(The World Bank, Environmental Improvement, and the Crisis of Development)
Bruce Rich. 1993; 376 pp.
ISBN 0-8070-4704-X
$30 ($33.75 postpaid) from Beacon Press, 25 Beacon Street, Boston, MA 02108; 617/742-2110

Stop Perverse Incentives

Finances that are counter-productive and encourage behavior that despoils the Earth and its human cultures are called perverse incentives. Here are three groups on the front line — warriors fighting financial perversity and promoting positive incentives for conservation-based development.

BankCheck: Juliette Majot, Editor. $25/ year (4 issues) from BankCheck, c/o International Rivers Network, 1847 Berkeley Way, Berkeley, CA 94703; 510/848-1155. The pit bulls at the World Bank's gates. The only critical newsletter.

Institute for Agricultural Trade Policy (IATP): 313 5th Street SE, Minneapolis, MN 55414; 612/379-5980. It may not sound muscular, but this institute cares for small farmers throughout the globe. Monitors the impact of NAFTA and GATT and other trade on the actual lives of real souls. They lobby heavy.

An End to Hunger?

The most thoughtful, informative, wide-ranging, complex and realistic book on hunger and its causes. Nourished by experience (Solon Barraclough worked on land tenure, hunger, agriculture and economics with the UN for twenty years), there are no graphs or models. Just the human computer, a bit baffled and a bit saddened, groping for a socio-political toolkit that will bring full stomachs to the planet's undernourished.
—Peter Warshall

•

I passed my report to a Chilean newspaper reporter. He visited the area, took pictures and published an article in a US magazine. He was subsequently jailed briefly for defamation of his country abroad.

Was the cause of this mini-famine climate, overpopulation, erroneous government policy, the highly unequal agrarian structure, the partially developed industrial structure of Chile, or the fluctuation of commodity prices on the world market? Was it the poverty and illiteracy of the peasants? Was it their powerlessness?

In fact it was all these things, and all were bound up in the operation of complex social systems interacting with fragile natural ecosystems. The causes of food insecurity can very seldom be traced to any single event or condition, nor are there simple recipes for doing away with hunger and poverty. Every situation, at the same time as it is determined by international and national phenomena, is to some extent unique.

•

Food security can be defined as sustained and assured access by all social groups and individuals to food adequate in quantity and quality to meet nutritional needs. A food system offering security should have the following characteristics: (a) capacity to produce, store, and import sufficient food to meet basic food needs for all groups; (b) maximum autonomy and self-determination (without implying autarky), reducing vulnerability to international market fluctuations and political pressures; (c) reliability, such that seasonal, cyclical and other variations in access to food are minimal; (d) sustainability such that the ecological system is protected and improved over time; and (e) equity, meaning, as a minimum, dependable access to adequate food for all social groups.

An End to Hunger?
(The Social Origins of Food Strategies)
Solon L. Barraclough. Zed Books, 1991;
320 pp. ISBN 0-86232-993-0
$19.95 ($22.95 postpaid) from Humanities Press International, 165 1st Avenue, Atlantic Highlands, NJ 07716; 908/872-1441

Ending Hunger

When I returned from Ethiopia, friends overwhelmed by TV images of swollen stomachs and 800 numbers, asked: Who's good? Who really helps? From personal experience and the experience of Claude Bart and Michael Scott, here are some gems.

Oxfam UK: *274 Branbury Road, Oxford OX2 7DZ, England; 011 44 086 531 1311.* ***Oxfam America:*** *26 West Street, Boston, MA 02111; 617/482-1211. In Ethiopia, they held my utmost respect. Practical in the face of the four horsemen. I trust I'll get good works for my money here.*

Bread for the World: *Membership $25/year (includes newsletter). 1100 Wayne Avenue, Suite 1000, Silver Spring, MD 20910; 301/608-2400, fax 301/608-2401. The best lobbying group with the best publications. When Clifton cut development and food security aid by 40 percent, Bread for the World tried to restore it by getting you to pressure your congressperson. Quick to respond and good-hearted, they have finely defined spiritual muscle.* ***Bread for the World Newsletter*** *and* ***Hunger 1994: Transforming the Politics of Hunger*** *($14.95) will tell you of empty stomachs here in America and overseas.*

Institute for Food and Development Policy: *Membership $30/year. 398 60th Street, Oakland, CA 94618; 800/888-3314. The producers of the great classic* ***Food First***, *still one of the best books on under-nutrition and the causes of world hunger. The avant garde on development, democracy and such issues as structural adjustments.*

American Friends Service Committee: *501 Cherry Street, Philadelphia, PA 19102; 215/241-7000. Supports development*

projects that are long-term and people-based. None of the "drop-in" and "go home" consultancies. They stay with a village for years until all the kinks of change have been witnessed and addressed.

Medicins Sans Frontieres: *8 Rue St. Sabin, F-755544, Paris, Cedex 11, France; 011 33 1 4021 2929. The doctors who go where it's needed — behind or on the battlefront.* —PW *[With the generous help of Claude Bart and Michael Scott]*

OTHER GREAT RESOURCES

Soil and Civilization: Edward Hyams. Harper & Row, 1952, 1976, HarperCollins Publishers. Out of print. The rise and fall of civilizations from the perspective of their topsoil. Here food and soil are seen as the long-term drivers of civilization. Read about the Nile and the Dust Bowl, the Euphrates.

Hunger Action Handbook: Leslie Withers & Tom Peterson, Editors. 1987, Seeds Magazine Press.

Food First (Beyond the Myth of Scarcity): Frances Moore Lappe & Joseph Collins. 1981, Institute for Food and Development Policy. The classic. What keeps starving people from feeding themselves? It is to humans what *Silent Spring* was to nature.

Hunger and Public Action: Jean Dreze & Amartya Sen. 1991, Oxford University Press. The most readable and important book from

the academy. Don't join an anti-hunger campaign until you've digested it.

Zed Books: 7 Cynthia Street, London N1 9JF, UK; 011 44 071 837 8466 or c/o Humanities Press International, 165 1st Avenue, Atlantic Highlands, NJ 07716; 908/872-1441. Best publisher on books on development and the environment.

The Mountain People

Hunger for food, for hope, for human contact. Watch them dissolve in a land of parched earth. One of the most riveting and reflective anthropological studies of one possible future global scenario: chaos. —PW

•

Most of us are unlikely to admit readily that we can sink as low as the Ik, but many of us do, and with far less cause. However, that is left for the reader to decide for himself; this story concerns the Ik, the Mountain People, and their struggle for survival. Although the experience was far from pleasant, and involved both physical and mental suffering, I am grateful for it. In spite of it all, and contrary to the first tidal wave of disillusionment, it has added to my respect for humanity and my hope that we who have been civilized into such empty beliefs as the essential beauty and goodness of humanity may discover ourselves before it is too late.

•

More and more it was only the young who could go far from the village as hunger became starvation. Yet while others starved, the young remained relatively active. Famine relief had been initiated down at Kasilé and those fit enough to make the trip set off, leaving the others behind. When they came back the contrast between them and the others was that between life and death. At this time people no longer sat on the *di*, they lay there waiting for nothing, the very old and the very young. Youths were too busy at this time to sit on their *di*, for collecting famine relief

The Mountain People
Colin M. Turnbull. Touchstone Books, 1987; 309 pp. ISBN 0-671-64098-4
$12 postpaid from Simon & Schuster/Order Dept., 200 Old Tappan Road, Old Tappan, NJ 07675; 800/223-2336

was virtually a full-time occupation, rather like hunting; it called for cunning and organization. When there was no relief to be had, the people who were well were all off foraging for what food they could find in the mountains or down in Kidepo.

Villages were villages of the dead and dying, and there was little difference between the two. People crawled rather than walked — the very young and the very old all crawled. . . . After a few feet some would lie down to rest, but they could not be sure of ever being able to sit up again, so they mostly stayed upright until they reached their destination. It was their destination that intrigued me, for really they were going nowhere, these semi-animate bags of skin and bone, they just wanted to be with others, and they stayed whenever they met. Perhaps it was the most important demonstration of sociality I ever saw among the Ik.

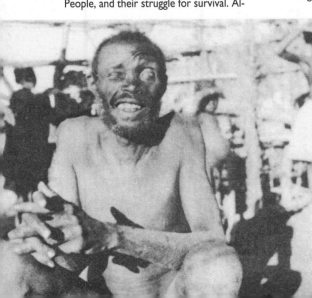

Blind Logwara . . . when he tried to reach a dead hyena for a share of the putrid meat, his fellow Ik trampled him underfoot. He thought it quite funny.

Environmental Conservation

I have bumped into this textbook in Africa and Latin America. Ray Dasmann is the sage to many culturally astute students of conservation-based development. I tip my hat each time I return to the photos chosen, diagrams drawn, or concepts explained. If, like most of us, you somehow didn't take "human ecology" in college or just discovered its importance, this is the gentle introduction to our lives as planetary and celebratory animals. Hard to beat. —PW

•

The conservation of nature is fundamental to human existence and is the concern of all people everywhere. It is not to be accomplished only by the setting aside of specially protected natural areas, but must be practiced in all places at all times. All areas must be protected areas to some degree, since even the most heavily urbanized areas provide suitable living spaces for many wild species.

•

With the increasing use of fossil fuels and the spread of industrial technology, the use of energy in the industrial world increased steadily, from the original 15,000 kilocalories per person per day to approximately 250,000 kilocalories in the United States in the middle 1970s. By that time most of the energy used was derived from petroleum, but during the 1960s and 1970s a growing percentage was derived from a nonsolar source, nuclear power.

It is worthwhile here to consider the question of basic energy needs as distinct from mere wants or "greeds." Every person must have food, and a means of keeping warm or cool through clothing or shelter, as well as the ability to transform unpalatable food to palatable food through cooking. These are basic needs, everywhere, and were accommodated easily within the 15,000 kilocalorie per day limit. They are still the basic needs for those living close to the earth and deriving their livelihood from the land. In industrial societies, however, organized the way they are today, basic needs cannot be so simply defined. The separation of home, work place, food supplies, and the sources of other essentials is so great in most urban communities that the possibility of traveling from one to the other by foot is ruled out. Even bicycles are not really useful if one lives in Queens and works in Manhattan, or must cross Los Angeles to get to the office or factory. Adequate transportation, with all of the energy use associated with it, becomes as basic as food itself, since it is the means for obtaining food.

Environmental Conservation
Raymond F. Dasmann. 1984; 486 pp.
ISBN 0-471-89141-X
$57.95 postpaid. John Wiley & Sons, Inc.,
1 Wiley Dr., Somerset, NJ 08873;
800/225-5945

Ecodevelopment: Old systems must be examined to find ways to improve yields without losing long-established balances, as in these rice paddies of Vietnam or tea plantations of Japan. The goal: self-reliance in partnership with nature.

See Restoration Forestry (p. 90).

Ecotrust

The model for communities going for the long haul, for lives embedded in conservation-based development. Ecotrust knows well that long-term earth care requires long-term institutions that will keep citizens directly interested in long-term watershed health. They created a nonprofit to help with mapping; a joint venture with Shorebank Corporation of Chicago that provides green incentive loans that other banks won't touch; a $1.6 million FDIC-insured EcoDeposit account to support local entrepreneurs who combine conservation with their businesses; and a Natural Capital Fund to help leverage the funding. Look to the Willapa Bay Alliance, the Nanakila Institute (a joint venture with the Haisla people to save the largest roadless temperate rainforest), Prince William Sound Science Center, and the well-known Clayoquot for the fruits of Ecotrust's commitment. A grand nexus of realism and heart. —PW

Ecotrust: 1200 Northwest Front Ave. #470, Portland, OR 97209; 503/227-6225.

•

The cardinal points on Ecotrust's compass are:

1. *Understanding* through ecosystem-level scientific research, monitoring of ecological, economic, and community trends, and education.

2. *Conservation* through protection, careful stewardship, and restoration of soils, waters, plants, animals, and natural ecological processes.

3. *Development* by providing technical, financial, and marketing assistance to environmental entrepreneurs.

4. *Policy Reform* by ensuring that local experience and needs guide governmental decision-making at all levels.

OTHER ATMOSPHERIC RESOURCES

Atmosphere Alliance: PO Box 10346, Olympia, WA 98502. $20 per year membership includes the excellent *No Sweat News* and all other Alliance publications.

Climate Change Dossier: Free quarterly bulletin in English, Spanish, French, Chinese, Japanese, or Urdu; UCC, UNEP, Geneva Executive Center, CP 365, 1219 Chatelaine, Switzerland. Easy-to-read factsheets: Why three hot summers don't mean global warming. Why the poor are most vulnerable. Climate and food security. Etc.

Global Warming Debate

Climate change could have the most devastating impact on our children's lives (especially those of the rural poor) and on biological diversity. We are poised at a moment when human industrial cycling surpasses the biosphere's in speed and volume of turnover. How sensitive is the planet's climate? How certain do we have to be before implementing a greenhouse policy? Is this science, or just scientists jumping onto the globalist bandwagon? What pieces of the puzzle need to be found?

I surveyed and rejected all the books on ozone and global warming or global cooling. They were not so much wrong as quickly out of date, or right for the wrong reasons. Then, from the scholarly arm of the National Geographic Society, came this well-spoken and beautifully illustrated "book" (actually an issue of their quarterly Research and Exploration). —PW

•

Degrees of Certainty
The 15-year-old often-reaffirmed U S National Academy of Sciences consensus estimate of 1.5 to 4.5°C global average warming if CO_2 were to double still reflects the best estimate from a wide range of current climate models and ancient climatic eras. The Earth has not been >1 to 2°C warmer than now during the 10,000-year era of human civilization. The previous ice age, in which mile-high ice sheets stretched from New York to Chicago to the Arctic, was "only" 5°C colder than the current 10,000-year-old interglacial epoch we now enjoy.

Humans have altered the natural greenhouse effect by adding 25% more CO_2, 100% more CH_4, and a host of other greenhouse gases such as N_2O and CFC since the Industrial Revolution. *CERTAIN*

Although no highly significant (i.e., at the of-

Global Warming Debate
(*Research and Exploration* Spring 1993: Vol. 9, No. 2)
Anthony R. de Souza, Editor.
$12.50 postpaid. Subscriptions $40/year (4 issues). National Geographic Society, 1145 17th Street NW, Washington, DC 20036; 800/638-4077

ten-cited 99% statistical confidence limit) cause-and-effect statements between the observed warming and the buildup of human-induced greenhouse gases can be credibly asserted for at least another decade or two, the likelihood that the 0.5°C 20th century warming trend is wholly a natural phenomenon is small (i.e., I would estimate perhaps a 10 to 20% chance.) *LIKELY*

Most forest species "migrate" at rates of at most 1 km/y, and would not be able to "keep up" with temperature changes at a rate of several degrees centigrade per century without human intervention to transplant them (i.e., ecological engineering). *VERY LIKELY*

Statues in a Louisville, Kentucky cemetery illustrate the effects of acid rain, created by the reaction between atmospheric moisture and fossil-fuel emissions. A black crust forms on the Madonna because it is sheltered, while the angel has no build up because of the scouring but nevertheless corrosive action of the rain.

At the Rio Earth Summit, about 18,000 nongovernmental organizations (NGOs) entered the fray. About 1,500 of them were actually accredited by ECOSOC (the UN Economic and Social Council).

Compare this to 1945, when the US government invited about forty NGOs to take part in United Nations organizing meetings in San Francisco. NGOs were listed as consultants. Every consultant brought associates, so there was plenty of lobbying.

The UN Charter did not originally mention human rights. It's said that only through the NGOs' efforts did human-rights guarantees become part of the Charter. The NGOs were organizations like the American Farm Bureau, Rotary, and NAACP — not much in the way of environmental groups.

With the tidal wave of citizens' groups now inundating the global stage, ECOSOC is reviewing the whole process of accreditation and what it means for NGOs to participate in the UN, a subject which has been fairly murky since that first meeting.

The UN has tentatively and very carefully opened its doors to wider NGO participation, basically under NGO pressure. But during the planning stages and at Rio, many UN delegates stood to benefit — they were unfamiliar with issues like biodiversity, forestry, and women's rights, and NGOs were often able to provide expertise. Since the 1,500 official NGOs could work on official texts, they were able to provide delegates with actual language and supporting rationale to present in debates. Many nations included NGO representatives in their Earth Summit delegations. To them, it was good evidence of their belief in grassroots political will.

At Rio, NGO lobbying was never confined to one's own country. On

any given issue, a few countries usually wanted to avoid aligning themselves with either the Northern Bloc or the Group of 77 (a coalition of Southern nations). For example, members of the Forest Treaty Working Group, an assortment of individuals and NGOs, would talk in the corridors to Mexican or Venezuelan delegates looking for compromise language or more sustainable approaches to forestry, and who were therefore eager (as eager as a UN delegate *can* be) to talk to us.

The North was trying to persuade the South not to cut down its forests, without offering any concessions or paying any persuasion money. The Group of 77, led by Malaysia, stressed sovereignty, saying that they could do what they pleased (basically meaning that the elites would sell off their timber to other elites, and never mind their own sustainable-forest NGOs). Looking for compromise, the Mexican delegate would often try to insert a phrase, or maybe an entire paragraph, from our suggestions into the negotiable sections.

All this has been viewed with some alarm by the UN. But the doors have remained open. If the UN remains a grand forum of global influence, then its citizenry will act globally as well as locally. Here's how:

Networking: It's great to see people compare notes and then end-run governments too inflexible or too mired in politics to move. At one preparatory meeting, Malaysians dealing with a recently arrived chemical company got together with a group who had just been dealing with their own sick children and the same chemical company in Louisiana. They exchanged stories, symptoms, strategies, and began to work together.

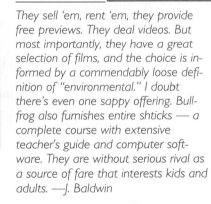

Learning: The Northern NGOs learned at first hand what kind of development must accompany environmental work, why overconsumption in our own backyards must be addressed before we speak about population control, and why equity and environmental justice must move to the top of the list.

Advocacy: UN delegates often represent their country's elite. At this point, the NGOs are the only advocates for grassroots, local communities, or indigenous interests.

Accountability: When a delegate makes grandiose statements about progress on human rights or the environment, not only have his or her own nation's NGOs heard the statement but also the NGO "bloc" from every other nation. Their members tend to remember, and to bring up these memories at appropriately embarrassing moments. —Sharyle Patton

The Video Project

Exceptional films and videos with an impressive list of award winners and videos like **The Panama Deception** *and the* **Glasnost Series** *(12 videos on modern Russia) available nowhere else. But their compassion is for a safe and sustainable world and I like* **Ancient Futures: Learning from Ladakh** *(p. 73) and* **A Thousand Cranes** *. Like Bullfrog Films, it's the Whole Earth Catalog animated. —PW*

The Video Project: 5332 College Avenue, Suite 101, Oakland, CA 94618; 800/475-2638

EcoLinking

For the environmental activist who isn't enthralled by virtual communities or online culture — but who might be very interested in an email list concerning birding, cancer clusters, or ocean drilling — **Ecolinking** *can be a one-step shopping spree. It takes you step by step through the fundamentals of buying and installing a modem, and connecting with online services. You also get thorough listings of environmental forums and databases available on EcoNet, Fidonet, Bitnet, Usenet, Internet, America OnLine, CompuServe, GEnie, the WELL, and commercial online research databases. Long lists of newsgroups and electronic archives, with precise subscription information, make this an indispensable resource for enviro-activists who are ready to use online media. —HLR*

•

A Selection of EcoNet Conferences:

en.cleanair Communication about air pollution; topics range from government policy to action ideas.

en.climate Discussion of pollution, its effects, and methods for dealing with it.

en.pollution Conference on pollution, including effects, sources, policy, and advocacy.

en.waste Discussion of waste management, from toxic pollution to actions planned against polluters.

en.bioanerobi Discussion of alternative methods of recycling waste products for fuel.

EcoLinking
(Everyone's Guide to Online Environmental Information)
Don Rittner. 1992; 352 pp.
ISBN 0-938151-35-5
$18.95 ($22.95 postpaid) from Peachpit Press Inc., 2414 6th Street, Berkeley, CA 94710; 800/283-9444

en.bioconversi Discussion of the use of woody and agricultural plants in energy production.

Bullfrog Films

They sell 'em, rent 'em, they provide free previews. They deal videos. But most importantly, they have a great selection of films, and the choice is informed by a commendably loose definition of "environmental." I doubt there's even one sappy offering. Bullfrog also furnishes entire shticks — a complete course with extensive teacher's guide and computer software. They are without serious rival as a source of fare that interests kids and adults. —J. Baldwin

•

TOAST. *12 Minutes/Grades 3-Adult; Produced by Earth Chronicles/A film by Daniel Hoffman*

One of the most effective energy films ever made, TOAST illustrates our underlying dependence on fossil fuels, and takes as its example the production and distribution of a commonplace item, bread. Using flowing images set to music, it documents all the fossil fuel inputs, from the oil well head (to make the fertilizer to grow the wheat, etc.) to the toaster. With Discussion Guide.

•

IN DEFENSE OF ANIMALS: A portrait of Peter Singer. *28 Minutes/Grades 9-Adult; Produced by Julie Akeret*

This is an excellent summation of both the philosophical and practical arguments that underpin one of the fastest growing political movements in this country and the

world. According to Peter Singer, the heart of the argument lies in the recognition that we should not discount the pain and suffering of another just because the being that is suffering is not human. Many believe this is a critical advance in the evolution of our moral thinking, and it is certainly time for all of us to familiarize ourselves with the arguments of the animal rights movement, arguments that are too frequently trivialized or deliberately misrepresented.

Bullfrog Films: PO Box 149, Oley, PA 19547; 800/543-3764

Millennium

This huge, handsome companion volume to a PBS television series is a coffee-table book with a vengeance. It is one thing to read the words, the stories of the people whose cultures are threatened, and another to see the look in their eyes. Laughing children in Himalayan villages, shamans in trances in Brazil: the most potent form of wealth in the world is people, and it isn't easy to deny that when you see this book. Anthropologist David Maybury-Lewis packs the 395 pages with insight and information about endangered cultural treasures. A brilliant text that is also a work of art. —HLR

•

That path is part of the Ancestor. When an Aborigine walks that songline and sings that song, he is part of that Ancestor and part of the continuing creation of the land that both exists and is being created. All this is what Aborigines mean when they refer to their land as sacred and explains why they are serious when they say they die when the land is taken from them.

A member of the Gabra of Kenya.

Millennium
(Tribal Wisdom and the Modern World) David Maybury-Lewis. Viking, 1992; 416 pp. ISBN 0-670-82935-8 $45 ($47 postpaid) from Penguin USA/ Consumer Sales, 120 Woodbine Street, Bergenfield, NJ 07621; 800/253-6476

A serious consideration of tribal ways of life should lead us to think carefully and critically about our own. What would it take for us to try to live in harmony with nature or to rehumanize our economic system? How can we mediate between the individual and the family, between genders and generations? Should we strive for a less fragmented view of physical reality or of our place in the scheme of things? These questions revolve around wholeness and harmony, around tolerance and pluralism. The answers are still emerging, but they too are variations on a grand theme that can be summed up in E. M. Forster's famous phrase: "only connect."

The project for the new millennium will be to reenergize civil society, the space between the state and the individual where those habits of the heart flourish that socialize the individual and humanize the state.

Cultural Survival

For twenty years, *Cultural Survival* has been the hub of a thousand spokes, a wheel trying to turn the world in the direction of preserving human diversity and helping pre-industrial peoples to escape getting runover by disease, destitution, despair, wars, and environmental damage.

The world and CS have gone through fits and starts as they persist in the daunting task of helping indigenous peoples and ethnic minorities deal as equals in their encounters with industrial societies and national bias. The millennial Nobel prize will go to the person who designs a peaceful amalgam of democracy and multiculturalism. *Cultural Survival* and

grassroots actions are the most likely places to nurture such an intern. *CS* has programs in resource management, applied anthropology, education, and public policy. —Peter Warshall

Cultural Survival
$45/Year (4 issues). 215 First Street, Cambridge, MA 02138; 617/621-3818

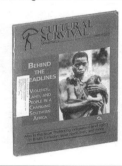

The Law of the Mother

Thumbnail sketches of thirty peoples dealing with their lives in protected areas. This book is the most readable summary of conflict resolution between indigenous peoples and conservation, including examples of the diverse tools needed in consensus building. Examples include: butterfly ranching as an alternative source of income; a fund to compensate farmers for elephants munching local lettuce; a project to turn hunters into antipoachers; or schemes to guarantee land rights. —PW

•

1. Build on the foundations of the local culture.

2. Give responsibility to local people.

3. Consider returning ownership of at least some protected areas to indigenous people.

4. Hire local people.

5. Link government development programs with protected areas.

6. Give priority to small-scale local development.

A dolphin funeral in Vung Tau, gateway to Con Dao National Park. In South Vietnam, marine mammals are given human burials at some special temples dedicated to cetaceans.

7. Involve local people in preparing management plans.

8. Have the courage to enforce restrictions.

9. Build conservation into the evolving new national cultures.

The Law of the Mother
(Protecting Indigenous Peoples in Protected Areas) Elizabeth Kempf, Editor. Sierra Club Books 1993; 296 pp. ISBN 0-87156-451-3 $25 ($28 postpaid) from Sierra Club Store Orders, 730 Polk Street, San Francisco, CA 94109; 800/935-1056

State of the Peoples

The cultural survival activist's handbook. The first part of this no-nonsense, sparsely illustrated guidebook consists of essays about indigenous groups that face cultural extinction — from Burma to Ethiopia to Minnesota. The remainder of the book is a survey of the status of 150 tribal peoples around the world. Thumbnail sketches of political and cultural threats to each group are accompanied by lists of resources and maps, for those in the cities of the industrialized world who want to know where and how to help these people fight for survival in the jungles, highlands, and deserts. —HLR

•

The Penan name specific trees, particularly productive stands of the staple sago palm. The key concept in naming and using such trees is the verb *molong*: to preserve or foster. Throughout the forest, each com-

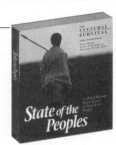

State of the Peoples
(A Global Human Rights Report on Societies in Danger) Marc Miller, Editor. 1993; 262 pp. ISBN 0-8070-0221-6 $18 ($21.75 postpaid) from Beacon Press, 25 Beacon Street, Boston, MA 02108; 617/742-2110

munity has a collection of thousands of trees and sago clumps that particular individuals or households molong. The molong system underlies a long-term harvesting strategy that assures the continued availability of resources.

Although the international campaign on behalf of the Penan focuses on the physical impact of logging, the dispossession caused by the industry is more complex. By transforming the landscape, logging destroys those things that are iconic of Penan society. When bulldozers clear roads through the forest, they scour away the surface of the land and obliterate recognizable features. Once the forest canopy is opened, an impenetrable mass of thorny vines and shrubs appears. These areas are virtual deserts with respect to the availability of game, and the dense cover makes movement difficult and access nearly impossible. The cultural density of that landscape — all the sites with biographical, social, and historical significance — is hidden, producing a sort of collective amnesia.

OTHER GREAT RESOURCES

The New Resource Wars: Al Gedicks, South End Press. Native and environmental struggles against multinational mining and energy corporations.

Genocide Watch: Helen Fein, Editor. Yale University Press. Why are bystanders passive? How do the media treat ethnic atrocities? Bahai in Iraq. Burundi. Bosnia. The Holocaust. Best academic collection.

Anti-Slavery Society (180 Brixton Rd, London SW9 6AT; 44-71-587-0573). The world's oldest human rights organization (1839).

A Cultural Survival Checklist

✔ Have we kept our land base? If a culture has lost it, we can expect trouble. The Kurds, the Jews, the Palestinians, the people of East Timor, and the Tibetans struggle to identify their spirit with a land.

✔ Have we kept our language? Native Americans are having a hard time with this one. Many kids have lost their native language (even though they have a land base). Immigrants are, almost by definition, people whose kids abjure their parents' language. Can a culture survive without its native tongue? Can people become immigrants in their own land?

✔ Do the people we marry join our culture? Do we join theirs? Or is "culture" simply a non-issue? If the kids marry out and drop the lineage, rather than absorbing new kin into the culture, the culture peters out.

✔ Have we kept our ceremonies, especially ritual foods? The last items to go are specialty foods and the "big" holy days. They can be fused, like Yaqui Easter ceremonies, into pandevotionalism. But the dialogue about purity and participation must not stop. Lose the cranky correctitude and there goes the tribe.

✔ Have we written a manual for eluding genocide? Too many cultures are caught unawares. Before they know it, all that's left are words in a history book. A survival manual includes how to conduct a successful diaspora, training specialists in refugee life, how to garner support in international politics, and how to preserve spiritual hope.
—Peter Warshall

South and Central American People

Cuzcatlan by Manilo Argueta (Random House).

Kafka in Salvadorian. Peasant life under the military.

South and Meso-American Indian Information Center (510/834-4263).

Best news source and networking group for the indigenous peoples of South and Central America. Organizes speaking tours of Amazonian indian delegations. Issues emergency human-rights alerts.

Global Alliance of the Indigenous Tribal Peoples of the Tropical Rainforests (510/524-0795).

The worldwide coordinating group for non-governmental organizations trying to restore to indigenous peoples the right to determine their own futures. An Earth Summit coordinator.

Coordinating Body for Indigenous People's Organization (Calle Alemania 836 y Mariana de Jésus, Quito, Ecuador).

Alliance of Indian organizations in Brazil, Peru, Ecuador, Colombia. Relays Amazonian perspectives to the rest of the world.

Indian Law Resource Center (202/547-2800 or 406/449-2031).

Free legal help in major cases involving Indian rights. Helps North American natives with the management of trust funds, the reform of discriminatory laws; works toward sovereignty in Central and South America.

I, Rigoberta Menchu

One of the most shattering books I've read in years. In monologues twenty-three-year-old Rigoberta Menchu describes her relationships with nature, life, death, and her community and reveals the cultural discrimination and genocide waged against Guatemalan Indian tribes today. Deeply personal, a gift of a human voice that whispers across the immense gap between the nature-based society of the Quiche Indians and our modern capitalistic societies. If you think you only have time to read one book about Central America, read this one, because it will demand of you to read more.
—Jeanne Carstensen

•

Before the seeds are sown in the ground, we perform a ceremony. We choose two or three of the biggest seeds and place them in a ring, candles representing earth, water, animals and the universe (that is, man). In our culture, the universe is man. The seed is honoured because it will be buried in something sacred — the earth — and because it will multiply and bear fruit the next year. We do it mainly because the seed is something pure, something sacred.

I, Rigoberta Menchu
Rigoberta Menchu.
1985; 252 pp. ISBN 0-86091-788-6
$13.95 ($16.45 postpaid). Routledge, Chapman and Hall/Order Dept., 29 W. 35th Street, New York, NY 10001-2291; 212/244-6412

Cultures in collision. Westernized Indian films have had a profound impact on young Ladakhis, making them feel ashamed of their own traditions and values.

Ancient Futures • Ladakh

Ancient Futures author Helena Norberg-Hodge is the planet's best example of excellence, skillful means, everyday compassion, and the patient path of cultural survival. —PW

Norberg-Hodge has had the dubious privilege of watching a sustainable society, elegantly coevolved with its environment, fall ill with the virus of development.

A Swedish linguist who went to Ladakh to collect folk stories, Norberg-Hodge was a little incredulous at the happiness, well-being, cooperation, and nonviolence of the Ladakhi people, despite the extremely harsh conditions of their existence. In 1978, the Indian government decided to promote tourism in Ladakh, and instituted development projects. Social deterioration followed with breathtaking speed.

Ancient Futures could stand as a cautionary tale. But the book is no mere epitaph; it is actually a colloquial ethnography of a remarkably sane society, a documentary critique of the Western model of development and a sound and modest proposal for the

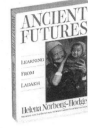

Ancient Futures
Helena Norberg-Hodge,
1991; 204 pp. ISBN 0-87156-643-5
$12 ($15 postpaid). Sierra Club Store Orders, 730 Polk Street, San Francisco, CA 94109; 800/935-1056

The Ladakh Project: PO Box 9475, Berkeley, CA 94709

creation, locally and globally, of a counterforce. —Stephanie Mills [Suggested by Peter Calthorpe]

•

I remember the first time I went with Sonam to visit his family in Hemis Shukpachan. As we sat around the kitchen stove, he described the tourist he'd seen in Leh. "They look so busy," he said. "They never seem to sit still. Just click, click, click . . . "He pretended to take a photograph, to the incomprehension of his audience. Then he patted his little sister on the head; imitating a tourist. " 'Here's a ball-point pen for you.' They're always rushing like this," he said, jumping up and running jerkily around the kitchen. "Why are they in such a hurry?"

Tibet

Their land conquered and spiritual leader exiled; resisting torture, political imprisonment, sterilization, and resource exploitation by the Chinese; and losing their common language, the Tibetans retain magnificent spiritual hope in the Dalai Lama and his seemingly endless wisdom. They also have strong international support for their spirit to return to Lhasa. —PW

The Anguish of Tibet. The best entry book, edited by Petra Kelly, Gert Bastian and Pat Aiello. Parallax Press.

Compassion In Exile. The superb video. (Lemle Pictures, 132 West 31st Street, NY NY 10001; 212/736-9606).

International Campaign for Tibet. The enviro, political, and human rights protection group. (202/628-4123).

The Tibet Fund. A nonprofit supporting Tibet refugee communities as well as Tibetan Buddhist religion and culture. (212/213-5010).

Tibet House. Works to preserve and present Tibet's cultural heritage through media and arts events. (212/213-5592).

In the Autumn of 1987, a Chinese birth control team set up their tent next to our monastery in Amdo (Northeastern Tibet). The villagers were informed that all women had to report to the tent for abortions and sterilizations or there would be grave consequences. Women who went peacefully to the tents and did not resist received medical care. The women who refused to go were taken by force, operated on, and given no medical care. Women nine months pregnant had their babies taken out.

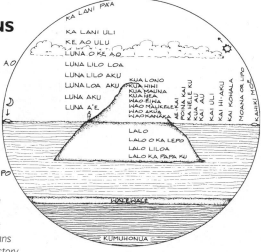

Hawaii

Most denizens of the Free World, even those who have vacationed on Waikiki Beach, know only the Hawaii of TV detective shows, in which the fast-driving, gun-toting hero and nearly all the villains and victims are Caucasian. There is also the Hawaii of American schoolbooks, where the Islands emerge from the void in 1941 as a stage set for Pearl Harbor and vanish again until attaining statehood in 1959. Native Hawaiians have always lived a quite different story of their homeland.

Man, Gods, and Nature traces the migrations of ancestral Polynesians from Java across the Pacific, to the islands at the "top" of the world. Michael Kioni Dudley reconstructs the Hawaiian world view that Western missionaries and landowners nearly succeeded in wiping off the face of the earth.

A Call for Hawaiian Sovereignty gets down to the historical and political nitty-gritty. Rather than hold the reader hostage to historical shame and guilt, the authors tell the Hawaiian story with dispassion and restraint. In assessing the future, they avoid any threat of militance, willing for one last time to trust North Americans' sense of fairness and justice. Between the lines, the emotional struggle is palpable. —Peter Akwai

•

The melting pot ideal may be fine for continental America. And it may be fine for foreigners coming to these islands to become Americans. But when Italian Americans or Japanese Americans, for example, lose themselves in American society, there are still Italians and Japanese in the homeland to preserve the national culture. There is no other homeland where Hawaiians are preserving their national culture. This is their only home. As Hawaiians mix in with others, Hawaiian culture, Hawaiian identity, and the Hawaiians as a people, become extinct. —*A Call for Hawaiian Sovereignty*

The Hawaiian structured his view of the world as a series of belts or levels reaching out from himself and his island. He named levels in the sky above, and within the earth beneath. He named levels of progress up the mountainside and belts around the island as one moved out to sea. —*Man, Gods, and Nature*

A Call for Hawaiian Sovereignty
Michael Kioni Dudley & Keoni Kealoha Agard. 1990; 187 pp. ISBN 1-878751-09-3
Man, Gods and Nature
Michael Kioni Dudley. 1991; 169 pp. ISBN 1-878751-15-8

Each $12.95 ($14.95 each postpaid) from Na Kane O Ka Malo Press, PO Box 970, Waipahu, HI 96794; 808/677-9513

Action groups

Big Island Rainforest Action Group. PO Box 341, Kurtistown, HI 96760. *Fighting geothermal development in the Wao Kele O Puna forest and a dozen other attacks on the remnants of island life.*

Ka La Hui. PO Box 4964, Hilo, HI 96720; 808/961-2888. *The organization for Hawaiian sovereignty, based on the Big Island.*

Hawaii Ecumenical Coalition. PO Box 711, Anahola, HI 96703; 808/822-7444. *Working to Hawaiianize the post-Iniki restoration of Kauai.*

The Conquest Continues: Endangered Holy Places

The Forest Service, the Feds, and some tribal councils have denied the validity of many sacred places with no ruined pyramids or rock cairns. For instance, the University of Arizona and the Vatican plunked their telescopes on the top of Mt. Graham (dzil n'chaa si an), the San Carlos Apache's most sacred mountain.

Dozens of such places are under siege. The law calls these unbuilt sites "intangible cultural properties." For people hammered by disease, land grabs, and military might, they are the source of hope, healing and power. What would we say to Israel putting gun turrets on Cavalry? A telescope through the cupola of St. Paul's Cathedral?

The American Indian Religious Freedom Coalition is working to help revise and strengthen the American Indian Religious Freedom Act. Native Americans and con-servation groups will work together as the revisions will also help preserve beautiful and biologically rich areas. Contact the Coalition c/o Native American Rights Fund. The Association of American Indian Affairs has been powerful in the defense of sacred lands of exceptional natural beauty and spiritual power. —Peter Warshall

Association of American Indian Affairs
245 5th Avenue #1801, New York, NY 10016; 212/689-8720

American Indian Religious Freedom Coalition
Information from Native American Rights Fund, 1506 Broadway, Boulder, CO 80302; 303/447-8760

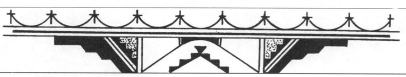

Zuni Conservation Project

The closest North American parallel to the Ladakh project (see p. 73) is the Zuni Sustainable Agriculture Project and Zuni Folk Varieties Project, publishers of *Zuni Farming for Today and Tomorrow*. Many Zunis and two Americans have put together a complex of tasks that sprout more hope every season. They are revitalizing hek:we (waffle gardens) along the Zuni River, funding a Zuni seed bank to preserve diversity, educating Zuni kids, replanting old variety peach orchards, installing soil and water management in the Nutria Irrigation Unit, and testing soils to improve kwa'kya:di' deyatchinanne (dryland farming or runoff field farming). Sound real? About as real as cultural strengthening can get.

•

Have you ever been to the grocery store and seen "Zuni Gold Popcorn" on the shelf? This is a brand being sold by a company in Nevada. How about "Hopi Blue Popcorn," trademarked by a company in Michigan? There is no evidence that these are truly Zuni or Hopi products, but the names of the tribes are being used to sell them to people all over the country.

Often the farm community that developed the crop and food is not asked for permission and is not given any of the profits. Some communities are responding. For example, Indian women from the White Earth Reservation in Minnesota formed the Ikwe Wild Rice Cooperative in 1987 in an effort to provide a surer income to their members harvesting wild rice in reservation lakes. They also wanted to counter the effects of some California companies that are growing large fields of rice and packaging and selling it as "wild rice," which it really is not.

For whatever reasons, Zuni seeds, Zuni foods, and even the name "Zuni" itself are used by people other than the Zuni. Many people in the Zuni community are familiar with this problem in the case of so-called "Zuni" jewelry being produced elsewhere and sold as a Zuni product. Zuni crafts people neither make the pieces or receive any benefits from such sales.

What do the Zuni people think about this in the case of agricultural products? Should Zuni seeds, foods and the Zuni name be shared with all people? What if those people want to make money from them?

Zuni Farming for Today and Tomorrow:
Daniela Soleri & David Cleveland, Editors. Sample copy $1 from Zuni Sustainable Agriculture Project, PO Drawer 630, Zuni, NM 87327; 505/782-5851.

Handbooks of North American Indians

If you have even the faintest interest in the ecological, spiritual, economic, and human history of the place you live, these volumes will be bibles of delight. Each one tells the history of a native people from archeological time until the date of publication. My native friends leaf the pages slowly, qualifying — approving or laughing — looking for family photos and renewed craft ideas. They even find words only their grandma spoke. Great price. —PW

As usual, peerless work. —SB

•

Papagos did not understand the concept of "representative government" in the same way in which that term is generally understood by non-Indians, including BIA administrators. Papagos were generally taught from the time of childhood onward that every human being was "his own man," so to speak, and that he could think for only himself and not for others. Each Papago was responsible for his own thoughts and actions and could not presume to know what lies in the hearts and minds of others. In this sense, then, the notions of "representing" someone else in tribal or community affairs was wholly foreign to Papagos.

In the 1970s, Papago tribal councilmen (both men and women) tended to run tribal council meetings as if they were old-fashioned village or community meetings. They were swayed by the opinions of others present at the council meeting rather than by abstract considerations of "representing" the "constituents" back home. Thus it was that for years in vote after vote of the council there were no dissenting ballots.

Handbooks of North American Indians
Vol. 4: History of Indian-White Relations. 1989; 852 pp. ISBN 0-87474-184-X.$49.25.
Vol. 5: Arctic. 1985; 845 pp. ISBN 0-87474-185-8. $31.25.
Vol. 6: Subarctic. 1981; 836 pp. l ISBN 0-87474-186-6. $27.25.
Vol. 7: Northwest Coast. 1990; 793 pp. ISBN 0-87474-187-4. $40.25.
Vol. 8: California. 1978; 800 pp. ISBN 0-87474-188-2. $27.25.
Vol. 9: Southwest. 1980; 700 pp. ISBN 0-87474-189-0. $25.25.
Vol. 10: Southwest. 1983; 884 pp. ISBN 0-87474-190-4. $27.25.
Vol. 11: Great Basin. 1986; 863 pp. ISBN 0-87474-191-2. $29.25.
Vol 15: Northeast. 1979; 924 pp. ISBN 0-87474-195-5. $29.25.
All prices postpaid from Smithsonian Institution Press/Dept. 900, Blue Ridge Summit, PA 17294; 800/782-4612

Quechan clay figures used in ceremony or for commerce.

NORTH AMERICA was conquered — not settled, not discovered. Half the continent's native tribes are extinct. Eighty percent of the existing languages (149) are no longer taught to children. As native cultures wobble, a robust renaissance has simultaneously dawned. Dozens of Native American writers, artists, videographers, musicians, and photographers have appeared on the horizon as prolific creators of spirit.

Five hundred years later, intermarriages, urban/reservation nomadics, alcohol and BIA junk food, teenage despair, Uncle Tomahawks fighting the traditionals, and the "wannabe" tribe of whites yearning for the spiritual wisdom of medicine people, have all tangled and tortured the lives and clarity of Native American cultures. The final perfection of the Conquest has many times been attained: division of a people against themselves, while the conquerers sit it out and watch. Exploit reservation resources or practice your love of the earth. It wracks the soul of Turtle Island. —Peter Warshall

Katherine Smith with rifle she used to resist relocation at Big Mountain. — Partial Recall

Partial Recall

A watershed publication in Native American history: reflections of Native Americans on photos and images portraying who Indians are supposed to be. —PW

Two Girls on Couch, c. 1910.

●

I like these girls. I am transfixed by this photo. From the moment I saw it, hanging on the wall, surrounded by other photographs of Indians, contemporaries from the turn of the century, I loved it. There they were, these girls surrounded by Curtis boys dripping dentalia and fur — the sepia kings, shot through spit and petroleum jelly, Lords of the Plains, Potentates of the Pot-

latch, the Last-Ofs. I take out my immediate distaste on them, but it's Curtis and the other pinhole illusionists I'm after. *Get a life,* I want to say to them. Quit taking out your fantasies on us. Just give me one in overalls and a cowboy hat. Then we can get serious about what was happening to these people.

—Rayna Green

Partial Recall
(Photographs of Native North Americans)
Lucy R. Lippard. The New Press, 1992; 199 pp. ISBN 1-56584-041-0
$19.95 ($23.45 postpaid) from W.W. Norton & Co./Order Dept., 800 Keystone Industrial Park, Scranton, PA 18512; 800/233-4830

Yaqui Deer Songs

This work is gentle, truthful, quiet, direct. A cooperative effort between a Euroamerican folklorist and a Yaqui poet to record, revive, mull over, and continue the spiritual heart of Yaqui life. A landmark book: it leaves behind that "authority" voice of Anglo-European brittle intellect. There is obvious friendship, like a Sonoran sun rising through the limbs of a chilled saguaro night. —PW

●

Over there, I, at the edge

of the flower-covered enchanted water,

on one wood branch,

I am brown,

dangling, hanging,

mad mountain lion.

Mountain lion is mad,

there in the wilderness,

is mad.

Here, during the concluding stanza, the deer will put down his headdress. The mountain lion sitting there will jump down on it, will pounce on it. He will drag the head around, and when he arrives there in

Practicing at Yoem Pueblo.

Yaqui Deer Songs
(A Native American Poetry)

Larry Evers & Felipe S. Molina. 1986; 239 pp. ISBN 0-8165-09956 $15.95 ($17.95 postpaid) from University of Arizona Press, 1230 N. Park Avenue #102, Tucson, AZ 85719; 602/621-1441

front of us he will lay brush, dry branches, and leaves on it. Then a coyote will arrive and will walk around him, and the mountain lion will punch him. It goes like that.

The Native American Renaissance

For years we reviewed the classics: Black Elk Speaks and Ishi. For years, Native Americans struggled with English and with the American media defining their identity for them. House Made of Dawn stopped that trend. Here are a few of the endless new Native American and mixed-blood novelists and poets carrying the power of oral storytelling into humorous, mystical, existential, loving and fist-in-your-face prose. From my perspective, buy 'em all. —PW [Thanks to Larry Evers.]

American Indian Myths & Legends. Richard Erdoes & Alfonso Ortiz. 1985, Pantheon Books. *One of the best collections of the "old" stories.*

Black Elk Speaks. John G. Neihardt. 1979, University of Nebraska Press. *The power of words can only build muscle if given to your people.*

Ishi in Two Worlds. Theodora Kroeber. 1976, University of California Press. *As close as anthropology ever got to putting a human face on the end of a 10,000 year period of hunter-gatherer history.*

Ceremony. Leslie Marmon Silko. 1977, Penguin Books. *The land itself and its katchina/animal personas help free a citizen from the scars of conquest and war.*

The Death of Jim Loney. James Welch. 1987, Penguin Books. *A stark portrait of a Native American determined to orchestrate his own death, in a modern/traditional ceremony.*

House Made of Dawn. N. Scott Momaday. 1977, HarperCollins Publishers. *The first great novel of the Native American renaissance.*

The Lone Ranger and Tonto Fistfight in Heaven. Sherman Alexie. 1993, Grove/Atlantic Monthly Press. *Punk black comedy on the postmodern rez.*

Love Medicine. Louise Erdrich. 1993, Henry Holt & Co. *The most charming of contemporary Native American writers, she weaves her story with surprises and heart.*

Woven Stone. Simon J. Ortiz. 1992, University of Arizona Press. *The best Native American criticism of colonialism written as poetry.*

Words and Place. 8 videotapes, $150 - $220 each from Norman Ross Publishing Inc., 330 W. 58th St., New York, NY 10019; 800/648-8850, fax 212/765-2393. For 7 day rentals: $37.50 - $52.50 per tape postpaid from AtlAtl, 2303 N. Central Ave, Suite 104, Phoenix, AZ 85004; 602/253-2731. *Videos from the southwest. Hopi Coyote stories, Leslie Marmon Silko, and Harold Littlebird reading Laguna tales and poems, and a conversation with Vine Deloria. Many more.*

Native American Public Broadcasting Consortium: PO Box 83111, Lincoln, NE 68501; 402/472-3522. *The main tributary of Native American voices into the Public Broadcasting System. Ask for their extensive catalog.*

The Conquest of Paradise: Kirkpatrick Sale. 1990, Plume Books. *The earthquake before them and the "new" world shrivels in terror. The most illuminating book on the columbian legacy.*

NOT ALL WOUNDS ARE REPARABLE.

Sometimes we can restore the physiology of an ecosystem — its cycles of water and nutrients — but not its species. Where whole mountains have been stripped by surface mining, the soil and much of the rock are gone. We can *rehabilitate* the landscape, find and furnish nutrient-rich materials like sewage sludge, create a new soil, and then plant the reconstruction. (Start now and you have 2 million acres of stripped earth to rehabilitate in the US alone.) This is more like postcollision plastic surgery than restoration: the land has a useful but completely different face.

If some soil remains in place, we can *reclaim* it; often we can restore its physiology with a few historical species. But very often, the new ecosystem only approximates the old. If the soil is intact, we can truly *restore* a system's original functions and species complex, by removing exotics, allowing natural disturbances to play their role, and replanting and reintroducing close genotypes. Restoring the buffalo commons of North America is one such dream.

All healers must decide: rehabilitate, reclaim, or restore? All healers must think in terms of decades and centuries. If you start with uranium tailings and dream of a piñon-juniper future, you have joined the eco-saints. Remember to read St. Francis! God bless. —Peter Warshall

The Restoration Nexus

The "bulletin board" of environmental restoration, Restoration & Management Notes *features articles plus abstracts from small publications and conferences. The best professional publication is* Restoration Ecology. *Both are from the best organization going: the Society for Ecological Restoration and Management. Join it! — there are local chapters. This is where the philosophy and politics of restoration are getting thrashed out.* —Richard Nilsen

•

Ecological restoration is not only the rehabilitation of the environment, it is a celebration of a new relationship with nature, and can be regarded as in some sense a new genre of ritual. We are already seeing this with events like the Land Institute's Prairie Festival in Kansas, Native Seeds/SEARCH's native plant festivals, and the burnings of grasslands here in the Midwest. For many people these activities have become exciting community events. These events show how restoration can become the occasion for fostering and expressing a new consciousness of ourselves as participating members of the land community.

•

We carry out restoration in six steps: scarification, stabilization, filling, planting and seeding, site protection, and monitoring. . . . Continued trampling of bareground sites has resulted in severely compacted soil on many social trails. Our first step on these sites is to scarify or loosen the soil to enhance root penetration and water percolation. Although all our work is labor-intensive, this step is perhaps the most tedious and least enjoyable. Each site is scarified to a depth of 10-15 cm with a pulaski (a single-bit ax with an adz-shaped hoe extending from the back, commonly used to dig fire lines) or shovel and then individual soil clods are broken up by hand. In areas that have lost more than five cm of soil, the crew then installs wood or rock silt bars, placing them within the impact and below the ground surface to reduce erosion.

•

Instant results make us look good fast, which is particularly tempting when we are dealing with clients, agencies, donors, and legislators. The temptation to maintain systems in a near-constant condition by high-frequency, low-intensity manipulations is often difficult to resist. Such micromanagement efforts may produce a result that continually looks like the desired "snapshot," but that involves labor-intensive and costly means that may bear little relation to natural ecosystem-maintenance mechanisms. Again, the question of appearance rather than function arises.

Restoration & Management Notes
$30/year (2 issues)
Restoration Ecology
$53/year (4 issues)
Both $64/year. Society for Ecological Restoration/University of Wisconsin Arboretum, 1207 Seminole Highway, Madison, WI 53711; 608/262-9547.

What may be preferable is a more patient, longer-term management program in which disturbances are rotated around through different areas within a landscape, so that any given area is disturbed less frequently but more severely than is now commonplace in restoration projects. This would require us to tolerate periods when portions of an area may be in an earlier successional stage than a particular snapshot depicted. —R&MN

Other Publications on Restoration

American Midland Naturalist: $75/year (4 issues). University of Notre Dame, Notre Dame, IN 46556. One of the best experimental-science journals available to the restoration community. It's not overly laden with technical jargon and unruly statistics. Worth having as a subscriber or through a college library.

Natural Areas Journal: Don Leopold, Editor. $25/year (4 issues). 108 Fox Street, Mukwonago, WI 53149. Reports from natural areas about rare-species management and monitoring as part of overall ecosystem management. Well written, good biblios on recent restoration issues.

Park Science: 4150 Southwest Fairhaven Drive, Corvallis, OR 97333. This newsletter has a solid commitment to scientific and restoration activities.

Environmental Conservation Journal: $197/year (4 issues). Elsevier Science Publishing Co., 655 6th Avenue, New York, NY 10010; 212/989-5800, fax 212/633-3990. The only journal that covers the whole Earth. Dedicated to counteracting enviro deterioration. Scan it for restoration articles.

Helping Nature Heal

It's a humane collection of vignettes on the (totally interdependent) restoration of mind, body, soul, and Earth by Whole Earth's wise man, Richard Nilsen. Theory and practice, at home, with love. —PW

•

Restoration work is not fixing beautiful machinery — replacing stolen parts, adding fresh lubricants, cobbling and welding and rewiring. It is accepting an abandoned responsibility. It is a humble and often joyful mending of biological ties, with a hope, clearly recognized, that working from this foundation we might, too, begin to mend human society.

•

Along the northern coast of California, salmon fishing has been a major source of protein and income as long as humans have lived here. By the late 1970s, the combination of growing fleet and dwindling salmon runs had many fishermen casting about for a new occupation. But the number of small one- and two-person trollers kept growing, and among the new members of the fleet were younger fishermen who were to become leaders in an exercise in consciousness-raising for the industry. In a very short time, these notoriously independent opera-

Helping Nature Heal
(An Introduction to Environmental Restoration)
Richard Nilsen, Editor. 1991; 152 pp.
ISBN 0-89815-425-1
$14.95 ($18.45 postpaid). Ten Speed Press, PO Box 7123, Berkeley, CA 94707; 800/841-2665

tors were to learn a new and reciprocal relationship to the resource which would allow them to continue in business.

Nat Bingham convinced commercial salmon fisherman to tax themselves in support of stream-repair projects that have helped to restore the salmon and preserve the livelihood of the fishermen.

•

So how do we go about repairing what has already been mucked up? For many of us, the first step is to slow down enough to observe that natural processes already at work, and to realize that restoration goes on for more than just our lifetime. It is both a big process and very discrete, and it begins with our actions in specific places.

Fire, key to the restoration of many ecosystems, dramatizes the need to conceive restoration goals in cinematographic rather than photographic terms. Shown here: prescribed burning of coastal heathland in Massachusetts. —R&MN

Bioscience: $52/year (membership includes 11 issues). American Institute for Biological Sciences, 730 11th Street NW, Washington, DC 20001; 202/628-1500. Pretty technical; scan for genetics and biodiversity.

Biological Conservation: $830/year (12 issues). Elsevier Science Publishing Co., 655 6th Avenue, New York, NY 10010; 212/989-5800, fax 212/633-3990.

Watershed Protection Techniques: Center for Watershed Protection, 1020 Elden Street, Suite 205, Herndon, VA 22076; 703/709-0040.

Land and Water: $14.40/year (6 issues). PO Box 1197, Fort Dodge, IA 50501; 515/576-3191, fax 515/576-2606. Heavy civil engineering, exotic grasses. This

is the arena for change. Viable alternatives to heavy-handed water- and earthworks are the future. Many good tools are advertised: BioLogs, Grasscrete, Geotextile. —PW [Suggested by Dave Egan]

OTHER GREAT RESOURCES

Environmental Restoration (Science and Strategies for Restoring the Earth): John Berger, Editor. 1990, Island Press. The best collection of technical papers on the widest range of topics; the path-restorer publication.

Restoration Ecology (A Synthetic Approach to Ecological Research): William R. Jordan, Michael E. Gilpin & John D. Aber. 1990, Cambridge University Press. The embryological theoretics of intentionally altering a piece of the Earth to emulate the structure and function of a historic ecosystem.

The Nature Conservancy

The Nature Conservancy: membership $15/year (includes 6 issues of *Nature Conservancy*). 1815 North Lynn Street, Arlington, VA 22209; 703/841-5300.

Your kids will thank The Nature Conservancy as God's gift to the Earth. NC has bought and manages more than 1,500 sanctuaries (five million acres plus), now with an effective and expanding program in Latin America. NC has done what a good government should have done. With more

The jaguar was revered by the Mayas who once flourished in the ancient city of Milpa.

than 550,000 members and a $170 million budget, America's single largest landholder deserves thanks from me, the next seven generations, and the endangered flowers and birds. They manage their purchases with (for my money) the best network of volunteer and professional land stewards. Some

NC preserves are the planet's best laboratories for restoration ecology, including crowd control. —PW

See also **Biological Conservation** (p. 100).

OTHER GREAT RESOURCES

Debt-for-Nature Exchange: Conservation International, 1015 18th Street NW #1000, Washington, DC 20036; 202/429-5660. To preserve land and cultures, a few international conservation organizations have bought national debt in exchange for land setasides. This is how it's done and how you can help.

The Conservation Easement Handbook (Managing Land Conservation & Historic Preservation Easement Programs): Janet Diehl & Thomas S. Barrett. 1988. The best access to good easements in urban environments.

Activist Groups, Saving Land

Ducks Unlimited. The 500,000-member Ducks Unlimited has been responsible for the preservation of more waterbird breeding grounds (especially marshlands) than any government or other group. Working internationally (ducks haven't learned about Canadian, US, and Mexican boundaries), Ducks Unlimited restores, manages, and purchases wetlands throughout North American waterfowl flyways. Their magazine is both intelligent and beautiful. —PW and Don Ryan

Isaak Walton League. A half-century old, the Isaak Walton League knows the meaning of sustainable works. This endowment was organized to help rebuild Outdoor America by the acquisition, for governmental agencies, of unique natural areas. With a Midwestern twang and a rooted morality, the League educates (Outdoor Ethics Newsletter) and celebrates (Outdoor America) the conservation and restoration of US natural treasures. —PW

The Trust for Public Land. Problem: a couple thousand acres of pristine scenery has been put up for sale. Realty developers are eyeing it hungrily, but it really ought to be a park. Can the state get the money together in time? The Trust for Public Land specializes in the quick move. They arrange to hold the land or historical site until it can be purchased for use as a public resource — a process that

typically takes considerable time. TPL is not an advocacy organization (you can't even join 'em!). But you can contribute financially to their important work. —JB

•

At the Audubon Society's request, TPL approached the landowner about selling the property. When the landowner resisted, the Audubon Society went to the public, talking-up their project, catching the attention of the media. They soon gained the support of a half a dozen local groups, including Quality Forward, the French Broad River Foundation, the League of Women Voters, the Sierra Club, and the Asheville Council of Garden Clubs. In May of 1988, the developer optioned the property to TPL.

Ducks Unlimited: One Waterfowl Way, Memphis, TN 38120; 901/758-3825.
Isaak Walton League of America Endowment: PO Box 824, Iowa City, IA 52244; 319/351-7037.
Trust for Public Land: 116 New Montgomery Street, 4th Floor, San Francisco, CA 94105; 415/495-4014.

Land-Saving Action

The last decade has seen a tremendous expansion of private-sector preservation of open-space lands. This book, with chapters by twenty-nine experts, embodies the experience that ten years has produced, and will serve as a bible for anyone who loves a piece of land enough to want to find out how to save it. —Richard Nilsen

•

Community support is vital in determining surrounding land users. The uses of the land neighboring the preserved agricultural land are of vital concern. A single farming operation, no matter how well laid out and managed, faces tremendous odds without compatible neighbors. Nuisance ordinances outlawing livestock operations and restricting spraying emerge in communities where too many farms have turned into ranchettes and other homesites for city folk. Protecting one parcel of agricultural land requires consideration of the guarantees that ensure that the surrounding land uses will stay compatible. Otherwise, that parcel is likely to become the preserved open space for adjacent development.

Land-Saving Action
Russell L. Brenneman & Sarah M. Bates, Editors. 1984; 249 pp. ISBN 0-933280-22-X $24.95 ($29.20 postpaid). Island Press, Box 7, Covelo, CA 95428; 800/828-1302

Preserving Family Lands

Preserving Family Lands (Essential Tax Strategies for the Landowner) Stephen J. Small. Landowner Planning Center, 1992; 99 pp. ISBN 0-9624557-1-7 $8.95 ($11.95 postpaid). Preserving Family Lands, PO Box 2242, Boston MA 02101

The two-pronged strategy: keep the taxman away; keep the land as it is. This is the field guide to estate taxes, gifts in the will, conservation easements and their tax consequences. Every conservation organization needs a copy, especially for the hardwood forestlands of the East. —PW

•

You may be entitled to an income tax deduction for protecting your property from development. That protection takes the form of a recorded restriction on your property, known as a "conservation easement" or a "conservation restriction." When you create a conservation easement and donate it to a charitable organization you still own your land; the size of the income tax deduction is based on the value of the development rights you give up. In addition, since you are reducing the value of your property, the value of your taxable estate drops, your estate tax drops, and your property tax should be lowered.

•

A second tax incentive for land conservation is a "remainder interest." With a remainder interest, a landowner retains the right to live on his or her land until death, and at death the land goes to the charitable organization.

•

A further possible approach to family land planning and estate planning involves giving your property to other family members while you are alive. A lot of incorrect thinking exists about this subject.

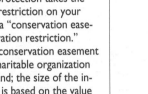

—Ducks Unlimited

Conflict Resolution

Ranging from the most necessary skill-ful means to pure hype, conflict resolution is for those with a distaste for pro-longed court litigation and costs and civil disobedience. Information sharing, facilitation, mediation, alternative dispute resolution, consensus building — the vowel-ful latinate phrases bring on a subtextual ache for tough Saxon words. Wanna duke it out? Can we shoot the shit instead?

Resolving Environmental Disputes has great vignettes and thoughts about the relevance of and place for mediation. The Conservation Foundation's RESOLVE (Center for Environmental Conflict Resolution) gives this book backbone. Breaking the Impasse considers the big picture, with a great bibliography and good thoughts on fairness, wisdom, zero-sum and integrative approaches. —PW

●

Storm King

The dispute: Opposition to Consolidated Edison Company of New York's plans to build a hydroelectric and pumped storage plant at the foot of Storm King Mountain in the Hudson River highlands first arose when the Scenic Hudson Preservation Conference was formed late in 1963. Over the years, the issues involved in the dispute spread from simply whether the plant would unacceptably mar the scenic beauty of the Hudson to broad questions of the total effect of several utility plants on the water quality and the fish life of the Hudson River.

Resolving Environmental Disputes
Gail Bingham, The Conservation Foundation. 1986; 284 pp. ISBN 0-89164-087-8
$15 ($17 postpaid). World Wildlife Fund, PO Box 4866, Hampden Station, Baltimore, MD 21211; 410/516-6951

The process: After a decade and a half of litigation and administrative hearings, attorneys for the environmental groups and Consolidated Edison discussed negotiating face to face and, in March 1979, asked Russell Train to mediate the dispute. Train spent several months laying the groundwork for negotiations and began them in August 1979. On December 1, 1980, 11 parties signed an agreement that ended the dispute.

The result: Consolidated Edison forfeited its construction license for Storm King and turned the land over to the Palisades Interstate Parkway Commission. To protect striped bass and other fish species, the utilities agreed to establish a fish hatchery and to reduce, for 10 years, their withdrawals of water from the river during the summer months. They further agreed not to build any new power plants without cooling towers above the George Washington Bridge for 25 years, to endow a river research organization, and to reimburse legal fees to the environmental groups. in return for these concessions, EPA dropped its de-

Breaking the Impasse
(Consensual Approaches to Resolving Public Disputes)
Lawrence Susskind & Jeffrey L. Cruikshank. Basic Books, 1987; 288 pp.
ISBN 0-465-00750-3
$15 ($17.75 postpaid). HarperCollins Publishers/Direct Mail, PO Box 588, Dunmore, PA 18512; 800/331-3761

mands for expensive cooling towers at several of the existing plants, and the environmental groups dropped legal and administrative challenges against the utilities. A year after the settlement, New York State issued discharge permits, incorporating the terms of the mediated settlement, to the utilities. All aspects of the settlement have been implemented. —*Resolving Environmental Disputes*

●

The "zero-sum" approach assumes that there are only limited gains available. Whatever one group wins, the other groups lose. Thus, the pluses to one side are balanced out by the minuses to the other side, yielding a total of zero — a "zero sum."

If a dispute concerns the allocation of a limited supply of water, for example, the negotiation will undoubtedly be framed as a zero-sum exercise: additional gallons gained by one party must be given up by others. In such a situation, the opening positions taken by the parties are crucial. An opening bid, so to speak, can "anchor" the final outcome. —*Breaking the Impasse*

Just What Is An EIR? • How To Write Quality EISs and EAs

In 1971, President Nixon signed the National Environmental Policy Act. It kind of slipped through in the new untested waters of earth-consciousness. It has been the most profound and important new element in participatory democracy since women gained the vote. Industrial elitists and neoclassical economists tried to squash environmental-impact reporting (EIR) by claiming it stopped progress. But EIRs simply improved the design of public projects like the Alaska pipeline, made developers more thoughtful about long-term consequences of their short-term profit motives, and everyone aware of the cumulative effects of our lives on the planet.

Just What Is An EIR? is a seasoned one hundred-page intro with perspectives from Sweden, the Netherlands, and England. It is excellent for town plans, sensitive areas, growth inducement, and alternatives. If you actually need to write or criticize an EIR, then How To is a step-by-step guide. No frills, essential.—PW

●

Be cautious about using the words *significant* or *significantly*. If you use either of these words, you must explain as precisely as you can, in terms of the context and intensity of the effects, exactly how you are using the term.

●

"Mitigation" includes:

(a) Avoiding the impact altogether by not taking a certain action or parts of an action.

(b) Minimizing impacts by limiting the degree or magnitude of the action and its implementation.

(c) Rectifying the impact by repairing, rehabilitating, or restoring the affected environment.

(d) Reducing or eliminating the impact over time by preservation and maintenance operations during the life of the action.

(e) Compensating for the impact by replacing or providing substitute resources or environments. —*How To*

●

"No Project" Alternative

Initially there was a good deal of resistance to preparing a "no project" alternative, at least in California. Many developers and project proponents (including government agencies) asked, "If our goal is to build a project, what possible good comes from planning *not* to build it?"

The "good" is this: by preparing an analysis of the "no project" alternative, it's actually possible to develop a clearer statement of the need for the project! The "no" alternative gives planners and decision makers a better framework for evaluating the "yes" alternatives. To the surprise of many environmental activists, the "no" alternative is sometimes more damaging to the environment than other project alternatives.

Just What Is An EIR
James A. Roberts. 1991; 208 pp.
ISBN 0-9630515-0-4
$14 postpaid. Global Environmental Management Service, 2862 Arden Way, Suite 215, Sacramento, CA 95825; 916/483-1564

How to Write Quality EISs and EAs
Larry H. Freeman. 1992; 84 pp.
ISBN 0-933427-98-0
$22.95 ($26.95 postpaid). Shipley Associates Attn: Products Dept., PO Box 460, Bountiful, Utah 84011; 801/299-4700

Each resource you analyze should have its own map showing the extent of the anaylsis.
—*How to Write Quality EISs and EAs.*

●

Now EIR offers the public a way to be involved in the decision-making process. Individuals or groups can help define what is to be studied, and they can suggest and analyze alternatives. They can present evidence about potential consequences and be involved in a way that has the double benefit of producing better projects and better-informed citizens.

The EIR process has not always been easy. Many well-meaning politicians and engineers have protested, "We never did it that way before; we have always built the 'best' plan and told the public what was decided." But now the 'best plan' must include elements defined by the public as well as what is important to experts and politicians. EIR has proved to be an excellent way to receive input from the public in an orderly and pro-

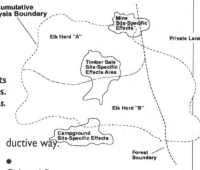

ductive way.

●

Cultural Resources

a. Will the proposal result in the alteration of or the destruction of a prehistoric or historic archaeological site?

b. Will the proposal result in adverse physical or aesthetic effects to a prehistoric or historic building, structure, or object?

c. Does the proposal have the potential to cause a physical change which would affect unique ethnic cultural values?

d. Will the proposal restrict existing religious or sacred uses within the potential impact area? —*Just What Is*

photo from *By Nature's Design*, see pg. 233

STREAMING WISDOM

Watershed Consciousness in the Twenty-First Century

—Peter Warshall

In our towns and cities, two of the essential sources of life — water to drink and soil to grow food — remain hidden from our eyes. The hills and valleys are coated with asphalt; ancient streams are buried beneath housing; and soil is filler between gas, water and electric piping. Watershed consciousness is, in part, an invitation to peel off (not discard) the layer of industrial and technological activity that hides us from the water and soils of our communities. It is an invitation to reveal where you live and how your body's plumbing and, in many ways, community heart, are connected to Nature's pathways.

A watershed is a gatherer — a living place that draws the sun and the rain together. Its surface of soils, rocks, and plantlife acts as a "commons" for this intermingling of sun and water. Physically, a watershed takes many shapes. It is drawn emblematically in the shape of a teardrop or a cupped leaf or a garden trowel, to depict the oblong dish-shape of the valley, with its hillslopes that gather runoff toward a central stream. But most watersheds do not faithfully copy the emblematic drawings. Uplifting or faulting or downwarping or layering give them a beautiful individuality. Human influences may distort or, as in city watersheds and strip-mining, completely destroy the original lay of the land. The bedrock texture of each watershed — its granite or shale, sand or limestone — holds (in a sense, cherishes) each watershed's fragile skin of soil. After the sun/water gathering has been accomplished, the watershed lets go: its unused water heads downstream or sky-up; its unabsorbed energy turns to heat or reflects back through the atmosphere. This seasonal and daily passage of solar fire, water flow, and the earth's metabolic breathing is as unique, in each watershed, as in each human on the planet.

For humans, the watershed (and its big cousin, the river basin) is a hydraulic commons — an aquatic contract that has no escape clause. The forested headwaters to the agricultural midstream valleys to the commercial and industrial centers at the river's mouth, good and bad news travels by way of water. Did my toilet flushing give downstream swimmers a gastrointestinal disease? Did the headwaters clear-cut kill the salmon industry at the river's mouth? Did my city's need for water drain off a river and close upriver farmland that fed me fresh vegetables? Did a toxic-waste dump leak into the groundwater table and poison people in the next county? Watershed consciousness is, in part, a campaign to advertise the mutual concerns and needs that bind upstream and downstream, instream and offstream peoples together.

This journey is right out your window — among the hills and valleys that surround you. It is the first excursion of thought into the place you live. It is not inner geography — the continual attempt to feel better by mapping the mysterious meanderings of our hearts and minds — nor is it whole Earth geography — the struggle to gain perspective of our place on the planet. It focuses on where your water comes from when you turn on the faucet; where it goes when you flush; what soils produce your food; who shares your water supply, including the fish and other non-human creatures. The watershed way is a middle way, singing a local song, somewhere close by, between Mind and Planet.

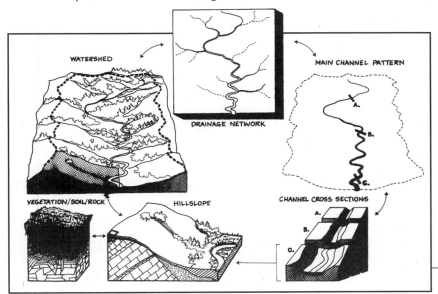

WATERSHED

MAIN CHANNEL PATTERN

DRAINAGE NETWORK

VEGETATION/SOIL/ROCK

HILLSLOPE

CHANNEL CROSS SECTIONS

THE HOME-REPAIR QUIZ

1. When you turn on your faucet, where does the water come from? (Can you trace it back to local storm systems?)
2. When you flush the toilet, where does the water go? (not just the treatment plant, but the final river or lake).
3. What soil series are you standing on?
4. How long is the growing season?
5. What are the major geological events that shaped your watershed (faults, uplifts, downwarps, volcanics, sea floods, etc.)? Does your community give them special attention: are they sacred, blessed, protected?
6. How did the original inhabitants eat, clothe, and shelter themselves? How did they celebrate the seasonal changes in times before you?
7. How many days until the moon is full?
8. From where you are sitting, point north.
9. What bioregions of the planet have the most similar climate, and culture, and analogous plants and animals? In other words, who are your Gaian cousins?
10. Name the major plant/animal associations that thrive in your bioregion. Name five resident and migratory birds; five grasses; five trees; five mammals and reptiles or amphibians. Which are native?
11. Name the plant or animal that is the "barometer" of environmental health for your bioregion. How's it doing? Endangered? Thriving? Has it become a symbol or totem of local power for your community?
12. Name the bioregions that grew each item of food on your dinner plate. Could you eat more locally? Support nearby farms?
13. Where does your garbage go? Is the landfill nearly full?
14. What heavenly events most influence life in your bioregion? (fire? lightning? hail? tornadoes? fog? blizzards? drought? permafrost? chubascos? spring thaw?)

—Peter Warshall, Leonard Charles, Jim Dodge, Lynn Milliman, and Victoria Stockley.

Entering the Watershed • Clean Water in Your Watershed

These two headwater books provide the tools to gather your hopes and information and community to confront the eternal frustrations of national politics. **Clean Water** *provides the best guide to how the process would ideally work — in a world without agency power plays, greed and connivance, and every other special-interest pressure that makes watershed protection real and tough. You learn the lingo: Best Management Practices (BMPs), Memorandums of Understanding (MOUs), monitoring protocols. The guide is oriented to surface runoff and smaller, more urban watersheds.* **Entering Your Watershed** *has no illusions. In a fighting tone it clearly lays out what watershed and ecosystem management must mean, in order to avoid the double speak of the Beltway, and explains how to organize to save benchmark watersheds, biological hot spots, riparian areas and healthy headwaters. It focuses more on whole river basins and more forested watersheds.* —PW

Entering the Watershed
(A New Approach to Save America's River Ecosystems)
Bob Doppelt, et al. 1993; 462 pp.
ISBN 1-55963-275-5
$27.50 ($31.75 postpaid) from Island Press, Box 7, Covelo, CA 95428; 800/828-1302

Clean Water in Your Watershed
(A Citizen's Guide to Watershed Protection)
$19.95 ($22.95 postpaid). Terrene Institute, 1717 K Street NW, Washington, DC 20006; 202/833-8317

•
[The Rapid Biotic and Ecosystem Response] approach differs significantly from the traditional piecemeal protection approaches that focus on discrete river segments with little sense of their importance to the problems or needs of the entire system. This approach also places the emphasis on preventing further degradation rather than on attempting to control or repair damage after it occurs. Prevention is more effective and cost-efficient than control or repair measures, which have failed in most cases.
—*Entering the Watershed*

•
Two types of critical areas are found in every watershed; the first type includes areas adjacent to or near the waterbody; the second includes areas that may contribute large amounts or high concentrations of pollutants to the watershed regardless of their location. Your group should consider the following critical areas:
• areas adjacent to waterbody;
• areas near a waterbody (within one-fourth mile);

• areas that contain direct discharges to a waterbody (pipes, ditches, tanks);
• areas that have intense land-use patterns, such as trailer parks and animal feedlots;
• areas that are used for higher risk purposes, and
• geologically vulnerable areas (natural or constructed), such as shallow soils overlying fractured limestone, bedrock, or areas where many test wells were drilled and abandoned. —*Clean Water*

Sensitive Chaos

Flowing forms our heart, cyclones, rivers and birdflight. We flowed as embryos, and our bones still spiral and loop with the markings of past eddy currents. Here is spiritual guidance in the greatest book of Jungian-Taoist fluid history. —Peter Warshall

●

Trains of vortices arise if a solid object is drawn in a straight line through stationary liquid.

In the open sea mighty vortices can arise in which the whole dynamic force of the suction centre becomes visible.

A photograph of a vortex taken under water reveals the spiralling surface between the water and the air which is being sucked in.

●

The activity of thinking is essentially an expression of flowing movement. Only when thinking dwells on a particular content, a particular form, does it order itself accordingly and create an idea. Every idea — like every organic form — arises in a process of flow, until the movement congeals into a form. Therefore we speak of a capacity to think fluently when someone is skilfully able to carry out this creation of form in thought, harmoniously co-ordinating the

Sensitive Chaos
(The Creation of Flowing Forms in Water & Air)
Theodor Schwenk. 1990; 232 pp.
ISBN 0-85440-304-3
$29.95 ($33.45 postpaid).
Anthroposophic Press, RR 4, Box 94A1, Hudson, NY 12534; 518/851-2054

stream of thoughts and progressing from one idea to another without digression — without creating "whirlpools."

●

In a stream: The wave form remains at the same spot with new water constantly flowing through it.

In the sea: The wave form wanders across the surface, the water itself remaining at the same place.

Through wave movements, of whatever kind, water reveals its extremely impressionable nature. A stone in the stream, a gentle breeze blowing over the surface of a

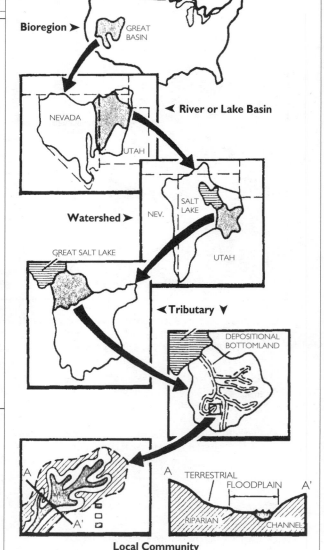

Trains of vortices arise if a solid object is drawn in a straight line through stationary liquid.

lake, the slightest thing will cause the water to respond immediately with a rhythmical movement. Two things are necessary for this rhythmical movement to come about: the water itself and some other activating force. Thus water is like a sense organ, which becomes "aware" of the smallest impacts and immediately brings the contrasting forces to a moving rhythmical balance.

●

As the sounds of the external world enter, whole vortex trains pass through the fluid of the internal ear. In connection with this a sorting out of rhythms takes place, by which the long wave trains of the low frequency low notes

reach the end of the basilar membrane, while the short, quick rhythms of the high notes fade away right at the start. On a minute scale and as an organic function, this is the counterpart to the great sorting out process of the different types of waves in the oceans of the earth.

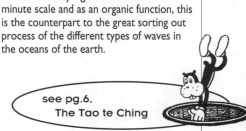

see pg.6,
The Tao te Ching

Cadillac Desert

The word river comes from rivalis, meaning rivals — and all over the West, humans are still throwing rocks at each other, from one bank to the other. As they say in the Valley, water flows downhill except when it flows uphill — toward money. Cadillac Desert condenses squalls of data into the most comprehensive tour of power magnates and megagallons. —PW

●

George Gillette, chairman of the Fort Berthold Indian Tribe Business Council, weeps as he watches Secretary of the Interior J.A. Krug sign a contract whereby the tribe sells 155,000 acres of its reservation's best land in North Dakota to the government for the Garrison Dam and Reservoir Project on May 20, 1948. Gillette said of the sale: "The members of the Tribal Council sign the contract with heavy hearts. . . . Right now, the future does not look good to us."

●

The simplest and cheapest way to solve Mexico's salinity crisis would have been for the U.S. government to buy out the Wellton-Mohawk farmers and retire their lands. Even today, a generous settlement probably would not cost more than a couple of hundred million dollars, and a tremendous source of salts would be removed. The solution

of choice at Wellton-Mohawk has been the construction of a reverse-osmosis desalination plant — ten times larger than any in the world — which, while consuming enough electricity to satisfy a city of forty thousand people, will treat the wastewater running out the drain canal. The legislation authorizing all of these works belongs in a class of Congressional sacred cows—whatever it costs to keep salinity levels down without retiring an acre of salt-ridden land is what Congress is willing to spend. The Yuma plant is now supposed to cost $293 million, a figure hardly anyone outside the Bureau believes. Energy costs could easily push the Yuma plant's cost to $1 billion or more over fifty years.

What Congress has chosen to do, in effect, is purify water at a cost exceeding $300 an acre-foot so that upriver irrigators can continue to grow surplus crops with federally subsidized water that costs them $3.50 an acre-foot.

Cadillac Desert
Marc Reisner. Penguin Books, 1993; 582 pp. ISBN 0-14-017824-4
$14 ($16 postpaid). Penguin USA/Consumer Sales, 120 Woodbine Street, Bergenfield, NJ 07621; 800/253-6476

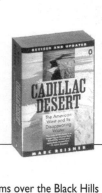

From Bioregion to Local Community

Bioregion ▶ GREAT BASIN

◀ River or Lake Basin

NEVADA UTAH

Watershed ▶ NEV. SALT LAKE

GREAT SALT LAKE UTAH

◀ Tributary ▼ DEPOSITIONAL BOTTOMLAND

A A' TERRESTRIAL FLOODPLAIN A A' RIPARIAN CHANNEL

Local Community

Water in Environmental Planning

The diamond text of clear watershed knowledge. Great vignettes. Important, at times difficult, aquatic math. Superlative chapter on floods. (I wish Luna Leopold's Water, the mathless paperback, was back in print.) —PW

Water in Environmental Planning
Thomas Dunne & Luna Leopold. 1978; 818 pp. ISBN 0-7167-0079-4
$51.95 ($54.95 postpaid). W.H. Freeman and Co., 4419 W. 1980 S., Salt Lake City, UT 84104; 800/488-5233

●

On the evening of June 9, 1972, a group of thunderstorms over the Black Hills of South Dakota poured more than 10 inches of rain within 6 hours onto an area of 60 sq. mi. Rivers draining the steep valleys of the region rose quickly, and around midnight devastating floods swept through campgrounds in the valley bottom and through towns and villages situated where the rivers drain from the hills onto the Great Plains. The largest of these towns is Rapid City, situated on Rapid Creek. . . .

Despite a warning broadcast by the mayor, most people stayed in their homes and were caught there when the flood hit the town. The river eventually rose 14 feet in about 4 hours, and 3.5 feet during one period of 15 minutes. Two hundred and thirty-seven people died in the flood, 3057 were injured, and the total cost of the damage was estimated by the Corps of Engineers to exceed $160,000,000 of which less than $300,000 was insured. Five thousand automobiles and 1335 homes were destroyed, while 2820 homes suffered major damage.

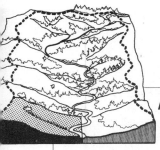

Mapping Your Watershed

Relax, take your time. The maps will begin to enter your dreams and change your percepts. I like walking Manhattan, spotting the old ponds as collapsed pockets of asphalt or feeling the divide between the East and Hudson Rivers.

Step 1: Gather your county soil map, the USGS map, and the road (highway) map. For history, find old maps and photos, especially low-altitude aerials. Start with any "outdoors" store and the Yellow Pages, under "Photographers — Aerial" and "Maps." Visit the local historical society and library.

Step 2: Trace the watershed divide(s).

Step 3: Color the streams by the number

of tributaries and star the high spots and unique spots.

Step 4: Overlay the human influences — storm sewers, outfalls, channelized stretches of creek, floodplains, and flood structures.

Step 5: Think of how to harmonize the ecostructure with the infrastructure. Think with friends.

USGS Topographic Maps and Low-Altitude Photographs

For your watershed mapping, you will want the basic contour maps at 1" = 2000' and 1" = 1 mile. The best sources are local map, blueprint, and outdoor stores.

The pictorial "maps" of North America are now diverse (infrared, radar, low-altitude aerial photographs) and becoming centralized. The newly devised search and inquiry

system for all US agency and commercial mapping comes by way of an extensive question-and-answer push-button phone journey run by the USGS Earth Science Information Center (phone 800/USA-MAPS).

The phone-tree leads you to aerial photography summary records, either as lists or plotted on maps (microfiched). The phone-tree can also lead you to more expensive detailed searches and special searches for side-looking airborne radar, which shows the topography beneath the trees. Agricultural Stabilization Conservation Service (ASCS) low-altitude aerials (some are 1" = 400') are available between $6 and $65. Call 801/975-3503, and they will call you back. Be sure you know latitude and longitude in degrees and seconds.

If still unsatisfied, try the EROS Data Center, via 800/USA-MAPS. —PW

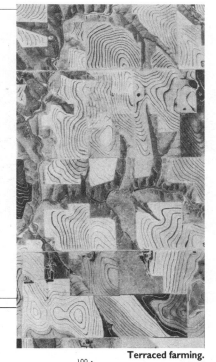

Terraced farming.
—ASCS

Terrain Analysis

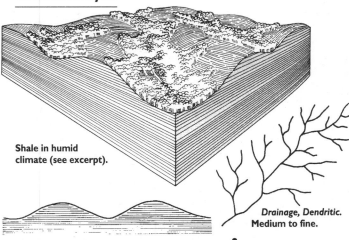

Shale in humid climate (see excerpt).

Topography, Soft Hills. A smooth, sag-and-swale topography occurs, appearing as soft hills and mounds. Sharp breaks in slopes are neither common nor stable. The attitude of the bedding layers does not affect the appearance of the topography.

Discover your bedrock and your landform. Look under humid shale or arid limestone, under glacial moraines or wind-laid landforms. Terrain Analysis will give you the Big Picture of your watershed and other areas with similar watersheds (watershed friends with similar lives and concerns). It will lay out the major conservation-based development issues: landslides or septic tanks, building slabs or bridges. Each area has a typical drainage basin, soil profile, landform description, aerial photo, and USGS contour map. It's out of print — photocopy your local landscape at the nearest library. —PW

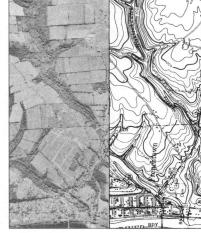

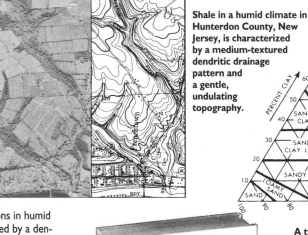

Drainage, Dendritic. Medium to fine.

Shale: Humid climate. Shale regions in humid climates are moderately dissected by a dendritic drainage pattern. The gently rolling uplands are cultivated or in forest cover. Even if cultivated, the slopes facing the drainage system generally remain wooded, providing rich wildlife habitats. Vegetative associations vary according to changes in microclimate and orientation. Few swamps and natural water bodies are found because of the extensive drainage system. The residual soils are fairly homogeneous over large areas and do not significantly determine changes in vegetative associations, except in major valleys. The overall landscape pattern forms a rather treelike corridor system, reflecting the drainage pattern and the steep, uncultivated slopes.

Traveling through a shale landscape in a humid climate exposes the viewer to a rolling topography covered with farms, pasture land, and some crops, with many subtle changes in scene but few regional views.

Shale in a humid climate in Hunterdon County, New Jersey, is characterized by a medium-textured dendritic drainage pattern and a gentle, undulating topography.

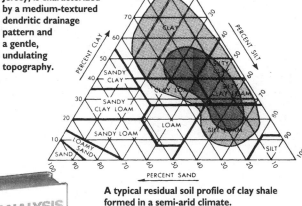

Terrain Analysis: Douglas S. Way. 1978, Dowden, Hutchinson & Ross, Inc. Out of Print.

The smooth, undulating topography offers limited visual spatial change; that is, hilltops tend to occur at the same elevation, and, though major valleys offer some degree of visual closure, the valley walls are not usually steep enough to create tight spatial enclosure.

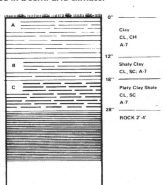

A typical residual soil profile of clay shale formed in a semi-arid climate.

		0"
A		Clay / CL, CH / A-7
B	12"	Shaly Clay / CL, SC; A-7
C	18"	Platy Clay Shale / CL, SC / A-7
	28"	ROCK 2'-4'

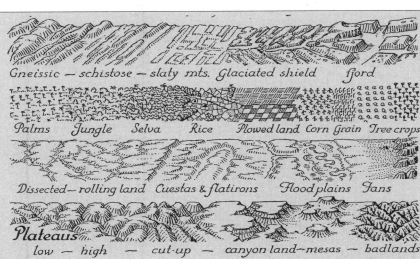

Gneissic — schistose — slaty mts. Glaciated shield   fjord

Palms   Jungle   Selva   Rice   Plowed land   Corn grain   Tree crops

Dissected — rolling land   Cuestas & flatirons   Flood plains   Fans

Plateaus
low — high — cut-up — canyon land — mesas — badlands

—Raisz Landform Maps

OTHER GREAT RESOURCES

After the Ice Age (The Return of Life to Glaciated North America): E. C. Pielou. 1992, University of Chicago Press. Our watersheds hold the history of the glaciers in their shapes and animals and plants. This tells the 10,000-year history of the northern watersheds. How the assemblage of life got to be.

Raisz Landform Maps: PO Box 773, Melrose, MA 02176; 617/868-3199. River-basin scale. The most beautiful of all North American maps by America's last great artist-cartographer. So easy to read, you cruise like an eagle over the land.

Go and look at the page on Maps (p. 14) and Boundaries of Home (p. 143)

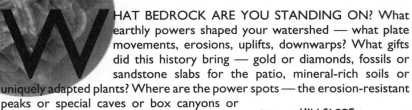

A prehistoric debris flow in altered volcanic rocks near the Pahsimeroi River, in Idaho.

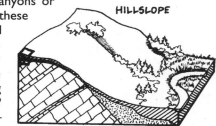

HILLSLOPE

WHAT BEDROCK ARE YOU STANDING ON? What earthly powers shaped your watershed — what plate movements, erosions, uplifts, downwarps? What gifts did this history bring — gold or diamonds, fossils or sandstone slabs for the patio, mineral-rich soils or uniquely adapted plants? Where are the power spots — the erosion-resistant peaks or special caves or box canyons or nearshore reefs? Is the geology of these power spots identical to the sacred places of native American residents? Does your community honor them? Have you listed the scars in your area made by mining or road cuts into Mother Earth? Have you studied the rock cuts — the architectural drawings of the stage of your life's drama? Have you identified the local geo-hazards — the landslides, soil creep, debris slides, seismic alignments, land subsidence zones or karst sinkholes? Have you tried to heal these stone-cold hurts? From beauty to beastliness, bedrock weaves. —PW

Geology Illustrated

An artist of aerial photography, Shelton uses four hundred of his finest photographs to illuminate the problems posed by asking: "How did it come about?" Not a traditional textbook, **Geology Illustrated** *is worth buying for the photos alone. It is a masterpiece, and by now, it's a classic.*
—Larry McCombs

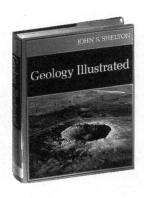

Geology Illustrated
John S. Shelton. 1966; 434 pp.
ISBN 0-7167-0229-0
$39.95 ($42.95 postpaid) from W.H. Freeman and Co., 4419 W. 1980 S., Salt Lake City, UT 84104; 800/488-5233

•

Prehistoric Landslides

Recognizing ancient landslides is a geological pastime that can be practiced in all but the flattest country. The skill thus acquired is not without practical value; indeed, lack of it may lead to disaster. Shortly after World War II, many persons began to build homes in the Palos Verdes Hills near Los Angeles. In the next few years 150 houses were built in an area from which there is a beautiful view of the sea, despite the fact that the land was clearly shown as an old

landslide on a United States Geological Survey map published in 1946. By 1956 the water from lawns, cesspools, and heavy rains — and possibly a redistribution of weight resulting from extensive grading — had reactivated the slide. Creeping along at 10 to 30mm a day, the variation being seasonal and apparently related to rainfall, 350 acres of ground began to crack and heave, tilting and breaking houses, rupturing roads and pipelines, and rendering the entire area uninhabitable. In three years the total horizontal movement exceeded 60 feet and the property damage was estimated at more than 10 million dollars.

•

[The photograph with this review] shows a prehistoric debris flow in altered volcanic rocks near the Pahsimeroi River, in Idaho. From its lobate lower end in the foreground the flow can be readily traced back up the canyon to an equally large steep-walled source area. A hummocky and wrinkled surface characterizes the ground that has moved. Some of its hollows are occupied by ponds and small lakes and normal stream drainage is not yet established over most of it, showing that the surface is little modified and that geologically it is a very recent feature. The smooth margin of the toe, where the mass moved out over the terraced valley floor, and the concentric repetition of this pattern in the hummocky surface of the thin, spreading lobe are evidences of viscous or plastic flow of fine debris. If there were a road-cut in the slide material, we would expect it to reveal a chaotic accumulation of fragments of the same rock that is exposed in the source area, probably in a matrix of fine-grained weathering products that are somewhat slippery when wet.

Geology Field Kit, etc.

A lot of rocks look alike. Geologists work by terrains. Out of context, a volcanic rock may actually appear to be a sedimentary rock. The fieldguides with color photos can help (the best is **Rocks and Minerals**), *but they can often lead to much confusion. It's best to know the terrain you're in — use the Roadside Geology series, the Geological Highway Maps, or local maps from the state or fed geological survey.*

The collective thoughts of earlier geologists diminish the false possibilities. As usual, a walk with a real live geologist surpasses all. **The Practical Geologist** *is a gateway paperback with lots of things to do.*

The fieldkit is simple: A Visine bottle or drip-cap equivalent, filled with a dilute hydrochloric-acid solution. (Swim-

knives). Finally, a Brunton combination compass/clinometer, or a compass and a clinometer, for a careful reading of the 60-percent slope you want to ascend. A sketchbook is indispensable. —PW

The Practical Geologist: Dougal Dixon & Raymond L. Bernor. Fireside Books, 1992; 160 pp. ISBN 0-671-74697-9. $15 postpaid. Simon & Schuster/Order Dept., 200 Old Tappan Road, Old Tappan, NJ 07675; 800/223-2336.

Geological Highway Maps: 1. Mid-Continent (KS, MO, OK, AK), 2. Southern Rockies (AZ, CO, NM, UT), 3. Pacific Southwest (CA, NV), 4. Mid-Atlantic (KY, WV, VA, MD, DE, TN, NC, SC), 5. Northern Rockies (ID, MT, WY), 6. Pacific Northwest (WA, OR), 7. Texas, 8. Alaska & Hawaii, 9. Southeast (AL, FL, GA, LA, MS), 10. Northeast (CT, ME, MA, NH, NJ, NY, PA, RI, VT), 11. Great Lakes (IL, IN, MI, OH, WI), 12. Northern Plains (MN, ND, SD, NE, IA) $9.90 each postpaid. Catalog free. American Association of Petroleum Geologists, PO Box 979, Tulsa, OK 74101; 918/584-2555.

Rocks & Minerals (Macmillan Field Guide): Douglas Helm & Colin Key. Collier Books, 1985; 192 pp. ISBN 0-02-079640-4. $12.95 postpaid. Macmillan Publishing Co., 100 Front Street, Riverside, NJ 08075-7500; 800/257-5755.

Brunton Cadet Pocket Transit: Item #37235. $38.25 ($41.25 postpaid). Forestry Suppliers, Inc., PO Box 8397, Jackson, MS 39284; 800/647-5368, fax 800/543-4203.

Geology Kit: Item #33329; $11.65 ($14.65 postpaid) from Forestry Suppliers, Inc., PO Box 8397, Jackson, MS 39284; 800/647-5368, fax 800/543-4203. *Includes magnifier, bottle, hardness testing tools, magnet, do-it-yourself clinometer, markers, ruler. Forestry Suppliers also has a good selection of hammers, compasses, and clinometers.*

ming-pool acid, aka muriatic acid, is concentrated. Dilute 1 part acid with 10 parts water. The bottle is crucial for distinguishing certain limestones.) A 2.5 pound geo-hammer (if you are walking short distances; get a lighter one for longer distances). A steel blade and a 10- to 20X hand lens (both blade and lens occur on some Swiss Army

xenolithic granite

xenolith
granite —
& Mineral

Roadside Geology Series

The best geo-fun for car nomadics. Coordinated with highway mileage markers, these books transform endless roadcuts and mountain peaks into millions of years of history. Each has an overview-intro and vocabulary. Turn down the radio and keep your sidekick scouting the terrain. —PW

Understanding the Sky

There is no better way to feel out local weather than in a small airplane (or reincarnated as a red-tailed hawk). This is the most lucid book on the messages of the clouds, the patterns of the local winds, thunderstorms, and thermal lore. The life-or-death nature of the information has produced good prose and great illustrations. Pagen also includes the big picture — how storm fronts carry your watershed news from the arctic or the equator. —PW

• *Unstable weather with light winds*
The smoke in the valley at A (see drawing above) gives an indication of wind speed and direction (light and along the valley) as well as the buoyancy of the air. The smoke breaks apart from the light turbulence and expands as it rises. Not much wind gradient is expected since not much wind exists. Thermals are present as can be told from the isolated cumulus clouds at B.

Rough air is expected everywhere due to the thermals, but strong turbulence is only encountered near the arid hot patch C and

Conditions on an unstable day (see excerpt).

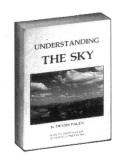

Understanding the Sky
(A Sport Pilot's Guide to Flying Conditions)
Dennis Pagen. 1992; 280 pp.
ISBN 0-936310-03-0
$19.95 ($21.85 postpaid) from Sport Aviation Publications, PO Box 101, Mingoville, PA 16823

the towering cumulus D. The thermals above C are small and intense while the thunderstorm D creates gusts which reach the ground and spread. As the thunderstorm marches up the valley it can bring stronger winds and trigger of dust devils in front of it.

Also see
Climate p.11

Acid Rain Study Kit

Are the frogs disappearing? Your city's marble statues crumbling? Want to give the kids or yourself the "acid test" because you don't know or trust the municipal authorities? Here's a kit to test rain, ponds, and household products. Good instructions, easy to do. —PW

Acid Rain Study Kit: Item #76610. $39.95 postpaid from Forestry Suppliers, Inc., PO Box 8397, Jackson, MS 39284; 800/647-5368, fax 800/543-4203.

Weather Equipment

You can now hook yourself up to the weather. Davis Instruments, Wind & Weather, and Forestry Suppliers have direct connects to your PC, with programs to display and graph daily and accumulated rainfall, dew point, humidity, wind direction and speed, and more. Some bugs are yet to be worked out. But a citizen's network of weather monitoring within your watershed, with monthly discussions of storms and winds, could revolutionize our understanding of local weather.

Wind & Weather also carries sundials, a multitude of weathervanes, and other pretty, old-fashioned stuff. —PW

Davis Instruments: Catalog free. 3465 Diablo Avenue, Hayward, CA 94545; 800/678-3669.

Wind & Weather: Catalog free. PO Box 2320, Mendocino, CA 95460; 800/922-9463.

Forestry Suppliers, Inc.: Catalog free. PO Box 8397, Jackson, MS 39284; 800/647-5368, fax 800/543-4203.

Left: Barometer with inlay mahogany case $195. — *Wind and Weather*

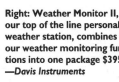

Right: Weather Monitor II, our top of the line personal weather station, combines all our weather monitoring functions into one package $395. —*Davis Instruments*

Stormtrack

No dilly-dallying on the front porch. Cruising the stormtrack is as spontaneous as natural history can get. If act locally, think globally ever had meaning, read this magazine and start your local chapter. —PW

•
My phone rang at 8 o'clock in the morning on January 19, 1990. It was the Texas Tech Tornado Chase Team who flew in from Lubbock on the early bird flight. They were ready to chase storms and wanted to know

the latest weather information. What?, I said. It's January! Sure, I realized a low pressure center was passing through the Dallas area today, and there was a chance of severe weather, but it was cold, rainy, and foggy. They said it was a new year, a new spring, and why not be the first to chase storms. And sure enough, a squall line moved through Dallas about mid-morning. Two down bursts caused extensive roof damage in south Dallas and yes, the first

STORMTRACK

TORNADO struck portions of Garland, around 11:30 am. The Tech team and mother nature signal the beginning of a new chase season. Ah, the chance of convection and chaser dedication.

The storm appeared even more surreal than before. The symmetry of its shape was silhouetted by twilight leaking around the north side under the altocumulus deck. The low clouds along the pseudo-warm

front were arranged in eerie bands that looked like fingers reaching toward the storm's bell-shaped updraft. Occasional lightning forked out of the downwind rain and hail core, but in many cases, never reached the ground. The mood inspired by the scene was reminiscent of "A Night on Bald Mountain" in Disney's "Fantasia."

Stormtrack: Tim Marshall, Editor. $10/year; 6 issues (Make checks payable to Tim Marshall) from 1336 Brazos Blvd., Lewisville, TX 75067.

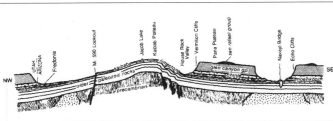

•
As seen from the junction of US 89 and 89a, the jumble of rocks between two faults marks a conspicuous break in Echo Cliffs, the route taken by US 89. A whole unit of the cliffs has been pushed up here. Erosion of soft mudstone and volcanic ash beds in the Chinle Formation of the lifted block provides access to the top of the cliffs. —*Roadside Geology of Arizona*

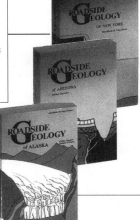

Roadside Geology Series
Currently available: AK, AZ, CO, ID, MT, NM, NY, No. CA, OR, PA, TX, UT, VA, VT & NH, WA, WY, Yellowstone Average prices $10-$16 ($12-$18 postpaid). Mountain Press Publishing Co., PO Box 2399, Missoula, MT 59806; 800/234-5308

water surface ▽

FLOW

Holes drilled
into boulders

Cable through
rootwad

**Side view of a boulder group
with an attached root wad to
provide cover.
—*Better Trout Habitat***

Better Trout Habitat • Adopting a Stream

*By the Millennium, there will be 10
million trout anglers. Many of them
simply love to stand by a creek, watch
the play of light on the water, catch,
and then release the writhing miracles.
This book understands that humans
do not have to "heal the stream," only
to provide the circumstances that allow the stream to heal itself.* **Better
Trout Habitat** *is a modest title for the
best layperson's guide to stream restoration and management. Fourteen
case studies are included.*

*Adopting A Stream remains the model
for the community-action aspects of
restoration, and as an introductory
bioregional guide to the Pacific Northwest.* **Better Trout Habitat** *is more
how-to-do-it in terms of stream flow,
channel shape, bottom texture.*
—Peter Warshall

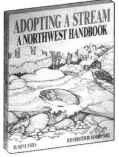

Adopting a Stream
(A Northwest Handbook)
Steve Yates. 1989; 126 pp.
ISBN 0-295-96796-X
$9.95 ($12.95 postpaid). University of
Washington Press, PO Box 50096, Seattle,
WA 98145; 800/441-4115

**Storm drain stencils remind citizens to
protect streams. —*Adopting a Stream***

OTHER GREAT RIVER RESOURCES

Trout Unlimited: $25/year (member-
ship). 800 Follin Lane SE #250, Vienna, VA
22180; 703/281-1100, fax 703/281-1825.

Rivers at Risk (The Concerned Citizen's Guide
to Hydropower): John D. Echeverria, Pope Barrow & Richard Roos-Collins. 1989, Island Press.

The Wild and Scenic Rivers of America:
Tim Palmer. 1993, Island Press.

The Restoration of Rivers and Streams:
James A. Gore. 1985, Butterworth Publishing.
Out of Print.

●
Irrigation Ditch/Spring Creek, Montana

Location	*Southwestern Montana*
Project Status	*Private*
Project Leader	*Dave Odell/Curlew Construction*
Landowner	*Private ranch*
Rehab. Length	*Ten miles*
Limiting Factor	*Lack of water depth, clean gravel, and bank vegetation*
Problem	*Overgrazing by livestock and siltation from irrigation return flows*
Prescription	*Fencing, channel narrowing, silt removal, log cabling, and revegetation with native shrubs*
Begin date	*1984 through 1987*
End date	*Ongoing*
Current status	*Fishery improving, natural reproduction occurring in creek*
Estimated cost	*$10,000 to $20,000 per mile for complete rehabilitation*

—*Better Trout Habitat*

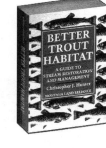

Better Trout Habitat
Christopher J. Hunter. 1991; 320 pp.
ISBN 0-933280-77-7
$24.95 ($29.20 postpaid). Island Press,
Box 7, Covelo, CA 95428; 800/828-1302

—*Adopting
a Stream*

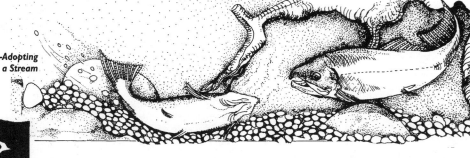

●

Because all streams are not created equal,
each rehabilitation project must be singular
and designed to improve one particular
stream, in one specific drainage, that is affected by the specific geologic and climatic
conditions that dominate that region. For
example, there have been many attempts to
rehabilitate Rocky Mountain streams using
habitat enhancement techniques developed
for midwestern streams. In-stream structures developed for meandering streams in
agricultural settings have been placed in
steep, sinuous forested streams with well-
armored beds. Most of these structures
were washed out, as were the banks they
were built into, during the first spring
freshet, because the stream rehabilitators
did not understand the natural forces that
create trout habitat. —*Better Trout Habitat*

American Rivers

*For twenty years, the nation's leading
river-saving organization has published
the "most endangered rivers" list, kept
tabs on Congress, checked out water
rights and instream flows, pumped up
private and corporate involvement and
coalitions, monitored urban rivers, researched incentives for river protection.
If you swim, fish, raft or just stare at
the eddies, American Rivers deserves
thanks. —PW*

RIVER NETWORK

*From River Network's headwaters, fine
educational pamphlets and grassroots
state partnerships flow without end.*

*For instance, protecting instream flows
is the essence of river stewardship.
(An instream flow is the amount of
water-flow left in a creek or river after
all the human diversions or stoppages
from dams.) The Network's* **Protecting
Instream Flows** *is the best way to get
your feet wet.* **People Protecting Rivers**
and **How to Save a River** *take us from
inspirational beauty to river reverence
to the how-they-did-it actions of river
protectors.*

American Rivers: $20/year (membership
and quarterly newsletter). 801 Pennsylvania
Ave. SE, Suite 400, Washington, DC 20003;
202/547-6900, fax 202/543-6142

●
Rio Grande/Rio Conchos River system
(Colorado, New Mexico, Texas and Mexico)
At the top of the endangered list is the Rio
Grande and its principal Mexican tributary,
the Rio Conchos. In Colorado and New
Mexico, the river has been degraded by
pollution from cyanide-leaching mining and
acid drainage, as well as agricultural diversions and nonpoint source pollution. In
some places along the Texas/Mexico border, the river is a virtual cesspool of untreated human waste, industrial pollutants,
and pesticides from both American and

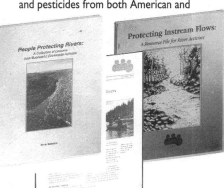

*For coverage of fundraising videos,
computer software, conferences and
the latest in strategies, the quarterly*
River Voices *nicely complements the
stronger political muscle of* **American
Rivers.** *—PW*

●
Most Americans don't give much thought
to flood insurance, unless they live in the
floodplain near a river or next to the
beach. The disastrous impacts of the fed-

Mexican sources. River-related cholera, ty-
phoid, hepatitis, and birth defects have created a human health crisis in both countries.

Columbia/Snake River system, including the
Yakima tributary *(Washington, Oregon, Idaho,
and Canada)* Although this river system
once sustained about 16 million wild
salmon, many of its stocks are now extinct
or endangered. It topped the 1992 most
endangered listing because of its alarming
declines in native salmon populations
brought on by the adverse effects of power
dams. In the past year, efforts to improve
the situation have been minimal.

Alsek and Tatshenshini River system *(Alaska
and Canada),* one of North America's most
spectacular wilderness systems, it is seriously threatened by creation of a proposed
massive open-pit copper mine in British
Columbia *(It's been saved! See related
articles on pages 2 and 3.)*

River Network: PO Box 8787, Portland,
OR 97207; 503/241-3506, 800/423-6747;
EcoNet: rivernet@igc.apc.org.

eral government's flood insurance program,
however, are worth noting. Over its 25-
year history, the flood insurance program
has promoted risky development too close
to the water's edge, led to degradation of
aquatic resources and drained the pockets
of American taxpayers creating one of the
nation's largest domestic liabilities. It was
supposed to do just the opposite.

During the 1980s Congress was forced to
pump more than $1 billion taxpayer dollars
into the NFIP to make up for premium
shortfalls, and in the wake of this summer's
Midwest floods, the NFIP was operating at
a $75 million deficit — with over $240 billion of policies outstanding! —*River Voices*

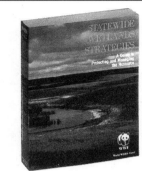

S uch beautiful muck so intimately tied to water!
-and the most productive patches of planet.
Restoration of wetlands balks our desire for control. Some
wetlands thrive on stability, others on disturbances. Wetland
plant succession follows no linear course, and nature-healers
can't usually predict what will happen from playing with
the heartbeat of water flows. Wetlands are pulsed ecosystems:
sometimes the water table pulses vertically, sometimes the
rain pulses seasonally, sometimes surface water arrives in
pulses from upslope or upstream; sometimes coastal waters
go in two directions with two water qualities. Humility is the
name of the game and nurturing a variety of fickle fluxing
plants and animals is the only grip allowed.
—PW

STREAM DEPOSITED (Fluvial) SEDIMENTS   STREAM/GLACIER DEPOSITED (Glaciofluvial) SEDIMENTS   GLACIAL DEPOSITED (Morainal) SEDIMENTS

Ground Water Level

Statewide Wetlands Strategies • Wetland Creation and Restoration

Have a wetland area in mind for restoration, but mucking about for ideas and process? Read **Statewide Wetlands Strategies** *and your bioregional section in* **Wetland Creation and Restoration**. *The former has particularly helpful sections on "Mechanisms for Protecting and Managing Wetlands" and "Wetlands Data Sources and Collection Methods" covering the thirty-five-plus federal laws, the fifteen or so statewide programs, and a baker's dozen of local strategies.* —PW

— *River of Grass*

The Everglades

The Everglades are the barometer of American environmental sincerity. These books love the word "ever-glades"; one feels the sound of "for-ever-glades" lapping among the cypress heads. The most lyrical celebration (with no photos) is Marjory Stoneman Douglas' **The Everglades: River of Grass**. *The best-illustrated and most complete introduction to the whole ecoystem is* **The Everglades Handbook**, *from Hurricane Andrew to Florida apple snails — or, more precisely, from the Kissimmee to Lake Okeechobee and downstream to Florida Bay; the prose is straightforward.* **Everglades: The Ecosystem and Its Restoration** *is a rare, totally authoritative compilation on the wetlands' status and trends, as well as the limited possibilities of restoration. It is the first major work concerned with an ecosystem's driving forces, history, ecological patterns and approaches to bioregional restoration. The prose is technical, and so rich that it is the only book in this catalog I would need a full four paragraphs to really describe.*

If you wonder why, despite admirable and persistent pressure by the Audubon Society and all these reasonable books, the everglades may implode, read **Double Whammy!**, *Carl Hiaasen's outrageous fish story of Florida's infatuation with the fast buck.* —PW

•

Miami was a small town still. Miss Hattie Carpenter, who taught the few high school students in the single grammar school, bicycling home to Brickell Hammock with a beefsteak in her basket, was chased by a panther. The streets were blinding white sand. The antisaloon ladies had made it a prohibition town, so that when the railroad crew came roaring in off the extension on a Saturday night they had to get drunk across the line in North Miami saloons. By morning, dead drunk, they would have been rolled across the line into Miami, with their pockets all pulled out. They would be arrested and jailed. In Monday morning's court, all Judge Frank B. Stoneman could do would be to sentence them back to work again. —*River of Grass*

The Everglades (River of Grass): Marjory Douglas. 1987; 448 pp. ISBN 0-910923-38-8 $17.95 ($19.95 postpaid). Pineapple Press, PO Drawer 16008, Southside Station, Sarasota, FL 34239; 813/952-1085

The Everglades Handbook (Understanding the Ecosystem): Thomas Lodge. 1994; 200 pp. ISBN 1-884015-06-9 $29.95 ($34.90 postpaid). St. Lucie Press, 100 E. Linton Blvd. Suite 403B, Delray Beach, FL 33483; 407/274-9906, fax 407/274-9927

Everglades (The Ecosystem and Its Restoration): Steve Davis & John Ogden. 1994; 826 pp. ISBN 0-9634030-2-8 $97.50 ($106.45 postpaid). St. Lucie Press, 100 E. Linton Blvd. Suite 403B, Delray Beach, FL 33483; 407/274-9906, fax 407/274-9927

Double Whammy: Carl Hiaasen. 1989; 320 pp. ISBN 0-446-35276-4 $5.50 ($8 postpaid). Little, Brown and Co./Order Dept., 200 West Street, Waltham, MA 02154; 800/343-9204

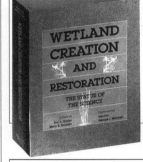

Statewide Wetlands Strategies
(A Guide to Protecting and Managing the Resource)
World Wildlife Fund Staff. 1992; 268 pp.
ISBN 1-55963-206-2
$40 ($44.25 postpaid). Island Press, Box 7, Covelo, CA 95428; 800/828-1302

Wetland Creation and Restoration
(The Status of the Science)
Jon Kusler & Mary Kentula. 1990; 591 pp.
ISBN 1-55963-044-2
$47.50 ($51.75 postpaid). Island Press, Box 7, Covelo, CA 95428; 800/828-1302

See also:
Constructed wetlands, page 163
Biomes (wetlands), page 61.
Ducks Unlimited, page 77.

Great Lakes: Great Legacy?

Our greatest lake cluster is in greatest trouble. The bird deformities warn us, the suffering humans tell us. Prevention must be given equal footing with cures. Environment must be given equal footing with economic sources (fish and transport) and economic sinks (ag runoff, sewage toxics, boat spills and leaks). This is the definitive introduction. —PW

•

Acid rain is not the only air-related problem. Clear evidence is now available that large quantities of toxic chemicals find their way into the Great Lakes ecosystem after having been carried perhaps several thousand miles by air currents. Thus, long-range deposition accounts for more than 90 percent of the dangerous polychlorinated biphenyls (PCBs) found in Lake Superior and is the *only* significant source of chemicals such as DDT and toxaphene, which are restricted in the United States and Canada but still used in Mexico and Central America.

By the process called "biomagnification," which passes along toxic substances in higher and higher levels as they proceed upward through the food web, contaminants that are almost undetectable in lake water may be magnified hundreds of thousands of times within the flesh of a Great Lakes fish. That is why it is often not safe to eat the fish that swim in the same water that one can drink.

Great Lakes: Great Legacy?
Theodora Colbern, Alex Davidson & Sharon Green et al. The Institute for Research on Public Policy, 1990; 301 pp. ISBN 0-89164-11-7 $20 ($23 postpaid). World Wildlife Fund, PO Box 4866, Hampden Station, Baltimore, MD 21211; 410/516-6951

Double-crested cormorant embryos from two northern Green Bay colonies. Birds are suffering from such defects as ascites (abdominal or subcutaneous edema), gastroschisis (stomach outside body), unmetabolized yolk sac, crossed bills, and hemorrhaging.

OTHER GREAT WETLAND RESOURCES

Adopting a Wetland (A Northwest Guide): Steve Yates. 1989, University of Washington Press. The best example of a bioregional education and action leaflet.

Wetlands: William Mitsch & James Gosselink. 1993, Van Nostrand Reinhold. The best technical text.

National Wetlands Newsletter: $25/year (4 issues). Environmental Law Institute, 16 P Street NW, Suite 200, Washington, DC 20036; 202/328-5150.

Lake Smarts: Steve McComas. 1993, Terrene Institute. Great (and only) access to tools for lake maintenance and detection of pollutants. Limited to the temperate lakes. A few tools (2,4-D and grass carp) are steps in the wrong direction.

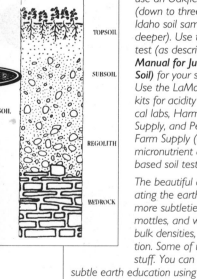

SOIL IS THE STAGE from which all things — good, beautiful, vicious, dull, outrageous and sorrowful — emerge. A teaspoon of soil contains twenty million fungi, five million bacteria, one million protozoa, and two hundred thousand algae. Amoebae slide over sand grains, hunting bacteria. Bacteria swim through microrivers scarfing nutrients. Viruses attack bacteria. Nematodes, the hyena-worms, devour almost anything. There are about 9,500 soil types in the United States; no one has ever tried to create sanctuaries for any of them.
—Peter Warshall

The Nature and Properties of Soils

*Soil is kaleidoscopic. A farmer sees fertility, groundwater, and tilth. An engineer sees bulk density and expansive clays. A maid sees dust. A home-site sewage consultant sees a filter, biotransformer and purifier. There's no one book, but **The Nature and Properties of Soils** is the old-time favorite college text for understanding gardens, agriculture and growing. —PW*

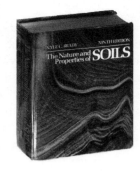

The Nature and Properties of Soils
Nyle C. Brady. 1989; 880 pp.
ISBN 0-02-313361-9
$76 postpaid. Macmillan Publishing Co., 100 Front Street, Riverside, NJ 08075-7500; 800/257-5755

●

Of the six major factors affecting the growth of plants, only light is not supplied by soils. The soil supplies water, air, and mechanical support for plant roots as well as heat to enhance chemical reactions. It also supplies seventeen plant nutrients that are essential for plant growth. These nutrients are slowly released from unavailable forms in the solid framework of minerals and organic matter to exchangeable cations associated with soil colloids and finally to readily available ions in the soil solution. The ability of soils to provide these ions in a proper balance determines their primary value to humankind.

Soil and Water Conservation Society

For half a century, the Society has insisted that Americans pay attention to their "natural capital" — worth more than Fort Knox to the nation's welfare. Yet over one million acres of prime farmland disappear to urban development every year; in the Great Plains and Pacific Northwest, 85 percent of the farms lose five tons of topsoil each year.

*The **Journal of Soil and Water Conservation**, the Society's journal, is unique: technical but fertile. —PW*

Soil and Water Conservation Society: membership $46/year (includes journal subscription). 7515 NE Ankeny Road, Ankeny, Iowa 50021; 800/843-7645.

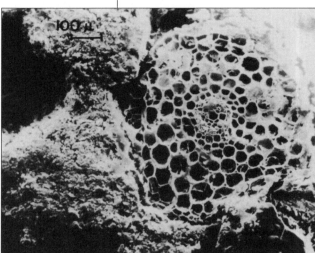

Scanning electron microscope of a cross section of peanut root surrounded by soil. Note the intimacy of contact.

●

"Feel" Method. The common field method of classifying a soil is by its *feel.* Probably as much can be judged about the texture and hence the class of a soil merely by rubbing it between the thumb and fingers as by any other superficial means. Usually it is helpful to wet the sample in order to estimate plasticity more accurately. The way a wet soil "slicks out"—that is, develops a continuous ribbon when pressed between the thumb and fingers—gives a good idea of the amount of clay present. The slicker the wet soil, the higher the clay content. The sand particles are gritty; the silt has a floury or talcum-powder feel when dry and is only slightly plastic and sticky when wet. Persistent cloddiness generally is imparted by silt and clay.

Soil Field Kit

Every citizen should be able to say a locally appropriate version of: "I live on a sandy loam that is about ten feet deep, sits on fractured granite, is acidic, and covers half my community." No one who speaks of the Earth should do so without knowing their own earth. Here's how: Look up the Soil Conservation Service in the phone book, or write Washington and ask for the soil map for your community. Go

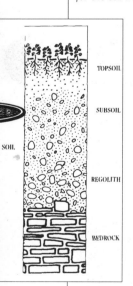

*out to the backyard or frontyard and dig a pit, or use an Oakfield sampler (down to three feet) or an Idaho soil sampler (for deeper). Use the "feel" test (as described in **The Manual for Judging Oregon Soil**) for your soil's texture. Use the LaMotte soil test kits for acidity or N-P-K. Local labs, Harmony Farm Supply, and Peaceful Valley Farm Supply (p. 99) offer micronutrient and other lab-based soil tests.*

The beautiful art of appreciating the earth has a lot more subtleties to it — soil mottles, and water table, bulk densities, root penetration. Some of us taste the stuff. You can achieve subtle earth education using

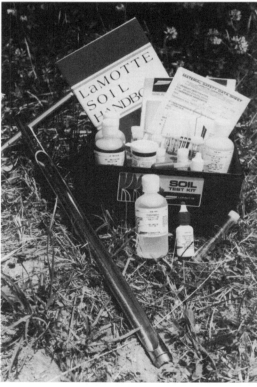

4% clay

29% clay

44% clay

—Manual for Judging Oregon Soils

the Munsell Soil Color Charts. (Note: "Sustain" comes from the Indo-European root for upholding from beneath: the soil matrix.) —PW

Soil Maps: Soil Conservation Service, PO Box 2890, Washington, DC 20013; 202/447-4543.
Manual for Judging Oregon Soil: OSU Extension Publication #6. $7.50 postpaid. Oregon State University Agricultural Communications, Publication Orders, Administrative Services 422, Corvallis, OR 97331-2119.

Soil Samplers: 20.5" length $47.49 from Harmony Farm Supply, PO Box 460, Graton, CA 95444; 707/823-9125, fax 707/823-1734. Various lengths & prices from Forestry Suppliers, Inc., PO Box 8397, Jackson, MS 39284; 800/647-5368, fax 800/543-4203.
LaMotte Soil Test Kit: N-P-K, 15 tests each; 30 pH tests. $34.95. Harmony Farm Supply (above).
Munsell Soil Color Charts: 8-chart set $88 postpaid. Forestry Suppliers, Inc. (above).

GREAT DIRTY RESOURCES

Soil Erosion (Crisis in America's Croplands?): Sandra S. Batie. 1983, World Wildlife Fund. Though a decade old, it's the only book on how to harmonize cash-flow problems (farm debt, land prices, market flux, Fed handouts) and soil conservation practices.

Dust Bowl (The Southern Plains in the 1930s): Donald Worster. 1982, Oxford University Press. The best book on how America fucked up and dusted its soil savings account. Our unabated obsession with financial capital could blow our natural capital once again.

Terrene Institute: 1717 K Street NW, Washington, DC 20006; 202/833-8317. Free catalog. In collaboration with the Environmental Protection Agency, they produce pamphlets and books on polluted runoff.

Biotechnical Slope Protection and Erosion Control: Donald H. Gray & Andrew T. Leiser. 1982, Krieger Publishing Company.

YOU CAN THINK OF THE WATERSHED as a leaf — a leaf cupped so all the water that touches it flows across its surface toward the tip. This surface waterflow is distinguished from "point" sources that travel in pipes to a single, unique opening, like the outfall pipe from a sewage plant. The "non-point" flow washes the landscape, taking with it loose soil (sediment), free chemicals such as nitrates from golf courses, and oil blotches from under your car. For clean water, the management of polluted runoff is as serious as sewage outfalls. But who's responsible? And how do you treat such a diffuse flow? Watershedologists now devise mini-wetlands to treat urban washwater; future governments will try to prevent sediment or pesticide from leaving private property. —PW

Water Resources Protection Technology

Here's the whole watershed catalog of tasks required to:
- *control increased runoff and decreased infiltration;*
- *manage erosion and sedimentation;*
- *protect drainage channels and grass waterways;*
- *stabilize stream channels and banks;*
- *minimize pollution from sewage.*

This honest guide to land-use mitigation explains advantages and disadvantages with designs and examples and cost implications. It has not been surpassed since 1981, but some companies cited no longer exist, and on-site sewage treatment and constructed wetlands for polluted runoff have greatly improved. —PW

Water Resources Protection Technology
J. T. Tourbier & Richard Westmacott. 1981; 178 pp. ISBN 0-87420-595-6
$36.95 postpaid. Urban Land Institute, 625 Indiana Ave. NW, Suite 400, Washington, DC 20004-2930; 800/321-5011

•
GROUP: Infiltration of runoff at source.
MEASURES: Modular paving.
PURPOSE: . . . [B]rick or concrete which, if laid on a permeable base, will allow water to infiltrate, either through the joints or through perforations.
ADVANTAGES: 1. Lattice concrete blocks permit establishment of grass.
2. . . . [S]mall section can be lifted for access to underground utilities.
3. A variety of patterns of paving can often be used.
4. These pavements are flexible and can withstand minor movements without cracking.
DISADVANTAGES: 1. Skilled labor is necessary to lay modular paving.
2. Unless a deep sub-base of porous material (crushed 2 in. stone) is laid, permeability may be poor. . . .
3. Lattice blocks and brick with wide joints are a poor walking surface.
IMPLEMENTATION & LEGAL IMPLICATIONS: Local regulations rarely permit developers to reduce the size of storm drains, even where substantial areas of porous pavement are used. This cuts out one of the main advantages of this measure for the developer.

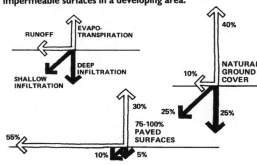

Typical hydrographic changes due to increasing the area of impermeable surfaces in a developing area.

Groundwork

This handsome handbook is the product of one of America's more than 3,000 resource conservation districts. With locally elected boards, but no power to make or enforce laws, RCDs function as the glue between governmental bureaucracies and private landowners in cooperative efforts to conserve soil and water. Superb line drawings of techniques and a succinct text make this pamphlet one to emulate. —Richard Nilsen

•
Willows are an effective and inexpensive way to armor active headcuts and gully banks.

Be sure to plant the willows right-side up. One almost foolproof method is to point

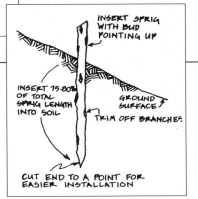

INSERT SPRIG WITH BUD POINTING UP

INSERT 75-80% OF TOTAL SPRIG LENGTH INTO SOIL

GROUND SURFACE

TRIM OFF BRANCHES

CUT END TO A POINT FOR EASIER INSTALLATION

the planting end of the sprig with an axe right after it is cut from the tree.

Willows spread easily—usually an advantage; but in some cases when an open channel is needed to carry stormflows, this can be a nuisance.

Upstream Solutions to Downstream Pollution

The Natural Resources Defense Council and Coast Alliance have teamed up to produce the best intro to citizen participation and polluted runoff, with great access to further resources. Beaches slimy? Great Lakes afloat with grunge? You care? Start here. —PW

•
Polluted runoff impairs more waterbodies than any other pollution source in the country. As evidenced by widespread beach closings, prohibitions on shellfish harvesting and the loss of biological diversity in coastal habitats, polluted runoff is a particularly serious problem for coastal areas. States' assessments of 75 percent of their estuarine waters indicate that 33 percent of these waters are impaired and 11 percent are threatened. The Coastal Nonpoint Pollution Control Program (otherwise known as Section 6217 of the Coastal Zone Act Reauthorization Amendments of 1990) is a potentially powerful and innovative new program to address the problem of polluted runoff. It requires all coastal states and territories with federally approved coastal zone management programs to establish effective, enforceable runoff prevention and control plans.

•
With over 8.5 million people living in Los Angeles County, Santa Monica Bay receives large amounts of urban runoff, from Malibu to the Palos Verdes Peninsula. Surface

Upstream Solutions to Downstream Pollution
(A Citizen's Guide to Protecting Seacoasts and the Great Lakes by Cleaning Up Polluted Runoff)
Sarah Chasis, et al. Natural Resources Defense Council, 1993; 127 pp. $7.50 ($8.95 postpaid). NRDC Publications, 40 West 20th Street, New York, NY 10011; 212/727-2700, fax 212/727-1773

runoff in the Los Angeles Basin is largely collected by more that 140 publicly owned storm drains flowing into the Bay. This storm drain system delivers 25 million gallons per day of untreated urban runoff during dry weather. During wet weather the volume of urban runoff increases significantly, reaching as much as 10 billion gallons per day. High levels of several harmful pollutants, affecting human health, aquatic life and the entire Santa Monica Bay ecosystem, are introduced by this flow and other sources.

Santa Monica Bay has been contaminated with higher levels of DDT and PCBs than the water bodies of any other urban area in the United States. PCBs have been detected at levels as high as 1,464 parts per billion (ppb) in White Croaker off Palos Verdes Peninsula; sadly, this high concentration of PCBs has changed little since 1975. Other commonly detected contaminants found in the tissues of fish in the Bay include arsenic, copper, selenium, zinc, mercury, silver, cadmium, and toluene.

One recent analysis of pollutant loadings into Santa Monica Bay from urban runoff measured some 65,085 pounds per year of lead and 2,110,241 pounds per year of oil and grease.

•
The anti-fouling agent tributyltin (TBT), used in boat paint, is one of the most toxic substances in the marine environment. One ounce can kill most organisms in 250 million gallons of water.

Fundamentals of Urban Runoff Management

Though the authors are terribly serious and bureaucratic in tone, they don't runoff at the mouth and they do flush out every important non-point pollution problem in urban watersheds. From rooftops to stormdrains to waterfront, no other book so thoroughly discusses the quality of urban water pollution and surface runoff, or engineered and social solutions to urban runoff pollution. Even more

important, one-half of the book is about how to implement your findings within the government arena. It's the sponge, mop, drycleaner, scrub brush, and decontaminant One-Stop Community Shop. —PW

Fundamentals of Urban Runoff Management
Richard H. Horner, et al.1994; 285 pp. $35 ($39 postpaid). Terrene Institute, 1717 K Street NW, Washington, DC 20006; 202/833-8317

Groundwork
(A Handbook for Erosion Control in North Coastal California)
Lisa Prunuske. 1987; 60 pp. $2 postpaid. Marin County Resource Conservation District, PO Box 219, Point Reyes Station, CA 94956; 415/663-1231

Geosurfing

I learned a new word in Malibu — "geosurfing." In a city of 250 land-slides and 26 miles of shoreline crammed with homes, each year brings a new story of cement founda-tion-pads slowly gliding toward the sea, or the sea curling its wave around a just-built home. The Living with the Shore Series, the best collection of geosurfing field guides, tracks the coast mile by mile and tells you where to leave nature alone. For coastal dwellers, these local guides are as im-portant as your address. **The Beaches are Moving** describes the mind-bog-gling exchange of beach sand, near-beach, surf, run-up and wave. Both are beautifully illustrated.
—Peter Warshall

•

1. Design to live with the flexible coastal environment. Don't fight nature with a "line of defense."
2. Consider all man-made structures near the shoreline temporary.

The Beaches Are Moving
(The Drowning of America's Shoreline)
Wallace Kaufman & Orrin Pilkey, Jr. 1983; 326 pp. ISBN 0-8223-0574-7
$14.95 ($17.95 postpaid) from Duke University Press, Box 90660 College Sta., Durham, NC 27708; 919/688-5134, fax 919/688-4574

3. Accept any engineering scheme for beach restoration or preservation as a last resort, and then only for metropolitan areas.
4. Base decisions affecting coastal develop-ment on the welfare of the public rather than the minority of shorefront property owners.
5. Let the lighthouse, beach cottage, motel, or hot dog stand fall when its time comes.
—Living with the Louisiana Shore

•

Although the sunbather lying sleepy and vulnerable on the warm sand seldom knows it, he is lying on one of the most in-

Living with the Shore
16 volumes: Lake Erie, Maine, Connecticut, Long Island's South Shore, New Jersey, Chesapeake Bay/Virginia, North Carolina's Barrier Islands, South Carolina, Georgia, East Florida, West Florida, Alabama/ Mississippi, Louisiana, Texas, California, Puget Sound/Georgia Strait.
Average prices $13.95 to $21.95 ($16.95 to $24.95 postpaid) from Duke University Press, Box 90660 College Sta., Durham, NC 27708; 919/688-5134, fax 919/688-4574

genious defensive structures in the world. In nature's endless interplay of force and material, the beach is a buffer zone, shock absorber, and biological way station be-tween the sea and the land. All this is made of wastes, materials cast off by the conti-nent, and in some cases by the life under the sea itself. In nature, of course, waste is mainly a matter of definition and point of view. The wastes that form the beaches are

not only vital in the coastal environment but are the first line of defense for the mainland from whence they issued.

•

A wave is like a bulge traveling across the ocean's surface. The bulge is not water it-self racing from place to place, but energy traveling like a ghost through the body of the sea. A wave may have birth, maturity, and death, but the energy it carries existed before the wave and lives on after its crash-ing death. —The Beaches Are Moving

See p. 54, Ocean Biomes, Sea Shepherd; and p.109, Ecoactivism.

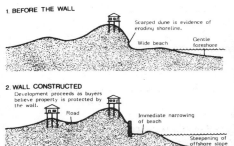

1. BEFORE THE WALL
Scarped dune is evidence of eroding shoreline.
Wide beach
Gentle foreshore

2. WALL CONSTRUCTED
Development proceeds as buyers believe property is protected by the wall.
Road
Immediate narrowing of beach
Steepening of offshore slope

3. TWO TO FORTY YEARS LATER
There is no beach. The wall is overwashed by storms, and wave energy is now undermining and steepening the offshore slope.

4. TEN TO SIXTY YEARS LATER (New Jerseyization)
Bigger, "better" reinforced seawall is put in.
As depth increases, wave size increases; therefore a higher wall is needed.

ULTIMATE RESULTS: Development is behind wall, no beach is available, and the sea floor is cluttered with fallen walls and groins.

The saga of a seawall. —Living with the South Carolina shore

Coastal Cleanup

Dumping plastics at sea has been banned by international treaty for more than five years. Yet high tides still bring in a harvest of plastic trash: six-pack holders, fishing line, Styrofoam pellets, plastic bags, and more. The sources are widespread: care-less beach visitors and overflow from land-based disposal sites, to offshore trash dumping from cargo ships, commercial fishing fleets and pleasure boats.

You can help by participating in the annual International Coastal Cleanup Days spon-sored by state and local parks, beach, or wildlife departments; find listings in the Center for Marine Conservation's **Coastal Connection**. Better yet, make every trip to the coast a cleanup day. —David Burnor

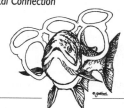

DON'T TEACH YOUR TRASH TO SWIM!

Coastal Connection: Quarterly, free from Center for Marine Conservation/Chesa-peake Field Office, 306A Buckroe Avenue, Hampton, VA 23664.

A Citizens Guide to Plastics in the Ocean: Kathryn J. O'Hara, et al. 1988; 131 pp. ISBN 0-9615294-2-3. Free from Center for Marine Conservation, 1725 DeSales Street NW, Washington, DC 20036; 202/429-5609.

The Society of the Plastics Industry: Infor-mation from 1275 K Street NW, Suite 400, Washington, DC 20005.

•

Plastics Indicated in Sperm Whale Death in North Carolina

The cause of the animal's stress and suffer-ing was determined quickly. Inside the di-gestive chamber located between the stom-ach and intestine were several assorted plastic items. One of them, an intact white plastic gallon bottle, was wedged securely in the opening to the small intestine . . . [forming] an effective plug that prevented the movement and digestion of food. Other items included another gallon plastic bottle; a balloon-sized plastic float used on large fishing trawl nets; about 35 feet of 3/8 inch nylon rope coiled into a wadded ball; sev-eral small unidentified pieces of plastic; one large intact plastic garbage bag, and one large chunk of unrefined natural rubber measuring 18 inches by 6 inches by 3 inches. —Coastal Connection

—The Society of the Plastics Industry

Ocean and Coastal Action

Hawaiian monk seal pup
—Center for Marine Conservation

Center for Marine Conservation (202/ 429-5609). To conserve the diversity and abundance of life in the oceans. Good works such as lobbying for advanced-de-sign tugboats escorting oil tankers, a zero-discharge program for solid wastes at sea, and implementation of the Monterey Bay National Marine Sanctuary (and exclusion of jet skis). They are in the main current with members of many official-sounding boards, such as the Pacific Fishery Man-agement Council's Groundfish Advisory Panel. Given rampant greed, CMC's voice casts a compassionate net. Wherever we cite ocean conservation, we cite CMC.

Coast Alliance (202/546-9554). The DC wave makers, inundating Congress with salty, right-on legislation to protect all American coasts, remove federal insurance subsidies that encourage coastal develop-ment, reduce pollution (especially of shore-line toxic sediments), control offshore gas and oil development, and on and on. Non-profit network center for coastal concern. Best publication is **And Two If By Sea** ($5).

Ocean Protection Initiative (212/727-2700). An important program within the Natural Resources Defense Council (page 78) to prevent oil spills, protect fisheries by negotiating high-seas regulation, curtail coastal pollution (see page 55), and sue the polluters. Sells a good intro called **Ebb Tide for Pollution**.

•

The harbor porpoise population in the Gulf of Maine is rapidly declining. The cause — fishing — is well known; however, virtually no measures have been undertaken to rem-edy the situation. Yet, more than two years after CMC and other organizations first submitted a petition to list the species as endangered, little has been accomplished to reduce mortality. Scientists estimate there are approximately 47,200 harbor porpoise in the Gulf of Maine; however, from 1990 to 1992, an estimated 1.9 to 1.1 percent of the population (900 to 2,400 animals) drowned annually in gillnets for mackerel.

•

Florida residents and visitors have been putting their names on the dotted line in support of increased federal funding for the Archie Carr National Wildlife Refuge, which would protect important beachfront habitat for sea turtles along Florida's Atlan-tic coast. Coordinated by CMC's Florida office over the summer, the petition drive has resulted in more than 1,500 signatures so far. —Marine Conservation News

stick in

pull up

pull back

Root seedling

slight bulge is root collar

hold seedling in hole with collar at ground level

pull out head and plunge in further back

push forward

heal in

and one last tug to see that it is firmly planted

The Earth Manual

Just like the man says: "Between well trimmed suburban lawns and the vast regions of mountain wilderness, there are millions of patches of land that are semi-wild. They may be wood lots, small forests, parks, a farm's 'back forty', or even an unattended corner of a big backyard — land touched by civilization but far from conquered. This book is about how to take care of such land: how to stop its erosion, heal its scars, cure its injured trees, increase its wildlife, restock it with shrubs and wildflowers, and otherwise work with (rather than against) the wildness of the land."

A book of gentle advice and easily absorbed wisdom. Great bibliography. —Peter Warshall

For beginners, it has the best exploration of small-scale restoration techniques. —Richard Nilsen

• If your problem is bank erosion, there are several steps you might take.

First of all, stop all physical injuries to the banks. In particular, stop grazing animals (cows, horses, and sheep) from breaking down

The Earth Manual
(How to Work on Wild Land Without Taming It)
Malcolm Margolin. 1985; 237 pp.
ISBN 0-930588-18-5
$16 ($17.05 postpaid) from Heyday Books, PO Box 9145, Berkeley, CA 94709

the banks to get to the water. You may have to fence off parts of the stream and, if necessary, even build a watering trough away from the stream's edge.

Next, you can build deflectors. Deflectors are basically piles of stone placed upstream from an eroding bank to absorb the force of the water.

• Contour trenches are simply ditches that you dig along a hillside, following a contour and running perpendicular to the flow of water. They catch water and allow it to sink into the ground before it can get a running start down the hill. Contour trenches are particularly valuable on hardened soil—like old logging roads—where water penetration is painfully slow.

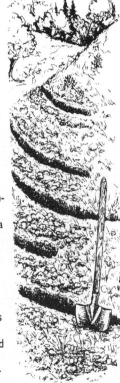

International Reforestation Suppliers

Reforestation tools and nursery equipment (also fire-fighting equipment and watershed measurement tools). Great service. —PW
[Suggested by Jack Monschke]

15" Deep Split Treebag

Our 15" Split Treebag continues to be our very best selling treebag. The split design allows for more comfort and a much easier ride on the hips, waist and backside. Constructed of the highest quality materials that are puncture and tear resistant, waterproof, mildew resistant, impervious to oil and grease and stays soft and pliable at low temperatures.

OST Bar
(Dibble Bar)
Widely used throughout the Southeast, the OST Bar is best suited for non-rocky, looser soils.

International Reforestation Suppliers: Catalog free from PO Box 5547, Eugene, OR 97405; 800/321-1037.

Native Seed Foundation

Not many readers will be able to purchase these seeds (wholesale only) of native shrubs of the northern Rockies. But this organization is interesting nonetheless as a model: "We are not a sophisticated organization which hires college graduates or anything. People are able to supplement their incomes by picking berries [for seeds] in the summer months. We get a lot of retired folks, families on welfare, housewives and kids, young people on vacation looking for a little extra money. We hire between 1-5 local men and boys to help with heavy processing work . . .

Native Seed Foundation: Information from Star Route, Dept. W, Moyie Springs, ID 83845; 208/267-7938.

We are proud that our product is a good one. We have some pretty good equipment now which is crucial for the fine work of cleaning all impurities from the seed and for guaranteeing a high germination rate to our customers."

If restoring clearcuts, burned forest, local biodiversity and sustainable economics is to happen, we will need more organizations like the Native Seed Foundation. —PW

Weed Wrench

Shrubs too hard to dig out with a spade? Tired of barriers of broom in California? Brazilian pepper trees in the Everglades? Banana puka on Molokai? Buy the weed wrench. Custom-designed to save your back and exorcise the exotic invaders. Variously sized jaws, with loveable long levers. —PW

Weed Wrench: $50 – $140 plus shipping. Free brochure. New Tribe, 5517 Riverbanks Road, Grants Pass, OR 97527; 503/476-9492.

Supertube

Goats or deer or rabbits eating your seedlings? Drought and wind wilting your forest restoration project? Up your luck with Supertube, the twin-walled tube that degrades after five to seven years, when the seedling has enough resilience to survive without it. Three to four inches in diameter and translucent, it comes in varying lengths and requires an anchoring stake. It's the most widely used tree shelter for replanting. —PW

See p. 105, Preserving Plant Knowledge; p. 83, Forestry Suppliers.

Supertube Tree Shelters: Free brochure from Treessentials, Riverview Station, PO Box 7097, St. Paul, MN 55107; 800/248-8239.

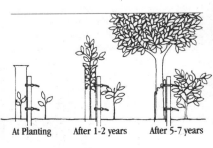

At Planting   After 1-2 years   After 5-7 years

H o w many trees

did it take to publish the *Millennium Whole Earth Catalog?*

Newsprint currently comes from tree flesh. 150,000 copies of this *Whole Earth Catalog* are being printed in the first run. Each copy weighs 3.25 pounds.

Step 1: Calculate the weight in paper (we will ignore the cover stock which is slightly heavier than newsprint):

150,000 copies x 3.25 pounds per copy = 487,500 pounds

Step 2: Subtract recycled postconsumer fiber. This *WEC* is printed on 100 percent recycled paper, but 85 percent of that is scraps and trimmings — the leftovers from trimming a roll of paper to the size required by some other book. Fifteen percent has actually been used at least once and then de-inked, returned to fiber, and recycled. We will subtract this postconsumer recycled fiber from the paper that required new timber harvests.

487,500 pounds of paper - 15 percent = 414,375 pounds of "new" paper

Step 3: Calculate the number of trees. Most American paper comes from pines that are cut when the tree weighs about 250 pounds.

Each yields about 125 pounds of paper. This means that the first printing of the *WEC* requires:

414,375 pounds ÷ 125 pounds per tree = 3,315 trees

Step 4: Lots of trees! To find how big a forest, we must estimate how much space 3,315 trees occupy. There's no hard and fast rule, but each tree usually occupies about 100 square feet of forest. The total square footage is:

3,315 trees x 100 sq. ft. = 331,500 square feet.

Most Americans think better in acres. To convert, we divide 331,500 square feet by the number of square feet in an acre (roughly 44,000 sq. ft./acre). The final answer is: 7.53 acres.

This answer gives us an order of magnitude. It's not one acre nor a hundred. It's in the neighborhood of ten acres — we'd have to know the actual forest and kind of trees, as well as the specific processing method to be more precise.

Step 5: Harper San Francisco and Point Foundation, in cooperation with Global ReLeaf (p. 92), will plant two trees for every one used to produce this book.

—Peter Warshall and Michael Stone

Restoration Forestry

This catalog of sustainable forestry lists 780 organizations, 120 universities that offer forestry degrees, 100 companies with "sustainably produced" wood, 230 forestry journals/periodicals, 100 model reforestation projects, 800 books, networks and other info sources, and 120 articles by the grassroots and the concerned. I even

Restoration Forestry
(An International Guide to Sustainable Forestry Practices Worldwide)
Michael Pilarski, Editor. 1994; 528 pp.
ISBN 1-882308-51-4
$26.95 ($30.45 postpaid). Kivaki Press, 585 E. 31st, Durango, CO 81301; 800/578-5904

found an address for my friend Ponderosa Pine (a human). —PW

The Fragmented Forest

This classic said the obvious: No piece of land is an island unto itself. For lots of reasons, Americans had done forgot. The author forces our eyes to perceive the "habitat islands" isolated by clearcuts or cities or farming, then to see how they can be connected by drainageways, mountain passes, valleys. He guides the landscape ecologist into seeing the pattern — the whole as greater than the sum of the parts. Though his book is limited (perhaps) by its bioregional intimacy (the coastal temperate rain forests of North America) and now stands in the company of newer insights, it was Harris who had the vision, and *The Fragmented Forest* holds it dear.
—PW

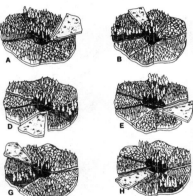

An old-growth patch surrounded by a long-rotation island that is cut in a programmed sequence to maximize average age difference between adjacent stands. Alternate stands are clearcut every 35 years but any single stand is cleared only once in 320 years.

All factors considered, an ideal old-growth area would occur on a moist site containing surface water and a stream. It would contain a topographic bench and a riparian strip dominated by hardwood species. This same riparian strip would connect it with at least two other stands. The site would be at a low elevation with a north or east aspect, but would ideally extend over a ridge top so that the ridge system could be used as a dispersal route and so some sunny, south-facing area would be included. The site would be as far removed from traffic and attendant risks such as wild crown fire as possible. It would be nearly surrounded by replacement stands that can serve as a buffer area and by at least two stands in early stages of growth to provide the full spectrum of successional stages in close proximity.

The Fragmented Forest
(Island Biogeography Theory and the Preservation of Biotic Diversity)
Larry D. Harris. University of Chicago Press, 1984; 211 pp. ISBN 0-226-31764-1
$13.50 ($16.50 postpaid). Chicago Distribution Center, 11030 S. Langley Avenue, Chicago, IL 60628; 800/621-2736

—**Cascade Holistic Economic Consultants**

The Forest and the Trees

Some books are about sustainable forests. Others are about sustainable forestry. This one is about a simple truth: trees take so long to grow that excellent forestry cannot withstand profiteering. Profiteering seems unstoppable; cathedral forests are desecrated. When greed is contained, this book will have a renaissance.
—PW

You don't need to be a professional forester to recognize bad forestry any more than you need to be a doctor to recognize ill health. If logging looks bad, it is bad. If a forest appears to be mismanaged, it is mismanaged. But a certain level of expertise is needed if you are going to be effective in doing something about it.

Good forestry is not a lucrative business. It never was and never will be, because it takes longer than a lifetime to grow high-quality timber, longer than anyone can wait for a return on investment. It takes 75 to 150 years to grow timber in sizes useful for lumber and plywood; it takes twice that long to grow high-quality wood for fine furniture and musical instruments. The large spruce trees in Alaska that are being cut and shipped to Japan for piano sounding boards, guitars, and exquisite residential paneling are often as much as 1,000 years old.

In recent years the Forest Service has turned its back on its tradition and substituted "dominant use" — timber protection — in its management of the nation's commercial timberland. Clearcutting has become the norm rather than the exception. If the agency is allowed to continue on its present course, the nation's old-growth forests will vanish forever, perhaps as soon as the end of this century. And when the old growth is gone, surely there will be a concerted effort by the timber industry to log the wilderness areas and parks as well.

Is this the direction in which we want to go? Or can we citizens, the owners of these old-growth forests, using the information in this book and others and the findings from the Forest Service's own research stations, succeed in convincing the agency to take a more prudent path?

OTHER GREAT RESOURCES

Fading Forests (North American Trees and the Threat of Exotic Pests): Faith Thompson Campbell & Scott E. Schlarbaum. 1994. $8.95 ($10.45 postpaid). NRDC Publications, 40 West 20th Street, New York, NY 10011; 212/727-2700, fax 212/727-1773. From Chile, Siberia or New Zealand can come a tree pest that would change the whole meaning of sustainable harvests. It has happened before. Here's the info on previous pestilence and the future.

Institute for Sustainable Forestry: Membership $25/year. PO Box 1580, Redway, CA 95560; 707/923-4719. The certifiers and designers of sustainable forestry.

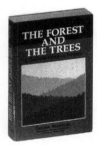

The Forest and the Trees
(A Guide to Excellent Forestry)
Gordon Robinson. 1988; 257 pp.
ISBN 0-933280-40-8
$22 ($26.25 postpaid). Island Press, Box 7, Covelo, CA 95428; 800/828-1302

this end up▶▶

Clearcut

A book for the President's night table; a time to reflect that 95 percent of our nation's original forests are no more. Save 5 percent of this heritage for future generations? Industrial pressure says: too much. **Clearcut** *says: enough is enough. One hundred stunning photos and twelve good essays make it the coffee table book for the Millennium.* —PW

•

Photographer Balthazar Korab tells of his personal struggle to understand, and then articulate through his photography, the agony wrought by industrialism to his adopted state of Michigan: In 1976, when working on an exhibit, "Man's presence in Michigan," I discovered with shock that millions of acres of white pines covered the state when white men arrived in the mid-1880s and by 1910 all but a few acres were cut down, without any effort to replant. Only 49 acres of old growth exist today, preserved by accidental circumstances in Hartwick Pines State Park. Most of the later reforestations show pitiful, unimaginative monotony. These shown here were probably planted by some Youth Corps during the Depression. . . . and today we listen to the inane debate of the politicians about the spotted owl versus jobs, while the clearcutting equipment is humming away. In a debate where nobody brings up the fact that when the white pines were gone the lumberjacks went on living by building cars. —Balthazar Korab

•

Industrial foresters attempt to apply principles of industrial management developed for production of such products as automobiles to what they call the "working forest." These principles include ever-increasing efficiency, lower labor costs (frequently translated to mean replacing human beings by machines), destroying craftsmanship and sense of community by hierarchical management, and attempts to constantly increase "worker productivity."

In some areas of California, when conifer trees are planted after clearcutting, the open areas are prime habitat for deciduous trees such as alders. Conifers will tend to grow through the canopy of trees and the deciduous trees will not live as long as the conifers. In order to give the commercially valuable conifers an early advantage over alders, industrial foresters like to aerially spray forests with herbicides that kill or defoliate the broadleaf trees. Aerial spraying of forests with herbicides was perfected during the 1960s in the war in Vietnam. The U.S. Air Force sprayed Agent Orange (a toxic concoction including 2-4-D) over

Clearcut
(The Tragedy of Industrial Forestry)
Bill Devall, Editor. Sierra Club Books/ Earth Island Press, 1994; 291 pp.
ISBN 0-87156-494-7
$50 ($57 postpaid). Sierra Club Store Orders, 730 Polk Street, San Francisco, CA 94109; 800/935-1056

an estimated one million acres of forest in Vietnam. After learning of this practice, critics invented the term *ecocide* to refer to the systematic destruction of a natural landscape for a limited or narrow goal — victory over the enemy.

Save America's Forests: Membership $25/ year. 4 Library Court SE, Washington, DC 20003; 202/544-9219. The shadow government of forest love, hidden in a little office off the Beltway, coordinates over 300 forest-loving protection and business groups. SAF lobbies Congress for an end to clearcutting, diverse forests on public lands, and decentralized citizen enforcement; they keep you informed with a great newsletter and citizen action guide.

AFSEEE (Association of Forest Service Employees for Environmental Ethics): Membership $20/year. PO Box 11615, Eugene, OR 97440; 503/484-2692. This organization gives federal employees some hope that truth will not be answered by job loss or stagnation. Their journal **Inner Voice** provides hope and pride to battered

agency workers trying to implement a fair deal for the long-term health of the public lands. For non-agency employees, this is the Internet of labor and the environment at its best. **Inner Voice** has some of the best understandings of bureaucracy, your trees and grass.

CHEC (Cascade Holistic Economic Consultants): **Different Drummer** magazine $21.95/year (4 issues). 14417 SE Laurie, Oak Grove, OR 97267; 503/652-7049.

Native Forest Network: Membership $20/ year. Western: PO Box 60271, Seattle, WA 98160; 206/545-3734, fax 206/ 632-6122, email spardee@igc.apc.org . Eastern: PO Box 57, Burlington, VT 05402; 802/863-0571, fax 802/863-2532, email peacejustice@igc.apc.org.

INNER VOICE
•

The government should establish administrative unit boundaries that make ecological sense. This includes transferring the Forest Service out of the Department of Agriculture to a new Department of Natural Resources and Environment along with the Park Service, and US Fish and Wildlife Service. Ecosystem Management is not agriculture.

We also recommend creating bioregional offices to combine, consolidate, and replace the current regional and supervisors' offices. For instance, the four National Forests in the Yellowstone area would be consolidated into one region, rather than divided between regions as they are today. This would provide the most efficient method, administratively, for doing ecosystem management.

Within each Bioregion, smaller administrative units should be established to coincide with watershed boundaries. Watershed unit offices would replace district offices and would carry out all Forest Service management functions except for planning, research, and policy-making — those would take place in the Bioregional Offices. The Watershed Unit would become the "heart and soul" of the Forest Service and receive the vast majority of the funding.

OTHER GREAT RESOURCES

An Analysis of the Timber Situation in the United States, 1989—2040: Richard Haynes. 1990, U. S. Forest Service. The Forest Service document on present and anticipated uses, supply, demand and price trends for our forests. You need this to understand the commercial fate of the forests and what needs change.

Global ReLeaf/American Forests

From America's oldest conservation organization, tree love grows. Their multi-branched approach includes:

• *the Global ReLeaf Heritage Forest projects, which restore public forests damaged by hurricanes, strip mining, fires, gypsy moths, anything. Among their twenty-one heartfelt projects are efforts to restore jack pines for the endangered Kirtland's warbler (Michigan) and acacia koa in the Hakalau forests (Hawaii) to save habitat destroyed by hurricanes;*

• *the Global ReLeaf International Program, in Latin America and Europe;*

• *the Forest Policy Center, with its list of great publications;*

• *Cool Communities — a project to reduce the urban heat-island effect and carbon dioxide;*

Global ReLeaf/American Forests
Membership $30/year from American Forests, PO Box 2000, Washington, DC 20013; 800/368-5748.

• *a National Register of Big Trees (since giants impress humans more than mixed-age forests).*

If your community wants to restore a forest or plant trees, call Global ReLeaf. Advocacy, action, and education for reforestation have deep roots and a huge canopy. —Peter Warshall

*Your membership also gets you **American Forests** — an excellent, absorbing bimonthly magazine.* —J. Baldwin

Man of the Trees

Richard St. Barbe Baker was a man ahead of his time — so far ahead that now, over a decade after his death, the reforestation concepts he was preaching sixty years ago are just beginning to enter the popular consciousness. He traveled the globe teaching people the importance of planting trees, and his description of forests as the lungs of the earth anticipated in a conceptual way the Gaia Theory debated today. It's fair to call him a pioneer of environmental restoration.

*The book **Man of the Trees** is a collection of St. Barbe Baker's short writings, taken from seven of his many books. The video of the same name is a documentary of his life; it includes a great sequence with him hugging a big tree as he explains that he does this daily as a way of gathering energy and charging up his batteries. Who knows — in another sixty years, maybe we'll understand that too.*
—Richard Nilsen

• *Today it is the duty of every thinking being to live and to serve not only his own day and generation, but also generations unborn, by helping to restore and maintain the green glory of the forests of the earth.*

Man of the Trees
(Selected Writings of Richard St. Barbe Baker)
Karen Gridley, Editor. 1993; 128 pp. ISBN 0-89815-549-5
$9.95 ($13.45 postpaid). Ten Speed Press, PO Box 7123, Berkeley, CA 94707; 800/841-2665

Man of the Trees (The Life of Richard St. Barbe Baker):
25m VHS video. Item #881. $19.98 ($23.73 postpaid).
Music for Little People, PO Box 1460, Redway, CA 95560; 800/727-2233.

Fire in America

America is rethinking fire — when we want it, how intense we want it, and when to suppress it. Ranchers and prairie-restorers, as well as some foresters, have rediscovered its benefits. But the Forest Service has exploited fear of fire to allow abusive logging, which they call "fuel reductions" or "salvage logging." And insurance companies have become neurotic about fire-prone chaparral (read: Malibu) — "We won't insure preventive burns to lower fuel loads, because they might escape and burn homes. But we will pay through the teeth when a more intense fire levels hundreds of homes."

***Fire In America** coolly wades through this historic transition. Perhaps more than you want to know, it is loaded with firefighting techniques, fire ecol-*ogy, fire politics, fire regimes. But it's as captivating as fire coals pulsing late at night. —PW

•

Fire is an event, not an element. It exists within a fire environment, without which it would perish. To modify that environment is to change the nature of fire. Equally, to change the nature of fire is to modify the fire environment. The fire regime fashioned by the industrial revolution is a novel one, and the assimilation of fire required new definitions and new prescriptions for fire's use and suppression.

•

A prominent function of rivers is to transport debris. A dam impounds the flow of sediment, and silting ultimately renders the dam useless. Similarly, a function of wildland fire is to decompose forest litter. But success in "damming" all wildland fires only impounds this litter with its nutrients into a large reservoir of fuels, slowing down the growth of many ecosystems and making possible future fires of catastrophic intensity. Both fire and flood protection seem to have reached a plateau. All of the obvious sites are protected, and the costs of noticeably improving the general system by further technological development appear exorbitant relative to potential benefits.

Reforming the Western Range

*The Big Picture of public-land grazing. This issue of **Different Drummer** offers solutions to range management (public and private) that are not Babbittry. A feedlot of law, ecology, history, economics, and positive thoughts.* —PW

•

The grazing permit system is the foundation for public range management. Three defects in the permit system caused these failures:

1. The permits originally issued by both the Forest Service and the BLM exceeded their land's carrying capacity.

2. Grazing permits limit the choices open to public land ranchers. Recreation, hunting, and fishing are viable alternatives to livestock grazing, yet permits preclude such options. Since public land ranchers are not allowed to sell their grazing rights to recreation groups, their only choice is to graze the land or lose their permit to someone else who will graze it.

3. Grazing permits give permittees strong incentives to overgraze public lands. They have no legal right to the public land, yet their own land value depends on the grazing preference limit in their permit.

•

Range condition data is susceptible to political manipulation. For example, to gain support for passage of the Federal Land Policy and Management Act (FLPMA) of 1976, the BLM claimed that range conditions had significantly declined over the previous ten years. In 1984, BLM reversed itself, claiming major improvements in both

Fire in America
(A Cultural History of Wildland and Rural Fire)
Stephen J. Pyne. 1982; 654 pp.
ISBN 0-317-03363-8 $14.95
($16.95 postpaid). The Phoenix Society, 11 Rust Hill Road, Levittown, PA 19056

Grassfire suppression with sprinklers, blankets, and buckets, Oklahoma, 1908. A water wagon typically accompanied such an operation to replenish the sprinklers.

his page gives you reforms for the ranch. But, remember: you buy the beef. If ranchers produce beef that despoils riparian and grassland recovery, that continues to kill non-target predators and birds, that eliminates wildlife and precludes public uses, then the best response is to boycott. If ranchers will not take responsibility for what happens to their cattle after the ranch — feedlot pollution, river pollution during grain production, sloppy slaughtering, and the employment of hormone and other chemical additives — why risk poisoning the nation's rivers or your body by buying beef?

The porterhouse feds — Democrats or Republicans — will not help. It's citizen action all the way to the barn. —Peter Warshall

☞ Bighorns forage on heavily grazed BLM cattle range near Cody, Wyoming, but if snow piles too high they may starve — while the cattle responsible for the lack of forage are fed hay. —*Waste of the West*

Prairies

The quiet documents of restoration. **Managing Change** *addresses the restoration of western riparian and grazing land. The other three pamphlets are tiny seeds of thought on prairie restoration. By the next* **Catalog**, *this hope will overwhelm the page with cowboy and enviro experience. The dialog has irreversibly changed.* —PW

•
The most obvious effects of a burn are easily seen. Fire rejuvenates a prairie; more plants flower, produce seed, grow taller, and are generally more robust than the previous year. Specifically, fire lengthens the growing season for most native prairie plants and shortens it for the Eurasian "weeds." Fire increases available nutrients through indirect stimulation of microbial activity in the soil, and by releasing a small amount of nutrients from the ash. Fire also controls invasion of shrubs and trees. —*How to Manage Small Prairie Fires*

•
Wherever you are, whatever your particular riparian grazing problem there are three basic ways to treat. From the least to the most complicated, they are:

Exclude livestock from the riparian area with stream corridor fencing.

Put riparian areas in separate pastures to get tight control over the season, duration and intensity of livestock use.

Herd or use some other grazing strategy to limit the season, duration, and intensity of grazing on riparian areas.

Managing Change (Livestock Grazing on Western Riparian Areas): Ed Chaney, Wayne Elmore & William S. Platts. Northwest Resource Information Center, 1993; 31 pp. Free from U. S. Environmental Protection Agency/Attn: Robert Goo, 401 M Street SW, Washington, DC 20460.

Prairie Restoration for the Beginner: Prairie Seed Source staff. 1988; 32 pp.
Prairie Propagation Handbook: Harold W. Rock. 1981; 74 pp.
Each $4.95 ($5.45 postpaid). Wehr Nature Center, 9701 W. College Avenue, Franklin, WI 53132.

How to Manage Small Prairie Wildfires: Wayne R. Pauly. 1985; 30 pp. $4 postpaid. Friends of Dane County Park, 4318 Robertson Road, Madison, WI 53714; 608/246-3896.

Top: Results of a century of season-long (June-October) continuous grazing.

Bottom: Results after excluding livestock for five years. —Managing Change

range condition and trend. FLPMA was supposed to have accomplished in eight brief years what would normally have taken nature a quarter-century to achieve.

The snail-like pace of improvement in range conditions lies at the heart of the environmental controversy surrounding public grazing lands. Symbolic of that controversy is the dismal state of western wetlands. Although data are incomplete, as much as 80 percent of all grazed riparian and wetland habitats on Forest Service and BLM lands are in depleted condition with no indication of recovery.

•
Proposed Reforms
1. Phase out all subsidies to ranchers as quickly as possible.
2. Completely eliminate use-it-or-lose-it rules.
3. Eliminate base property requirements so that anyone can buy permits from existing ranchers even if they own no land.
4. Reverse the historic policies that favor small allotments that promote overgrazing and are economically unsustainable.
5. Dissolve community allotments into individual allotments or make the associations that run them responsible for the actions of their members.

Reforming the Western Range
(*Different Drummer*, Spring 1994)
Randal O'Toole, Editor. Single copy $5.95 postpaid; $21.95/year (4 issues). Cascade Holistic Economic Consultants, 14417 SE Laurie, Oak Grove, OR 97267; 503/652-7049

6. Reward the best ranchers with permits that last longer than the standard ten years.
7. Allow national forests and BLM districts to set their own grazing fees.
8. Allow the Forest Service and BLM districts to set their own grazing fees.
9. Fund the agencies out of their net income, not out of tax dollars.
10. Create a biodiversity trust fund that will give managers and landowners incentives to protect plant and animal diversity.

How Not to Be Cowed • Waste of the West

The Natural Resources Defense Council's **How Not to Be Cowed** *is the "toolbox" for activists challenging BLM allotments or seeking to take responsibility for the land owned by all of us (hikers, hunters, anglers, photographers, river runners, native plant enthusiasts, biologists . . .).* **Waste of the West** *is the best muckraker's cry for saving the grass. Not liked by anyone in ranching circles.* —PW

•
This is not just a dispute over cows and sheep. It's a fight over who controls the public lands. To tip the balance our way, we'll need a vast infusion of concern, interest, and action by all who care about these treasures.

•
Issues to Raise on Any Grazing-Related Decision:
Determine whether the number of livestock proposed in a plan or permit represents an increase or a reduction in comparison to the "actual use" made for the allotment in recent years.

Insist that BLM prepare an EA or an EIS in order to evaluate the potential environmental impacts of proposed range "improvement" projects.

Ask BLM to state the cost of the project and whether funds will realistically be available to carry it out.

Ask BLM to document soil conditions in grazed areas, including erosion and soil compaction.

Ask BLM to document the availability of ephemeral forage *each* season they propose to graze it.

Insist that BLM demonstrate—and obtain the Fish and Wildlife Service's concurrence—that ephemeral grazing will not harm sensitive plant and wildlife species.

Has BLM gathered the necessary data to show that state water quality improvement standards are being met?

Request copies of water quality monitoring data and standards. —*How Not to Be Cowed*

How Not to Be Cowed
Johanna Wald. Natural Resources Defense Council & Southern Utah Wilderness Alliance, 1991; 70 pp. $3 postpaid. SUWA, 1471 South 1100 East, Salt Lake City, UT 84105; 801/486-3161

Waste of the West
(Public Lands Ranching)
Lynn Jacobs. 1991; 602 pp.
ISBN 0-9629386-0-2 $28 postpaid. Lynn Jacobs, PO Box 5784, Tucson, AZ 85703

Michael Ableman

The problems of our farmland and production of our food no longer belong exclusively to the 2 percent of the population we call farmers. When we rejoin the food process we begin to see ourselves as farmers, and the whole planet as our farm to be nurtured and cared for. And when we rejoin the food process we rejoin the environmental process as well: we begin to understand more precisely what part of our planet belongs to us for food, for fiber, and for fuel, and what part must be left sacred to nature.
—Michael Ableman, **From the Good Earth**: A Celebration of Growing Food Around the World

SUSTAINABLE AGRICULTURE STARTS WITH A MOMENT OF HESITATION, the stop-time in the movement of a piece of toast to the mouth, a space for words of grace. Thank the soil that nurtured the crop; the seeds that germinated; the water that sustained growth; the sun for its energy; the farmer and picker and quality grader and trucker for their toil; the factory hands for processing the grains and composing the bread; the retailer for ordering the right brands. Saying grace is paying homage to the props of our vitality. "To sustain" literally means to support from below.

The contrast of sustainable and non-sustainable ag is clear. On one hand, the oversimplified monoculture of agbiz covers its fields with huge quantities of petroleum-based fertilizers, herbicides, and pesticides. Its machines tend to compact and disrupt the soil, increasing erosion on slopes. Its water is imported from deep groundwater or from rivers hundreds of miles away; the runoff is loaded with pollutants. On the other hand, the complex agroecology of organic farming minimizes chemical use. Manures, green cover crops, mixed crop/livestock rotations, and biological disease management and pest management nurture the soil's tilth, prevent soil depletion, and keep the nutrient cycle closed to obviate off-site damage. Agbiz survives because of low labor use, high yields (not nutrition or good taste), vertical and lateral corporate integration, and price supports. Agbiz's emblem is the duck with a twisted bill from selenium poisoning. Organic farming's emblem is a superb-tasting tomato.

The transition to sustainable ag has two paths: diversified farming and low-input farming. Many North American farmers are well down one or both of these paths. Diversified farming simply adds more kinds of crops, trees, livestock, rotations, and "green" market products. Low-input farming simply reduces energy, water, agrochemicals, plowing, and slope cultivation. Both lead to lower environmental impacts, lower price supports—and, at times, a small reduction in yields. But, as sustainability requires, the overall economic ecological cost balance improves.

To join the practice of sustainable ag, you need not be a farmer. Are you tired of simulated tomatoes or chemical-loaded milk? Shop at farmers' markets and fruit stands to support and influence your local good farmers. You can pressure the retailer, the health and safety labelers, and the farmers to improve food health. You can work with farm laborers, who suffer the most severely from ingesting agrochemicals, or become an expert in toxics and enter the regulatory health and safety administrations. You can join an environmental group concerned with the offsite impacts of ag erosion or toxics on downstream peoples or in-stream fish.

In the next pages, Richard Nilsen and Karen Van Epen have green-thumbed the best tools for sustainable ag. After weeding and pruning the mass of material, we harvest the same ol' ancient advice: If you want a good tomato, find a spot near the window or a corner of the yard, and grow your own. Before you eat, say grace. —Peter Warshall

As the photos from his book on pages 94 to 99 demonstrate, Michael Ableman is a widely traveled master photographer. As the quote preceding Peter Warshall's introductory essay testifies, he is a poetic visionary. He is also an organic farmer whose fertile and productive land is now surrounded by suburbs. Who better to show us the traditional, industrial, and sustainable forms of agriculture, pointing out the new way to farm? —Karen Van Epen

From the Good Earth: A Celebration of Growing Food Around the World: Michael Ableman, 1993; 168 pp. ISBN 0-8109-2517-6. $27.50 ($30.50) postpaid from Harry N. Abrams, Inc., 100 5th Ave., New York, NY 10011; 800/345-1359.

Agroecology

The agricultural establishment has spent an inordinate amount of energy supporting the claim that alternative agriculture is old-fashioned and inefficient. Miguel Altieri and company were the first ones to organize all the evidence, showing that a solid foundation does underpin the concepts of agroecology.

An environmentally and socially sensitive approach, agroecology considers the ecological sustainability of the whole system, rather than the production of a specific crop. It recognizes that good farming involves management of many intricately intertwined resources—that there's more to it than just maximizing the yield of the target crop.

To illustrate agroecological principles, the authors draw on examples from traditional Third World farmers and small farms in Europe and the US. They provide a simple synthesis of research on novel agroecosystems and an analysis of ecologically based farms.

Agroecology
(The Scientific Basis of Alternative Agriculture)
Miguel A. Altieri, Editor 1987; 227 pp.
ISBN 0-8133-7284-4
$39 ($43 postpaid) from Westview Press, 5500 Central Avenue, Boulder, CO 80301; 303/444-3541

Not just another dry scientific treatise, this seminal work speaks in an elegant tone that lifts science to the level of philosophy. —Karen Van Epen

●

One of the major reasons that farmers throughout the world choose to use polycultures is that frequently more yield can be harvested from a given area sown in polyculture than from an equivalent area sown in separate patches of monocultures. This increased land-use efficiency is important in areas of the world where farms are small because of socioeconomic conditions and where crop production is limited to the amount of land that can be cleared, prepared and weeded (usually by hand) in a limited amount of time.

The Unsettling of America

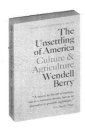

The Unsettling of America
(Culture & Agriculture)
Wendell Berry. Sierra Club Books, 1986; 228 pp. ISBN 0-87156-772-5
$9 ($12 postpaid) from Sierra Club Store Orders, 730 Polk Street, San Francisco, CA 94109; 800/935-1056

Our land is more undone by our agriculture than by any other mischief. Farmer/poet/essayist Wendell Berry speaks to the matter with plain speech — it rasps the brain, leaves memory of the thought. Don't say it is no longer possible to do our farming right. Berry is. —Stewart Brand

●

We need wilderness as a standard of civilization and as a cultural model. Only by preserving areas where nature's processes are undisturbed can we preserve an accurate sense of the impact of civilization upon its natural sources. Only if we know how the land *was* can we tell how it *is*.

Family Farming

The best analysis I've seen of American agriculture — clearheaded, informative, practical, and well written. This honest book acknowledges the mistakes and shortcomings of family farms, while arguing for their preservation. Those interested in sustainable agriculture will find this a plausible view of how we get from here to there. —David Orr

●

Public policy should make ownership the just reward of good land use, and good land use the obligation of owners.

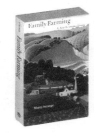

Family Farming
(A New Economic Vision)
Marty Strange. Bison Books, 1989; 311 pp.
ISBN 0-8032-9194-9
$7.50 ($9.50 postpaid) from Institute for Food and Development Policy, 398 60th Street, Oakland, CA 94618; 800/888-3314

OTHER GREAT RESOURCES

Seed to Civilization: The Story of Food: by Charles B. Heiser, revised 1990. Harvard U. Press, 228 pp, softcover. An eminent ethnobotanist regales us with facts and anecdotes about how humans have produced and eaten food since prehistoric times.

From the Ground Up: Rethinking Industrial Agriculture: by Goering et al., 1993.

ISEC, 120 pp, softcover. A pointed critique of modern agriculture, this advocates decentralization and reconsideration of traditional ag practices.

Food for the Future:Conditions and Contradictions of Sustainability Patricia Allen, Editor. John Wiley & Sons, 1993; 328 pp, softcover

Michael Ableman

At Nature's Pace

"Pure, unmitigated, unashamed anger" about the decline of our rural society drove Gene Logsdon to write this book. Even so, he has managed to include a good measure of optimism and humanity in these pages.

Logsdon knows what he's talking about. He's an experienced farmer from the heartland who has been writing on farm issues for many fruitful years. Equally at home with university deans and Amish plowmen, he helps us understand that healthy agricultural practices transcend technological efficiency. His observations on crop subsidies, ag education, technology and mechanization, or the harmonies of cutting firewood, offer practical examples and valuable metaphors for the development of sustainable human life on Earth. —David Katz

•
I can give three reasons for my prediction that the number of food and fiber producers ("food and fiber producer" is the only definition of farmer that works) is about to increase. One: historically, in all the past civilizations I have studied, the denser the population becomes, the smaller and more numerous the farms become. Two: financially, the economies of scale that apparently rule manufacturing do not really apply to any sustainable kind of food production; when you count all the costs, it is cheaper to raise a zucchini in your garden than on your megafarm. And three: socially people are beginning to understand they really are what they eat and are demanding quality food, which megafarms can't supply.

At Nature's Pace
(Farming and the American Dream)
Gene Logsdon. Pantheon Books, 1994;
208 pp. ISBN 0-679-42741-4
$23 ($25 postpaid) from Random House/
Order Dept., 400 Hahn Road,
Westminster, MD 21157; 800/733-3000

T he endless balancing acts of civilization get played out on the land. Here starvation, there economic collapse from oversupply. Here urban claustrophobia, there rural loneliness. Human life dangles on a few threads — sunshine, rainfall and topsoil. From these come plants, and the kind of relationship we have with green things defines who we are. —Richard Nilsen

Sustainable Agricultural Systems

The closest thing so far to an encyclopedia on the subject, this is both a major reference and a comprehensive reader. It's all in here, from history & social issues to the specific components of sustainable ag systems in the temperate & tropic zones. —Karen Van Epen

International Federation of Organic Agriculture Movements (IFOAM): Ökozentrum Imsbach, D66636 Tholey-Theley, Germany; Phone: 49-6853-5190, Fax: 49-6853-3011. For twenty years the most important forum for sustainable agriculture groups around the world. Their publications include a member directory, handbooks of standards, and proceedings of their valuable conferences.

Community Alliance with Family Farmers (CAFF): Membership $25/year. PO Box 464, Davis, CA 95617; 916/756-8518. Working to promote social justice and environmental responsibility, this alliance of family farmers and eco-activists sponsors the Lighthouse Farm Network and other programs. LFN provides technical and peer support to farmers seeking more ecological ag methods.

International Alliance for Sustainable Agriculture (IASA): Membership $25/year from IASA, 1701 University Avenue SE, Minneapolis, MN 55414; 612/331-1099. IASA concentrates on education, publications and networks to support sustainable ag.

Ethics and Agriculture

Agriculture is changing around the world; how we think about it is changing as well. No longer content to let the "experts" and the farm lobby determine farm policy, people everywhere are demanding to understand the true costs incurred when food is produced. Whether the issues are pesticides, biotechnology, or the growth of corporate agribusiness, the connections between the technology of farming, the health of our rural communities, and the taste of our food are becoming evident. This book can help you understand the nature of those connections.

The sixty authors who contributed to this thick compendium explore a wide range of ideas and points of view about many of the ethical issues we face. The result is a very useful reference for finding material on farm structure, biotechnology, food price issues, soil conservation, land trusting, pesticide policy and myriad other subjects. —DK

•
Sustainable agriculturalists contend that agriculture is not practiced and cannot be understood, taught, or researched in isolation. Individual plants, and animals, fields, farms and agriculture as a whole exist as part of a biological, social, and economic system and can be truly comprehended only by way of an ecological or holistic perspective — one that recognizes the whole to be greater than the sum of its parts, one that insists that the parts cannot be understood without understanding the whole. The task of shifting world views is tremendous and may well require major reorganization of agriculture departments, programs, and evaluation criteria.

Ethics and Agriculture
(An Anthology on Current Issues in World Context)
Charles V. Blatz, Editor. 1991; 673 pp.
ISBN 0-89301-134-7
$24.95 ($28.95 postpaid) from University of Idaho Press, 16 Brink Hall, Moscow, ID 83843; 208/885-5939

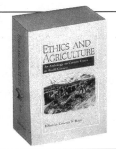

Meeting the Expectations of the Land

The ideas here are visionary in that they look both forward and backward in time, but lest you think the book advocates a retreat to agricultural animism, it is worth emphasizing that these ideas are also very practical. You won't find them in use on most American farms today because there the emphasis has been on productivity and profits.

Profits? Even if your news from the farm comes only from the TV, you know you can forget about "profits" in farming. And productivity? Sure, that's there, but it is the same kind you find in a coal mine: you shut it down when the coal is gone and move on. When the topsoil is gone, or the soil is salted out from irrigation, where do you go?

You go to a kind of agriculture that can sustain; not only the land, but also the life on it and in it, as well as the people who work it and those who depend on them for food. This book is full of clues to how that kind of agriculture will work, by people like Gene Logsdon, John Todd and Gary Snyder. —Richard Nilsen

•
I once asked an Amish farmer who had only twenty-six acres why he didn't acquire a bit more land. He looked around at his ten fine cows, his sons hoeing the corn with him, his spring water running continuously by gravity through house and barn, his few fat hogs, his sturdy buildings, his good wife heaping the table with food, his fine flock of hens, his plot of tobacco and acre of strawberries, his handmade hickory chairs (which he sold for all the extra cash he really needed), and he said, "Well, I'm just not smart enough to farm anymore than this *well*." I have a hunch no one could.

Meeting the Expectations of the Land
(Essays in Sustainable Agriculture and Stewardship)
Wes Jackson, Wendell Berry, & Bruce Colman, Editors. North Point Press, 1984;
250 pp. ISBN 0-86547-172-X
$12.50 ($16.75 postpaid) from Putnam Publishing Group/Order Dept., PO Box 506, East Rutherford, NJ 07073; 800/631-8571

Sustainable Agricultural Systems
Clive A. Edwards. 1990; 696 pp.
ISBN 0-935734-21-X
$60 ($64.25 postpaid) from Soil and Water Conservation Society, 7515 NE Ankeny Road, Ankeny, IA 50021; 800/843-7645

•
When animals are confined, manure can be managed to use the nutrients more efficiently. Management strategy should be to minimize the loss of nutrients during collection, storage, and application and to apply manure uniformly to maximize nutrient use by crops. As in a pasture system, nitrogen is the nutrient that is most readily lost from manure in confinement. Therefore, manure should be collected as quickly as possible and properly stored or applied to fields to reduce ammonia volatilization. Safley and associates reported a 23 percent loss of nitrogen from dairy manure from the time of defecation in the barnlot until removal from storage (stored as liquid in above-ground tanks or earthen lagoons). Most of the loss occurred during the 24-hour period between barnlot cleanings.

Michael Ableman

See The Journal of Soil and Water Conservation on p. 88.

Soil and Water Quality

Agricultural practices can wreak havoc with our nation's wealth of rich soil and abundant water. Every day the news makes us more aware of the increased degradation of our resources: polluted wells, flooded river channels, reduced farm productivity, poisoned wildlife. The National Research Council documents and quantifies these problems here, offering an agenda for long-term conservation. —Karen Van Epen

•

National policy should seek to (1) conserve and enhance soil quality as a fundamental first step to environmental improvement; (2) increase nutrient, pesticide, and irrigation use efficiencies in farming systems; (3) increase the resistance of farming systems to erosion and runoff; and (4) make greater use of field and landscape buffer zones.

•

Although erosion processes can be complex, the principles of controlling erosion are relatively simple. Effective water erosion control requires simultaneous efforts to increase the degree to which and the length of the season during which the soil is covered by plants or plant residues and to decrease the volume and energy of runoff water. Effective wind erosion control also depends on increased amounts of soil cover and reductions in the energy of wind that is in contact with soil particles.

Soil and Water Quality
(An Agenda for Agriculture)
National Research Council Committee on Long-Range Soil and Water Conservation Policy. 1993; 420 pp. ISBN 0-309-04933-4 $59.95 ($63.95 postpaid) from National Academy Press, Box 285, Washington, DC 20055; 800/624-6242

Spanish in the Field

It's a fact of life that most farmworkers in the West speak Spanish. Sign language and Spanglish just don't cover the fine points of pruning, mechanics or soil preparation, making it hard on English-only farmers. Organized around farm tasks and situations, this set can quickly bring you up to speed. —Howard Beeman

Spanish in the Field
(Practical Spanish for Ranchers, Farmers, or Vintners)
Carmen P. Clough. 1983; 256 pp.
ISBN 0-932857-02-7
$23.95 ($27.95 postpaid)
Book, dictionary and 4 audio tapes, ISBN 0-914330-59-4, $59.95 ($63.95 postpaid); AgAccess, PO Box 2008, Davis, CA 95617; phone 916/756-7177, fax 916/756-7188

BOOKS

Preserving Family Lands: Essential Tax Strategies for the Landowner: Steven Small, 1992. Landowner Planning Center, PO Box 4508, Boston, MA 02101-4508; 617/728-9799. How to avoid the pitfalls.

Fertile Soil: A Grower's Guide to Organic & Inorganic Fertilizers: Robert Parnes, 1990. AgAccess. Hard-to-find information.

Alternative Agriculture: 1989, National Academy Press. An overview of alternative farming practices and a report on specific techniques.

The New Farm Magazine of Regenerative Agriculture: PO Box 7306, Red Oak, IA 51591; 800/365-3276. Consistently the place to find the practical answers about how to put people, profit and biological permanence back into farming.

Passing Down the Farm: The Farm Crisis

Even the most successful family farm has to deal with the problems of one generation handing off to the next. Grandpa and Dad tend to be rugged individualists who know just how to do everything. Where do the younger folks fit in? And what about the pressure to cash in from off-farm family members, who may neither benefit from nor appreciate the intangible advantages of farm life?

We are all entangled in the complexities of family life, but with a multimillion-dollar business in the mix, things can get really difficult. Very reassuring to find this map through the maze, from some people who have seen it all. —Karen Van Epen

•

Farm ownership can be like sailing in rough weather. The wind and the speed are exhilarating but only if you're in control. With the family involved intimately in the operation, the deck can get crowded with a sometimes unruly mob. It's bad enough when the crew isn't organized to work together, but it can get downright dangerous when people start fighting over control of the helm.

Small wonder everybody starts dreaming about solitude and peace.

Families who own farms travel together, out in some pretty rough weather. They do it day after day, season after season. It's tough to be stoic — let alone enthusiastic — when your own crew seems determined to turn you broadside to the waves. For those farming families who manage themselves well, the journey can be an enticing, if risky, challenge. For those who are poorly organized, however — as far too many are — the experience can be hell.

Passing Down the Farm
(The *Other* Farm Crisis)
Donald J. Jonovic & Wayne D. Messick.
1991; 209 pp. ISBN 0-915607-08-5
$24.95 ($28.95 postpaid) from Jamieson Press, PO Box 909, Cleveland, OH 44120; 216-752-7970

Saving the Farm: A Handbook for Conserving Agricultural Land

Our continually expanding cities gobble up farms at an alarming rate. That process involves so many commissions and regulations that even well-informed activist groups have trouble negotiating the labyrinth.

The American Farmland Trust is the foremost authority on preserving agricultural lands. Their handbook pinpoints resource information and organizations. Based upon the Trust's experience in California, it shows us how to implement conservation programs by networking with local government agencies. Private options for land conservation are also covered. Detailed, easy-to-follow, effective strategies are outlined in a meticulously organized format. Indispensable for local governments, landowners, and private organizations interested in land use issues. —Karen Van Epen

•

A conservation easement is a voluntary agreement between a landowner and a qualified conservation organization. This agreement legally restricts uses of the land, such as building houses on it, that would reduce or destroy its potential for agricultural production. A conservation easement can also be use to conserve other natural resources, such as soil, water quality, wildlife and scenic values of the land. The principal objective of an agricultural conservation easement is to safeguard the productivity of the farmland, and the integrity of the agricultural operation.

Saving the Farm
(A Handbook for Conserving Agricultural Land)
American Farmland Trust. 1990.
$20 ($22.50 postpaid) from American Farmland Trust Western Office, 1949 5th Street, Suite 101, Davis, CA 95616; 916/753-1073

Farming in Nature's Image

It's an American tradition that the most original thinking comes from those outside the academic pale. Since 1976, the Land Institute in Kansas has been investigating a system of agriculture based on the concept that farms should mimic the ecosystems in which they exist. Research has centered primarily around temperate grain production using perennial seed crops, with the prairie as a model.

Some potential problems attend a polyculture of perennial crops. Must we sacrifice high yields? How to calculate soil nutrient losses? The Institute tackles such questions in the search for long-range solutions to the problems of modern agriculture.

The Institute does not confine itself to this research, however. Its chief spokesman, Wes Jackson, is one of the most eloquent and persuasive pro- *ponents of sustainable agriculture. This volume includes the arguments leveled by Jackson and others against industrial agriculture, following up with this new approach to solving these problems. —Karen Van Epen*

•

Over a short 100 years of applying monoculture farming to the native prairies of North America, 50 percent of the topsoil's latent productivity has slipped away. In contrast, the native prairie built and maintained soil and supported large populations of grazers. Perhaps before the remaining 50 percent of latent soil productivity is used up, a model for the future of North America's breadbasket, a model that mimics the native vegetation, should be considered.

•

Our agricultural science institutions are now and have always been closely aligned with industry. From their inception, the public agricultural research institutions in

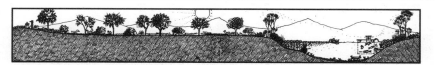

Michael Ableman

Slide to the Garden Pages and check out Pest Control. p.166

Permaculture

This is the book everybody was looking for twenty years ago. The one that explains how to grow food, fix broken land, and devise a better society — anywhere you happen to live. Couldn't find it then because the only folks doing decentralized, ecologically sustainable agricultural systems in those days were scattered around the Third World, and they didn't publish. Well, here it is — a treasure-house of keen observation, responsive design, patience, and hope. —Richard Nilsen

•

Mollisonian Permaculture Principles:

1. Work with nature, rather than against the natural elements, forces, pressures, processes, agencies, and evolutions, so that we assist rather than impede natural developments.

2. The problem is the solution; everything works both ways. It is only how we see things that makes them advantageous or not (if the wind blows cold, let us use both its strength and its coolness to advantage). A corollary of this principle is that everything is a positive resource; it is just up to us to work out *how* we may use it as such.

3. Make the least change for the greatest possible effect.

Permaculture
(A Designers' Manual)
Bill Mollison. Tagari Publications, Australia, 1988; 575 pp. ISBN 0-908228-01-5
$55 ($59 postpaid) from AgAccess, PO Box 2008, Davis, CA 95617; phone 916/756-7177, fax 916/756-7188

the United States have approached their work from the vantage point of the industrialist entrepreneur. This view dictates that solutions be compatible with the goal of maximizing profitability via maximum production and minimum labor. It follows from the premise that the country has plentiful resources and a shortage of labor.

•

Breeding Perennial Seed Crops. Two distinct approaches are possible in the modern development of perennial grains. One approach starts with annual grain crops and attempts to turn them into perennials via wide hybridization with perennial relatives. The rationale for this approach is that annual crops have proven themselves to have already undergone selection and domestication over the last several thousand years. Hence, they already show such agronomically favorable characteristics as edibility, high yield, large seed size, ease of threshing, synchronous maturity, and resistance to shattering and lodging (falling over). Wild perennials, on the other hand, rarely display these traits.

Organic Farming

Organic farming is more sophisticated and complex than conventional agribusiness with its "out of the bottle" solutions.

This, the most practical of the general books on organic farming, illuminates the real techniques. Not just another overview, it features long, detailed chapters on specifics — manure management, crop rotation design, soil health, weed management, and grassland and fodder crops. Valuable to farmers everywhere, this wide-ranging resource from the UK also covers switching to organics, livestock husbandry, marketing, and potential financial returns. Nicolas Lampkin describes the cropping systems of many different farms, to give us a feel for the infinite combinations of soil, weather, and personal inclination that shape them. —Karen Van Epen

•

The crops grown today have evolved over millions of years to utilise the nutrients made available in the soil by the activity of soil microorganisms. They have developed symbiotic relationships with the soil fauna and flora, the most notable examples being Rhizobia bacteria which live in nodules on the roots of legumes and fix nitrogen from the atmosphere, and the mycorrhizae, small fungal threads which penetrate plant roots. and allow nutrients to be transferred directly from the soil into the plant's root system. The use of readily available, soluble mineral fertilisers by-passes or short circuits the biological processes to which the plants have become adapted and makes the nutrients directly available to the growing crop.

Organic Farming
Nicolas Lampkin. Farming Press UK, 1990; 720 pp. ISBN 0-85236-191-2
$51.25 ($55.25 postpaid) from AgAccess, PO Box 2008, Davis, CA 95617; phone 916/756-7177, fax 916/756-7188

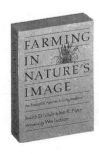

Farming in Nature's Image
(An Ecological Approach to Agriculture)
Judith D. Soule & Jon K. Piper. 1992; 286 pp. ISBN 0-933280-88-2
$19.95 ($24.20 postpaid) from Island Press, Box 7, Covelo, CA 95428; 800/828-1302

Healthy Harvest

Every sector of sustainable agriculture worldwide is included in this directory: ag production, education, horticulture, pest management, marketing, food distribution, politics, reforestation, international development, certification, appropriate technology, intentional communities, publications, and more. —Karen Van Epen

•

Manor House Agriculture Center: Private Bag, Kitale, KENYA ; Davies W. Nakitare (254)-325-20488
The Center was started in 1985 to teach bio-intensive agriculture to local women. In 1986, the Center opened its doors to local school dropouts. The Center offers all a two-year course in bio-intensive agriculture. Their goal is to stress the sustainable agriculture concept in rural communities through the training of young Kenyan school dropouts . Two English and/or Kiswahili speaking volunteers needed for one or two years.

Many Hands Organic Farm: R.F.D. 2, Barre, MA 01005; Julie Rawson/Jack Kitteredge, Owners; (508)355-2853
Many Hands Organic Farm is a 55-acre NOFA/Mass certified organic farm in Central Massachusetts. A family operation, our four children, aged 9-13 are an essential part of our work force. We grow two acres of vegetables, one acre of small fruits, free range hogs, chickens, turkeys, geese, and ducks for market. We also have a milk cow. We are seeking an apprentice for April-November. We pay $50/week plus room and board. We also are headquarters for NOFA/Mass, the NOFA Summer Conference and The Natural Farmer Quarterly.

Maple Farm: Old Hardwick Road Barre, MA 01005; Peter Wartiainen, Jr. (617)355-4092
Maple Farm is an organic homestead with roosters, 500 hens, four pigs, bees, vegetables, disease-free apples, strawberries, blueberries, and raspberries. The farm produces cider and maple syrup. Two-wheel tractors, rototillers, chainsaws, dehydrator, and a wood splitter are among farm equipment used. There is a green house in operation. Apprentices are accepted year-round.

Maplewood Organic Farm: 132 Belchertown Road, Amherst, MA 01002; David Holm, Farm Manager. (413)256-0926; (413)253-9472

Marsh Haven Farm: 47815 Floras Lake Loop, Langlois, OR 97450. E. Mulligan. Organic strawberries, blueberries, flowers, herbs, and selected row crops. Bed and breakfast in a beautiful 115 year old farmhouse on the wild Oregon coast.

Healthy Harvest
(A Global Directory of Sustainable Agriculture & Horticulture Organizations 1992); 194 pp. ISBN 0-932857-09-4
$19.95 ($23.95 postpaid) from AgAccess, PO Box 2008, Davis, CA 95617; phone 916/756-7177, fax 916/756-7188

GROUPS

American Farmland Trust: 1920 N St., N.W., Suite 400, Washington, D.C. 20036; 202/ 659-5170. Dedicated to the conservation of the nation's best farmland through public education, policy development, and private land conservation transactions.

Land Stewardship Project: 14758 Ostlund Trail N., Marine, MN 55047; 612/433-2770. Excellent publications by and for farmers about innovative, sustainable farm practices in the Midwest.

Kerr Center for Sustainable Agriculture: P.O. Box 588, Poteau, OK 74953; 918/647-9123. Technical assistance and publications on ecologically/economically sound methods of producing food and sustaining farm livelihood.

Land Institute: 2440 E. Water Well Road, Salina, KS 67401; 913/823-5376, fax 913/823-8728. A research & education non-profit dedicated to sustainable agriculture and good stewardship of the earth.

Organic Farming Research Foundation: Box 440, Santa Cruz, CA 95061; 408/426-6606. Bob Scowcroft, Executive Director. Directed primarily by organic farmers, it funds innovative on-farm research and disseminates information. Write for grant guidelines and info.

The Bio-Dynamic Farming & Gardening Association: PO Box 550, Kimberton, PA 19442; 800/516-7797. Begun in 1924 by Rudolf Steiner in Switzerland. Combines the earthy and the metaphysical to produce very healthy plants and animals.

Michael Ableman

Check Getting Started in
Telecommunications on
page 260.

Getting the Real Stuff: Organic Food

What is "*organic*"? Over the last twenty years, as the organic farming movement found its footing to become an important supplier of food, many different definitions of the term have been proposed and used.

Organic farmers manage their farms as whole systems, using biological methods to improve soil fertility and promote ecological stability in the fields. Chemical fertilizers and pesticides have no utility or application in this approach. The fact that organic farmers don't use these chemicals is often considered the definitive aspect of organic farming, but in fact what defines organic farming is this whole-systems approach.

Consumers have often been confused about which food is "really" organic. Occasionally bogus food has been sold as organic. Certification procedures for growers were left to a host of private and non-profit groups scattered around the world, with the lead taken by organic farmer organizations like the California Certified Organic Farmers, which developed detailed certification and labeling programs.

As consumers became better acquainted with organic food and pesticide issues in the late Eighties, some commercial laboratories sold testing services so supermarkets could claim "no detectable pesticide residues," without addressing the issue of how the food was actually grown. Various state governments, responding to pressure from activists and taking their cues from statewide organic farming groups, began passing regulations governing the use of the term "organic." More than twenty-three states passed organic laws of one type or another, from the comprehensive, detailed programs of California and Texas, to Maryland's one-paragraph statute.

In October 1993, the federal Organic Foods Production Act went into effect, although it has a long way to go before being fully implemented. Thanks to the experience and input of the farmer groups who pioneered certification, the Act defines organic food by how it is grown, not by food safety standards. It sets minimum production standards for all food sold as organic, and requires a three-year transition period to clear the soil of chemicals. The law mandates a certification program and establishes a National Organic Standards Board.

Passed in the last days of the Bush administration, the law failed to provide for the appropriation of funds to set up the Standards Board, and the USDA did nothing to get the Act running. The Clinton administration is now talking a good organic line, but the USDA is moving very slowly to supply the staff needed. Only minimal funding is available to implement the provisions of the Act so it can begin to provide a workable standard for the organic food market.

Some long-time leaders of the organic movement have voiced concerns that leaving the business of organic certification in the hands of government is not such a good idea. As the bureaucrats take over, there is the danger that organic farming will end up being defined according to a list of allowable materials, without thought for overall ecosystem health or the quality of the food being produced.

Already there have been calls to tax organic producers to pay for the certification process. The response to this has been the suggestion that all chemicals used on farms should carry a special "eco-tax" commensurate with their effect on the ecosystem both on and off the farm.

Along with these new national standards comes the possibility that the very large, well-capitalized "mega-farms" that now dominate American food production will enter the organic market and blow away the small family farms that have been the mainstay of the organic market. This would be especially tragic in view of the fact that the growth of the organic market has enabled small farmers across the county to enjoy a small measure of prosperity these last few years. —David Katz

CERTIFICATION ORGANIZATIONS

California Certified Organic Farmers (CCOF): 303 Potrero St. Suite 51, Santa Cruz, CA 95060; 408/423-2263, fax 408/423-4528. A democratic association of chartered grassroots chapters, this twenty-year-old group is the model for the nation. CCOF represents over 600 growers cultivating more than 70,000 acres. Their excellent program has spawned such detailed publications as Certification Handbook and the List of Growers Crop Index (see Directories).

Texas Department of Agriculture: Consumer Services Division, PO Box 12847, Austin, TX 78711; 512/475-1641, fax 512/ 453-7643. Texas boasts the best and most extensive state-run organic certification program.

Oregon Tilth: P.O. Box 218, Tualatin, OR 97062; 503/691-2514. Founded in 1974, this organization operates a very good certification program. They also publish a newsletter and conduct all kinds of educational activities.

Organic Crop Improvement Association (OCIA): 3185 Twp. Rd. 179, Bellefontaine, OH 43311; 513/592-4983, fax 513/593-3831. A farmer-owned and-operated international grassroots certification program with fifty-eight chapters. Food processing companies getting supplies from distant sources often use this widely recognized group to certify that the crops are indeed organic. Lots of support services for farmers through the regional chapters.

Quality Assurance International: 12526 High Bluff Drive, Suite 300, San Diego, CA 92130; 619/792-3531, fax 619/755-8348. An independent, for-profit service whose purpose is to verify the authenticity of organically grown and processed foods worldwide.

Organic Growers and Buyers Association: PO Box 9747, Mineapolis, MN 55440; 612/378-8355, fax 612/636-4135. Working for more than twelve years developing organic standards and certifying producers. In addition to supplying inspection and certification services worldwide, they also offer programs to help farmers make the switch to organic methods.

Farm Verified Organic, Inc.: RR 1, Box 40A, Medina, ND 58467; 701/486-3578, fax 701/486-3580. In business since 1979, this private certification organization will certify a grower or processing company anywhere in the world.

Organic Foods Production Association of North America (OFPANA): PO Box 1078, Greenfield, MA 01302; 413/774-7511, fax 413/774-6432. The leading trade organization linking growers, manufacturers, consultants, distributors, retailers, and consumers. Their mission is to promote organics and protect the integrity of organic standards. Newsletter and lots of organizing activities and materials related to standards, laws, government policy and commerce in the organic food biz.

Independent Organic Inspectors Association (IOI): Tr. 3, Box 162-C, Winona, MN 55987 Phone/FAX (507) 454-8310. A relatively new professional association of organic farm and processing inspectors and supporting members, dedicated to maintaining high standards of organic inspection and inspector integrity.

Online Resources

EcoNet: 18 de Boom Street, San Francisco, CA 94107; 415/442-0220, fax 415/546-1794. An international computer-based communications system committed to serving organizations and individuals working for environmental preservation and sustainability. This is the perfect place to meet and communicate online with people working in sustainable ag all over the world. One of the least expensive bulletin board services, EcoNet has a number of agricultural conferences and is working to expand their services in this area. The system lets you use the Internet, fax and telex anywhere in the world, and log into most Email networks.

ALF (Agricultural Library Forum): National Agricultural Library, 10301 Baltimore Blvd. Beltsville, MD 20705; 301/344-2113, modem 301/344-8510. For the price of a phone call, this bulletin board provides access to the incredible resources of our National Agricultural Library: technical info specialists, extension workers, and researchers. Bulletin areas include downloading and/or using archived data, agricultural and aquacultural topics titles, ag calendar, and water quality information.

AGEBB (UMC Coop Extension): Ron Bell, 325 Mumford Hall-UMC, Columbia, MO 65211. tel: 314/882-4827. modem: 314/882-8289. Sponsored by the U. of MO Coop Extension, this service features a message system, bulletins, online hay directory, public domain software library, extension templates, market analysis, market listings and crop performance testing.

ATI-NET: CSU Fresno, Fresno, CA 97340-0115; 209/278-4872. Modem 209/278-4265 (1200 bps); 209/278-4615 (2400 bps). Internet address: caticsof.cati.csufresno.edu or 129.8.100.15 The Advanced Technology Information Network, California State University, Fresno, disseminates ag info including market reports (updated every fifteen minutes from the USDA), Foreign Ag Service and TOP trade leads, USDA news, extensive job listings, Email, California weather, and more. There are now twenty-one local CA phone numbers for log-on.

NBIAP: modem 800/624-2723, 703/231-3858. Cost: 1/2 hour toll-free per 24 hours. The National Biological Assessment Program facilitates the safe evaluation of genetically modified organisms in the environment. The bulletins area contains news reports on recent developments and databases of regulations and guidelines, information sources, current literature, companies, job listings, and more.

WHO'S DOING IT?

CCOF Certification Handbook and **List of Growers Crop Index:** $10 each from CCOF (see "Certification Organizations," above). The most detailed guides to certification, procedures, practices, and materials. Emulated nationally.

National Directory of Organic Wholesalers: Published yearly by CAFF (see p. 97). A guide for farmers seeking wholesalers and marketing tips, and for retailers looking for product.

Texas Organic Resource Directory: Natural Food Associates, P.O. Box 210, Atlanta, TX 75551; 800/594-2136 An industry reference book of growers and farm supplies.

Organic Market Guide: New Jersey Region, $9.95 from agAccess. Directory to farmers, retailers, wholesalers, processors, farm and garden supplies, landscapers and nurseries, resource organizations, and publications.

Directory of Organic Agriculture: Box 116, Collingwood, Ontario L9Y 3Z2, Canada; 705/4440923, fax 705/444-0380. Compendium of fifteen hundred growers, products and educational services.

Agricultural Resources

on Line

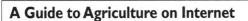

Michael Ableman

Over the last ten years there have been numerous attempts, some successful and some not, to use electronic systems to deliver information to farmers and others in agriculture. Farmers have been slow to adopt computer technology; more importantly, some of these services have misunderstood the market and the nature of electronic information.

Most of the for-profit ventures have failed or are struggling. However, a number of government-sponsored efforts, mostly at the state level, are beginning to take hold. Initially most of the systems offered market information (almost always about commodity markets) or weather. Now a much wider variety of information resources is available on-line. EcoNet and the Well offer conferences on agricultural topics, and regional services are popping up all over. —DK

A Guide to Agriculture on Internet

A great self-study guide to retrieving agricultural information using the basic services offered by Internet. Clearly written, it provides step-by-step instructions, lots of explanatory material and definitions of terms. The author includes a good quick-reference section, extensive lists of user groups and other resources, and an instructor's and student's guide complete with lessons and quizzes. —DK

•
Internet is vast and you will get lost. A clearly defined objective is essential to guide your information retrieval efforts. On the other hand, you will probably find that your questions will change as you come upon new pieces of information. Like an explorer, you need a compass to keep you going in the right direction (the search objective) and the expectation that you will have to wander around obstacles (reading related material, finding the location of sources).

•
Let's use our grower example to demonstrate a search.

Search Strategy = Sieve
Using the Internet Resource Guide on page 45, she logs onto every resource listed and spends an hour or two familiarizing herself with the commands used by each system. While logged in, she also tries to determine where useful information might be located.

Search Strategy = Targeted Search
After reviewing all of the known resources she finds that the Almanac mail server at Oregon State University is a rich source of sustainable agriculture information. She also identifies PEN pages as a good resource.

Search Strategy = Sample
She decides to log onto PENpages and try searching under the keywords "orchard," "orchard floor," "cover crop," "grove," "weed," "weed control." She soon finds that the single words "weed," "orchard," and "cover" work best.

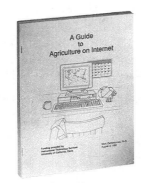

A Guide to Agriculture on Internet
Mark Campidonica. UC Davis, 16.95; $16.95 ($20.95 postpaid) from AgAccess, PO Box 2008, Davis, CA 95617; 916/756-7177, fax 916/756-7188, email *agaccess@igc.org*

AgAccess

*It takes considerable hubris to bill yourself as **the** Agricultural Information Source, but that's just what AgAccess has grown to be since its modest start in 1984. Now universities, corporations and even governments have joined the folks calling AgAccess for the information they need. AgAccess stocks or can obtain more than fourteen thousand books — virtually every ag and ag-related book in print. They'll even hunt down out-of-print books for you and for a suitable stipend, their experts and consultants will research any ag subject. But the best part of this most useful and well-organized service is the AgAccess bookstore in Davis, CA. There you can meet the congenial crew and the always-interesting customers while you peruse the tasty offerings (allow at least an hour). I'll bet you don't leave empty-handed even if you aren't a gardener or farmer. —J. Baldwin*

•
Backyard Market Gardening: the Entrepreneur's Guide to Selling What You Grow

Andrew W. Lee, 1992. An informative guide, absolutely packed with solid advice & tips gleaned from many years of market gardening. Lee details how he arrived at the successful way he runs his operation including cultivation methods, indispensable tools of the trade, and the focus of the book:

marketing. Much attention is paid to increasing sales & profits.

•
Growing Great Garlic
Ron Engeland, 1991. A highly readable guide that includes all you need to know about this enigmatic crop. The author, an organic farmer who has grown 200 strains of garlic over the last fifteen years, covers all pertinent topics ranging from crop history, to cultivation, pests, storage and marketing. He presents an exhaustive description, with good illustrations, of the several distinct varieties of garlic and their preferred climatic and soil conditions.

•
Raising & Sustaining Productivity of Smallholder Farming Systems in the Tropics
Willem C. Beets, 1990. In this massive, multi-disciplinary handbook of sustainable ag development, the author stresses self-reliance, environmental balance, and long-term planning. He uses the experience gained in his many years of fieldwork to construct a theoretical framework for raising overall productivity of farming systems.

•
Greener Pastures on Your Side of the Fence
Bill Murphy, 1991. Murphy claims very persuasively that controlled grazing management can double or triple productivity for conventionally managed permanent pasture. Practical & well delineated, his book details pasture ecology, animal grazing habits, paddock layout & fencing, livestock production, feed planning, & more. Management suggestions are made for improving many different grazing situations.

•
Oriental Vegetables
Joy Larkcom, 1991.
Thorough, specific and well illustrated, this is a superb book. Larkcom has spent ten years in research in her own organic garden and in Asia. She reports details of history, varieties, use, pests, harvest, storage, & cuisine for over one hundred Asian vegetables & herbs. Most important, she describes traditional & modern cultivation techniques for large- & small-scale operations.

AgAccess: 603 Fourth Street, Davis, CA 95616; 916/756-7177, fax 916/756-7188, email agaccess@igc.org

Ghost Bears

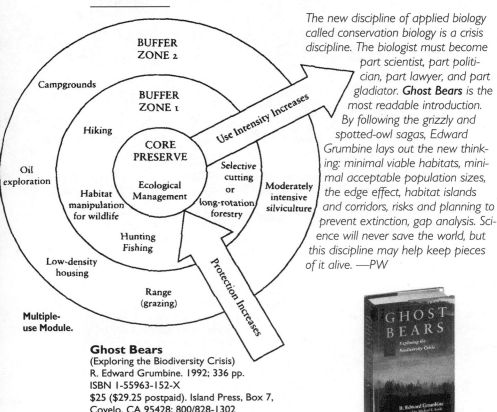

Multiple-use Module.

The new discipline of applied biology called conservation biology is a crisis discipline. The biologist must become part scientist, part politician, part lawyer, and part gladiator. Ghost Bears is the most readable introduction. By following the grizzly and spotted-owl sagas, Edward Grumbine lays out the new thinking: minimal viable habitats, minimal acceptable population sizes, the edge effect, habitat islands and corridors, risks and planning to prevent extinction, gap analysis. Science will never save the world, but this discipline may help keep pieces of it alive. —PW

Ghost Bears
(Exploring the Biodiversity Crisis)
R. Edward Grumbine. 1992; 336 pp.
ISBN 1-55963-152-X
$25 ($29.25 postpaid). Island Press, Box 7, Covelo, CA 95428; 800/828-1302

In this Multiple-use Module (MUM), an inviolate core preserve is surrounded by a gradation of multiple-use buffer zones. Intensity of use increases outward through the buffer zones, while intensity of protection increases inward. Important functions of a MUM are to (1) insulate sensitive elements in reserves from intensive land use and other human activities, (2) provide marginal habitat for animals inhabiting a reserve, which would increase effective reserve size, and (3) provide for an assortment of human uses with minimal conflict.

Conservation biology is the science that studies biodiversity and the dynamics of extinction. Much of this work focuses on how genes, species, and landscapes interact, and how human activities affect changes in ecosystem components, patterns, and processes. What species are vulnerable to anthropogenic change and why? Can we act to protect them, and if so, how? What are the implications of the biodiversity crisis for people and other life forms? These are some of the questions that fascinate and frustrate conservation biologists.

Conservation biology is an applied science. It differs from other natural-resource fields such as wildlife management, fisheries, and forestry by accenting ecology over economics. Most traditional resource management is reductionist, mainly concerned with species of direct utilitarian interest: How can humans have bucks to bag, trees to harvest, salmon to catch? Conservation biologists, in contrast, consider the entire biodiversity hierarchy at diverse scales of space and time and generally "attach less weight to aesthetics, maximum yields, and profitability, and more to the long-range viability of whole systems and species."

Wildlife biologists have traditionally viewed edges as positive influences on species and ecosystems. As the saying goes, The more edge the better. But recent studies of the effects of habitat fragmentation prove that not all species benefit from edges. Forest songbirds that require large breeding territories in forest interiors have shown long-term population declines in highly fragmented eastern deciduous forests. Nest predation and parasitism increase dramatically near the inside edges of habitat patches. Much of this is because of increased populations of raccoons, skunks, opossums, and other middle-sized omnivores that thrive in fragmented landscapes and invade native-habitat patches.

Books of the Big Outside

This quarterly catalog is an earth-child of the Whole Earth. Over 400 books, maps, CDs, and cassettes covering conservation biology, wildlife protection, wilderness and land ethics, eco-philosophy and eco-psychology, natural history, kids' books make it a one-stop bookstore for most every hip and important aspect of the big outdoors. Many of the books here are remaindered or out of print — you can't find them elsewhere. All are reviewed by Dave Foreman, whose depth of understanding of America's eco-activist history has yet to receive adequate praise. There's even an Uncle Dave's Top Fifty. Beers up! Backpacks on! Which book for the trek? —PW

OTHER GREAT RESOURCES

The Big Outside (A Descriptive Inventory of the Big Wilderness Areas of the United States): Dave Foreman. 1992, Crown Publishing Group. An inventory of the last 385 "wilderness"-like areas of North America. Urgent inspiration to preserve what little is left.

Essentials of Conservation Biology: Richard B. Primack. 1993, Sinauer Associates. The best introductory college text.

The Michael Soule Series. The force majeure of conservation biology, Soule has edited the major technical and essay books. Titles include:

Viable Populations for Conservation: Michael Soule. 1987, Cambridge University Press.

Conservation Biology: Michael Soule. 1986, Sinauer Associates.

Research Priorities for Conservation Biology: Michael Soule. 1989, Island Press.

All are available from Books of the Big Outside.

• *The Great Bear: Contemporary Writings on the Grizzly.* Edited by John Murray. GRIZ demands our attention. In this fine collection, Ed Abbey, Doug Peacock, Bill Kitteredge, Rick Bass, Aldo Leopold, Frank Craighead Jr., Bud Guthrie, Adolph Murie, and others focus their attention on the Great Bear. This is clearly as fine an anthology of wildlife writing as ever published. Royalties are donated to The Nature Conservancy for the Pine Butte Swamp Grizzly Bear Preserve in Montana. Northwest Alaska Publishing, 1992, paperback, was $14.95, now special discount $10.00.

• *Animal Dreams by Barbara Kingsolver*
A stunning novel about the hidden horror of mining contamination in an Arizona company town, and the strong women who stand up to it. 342 pages. HarperPerennial, 1991. Paperback, $12.00.

Books of the Big Outside: Catalog free from Ned Ludd Books, PO Box 5141, Tucson, AZ 85703; 602/628-9610.

Wild Earth

In a decade when enviro mags stick and sink in the tar pits of Bubbaland boosterism, Wild Earth floats up like the condor. It is the populist arm of the conservation biology movement, speaking outrageously reasonable ethics, eco-poetry, actions to bring back the wolf, refreshing analyses of Congress and Clintonia. Biodiversity mavens: Wild Earth is forever reminding us: if you don't like the news, go out and make your own.—PW

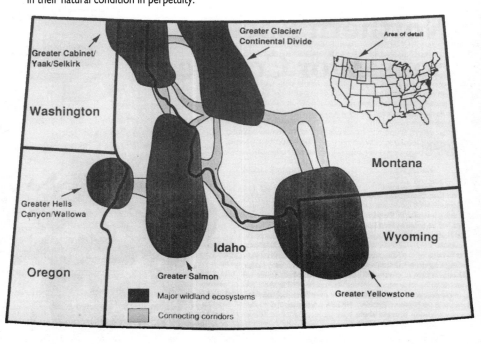

U.S. portion of the Northern Rockies Bioregion, its five major ecosystems and connecting corridors.

Wild Earth
Dave Foreman, Editor.
$25/year (4 issues). PO Box 455, Richmond, VT 05477; 802/434-4077

• Traditionally, wilderness legislation has passed Congress based on several anti-wilderness precepts. First, all designations are made according to arbitrary political boundaries, such as state lines or administrative boundaries. Second, lands eligible for Wilderness designation are lands in which extractive industry has no interest or prior claims. Third, Wilderness designations conform to subjective determinations of what constitutes nice scenery and recreational opportunity. This often means high alpine "rocks and ice," allowing for the "snapshot" approach to wildlands protection, since these high alpine areas are predictable in appearance over several decades. And fourth, any analysis of the economic values of the landscape assesses only the commercial extractive values, such as timber jobs and the local tax base. Virtually no assessment is made of the economic value of wildlands left in their natural condition in perpetuity.

The key purpose of the Northern Rockies Ecosystem Protection Act is protection of native biodiversity. It would protect five major ecosystems allowing for genetic interchange and landscape-scale disturbances such as wildfires, which can occur across millions of acres in just one season.

Wildlife Damage Review • The Predator Project • Humane Society

Animal Damage Control is an obsolete agency that hangs in there by sheer inertia. With pitiful bravado, they pretend the West is still a shoot-out between marauding coyotes and poor sheep ranchers with helpless sheep. Watch both hands: one holds the poison pellets, the other is in the taxpayer's pocket.

The Wildlife Damage Review is the heartful, mindful advance guard in the endeavor to reduce unnecessary pain from traps and poisons, to stop bear-

baiting, coyote-killing festivals, and to spread the word on the actual state of wildlife. Join and purchase *Waste, Fraud and Abuse in the ADC.*

The Predator Project tracks money. Its slogan: North America needs predators for intact ecosystems. If you live in one of the seventeen western states, their **ADC: How Your Tax Dollars Subsidize Agribusiness by Killing and Harassing Wildlife** *($10) is an indispensable guide to shutting the financial faucet.*

With its 1.6 million members, the **Humane Society** *monitors a broader hate-field of animal abuse (domestic, laboratory, and wild). Experts in cruelty investigation, they can provide local help. —PW*

Wildlife Damage Review: $25/year (membership and magazine, 4 issues). PO Box 85218, Tucson, AZ 85754; 602/884-0883.

The Predator Project: $15/year (membership). PO Box 6733, Bozeman, MT 59771; 406/587-3389.

Humane Society of the United States: 2100 L Street, NW, Washington, DC 20037; 202/452-1100.

Landscaping for Wildlife

The Minnesota Department of Natural Resources has produced an outstanding how-to wildlife-landscaping book. It also covers Wisconsin, Iowa, Michigan and Northern Illinois, Indiana and Ohio. People who live elsewhere should consider buying the book anyway — it's cheap, and there are enough glorious animal pictures to make it a great bedtime book for children.

Landscaping for Wildlife presents a mountain of detail made comprehensible and accessible, plus directions and plans for backyards, farmsteads and whole woodlands. It's good enough even to be used as a lever — show it to your Dept. of Natural Resources and ask politely why your state doesn't have a book like this. —Richard Nilsen

•

One of the greatest opportunities that exists for homeowners to help wildlife is within the boundaries of their own yards! In most yards that have been landscaped in the past, wildlife benefits were accidental or incidental. Only the most adaptable species like robins, house sparrows and European starlings thrived in such habitats. More than

100 wildlife species, however, may use a well-planned backyard habitat at one time or another.

•

In extreme circumstances where snags are lacking, you can create snags in a woodlot by girdling several diseased or deformed trees. The best trees for creation of snags are oak, sugar maple, basswood, ash and elm. Girdling involves cutting a ring around the trunk through the bark and well into the sapwood so that the cambium layer between the bark and wood is completely severed.

Landscaping for Wildlife
Carrol L. Henderson. 1987; 144 pp. $8.95 ($10.95 postpaid). Minnesota Bookstore/Documents Division, 117 University Avenue, St. Paul, MN 55155; 612/297-3000

Backside of Garden

Key: 1. 'Dropmore' Scarlet Trumpet Honeysuckle
2. Scarlet Runner Bean
3. Split Rail Fence Support For Vines

Figure 19. Hummingbird garden for sunny to partially shaded sites.

Wildlife Habitat Enhancement Council

Corporations control lots of land, and often have little idea what's happening on it (think of the miles of powerline right-of-ways stretching across the landscape). This two-year-old organization is a cooperative venture between some very large US corporations and some very mainline conservation groups. The goals appear to be restoring landholdings to environmental usefulness, making the public happy, and polishing tarnished images a bit. Let's see, that's win, win, win. If you live next to some BIG neighbors, these folks might be able to help you meet them. —Richard Nilsen

•

Case Study: Delaware, Maryland and Virginia. *Company:* Delmarva Power & Light, Vienna Power Plant. *Habitat:* The Nanticoke River, a Chesapeake Bay tributary. *Project:* Delmarva Power constructed a $50,000 brooding pond on its Vienna Power Plant grounds to help save the dwindling striped bass population in the Chesapeake Bay and its tributaries. Since 1985, Delmarva Power has released more than 40,000 striped bass fingerlings or rockfish into the Nanticoke River in Maryland.

Wildlife Habitat Enhancement Council
1010 Wayne Avenue, Suite 290, Silver Spring, MD 20910; 301/588-8994, fax 301/588-4629

Care of the Wild, Feathered and Furred

A good way to graduate from bunny love to rabbit understanding is to take care of one that is injured. It takes more than a good heart and regard for God's creatures, it takes knowledge and skill. Here's where to get plenty of both; how to feed 'em, house 'em, and make repairs. —J. Baldwin

•

Botulism or "limber neck" is a kind of food poisoning that sometimes decimates whole populations of water birds, particularly ducks and geese. The seriousness of avian botulism increases as man continues to develop a million acres a year in the U.S. Botulism can kill fifty thousand ducks, as happened in a California slough in 1871. You may remember that photo of a mountain of dead ducks about to be cremated.

Botulism is caused by a toxin released from a bacterium that thrives in the gut of inver-

tebrates, particularly maggots. Recent research indicates that birds acquire botulism by eating maggots living in the lethal toxins of other dead birds, and that it is not found, as originally presumed, in living vegetation or organically rich mud. When a bird is found suffering from botulism it is usually in critical condition. Paralysis prevents the nerves from transmitting messages to the muscle tissues. Flush out the intestinal tract with an Epsom salt solution administered orally. If it is a large bird such as a duck, a small basting syringe may be used. Otherwise fifteen-minute intervals of dosing with milk of magnesia from an eyedropper will be necessary. When using Epsom salts a bird must be given water to replace the dehydration which occurs within twenty minutes. Birds flushed out every six hours with this solution seem to improve.

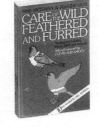

Care of the Wild, Feathered and Furred
(Treating and Feeding Injured Birds and Animals) Mae Hickman & Maxine Guy. 1993; 143 pp. ISBN 0-935576-45-2 $14.95 postpaid. Michael Kesend Publishing, 1025 Fifth Avenue, New York, NY 11028; 212/249-5150

Bind the gauze over the sutured area with two long strips of tape, continuing the tape around the bird's body so the gauze will remain in place.

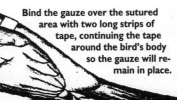

Ethnobotany and Vanishing Knowledge

Before Western medical research paid attention to a folk tradition and extracted quinine from the bark of cinchona trees, many people died needlessly from malaria. Perhaps similar words will be said about cancer someday — unless that cancer cure is never discovered because the tropical tree that produced it became extinct yesterday or the last shaman who knew how to use it died this morning.

A catastrophic loss of knowledge is taking place as the old-growth environments — ancient living laboratories for biopharmaceutical evolution — die out. Plant medicines for the body, mind, and soul are becoming extinct as their host environments are destroyed. And the people who know how to use the healing plants, the heirs to empirically based, highly pragmatic traditions thousands of years old, are dying too, without leaving successors.

It took tens of millions of years for medicinal plant compounds to evolve, tens of thousands of years for people to learn how to use them, and both the plants and the knowledge might be gone within twenty years. Gathering such knowledge in the first place must have been a painstaking and hazardous process for early generations of experimental shamans, requiring remarkable bravery as well as ironclad devotion to the experimental method in order to sift through the abundant variety of plants, many of them fatally toxic, to find the ones with specifically useful effects.

The shaman's knowledge was a cultural library for the tribal group. Each shaman learned, applied, and passed along knowledge of botany and bonesetting, hunting lore and agronomy, pharmacy and storytelling, spiritual and social wisdom vital to the welfare of the tribe, knowledge related not only to healing but to warfare, to relocating the village or settling family disputes, or any of the critical decisions that maintain the life of the culture in relationship to its environment. The plant teachers were used for guidance and decision making and to remain in balance with the natural world.

In the past, when Western medical researchers paid attention to this knowledge, the payoff was spectacular: "folk medicines" such as digitoxin and digoxin (heart failure), ergotamine (migraine), salicin (inflammation and pain), morphine (pain), vin-caleukoblastine and vincristine (Hodgkin's disease and childhood leukemia), and more than one hundred other antibiotics, anti-tumor agents, immune-system stimulants, tranquilizers, sedatives, anaesthetics, contraceptives, laxatives, and pain relievers.

According to the World Health Organization, approximately 70 percent of the world's population relies on the use of plant extracts within the context of "traditional medicine" as their primary source of health care. At the same time, American consumers paid more than $8 billion in 1985 for prescriptions whose active constituents were extracted from plants.

Networks of determined amateurs are working to save a remnant of the old-growth environments, the old knowledge, and the cultures who hold the keys to that knowledge, before it all goes up in smoke or smothers in concrete. Ethnobotanical preservation and cultural survival are two allied responses to connected crises. There have been successes. Plants have been rescued from extinction; the role of plant knowledge in pharmaceutical medicine is becoming more widely known; the cultures and individuals who hold the knowledge have found allies and resources in their struggles.

Plants have powers. And humans must approach plants humbly, if those powers are to be used wisely. Every plant-using culture understands these principles. Yet, to people who have been taught that the universe is a lifeless machine, the powers of life-forms are nothing more than superstitious beliefs.

The plants have much to teach us. They are asking for our help. Here's what you need to know, the tools you need to assemble, the tasks that need to be done, the communities of colleagues who need your help. Every action, every thought is a seed. Every small ethnobotanical victory today is a gift to future generations. —HLR

OTHER GREAT RESOURCES

N.R. Farnsworth, 1988. "Screening Plants for New Medicines," *National Forum on Biodiversity*, E.O. Wilson and F.M. Peters, eds., Washington, D.C.: National Academy Press.

Kamainja on the Suriname-Brazil border drips *Go-lo-be* fungus sap into an aching ear.
—*The Shaman's Apprentice* (p. 104).

Botanical Preservation Corps: Training in Field Ethnobotany

Saving as much as possible of the remaining traditional cultures and their habitats is an urgent task, and an enormous one. Governments and well-funded international organizations must be involved in much of this work. Saving the plants themselves is a task in which dedicated, well-trained amateurs can make headway. But you have to know what you are doing.

Small networks of collectors are helping to ensure the survival of ethnobotanical resources native to Asia, Africa, Central and South America. Dedicated travelers, botanists, anthropologists, and ecologists can learn how to help locate seeds and specimens, how to prepare and ship them, and how to collect indigenous folk medicines for identification.

If you are interested in participating in ethnobotanical rescue training sessions (emphasizing, but not limited to, psychoactive plants), send a self-addressed, stamped envelope to Botanical Preservation Corps, PO Box 1368, Sebastopol, CA 95473.

Ethnobotany is traditionally a field in which amateurs have made significant contributions. We have a small win- dow for action. Let's take the opportunity. Many people, each doing a small part, can accomplish great deeds. Our grandchildren will thank us for it.
—HLR

Preparing seeds for shipment

Gather pulpy or fleshy fruits when very ripe, preferably groundfalls which are slightly fermented but not yet decomposing. Larger fruits can be mashed in a bucket of water, left to ferment a couple days, then rubbed well to separate the good seeds, which sink. Hard-fleshed berries are trickier. I managed to easily de-pulp a large batch of Heliconia once in Ecuador by rotting the small, freshly picked fruits in a sealed plastic bag. Several days later, the slimy pulp was rubbed off by transferring them into a burlap sack and treading it underfoot on a flat rock along a stream.

Many tropical seeds perish upon drying. Care must be taken to preserve a degree of moisture after cleaning and treating them. Even so, many such seeds have a very short viable life, so I try to use the time spent in transit to maintain maximum viability and in some cases to even germinate during shipping.

Surface-dry the seeds in shade from four to six hours. Place them in a plastic bag with fine holes. Soak some peat moss or fine charcoal in 1 percent sodium hypochlorite

Ethnobotanical Research Field Kit *by Rob Montgomery*

Tupperware-type containers. Will keep anything dry. Deep sandwich-sized ones are great. These snap-lid containers are rare, practical, and much-appreciated gifts to bestow upon helpers and hosts in humid tropics. From variety stores.

Strapping tape. The kind with reinforcing fibers in it. Very useful (and very hard to find outback) for parcel shipments, mending, and as a rope substitute when rolled sideways into a "string." From hardware stores.

Superglue. Not only wonderful for quick mends of equipment, cyanoacrylate glues are also excellent for emergency microsurgery. Sounds weird, but superglue will close up surface-dry wounds in spots nothing else can — like hair-coated injuries. Just squirt the glue in the wound liberally. It works like stitches, and is similar to products now used in hospitals. Just the thing to use on tropical botfly stings (not uncommon; they lay disgusting larvae beneath the skin). Seal up their airhole with Superglue. From variety stores.

Seed containers. Plastic film canisters are ideal, and often free. Paper envelopes for coin collectors work great too. Wedding-invitation envelopes work in a pinch. From stationery stores.

Ziploc-type bags. Bring dozens of these; they're hard to find outback. Sandwich- and gallon-size are the most useful. From grocery stores.

Moss. To ship live plants back, you need to wrap their bare roots with moisturizing and sterile moss — not soil. Using wild native moss is prohibited. Peat moss is elegantly convenient to carry in the form of Jiffy Pellets, those little disks that swell with water. One of these moistened with 1 percent bleach will coat many batches of perishable seeds needing humidity in transit. Just toss into Ziploc bags. Sphagnum moss can be compacted easily for storage, and unpacked and moistened to wrap roots and other propagative parts. From garden stores.

Superthrive. This is a brand-name product made of liquid B-vitamins; it is real magic in reducing plant trauma and enhancing seed viability. A tincture diluted 50 drops per cup should be misted on entire plant, seeds, and any material in direct contact with them. From garden stores.

Notebooks. The idea here is to assign an accession number for every specimen, and then enter whatever data you compile for that specimen in a notebook — locality, date, description, photo, etc. — under that number, which follows both the specimen and the data, whether or not the plant or seed is identified. Often, identification isn't determined by a professional until later on. Use convenient pocket-size notebooks on site, then transfer the data to a larger hardbound book while the notes are fresh. From stationery stores.

Labels. You need several sizes of adhesive office labels and strong manila tags with reinforced holes for plant and seed labels. From stationery stores.

Waterproof pens. They need to be really waterproof. Try spilling coffee or dripping forehead sweat on a test label or page before using on a trip. Also test to see if alcohol dissolves it. From department or stationery stores. "Sharpie" finepoint is particularly recommended.

Plant press. The classical, cumbersome wooden one is for the truly devoted. A very usable makeshift press can be whipped up using universally available newspapers. Fresh plants are inserted between doubled newspaper pages, with their accession number written right on the paper, then rolled up tightly like a carpet. Additional specimens are added and the roll gets larger. Store in a leakproof plastic bag and keep moist with alcohol. Later, unroll and dry the materials using a herbarium press as soon as possible. Try borrowing one from the nearest university's botany department; always donate duplicate specimens to them in return for the loan.

Machete. With sheath and file. Shortest blade length is more portable. Bring along 3/4" triangular file for sharpening. From hardware or camping stores.

Serrated knife. Alternative to large machete. Indispensable for cutting, sawing, chopping, and even digging. Best kind is the special curved Japanese gardener's 6" sickle, but any strong, broad-serrated knife will work. From garden and hardware stores.

Fungicide. For seed shipments. Should be rated low in toxicity (on label) and be a dazzling color to impress quarantine inspectors. Copper sulphate or sulphur products are suitable. Common bleach is fine, too. Dilute Clorox in 3 parts water, dip seeds for 15 minutes, dry and toss into moss. Or use sodium hypochlorite tablets, which can also purify drinking water. From camping stores and garden stores.

Alcohol. For pickling specimens, formaldehyde works best, but it is very toxic. Use alcohol to help preserve plants before full drying. It is hard to imagine collecting plants somewhere that 70-percent distilled booze or moonshine cannot be found. Or you can use rubbing alcohol.

Strainer. Helpful to de-pulp seeds. Best for ease of hauling is an unbreakable 6" plastic sandbox toy or a 3" tea strainer with handle cut off.

Flashlight. Best type is waterproof MiniMag brand. Take extra batteries and bulb, which are hard to find. From camping stores.

Personal gear. Never, ever take camouflage or army-surplus style clothing and gear such as a camouflaged compass or mess kit. You will be suspicious-looking enough and little details can be damning.

Trade items. Consider low-impact non-disposables that are hard to get — batteries, plastic containers, etc. Stainless-steel fishhooks are easy to carry and very much appreciated. Officials must be dealt with at every level from jungle checkpoints to immigration to traffic cops. The diplomatic exchange of the right gift can smooth small requests such as guarding extra gear, visa extension, or overlooking an infraction, but only if you're at ease with the procedure. Embossed-name, hometown police uniform buttons are good — promise the local official you'll bring back theirs in trade.

Optional Equipment

Instant camera. Lets you see your shot and be sure it's good. Plant collectors' features: close-up ability, time-release shutter for low-light forests. Bring lots of film and flashbulbs.

Map pipe. Precut a 3"-diameter ABS plastic pipe to fit a standard rolled-up map, and fit with a removable cap at each end. It'll keep all your maps undamaged. From hardware stores.

Altimeter. Useful when searching for plants with known elevation range. A pocket altimeter (0-4500m range, 50m increments), from good backpacking stores.

Hand lens. A Bausch & Lomb folding pocket lens with 20-power magnification is very rewarding, and works wonders on virtually everything — fifteen minutes of marveling on one single, tiny vista will transmit semesters of esoteric wisdom. From stationery or nature stores.

Tape recorder. Try recording essential field data in a rainforest (remember why they call it that) and you can appreciate the luxury of voice-activated, pocket-size, micro-cassette recorders. Just speak in your collection number and every detail you wish. Transcribe later. From electronics stores.

solution (household bleach is 3-4 percent). I carry compressed jiffy pots; one is enough for most of a day's work. Squeeze the moss as dry as possible. Let it or the charcoal surface dry for four to six hours as well — do this simultaneously when treating the seeds. Place a small amount in each bag (1 tsp. per 30-50 seeds). This should hold them in good condition for two to four weeks. If a long time will elapse before planting, check occasionally to make sure the seeds are not too moist.

Earlier this year, I sent two shipments of a fruiting palm seed (*Zallaca zallaca*, salak) to friends in Brasil. Salak has a notorious viability: reported as 50 percent at 3 days, 0 percent in one week. The first shipment arrived in 20 days with 100 percent germination, the second 4 weeks later for a total of 56 days with only one seed not germinating (95 percent). The salak seeds were treated and packed as described above.

•

Tiny seeds may be mailed in airmail letters. Small seeds should be placed into a series of small packets taped evenly on stiff paper and wrapped with enough padding to prevent crushing but still feel like a regular letter. One professional botanist mails seeds and even seedlings and cuttings perfectly packaged to seem like academic printed matter. Separate mailings like these back up the regular imported stock to ensure some specimens make it. —Rob Montgomery

Rosetta Folios and Books

It is possible to obtain plants of ethnobotanical, medicinal, and spiritual interest, entirely legally, from mail-order suppliers such as " . . . of the jungle" (below), but it is not as easy to find out how indigenous people use those plants, how to prepare them for use, and other key information.

Rosetta is a service that provides quality books and obscure, out-of-print research references in the field of ethnobotany and psychopharmacological culture. Folio Set 1 includes five articles about San Pedro cacti, a piece of art from the Chavin culture of ancient South America that provides clear evidence that the medicine has been in use for several thousand years, and a "San Pedro Owner's Manual." — HLR

●

Journal of Ethnopharmacology, 11 (1984) 123-133. Elsevier Scientific Publishers Ireland Ltd.

The Healing Practices of a Peruvian Shaman

. . . Like that of the other plant specialists I met in the area, Don Emilio's most common recipe for the preparation of *ayahuasca* consists of boiling together about 30 pieces, 30-40 cm long of the crushed

Rosetta Folios and Books
Catalog $1. PO Box 4611, Berkeley, CA 94704.

stems of *Banisteriopsis caapi* with 200 leaves of *charcruna* or *yage* (*Psychotria viridis*). Between 12 and 15 l. of water are added to the mixture, and it is allowed to boil until it is reduced to about 1 l. that is separated into another pot. The operation is repeated seven times, and the extract collected is boiled again until only approx. 500 ml. of a syrup-like liquid is left, enough for about 12 doses. The whole process takes 12 h, from six in the morning to six in the evening.

Don Emilio, like other plant specialists, claims to know several kinds of *ayahuasca*. Unfortunately I was not able to collect voucher specimens of these varieties this time. He stressed the necessity of adding the *Psychotria viridis* (apparently he also uses *P. carthaginensis*); otherwise no visions will occur. The *chacruna*, Don Emilio explains, is like the "mirror" of *ayahuasca*. It is known (Schultes and Hofmann, 1980 p. 170) that the effect of the tryptamines present in the *P. viridis* (as in the case of *Diplopterys cabrerana* and others) are enhanced due to the inhibiting effect towards monoamine oxidase (MAO) of the ß-carbolines harmine and harmaline present in the *ayahuasca* vine (Gorkin, 1966, Pletscher, 1966).

. . . of the jungle

This lovingly amateurish hand-stapled catalog reflects the nature of the operation — knowledgeable plant devotees who distribute seeds and rooted specimens of legal ethnobotanical plants. Don't ask them for information about using the plants: the law frowns on that. Ethnobotanists who quietly supply major arboretums around the world with specimens of rare, useful plants, they see this catalog as a way of taking direct action in dire times. — HLR

●

As always, the plants remain the real teachers. They are heuristic by nature, enabling seekers of truth to find their own answers. Growing a plant can be a profound spiritual exchange. . . .

●

Brunsfelsia jamaicensis, (Solanaceae). Endangered species from cloudforests in Jamaica's Blue Mountains. Long tubular corollas with narrow necks and wide undulating edges. One of the most fragrant of all scents, exhaled in little breaths during the evening. Reminiscent of vanilla and clove. We keep several in 1 gallon pots, rotating the ones

. . . of the jungle
Catalog free. PO Box 1801, Sebastopol, CA 95473.

in bloom into the bedroom for pleasure making. Treelet $22.00

●

Hydrocotyle asiatica "Gotu Kola," (Umbelliferae). Tropical creeping herb famed as Chinese longevity and brain tonic. Good terrarium specimen or as groundcover for plants in containers. Spreads vigorously with warmth, sun and moisture. Commercial Gotu Kola often is dredged from open sewage ditches in India, so home-grown is highly recommended. Easy to grow. Plant $10

●

Iochroma sp. "Borrachero" (Solanaceae). Scandent shrub with electric-blue/violet, tubular flower clusters. Elder shamans of Colombia's Sibundoy Valley will seldom speak of this sacred medicinal, yet they all have carefully tended bushes in their secret gardens. Outstanding specimen plant of significant ethnopharmacologic status. Treelet $15.00

Shaman's Apprentice Program

*This undertaking by Conservation International carries on the work described in **Tales of a Shaman's Apprentice**. Its aim is to bridge the preliterate and literate generations of the Tirio tribe on the Surinam-Brazil border and the Bri-bri in Costa Rica, and to preserve indigenous ethnobotanical knowledge, assisting older tribal members in assembling this knowledge and passing it on to the younger generation.*

For information about membership in Conservation International, write: 1015 18th Street NW, Suite 1000, Washington, DC 20036; 202-429-5660. —MKS

Tales of a Shaman's Apprentice

Tales of a Shaman's Apprentice
(An Ethnobotanist Searches for New Medicines in the Amazonian Rain Forest)
Mark Plotkin. Viking, 1993; 318 pp. ISBN 0-670-83137-9 $22 ($24 postpaid) from Penguin USA/Cash Sales, 120 Woodbine Street, Bergenfield, NJ 07621; 800/253-6476

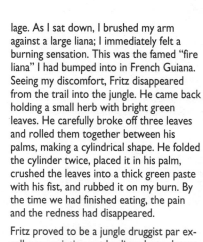

Witch doctor of the Wayana tribe, upper Tapanahony River, southeast Suriname. Some of the plants he is holding are from the frankincense family and are used to treat colds.

Plant people recognize each other not only by a shared enthusiasm for the myriad forms, colors, growth patterns, and useful properties of their favorite living things, but also by the shared shape of lives lived in relation to plants. This is the story of encounters between a Harvard-educated plant person and the leading plant experts of the Americas: the shamans and healers of the tropical-forest societies of South America. Despite his alien background, these experts saw Dr. Plotkin as a colleague in plant studies and shared their hard-won knowledge with him. Plant people will find their kindred in this book. They will also hear tales drawn from several centuries of seeking plants and plant extracts that heal, kill, stimulate, stun, lubricate, bounce, etc. And, if they hope to someday have occasion to visit with their South American colleagues, they will pick up a few tips for the trail. —Bret Blosser

●

After walking for several hours and looking at a number of plants, we decided to stop for lunch. I was carrying a daypack into which Fritz had put two pieces of smoked fish he had been given in the vil-

lage. As I sat down, I brushed my arm against a large liana; I immediately felt a burning sensation. This was the famed "fire liana" I had bumped into in French Guiana. Seeing my discomfort, Fritz disappeared from the trail into the jungle. He came back holding a small herb with bright green leaves. He carefully broke off three leaves and rolled them together between his palms, making a cylindrical shape. He folded the cylinder twice, placed it in his palm, crushed the leaves into a thick green paste with his fist, and rubbed it on my burn. By the time we had finished eating, the pain and the redness had disappeared.

Fritz proved to be a jungle druggist par excellence, pointing out healing plants almost every step of the way. We collected the triangular-leaved *mispel* herb, eaten to treat gonorrhea; the fetid wood of the *jarakopi* tree, brewed into a tea to relieve fevers; and the green, heart-shaped leaves of a delicate little herb called *konsaka wiriri*, which is literally used from head to toe as a treatment for both headache and athlete's foot. Fritz also pointed out the *mokomoko*, a shrub with leaves shaped like arrowheads, which is found only at the edge of the river. The sap of the *mokomoko* is dripped into cuts and other wounds to stanch blood flow. Fritz warned that this is a painful remedy because the plant fluid burns when applied.

But one plant stood out from all the others in terms of healing properties. It was a small green herb growing at the edge of the trail; the plant's unremarkable appearance gave no indication of its curative potential. Pulling the herb up by the roots, Fritz explained that you take a tea of the leaves twice a day — "*te joe habe toomsi soekroe na broedoe*" — when you have too much sugar in the blood. It took a minute for me to realize the malady Fritz was describing was diabetes. I asked him to explain how tribal peoples living deep in the rain forest were able to diagnose excessive sugar in the bloodstream.

"Simple," he replied. "You taste the urine."

Seeds of Change

Author Kenny Ausubel, who in 1989 formed an organic seed company (also called "Seeds of Change"), delineates how the breadth and resilience of our food supply — not to mention such whimsical concerns as taste and nutrition — are being sacrificed for perceived practical advantages in things like crop yield, packing suitability, and shipping schedules. More ominous are the agendas of a number of the vertically integrated companies that not only make the pesticides and petrochemical fertilizers, but sell most of the seeds used by US farmers as well — seeds they've deliberately altered to tolerate huge quantities of chemicals.

Balancing its sober warning of impending catastrophe, the book also celebrates the riotously myriad world of seed diversity propagated by Seeds of Change. Eight hundred different kinds of plants are cultivated at the company's farm in New Mexico's Gila Valley. The organization's mission is to "create a botanical ark, a genetic shelterbelt against an erosing future." To this end, the company has eighty growers in twenty-seven states providing them with certified organic seeds, many of them "heirlooms" handed down through generations.

Ausubel believes that organic backyard gardeners, planting their own idiosyncratic array of fruits and vegetables, are key to reversing the march of homogeneity and holding off the biological holocaust. Reading his vivid descriptions of the hundreds of luscious vegetables you'll never find in a supermarket, from Red Russian kale to Calabash tomatoes to Nantes carrots, will inspire you to go out there and grow your own.
—Laurie Benenson

Seeds of Change
(The Living Treasure)
Kenny Ausubel, Harper San Francisco, 1994; 256 pp.
ISBN 0-06-250008-2
$18 ($20.75 postpaid) from HarperCollins Publishers/Direct Mail, P. O. Box 588, Dunmore, PA 18512; 800/331-3761

●

The Gila farm tested around a hundred watermelons last year and is testing a hundred and fifty in 1993. The Early Moonbeam is a ravishing favorite, yellow-fleshed and thin-skinned. Its excellent flavor is a summer romance. "Another prize of the south," says Rich, licking his lips, "is the Black Diamond. These melons can get to be forty-five pounds, and I know that sounds gargantuan and outrageous. How can you eat something that big? But if you had ever sat down on a hot day with ten people around a forty-five-pound Black Diamond whose every bite was delicious right down to the rind, you might want to grow it too."

●

Poised on the two-headed cusp of the biotechnology revolution, the seed genetics industry comprehends the depth of public controversy it could provoke. Scientists are reporting to work today at the gene bank and the cell library. Using tissue culture technology, they take cellular samples of a plant and grow it out in the laboratory. They cook up large batches of plant embryos and bathe them in liquid fertilizers and pesticides. Then they ready them for sale to farmers and gardeners, eliminating all the chancy, costly, time-consuming vagaries of agriculture and seed production. How will the twenty-first century Norman Rockwell picture eager gardeners poring over their spring seed catalogs in gleeful anticipation of embryo-planting season?

Enduring Seeds

In his third book, ethnobotanist Gary Nabhan continues his exploration of Native American farmers and their crops. Nabhan collects seeds from these farmers and distributes them to Native Americans and others willing to grow and thus preserve these often rare and endangered varieties. He is also a good writer, and this time travels far beyond the Sonoran desert bioregion. This collection of essays is filled with good stories of interesting people in out-of-the-way places. It is history with roots in the soils of the present. —RN

●

Modern agriculture has let temporary cheap petro-chemicals and water substitute for the natural intelligence — the stored genetic and ecological information — in self-adjusting biological communities.

●

For centuries, local seed-saving was the norm. Ethnobotanist Janis Alcorn has described how traditional farmers follow unwritten "scripts," learned by hand and mouth from their elders, that keep agricultural practices relatively consistent from generation to generation. Most land-based cultures have such scripts that guide plant selection and seed-saving. Each individual farmer might edit this script to fit his or her peculiar farming conditions, but the general scheme is passed on to the farmer's descendants. Thus, the crop traits emerging through natural selection in a given locality are retained or elaborated by recurrent cultural selection.

●

Some native farmers don't necessarily plant the same kind of corn every season, but vary their selection depending upon the weather. By having caches of other seedstocks for particular weather conditions, farmers can hedge their bets. Anthropologist Tim Dunnigan has told me of this kind of crop switching among Mexico's Mountain Pima, relatives of the Pima and Tohono O'odham of Arizona. They keep several varieties of maize on hand, including a quick-maturing corn in case spring drought should delay planting, thus short-

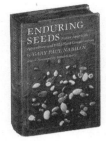

Enduring Seeds
(Native American Agriculture and Wild Plant Conservation)
Gary Paul Nabhan. North Point Press, 1989; 225 pp. ISBN 0-86547-344-7
$11.95 ($13.95 postpaid). Putnam Publishing Group/Order Dept., PO Box 506, East Rutherford, NJ 07073; 800/631-8571

ening the growing season. Other Mountain Pima maize varieties can be planted earlier in cool, wet springs, but need five months to mature.

●

Why, [anthropologist Edward] Spicer asked, have some peoples succumbed to acculturation and assimilation, while others have endured culturally? When he began to compare the cultural traits of nine enduring ethnic groups, Spicer quickly found that easy assumptions — that the "keepers" forbid intermarriage with other cultures, or defended their homeland against all odds, or maintained a language to encode secrets indecipherable to outsiders — all fell by the wayside. Most of the enduring peoples had lost some of their genetic identity, some of their original territory, and often, much of their native language . . . .

What counted, Spicer found, was that if enough members of a community express an affinity to shared symbols and values through time, across the generations, their culture will remain viable. This common covenant must be constantly transmitted and reinforced by the legends, codes of behavior, ceremonial songs and dances, rituals, vigils, and homages to places sacred to that particular culture. Once inoculated with the values held within their community, children acquired a certain resistance to the trappings of the dominant culture. Perhaps these values act as "cultural antibodies," which react to outside influences in such a way as to overcome their negative effects.

Biodiversity Prospecting

Biodiversity prospecting is the name for one of the most important new models of sustainable business—a way to discover dramatically useful biological tools for pharmaceutical and agricultural applications while preserving the wildland habitat where these riches are found. There are ways to misuse ethnobotany, and the most well-meaning ventures can cause more damage than good if they aren't set up properly. This report by World Resources Institute, Rainforest Alliance, and African Centre for Technology Studies sets out guidelines for researchers, entrepreneurs, and policymakers who are creating the methodology, business, and legislative underpinnings of this new kind of sustainable technology. —HLR

●

If a rancher sells a cow to a slaughterhouse,

he gets the profits (less any tax imposed by the government to cover public services to the rancher). But if the rancher sells the genes of a tree on his ranch, he has sold a piece of common national property.

Shouldn't some of the returns from such a sale be distributed more broadly and be nationally regulated? And does a transaction tax represent a fair contribution to the enormous national cost of maintaining the whole tree population? (Recall that the genetic material on the individual's ranch might not be able to survive if other populations of that species and supporting species were not thriving outside the boundaries of the ranch.) The problem is that if the profits are broadly distributed, individual farmers may receive so little that they will not value the tree. The solution — at least in part — is for ranchers to sell *services.* Getting the sample and insuring the survival and health of the tree from which it came are part of these services. However, if these services require subsidy from the

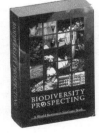

Biodiversity Prospecting
(Using Genetic Resources for Sustainable Development)
World Resources Institute. 1993; 340 pp. ISBN 0-915825-89-9
$29.95 ($32.95 postpaid) from WRI Publications, PO Box 4852 Hampden Station, Baltimore, MD 21211; 800/822-0504

public sector, as is the case with the tree's genes, then the commercial agreement should insure a return to the public. The INBio-Merck and Co. agreement discussed below contains this element explicitly.

Lilies of the Hearth

*Women and plants have been close associates throughout human history, but being the relatively quieter types, this hasn't been much talked about. Jennifer Bennett, the gardening editor of Canada's **Harrowsmith**, has spent years collecting anecdotes, myths, medieval references, rites, herbal practices, and even correspondence between proper English lady gardeners. In Lilies of the Hearth, she focuses largely on European and Mediterranean societies of the past several thousand years, and their North American descendants (but then these are the women who have written or been written about). Combined, these fragments make a densely detailed tapestry of evidence that women have represented, nurtured, and repeatedly altered the place of nature in culture. Women have in turn been altered by it: Our social standing and perceived value has fluctuated with our botanical stereotypes, especially in the two hundred years of witchhunts (we knew too much about medicinal and magical*

Lilies of the Hearth
(The Historical Relationship Between Women & Plants)
Jennifer Bennett. 1991; 192 pp.
ISBN 0-921820-27-5
$14.95 ($14.95 postpaid) from Firefly Books Ltd., 250 Sparks Avenue, Willowdale, Ont M2H 2S4 Canada; 416/499-8412

plants), and the Victorian era, during which we were modeled after delicate flowers, easily wilted.
— Kathleen Harrison

•

Persephone's symbol was the pomegranate, because as a result of eating its seeds, she was committed to an eternal marriage with Hades in the underworld. (The pomegranate is an emblem of red, womblike, seed-filled fertility and, like the apple, recurs throughout the history of women and plants. It is interesting that the pomegranate has recently been found to contain small quantities of the female hormone progesterone.)

Plant Fiber Cordage

Jim Riggs begins this video by explaining how the world of aboriginal peoples was literally held together by cordage. He shows how to identify, harvest, extract fibers, and make cordage from dogbane (Apocynum cannibinum), stinging nettle (Urtica dioica), and milkweed (Asolepias speciosa).

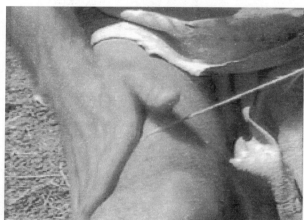

Jim shows how to make a one-ply cord: One bundle of fibers (half a stalk) is rolled on the thigh to give it a twist (the twist imparts more strength). For greater strength, Jim shows an easy way to make the cord into two-ply: Hold the cord stretched in front of oneself. Grasp the middle with one's teeth. Maintaining tautness, bring the two ends together. With ends held together, release one's teeth; the cord twists itself into two-ply. Rolling the cord on one's thigh tightens up the twist. Other methods of making two- and four-ply cordage are also covered.

When Jim demonstrates, his hands are filmed from over his shoulder; thus viewers have the same perspective Jim does, and the same one they have when looking at their own hands. This video does a superb teaching job.
—Julie Summers

Plant Fiber Cordage
Video by Jim Riggs. 1990.
$29.95 ($32.95 postpaid) from Northwestern Video Productions, PO Box 251, Roseburg, OR 97470; 503/673-3294

Tree-Free Paper
BY JOHN STAHL

THOMAS JEFFERSON'S draft of the Declaration of Independence, released by the Continental Congress on July 4, 1776, was written on paper made from hemp.

The supply of wood for papermaking is not inexhaustible. As early as 1916, the federal government understood that the trees were running out; Bulletin 404 recommended the cultivation of hemp as an alternative source of fiber for papermaking. The USDA figured out that the supply of trees could barely last a century. Now we're running out of trees. We see the local logging industry fading away because all the easy trees have been taken and there aren't that many left to harvest.

I've been experimenting with alternative fibers. Hemp is definitely one of them, though not the only one. I want to mention one other fiber right away: kenaf.

Kenaf is legal (no psychoactive element) and politically safe, and it is an excellent fiber.

It's easy to grow, it's easy to work with, it makes abundant crops, and it makes wonderful paper. A variety of hibiscus — *Hibiscus cannabinum* — kenaf is similar to hemp: a very tough, fibrous plant. It grows like hemp as an annual.

Paper is made from cellulose. Most plant material contains cellulose; however, there's only 30 percent cellulose in wood — at best. The rest is impurities — chiefly lignins and various other junk, which has to be cleaned out through the use of toxic chemicals. And the cellulose is then bleached with chlorine. You go through this incredibly toxic process to extract such a small amount of cellulose from wood. Hemp and kenaf are much richer sources of cellulose.

The Emperor Wears No Clothes

The premier book on hemp by the George Washington Carver of the hemp movement. Herer is also the founder of HEMP (Help Eliminate Marijuana Prohibition), a great source of information on the plant's commercial uses. — Alan Mason

The Emperor Wears No Clothes
Jack Herer. Queen of Clubs, 180 pp.
ISBN 1-878125-00-1
$19.95 ($24.95 postpaid) from Quick Trading Company, PO Box 429477, San Francisco, CA 94142-9477; 800/428-7825, ext 102

HEMP— Lifeline to the Future

*A little hard to read, but packed with a huge amount of information on the history and uses of hemp. Conrad edited **The Emperor Wears No Clothes**, and founded BACH (Business Alliance for Commercial Hemp), another information and lobbying group. — Alan Mason*

Hemp—Lifeline to the Future
Chris Conrad. 312 pp.
$12.95 ($17.95 postpaid) from Quick Trading Company, PO Box 429477, San Francisco, CA 94142-9477; 800/428-7825, ext 102

Indoor Marijuana Horticulture

Smoking and then growing marijuana once introduced a generation of Americans to gardening. Today it is illegal to grow marijuana in America. Between drug law enforcement and the neighbor kid down the block, growers today are becoming experts at high-tech indoor cultivation. High-intensity discharge lights, hydroponic cultivation and even computer-controlled indoor environments are all available. Indoor Marijuana Horticulture is the best introduction to the wonderful world of electricity that makes total indoor growing possible — fans, lights, timers, moisture meters, and CO_2 enrichment systems.

Commercial marijuana growing tends to be armed, dangerous, and locked in a symbiotic bear-hug with government.

There but for the police would go the price and market share to the likes of Philip Morris, R. J. Reynolds, and individual growers. There but for the illegal growers would go the need for an entire paramilitary bureaucracy fighting a war it can never win. Meanwhile the Fourth Amendment continues to get whittled away at, and nobody gets the tax revenues from a multi-billion-dollar industry. —RN

•

Technological breakthroughs and scientific research have shed bright light on indoor horiculture, by producing the *1000 watt metal halide* and *1000 watt High Pressure (HP) sodium, High Intensity Discharge (HID) lamps.* Now, a reasonably priced artificial light source, providing the color spectrum and intensity necessary for marijuana growth, is on the market. With the HID

Indoor Marijuana Horticulture
Jorge Cervantes. Interport, 1984; 288 pp.
$21.95 ($26.95 postpaid) from Quick Trading Company, PO Box 429477, San Francisco, CA 94142-9477; 800/428-7825, ext 102

lamps, a gardener may totally control the indoor environment. Together, these two types of HID lamps provide sufficient intensity, of the proper colors in the spectrum, to grow incredibly potent marijuana.

•

Caution: a hot HID may explode if touched by a single drop of cold water. Be very careful and make sure to move the HID out of the way when servicing garden.

The Science and Romance of Selected Herbs used in Medicine and Religious Ceremony

African ethnobotany is little understood by Europeans, and even less investigated by American botanists. Anthony Andoh, an ethnobotanist from Ghana, trained at London's Kew Gardens, has compiled and self-published a unique work that reflects a lifetime of studying plants and their many dimensions.

Andoh's focus is on the magico-spiritual plants used in the ancient Ifa religions of West Africa. When the imported slaves brought this divinatory plant-based religion to the New World, it absorbed the Roman Catholic saints and symbols, people of Spanish, Portuguese and Native American descent, and became Santeria, still a very active faith, particularly in the Caribbean and Brazil. The practitioners had to find plants that corresponded in their qualities to the African plants traditionally used, and therefore did extensive intuitive ethnobotanizing. —Kathleen Harrison

•

MELIA AZADERACH L. (meliaceae)

Common/Vernacular Names: *English:* China berry, Persian lilac, West Indian lilac, Bead tree, Pride of India, Hog bush, Bastard cedar, Tree of Paradise; *Spanish:* Paraiso, Lila, Pasilli, Arbol Santo; *Africa:* Nassara, Eke-oyinbo, Itchin-kurdi (Nigeria); *China:* Lien, K'n-lien, Sen-shu. . . .

Legend, Lore and Romance: This is one of the important ingredients of the "Omiero," the sacred elixir of initiation ceremonies. . . .

The active principle of this plant is the yellowish-white body soluble in alcohol and scarcely soluble in cold water, though it is more likely to be a substance still to be isolated which happens to be extracted with

the resinous body. This explains the reason for the plant's use as a fish poison, for example, in China, by a water soluble substance, and why a water infusion is used as a vermifuge in India. This unknown substance is destroyed by boiling. An overdose of the extract produces symptoms like those of *Atropa Belladonna* poisoning, and after stupor, death may follow. Recently, a toxic alkaloid, tazetine ($C_{18}H_{21}NO_5$) has been reported in the fruit and bark. The crushed, dried fruit has yielded azadirachtin, which is known to inhibit feeding of the desert locusts.

The Science and Romance of Selected Herbs Used in Medicine and Religious Ceremony
Anthony K. Andoh. 1986; 350 pp. ISBN 0-916299-01-5
$27.95 ($30.95 postpaid) from North Scale Institute, 2205 Taraval St., San Francisco, CA 94116; 415/759-9491

OTHER GREAT RESOURCES

Where the Gods Reign: Richard Evans Schultes. 1988, Synergetic Press.

Psychedelic Shamanism: Jim DeKorne. 1994, Loompanics Unltd.

See Spirituality
(pp. 32-36).

The sincerity and absolute faith in the revelatory power of the mushrooms is evident in these photographs of Maria Sabina, who, during the night-long chanting and clapping ceremony, feels herself fully in contact with the other world which the mushrooms have allowed her to visit.
—*Plants of the Gods*

Plants of the Gods • Medicines from the Earth

Richard Evans Schultes has been the nexus of almost everything interesting and supportive concerned with economic and cultural uses of plants. Plants of the Gods gives precise and illuminating portraits of the many peoples of the Earth who pay homage to and gain insights with the aid of psychedelic plants: an exquisite, thoroughly scholarly book. Medicines from the Earth has 250 of the plants most used for complaints and ailments. Cross-referenced by plant, illness, preparation (teas, compresses, etc.); best season to collect; and chemical

constituents discovered by pharmacologists. It's the best modern "herbal." —PW

•

Dated somewhere between 200 B.C. and A.D. 100, the beautiful ceramic artifact from Colima, Mexico (above) shows celebrants dancing around a mushroom effigy. From this artifact and the relative size and position of the fungus, it would appear that the mushroom represents something akin to the World Tree, the *axis mundi*. The mushroom, with its peaked cap, could well be *Psilocybe mexicana* or a close relative of this species. —*Plants of the Gods*

Plants of the Gods
(Their Sacred, Healing, and Hallucinogenic Powers)
Richard Evans Schultes & Albert Hoffmann. Healing Arts Press, 1979, 1992; 192 pp. ISBN 0-89281-406-3
$19.95 ($22.95 postpaid) from American International Distribution Corp., 64 Depot Rd., Colchester, VT 05446; 800/445-6638

Pharmacotheon: Entheogenic Drugs, Their Plant Sources and History

This work is, as Albert Hofmann emphasizes in his introduction, scientific and comprehensive. It would stand as a major contribution to the scholarship on entheogens (the term Ott advocates in place of "hallucinogens") if it contained only a review of the history of the field; a critique of the major controversies; an encyclopedic overview of the current state of our knowledge; a thorough introduction to the literature; a Merck-like index of the pharmacology and chemistry of 50 entheogens; and the most current and complete bibliography of the historical, anthropological, botanical, chemical, and pharmacological literature to date. Ott, however, has taken advantage of the unique literary freedom of the self-publisher. He introduces his work with an impassioned analysis of Western society's stance against ecstasy and euphoria. Throughout the book, he refers to his own experiences and to the experiences of his colleagues with entheogens breaking the hoary taboo against mingling the scientific with the subjective; in doing so, he speaks to us in a voice of unfamiliar and unsettling authority.

Those new to this topic will skip over pages dominated by vital botanical and chemical details in Latin and Greek, but will be drawn in when they come across Ott's arguments for the identities of the sacraments of the Rig Veda and the Eleusinian Mysteries, tales of nineteenth- and twentieth-century pioneering encounters with entheogens, and reports of careful experiments with obscure plant teachers. —Bret Blosser

•

In the most exciting recent development in the study of LSD and other ergoline entheogens, R. Gordon Wasson, Albert Hofmann and Carl A. P. Ruck have advanced a startling new theory concerning the Eleusinian Mysteries of ancient Greece. . . .

The Eleusinian Mystery was an annual celebration of a fertility cult, over which the goddess Demeter presided. Anyone speaking Greek could be initiated into the cult, but only once in a lifetime. The "Greater Mystery" was celebrated in the autumn, in a sanctuary at Eleusis, bordering the Rarian Plain near Athens. For nearly 2000 years the annual celebration was held, but never was the secret of the Mystery revealed. Initiates passed the night together in the dark-

Pharmacotheon
(Entheogenic Drugs, Their Plant Sources and History)
Jonathan Ott. Natural Products Co., 1993; 639 pp. ISBN 0-9614234-3-9
$40 ($44 postpaid) from AgAccess, PO Box 2008, Davis, CA 95617; 916/756-7177; Fax: 916/756-7188

ened telesterion or initiation hall, where they beheld a great vision which was "new, astonishing, inaccessible to rational cognition." Of the experience, they could only say that they had seen *ta hiera*, "the holy" — it was forbidden by law, under penalty of death, to say more (Wasson, et al. 1978).

•

It is the thesis of *The Road to Eleusis* that Demeter's potion, the *kykeon*, was entheogenic, and elicited the ineffable vision experienced each year by thousands of initiates. According to the theory, it was ergot growing on the barley added to the *kykeon* which accounted for the potion's entheogenic properties.

Medicines from the Earth
(A Guide to Healing Plants)
William A. Thomson, Editor. 1984, HarperCollins Publishers, Out of Print

•

It has been estimated that fewer than 10 percent of the world's flora has even been superficially examined from a chemical and pharmacological point of view. Thus, the potential for new medicinal agents has hardly been tapped.
—*Medicines from the Earth*

BriefBook: Biotechnology, Microbes & the Environment

This informative read shares a great perspective on microbes and the microbial aspects of biotech. There's also a breezy run-through of the politics and a good list of journals and sources (prior to 1990). Biotechnology does not address genetic manipulation of higher organisms or other related issues. —PW

•

To date, the small-scale field tests of genetically engineered microbes have, more than anything else, supported what the overwhelming majority of experts suspected would happen: The indigenous bugs beat out their much-ballyhooed brethren. Companies' claims notwithstanding, genetically engineered microbes definitely will not dot the shelves of farmers' sheds for some time. No better example of this can be found than what happened to a biotech version of a *Rhizobium meliloti* released on April 19, 1988, in Pepin County, Wis. Having altered the genes and enhanced the bacterium's nitrogen-fixing capability, Biotechnica Agriculture, a Cambridge, Mass.-based biotech

firm, hoped to enhance yields of alfalfa by as much as 17%, an improvement Biotechnica had demonstrated in the greenhouse. The test was the first open-air release of biotech-altered microbes in the Midwest, and the second in the United States.

So what happened?

Biotechnica's *Rhizobia* got so thoroughly outcompeted by local microbial residents that Biotechnica scientists could barely find them in the test plot soil.

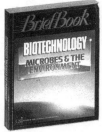

The worst-case scenario goes something like this: Put out in nature some mild-mannered bugs with some potent biological trick such as efficiently eating some toxic chemical spliced into them and they compete pretty well. These gene-spliced bugs begin to produce methane as a by-product. Then they exchange genes in a Bacterial Bazaar, and the genes for toxic taste buds get passed to some tough local bacteria that now start punching like Mike Tyson. In turn, this starts a ripple effect of toxic chemical consumption and methane

pollution that creates chaos in Bacterial Bazaars. Eventually, the big bacterial buffer that maintains all ecosystems begins to break down. Like an elegant, handcrafted gown losing a thread, the whole thing frays and comes apart, and there is no replacement for Earth's microbial gown.

Whatever is said about possible microbial mayhem, the irony remains that no one will ever know ahead of time when or where a microbial mishap will occur. You can say this: It will be at the right place and the right time for the microbe, which doesn't give a hoot about human interpretations of its behavior.

BriefBook: Biotechnology, Microbes & the Environment
Steven C. Witt. 1990; 219 pp.
ISBN 0-912005-04-1
$17.50 ($20.50 postpaid). Center for Science Information, 63 Homestead Street, San Francisco, CA 94114; 415/824-3192, fax 415/824-0201

Perils Amidst the Promise • Biotechnology's Bitter Harvest

The hope that biotechnology would be environmentally friendly and improve economic equities has faded all too fast. Little work has been done on genetically engineered predators to reduce crop pests. Instead, the money has gone to new crops that are more herbicide-resistant — allowing more use of herbicides. These two pamphlets put "sustainable ag" and "biotech ag" into the ring. They duke it out with thoughtful critiques of fed subsidies and ecological issues. They do not address human and animal health issues (see Superpigs for that). —PW

•

The widespread commercialization of transgenic versions of the full spectrum of food and fiber crops poses serious environmental risks that can be considered in several broad categories. These include the possibilities that:

• transgenic crops themselves will become weeds. Weeds — a term that will be used broadly in this report to cover plants unwanted in farms, lawns, roadside, and unmanaged ecosystems — are billion-dollar problems. In 1991 alone, farmers and others spent over $4 billion to control weeds in the United States.

• transgenic crops will serve as a conduit through which new genes move to wild plants, which could then become weeds. Like the crops themselves that become weeds, these plants could require expensive control programs. In addition, the novel transgenes may affect wild ecosystems in ways that are difficult to evaluate.

• plants engineered to contain virus particles will facilitate the creation of new viruses. New viral pathogens that affect economically important crops could require significant control costs.

Perils Amidst the Promise
(Ecological Risk of Transgenic Crops in a Global Market)
Jane Rissler & Margaret Mellon. 1993; 92 pp.
$14.40 postpaid. Union of Concerned Scientists, 26 Church Street, Cambridge, MA 0238; 617/547-5552

Biotechnology's Bitter Harvest
(Herbicide-Tolerant Crops and the Threat to Sustainable Agriculture)
Rebecca Goldburg, Jane Rissler, et al. 1990; 72 pp. $6 ($9.25 postpaid). National Wildlife Federation, 8925 Leesburg Pike, Vienna, VA 22184; 800/432-6564

• plants engineered to express potentially toxic substances like drugs and pesticides will present risks to other organisms that are not the intended targets of the new chemicals. For example, drug-producing plants might poison birds feeding in cornfields.
—*Perils Amidst the Promise*

•

The Forest Service is developing herbicide-tolerant trees at the same time as a lawsuit settlement has forced the Pacific Northwest management region of the Forest Service, and the northwest office of the Bureau of Land Management, to prepare environmental impact statements that consider the effects of vegetation management practices on natural ecosystems, as well as timber production. The Forest Service's final impact statement promotes *reduction* of herbicide use as the preferred alternative for vegetation management.

Herbicide-tolerant trees may make short-term economic sense for foresters, but

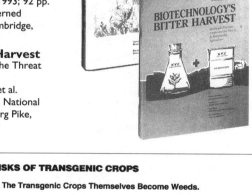

RISKS OF TRANSGENIC CROPS

1. The Transgenic Crops Themselves Become Weeds.

Transgenic Crop → New Transgenic Weed

2. The Transgenic Crops Transfer Pollen to Wild Relatives That Become Weeds.

Transgenic Crop / Transgenic pollen / Wild Plant Relative → New Transgenic Weed

they are incompatible with land stewardship and long-term economic productivity. Using them in government forests would be a strong expression of timber primacy — the idea that our national forests are managed for timber production, not conservation and recreation.
—*Biotechnology's Bitter Harvest*

Superpigs and Wondercorn

Corporate responsibility is not trivial when it comes to biotechnology. Some think of biotechnics as playing God. Others as a "natural" outcome of evolution. All agree that the technocrats, investors, and researchers have enormous powers never confronted before in human history.

This is the best overview of the biopolitical and scientific applications for biotechnology. Superpigs' author is a Humane Society vice president and an extremely thoughtful biologist. The opposition calls him an alarmist and a moralist. So was Paul Revere. —PW

•

Over the past decade and a half, the biotechnology industry has become the fastest growing industry in recorded history. Venture capitalists have invested in both small and large companies that promise great profits from new, genetically engineered products and services. By 1984, investment in genetic engineering had already exceeded $2.5 billion, with the total global investment estimated at $40 billion by the year 2000, according to analyst J. Elkington. Sales of biotechnology products in the United States reached $1.11 billion in 1989 and are expected to surpass $40 billion by the year 2000. In January 1991 the Bush administration boosted funding for its program for biotechnology research to $4 billion.

•

Biotech is already a threat to the agricultural economies of some third-world countries. One example is the synthetic production of aromatic oils and essences like vanilla in the United States, which is in direct competition with African and other third-world countries whose economies are dependent on the export of the natural forms of these products.

Superpigs and Wondercorn
(The Brave New World of Biotechnology and Where It All May Lead)
Michael W. Fox. 1992; 256 pp.
ISBN 1-55821-182-9
$21.95 ($24.45 postpaid). Lyons & Burford Publishers, 31 W. 21st Street, New York, NY 10010; 212/620-9580

OTHER GREAT RESOURCES

Foundation for Economic Trends: 1130 17th Street NW, Suite 300, Washington, DC 20036; 202/466-2823, fax 202/775-0074. Jeremy Rifkin's organization is known for blistering biotech critiques, and for lawsuits.

The Gene Hunters (Biotechnology and the Scramble for Seeds): Calestous Juma. 1990, Princeton University Press. What will biotech mean for world politics? Biological warfare using genetic information? Here's an African perspective.

Walden, and On the Duty of Civil Disobedience

Emerson looked at Thoreau through the jailhouse bars. Why are you in there? he asked. Why are you out there? he answered. No two books cut closer to the American grain: one transcendent, the other pious.
—Peter Warshall

•

I learned this, at least, by my experiment: that if one advances confidently in the direction of his dreams, and endeavors to live the life which he has imagined, he will meet with a success unexpected in common hours.

•

I rejoice that there are owls. Let them do the idiotic and maniacal hooting for men. It is a sound admirably suited to swamps and twilight woods which no day illustrates, suggesting a vast and undeveloped nature which men have not recognized. They represent the stark twilight and unsatisfied thoughts which all have. All day the sun has shown on the surface of some savage swamp, where the single spruce stands hung with usnea lichens, and small hawks circulate above, and the chickadee lisps amid the evergreens, and the partridge and rabbit skulk beneath; but now a more dismal and fitting day dawns, and a different

Walden, and On the Duty of Civil Disobedience
Henry David Thoreau. 1970; 271 pp. ISBN 0-06-080615-X
$5 ($7.75 postpaid). HarperCollins Publishers/Direct Mail, PO Box 588, Dunmore, PA 18512; 800/331-3761

race of creatures awakes to express the meaning of Nature there. —*Walden*

•

Under the name of Order and Civil Government, we are all made at last to pay homage to and support our own meanness. After the first blush of sin comes its indifference; and from immoral it becomes, as it were, unmoral, and not quite unnecessary to that life which we have made.
—*Civil Disobedience*

Ecodefense

*Inspired by Ed Abbey's **Monkey Wrench Gang**, the authors describe proven techniques of tree-spiking, road-spiking, heavy-equipment-disabling, fence-cutting, trap-clearing, lock-jamming, billboard-trashing, and sundry skills of propaganda, camouflage, sneaking around, escape and evasion, and the like. It is best not to skim and try, but really study before trying — for two reasons. One is that monkeywrenching mostly takes place in country where retribution is not only in the courts but also by direct action: you get the shit beat out of you. The second is that monkeywrenching the wrong target is grotesquely counterproductive; you not only have to be right every single time, but conspicuously right — or you're just another random vandal making everyone else feel sick about being alive. The book constantly warns about knowing your target cold before making a move, and if in doubt, don't. —SB*

•

Try to break down the power of the billboard ad by *answering* it, looking at the space available and the way in which the words and images lend themselves to addition, alteration or comment. Humor is extremely effective in exposing the advertiser's real intentions — turning the ad's message back on itself. (Be sure to avoid spelling mistakes!)

If the offending billboard proves too high to reach, you can either get a ladder (which isn't particularly convenient) or build a spray can extension rod:

Obtain a broom handle or another solid, strong but lightweight wooden pole (see illustration, #1). At one end, cut out a wedge, half the width of the pole. Fit a flat metal bar to the remaining wood (#2).

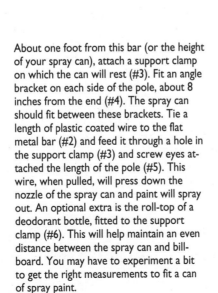

About one foot from this bar (or the height of your spray can), attach a support clamp on which the can will rest (#3). Fit an angle bracket on each side of the pole, about 8 inches from the end (#4). The spray can should fit between these brackets. Tie a length of plastic coated wire to the flat metal bar (#2) and feed it through a hole in the support clamp (#3) and screw eyes attached the length of the pole (#5). This wire, when pulled, will press down the nozzle of the spray can and paint will spray out. An optional extra is the roll-top of a deodorant bottle, fitted to the support clamp (#6). This will help maintain an even distance between the spray can and billboard. You may have to experiment a bit to get the right measurements to fit a can of spray paint.

Although these spray can extension rods are clumsy to use at first, with practice they become very effective.

Ecodefense
(A Field Guide to Monkeywrenching)
Dave Foreman & Bill Haywood. Abbzug Press, 1993; 350 pp. ISBN 0-9637751-0-3
$20 ($22.50 postpaid). Ned Ludd Books, PO Box 5141, Tucson, AZ 85703; 602/628-9610

*W*hen **LEGAL OPTIONS** have been **subverted**, when <u>government</u> once again puts a *fox* to <u>guarding</u> the *chickens*, when *time's a-wastin'*, the only remaining answer may be *immediate, possibly "*<u>illegal</u>*" action.* If the <u>ACTS</u> are well chosen and carried out with intelligence and *theater*, the public is at least **awakened**, if not totally <u>OUTRAGED</u>. Straight folks, and of course those targeted, engage in much *hand-wringing* and talk of **TERRORism**. But a look at the recent past will show that *courageous Earth First!-ers* and *Greenpeace squads* and *Sea Shepherd sailors* have often been the *first* to **stir up** what later became major causes championed by less **CONTROVERSIAL** organizations with offices in <u>Washington</u>. I'm glad there are folks out there *with the GUTS to do this* sort of thing. —JB!

Earth First!

"No compromise in the defense of Mother Earth!" Face it, with mainline America nostalgic for commies, they're going to pick on green-symps. Earth First! is up agin it. Hard times: If you believe property rights means caring for the earth you own, you're subversive. If you believe in reducing the pain and suffering of nonhuman creatures, you're primitive and subversive.

Yet Earth First! tickles an underground envy and respect from the Big Boys that bust 'em. In the theater of ecopolitics, direct action against machinery (not people) can be the final act. You can subscribe to the newspaper — hopefully without an IRS check. You can buy the needy outrageous stuff through Books of the Big Outside (p. 100).

Earth First!:
$25/year, includes 8 issues of *Earth First! Journal*, from PO Box 1415, Eugene, OR 97440; 503/741-9191, fax 503/741-9192

Sea Shepherd Conservation Society: Membership $25/year from 3107A Washington Boulevard, Marina Del Rey, CA 90292; 310/301/7325, fax 310/574-3161

Greenpeace: Membership $30/year from 1436 U Street NW, Washington, DC 20009; 202/462-1177

Sea Shepherd

There is no 911 on the high seas: no way to bring in The Law, no way to stop the deaths of fish in miles of illegal netting and no way to halt the radar-directed Darth Vaders from the outlaw empire of Norway from killing whales. Time for the Lone Ranger and Tonto — who, under the circumstances, are Sea Shepherd. Now equipped with a Yellow Submarine and more moxie than a football stadium of white sharks, they are the only law around on the salty frontier. They are, of course, being prosecuted and harassed by Canada (among others).

Greenpeace

Direct action in twenty-four countries, operating in the gray area where there may be international law, but there are no global enviro-cops. Greenpeace treads that line: Who is within and who without the law, when it comes to ozone, nuclear waste, the global waste trade, planetary warming, protecting open-ocean marine mammals? The winds know no boundaries: ask Chernobyl. They are prone at times to violent enthusiasms ("Chlorine-Free by '93"), but Greenpeace offers the most extensive activist-net for the international scene. There is no better global group for political organizing and digging in for the fight.

It will take hard work to join German Greenpeace to American Greenpeace. It's worth the effort. Target your checks to help the new citizen-based linkages for managing the global cow or transnationals. And join their boycotts. —PW

Local Action: The United States

In the theater of power, the grassroots shies from Beltway careerists with $100,000+ salaries and fancy brochures printed on virgin tree flesh. Nevertheless, the "corporate-style" groups remain the say-it-nice ambassadors to mainstream America, to White House shenanigans, and to numerous deep pockets. Their main goal and major hope for revival should be a concerted, concentrated effort to break the "takings" issue, dissolve the doublespeak of the wise-guys movement, return honesty to the resource agencies, and find a spirituality in the American grain. The grassroots and a more muscular Beltway could come together by punishing the political parties. They need to work together to swing specific elections on enviro issues. People of color, enviros and labor have begun to see common issues and trade-offs. If the enviros don't swing a few votes, the Big Boys and Gals won't notice. Politicos are simply into perpetuation.
—Peter Warshall

Grassroots Toolkit

Student Environmental Action Coalition

Think student action is dead? Nonsense. SEAC's hot and (compared to old farts) doesn't give a damn for pigeonholes. People-of-color coalitions and discussions of homophobia mix right in with fights for ancient forests and Mr. Monkeywrench. Their regional updates show an amazing number of students fighting for environmental and social justice. Threshold, *their magazine of movement, is printed in soy-based inks on recycled paper. Compare that integrity to a slick Beltway rag! Do the wild thing and join just to help Generation X.*

Public Employees for Environmental Responsibility (PEER)

Government employees and contractors are often the front line of defense. Their personal decisions increase or decrease, stop or encourage environmental harm or death. Some agencies like the Forest Service are exquisitely corrupt, bumping employees that tell the truth, manipulating reports after employees spent months trying to write the truth, using advancement carrots and job-stagnation sticks.

PEER is a wonderful empowerment organization, the first penetration into a byzantine, smoke-and-mirror bureaucracy. You don't have to be an employee (or employed) to join. If you believe in free speech for everyone, open government, free information flow, and breaking the destructive complicity of mid- and high-level managers, then PEER's the place. Started by Jeff DeBonis (see AFSEE, p. 91).

Friends of the Earth

FOE is global, with 143 worldwide affiliates. It pressures US agencies to take social and conservation costs into account in their trade policies. It keeps muscling for better policies on ozone, global warming, corporate accountability, nuclear weapons and toxic safety. If an issue crosses political borders, FOE crosses them too. FOE has fused with the Oceanic Society and Environmental Policy Institute. This may be just the tentative embryonic stage of a more robust global civilian network to counteract the less earth-sensitive megacorps.

Earth Island Institute

David Brower's smorgasbord of thirty sustainable, biodiverse, restorative, and just endeavors. Pick your project — saving Lake Baikal, the Tibetan Plateau, or the inner city of Berkeley — to give muscle to their burgeoning ideals. —PW

Student Environmental Action Coalition: PO Box 1168, Chapel Hill, NC 27514-1168; 916/967-4600, Internet: seac@unc.bitnet, fax 916/967-4648.

Public Employees for Environmental Responsibility: 810 First Street NE, Suite 680, Washington, DC 20002; 202/408-0041, fax 202/842-4716.

Friends of the Earth International: 218 D Street SE, Washington, DC 20003; 202/783-7400.

Earth Island Institute: 300 Broadway, Suite 28, San Francisco, CA 94133; 415/788-3666, Internet: earthisland@igc.apc.org.

INDEX TO MWEC's ECOACTIVISM

The Beltway

Sierra Club

A hundred and two years old, with more than a half-million members, the Sierra Club needs to play poker for earth-keeps. They need to let congressmen know that Sierra can lose them their seats; they need to compromise less and to let their local chapters experiment more at playing hardball. Times are tougher for the planet than SC seems to admit, and Sierra is grossly self-promotional. But John Muir would not want any members to abandon ship.

National Audubon Society

The heart of Audubon has always been grassroots, outdoor, naturalist education. The politics have always been avian. (Audubon started as a fight to keep egret plumes off women's hats.) So it is surprising that the Society is so out of touch; other bird magazines have stolen the dawn song.

With so many birds in trouble, you would think the AS could settle down to a focused cockfight with the White House. On the other hand, Audubon has allowed its local chapters great freedom to educate or fight with less circumspection. Direct your funds to specific local projects. Audubon has some wonderful staff, like Brock Evans, and a dedication to the Everglades that rightly keeps some of its membership loyal.

The Wilderness Society

With a strong background of protecting wildlands and wildlife, they are the ideal spearhead to shape the new West with conservation-based development, realignment of labor, recreationalists, and enviros, and clear economic/ecologic refutations of the wise-use movement. They could learn a bit from The Wildlands Project and could use the assistance of their former staff now dwelling in Clintonia. (To show you how ineffective Beltway enviros can become: they lost Jim Baca.) The WS represents the front line and deserves membership backup.

Defenders of Wildlife

Not really in the moneybuckets like other Beltway groups, DoW's fight is focused on protecting species and habitats. They are a fine link between smaller groups and bigger groups who need a strategy to improve (not corrode) the implementation of the Endangered Species Act. Undercover work, consensus work among the enviros, and legal imagination could be the cards in their hand. —PW

Sierra Club: 730 Polk Street, San Francisco, CA 94109; 415/776-2211, fax 415/776-0350.

Audubon Society: 613 Riversville Rd., Greenwich, CT 06831; 203/869-2017, fax 203/869-4437.

The Wilderness Society: PO Box 296, Federalsburg, MD 21632-1296; 212/833-2300.

Defenders of Wildlife: 1101 14th Street NW, Suite 1400, Washington, DC 20005; 202/682-9400.

—S.N.E.E.J.

Environmental Justice

Southwest Network for Environmental and Economic Justice

Communities of color have been sacrificial areas — zones for landfills with toxic wastes and uranium tailings, for petrochemical factories, for other high-risk industries (like lead smelters), for high exposure/slow health-official response/meagre compensation and insurance payments. Environmental racism.

But not for long! Solid coalitions are forming. Lessons on how to operate multi-racial and multi-ethnic organizations are paying off. It took the revenge of a polluted and destroyed Mother Nature to galvanize enviros with the Rainbow Coalition. —PW

Toxic Waste and Race in the United States: $20 postpaid. United Church of Christ Commission for Racial Justice, 700 Prospect Avenue, Cleveland, OH 44115.

Race, Poverty and the Environment: Urban Habitat Program. $15/year (4 issues). Earth Island Institute, 300 Broadway, Suite 28, San Francisco, CA 94133; 415/788-3666, Internet: earthisland@igc.apc.org.

Southwest Network for Environmental and Economic Justice: PO Box 7399, Albuquerque, NM 87194-7399; 505/242-0416, fax 505/242-5606.

About as solidly local and strong as any multiracial, multicultural organization of students, youth, and community organizations trying to attain environmental and social justice can get. In the name of our mother, earth.

Confronting Environmental Racism (Voices from the Grassroots): Robert D. Bullard, Editor. 1993; 259 pp. ISBN 0-89608-446-9. $16 ($19 postpaid). South End Press, PO Box 741, Monroe, ME 04951; 800/533-8478.

ENVIRONMENTAL DIRECTORIES

Whether your interests run to saving elephants or bluebirds, some like-minded group out there probably shares your concerns. Of the many guides to such groups, we find these the most useful. —David Burnor

1994 Conservation Directory: Item # 7956. $20 ($24.85 postpaid). National Wildlife Federation, 8925 Leesburg Pike, Vienna, VA 22184; 800/432-6564. International and governmental agencies, citizens' groups, schools, and online databases.

Who Is Who in Service to the Earth: Hans J. Keller, Editor, 1993. ISBN 0-9628405-2-1. $30 ($32.50 postpaid). VisionLink Education Foundation, 47 Calhoun Rd., Waynesville, NC 28786; 704/926-2200, fax 704/926-9041. Cross-referenced by organizations, projects, names, and key words.

The Encyclopedia of Associations: Gale Research Inc. Check your local library. Has the most extensive, though least discriminate, listings. Updated annually.

High Country News

The model for eco-media reporting. Even when you disagree, the interest in what is said remains. If conservation-based livelihoods are in our future, the dialog, news and weather vanes will come from eco-regional reporting in styles like High Country News. —PW

High Country News
Betsy Marston, Editor.
$28/year (20 issues). High Country Foundation/HCN, Box 1090, Paonia, CO 81428; 303/527-4898

•

For three decades, the Columbia River Scaling and Grading Bureau (CRSB) has been one of the largest companies of its type in the West. CRSB employees "scale" logs on trucks that roll off national forests in Alaska, California, Oregon and Washington — that is, they measure and inspect the logs, estimate the percentage of rot and defect in them, and come up with a figure of how much marketable timber they contain. From these figures, the forest service determines how much money it — and in turn, we taxpayers — are paid for the logs.

But for decades apparently, CRSB has been ripping us off.

TIMBER THEFT

—*High Country News*

Unequal Protection (Environmental Justice and Communities of Color): Robert D. Bullard, Editor. 1994; 392 pp. ISBN 0-87156-450-5. $25 ($28 postpaid). Sierra Club Store Orders, 730 Polk Street, San Francisco, CA 94109; 800/935-1056.

Walleye Warriors (An Effective Alliance Against Racism and for the Earth): Rick Whaley & Walter Bresette. 1994; 272 pp. ISBN 0-86571-257-3. $17.95 ($20.45 postpaid). New Society Publishers, 4527 Springfield Avenue, Philadelphia, PA 19143; 800/333-9093.
A multiracial alliance fights racism and greed to keep Anishinabe (Chippewa) fishing rights from defeat.

THIS IS PURELY AN ECONOMIC ISSUE...

—*Walleye Warriors*

—*World Watch*

The Greenpeace Guide to Anti-Environmental Organizations

Here's a sad litany of organized environmental foes and their goals. Their names are benign; some even suggest that they are save-the-world groups. Their financial supporters include corporations making lots of pro-environment noises these days. This little book reveals their villainy.
—J. Baldwin

•

Citizens for the Environment (CFE) 470 L'Enfant Plaza SW, Washington DC 20024; 202 488 7255

Citizens for the Environment describes itself as a "grassroots environmental group that promotes market-based methods for protecting our

The Greenpeace Guide to Anti-Environmental Organizations
Carl Deal. 1993; 110 pp. ISBN 1-878825-15-4 $5 ($7 postpaid). Odonian Press, Box 7776, Berkeley, CA 94707; 800/798-5786

environment." Despite this claim, it has no citizen membership of its own. Founded in 1990 as an offshoot of Citizens for a Sound Economy (a right-wing "consumer" group), CFE is a think tank and lobbying group that advocates strict deregulation of corporations as the solution to environmental problems.

It rallied opposition to the Clean Air Act of 1990 and to California's Proposition 128 ("Big Green"), a broad environmental package to improve state regulation of toxins. Congress passed the Clean Air Act, but Proposition 128 was defeated.

CFE scientist Jo Kwong urges the public to "discard the hype" circulated by environmentalists. She identifies sixteen environmental problems that she says are a sham. These "myths" — acid rain, natural-resource depletion and shrinking landfill space — "dictate public policy" Kwong complains.

CFE argues that industry has always played a positive role in protecting the environment. "The introduction of free-market economics — which occurred about the same time as the American Revolution — enabled us to grow wealthier, which in turn gave us the technology to grow healthier." CFE President Stephen Gold told an EPA conference, "Two centuries later, we've reduced and even eliminated many of our previous environmental threats." Gold concludes that natural resources will be preserved by future generations only "by channeling the powerful forces of the marketplace — that invisible hand — to enable

World Watch

*This is one of three places Worldwatch Institute appears in this Catalog (see p. 68 for **Vital Signs** and p. 304 for **State of the World**). If these other publications can be qualified in small ways, **World Watch** cannot. By Whole Earth staff consensus, it is the most thoughtful and wide-ranging whole-earth enviro-mag — with no ads. Some sample contents: What do the deaths of birds all over the biosphere tell us? Eco-communications by computer. How to help indigenous people make maps to show that they "own" the land they live on. Can China kick its coal habit — a habit which may undo any progress in global warming? Why does LA recycle better than New York?* —PW

World Watch
Ed Ayres, Editor.
$15/year (6 issues). Worldwatch Institute, 1776 Massachusetts Avenue NW, Washington, DC 20036-1904

this country to enter the next century cleaner and healthier than before."

Funding
CFE's parent, Citizens for a Sound Economy, is partially funded by:
Alcan Aluminim • American Petroleum Institute • Ameritech • Amoco • Association of International Automobile Manufacturers • Boeing • Chevron • Coors • General Electric • General Motors • Georgia-Pacific • Honda North America • Kobe Steel • Mobil • Nissan • John M. Olin Foundation • Phillip Morris • Rockwell International • Sarah Scaife Foundation • Sony • Toyota • Union Carbide • Xerox

OTHER GREAT GREENTALK

Garbage: Patricia Poore, Editor. $39/year (4 issues). Dovetale Publishers, 2 Main Street, Gloucester, MA 01930-9941; 800/274-9909. The up-in-your-face enviro mag, streetwise and wise-ass. I like their way of thought and marvel at the enviro-hype ads that obviously pay the bills. Who knows if they're as "practical" as claimed? They do more research and argue well.

Common Ground: The Conservation Fund, 1880 N. Kent Street, Suite 1120, Arlington, VA 22209; 703/525-6300. This bimonthly has interesting information that you won't find anywhere else: state actions, corporate notes, eco-organization profiles and updates, readings and more.

Ambio: $44/year (8 issues). Allen Press, 1041 New Hampshire Road, PO Box 18917, Lawrence, KS 66044. It's Swedish, international, and smart.

The Ecologist: $34/year (6 issues) from MIT Press Journals/Circulation Dept., 55 Hayward Street, Cambridge, MA 02142; 617/253-2889 (fax 617/258-6779). A nice mix of careful and radical. Strong point of view, lots of good ideas, and considerable effect. A British magazine.

ORION: George K. Russell, Editor. $18/year (4 issues). Myrin Institute/ORION Subscriptions Dept., 136 E. 64th Street, New York, NY 10021; 212/785-6475. The most beautiful greentalk magazine in prose and photos, deep in the tradition of literary/philosophical natural history.

NOT IN MY BACKYARD! is the justifiably outraged response to nasty stuff being dumped where you live. But where do *your* nasties go? Do you even know what they are? Just making the mattress you sleep on also made a mess somewhere for somebody else. Community-level toxics are a serious problem with much opportunity for injustice, but we all share responsibility. It will take all of us to clean the place up. —J. Baldwin

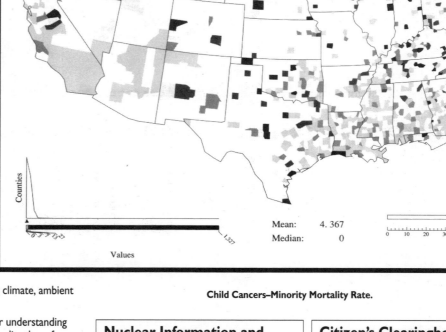

Mean: 4.367
Median: 0

Child Cancers–Minority Mortality Rate.

The Truth About Where You Live

This book surveys the incidence of mortality and disease by locale, and maps the results county by county across the USA in irrefutable, appalling, worrisome detail. I can almost guarantee you will find unwelcome surprises here. It's accompanied by suitable explanations and a long-past-due call to arms. This is magnum ammunition for activists. I can just hear you furiously thumbing pages to find out how your area is rated. (Mine is so-so.) As R. Crumb says, "There's no peace for the living." —JB

• Epidemiologists untangle such questions by classifying the causes of disease according to three factors:

Agents of disease are specific factors that contribute to ill health — bacteria, viruses, toxic chemicals, ionizing radiation, cholesterol and others.

Host factors (or intrinsic factors) are personal characteristics that influence susceptibility or response — age, sex, social class, ethnicity, genes, behavior, nutritional state, heightened chemical sensitivity due to previous exposures, and the like.

Environmental factors (or extrinsic factors) include any aspect of the physical, biological, or societal environment that influences the existence of an agent and exposure or susceptibility to it — food sources, occupation, economic conditions, government regulations, housing climate, ambient pollution, and so forth.

This is a useful scheme for understanding causes of disease, but in reality these factors interact in a way that demands an appreciation of ecological interrelationships.

The Truth About Where You Live
(An Atlas for Action on Toxins and Mortality)
Benjamin A. Goldman. Times Books, 1991; 416 pp. ISBN 0-8129-1898-3
$17 ($19 postpaid) from Random House/Order Dept., 400 Hahn Road, Westminster, MD 21157; 800/733-3000

Preventing Industrial Toxic Hazards

Here's a workbook for keeping toxic wastes out of your, or somebody else's, community, with an emphasis on reduction at the source. It presents strategies and tactics for accomplishing this, complete with worksheets (so you won't leave out anything important), reproductions of official forms, and a discussion of laws and citizens' rights — virtually everything needed for an effective campaign. You furnish the information required to fill in the blanks and enough outrage to get things moving. The previous edition proved to be a formidable weapon in the hands of ordinary people tired of being dumped upon. This new one is even better. —JB

•

"Our TRI [Toxic Release Inventory] data show that we have reduced our emissions since the 1987, 1988, 1989, or 1990 reporting years"

This type of claim is commonly made, and in fact the TRI emissions numbers in many cases do show some reductions. However, these "paper" reductions in TRI figures most often cannot necessarily be attributed to true source reduction activity. A National Wildlife Federation study has revealed that most of the largest decreases in toxic emissions have resulted from changes in reporting requirements (such as chemical reporting thresholds and chemical delistings); analytical methods (calculation changes); and production level variations (volume reductions, such as lowered production) — not from source reduction, waste minimization, recycling or treatment. Although there are some good examples of emissions decreases due to genuine source reduction practices, you are still advised to request specific information on how the reductions were achieved.

Preventing Industrial Toxic Hazards
(A Guide for Communities)
Marian Wise & Lauren Kenworthy. 1993; 199 pp. ISBN 0-918780-60-8
$25 ($28 postpaid) from INFORM, Inc., 381 Park Avenue South, New York, NY 10016; 212/689-4040

Nuclear Information and Resource Service

The dishonesty of the nuclear lobby is balanced by this hard-working organization. Membership gets you the Nuclear Monitor newsletter and a constantly updated watchdog report on every nuclear facility in the USA. Alerts by snail- and email call you to action, which they'll assist. —JB

NIRS
Membership $35/year. 1424 16th Street NW, Suite 601, Washington, DC 20036; 202/328-0002,
email nirsnet@aol.com or nirsnet@igc.apc.org

Microwave News • VDT News

Microwave News is probably the last independent source of science-based information on the sources and effects of the non-ionizing radiation constantly bombarding us. VDT News watches the ramparts of computer safety. Expensive, but lots less than you'd pay to collect the info yourself. —JB

VDT News
Lewis Slesin, Editor.
$127/year (6 issues).

Microwave News
Lewis Slesin, Editor.
$285/year (6 issues). Both from PO Box 1799, Grand Central Sta., New York, NY 10163; 212/517-2800

Citizen's Clearinghouse for Hazardous Waste, Inc.

Twelve years of often-successful infighting have made this outfit a formidable foe of polluters and scatterers of foul substances. Membership gets you a lively newsletter called Everyone's Backyard. and a catalog offering an arsenal of action manuals intended for inexperienced citizens up in arms. —JB

Citizen's Clearinghouse for Hazardous Wastes, Inc.
Membership $25/year. PO Box 6806, Falls Church, VA 22040; 703/237-2249.

Toxic Trade Update

Villainous dumping of toxic wastes on populations that don't have political power or effective laws to hold it off is what this quarterly is mostly about. Grim, true, and infuriating, it makes plain where some hard work must be done. —JB

Toxic Trade Update
Available in English, French or Spanish.
$20/year (4 issues) from Greenpeace Toxic Trade Campaign, 1436 U Street NW, Washington, DC 20009

"THE GOAL isn't just a recycling *program*; we want it to be the way people normally do things around here." —Linda Christopher, Garbage Reincarnation, Santa Rosa, CA.

Can we afford a society-wide system that recycles or reuses nearly everything? Is it even possible? How a near-total reuse/recycle system will be achieved, how it is to be paid for (we know *who* is going to pay for it), and how close we will come to perfection are all being decided right now in the ponderous, untidy techno-political dance that eventually gets things settled in this country.

It's obvious that a comprehensive recycling system will have to be put in place sooner or later, and that it must be essentially eternal. (Recycling that can't be kept up indefinitely merely postpones doom.) Activists should remember that getting the job started is more important than sinner-smiting and unattainable perfection; managers should note that responding to citizen protest is not the same as corporate responsibility; politicians should heed Buckminster Fuller's admonition that in matters of this sort, the true cost is what it'll cost if we *don't* act. All of us should keep in mind that, as with pollution, recycling and re-use is best handled by not making a wasteful mess in the first place. —J. Baldwin

Rubbish!

The material evidence of our civilization, lovingly preserved in landfill, diverges considerably from our image of ourselves. This book is full of amazing news gathered in two decades by the Tucson-based Garbage Project. The debris accumulation in Troy raised the city 4.7 feet per century. New York City has risen 6 to 30 feet since its founding. The methane generated in landfills is being used in some places as a power source, but there is relatively little actual rotting going on in landfills, and "biodegradable" products (including even fresh food) are preserved perfectly for decades.

The urban poor in Mexico City "consume proportionally more candy — pound for pound, the most expensive type of food in the city — than their more affluent neighbors." People my age may remember paper and scrap drives during World War II in America and Britain. It turns out they produced such surpluses that much of it was quietly landfilled, but the programs were kept on for "morale" reasons. In modern recycling, by far the most eco-

nomically lucrative yield is aluminum from beverage cans. Tires can't be landfilled; they always pop to the top.

Environmentalists have persuaded the American public that landfill is made up of 20-30 percent fast-food packaging, 25-40 percent expanded foam, and 25-45 percent disposable diapers. ("The Disposable Diaper Myth" in WER *#60, Fall 1988, declared in a tone of outrage that 3-4 percent of landfill was diapers.) The actual figures: 0.59-1.28 percent disposable diapers; 1 percent foam; 0.33 percent fast-food packaging. The real villains are paper (40 percent); construction debris (12 percent); and food and yard waste (7 percent). —SB*

New York's garbage is trucked as far away as New Mexico.

Salvaging the Land of Plenty

The subtitle of this realistic book is "Garbage and the American Dream," but it isn't the usual grim jeremiad. A cool, academic look at how we got into the mess we're (literally) in makes the intricate processes of incremental change seem obvious in hindsight. The analysis instills a sense of the rate of change and the array of interlocking forces that hustle things along toward intractable global nastiness. Next comes a hard look at the current situation. The absence of simplification is refreshing and sets the stage for Part III with its abrasive chapter headings: Can Technology Fix it?; Can Science Sort It Out? The conclusions require, as they must, a change in all of us — which is easily said. Fortunately, after all the talk the author makes some good suggestions for moves that could bring about the desired results. That's unusual in this sort of book. So is the author's lively writing style. If you read just one book to bring you up to date on the subject, this is it. —J. Baldwin

The choice between economic and environmental goods, however, is a false one. The idea that protecting the environment hurts the economy seems to make sense if we look at environmental protection chiefly as development forgone, or if we merely count up the costs of pollution control. However, this sort of calculation leaves out more than it includes, such as safeguards for health; conservation of resources and protection of species for future consumption; preservation of natural beauty as a basis for tourism; savings by industry from reductions in materials input and wastes; and both jobs and profits flowing from new services predicated on conservation of resources. In 1992, the U.S. environmental-services industry counted nearly seventy thousand businesses, with an income of $134 billion, employing over a million workers.

Preserving natural habitats for tourists, rather than exploiting forests for timber, land for minerals, rivers and streams for irrigation, or prairies for meat production, also encourages use rather than appropriation and consumption. Because tourism can be sustained indefinitely, generating jobs and income in the long term, it represents a much better investment than the alternative of materials extraction which will end when old-growth mining slag lies heaped across mountainsides, forests are fields of stumps, and soil erosion has made of rolling plains a landscape of dirt and sawgrass.

Again, looking at the way we go through housing stock, enormous savings — with potentially high aesthetic payoffs — would result from revising tax and subsidy policies to favor renovation rather than construction of new housing tracts.

Salvaging the Land of Plenty
(Garbage and the American Dream)
Jennifer Seymour Whitaker. 1994; 336 pp.
ISBN 0-688-10130-5
$25 ($26.50 postpaid). William Morrow
and Co./Wilmore Warehouse, 39 Plymouth Street, Fairfield, NJ 07004

OTHER GREAT RESOURCES

BioCycle: $63/year (12 issues) from the JG Press, 419 State Avenue, Emmaus, PA 18049; 215/967-4135. This journal is close to my feces-fertilizer-farm-food-feces revolving vision. Herein, the creators of America's long-term wealth. —Peter Warshall

Silent Spring: Rachel Carson. 1962, Houghton Mifflin Company. Where wide awareness of toxics started. It's still a good cautionary read. —JB

Rubbish!
(The Archaeology of Garbage)
William Rathje & Cullen Murphy.
HarperPerennial, 1992; 256 pp.
ISBN 0-06-092228-1
$12 ($14.75 postpaid). HarperCollins
Publishers/Direct Mail, PO Box 588,
Dunmore, PA 18512; 800/331-3761

In the United States, the skillful packaging of food products cuts down markedly on the wastage of foods. Packaging and the development of a modern, corporate-driven food industry are among the most important reasons why U.S. households, on average, produce fully a third less garbage than do households in Mexico City, where a higher percentage of food is bought fresh, and a larger volume of garbage inevitably results.

Wasting Away

"It's all a nasty business," comments Kevin Lynch, referring to his somewhat repellent subject of waste. In this wonderfully adroit, posthumously published book, he addresses every meaning and implication of the word, ranging widely enough to encompass potlatching, used tires, neighborhood destruction (he was a noted city planner), the Marxist view, and death. He doesn't dodge the philosophically thorny question, is it even possible to have a society that doesn't waste? His argument buttressed by the results of a public questionnaire on various aspects of waste, Mr. Lynch concludes that waste is part of the human condition, and we'd best get good at managing it. As a thorough exploration of a concept, the book is a delight; at once enlightening, admonishing, and occasionally annoying. In other words, realistic. —J. Baldwin

Wallace Stegner recounts the beauty, mystery and pain of what he found in the rural dump of his childhood: the discarded volumes of Shakespeare, the skeleton of his own pony. The dump was a history of his settlement, a source of treasures that he rescued only to see them returned by his family: "I learned more from that dump than I did from school."

In our minds waste, decline, and death are linked. No wonder dirt arouses such feelings. It is uncontrolled, malicious, a reminder of our ends. All the words for waste are evil magic; they force attention.

And yet these things have hidden attractions. We are fascinated by destruction and disorder. Disorder spoils our patterns but supplies material for new patterns, and we are the pattern makers. Waste is full of novel forms, and carries subtle signs of its origin and former use. Its ambiguities are poetic. Waste heaps are information sources, into which we poke with prurient fingers. We can find morbid satisfactions in decay. There we can be nostalgic for the past, and yet rejoice in our survival.

Wasting Away
Kevin Lynch. Sierra Club Books, 1991;
270 pp. ISBN 0-87156-675-3
$30 ($33 postpaid) from Sierra Club Store
Orders, 730 Polk Street, San Francisco, CA
94109; 800/935-1056

The Garbage Primer • The Plastic Waste Primer

The League of Women Voters offers these concise, dispassionate overviews of the several ways of dealing with garbage and plastic, hoping you'll do the right thing when controversial bond issues appear on the ballot. It's a pleasure to read about these things unencumbered by cries of woe, doom, and retribution.
—J. Baldwin

1000 paper vs 1000 plastic grocery sacks. While reusables are preferred, impact on landfill capacity is one of many factors to consider when comparing the relative merits of disposable materials.

The Plastic Waste Primer
League of Women Voters. 1993; 137 pp.
ISBN 1-55821-229-9
$10.95 ($13.45 postpaid).

The Garbage Primer
League of Women Voters. 1993; 181 pp.
ISBN 1-55821-250-7
$12.95 ($15.45 postpaid).

Both from Lyons & Burford Publishers, 31 W. 21st Street, New York, NY 10010; 212/620-9580

Business Recycling Manual

Think of this workbook as an able assistant helping you to start recycling in your place of business. The Institute for Local Self-Reliance explains and outlines an adaptable, battle-proven program. They encourage successful implementation with worksheets that act as checklists and credibility-enhancers. A glossary and bibliography will ensure your efforts appear professional. Just add appropriate numbers, a slug of determined hubris, and serve hot. —JB

• Worksheet #10, Recycling Cost Analysis, can be used to compare the costs of operating various recycling programs to help determine which recycling project design would be the most cost effective. As you work through this worksheet, bear two things in mind:

1. Don't underestimate the costs of your current waste disposal system.

2. All factors involved are not equally or easily quantifiable.

• The key to a successful waste audit is to see each operation — no matter how familiar you are with it — through the eyes of a recycler. Think of the different operations as waste generating stations.

Business Recycling Manual
INFORM, Inc. and Recourse Systems Staff. 1991; 196 pp.
ISBN 0-918780-57-8
$85 ($90 postpaid) from INFORM, Inc., 381 Park Avenue S., New York, NY 10016; 212/689-4040

A bottle crusher mounted atop a 55 gallon drum can be used on site to reduce glass volume.

Compendium for Integrated Waste Management

You'd never guess from the soporific title that this book provides forty-four easily used, graded evaluations of the best K–12 curricula in waste management. Start 'em young, and they'll shame their parents into being good citizens.
—JB [Suggested by Linda Christopher]

Garbage Reincarnation
Sonoma County
Community Recycling
P.O. Box 1375
Santa Rosa, CA 95402
(707) 584-8666 Linda Christopher

Call for cost information.

This Instructional Aids Packet is divided into four sections related to materials conservation and solid waste management. The four sections are: Solid Waste, Everything Goes Somewhere, Recycling in the Classroom and the Home, and Community Involvement. 51 pages. Updated version to be released in December 1993.

Grades K-6.

Report Card

General Content	A-
	B
Presentation	B+
Pedagogy	B
Teacher Usability	C+
Solid Waste	

Discipline Emphasis 0 1 2 3 4
Science
History/Social Science
Health
Mathematics
Performing/Fine Arts
Language Arts
Industrial/Vocational Education
Foreign Language

Environmental Education Compendium for Integrated Waste Management
Kathy Love, Editor. Free from Schools Program, California Integrated Waste Management Board, 8800 Cal Center Drive, Sacramento, CA 95826; 916/255-2200

Beyond 40 Percent

Here's documented proof of successful recycling programs from seventeen communities of assorted sizes. There's no reason that your burg couldn't do as well as the least inspiring example — 30 percent of the municipal garbage stream recycled. One city has managed 50 percent! This is the next step beyond can squashing. —JB

• Many of the costs associated with recycling are included in the total cost of sanitation services for the Village. The same crews collect recyclable materials and garbage with the same trucks on the same days, so there are no additional collection costs for recycling. In fact, the revenues received and landfill cost per stop avoided by adding recycling to sanitation services have actually reduced the overall costs of sanitation services.

Beyond 40 Percent
(Record-Setting Recycling and Composting Programs)
Institute for Local Self-Reliance Staff. 1991; 264 pp.
ISBN 1-55963-073-6
$25 ($29.25 postpaid).
Island Press, Box 7, Covelo, CA 95428; 800/828-1302

Solid Waste Generation and Collection
(Annual Tonnages for 1989)

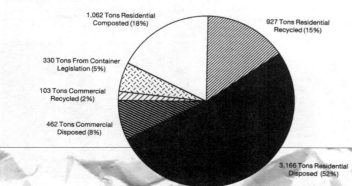

1,062 Tons Residential Composted (18%)
927 Tons Residential Recycled (15%)
330 Tons From Container Legislation (5%)
103 Tons Commercial Recycled (2%)
462 Tons Commercial Disposed (8%)
3,166 Tons Residential Disposed (52%)

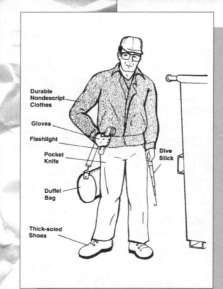

Durable Nondescript Clothes
Gloves
Flashlight
Pocket Knife
Duffel Bag
Thick-soled Shoes
Dive Stick

The Art and Science of Dumpster Diving:
John Hoffman. 1992, Loompanics Unlimited.

Competing with street hunter-gatherers and dodging cops, dumpster divers recycle, reuse, and resell. Here's how. —JB

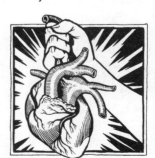

Sell Yourself to Science: Jim Hogshire.
1992, Loompanics.

Recycle pieces of yourself or loved ones, for cash, after, or even before, expiring. Sell secretions (sperm, milk) and excess (hair), too. Parting (out) is such sweet sorrow. —J. (why-are-you-looking-at-me-that-way, dear?) Baldwin

"Garbage Represents a Design Failure in the Disposal System"

Urban Ore, Inc., is a twelve-year-old, vigorously successful recycling/ reuse operation in Berkeley, CA. It's an MRF — Materials Recovery Facility, or "merf". Urban Ore's twenty-person crew generates annual revenues of about $1.2 million, while reducing landfill by several thousand tons. MRFs are spreading rapidly across the country; a similar operation (that needs your support) may be nearby you. MRFs are under fire from garbage contractors (a notoriously politicized bunch) whose need to deter competition takes precedence over the good of environment and society. Many garbage haulers are trying to get laws passed to legally call *all* discards garbage, thus destroying MRF enterprises such as Urban Ore. You need a cause? This fight's just heatin' up.

Most of this report is derived from *Total Recycling: Realistic Ways to Approach the Ideal,* a book by Urban Ore founders Daniel Knapp, Ph.D., and Mary Lou Van Deventer, coming soon from the University of California Press. Urban Ore Information Services Manager David Stern furnished news of the latest developments. Those people work hard.
—J. Baldwin

Sink and tub department shows typically wide selection. Reused plumbing fixtures permit upgrading that could not be afforded with new hardware. (Studies show that Urban Ore's operation has had little effect on local new retail sales of similar items.)

HOW TO DESIGN TOTAL RECYCLING SYSTEMS

TOTAL RECYCLING IS A BIG VISION — it means of anything we can no longer use. It means wasting and attitudes that permit waste are unacceptable. It has been considered presumptuous even to think of such a thing — until now. Now it is necessary.

But in a world of sound bites and attention spans shortened by television, big visions must be reduced to microbits to be seen at all. Which is okay, so long as the microbits expand on command. The following principles are presented as microbits that could be expanded into a huge industry called total recycling:

Waste isn't waste until it's wasted. Conventional disposal systems waste resources by mixing unlike things together, often in the name of efficiency. The first step in avoiding waste is avoiding mixing.

Recyclers handle discards, not wastes. Discards can be recycled or wasted. We will always have discards, but we can deny people the option of wasting them.

Recycling upgrades discards to resources instead of downgrading them to garbage. Garbage represents a design failure in the disposal system. Recyclers sometimes waste things, but their ultimate goal is to waste nothing.

Recycling manages the supply of discards, not the "solid waste stream." The term "waste management" should be reserved for the garbage disposal industry.

Recycling is a form of disposal. Disposal by recycling is not destruction; it is orderly placement. Auction houses also dispose of things, as do estate sales. Only the garbage system disposes of things by destroying their value.

Disposal fees can power recycling disposal just as they do garbage disposal. There are fees for disposal services rendered. Recyclers must be allowed and encouraged to compete with garbage interests for disposal fees. This will unlock the potential for recycling businesses to handle vast quantities of material and eventually to replace the garbage system.

All of what now becomes garbage can be sorted into twelve master categories of recyclable materials known as The Clean Dozen™: Reusable goods, Paper, Metals, Glass, Textiles, Plastics, Plant debris, Putrescibles, Wood, Ceramics, Soils, and Chemicals. Experience has shown the Clean Dozen to be a useful categorization. Total Recycling must include all twelve. Fifty percent of total recycling is achievable now. It will take more time to do better, but it's going to happen. Because it must.

Urban Ore now has a consulting service to help others start MRFs. They have a growing database for sharing their experience and information. Contact Urban Ore Information Services at 510/559-4454, fax 510/528-1540.

Window shopping. You may find odd and obsolete sizes here, sometimes with decorative motifs that are not commercially available today. Add a bit of imagination to get an inexpensive cold frame, light table, or porch wind deflector.

Machines could never do the sorting and choosing accomplished quickly by trained people. Urban Ore has about twenty who decide what goes where. Without them, this obviously useful truckload might have ended up in a landfill.

Doors? Yeah, they have doors — enough to supply a local artist who made an entire cabin from doors (all of which can be opened). The Urban Ore crew sorts everything to make your choice easier, providing help to novices — just like in a regular store, which Urban Ore's sales department increasingly resembles.

IT'S TIME TO QUIT FOOLING AROUND. The mandate is this: Use less energy. Use less everything. Use less anything. No matter what it is — whether it's recycled, renewable, sustainable, natural, handmade, economical, or even free — use less, or do things in a way that uses none at all. Everything that is made, shipped, utilized, and discarded eats energy at each phase of its existence. What you're after is performance — getting a job done. Using more energy or resource than is necessary to do that job (in other words, being wasteful) is a mark of ineptitude, laziness, or stupidity, and is inelegant, uncool, and ultimately dangerous. Efficiency usually costs much less than developing new sources. Efficiency — doing the most with the least — is the only hope for distributing the Earth's resources fairly. —J. Baldwin

Energy Efficiency and Human Activity

Authors Lee Schipper and Stephen Meyers have been developing "the numbers" for more than a decade, using impeccable methodology and logic. No hint of politics or emotion saps the credibility of their analyses and recommendations. There is no hint of shallow popularization, either, but skillful organization and good writing have made it uncommonly readable. A nononsense prologue by John Holdren provides a helpful review of the issues before the action starts. The book is homework for understanding energy matters throughout the world, including in the former Soviet Union. —JB

Energy Efficiency and Human Activity
(Past Trends, Future Prospects)
Lee Schipper & Stephen Meyers.
1992; 385 pp. ISBN 0-521-43297-9
$49.95 ($51.95 postpaid).
Cambridge University Press, 110
Midland Avenue, Port Chester, NY
10573; 800/872-7423 (outside
N.Y.) 800/227-0247 (N.Y. only)

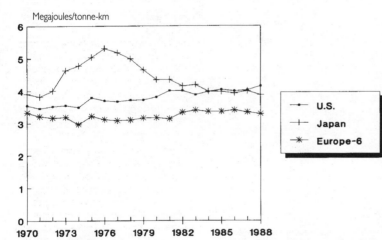

Megajoules/tonne-km

Legend:
- U.S.
- Japan
- Europe-6

Fig. 4.23. Truck freight energy intensity; OECD countries; 1970–1988

In the United States, the data show that average fuel use per km was the same in 1988 as in 1973 for both medium and heavy (tractor-trailer) trucks. It appears that improvement in technical efficiency was offset by several factors. One was the increase in operating speeds on major intercity highways. Another was increasing traffic congestion in urban areas. The overall increase in energy per tonne-km was apparently due to factors related to the operation of

trucking fleets and the nature of freight carried. Despite deregulation of the trucking industry there is evidence that there was an increase in empty backhauls (Mintz, 1991), resulting in reduced tonnage per distance traveled. In addition, it appears that the weight carried per volume of truck capacity declined. One reason for this is increased packaging for many goods (packaging is light-weight but takes up truck capacity).

Woodburning

Used to be that wood heat was unquestionably correct among most of the environmentally righteous. Now it is clear that mindlessly correct would have been closer to the truth: wood isn't renewable energy unless users plant — and nurture — as many trees as they burn, as fast as they burn them. Few do. Though it doesn't add to overall CO₂ emissions, wood is a very dirty fuel if not consumed in newer, code-meeting high-efficiency stoves. Even the best of those is none too tidy.

If you must burn wood, I recommend (with some trepidation) that you seek an EPA-approved, non-catalytic stove. Catalytic stoves are a bit cleaner, but they require periodic replacement of the expensive converter — a device that is fatally damaged by such innocent acts as starting a fire with the Sunday comics. Pellet stoves are convenient, but they're expensive to buy, can be expensive to feed, and they require electricity to operate. It is not yet clear whether the pellets are environmentally wonderful. No matter which you choose, insulate the building; no point wasting anything, even scraps. —JB

The Sunshine Revolution

This is the most interesting introduction to solar energy I've ever encountered. The handsome book is from Norway, giving a refreshing international viewpoint to US readers numbed by the images and half-truths tiresomely repeated in so many of our publications. It's easy to make solar schemes work tolerably (if not well) in Arizona; north-dwellers have to be sharp. The presentation is thorough and easily understood. It should be especially useful to schoolteachers and others

who need to be confidently knowledgeable in basic solar energy matters — politics and all. —JB

The Sunshine Revolution
Harald N. Røstvik. SUN-LAB
Publishers, 1992; 188 pp.
ISBN 82-91052-03-4
$39 ($45.95 postpaid). Real
Goods Trading Corp., 966
Mazzoni Street, Ukiah, CA
95482; 800/762-7325

Wind Power for Home and Business

This fine book collects and organizes decades of experience — good and bad, funky and slick. Names are named. Facts, tips, legends, physics, and effective practice are augmented by tables, illustrations, formulas, and a

source list. Economics are particularly well attended. I wish this had been available twenty years ago when we were learning everything the hard way. This book is all the book-learning a wind-harnesser needs to know, and most welcome it is, too. —JB

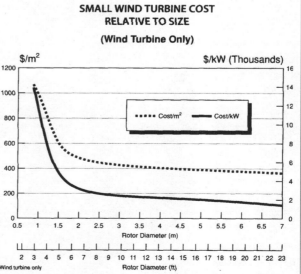

SMALL WIND TURBINE COST RELATIVE TO SIZE

(Wind Turbine Only)

$/m² — $/kW (Thousands)

Legend:
- Cost/m²
- Cost/kW

Rotor Diameter (m)

Wind turbine only — Rotor Diameter (ft)

Figure 5-1. Relative cost of small wind turbines. The relative cost of small wind machines generally declines with increasing size.

Wind Power for Home and Business
(Renewable Energy for the 1990s and Beyond)
Paul Gipe. 1993; 413 pp.
ISBN 0-930031-64-4
$35 ($39.95 postpaid) from
Real Goods Trading Corp.,
966 Mazzoni Street, Ukiah,
CA 95482; 800/762-7325

ꙿOU NEED TO KNOW about these folks — instead of merely complaining and blaming, they're actually changing the world. I'll eliminate the middleman and let them speak for themselves:

Rocky Mountain Institute is a non-profit research and educational foundation with a vision across boundaries.

Seeking ideas that transcend ideology, and harnessing the problem-solving power of free-market economies, our goal is to foster the efficient and sustainable use of resources as a path to global security.

Rocky Mountain Institute believes that people can solve complex problems through collective action and their own common sense, and that understanding interconnections between resource issues can often solve many problems at once.

We focus our work in seven areas — Agriculture, Economic Renewal, Energy, Green Development, Security, Transportation, and Water — and carry on international outreach and technical exchange programs.

Big Power looked a bit silly after Amory Lovins published his now-famous 1976 paper, *The Road Not Taken*, and the elaborating 1977 book, *Soft Energy Paths*. Amory argued that growth — especially of energy use — was not necessary for prosperity. He demanded credibility by using the same numbers as his corporate opponents, who had not been paying attention to changes in technology, economics, and public attitudes. The numbers showed that saving energy is cheaper than making energy. He dubbed the saved electrical energy "Negawatts."

Amory showed that negawatts could pare demand to the point where renewable energy sources could furnish all the energy needed for everyone to live decently. Oil imports (and oil wars) would be eliminated, along with risky drilling offshore and in the fragile Alaska Wildlife Refuge. Nuclear power plants would be unnecessary. Acid rain, greenhouse gas emissions, and environmental degradation would be greatly reduced. Reduced dependence on imported energy and on vulnerable, centralized power plants would improve national security. And those are just a few of the advantages.

Such extreme talk attracted vigorous attack, but Amory fended off his foes by treating them less as enemies than as unenlightened folks in need of education. That was an unusual strategy in those confrontational times, but it has been remarkably effective (as well as refreshing). Many foes became clients.

Amory and Hunter Lovins fired up RMI in 1982, as a means of applying the basic logic of their energy efficiency work to all resources, and spreading the knowledge worldwide. The nonprofit enterprise was an immediate success, and continues to grow. The Institute regularly advises major corporations, power companies, managers of cities large and small, and the federal government (including the military) at the highest levels. Amory also consults with many foreign governments — true citizen diplomacy. Institute director L. Hunter Lovins, Amory, and a number of the researchers spend a lot of time on the road giving lectures and workshops all over the world.

The corporate headquarters in Snowmass, Colorado is both the Lovins' home and the main office for more than forty researchers and staff. It's a working demonstration of RMI values: photovoltaic panels provide most of the electricity; surplus is sold to the utility. The place uses about 10 percent of the power a conventional building would require — making the use of photovoltaics a reasonable choice. Water use is about 50 percent of what's considered normal for a building of this size and use.

The solar design is cool in summer, yet stays cozy in winter even when the temperatures drop to -30°F. A semitropical indoor garden produces bananas, flowers and veggies, cleans the air, smells good, and provides habitat for a delightfully sneaky iguana. The grow-ing conditions are good — in the morning you can hear the solar-powered greenhouse fan flupping the banana leaves that have edged toward it overnight. The horde of visitors may take a (quiet) self-guided tour of the building. The Tour Guide and the source list for the hardware used in the house are offered on the RMI publications list (right). The same techniques and equipment could be used in larger, or more modest, structures.

Unlike many environmentally in-spired organizations (including Whole Earth, I blush to confess), RMI has reduced commuting for its people by acquiring nearby homes for some of them. (Amory, of course, only has to commute fifty feet past the iguana.) This simple move reduces traffic congestion, noise, risk, and emissions. There's less demand for fuel, and no need for a fancy parking lot. Driving costs shrink because noncommuting cars eat less, last longer, and attract lower insurance rates. The Institute's people are living better on less en-ergy, at less cost, with no loss of amenity.

RMI is an inspiring example of good scholarship, tough discipline, and high spirits from talented people. They're making a real difference. In just twelve years, this modest group has become the world's most effec-tive organization encouraging the intelligent use of resources. They're working for all of us. Make use of what they've learned, and support them when you can. —J. Baldwin

RMI Publications

Rocky Mountain Institute's extensive publi-cations list includes books, reports, reprints of articles by and about RMI, videos, plus T-shirts and the like. It's free. Here are a few of the offerings therein:

A yearly contribution of $10 helps RMI bring you the encouraging **Rocky Moun-tain Institute Newsletter**. *Send more if you can — they use it well. RMI doesn't live high on the hog, and is as efficient with money as it is with energy. Even the fundraising is efficient: "We put all our begs in one askit," they say, eliminating re-petitive mail. If you can't contribute, at least spread the word.*

Visitor's Guide: *A descriptive tour guide to RMI headquarters, plus a where-to-get-it list of the technology used.*

Reinventing the Wheels: *The RMI Trans-portation project presents an analysis and design criteria for an advanced automobile that could be built today without techno-logical breakthroughs. Would you buy a roomy, peppy car that could carry a family safely and comfortably coast to coast on ten gallons of fuel? "Here comes the big-*

The RMI building serves as a home, headquarters for about forty-five staff members and volun-teers, and a semi-tropical garden (with iguana). The solar structure uses only 10 per-cent of the energy needed by a con-ventional building of the same utility. Yes, that's a renew-able-energy hot tub in the foreground.

gest change in industrial structure since the microchip." A more technical paper and a video are also available.

The Energy Efficient Home: *A revision and update of the very useful* **Practical Home Energy Savings**. *Ways of cutting home en-ergy and water use are detailed, right down to brand names. It's organized well enough to serve as the basic text for the energy course that should be part of everyone's education. I highly recommend it, especially for those involved with new construction. For larger projects, see Green Development Services (below).*

The Community Energy Workbook *offers extensive, detailed instructions for organiz-ing and educating a community to be more self-reliant. An intelligent energy policy is among the measures that keep local money in the local economy. Unusu-ally well detailed by field experience, the book could serve as a model for any orga-nizing effort.*

Water Efficiency for Your Home *will help you begin to implement your responsibility as a water user. RMI's more comprehen-sive water publications are listed in back, each with a brief description. They reveal brand names, test results, and proven strategies for setting water policy at local and regional levels. "Negagallons!"*

For larger projects, consider RMI's Green Development Services. They "work with ar-chitects, builders, developers and property managers to encourage cost-effective state-of-the-art construction that saves energy, materials and water, produces comfortable and healthful interior spaces, preserves habitats and cultural resources, re-duces traffic, and limits harmful and thought-less sprawl." This sort of comprehensive ap-proach to design will be repaid in the long run, and those who must use the facility or be affected by it will thank you. —JB

Rocky Mountain Institute: $10/year (membership includes newsletter). 1739 Snowmass Creek Road, Snowmass, CO 81654-9199; 303/927-3851, fax 303/927-4178.

RMI Publications List and **RMI Visitor's Guide:** Free.
Reinventing the Wheels:
Contact RMI for price.
The Energy-Efficient Home:
$9.75 postpaid.
The Community Energy Workbook:
$25 postpaid.
Water Efficiency in Your Home:
$1 postpaid.

ANOTHER GREAT E SOURCE

E Source: 1033 Walnut, Boulder, CO 80302; 303/440-8500, fax 303/440-8502 (formerly Competitek) is a for-profit subsidiary of non-profit RMI. It's the world's leading source of information on advanced techniques for elec-tric efficiency. Big energy users, energy policymakers, utilities, corporations, and gov-ernments large and small pay a membership fee for advice and the latest information. E Source's remarkable track record keeps the membership growing.

A house in a shaded location can utilize a "power shed" to position photovoltaic panels in the sun. Batteries and controls are close (for efficiency), snug, and safe inside.

Home Power

As "alternative energy" has entered the mainstream, **Home Power** has not only survived; it has flourished. Astute editorial policy has evolved a more professional, less funky character, matching the growing public acceptance of low-energy living, off or on the grid. The articles present what you need to know, whether you are a professional or just interested in learning. In-group jargon is avoided; intelligence is assumed. The issue I hold (April/May '94) includes an article on European electric vehicles (including crash tests of an electric pipsqueak vs. big Audi, with unexpected results), and a definitive article on solar water pumping is by the acknowledged master of the subject, Windy Dankoff, PVSS [(505)-351-2100]. Ultra-experienced Al Rutan, the Methane Man, shows off his portable digester, too. And there are the usual lively pages of reader comment. There's lots more.

Extensive, interesting advertising gives readers such good access to the best suppliers and publications that there is no point in us repeating all that in this section. Yet the magazine's heart remains pure. Staff and subscribers mercilessly test products under real-life conditions, calling out the ones that don't work whether they are among the advertisers or not. Such courage has made the magazine a leader and reality check as well as a reporter. I'm not alone in finding **Home Power** to be essential and trustable.
—J. Baldwin

Home Power
$15/year (6 issues). PO Box 520, Ashland, OR 97520; 916/475-0830, BBS 707/822-8640

APT Powercenters

Big News: Ananda Power Technologies' Powercenters are the first to have Underwriters Laboratories (UL) approval as control panels for photovoltaic or other on-site power systems. Powercenters are very cleverly engineered, and constructed for durability and foolproof operation. Servicing is commendably easy — a sure sign of careful design. Prospective customers dismayed by the price should note that a Powercenter is enclosed in a single compact box, greatly simplifying installation and code approval. The UL label should smooth the path to

loan approval, too — finance officers have been rightly leery of the disorganized agglomerations of hardware previously needed for control duties. Professionalism comes to photovoltaics at last! —JB

Harris Hydroelectric

Hydro-Power for Home Use

Works with Heads as low as 10 feet.	Prices start as low as $695.

632 Swanton Road
Davenport, CA 95017
408-425-7652

"The best Alternator-based MicroHydro generator I've ever seen."
Bob-O Schultze, Hydroelectric Editor, Home Power Magazine

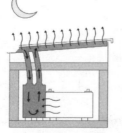

Solar cookers ready to shine in HP's Solar Cooking Contest.

VIEW WITH INTERIOR DOOR OPEN
SHOWING CUSTOMER TERMINATION AREA, CONTROL COMPONENTS, AND FACTORY WIRING

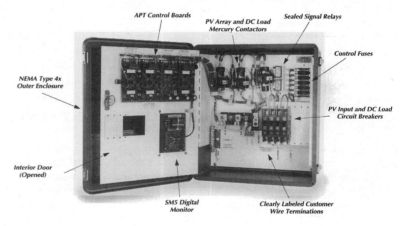

APT Control Boards
PV Array and DC Load Mercury Contactors
Sealed Signal Relays
Control Fuses
NEMA Type 4x Outer Enclosure
PV Input and DC Load Circuit Breakers
Interior Door (Opened)
SM5 Digital Monitor
Clearly Labeled Customer Wire Terminations

APT Powercenters:
$695–$1,595.
Ananda Power Technologies,
14618 Tyler Foote Road, Nevada City, CA 95959; 916/292-3834, fax 916/292-3330.

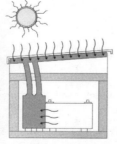

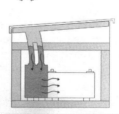

SUMMER DAY COOLING
During hot summer days, water in the patented Zomeworks system absorbs heat from batteries, equipment, and solar gain.

SUMMER NIGHT COOLING
During summer nights, warm water rises to the lid, radiates its heat to the cold night sky, and sinks back into the enclosure. This thermosiphon action removes heat from the system throughout the night.

WINTER/NIGHT FREEZE PROTECTION
During very cold weather, water in the tank freezes, releasing 1 kWh of heat into the enclosure for each 3 gallons of water in the system. For additional protection in extremely cold climates, an optional variable output heater can be used to reverse this phase change, extending the freeze protection cycle indefinitely.

How **COOL CELL** works to moderate the temperature in an equipment enclosure

Zomeworks

It's easy to spot Zomeworks products. They fulfill basic needs, such as water-heating or sun-tracking, with elegant, sturdy designs, many of which are original inventions. Zomeworks works work.

Founder and chief designer Steve Baer says this sort of quality is to be expected from a group that has supported itself entirely by producing and selling innovative solar hardware, rather than parasitizing the government. To survive twenty-five years in a

developing marketplace, you have to be good. I consider Zomeworks to be more than a provider of worthy products; they are an inspiring example of an enterprise succeeding in a field notorious for poor products and consequent miserable demises. —JB

Zomeworks: PO Box 25805, 1011A Sawmill Road NW, Albuquerque, NM 87125; 800/279-6342, fax 505/243-5187.

Real Goods

We last reported on the Real Goods Trading Corporation in 1990, when it was becoming clear that the funky little counterculture-supply store was maturing into the world's largest, most comprehensive purveyor of renewable energy hardware. That year, they grossed about $2 million. In 1993, they boasted revenues approaching $12 million (before taxes), with common stock being traded on the Pacific Stock Exchange. The company continues to grow vigorously, recently acquiring Earth Care Paper Company, and opening a midwest retail store in Amherst, WI.

The rapid growth of Real Goods has not been without its problems and detractors. To my mind, most of the valid complaints are the classic ones that attend any rapidly expanding enterprise that grows beyond Mom & Pop dimensions and capabilities: toes get stepped upon in the tumult, jealousies arise, smaller rivals are outcompeted, some management experiments fail, certain corporate policies are outgrown — sometimes with messy consequences. Overall, though, Real Goods seems to be doing much that is good. Here are a few reasons why I think so. (Hm. I'd better add here that I am not a Real Goods stockholder, do not command a discount, and am often seen among the complainers.)

Real Goods does more than sell stuff: it also operates the Institute for Independent Living, a series of workshops offering training in the several skills needed for renewable-energy work, as a professional or on your own spread. Of course, this sells more goods, but the graduates often go on to become teachers; that benefits everyone.

A lively free newspaper, the **Real Goods News**, preaches comfort to the saved and spreads the word to the heathen hordes. What isn't ads is mostly gab from critics, commenters, curmudgeons (including me), installers, teachers, and folks at the front lines of off-the-grid living. With a whopping 200,000 circulation, the paper is hastening the day when energy-efficient building is considered normal building.

A corporate headquarters complex has been designed, by architect/ teacher Sim Van der Ryn (p. 230), and land has been selected near Hopland, CA. Work should be under way as you read this. It will be a demonstration of sensitive land use and will, of course, show much of the Real Goods catalog in action. The installation should spur increased commercial application of solar designs.

Real Goods had a hand in the Greening of the White House, a stab at making that ostentatious abode less of a conspicuous consumer.

And there's the deservedly famous **Solar Living Sourcebook.** The new one (8th edition) augments the Real Goods tradition of providing a basic energy education along with product descriptions. It could well serve as the text for an entry-level course in applied energy efficiency. With 250,000 in print, the 600-page **Sourcebook** has had a powerful effect, increasing people's awareness that intelligent energy use is not the faddish fantasy of a few environmentalist nuts.

The bottom line is this. One person — John Schaeffer, with lots of help from colleagues, employees, and manufacturers — has organized a company that has made solar hardware comprehensible and available to ordinary folks, on a scale that can be regarded as significant, for the first time. Real Goods claims the hardware it has sold has prevented more than 645 million pounds of CO_2 from being generated. Their goal is a billion pounds by 2000. Looks like they'll exceed that easily. How are you doing? —J. Baldwin

**Real Goods
Trading Corporation:**
966 Mazzoni Street,
Ukiah, CA 95482; 800/762-7325.

Solar Living Sourcebook: $19. **Book of Light:** $5. Add $4.95 shipping charge per order. $40 lifetime membership in The Real Goods Hard Corps includes 5% discount on purchases, **Real Goods News**, **Real Stuff Newsletter**, and a copy of **Solar Living Sourcebook.**

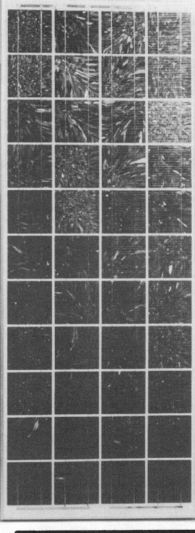

The Pocket Socket is smaller, lighter, and less expensive than any other inverter. It will power a 100-watt appliance. You can use these inverters to run small TVs and VCRs, computers, a camcorder charger or any other appliance that uses less than 100 watts. Both use a standard cigarette lighter plug. The Pocket Socket has a replaceable 14-amp fuse for reverse polarity and catastrophic overload protection.

27-101   Pocket Socket Inverter $79

The Book of Light

One of the easiest and most effective ways you can be a better environmental citizen is to replace (where appropriate) your dramatically inefficient, energy-sucking incandescent light bulbs. They typically transform the incoming energy into about 6 percent light and 94 percent heat that you may not want. You'll not only reduce fossil and nuclear fuelburning and the pollution thereof, and you'll not only save money; with a bit of luck you'll make money! Real Goods has become the retail outlet for Rising Sun, the world's largest distributor of low-energy lighting. **The Book of Light** contains what you need to know to make the right purchase, detailed right down to full-size paper cut-outs of various bulbs so you can see which ones fit your fixtures. —JB

Burns 736 lbs. of coal.

Burns 177 lbs. of coal.

OTHER GREAT RESOURCES

Rising Sun Enterprises, Inc.: PO Box 586, Old Snowmass, CO 81654; 303/927-8051. Wholesale only — for retail mail order of Rising Sun products, contact Real Goods. This pioneering corporation sells energy-efficient bulbs wholesale. Their consulting service makes sure you do the best thing.

THE two-hundred-and-twenty fortunate families of the Village Homes development live in what most folks would call a park. Trees and gardens are everywhere, *redolent* with ripening edibles. All the homes are solar, with energy bills about half those of houses in conventional developments nearby. The small lots are augmented by the mutually owned community garden, expansive village green, swimming pool, and bike paths; these connect all the homes to one another and to the nearby town of Davis, CA. Inhabitants pay monthly dues to a strong neighborhood association that sets policy and sees to the maintenance. Crime is low and neighborliness is rampant. The place is quiet and it smells good. It's a nice place to live. Even teens like it.

This astonishingly attractive, environmentally wonderful community is so popular that homes change hands, unadvertised, for 20 percent more than others of similar class nearby. Visitors resist leaving. The developer made money. Yet after eighteen years of success, no new project like it has been attempted anywhere. Lazy developers, stodgy bankers, and cowardly bureaucrats provide the obstructions, as usual. But an imaginative and persistant developer, Mike Corbett, has shown us that they can be dealt with. Your move. —J. Baldwin

Special thanks to Judy Corbett, Virginia Thigpen, and Richard Nilsen for information and assistance. Photos by Don Ryan.

Houses front on bike paths, the real streets of Village Homes. The paths allow safe travel to any other house without crossing a street. Their connection to town makes most auto use unnecessary.

Alley-like cul-de-sacs eliminate through traffic. Street parking is not allowed. Shaded, narrow pavement reduces heat gain, helping to keep the neighborhood about ten degrees cooler than others nearby. Houses are comfortable without air conditioning.

Drainage "swales" hold rain runoff, making storm sewers obsolete while recharging the local water table. Temporary ponds are absorbed before mosquitoes can breed. Some swales serve as playgrounds during the dry season.

J. R. R. Tolkien street names invite the local "Hobbittown" nickname. It's used with respect.

*W*HATEVER COMMUNITY IS, WE HANKER FOR IT ANYWHERE AND SOMEHOW.

The best definition of community I've heard is this: It's a space, or place, where you work with people you don't necessarily like or always agree with, to make *It* better.

What are we, finally, to do about *It*? Not I the lone hero or the *dei ex machinae* in the capitols, but we here.

Hoary as the advice may seem, it's never too late to try nonviolence, cooperation, compassion for all beings, lives outwardly simple and inwardly rich. In Community we may find our myriad ways out of Dystopia.

The ways and means, the art of community, have been refined in the last decades. Many practically tested souls are eager to share their knowledge and a lively sense of renewed possibility. Great hopes occupy real ground in these small groups. Conflict, rightly joined, can bring clarity, not carnage.

—Stephanie Mills

—The Gaia Atlas of Cities (see p.130)

The Call of Service

A famous psychiatrist and writer, Robert Coles still volunteers in a ghetto elementary school; he teaches courses requiring community service, and introduces Tolstoy and Toni Morrison into the Harvard Medical School curriculum. His exploration of service — its motivations, satisfactions, frustrations, hazards, consequences — is sophisticated and useful, but the heart of this large-hearted book is its stories about

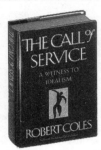

The Call of Service
Robert Coles. 1993; 306 pp.
ISBN 0-395-63647-7
$22.95 ($24.70 postpaid) from Houghton Mifflin Co./Mail Order Dept., Wayside Road, Burlington, MA 01803; 800/225-3362

service given and received. Coles' stories are also models for doing service: slow down, fret less about theory or results, pay careful attention to persons, to each person. Therein lie community, healing, and growth.
—Michael K. Stone

•

Less than a day later the long-time guest died, and shortly after his funeral (arranged by the Catholic Worker community) his modest estate went to the only "family" he had known all through his adult life. But for Frank Donovan and others at the Catholic Worker community, I think it fair to say, this man's greatest legacy was his insistence on making clear with words what he had felt so long. Indeed, the outbursts he inflicted on others and on himself were a measure of trust. Here was a place where the accumulated suffering of a life was offered a safe moment's expression. He was not given indulgence or interpretation, but the firm, rallying attention of volunteers who had no interest in being police or psychotherapists. They were companions in the literal meaning of the word: People who sat with others and shared bread with them.

The Small Community

People could probably have very interesting times, lifetimes, even, following the precepts laid out in this good old (1942) book. There are definite ways and means of developing community, it says — certain things are known, and there are rules to play by.

Morgan provides a spare but definitive guidebook. He covers a lot of ground, talking about the appropriate scale of communities, economic self-reliance, skill banks, the importance and liabilities of regional planning, and provision for the community welfare, among many other topics. —SM

•

Where community life is dissolved and the only remaining sense of social identity is with vast societies, such as great nations, serious-minded young people who wish to be socially effective often measure their small powers against national or world movements, and develop a feeling of frustration and futility. On the other hand, where there are members of small communities they have opportunities to deal with problems within their grasp. They can be realists and can be effective within the community, and so can have a feeling of validity denied them when their primary relations are to vast social aggregations.

•

Many times in history urban civilizations have broken down, leaving society to rebuild, largely from the village level. Should

there be a breakdown in the present social order, the small community is the seed bed from which a new order would have to grow. If it now deteriorates by neglect and by being robbed of its best quality, the new order will not be excellent. Whoever increases the excellence and stability of small communities sets limits to social retrogression.

The Small Community
Arthur Morgan. 1942, 1984;
336 pp. ISBN 0-910420-28-9
$10 ($13 postpaid) from Community Service Inc., PO Box 243, Yellow Springs, OH 45387; 513/767-2161

OTHER GREAT RESOURCES

Communalism: Kenneth Rexroth (Seabury Press, 1974).

Commitment and Community: Rosabeth Kanter (Harvard University Press, 1972).

Communitas: Paul and Percival Goodman (Columbia University Press, 1990).

Sex, Economy, Freedom and Community: Wendell Berry (Pantheon, 1993).

Mutual Aid

In the late nineteenth century, the vulgarization of Darwin's thought into a Hobbesian "struggle for existence" began to dismay Petr Kropotkin, a Russian prince-turned-geographer-turned-anarchist-turned-prisoner-turned-exile. After having considered real-life observations made during his surveys in Siberia, as well as his scholarly researches, Kropotkin took to print in The Nineteenth Century *to reply to Thomas Huxley's interpretation of the* Origin of Species *portraying nature as "a continuous free fight."*

In Mutual Aid, *Kropotkin carefully and warmly relates instances of cooperation in all animal societies, including our own.*

Mutual Aid's *reclaiming of conveniently omitted history is inspiring, particularly the material on medieval free cities. With infrastructure shaped by craftsmen's ethics — the guild charters — these cities sound very much like Utopia. Their citizens worked together in all manner of ways to support their communes — not from altruism, which is a rather modern concept, or necessity, but because such decency elegantly achieved stability and sufficiency. It took considerable ruthlessness on the part of nation states to subjugate these cities and destroy their autonomy.*

Kropotkin found, in human and natural history, not a disposition to unremitting strife and aggression but an instinct for cooperation, and the balance and freedom that it provides. —SM

•

Happily enough, competition is not the rule either in the animal world or in mankind. It is limited among animals to exceptional periods, and natural selection finds better fields for its activity. Better conditions are created by the *elimination of competition* by means of mutual aid and mutual support. . . . Most of our birds slowly move southwards as the winter comes, or gather in numberless societies and undertake long journeys — and thus avoid competition. Many rodents fall asleep when the time comes that competition should set in. . . . And when animals can neither fall asleep, nor migrate, nor lay in stores, nor themselves grow their food like the ants, they do what the titmouse does, and what Wallace (*Darwinism*, ch. v.) has so charmingly described: they resort to new kinds of food—and thus, again, avoid competition.

•

A fearful snowstorm, blowing across the

Mutual Aid
(A Factor of Evolution)
Petr Kropotkin. 1902, 1976;
362 pp. ISBN 0-87558-024-6
$6.95 ($8.95 postpaid) from Porter Sargent Publishers, 11 Beacon Street, Suite 1400, Boston, MA 02108

Channel, raged on the flat, sandy coast of a tiny village in Kent, and a small smack, laden with oranges, stranded on the sands near by. In these shallow waters only a flat-bottomed lifeboat of a simplified type can be kept, and to launch it during such a storm was to face an almost certain disaster. And yet the men went out, fought for hours against the wind, and the boat capsized twice. One man was drowned, the others were cast ashore. One of these last, a refined coastguard, was found next morning, badly bruised and half frozen in the snow. I asked him, how they came to make that desperate attempt? "I don't know myself," was his reply. "*There* was the wreck; all the people from the village stood on the beach, and all said it would be foolish to go out; we never should work through the surf. We saw five or six men clinging to the mast, making desperate signals. We all felt that something must be done, but what could we do? One hour passed, two hours, and we all stood there. We all felt most uncomfortable. Then, all of a sudden, through the storm, it seemed to us as if we heard their cries — they had a boy with them. We could not stand that any longer. All at once we said, 'We must go!' The women said so too; they would have treated us as cowards if we had not gone, although next day they said we had been fools to go. As one man, we rushed to the boat, and went."

Creating Community Anywhere

Our society is now pioneering new forms of community, more innovative and diverse than either traditional neighborhoods and small-town communities or the idealistic communities of the sixties and seventies. Authors Shaffer and Anundsen define this new breed of community as occurring in "the dynamic whole that emerges when a group of people participate in common practices; depend upon one another; make decisions together; identify themselves as part of something larger than the sum of their individual relationships; and commit themselves for the long term to their own, one another's, and the group's well-being." We can find community in workplace teams, neighborhood associations, social clubs, support groups, men's and women's groups, salons, ritual and creativity groups, and electronic networks.

With conviction and compassion, the authors describe how all kinds of communities have dealt with the "shadow" — scapegoating leaders, shunning members who bring up serious problems, manipulation and power plays, and more. Also: good communication

in meetings; fair, productive decision-making; using inevitable conflicts to deepen friendship. A worthy resource for any community.
—Diana Leafe Christian

●

Any system of governance operates according to a particular set of power dynamics. . . . In your community, you can choose to make your power dynamics conscious and continually refine them to match your agreed-upon values and vision. If you instead choose to let power dynamics develop below the level of group awareness, you take the chance that they will mirror the values that each of you learned in your family of origin rather than those you now hold. You also risk falling into either the harmony trap, the equality trap, or both.

●

You can turn your meetings into regular opportunities for becoming more conscious and effective as a community — and more deeply bonded. Every meeting serves as a microcosm of community. Each is an organic whole within the whole that takes on a life of its own but also reflects the spirit of the larger community as well as that of the individuals who comprise it.

Creating Community Anywhere
Carolyn R. Shaffer & Kristin Anundsen. Jeremy P. Tarcher Inc., 1993; 352 pp.
ISBN 0-87477-746-1
$15.95 ($17.95 postpaid) from Putnam Publishing Group/Order Dept., PO Box 506, East Rutherford, NJ 07073; 800/631-8571

The Great Good Place

The routines of everyday institutions of community — the often-unacknowledged "third places" (after home and work) — are what make civilization. Coffee shops and general stores work through exactly the same dynamics that make the online salon, the WELL, work as a hangout.

Great good places are not so much built as raised; they will grow naturally if you don't prevent them. The author says that democracy emerges chiefly out of these kinds of community centers; I believe him. —Kevin Kelly

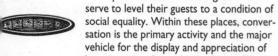

●

Third places exist on neutral ground and serve to level their guests to a condition of social equality. Within these places, conversation is the primary activity and the major vehicle for the display and appreciation of human personality and individuality. Third places are taken for granted and most have a low profile. Since the formal institutions of society make stronger claims on the individual, third places are normally open in the off hours, as well as at other times. The character of a third place is determined most of all by its regular clientele and is marked by a playful mood, which contrasts with people's more serious involvement in other spheres. Through a radically different kind of setting from the home, the third place is remarkably similar to a good home in the psychological comfort and support that it extends.

●

What the tavern offered long before television or newspapers was a source of news *along with* the opportunity to question, protest, sound out, supplement, and form opinion locally and collectively. And these active and individual forms of participation are essential to a government of the people.

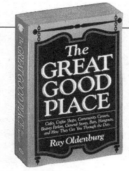

The Great Good Place
Ray Oldenburg. Athena, 1991; 338 pp. ISBN 1-55778-458-2
$14.95 ($16.95 postpaid) from Paragon House/Order Dept., 90 Fifth Avenue, New York, NY 10011; 800/727-2466

●

The tremendous advantage enjoyed by societies with a well-developed informal public life is that, within them, poverty carries few burdens other than that of having to live a rather Spartan existence. But there is no stigma and little deprivation of experience. There is an engaging and sustaining public life to supplement and complement home and work routines. For those on tight budgets who live in some degree of austerity, it compensates for the lack of things owned privately. For the affluent, it offers much that money can't buy.

●

The activity that goes on in third places is largely unplanned, unscheduled, unorganized, and unstructured. Here, however, is the charm. It is just these deviations from the middle-class penchant for organization that give the third place much of its character and allure and that allow it to offer a radical departure from the routines of home and work.

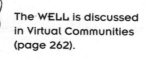

The WELL is discussed in Virtual Communities (page 262).

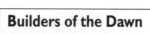

Builders of the Dawn

Intentional communities still thrive, in diverse social, economic, and architectural arrangements. Thousands of people still put their lives on the line in quest of new ways to live and work cooperatively. Their successes and failures offer essential information to people contemplating joining or starting an intentional community.

The authors, unabashed enthusiasts for their subject, make no attempt to provide systematic social science. They visited thirty North American intentional communities, and wrote about the variety, the ups and downs, the values, the most useful social tools they found. The lessons on social dynamics are valuable for those who can use them, or for those who are simply curious about the state of the art in social experimentation. —HLR

Builders of the Dawn
Corrine McLaughlin & Gordon Davidson. 1990; 372 pp. ISBN 0-913990-68-X
$17.95 ($20.95 postpaid) from The Book Publishing Company, PO Box 99, Summertown, TN 38483; 615/964-3571

●

The impact of the community movement today is not due to one particularly successful prototype of community but rather to the diversity of new communities and the strength of their combined innovations in so many areas of human life, from new techniques for conflict resolution and good communication to alternative forms of energy and health care. These workable solutions to real life problems have wide appeal.

To study communities is to examine in microcosm the problems, and some of the solutions, in creating a new social structure for humanity. Many different personality types live together in a given community, and they may even share certain values. The main task of community living is to create unity out of human diversity.

The Simple Life

Since Colonial times, numerous ideologies of and attempts at simple living in community have flamed briefly, only to be overwhelmed by the materialism and privatism that seem far more native to the American character. Nevertheless, plain living in other than kin-groups is an idea that can't be conquered, and in chronicling its history Shi relates a considerable sweep of this nation's history and higher yearnings. —Stephanie Mills

The Simple Life
David Shi. 1986; 352 pp.
ISBN 0-19-504013-9
$11.95 ($13.95 postpaid) from Oxford University Press/Order Dept., 2001 Evans Road, Cary, NC 27513; 800/451-7556

CONSENSUS DECISION MAKING, in its true form, is a most radical spiritual practice. Even in groups with the prerequisite common interest, a manner of decisionmaking founded on the conviction that every person has a piece of the truth and every person is equal to every other, and must be listened to with fitting respect, demands — and eventually elicits — a new kind of self. It's a way of finding workable agreements without knightly clashes or backroom deals.

Thus it goes against the grain of our modes of discourse and thinking. The goal is not for me to come up with such a clever solution to a problem that everyone else in the group will fall right down oohing and ahing whereupon my notion prevails (thereby leaving the silent majority or minority a little disenfranchised, if not positively rebellious). The goal is for a group of absolute peers to arrive, by careful, respectful, open and attentive discussion, at the best possible decision that can be made at that time.

Consensus develops a powerful sense of community in a group that shares values and a purpose. It takes time — good and careful work usually does. As you might expect, the outcomes are satisfying, comely, and durable. Cutting one's ideas loose from one's ego by faith that nothing is wasted in consensus process fosters a gentle possibility of enlightenment.

—Stephanie Mills

Meeting Facilitation

*Ten pages of advice that can save you and your group a world of hurt, to say nothing of a great deal of time. **Meeting Facilitation** is simple, but not easy. It's profoundly different from presiding. Berit Lakey tells how with simplicity and brevity. Keep this handy and review it frequently. —SM*

•
Agenda Review
1. Go through the whole agenda in headline form, giving a brief idea of what is to be covered and how.

2. Briefly explain the rationale behind the order of the proposed agenda.

3. Then, and not before, ask for questions and comments.

4. Don't be defensive about the agenda you have proposed, but don't change everything at the suggestion of one person — check it out with the group first.

5. If major additions are proposed, make the group aware that adjustments must be made because of the limited time available,

Meeting Facilitation
(The No-Magic Method)
Berit Lakey. 1975; 11 pp.
ISBN 0-86571-027-9
75¢ ($3.25 postpaid) from New Society Publishers, 4527 Springfield Avenue, Philadelphia, PA 19143; 800/333-9093

like taking something out, postponing something until later, etc.

6. If an item that some people do not want to deal with is suggested for discussion, consider that there is no consensus and it cannot be included at that time.

7. Remember that your responsibility as facilitator is to the whole group and not to each individual.

On Conflict and Consensus

This manual provides instructions in a method of consensus that subjects a participant's move to block consensus to the judgment of the group as a whole. Fine exposition of the shared principles that must undergird a group's consensus decisionmaking, as well as specific advice on agenda setting, meeting conduct, and roles that may usefully be filled (Public Scribe, Advocate, Notetaker, Doorkeeper, Timekeeper, and Peacekeeper, for instance.) —SM

•
Formal Consensus is a specific kind of decisionmaking. It must be defined by the group using it. It provides a foundation, structure, and collection of techniques for efficient and productive group discussions. The foundation is the commonly-held principles and decisions which created the group originally. The structure is predetermined, although flexible. The agenda is for-

On Conflict and Consensus
(A Handbook on Formal Consensus Decisionmaking)
C. T. Lawrence Butler
& Amy Rothstein. 1991; 63 pp.
$12.50 ($14 postpaid) from Food Not Bombs Publishing, 295 Forest Avenue #314, Portland, ME 04101

mal and extremely important. The roles, techniques, and skills necessary for smooth operation must be accessible to and developed in all members. Evaluation of the process must happen on a consistent and frequent basis, as a tool for self-education and self-management. Above all, Formal Consensus must be taught. It is unreasonable to

Building United Judgment • A Manual for Group Facilitators

Two comprehensive, tried-and-true texts form the basic kit for adopting and practicing consensus process.

Building United Judgment explains the fundaments of consensus and the values that support it. A Manual for Group Facilitators addresses the technique of meeting facilitation. It's very savvy about group dynamics and simple physical things that can be done to make any working meeting more satisfying. It might also be called a manual for servant leadership.
—SM

•
Advantages for Group Facilitators
1. *Quality of the decision.* Since the decision must be acceptable to a variety of people, it is more likely to be examined carefully and to meet complex standards of workability, desirability, and integrity.

2. *Creativity.* Rather than a quick choice for the favorite of two, or a few, options, a decision which attempts to meet everyone's needs will require the group to produce and consider a wide range of proposals. Often more imaginative and creative possibilities are discovered.

3. *Commitment and satisfaction.* The struggle to reach consensus requires more intense involvement from group members. In majority rule, dissenting group members are often committed to the decision merely by contract. In consensus, commitment arises from involvement as well as from satisfaction.

•
The decision to block consensus is a momentous one. If you as an individual block a decision that the rest of the group supports, you are saying that you feel the decision is so seriously wrong that you will

not permit the group to proceed on it. Your reason may be on moral or practical grounds, or based on personal feelings or on the needs of group members or people whom the group affects. It is important not to take your power to block consensus lightly. However, if after careful consideration, you strongly believe that the decision would be a wrong one, then it is your responsibility to block consensus.
—Building United Judgment

•
One need not be labeled "facilitator" in order to employ facilitation techniques in a group. Any group member can call the group back to the subject of the discussion, interrupt patterns of conflict or misunderstanding between other parties, offer clarifying comments, summarize activities or give evaluative feedback. In some groups, these responsibilities are shared by many or all of the members. Other groups, whose members are less skillful at group process, will expect the facilitator to perform this function alone.
—A Manual for Group Facilitators

Building United Judgment
(A Handbook for Consensus Decision Making)
Center for Conflict Resolution. 1981; 124 pp. ISBN 0-941492-01-X

A Manual for Group Facilitators
Center for Conflict Resolution. 1978; 90 pp.
ISBN 0-941492-00-1
Each $12.95 ($15.45 postpaid) from New Society Publishers, 4527 Springfield Avenue, Philadelphia, PA 19143; 800/333-9093

Facilitation Training

Facilitation isn't exactly counter-intuitive, but it's deeply counter-cultural. Personal instruction, observing a proficient facilitator, and role-playing in workshops all can launch you into opportunities to be of real service in groups pursuing a common purpose and, ideally, a greater good. C.T. Lawrence Butler and Caroline Estes are masters of this art.
—SM

For further information, contact:

C. T. Butler, c/o Food Not Bombs Publishing, 295 Forest Ave., #314, Portland, ME 04101; 207/828-0401, or Caroline Estes, c/o Alpha Farm, Deadwood, OR 97430; 503/964-5102.

ANOTHER GREAT RESOURCE

Tools for Change Reader: Margo Adair and Sharon Howell. Information from Tools for Change, PO Box 14141, San Francisco, CA 94114.

expect people to already be familiar with this process. Generally, cooperative, nonviolent conflict resolution does not exist in modern North American society. These skills must be developed in what is primarily a competitive environment. Only time will tell if, in fact, this model will flourish and prove itself effective and worthwhile.

It may be that the reason our hankering for community has intensified lately is not only that we've lost our extended families and no longer reciprocate with our neighbors, but that the community of species to which we belong and the ecosystems that are our real neighborhoods are now decimated. There's much that's particular to our species that's critical to understand, of course, and most of what follows in these pages addresses the relationships of humans in groups, of individuals to groups, of nonviolent aggregates of homo sappys, generally, attempting to pursue some common good.

To better the good, we need to understand that we're part of a larger system that's creative without benefit of intellect or altruism: Nature, our nature, call it "the Way." The essential teaching of the living world can't be book-learnt, only known directly. Seeking and noting its traces — in the rangy wild vitality of a vacant lot, in the pineal funk that descends as the winter days grow short, in the mysterious ability of a nicked finger to heal from within — reminds us that we're still biology and we can still belong. —Stephanie Mills

World As Lover, World As Self

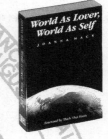

This is a profoundly important, passionate book, one that truth-seekers, spiritually-motivated political activists, and ordinary citizens with their eyes open will find indispensable. It's roughly equal parts autobiography, textbook, philosophical treatise, cheerleading manual, and blueprint for living in and changing a degraded world. The crux of the text is the Buddha's teaching of pattica samuppada. Reduced to deceptively simple terms, this says that everything in the world — every object, feeling,

World As Lover, World As Self
Joanna Macy. 1991; 272 pp.
ISBN 0-938077-27-9
$15 ($18.50 postpaid) from Parallax Press, PO Box 7355, Berkeley, CA 94707; 510/525-0101

Sacred Land, Sacred Sex: Rapture of the Deep

This compendious, scholarly, confessional book is a wildling. Anyone looking for a critical explanation of European civ's ecocidal tendencies and the ancient (Taoist) and modern (contemporary nature ritual) countertendencies would be well advised to acquire a copy and to spend some real time with it. Author Dolores LaChapelle is one of the most startling — and sensible — thinkers-on-the-page that you may ever meet. She omits nothing, from sketches of the colonization of the New World, to an exaltation of D. H. Lawrence as true nature poet, to basic instructions for making seasonal and earth-calendrical ritual, to the practice of sacred sex, to the way the gourd taught humans agriculture, to revelatory deep-powder skiing and mountaineering stories. —SM

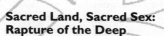

Most traditional cultures had festivals to mark each of these 8 important stages of the year.

•

THE SEVEN DEADLY DELUSIONS

1) Ideas and ideal — dating back to Plato.

2) The false dichotomy of spirit vs nature.

3) Eurocentrism — that Europeans discovered everything first and know how to run the world better than any other culture.

4) Noosphere — that humans create the mind/wisdom of the earth.

5) Anthropocentrism — that man is the most significant entity in the universe; therefore the entire earth is for human "use."

Sacred Land, Sacred Sex: Rapture of the Deep
(Concerning Deep Ecology and Celebrating Life)
Dolores LaChapelle. 1988; 382 pp.
ISBN 1-882308-11-5
$24.95 ($28.45 postpaid) from Kivaki Press, 585 E. 31st, Durango, CO 81301; 800/578-5904

6) Perfectionism.

7) Tragic heroism.

•

In all European languages, locked as they are into the Greek grammar, we have a subject, (that which does the action), the verb (what is done), and the object (that which it is done to). Since, for the newly literate Greek, there was no longer any implicit meaning in each letter or syllable of the sentence, he, himself, the writer or

reader, gave the meaning. For example, as Havelock explains: "In phonetic reading, these counterparts are elements of sound usually meaningless in themselves, though the brain of him who is visually scanning the script..." etc. Thus we see how the writer or reader must of necessity give the meaning. From this it is only a short step to the illusion that man gives meaning to the rest of the world. Without the knower, (the reader or writer), the rest of the world has no meaning.

•

How can we begin to reweave the fabric of our broken, fragmented world? The first step is to fully acknowledge that we humans can't do it. The Tewa Chant, above, asks that the greater beings of our place do it for us: the white light of morning, the red light of evening and the rainbow; therefore, the first step is to set up structure which will invite the changing light of the sun or the moon or the storm or the sudden clearing; the light of the different seasons; and the various animals or plants that come with those seasons in each place. Once we do this, we begin to recognize the relationship between nature within us, the "inscape" and nature outside of us, the landscape. By ritual use of these structures through the seasons we begin to discover that there's no one thing that causes everything else; we find that truly everything in the bioregion is interrelated. The entire bioregion is a single organism or, in Needham's words, "the web that has no weaver."

emotion, action — is influenced by a huge, all-inclusive web of factors. Any change in the condition of any one thing in this web affects everything else, by virtue of their interconnectedness.

Author Joanna Macy swoops from lofty contemplation through chatty passages of autobiography to practical, day-to-day applications of insight. She spent too many years working with the Peace Corps to be fond of ideas that only look good on paper. She presents concrete examples of systems theory — pattica samuppada in action at the personal, communal, national, and global levels. Most poignant in Macy's writings is her advocacy for beings of other species and for the future. She advances the logic of interconnectedness across boundaries of time and space, and establishes as obvious and unshakable the responsibility humans of the present have to the earth's entire population. —David Schneider

•

So long as we see ourselves as essentially separate, competitive, and ego-identified beings, it is difficult to respect the validity of our social despair, deriving as it does from interconnectedness. Both our capacity to grieve for others and our power to cope with this grief spring from the great matrix of relationships in which we take our being. We are, as open systems, sustained by flows of energy and information that extend beyond the reach of conscious ego.

•

The process of development is perceived as being multidimensional. One's personal awakening is integral to the awakening of one's village, and both play integral roles in the awakening of one's country and one's world.

The Practice of the Wild

Like Gary Snyder's poetry, the prose in this collection of essays is usually outside, going about its business. Being grounded in a sense of place lessens the chasm between thinking and acting. Spanning the last fifteen years, these essays offer a bioregional route through the debris accumulated from the clash between human civilization and the world's wild places. —Richard Nilsen

•

Bioregionalism is the entry of place into the dialectic of history.

•

We (who stand aside) stand on the lateral moraine of the glacier eased along by Newton and Descartes. The revivified Goddess Gaia glacier is coming down another valley, from our distant pagan past, and another arm of ice is sliding in from another angle: the no-nonsense meditation view of Bud-

dhism with its emphasis on compassion and insight in an empty universe. Someday they will probably all converge, and yet carry (like the magnificent Baltoro glacier in the Karakoram) streaks on each section that testify to their place of origin. Some historians would say that "thinkers" are behind the ideas and mythologies that people live by. I think it also goes back to maize, reindeer, squash, sweet potatoes, and rice. And their songs.

It is appropriate to feel loyalty to a given glacier; it is advisable to investigate the whole water cycle; and it is rare and marvelous to know that glaciers do not always flow and that mountains are constantly walking.

•

Sometimes it seems unlikely that a society as a whole can make wise choices. Yet there is no choice but to call for the "recovery of the commons" — and this in a modern world which doesn't quite realize

what it has lost. Take back, like the night, that which is shared by all of us, that which is our larger being. There will be no "tragedy of the commons" greater than this: if we do not recover the commons — regain personal, local, community, and peoples' direct involvement in sharing (in *being*) the web of the wild world — that world will keep slipping away. Eventually our complicated industrial capitalist/socialist mixes will bring down much of the living system that supports us.

•

The commons is a curious and elegant social institution within which human beings once lived free political lives while weaving through natural systems. The commons is a level of organization of human society that includes the nonhuman. The level above the local commons is the bioregion. Understanding the commons and its role within the larger regional culture is one more step toward integrating ecology with economy.

The Practice of the Wild
Gary Snyder. Farrar Straus Giroux, 1990; 208 pp. ISBN 0-86547-454-0
$11 ($13 postpaid) from Putnam Publishing Group/Order Dept., PO Box 506, East Rutherford, NJ 07073; 800/631-8571

A BAD RELATIONSHIP IS A LOT OF WORK — avoiding the person, feeling terrible about yourself, thinking up excuses not to make amends. Whites in general in the United States have had just such a relationship with people of color since before the nation was founded, and it's damaging all of us.

It takes less energy in the long run to set the relationship right. The work begins one on one.

When you make just one friend who is different from you, you feel easier about every other person in that group. When you become interested in a people — in their culture, their history, the ways they have been oppressed — because you are interested in your friend, you become an ally bound by love. You use the passion and insight you gain as solid ground on which to challenge not only institutionalized racism (such as the way the death penalty is currently enforced), but also the smaller, constant insults of everyday racism.

Expect this to be difficult. Budget yourself a lot of mistakes. It is not simple to make, much less preserve, a real, peer friendship with someone you may have been brought up to live apart from, to look down on, to fear. You may be looking across class as well as race barriers to find people of color to be friends with — at the man bussing your dishes, the woman taking care of your neighbor's kids. Things will get uncomfortable. But holding on when you want to give up will be one of the greatest challenges you can make to racism.

Don't forget to stay close to other white people as you do this. You may find yourself wanting to distance yourself, believing that they are the problem, not you. But all of us in the U.S. have been steeped in racism our entire lives. We live in a society that economically benefits some members while exploiting the majority. This system perpetuates itself only by separating people through many, many divisions along lines of sex, age, class, race, sexual orientation, physical ability — systematically mistreating some and "rewarding" others. Everybody gets hurt.

To be divided from other human beings is a painful thing. But nobody asked for this. That doesn't mean that nobody ever did anything wrong — only that good people (which is everyone) were taught to hate and fear. Often we learned these lessons at the knee of people we loved and respected — or had them pounded into us, or humiliated into us. (You stood up against it until you couldn't anymore.) We can undo the damage by getting good information to counteract the junk, examining the emotional glue that holds the misinformation in place, and building alliances wherever we can. Making friends with people who are different from us is a truly subversive act. —Ann Bartz

National Coalition Building Institute

In the United States, where hardly anybody in the middle class and so in the larger media context in which we live talks realistically about racism, classism, and other imbalances of power, it is a relief to come across people who will.

When we talk about "community," or "peace," or "social justice," we are most practically talking about eliminating just these barriers between human beings. Where the National Coalition Building Institute succeeds is first in realizing that that's possible, and second in recognizing the emotional component that travels hand in hand with the misinformation of prejudice.

NCBI trains anybody who wants to learn to be a leader in building alliances among people of different races, sexes, classes, ages, religions, sexual orientations, or physical abilities. Trainees look at their own group

issues and then work together in local teams in the workplace or community. They've been all over the world since 1984, and have already had an impact on governments, schools, unions, and police departments. —AB

●
In 1988 NCBI trained a critical team of leaders who work in Catholic/Protestant reconciliation in Northern Ireland. Since then, over 100 Catholic and Protestant leaders have formed an NCBI chapter, housed at the University of Ulster in Derry, to lead NCBI programs throughout Northern Ireland. • In 1988 and again in 1989, the Department of Education of the University of Port Elizabeth in South Africa invited NCBI to train a racially diverse team of educators, who have begun to train teams of White and Black young people using NCBI models. • In 1992, NCBI led the first workshop of its kind in N.Y.C. between Chinese and Tibetan leaders. • Several hundred elementary school children in a dozen public school systems have been success-

National Coalition Building Institute
Information from 1825 K St. NW, Suite 715, Washington, DC 20006; 202/785-9400, Fax: 202/785-3385

fully trained by NCBI to be prejudice reduction leaders in their schools. The children are trained to settle playground disputes, take coalition building principles into their classrooms and homes, and lead other children in prejudice reduction exercises. —*NCBI literature*

Cultural Etiquette

Many white people don't have any idea that something they're doing is coming across as racist to a person of color. This book and your own good thinking will help you avoid unaware racism. —AB

●
Dreadlocks, locks, dreads, natty dreads, etc., is an ancient traditional way that African people sometimes wear their hair. It is not braided, it is "locked." Locking is the natural tendency of African hair to knit and bond to itself. It locks by itself, we don't have to do anything to it to make it lock. It is permanent, once locked, it cannot come undone. It gets washed just as regularly as anyone else's hair. No, you may not touch it, don't ask.

Internalized Racism
Suzanne Lipsky. Rational Island Publishers, 1987; 17 pp. $1.00 from Rational Island Publishers, Box 2081, Main Office Station, Seattle, WA 98111

Cultural Etiquette
(A Guide for the Well Intentioned)
Amosa Three Rivers. 1991; 28 pp.
$5 postpaid from Market Wimmin, Box 28, Indian Valley, VA 24105

Internalized Racism

Messages of inferiority and devaluation from an oppressive society find their mark in the hearts of people of color who come to devalue themselves and each other. Internalized racism is at the root of black-on-black crime, any feeling that lighter skin and straighter hair are somehow more beautiful, Asian people surgically altering the epicanthal folds above their eyes, and alcoholism among Native Americans, to name but a few manifestations. —AB

●
Distress patterns, created by oppression and racism from the outside, have been played out in the only two places it has seemed "safe" to do so. First, upon members of our own group — particularly upon those over whom we have some degree of power or control, our children. Second, upon ourselves through all manner of self-

invalidation, self-doubt, isolation, fear, feelings of powerlessness and despair.

As part of our liberation work, we know that we must seek out and direct the attention of ourselves and the world to the strength, intelligence, greatness, power and success of our people and our culture.

OTHER GREAT RESOURCES

Race (How Blacks and Whites Think and Feel About the American Obsession): Studs Terkel. 1992. Anchor Press, Bantam Doubleday Dell.

Rational Island Publishers publishes a host of great resources for whites and people of color, including journals on the liberation of Asians and Asian Americans, Latinos/as, African Americans, Arabs and Arab Americans, Native Americans, the working class, the middle class, the owning class, parents, young people, men, women, teachers, and people with disabilities. Box 2081, Main Office Station, Seattle, WA 98111, for a list and prices.

Sustainable Cities

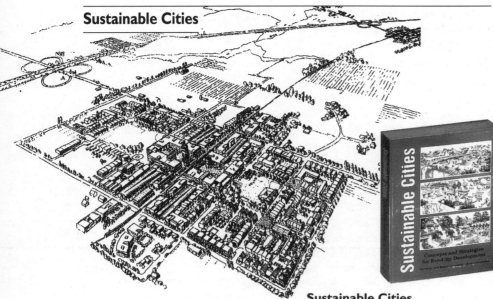

In a profoundly anti-urban society, it is refreshing to find a book written by people with a city-positive attitude. This resource is a product of the "new partnership" between the forces for urban growth and the movement for a sustainable environment. An anthology of essays by environmentalists, developers, architects, planners, and politicians, it does a good job of covering the emerging principles of eco-city design, planning, politics, and economics; however, the book's main contribution is its coverage of projects that are currently underway in Los Angeles and across the country. It also offers an extensive resource guide to organizations and publications on every aspect of the sustainable city, including permaculture, community building, resource-efficient architecture, and livelihoods. —Ray Tomalty

Sustainable Cities
Bob Walter, Lois Arkin
& Richard Crenshaw.
1992; 354 pp. ISBN 0-9633511-0-9
$20 ($23.50 postpaid) from Eco-Home
Media, 4344 Russell Avenue, Los Angeles,
CA 90027; 213/662-5207

•

The trend over the past 40 years has been to integrate more parking into the land use, whether residential, commercial, or industrial, and to favor off-site parking over on-street parking. So much is typically required, that if any change were to be made, many empty spaces would result. In the Los Angeles area, this has resulted in the peculiar situation in which Air Quality Regulation 15, limiting the number of vehicles used to bring people to work, now creates an imbalance in which the parking spaces required by most zoning codes are not all used. If carpooling is to be encouraged, then this should be reflected in regulations that call for fewer employee parking places.

The Urban Ecologist

This newsletter is a valuable resource for those who are committed to improving life in their city, suburb, or eco-village off the subway. The organization that puts it together, Urban Ecology, is a river of eco-city passion and commitment. The articles and news bits from urban activists all over the world cover all fronts: urban nature, housing, transportation, economics, advocacy strategy. These people know their sidewalks and the waters that run under them.
—Whitney Smith

The Urban Ecologist
$30/year (membership includes 4 issues).
Urban Ecology, PO Box 10144, Berkeley,
CA 94709; 415/549-1724

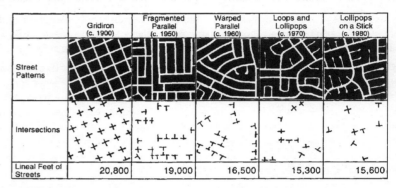

	Gridiron (c. 1900)	Fragmented Parallel (c. 1950)	Warped Parallel (c. 1960)	Loops and Lollipops (c. 1970)	Lollipops on a Stick (c. 1980)
Street Patterns					
Intersections					
Lineal Feet of Streets	20,800	19,000	16,500	15,300	15,600

Neighborhood Street Patterns: **Different street designs create vastly different urban communities. The traditional gridiron, though often insensitive to contour and ecological features, created a fine-grained, well-connected and diverse urban fabric. Suburban patterns have less street frontage and far fewer intersections and neighborhood access points. Within these communities automobile traffic gets channeled to a few intersections and arterials, and it is difficult to bicycle or walk from one point to another.**

•

As the nation's 39,000 shopping centers and malls age, a growing number are being torn down and recycled into housing or more ecologically appropriate mixed-use developments. . . . Nationwide, the Chicago-based Real Estate Research Corporation has estimated that 10-15 percent of the nation's malls will be abandoned and ripe for redevelopment in the coming years.

Ecocity Berkeley

Ecocity Berkeley
Richard Register. 1987;
144 pp. ISBN 1-55643-009-4
$10.95 ($13.45 postpaid) from
North Atlantic Books, PO Box 12327,
Berkeley, CA 94701; 510/559-8277

Richard Register has been at the forefront of the movement to rebuild North American cities along ecological lines. He designed this book to help that process, asking us to think and dream a little together. Part one details many of the new design ideas gaining wide acceptance as antidotes to the ecological and social destruction wrought by urban sprawl: compact, diverse, liveable cities based on mixed land uses and proximity rather than mobility. Part two applies these ideas to Berkeley, CA in what amounts to a 140-year plan for transforming the city into an ecotopia. A rich scenery of illustrations helps us visualize our way along this path. —Ray Tomalty

•

Where trees and buildings block sun and air movement, the microclimate is generally much cooler and more moist. Tall buildings are often said to "cause" windy streets. But this is no more true than saying redwood trees, the tallest in nature, cause windy canyons. In fact, the stillness at the base of these giants is almost spooky sometimes. The relationship between buildings and streets — and open parking lots and parks — and the direction of the winds relative to the layout of the streets determines whether the streets are swept by the wind or not.

•

If American building codes, city ordinances and zoning — even solar access and personal liability laws — were applied retroactively to the wonderful old cities of Europe, the Second World War would look friendly by comparison: it would *all* have to go. Too many people live in spaces too small and odd-shaped served by too little electricity — not enough safety measure: too few walls around canals, often no banisters on steps which are usually too steep or narrow, too few giant signs for speeding cars, wide roads, bright city lights at night. The narrow streets of the old city centers would run afoul of solar access regulations. Many trees, especially fruit and nut trees, would have to be eliminated. Their crime: producing nutritious food that can fall with a squish into the public domain.

Downwind

Greening cities is more than just a matter of generic street trees and astroturf-like median strips. It's about retrieving a sense of the original biotic community that hosted the city's formation, discerning that first community's lingering presence, and celebrating it, the round of the seasons, and the many opportunities for real good work that cities present. *Downwind*, edited in and for Chicago's environs by Beatrice Briggs, ace urban bioregional organizer, handily abets those activities and more with a calendar of field trips and other events

and salutary editorials. An example for other city bioregionalists to follow and a must-read for residents of the Wild Onion bioregion.
—Stephanie Mills

•

To say that Chicago has only two seasons, winter and road construction, almost always gets a laugh, but such comments entirely disregard the nuanced turning of the wheel of the year in this bioregion. Like children who are unfairly labeled "stupid" in school, we come to believe the untrue things said about our home place. Soon we too start saying mean, critical, derogatory things, mostly because we do not know

Downwind
$10/year from Wild Onion Alliance, 3432
N. Bosworth Street, Chicago, IL 60657

how to do anything else. What, through either ignorance or fear, we cannot praise, we put down. We do it to each other. We do it to ourselves. We do it to the place we live. Pretty soon we find ourselves stuck with self esteem problems, a fragile social network and a steadily deteriorating ecosystem.

The alternative to such verbal trashing is not to witlessly proclaim, "I Love Chicago," but to be far more place-specific and less human-centered in our boosterism.

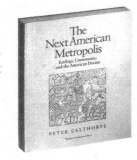

Secondary Area
Residential
Public/Open Space
2000 feet
Transit Stop
Core Commercial
Office/Employment
Arterial

The Next American Metropolis

In this handsome and probably influential book, Peter Calthorpe (architect and planner of Pedestrian Pockets fame) adjusts his TOD (Transit-Oriented Development) concept, seeking to balance human concerns, technics, and the purely environmental.

His position has drawn critical fire — not surprising when the line between balance and compromise is hard to draw. Not all houses face south, for example, but they are superinsulated, and the streets serve neighborhoods nicely. I remain neutral until his projects now under construction are completed and inhabited by people going about their daily lives.

The book commences with a sharp treatise outlining the forces that have engendered existing, undesirable urban and suburban development. Alternatives are suggested, buttressed with

*supporting logic. Next comes a very useful set of guidelines, prescribing the many parts and features that must be woven into a dynamic community. The last third of the book presents applications of the principles and guidelines. If the Next American Metropolis gets built, this book will have helped it happen.
—J. Baldwin*

●

Urban Growth Boundaries (UGB) should be established at the edge of metropolitan regions to protect significant natural resources and provide separation between existing towns and cities. Lands within the UGB should be transit accessible, contiguous to existing development, and planned for long-term urbanization.

Oregon is one of the few states that has

enabling legislation for UGBs. Fundamental to such a device are regional governing bodies that have the power to establish and protect limits to growth. The problem of a single jurisdiction establishing such a line is that a simple change of the elected board can reverse or revise the line. A UGB typically has to be created in the context of multiple jurisdictions being meaningful. One alternative to state-level empowerment or regional governments is a joint power agreement between several jurisdictions. If, for example, a county and several cities were to agree upon a boundary and corresponding holding capacities, any change would require unanimous agreement — an unlikely political event, short of a new regional consensus.

The placement and configuration of a UGB is a complex, site-specific task. It is important that the boundary be large enough to absord a reasonable amount of growth for a significant period of time. It should not be

The Next American Metropolis
Peter Calthorpe. 1993; 175 pp.
ISBN 1-878271-68-7
$24.95 ($28.45 postpaid) from Princeton Architectural Press, 37 E. 7th Street, New York, NY 10003; 800/458-1131

a mechanism for down-sizing lands imminently vulnerable to development. It is a long-term tool to direct growth and regional form. One of its purposes is to prevent investments from being squandered on land speculation in inapropriate areas. It can serve to keep development intelligent and efforts focused on coherent sites. Such a boundary must respect and protect major environmental assets and integrate the needs of transit. This transit criterion means that there should not be gaps in the urban fabric, and that all areas within the UGB be transit accessible.

A Pattern Language

This project is overwhelmingly ambitious — to establish a language for talking about what people really need from buildings and communities, drawing from many epochs and cultures but focusing on our own. The genius of Alexander et al. is that they simply ignore the stylistic fadmongering that passes for architectural thought, and get on with sensible, useful, highly distilled wisdom about what works and what doesn't. They're not shy about laying down rules of thumb ("Balconies and porches which are less than six feet deep are hardly ever used"), often with research citations to back them up, and charming, pointed illustrations.

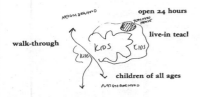

open 24 hours
live-in teacl
walk-through
children of all ages

In every neighborhood, build a children's home — a second home for children — a large rambling house or workplace — a place where children can stay for an hour or two, or for a week. At least one of the people who run it must live on the premises; it must be open 24 hours a day; open to children of all ages; and it must be clear, from the way it is run, that it is a second family for the children — not just a place where baby-sitting is available.

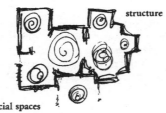

A Pattern Language
Christopher Alexander,
Sara Ishikawa, & Murray Silverstein.
1977; 1171 pp. ISBN 0-19-501919-9
$49.95 ($51.95 postpaid) from Oxford University Press/Order Dept., 2001 Evans Road, Cary, NC 27513; 800/451-7556

The most important book in architecture and planning for many decades, a landmark whose clarity and humanity give hope that our private and public spaces can yet be made gracefully habitable. —Ernest Callenbach

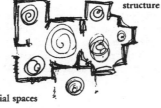

structure
social spaces

On no account allow the engineering to dictate the building's form. Place the load bearing elements — the columns and the walls and floors — according to the social spaces of the building; never modify the social spaces to conform to the engineering structures of the building.

Planners Network

*This simple newsletter lists conferences, undeservedly obscure not-so-specialist publications, fellowships and queries. Planners Network looks like a handy source of insight into contemporary socialism, with a small s.
—Stephanie Mills*

●

INCLUSIVE COMMUNITIES: *NIMBY Report* is a new monthly publication (likely free) from the American Friends Service Committee (1501 Cherry St., Philadelphia, PA 19102, 215/241-7000) on issues and resources aimed at fostering inclusive communities. It's edited by Kale Williams, 305 S. Green St., Chicago, IL 60607, 312/258-8010.

HOUSING DATA SOURCE: HUD User's (Box 6091, Rockville, MD 20850, 800/245-2691) *Directory of Information Resources in Housing and Urban Development* is now available in a third edition, with listings on 145 public agencies, research institutions,

Planners Network
Membership $25/year from Planners Network, 1601 Connecticut Avenue NW, Washington DC, 20009

trade and professional associations, advocacy groups, and clearinghouses. Also included are listings for 44 online databases. Copies are $26.

The Geography of Nowhere

With this book, James Howard Kunstler has become the Hunter Thompson of planning and urban design. A difficult achievement with a topic as juicy as politics, but with planning it takes a work of genius — and that's what this book is. Not only does Kunstler turn the dry world of land use planning and development into a circus (which it secretly is), but he also transforms the history (drier yet) into an action thriller. He tracks the history of our physical

world in the most concise manner I have ever encountered, describing "our new communities" in case studies that read like the porno novelettes they really are. —Peter Calthorpe

●

As Randall Arendt realized, . . . typical zoning laws not only failed to protect the landscape, they virtually *mandated* sprawl. To reproduce anything resembling a traditional New England village had become illegal, a violation of all codes, acreage

The Geography of Nowhere
James Howard Kunstler. 1993; 303 pp.
ISBN 0-671-70774-4
$23 postpaid from Simon & Schuster/Order Dept., 200 Old Tappan Road, Old Tappan, NJ 07675; 800/223-2336

requirements, setbacks, street widths, and laws insisting on the separation of uses. So, towns ended up splattered all over the countryside while the countryside lost its rural character. All you could build in contemporary New England was Los Angeles.

The Community Garden Book

Community gardening is a popular and spreading practice, but few books are in print on the subject. The Community Garden Book, published a decade ago, remains the best single source. Author Larry Sommers covers nearly everything a person or group would need to start a community garden: getting land, organizing and working as a group, designing a site, relating intelligently to the local earth, water, fire, and air, economics of a garden, vandalism, hooking up with other gardens, sources for material, funding, and so on.

Things have shifted some since this book was written — protecting yourself from drive-by shootings in drug-infested areas is a subject Mr. Sommers doesn't cover, for instance — but the writing and illustrations are clear, to the point, and cheerful.
—David Schneider

The Community Garden Book
Larry Sommers. 1980; 121 pp.
ISBN 0-915873-01-X
$5.95 ($8.95 postpaid) from National Gardening Association, 180 Flynn Avenue, Burlington, VT 05401; 802/863-1308

●

The city of Philadelphia allows garden groups to hook up to fire hydrants for garden water if they get special permits first. Sally McCabe, garden coordinator, says "Users must sign an agreement not to abuse the privilege and to use hydrants only to fill storage drums. The groups must buy their own special hose adaptor and a wrench to turn the water on and off."

●

Raised beds allow the gardener to use topsoil, concentrate fertilizers, organic matter and water in a small, intensely-planted area. They help conserve resources while focusing soil-building efforts on defined areas. . . .

The raised bed layout provides order and definition to the site, making it easier for gardeners of all skill levels to maintain their areas.

Let's Grow!

Because so many intentional and residentially based communities include children, and because children bring fresh minds and senses to a garden, and because they are indefatigable if somewhat distractable workers, my scan of resources for community gardens includes a quick review of the literature of gardening for children — a literature that is excellent and burgeoning. I include books for adults to use in talking about and teaching gardening to children, and books aimed right at children themselves.

My favorite of the books for adults is Let's Grow! The "lessons" are simple, practical, and inspiring: weeding, amending soil, picking fruit; nothing seems missing. The children in these photographs are in bliss. No one could have faked or posed this stuff.
—DS

Let's Grow!
(72 Gardening Adventures with Children) Linda Tilgner. Garden Way Publishing, 1988; 208 pp. ISBN 0-88266-470-0 $10.95 ($14.20 postpaid) from Storey Communications, Schoolhouse Road, Pownal, VT 05261; 800/827-8673

American Community Gardening Association

This association exists to promote community gardening in the US. Their journal, Community Greening Review, tracks ripples, waves, and splashes in the pool of American community gardening. Each issue contains a detailed "how to" section, as well as in-depth looks at projects in progress (Denver, Cleveland, Louisville, Omaha, and Atlanta were discussed in recent issues). Excellent networkers, the authors and editors make a point of directing readers toward helpful people and organizations. A rich resource.
—DS

●

Operation GreenThumb
GreenThumb leases city-owned vacant property to non-profit organizations for the establishment of community vegetable and flower gardens.

GreenThumb's staff of eight works with garden sponsors by training them in garden design and horticultural techniques. The

American Community Gardening Association
Membership $25/year (includes annual *Community Greening Review*), 325 Walnut Street, Philadelphia, PA 19106; 215/625-8280

Lugging water a long distance at 8 pounds per gallon should be a last resort, even with willing porters.

Grow It!

Among the books written specifically for (literate) children, Grow It! stands out. Grow It! is done in a heavily illustrated, nearly comic-book style that gets through to me real well. I learned a good deal from this small, inexpensive, information-rich book.
—DS

Grow It!
(An Indoor-Outdoor Gardening Guide for Kids) Erika Markmann. 1991; 48 pp.
ISBN 0-679-81528-7, $6.95 ($8.95 postpaid) from Random House/Order Dept., 400 Hahn Road, Westminster, MD 21157; 800/733-3000

This pot has a secret water compartment.

Clay pots

gravel   moist soil or peat moss

OTHER GREAT RESOURCES

Four more good gardening books for or about children:

Plants for Play (A Plant Selection Guide for Children's Outdoor Environments). Robin C. Moore. 1993, MIG Communications.

The Amazing Dirt Book. Paulette Bourgeois. 1990, Addison-Wesley Publishing Co.

Kids Gardening: A Kid's Guide to Messing Around in the Dirt. Kim G. & Kevin Raferty. 1989, Klutz Press.

The Growing Classroom: Garden-Based Science. Roberta Jaffe & Gary Appel. 1990, Addison-Wesley Publishing Co.

National Gardening Association. 180 Flynn Avenue, Burlington, VT 05401; 802/863-1308.

Brooklyn Botanic Garden. 1000 Washington Avenue, Brooklyn, NY 11225-1099; 718/941-4044.

The Life Lab Science Program. 1156 High Street, Santa Cruz, CA 95064; 408/459-2001.

Cornell Cooperative Extension, New York City Urban Horticulture Program. 15 E. 26th Street, 5th Floor, New York, NY 10010; 212/340-2930.

Farms of Tomorrow

Community gardening extended in scale becomes community farming. Community-supported agriculture or CSA, as the growing movement is called, harkens back to earlier days of agriculture, perhaps even the first days. Farms of Tomorrow *is an excellent introduction to the thinking and practices of CSA. With farming, situations are local; there is no one way to do CSA. This book documents a half-dozen different approaches.*
—David Schneider

•

We have no choice about whether to farm or not, as we have a choice about whether to produce TV sets or not. So we have to either farm or support farmers, every one of us, at any cost. We cannot give it up because it is inconvenient or unprofitable.

•

Since our existence is primarily dependent on farming, we cannot entrust this essential activity solely to the farming population — just 2% of Americans. As farming becomes more and more remote from the life of the

Farms of Tomorrow
(Community Supported Farms, Farm Supported Communities)
Trauger Groh & Steven McFadden. 1990; 176 pp. ISBN 0-938250-28-0
$12 ($14.75 postpaid) from Bio Dynamic Farming & Gardening Association, PO Box 550, Kimberton, PA 19442

average person, it becomes less and less able to provide clean, healthy, lifegiving food or a clean, healthy, lifegiving environment. A small minority of farmers, laden with debt and overburdened with responsibility, cannot possibly meet the needs of all the people.

AIDS Memorial Grove

Community gardens need not be rooted in residence. The AIDS Memorial Grove in San Francisco's Golden Gate Park doesn't relate to addresses. The Grove memorializes those who have died from AIDS; it is a community garden based on planting life in the face of death. The Grove is a garden of the HIV community, or of the gay community, or of anyone sympathetic to either community. These folks are staking out, refurbishing, and re-invigorating an obscure section of a world-class park. Golden Gate Park, like most parks these days, is desperately underfunded, so this is a boon for the park and the city as well.
—DS

American Horticultural Therapy Association

"Community" is a term that seems to dilate and contract as needed; community gardening is thus a flexible concept also.

The American Horticultural Therapy Association promotes gardening as therapy. They work with communities of disabled and disadvantaged persons: workers in vocational rehabilitation, handicapped children, communities of prison inmates. An elegant application of the sanity of gardening.
—DS

American Horticultural Therapy Association: 362A Christopher Avenue, Gaithersburg, MD 20879; 301/948-3010.

The AIDS Memorial Grove, Urban Resource Systems. 783 Buena Vista West, San Francisco, CA 94117; 415/621-3260

groups attend a series of design, construction and planting workshops, after which they are issued tools, material to build fences, lumber to build raised beds, picnic tables and benches, soil, ornamental and fruit trees and shrubs, seeds and bulbs.

GreenThumb currently leases more than 1,000 different lots totaling approximately 125 acres to more than 600 community groups in 39 of New York's 59 Community Planning Boards.

For more information contact: Operation GreenThumb, Department of General Services, 49 Chambers St. Room 1020, New York, NY 10007; 212-233-2926

To Dwell Is to Garden

This book proposes to be a history of Boston's community gardens. In truth, author Sam Bass Warner, Jr., has written an engaging modern history of community gardens, including Boston's. Warner argues incisively that community gardening is always a political statement. Perhaps as a result of his own participation in gardens, Warner's book is both learned and intimate.
—DS

•

I was seeking the origins of community gardens by asking a question about a pattern of land use: where else, and at what earlier times, did landless people cultivate small garden plots in grouped parcels separated from their homes? The answer turned up in a nasty bit of English history. At about the time of the American Revolution the farmers and landlords of England divided and fenced the common lands of the villages,

To Dwell Is to Garden
(A History of Boston's Community Gardens)
Sam Bass Warner, Jr., Photographs by Hansi Durlach. 1987;
128 pp. ISBN 1-55553-007-9
$21.95 ($24.95 postpaid) from Northeastern University Press, 360 Huntington Avenue, Suite 272, Boston, MA 02115; 617/373-5480

thereby driving thousands of country families into poverty and on to public relief. Community gardens, vegetable plots offered at very low rents, then commenced as a philanthropic experiment undertaken in the hope of reducing the costs of public welfare!

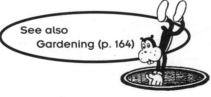
See also
Gardening (p. 164)

OTHER GREAT RESOURCES

Department of Horticulture, Kansas State University: 226 Waters Hall, Manhattan, KS 66506-4002; 913/532-6170

Kansas State University offers a degree in Horticultural Therapy.

Findhorn Garden: HarperPerennials.

The Findhorn Garden was possibly the most extreme development in community gardens — a group who, beginning in the 1960s, grew fantastic plants from supposedly barren soil in the harsh climate of Scotland. Their secret? They took a lot of divine guidance, and they took it from the plant "devas" themselves. Much of their vegetal advice is recorded here. I found the book in the Witchcraft section of my local ag library. That in itself should recommend it.

Seed collectors, seed savers, and seed traders form another nonresidential gardening community. (See p. 104 for good professional and amateur seed-related ventures.) Collecting indigenous seeds keeps floral community alive; it also preserves plants of significance to local cultures. Trading seeds fosters a larger horticultural community. Both saving and trading seeds move us beyond concerns for individual species to a larger concern for our ecological "self." —DS

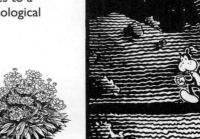

The Gaia Atlas of Cities

The physical, and sometimes the psychological, consequences of centralizing pop-ulations in cities have been devastating for Gaia and millions of human beings. Yet this smart, useful book understands and celebrates the appeal of civilization, and the kinds of excellence that seem to flourish in big burgs.

Writing of cities as if they were (or should be) responsible actors, Herbert Girardet proposes a morality for them: "circular metabolism": zero waste. His perspective on how this might come about is illustrated with some surprisingly happy news from situations one might have stereotyped as hopeless.
—Stephanie Mills

●
All over the developing world people succumb to the magnetic pull of urban centres. This is far from irrational — average earnings in the city can be three to four times greater than in the country, though this figure does not include the monetary value of food self-sufficiency that rural people enjoy. Cities, despite their difficulties, seem to offer opportunity. Disease may be a problem, but doctors are easier to find; worldwide the number of children surviving infanthood is significantly higher in cities than in the countryside.

Few are drawn to cities just by the lure of "bright lights" and great expectations, but the excitement of city life and freedom from the constraints of village life are significant "pull" factors.

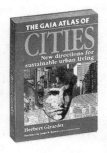

The Gaia Atlas of Cities
Herbert Girardet.
Doubleday & Co., 1993;
191 pp. ISBN 0-385-41915-5
$16 ($18.50 postpaid) from
Bantam, Doubleday, Dell/
Fulfillment Dept., 2451 S. Wolf
Road, Des Plaines, IL 60018;
800/223-6834

CityWatch

This hard-hitting zine, out of Asheville, North Carolina, offers photoessays, success stories, crusades-in-progress, resources, information, and advice, by and for citizen activists who are rebuilding cities all around the US. —HLR

●
On July fourth, Asheville celebrated the opening of Pack Place, anchor of a possible park running from Vance Monument to City Hall. Such parks have given middle class people good reasons for staying put and lending a hand, rather than jumping out to the suburbs.

Pack Place, Asheville, NC.

City Watch
Julian Price, Editor.
Published several times a year. Free or donation. PO Box 3105, Asheville, NC 28802; 704/253-2683

Institute for Local Self-Reliance

ILSR's goal: self-reliant urban communities that can generate income from within rather than suck the resources from rural communities. They've established a good reputation in waste-recycling, and they're active in other areas as well. —Peter Warshall

●
Democratic control of local government and local economic development are the cornerstones of local self-reliance. The Institute works to strengthen these. Small, local organizations are more in touch with nitty-gritty realities than large bureaucracies. When government is face to face with its electorate, it is most readily accountable to it. Locally owned businesses are more sensitive to their communities than those distantly headquartered.

We rally these diverse constituencies to eliminate waste and thereby increase efficiency. By extracting the maximum value from local resources — from waste to solar energy and plant matter — we seek to build locally owned, productive capacity within communities.

Technical Assistance
The Institute's ongoing research is continuously tested and applied in real life, local settings. The data we collect provides the basis for the staff's technical assistance for citizen groups, local officials, entrepreneurs, and small businesses. We disseminate and apply the results of our research in:

• assistance to community groups and local governments in planning processes;

• seminars, workshops, regional conferences;

• national and regional networks;

• expert witness testimony at public hearings; and

• linking the private and public sector to launch sustainable economic development projects. —ILSR brochure

Institute for Local Self-Reliance:
2425 18th Street NW, Washington, DC 20009; 202/232-4108

Saving Cities, Saving Money

In this era of municipal budget-slashing, environmentalists have a wonderfully effective new tool: urban communities designed as sustainable ecosystems can pay off in maintenance savings.

Saving Cities, Saving Money is full of resources and case histories of cost-saving energy conservation, recycling, pollution management and, land use planning programs that actually work for someone, somewhere. —HLR

●
In 1989, Aarhus became the first Scandinavian city to announce a strong energy policy: it resolved to cut its energy use in half by the year 2010.

Essential to Aarhus's energy plan is an expansion of district heating, a technology not yet widely employed in the New World. Like many Scandanavian cities, this one pipes hot water from fuel-burning electrical power stations into neighborhoods, harvesting heat that would otherwise be a wasted byproduct (cogeneration). Aarhus estimates that its existing heating service already saves 200,000 tons of oil a year. By 1995, the Studstrup Power Station will supply virtually the entire metropolis.

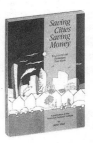

Saving Cities, Saving Money
John Hart. 1992; 116 pp.
ISBN 0-932857-08-6
$15.95 ($19.95 postpaid) from AgAccess, PO Box 2008, Davis, CA 95617; Phone: 916/756-7177/FAX: 916/756-7188

Center for Neighborhood Technology

Since 1978, CNT has been grappling with the jobs-and-justice realities of life in decaying urban neighborhoods. Having earned a national reputation for its demonstration projects in energy conservation, the Center is now focusing on policies, technologies, and grassroots coalition-building strategies to create a sustainable Chicago.

The Neighborhood Works, CNT's award-winning magazine, covers community approaches in housing, energy, environment, transportation, and economic development. CNT also has published a distinguished array of handbooks on such diverse topics as school reform and ecologically sound dry cleaning. Write for a list of what's currently available. —Beatrice Briggs

●
When Mather Air Force Base in Sacramento, Calif., was named for closure in 1989, the local congressman appointed a commission to oversee the base's conversion. Acting nearly as rapidly, a network of community activists organized the Peace, Environment, Justice Conversion Coalition to push for a democratic planning process that identified new civilian uses which met critical local needs. Potential community polarization was avoided when several of the coalition's leaders were subsequently appointed to slots on the official commission. After three years' work, the commission came up with a mixed reuse plan including affordable housing and open space surrounding an airport devoted to air freight and general aviation.

It is clear from past and present experience that military base conversion is both a threat and an opportunity for affected communities.

Neighborhood Works Newsletter
$30/year (6 issues) from Center For Neighborhood Technology, 2125 W. North Avenue, Chicago, IL 60647

Mad Housers

Mad Housers is a volunteer group that builds homes for the homeless and gives them away. These huts are small (48 sq. ft.), have no electricity or running water and are not "up to code" precisely because city rules make it impossible to build minimal low-cost housing. These homes are not meant to be a permanent solution, but to provide protection from the elements, warmth (a stove), and privacy; they are located in out-of-the-way places in hopes that the occupants will be left at peace. Hut dwellers quickly transform this raw space into cozy homes with carpet, paint, and furniture.

Mad Housers began in Atlanta in 1986 and in Chicago in 1991. For many homeless, these small homes have proven to be a better solution

MAD HOUSER HUT

than either shelters or public housing because institutional housing lacks privacy and security. For volunteers there is a chance to learn construction skills and to get to know homeless clients.
—Tor Faegre

Mad Housers Chapter Starter Kit: $8 postpaid. Mad Housers, PO Box 52657, Atlanta, GA 30355.

Shooting Back (A Photographic View of Life by Homeless Children): Jim Hubbard, Editor. 1991; 120 pp. ISBN 0-8118-0019-9 $14.95 ($18.45 postpaid). Chronicle Books/Order Dept., 275 Fifth Street, San Francisco, CA 94103; 800/722-6657

Transitory Gardens, Uprooted Lives: Diana Balmori & Margaret Morton. 1993; 160 pp. ISBN 0-300-05772-5 $25 ($28 postpaid). Yale University Press/Order Dept., PO Box 209040, New Haven, CT 06520; 203/432-0940

Homeless (Portraits of Americans in Hard Times): Howard Schatz. 1993; ISBN 0-8118-0512-3 $22.95 ($26.45 postpaid) from Chronicle Books/Order Dept., 275 Fifth Street, San Francisco, CA 94103; 800/722-6657

Collaborative Communities

US interest in cohousing was largely ignited by the conceptually exciting but narrowly focused **Cohousing**. This more comprehensive book identifies cohousing as just one of many community/neighborhood schemes that exist, are under construction, or are being planned here and abroad. It's a rousing assortment, wonderfully informed by the wide variety of people involved. A selection of closely examined examples is enlivened by photographs and drawings of the layout of both community and housing units. The nasty questions of organization, finance, and bureaucracy are answered from often-difficult experience. While not quite as enticing a presentation as **Cohousing**, this book will nonetheless add to the growing interest in this sort of living. Its wise, realistic information and advice will help build the deliberate communities that so many people are finding attractive. —J. Baldwin

•
The urban neighborhood is a way to tie cohousing to the larger community, en-

hancing both. The idea is to integrate housing, business, and commercial services in an old-fashioned market town. The kinds of neighborhoods that people used to live in were very much an inspiration for cohousing, and the urban neighborhood attempts to recreate a similar concept on a larger scale. The first phases of the residences have been completed in two ambitious developments near Copenhagen.

•
Each member, stake in hand, walked the site and stopped where he or she thought the center of the house should be. The stake was pounded in. A 50-foot rope was tied to the stake, and a circle was drawn, with the stake as its center. The result was seven round sites, each with a 100-foot circumference, about 8,000 square feet. By using a circle, they did not need to lay out four stakes. Surprisingly, this method worked well; there was no overlap of circles because each person had chosen a different site.

There are seven homes on the 8-acre site.

Collaborative Communities (Cohousing, Central Living, and Other New Forms of Housing With Shared Facilities) Dorit Fromm. 1991; 296 pp. ISBN 0-442-23785-5 $46.95 ($49.45 postpaid). Van Nostrand Reinhold/Order Dept., 7625 Empire Drive, Florence, KY 41042; 800/842-3636

The 7 "leftover" acres are held in common. The parking area is to one side, and there is a short walk to the homes.

When the sites had been figured out, they went to a lawyer and asked, "How do we do that?"

Address Unknown

A stark, plainspoken book that explains the demographics, dynamics, and causes of homelessness, an estate within uncomfortably easy reach of many today. Wright explains the social and economic trends that have led to this growing disgrace. His proposals sound like temperate and reasonable solutions, too. It's not easy. Many homeless people are difficult, and multiply afflicted. But the homeless are not the problem; the failure of institutional and individual conscience is. —Stephanie Mills

Address Unknown (The Homeless in America) James Wright. 1989; 170 pp. ISBN 0-202-30365-9 $18.95 ($22.45 postpaid). Aldine de Gruyter/Order Dept., 200 Saw Mill River Road, Hawthorne, NY 10532; 914/747-0110

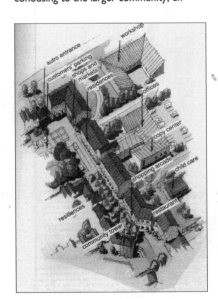

The urban neighborhood combines housing, local shops, day care, and small businesses located along pedestrian streets, with parking at the periphery.

The CoHousing Company • The CoHousing Network

In addition to authoring **Cohousing**, Kathryn McCamant and Charles Durrett maintain the CoHousing Company, a development company dedicated to building CoHousing communities. They give introductory slide lectures and workshops and maintain a national referral network of people interested in cohousing life. This last is important: it takes a determined and clever group to actually build cohousing. Once the group is together, the CoHousing Company staff assists the whole complex process of acquiring land, financing everything, getting the permits, and designing the project — all things that would be very difficult to do on your own (unless you were already a developer).

The CoHousing Network nurtures, incites, and cross-pollinates the movement. Their newsletter, **CoHousing**, tells all. —JB

The first thing to consider when designing a kitchen for a CoHousing community is that the focus is not just on meal preparation and service as is the case in most commercial kitchens. Rather, there is a social element that must be addressed. The act of food preparation takes place within the larger context of the community's gathering. While there is a need to create an efficient, functional food preparation and service space, there is the added desire to create a comfortable, homelike atmosphere

where conversations flow easily. The common house kitchen should be a place where sharing of culinary insights is enhanced and the "cooks" are not isolated from the rest of the community activity.

CoHousing Network: Membership $20/ year (includes newsletter). 1620 Belvedere Avenue, Berkeley, CA 94702.

CoHousing Company: 1250 Addison #113, Berkeley, CA 94702; 510/549-9980.

Floods, earthquakes, wildfires, tornados, hurricanes…
— "acts of God" to courts of law and insurance underwriters — can devastate communities. They can also inspire the highest levels of human cooperation, courage and selflessness.

Particular disasters often strike with little warning, but the fact of disaster somewhere, some time, is assured. Readiness is all. Disaster response experts agree that community preparation begins with each individual household. The most neighborly gesture is to reduce your contribution to the local burden: remove fire hazards, fasten buildings to their foundations, secure utility connections, lay in a store of emergency supplies (see "Safe and Secure Household," p. 161). Increase your odds of being a helper instead of a victim.

Then join forces and create a neighborhood plan: identify who has special skills or training; who is likely to be home (and, conceivably, trapped) during the day or night; who has disabilities or special needs; who owns a four-wheel-drive vehicle, a swimming-pool water source, or a ham radio. Give advance permission and instructions to shut off utilities, pick up children from school, or contact relatives. For help in organizing a neighborhood, see the two publications by the California Governor's Office of Emergency Services (below).

At the community level, agencies and nonprofits are learning to pool resources and clarify authority and responsibilities *before* a disaster. My county's Interagency Disaster Response Administration, combines public health and safety agencies with the Red Cross, Volunteer Center,

Salvation Army, Community Food Bank and Humane Society. The Federal Emergency Management Agency, through its Emergency Management Institute, offers classroom training and home study courses in emergency management, volunteer coordination and emergency data systems. For further information and referrals to agencies and programs in your state, call FEMA.
—Michael K. Stone

Disaster Preparedness Resources for Community-Based Organizations and Specific Populations: $5 postpaid.
Organizing Neighborhoods for Earthquake Preparedness: $7 postpaid.
Both from ABAG, PO Box 2050, Oakland, CA 94614; 510/464-7900.
FEMA: 16825 S. Seton Avenue, Emmitsburg, MD 21727; 800/238-3358.

A Neighborhood Disaster Toolbox

Gas-powered saws. Hand saws. Axes. Ladders. Crow bars and pry bars. Bolt cutters. Wrenches for gas valves. Flashlights, miners' lights, lanterns, extra batteries. Portable generator, power tools, work lights. Jacks, blocks, and shoring material such as 4 x 4 lumber. Rope. Sand bags. Shovels, work gloves, boots. Loud hailers. Buckets. "Water thief" to adapt a garden hose to any faucet.

A neighborhood inventory will determine which tools are already available, and who knows how to use them. Neighbors can jointly purchase expensive or one-to-a-neighborhood items like a generator, Multipurpose Tool or Handyman Jack. Toolbox location should combine theft and disaster resistance with easy access, and should have an official keeper.
—MKS

Handyman Jack: $42-$49, Information free from Harrah Mfg. Co., PO Box 228, Bloomfield, IN 47424; 812/384-4441.

Buy a bunch of "bottle jacks" (about $12. for a two-ton model at a discount auto-parts store). The small collapsed size permits clever placing. The Handyman Jack will lift or spread 7,000 pounds three feet; its range can be extended with a length of 2" pipe.
—J. Baldwin

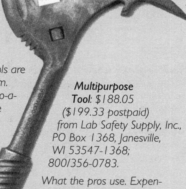

Multipurpose Tool: $188.05 ($199.33 postpaid) from Lab Safety Supply, Inc., PO Box 1368, Janesville, WI 53547-1368; 800/356-0783.

What the pros use. Expensive, but well designed; the non-sparking feature permits hacking away in the presence of explosive fumes. With a bunch of these, the Sabine Women might have changed history! —JB

Wildland Firefighting

If you appreciate looking at a definitive text, or if you are on a planning commission, rural town council, or the executive committee of a homeowners' association, you need to see this book.

Anyone planning to build a home who spends an evening with this book and doesn't make some design changes in the house plans is either already a fireman, or daft. **Wildland Firefighting** *is all about the tools and militarily precise routines that allow fire crews to function safely and effectively as a team.* —Richard Nilsen

•
Two fire seasons impact the southeastern states. The spring fire season is influenced by Hudson Bay High pressures when cold, dry air from Canada and the lake states moves south and east into the region. The

Wildland Firefighting
(Fire Behavior, Tactics & Command)
Donald G. Perry. 1990; 412 pp.
ISBN 0-941943-02-X
$29.95 ($33.95 postpaid) from Fire Publications Inc., 9072 Artesia Boulevard/Suite 7, Bellflower, CA 90706; 310/866-1664

spring fire season is associated with gusty, erratic winds. . . .

The Bermuda High may influence the southeast by limiting the flow of moist air from the Gulf of Mexico. Like the Pacific or Great Basin highs, the Bermuda High can produce high-pressure subsidence and a general drying of the region.

Peace of Mind in Earthquake Country

Stewart Brand's review of the first edition of our favorite earthquake book offered advice on ". . . where to locate, evaluating sites and buildings, insurance, design, and where to run." Homeowners and buyers in earthquake-prone locations need to know this stuff. Non-Californians need not be smug, there have been serious earthquakes over the past 200 years in many places, particularly South Carolina and Missouri. Boston, even! —JB

•
Plywood sheathing — shear-wall bracing — when properly and adequately nailed is superior to any other type of bracing for a small wood-frame structure. It provides tremendous strength against damaging deformations of the walls during an earthquake, and it greatly enhances the dispersal of the earthquake forces back to the foundation. Plywood shear-wall bracing is commonly found in earthquake country both as an exterior architectural feature (with battens, for example) and as a backing for stucco or some other exterior facing.

Peace of Mind in Earthquake Country
Peter I. Yanev. 1991; 218 pp.
ISBN 0-87701-771-9
$14.95 ($18.45 postpaid) from Chronicle Books/Order Dept., 275 Fifth Street, San Francisco, CA 94103; 800/722-6657

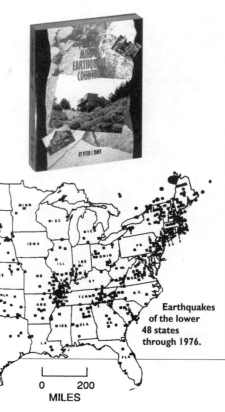

Legend
• Intensity V - VI (except California)
• Intensity VII
• Intensity VIIII
• Intensity IX
● Intensity X - XII

Earthquakes of the lower 48 states through 1976.

0   200
MILES

CITIES ARE TOUGH, getting tougher. Hard to imagine that anything less than miraculous could render them convivial again. Religion, while famous for associating itself with miracles, can be disappointingly unproductive of fundamental changes. It's like the little girl with the curl. When good, very, very good. When bad, horrid.

Very good are these instances of religious congregations and institutions dauntlessly,

The Lord's Supper, 1951   Fritz Eichenberg

doggedly, selflessly, and soulfully effecting daily miracles of compassion and recovery in settings so large, complex and troubled that to begin trying to help could break (or make) your heart. The secret, perhaps, is faith, whether it be in the divine or in the value of right action. Good and bad, there's a long tradition of the temple being at the heart of the city, now flourishing helpfully in these millennial times.

—Stephanie Mills

Revolution of the Heart

Every time I learn more about the Catholic Worker, I realize again that an unprecedented standard of decency has been established by this anarchist Christian movement. Founded in the thirties to live out the radical love portrayed in the gospel, the Catholic Worker, through its Houses of Hospitality, has seeded intentional communities of service among the urban poor.

This thoughtful collection examines the history of the Catholic Worker, the thought of its founders, and the ramifications of its practices — voluntary poverty, direct personal service, nonviolence. Descriptions of the daily practice of nonviolence in the hospitality houses that feed and shelter the homeless, sometimes violent themselves, are arresting and instructive.

An appendix lists more than one hundred Catholic Worker Hospitality Houses in the US. —SM

•

If Maurin's hope that personal and community witness could redirect, even dismantle, the power of modernity seems naive, his

Revolution of the Heart
(Essays on the Catholic Worker)
Patrick G. Coy, Editor. Temple University Press, 1988; 394 pp. ISBN 0-86571-262-X
$16.95 ($19.45 postpaid) from New Society Publishers, 4527 Springfield Avenue, Philadelphia, PA 19143; 800/333-9093

vision of the new social order was not superficial. If anything, Maurin was willing to confront what contemporary society, at its own peril, labors so hard to forget: the need for meaningful work; the development of the interior life; the connection between purpose and the mysteries of life found on the land and in worship; the importance of community; the reality of death.

For the powerful and the passive Maurin had the ability to function as a dangerous memory, to shock the contemporary world into a reassessment of its values and

No Hiding Place

An oral history of the original, particular responses of the remarkable Glide Memorial Church to the scourges of addiction, abuse, and HIV/AIDS besetting the people of San Francisco's seamy Tenderloin district.

With Janice Mirikitani, his wife, Cecil Williams has worked tirelessly for decades to make Glide of maximum service to its extended family. He's a true pastor and an inspired preacher; much of the book sounds like a fine sermon. This good book demonstrates that resurrection can occur in the most battered lives. —SM

No Hiding Place
Cecil Williams & Rebecca Laird. 1993; 240 pp. ISBN 0-06-250988-8
$10.00 ($12.75 postpaid) from HarperCollins Publishers/Direct Mail, PO Box 588, Dunmore, PA 18512; 800/331-3761

directions, to question "business as usual" in the midst of holocaust.

•

The Catholic Worker possesses an added resource in its attempt to live nonviolently with the urban poor: community life. Workers generally live in the same house with guests, and a certain sharing of lives naturally results. In addition, many Worker houses are intentional communities. That is, efforts are made to attend to and nurture life *within* the Worker community itself. Although long-term commitment requirements are usually fluid (given the anarchistic roots of the movement), many communities have expectations of their members in terms of pooling economic resources, emotional sharing, and a common spiritual life. Living in community, with its emphasis on vulnerability in relationship, is understood to be itself an act of resistance to the status quo of violence and rugged individualism that so marks U.S. society. In a fundamental sense, Worker communities are thereby engaged in Maurin's ever-present challenge: to build a new society within the shell of the old.

"I've been talking on Sundays about 'toxic hustling.' Toxic hustling is trying to sell others the lies we have told ourselves. Toxic hustling is the opposite of living by the Spirit and the truth. Toxic hustling is pretending, denying, and conning.

"I realized this week that I've been hustling some of y'all by asking 'How are you doing?' when I see you around here. I've been pretending to listen to your answers. I've nodded and smiled, but my mind has been on other things. That's hustling. I want to tell the truth. I'm not all that good either. I'm still working on me. Always will be. I'm going to work to be honest when I meet you day by day. If I don't have time to talk, I'm going to say hello and go on my way. Y'all help me now. If you hear me ask you 'How are you?' and then I act faraway, you call me on it. Say, 'Cecil, are you listening to me?' I'm always calling you folks on your hustling; I need you to do the same for me. I'm recovering, too."

Green Cathedral

Megacities are here to stay. So is religion, Judeo-Christian style. So, perhaps, is Western Civ. Ecology and ecosystems, on the other hand, seem to be on the ropes, as do masses of human beings marginalized by the brutal economics of our time. What's a Mother Church to do? Spawn a green Dean.

St. John the Divine, the mammoth NYC edifice that recently celebrated its hundredth anniversary, is thriving under the leadership of the Very Reverend James Parks Morton. Dean Morton has broadened ecumenism to include ecological concern; among the cathedral's dozens of innovative programs are high-level scientific colloquia, recycling programs, and the Joint Appeal by Religion and Science for the Environment (see below).

St. John the Divine exemplifies the shining possibilities for religious institutions to serve life, in all its forms and in myriad ways. It's a dramatic example of religious courage, creativity, and inclusiveness that suggests possibilities for any church in any town. You don't need a cathedral to get started. —SM

A Directory of Environmental Activities and Resources in the North American Religious Community:
The Joint Appeal by Religion and Science for the Environment, 1992. $14.90 postpaid from Kurtztown Publishing, PO Box 346, Kurtztown, PA 19530; 800/523-8221.

Virtual Unreality

(heard on XELO, Juarez)

"Good evening. This is Brother Bishop, coming to you once again from our studios here at Bishop Tabernacle in Del Rio. I'd like to share with you an inspirational story.

"Following a tent meeting in Arthurville Sunday last, a couple of folks came up to the pulpit and asked for my help. Seems there was a sister from that congregation who had suddenly stopped attending services after the death of her son, and I was asked if I could find it in my heart to visit the woman. I said that of course I would go to see the sister. This is, after all, an outreach ministry.

"I followed directions down through a patch of woods, across a rickety wooden bridge, to a little house in a clearing. You could tell this had once been a fine, fine home, but the paint was beginning to peel, and the roof needed fixing. When I knocked, a little voice said 'Come in, Brother Bishop,' though I don't know how she knew my name.

"Once inside, I spied a small, frail woman, rocking slowly back and forth in an old rocker. Every once in a while a tear would dribble down her cheek.

"I said 'Sister, the folks from the church sent me down here to see if I can be of any consolation to you in your time of grief.'

"And here is what she replied: 'Brother Bishop' (and I still don't know how she knowed my name), 'Brother Bishop, I had a young son, a fine son, the light of my earthly life, and he was killed suddenly in a car wreck, before I had time to show him his way to Jesus Christ, and I just know, because of my negligence, that he is rotting away in Hell today.'

"Now, just what do you tell a woman like that? I told her the only thing I could. I said 'Sister, you just wait until you get to heaven, and the Lord will blot out your memory.'

—JD Smith

POWERFUL TOOLS CAN CUT BOTH WAYS. Information processing and communications technologies, many of which empower us in other ways, have rendered us vulnerable to commercial or state-sponsored snooping. Credit cards, bar codes, databases, pattern-recognition algorithms, voiceprints, satellite sensors, email, videocams, personal computers, embedded computers, and supercomputers have caught us all in an electronic net of our own convenience, unknowingly exposing our most intimate secrets when we buy groceries or subscribe to a magazine.

Privacy — the boundary between individual and community — is the site of the next conflict between the rights of citizens and the power of the state. Fortunately, there are ways for citizens to redefine their perimeter. Here they are. — HLR

PRIVACY IN THE MILLENNIUM

by Gary T. Marx

The head of a computer database company providing reports on potential tenants to landlords says, "The more you know about somebody else, the better off everybody is." That highly questionable observation ignores the strategic, aesthetic, diplomatic, and self-definitional aspects of personal information. Yet it is increasingly easy to know "more" about others without their knowledge or consent. Whole new industries have emerged, selling surveillance technology and personal information to marketers, employers, insurers, landlords, government, and individuals. The United States, unlike European countries, treats most personal information as if it were just another commodity to be bought and sold like toothpaste.

What new challenges to privacy will the next decade bring? Eight technologies for surveillance are now being developed or advocated:

• DNA screening and monitoring. Beyond identifying persons likely to develop serious illnesses or to have children at risk of illness, this may lead to claims to identify tendencies to alcoholism, homosexuality, and poor work habits . . .

• A national health insurance system could merge all individual medical data onto a single smart card. Beneficiaries would be required to have the card as a condition of enrollment. (Of course you won't have to enroll — so this can be defined as voluntary.)

• Vehicle and personal tracking systems could collect tolls or determine location.

• Spy satellites, capable of producing images of objects as small as a baseball, may become commercially available.

• Smart image-recognition systems could permit computer scanning of faces in large crowds to locate persons of interest.

• Wireless portable personal communication devices would lend themselves to interception, and to place and time tracking — for billing purposes.

• Smart homes in which data (electricity, communications, temperature) flows into and out of the home could be part of an integrated system available to monitors.

• Electronic highways could integrate commercial, entertainment, and communications transactions. Even if much of this is protected by an encryption system provided by government, one must ask whether the government can be trusted to invade privacy only with an appropriate court order. If the conclusion is no, then government-sponsored encryption, offered as a privacy protection device, becomes a threat to privacy.

Apart from incursions by new technologies, we are likely to see the continued blurring and crossing of the line between public and private places and between work, travel, and home. These have traditionally helped to maintain privacy. "Public" places such as shopping malls, theme parks, university campuses, large apartment and housing complexes, and industrial parks are increasingly legally defined as private places permitting whatever surveillance their owners deem appropriate. Fast-track employees who are given car phones, beepers, and home fax machines and computers by the company are always on the job — evenings, weekends, and vacations — and their communications and location are accessible to their employer.

Finally: if we think of privacy invasion as not only taking something from the individual, but covertly intruding upon the individual, our attention should also be focused on evolving technologies for subliminal communication through radio, television, and computer screens; aromatic engineering that attempts to affect behavior; dietary engineering, which attempts to affect behavior through food combinations and chemical additives; and microwave harassment and mind-control efforts.

"Privacy is the most comprehensive of all rights . . . the right to one's personality," wrote Louis Brandeis for the Harvard Law Review in the 1890s. But Judge Thomas Cooley, an obscure contemporary of Brandeis, probably put it better: "Privacy is the right to be let alone."

Unfortunately, our founding fathers neglected to mention privacy specifically in either the Constitution or the Bill of Rights. The Fourth Amendment does protect you from "unreasonable searches and seizures," but it doesn't prevent your boss from bugging the company bathroom, a federal employer from demanding a urine sample, or your nosy neighbor from monitoring your cordless phone conversations with a police scanner. In sum, your safeguards against government, corporate, and freelance snoopers are pretty slim, dependent on a handful of narrow federal and state laws and scattered court precedents. California and a few other states embed broad privacy protections right up front in their constitutions, but this is an exception, not the rule.

If you want to protect your credit rating, prevent your boss from rifling your email, or keep the government out of your bladder, peruse this compendium of vital privacy resources. There's something here for everyone, from the casual reader to the privacy buff. —Robert Luhn

Privacy for Sale

What happens to that "confidential" credit form you fill out? To that worker's-compensation claim? **Business Week** *reporter Jeffrey Rothfeder knows, and it isn't pretty. Rothfeder's book exposes the information underground — the marketplace where credit agencies, the IRS, private investigators, direct marketers, and other "data cowboys" legally and illegally acquire and sell sensitive personal information. To demonstrate the laxity of existing safeguards, the author easily nabs copies of both Dan Quayle's and Dan Rather's credit reports. This wry book is a cautionary tale of how private and government databases threaten personal privacy, the economy, and more.* —RL

Privacy for Sale
(How Computerization Has Made Everyone's Life an Open Secret)
Jeffrey Rothfeder. 1992; 224 pp.
ISBN 0-671-73492-X
$22 postpaid from Simon & Schuster/Order Dept., 200 Old Tappan Road, Old Tappan, NJ 07675; 800/223-2336

Your Right to Privacy

This omnibus pocket guide from the ACLU covers just about every privacy issue under the sun: what an employer may disclose from your personnel records, confidentiality of AIDS tests, who may ask for your Social Security number, how to correct government records, and how to deal with sneaky private investigators. "If there's enough money, you can get anything," boasts one anonymous PI in the book. "You have to find the weak link in the chain and go for it." The

book gives advice in an accessible question-and-answer format, and includes just enough history to give you the proper context. If you buy only one book on the subject, buy this one. — RL

Your Right to Privacy
(A Basic Guide to Legal Rights in an Information Society)
Evan Hendricks, Trudy Hayden & Jack D. Novik. 1990; 208 pp.
ISBN 0-8093-1632-3
$7.95 ($9.95 postpaid) from Southern Illinois University Press, PO Box 3697, Carbondale, IL 62902; 618/453-6619

Our Vanishing Privacy

Big Brother isn't a dictator on a huge screen, but a million grocery clerks with bar-code readers. Robert Ellis Smith, publisher of **Privacy Journal** *(p. 136), has written a short primer on the threats to privacy in the 1990s and means of defense available to citizens — the technical and legal aspects of drug testing, the abuse of Social Security numbers, genetic finger-printing, "Caller ID" telephone services, computerized data-collecting, and other new technologies that help people peek into our personal lives. Medical records, credit histories, even the records of grocery purchases, are fodder for those who would invade our privacy not to control us politically, but to sell us products: read the excerpt below and tell me you'll ever be completely comfortable with a bowl of oatmeal again.* —HLR

•

Have you heard about "target marketing"? Some call it "database marketing"; others

Don't Bug Me (The Latest High-Tech Spy Methods): M.L. Shannon. 1992, Paladin Press. A useful companion to Lee Lapin's works, this shows you how to protect yourself from electronic eavesdropping.

The Law of Privacy in a Nutshell: Robert Ellis Smith. $14.50 postpaid from Privacy Journal, PO Box 28577, Providence, RI 02908; 401/274-7861. Not for casual readers, but if you have an interest in the law and the historical underpinnings of privacy rights (from torts to "fair information" practices), this book is for you.

Protectors of Privilege (Red Squads & Police Repression in Urban America): Frank Donner. 1992, University of California Press. A thoroughly researched book on repressive police tactics over the last thirty years, with much coverage devoted to covert surveillance, and the illegal compilation and distribution of dossiers.

Cloak and Gavel (FBI Wiretaps, Bugs,

Informers, and the Supreme Court): Alexander Charns. 1992, University of Illinois Press. How Hoover's FBI bugged, harassed, and otherwise attempted to manipulate the Supreme Court during the fifties and sixties.

Confidential Information Sources (Public and Private): John Carroll. 1991, Butterworth Publishers. Private and public databases — who maintains what data on whom and what rules (if any) regulate how that information is disseminated. A slow read, but a valuable sourcebook.

The IRS and the Freedom of Information and Privacy Acts of 1974: Marcus Farbenblum. 1991, McFarland & Co. This readable guide details how the IRS withholds records and obscures its own procedures — and how you can make the IRS "tell you everything you have a right to know."

How to Achieve Personal and Financial Privacy In A Public Age: Mark Nestman. 1993, Low Profile Inc. (LPP Ltd.).

---

call it "targeting by taste." Whatever it's called, there is a startling change taking place in the way wholesalers and retailers try to get their products in the hands of consumers.

No longer are they content to advertise in mass media — spending millions of dollars for messages that may fall on deaf ears — and hope that customers will find their way to stores where thousands of items are displayed. Manufacturers and many retail outlets now want to target customers directly and lock them into consistent buying patterns.

The way to do this, of course, is to use precise lists for mail or telephone solicitation or to identify customers loyal to your brand and somehow manipulate them into buying your products over and over. The only way to accomplish this successfully is to know everything possible about your customers: their age, income, ethnicity, family size, credit cards, and buying habits.

Some target marketers, like Quaker Oats Co., want to know their customers' political and social views. In one massive direct-marketing campaign, Quaker Oats asked customers, including many children, their views on drug testing, school prayer, and gun control, on the theory that their responses indicate whether they are traditionalist or are open to new ideas. Kids and adults who ordered the Cap'n Crunch Dick Tracy Wrist Watch Radio through a Quaker Oats offer in cereal boxes were sent an intrusive questionnaire that asked about these three political issues, plus street address, income, what credit cards the family uses, the names, ages, and preferences of smokers in the household, and who has what diseases in the family. It also asked the wrist-watch radio users to agree or disagree strongly or moderately with the statement: "My dog is like my baby."

The company used the data to market other products directly to the family, based on its preferences. It then tracked the purchases so that it could reinforce patterns by marketing the identical products and allied products in the future. Customers will receive different levels of discounts depending on their family characteristics. Quaker Oats planned to "overlay" television, radio, and newspaper advertising and monitor the varying responses, thus completing the manipulation of the buyer.

Our Vanishing Privacy

(And What You Can Do to Protect Yours)
Robert Ellis Smith. 1993; 136 pp.
ISBN 1-55950-100-6
$12.95 ($16.95 postpaid) from Loompanics Unlimited, PO Box 1197, Port Townsend, WA 98368

Privacy: How to Get It, How to Enjoy It

A Mulligan stew of privacy advice, philosophy, resources, humor, with a little conspiracy paranoia thrown in for good measure. But as you read story after story — the "little Einstein" who hacked into twenty-one Canadian computer systems, banks that blithely (and illegally) share depositor information with just about anyone — you begin to see the author's point of view.

Privacy's pithy chapters identify key privacy abuses (from credit-card scams to the twenty-four federal agencies that gather intelligence on Americans), offer pointed remedies, explain obscure laws that can help you keep a low profile, and suggest further reading. Sometimes the advice is spot-on ("consider the use of mail-drop services") and sometimes downright weird ("you and your friends might try learning an obscure foreign language to promote privacy"). Either way, it's a fascinating, eclectic read.

*Eden Press offers half a dozen other privacy books, from **Personal and Business Privacy** to **100 Ways to Disappear and Live Free**. For the privacy anarchist within.— RL*

Privacy
(How to Get It, How to Enjoy It)
Bill Kaysing & Cathy Clark. 1977, 1991; 128 pp. $18.95 ($21.95 postpaid) from Eden Press, P.O. Box 8410, Fountain Valley, CA 92728; phone 800/338-8484, fax 714/556-0721

How to Get Anything on Anybody

Want to learn how the pros tap a phone, surreptitiously videotape someone, tail a subject, or crack a "secure" computer? This ultimate hardware catalog/how-to-manual for professional snoops even notes where you can buy neat-o spy stuff. It's also a boon for the less nosy, says author Lapin, because "the first time someone kicks you right in the privacy act" you'll be prepared. "Law-enforcement agencies are only the tip of the electronic-eavesdropping iceberg. Most bugs are planted by people to spy on their spouses or to gain an advantage in business."
— RL

How to Get Anything on Anybody
(The Encyclopedia of Personal Surveillance)
Lee Lapin. Paladin Press, 1991; Vol. I: $30 ($33 postpaid); Vol. II: $35 ($38 postpaid). Eden Press, P.O. Box 8410, Fountain Valley, CA 92728; 800/338-8484 (fax 714/556-0721)

Undercover

Gary Marx knows about undercover police at first hand. When the MIT sociology professor was a student at UC Berkeley, his student organization promoting racial equality was nearly destroyed when its treasurer — a police agent — embezzled the group's funds. But Marx's book looks beyond political policing and tackles a tougher question: In the face of rising crime and political corruption, when is undercover police surveillance warranted? Marx examines this and many other uncomfortable questions in this extensively researched, surprisingly readable and lively book for academics and policy analysts, and arrives at a rather startling conclusion: "In starting this book, I viewed undercover tactics as an unnecessary evil. But in the course of research I have concluded, however reluctantly, that in the United States they are a necessary evil." Specialists, and some general-interest readers, will find Marx's work absorbing. —RL

•

In a 1791 book, *Panopticon or the Inspection House,* Jeremy Bentham offered a plan for the perfect prison. There was to be constant inspection of both prisoners and keepers; cells were to be constructed with bars (rather than opaque doors) around a central inspection tower. His ideas helped give rise to the maximum-security prison, which today is characterized by perimeter security, thick walls with guard towers, spotlights, and a high degree of electronic surveillance. Many of the kinds of controls found in prison are diffusing into the society at large. It is important to ask if recent developments in technology, culture, and social organization are not pushing us toward becoming a maximum-security society.

The maximum-security society is composed of five interrelated subsocieties:

1. a dossier society, in which computerized records play a major role

2. an actuarial or predictive society, in which decisions are increasingly made on the basis of predictions about our future behavior as a result of our membership in aggregate categories

3. an engineered society in which our choices are increasingly limited and determined by the physical and social environment

4. a transparent or porous society, in which the boundaries that traditionally protected privacy are weakened

5. a self-monitored society in which auto-surveillance plays a prominent role.

In such a society, the line between the public and private is obliterated; we are under constant observation, everything goes on a permanent record, and much of what we say, do, and even feel may be known and recorded by others we do not know. Data from widely separated geographical areas, organizations, and time periods can be merged and analyzed easily. Control is embedded and preventive; informers, dossiers, and classification are prominent. The society becomes, in Erving Goffman's words, a "total institution," and there is no longer a backstage.

Undercover

(Police Surveillance in America)
Gary T. Marx. University of California Press, 1988; 283 pp.
ISBN 0-520-06969-2
$13 ($16 postpaid) from California/Princeton Fulfillment Services, 1445 Lower Ferry Road, Ewing, NJ 08618; 800/777-4726

More Privacy Tools

by Robert Luhn

REPORTS AND PAMPHLETS

If an Agent Knocks

This bargain pamphlet is the ultimate how-to privacy guide. A simple question-and-answer format shows what to do if a federal agent tries to question you, the scoop on agencies that gather political intelligence, how the feds infiltrate political organizations, and much more.

In English and Spanish..

How to Use Freedom of Information Statutes

This informative guide shows you how to use the Freedom of Information Act (FOIA) and California Public Records Act to gain access to files maintained on you by the government. You learn what's open and what's exempt, and how to make a request (sample letters are included); relevant addresses and copies of the two acts in question are included.

Your Right to Privacy

This special Congressional Quarterly report is an excellent introduction to personal and workplace privacy, with a summary of federal privacy laws, a table detailing privacy laws by state, and tips on how to protect yourself.

Privacy Law in the United States: Failing to Make the Grade

This 32-page report by the US Privacy Council and Computer Professionals for Social Responsibility (CPSR) spotlights huge gaps in American privacy laws and lax enforcement by federal agencies, and argues persuasively for the creation of a national data-protection board. Somewhat technical, but a good source.

Privacy International

Like Amnesty International, Privacy International is a global organization dedicated to fostering human rights — in this case, privacy rights. PI's first task is to sound the alarm over privacy abuses around the world and to push for the adoption of practices that "guard against malicious or dangerous use of technology." PI raises awareness about privacy assaults and repressive surveillance practices, coordinates privacy advocates internationally and, like Amnesty International, monitors and reports abuses country by country. Members also receive the International Privacy Bulletin, a quarterly newsletter with privacy reports from around the world, legislative updates, and news on related civil liberties issues.

NEWSLETTERS AND JOURNALS

Privacy Journal

This indispensable eight-page monthly digest covers key privacy stories, legislation, abuses, and trends in the US and abroad, with a particular focus on computerized information and telecommunications. Publisher and gadfly Robert Ellis Smith has been putting out PJ for nearly twenty years, frequently testifies before Congress on privacy legislation, and is a constant thorn in the side of credit bureaus. This accessible guide will inspire you to get mad. PJ also publishes useful reference books and studies.

Privacy Times

This biweekly ten-page newsletter is more

HOW TO USE YOUR SOCIAL SECURITY NUMBER

by Simson Garfinkel

BUSINESSES IN THIS COUNTRY are increasingly using Social Security numbers for identification — or proof of identity. Banks, credit-card companies, insurance firms, and health care organizations will frequently divulge reams of "confidential" information over the telephone to any voice that speaks a name and Social Security number. Someone who knows your Social Security number can effectively invade your privacy or make your life very difficult.

To make matters worse, information that is wrong or misleading is often repeated, reinforced and sold from vendor to vendor. Even if the original mistake is tracked down and corrected, it can be nearly impossible to find all the copies — and to persuade the new "owners" of the information to change their records.

What You Can Do

For starters, you don't have to give your Social Security number to everybody who asks you for it. Although certain government agencies are empowered by law to demand your SSN, they are required to state the specific law that grants them that power when they ask you for your number. Private businesses may ask you for your SSN but they cannot legally compel you to provide the number (although, as the Social Security Administration says, private firms are not required to do business with **you,** either).

Although an employer needs to know your Social Security number in order to pay you, you should be suspicious of employers who ask your SSN before you have started working for them. (It should be noted, however, that credit reporting companies are increasingly marketing their services to employers for pre-employment screening.)

Here are a few simple steps that most people can take to protect their privacy and limit their risk of fraud and harassment:

1. Keep your Social Security number off your driver's license if possible. Several states give you no choice about this. In the other states and Puerto Rico, however, the SSN is either optional or does not appear — although some of these other states will happily use your SSN as your driver's license number if you provide it.

2. Request a statement of your earnings from the Social Security Administration every three years. Misfiled or misreported earnings can be corrected up to three years, three months and fifteen days after a mistake is made, saving you lots of trouble at retirement. Furthermore, an earnings statement tells you if someone else is reporting earnings under your SSN.

To get your statement, you need to fill out a "Request For Earnings and Benefit Estimate Statement" card which can be ordered by telephone from the Social Security Administration's toll-free number, 800-772-1213.

3. If you are rejected for credit, an apartment, a job or insurance because of a credit report, get a copy of that report. If there is invalid information on it, correct it.

If you have been denied credit within the last thirty days, the credit reporting agency is obligated under the Fair Credit Reporting Act (FCRA) to provide you with a copy of your credit report for free. The report will include the names of all businesses that have asked for your report within the past two years and the reason they gave for looking at your file.

Two of the largest consumer reporting agencies are TRW (which acquired Chilton) and Equifax (formerly Credit Bureau, Inc., or CBI). Their addresses are:

> *TRW:* PO Box 5450, Orange, CA 92667, 714/991-5100.

> *Equifax:* 5500 Peachtree Dunwoody, Suite 600, Atlanta, GA 30358; 404/252-1134.

If you disagree with anything in your report, the credit bureau is required to reinvestigate the facts in dispute. If there is still disagreement after the bureau reinvestigates, you have the right to insert a statement in your report with your version of the story.

4. Be cagey with your Social Security number. While some people, like banks and employers, have a legitimate reason to know your SSN, many other businesses that ask for it haven't. Agencies that collect blood often ask for SSNs from donors, although blood is almost always accepted even if the SSN is not provided. Since blood in this country is screened for HIV and other diseases, the possibility exists that the SSNs of pints that test positive (either rightly or due to false positives) may turn up in databases, either legitimate or clandestine ones.

"Many police departments sponsor burglary-prevention programs by which citizens may label their belongings. Virtually all police departments advise citizens to use their Social Security numbers as identifiers, even though house burglars are precisely the persons one would not want to have one's SSN," writes Robert Smith in the *Privacy Journal*'s Report on the Collection and Use of Social Security Numbers.

5. Request that companies not use your SSN for account numbers. When asked for your SSN, leave the request blank, if possible. When my health-insurance company assigned me my SSN as my account number, I asked them to change it, and they did. Every organization that uses a different number to keep track of you makes it that much harder for somebody else to use those numbers to gain access to your files or otherwise complicate your life.

news-oriented and more timely than **Privacy Journal***, with in-depth coverage of such topics as why the Bush administration tried to shut down the FOIA office, and summaries of recent court rulings affecting privacy.*

AUDIO AND VIDEO

The Privacy Project

This engaging thirteen-part series, originally produced for Western Public Radio, is now available on cassette. The half-hour episodes combine humor, hard-nosed advice, and interviews with privacy experts. An excellent introduction to privacy issues. The company also sells audio tapes of recent Computers, Freedom & Privacy conferences.

The Complete Video Library of Computers, Freedom & Privacy

This video collection from various CFP conferences features legal, computer, privacy, and ethics experts debating key privacy issues. See Laurence Tribe on "The Constitution in Cyberspace," the Secret Service on

law enforcement problems, Gary Marx on computer surveillance, the FBI on phone tapping, and more.

If an Agent Knocks
$1 postpaid. Center for Constitutional Rights, 666 Broadway, New York, NY 10012; 212/614-6464.

How to Use Freedom of Information Statutes
$12 postpaid. Freedom of Information Project, 102 Banks Street, San Francisco, CA 94110.

Your Right to Privacy
January 20, 1989 Editorial Research Report. $7 postpaid. Congressional Quarterly Inc., 1414 22nd Street NW, Washington, DC 20037; 202/822-1439.

Privacy Law in the United States: Failing to Make the Grade
US Privacy Council and Computer Professionals for Social Responsibility. $10 postpaid. Computer Professionals for Social Responsibility, PO Box 717, Palo Alto, CA 94301; 415/322-3778.

Privacy International
$50/year (membership). CPSR, 666 Pennsylvania Avenue SE, Washington, DC 20003.

Privacy Journal
$109/year (12 issues) (call for individual discount rates). PO Box 28577, Providence, RI 02908; 401/274-7861.

Privacy Times
$250 ($225 prepaid)/year (24 issues). Privacy Times, PO Box 21501, Washington, DC 20009; 202/829-3660.

The Privacy Project
13-part Western Public Radio Series. $11/tape; $75 for all 13. Pacifica Radio Archive, 3729 Cahuenga Blvd., North Hollywood, CA 91604; 800/735-0230.

The Complete Video Library of Computers, Freedom & Privacy
$55/tape; $385-$480 for complete set. Freedom & Privacy Video Project, PO Box 912, Topanga, CA 90290; 800/235-4922.

CITIZEN ENCRYPTION
by Steven Levy

"When privacy is outlawed," says software author Phil Zimmermann, "only outlaws will have privacy." He is addressing the issue which has become the flash point of technoculture: citizen encryption. "Encryption" is still esoteric technology to most people, but it might turn out to be the militia rifle of the privacy wars. As a result of a brilliant breakthrough by non-spookish hackers and mathematicians, cryptography has suddenly emerged as a people's technology, liberated from the top-secret vaults of diplomacy and military tactics. And not a moment too soon — the information age has rendered our communications vulnerable to eavesdroppers (official and otherwise), and allowed megabytes of our personal data to accumulate in databases we don't control. But if we encrypt, snoopers can't get at the stuff. Crypto is the silver bullet to protect our conversations and safeguard the details of our lives; it's the means by which we can take back our privacy from Big Brother and his countless cousins.

Today, encryption can be used to protect the privacy of voice communications and electronic mail. The digital trails so many of us leave when we use credit cards, ATM cards, and smart cards are another area of vulnerability: most people don't realize that paying for bar-scanned groceries with a credit card creates a database linking information about how many bottles of liquor, which magazines, what kind of food you purchase to other information such as your name, address, Social Security number, credit status. This information is valuable to marketers and to political groups collecting information about friends and enemies. Citizen encryption would make "anonymous digital cash" possible — giving us the convenience of electronic transactions without the side effects of malevolent snooping.

The catch? Uncle Sam doesn't like it. Spy institutions and law enforcement agencies have nightmares about "crypto anarchy," when access to strong encryption ensures that **they can't snoop our communications.** So the government has been fighting to suppress strong crypto. The first shot in this conflict came in the spring of 1994, when the Clinton Administration began urging a compromise known as the "Clipper Chip" — a scheme that supposedly provides a degree of protection but includes a "back door" that provides the government the keys to unscramble the messages and conversations. Two main groups oppose Clipper: manufacturers unable to offer customers state-of-the-art protection and privacy advocates who see the scheme as an attempt to limit the ability of citizens to speak to each other without the specter of a third party's unwelcome ear. And a third group of crypto civil disobedients — cypherpunks — have devoted themselves to spreading strong protection tools throughout the infosphere — so that even an outright government ban on strong crypto would be too little, too late.

The outcome of the crypto wars will determine whether civil rights will survive cyberspace. While crypto technology is arcane, its uses could influence every part of our lives.

EXPLANATION OF PUBLIC KEY CRYPTO

The breakthrough that enabled crypto to spread to the masses is "public key" cryptography, invented by Whitfield Diffie and Martin Hellman in the mid-1970s. Its main implementation, devised by three MIT cryptographers, is a patented system called RSA.

Conventional crypto systems begin with a "plaintext" message that the sender scrambles by use of a "key" into an unintelligible "ciphertext" and then passes it on. The recipient translates this jumble back into plaintext by use of the same key. The problem is that it's difficult to get the key from the user to the sender, and protect it thereafter.

Public key cryptography solves the problem by using a matched set of two keys — a "private" key and a "public" key. The private key is known only to the holder, but the public key can be widely distributed without compromising security. Having someone's public key gives you no advantage in trying to crack their codes — you need both to unscramble a message.

If I want to send a private message to Howard Rheingold, I first get his public key (this may be widely available) and use it to scramble the message into ciphertext. From that point on, the only person in the world who can unscramble that message is the one holding the matching private key — Rheingold. When Howard sends a message back to me, he'll use **my** public key to scramble the message, knowing that I am the only one who will read it. This allows people to communicate privately with many others, even those they have never met.

Applied Cryptography

Budding cypherpunks and others simply interested in the nuts and bolts of crypto should check out this book that has become the bible of code hackers. Though directed to those who know their way around an algorithm, the book also gives a more casual user an eye-popping initiation into the gestalt of industrial-strength crypto.

Bruce Schneier doesn't hesitate to inject pithy opinions and political content into the mix, either; straight away he states: "Encryption is too important to be left to the government." Then he provides the most comprehensive citizen's view yet on how to do it yourself.

Applied Cryptography includes source code for some popular encryption schemes, including some regarded too powerful to export. In other words, if you type into your computer some of the codes Schneier includes here, your hard disk immediately becomes, in the government's view, a form of munitions — and, in theory at least, you can get jailed for carting your laptop across a border! What better lesson that crypto in the hands of the people is powerful stuff — and impossible to control. —SL

Applied Cryptography
Bruce Schneier. 1994; 618 pp.
ISBN 0-471-59756-2
$44.95 postpaid. John Wiley & Sons Inc.,
1 Wiley Drive, Somerset, NJ 08873;
800/USWILEY

●

Dictionary Attacks and Salt

Even a file of passwords encrypted with a one-way function is vulnerable. In his spare time, Mallet compiles a list of the 100,000 most common passwords. He operates on all 100,000 of them with the one-way function and stores the results. If each password has about eight bytes, the resulting file will be no more than 800K; it will fit on a single floppy disk. Now, Mallet steals the encrypted password file. He compares the encrypted password with his file of encrypted possible passwords and sees what matches.

This is a **dictionary attack,** and it's surprisingly successful. **Salt** is a way to make it more difficult.

Salt is a random string that is concatenated with the password before being operated on by the one-way function. Then, both the salt value and the result of the one-way function are stored in the database. If the number of possible salt values is large enough, this practically eliminates a dictionary attack against commonly used passwords.

A lot of salt is needed. Most UNIX systems use only twelve bits of salt. Even with that, Daniel Klein developed a password-guessing program that cracks 21% of the passwords on a given system in about a week [482]. David Feldmeier and Philip Karn compiled a list of about 732,000 common passwords concatenated with each of 4096 possible salt values. They estimate that 30% of passwords on a given system can be broken with this list [346].

Salt isn't a panacea; increasing the number of salt bits won't solve everything. Salt only protects against general dictionary attacks on a password file, not against a concerted attack on a single password. It obscures people who have the same password on multiple machines, but doesn't make poorly chosen passwords any better.

Crypto Software for the People

The crypto revolution has hit freeware. The most popular program is Phil Zimmermann's PGP — short for "pretty good privacy." As its name implies, PGP offers a strong measure of security for communications sent over the Net, as well as a wonderful hands-on education on the workings of public-key software. This public-key program is the software of choice of cypherpunks worldwide, much to the chagrin of the US government; the feds have registered their alarm at its ability to pass beyond our borders. PGP is, in a sense, outlaw-ware: RSA Data Security, Inc., owner of the public-key copyrights, charges that PGP infringes upon its intellectual property. Despite this, it is possibly the most widely used public-key crypto system in the world.

Unlike PGP, Mark Riorden's public-key program RIPEM is officially licensed by RSA. As long as you don't use it for commerical purposes, you can use it for free. Both PGP and RIPEM are available in Mac and DOS versions; however, RIPEM is not as fully implemented as PGP, though Riorden continues to update it.

If you want public-key software for commercial purposes, you should go to the source — RSA Data Security. If you simply want to protect the information on your hard disk, you don't need public-key crypto: dozens of programs use faster systems based on other algorithms. Bruce Schneier recommends the Kent-Marsh programs for both the Mac and DOS. —SL

RSA Data Security Inc.: 10 Dolphin Drive, Redwood City, CA 94065

PGP (Phillip Zimmermann): The download sites change; consult the usenet newsgroup *alt.security.pgp* and ask which sites currently provide software.

RIPEM (Marc Riorden) via ftp from *ripem.msu.edu.*

OTHER GREAT RESOURCES

The Codebreakers: David Kahn. 1967, Macmillan. The seminal work on the history of (pre-public-key) crypto, as thrilling as a spy novel and as challenging as a cryptogram.

Ender's Game: Orson Scott Card. 1985, Tor Books. This stunning sci-fi novel is a cypherpunk favorite because of its imaginative yet realistic use of crypto scenarios.

See also: Electronic Democracy, p.288 and "Citizen Organizations on the Electronic Frontier," p.291

idle and not-so-idle conversations can lead to interesting developments: new intellectual eras, revolutions, countercultures that become the mainstream, formerly abstruse subjects clarified by sustained group attention and discussion. We're talking, listening animals, and when we engage our minds before we put our mouths in gear, what we say among ourselves is usually worthwhile, to say nothing of being hugely entertaining, live and in-person.

Small groups can be great at supporting their members while questioning and supplanting remote distantly done authority. As the late great Margaret Mead put it: "Never doubt that a small group of thoughtful, committed citizens can change the world. Indeed, it's the only thing that ever has." —Stephanie Mills

Study Circles Resource Center

The Study Circle is a semiformal method for group discussion of some pressing social concern; racism, sexual harassment, civil rights for gays and lesbians are among the topics of this outfit's concise discussion guides.

A study circle requires an organizer, a leader, and participants willing to commit three or more evenings to civil conversation and deliberation about the topic at hand.

The Study Circles Resource Center provides how-to literature on organizing and leading study circles. SCRC's quarterly newsletter reports on this rapidly burgeoning practice of adult collaborative learning. It's a citizenship gym with open membership, a way to tone up those rights-and-responsibilities muscles. —SM

Study Circles Resource Center:
Information from PO Box 2031, Pomfret, CT 06258; 203/928-2616, Fax: 203/928-3713

People are sometimes baffled by the necessity to promote such a simple idea as discussion. After all, people talk all the time don't they? Well, yes and no. Though the study circle is a simple concept, it is also refreshingly different from other kinds of talking. We often observe or hear from those who have experienced the study circle "Aha!" that happens when people realize that they are talking about the same old issues in a distinctly different way. At the end of one study circle session, a new participant offered, "This must be what it feels like to be a citizen."

Comparison of dialogue and debate

Dialogue is collaborative: two or more sides work together toward common understanding.

Debate is oppositional: two sides oppose each other and attempt to prove each other wrong.

Dialogue enlarges and possibly changes a participant's point of view.
Debate affirms a participant's own point of view.

Dialogue reveals assumptions for reevaluation.
Debate defends assumptions as truth.
—Focus on Study Circles

Revolution from Within

Gloria Steinem, perhaps our most exemplary servant-leader, turned her midlife crisis into philosopher's gold. An honest, compassionate engagement with one's own inner life and history, she found, is the indispensable complement to fair and effective work with groups of individuals seeking justice and positive social change. Self-esteem, counsels Steinem, is the essential element in personal and societal liberation.

The small group proves to be a critical tool. In her afterword, Steinem gives a simple format for organizing an updated version of the feminist consciousness-raising group, a small, regular gathering of persons interested in self exploration, mutual support, and action to improve the larger situation. It is nonviolent, humane revolutionary practice moving in the only authentic direction — from the examined self through conscious community to the suffering society as a whole. —SM

Perhaps our first job is to envision a full-circle, extended-family-size group and know we have a *right* to it. Otherwise, we will go right on turning to big organizations, narrow interest groups, and nuclear family units that can't take the pressure of all our hopes and needs. Look at it this way: if each cell within our bodies is a whole and indivisible version of those bodies, and each of us is a whole and indivisible cell of the body politic, then each of us has an organic need to be part of a group in which we can be our whole and indivisible selves.

So, as a result of what I've learned from readers of this book, here is a suggestion for a goal by the year 2000: *A national honeycomb of diverse, small, personal/political groups that are committed to each member's welfare through both inner and outer change, self-realization and social justice.* It doesn't matter whether we call them testifying or soul sessions as in the civil rights movement; consciousness-raising or rap groups as in early feminism; covens, quilting bees, or women's circles as in women's history; or revolutionary cells, men's groups, councils of grandmothers, or "speaking bitter-

Revolution from Within
Gloria Steinem. 1992; 421 pp.
ISBN 0-316-81247-1
$11.95 ($14.95 postpaid) from Little, Brown and Co./Order Dept., 200 West Street, Waltham, MA 02154; 800/343-

ness" groups as in various movements and cultures. Perhaps they will have an entirely new name... I think of them just as "revolutionary groups," for a revolution is also a full circle. The important thing is that they are free, diverse, no bigger than an extended family — and everywhere.

This isn't as large an order as it sounds. If two white male alcoholics could start a national network of meetings that are free, leaderless, and accessible, so can we.

Neighborhood Salon Association

A 1991 Utne Reader issue described salons and their variants and offered to connect readers with others expressing similar interests in nearby zip codes. Utne got more than eight thousand responses, grouped them into five hundred geographical clusters, and voilá, the modern salon movement was born. At last count, more than three hundred Utne-inspired salons, study circles and councils remain active, connected loosely through the Neighborhood Salon Association. For $12, NSA members get a list of potential salonites in their area, placement in an Internet email salon, and **The Salon-Keeper's Companion,** *a guide to starting and conducting a salon. You can certainly start your salon without the help of NSA or anyone else, but here's the place to turn for ideas and contacts with those who have gone before.* —Michael K. Stone

Breaking bread together is a time-honored social lubricant, but food can also get in the way of focused group conversation. Whether you gather for breakfast, lunch or dinner, it's usually best to start the discussion first and break later for eating. Most salon-keepers we've talked to feel that the best conversation happens without alcohol.
—The Salon-Keeper's Companion

Neighborhood Salon Association:
Lifetime membership $12.
c/o Utne Reader, 1624 Harmon Pl., Minneapolis, MN 55403; 612/338-5040.
Email salons@utnereader.com or utnereader@igc.apc.org

The Practice of Council

Council is a method for group discussion and communion around issues and problems — including vibes and behavior — of common concern. The emphasis is on devout listening and spontaneous speaking. The experience, they say, is like a group meditation, a rapt attention to the truth voiced by each participant in turn. There is ceremonial form to this, and — sometimes — transcendent content. Shadows, too, naturally, but the hope is that the detachment learned through opening to the group will render those projections less adhesive.

Listening from the heart is prerequisite for speaking from the heart, and these two activities may form the fundamental discipline that will guide us through the nineties. Millennium, ho!
—SM

When exploring strongly held underlying values, alterations of the usual form of Council are often helpful. One simple variant is to place the talking stick in the center of the circle (say after completing one round in the usual fashion), where it can be retrieved by anyone wanting to speak again

The Practice of Council
Jack Zimmerman & Virginia Coyle. 1993; 22 pp. $3 postpaid from Ojai Foundation, PO Box 1620, Ojai, CA 93023; 805/646-8343

and then returned to the center. In this way the attentive listening and spirit of Council are maintained while those particularly impassioned can deepen their interaction without the necessity of hearing from the entire circle.

Another form well-suited to the extended exploration of a complex or demanding issue, particularly when the circle is large, is the "fishbowl," or "web." In this process, which also lends itself admirably to decision making, a few pillows or chairs (four is usually suitable) are placed in the center of the circle along with the talking stick. As the Council starts, anyone can fill the empty seats and make their statement. Then that person passes the stick to the next person in the center and returns to the large circle, leaving a space for others stirred to speak. People are allowed to return to the fishbowl a second or even a third time, but are asked to self-regulate if there remain others who as yet haven't contributed.

Getting to Yes

This book on negotiation comes as a great personal relief to me and may well to you. I've always avoided situations that involved bargaining because of all the dishonesty that seemed to be required. When I was forced, by life, to bargain anyway, I usually did poorly, which reinforced my reluctance. All that is now cured by this modest 163 pages of exceptional insight and clarity.

The point is to negotiate on principle, not pressure — on mutual search for mutually discernible objectivity, patiently and firmly putting aside every other gambit. The book is a landmark, already a bible for international negotiators but just as useful for deciding which movie to see tonight or which school to send the family scion to.

Getting to Yes is a model in every way of ideal how-to writing. —SB

•

A good case can be made for changing Woodrow Wilson's appealing slogan "Open covenants openly arrived at" to "Open covenants privately arrived at." No matter how many people are involved in a negotiation, important decisions are typically made when no more than two people are in the room.

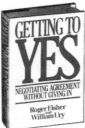

Getting to Yes
Roger Fisher, William Ury & Bruce Patton.
Penguin Books, 1981; 208 pp.
ISBN 0-14-015735-2 $11 ($13 postpaid)
from Penguin USA/Consumer Sales, 120
Woodbine Street, Bergenfield, NJ 07621;
800/253-6476

•

A variation on the procedure of "one cuts, the other chooses" is for the parties to negotiate what they think is a fair arrangement before they go on to decide their respective roles in it. In a divorce negotiation, for example, before deciding which parent will get custody of the children, the parents might agree on the visiting rights of the other parent. This gives both an incentive to agree on visitation rights each will think fair.

The Listening Project

A wise, simple, brilliant method for defusing community conflict and engendering creative unity. The basic idea is not to confront popular or institutionalized prejudice with righteous protest and a media blitz, but to go into divided communities and question people about the real content of their opinions, and to listen — attentively and respectfully — to the concerns that emerge. Then you find the premises for organizing the whole community (not just a faction) to make it better.

Originated by Herb Walters of the Rural Southern Voice for Peace (which makes its home at Celo, an intentional community in North Carolina), the Listening Project has brought a measure of peace and progress to venues as widely scattered as Harlan County, the Honduran-Nicaraguan border, and the Pacific island nation of Palau.

David Grant, writing in Exquisite Corpse, calls it "Dharma Combat":

"Right now we're listening to death penalty proponents. Asking if they'd like to pull the switch. I'm listening best I can to my own soul (soul, bro'…daddy's brand new funky chicken bag). Doing my best to listen, to be there, compassionately attending, as my lovely barbarians, without and within, revive and revive. Listening projects without end."

A remarkably compelling idea. —SM

The Listening Project
Information from Rural Southern Voice for
Peace, 1898 Hannah Branch Road,
Burnsville, NC 28714; 704/675-5933;
Fax: 704/675-9335

Neighbor Law

Life's a lot easier when you're on friendly terms with your neighbors, but sometimes conflicts happen. They may be over the dog next door barking away at 6 A.M., or the branches jutting over the back fence into your clothesline, or just something irritating like the broken down Corvair rotting on the front lawn across the street.

We want to live in a comfortable community, and we have certain legal rights that guarantee that comfort. Attorney Cora Jordan explains, in plain English, the laws regarding the resolution of neighbor disputes. She covers the most common neighborly conflicts — those over noise, trees, fences and boundaries — and outlines options and strategies, from negotiating in a friendly way to taking your case to court. Best of all, the book encourages communication and good neighborly relations whenever possible.
—Mike Ashenfelder

•

If your neighbor thinks your complaints are unreasonable and does nothing to remedy the situation, you have a choice: go to court or suggest mediation. Because most legal mechanisms will cost time, money and any future good relationship, trying mediation first is a worthwhile effort to keep the dispute just between you and your neighbor, and to arrive at your own solution.

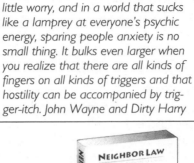

Neighbor Law
(Fences, Trees, Boundaries & Noise)
Cora Jordan. 1991; 320 pp.
ISBN 0-87337-158-5 $14.95 ($18.95 postpaid) from Nolo Press, 950 Parker Street, Berkeley, CA 94710; 800/992-6656 or 510/549-1976

In mediation, you work out your own agreement with the help of a trained, neutral third party (mediator). One reason mediation between neighbors is so successful is because sometimes both neighbors simply need to have their say. Often, both have complaints about other issues. Once they are aired, a compromise involving everything in dispute is possible.

Community Boards of San Francisco

Community Boards has developed techniques to help neighbors tackle the knottiest local disputes. With the aid of community conciliation panels, disputants stay out of court and build foundations for reestablishing neighborliness after the conflict has subsided. Community Boards' Conciliation Handbook, available in English and Spanish, gives you the fundamentals for starting a program of your own. The organization also offers excellent training sessions across the country, produces elementary- and secondary-school conflict-resolution curricula, and

publishes Dispute Resolution Access, a twice-yearly roundup of the best new research on dispute resolution at all levels, interpersonal to international.

Dispute Resolution Access: $15/year for individuals, $25/year for organizations; 2 issues.

Conciliation Handbook: 1993; 47 pp.
Order # MI, $18 ($21 postpaid)

Both from The Community Board Program, 1540 Market St., Suite 490, San Francisco, CA 94102.

Getting Past No

Getting Past No
(Negotiating Your Way from
Confrontation to Cooperation)
William Ury. Bantam Books, 1991; 189 pp.
ISBN 0-553-37131-2 $9.95 ($12.45 post-paid) from Bantam, Doubleday, Dell/
Fulfillment Dept., 2451 S. Wolf Road,

I wish I'd cracked this book before I faxed Howard Rheingold my non-negotiable-sounding demands for help getting my work done. At the very least, it would have saved us both a little worry, and in a world that sucks like a lamprey at everyone's psychic energy, sparing people anxiety is no small thing. It bulks even larger when you realize that there are all kinds of fingers on all kinds of triggers and that hostility can be accompanied by trigger-itch. John Wayne and Dirty Harry

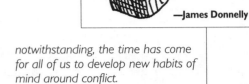
—James Donnelly

notwithstanding, the time has come for all of us to develop new habits of mind around conflict.

William Ury offers pithy, practical, systematic advice for developing co-operation, for engaging in joint problem solving rather than bitter competition. Anyone can begin, anywhere, like Howard did in his response to my fax. Unfazed, he sought to discern and serve our respective interests. So I stayed on the project. Ever so much better than going away mad and minus an agreement that served us both. This sort of agreement is what Getting Past No can teach you to achieve. It's work, as Ury acknowledges, and a novel satisfaction. Different from getting your gun off. —Stephanie Mills

•

The single most important skill in negotiation is the ability to put yourself in the other side's shoes.

•

The key word in agreement is "yes." "Yes" is a magic word, a powerful tool for disarming the other side. Look for occasions when you can say yes to them without making a concession. "Yes, you have a point there." "Yes, I agree with you." Say yes as often as possible…

Each yes you elicit from the other side further reduces tension. As you accumulate agreement, even if only on what they are saying, you create an atmosphere in which they are more likely to say yes to a substantive proposal.

•

Your counterpart can easily answer no to questions prefaced by "is," "isn't," "can," or "can't." So ask a question that cannot be answered by no. In other words, make it open-ended. Preface your question with "how," "why," "why not," "what," or "who." Your counterpart cannot easily answer no to questions such as "What's the purpose of this policy?" "Who has the authority to grant an exception?" and "How would you advise me to proceed?"

— *Communities Magazine*

ROUP LIVING — reversing the disintegration of households to their least divisible units (single parents, solitary elders) — could be the most elegant solution to a whole gang of problems: the affordable-housing shortage, the dispersal of kin groups, toxic fallout from the implosions of nuclear families, fear of growing old and dying alone, boredom, trying to make ends meet all by yourself, ghettoizing children needing real-time settings for mutual aid and personal growth.

Lest you think that communes went the way of all sixties flesh, consider this: the number of intentional communities in the US is growing. While part of that growth may stem from necessity, it's being fostered with hard-won intelligence and undiminished conviction by the newsletters and federations reviewed here. While some of this is novel, it's mostly just the contemporary version of the way our species lived until about three thousand years ago. So while the capacity for intimate relationship with a clan-sized group may have gotten flabby in the last few millennia, the occasions for strengthening it are proliferating now. —Stephanie Mills

The Federation of Egalitarian Communities

Membership is restricted to secular communities that hold land, labor, income, and other resources in common and practice democratic decision-making. But you don't have to be a member to avail yourself of FEC's "Systems and Structures Packet": 1,000 pages of by-laws, membership agreements, visitor and pet policies, property codes, economic and labor agreements, to use as models for your own. —MKS

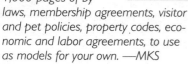

The Federation of Egalitarian Communities: Route 3, Box 6B2, Tecumseh, MO 65760; 417/679-4682.

Communities Magazine

*This quarterly updates the **Directory of Intentional Communities** and offers pertinent news and a bulletin board for communities seeking members and vice versa. Articles discuss community experiences (good and bad) and mutual help. The idealistic tone is tempered by the writers' willingness to speak frankly about failed efforts.*

Communities also addresses an audience beyond the communities movement. By now, that movement represents a series of long-term experiments in leadership styles, decisionmaking, and conflict resolution. Those experiments' results are tools any of us can apply to our own organizations, families, and workplaces. —MKS

●
Collectivization of life in general gradually eroded people's personal motivation to do anything creative, unusual, risky, beautiful. In the early days it was not that way so much — many people did explore different kinds of artistic, musical and recreational activities, and there was a spirit of fun and excitement to the scene. But, over time, this faded. Though other things no doubt affected people's morale as well, I believe that our communistic approach to life effectively immobilized people. It was an interesting coincidence that, at about the same time that some of us at Kerista were becoming aware of, and uncomfortable about, this problem, the Soviet empire was crumbling and the world was getting a very clear understanding of the incompatibility of communism and personal motivation — and the social gains that derive from individual creativity.

Communities Magazine
Diana Leafe Christian, Managing Editor. $18/year (4 issues); sample issue $5. 1118 Round Butte Drive, Fort Collins, CO 80524; 303/224-9080

Directory of Intentional Communities

The communities movement's diversity is as impressive as its growth: communities just hatched and communities still thriving after thirty years; egalitarian, authoritarian, secular, spiritual, urban and rural communities; communes with a sixties ethos and CoHousing associations of suit-and-tie professionals.

The Fellowship for Intentional Community offers information exchanges, conferences, publications, and other opportunities to support and learn from one another.

*In the fellowship's **Directory**, each of 500 North American communities speaks for itself, offering glimpses into its style and atmosphere along with basic data. The book also includes access information, comparative maps and charts of major features, 200+ resources, and articles addressing important considerations.*

This book is the very best resource if you're seeking a community, planning a "communities tour," or looking for inspiration from a lively and diverse movement. —Michael K. Stone

●
The EcoVillage at Ithaca; CRESP, Anabel Taylor Hall; Cornell University; Ithaca, NY 14853; (607)255-8276.

Located in the beautiful rolling hills of New York's Finger Lakes Region, EcoVillage at Ithaca is actively seeking new resident members.
Our goal is to build a replicable model of a cooperative, environmentally sensitive

Directory of Intentional Communities
1992; 328 pp. ISBN 0-9602714-2-7. New edition due fall, 1994, $19 postpaid, $21 outside US, from F.I.C. Directory, Twin Oaks, Rt. 4, Box 169, Louisa, VA 23963

community clustered in six neighborhoods of 25-30 attached houses each. The design provides for a pedestrian village surrounded by expansive gardens, orchards, woods, wetlands, ponds, and sustainable agricultural areas. Our plan incorporates energy-efficient, healthy housing with passive solar design features. Planning is underway for a biological waste treatment system that will also supplement village energy needs.

EcoVillage has purchased 176 acres of land located 1-1/2 miles from downtown Ithaca, and 3-1/2 miles from Cornell University and Ithaca College, with access to local services. Using the Cohousing model pioneered in Denmark, twenty households have been meeting for a year to plan the first neighborhood. Each neighborhood will feature cooperative dining in a common house which may include a day care facility, recreation area, workshop, guest quarters, and laundry room. The first resident group plans to move in 1995. As a living laboratory and teaching center, EcoVillage will showcase systems that can be replicated nationally and internationally. We hope that you will join us. SASE requested. 7/27/93

Growing Community

This newsletter, for people thinking about starting new communities, is a model of concise, pertinent advice. Not much rhapsodizing about the joys of community living, just practical information and indispensable resources and coverage of issues you had better anticipate before launching your brave new community (the need for adequate lead time; legal, land use, and zoning questions; policies for adding or dismissing members; finances; work assignments). The wheels needed to keep a community moving have been repeatedly invented. You'll spend less time redesigning those wheels if you take these lessons to heart. —MKS

●
The *most* important decisions facing any community are about who should join it. Who the members are affects every single aspect of community life. (A rigorous admission policy is highly correlated to community stability, according to two studies.)

Diggers and Dreamers: Information from Federation of Egalitarian Communities, c/o Redfield Community, Winslow, Buckinghamshire MK18 3IZ, UK. This British version of *The Directory of Intentional Communities* is uneven, but useful for comparing British and North American communities.

Experienced communitarians strongly advise that unless there is a natural affinity with a prospective member, all the group processing in the world will not create harmony. The consciousness of potential members is considerably more important than, say, their highly desirable gardening or mechanical skill. Even one person who is regularly "off" can disrupt the group and wear on everyone's patience.

Communities should try to attract members with a strong sense of self-worth, advised Virginia Satir, the late family therapist. She warned that members with low self-esteem will constantly need the approval and support of other members, draining off energy that is needed to build the community. As one Findhorn member says, "If a person looks like they're going to take more energy than they can give, you can't afford it."

Growing Community
Diana Leafe Christian, Editor. $21/year (4 issues); sample issue $3. 1118 Round Butte Drive, Fort Collins, CO 80524; 303/490-1550

REDEEMABLE FOR MEALS UP TO A VALUE OF TEN DOLLARS

10 VALID AFTER $10

HELP MOVE THE DELI

THE DELI ✦ MAIN STREET ✦ GREAT BARRINGTON

1 2 3 4 5 6 7 8 9 10

Tom Greco's *New Money for Healthy Communities* — comprehensive, scholarly, set in a broad Gaian context — is the basic resource on community-issued money. —Stephanie Mills

Trading Without Money

"Oh, barter," you say. Well, not really. Bartering is too limiting; that's why money was invented. But the problem with (official) money is that most of us can't get enough of it to buy all the things we need.

However, communities can create money substitutes for themselves — exchange media that make it possible to mobilize local resources that, for lack of money, may now be idle. It's been done, in various ways, around the world. (During the Great Depression, American communities issued "scrip.")

Among the most successful current approaches are the international credit system LETS (Local Exchange Trading System), a local currency called Ithaca HOURS, and a credit system for the exchange of services that uses Time Dollars. Australia has more than 160 active LETS systems, New Zealand has about 70, Great Britain 60, and Canada 15, with more popping up all the time. While the US has only a few LETS systems, more than 85 Time Dollar programs operate in 26 states.

LETS members agree to trade goods and services among themselves, but instead of paying cash, they keep a record of accounts. Ithaca HOURS, paper notes that

A Deli Dollar $10 Note. —New Money for Healthy Communities

circulate around town, can be used to buy restaurant meals, records, movie tickets, among numerous goods and services. Time Dollars represent bankable credits for hours worked in services like child care, helping elders, or tutoring students. The provider can later claim services when he or she needs help.

Even in the best of times, most communities have underutilized skills, talents, and resources. Local exchange systems can provide the missing element for economic resurgence.
—Thomas H. Greco, Jr.

Local Exchange Trading System (LETS): Landsman Community Services, Ltd., 1660 Embleton Crescent, Courtenay, BC V9N 6N8, Canada; 604/338-0213, fax 604/338-7242.

Ithaca Money Newsletter: Paul Glover, Editor. $25 (Money Kit and newsletter). Box 6578, Ithaca, NY 14851; 607/273-8025.

Time Dollar Network: PO Box 42160, Washington, DC 20015; 202/868-5200.

New Money for Healthy Communities: Thomas H. Greco, Jr. 1994, Thomas H. Greco, Jr., publisher, 602/577-2187.

Building Sustainable Communities

Architects tend to see sustainability in terms of amenity and plan, well integrated with nature. Economists and sociologists are more concerned with the economic basis for community.

*Of course, both must be heard. This book is based on seminars held by the E. F. Schumacher Society (see **Small is Beautiful**, p. 26). Some interesting principles are debated, most having to do with self-government — true Democracy. You know in your heart it's right. But you also know that The Establishment is unlikely to assist. This book is a reminder of what it is we really need to do.* —J. Baldwin

●

As working members develop the capacity to self-organize and self-administer, the managerial role becomes more one of general overseeing and planning and of following guidelines laid down by the board and by the membership as a whole. In a number of cases, however, cooperatives have started out with an unrealistic sense of their capabilities and without sufficient understanding of the need for clear job definitions and responsibilities. The tendency is often to rebel against expertise and hierarchy and to deny the validity of both. But hierarchy is legitimate so long as final authority rests not with the top figure in the hierarchy but with the whole. And expertise is necessary and does not prevent democratic management so long as it is not mystified and information needed to make basic policy decisions is disseminated throughout the organization.

Building Sustainable Communities
(Tools and Concepts for Self-Reliant Economic Change) Ward Morehouse, Editor. Bootstrap Press, 1989; 196 pp. ISBN 0-942850-11-4 $13.50 ($17 postpaid) from Intermediate Technology Development Group, 777 United Nations Plaza, Suite 3C, New York, NY 10017; 212/953-6920

Whole Co-op Catalog

Co-ops range in size from Sunkist to the Oryana Natural Foods Cooperative, on whose board I now serve. (What is a nice, innumerate liberal artiste like moi doing staring at a monthly financial report?) Co-ops are member-owned enterprises created to meet certain needs that the invisible hand of the marketplace has failed to consider. Such as natural foods, or recreational equipment, or affordable apartment housing.

*With access to hundreds of different publications, videos, slide shows, and networks, the **Whole Co-op Catalog** addresses every facet of cooperatives — accounting, failures, successes, start-ups, bulk foods, meeting conduct. Nice inventory from specialty to basic. Self-help, next to none of it intrapsychic.* —SM

●

General/Management/Operations

B-01 Food Co-op Handbook
The Co-op Handbook Collective, Cooperative Publishing, 1983 (revised). A study of food co-op history, organization, and operations. *The handbook* includes sections on decision making, legal issues, growth, wholesaling, retailing, and the politics of food. 326 pages. 1983. $7.95

B-03 The Cooperative Audit
Intra Community Co-op (now NorthFarm). A self-evaluation of food co-op business performance and cooperative organization. A tool for retail co-ops that provides information for effective management. A must for boards and managers, to improve their co-op's organizational clarity and efficiency.

Plus Organizational Profiles. Test the results of the activities and performance of retail food co-ops with this objective and easy-to-understand evaluation. 57 pages. 1982. $6.50

The Whole Co-op Catalog

TWIN PINES

Whole Co-op Catalog
Free from Twin Pines Cooperative Foundation, 1442 A Walnut Street #415, Berkeley, CA 94709; 510/538-0454

Cooperative/Credit Union Dictionary and Reference

A useful volume for anyone interested in the history, practice, and terms of economic cooperation. Entries on co-ops of every size, purpose, and scale, plus capsule biographies of generally unsung movement pioneers. There's vitality, ingenuity, and effectiveness, to say nothing of years of committee meetings and a hell of a lot of scut work in functioning cooperatives. They won't make the five o'clock news, but they are making a difference. —SM

●

Co-Operative Movement — Definition: "The Co-operative Movement is an education in democracy, in thrift, and in the general conduct of business. It makes for altruism as against selfishness; it gives people self-respect when they find that they are, after all, able to do something in the way of managing their own social and economic affairs, when the truth comes home to them that business ability is not something to be found in only a few human beings, but that there is a certain amount of it in everybody. From this experience they acquire confidence in themselves, have respect for themselves, develop an awareness of their duties and obligations to themselves and to other members of the human race." (E. Forrest Scharf, Saskatchewan).

Cooperative/Credit Union Dictionary and Reference
Jack McLanahan & Connie McLanahan. 1990; 410 pp. ISBN 0-9625894-1-1 $14.50 ($17 postpaid) from Cooperative Alumni Assn. Inc., 250 Rainbow Lane, Richmond, KY 40475; 606/623-0695

We Build the Road As We Travel

The Mondragon cooperatives in Spain's Basque country offer a mind-boggling example of how far worker ownership and worker control can go: 21,000 workers; sales of $1.6 billion; a bank with assets of $2.9 billion; Ulgor, Spain's largest appliance manufacturer; Lagun-Aro, a social security and insurance organization; Eroski, a multi-hundred-million-dollar retail co-op; Hezibide Elkartea, a collection of schools from elementary to university level, totaling 45,000 students; and Ikerlan, an advanced technology research center. It's communitarian capitalism that works big-time. —HLR

We Build the Road As We Travel
(Mondragon, A Cooperative Social System) Roy Morrison. 1991; 276 pp. ISBN 0-86571-173-9 $16.95 ($19.45 postpaid) from New Society Publishers, 4527 Springfield Avenue, Philadelphia, PA 19143; 800/333-9093

Community and the Politics of Place

This slim book provides a lively tour through the thought of Jefferson and the Federalists, the nineteenth-century populists, the closing of the Western frontier, and the insights of Wendell Berry, Hannah Arendt, and others.

The author reconsiders some basic premises. He redefines the concept of civic virtue as the assumption of responsibility for particular places. He considers shared inhabitation as both the motive and the goal of the polis. His single most effective notion may be that cities once more become regional hubs: "A politics of inhabitation may well be one in which cities and their hinterlands, together, are understood as a basic political unit."
—Freeman House

•

This sharing of responsibility between the human and the natural extends also to the question of the scope or scale of the political entity. Over what domain is political will to be exercised? In our time, we have come to assume that answering this question is strictly a human responsibility. So humans draw lines on the land, marking off nations, states, and counties. But as the challenge of inhabitation makes itself felt in the political sphere, it becomes clear that this drawing of lines should not, perhaps, be

Community and the Politics of Place
Daniel Kemmis. 1990; 150 pp.
ISBN 0-8061-2477-6
$9.95 ($12.45 postpaid) from University of Oklahoma Press/Order Dept., PO Box 787, Norman, OK 73070-0787; 800/627-7377

left entirely to human choice. Too often, the lines cut across natural units of inhabitation, leaving inhabitants cut off from each other in terms of their capacity to act together politically — to will a common world.

•

It is important to keep in mind that the concept of "place" enters into this situation in a literal as well as a metaphorical way. The pulp mill and the local environmental group were brought to the point of collaboration because both of them had a stake in what happened to a particular place. They had different stakes, and had they been left to themselves, they would have done different things with the place, but in the end it was one and the same place. Neither party wanted to leave the place, and both recognized that what Lester

From *Small Town America* (The Missouri Photo Workshops 1949 – 1991), by Cliff and Vi Edom and Verna Mae Edom Smith. 1993, Fulcrum Publishing.

Thurow says of territoriality in such a case is true: neither side could gain a decisive or lasting victory over the other. . . . They were [therefore] thrown back on collaboration (on citizenship). But what holds people together long enough to discover their power as citizens is their common inhabiting of a single place. No matter how diverse and complex the patterns of live-lihood may be that arise within the river system, no matter how many the perspectives from which people view the basin, no matter how diversely they value it, it is, finally, one and the same river for everyone. There are not many rivers, one for each of us, but only this one river, and if we all want to stay here, in some kind of relation to the river, then we have to learn, somehow, to live together.

Small Town

*A mixture of fairly technical analysis with naked emotional concern, **Small Town** has been around for years. It is a kind of professional journal for those who care about preserving small towns.*
—Fred Fuller

Small Town
Kenneth Munsell, Editor.
$30/year (6 issues) from Small Town Institute, PO Box 517, Ellensburg, WA 98926; 509/925-1830

•

Throughout a transportation corridor's evolution, two forces of landscape change are held in tension. The first is a growing complexity caused by the accumulation of remnants from old landscapes that are not thoroughly erased by succeeding landscapes. These remnants of past lifestyles cling to the roadside, ensuring that each contemporary cultural landscape will be an amalgam of past landscapes.

The second force of change is an increasing simplicity caused by the shaping agents of succeeding landscapes which have become more centrally controlled. The railroad was the first agent of national landscape uniformity, bringing the metropolis and industrial America to the doorstep of small towns throughout the nation. Control over local economies, and thus over one aspect of local identity, was transferred from thousands of small towns to distant corporate headquarters. Likewise, the automobile especially accelerated corporate America's homogenizing effects, creating highway landscapes that are nationally recognizable and placeless in their sameness.

The Small Town Planning Handbook

I wish I'd had this book when I was helping write a new comprehensive (not master) plan for our town. It's from the mainstream American Planning Association, but it rights many past wrongs, principally that most planners try to impose urban-planning dogma on small towns. I like the fact that it starts out by listing five good reasons not to plan. It also tells how local citizens can write a plan by themselves.

This book can help you translate your revolutionary ideas into language the bureaucracy can understand.
—Fred Fuller

•

Planning is the mark of good community sense and intelligent thought. It makes sense for a community to plan when changes are occurring and if the citizens wish to be a part of those changes. It makes even better sense to plan when changes are pending. Planning enables people to influence changes in the appearance, economy, and social life of their community. By planning, the community will begin to realize that the economy, the housing base, the unique environment, and the historic characteristics are closely related to those annoying or pressing problems such as traffic congestion, water pressure, flooding, and the lack of adequate employment. . . .

The Small Town Planning Handbook
Thomas L. Daniels & John W. Keller. 1988; 170 pp. ISBN 0-918286-53-0
$28.95 ($33.95 postpaid) from Planners Press Bookstore, 1313 E. 60th Street, Chicago, IL 60637; 312/955-9100

Planning will assist the community in thinking regionally. The more a community becomes involved in the planning process, the more quickly it will realize that local problems, as well as local assets, are not unique. Before long, those who participate in the planning process will come to think of the region as the community. Many problems are larger and more complex than originally anticipated, and often these problems are shared with the county and the community next door. Indeed, it may become apparent that the solution to some problems requires cooperative efforts among communities.

Involving Citizens in Community Decision Making

This manual is about how to incorporate citizens into planning and decision-making processes from the git-go. It's published by the Program for Community Problem Solving, a clearinghouse created "to help communities develop a civic culture that nurtures and supports community problem solving." PCPS offers presentations, training, coaching, and occasional facilitation and mediation, as well as additional publications. —Stephanie Mills

•

Here are some of the things professional mediators look for in assessing the potential for resolving an issue:

• The groups or interests involved in the conflict have reached the point where they recognize that the costs of continuing the conflict exceed the benefits of keeping the conflict going.

• All parties to the conflict acknowledge the legitimacy of all the other groups or interests.

• The parties are well-enough organized that their representatives can make commitments on behalf of the group.

• Everybody believes that there is some chance, no matter how slim, for resolution.

• Everybody understands that if they engage in this process, it's "for real"; if they're ever going to deal, this is the time to do it.

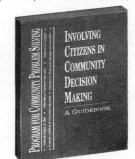

Involving Citizens in Community Decision Making
James L. Creighton. 1992; 227 pp.
$40 postpaid from Program for Community Problem Solving, 915 15th Street #660 NW, Washington, DC 20005; 202/783-2961

> **B**IOREGIONS are more tangible and articulate than states or nation states. People are beginning to understand their bioregions, their watersheds, as ecological communities. These can reward our efforts to heal them with sustenance. Such "reinhabitation" is bound to be different in every different place. *E pluribus pluribus* is the basic idea. —Stephanie Mills

Watershed Governance

"Policymakers and opinion leaders generally agree that the traditional way of doing business — managing by political boundaries — must give way to managing by hydrologic boundaries," says a recent issue of the **Grand Traverse Bay Watershed Initiative News**. Township governments of five counties are linked with citizens' groups, businesses, and local agencies in an informal partnership to protect the bay's water quality. The Watershed Initiative has launched a **Stewardship Quarterly**, and, with the help of a regional land conservancy, published an inhabitant's guide to the bay's largest tributary. It's all very cautious and respectful of private property, but a quantum leap in seeing land and water as seamless and watersheds as meaningful units of perception.

Flowing from a glacier on Mt. Rainier to Puget Sound, the Nisqually River has a council that includes representatives from cities in the watershed, from the Nisqually Indian Tribe, from state and federal agencies, and from a public utility.

The council *"has erected signs wherever state and county roads cross the Nisqually basin boundaries. These signs help build an awareness of the extent of the watershed."* There's a basin watch similar in concept to Neighborhood Watch, education and publication projects, a land trust, and water quality monitoring. An exemplary program, but not unique — more like the shape of things to come. —SM

Stewardship Quarterly: Rebecca Martin, Editor. Information from Fen's Rim Publications, Inc., 102 Dexter Street, Elk Rapids, MI 49629; 616/264-6800

Nisqually River Council: PO Box 1076, Yelm, WA 98597; 206/459-6780

Grand Traverse Bay Watershed Iniative News: C/o Northwest Michigan Council of Governments, PO Box 506, Traverse City, MI 49685

OTHER GREAT RESOURCES

Clean Water in Your Watershed: Information from Terrene Institute as reviewed for Watershed Home (page 79).

E. F. Schumacher Society: Box 76, R.D. 3, Great Barrington, MA 02130; 413/528-1737.

The Northern Forest Forum

This serious, superlative tabloid addresses a constellation of questions bearing on the fate of New England's forests, and thus the future of the region's ecological and human communities. Editor Jamie Sayen covers local symposia and councils that are generating intelligence on the status of biodiversity and land preservation strategies. He also seeks dialog with folks such as commercial forest owners. This periodical's a must for residents of this bioregion. —SM

The Northern Forest Forum
Jamie Sayen, Editor.
$12/year (6 issues) from Earth Island Institute, PO Box 6, Lancaster, NH 03584

●

Public support for wolf recovery is growing across the United States. Public opinion surveys have shown strong approval for recovery efforts in Minnesota, Wisconsin, Michigan, Yellowstone National Park, and elsewhere. The Michigan survey showed that "deer hunters revealed the greatest sympathy, concern, ecological appreciation and outdoor recreational interest in the wolf of any group examined." Even the Arizona Cattle Grower's Association has lent its support to the recovery of the Mexican wolf.

Based on positive attitudes elsewhere, Northern Forest residents would also be likely to approve of a wolf recovery study. But they have never been asked what they think.

Does the Northern Forest have adequate wolf habitat? According to the *Recovery Plan for the Eastern Timber Wolf*, the most important habitat requirements for wolf survival are: "(1) large tracts of wild land with low human densities and minimal accessibility by humans, and (2) the availability of adequate wild prey, largely ungulates (deer and moose) and beaver." Although more study is needed, the potential recovery sites in the Northern Forest that were identified by the USFWS — northern Maine and New Hampshire and the Adirondacks — appear to meet these requirements.

Forests of the East

So you thought only the Pacific Slope was being clearcut? Think on this: America was all old-growth forest except for the parts that were prairie or desert. People in the Midwest are rallying to save their woods — the climax ecosystem that's the living heart of bioregional culture to come.

Heartwood is a regional forest activist group working to protect the native forests of the Central Hardwood Region, with co-ordinators in Arkansas, Kentucky, Illinois, Indiana, Missouri, Ohio, Tennessee, and West Virginia. They publish a lively and appealing newsletter and, when necessary, stalk the halls of Congress.

The Midwest Sierra Club publishes **The Forest Networker,** *carrying news of the regional forests of the Midwest, digested from various sources and bridging some of the territory between Heartwood and North Woods.*

The Superior Wilderness Action Network is coordinating efforts to produce a "scientifically guided proposal for a biodiversity reserve system across the Upper Great Lakes Bioregion." Their first "Occasional Paper" is a masterpiece of concise expository prose.

Northwoods Wilderness Recovery focuses on northeast Wisconsin and Michigan's Upper Peninsula, and is concurrently developing a wilderness reserve proposal and taking action to defend the territories that would make up such a reserve. —SM

Heartwood: membership $35/year. PO Box 402, Paoli, IN 47454-0402

The Forest Networker:
214 N. Henry Street, Madison, WI 53703

Superior Wilderness Action Network:
c/o Biology Dept., University of Wisconsin/ Oshkosh, Oshkosh, WI 54901

Northwoods Wilderness Recovery:
PO Box 107, Houghton, MI 49931

Boundaries of Home

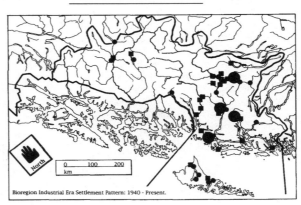

Bioregion Industrial Era Settlement Pattern: 1940 - Present.

The editor's introduction ascribes too much evil intent to those among us who are not bioregionalists. Straw men rise left and right. Anger swirls like the mists, paranoia flows like blood.

But at this book's heart you will find a dozen or so fine storytellers. Among the adventures: enthusiastic, front-line amateurs encounter Geographic Information Systems (also discussed on p. 14). GIS' unavoidable limitations are revealed. In another tale, Stuart Allan (of Raven Maps) discovers four principles of map design that have applications far beyond the scope he modestly claims. The editor himself leads us step by step in a discovery of his bioregion in coastal British Columbia. We are laden heavily with access and annotation.

The tone of the contributors' chapters — 80 percent of the book — is uniformly realistic, positive, and useful. —Don Ryan

●

By sifting through maps that meticulously divide the world into pieces, and then layering this abstraction back into descriptions of whole ecosystems, you will spare yourself great energy and expense. Imagine the horror of government agencies who are inundated with people who want access to the knowledge their taxes have provided.

Boundaries of Home
Doug Aberley, Editor. 1993; 138 pp. ISBN 0-86571-272-7
$9.95 ($12.45 postpaid) from New Society Publishers, 4527 Springfield Avenue, Philadelphia, PA 19143; 800/333-9093

And imagine if map-borne information generated for exploitation of land and life is redirected to an equally proficient quest for social justice and integration of human cultures with place!

●

We have no word in English to express *Heimat* in German, or *bro* or *cynefin* in Welsh, meaning familiar territory. But Common Ground is offering the word "parish" as a substitute. A parish, often based on ancient ecclesiastical delineations, is the smallest political and administrative unit recognized by central government in the United Kingdom. But Common Ground is using the word in a looser sense to mean the locality to which people feel a sense of belonging and which belongs to them. People can draw their own lines, or use old ecclesiastical or newer civil parish or community council boundaries.

ALL-GIRL PRAIRIE!

Dakota (A Spiritual Geography): Kathleen Norris. Ticknor & Fields, 1993.

Where the Buffalo Roam: Anne Matthews. Grove Weidenfeld, 1992.

Kill the Cowboy: Sharman Apt Russell. Addison-Wesley, 1993.

A Thousand Acres: Jane Smiley. Random House, 1991.

Upriver Downriver

Bioregionalism is about (among other things) manifesting contemporary cultures-of-place, encompassing everything from literature to livelihood, all informed with the lore of the land. Reinhabitation is all in the details. Upriver Downriver is an irregular, arresting, enlightening and, in its way, classy periodical. Lots of fine original work here, in every genre that can go on a piece of paper, from well-known and due-to-be-known outdoor literati of the Shasta bioregion. —SM

Upriver Downriver
Freeman House & Seth Zuckerman, Editors. $10 (4 issues). PO Box 103, Petrolia, CA 95558

•
Poetry Contest
Defenders of Poetry (Jack Spicer Troupe/ Wolverine Patrol) is offering a $100 award for an outstanding original poem on tan oak (Lithocarpus densiflorus), a.k.a. tanoak, tanbark oak. In addition to the usual poetic virtues of lucidity and grace, the poem should display particular insight into the biology/ecology/mythology of tan oak.

•
This is the sixteenth issue of *Upriver Downriver*. We think of it as an extended correspondence among people who live in northern california, a place we regard as a distinct biologic/cultural region. We consider the region a community of life, and therefore feel it is important to resist the further destruction of its natural systems and to begin repairing the damage already done. Our primary concern as a publication is to provide reliable information and useful ideas about life in this region, and to do so with a seriousness refreshed by a sense of humor. May our hearts prove bigger than our mouths.

Heartland Journal

Since 1979, Heartland Journal has tracked human rights, civil rights, women's rights, Indian rights, urban ecology, environmental justice, alternative health care, local and national electoral politics, Central America, perestroika, the Gulf War, bioregionalism, etc. This tabloid also serves book, film, and movie reviews, recipes, and articles on sport, bodymind awareness, fitness and health for the compleat activist.

The handsome design both evokes and provokes the emerging spirituality of sustainability and justice.
—Beatrice Briggs

Heartland
Michael James & Kathleen Hogan, Editors. $15/year (6 issues; free in the upper Midwest) from New Heartland Cafe, Inc./Subscriptions, 7000 N. Glenwood, Chicago, IL 60626; 312/465-8005

•
How do we get from A to Z? How do we find, or create, Atlantis, Camelot or Shangrila? Certainly not by osmosis and not by good thoughts alone. We will help determine the future by conscious and principled acts and actions, individually and together. A real life concert, minute by minute, hour by hour, day by day, year by year for a long time. We must nurture a long range vision, with ongoing development of plans that unfold a bit at a time, for a long time.

Northern Lights

*This graphically sophisticated newsprint magazine celebrates the life, art, and places of the Northern Rockies. It handsomely occupies a niche between the political/environmental news from this region found in **High Country News** and those slick, puffball regional magazines that hype lifestyle and real estate. The mix here is essays, art, and fiction, and though published by a nonprofit institute dedicated to reducing regional conflicts and uniting "the political right and left behind commonly held public values," it is not afraid to tackle controversy. **Northern Lights** elegantly gives lie to the notion that in America, culture is a bicoastal phenomenon. —Richard Nilsen*

The New Catalyst

This tabloid out of BC has shifted its attention somewhat, from reinhabitory alternatives to defending the bioregion from transnational outfits looking to mine its ecosystems. Recent issues carried excellent advice on how to defend the defenders from SLAPP (Strategic Lawsuits Against Public Participation) suits and some solid investigative journalism on the PR scam called Sustainable Development. —SM

•
• Don't tangle with a transnational on its chosen grounds. Your strength is democracy; their strength is wealth. Both can impact political decision-making.

• Keep decision-making public and open. Resist intimidation by refusing to be intimidated; speak out and defend democracy.

• Your most valuable resource is the time devoted by ordinary citizens. Your opponent can't buy off a volunteer.

• Choose a group of representatives, not just one person. Find strength in diversity. Have a team attend every meeting and interview. Not only will you have more than one speaker, you will have more than one listener.

• Professionals prefer open houses, rather than public meetings. There, in a controlled setting, they can focus on individuals for one-on-one pressure with no records kept of offers or commitments.

The New Catalyst
Judith Plant, Editor. $5 (to cover postage; 4 issues) from Catalyst Education Society, PO Box 189, Gabriola Island, BC Canada V0R 1XO; 604/247-9737 (in Canada: 800/567-6772)

• Maintain control. Be leery of a "free lunch" and experts who "volunteer" to help. Develop your own range of trusted advisors who have no self-interest in prolonging the relationship.

• Keep to the highroad. The opposition will try to engage you in petty scraps where only you and your credibility can lose. If you consider a tactic only to pay back the other side, it's probably the wrong thing to do.

• Corporations rely on whatever money can buy, including public relations consultants, lawyers, and access to the mainstream media. Community cohesion is a powerful ally, and frequent target. Be aware that tactics may include inciting conflict within the community, personal threats, exhausting processes, and strategic lawsuits.

Rain

This skinny but always meaty mag has been around for almost as long as **WER***. It got its start as an alternative-energy information source, then segued into more community-oriented interests. Over the years,* **Rain** *has flourished, faded, and flourished once again; these days, it is one of the best sources for community-building concepts and tools. I learn something essential in every issue. —J. Baldwin*

Rain
Greg Bryant & Danielle Janes, Editors. $20/year (4 issues). PO Box 30097, Eugene, OR 97403-1097

Northern Lights
Membership $25/year (includes 4 issues). PO Box 8084, Missoula, Montana 59807-8084; 406/721-7415

•
On the day my grandmother died, the black and shining wet frog with golden eyes leapt against the wall, hitting it with a force that broke its spine. The grief for my grandmother was still too large for weeping, so I held the frog in my palm and cried for it.

With fascination, I had watched the amphibious development of the frog, rescued from science-worshiping people. It seemed to reflect my own human growing, the way an egg divides, the pushing out of legs, how my own gill slit in the womb before birth vanished back into my still-wet skin. Like the frog, my grandmother and I lived between the elements, born to two worlds, Indian and white. And that white world was one that had come down, for Indian people, like a wall we were thrown against, a wall that turned our lives inside out, broke the spine of our societies.

Planet Drum Foundation

*Since its start in 1974, Planet Drum has been a major influence in developing interest and action in bioregionalism and "reinhabitation." They are "now working to foster exchange among bioregional groups and projects — the growing number of people exploring cultural, environmental, and economic forms appropriate to the places where you live." You get the (increasingly international) news in their often provocative review, **Raise the Stakes**, sharply edited by the not-always-polite Peter Berg. It occasionally features a valuable updated directory of bioregional organizations. Other Planet Drum publications include "bundles" of essays, posters, poems, and other materials celebrating individual bioregions, and a small selection of important books. This outfit is one to watch — their insights have often been years ahead of the rest of us. —JB*

Planet Drum Foundation

Membership $15/year (includes two issues of *Raise the Stakes*, one bonus publication, 25 percent discount on all books, access to workshop facilities). PO Box 31251, San Francisco, CA 94131, Shasta Bioregion, USA

HOME!

*When people ask "What is bioregionalism all about?", this is the book I press into their hands. **Home!** contains essays by some of the movement's most articulate exponents, sensibly arranged in five sections and followed by an annotated bibliography. Tucked among the essays are additional pithy quotations, illuminating excerpts, poetry, and artwork. This anthology captures the intellectual and aesthetic legacy of the first decade or so of contemporary bioregionalism and provides the seed energy for the ongoing unfolding of the theory and practice of reinhabiting the North American continent. Welcome home.*
—Beatrice Briggs

Home!

Van Andruss, Christopher Plant, Judith Plant & Eleanor Wright, Editors. 1990; 181 pp. ISBN 0-86571-188-7 $14.95 ($17.45 postpaid) from New Society Publishers, 4527 Springfield Avenue, Philadelphia, PA 19143; 800/333-9093

●
The bioregionalist faith as it is fleshed out in these pages is that given a little push by clear ideas, local organizing, and that which can be learned from digging in the dirt, humans can and will come together to work for the restoration of life — home life — and the regeneration of its wild diversity.

It is life's earthly beauty and its daily consummations, not the cheap glamor of political or technical dominance, that draws bioregionalists on.

●
A second element of bioregionalism is anarchy. I hesitate using that fine word because it's been so distorted by reactionary shitheads to scare people that its connotative associations have become bloody chaos and fiends amok, rather than political decentralization, self-determination, and commitment to social equity. Anarchy doesn't mean out of control; it means out of *their* control. Anarchy is based upon a sense of interdependent self-reliance, the conviction that we as a community, or a tight, small-scale federation of communities, can mind our own business, and can make decisions regarding our individual and communal lives and gladly accept the responsibilities and consequences of those decisions. Further, by consolidating decision making at a local, face-to-face level without having to constantly push information through insane bureaucratic hierarchies, we can act more quickly in relation to natural systems and, since we live there, hopefully with more knowledge and care.

—Northern Lights

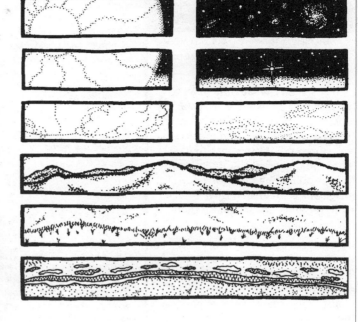

●
Such a treaty, or some such spiritual bond, between ourselves and the natural world, is needed, a bonding based on the principle of mutual enhancement. The river and its valley are neither our enemy to be conquered, nor our servant to be controlled, nor our lover to be seduced. The river is a pervasive presence beyond all these. It is the ultimate psychic as well as the physical context out of which we emerge into being and by which we are nourished, guided, healed, and fulfilled. As the gulls soaring above the river in its estuary region, as the blossoms along its banks, the fish within its waters, so, too, the river is a celebration of existence, of life lived in intimate association with the sky, the winds from every direction, the sunlight. The river is the binding presence throughout the valley community. We do not live primarily in Poughkeepsie or Peekskill, Newburgh or Yonkers. We live primarily along the river or in the valley. We are river people and valley people. That fact determines more than anything else the way we live, the foods we eat, the clothes we wear, how we travel. It also provides the content and context for celebrating life in its most sublime meaning.

Turtle Island Office • Turtle Island Bioregional Gatherings

Turtle Island Office serves as the primary information clearinghouse for the North American bioregional movement. TIO coordinates twelve bioregional resource centers, housed by well-established bioregional groups who share libraries of different bioregional organizing approaches and styles across the continent.

Every other year, the Turtle Island bioregionalists gather for a week to greet old friends, make new ones, discuss ways and means of advancing the cause, eat good food, entertain one another, and in general feel at home for a while in what one participant characterized as a "ceremonial village." The common denominator at these gatherings is a desire to know the truth in the nouns of the life-place: plants, persons, patterns. Registration fees are modest. —SM

●
Cascadia: A group here, interested in issues of sustainability, both locally and globally, started a quarterly newsletter, *The Cascadia Link*. They would like to network with bioregionalists. "We envision bioregional governance emerging initially through a Network of NGOs . . . and a working relationship between core groups. We are reaching out to establish an on-going dialogue with you, beyond the newsletter, via computer networking or other ways." Cascadia LINK 503/226-7807; Email: Cascadiaproj (PeaceNet).
—Turtle Island News

Turtle Island Office: 494 Broadway, New York, NY 10012; 212/226-7171

Bioregional groups run on a shoestring. When making your contacts, bear in mind that there may not even be an office, let alone a staff, so have patience! —SM

If you're unusually well informed about your neighborhood, The Home Repair Quiz (p. 79) will make you feel really really good about yourself.

Bioregional matters are knowledgeably addressed and lucidly presented in High Country News (p. 111).

ousehold is (with luck) who, what, and where you come home to — for a while; statistics show that each year, about 94 million US citizens change their addresses.

Families aren't what they used to be, either. The mom, pop, two kids, and one cocker spaniel sort of family is now in the minority, though you'd never guess that from looking at all the oversized houses still being built for now-imaginary Bumsteads, their slow-growing children, and their Methuselahn dog.

Big changes are occurring as demographics shift, economics flicker, and good two-by-fours get harder to afford or even find. Major adjustments have happened before, and there's more to come. You're involved. Here are some items that may help that involvement be a bit more voluntary.

—J. Baldwin

Right Where You Live

House buyers are the intended readership of this book, but it serves equally well as a primer for house designers and remodelers. Constance Brady examines good features and bad in an easygoing, conversational style that is readable even for kids — a nice way to get them into the process. For practice, try testing your present digs against the criteria presented here (you might want to move). The kitchen chapter is particularly good. This book has been around since 1979. It's still in print for good reason. —JB

•
A flow diagram is used to program the design of most commercial kitchens. It is an assembly line that works straight through from delivery of food, to preparation and serving, back to washing and storing of dishes. Not only is it not triangular, it is obvious that it is another path, a footpath! When cooking is seen as a journey through all the operations of food assembly, it becomes apparent we can deal with it in a businesslike manner.

STORAGE: BOWLS AND PANS BELOW, REPEATABLES ABOVE

Food path diagram applied to a residential kitchen.

Right Where You Live
(An Illustrated Guide to the Secrets of Finding a Home That Fits You)
Constance Brady. 1979; 187 pp.
ISBN 0-686-35975-5
$9.95 postpaid. Conarc, Box 339, Bethel Island, CA 94511; 510/684-3362

The Greener Pastures Institute

This fledgling organization is dedicated to redistributing the population more evenly across the land. They decry the tendency for the population to gather into huge, land-eating agglomerations infested with crime and poverty. They encourage smaller cities and towns for human and ecological reasons. Life goes better in smaller places. Many of us already know that, but seem to end up trapped in megalopolis anyway.

The Institute offers videos, tapes, seminars, and other encouragement to those who would escape to a better life. **The Greener Pastures Gazette** *is a bit slim, but always has good information and advice, as a clearinghouse should. If life in the city has lost its charm, this paper might literally get you moving.* —JB

According to an American Demographics Magazine report, rural dwellers spend $23,106 a year compared to urban dwellers' $28,584.

The savings would be much more except that statisticians factor in long distance travel expenses by farmers who can't make it on the land alone and have to commute to city jobs. (Few Greener Pastures readers, I hope, will be falling in to THIS trap!)

Rarely discussed (and almost never published), however, are the hidden savings of living in smaller cities and towns.

That's partly because the supposed experts either haven't lived in the countryside or are unfamiliar with the kinds of innovative lifestyles that are possible there that save money.

The Greener Pastures Gazette
Bill Seavey, Editor.
$25/year (4 issues). PO Box 1122, Sierra Madre, CA 91025; 800/688-6352

Redesigning the American Dream

Do you dream of living in a single-family home? You might find this eloquent argument against the idea provocative. Architect Dolores Hayden shows that the traditional home is often inappropriate for the rising number of single-parent families, families with more than one adult wage-earner, and the elderly. It's better to further develop existing housing with "granny units" and cleverly refurbished neighborhoods. The author shows rare sensitivity to the role (some would say plight) of women; she considers women's needs in virtually every proposed design. I found the level of research and analysis to be deeper than in other books on the subject. Easy to read, too — there's no academic poopadoodle at all. —JB

Redesigning the American Dream
(The Future of Housing, Work, and Family Life)
Dolores Hayden. 1986; 270 pp.
ISBN 0-393-30317-9
$10.95 postpaid. W. W. Norton & Co./Order Dept., 800 Keystone Industrial Park, Scranton, PA 18512; 800/233-4830

•
Access to the public domain is especially difficult for older women. After age sixty-five, many women reap the results of a lifetime of low earnings, limited mobility, and self-sacrifice. In a study of 82,000 widows in Chicago, Helena Lopata found that over

half of them did not go to public places, and over a fifth did not even go visiting. While 82 percent were not in a position to offer transportation to others, 45 percent had no one, of any age, to rely on for transportation.

Nina West Homes for single parents and their children. The child-care center is at the back of the site on the ground level; the corridor between apartments also serves as a children's play area. Kitchen windows offer easy observation of the corridor, and intercoms link units for easier baby-sitting.

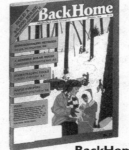

see also
Caretaker's Gazette and Country Careers p. 308

BackHome

This magazine attends pickup trucks, chickens, tomatoes, sawmills, home schooling, maple syrupping — all the stuff you need to know to live a good, but not necessarily more simple, life in the country. Written by unpretentious folks who are living the life portrayed, it's an improvement on sixties efforts that tended to be unrealistic hype and dream. Already-theres and wannabes alike will find plenty of ideas and good information. —JB

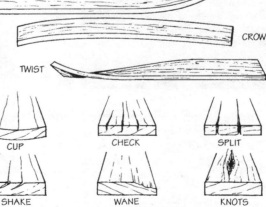

THINGS TO LOOK FOR

BOW
CROWN
TWIST
CUP
CHECK
SPLIT
SHAKE
WANE
KNOTS

Bow: A curve in the flat surface of a board, running lengthwise.
Crown: A lengthwise curve in the edge of a board, also known as crook.
Twist: A curve in two directions in the same board.
Cup: The curling of a board's edges, creating a lengthwise high spot in the surface.
Check: Small separations in the grain of the wood, causing a cosmetic defect.
Split: Penetrating separations in the wood's grain, sometimes completely through the board. Usually a structural defect.
Shake: A check that follows the path between growth rings, causing a structural defect if it's deep enough.
Wane: A sawing, more than a drying defect, wane is the lack of an edge corner because of cutting too close to the edge of the log, with subsequent bark loss.
Knots: These come loose and may pop out with movement of the wood as it dries. They're only a cosmetic blemish when numerous.

BackHome
Richard Freudenberger, Editor.
$16/year (4 issues). PO Box 70, Hendersonville, NC 28793; 800/992-2546

Finding & Buying Your Place in the Country

We've liked this book a lot since it first appeared in 1974. Here's the third edition, thoroughly updated and better than ever. The book continues to be a great example of doing things right; not only is the minutely detailed information exactly what you need, it's reinforced with caveat, sage advice, demystification, and a good education in the often shady real estate game. Supporting the main event is a glossary of arcane terms, a selection of sample forms, and a useful bibliography (much available for free) of homework. Most of the information pertains to non-country places too. It's one of those rare books that would be difficult to improve. —J. Baldwin

•

Don't be afraid of the tax assessor or his or her office. All files are open to the public, and the chances are that the person who appraised your land will be in the office and available for discussion. Ask what factors the assessor considered in appraising the property, including improvements, recent sales in the area and the price being asked by the seller for the property. The assessor can give you a rough estimate of how much your taxes will probably increase, based on the amount you intend to pay for the land.

In a subtle way, ask if the assessor thinks the seller's asking price is reasonable. His or her answer and analysis of the property might give you some valuable information to use when negotiating the purchase price.

•

The importance of understanding easements and knowing when and where they are located cannot be overstressed. Beware of the real estate agent who tells you, "Don't worry about getting an easement. The former owner of this land has been using it for years. Everybody is real friendly. Nobody here ever gets easements." Tell the agent that if nobody cares if you use the road, then he or she should have no problem getting the landowners to sign deeds granting such an easement formally.

Think about the future. The people who now own the land you cross might not care whether you do so, but the next owners

might not be so gracious. Or the present owners might not like your looks and decide they are not going to treat you as they did the last owners. All they have to do is put up gates and tell you not to cross their land if you don't have deeded access. These situations are very common in the history of real estate disputes.

•

If you are moving to an isolated area, your neighbors might be more important to you than if you are living close to town.

If you have children, you will probably want neighbors with children in the same age group, particularly if you plan to live there permanently. On the other hand, if you don't have any children, you may not want any nearby children who will climb your apple trees, or adolescents, who will race their cars. If most of your neighbors are young couples, you should expect an increase in the number of children in the area.

A unique problem with neighbors occurs in some areas where ranching is practiced. Many states still observe the "open range" law, which permits animal owners to let their livestock roam free. The burden of fencing in land is on any landowner who does not want the wandering herds to enter his or her property. Thus, if you buy a place next to a cattle ranch and you don't want cows wandering through your land, you will have to build a fence to keep them out. This is a costly project and should be figured in your purchase price.

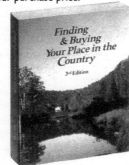

**Finding & Buying
Your Place in the Country**
Les Scher & Carol Scher. 1992;
407 pp. ISBN 0-79310-395-9
$24.95 ($28.95 postpaid). Dearborn
Financial Publishing, 520 N. Dearborn,
Chicago, IL 60610; 800/829-7934

Your New House

This is the best collection of things to desire, think about and beware when buying or building an abode. Alan and Denise Fields present their advice in an upbeat, witty (some would say smartypants) manner that acts as an antidote to the depression so easily engendered by having to deal with a maze of predatory realtors, builders, and bankers. Here and there "Money Bomb" symbols warn where things could turn expensive unless controlled carefully. There are lists of resources, product reviews, and even a 900 number for updates. I've not seen so much of this information made so easily readable. —JB

•

Fortunately, for today's home buyers, the eco-house has metamorphosed into something much more palatable than the geodesic dome. Many of today's eco-houses are

cleverly disguised to look like real houses. From the exterior, they are normal. Look under the roof, however, and you'll note a few changes...

The Drawbacks to the Eco-Home.

1. Unskilled laborers must learn new tricks — at your expense. Many eco-products require special installation methods. Unfortunately, this is sometimes above the skill level of many sub-contractors. As a result, there may be time delays and cost overruns as they learn steel framing or the installation of plastic wood.

2. A few of these products are still in the experimental stage. All the bugs haven't been quite worked out from some eco-friendly products. In the real world, you may not have access to these products in certain areas of the country.

Moving Successfully

You'd think it'd be simple to have someone come in, pack your stuff (without forgetting anything) and load it into a truck (carefully, so nothing breaks), drive it (smoothly, so that nothing breaks) to the new place (arriving at the time agreed), unload it into all the proper rooms, unpack the boxes, (still being careful so nothing breaks) and, um, well, sheesh. If that was easy to do, you'd be doing it yourself, right? There are tricks to the enterprise (especially if moving abroad) whether you do it or hire it done. They're all right here, in this book. —JB

•

Phone books are also heavy, but you might want to hold on to your local telephone directory — the one you depend on most for numbers. In your new home, you may find yourself in need of your old town hall or health department number.

•

Incidentally, since a lot of your goods will already have been packed in boxes when the movers arrive, it would not be practical for them to open each box and examine the contents. Instead, the movers mark the boxes "PBO", meaning "packed by owner." Ostensibly, this would make you liable if damage occurs, but in fact, if the movers take the box on the truck and the contents are damaged, the company will be liable.

**Moving
Successfully**
Tom Philbin. 1994;
106 pp. ISBN 0-89043-536-7
$14.95 ($17.45 postpaid). Consumer
Reports Books, 9180 LeSaint Drive,
Fairfield, OH 45014; 513/860-1178

The Complete House Inspection Book

You should always inspect a building before you buy it. Yeah, you. The bank will probably insist upon a certified or otherwise-approved inspector, but you should do your own, or at least accompany the professional. They can be wrong. They may miss something. They may not be on your side. If you tag along, you will be sure to learn things you need to know that may not appear on the report. This book gives you the basics. —JB

•

Galvanized-steel pipe is designed for a service life of seventeen years, in normal use. Of course, in areas where corrosion and mineral factors are low, galvanized steel has lasted for the better part of a century. In other locations, steel pipe has been nearly closed by corrosion within fifteen years.

Unsatisfactory

Satisfactory

•

If the conductors (wires) are silver, they are probably aluminum. At this point, I must sound a WARNING! Aluminum wiring has had a record of failure over the years. Much aluminum wiring was manufactured and installed during and shortly after World War II and the Korean conflict to conserve strategic copper. If this material was installed without taking proper precautions, it can cause overheating wherever it is connected to a receptacle, panel, or fixture.

**The Complete House
Inspection Book**
Don Fredriksson. Fawcett Books,
1988; 137 pp. ISBN 0-449-90263-3
$9.95 ($11.95 postpaid). Random
House/Order Dept., 400 Hahn Road,
Westminster, MD 21157; 800/733-3000

**If you are unable to use water,
another way to test the slab
pitch is with your rubber ball.**

OTHER GREAT RESOURCES

**How to Buy
Land Cheap:**
Edward Preston.
1991,
Loompanics
Unlimited.
You can.
Here's how.
Good luck.

Your New House
(The Alert Consumer's
Guide to Buying and
Building a Quality Home)
Alan & Denise Fields.
1993; 253 pp.
ISBN 0-9626556-2-7
$11.95 ($14.95 postpaid). Windsor Peak
Press, 1223 Peakview Circle, Suite 9000,
Boulder, CO 80302; 800/888-0385

—80' diameter Dyna Dome church being built by parishioners —Shelter.

Shelter

First published in 1973, this book is a celebration of indigenous, hand-made, personal-statement building, ancient to contemporary. It should be the first book a first-year architecture student sees. The passing years haven't tarnished it much, though the sixties-seventies viewpoint feels a bit dated. All photographs with brief commentary. —J. Baldwin

Shelter
Lloyd Kahn, Editor. Shelter Publications, 1973; 176 pp. ISBN 0-89815-364-6 $16.95 ($19.95 postpaid). Home Book Service, PO Box 650, Bolinas, CA 94924

Ronyoon, Burma.
Building a temporary theatre.

—1200 square-foot design by Fredrick Phillips, architect.

New Compact House Designs

Twenty-seven award-winning plans for houses of 1,250 square feet or less. Most are more interesting than typical developer designs, and all meet code. A few are downright enchanting. —JB

New Compact House Designs
Don Metz, Editor. 1991; 188 pp. ISBN 0-88266-666-5 $17.95 ($21.20 postpaid). Storey Communications, Schoolhouse Road, Pownal, VT 05261; 800/827-8673

Yesterday's Houses of Tomorrow

Housebuilding remains the only major handcraft enterprise in our industrial society. Lacking the economic and performance advantages of mass production, but gaining little advantage from on-site construction, houses are unnecessarily expensive to buy and maintain. Virtually all are biodegradable — an undesirable feature that's hard to square with the hatred of planned obsolescence expressed by so many homeowners. Except for mechanical components, today's house-tech is basically nineteenth- or even eighteenth-century.

This fascinating book presents exciting examples of innovative housing built between 1850 and 1950. Not surprisingly, few are by architects: they tend to have a vested interest in current practice. The move to high-tech housing has yet to be made in the US.

Wanna bet our housing industry suffers the same fate as Detroit before it woke up — and for the same reasons? —JB

●

The Aluminaire gave many Americans their first real glimpse of an International Style dwelling; sleek, low-maintenance surfaces; large windows making maximum use of natural daylight; built-ins; and a compact, efficient floor plan. Even if the startling, machinelike appearance of the house was not embraced by the majority of new homeowners and their architects, many of the Aluminaire's features began to appear in American houses in the late 1930s and 1940s.

Yesterday's Houses of Tomorrow
H. Ward Jandl, John A. Burns & Michael J. Y. Auer. 1992; 224 pp. ISBN 0-89133-186-7 $29.95 ($33.95 postpaid). Preservation Press, 1785 Massachusetts Avenue NW, Washington, DC 20036; 800/766-6847

Small Houses

The best way to be energy- and resources-efficient is to not use so much energy and resources in the first place. The only good reason to have a big house is if you have a lot of kids, relatives, or friends that need to be there often. Otherwise, you're probably building for old-mode prestige, or warehousing a collection of possibly nifty, but probably tiresome-by-now stuff. You must enjoy — or ignore — housework.

Small houses take less work to make and less time to maintain and are potentially cheaper. They need not be cramped, tacky, or otherwise annoying — but clever design is a must. Think built-ins. Think yacht. Just think. I've seen abundant proof that a really nice, efficient house for two people can be had for well under $100,000 even in California. This book is part of the proof. —JB

●

Today, contemporary, residential architecture (and most other architecture as well) is an embarrassment to the craftsman, enormously costly to the client, and a compromise to the architect, who is removed from the construction itself and is at the mercy of cost and bids. I believe that, given a good crew of interested craftsmen, economical, sensible and delightful solutions to problems can be evolved on the site with common tools, materials and good sense — better and more appropriate solutions than those drawn up before the fact, in the office. — David Sellers, architect, Warren, VT.

●

The house is an ongoing project, as there are no bankers or mortgages involved, and living in it unfinished has given me more and better ideas of space than I otherwise would have had. —Nancy Barrett, homeowner.

Small Houses
Fine Homebuilding. 1992; 160 pp. ISBN 1-56158-046-5 $24.95 ($27.95 postpaid). The Taunton Press, Box 5506, Newtown, CT 06470-5506; 800/283-7252

With no money in the budget for design time, David Sellers quickly built a small model for his client's approval. It was used during some of the framing, but was destroyed before most of the house (top) went up.

OTHER GREAT RESOURCES

Handmade Houseboats: Russell Conder. 1992, International Marine Publishing. The tempting and practical aspects of houseboat living are here mixed in a manner hard to resist.

Architecture Without Architects: Bernard Rudofsky. 1965, 1987, University of New Mexico Press.

The Prodigious Builders: Bernard Rudofsky. 1977, Irvington Publishers. Classic photo studies of indigenous, amazing architecture, sure to change how you think about buildings.

Most people are familiar with the typical "stick building" — you probably live in one. On this page, we glimpse some less-familiar techniques and materials that are slowly becoming more common. As energy costs rise and wood becomes scarce and expensive, expect to see more of this sort of thing. While there is much to celebrate, be realistic about the economics — walls are only about 20 percent of the cost of most houses. —J. Baldwin

Adobe and Rammed Earth Buildings • The Adobe Journal

Building with local materials is a major path to resource efficiency. Not usually thought of as appropriate for, say, Wisconsin, adobe and rammed earth (pisé) can be used almost anywhere there is suitable soil, the building code permits, and the climate (and the site) isn't downright liquid. A wide range of styles can be built, but you'd better like wide windowsills. The silence of earth walls is uncanny. The inciting, photograph-laden **Adobe and Rammed Earth Buildings** *is more than a primer: the author addresses engineering and design, too. The* **Adobe Journal** *is a good place to keep up with the latest ideas. —JB*

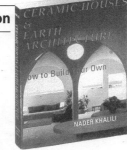

Adobe and Rammed Earth Buildings
Paul Graham McHenry, Jr. 1984; 217 pp. ISBN 0-8165-1124-1
$24.95 ($26.95 postpaid). University of Arizona Press, 1230 N. Park Avenue #102, Tucson, AZ 85719; 602/621-1441

The Adobe Journal
Michael Moquin, Editor
$15/year (4 issues). PO Box 7725, Albuquerque, NM 87194; 505/243-7801

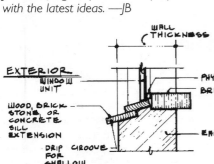

—Adobe wall anchor.

Straw Bale Construction

Straw? Egad! Straw bale wall construction has come a long way since the early days; it's now supported by much careful development effort from reputable individuals and institutions. The advantages are many, but your banker might need convincing.

Plastered Straw Bale Construction *provides the know-how. Out on Bale is the resource center with workshops, seminars and other information. Send an SASE for a current list. —JB*

Plastered Straw Bale Construction
David Bainbridge with Athena & Bill Steen. The Canelo Project, 1992; 46 pp.
$7.50 ($11.50 postpaid). AgAccess, PO Box 2008, Davis, CA 95617; 916/756-7177, fax 916/756-7188

Out On Bale (un) Ltd.:
1037 E. Linden Street, Tucson, AZ 85719; 602/624-1673.

Lay dry bales in staggered courses
Pin with hardwood dowel or rebar
Metal headers of angle iron
Wood frames
Wire mesh
Plaster outside
Plaster inside

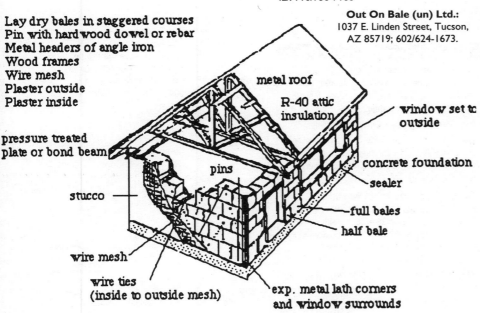

Ceramic Houses • The Geltaftan Foundation

What happens if you fire an adobe house as if it were a huge ceramic pot? Turns out that firing imparts strength, quiet, earthquake resistance, and remarkable permanence. Is it practical? Yes. Hell (so to speak), you could even glaze it! This remarkably intense book engenders the right attitude as well as a feel for the procedures involved. It's just plain super in every way. (You can help this work along and keep up with latest developments by joining The Geltaftan Foundation.) —JB

Ceramic Houses and Earth Architecture
Nader Khalili. Burning Gate Press, 1991; 238 pp. ISBN 1-878179-02-0
$21.95 ($24.95 postpaid). SCB Distributors, 15612 S. New Century Drive, Gardena, CA 90248; 800/729-6423

The Geltaftan Foundation: 10376 Shangri-la Avenue, Hesperia, CA 92345.

Steam rises from the old adobe structure for many hours as the fire continues to burn inside. The firing process also makes the vermin-infested house hygienic.

Earthships

As defined — and built! — here, an Earthship is of the earth, heated and cooled by natural systems, raising its own food, managing its own water supply, and not making a mess, while providing good shelter for its occupants. It is made by hand from simple materials, including detritus of our industrial society — tires and cans, for instance. Earthships demonstrate that the result need not be funky like sixties hippy hovels, though obviously the aesthetic tends to the unconventional. It's fair to call them affordable, but they're not for everyone. The hubris is wonderful.

Volume I lays out the basic vision. Volume II adds spiritual and engineering details. Volume III shows more details, what's been learned as the number of Earthships grows, and what the potential might be. Earthships have become a veritable movement, and an interesting one at that. To my mind, the Earthship spirit is more important than the ships themselves. —JB

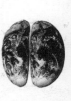

Earthship in Taos, New Mexico.

Earthship
Michael Reynolds. 1990, 1993
Each volume $24.95 ($26.95 postpaid). Solar Survival Press, PO Box 1041, Taos, NM 87571; 505/758-9870

Concrete requires more energy to produce than any other building material, so the Greenhome used precast panels containing half the concrete of conventional poured-in-place foundations. Each panel was 8 by 16 feet, weighed three tons and had to be craned into position.

Design With Nature

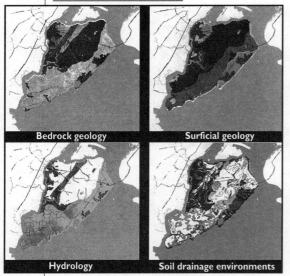

Bedrock geology | Surficial geology

Hydrology | Soil drainage environments

Ian McHarg's 1969 pioneering work may be venerable, but the methods it outlines remain remarkably useful. The basic idea is this: A site is analyzed by determining the ecologies of the flora and fauna present, the topography, hydrology, demographics and any other relevant constraint. Each is mapped in a different color onto a transparent sheet. When the sheets are stacked, the areas where development will have the least impact are revealed. The book is justly famous for the attitude of care and respect for nature it engenders. —JB

Design with Nature
Ian L. McHarg. 1991; 208 pp.
ISBN 0-471-55797-8
$59.95 postpaid. John Wiley & Sons, Inc.,
1 Wiley Dr., Somerset, NJ 08875;
800/225-5945

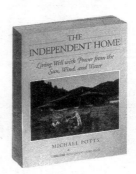

See also:
A Pattern Language, p. 127

The Independent Home

Here's what it's like to be "off the grid," made real by examples of people actually living the alternative-energy life proposed twenty years ago. A good life it is, too — now frontier-funky only if you like it that way. The book is a great mix of philosophy, what-works-best instruction, tips, and cautions you'll need to retrofit or build your energy-independent home right now. Dependable knowledge is available. The hardware is not only available, it has been developed (to code) and priced to the point where you can get a bank loan on it. If you're considering home energy independence, this book is your first homework. —JB, who reminds you that. . . .

Your independent home isn't independent of other people or of the environment you are trying to help. Please be careful of where you put the house, and be especially aware of the de-

mands and effects of the vehicle that totes your tail and your stuff thereto and therefrom.

•

If we take energy for granted, we think nothing of leaving a light on so that a room will be "friendlier" when we enter it; appliance engineers have taken the cue, and designed our appliances so that they are never really off. Futurist-designers proudly tell us that microprocessors, the little silicon computers that make microwaves and televisions smart, will soon be found in all our appliances. Off-gridders ask: Do you really need a clock in your coffeepot? We know that fewer than 20 percent of con-

The Independent Home
(Living Well with Power from the Sun, Wind and Water)
Michael Potts. Chelsea Green/Real Goods Independent Living Books, 1993; 320 pp.
ISBN 0-930031-65-2
$18 ($22.95 postpaid). Real Goods Trading Corp., 966 Mazzoni Street, Ukiah, CA 95482; 800/762-7325

Greenhome

The challenge was to make an affordable, energy-efficient, market-acceptable house out of environmentally benign materials — in Canada, where it gets colder than you'd believe.

Where most eco-house books merely prescribe, this one shows what a clever and resourceful design team actually did, complete with brand names and phone numbers. Even better, the reasoning behind their decision is revealed in detail, teaching you how to think about such things. Well done and most welcome (despite the anachronistic aesthetics) to anyone about to build in a similar climate. —JB

•

"The energy rating," says John, "is simply a calculation based on total solar heat-gain through the window, minus heat loss by convection, conduction and infiltration out through the window. It's given in watts per square metre, prorated over the entire heating season." For a while, Ontario Hydro was awarding $5 per square foot of window to any new homeowner installing windows with an energy rating greater than minus 11 (only if the new homeowner also happened to be heating with electricity, of course), which means the window loses less than 11 watts per square metre of glass. The Dorwin window has an energy rating of plus 1; a Dorwin window will actually gain 1 watt per square metre of window area each winter.

sumers use their VCRs to time-shift programs by recording them automatically and playing them back when convenient, but every VCR with a clock frivolously guzzles electrons twenty-four hours a day.

What does it feel like to use no electricity? When the power fails, we know. Afterwards, owners of grid-powered houses must scurry around resetting clocks.

•

I'm trying to strike some decent balance between technical achievement and independence. To live like this, you've got to be committed to being different.

Greenhome
Wayne Grady. Camden House Publishing, 1993; 208 pp. ISBN 0-921820-69-0
$15.95 ($16.95 postpaid). Firefly Books, Ltd., 250 Sparks Avenue, Willowdale, Ont M2H 2S4 Canada; 800/387-5085

Sunwings

Add a greenhouse to your househouse. Done well, you'll gain lots of solar heat in winter (and too much in summer if you aren't careful to design it correctly), plus veggies and nice flowers all year. Statistics show that most add-on sunspaces are used more for living than for serious gardening, which isn't surprising; even on a cool, cloudy day, a well-executed sunspace will heat up to an enticingly comfy temperature. Our grandparents called them sun porches, and spent a lot of time in them.

Statistics also show that poor design is common. I have heard horror stories featuring damp-ruined structure in the main house, increased heating bills, and roasted shingles.

Do it right. This book tells how. —JB

Sunwings
(The Harrowsmith Guide to Solar Addition Architecture)
Merilyn Mohr. Camden House Publishing, 1985; 151 pp. ISBN 0-920656-37-4
$4.99 ($5.99 postpaid). Firefly Books, Ltd., 250 Sparks Avenue, Willowdale, Ont M2H 2S4 Canada; 800/387-5085

SOLID ROOF TO REDUCE HEAT LOSS

OPERABLE PANES FOR VENTILATION

VERTICAL GLAZING TO PREVENT OVERHEATING

BACKUP HEATING SYSTEM TO MAINTAIN COMFORT LEVEL

Snow insulates Carl Bates's house, and the undisturbed woods protect it from wintry gales. Only windows and chimneys rise about the snowy hillside.

OTHER GREAT RESOURCES

The New Solar Electric Home
(The Photovoltaics How-To Handbook):
Joel Davidson. 1987, aatec Publications. Still our favorite photovoltaic primer.

Passive Solar Design Strategies: 1090 Vermont Avenue NW, Suite 1200, Washington, DC 20005; 202/371-0357. Site-specific technical assistance for designers and builders of energy-efficient structures.

The Center for Maximum Potential Building Systems ("Max's Pot"): 8064 F.M. 969, Austin, TX 78724; 512/928-4786. For about twenty years, this energetic, frontline outfit has been an innovative leader in architecture utilizing local materials, arid-land farming practices, and the social structures pertaining thereto. Pliny Fisk III, prop.

Solarium Sunwing
Instead of maximizing solar heat gain or sunlight, solarium design concentrates on human comfort, combining the principles of energy efficiency with passive solar collection.

JOISTS OVER GIRDERS   JOISTS FLUSH WITH GIRDERS

Girders
—Well-Built House

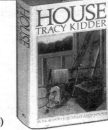

House • The Well-Built House

Like the needle of the acupuncturist, *House* is accurately, painfully, exquisitely, right. On the surface, it chronicles the building of a home from conception to move in. But what it's really about is the subtle class struggles that go on between people who are "professionals" and those "in the professions"; in this case the owners are a lawyer and a Ph.D. educator confronting equally educated carpenters. Egos are flaunted. Misunderstandings worthy of a tempestuous marriage illuminate the scene with snarls, huffs and laughs. Compromises are made; just as in real life. The house gets built. *The Well-Built House* is the same story told by one of the carpenters. This is good stuff to know if you're involved with architects and housemakers. —JB

"Actually, I wanted it August first," says Jonathan "But I guess that's impossible. Why four months?"

"Our labor is four and a half months of solid time," Jim repeats. "And there are a couple of vacations in there."

"Why a couple of vacations in there?" says Jonathan, tilting his head. "The farmers I know, the builders I know, take their vacations in the winter."

"Okay," says Jim. He's raised his chin. He purses his lips now and stares at the wall on Jonathan's right.

"Hey, it's none of my business. But it affects me."

"If you've got money," says Jim, turning back to Jonathan, whose face still bears the tan he got on his late-winter vacation in Florida, "you take time off in the winter. If you don't have money, you take time off in the summer." —*House*

The Apple Corps Guide to the Well-Built House
Jim Locke. 1988; 276 pp.
ISBN 0-395-62951-9
$11.95 ($14.45 postpaid). Houghton Mifflin Co./Mail Order Dept., Wayside Road, Burlington, MA 01803; 800/225-3362

House
Tracy Kidder.
1985; 352 pp.
ISBN 0-380-71114-1
$12.00 ($13.50 postpaid)
from Avon Books,
PO Box 767, Dresden,
TN 38225; 800/223-0690

Design Works

Design Works Kits: 3D Home Kit $29.95 ($33.95 postpaid); Solar Card $12.95 ($16.95 postpaid); Architect's

Design Works, 11 Hitching Post Road, Amherst, MA 01002; 413/549-4763.

Solar Card

This company sells a fine assortment of products that can help you design your home or any other modest building. You can make models with one of Design Works' 3D Home Kits. They have all manner of siding, windows, furniture, and most other items you'll need — even scale people. I consider these kits highly useful because you can't lie to yourself or others with a model. On the other hand, any kit reflects the taste of the kitmaker, and tends to subtly encourage designs that can be easily made with the kit. Don't forget.

My favorite Design Works product is their Solar Card. Is your neighbor's tree going to shade out your solar hot-water heater in February? Will your proposed garden get enough sun for tomatoes? You can find out easily by viewing the selected surroundings through the fine date-and-time lines printed on the Solar Card. The thing is a bit awkward to use, but it's cheap and it works. Tell them your city and state when ordering. —JB

Drafting

When I first got this book I kept mumbling "Arrgh, I wish I'd had this book last year" or some such remark born of unhappy memories of past disaster. Mr. Syvanen has a knack for explaining things you don't see explained elsewhere. Beginnership is assumed. —JB

Drafting
Bob Syvanen. 1993; 112 pp.   ISBN 1-56440-250-9
$12.95 ($15.95 postpaid). Globe Pequot Press, 6 Business Park Road, PO Box 833, Old Saybrook, CT 06475; 800/243-0495

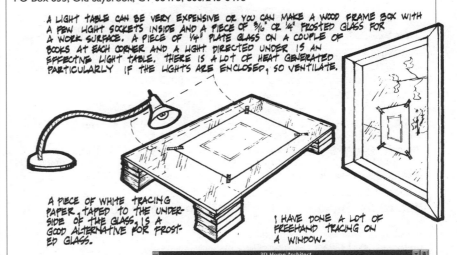

A LIGHT TABLE CAN BE VERY EXPENSIVE OR YOU CAN MAKE A WOOD FRAME BOX WITH A FEW LIGHT SOCKETS INSIDE AND A PIECE OF 3/16" OR 1/4" FROSTED GLASS FOR A WORK SURFACE. A PIECE OF 1/4" PLATE GLASS ON A COUPLE OF BOOKS AT EACH CORNER AND A LIGHT DIRECTED UNDER IS AN EFFECTIVE LIGHT TABLE. THERE IS A LOT OF HEAT GENERATED PARTICULARLY IF THE LIGHTS ARE ENCLOSED, SO VENTILATE.

A PIECE OF WHITE TRACING PAPER, TAPED TO THE UNDERSIDE OF THE GLASS, IS A GOOD ALTERNATIVE FOR FROSTED GLASS.

I HAVE DONE A LOT OF FREEHAND TRACING ON A WINDOW.

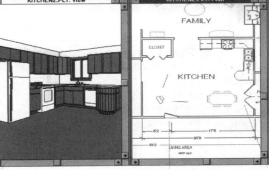

3D Home Architect

This affordable amateur's CAD (computer-aided design) software is relatively easy to learn and use — in contrast to many competitors and most complex professional CAD setups. A bit of practice will have you drawing without knowing how to draw. A "toolbox" of procedures awaits your command at the top of the screen. A huge inventory of furniture and architectural feature symbols lets you design rooms as you wish, but not in ways that are ridiculous to build (and not in curved plans, unfortunately). A click instantly puts your floor plans into a choice of zoomable 3D views that you can mess with on screen (including trying out different color schemes). Your changes will automatically change the original floor plan, too. An "inspector" is available to call in for comment.

The program will prepare a materials list for cost estimating. The software includes fifty professionally done plans for your edification while you develop your own designs. You'll need a PC with Windows 3.1 and a mouse (alas, no Mac version). What you perpetrate can be exported to professional CAD programs. Very cool, and great fun. —JB

3D Home Architect
IBM PC 386 or better, VGA monitor, 4 MB RAM, Windows 3.1, $59.95 postpaid from Brøderbund Software, PO Box 6121, Novato, CA 94948; 800/521-6263

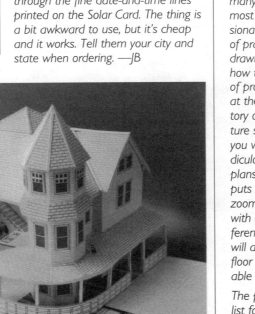

3D Home Kit

Homing Instinct

You can merely occupy a house, or you can make it a home that is unique and satisfyingly yours: home as self-portrait. Here is how to think about designing your (conventional) home from scratch or by remodeling — then go beyond the talk to make it happen (though you certainly won't be finished with the learning). At the book's heart is what amounts to the curriculum of the famed Yestermorrow Design/Build School in Warren, Vermont, which the author founded. As is true of any architect-client relationship, his approach may or may not be what you need. If it's to your taste, you'll find the book useful. If it isn't your style, the book can still serve as a review. It starts at square one. —J. Baldwin (Suggested by John Ringel, a Jersey Devil.)

From the delivery truck the trusses are first delivered to this position

Then they can be moved to this position

Finally, each one is carefully installed in this position

Note: these must be braced against falling down.

The whole reason for using trusses is to reduce labor costs by speeding erection

Before the trusses arrive, the sheathing must be installed to prevent racking from trusses laid on frame.

"I'm just going to have to use the same old conventional way of doing things. They were developed to be affordable and they still are. What's the matter with tradition? If it ain't broke, don't fix it. My budget is small and I can't afford to be politically correct."

"But now we're *creating* the tradition," counters another student. "Why must we build stupidly just because others have? If vernacular architecture means houses designed in response to the culture and surroundings of the occupants, then current

Today's practice of purchasing homes as if they were products continues to propel us in a nonsustainable direction. Only when people reinvolve themselves in the making of their homes can the act of dwelling reflect a new and ethically sound global awareness.

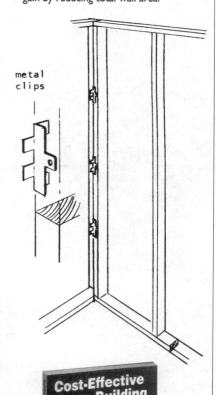

Homing Instinct
(Using Your Lifestyle to Design and Build Your Home)
John Connell. Warner Books, 1993; 416 pp.
ISBN 0-446-51607-4
$35 ($37.50 postpaid) from Little, Brown & Co./Order Dept., 200 West Street, Waltham, MA 02154; 800/343-9204

vernacular needs some updating. I would rather build a small, well-made home than a big stupid one. When we're gone, which do you think will get torn down first?"

OTHER GREAT RESOURCES

Healthy House Building: Healthy House Institute, 7471 N. Shiloh Road, Unionville, IN 47468; 812/332-5073. Here's how to design and build a steel-framed, non-toxic house. There's a video, too.

Builders Booksource: 1817 4th Street, Berkeley, CA 94710; 800/843-2028, 510/845-6874. A very fine specialized bookstore that carries at least one book on every imaginable aspect of building. If you have special needs, ask them for a reference. Bet they have it.

Fine Homebuilding: $29/year (7 issues). The Taunton Press, Box 5506, Newtown, CT 06470-5506; 800/283-7252. Intriguing, inspiring, informative, and just plain fascinating, this is the best building magazine around.

Environmental Building News: $60/year (6 issues). RR1, Box 161, Brattleboro, VT 05301; 802/257-7300, fax 802/257-7304. This newsletter is a good place to keep up with the latest developments in low-impact building.

Cost-Effective Home Building

You'd think that Optimum Value Engineering (OVE) would be common practice, but the building trades are technologically about a century behind the rest of society. The suggestions here will cut costs, but they also tend to cut innovation and delight; they're a challenge to an architect with fancy predilections. In any case, the booklet shows that overbuilding is not necessarily a requirement of good quality, and is often stupid. —JB

A 7'-6" ceiling height often eliminates one step in two-story construction, thereby providing more space for locating stairways. In addition, the lower ceiling height provides an enhanced exterior profile and tends to increase the apparent room size on the interior, because the scale of horizontal-to-vertical dimensions is greater (especially significant in smaller homes). A 7'-6" ceiling height also reduces heat loss and heat gain by reducing total wall area.

Before You Build • Building Your Own House • Building Your Own House II (Interiors)

These books were originally used as textbooks for a school teaching build-it-yourself skills. Robert Roskind, who has enormous experience with neophyte builders, is always at your elbow like a cool, friendly uncle — an uncle who has seen the elephant. He knows what your problems are likely to be; when you say "Sheesh! What do I do now?" the answer is right there in the next sentence. I strongly recommend reading all three books even if someone else is going to do the building. —JB

Foot fulcrum

— Building Your Own House II

Before You Build
1981; 240 pp. ISBN 0-89815-036-1
$12.95 ($16.45 postpaid)

Building Your Own House I
1984; 438 pp. ISBN 0-89815-110-4
$19.95 ($23.45 postpaid).

Building Your Own House II
(Interiors)
1991; 288 pp. ISBN 0-89815-358-1
$14.95 ($18.45 postpaid).

All by Robert Roskind, from Ten Speed Press, PO Box 7123, Berkeley, CA 94707; 800/841-2665

metal clips

Applying the Drywall

Margin of Error: 1/4"
Most Common Mistakes
Not getting insulation and utilities inspected before covering with drywall.

Not getting nail pattern inspected if necessary (check local code) before covering nails with compound and tape.

Driving the nails or screws so deep that they break the paper on the panels.

Not using drywall nails or screws.

Not butting two panels of drywall at the beveled factory edge (although this is unavoidable at the ends).

Not butting panels at the center of a stud or rafter.

Applying the drywall sheets with the wrong side exposed.

Creating more seams than are necessary — for example by using small scraps.
—*Building Your Own House II, Interiors*

BEFORE YOU BUILD
A Precontruction Guide

BUILDING YOUR OWN HOUSE II

BUILDING YOUR OWN HOUSE

Finish Sander — *Building Your Own House*

Cost-Effective Home Building
(A Design and Construction Handbook)
NAHB Research Center. 1993; 128 pp.
ISBN 0-86718-391-8
$20 ($24 postpaid). Home Builder Press Bookstore, 1201 15th Street NW, Washington, DC 20005; 800/223-2665

Journal of Light Construction

To find the difference between what's hype and what's real, ask the person who actually builds — in this case, traditional architecture. Savvy articles solve technical problems arising from energy-efficiency schemes, new materials, and the latest construction techniques. A feeling of pride in doing things right pervades the articles and the lively, occasionally acrimonious letters' column where controversies get settled by folks who have learned the hard way. The advertising — always an indicator of what's available — will keep your hardware and software current. Good writing and lots of pictures make the experience of the pros accessible to amateurs. —JB

Journal of Light Construction
$32.50/year (12 issues). PO Box 687, Mt. Morris, IL 61054; 800/375-5981

Renovation

If I owned a hardware store or ran the local lumberyard, I'd buy a desk copy of this book for do-it-yourself customers to paw through. The ones who should have done some home-work before they walked in can here learn the names of the things they need. Those with questions about the best way to do something will find the explanation of methods well-integrated in text, line illustra-tion, and photographs. Both groups will return to the sales desk informed and encouraged.

*What makes **Renovation** shine is experience and teamwork. The illustrator used to be a contractor. The photographer had previously remodeled a loft and wasn't afraid to lug her camera into grungy buildings. The author renovated three houses and had a hand in the beginnings of **Fine Homebuilding** magazine. The book probably won't have any serious competi-tion for years to come.*
—Richard Nilsen

Still true after twelve years. —JB

•

Jacking houses is scary, and should be: there are tremendous loads in-volved. But it can be done safely if you proceed slowly and observe the following precautions:

1. Wear a hard hat. Get a tetanus shot. Set up adequate light. *Always have help within shouting distance. . . .*

5. *Important:* Never jack more than you must, and raise all jacks in equal increments — say, 1/8 in. at a time.

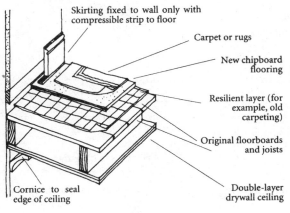

Left, a hydraulic jack atop cribbing; right, a screw jack atop a concrete pier block

Renovation
Michael W. Litchfield. 1990; 566 pp. ISBN 0-13-159336-6 $36 ($39 postpaid). Prentice Hall Press/Order Processing Center, PO Box 11071, Des Moines, IA 50336-1071; 800/947-7700, fax 514/284-2607

Eco-Renovation

Yup. Renovation for efficiency and less impact upon you and your surroundings. Tight organization makes it easy to find what you need. "Priority For Action" lists show you where to start. —JB

Skirting fixed to wall only with compressible strip to floor

Carpet or rugs

New chipboard flooring

Resilient layer (for example, old carpeting)

Original floorboards and joists

Cornice to seal edge of ceiling

Double-layer drywall ceiling

Eco-Renovation
(The Ecological Home Improvement Guide) Edward Harland. Real Goods Independent Liv-ing Books, 1993; 263 pp. ISBN 0-930031-66-0 $16.95 ($20.90 post-paid). Real Goods Trad-ing Corp., 966 Mazzoni Street, Ukiah, CA 95482; 800/762-7325

The Cost Cuts Manual

"Why don't the poor do something for them-selves?" That hoary excuse gets two (grimy) gloves in the face in this manual of proven building rehabilitation technique. Beset by ripoff in high places, racism, and demoralizing bureaucratic hassles, rehab work is frustratingly ineffective in furnishing low-cost housing to those who need it. The Enterprise Foundation assists groups engaged in rehab efforts across the country. They present their strategies and tactics in this manual, and you can tell that it's information hard-won. It's dirty hands, all the way; no bullshit — just what works, presented in sufficient (illustrated) detail to invite replica-tion. Competent and spirited.

*There's a free **Cost Cuts** newsletter, too.* —JB

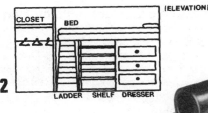

[FLOOR PLAN]

CLOSET

BED

WINDOW

DOOR

1

Two ideas create space instantly: 1. Keep one side of the bed against the wall. 2. Elevate the bed. Idea No. 2 of-fers the best use of a small space, so try it whenever you can

[ELEVATION]

CLOSET   BED

LADDER SHELF DRESSER

2

The Cost Cuts Manual
(Nailing Down Savings for Least-Cost Housing) Robert M. Santucci, Jim Thomas, et al. 1988; 336 pp. ISBN 0-942901-00-2 $10 ($14 postpaid). Enterprise Foundation, 10227 Wincopin Circle, Ameri-can City Building, Suite 500, Columbia, MD, 21004; 410/964-1230

A Consumer's Guide to Home Improvement, Renovation & Repair

*An amateur's version of **The Cost Cuts Manual**, this book is the best of its kind. The authors have accurately aimed it at the homeowner's needs and probable level of expe-rience (little, if any), but I'll bet even the most seasoned professionals will find stuff they didn't know. There's even a chart showing the best season to buy certain items. Mine is dog-eared.* —JB

A Consumer's Guide to Home Improvement, Renovation & Repair
Robert M. Santucci, Brooke C. Stoddard & Peter Werwath. 1990; 270 pp. ISBN 0-471-51923-5 $19.95 postpaid. John Wiley & Sons, Inc., 1 Wiley Dr., Somerset, NJ 08875; 800/225-5945

TABLE 15.2 New Driveway Options

THE PROJECT Construct a driveway 10' wide by 25' long to meet an existing street apron.

Options	Cost/sq ft Contracted	Cost/sq ft DIY	Project Cost Contracted	Project Cost DIY	Difficulty Level DIY Advice	Comments and Recommendations
Crushed Gravel Install 6" of washed, crushed gravel in 2" × 4" treated pine edging.	$1.25	$0.71	$312	$177	**1** Easiest DIY.	Should be used more often. Quick, easy to maintain, low cost, with low environmental impact (doesn't contribute to storm runoff).
Ribbons of Concrete Install 24"-wide, 4"-thick concrete ribbons over 4" gravel base with a broom finish.	$3.60	$1.42	$360 CC	$140 CC	**2**	Concrete ribbons balance the strength of poured concrete with the low cost of minimum coverage. Easy DIY job.
Soil Cement Install 6" of clay base mixed with 8%–10% portland cement, compacted.	$1.90	$1.22	$475	$305	**1** A rototiller and a rented compactor can make this a weekend job.	Not recommended in northern climates.
Asphalt Install 2" of binder, 1" top coat over 4" gravel base.	$2.50		$625 VB		DIY not recommended.	About the same life-cycle costs as concrete, but lower initial cost.
Poured Concrete Install 4" slab over 4" gravel base with a broom finish	$3.40	$1.42	$850 VB	$355 VB	**3** Placing and finishing concrete is hard and demanding.	High cost, long life; use air-entrained concrete.

The Sourcebook for Sustainable Design

This sourcebook of environmentally least-despicable building materials and hardware is by far the best and most useful I've ever seen. Among the many categories are composting toilets, wood substitutes, pipe and brick made of recycled materials, and unusual insulation — described, not merely listed. Each category is led by a brief discussion of the environmental aspects involved, plus the information you need to make, defend and order good choices. Like our **Whole Earth Catalog***s, the* **Sourcebook** *gains credibility by pointing to, but not selling. It is not excessive to say that all architects, designers, specifiers, contractors and students thereof need a copy of this remarkable book. Ignorance is no longer an excuse for doing things the old, wasteful way. —J. Baldwin*

●

Wood is one of the oldest and most versatile of building materials, and continues to play a major part in almost every building project. Properly managed as a renewable resource, it should continue to be a basic construction material indefinitely. Guidelines for ensuring that this will be the case include the following:

Sourcebook for Sustainable Design
Andrew St. John, Editor. 1992; 140 pp. $25 ($28 postpaid). Boston Society of Architects, 52 Broad Street, Boston, MA 02109; 617/951-1433 ext 221

1. Find alternatives to old-growth timber for all wood uses.

2. Use woods whose origins are known to be "sustainable" or "well-managed."

3. If a client demands rarer woods, use veneers instead of solid wood. Veneers provide more effective use of the whole tree, and the substrate can be made from sawmill scrap or waste.

4. Write for a subscription to *Wood Report* to Earth Access, 87 Cherry Street, Cambridge, MA 02139.

5. If formaldehyde emissions are a strong consideration, specify low-emitting UF-bonded panel products or phenol-bonded products.

Resource Conservation Technology

Building materials are changing. Once you get past the basic stuff — nails, studs, and plates, even beyond drywall screws and hurricane ties and housewrap — you run into a domain of synthetics and alloys and something called Ethylene Propylene Diene Monomer. These are products originally developed for the new era of factory-built houses — especially those being made in efficiency-conscious northern Europe and Japan.

Are materials engineered for the controlled conditions of the factory floor applicable out on your building site? Emphatically yes! The producers of these new materials have developed products for window and door sealing, for gap bridging at sills and rough openings, and liners and coatings and caulks enough to tempt me to start another house just to get it right.

You can get this stuff through this catalog — along with sun-control awnings and blinds, ultra-low-flush toilets in three (!) price ranges, drain-

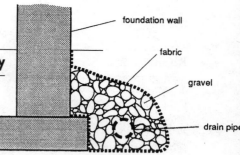

Using polypropylene liner protection fabric as filter fabric to keep soil from clogging foundation drain.

age management products like nylon mesh matting and filter fabric, and pond lining, and custom-made, seamless EPDM rubber roofing (proven great for earth-sheltered houses). And they show you right in the catalog how to install the materials.

Quantities available range from homeowner scale to contractor-size lots, and although the materials are not directly comparable to those found at your local hardware store, you're likely to find better stuff, cheaper, here. —Don Ryan

Resource Conservation Technology, Inc.: Catalog $5. 2633 N. Calvert Street, Baltimore, MD 21218; 410/366-1146.

Guide to Resource Efficient Building Elements

You'll find lumber made from recycled plastics, foam concrete, and lightweight-panel building systems in this interesting reference, but not at your local Homedreck Supply. I suspect most readers don't know most of this stuff exists. It does, and you're going to see more of it soon. —JB

Guide to Resource Efficient Building Elements
Center for Resourceful Building Technology, 1994; 94 pp. $25 postpaid. CRBT, PO Box 3866, Missoula, MT 59806; 406/549-7678, fax 406/549-4100

●

air Krete, Inc.
P.O. Box 380, Weedsport, NY 13166 (315) 834-6609

An ultralight cementitious foam insulation with cellular structure.

Applications:
Designed for installation in cavity fill applications. Can be installed in any cavity through a 1" to 3" diameter hole. Can be used in both new and existing wood or steel stud construction. In new construction, foam is trowled into open stud cavities.

R-Value:
3.9 per inch at standard installed density of 2 lbs/ft³.

Fire Rating:
Zero flame spread, zero fuel contribution.

Comments:
Is 98% inorganic, chemically stable, and contains no formaldehyde or asbestos. Good acoustical absorbance. Will not support compressive loads at "standard" density. 2 to 4 weeks curing time. air Krete licenses manufacturing around the nation.

Environmental by Design

Environmentally hip interior designers can now specify materials and products that are relatively benign (perfection isn't possible) to their sources, workers, and users, before expiring gracefully someday. This welcome sourcebook provides the logic behind the criteria used to judge each type of product, then describes the features of individual brands and where to obtain them. Plenty of educational chat helps you choose. The book's very existence is proof that being a good environmental citizen makes new jobs. —JB

Environmental by Design
Kim Leclair & David Rousseau. 1992; 261 pp. ISBN 0-88179-086-6 $19.95 ($23.45 postpaid). Hartley & Marks, Inc., PO Box 147, Point Roberts, WA 98281; 206/945-2017

Building with Junk and Other Good Stuff

This book may be offensive to banks and developers; its anarchic spirit encourages individual action and sass. The author is a master scrounger (recycler in ecospeak) and make-do person, yet he is aware of energy matters as well as unhealthy materials and building practices. His writing makes you feel like you're hatching a plot with your Cousin Jim. Nothing illegal, but he's certainly out to circumvent and exploit The System. The advice is thorough, true, and full of droll wit. Before you give up on that unaffordable dream house, better give this a read. —JB

●

Laminated safety glass, which is two pieces of glass stuck onto either side of a film of plastic, is all over the place, including auto salvage yards. . . . A good craftsman with routers, etc. or someone with a lot of time, patience, determination and a chisel can do some pretty astounding things with windshields and curved glass pieces for protruding windows, furniture bases, light fixtures, etc.

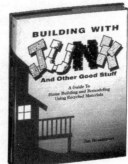

Building with Junk and Other Good Stuff
Jim Broadstreet. 1990; 168 pp. ISBN 1-55950-036-0 $19.95 ($23.95 postpaid). Loompanics Unlimited, PO Box 1197, Port Townsend, WA 98368

Appropriate Building Materials

That's Appropriate as in Appropriate Technology. Many of the items in this book of low-cost building materials and methods would give a US building inspector a seizure. But elsewhere in the world — which is most of it, remember — these things are done every day. Good to know, because you never know . . . —JB

●

Steel Flitch Plate Connections
Mild steel sheets up to 1mm thickness can be easily penetrated by normal round

Appropriate Building Materials
Roland Stulz & Kiran Mukerji. 1988; 430 pp. ISBN 0-94688-28-1 $28.50 postpaid. Intermediate Technology Development Group, 777 United Nations Plaza, Suite 3C, New York, NY 10017; 212/953-6920

wire steel nails without pre-drilling. Thicker sheets require drilling or the use of hard steel nails. Tests have shown that for most applications and timber species two 1 mm plates provide sufficient strength of the connections . . . Stronger timbers may require flitch plates of larger areas to achieve appropriate design stresses.

The ability of the nailed flitch plate connection to sustain loads after initial failure is a characteristic which could prove valuable in areas where buildings may be subjected to earthquakes and high winds.

Simpson Strong-Tie Connectors

Most folks who work with lumber know that a "joist hanger" is a metal cradle that joins floor beams. That commoner has many lesser-known cousins. The variety is a wonder to behold. Inspiring, too — we whipped out a bunch of heavy picnic tables in about half the time it would have taken using old-mode joining methods that don't work well with today's crappy lumber, anyway. Simpson makes special earthquake and hurricane bracing — widespread use of which could have reduced the damage in recent disasters. You can even get ornamental versions for exposed locations. Your dealer has the impressive catalog. —JB

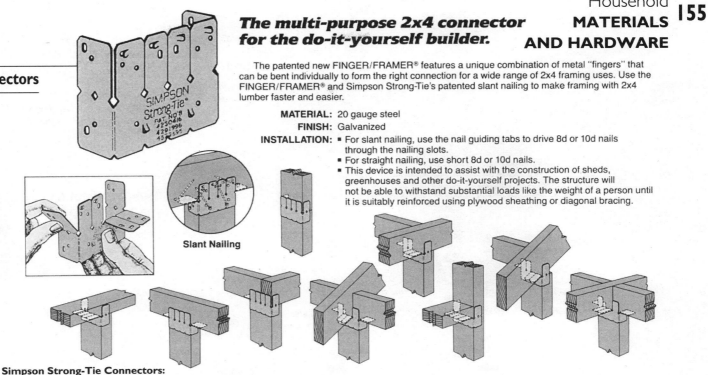

Slant Nailing

The multi-purpose 2x4 connector for the do-it-yourself builder.

The patented new FINGER/FRAMER® features a unique combination of metal "fingers" that can be bent individually to form the right connection for a wide range of 2x4 framing uses. Use the FINGER/FRAMER® and Simpson Strong-Tie's patented slant nailing to make framing with 2x4 lumber faster and easier.

MATERIAL: 20 gauge steel
FINISH: Galvanized
INSTALLATION: ▪ For slant nailing, use the nail guiding tabs to drive 8d or 10d nails through the nailing slots.
▪ For straight nailing, use short 8d or 10d nails.
▪ This device is intended to assist with the construction of sheds, greenhouses and other do-it-yourself projects. The structure will not be able to withstand substantial loads like the weight of a person until it is suitably reinforced using plywood sheathing or diagonal bracing.

Simpson Strong-Tie Connectors:
For the name of your nearest dealer call 510/562-7775.

Country Store Catalogs

Like the Amish community it serves, Lehman's Hardware and Appliances is gentle, bucolic, and competent. Not a trace of tourist-fake nostalgia in the farm kitchen gear: gas refrigerators, wood cookstoves, and 50 gallon cannibal cauldrons. You can still get Flexible Flyer sleds here! Cumberland General Store has similar country stuff, plus a wonderful selection of horse-drawn buggies and wagons. The Vermont Country Store specializes in old-style cotton clothes and household goodies. They still make 'em like they used to. —JB*

"Even grown-ups ought to find a use for these," says nine-year-old Brandon Amstutz from his perch on "Our Best Medium" wagon.

Our Best Wagons

Small-Slightly larger than our Berlin Flyer but much stronger — hauls up to 600 lb or three times the Flyer's (and most other wagons') capacity.
Medium-The bestseller of **Our Best** line. Large bed holds two children with playing space or one child and gear. It's the best combination of size and maneuverability. (Withstands an 800 lb payload yet easily fits through a standard door.) Shown with optional air filled tires.
Large-World's largest production model — 4 ft by 2 ft! Hauls anything from the family St. Bernard to groceries for a month to the head of the household! In spite of its size, older children, teenagers and adults can easily pull it. The 16" air-filled wheels conquer obstructions and uneven terrain (8" ground clearance).

Lehman's Hardware and Appliances:
Catalog $2 from One Lehman Circle, PO Box 41, Kidron, OH 44636; 216/857-5757, fax 216/857-5785.

Wrens control insects and sing melodiously

Budget Bluebird House

...y 1" hole keeps out ...esirable competing birds. ...p design protects young ...n predators. Extra long ...rhang protects from ...ther. Amish-made log ...n of 7/8" rotproof cedar, ...H, 3 lb, USA made. **#LC-** ...; $16.95

Now, as in Lincoln's day, log homes are most practical. Ideal for fencerows, other multiple installations. Amish made, 7/8" cedar, 10"H, 4 lb. **#LC-BB;** $19.95 ea, 2 for $13.95 ea, 6 for

Cumberland General Store:
Catalog $3 from Rte 3 Box 81, Crossville, TN 38555; 800/334-4640.

1840's Hurricane Lamp Is Back In Black Enamel & Solid Brass

Using the original 1840 molds, the R. E. Dietz Company is once again manufacturing the hurricane lamp. We offer two styles: Captain's lantern is solid brass with a gleaming polished finish. Shipmate's lantern has a black baked enamel finish with shiny brass plated trim. Named for exceptional performance under the most adverse weather conditions, they are both functional and decorative indoors and out. Both use regular kerosene or charcoal lighter fluid (odorless and smokeless) which burn cleaner than lamp oil. No.19535 **Black Hurricane Lamp $18.95.** No.20162 **Brass Hurricane Lamp $39.95.** Ship. wt. 3 lbs. each.

The Vermont Country Store: Catalog free. PO Box 3000, Manchester Center, VT 05255-3000; 802/362-2400, fax 802/362-0285.

Old-fashioned wooden hay fork

Handsome examples of a nearly lost art

Outstanding strength to weight ratio (all weigh under 4 lb). No other fork better for loading fresh-cut hay. Folks that use bales will find they make attractive wall hangings.

Factory made-In continuous production for over 100 years! Riven from a single piece of select ash. Sanded smooth and steamed to hold its shape permanently. USA made.
#760-303 (66"L, 3 tines, 2 lb); $53.95
#760-304 (66"L, 4 tines, 2 1/2 lb); $59.95
#760-302 "Mini Decorative" (A childsize 3-tine that matches Mini Rake. 36"L, 1 lb); $23.00

Livos Non-Toxic Home Products • Auro Natural Plant Chemistry

These vendors will probably wince when they see themselves reviewed together here — it has been my experience that their salespeople tend to engage in a bit of mutual sniping. Fact is that they both sell paints, pigments, wood preservatives, adhesives, waxes, and even kids' art supplies. Both claim to use only natural, non-toxic materials, such as lemon oil and natural earth pigments. (Note: this does not mean that you can drink the stuff.) Colors tend to the earthy; smells tend to the nice. Assiduous use of these products eliminates many chemical sensitivity sources in the home. Paint performance seems to be acceptable, though under severe conditions (yacht duty, for instance) not up to the standards of heavy-duty products containing foul substances.

For most uses at home or the office, these products do very well; I've heard few complaints and would not hesitate to use either brand. —JB

Livos Non-Toxic Home Products:
Catalog free. 1365 Rufina Circle, Santa Fe, NM 87501; 505/438-3448.

Auro Natural Plant Chemistry: Catalog free. PO Box 857, Davis, CA 95617-0857; 916/753-3104

Hendricksen Natürlich Flooring and Interiors

INTRODUCTORY SAMPLE BOARD

Hi-tech floorcoverings (and floors) may successfully repel the foe, but they can poison sensitive folks (and possibly everyone) with a cocktail of noxious exudates. Hendricksen sells "natural" carpet, in wool that can even be undyed; several types of sisal; coir (from coconuts); and real linoleum. (Did you know that linoleum is made from materials such as pine resin, linseed oil and cork?) Prices seem competitive with many synthetics. I can't vouch for durability except for the linoleum: my parents' home had linoleum-covered bathroom and kitchen floors and counters that still looked new after forty-five years. —JB

DIAMOND SISAL
12'0"W

MANDALA JUTE

Hendericksen Natürlich Flooring and Interiors: Catalog free. PO Box 1677, Sebastopol, CA 95473; 707/824-0914.

CLASSIC
15'2"W

IMPRE...
12'0"...

Flexible Flyer Eagle — The original "steerable" sled

The same quality and craftsmanship that made Flexible Flyer the best sled in 1889 make it the best today! ...to take it with high quality hardwood bed ...ough tempered steel frame. The world's ... steerable sled, the Flexible Flyer remains a ...c example of American ingenuity. USA ...e (of course).

Helpful Hint-Make your sled *scream* down hills! Sand paint from runner bottoms. Then, rub on a heavy coat of candle wax. Recoat after every use to prevent rust and cut friction.

Sizes up to five feet long for breathtaking speed! Truly steerable, it's far safer than uncontrollable "straight runner" sleds.

The Classic Racer-Eye-catching red with black trim and bumper in the tradition of European sports cars. Flyer's sportiest! Triple pivot steering earned it the "King of the Hill" title. (Competing sleds, if steerable, use double pivots.)
#F648 (48"L, 10 lb) $60.95
#F654 (54"L, 13 lb) $68.95
#F660 (60"L, 14 lb) $74.95

PRUSSIAN KING
13'2"W

ROMAN EMPIRE
12'0"W

ARABIAN DESERT
12'W

LINOLEUM
79'W

*J*ust thought we'd rattle your chain with a selection of tools not usually carried at homeowner hardware stores. Hide my checkbook! —J. Baldwin

The Ultimate Ulmia Bench is perfect for every cabinetmaking project.
—Woodcraft

Fein Sander: $189 ($192.50 postpaid). The Sanding Catalogue, PO Box 3737, Hickory, NC 28603-3737; 800/228-0000, 704/326-0380.

Designing? You must see the Bucky Fuller stuff on page 36.

Designing? You must see the Bucky Fuller stuff on page 36.

Ryobi Detail Sander: $44.95 ($48.45 postpaid). The Sanding Catalogue, PO Box 3737, Hickory, NC 28603-3737; 800/228-0000 or 704/326-0380, or at your local Ryobi dealer.

Ryobi Detail Sander • Fein Sander

Either of these nifty machines will neatly sand heretofore difficult ledges and inside corners, with no danger of chatter and mar. (Practice first on scraps, though.) The Ryobi is light, buzzy, and priced right. The Fein is heavy-duty professional, can be used as a center-of-panel saw, and is priced accordingly. Woodworkers rejoice.

Can-Do Clamp

A trick double-swivel jaw holds (on both sides) pieces of different thickness and depth at an implacable 90 degrees. It's the best.

Can-Do Clamp: $24.95 postpaid from MLCS Ltd., PO Box 4053, Rydal, PA 19046; 800/533-9298, 215/938-5060, fax 215/938-5070.

Lumber Jack

This tool is more necessity than gadget when today's deplorably warpy wood must be forced into place. Works in any position. Three sizes. Clever lever.

Lumber Jack: Model 100, for use on material 1 1/4" - 1 3/4" wide, $89.95 ($94.40 postpaid); Model 400, 3 - 3 3/4" wide, $129.95 ($134.90 postpaid); Model 600, 5 - 5 3/4" wide, $149.95 ($154.90 postpaid). T.C. Manufacturing, PO Box 122, Frederickstown, OH 43019; 800/253-5669, fax 614/694-1953.

The Sanding Catalogue

You are expecting maybe forty pages of enticing color photographs of little squares of sandpaper? Well, uh, yes, sort of; the gritty paper is there in every form imaginable, but so are the devices that use it. Many of these are ingenious, of recent birth, and not apparent at your local store. Everything is described usefully. The entire selection is a welcome boon, even to experienced woodworkers.

The Sanding Catalogue: Free. PO Box 3737, Hickory, NC 28603-3737; 800/228-0000, 704/326-0380.

D'versiBIT®

To induce preternaturally insolent wires to go from here to there through a complex wall, try one of these six-foot-long, springy, whippy bits. A tie-hole in the tip snakes the wire as you back out. NB: Gentle practice is required to prevent an expensive SNAP!

D'versiBIT®: $20-$40 at building trades supply houses. Information from Greenlee Textron, 4411 Boeing Drive, Rockford, IL, 61109; 800/435-0786.

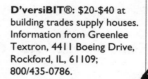

Fig. 1   **Fig. 2**   **Fig. 3**   **Fig. 4**

ClampTite™

1-WRAP   2-WRAPS

Mercilessly tightens baling-type wire into a binding "hose clamp" — diameter limited only by your wire supply. Super-strong; super-useful.

ClampTite™: Plated $29.95 ($32.45 postpaid), Stainless Steel $39.95 ($42.55 postpaid). PO Box 414, Shady Cove, OR 97539; 800/962-2901, fax 503/826-4466.

Woodworking Supplies

When I need a woodworking something that is not available locally, I look in these catalogs first. Woodcraft and Garret Wade tend to the exotic; some of their handcrafting tools could pass as jewelry. There is some overlap between the rivals, but much that is unique, too. I peruse both — sometimes just for inspiration. Woodworker's Supply is the more prosaic stuff for the professional-job shop. They stock a huge assortment of power tools, including the big ones used in production. Amateurs will welcome the heavy-duty versions of home shop stuff, and the truly labor-saving hardware. All these catalogs offer the full descriptions necessary for making the right choices.

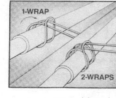

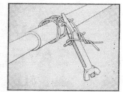

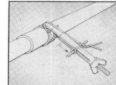

Calibrated Flexible Rule
This new tool allows you to copy curved designs and transfer them without measuring. Made from a lead core, encased in a vinyl body. —Woodworker's Supply.

Garrett Wade Tools: Catalog free. 161 Avenue of the Americas, New York, NY 10013; 800/221-2942.

Woodcraft: Catalog free. 210 County Industrial Park, PO Box 1686, Parkersburg, WV 26102-1686; 800/535-4482.

Woodworker's Supply: Catalog free. 5604 Alameda Place NE, Albuquerque, NM 87113; 800/645-9292.

Instant Accuracy for Delta 14" Bandsaws. Using compact and rugged, lubricated for life all-ball-bearing guides at the sides and the rear of the blade, these sets of upper and lower guides give an incredible boost to the performance of Delta's 14" bandsaws. —Woodworker's Supply

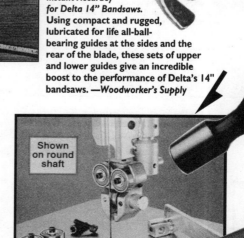

Shown on round shaft

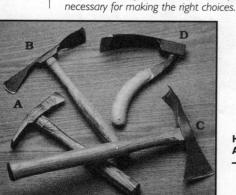

Hickory Handled: (A) Small Adz. (B) Medium Adz. (C) Large Adz. (D) Hollowing Adz. —Woodcraft

Hickory-handled hammers and Japanese square-head hammer. —Garrett Wade

McFeely's

Among the usual woodworker paraphernalia, this catalog features "square drive" screws of various ilk. The square-driven system deters the fatal slips that inevitably accompany Phillips and common straight-slot screwdriver use, especially if power drivers are employed. These screws are stronger than similar-looking dry-wall screws, and better in every way than those silly tapered traditional wood screws. For many applications, you don't even need to drill a hole. I use them a lot. To know them is to love them.
[Suggested by Roger Knights]

McFeely's: Catalog free. 1620 Wythe Road, PO Box 3, Lynchburg, VA 24505-0003; 800/443-7937.

Why Square Drive? 🄱

Features:
1. Square Recess for maximum driving torque -reduces driver bit "cam–out".
2. Heat treated steel for dependable strength.
3. Sharp thread angle cuts into wood to prevent cracking or bursting.
4. Optimized thread depth to thread spacing ratio to minimize crumbling between threads.
5. Thread surface is nearly perpendicular to the thread axis to provide the greatest resistance to pullout.
6. Minimum body diameter causes least possible material distortion.
7. Sharp point provides easy penetration and a full thread within just one revolution.

Deburring Tool

The swiveled, handled, hardened blade dulls sharpies when applied scraper-fashion to the threatening edge (the "burr"), especially the nasty inner rims of fresh-sliced pipe and tube.

Deburring Tool: Catalog #70415, $11.40 postpaid. The Mill-Rose Co., 7995 Tyler Blvd., Mentor, OH 44060; 800/321-3598.

Trend-lines

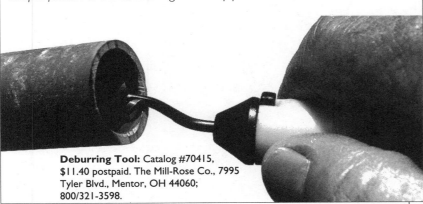

The good prices on this respectable assortment of woodworking machinery and hardware may even beat local sales. What your local hardware store ought to be, but probably isn't.

Trend-lines: Catalog free. 375 Beacham Street, Chelsea, MA 02159; 800/767-9999.

Roto Mite Spiral Cut: Save hours of labor cutting outlet openings. Just 2.5 lbs., the Roto Mite features easy one-hand control and virtually dustless operation.

Milwaukee Job Saw

This handy handle accepts any blade made for the esteemed Milwaukee Sawzall®, for quiet, delicate (and laborious) hand-sawing. Fits on a pole, too.

Milwaukee Job Saw: About $11 at local hardware stores.

Bucket Boss

A wide, heavy-duty Cordura belt with pockets of various sizes transforms a standard five-gallon bucket into a great tool-tote. I have two in service.

Bucket Boss: $21.99 ($25.49 postpaid). Portable Products, 56 E. Plato Blvd., St. Paul, MN 55107; 800/688-2677.

Electric Screwdrivers

Mine is a Black & Decker Model 9074/SD2000, which I like. What's wrong with hand-power? Humans are not built to make certain motions over and over; millions of sport and on-the-job repetitive-motion injuries (carpal tunnel syndrome, for instance) are ample evidence. I have no doubt that in the old days many permanent injuries were inflicted by traditional hand tool use. OK, how 'bout the push-pull mechanical Yankee screwdrivers? They are awkward (the bigger ones need two feet of clearance), no good at screw removing, and cost twice as much as a good electric. You don't need either Yankee or electric unless you do a lot of, uh, screwing.

Black & Decker Electric Screwdriver: Model 9074/SD2000. Available — hard to avoid, even — at hardware stores everywhere. Or call B & D for dealer information: 800/762-6672.

Wood Finishing Supply

French Polishing
These products were developed by Les Produits des Ancies Ebenistes in France to meet the needs of professional cabinetmakers, furniture restorers, antique wholesalers and dealers.

It's rare that a woodworker can just go downtown and buy most of the items in this well-considered selection of materials and tools for fine finishing and detailing. When was the last time you saw Rottenstone and Ground Rabbit Skin Glue at Kmart?

Behlen's Water Base Urethane Finish: A quick drying, clear topcoat formulated from waterborne urethanes and copolymers. It produces a finish that is mar and solvent resistant, and may be applied by brush (foam or nylon bristle) or sprayed with conventional or HVLP spray equipment.

See *The Science of Structures and Materials* on page 233.

Wood Finishing Supply: Catalog free. 5604 Alameda Place NE, Albuquerque, NM 87113; 800/645-9292.

Knipex Alligator Pliers

Alligators grip harder the more you pull — no need to squeeze. That, and slimmer size make them more useful than the deservedly popular ChannelLocks. I love 'em.

Knipex Alligator Pliers: 10" $24.60; 12" $37.80. Anglo-American Enterprises Corp., 403 Kennedy Blvd., Somerdale, NY 08083; 800/223-8600, 609/784-8600.

Stop Table-Wobble Forever!

End the annoying wobble of tables with Superlevel™. This unique piece of hardware uses the table's weight to keep all feet firmly on the ground even on rough surfaces.
—*Woodworker's Supply.*

The Offset Broad Hatchet is a traditional tool for shaping beams. —*Garrett Wade.*

The Workshop Book

Thingmakers inevitably make places in which to make things. As time passes, that place becomes a shop — at first a collection of tools in a space, eventually a finely tuned capability, an extension of the maker's mind. Like kitchens, seasoned shops mirror the personalities of their creators.

This handsome book lets you get rather more than just a peek inside a selection of interesting shops of various sorts — my mobile prototyping shop among them. Sizes range from grand dreamshop to retractable-into-closet. Incisive interviews with their owner-builders reveal the logic and the subtleties. Excellent photographs show you around. A home without at least a few organized tools is helpless.
—J. Baldwin

The Workshop Book
Scott Landis. 1991; 216 pp. ISBN 0-942391-37-3 $34.95 ($37.95 postpaid). The Taunton Press, Box 5506, Newtown, CT 06470-5506; 800/283-7252

Baldwin's color-coded tool identification system is useful for directing visiting gofers, e.g. "The wrench is in the red cabinet." Drawers are lined with indoor/outdoor carpeting, which protects the tools and keeps them quiet on the road. (Old chair springs keep the files from filing each other.) After repeated soakings in WD-40, the carpet lining helps prevent rust.

The Woodworkers Guide to Making and Using Jigs, Fixtures and Setups

As woodworkers graduate from Birdhouse 101, they often become involved in projects requiring lots of identical moves on common shop machinery. This book shows how to fabricate the hardware necessary to achieve that worthy goal. It's straightforward stuff, craftily presented, but beginners probably should do those birdhouses first. —JB

• The mortising machine looks complex, but it really is quite simple to assemble. An organized woodworker could do it in a few hours. You can buy a machine like this for about $600. As of this writing, the shop-made version will cost about $150. . . .

The mortising machine shown here employs a router and two sliding tables to make the cuts. One table holds the work and moves it in and out in relation to the cutter, controlling mortise depth. The other table holds the router and moves from side to side, controlling mortise width.

The Woodworkers Guide to Making and Using Jigs, Fixtures and Setups
David Schiff & Kenneth S. Burton, Jr. 1992; 450 pp. ISBN 0-87596-137-1 $26.95 postpaid. Rodale Press, 33 E. Minor Street, Emmaus, PA 18098; 800/441-7761

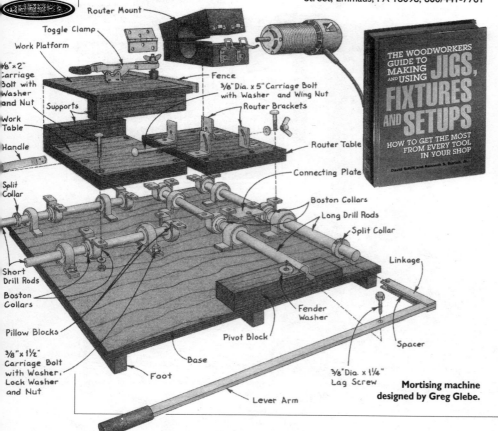

OVERALL VIEW

Router Mount
Toggle Clamp
Work Platform
3/8" x 2" Carriage Bolt with Washer and Nut
Supports
Work Table
Handle
Fence
3/8" Dia. x 5" Carriage Bolt with Washer and Wing Nut
Router Brackets
Router Table
Connecting Plate
Split Collar
Boston Collars
Long Drill Rods
Split Collar
Linkage
Short Drill Rods
Boston Collars
Pillow Blocks
Fender Washer
Pivot Block
Spacer
3/8" x 1½" Carriage Bolt with Washer, Lock Washer and Nut
Base
Foot
3/8" Dia. x 1¼" Lag Screw
Lever Arm

Mortising machine designed by Greg Glebe.

Improvements

Problem-solvers are most of what's in this assortment of unusual hardware, gadgets, nostrums, and, yes, a few doodads. The catalog answers a surprising number of those "I wonder where you get that?" questions. —JB

• **Now Electric Cords Won't Unplug Themselves!**

Almost every time you drag a weed trimmer through the bushes (or a power saw around a sawhorse), the electric plug gets snagged and pulls out the extension cord. More time wasted, more frustration.

Connect-A-Plug™ prevents accidental disconnection of electrical cords. It keeps two together within its strong polypropylene body — they won't pull apart. You get *two:* use one in your shop, the other for outdoor tools.

35600— Connect-A-Plug 2/$6.99

• **Thermostatic Blower "Booster" Delivers Up To 80% Greater Air Flow Out of Your Register . . . Heat Or A/C**

If the blower on your furnace or air conditioner doesn't reach a particular room, you know it's going to be cooler than the others in winter, or warmer in summer. Give that blower a boost! This automatic Register Airflow Booster 2 *pulls up to 80% greater air flow* out of your register. Built-in, energy-saving, electronic sensor turns the quiet fan on automatically when your blower goes on; sensitivity can be adjusted to compensate for poor register air flow.

Fits up to 12" x 6" *floor or wall* registers. "On-off-automatic" and "summer-winter" rocker switches; 6' 2-prong cord. Strong ABS housing. CSA and UL-listed.

49254 - Blower-Booster 2™ $49.99

• **Mini-Torch Heats To 2300° F, Lights With A Push Of A Button!**

That's hot enough to melt aluminum, copper, or gold, so it easily melts silver solder, thaws pipes or softens plastics and old paint (carefully used).

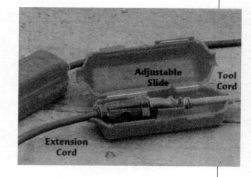

To ignite, just turn the gas nozzle to "open" and press the ignition button . . . works just like a piezo-electric cigarette lighter. No need for wicks, matches, or flints. It uses *butane fuel*, so refills for pennies, and it has a burn rate of up to two hours before refilling is required. Yet, it weighs only eight ounces and is only 5 3/4" long. Butane not included.

101212 - Mini-Torch $39.99

Improvements Catalog: Free from Leichtung Workshops, 4944 Commerce Pkwy., Cleveland, OH 44128-5985; 800/642-2112.

Energy-Efficient and Environmental Landscaping

Seasonal shade planting, windbreaks, water-efficient planting (xeriscape), and lawns are worked over well in this manual. You might be surprised at how much landscaping can affect your heating and cooling bill: the right trees and plants can reduce air-conditioning need by half. Windbreaks can do the same for winter heating loads. Here's how to do all that and look nice, too. —JB

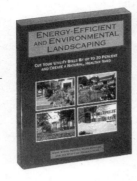

Energy-Efficient and Environmental Landscaping
Green Living Staff. 1994; 240 pp. ISBN 0-9638784-0-9
$17.95 ($19.95 postpaid). Appropriate Solutions Press, Dover Road, Box 39, South Newfane, VT 05351; 802/348-7441

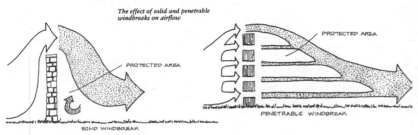

The effect of solid and penetrable windbreaks on airflow

PROTECTED AREA
PROTECTED AREA
PENETRABLE WINDBREAK
SOLID WINDBREAK

Alden Ponds

Want a small pond (complete with appropriate denizens) in your yard, but don't want to hunt around for everything you'll need? Here's where to get the (recycled) pond liner material and other supplies. Your downspouts can supply the water. (Obviously, there are cheaper ways to make ponds, but few that are easier and thus more likely to get done.) —JB

Alden Ponds: Catalog free. PO Box 395, Brentwood, NY 11717; 516/273-0255.

The Secret Garden

The microscopic world is at least as complex and mysterious as the outer reaches of the universe, and (relatively) easier to study. David Boudanis paints a vivid picture of what is going on in our gardens, under our noses and feet. The most far-fetched science fiction is not so far off, after all. Fantastically colored photo-electron micrographs of these fabulous tiny beasts and beauties accompany two parallel narratives, human and miniature. —Karen Van Epen

The Secret Garden
David Bodanis.
Touchstone Books, 1993; 187 pp. ISBN 0-671-86861-6
$14 postpaid. Simon & Schuster/Order Dept., 200 Old Tappan Road, Old Tappan, NJ 07675; 800/223-2336

Beetles are among the most successful life forms on the planet. This one is emerging from a grain of wheat.

The Natural Lawn & Alternatives

"Why struggle with lawn when there are scores of interesting plants that thrive on low light?" Why indeed? The chapter that encourages you to think that way outlines but one of many alternatives to grass. Of course, grass is still an option: new varieties are hardier and require less care (and suspicious chemicals). This little guidebook tells all. —JB

The Natural Lawn
Margaret Roach, Editor. 1993; 96 pp. ISBN 0-9453528-0-8
$6.95 ($10.70 postpaid). Brooklyn Botanic Garden Association, 1000 Washington Avenue, Brooklyn, NY 11225-1099; 718/941-4044

Clockwise from top left: *Hosta 'Kabitan', Asarum canadense, Hosta 'Louisa'* and *Pachysandra procumbens, allegheny spurge.*

Gazing Balls

They're called mirror balls or gazing balls. The glass spheres are intended to sit on a low pedestal in the garden, reflecting flowers, sky, sun and the passing scene. Choose a color for the effect you wish (here in the sun-fried California landscape, gold is especially nice). This is the first time I've seen them for sale west of the original thirteen colonies, and even there, satisfying fat ones like these twelve-inchers are not easy to find. Some folks feel that gazing balls also reflect a taste tending to the pink plastic flamingo; but for about a century now, many folks have regarded them as a rare garden-enhancing treat. Not suitable for neighborhoods infested with BB guns. —JB

Gazing Balls: In silver, mauve, blue, green, or gold. Each $47.50 ($53.50 postpaid). Wind & Weather, PO Box 2320, Mendocino, CA 95460; 800/922-9463.

The Natural House Book

No paranoia-inducing diatribes from this author, and no smug admonitions to strive for an impossible level of environmental correctness in your home. We get an encouraging look at the design and materials choices that'll help make a joyful, healthy home. The author makes it clear that the use of "natural materials" does not necessarily mean better health or reduced environmental impact — a point often missed. This book glows with wonderful examples (from all over the world) of things done imaginatively and well. The psychological effects of color, light, smell and space are enthusiastically stirred into the brew. There's even a discussion of feng shui (Geomancy).

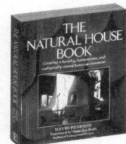

The Natural House Book
David Pearson. Fireside Books, 1989; 287 pp. ISBN 0-671-66635-5 $20 postpaid. Simon & Schuster/ Order Dept., 200 Old Tappan Road, Old Tappan, NJ 07675; 800/223-2336

This book is popular for good reason. It's certainly the best I've seen on the subject. —J. Baldwin

Sustaining the Earth

Debra Dadd-Redalia was one of the first to untangle the truth about which products are safe for the environment, and you. She's still at it, and still doing a great job of gathering information that would be very difficult for you to gather yourself. There is some overlap between this book, her previous publications, and *The Green Consumer*, but there's a lot of new material, too. Reading both will probably make you the local expert. —JB

Sustaining the Earth
Debra Dadd-Redalia. Hearst Books, 1994; 352 pp. ISBN 0-688-12335-X $15 ($16.50 postpaid). William Morrow and Co./Wilmore Warehouse, 39 Plymouth Street, Fairfield, NJ 07004

•

The FDA claims irradiation of food is safe and has already authorized the irradiation of fruits, vegetables, pork, chicken, herbs, spices, teas, and seeds. So far, spices are the most widely irradiated food in the United States. The FDA requires whole foods that have been irradiated to display on the label an international logo of a flower in a circle, but this is not a warning label, nor is any wording required to indicate the product is irradiated. However, when used as an ingredient in processed foods or in spice blends, the fact that a food has been irradiated does not have to be indicated on the label. Irradiated foods can also be used in restaurant foods, school cafeteria foods, or institutional foods without notification.

OTHER GREAT RESOURCES

Green Alternatives: $18/year (6 issues). 38 Montgomery Street, Rhinebeck, NY 12572; 914/876-6525. This magazine, like many others, discusses and advertises Green consumer products and procedures. The difference? A cool, straightforward editorial policy avoids mindless alarmist fluff and irritating political correctness.

The Green Consumer • The Green Consumer Letter

The Green Consumer is among the best question-answerers for consumers who would like to consume less destructively. Names are named, but the book is more a primer in basic principles by which to judge any item, not just those attended here. *The Green Consumer Letter* reports the latest findings and controversies. It's a lot sassier and inevitably more current than the book. —JB

•

What about those high-tech electronic flea collars advertised in magazines as environmentally preferable? Forget about them. As the EPA's Dennis Edwards puts it, "We'd be delighted if one did work, but as yet they don't."

•

The bottled-water industry is mopping up following 1991 findings by the Food and Drug Administration that the purity of its products leaves a lot to be desired. Among the findings: 31 percent of samples tested were tainted with bacteria. This, for water that sells for 200 to 1000 times more than tap water.

The Green Consumer
Joel Makower, John Elkington & Julia Hailes. Penguin Books, 1993; 320 pp. ISBN 0-14-017711-6 $11 ($13 postpaid). Penguin USA/ Consumer Sales, 120 Woodbine Street, Bergenfield, NJ 07621; 800/253-6476

The Green Consumer Letter: 1526 Connecticut Avenue NW, Washington, DC 20036; 800/955-GREEN or 202/332-1700.

The fact is, tap water turns out to be the source for about a third of the bottled water sold in the Unites States.

Household Ecoteam Program

Those who have tried to minimize their consumerism (how very appropriate that word is!) may have found that the Many-Things-You-Can-Do books just increase frustration. This workbook helps you organize your household into an Ecoteam. This step-by-step program can significantly improve your performance as a good environmental citizen. Monthly results from each Ecoteam are added to others in the community; those results are added to national and global totals. A feedback report shows you the morale-boosting accomplishments. To date, 7,000 households in 12 countries have participated. Those in the US reduced their garbage by 42 percent, water

Household Ecoteam Program
Membership $38 postpaid; includes the Household Ecoteam Workbook and newsletters. Global Action Plan, PO Box 428, Woodstock, NY 12498; 914/679-4830, fax 914/679-4834

use by 25 percent, and motor fuel by 16 percent, and saved an average of $401 — not bad for the first six months! —JB

Home heating and cooling

This is the biggest single energy use in the home, accounting on average for 59% of overall home energy use. Here are some things you can do to save energy, money, and the air around us:

◆ **Turn the thermostat down on your heating system; turn it up on your cooling system.**

Estimates are that you can save 2% on your heating for every degree you turn your thermostat down.

I am doing	____°F
More I will do	____°F
Not applicable	☐

Action step for this month: Agree within your household on the temperature at which to set the thermostat.

Action step done	☐
Date	_____ ◆

◆ **Turn down the thermostat at night or when you leave the house.**

This doesn't save as much as a steady turn down, because you will have to warm the space back up later, but the savings can still be substantial. A thermostat with a timer can make this process easy.

I am doing	____°F
More I will do	____°F
Not applicable	☐

Action step for this month: Agree within your household on the amount to turn down the thermostat at night. Optionally, purchase and install a timed thermostat.

Action step done	☐
Date	_____ ◆

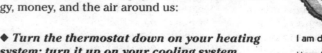

Defender Foam Systems

Add nontoxic Silv-ex concentrate to ordinary water and you get a persistent, damp foam that resists ignition for up to six hours. Much more effective than water for firefighting, Silv-ex saved many structures in the 1988 Yellowstone Park fire. Defender sells the foam, and a small pump system that can suck from any standing water source till the real firefighters come. —J. Baldwin

Defender Foam Systems: $1100 – $1600. Free brochure. Brushfire Hydrant Co., 1818-B Mount Diablo Boulevard, Walnut Creek, CA 94596; 510/932-5080.

Safer Home Test Kit

This is a set of simple tests and monitors that indicate dangerous levels of radon, lead (in paint, pipes and crockery, but not directly in water), microwave leakage, carbon monoxide (from stoves, heaters and engines), and ultraviolet radiation (as on a beach or through sunglasses). A formaldehyde test is available at an extra cost. Remember that amateur findings must be regarded as tentative. —JB

Safer Home Test Kit: $58 ($65.75 postpaid). 7th Generation/Order Dept., 49 Hercules, Colchester, VT 05446-1672; 800/456-1197.

Moving Heavy Things

This marvelous little primer brings to mere mortals the secrets of manipulating weighty objects without damage to mover or movee. The book encourages the proper spirit and thus independence; every household should have one. —JB

Moving Heavy Things
Jan Adkins. 1980; 48 pp.
ISBN 0-395-29206-9
$15.95 ($18.45 postpaid). Houghton Mifflin Co./Mail Order Dept., Wayside Road, Burlington, MA 01803; 800/225-3362

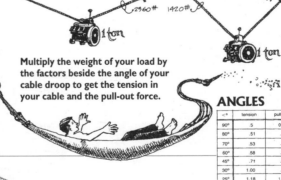

Multiply the weight of your load by the factors beside the angle of your cable droop to get the tension in your cable and the pull-out force.

ANGLES

<°	tension	pull-out
90°	.5	0
80°	.51	.10
70°	.53	.18
60°	.58	.29
45°	.71	.50
30°	1.00	.87
25°	1.18	1.07
20°	1.46	1.37
15°	1.93	1.86
10°	2.88	2.83
5°	5.74	5.72

Storm Whistle

Even a kid can elicit an ear-shattering shriek from this whistle, claimed to be the world's loudest. You can literally hear it a mile away under normal conditions. —JB

Storm Whistle: $5.95 in sporting goods and drug stores, or $7.95 postpaid from All Weather Safety Whistle Co., PO Box 8615, St. Louis, MO 63126; 314/436-3332.

The Extractor

Assuming you've practiced a few times, you can select the proper tip and have super suction on the snakebite (or insect sting) in less than a minute, with no infection risk. This thing could raise a hickey on a rhino! —JB

The Extractor™: $11.95 postpaid. Sawyer Products, PO Box 188, Safety Harbor, FL 34695; 800/356-7811.

Magna-Point Tweezers

A powerful magnifier mounted on fine-point, high-traction tweezers makes short work of most splinters, especially on your own anatomy. —JB

Magna-Point Tweezers: $9.95 ($11.95 postpaid). Miracle Point, PO Box 71, Crystal Lake, IL 60014.

On Duty Emergency Tool

Firefighters designed this pry bar/digging claw/water and gas shutoff wrench. —JB

On Duty Emergency Tool: $14.95 postpaid. On Duty, Inc., 13176 Oak Crest Drive, Yucaipa, CA 92399; 800/866-3889.

Consumer Reports (May 1994) p. 307: Home security alarm products are changing so fast that we have not included any here. Virtually all books are obsolete. The latest basic equipment is now cheaper and a lot easier to install; consult a reputable dealer/installer. The May 1994 issue of *Consumer Reports* has a good piece on security door hardware.

The Safety Zone Catalog: Hanover, PA 19333-0019; 800/999-3030. An interesting assortment of items (including a few of questionable merit) intended to help make your life safer.

⇦ **OTHER GREAT RESOURCES** ⇨

The Wary Canary: $20/year (4 issues). PO Box 2204, Fort Collins, CO 80522; 303/224-0083. Miners used to carry canaries to warn them of (forgive me) foul air — the luckless, hypersensitive birds fell off the perch before a human could detect danger. This newsletter serves today's canaries, the unfortunate folks suffering from Multiple Chemical Sensitivities (MCS). Their needs are helping to raise air and water quality standards for all of us.

The Drinking Water Book • Think Before You Drink

Good drinking water requires a good watershed to prevent polluted runoff, a good treatment system to deal with the peculiarities of your local water, and a good distribution system so that leaks and pipe leachates don't restore pollutants. **Think Before You Drink** *seeks to eliminate your need for bottled water or filters, at costs that are ultimately less per household. It addresses watershed, waterworks, community.*

Rampant individualism and skepticism of authority (the water department) have led many citizens to give up on community solutions in favor of custom-designed home water treatment. Some problems (like volatile organics and radon in your shower water) are difficult to manage without in-pipe filtering. Others, like calcium salts, are controversial. Others, like odor and taste, are easy. Bottled waters are not always the solution. **The Drinking Water Book** *is fine access to home health with an easy how-to format. It has some mistakes (like blaming nitrates on metheglobinemia), but they are minor.*

To help you custom-design, Real Goods has access to one of the better water-testing labs at a reasonable price. —PW

•
The Center for Disease Control, in a recent report, found that over 900,000 people become sick in the United States per year from contaminated water. The 1993 Milwaukee disease outbreak alone reportedly affected over 370,000 people. As the Milwaukee disease outbreak and many other cases highlight, AIDS patients, the elderly, young infants, and people that have compromised immune systems are put at greatest risk by these contamination problems, and in many cases have died from drinking water contamination.

•
Trihalomethanes and other disinfection by-products (DBPs) are formed when chlorine or other similar disinfectants are used to disinfect water that has not been treated to remove organic matter before disinfection. They are found in the drinking water of over 100 million Americans. A recent study by doctors from Harvard and Wisconsin, published in a prestigious journal, found that DBPs may be responsible for 10,700 or more rectal and bladder cancers per year. —Think Before You Drink

•
Radon is a known cancer-causing agent. When present in household water, it evaporates easily into the air and is inhaled. The effects of radon inhalation are now believed to be more dangerous than those of any other environmental hazard.

•
One type of organic chemical is particularly dangerous. Volatile organic chemicals, or VOCs, are absorbed through your skin when you come into contact with water, as in a shower or bath. Further, hot water allows these chemicals to evaporate rapidly, and they are harmful if inhaled. VOCs can be in any tap water, regardless of where you live or what your source of water is. If your tap water should contain significant levels of these kinds of chemicals, they will be a health threat from skin contact with the water even if you don't drink it. —The Drinking Water Book

Showerhead filters are usually available through water purification dealers. Some shower filters are filled exclusively with a redox medium (which removes chlorine more efficiently than carbon does), but redox can't remove radon. So if you buy a showerhead filter for radon removal, be sure it includes carbon in its filtering medium.
—The Drinking Water Book

The Drinking Water Book
(A Complete Guide to Safe Drinking Water)
Colin Ingram. 1991; 195 pp.
ISBN 0-89815-436-7

$11.95 ($15.45 postpaid). Ten Speed Press, PO Box 7123, Berkeley, CA 94707; 800/841-2665

Think Before You Drink
(The Failure of the Nation's Drinking Water System to Protect Public Health)
Erik D. Olson.

$7.50 ($8.95 postpaid). Natural Resources Defense Council/NRDC Publications, 40 West 20th Street, New York, NY 10011; 212/727-2700

ERE'S A FIRST: this *Whole Earth Catalog* displays no water conservation toilets, shower heads, or faucets. No need — they're everywhere. If you're still the evil waterwaster of yesteryear, buy the quarterly update of Real Goods' catalog — it has all you need.

Two reminders: check the new low flow clothes-washers, and read *Captain Hydro* (in English and Spanish from East Bay Municipal Water District, 510/835-3000 or 800/233-2683) to your kids.

—Peter Warshall

Planning for an Individual Water System

The water system you want will depend on the volume you need (fire protection, gardens, and the household), the water source (well, pond, roof), water quality, water transport (gravity or electric pumps), and the trade-off between labor and capital investment (do you want a hand-pump or automatic-backwash filter?). After twenty years and four editions, no other book comes near **Planning** *as a*

do-it-yourself manual with great illustrations and safety tips, and a great price. —PW

Planning for an Individual Water System
1982; 160 pp. ISBN 0-89606-097-7
$13 ($16 postpaid). American Association for Vocational Instructional Materials, 220 Smithonia Road, Winterville, GA 30683
800/228-4689

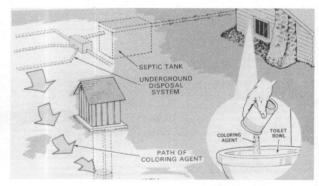

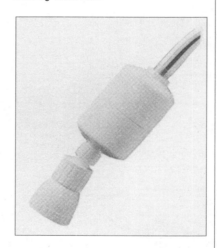

Below: Here is a sample of misleading claims from a recent advertisement, which uses a chart to compare the manufacturer's Reverse Osmosis unit ("Brand X") with bottled water and carbon filters.

In promoting its own RO system, this manufacturer has stretched the truth quite a bit. For example, the chart shows that Brand X RO removes bacteria and viruses. This isn't accurate. While ROs do remove some microorganisms, they cannot remove them all and manufacturers cannot legally make this claim. ROs are also notoriously poor at removing nitrates from the water, yet the chart claims that Brand X can remove them.

	Rust	Pesticides	Chlorine	Odors	Nitrates	Lead	Radium	Sodium	Asbestos	Bacteria	Virus
Bottled Water	X	X	X	X	?	?	?	?	?	?	?
	FDA bottled water standards are the same as EPA tap water standards										
Carbon Filter	X	X	X	X	–	–	–	–	–	–	–
	Carbon filters can be a breeding ground for bacteria										
BRAND X Reverse Osmosis	X	X	X	X	X	X	X	X	X	X	X
	BRAND X reverse osmosis is effective against almost all types of contaminants										

Note: This chart is an example of a misleading claim. —The Drinking Water Book

REAL GOODS, the source put forth for so many items mentioned on this spread, is itself reviewed on p. 119.

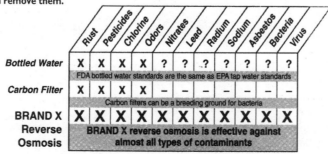

THE NEXT WHOLE EARTH VISION IS TOTAL REUSE — no more outfalls anywhere, ever. The technology is here to drastically reduce sewage in edge cities, municipalities and (surely) in neighborhoods and independent homes. For independent homes, Real Goods has news on the ultra in toilets, graywater soaps, and "off-the-aqueduct" homesite sewage. For communities, here are some sound-bites and news. —Peter Warshall

Wetlands can polish primary treated wastewater to better levels than most systems based on mechanics and energy. They have not received adequate attention because they require more real estate — and changes in the mentality of civil engineers. My first constructed wetland is twenty years old; it now holds the American record for the most kinds of birds ever recorded at a total recycling sewage plant (over 290!). No layperson's guide is available. But: think a million times before you let anyone discharge your effluent directly into a river, lake, or sea without a wetland in between. Here are some tech intros:

Constructed Wetlands (and Aquatic Plant Systems for Municipal Wastewater Treatment —

EPA Design Manual): 1988; 83 pp. EPA/625/1-88/ 022. Free. EPA Publications & Information Center, PO Box 42419, Cincinnati, OH 45242; 513/ 569-7597. A good intro with good examples.

Wastewater Engineering: Metcalf and Eddy. 1981, McGraw-Hill. This is the text that finally spanned the alternative and the mainstream. If you need to think about your town and what happens when you flush the toilet, this is the encyclopedia.

Ecological Engineering for Wastewater Treatment (2nd edition): C. Etnier & B. Gutersom, Editors. 1994, Lewis Publishers. — PW

National Small Flows Clearinghouse

If you need help with alternative wastewater issues or technical assistance for small-community wastewater systems, turn this faucet. The Clearinghouse produces the best technical quarterly (**Small Flows**), a load of free info, a computer bulletin board (800/ 544-1936), databases, and seminars. If you wonder when to pump your septic tank, or what kind of toilet paper best feeds its microbes, or how pressure sewers could save your town millions, this is the information aqueduct. For a great introductory poster on alternatives for small communities, spend two bucks and request #WWBLPEO2. —PW

National Small Flows Clearinghouse: West Virginia University, PO Box 6064, Morgantown, WV 26506-6064; 800/624-8301

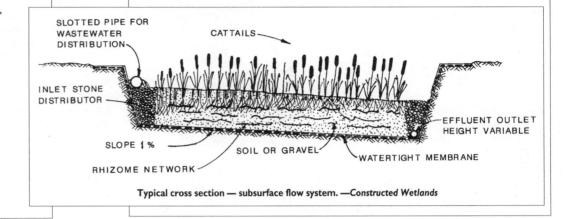

Typical cross section — subsurface flow system. —Constructed Wetlands

Waterless Toilets

Hey! If you're out in the country, an outhouse can work just fine. But the National Sanitation Foundation has approved an in-house waterless toilet (the Sun-Mar Composting toilet) that uses peat moss and the electric power of a small light bulb to prevent the horror show: ponded feces and urine. Sun-Mar has a non-electric and Real Goods a truly low-flow (quart) water closet. The best guide for building your own is **Guide to Building Your Own Compact Composter**. New on the market are solar-powered compost toilets; contact Bob Bland at Foresees, Inc. —PW

Sun-Mar: 5035 North Service Road C-9, Burlington, ONT L7L 5V2 Canada; 800/461-2461.

Guide to Building Your Own Compact Composter: Sietz Leeflang & Dion van Oirschot. 1991; 28 pp. $32 postpaid by US check, $24 by cash. De Twaalf Ambachten, De Bleken 2, 5282 HB Boxtel, The Netherlands.

Forsees, Inc.: 1525 Airport Road, Hot Springs, AR 71913; 800/338-3581.

Real Goods Trading Corp.: 966 Mazzoni Street, Ukiah, CA 95482; 800/762-7325.

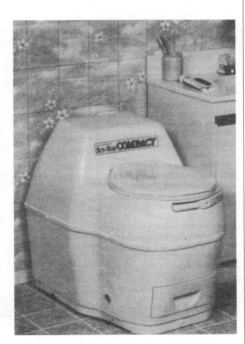

For those who don't need the larger capacity of the XL and have access to 120V power this is the recommended unit. For 1 person in full-time residential use, or 2-4 in intermittent cottage use. Sun-Mar Compact $1149

The Compact Composter needs only be emptied once ever 2 to 3 years. The amount of humus recovered depends on the amount of added kitchen wastes.

Graywater

Eighteen years after I wrote **Septic Tank Practices**, the first outlaw graywater leaflet in California, the state adopted a graywater code. Whew! Things are happening.

My new edition of **Septic Tank Practices**, Robert Kourik's **Gray Water Use in the Landscape**, and Real Goods will keep you up to date. —PW

Always cut into your existing plumbing after (down hill from) the vent pipe(s). If you're cutting into metal pipe, you must use a no-hub connector and tighten the two hose clamps carefully.

#1 existing pipe from gray water source

#2 trap

#3 vent pipe

#4 no-hub connector (with two hose clamps)

Gray Water Use In The Landscape
Robert Kourik. 1988; 28 pp. ISBN 0-9615848-1-5. $6 postpaid. Metamorphic Press, PO Box 1841, Santa Rosa, CA 95402; 707/874-2606.

Septic Tank Practices
Peter Warshall. Call or write: Real Goods Trading Corp. (See address under Waterless Toilets).

#5 sanitary wye (ABS)

#6 street 1/2 bend (ABS)

#7 piece of ABS pipe as connector

#8 PVC ball valve

#10 existing pipe to sewer/septic

—Gray Water Use

ORENCO: 2826 Colonial Road, Roseburg, OR 97470; 503/673-0165. The best source for intermittent sand filters and every other gizmo to custom-design your septic tank to the most unlikely habitats (slopes, landslides, beaches, shallow soils, clays). Great service. Great teachers.

Ocean Arks: 1 Locust Street, Salmus, MA 02546; 508/540-6801. New England artiste/wastewater solar aquatics specialists. They team up with civil engineers.

We All Live Downstream: Pat Costner. 1990, Waterworks Publishing Company. Best populist stream of info on pollution and home systems.

Water Books Catalog: Free from AgAccess, PO Box 2008, Davis, CA 95617; phone 916/ 756-7177, fax 916/756-7188.

The Meaning of Gardens

We make gardens for all reasons, following the muses of faith, power, ordering, cultural and personal expression, and healing. This exploration considers the why, not the how.
—Karen Van Epen

•

Every garden, even one just made, is a place haunted by spirits that whisper to our memory. The garden is thus nostalgic, reactionary. But just as strongly every time a garden is born, there is the hope that the world will be made better by it, an unselfconscious but radically utopian belief. Meaning resides in the power of the garden to express, clarify, and reconcile oppositions and transform them into inspirations.

•

My grandfather, on the other hand, a quiet tailor who had escaped religious persecution in Poland, spent considerable time in his garden—at least that is how I remember it. The same mild-manneredness he expended on a hem also found its subject in his backyard. I recall in particular fecund tomato plants, giant bushes of blue and yellow-green hydrangeas, and a central feature (was it round?) of brilliantly colorful annuals.

The families who are sharing their land have expressed an admiration for the Hmong gardeners' hard work and talents. The corn farmer, Ron, told me, "They are the most conscientious workers I have known." He has continued the arrangement for a second year and third year.

The Meaning of Gardens
Mark Francis & Randolph T. Hester, Jr., Editors. 1992; 283 pp. ISBN 0-262-56061-5 $24.95 ($27.95 postpaid) from The MIT Press/Order Dept., 55 Hayward Street, Cambridge, MA 02142; 800/356-0343

OTHER GREAT RESOURCES

Gardening By Mail: Barbara Barton. 1994, Houghton Mifflin Co. Leave it to a gardening librarian to collect every address you could need — nurseries and seed companies, garden suppliers, societies, libraries, periodicals — all in one superlative reference.

Landscaping for Wildlife: Carrol L. Henderson, 1987. Minnesota Bookstore/Documents Division, 117 University Avenue, St. Paul, MN 55155; 612/297-3000. A wealth of ideas, plans, and detail. Helpful to non-Minnesotans, too.

Redesigning the American Lawn: F. Herbert Bormann, Diana Balmori, and Gordon T. Geballe. 1993, Yale University Press. Symbols of suburbia, lawns can be transformed to enhance the neighborhood.

Fine Gardening: Betsy Levine, Editor. The Taunton Press, Box 5506, Newtown, CT 06470-5506; 800/283-7252. Beautifully illustrated profiles of unique gardens and gardeners make this the best of the ornamental-garden magazines.

National Gardening Association: 180 Flynn Avenue, Burlington, VT 05401; 802/863-1308. The great publications from these folks are the next best thing to a friendly neighborhood full of experienced gardeners.

Noah's Garden

Sara Stein discovered how gardening ruins life for wildlife — and reversed herself, redoing years and acres of work. If you've felt the desire to quit trying to save the world and retire to cultivate your own garden, take heart. You can do both. Perhaps you must do both. —Hank Roberts

•

I'm lucky to have spent my childhood summers among woods, streams, meadows, and marshes, but most suburbanites have never searched for frogs' eggs, caught fireflies in a jar, or peeked into a grassy nest of adorable baby mice. As the years pass, fewer and fewer people will long for the call of bullfrogs. Today's children, growing up on lawns and pavements, will not even have nostalgia to guide them, and soon the animals will be not only missing but forgotten.

•

I realize now that to help one's garden overmuch is to hinder it. I must have been living in another world when I wrote, only a few years ago and with considerable satisfaction, of the view from my window of our gardens "bare to their bones, neat and clean, nicely edged, weed-free." Now I see that there is teeming life down there that, neatly and cleanly, I was starving. Why was I not replacing in their beds the limp bodies of weeds I had uprooted? What was I doing cutting flowers to the ground, raking them away, bagging grass clippings, blowing autumn leaves from underneath the hedge? I was robbing the life savings from my garden beds, exposing them to the elements to leach their lifeblood away.

Noah's Garden
Sara Stein. 1993; 294 pp. ISBN 0-395-65373-8 $21.95 ($23.45 postpaid). Houghton Mifflin Co./Mail Order Dept., Wayside Road, Burlington, MA 01803; 800/225-3362

Color in Your Garden

Have you ever watched somebody do something they were really good at and then asked them to explain how they did it? Words often fail. Arranging color in a garden is like that: it involves positioning plants both in space and in time, through changes of bloom and season. Penelope Hobhouse succeeds at sharing years of gardening experience and at explaining the whys of her very refined sense of what goes with what. She begins with a color wheel and basic theory, and moves on to chapters like "Clear Yellows," "Pinks and Mauves," and "Hot Colors." Each chapter has a plant catalog arranged by season. The color photography is exceptional. —Richard Nilsen

•

There are both painters and gardeners who seem instinctively to understand color, placing pigments on a canvas or plants in a flowerbed with unerring discretion, which, often, they find difficult to explain. For most of us, however, understanding and appreciation come from a combination of observing what actually happens in nature with a study of theory.

•

The texture of a red petal, calyx or leaf surface affects the 'redness' we see; shining satiny tulips appear much lighter and brighter than the velvet of some rose petals, although the colors of the two may well match on a chart. One flower-petal in rain might become richer and more shining, another becomes sodden and dull. From a distance red flowers retain

their strong eye-catching and advancing quality and do not blend quickly with their own complementary green leaves to look pale yellow at a distance.

Color in Your Garden
Penelope Hobhouse. 1985; 240 pp. ISBN 0-316-36748-6 $45 ($49.40 postpaid) from Little, Brown and Co./Order Dept., 200 West Street, Waltham, MA 02154; 800/343-9204

Reader's Digest Illustrated Guide to Gardening

The vast resources of Reader's Digest produced an impressive book. The illustrations alone involved forty-four different artists. With step-by-step captions, they are frequently all that is needed to explain garden chores. The text explains more details than most people would have time for in a lifetime of gardening. My one reservation is the heavy reliance placed on synthetic pesticides and weedkillers — watch out here, or they will have you out there spraying everything from methoxychlor to paraquat. —RN

Reader's Digest Illustrated Guide to Gardening
Carroll C. Calkins, Editor. Reader's Digest Association, Inc. 1978; 672 pp. ISBN 0-394-21707-1 $30 ($32 postpaid) from Random House/Order Dept., 400 Hahn Road, Westminster, MD 21157; 800/733-3000

Xeriscape Gardening

It turns out that gardeners outside the drought-prone West need to watch their water consumption, too. This comprehensive book lays out the basics of low-water gardening, then presents more than 150 pages of suitable plants arranged in annotated regional lists. —Karen Van Epen

Xeriscape Gardening
(Water Conservation for the American Landscape)
Connie Ellefson, Tom Stephens & Doug Welsh. 1992; 320 pp. ISBN 0-02-614125-6
$30 postpaid from Macmillan Publishing Co., 100 Front Street, Riverside, NJ 08075-7500; 800/257-5755

●

Cobblestone runoffs. Instead of the unattractive solid concrete splash blocks at downspouts, try using a shallow swale with three- to six-inch diameter cobblestones extending to the edge of the planting bed and lawn or turf area. The cobblestones should be placed on a solid black plastic or Visqueen sheet for the first five to eight feet away from the house or building.

●

Judith Phillips, native plant propagator, in Albuquerque, New Mexico, emphasizes the need for extremely local information. She remarked that she was struck recently about how differently she and another grower in Santa Fe, just sixty miles north, at the edge of the Sangre de Cristo Mountains, regarded the water needs of several plants.

How to Grow More Vegetables

John Jeavons did not invent the bio-dynamic/French intensive method of gardening, but he clearly qualifies as its chief popularizer, and this book boils the technique down to its simplest terms. It is organic gardening using hand labor, raised beds, close spacing between plants to eliminate weeds and conserve soil moisture, and heavy feeding and composting. It can produce very large yields in very small spaces. It is therefore applicable to many diverse situations. —Richard Nilsen

●

A good growing bed will be 4 to 12 inches higher than the original surface of the soil. A good soil contains 50% air space. (In fact, adequate air is one of the missing ingredients in most soil preparation processes.)

How to Grow More Vegetables
(Than You Ever Thought Possible on Less Land Than You Can Imagine)
John Jeavons. 1991; 192 pp.
ISBN 0-89815-415-4
$14.95 ($18.45 postpaid)
Both from Ten Speed Press, PO Box 7123, Berkeley, CA 94707; 800/841-2665

The increased air space allows for an increase in the diffusion of oxygen (which the roots and microbes depend on) into the soil, and the diffusion of carbon dioxide (which the leaves depend on) out of the soil. This increased "breathing" ability of a double-dug bed is a key to improved plant health.

The Complete Book of Edible Landscaping

Titles with the "the complete book of" in them make me leery. In this case the phrase is deserved, for in addition to garden planning, construction, and maintenance, an exhaustive alphabetical treatment of 120 edible species tells everything from where they grow to how to cook them. The art described here is in combining utility with beauty to produce a garden that looks good enough to eat. —RN

●

Preserving and Preparing
Raw or Boiled Shoots: For all types of bamboo peel the outer layer to expose the white flesh. Cut small-diameter shoots into rings one node at a time, cut large shoots into slices. If the shoots are sweet they are edible raw in salads or with dips as an appetizer. However, most shoots are bitter until

parboiled for 15 to 20 minutes. Change the water after the first 10 minutes, and drain shoots when you are done parboiling them. To serve immediately, cook until tender, or preserve for later use. The raw shoots deteriorate very quickly, so process or serve them on the day they are harvested.

The Complete Book of Edible Landscaping
Rosalind Creasy. Sierra Club Books, 1982; 379 pp. ISBN 0-87156-278-2
$22 ($25 postpaid) from Sierra Club Store Orders, 730 Polk Street, San Francisco, CA 94109; 800/935-1056

ANOTHER GREAT RESOURCE

Lazy Bed Gardening
(The Quick and Dirty Guide): John Jeavons & Carol Cox. 1993, Ten Speed. A streamlined version of *How to Grow More Vegetables* (above).

Regional Gardening Books

Most of the really important secrets of successful gardening revolve around microclimate: what to plant when. You can thank your lucky stars and local garden devas for these gems of regional lore, thick with what and when for your neighborhood. —Karen Van Epen

Sunset Western Garden Book: 1988, Sunset Books. The premiere regional gardening book, this sets the standard, as yet unmatched for any other region.
Golden Gate Gardening: Pam Peirce. 1993, AgAccess. For the mostly mild, damp, cool conditions of the San Francisco Bay Area and Coastal California.
What Grows Here? Mountain Gardening in Northern California: 1992, Carol Young. Techniques for ornamentals and edibles, including fruit.
Desert Gardening: Fruit & Vegetables: George Brookbank. 1991, Fisher Books. Extreme variations of temperature make these gardens very tricky.
The Low Water Flower Gardener: Eric A. Johnson & Scott Millard. 1993, Ironwood Press. It's all very well to talk about what won't die from lack of water, but quite another thing to know what will actually thrive and flower.
Cold Climate Gardening: Lewis Hill. 1987, Garden Way. Specifics on all aspects of gardening (not just season extension) in the icebox areas.

Designing and Maintaining Your Edible Landscape Naturally

Edible landscaping is a new term for an old idea. It is a reaction to the lawns and shrubs that make many suburban yards look so boring. The idea is to integrate food plants into the landscape — specifically, to liberate fruits and vegetables from the rectangular prisons at the back of the lot.

What used to be common wisdom was lost when people stopped growing any of their own food, and ran out of time even to be in their gardens, let alone work them. That is changing, and these books suggest that vegetable gardening can also be aesthetic.

Robert Kourik has produced a classic homemade book in the best sense of the term. His mind works referentially, and fortunately by publishing his own book he didn't have to meet up with a linear-minded editor eager to streamline his work. The book is massive, detailed, totally indexed, full of charts and graphs that allow the comparisons and decisionmaking that land-

scape designing is all about. There is extensive information on selecting fruit-tree varieties and appropriate rootstocks.

Like all gardening books, this one is written with a sense of place (northern California) in mind. But Kourik is aware that your garden, right down to its microclimates, is unique. —RN

●

The amount of effort needed to sustain a landscape or garden is, perhaps, the single most important design consideration. Planting happens quickly, at the peak of the gardener's enthusiasm. Maintenance usually ends up being crammed into busy, everyday life.

●

Another way to understand the sunlight patterns and the microclimates of your yard is simply to grow vegetables. Instead of designing a landscape just after moving into your new home, wait and observe the yard through a complete cycle of seasons. For at least a year, grow edibles in a number of spots that seem to have beneficial

sunlight and climate. You will probably get a very good feel for the nuances of sunshine patterns, frost pockets, windy spots, wet soils, rocky soils, and other important information before designing your edible landscape. The placement of your first edibles may turn out to be ill-advised or just right.

Designing and Maintaining Your Edible Landscape Naturally
Robert Kourik. Metamorphic Press, 1986; 400 pp. ISBN 0-9615848-0-7
$20 ($24 postpaid). Edible Landscape, PO Box 1841, Santa Rosa, CA 95402

To capture a spider, invert a glass or jar over it, slip an index card underneath, carry the spider outside and release it.

Common-Sense Pest Control

Ants or cockroaches or weevils over-running your kitchen? To control them without toxic chemicals, you will probably have to pay more attention to the problem than if you were willing to spray a kill'em-all pesticide. To really know what you're doing, you need specific information about the life cycle of the pest you're dealing with. Detailed knowledge is the key to integrated pest management (IPM, as the breakthrough technique is dubbed).

Common-Sense Pest Control will fill the bill for years to come. It is a first-rate, encyclopedic reference presented in nontechnical language. Written by three pioneers of IPM, the volume is packed with truly safe techniques for managing all kinds of plant and animal pests. The authors supply the necessary level of fine detail for avid readers and scientists, while giving quick answers for people in a hurry.

The Olkowskis and Sheila Daar have been battling for decades to improve pest management methods and reduce worldwide use of poisonous chemicals.

To further the same goals, these three founded the Bio-Integral Resource Center (BIRC; see Other Great Resources). —Karen Van Epen

•

Ant Barriers. As discussed earlier, in some areas of the country certain ant species protect aphids from their natural enemies

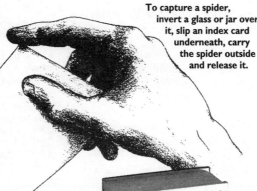

Common-Sense Pest Control
(Least-toxic solutions for your home, garden, pets, and community)
William Olkowski, Sheila Daar, & Helga Olkowski. 1991; 715 pp.
ISBN 0-942391-63-2
$39.95 ($43.95 postpaid) from The Taunton Press, Box 5506, Newtown, CT 06470-5506; 800/283-7252

to ensure that the aphids continue to excrete the honeydew the ants feed upon. If you see ants on aphid-infested plants, assume they are playing this protective role. The application of a band of sticky material (such as Stickem™ or Tanglefoot™, available at nurseries) to stalks of roses and other woody plants keeps the ants away. Be certain the foliage of the banded plant is not touching anything the ants can use as a bridge to the plant foliage.

•

Bedbugs at any stage of development are capable of withstanding starvation for 80 to 140 days; however, older stages are most starvation-resistant. With adequate food and normal development, the adult stage lives about 10 months. In unheated buildings without food, adults can live a year or longer. (It is an interesting characteristic of many blood-feeding organisms that they can actually live longer without food.)

Pests of Landscape Trees and Shrubs

*This first comprehensive guide to using IPM for woody landscape plants is directed at landscape professionals and homeowners. It tells how to identify, monitor, and manage the whole pest spectrum: insects, pathogens, nematodes, and weeds. The excellent color photos (over 300) are sharp enough to show minute details. In IPM, it really is important to be able to distinguish between two species of whitefly.
—Jill Hannum*

*This landmark book is cause for celebration, as it has potential to substantially reduce the toxic chemicals on our home turf, and in parks and commons across the country.
—KVE*

•

It may be beneficial to introduce mycorrhizae when planting new species that have not previously grown at that site. One way to do this is to collect soil or litter — if it is known to be free of pathogens — from around established older plants of that species and rake it into the soil around the young plants to be innoculated.

•

Commercial suppliers of *Trichogramma* normally ship the parasite in the form of parasitized caterpillar eggs glued to a piece of cardboard. The wasps, which complete their immature stage within the caterpillar eggs, should emerge as adults soon after the shipment arrives. *Trichogramma* are more likely to be effective if they are allowed to emerge in containers *lightly* streaked with honey diluted with water and permitted to feed for 24 hours before release.

Pests of Landscape Trees and Shrubs
(An Integrated Pest Management Guide)
Steve Dreistadt & M. L. Flint, Editors.
1994; 336 pp. ISBN 1-879-906-18-X
$32 postpaid from ANR Publications, University of California, 6701 San Pablo Avenue, Oakland, CA 94608-1239; 510/642-2431

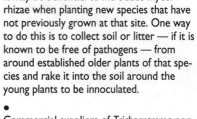

Environmentally Friendly Gardening

There's been a revolution in backyard vegetable gardening, and this book can help us profit from it. Pam Peirce interprets the new principles and techniques of non-chemical pest control for home gardeners. She uses good, crop-specific color photos to show us the guilty culprits, the good guys, and the problems caused by poor growing conditions. —KVE

Environmentally Friendly Gardening
(Controlling Vegetable Pests)
Cindy Putnam, Editor. Ortho Information Services, 1991; 160 pp. ISBN 0-89721-230-4
$12.95 ($14.95 postpaid) from Brent Lovell Associates, 3811 Pinot Court, Pleasanton, CA 94566; 800/732-0121

OTHER GREAT RESOURCES

Bio-Integral Resource Center (BIRC): PO Box 7414, Berkeley, CA 94707; 510/524-1758. A nonprofit educational organization, BIRC provides publications and services for environmentally sound pest control. The group also publishes a magazine for the layperson, *Common Sense Pest Control Quarterly*, and an international journal for pest control professionals.

Suppliers of Beneficial Organisms in North America: Charles D. Hunter. Free from California Environmental Protection Agency/Dept. of Pesticide Regulation, 1020 N Street, Room 161, Sacramento, CA 95814; 916/324-4100. A great directory listing 95 suppliers of over 125 organisms.

Pests of the Garden and Small Farm

*For most people, the major exposure to pesticides occurs in their own gardens. "Each year in California, home gardeners use about one pound of pesticide for every man, woman and child in the state," says author Mary Louise Flint. This richly illustrated book is filled with all the details about what you can do instead — for insects, plant diseases, nematodes and weeds. It's worth buying just to have good pictures of so many little critters finally gathered all in one place. It is keyed to California, but most of the species discussed occur throughout North America; the techniques (like soil solarization — cooking weed seeds and fungi to death in the soil under plastic sheets) will work anywhere.
—Richard Nilsen*

*Dr. Flint heads the IPM Manual Group, whose work has been a prime factor in the shift of farmers toward more sustainable agriculture. ANR carries their excellent manuals for commercial-scale management of alfalfa hay, apples & pears, almonds, citrus, cole crops & lettuce, cotton, potatoes, rice, tomato, small grains, and walnuts.
—KVE*

•

Most biological control occurs naturally without assistance from the grower or gardener. Often its importance is not appreciated until a broad spectrum pesticide, which kills certain natural enemies as well a targeted pests, is applied and a new pest — suddenly released from biological control — becomes a serious problem. This type of phenomenon, known as secondary pest outbreak, occasionally occurs in gardens. One example might be the sudden out-

break of aphid, scale, mite, or whitefly populations throughout a garden soon after a large tree has been sprayed with a broad spectrum insecticide such as carbaryl; not only are the pest insects in the tree destroyed, but also the insect parasites and other natural enemies in, beneath, and adjacent to the tree canopy.

•

Check your vegetable plants or orchard trees at least once a week . . . for signs of pests and pest damage. In orchards, pick a few leaves on each side of the tree to check for pests, pest damage, or disorders, check the trunk for injury, oozing sap or migrating insects. In vegetable crops, walk through the furrow turning over leaves on every few plants to check for signs of insects or disease.

Pests of the Garden and Small Farm
(A Grower's Guide to Using Less Pesticide)
Mary Louise Flint. 1990; 276 pp.
ISBN 0-931876-89-3
$30 postpaid from ANR Publications, University of California, 6701 San Pablo Avenue, Oakland, CA 94608-1239; 510/642-2431

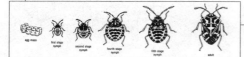

Development of a stink bug species, the harlequin bug, showing gradual metamorphosis with wing development.

The Complete Book of the Greenhouse

THE EXTERIOR, FROM THE ITALIAN TERRACE.

Obsessed with their cucumbers, the Brits really know their way around a greenhouse. So for once we can be delighted, rather than dismayed, to learn that a practical gardening book is English. Ian Walls' classic reference has been in print for twenty years, and he has ironed out all the kinks. He explains the design and operation of greenhouses, supplying crucial details about growing ornamentals, vegetables, and fruit. —Karen Van Epen

•

As the sun is never in the same position for long, any conventionally shaped greenhouse receives the maximum amount of light only for the very short period when the sun's rays penetrate the glass at 90° to the sun's rays. Modern types of round or geodesic greenhouses have been designed expressly to allow maximum light transmission over a period.

•

Cucumbers require regular watering, a regular supply of nutrients and good environmental control if they are to be a highly

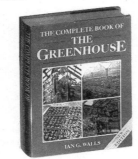

The Complete Book of the Greenhouse
Ian G. Walls. Ward Lock UK, 1993; 256 pp.
ISBN 0-7063-7186-0
$29.95 postpaid from Sterling Publishing
Co., 387 Park Avenue S., New York, NY
10016; 800/367-9692

successful or economically viable crop. Constant visual assessment of the nutrient situation is necessary. For short-season crops grown in properly made up beds supplementary feeding may not be needed. Guidance on this matter can be forthcoming from having an analysis made of the soil used for the soil/manure bed.

Start with the Soil

Stupendous crops of glowingly healthy plants do indeed start with the soil. Grace Gershuny is a master at explaining how to create the fragrant, dark, crumbly stuff that will make you proud of your garden. She does an excellent job of explaining how to care for the "soil community" of small and invisible organisms who contribute to the health of your plants. No mysticism, lots of specifics on managing soils for different situations: vegetables, flowers, lawns, trees, container plants. The book includes good, simple, well-illustrated explanations of the methods & benefits of composting and green manures. —KVE

•

Just as wine can vary widely in quality, so can humus. Its qualities will reflect different origins and composition. And just as different wines are suitable for different culinary purposes, the various types of humus serve varying soil functions.

•

Perennial weeds are frequently deep-rooted, helping break up hardpans, aerate the subsoil, and bring up mineral nutrients from areas too deep for crop roots. When the weeds die and decompose, these nutrients become available for other plants. Some plants are such reliable mineral accumulators that prospectors can use them to indicate a possible source of deposits such as copper and selenium.

blossom-end rot

weak stems

dry buds

curled leaves

stunted roots

This tomato plant shows signs of distress that point to a calcium deficiency.

Start with the Soil
Grace Gershuny. 1993; 274 pp.
ISBN 0-87596-567-9
$24.95 postpaid from Rodale Press,
33 E. Minor Street, Emmaus, PA
18098; 800/441-7761

The Rodale Book of Composting

The single best thing you can do for your garden is to improve the soil. And the simplest way to do that is to make compost. This manual answers almost every question you might have about the alchemy of transforming garbage into magical humus. Methods and materials are discussed, as well as how and when to use the finished product.

The authors don't stop with backyards, either. They supply more information about large-scale municipal or on-farm systems than you will find anywhere else. —KVE

**The Rodale
Book of Composting**
Deborah L. Martin & Grace Gershuny,
Editors. 1992; 278 pp. ISBN 0-87857-991-5
$23.95 postpaid from Rodale Press,
33 E. Minor Street, Emmaus, PA 18098;
800/441-7761

•

It is not possible to stress too heavily the "soil bank account" theory of fertilizing. The real purpose of the organic method is to build permanent fertility into the soil by adding to its natural rock mineral reserves and to its humus content. Practically all the natural fertilizers are carriers of insoluble plant food. They start working quickly, but they don't drop their load of food all at once, as does a soluble fertilizer. An insoluble fertilizer will work for you for months and years.

grass clippings

fallen leaves   weeds

wood ashes   kitchen scraps

twigs and wood chips   pet and human hair

shredded newspapers   garden residue

lint and sweepings

Worms Eat My Garbage

Worms Eat My Garbage
Mary Appelhof. 1982; 100 pp.
ISBN 0-942256-03-4
$8.95 ($10.45 postpaid) from Flower Press,
10332 Shaver Road, Kalamazoo, MI 49002;
616/327-0108

Before climbing onto a new bandwagon, especially one that involves as much trudging and toting as recycling does, it's a good idea to ask yourself, "Is anybody already doing this a simpler way?"

Take composting. You have smelly organic kitchen garbage, and you want great fertilizer for your garden. What else besides composting with your muscles can accomplish this transformation?

Worms can. Their castings are prized fertilizer, and they will live in an old box by the back door (or in the basement during a freezing winter when compost heaps stop working). This book tells you how. —Richard Nilsen

•

What kind of garbage and what do I do with it?

Any vegetable waste that you generate during food preparation can be used. Spoiled food from the refrigerator, such as baked beans, moldy cottage cheese, and leftover casserole also can go into a worm bin, enhancing the texture of the final vermicompost. Tea leaves, and even tea bags and coffee filters are suitable. Egg shells can go in as they are, and I have found as many as 50 worms curled up in one egg shell.

OTHER GREAT RESOURCES

Organic Gardening: $25/year (9 issues). PO Box 7320, Red Oak, IA 51591; 800/666-2206. The updated format and beautifully illustrated, fact-jammed articles put this old-timer way ahead of the competition. Not crazy after all these years.

HortIdeas: $15/year (12 issues). 460 Black Lick Road, Gravel Switch, KY 40328. The Williamses read through and report on all the latest horticultural information, with a good eye for the newest, most useful techniques, plants, tools, and books.

Four Season Harvest: Eliot Coleman. 1992, Chelsea Green. The secrets of season extension are revealed and demystified by garden master Coleman.

Gardener's Supply: 128 Intervale Road, Burlington, VT 05401; 800/863-1700. Big, colorful and informative, this catalog features believable testimonials from satisfied buyers of propagation equipment, tools, greenhouses, and all.

Gardens Alive!: 5100 Schenley Place, Lawrenceburg, IN 47025; 812/537-8650. Organic pest management and garden supplies.

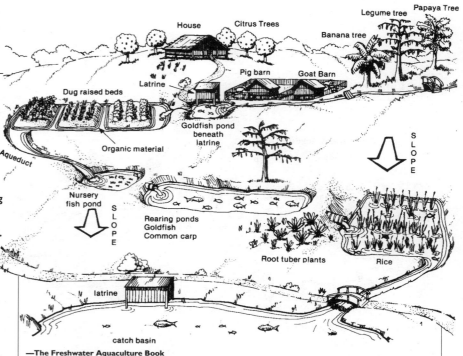

Garden Way Livestock Books

The classic series about raising livestock on a small to semicommercial scale. Garden Way offers a book apiece on rabbits, sheep, milk-goats, poultry, ducks, turkeys, dairy cattle, beef cattle, and pigs. Also a general book on livestock health. Each is clear, concise, and easy to read. —David Schneider

Garden Way Livestock Books: Publications list free. Storey Communications, Schoolhouse Road, Pownal, VT 05261; 800/827-8673

Simple method of killing a rabbit with a quick snap of its neck.

Cut around hock and slit from leg to leg. Then pull the skin down over the carcass the way you would peel off a pullover sweater.

Backyard Livestock

This wide-ranging book on animal husbandry has a useful section on each of the standard livestock animals. Chapters include advice on breeds, feeds, equipment, housing, health, management and butchering. —DS

Backyard Livestock (Raising Good, Natural Food for Your Family) Steven Thomas & George Looby. 1990; 229 pp. ISBN 0-88150-182-4 $14.95 ($17.45 postpaid) from the Countryman Press, PO Box 175, Woodstock, VT 05091; 800/245-4151

OTHER SMALL-LIVESTOCK RESOURCES

Caprine Supply Catalog: Free. PO Box Y, Desoto, KS 66018.

Stromberg's Poultry Supply Catalog: $1. Stromberg's Pets and Chicks Unlimited, Pine River, MN 56474.

Cheesemakers Supply Catalog: $1. New England Cheesemaking Supply Co., 85 Main Street, Ashfield, MA 01330; phone 413/628-3808, fax 413/628-4061.

—The Freshwater Aquaculture Book

Aquaculture • The Freshwater Aquaculture Book

British Fishing News Books, a division of Blackwell Scientific Publications, seems to be dedicating itself to making handsome aquaculture books on specific topics. The **Aquaculture Training Manual** *is a good example of the high-quality work this press produces.*

Aquaculture is to water what agriculture is to Earth and, as such, is nearly an impossibly large topic. With **The Freshwater Aquaculture Book**, *Bill McLarney provides the definitive how-to text on a relatively small scale. His audience ranges from the average rural household with pond or stream nearby, to medium-size commercial operations.* —DS

Aquaculture Training Manual Donald Swift. Fishing News Books, 1993; 158 pp. ISBN 0-85238-194-8 $29.95 ($34.45 postpaid) from Blackwell Scientific Publications, 238 Main Street, Cambridge, MA 02142; 800/759-6102

The Freshwater Aquaculture Book William McLarney. 1984; 583 pp. ISBN 0-88179-018-4 $40 ($43.50 postpaid) from Hartley & Marks, Inc., P.O. Box 147, Point Roberts, WA 98281; 206/945-2017

The How-To-Do-It Book of Beekeeping

Apiculture has been, and will be, around a long time — humans have a lot of uses for wax, and they dote on honey. According to former WEC editor Dick Fugett, all the major technological advances in beekeeping had been made one hundred years ago.

However, the literature on the subject keeps growing. Perhaps this is because bee people are something like baseball people: their obsessions are productive of smart prose. This delightful book covers every aspect of the craft with humor, and in detail. —DS

•

You cannot be tending an apiary and talking at the same time unless, of course, you are talking to the bees. They do not hear you, but that is not to the point. You talk to them anyway, simply as an expression of your kinship with them. It is in this sense like saying prayers. The question whether or not one's prayers are 'heard' is largely irrelevant.

Inserting an escape screen.

The How-To-Do-It Book of Beekeeping Richard Taylor. Linden Books, 1977; 251 pp. ISBN 0-9603288-2-3 $8.95 ($12.95 postpaid) from AgAccess, PO Box 2008, Davis, CA 95617; phone 916/756-7177, fax 916/756-7188

Killer Bees

One of the most notorious bits of modern species invasion involves bees. Wanting the huge honey loads of African bees, a Brazilian geneticist named Warwick Kerr imported some queens in 1956, and thus began "conquest" of the Americas by these fierce insects.

Mark Winston traces the ecological and economic impacts of the invasion. He also points out successful adaptations by beekeepers, livestock owners and the general public. An authoritative book, by one of the early researchers (he's got stings to complement his academic credentials). —DS

Killer Bees Mark L. Winston. 1992; 162 pp. ISBN 0-674-50353-8 $10.95 ($13.95 postpaid) from Harvard University Press/ Customer Service, 79 Garden Street, Cambridge, MA 02138; 800/448-2242

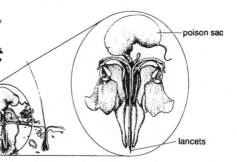

poison sac

lancets

A honeybee sting in action. Note the large poison sac and the barbed lancets that anchor the sting in the flesh as the bee pulls away and dies.

OTHER GREAT BEE SOURCES

The Beekeeper's Handbook: Diana Sammataro & Alphones Avitabile. 1986, Macmillan Publishing Co. Out of print. Considered by many to be one of the most thorough and accessible beginners' books, it would benefit the beekeeping world if this were put back in print.

The New Comb Honey Book: Richard Taylor. 1982, Linden Books.

Mastering the Art of Beekeeping: Ormond & Harry Aebi. 1982, Prism Press/ AgAccess. Gorgeous drawings, inspired, chatty text.

The ABC and XYZ of Bee Culture: Amos Ives Root, Roger Morse & Kim Flottum. 1990, A. I. Root Co. Literally an encyclopedia, loaded and indispensible to a serious beekeeper. Not a beginner's book.

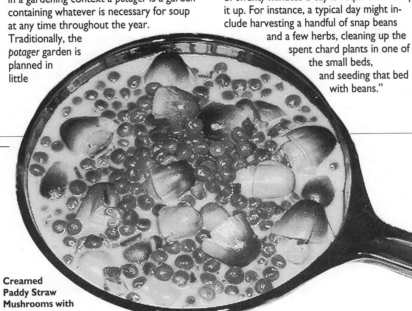

Cooking from the Garden

The notion of turning pages and salivating is a bit new, but this book did that for me. It is actually several books rolled into one. The price and full-page color photography make it suitable for the food-as-art coffee table. The information on gardening techniques, and what varieties gardeners around America are growing, make this a fascinating gardening book. And the recipes, which come from all over the world and which use vegetables but are by no means only vegetarian — well, that's where the drooling comes in.

This enormous book is really a state-of-the-art survey of America's gardens and kitchens. The link between the two is not new but very old, and by artfully re-establishing it, Rosalind Creasy is providing that awareness so essential before the public can demand and get food that is not only tastier, but safe to eat.

The book is filled with profiles of people from both ends of the food

spectrum — market gardeners, specialty growers, seed dealers, and chefs — and Creasy is always asking not just "what are you growing or using?", but "how do you cook it?" The recipes come pouring in from everywhere, because every gardener is a cook and, by implication, every cook should be a gardener, or at least care more about where the ingredients come from. Creasy's first book, **The Complete Book of Edible Landscaping** (p. 165), put vegetables outside the kitchen door, and even into the front yard; this book puts them in the soil, the kitchen, and the imagination. —Richard Nilsen

●

Potage is the French word for soup, and in a gardening context a *potager* is a garden containing whatever is necessary for soup at any time throughout the year. Traditionally, the *potager* garden is planned in little

Cooking from the Garden
Rosalind Creasy, 1988; 547 pp.
ISBN 0-87156-588-9
$25 ($28 postpaid) from Sierra Club Store Orders, 730 Polk Street, San Francisco, CA 94109; 800/935-1056

three- or four-foot-square or rectangular plots, which rotate with the seasons, along with a nursery area for young seedlings. . . .

As Georgeanne put it, "This garden fits into your life; it doesn't dominate it. Once the garden area is prepared, an average of twenty minutes a day is required to keep it up. For instance, a typical day might include harvesting a handful of snap beans and a few herbs, cleaning up the spent chard plants in one of the small beds, and seeding that bed with beans."

Taming the Wild Mushroom

Yum! The best cookbook for the twelve most popular mushrooms on the market. Oyster mushroom fritters, chanterelle popovers, enokitake and endive salad, marinated matsutake salad. Yum! (See also **Edible Wild Mushrooms of North America** by David Fischer and Alan Besette for more recipes from wild-foraged mushrooms.) —PW

●

Due to its vibrant color, apricot like fragrance, and fruity flavor, the Chanterelle is one of the most popular of wild edible mushrooms. Its texture is delicately chewy and crunchy and holds up well in cooking. Like fruit, it is excellent with poultry of all kinds, with cheese and cream sauces, in soups and casseroles, and with eggs. To enhance its flavor, which can have peppery undertones, try combining Chanterelles with nutmeats, dried apricots, apples, or peaches. Due to the Chanterelle's sturdiness, it is excellent in baked dishes. Additionally, its color provides a nice decorative touch to meals.

Creamed Paddy Straw Mushrooms with Baby Peas.

Taming the Wild Mushroom
(A Culinary Guide to Market Foraging)
Arleen Rainis Bessette & Alan E. Bessette.
1993; 113 pp. ISBN 0-292-70798-3
$24.95 ($26.95 postpaid) from University of Texas Press, PO Box 7819, Austin, TX 78713-7819; 800/252-3206

Fungi Perfecti • Growing Gourmet & Medicinal Mushrooms • The Mushroom Cultivator

If you're a gardener and want a delicious mushroom crop, an indoor mushroomer with a craving for a golden oyster patch, or a professional cultivator in need of equipment, advice or a seminar, these are prime forage.

Cultivator has sixteen edible and psychoactive species; Growing Gourmet has twenty-five medicinal and best-tasting edible species. Growing Gourmet is, in addition, the break-through book on using mushrooms for environmental improvements and mushroom permaculture.

Fungi Perfecti is the central source for field guides and needs for all the cultivation styles mentioned above. FP also sells a wonderful Children's Mushroom Garden. —PW

Shitake mushrooms fruiting from blocks of supplemented alder sawdust

The Mushroom Cultivator
Paul Stamets & J. S. Chilton. Agarikon Press, 1983; 416 pp. ISBN 0-9610798-0-0
$29.95 ($34.95 postpaid).

Growing Gourmet & Medicinal Mushrooms
Paul Stamets. Mycomedia/Ten Speed Press, 1993; 552 pp.
ISBN 0-89815-608-4. $49.95 ($54.95 postpaid).

Both from **Fungi Perfecti:** PO Box 7634, Olympia, WA 98507; 206/426-9292.

Herbal Renaissance

Herbalist Steven Foster has broken the mold with this excellent new volume, unique in several aspects. In addition to cultural information for home gardeners, it covers commercial-scale growing, a topic not covered anywhere else. Knowledgeable about both medicinal and culinary uses of herbs, Foster has traveled and studied widely. The information he shares with us is from his own direct experience, extremely valuable to professionals and regular folks, too. Much of this is new research, not to be found in other herbals, such as details about Native American and Chinese medicinal plants. —Karen Van Epen

●

Seeds may rot in a cold, damp soil, as happened to my basil planted in the spring of 1978. We had over twenty-five days of rain that June. The soil surface became crusty on the few sunny days we had, and the seed was sealed in the ground, rotting before it could germinate. Seed may also slip up to the soil's surface after a rain because of the slippery coat produced by the mucilage in the seed.

●

Ironically, while the rest of the world is increasing therapeutic application of peppermint oil, the FDA, in its ongoing over-the-counter (OTC) drug-review process, has removed peppermint from its list of effective digestive aids. During the OTC review process, manufacturers submit new data on safety and efficacy to support new OTC drugs. Since no company came forward with information on peppermint, it was simply dropped from the list of safe and effective remedies.

Herbal Renaissance
Steven Foster.
1984; 234 pp.
ISBN 0-87905-523-5
$16.95 ($18.95 postpaid) from Gibbs Smith Publisher, PO Box 667, Layton, UT 84041; 801/544-9800

A NEW GENERATION OF MEDICAL computing systems will serve layfolk as well as doctors. Providing customized health information without arcane technical knowledge or sophisticated hardware, these new systems will play an important part in our effort to reinvent health care.

The self-care movement goes back, of course, at least to the early seventies. But the emergence of the new generation of electronic tools will enable the layperson to do what only the most dedicated and diligent could do before. Recent professional meetings have focused on a new field of medical computing, Consumer Health Informatics (CHI). It now seems clear that CHI systems will support consumers' desire to play an upgraded role in their own health maintenance and treatment.

Recent CHI system demos have included a home health workstation for people with AIDS (the CHESS program), an interactive system that helps men with enlarged prostates decide whether to have surgery (the Dartmouth-Sony decision support videodisks), a psychological spreadsheet for people experiencing high-stress life events (the Therapeutic Learning Inventory), a personal health information system for home use (Healthdesk), a voicemail-based self-help network (Talknet), consumer-initiated searches of the medical literature, a wide variety of health-oriented BBSs, and increasingly useful and accessible health forums and other information resources on CompuServe, America Online, the Internet, and other computer networks. Also proposed or in development: consumer-provider email/voicemail links, patient interfaces for computerized medical records, diverse online and interactive networks, databases, and other resources.

Many recent CHI meetings have been interrupted by stunned silence as we grasped some of the long-term consequences.

Certain widely held assumptions must be abandoned: that we can safely ignore our own health until we have a breakdown experience, then count on the doctor to bail us out; that only doctors can know about medicine. We have to provide ourselves, and especially our children, with tools, skills, information, and support to assume the role of primary practitioner.

Our present "map" of health care, developed nearly a century ago, divides health care into three categories: primary (front-line health professionals), secondary (community hospitals and specialists), and tertiary care (academic medical centers). The realm of lay medicine has been overlooked. We have ignored (and often actively rejected) our biggest health resource of all — our ability, as informed layfolk, to prevent or manage our own health problems.

CHI systems will help us reconnect self-help and self-care with professional medical care. The health-active consumer, the concerned family member, the neighborhood natural helper, the corporate wellness professional, the self-help-group coordinator, the network sysop, and perhaps other key players — working in cooperation with a new generation of supportive health professionals — will be the real primary practitioners.
—Tom Ferguson, M.D.

For information on future conferences and publications on consumer health informatics, send a self-addressed, stamped envelope to:

CHI Info c/o MailComm Plus, 2729 Exposition Boulevard, Austin, TX 78703; 512/472-1296.

FROM INDUSTRIAL-AGE MEDICINE TO INFORMATION-AGE HEALTH CARE

With the support of effective CHI systems, a person with a health concern should be able to manage it on the highest possible level of this new "map" of the health care system.

1. Individual Self-Care. When people first become aware of a health concern or problem, they first attempt to prevent, diagnose, manage and/or treat it on their own. In most cases they are able to do so.

2. Friends & Family. When individual self-care doesn't do the trick, people turn to family, friends, and neighbors for advice, information, and support. Much additional care will be provided at this level as more layfolk are encouraged to see themselves not only as consumers of health care, but as key providers.

3. Self-help Groups and Networks. When the help above is not sufficient, people turn to experienced self-helpers, mutual aid networks, and "natural helpers."

4. The Health Professional as Facilitator. Many unnecessary clinical visits occur because consumers can't get information or advice by phone or email. Electronic communication between layfolk and professionals could cut costs while improving care. Health professionals would have to put aside their "authority" role and serve as advisors, facilitators, and supporters of self-provided care. The assumption would be that even though professional consultation was needed, clients could successfully manage most aspects of most health problems on their own. Resolution of legal liability issues would make health professionals more comfortable with this new role.

5. The Health Professional as Partner. Serious or chronic problems would require occasional or regular contact between patients, families, and health professionals — by some combination of telephone or electronic link and/or clinic, home, or hospital visits.

6. The Health Professional as Authority. In emergency situations, when the person needing care is unconscious or incapacitated, or in cases where the client chooses certain high-tech interventions, layfolk might ask health professionals to make the key medical decisions — at least on a temporary basis. —TF

Health in the Information Age

In this audio tape, Ferguson proposes that we are in the early stages of a medical Reformation as profound as the religious Reformation of Luther's day. The current medical Reformation is transforming a professional elite from authorities to facilitators, and establishing the legitimacy of lay opinion and self-determination in a field formerly considered the exclusive domain of experts.

He traces the current health information explosion from the mid-seventies to the present, then takes us through the six levels of the emerging Information Age health care system (see facing page). The message here is that professional health care is an important but diminishing part of health care. Self-care, mostly invisible till now and often ignored or actively discouraged by health professionals, is becoming more visible and important by leaps and bounds. And health-responsible behavior turns out to be more closely related to individual fulfillment and personal growth than to blindly following "doctor's orders."
—Elaine Davenport

●

Who do people ask for help when faced with medical, psychological, or marital problems? They almost always ask women. Women are the main providers of lay health care. This is one of the reasons self-help and self-care have been largely ignored: they were considered women's work and not part of the real (i.e. doctor-centered) medical economy.

●

The primary goal of the old health care system was to empower the health professional. The primary goal of the new health care system will be to empower the client.

●

The take-home lesson of the new health care system is that we each have the right—and the responsibility — to fully empower ourselves. No one can give us a 1-2-3 formula that is exactly right for our unique situation. There is always a choice of options. And we are the ones who should make the final choices.

Health in the Information Age: Tom Ferguson, M.D. 90-minute tape. $16.95 postpaid. Writer's AudioShop, 204 E. 35th Street, Austin, TX 78705; 800/88-WRITE or 512/476-1616.

Lee Hancock's List

This is the definitive annotated list of health resources on the Internet. Officially known as the Internet/BitNet Health Science Resources List, it can be browsed on various gophers.

Lee's AIDS listings provide access to state-of-the-art research — the information is much more current than anything in the printed literature.

Many FTP sites listed have a good selection of patient education materials. Or you can read the latest bulletins, direct from the researchers.

The current edition prints out to 91 pages. Many of the listings are for medical professionals, but a great many more will be useful to self-helpers. Lee updates his list several times a year and would be happy to hear about additional or updated listings for future editions. —TF

●

Electronic Publications:
ALS Digest (Bob Broedel, Editor)

To subscribe, unsubscribe, or to contribute notes, please send e-mail to bro@huey.met.fsu.edu (Bob Broedel). (Amyotrophic Lateral Sclerosis or "Lou Gehrig's Disease") This includes ALS patients, patient supporters, physicians, support groups, research centers, etc.

The Blind News Digest

The Blind News Digest is an electronic-mail only digest of articles dealing with blindness or any type of vision impairment. To subscribe send an e-mail message to: wtm@bunker.shelisc-br.com, Listserv: BLINDNEWS list at NDSUVM1

Internet Data Archives:
CancerNet
A quick and easy way to obtain, through electronic mail, recommended treatment guidelines from the National Cancer Institute's Physician Data Query (PDQ) system in English or Spanish. For directions for accessing CancerNet, you may call (301) 496-7403 or send an e-mail message to cheryl@icicb.nci.hih.gov on the Internet.

Lee Hancock, Educational Technologist: Archie R. Dykes Library, University of Kansas Medical Center, 3901 Rainbow Boulevard, Kansas City, KS 66160-7181; 913/588-7144, Internet: LEO7144@UKANVM.CC.UKANS.EDU

Internet/Bitnet Health Science Resources List: Send SASE for current ordering information. 3580 Rainbow Boulevard #826, Kansas City, KS 66103

Internet/Bitnet Health Science Resources List: Available through FTP at FTP.SURA.NET in directory PUB/NIC as file MEDICAL.RESOURCES.XX (XX=Date of last update).

OTHER GREAT RESOURCES

The CHESS Project: Room 1119, 610 Walnut Street, University of Wisconsin, Madison, WI 53705; 608/263-0492. This state-of-the-art CHI system is essentially a home health workstation plus email support network for people with AIDS, breast cancer, or another health crisis. Designed to be used by local governmental agencies, HMOs, and hospitals, the current version runs on an inexpensive 286 IBM clone.

The Dartmouth-Sony Series of Decision-Support Videodisks: Foundation for Informed Medical Decision Making, PO Box C-17, Hanover, NH 03755; 603/650-1180. These interactive multimedia programs help consumers make key decisions on treatment of enlarged prostate, low back pain, breast cancer, and mild hypertension.

The Therapeutic Learning Program: Interactive Health Systems, Suite 210, 525 Broadway, Santa Monica CA 90401; 310/451-8111. This psychological spreadsheet provides many of the same benefits as brief psychotherapy; 96 percent positive ratings from users.

HealthDesk: 1801 5th Street, Berkeley, CA 94710. 510/843-8110, fax 510/845-8305. This Windows program is a sort of combination family medical record and hypertext health encyclopedia. Add-on modules will allow in-depth resources on topics of special interest.

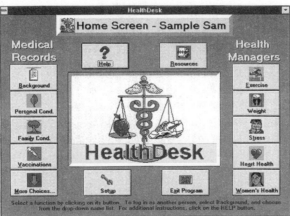

Talknet: Farrokh Alemi, Ph.D., Health Administration Program, Cleveland State University, Cleveland OH 44115; 216/687-4749, 216/229-2121, fax: 216/687-9317. A pioneering use of voicemail as a vehicle for self-help and professional-client communication.

Dial-Health: Access numbers for modem communication: 410/381-4256, 301/251-6157, 703/451-3932, 510/528-2900. This on-line service provides users with health information and networking. It contains 14,000 health-related articles, daily news from *USA Today*, electronic mail capabilities, an extensive database of hospitals, doctors, and information on the latest health products.

Mindware Catalog: 1803 Mission Street, Suite 414, Santa Cruz, CA 95060; 800/447-0477. A catalog of computer programs and CD-ROMs in the general area of self-help, success, and self-improvement.

Health Information Brokers

It's getting easier and easier to search the popular and professional medical literature. The groups below do customized online medical searches for a fee; some can help you learn to do searches on your own. —TF

Planetree Health Resource Center: 2040 Webster Street, San Francisco, CA 94115. 415/923-3680.

The Center For Medical Consumers: 237 Thompson Street, New York, NY 10012; 212/674-1705.

HRI Services (Health Research and Information), 4527 Montgomery Drive, Suite E, Santa Rosa, CA 95409. Voice 707/539-3967, fax 707/539-8234.

The Health Resource: 564 Locust Street, Conway, AR 72032; 501/329-5272.

AIC Services: PO Box 8030, Ann Arbor, MI 48107; 313/996-5553.

Medsearch Unlimited: 4515 Merrie Lane, Bell Aire, TX 77401; 800/748-6866.

Consumer Health Informatics

Includes a summary of conclusions reached by CHI systems experts and developers. Also: an extensive selection of conference handouts, contacts and mailing lists, listings of developers and researchers, key articles, and vision statements by developers and early CHI users. —TF

●

On Wednesday and Sunday nights, there are open Alcoholic Anonymous meetings that people from across the country attend on CompuServe. A diabetes group meets Thursday evenings, and the closed incest survivor's group is on Friday. Yet those participating in such national meetings never leave their homes. People are using their home computers to go beyond the bounds of traditional face-to-face groups to share common concerns, practical information, emotional support, and advocacy plans via electronic networks and communities. But on-line self-help groups are only one example of the opportunities available for mutual help and information "on-line."

●

Ultimately the best measure of the effectiveness of CHESS comes from users, like the HIV-positive man who left this message in the Discussion Group:

"I'm proud to say I've gotten as far as I have in the past couple of months because of this CHESS program. I feel as if I've grown by giant leaps and bounds, as if a whole new person has come out from inside me, it was always there but never came out, something like a spring flower. Thanks for all your great support and advice. I know I'm only at the beginning of my growing stage but I'm hoping for a good growing season. Coming out so honest to this machine is what I feel has broken the barrier I had set up for myself, then this machine came alive and became real, and now suddenly these real people really know me, WOW! I'm finally started going to groups and meeting lots of new people, and getting my life going again."

Consumer Health Informatics (Proceedings of the First National Conference on Consumer Health Informatics) Tom Ferguson, Editor. 1993; Self-Care Productions $24.95 ($33.45 postpaid) from Mailcomm Plus, 2729 Exposition Blvd., Austin, TX 78703; 512/472-1296

Finding or Forming Your Own Self-Help Network (Face-to-Face or Online)

By Edward J. Madara and Tom Ferguson, M.D.

SELF-HELP NETWORKS ARE LIKE SURROGATE FAMILIES: members share common problems and help each other toward mutual goals. The support they provide is available for free and, in most cases, around the clock. A surprisingly large proportion of self-help activity takes place late at night — through personal visits, phone calls, email or online computer networking.

In our increasingly fast-paced society, the traditional supports — the nuclear and extended family, the neighborhood, and the community — seem to be falling away. It is no coincidence that at the same time that these traditional links are disappearing self-help networks are growing rapidly.

"Families of choice" can help provide a lifesaving buffer against the stresses and challenges of life. The tips and personal experiences we share as group members can help us build our self-confidence and develop the coping skills we need to manage our health problems — and other life situations. Research is beginning to show a dramatic correlation between support group participation and improvements in both physical and mental health.

Becoming involved in a support group can allow you to plug into a powerful network of proactive people with similar concerns. Self-helpers offer the kind of hard-earned wisdom and intense personal knowledge that can be born only from living with a problem. They are thus often able to offer a much wider and deeper range of potential strategies and guidelines than medical and helping professionals, whose expertise is often limited to the technical, pathological, and pharmacological aspects of a condition. And unlike most professionally oriented medical institutions, which often push people into the role of dependent patient, self-help networks typically encourage members to build their competence and to hold on to their power.

Self-help networks can also serve as an effective interface between the person needing help and the professional health care system, destigmatizing problems, explaining treatment benefits, helping newcomers understand when professional help really can be useful and the best way to go about getting it, and providing access to the best information on their focus topic.

Finding or forming a network on the topic of your own special interest may be easier than you think. The first step is to find out what groups already exist, locally and nationally. The resources on page 173 provide a good starting place, but don't stop there. Let friends know what you're looking for. Use your networking skills. Many of the newer, smaller groups and networks are extremely informal and may not be advertised or listed in the standard directories.

Choosing a self-help network is much like choosing a potential romantic partner: look for the one that feels right, that provides the best match between you as an individual and the values and focus of the group.

If you don't find the group of your dreams, consider starting your own. But don't try to do it alone. Identify and communicate with other potential group founders through personal contacts and/or informal consultation. Reach out into the community with flyers and letters; leave online messages on the most appropriate bulletin boards or networks.

Most experienced group founders suggest starting with a core group of two to five people. Identify and contact any existing group that could serve as a model, providing information and guidance.

The next step is to see if anybody shows up. Be ready to rethink the focus of the group or perhaps divide into subgroups. Avoid trying to do everything yourself, as this may result in the other members perceiving the group as "yours," not "theirs." The key to success is making sure the members of the group feel as if they own the group. Members who feel this way will be much more active and involved — and will take on added responsibility to make sure the group survives.

An especially exciting new development is the spread of self-help networks via electronic networks. Online self-help removes such barriers to participation as difficulty getting to meetings or lack of available and interested neighbors who share your concern.

Most online self-help systems are available around the clock. And computer self-help can be a great equalizer: such trappings as dress, looks, health status, and accent can't get in the way. While newcomers sometimes miss nonverbal communication, more experienced hands find that dealing with this is simply a matter of learning to operate in a new medium.

Online self-help networks include NAPWA-Link, a bulletin board run by the National Association of People With AIDS; an active forum on Prodigy run by the Crohn's Disease and Colitis Foundation of America; the WID-Net, developed by the World Institute on Disability; the New Parents Network; and several different networks on chronic fatigue syndrome. America Online and CompuServe both have active self-help forums. America Online recently added a self-help section run by the National Alliance for the Mentally Ill.

Online self-help links can be local as well as national and international. The Cleveland Freenet offers an online health clinic, health fairs and health education. Such locally based networks are natural breeding grounds for locally oriented self-help groups.

jump to:
Virtual Communities
p. 262

The Self-Help Sourcebook

This book is the best national listing of self-help organizations; it is an invaluable tool for self-helpers, and an essential reference for every library, therapist's office, social service agency, and community resource center. It includes much advice on finding or forming the support group that's right for you, and an excellent section for professionals who would like to understand how to work more effectively with self-help groups.
—Tom Ferguson, M.D.

A.I.D.S.

National Association of People with A.I.D.S.
National. 102 affiliated groups. Founded 1986. Network of persons with AIDS. Information-sharing, collective voice for health, social & political concerns. Phone mail & electronics network, speakers bureau. Monthly newsletter $55 annual subscription. Write: 1413 K St., NW, #10, Washington, DC 20005-3405. Call 202/898-0414 (day).

CAREGIVERS

Well Spouse Foundation
Int'l. 60 chapters. Founded 1988. Emotional support for people married to a chronically ill spouse. Works on advocacy for long-term care. Quarterly newsletter, pen pals,

conferences. Guidelines & assistance available for starting groups. Write: P.O. Box 28876, San Diego, CA 92198-0876. Call 619/673-9043.

LIFE-THREATENING ILLNESS

The Center for Attitudinal Healing
National. 70+ affiliates. Founded 1975. Support programs for children, adolescents & adults facing their own, or a family member's, life-threatening illness. All services free of charge. Quarterly newsletter. Write: 19 Main St., Tiburon, CA 94920. Call 415/435-5022.

SMOKING

Nicotine Anonymous World Services
Int'l. 500 + groups. Founded 1985. Self-help group using the 12-step program of recovery for people who want to help themselves & others recover from nicotine addiction & live free of nicotine in all forms. Newsletter. Assistance available for starting groups. Write: 2118 Greenwich St., San Francisco, CA 94123. Call 415/922-8575.

STROKE

Courage Stroke Network
National. 808 groups. Founded 1979. Promotes development of support groups. Provides leadership consultation. Information, referral & public education. "Stroke Connection" newsletter. Annual seminar. Peer counselor training. Group develop-

ment guidelines ($12.95/members; $16.95 non-members + postage/handling). Write: c/o Courage Center, 3915 Golden Valley Rd., Golden Valley, MN 55422. Call 800/553-6321 or 612/520-0464.

CRIME VICTIMS/OFFENDERS

National Organization for Victim Assistance. *National. 2500 organizations & members. Founded 1975.* Support & advocacy for crime victims. Newsletter, information & referrals, phone help, conferences, group development guidelines. Dues $30/individuals; $100/organization. Write 1757 Park Rd., NW, Washington, DC 20010. Call 202/232-6682; fax 202/462 2255.

MARRIAGE/FAMILY

Association of Couples for Marriage Enrichment; *National network. Founded 1973.* Network of couples who want to enhance their own relationship as well as help strengthen marriages of other couples. Support groups, retreats, workshops. Bi-monthly newsletter. Leadership training, conferences. Group development guidelines. Write: ACME, PO Box 10596, Winston-Salem, NC 27108. Call 919/724-1526.

MESSINESS

Messies Anonymous
National. 45 Groups. Founded 1981. Aims to improve the quality of life of disorganized homemakers by providing motivation & a program for change to help members improve self-image as control of house & life is obtained. Quarterly newsletter $5. Optional dues. Write: 5025 SW 114th Ave., Miami, FL 33165. Call 305/271-8404.

The Self-Help Sourcebook
(Finding and Forming Mutual Aid Self-Help Groups)
Barbara J. White & Edward J. Madara, Editors. 1986, 1992; 222 pp.
ISBN 0-9634322-0-6
$9 from Sourcebook, St. Clares-Riverside Medical Center, Denville, NJ 07834

Common Concern Program

If you can't find a group dealing with your particular concern and would like to start your own, the Common Concern Program is a terrific resource.

These booklets and tapes can help turn five to ten people with a common issue into a fully functioning mutual support group. Six audiotapes and a coordinator's manual teach you how to recruit and select group members and assist you in setting up the first meeting. A different group member presides over each meeting while the group listens to a tape and follows with a discussion. Members learn basic group leadership, listening, and communications skills, and get help with members who either monopolize the conversation or never say anything. Specialized tapes are also available on such subjects as incest survivors, recent widows, and recently divorced women. —Lewis Engel

The overall program is built around six basic talk tools:

1. **Questions**. There's more to these ordinary, everyday responses than you might guess.

2. **Advisements**. The various forms of guiding each other, commonly called "advice," can help or hinder the helping process.

3. **Wait-times**. You may be surprised to learn that these silent pauses have dramatic effects on conversations.

Common Concern Program
(Forming and Enhancing Self-Help Support Groups)
Master Tapes & Coodinator's Manual $79.95 ($83.95 postpaid); Leader's Guide $5.95 (order one for each group member); Specializing Tapes $11.95 each from New Harbinger Publications, 5674 Shattuck Avenue, Oakland, CA 94609; 800/748-6273

4. **Reflections**. Used rarely in everyday conversations and frequently in therapists' offices, these are excellent for showing empathy and understanding.

5. **Interpretations**. These powerful but tricky tools try to tell us what we are and why we are that way.

6. **Self-Disclosures**. These are the key to revealing yourself to others and increasing group closeness.

The program helps you learn how these talk tools are typically overused, underused, and abused.

The American Self-Help Clearinghouse

This organization is an excellent source of advice on both face-to-face and online self-help. Callers to the center's help line receive information about national groups in their area of interest. If there is no group in your area, the center will provide advice on finding like-minded people in your community and continuing advice to those working to establish their own mutual support network. They have helped callers organize hundreds of new groups in recent years. Their free brochure, Ideas and Considerations for Starting a Self-Help Group, is available on request with an SASE. —TF

The American Self-Help Clearinghouse: St. Clares-Riverside Medical Center, Denville, NJ 07834; 201/625-7101.

Advisements can be a valuable tool in support groups, but they're frequently overused, misused, and abused.

Advisements tend to be used frequently because:

• Giving advice makes us feel we're helpful, caring, and knowledgeable people.

• Giving advice requires less effort than many other talk tools used for helping.

• Some people don't realize there are other ways to help besides advisement.

• Some people find it's hard to listen to other persons' problems so they give a quick shot of advice to end the conversation.

Healing and the Mind • Mind/Body Medicine

*If you have never seen Bill Moyers'
five-part television series* Healing and
the Mind, *here are videos, audiocassettes, and a book, all demonstrating
how difficult it is to miss anything in
this age of multimedia. The video- and
audiocassettes cover identical broadcast material; the book provides full
transcriptions of Moyers' interviews
(and insight into how much editing is
necessary to squeeze a subject into a
one-hour format).*

*The best first choice, though, is
another book entirely —* Mind/Body
Medicine, *from the nonprofit Consumers Union, publishers of* Consumer
Reports. *Like the Moyers series, it was
funded by the Fetzer Institute, but it
covers the same ground in much
greater detail. Each chapter is by a
different expert (the last chapter is
by* MWEC *medical editor Tom
Ferguson).*

*The other thing worth owning from this
smorgasbord of choices is the first of
the Moyers videos,* The Mystery of
Chi. *It functions as a beautiful travelogue through China (the only segment
of the series to venture outside the
United States) and contains footage
that needs to be seen to be believed.
As someone using Western allopathic
medicine, Chinese medicine and homeopathy on my own mind/body, I
have a few bones to pick with Moyers'
guide and interpreter, American M.D.
David Eisenberg (he is so busy covering his Western medical professional
ass that if you close your eyes and attend to his choice of language, you
might think you are listening to testimony from a Senate confirmation
hearing) but the work's larger contribution is clearly positive: this is where
America wakes up and smells the
ginseng.*

*For people who have been paying attention to alternative medicine for the
last twenty years, there is little news in
any of this material. For those who
haven't, it's a cornucopia. Throughout
his distinguished career, Moyers has
always aimed for and connected with
the great American middle. His folksy
"I'm just a Babtist ploughboy from
Marshall, Texas" approach still
works, because he combines*

*childish wonder, grown-up skepticism
and a compassionate heart. No one
else in broadcast journalism even
comes close. He is the great American
popularizer. —Richard Nilsen*

Michael Lerner: There's a wonderful line
from Goethe that goes something like,
"Whoever said that we have only two beings wrestling within us underestimated the
number by a considerable amount." We all
have many, many facets that are jostling
about inside us. The process of really coming to grips with all those different aspects
of our personalities and beginning to
integrate them and bring them forth
is a lifelong task.

Dr. Xie: Chinese medicine stresses the human capability to resist disease. Therefore,
many treatments are designed to motivate
this capability — once it is motivated, some
diseases can be cured easily. That's the key
point of Chinese treatment.

In gaining a sense of control over our medical treatments, in making conscious choices
about how we spend our lives, and in allowing others into our sufferings, we are
releasing innate healing capacities that make
us nature's allies in our own recovery.

Jon Kabat-Zinn: A lot of people are running
around on the planet, trying to get somewhere, and they're very unhappy and relatively unhealthy. But you could actually feel
comfortable in your body right now, just
the way it is, whether you had heart disease, or cancer, or, for that matter, even
AIDS or an HIV diagnosis. The only time
that any of us have to grow or change or
feel or learn anything is in the present moment. But we're continually missing our
present moments, almost willfully, by not
paying attention. Instead of being on automatic pilot, we can explore what's possible
if we start to kindle the flame of being fully
alive.

Moyers: I never thought I would be hearing
this kind of talk in a major American hospital. —Healing and the Mind

Many joggers say they experience a "high"
after running four or five miles. By using a
relaxation response technique while you
exercise, it is possible to experience this
mild euphoria in the first or second mile.

There is no way to fail, because you are not
trying to get anywhere or feel anything particular in the first place. As long as you are
willing to breathe and be in the state you are
already in, you are practicing mindfulness.

In *patient-controlled analgesia* (PCA) a pump
provides a small dose of medication, usually
morphine, into your IV when you push a
button. This system puts the patient in
charge of pain control and does away with
the sometimes agonizing wait for a nurse
to supply a new dosage of painkiller every
time the drug runs out. By allowing a
nearly constant level of morphine in the
blood and reducing patient anxiety, this
device has revolutionized postoperative
pain management. —Mind/Body Medicine

Healing and the Mind
Bill Moyers. Doubleday & Co., 1993; 369
pp. ISBN 0-385-46870-9
$25 ($27.50 postpaid) from Bantam,
Doubleday, Dell/Fulfillment Dept., 2451 S.
Wolf Road, Des Plaines, IL 60018;
800/223-6834

Healing and the Mind
audiocassette version
Bantam Audio Publishing, 1993;
ISBN 0-553-47134-1
$25 ($27.50 postpaid) from Bantam,
Doubleday, Dell/Fulfillment Dept.,
2451 S. Wolf Road, Des Plaines, IL 60018;
800/223-6834

Healing and the Mind
videocassette version
Set $129.95 ($137.45 postpaid); individual
videos $29.95 ($33.45 postpaid).
*Vol. 1: The Mystery of Chi; 2: Mind-Body Connection; 3: Healing From Within; 4: The Art of
Healing; 5: Wounded Healers.*
All from Ambrose Video Publishing, Inc.,
PO Box 2054, South Burlington, VT 05407;
800/633-1999

Mind/Body Medicine
(How to Use Your Mind for Better Health)
Daniel Goleman & Joel Gurin. 1993; 482 pp.
ISBN 0-89043-580-4
$24.95 ($27.45 postpaid) from Consumer
Reports Books, 9180 LeSaint Drive,
    Fairfield, OH 45014; 513/860-1178

Full Catastrophe Living

The title comes from Zorba the Greek:

*— Zorba, have you ever been
married?*

*— Of course I've been married. Wife,
house, kids, everything … the full
catastrophe!*

Like Zorba, *this book conveys the positive force that informs the most
crazymaking aspects of our lives. The
author proposes
that one skillful
way of taking
control of our
situation is to establish a regular
daily practice.
He then provides a rich
collection of
examples and
guidelines to
help us do
exactly that.*

*This extraordinary guide to
stress management, mindfulness, and meditation practice
will be of special
interest to those
experiencing
burnout or breakdown. But I know
few people who would not benefit
at some level.*

*Sincerely felt and artfully
presented, this is one of the
best books ever written on the
art and craft of psychological
self-care.—Tom Ferguson, M.D.*

Seven attitudinal factors constitute the major pillars of mindfulness practice as we
teach it at the stress clinic. They are nonjudging, patience, a beginner's mind, trust,
non-striving, acceptance, and letting go.

One measure of your commitment is
whether you can bring yourself to shut off
your telephone for the time you will be
practicing or to let someone else answer it
and take messages. It is a great letting go in
and of itself only to be home for yourself at
those times, and great peace can follow
from this alone.

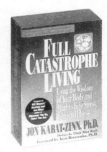

Full Catastrophe Living
Jon Kabat-Zinn. Delacorte Press, 1990;
467 pp. ISBN 0-385-30312-2
$12.95 ($15.45 postpaid) from Bantam,
Doubleday, Dell/Fulfillment Dept.,
2451 S. Wolf Road, Des Plaines, IL 60018;
800/223-6834

Holly Lane, *Valetudinarian Aided by the Labors of Plants and Bugs, 1991*

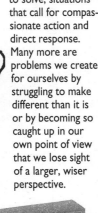

A Path with Heart

Jack Kornfield tells his own story of personal healing through a combination of psychotherapy and meditative practices and translates many ideas of the Buddhist meditation tradition into an understandable American idiom. He breaks important new ground in suggesting that Western meditation students can benefit from simultaneous therapy. An especially good book to read while establishing or practicing a regular meditative routine.
—TF

•

There are two kinds of difficulties. Some are clearly problems to solve, situations that call for compassionate action and direct response. Many more are problems we create for ourselves by struggling to make different than it is or by becoming so caught up in our own point of view that we lose sight of a larger, wiser perspective.

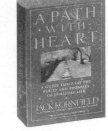

A Path with Heart
Jack Kornfield. Bantam Books, 1993;
352 pp. ISBN 0-553-37211-4
$11.95 ($14.45 postpaid) from Bantam, Doubleday, Dell/Fulfillment Dept., 2451 S. Wolf Road, Des Plaines, IL 60018;
800/223-6834

Mind-Body Toolkit

Hazelden

A fat 72-page catalog of books and tapes on healing and recovery in the twelve-step tradition. Subjects covered include alcohol, chemical dependence, children of dysfunctional families, chronic illness, co-dependence, compulsive sexual behavior, depression, families of alcoholics, kids, overeating, overweight, parents and children, relationships, sexual abuse, smoking, women's and men's issues, and much more. A thoughtful and knowledgeable selection of books from a variety of publishers. This venerable nonprofit is a trusted source of information on resources for recovery. —TF

The Hazelden Catalog: Free from The Hazelden Foundation, PO Box 176, Center City, MN 55012; 800/328-9000.

Seiza Bench
A rugged bench handcrafted from beautiful deep-grained hardwoods. It comes finely sanded and ready for finishing.
Measures 18" x 8" x 7".   #7001 $36.00

Healthy Pleasures

This revolutionary book proposes that the pursuit of pleasure can be an effective pathway to well-being, fulfillment, and better health. Robert Ornstein and David Sobel have combed the medical literature for evidence that we can make real and lasting life changes by emphasizing the things that bring us the most enjoyment: eating, drinking, sleeping, sex, learning, exercise, nature, music, pets, friends, family, relaxation, touching. Self-care needn't be just a matter of micromanaging your fiber intake or forcing yourself to adopt a series of nearly impossible regimens. —TF

•

Sexual fulfillment may help reduce the impact of certain stresses in a marriage. In one fascinating study, married couples monitored sexual intercourse and arguments on a daily basis. The result could be dubbed the "F Index": *the frequency of fornication minus the frequency of fights.* The higher the F index, the happier the marriage. For example, if a couple fights ten times per month but engages in sex twelve times per month, their F index is +2, which points towards happiness. Conversely, a couple that fights only four times monthly but has sex only twice, has an F index of -2 and is probably less happily married.

Falling Apart

Falling Apart
Michael Epstein & Sue Hosking. 1992;
312 pp. ISBN 0-916360-51-2
$12.95 ($15.20 postpaid) from CRCS Publications, PO Box 1460, Sebastopol, CA 95473; 707/829-0735

DharmaCrafts

A good source of meditation pillows, benches, books, and other supplies. —TF

DharmaCrafts (A Catalog of Meditation Supplies): Free from 199 Auburn Street, Cambridge, MA 02139; 617/492-4793.

•

Psychologist Sidney Jourand roamed cafes [in England, the United States, France and Puerto Rico] recording how many times people touched each other. In San Juan, Puerto Rico, he tallied 180 contacts per hour. In a café in Paris, couples touched at a rate of 110. In Gainesville, Florida, twosomes touched only twice an hour. And in London, England, the men and women *never* touched.

•

Controlled studies suggest that laughter can, indeed, raise pain thresholds. Student volunteers listening to twenty minutes of Lily Tomlin joking about Alexander Graham Bell were far less sensitive to pain than their peers who listened to a dull lecture titled "Ethics and the Sociology of Peer Review."

Healthy Pleasures
Robert Ornstein & David Sobel. 1990;
301 pp. ISBN 0-201-52385-X
$9.95 ($12.95 postpaid) from Addison-Wesley Publishing Co./Order Dept., 1 Jacob Way, Reading, MA 01867;
800/447-2226

Worker's Comp claims for stress-related illness have gone up 700 percent in the last decade.

Falling Apart gives you stress and breakdown facts using case studies to make points and describe processes and solutions. It tells what signs to look for, how to change behavior patterns, and what to do if a breakdown occurs.

Perhaps the most important point this book makes is to learn what your own warning signs are and to do something about them, now. To improve your quality of life, you must learn to eliminate or deal with many of its stresses.
—Susan Erkel Ryan

•

Ten Signs of Stress:
1. Crying easily.
2. Depression.
3. Low confidence.
4. Irritability.
5. Poor memory.
6. Muddled thoughts.
7. Exhaustion.
8. Loss of interest in sex.
9. Sleeping problems.
10. Fear of social situations.

OTHER GREAT RESOURCES

Advances (The Journal of Mind-Body Health): $39/year (4 issues) from Fetzer Institute, PO Box 3000, Denville, NJ 07834; 800/875-2997.

At a Journal Workshop: Ira Progoff. 1975, 1992, Jeremy P. Tarcher Inc. An excellent guide to keeping a psychological journal.

Mental Medicine Update: Robert Ornstein & David Sobel, eds. $39/year (3 issues) from ISHK Book Service, PO Box 381062, Boston, MA 02238; 800/222-4745. A readable, inexpensive review of recent studies on the effects of mind and mood on the body.

The Future of the Body: Michael Murphy. 1993, Perigee. Astonishing and scientific look at the upper limits of human potential.

The Intuitive Body (Aikido as a Clairsentient Process): Wendy Palmer. 1994, North Atlantic Books. Training Intuition as a means of mind-body awareness.

The Intuitive Body (Aikido as a Clairsentient Process): 70-minute video by Wendy Palmer. 1991, North Atlantic Books. Aikido teaches harmony and blending as an alternative to conflict; this video shows how to do it.

Body, Spirit, and Democracy: Don Hanlon Johnson. 1994, North Atlantic Books. About "embodiment" in personal and political contexts.

In certain circles, to describe a book as "self-help" is to dismiss it. Many people assume that all such books are superficial, overly simple, and overgeneralized. And many otherwise thoughtful professionals adopt a tone that implies that while these books might be useful for the less critical, an intelligent, reflective reader would not be interested.

Such attitudes greatly underestimate the genre. Self-help books are tools. They are tools that many take up when their own attempts to deal with psychological or physical problems don't work. Or when the help of experts is less than helpful, or when it actually makes things worse. A self-help approach can be an excellent supplement to psychotherapy. Self-help embodies a deep and admirable aspect of the American tradition of self-reliance — a tradition that says you don't necessarily need a mechanic to fix your car, a plumber to fix a leak, or a psychotherapist to solve a problem in living. (The Whole Earth Catalog itself is an example of that tradition.)

Like carpentry tools, some self-help books are finely crafted, some are badly made, and some, though not beautiful, will do the job for which they were designed. Even a book with glaring imperfections can be useful if it is written in terms that make sense to you. Reading about others who have suffered from similar difficulties, and realizing you are not the only one struggling with that problem, can provide great comfort. The best of these books can give readers a sense that they are on (or can get on) a path toward overcoming their problems — and can show how to take the next step.

—Lewis Engel

Listening to Prozac

The development of powerful new drugs with fewer side effects (Prozac being the best known) has enabled millions of patients to overcome longstanding problems that were unaffected by psychotherapy.

These drugs don't help everyone, but when they work, they help with an incredibly wide spectrum of problems: acute, chronic, post-partum, and seasonal depression; anxiety, shyness, binge eating, anorexia, and panic attacks; obsessive-compulsive disorder, compulsive masturbation, stage fright, kleptomania, compulsion to gamble, and alcohol and drug addiction.

Are all these very different problems actually just symptoms of the same biochemical imbalance? If it is a chemical problem, why do the writers in the field stress the importance of psychotherapy along with medicine?

***Listening to Prozac** is the book to read if you want to think about the broad psychological, philosophical, anthropological, and sociological issues raised by these potent new drugs. —LE*

•

Within weeks of starting Prozac, Tess settled into a satisfying dating routine with men. She had missed out on dating in her teens and twenties. Now she reveled in the attention she received. She seemed even to enjoy the trial-and-error process of learning contemporary courtship rituals, gauging norms for sexual involvement, weighing the import of men's professed infatuation with her.

What You Need to Know About Psychiatric Drugs

Psychiatric drugs are both over- and underprescribed. Any licensed physician can prescribe them, and they are often given out (particularly to women) when counseling or marital therapy would be a much better alternative. On the other hand, many people, in and out of therapy, are not given medication even though they are suffering terribly — because of irrational fear of addiction or a puritanical conviction, by physicians and laypeople alike, that taking medicine is the easy way out.

This excellent reference can help with both problems.

The first half describes common psychological problems and gives guidance as to whether medication could be helpful. It also explains which drugs are used inappropriately, and why. The book's second half gives detailed listings of commonly prescribed psychiatric drugs, presented in an easy-to-understand graphic format, including side effects and negative interactions with other drugs.

*If a doctor or therapist has recommended that you or someone close to you take a psychiatric drug, this book is necessary reading.
—LE*

What You Need to Know About Psychiatric Drugs
Stuart Yudofsky, Robert E. Hales, & Tom Ferguson. Ballantine Books, 1991; 672 pp. ISBN 0-345-37334-0
$14 ($16 postpaid) from Random House/ Order Dept., 400 Hahn Road, Westminster, MD 21157; 800/733-3000

•

Questions to Ask Before Taking Any Psychiatric Drug

• Exactly what is the psychological problem that you (or your family member or friend) are facing? Is your problem a sign or a symptom of a medical illness or a primary psychiatric disorder? If it is a psychiatric disorder, what is the official American Psychiatric Association diagnosis of your condition?

• What are the most effective nondrug therapies for this condition?

• Can a psychiatric prescription drug help to alleviate, manage, or solve this problem?

• Can nondrug therapies be used instead of drug therapy? Can they be used as a supplement to drug therapy?

• What are the positive (therapeutic) effects this drug may provide?

• How likely is it that this drug actually will provide these effects?

OTHER GREAT RESOURCES

New Harbinger Publications: High-quality, cognitively oriented self-help books and tapes. Catalog free. 5674 Shattuck Avenue, Oakland, CA 94609; 800/748-6273.

Hidden Guilt: Lewis Engel & Tom Ferguson. 1991, Pocket Books, Simon & Schuster. A new approach to understanding how deeply ingrained childhood beliefs can lead to self-sabotage. Includes advice on how to tap into your own internal guidance for solving your psychological problems.

Trauma and Recovery

People who suffer trauma are often surprised by how long the effects last. They startle easily; they have nightmares and flashbacks; they may avoid anything — like sex, in the case of incest victims — that reminds them of the original wound. Faith in a benign universe has been ruptured, and so has a basic trust in the human community. Their suffering can be made worse by a society that stigmatizes and isolates victims.

Judith Herman, a psychiatrist at Harvard, draws on the words and experiences of survivors of all sorts of trauma and places their wounds in a social context. She links the private disasters that befall women (like rape) with the more public wounds suffered by men in war: they create the same symptoms.

The book's description of the psychological effects of trauma is reassuring to the trauma victim because it makes it clear that they are a universal response to horror, not a sign

Trauma and Recovery
(The Aftermath of Violence — From Domestic Abuse to Political Terror)
Judith L. Herman. Basic Books, 1992; 276 pp. ISBN 0-465-08766-3
$14 ($16.75 postpaid) from HarperCollins Publishers/Direct Mail, PO Box 588, Dunmore, PA 18512; 800/331-3761

*of individual insanity. I especially loved the last chapters on the three stages of recovery from post-traumatic stress disorder. The first step involves re-creating safety — getting out of the battering marriage, stopping the drug addiction or the crazy sexual relationships. Once things are stabilized, you can join a trauma-focused group and remember, mourn, and integrate; when you have opened to the pain, you can restore your damaged connections to the rest of the human community — learn to trust again, and learn things blocked for years by the isolation and distrust that trauma fosters.
—Katy Butler*

Re-Evaluation Counseling

Discovering co-counseling was like being handed the keys to the immediate, tangible political and emotional universe. It puts individual difficulties into a larger social context and provides the best tools I've seen anywhere for overcoming them. In co-counseling classes, people of all ages and backgrounds, in communities all over the US and in many other countries, learn to take turns listening to each other (instead of paying, say, a therapist) to liberate their intelligence from the rigidifying effects of early hurts through the physical release of feelings — crying, laughing, shaking, etc.

*As people think better, they are better able to act on their own behalf and against injustice. The basic theory and practice of co-counseling (known more formally as Re-Evaluation Counseling) extend themselves beautifully to the elimination of racism, sexism, classism — every lid on human flowering.
—Ann Bartz*

For information on co-counseling contact:
The Re-Evaluation Counseling Communities, 719 2nd Avenue N, Seattle, WA 98109; 206/284-0311.
Present Time (the Journal of Re-Evaluation Counseling): $10/year (4 issues; sample copy $2.50). Rational Island Publishers, PO Box 2081/Main Office Station, Seattle, WA 98111; 206/284-0311.

I had never seen a patient's social life reshaped so rapidly and dramatically. Low self-worth, competitiveness, jealousy, poor interpersonal skills, shyness, fear of intimacy — the usual causes of social awkwardness — are so deeply ingrained and so difficult to influence that ordinarily change comes gradually if at all. But Tess blossomed all at once.

●

After about eight months off medication, Tess told me she was slipping. "I'm not myself," she said. New union negotiations were under way, and she felt she could use the sense of stability, the invulnerability to attack, that Prozac gave her. Here was a dilemma for me. Ought I to provide medication to someone who was not depressed?

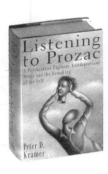

Listening to Prozac
(A Psychiatrist Explores Antidepressant Drugs and the Remaking of the Self)
Peter Kramer. Viking, 1993; 409 pp.
ISBN 0-14-015940-1
$11.95 ($13.95 postpaid) from Penguin USA/Consumer Sales, 120 Woodbine Street, Bergenfield, NJ 07621; 800/253-6476

I could give myself reason enough — construe it that Tess was sliding into relapse, which perhaps she was. In truth, I assumed I would be medicating Tess's chronic condition, call it what you will: heightened awareness of the needs of others, sensitivity to conflict, residual damage to self-esteem — all odd indications for medication. I discussed the dilemma with her, but then I did not hesitate to write the prescription. Who was I to withhold from her the bounties of science? Tess responded again as she had hoped she would, with renewed confidence, self-assurance, and social comfort.

●

I wondered whether we were ready for "cosmetic psychopharmacology." It was my musings about whether it would be kosher to medicate a patient like Tess in the absence of depression that led me to coin the phrase. Some people might prefer pharmacologic to psychologic self-actualization. Psychic steroids for mental gymnastics, medicinal attacks on the humors, antiwallflower compound — these might be hard to resist. Since you only live once, why not do it as a blonde? Why not as a peppy blonde? Now that questions of personality and social stance have entered the arena of medication, we as a society will have to decide how comfortable we are with using chemicals to modify personality in useful, attractive ways. We may mask the issue by defining less and less severe mood states as pathology, in effect saying, "If it responds to an antidepressant, it's depression." Already, it seems to me, psychiatric diagnosis had been subject to a sort of "diagnostic bracket creep": the expansion of categories to match the scope of relevant medications.

You Mean I Don't Have to Feel This Way?

Antidepressants freed the author's daughter from ten years of recurrent, disabling depressions and allowed her to live a happy and fulfilling life.

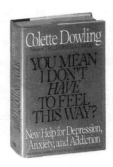

You Mean I Don't Have to Feel This Way?
(New Help for Depression, Anxiety, and Addiction)
Colette Dowling. Bantam Books, 1991; 293 pp. ISBN 0-553-37169-X
$11.95 ($14.45 postpaid) from Bantam, Doubleday, Dell/Fulfillment Dept., 2451 S. Wolf Road, Des Plaines, IL 60018; 800/223-6834

Inspired to research the world of psychiatric drugs, review the relevant journals and talk with leaders in the field, Colette Dowling produced a hope-filled book. —LE

●

Before Gabrielle was evaluated, she had said to me at the end of one of her bad days, "I wish there were a pill." And then, with a little smile, she'd added, "Of course, I know that's a copout."

●

If mood disorders are biological in origin, why is psychotherapy necessary at all? . . .

Frederick Goodwin, M.D., of the NIMH, notes that while biology is at their core, these illnesses manifest in ways that "are behavioral and psychological, with changes in perception, attitudes, personality, mood, and cognition. Therapy can be of unique value to persons undergoing such devastating changes in the way they perceive themselves and are perceived by others."

The Feeling Good Handbook

While important new developments in the medical treatment of psychological problems have taken place over the last several decades, there have also been important developments in non-drug treatment. One of these new therapeutic approaches, Cognitive Therapy, has become a major influence in psychotherapy. Instead of focusing on the resolution of deep unconscious conflicts, Cognitive Therapy holds that your thoughts, attitudes, and beliefs create your moods. Originally developed to combat depression, Cognitive Therapy has now developed approaches for a variety of psychological problems. Cognitive Therapy is typically short-term and highly focused,

●

A panic attack is usually triggered by a negative thought or a frightening daydream. Once a panic attack develops, your thoughts, feelings, and physical symptoms feed each other in a vicious cycle. . . . Your panic is triggered by your negative thoughts. Your heart pounds and your thoughts race as adrenaline pours into your blood. These sensations alarm you and you think, "Gee, something must really be wrong." This thought creates even more fear and frightening physical symptoms.

At the same time, your negative thoughts and feelings feed each other. You feel so anxious and tense that it seems that something dreadful must be wrong. After all, why would you feel so frightened if you weren't in real danger? This is called "emotional reasoning," because you take your emotions as evidence for the way things really are.

Finally, your actions also make things worse. If you think you're dying or cracking up, you may crawl into bed with the lights off and try to hang on for dear life. This is like a sensory deprivation experiment, and it lets your fantasies run wild! You feel abnormal and impaired. This convinces you that there must be something terribly wrong.

and requires that the patient do homework between sessions.

The Feeling Good Handbook is an informative, readable self-help tool for the layperson. It covers the treatment's application to depression, anxiety, panic, phobias, procrastination and relationship problems. Set up as a workbook, it presents the concepts and techniques of Cognitive Therapy through exercises, self-tests, and forms. —LE

The Feeling Good Handbook
David D. Burns. Plume Books, 1990;
ISBN 0-452-26174-0
$14 ($16 postpaid) from Penguin USA/Consumer Sales, 120 Woodbine Street, Bergenfield, NJ 07621; 800/253-6476

E M D R
(EYE MOVEMENT DESENSITIZATION AND REPROCESSING)

Intractable nightmares, flashbacks, and intrusive memories have long afflicted people who suffered trauma — in warfare, and through rape, incest, mugging, and torture. Nothing has seemed to help much. Psychotherapists were frustrated, and neurobiologists speculated that a single instance of overwhelming terror could create permanent changes in brain chemistry. But in 1987, a California psychologist named Francine Shapiro came across an odd technique that rapidly takes the charge out of traumatic memories.

The client calls to mind the trauma and its related images, thoughts, and body feelings. Then the therapist moves her fingers back and forth across the client's field of vision about thirty times, making the client's eyes track back and forth. At this point, something mysterious occurs. Images, memories, associations, thoughts, emotions flip rapidly through the client's mind, like Freudian free association at breakneck speed. Seemingly

hardwired thought patterns — "It was my fault," "I'm helpless" — turn out to be software, after all. Afterward, many clients find that their nightmares and intrusive memories go away.

Some caveats: This is not a self-help tool. It requires a trained and licensed psychotherapist because it can bring back memories with overwhelming vividness. It works most dramatically with otherwise healthy people who have suffered a single trauma. It takes more time — from four sessions to a year or more — for people who have been repeatedly traumatized.

EMDR doesn't work for everybody, and it can't do everything. Incest survivors, for example, may need to learn about assertiveness or sexuality, or job and social skills, once they are no longer preoccupied with past horrors. But EMDR can clear a space in the brain so that new learning can take place. Weekend trainings cost about $300 and are open only to licensed therapists. —Katy Butler

For information on EMDR: 408/372-3900; PO Box 51010, Pacific Grove, CA 93950-6010.

WHEN YOU NEED MORE THAN SELF-HELP

Sometimes a couple's problems are too serious for self-help. When this is the case, a third person, who can be objective and see the big picture can make a huge difference.

The best referral source is your individual therapist, a friend, doctor, or member of the clergy. Or call the American Association of Marriage and Family Therapy (800/374-2638) for a list of AAMFT-certified counselors in your zip code, and for their pamphlet, the *Consumer's Guide to Marriage and Family Therapy*. The American Psychiatric Association (202/682-6000) and the American Psychological Association (202/336-5800) will provide referrals to regional associations and to counselors in your area.

Shop around; find the right person. Important criteria in making a decision are that *both* partners feel safe with the counselor, that both feel he or she understands them, and that the counselor has had extensive experience in couples counseling. It is a big plus if the counselor has been married or been in a long-term relationship.
—Brandy and Lewis Engel

See The Association of Couples for Marriage Enrichment (p.173).

Getting the Love You Want: A Guide for Couples

The author claims that we choose people we hope will help us heal our childhood wounds. We look for someone about whom we can say, "Finally, this one will understand me/love me enough/let me be my true self." But, unconsciously, we seek out people who possess both the positive and the negative traits of our original caretakers.

Why the negative? So we can re-create the conditions of our upbringing — in order to correct them. Since this task is unconscious, we often reactivate old injuries and want to either fight or flee. But it doesn't have to be that way. This book offers a series of well-planned exercises to help us resolve those childhood issues with our partners, rather than repeat them. —BE

After the Honeymoon

If you are convinced that the right way to act in an intimate relationship is to put your best foot forward rather than to be self-centered, jealous, or boastful; to consistently abide by the rules of good communication rather than be angry, withholding, or irrational; and to be self-confident and mature rather than wounded, dependent, and afraid of intimacy, then read this book.

Dan Wile not only encourages us to be our true selves, but also to regard what we might consider our shortcomings and mistakes as sources of information crucial to learning to love ourselves, to filling in gaps in our personalities, to becoming more intimate, and to having more fun. —BE

●

Fight fact 10: people need to know that an argument may be the only entry point to a needed conversation.

Everyone knows that people say many things in fights that they don't mean. And everyone knows that fights may be the only times that people are able to say certain things that they *do* mean. People don't sufficiently appreciate, however, how this latter fact can be turned to advantage.

Joseph's complaint that Karen thinks only about herself could lead later on to a conversation in which they discover that:

Joseph misses their not talking much together anymore.

Karen does also.

It's easy for them to get caught up in the rush of everyday activities and forget to talk.

And they are already feeling much better.

After the Honeymoon
(How Conflict Can Improve Your Relationship)
Daniel B. Wile. 1988; ISBN 0-471-85347-X
$17.95 postpaid from John Wiley & Sons, 1 Wiley Dr., Somerset, NJ 08873; 800/225-5945

now that they *are* talking, even though what they're talking about is how they haven't been talking.

Joseph's angry statement that Karen never thinks of anybody but herself could be used as an entry point to this important conversation.

●

Some people say that you should become independent *before* beginning a relationship. "Dependence dooms relationships," they say. "You've got to stop trying to turn your partner into a parent. You've got to stop being so dependent."

I have a different view.
I believe that:

Learning to become independent is what relationships can help accomplish rather than what must be done prior to beginning them.

At the same time, relationships are good places to accomplish the opposite task: learning to become successfully dependent. Dependency isn't a deficiency that needs to be overcome but a skill that needs to be developed. Dependence is too important a task to be left to children.

In other words, relationships are good places to develop skill in being both dependent *and* independent.

Getting the Love You Want
(A Guide for Couples)
Harville Hendrix.
HarperPerennial, 1988;
256 pp. ISBN 0-06-097292-0
$13 ($15.75 postpaid) from HarperCollins Publishers/Direct Mail, PO Box 588, Dunmore, PA 18512; 800/331-3761

Iguana Hold Your Hand

(heard in San Francisco)

"I've had enough of men. They have too much skin, all in the wrong places, but I married two of them.

"The first one couldn't make up his mind. I'd ask him what he wanted for breakfast and he'd say, oh, he didn't care, but what he really meant was that he wanted fluffy scrambled eggs and toast with the crust cut off like Mommy made, and when I cooked anything different he would pout. We never went anywhere together because we just couldn't decide where to go.

"I finally dumped him the day I was putting laundry away and came across a pair of dark blue pantyhose that weren't mine. When he came home from the car parts store that night I had the pantyhose sitting on his supper plate, and after hemming and hawing awhile, he fished some pictures out of his wallet and showed me a photo of him and his bowling team all dressed up as women. At the time it was just too fucking weird for me to handle. I told him to tuck his dick between his legs and go suck off his momma, then booted his ass out.

"I met my second husband right over there by the jukebox. He was picking out some tunes and I wandered over to give him some advice and he told me to mind my own business, that he knew exactly what he wanted to play, and I fell in love. By closing time I had him on the hook. Two days later we took his hog up to Tahoe and got married.

"His real name was Andrew, but the guys in his club called him The Bog, 'cause he worked over at Del Monte fishing pickles and he smelled like his job. He was awful good to me, but he drank too much. One night he came home from Oakland and laid down on the couch and died, just like that. Doctor said the pickle fumes and the booze thinned out his blood too much. I gave the Harley to his baby brother, who sold it to buy toot. If I ever catch the little fucker I'll kill him.

"So I bought an iguana to keep me company, and called it Boggy. She lived on top of the television in my bedroom, where it was nice and warm. I left the window cracked a little so she could get out on the fire escape and lay around in the sun while I was tending bar.

"About a year after The Bog crapped out on me, I was doing the day shift in here and this cutesy-butt drugstore cowboy shows up and starts coming on to me. I figure what the hell, better use it before it grows shut, so I kinda lead him on, buy him a few shots, and at five we dance a few slow ones and go up to the apartment, where we smoke a couple of fat ones and do a fifth of Cuervo gold to warm up.

"We get in the bedroom and he starts peeling off his jeans, gets them down around his knees, just as Boggy comes back from sunning. The cowboy spots her and freaks, slams her head in the window and snaps her backbone, just like that. Me, I get pissed at the ignorance, and toss the asshole out on the street wearing just his pants.

"That is the last man I'll ever have anything to do with. These are his boots I'm wearing. Like them?"
—JD Smith

Going the Distance

Psychologists Barbach and Geisinger have provided those who are looking for a life mate a carefully drawn, highly detailed road map of the couples' journey.

Going the Distance has the characteristics of a good reference book; it is a compendium of sound principles, illuminating case histories, and clear

advice. It is organized around the progressive stages of an intimate relationship: choosing a prospective mate, courtship, and on through the stages of commitment and renewal — easy to consult for specific help at each step. This is a good resource for those of us already on the path and those wanting to get started. —BE

●

Clearly, courtship serves an essential purpose: it can and should provide us with a microcosm of the future relationship. Its duration permits real life to have its proper impact on the romanticized, getting-to-know-you stage. Within this period we are given the invaluable opportunity to assess our future life mates more thoroughly, to learn more about whether we work well as a team, whether our values are congruent, whether we negotiate our differences well, whether we are sexually compatible, whether we enjoy each other's company and whether we can agree on life plans. We are able to "sample" the various dimensions of our partners: to see them under stress, to see how they handle relationships with their friends and family, to discover conflicting interests and possible personality clashes. Most importantly, perhaps, we can

find out whether mutual trust, the pivot point of all good relationships, is able to grow and develop.

●

Like any living thing, a relationship goes through many cycles of growth and rest during its course. If it is to continue to maintain its interest and its usefulness to the partners over the years, it will always benefit from being renewed.

Set aside time once a year to celebrate the relationship you have created together. Recommitting yourselves to each other can have a spiritual and symbolic importance that rejuvenates the relationship and reminds you both of the sanctity of your bond. This renewal celebration can take place on the anniversary of your marriage, of the day you first met, of the day you first made love to each other or declared your love for one another.

●

The key to eliciting a change in your partner's behavior lies in a totally different process: One based upon changing *yourself*. Since you are the designated authority over only one person, *you* are the only person you can effectively change. However, when your intentions and efforts are creatively and consciously *self*-focused, the *incidental*

effect on your partner's behavior can be decisive.

●

Courtship is about *mating*, not dating. It is entirely possible for two people to date for months or even years without courting, and two people do not always enter courtship at the same time. One partner may have a more casual attitude about the relationship while the other has a greater desire to deepen and advance its purpose.

Going the Distance
(Finding and Keeping Lifelong Love)
Lonnie Barbach & David L. Geisinger. Plume Books, 1993; 320 pp. ISBN 0-452-26948-2
$10 ($12 postpaid) from Penguin USA/ Consumer Sales, 120 Woodbine Street, Bergenfield, NJ 07621; 800/253-6476

Men Are from Mars, Women Are from Venus

The author suggests that the remedy to frustrating, alienating interactions between male and female partners is to remember that s/he is as comprehensively different from you as someone from another planet.

For example, Gray explains why women feel frustrated that a man's immediate response to their complaining about something is to offer a solution. Gray holds that when women (Venusians) share problems, they want to achieve a sense of sympathy and closeness. When men (Martians) hear a problem, they assume their partner wants help — so they propose a solution. Thus, even though both parties are doing their best, the result is disappointment.

Gray's ideas might help a lot of men and women to avoid needless conflict. —BE

●

Autonomy is a symbol of efficiency, power, and competence.

Understanding this Martian characteristic can help women understand why men resist so much being corrected or being told what to do. To offer a man unsolicited advice is to presume that he doesn't know what to do or that he can't do it on his own. Men are very touchy about this, because the issue of competence is so very important to them.

●

Men and women generally are unaware that they have different emotional needs. As a result, they do not instinctively know how to support each other. Men typically give in relationships what men want, while women give what women want. Each mistakenly assumes that the other has the same needs and desires. As a result they both end up dissatisfied and resentful.

Men Are from Mars, Women Are from Venus
John Gray. HarperPerennial, 1992; 256 pp. ISBN 0-06-092416-0
$12 ($14.75 postpaid) from HarperCollins Publishers/Direct Mail, PO Box 588, Dunmore, PA 18512; 800/331-3761

Coming Apart

When an intimate relationship ends, the participants usually try to fix blame — on their partner, on themselves, or vacillating between the two. On top of their loss, they feel like failures.

Coming Apart offers a way out of the blame-frame. In fact, rather than viewing divorce as an unequivocal tragedy, the author suggests that it is the natural and best ending to some relationships.

The author, a marriage counselor, provides guidelines for assessing developmental gains and dealing with the pain of loss in an unworkable relationship. She encourages the reader to recognize that the powerful, persistent feelings that arise in splitting up are normal and expectable, and thus to feel less defeated, ashamed and confused. —BE

●

I am certainly not saying that we should take the mystery, or the magic or romance, out of falling in love; but we certainly do need to take the mystery out of falling OUT of love. When a relationship ends, it is vital to look at it through reality-colored glasses and ask: "What was it really about?" "What were we doing together, anyway?" We need to see what happened so that we don't feel guilty, so that we learn for the future, so that we can love again.

●

Angry and, in particular, violent feelings are very scary. We usually want to inhibit them or disown them. They certainly don't fall into the category of any feelings our mothers ever told us were acceptable. But in order to heal from the devastating wound that ending a relationship is, it is important that we also experience these vile, rotten, intense and unacceptable emotions.

In order to get beyond them, it's important to go through them, to give them full rein, to allow them expression — but in some way which is not, in fact, destructive, so that we can get beyond them.

A very good vehicle for this is what I call The Poison Pen Letter. In this exercise, you write a letter to your partner in which you express the full intensity of your rage, your most vile intentions about him or her, and your most self-indulgent wishes for his or her demise.

The purpose of The Poison Pen Letter is to allow you to give expression in fantasy to these intense feelings without harming yourself or anyone else.

●

So now, write a letter of apology to your old sweetheart, partner, husband, wife, or mate for all your crimes. In this letter, be absolutely ruthlessly honest in identifying what went wrong, and be absolutely crystal clear in your apology. This is a letter for your benefit. Its purpose is to cleanse your consciousness and it need never be shown to your partner.

Coming Apart
Daphne R. Kingma. 1991; 189 pp. ISBN 0-943233-00-3
$8.95 ($12.20 postpaid) from Conari Press, 1144 65th Street, Suite B, Emeryville, CA 94608; 800/685-9595

OTHER GREAT RESOURCES

American Association of Marriage and Family Therapy: 1100 17th Street NW, Washington, DC 20036; 800/374-2638.

American Psychiatric Association: 1400 K Street NW, Washington, DC 20005; 202/682-6000.

American Psychological Association: 1st Street NE, Washington, DC 20002; 202/336-5800.

Before You Call the Doctor

Here's a clear, comprehensive guide to self-care for a wide range of common symptoms and ailments. Each entry gives a concise overview of the condition, guidelines for what to do at home, and a concise list of symptoms and circumstances that indicate professional attention.

Doctors sometimes speak of three types of patients: those who come to the doctor's office when they could manage their problem on their own, those who don't come in when they should, and those who seek professional care only when it's needed. This book can help you stay in the third category.
—TF

•

Nosebleeds

What's Going On? Most nosebleeds are caused by picking the nose or blowing it frequently due to colds or allergies. The dry air in air-conditioned buildings and airplanes increases the likelihood of nosebleeds because the relative humidity dries out the protective layer of nasal mucus that covers the tiny blood vessels in the nose ("capillaries"), increasing the risk of bleeding from the minor trauma of picking and bleeding.

Before You Call the Doctor
Anne Simons, Bobbie Hasselbring & Michael Castleman. Fawcett Columbine Books, 1993; 688 pp. ISBN 0-449-90493-8
$15 ($17 postpaid) from Random House/ Order Dept., 400 Hahn Road, Westminster, MD 21157; 800/733-3000

Before You Call the Doctor. If blood is coming from only one nostril, press against the nostril firmly. If both nostrils are bleeding, pinch the fleshy part of the nose together. In either event, maintain pressure for five to ten minutes to allow time for the blood to clot. Do not stop pinching before five minutes. The vast majority of recurrences are the result of impatience. Just keep applying pressure for five to ten minutes. If bleeding continues, apply pressure for another ten minutes.

When to call the Doctor. Consult a physician if bleeding cannot be stopped by pinching or packing.

The Mouth, Nose, and Throat.

Healthwise Handbook • Healthwise for Life

This medical textbook for the layperson provides guidelines for dealing with common health concerns. Useful sections on basic self-care and home health management skills (home physical, choosing and working with your doctor, preparing for an office visit, first aid) make **Healthwise Handbook** *a good basic crash course in self-management.* **Healthwise for Life** *focuses on health issues common among older people.*
—TF

•

Fishhook Removal

Step A: Tie a piece of fishing line to the hook near the skin surface.

Step B: Grasp the eye of the hook with one hand and press down about 1/8 inch to disengage the barb.

Step C: While still pressing the hook down (barb disengaged), jerk the line parallel to the skin surface so that the hook shaft leads the barb out of the skin.

If the fishhook is deeply embedded, another option is to push the hook the rest of the way through the skin, snip off the barb, and remove the hook.

Wash the wound thoroughly. Use soap if available. Treat as you would a puncture wound.

Do not try to remove a fishhook from the eye.
—*Healthwise Handbook*

Step A

Step B

Step C

Healthwise Handbook
Donald Kemper. 1994; 306 pp. ISBN 1-877930-04-0

Healthwise for Life
Molly Mettler & Donald Kemper. 1992; 380 pp. ISBN 1-877930-02-4

Each $14.95 ($16.45 postpaid) from Healthwise Inc., PO Box 1989, Boise, ID 83701; 208/345-1161

SelfCare Catalog

Founded by **MWEC** *medical editor Tom Ferguson back in the 1970s, this catalog of medical and self-help tools has changed with the times while consistently offering the latest and best self-help tools. The expected items are devices for home workouts, sports medicine, massage, stress relief, pain management, back care, and biofeedback. You can also order a state-of-the-art eardrum thermometer, a home otoscope for checking your kid's ears, sun-protective clothing, Gore-Tex dental floss, a surgical-quality splinter removal kit, and the ultimate back-support pillow for your car.*

Each new catalog introduces new (and sometimes untried) products; the editors rely on reader feedback to cull the dogs and keep the winners. SelfCare offers a $500 award to readers who recommend useful new products. —J. Baldwin

•

The patented Active Ankle Brace keeps you up and about despite an injured ankle. Its solid plastic "U" frame decreases side-to-side stress, protecting against further injury, while pivoting hinges allow full front-to-back flexing, promoting early activity after injury and faster rehabilitation. Wear with any footwear: your everyday shoes, running shoes, even ski boots. Fits either foot. Specify men's or women's, and shoe size.
Active Ankle Brace A3151 $36.95.

•

Detect Ear Infections Before Your Child Feels Any Pain. Ear infections are nearly as common as colds among young children. . . . and more painful! Monitor your child's ears to detect infections before they feel any pain. Earscope comes with case, instruction booklet, and three tips (adult, youth, baby). Uses two AAA batteries (included).
Family Earscope A1104 $25. Additional set of 3 Tips SP104 $5.

SelfCare Catalog
Free. 5850 Shellmound Street, Emeryville, CA 94662; phone 800/345-3371, fax 800/345-4021

Choices in Healing

A balanced and responsible approach to alternative and psychological cancer therapies. The author believes that people with cancer should be under the care of well-trained oncologists — and that oncologists should encourage patients to pursue alternative cancer treatments.

Very detailed, and very broad in its range of information about those alternative approaches, **Choices in Healing** *is the definitive sourcebook for such further explorations.*

NB: Michael Lerner offers a week-long residential program for people with cancer (all kinds) who are receiving mainstream medical care but want to do something more. For information, contact Commonweal Cancer Help Program, Waz Thomas, Coordinator, PO Box 316, Bolinas, CA 94924; 415/868-0970. —TF

•

This inner work of healing can be done by the patient himself; with a support group; with a psychotherapist; with a minister, rabbi or spiritual counselor; with a network

Choices in Healing
(Integrating the Best of Conventional and Complementary Approaches to Cancer)
Michael Lerner. 1994; 608 pp.
ISBN 0-262-12180-8
$24.95 ($27.95 postpaid) from The MIT Press/Order Dept., 55 Hayward Street, Cambridge, MA 02142; 800/356-0343

of supportive friends; within one's family; at work; and in a thousand uniquely personal ways. It certainly *expands* life to seek this kind of healing and it may possibly *extend* life for some people by stimulating the immune function and other resilience factors. The search for healing can also transform one's relationship with events that used to feel stressful, so that they feel less stressful. Stress, as we have seen, is known to enhance the growth of many cancers.

No Time to Wait

A superb resource for anyone who is HIV-positive, whether they have developed symptoms or not; equally useful for partners, friends, and family. **No Time to Wait** *provides understanding of the immune system, and describes treatment options — natural botanicals, Chinese medicine, antivirals, immune modulators, and prophylactic therapies. There's also good coverage of nutrition and stress reduction techniques. An excellent resource supplement introduces additional information sources and support services.* —Tracey Cosgrove

•

The more natural treatment interventions usually take longer than mainstream approaches. If a natural-treatment intervention doesn't work after three months, I would definitely give it more time. Most natural-treatment interventions take six months to a year to show results. If you don't have the time to wait for those results, you should be on a more aggressive treatment, boosting your cells, controlling HIV, and *then* substituting the more natural treatments.

No Time to Wait
(A Complete Guide to Treating, Managing, and Living with HIV Infection)
Nick Siano & Suzanne Lipsett. 1993; 367 pp. ISBN 0-553-37176-2
$12.95 ($15.45 postpaid) from Bantam, Doubleday, Dell/Fulfillment Dept., 2451 S. Wolf Road, Des Plaines, IL 60018; 800/223-6834

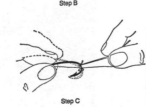

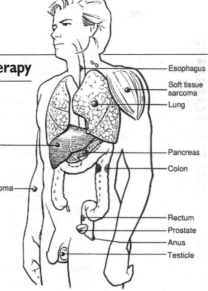

Everyone's Guide to Cancer Therapy

*A comprehensive explanation of most cancer diagnoses, with a good overview of conventional therapies. The book's genius is in its organization. Information is grouped by type of cancer, detailing the methods typically used to treat that type in its various stages. (The clear explanation of the stage-definition process was a revelation.) Broad explanations of different treatment methods include such exotic techniques as biological therapy (immunotherapy), laser therapy, and hyperthermia. There's a somewhat tightlipped chapter on "questionable and unproven" therapies, too. For the newly diagnosed patient, especially one facing difficult treatment choices, this book is indispensable.
—Phil Catalfo*

●

Sixty percent of esophageal cancers appear in the cells lining the esophageal tube (squamous cells), usually in the upper two-thirds of the esophagus. About 40 percent develop in the glands (adenocarcinoma) in the lower third. One to 2 percent are relatively rare tumors, such as melanoma, primary lymphomas or tumors in the smooth muscles, among others.

How It Spreads. Carcinoma of the esophagus usually starts on the surface layer, invades the surrounding tissue and grows to cause an obstruction that makes swallowing difficult. It spreads through the lymph system to lymph nodes. The most common sites for metastases are the lymph nodes, lungs, liver, brain, adrenal glands and bones.

Everyone's Guide to Cancer Therapy
Malin Dollinger & Ernest Rosenbaum. 1991, 1994; 624 pp. ISBN 0-8362-2427-2

$19.95 ($21.95 postpaid) from Andrews & McMeel, PO Box 419242, Kansas City, MO 64141; 800/826-4216

At the Will of the Body

This brief memoir of two serious illnesses (a heart attack and cancer) provides deep insight into the ways doctors (who think in terms of formulas, numbers, and procedures) and ill people (who are more concerned with feelings and relationships) work at cross-purposes, and inevitably misunderstand one another. Our ingrained dependence on professional care and happy outcomes can undermine our ability to mount an appropriate response to our own illnesses.

*Arthur Frank joins such writers and thinkers as Norman Cousins, Oliver Sacks, Arthur Kleinmen, and Rachel Naomi Remen in the creation of an important genre of writing that defines the experience of illness as a wisdom tradition of its own. **At the Will of the Body** is one of the best of the breed.*
—TF

●

I want to keep running, but someday I will have to stop. I do not know what that day will be like. If I have recovered well but not too much, I will remember a poem I keep over my desk by the late Raymond Carver, called "Gravy." A man, an alcoholic, is about to die, but he changes his habits and lives for ten years. Then he gets a brain disease and again is dying. He tells his friends not to mourn:

"I've had ten years longer than I or anyone expected. Pure gravy. And don't you forget it."

I try not to.

At the Will of the Body
(Reflections on Illness)
Arthur Frank. 1992; 160 pp.
ISBN 0-395-62430-4

$8.95 ($10 postpaid) from Houghton Mifflin Co./Mail Order Dept., Wayside Road, Burlington, MA 01803; 800/225-3362

Building Partnerships in Hospital Care

The author was one of the architects of the care-partner model developed at the Planetree Model Hospital Unit (reviewed below). The model's basis is a three-way partnership among patient, family or friends, and key members of the health care team. The patient is the team's director; patients too ill to play this role can appoint a friend as a spokesperson.

Family members are trained to provide support and nursing care for their hospitalized loved ones. Once the patient is discharged, the care partners help to coordinate self-care at home.

This book can help families deal with the frequently dehumanizing, discouraging aspects of hospitalization. It encourages a level of medical self-responsibility and interpersonal innovation that can help transform an ordeal

into a process of enrichment and renewal. It's an important model for health care reform. —TF

Building Partnerships in Hospital Care
Mary D. Scheller. 1990; 315 pp.
ISBN 0-923521-07-0

$10.95 ($13.95 postpaid) from Bull Publishing Co., PO Box 208, Palo Alto, CA 94302-0208; 800/676-2855

Graedons' Best Medicine

This unique, well-written guide to popular pharmacology recommends the most effective medicines for many ailments. While most such guides stick to a single treatment approach (herbal remedies, vitamins, over-the-counter or prescription drugs), the authors consider all of these — just as most people do in self-care.

Where else could you discover that paper-filtered coffee may be healthier than the perked variety? Or that taking an aspirin tablet half an hour before your daily dose of niacin may reduce the discomfort of the "niacin flush?" Along with such odd but useful tips, the authors have put together the best advice I've seen on stocking your home medicine chest.

The Graedons use a system of one-to five-star efficacy ratings: chamomile tea and Pepto-Bismol both receive four stars for upset stomach. Advil gets two stars for pain, while Rogaine squeaks by with one, for baldness. Aspirin is the only drug to receive the five-star rating.

Graedons' Best Medicine
(From Herbal Remedies to High-Tech Rx)
Joe and Teresa Graedon. Bantam, 1991. 444 pp. ISBN 0-553-35274-1

$15.95 ($18.45 postpaid) from Bantam, Doubleday, Dell/Fulfillment Dept., 2451 S. Wolf Road, Des Plaines, IL 60018; 800/223-6834

The Graedons host a nationally syndicated radio show addressing drug-related topics. Tapes of programs are available. For a list of topics, write or call MIR Productions, 3500 Westgate Drive, Suite 101, Durham NC 27707; 919/419-4484. —TF

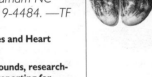

Earlobe Creases and Heart Disease

As crazy as it sounds, researchers have been reporting for years that diagonal earlobe creases which run at a forty-five-degree angle are strongly associated with cardiovascular disease. Don't panic if you find one, but check in with a cardiologist for a more scientific workup.

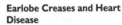

Planetree Model Hospital Alliance

Contrary to prevailing assumptions, you don't need to leave your brain at the door when you check into a hospital. Self-care on the wards is possible, advisable, and beneficial. No one has done a better job than Planetree of humanizing, personalizing and demystifying medicine and pointing the way toward the hospital of the future.

Patients on the Planetree unit set their own daily schedules, administer their own medications, and routinely read and write in their own medical records. Personal choices in visiting hours, furnishings, and clothing are encouraged. There is a special kitchen where family members can prepare food for their ailing loved ones, and a patient lounge

with a videotape library and visiting musicians. Patients choose a primary nurse from the staff to serve as their main caregiver, advocate, health educator, and friend throughout their stay.

Planetree also operates one of the country's most sophisticated consumer health information libraries. With their help, patrons can locate health and medical information, drawing on an extensive selection of sources. For a modest fee, Planetree can compile a customized information packet on virtually any medical or health topic, or perform a customized computer search of pertinent literature. —TF

Planetree: 2040 Webster, San Francisco, CA 94115; 415/923-3681.

Home Medical Reference

As a medical librarian at the Planetree Health Resource Center (p. 181), I'm frequently asked for advice on choosing a good medical reference book to have at home. Of the available guides to orthodox (M.D.-variety) medicine, these are the three I most frequently find myself recommending. You should also be able to find these books (and many others) at your local public, university, or hospital library.

Current Medical Diagnosis and Treatment 1994: *This clearly written, concise medical textbook is well organized and uses minimal medical jargon. Annual revisions make this one of the few medical books that keeps up with new diagnoses and therapies.*

Current Medical Diagnosis and Treatment

Lawrence M. Tierney. 1993; 1418 pp. ISBN 0-8385-1375-1 $39.95 postpaid. Appleton and Lange, 25 Van Zant Street, Norwalk, CT 06855; 203/838-4400

American Medical Association Encyclopedia of Medicine: *This comprehensive home reference comprises a medical dictionary, anatomy guide, drug handbook, and A-to-Z approach to understanding the human body. Illustrations and charts are useful supplements to the text. The book provides a good overall review of body systems and a summary of the whole range of established diseases.*

The American Medical Association Encyclopedia of Medicine

AMA Staff. 1989; ISBN 0-394-56528-2 $45 ($47 postpaid). Random House/ Order Dept., 400 Hahn Road, Westminster, MD 21157; 800/733-3000

Complete Guide to Symptoms, Illness, and Surgery: *This handy book offers one- to two-page information capsules of common symptoms, diagnoses, and surgical procedures. Not as much detail as the books above, but a good first stop in getting a convenient quick fix on a condition that may be new to you. Other "Complete Guide" titles in this series provide similar summaries for people over fifty, kids, medical tests, drugs, sports injuries, and vitamins/food supplements.*
—Tracey Cosgrove

Complete Guide to Symptoms, Illness and Surgery

Griffith H. Winter. The Body Press, 1989; 896 pp. ISBN 0-399-51709-X $15.95 ($17.95 postpaid). Putnam Publishing Group/Order Dept., PO Box 506, East Rutherford, NJ 07073; 800/631-8571

Substance Abuse Intervention

Everyone uses mind-altering substances at least occasionally. Around one person in ten is unable to self-regulate substance use. Chronic abuse harms people financially, legally, in their professional lives. Addiction is characterized by a continuing pattern of episodes of abuse, loss of control over frequency and amount of chemical use, and/or a repetitive pattern of adverse consequences. If someone you know has a problem and you want to help:

1. Find a professional to talk to about it, or a knowledgeable friend (preferably one who is not involved with the person who has a problem). It's important to determine whether it is a problem or a matter of perception. Not all use of a substance is abuse, unless the person is operating hazardous machinery.

On page two of the white pages of every telephone directory is a list of crisis lines.

2. If you determine that an abuse or an addiction problem exists, try to point out, nonjudgmentally, examples of behavior that indicates a problem — DWI arrests, missing work, abusive behavior.

3. If that doesn't work, intervention by several people can be more effective than by one individual. Interventions are often done by a trained substance-abuse therapist and a group that can comprise spouses, siblings, parents, other loved ones, employers — people close to the person with the problem, with specific knowledge of the way the person is acting self- or otherwise destructively. The interveners should have rehearsed what they are going to say, and checked out treatment options before the intervention.

4. Usually, the interveners arrange a surprise meeting outside the security of the person's home. The group's chosen facilitator will say "George, we want to talk with you about something we feel is serious, and we want you to hear what we have to say." Ask the person not to respond until everyone has had their say. Then one by one, the group members explain why they think there is a problem, citing specific behavior.

The intervention should end with an ultimatum. A spouse could say: "I love you, but I'm very concerned about this behavior. You need to get treatment, or I am going to have to leave."

5. Some people need hospital detoxification, depending on the substance, the person, and the situation. Withdrawal from substances that cause physical dependence — alcohol, barbiturates, tranquillizers — can be life-threatening if withdrawal occurs suddenly, without medication.

6. Once a person is detoxified, however it occurs, the hardest part of the treatment begins — preventing relapse. A combination of education, counseling, and continuing support is best. That's the benefit of support groups, such as twelve-step groups and their rare alternatives. Recovering addicts have experience and important information to share, and the company of people who are not active users can be equally important.

The Alcoholics Anonymous model dominates chemical-dependency treatment. Some people have problems with twelve-step programs because they cannot accept the religious/spiritual principles involved. Two alternative groups that can be found in larger urban centers are S.O.S. (Secular Organizations for Sobriety) and Rational Recovery.

S.O.S.: Call 716/834-2922 for information on local meetings.
Rational Recovery: Call 916/621-4374 for information.
AA is everywhere; check your telephone book.

—Eugene Schoenfeld, M.D., M.P.H.

OTHER GREAT BOOKS ON MEDICAL SELF-CARE

CANCER

From Victim to Victor: Harold H. Benjamin & Richard Turbo. 1987, Dell Publishing. A short, easy-to-read, medically-conservative pep talk for newly diagnosed cancer patients and their families. It's a good first book to read after receiving a diagnosis of cancer.

Peace, Love, and Healing • Love, Medicine, and Miracles • How to Live Between Office Visits: Bernie Siegel. 1990, 1991, 1993, HarperCollins. People seem to either love Dr. Bernie Siegel or hate him; those who hate him are generally physicians who do not have cancer. These were the most frequently recommended books for inclusion in this section.

Cancer Therapy: Ralph W. Moss. 1992, Equinox Press. Another thorough and well-documented guide to alternative therapies.

Cancer as a Turning Point: Lawrence LeShan. 1989, Penguin Books. Considering a diagnosis of cancer as an invitation to re-examine your life. LeShan, the George Washington of psychological approaches to cancer, is still one of the field's most advanced and respected thinkers.

Understanding Cancer: Mark Renneker. Out of print.

DEATH AND DYING

Midwives to the Dying: Miriam Schneider & Jan Selliken Bernard. Angel's Word, 1992. How to support the physical, emotional, and spiritual needs of dying loved ones and the people caring for them.

Final Exit: Derek Humphry. 1991, Dell. A controversial book on death with dignity via suicide. Those who choose this path need to be well informed about possible implications of their decision. This frank book also contains a great deal of useful information on how *not* to commit suicide.

DRUGS

Essential Guide to Prescription Drugs, 1994: James W. Long. 1994, HarperCollins. This annually updated guide to the 250 most commonly prescribed drugs. Provides a good overview of the basics you need to know about your medications, such as side effects, interactions, expected benefits, and long-term effects.

ENVIRONMENTAL HEALTH

NYU Medical Center Family Guide to Staying Healthy in a Risky Environment: Arthur C. Upton et al. 1993, Simon & Schuster. A good overview, with tips for avoiding and preventing problems and guidelines for seeking medical advice.

HEART DISEASE

Dr. Dean Ornish's Program for Reversing Heart Disease: Dean Ornish. 1990, Random House. Self-care techniques (meditation, yoga, visualization, social support, exercise, diet, and more). Ornish and colleagues were the first researchers to prove that lifestyle strategies could not only prevent but actually reverse coronary artery disease.

HIGH BLOOD PRESSURE

The H.A.R.T. Program (Lower Your Blood Pressure Without Drugs): D. Ariel Kerman & Richard Turbo. 1992, HarperCollins. A superb guide to self-care for people with hypertension. How to control your condition without drugs if humanly possible (it usually is). Everyone with high blood pressure should read this book.

MEN'S HEALTH

Understanding Male Sexual Health: Dorothy Baldwin. 1993, Hipocrene Books. Diagnosing and managing male sexual problems, complete with detailed self-care advice.

NATURAL MEDICINE

Natural Health, Natural Medicine: Andrew Weil. 1990, Houghton Mifflin. A thoughtful how-to manual. Especially good on home remedies and self-care techniques for common health problems.

REFERENCE

What to Do When You Can't Afford Health Care: Matthew Lesko et al. 1993, Information USA. An amazing collection of resources with information about thousands of health conditions, guidelines for finding low-cost or free health care services, and legal advice on consumer health complaints.

SELF-CARE FLOWCHARTS

Take Care of Yourself • Take Care of Your Child: Donald Vickery & James Fries. 1990, 1993, Addison-Wesley. Simple, straightforward decisionmaking flowcharts serve as useful aids to self-care and decisions about professional care for common medical problems. The companion volume features flowcharts for the common medical problems of children.

WOMEN'S HEALTH

The New Our Bodies, Ourselves (A Book For Women): Boston Women's Health Collective. 1992, Simon & Schuster. Reviewed on p. 184.

DEADER'N HELL, BUDDY

Intoxicated by My Illness: Anatole Broyard. 1993, Clarkson Potter. This memoir of the author's final fourteen months is as edifying as it is electrifying. A gifted writer confronts the ultimate deadline.

—Tracey Cosgrove and Tom Ferguson, M.D.

Jane Brody's Good Food Book • Jane Brody's Nutrition Book

True confession: I read page one of Good Food while dining in a restaurant on exactly those things the author discourages: fats, sugars and empty calories. Second true confession: one week after reading several chapters, my eating and shopping habits had shifted. I became more mindful of not only what I ate but when and how I ate it — a testimony to Jane Brody's talent for convincing us we can change our diets over time and, best of all, enjoy the journey.

Good Food is a well-organized tome of hard-core nutrition data, recipes and food lore. Periodically, she transports us back in history to pursue the origins of foodstuffs and to see why certain ones never made it onto our grandmothers' grocery lists. In addition to shopping and storage advice, she has wisely included a chapter on eating out that gently guides us not only through menu obstacles in restaurants but helps us survive hotel room service and airline meals.

The revised edition of her Nutrition Book is an excellent kitchen-shelf companion to Good Food. With straightforward information and cleanly rendered charts, it is still one of the best quick references I've found.
—Linda Morgan

•

I usually order [breakfast room service] the night before to arrive after I have returned from my morning run and have showered. I have found that specific requests are nearly always honored: an omelet made with one egg yolk and two whites; whole wheat toast, unbuttered; skim milk for my cereal and coffee; oatmeal cooked in skim milk; berries without cream; and so forth. And if my day's schedule looks like there's no time for lunch, along with my breakfast I sometimes order a sandwich that will keep in my briefcase until lunchtime.

•

Popcorn kernels have more hard starch than other types [of corn], which helps them "explode" when heated. No, popcorn was not the invention of Metro-Goldwyn-Mayer. Actually, the Incas cultivated it and used it to decorate bodies for burial, and the Indians who greeted Columbus were wearing necklaces of strung popcorn. The Indians who attended the first Thanksgiving dinner supposedly arrived bearing bowls of popcorn, thus starting a national passion long before there was a nation.

•

Even with whole-wheat flour products, the nutrient level can vary depending upon how the flour is milled and processed. You get the most nutrients — and the best flavor — from stone-ground whole-wheat flour. If not in the "health food" or regular flour section of your supermarket, you'll find it in health stores. It is one health food that is worth the extra expense. It is coarsely ground between rotating millstones much like the ones used in centuries past. Stone-ground graham flour is whole-wheat flour in which the starchy part of the wheat kernel is finely ground but the bran is left coars and flaky. Second best is ordinary whole-wheat flour, which is less coarse than the stone-ground variety and may contain flour additives (like malted barley flour). You can also buy whole-wheat pastry flour, made from soft whole wheat that is finely milled. —*Good Food*

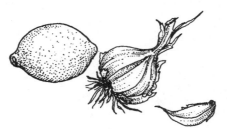

CREAMY VINAIGRETTE

about 1¼ cups

⅔ cup plain low-fat yogurt
⅓ cup apple cider vinegar
2 tablespoons olive oil
1 tablespoon Dijon mustard
1 tablespoon fresh lemon juice
1 very large clove garlic, crushed
1 tablespoon reduced-sodium soy sauce (optional)
¼ teaspoon dried dillweed

Combine all the vinaigrette ingredients in a bowl or jar with a tight-fitting lid, whisking or shaking them to blend them well.

Jane Brody's Good Food Book
Jane Brody. Bantam Books, 1987; 736 pp. ISBN 0-553-34618-0

Jane Brody's Nutrition Book
Jane Brody. Bantam Books, 1982; 576 pp. ISBN 0-553-34421-8
$15 each ($17.50 postpaid).
Bantam, Doubleday, Dell/ Fulfillment Dept., 2451 S. Wolf Road, Des Plaines, IL 60018; 800/223-6834

The McDougall Program • The New McDougall Cookbook • Eat More, Weigh Less

I've been overweight all my life and have tried many diets. None worked. Then my wife began the McDougall diet. She lost weight and the food tasted fine.

My friend, nutrition expert Betty Kamen, tells me that McDougall's program is nutritionally sound, based on solid research. For the evidence supporting McDougall's plan, start with The McDougall Program. If you're already persuaded, jump straight to The New McDougall Cookbook, which contains a summary of his dietary principles and a few hundred easily prepared recipes.

Dr. Dean Ornish's Eat More, Weigh Less is another, less doctrinaire low-fat program, with intricate recipes created by gourmet chefs. Many of the recipes are outstanding. They include the nutritional content, something lacking in McDougall's recipes. —Roger Karraker

•

Meats, fish, eggs, dairy products, lard, vegetable oils, and refined foods all fail as health-supporting foods for human nutrition. The fact that they are lacking in complex carbohydrates, fibers, many vitamins, and essential minerals is a serious concern, but one can usually obtain enough of the necessary nutrients in other foods to survive. The problem is that these foods contain excessive amounts of the potentially good nutrients, and harmful quantities of fundamentally unhealthy non-nutrients. A diet centering around these foods continuously assails us with imbalances and excesses of many kinds, and the body soon reacts with signs of distress that we recognize as diseases. —*McDougall Program*

The McDougall Program
John A. McDougall. Plume Books, 1990; 436 pp. ISBN 0-452-26639-4
$12 ($14 postpaid). Penguin USA/ Consumer Sales, 120 Woodbine Street, Bergenfield, NJ 07621; 800/253-6476

The New McDougall Cookbook
John A. McDougall & Mary McDougall. Dutton, 1993; 405 pp. ISBN 0-525-93610-6
$24 ($26 postpaid). Penguin USA/ Consumer Sales, 120 Woodbine Street, Bergenfield, NJ 07621; 800/253-6476

Eat More, Weigh Less
Dean Ornish. 1993; 425 pp. ISBN 0-06-016838-2
$25 ($27.75 postpaid). HarperCollins Publishers/Direct Mail, PO Box 588, Dunmore, PA 18512; 800/331-3761

OTHER GREAT RESOURCES

Diet for a Small Planet: Francis M. Lappé. 1991, Ballantine Books. Chock-full of vegetarian recipes and well-annotated facts on nutrition, the twentieth anniversary edition of this internationally respected book now serves a new generation of health-conscious readers. —Cynthia Dyer-Bennet

Food and the Gut Reaction (Intestinal Health Through Diet): Elaine Gottschall. 1987, Kirkton Press, 942 Military St., Suite A, Port Huron, MI 48060; 800/332-3663. This book is aimed at the thousands of people in our society who suffer from chronic gut problems like ulcerative colitis, Crohn's disease, or celiac disease. —Flash Gordon, M.D.

University of California at Berkeley Wellness Letter: PO Box 420149, Palm Coast, FL 32142. About 40 to 60 percent of each issue is devoted to nutrition.

AS FAR AS THE HEALTH care profession is concerned, the standard design of the human body is male.

This despite that fact that women make up more than half the population.

This despite the fact that women consume as much health care as men — they use more prescription drugs, they undergo more unnecessary surgery (notably hysterectomies and cesarean sections), and they are far more likely to be referred for psychotherapy.

By the time we hit kindergarten, of course, most of us realize: women's bodies are *different* from men's bodies. Men do not have uteri or ovaries. Men do not secrete estrogen or progesterone in significant quantites. Men are not prone to premenstrual syndrome, dysmennorhea, fibroids, ovarian cysts, or breast cancer.

This does not account for the gender biases within health care.

Women's health issues are marginalized by the medical industry. Even the normal female conditions associated with aging are treated according to the disease model. Menopause, for example, has been called an "estrogen deficiency disorder." Ever hear of the *disease* of male pattern baldness?

Medical research is almost exclusively slanted toward men — consider the systematic exclusion of women from the clinical trials of new drugs on the grounds that menstrual cycle fluctuations or possible pregnancy complications might interfere with the research. It is only logical to assume that the metabolic differences between the two sexes will have a significant effect on the drug's assimilation, yet this is rarely factored into the experimental design.

Physicians are less likely to diagnose certain kinds of diseases in women than they are in men — a trend accentuated by the tendency of many women to use their gynecologist as their primary-care physician. Long after the vectors of HIV infection were deduced, AIDS in women continued to go undiagnosed and ignored. And although each year 500,000 women die of diseases of the heart and blood vessels, coronary artery disease is less likely to be diagnosed in women than it is in men because of the perception that it is, somehow, a male disease. Once diagnosed, diseases are less often treated: one recent study demonstrated that women with kidney disease severe enough to require dialysis were 30 percent less likely to receive kidney transplants than men.

Public attention has brought some changes. In 1992, the National Institutes of Health undertook a ten-year, $500 million project, The Women's Health Initiative. Support is growing today for a medical specialty in women's health beyond gynecology and obstetrics. And widely varied self-help resources for women have also become available. In the new millennium, perhaps women will finally get the health care they deserve.

—Patrizia DiLucchio

How Not to Get Pregnant

There are only two surefire ways to avoid pregnancy: abstinence or hysterectomy. Neither of these is discussed in this book.

What is discussed in this book, however, are numerous contraceptive strategies — natural family planning, the new low-dose estrogen birth control pills, the intrauterine device (sadly unavailable in American markets), barrier methods (condoms, diaphragms, contraceptive foam, and sponges), vasectomy, tubal ligation, and the newer methods like quarterly Depo-provera shots and Norplant — one of which may be right for you. —PDiL

•

When Robert Redford or James Bond make love to a woman on the screen, it all seems so easy, so joyful, and so utterly free of any responsibility. Bond does not have to interrupt his foreplay to go to the hotel room dresser to get out a condom, nor does his partner for the evening have to check her basal body temperature chart to see if it is safe. Nor is she seen in the morning remembering to take her birth control pill. Bond is not seen showing up at the urology clinic with pus dripping out of his penis from a sexually transmitted disease, nor is his female companion for that evening shown eight years later undergoing a complicated microsurgical operation to try to open up tubes that were blocked from an infection she got because she failed to make her strange lover wear a condom, or was using the wrong IUD. All around us our society is hyping up sex and making it seem like we are truly free from any need of forethought or contraceptive planning.

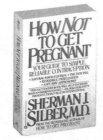

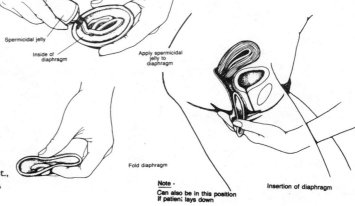

How Not to Get Pregnant
Sherman J. Silber. 1987; 323 pp.
ISBN 0-446-39088-7
$9.95 ($12.45 postpaid) from
Little, Brown & Co./Order Dept.,
200 West Street, Waltham, MA
02154; 800/343-9204

Spermicidal jelly

Inside of diaphragm

Apply spermicidal jelly to diaphragm

Fold diaphragm

Note -
Can also be in this position
if patient lays down

Insertion of diaphragm

The Female Heart

Although coronary heart disease has been the number-one killer of both women and men in this country since 1910, women and their physicians have consistently ignored or neglected its warning signs. The result? Thirty-five percent of all heart attacks in women go unreported or ignored, and women are twice as likely as men to die after their first heart attack.

*Specifically designed for women, **The Female Heart** contains information about both normal and abnormal heart function, women at risk, the effects of pregnancy, menopause, and estrogen replacement therapy on the heart, and lifestyle changes women can make to help their hearts function optimally. Buy it, read it, and add it to your library. —PDiL*

The Female Heart
(The Truth About Women
and Heart Disease)
Marianne J. Legato. 1991; 252 pp.
ISBN 0-380-72003-5
$10 ($11.50 postpaid) from Avon Books,
PO Box 767, Dresden, TN 38225;
800/223-0690

•

Until age fifty-five, women usually have lower blood pressures than men of the same age. After that, the tables suddenly turn. Between fifty-five and sixty-five women run the same risk as men of developing high blood pressure, but by age sixty-five they are even more likely than men to become hypertensive. Although hypertension appears to be a late-onset disease, it can also occur in children and even in infants.

The New Our Bodies, Ourselves

*The grandmother of all self-help books, **Our Bodies, Ourselves** is the most complete sourcebook available today on women's health. Such subjects as the new Reality female condom, Norplant, RU-486, the French abortion pill, breast reconstruction after mastectomy, chronic fatigue syndrome, interstitial cystitis, and environmental sensitivities are presented in the context of larger public health questions on how the medical care system can be altered to better meet women's needs. A veritable owner's manual for everyone with a female body. —PDiL*

•

From *in vitro* fertilization and sex preselection to embryo transfer, scientists and physicians are working hard on new technologies that could drastically change women's relationship to childbearing. . . . Most of the money that goes into developing these technologies would be better spent on preventive measures and basic health care services for all women. What's more, white, professional, affluent men make up the overwhelming number of the scientists who research these technologies, the physicians who apply them, the legislators who approve and fund the research and the drug company directors who translate them into products to be advertised, sold, and profited from.

PMS Self Help Book

Suppose for one week out of every month you had to take a drug that made your body bloat up with five to eight pounds of extra water, that racked your abdomen with nausea and cramps, that made you quarrelsome, jumpy, and prone to tears. This is what premenstrual syndrome feels like.

Susan M. Lark's helpful book will assist

Above and left: Neurolymphatic point relieves cramps, low back pain. Massage each area shown in the photographs for 20 to 30 seconds.

you to identify and organize your particular set of symptoms. It gives specific information on nutrition, stress reduction, exercise, and yoga that will assist you in putting together an effective treatment program. The bonus? You'll feel like yourself all month long. —PDiL

PMS Self
Help Book
Susan M. Lark.
1984; 239 pp. ISBN
0-89087-587-1
$16.95 ($20.45
postpaid) from
Celestial Arts
Publishing, PO Box
7123, Berkeley,
CA 94707; 800/
841-2665

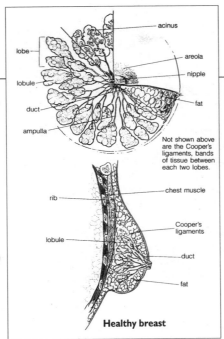

lobe
acinus
areola
nipple
lobule
fat
duct
ampulla

Not shown above are the Cooper's ligaments, bands of tissue between each two lobes.

rib
chest muscle
Cooper's ligaments
lobule
duct
fat

Healthy breast

Women's Cancers

In 1992, approximately 180,000 women in the United States were diagnosed with breast cancer; of this total, 46,000 died. An additional 50,000 women had abnormal Pap smears, some proportion of which progressed to cervical cancer.

Cancer is every woman's worst nightmare.

Many good resources are available on the subject of women's malignancies. However, Kerry A. McGinn and Pamela J. Haylock (both registered nurses working in oncology) have put together most of the information you should ever need: cellular descriptions of the disease; treatment protocols; advice on prevention strategies if you are at risk for developing breast, pelvic, uterine, ovarian, or other cancers. Though no book on cancer can be described as comforting, the tone of this book — written by women for women — is reassuring. —PDiL

●

Chemotherapy is a different experience for every woman. How she responds to chemo depends not only on the regimen itself — there are all kinds and combinations of drugs and ways

of receiving them — but also on how the woman's body and mind respond. While chemo hits some women really hard, and many feel flu-ish part of the time, plenty of others breeze through it with a little tiredness and an occasional nap.

Women's Cancers
Kerry McGinn & Pamela Haylock. 1993; 432 pp.
ISBN 0-89793-103-3
$14.95 ($17.45 postpaid) from Hunter House, 2200 Central Avenue, #202, Alameda, CA 94501; 510/865-5282

The New Our Bodies, Ourselves
Boston Women's Health Book Collective. Touchstone Books, 1984, 1992; 751 pp.
ISBN 0-671-79176-1
$20 postpaid from Simon & Schuster/Order Dept., 200 Old Tappan Road, Old Tappan, NJ 07675; 800/223-2336

Women and Madness

Who decides if a woman is mentally ill? Who decides the nature of her illness?

For most of this century, the medical model that has dominated psychotherapy has relied primarily on clinical theories of personality depicting women as essentially passive, dependent, even masochistic, childlike, and sometimes hysterical. Treatment has emphasized the importance of adjusting to life circumstances rather than trying to change them, undercutting the legitimacy of the complaints.

In this classic examination of how sex-role stereotypes are used to define mental illness, Phyllis Chesler concludes that women have suffered for centuries from a double standard that punishes anyone who veers even slightly from "feminine" roles by labeling them as imbalanced.

Women and Madness was first published in 1972. While quite a lot has changed, we still have a long way to go. —PDiL

Women and Madness
Phyllis Chesler. 1989; 359 pp.
ISBN 0-15-698295-1
$9.95 ($12.45 postpaid) from Harcourt Brace Trade Dept., 6277 Sea Harbor Drive, Orlando, FL 32887-4300; 800/543-1918

●

The female "career" as a psychiatric patient in America seems to follow a certain pattern as a function of age, marital status, social class, race, and most certainly "attractiveness" (of course, this last is hard to document). . . . In terms of age, women are most concentrated in outpatient facilities between the ages of twenty and thirty-four . . . women's "prettiest" and childbearing years. Even if they are unhappy or functioning at low levels, their childrearing responsibilities and/or sexually youthful appearance keep them within the "outside" patriarchal institutions such as marriage and private psychotherapy.

The Invisible Epidemic

*Fact: Women are the fastest-growing sector of both people with AIDS and people with HIV. Yet, from the beginning of the AIDS pandemic, the threat to women has been ignored and underestimated in ways that offer chilling insight into the gender biases in health care and medical research. **The Invisible Epidemic** traces the chronology of HIV as it has affected women in the United States. Comparisons to Randy Shilts's **And the Band Played On** are unavoidable, but while Shilts focused on the devastating impact of the disease upon gay men, Corea tells the parallel story of HIV's ruthless attack upon women. Gyncological manifestations were not part of the AIDS definition until cervical cancer was belatedly added to the list of AIDS-defining diseases in 1992. Nor, to this day, have any studies attempted to isolate the virus from menstrual blood. Corea's book makes it clear that AIDS is not only a medical emergency, but a social crisis that leaves unanswered questions for all women. —PDiL*

●

None of the physicians or scientists talked about the women with AIDS as being sick

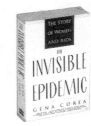

The Invisible Epidemic
(The Story of Women and AIDS)
Gena Corea. 1992; 356 pp.
ISBN 0-06-092191-9
$12 ($14.75 postpaid) from HarperCollins Publishers/Direct Mail, PO Box 588, Dunmore, PA 18512; 800/331-3761

themselves. They all saw women simply as vectors of disease to men and fetuses, as organisms, like insects, that transmit a pathogen. Women were discussed in perinatal and prostitute studies: Those innocent babies getting it from those irresponsible moms. Those bad women in prostitution giving it not only to innocent men — the johns — but to "good" women, the johns' wives. As if this guy in the middle had nothing to do with it. And the reason that it mattered that the "good" women were getting AIDS, according to the physician-experts, was not that they would suffer from the disease but that they would give it to the innocent man's innocent babies.

Making Sense of Menopause

Two things recommend this book among the many excellent resources available on the subject. First, Cone is an intelligent woman who does not have a medical background; when the change hit, she began canvassing bookstores, libraries and periodical shelves for information. As a result, her book is refreshingly free of medical jargon. Second, she takes no sides. Controversial topics like hormone replacement therapy are presented side-by-side with alternative therapies for menopause so that each reader may make her own decision. Filled with stories culled from over 150 interviews, this book does not tell readers what to do; rather, it empowers women to find the choice that works best for them. —PDiL

●

I was out for dinner, playing corporate wife, and found myself sitting at a table of five men, all in their late forties. After we had dispensed with the usual pleasantries and business had been discussed ad nauseam one of the men turned to me and asked about the subject of my book. When I replied I was writing about menopause, he was a little surprised. Nevertheless, he bravely plunged ahead and asked why I had chosen the subject. By that time, general conversation had come to a screeching halt, and all eyes were focused in my direction. I said it was because I had started menopause two years ago and could not find enough information on the subject. Well, every jaw at the table, except my husband's, of course, dropped. "But you can't be." "You're too young, ha ha." "Did you say menopause?" "Is it a humorous book?" This articulate group of marketing geniuses was unable to put together a single comprehensible response.

Making Sense of Menopause
Faye Kitchener Cone. 1993; 384 pp.
ISBN 0-671-78638-5
$13 postpaid from Simon & Schuster/Order Dept., 200 Old Tappan Road, Old Tappan, NJ 07675; 800/223-2336

OTHER GREAT RESOURCES

Women and HIV AIDS: An international perspective for health professionals, educators, researchers, journalists, policymakers — and you. Marge Berer & Sunandra Ray. HarperSanFrancisco, 1993.

Menopause Without Medicine: A comprehensive review of therapies to treat or prevent the symptoms naturally. Linda Ojeda. Hunter House, 1992.

I T COULD BE argued that childbirth is the ultimate feminist statement. Simply put: while a woman can probably do most everything a man can do, men cannot bear children.*

Normal variations exist throughout pregnancy, birth, and postpartum. It was only as recently as twenty years ago that the natural process of birth came to be regarded as a medical procedure to be managed, regulated and controlled. But pregnancy is not an illness; it's a normal physiological function. While advances in obstetrics have significantly lowered morbidity and mortality rates, it must be kept in mind that doctors are trained to anticipate worst-case scenarios. Most pregnancies are low-risk and will never require intensive interventions. The current trend is toward letting nature take its course: breathing and relaxation techniques, alternative birthing centers, fathers who catch the newborn and cut its cord — these have become the norm. Other options (home birth versus the usual hospital stay, or a midwife versus an attending physician) are also being explored by the consumer-wise expectant mother.

Relax. Enjoy your pregnancy. Believe me: there will be plenty of time to worry when your child becomes a teenager and wants to borrow the car.
—Patrizia DiLucchio

* Given the rapid developments in reproductive technology, this may change someday soon.

How to Get Pregnant with the New Technology

For the childless couple seeking to start a family, the anguish of infertility can be heartbreaking — betrayal at the most basic of biological levels. Studies say that 25 percent of couples in their thirties have been unable to have a baby. In the past the options were childlessness and adoption. Now, Sherman Silber — a physician, researcher, and acknowledged expert in the field of fertility — offers the hope of a biological pregnancy.

In straightforward, reassuring prose, *How to Get Pregnant* explains the mysteries of fertility, delving into recent advances in in vitro fertilization, surrogate pregnancy, micromanipulation, Gamete Intra Fallopian Transfer, and myriad other techniques and strategies.

Childlessness need no longer be a life sentence. The new technology offers great hope, and more than a few good answers. —Ben Trumble

How to Get Pregnant with the New Technology
Sherman J. Silber. 1991; 390 pp.
ISBN 0-446-39322-3
$12.99 ($15.49 postpaid) from Little, Brown & Co./Order Dept., 200 West Street, Waltham, MA 02154; 800/343-9204

Spiritual Midwifery

Ina May Gaskin got her start in the birthing business as the premier midwife providing prenatal care and attending births for a commune of 1,200 in southern Tennessee called The Farm. Gaskin may be the closest thing to a white witch postwar America has yet produced; *Spiritual Midwifery* is the classic in its field. Meticulous in its observation of physiological detail, impeccable in its attention to safe procedure, this book also honors another dimension of the birthing process, one that is seldom covered in obstetrical textbooks. Almost every woman with whom I have ever reminisced about the birth experience has remarked upon it: the mysticism of birth. Properly observed, giving birth can be an epiphanic experience, one where ego boundaries shimmer and break down.

A good birth is one that utilizes this spiritual energy in the physical process of delivery. To this end, Gaskin recontextualizes potentially negative stimuli — perhaps a little too carefully. Her laboring mothers do not have "contractions," they have "rushes." Fathers are not only encouraged to be present but are actually obligated to do their bit to ripen the cervix by kissing and petting with their laboring wives. Women who verbalize anxiety or physical discomfort are taken firmly in hand, told, "Shut up and shape up." All of which strikes me as a bit smarmy — labor hurts, after all, and what's a little healthy venting among friends? Never mind. There is so much that's useful in this book that a little gratuitous Pollyannaism hardly gets in the way. —PDiL

•

When I started pushing, it was with my whole thing. With the first push, the water

Your Baby, Your Way

Sheila Kitzinger is probably the world's preeminent childbirth educator. Here, she counsels the careful consumer approach to the bewildering assortment of options available in pregnancy and childbirth. The essence of parenthood is, after all, knowing how to make wise choices — and the number of choices you have to make goes up exponentially when you're giving informed consent not only for yourself, but also for your minor children.

Kitzinger gives firm grounding in the decisionmaking process. Chapters on drugs and health, food choices, exercise, environmental effects, pain control during labor, and natural vs. obstetrically directed childbirth help the expectant mother tailor the birth plan that will most exactly fit her own highly individualized needs.
—PDiL

•

In practice many women find that they are subjected to crude emotional blackmail. A woman is threatened, for example, that if she does not "toe the line" and deliver in the hospital, or agree to induction because she has reached forty-two weeks, she is risking the baby's life. (Home birth and induction are both subjects of a good deal of obstetric bullying.) A particular decision may introduce an unacceptable risk to the baby, and it is for the woman to consider the pros and cons of this in the light of her own beliefs and values. Ultimately, this is not a medical but a moral decision. No one else has the right to take that responsibility from her if she makes the decision to accept it.

Your Baby, Your Way
(Making Pregnancy Decisions and Birth Plans)
Sheila Kitzinger. Pantheon, 1987; 352 pp.
ISBN 0-394-75249-X
$15 ($17 postpaid) from Random House/ Order Dept., 400 Hahn Road, Westminster, MD 21157; 800/733-3000

See Women's Health on page 184.

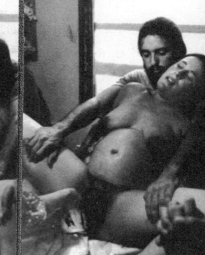

bag broke and got Kathryn in the face. We laughed. "See, you didn't need us to do it," the midwives said. Douglas held up a mirror for me to see my puss and I was amazed. It looked very psychedelic, like the big pink petals of a flower opening up. It was really beautiful. It surprised me and I felt like I had a new respect for my body. I remembered and told everyone how the story of Buddha says he was born from a lotus blossom. Everybody, every Buddha, is born that way. Just a few pushes later he came out, all purple and yelling. He was beautiful, real strong and healthy-looking. I was really grateful to see him. I wanted to hold him right away but I still had to get the placenta out and both of us had to get fixed up. I kept looking at him. He was right there. I was awake all night, too energized to sleep, and whenever I'd think, "How is he? Is he okay?" he'd open his eyes and look at me.

The Premature Baby Book

Consider the numbers: every year in the United States, 50,000 premature babies are born who weigh less than three pounds. The mother who is unable to bring a baby to full term often feels shock and sorrow, as though her body has betrayed her. By the time she has reached the end of her second trimester — the time when a live premature birth becomes a possibility — the morning sickness and hormonally induced anxieties of the early months have receded. She is physically and emotionally unprepared for the trauma of what can come next. In a sense, giving birth does not end her pregnancy — it merely transfers her baby from the warmth of its mother's womb to the harsh, sterile, mechanical environment of the neonatal intensive-care nursery. This fourth trimester, as some have called it, can turn her life into a nightmare.

The Premature Baby Book is a comprehensive resource designed to assist parents in coping with the contingencies of early birth. It contains sections not only on what to expect during your baby's hospital stay, but also on what to expect when you bring your baby home, what to expect developmentally, and on such practical matters as breast-feeding and where to find diapers and clothes that will fit. The personal accounts by parents who have been there are particularly helpful. *—PDiL*

•

The constant focus on the baby's medical condition can be depersonalizing. Said one mother, "Doctors were in and out of my room that first day telling me what was wrong with my baby and what complications they expected. Then a nurse from the NBICU (Newborn Intensive Care Unit) came in smiling and said, 'Congratulations, you have a lovely little girl!' She gave me a picture of Katy and a copy of her footprints. For the first time I felt like I'd really had a baby and not just a medical problem." Said another mother, "My way of coping was to immerse myself in the medical details of my son's care. One day a resident commented to me, 'He really is a little *person*, you know.' I realized then how I'd been using the medical aspects to keep my distance from the baby."

Above
Timothy at 1 pound, 13 ounces.

Left
Timothy at 9 months.

The Premature Baby Book
(A Parents' Guide to Coping and Caring in the First Years)
Helen Harrison. St. Martin's Press, 1983; 273 pp. ISBN 0-312-63649-0
$18.95 ($22.95 postpaid) from Publishers Book & Audio, PO Box 070059, Staten Island, NY 10307; 800/288-2131

Childbirth Wisdom

Long before Hippocrates began compiling the knowledge that is the basis for modern medicine, far older societies were accumulating and passing down a legacy of folk wisdom whose applications are still relevant for childbirth today. **Childbirth Wisdom***, an anthropological look at birthing lore from nearly five hundred traditional cultures (with the footnotes to prove it), provides the modern reader with an intriguing contrast to the outlook of modern obstetrics. Take birthweight: in postwar America, birthweight is one measure used to determine a newborn's relative health: the bigger the better, as we see it. But in tribal societies, expectant mothers carefully moderate their dietary intake so that their babies will not be difficult to birth.*

Now. A seven-pound baby is not unhealthy — and the difference between giving birth to a seven-pound baby and to a nine-pound baby may be one of many hours.

It kind of makes you wonder. —PDiL

Childbirth Wisdom
(From the World's Oldest Societies)
Judith Goldsmith. Congdon & Weed, 1984. ISBN 0-312-92094-6
$10.95 ($13.95 postpaid) from East West Natural Health Books, 17 Station Street, Brookline, MA 02147; 617/232-1000

•

The majority of tribal women birth either alone or with close family members in attendance, although a few tribes view birth as a social event.

One of these tribes is the Javanese of Surinam. Here, the woman's mother and sisters, other close female relatives, and the *dukun* (midwife) are all present at the birth. Neighbors also attend, to watch or prepare food for the coming *slametans* (birth celebrations). The only man present is the husband, who sits behind his wife with his legs around her, helping to push the baby out. "On the whole," one researcher notes, "childbirth is a rather gay occasion and women like very much to attend it. There is always something funny to laugh at, 'it is more amusing than the movies,' they said. One cause of great merriment is the behavior of the father. Sometimes he is very young and more scared than his wife. Sometimes he screams every time when she does. Sometimes he is not strong enough to push, and both topple over. But it is considered to be most amusing of all when wife and husband begin to quarrel. The woman will usually start by scolding her husband that it is all his fault. He, in turn, often answers with bawdy remarks and jokes, and it is a great disappointment to the onlookers if he is too young or too shy to do so."

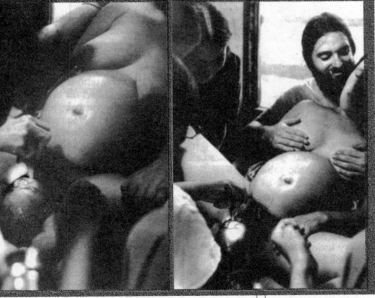

Spiritual Midwifery
Ina May Gaskin. 3rd ed. 1990; 480 pp. ISBN 0-913990-63-9
$16.95 ($18.43 postpaid) from The Book Publishing Company, PO Box 99, Summertown, TN 38743; 615/964-3571

What to Expect When You're Expecting

Remember in **Gone With the Wind** *where Butterfly McQueen tells Vivien Leigh: "I don't know nothin' about birthing babies"? If only Butterfly had read this book, Scarlet and Rhett might be living happily ever after. This pregnancy guide is a veritable encyclopedia of accurate, up-to-date facts covering all aspects of pregnancy from the planning stage to postpartum, chronologically arranged in a month-by-month format for easy reference. Nutrition, lifestyle and psychosocial aspects of pregnancy share equal billing with medical complications. Special sections address the first six weeks of postpartum (the fourth trimester), fathers' experiences, and preparing for your next baby. An appendix lists all common tests performed during pregnancy. If you're having a baby, and you have time to read only one book, this should be it. —PDiL*

•

Do-It-Yourself Labor Induction?

One study showed that women who, from 39 weeks on, stimulated their nipples for three hours or more daily were much less likely to carry past their due dates. In the study women stimulated the nipple, areola, and breast with the balls of their fingertips, 15 minutes a breast, alternating breasts, for one hour three times a day. Creams or lotions were optional as was a husband's help. The problem is that not only is this technique time- and energy-consuming, but without careful medical supervision, it can be risky. It can produce very strong contractions (much as oxytocin can), which could lead to trouble. *So do not try this technique unless your practitioner recommends it.*

What to Expect When You're Expecting
Arlene Eisenberg, Heidi E. Murkoff, & Sandee E. Hathaway. 1984, 1991; 455 pp. ISBN 0-89480-829-X
$10.95 ($13.95 postpaid) from Workman Publishing, 708 Broadway, New York, NY 10003; 800/722-7202

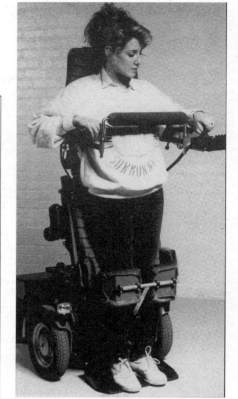

BBSs, disability magazines, and 800 numbers have made it easier to find information on any aspect of disability. Catalogs specializing in products for disabled people abound. But if information wants to be free, equipment still wants to be expensive. Unless you have help from a government agency or an insurance company, you'll have to shop for the equipment you need very carefully. Always check as many sources as you can. Don't let *anyone* — doctors, therapists, social workers — get you things you haven't tried. Talk with other people with your disability; they're the real experts. If you don't know anyone with your disability, find them through magazines, BBSs, and independent living centers. —Mark O'Brien

CripZen: A Manual For Survival

I've read books on what it's like to be paralyzed, but this is the first book I've seen on how to take the shit disability hands out daily. Not only how to take it, but also how to survive it with grace and sanity. Chapters on drugs, sex, meditation and "Crip Lit" illuminate the zen of crip with honesty and understanding. Drawing upon his forty years with polio and extensive studies in religion and psychology, Milam has written a tough, funny, surprising guide for the newly disabled. Even though I'm an old-timer, I learned much from this book about my demons of denial, rage and self-pity. This is the book I'd recommend to anyone planning to become paralyzed. —MO

•

To paraphrase one of my favorite bumperstickers, *Crips Need Love Too.* You will be hurting yourself if you let shame, fear, and self-destructive attitudes keep you tied down. It might help you if I tell you about Friend Larry, who lives in a small suburb outside Detroit. After fretting for six months, he finally placed an ad in a local gay newspaper:

*Help the handicapped!
Severely disabled fifty-three-year-old man wants male lover.
Telephone XXX-XXXX.*

Truth in advertising always works best. A non-specific illness had left Larry with the use of the right side of his body. He was, at least by society's lights, "severely disabled." The ad was honest. Perhaps that is why it

CripZen
(A Manual For Survival)
Lorenzo W. Milam. 1993; 254 pp.
ISBN 0-917320-03-4
$12.95 ($14.95 postpaid) from Mho & Mho Works, PO Box 33135, San Diego, CA 92163

brought in over twenty calls. After evaluating the callers, Larry met with (and interviewed) three of the most promising. Imagine having over twenty people go to so much trouble to be with you.

•

Pain and fatigue sap what's left of your body, depression sweeps down again and brings such an aching woe that time ceases moving. Drinking is stupid, the drugs they offer you turn you into a beast — and you can't pay for them anyway on your tiny allowance. Regret keeps gnawing at you (why didn't I stop when there was time?) again and again and again — and you've found out the hard way that they have built a social service system not meant to help or rehabilitate — but rather to brutalize, defeat, mock, humiliate, degrade, and finally (is this what they really want?) to kill. They never promised us a rose garden, but they never promised us a shitheap either.

HEATH Resource Directory

While this guide from HEATH (Higher Education and the Handicapped) offers much about organizations that help disabled people enter college, it's also a goldmine of other necessary information on disability. Want to know how to tune in to the radio network for the blind? Learn about epilepsy? Find magazines written by and for the disabled? It's all here with phone numbers, addresses and descriptions. This is the book to begin with when you need information on disability. —MO

HEATH Resource Directory
Ann R. Davie, Editor.
American Council on Education.
Free from HEATH Resource Center,
DuPont Circle NW, Suite 800, Washington,
DC 20036; 800/544-3284

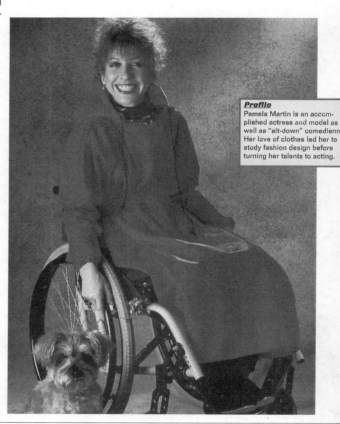
The Med Group's Permobil.

Avenues Unlimited

Fashion for the wheelchair set. Specially engineered clothes for the "chair users" that are cleverly practical, yet look snazzy — even suave. The models, who are all chair users in real life, are so elegant in these threads they make the wheelchair look like a hip fashion accessory.
—Kevin Kelly

Profile
Pamela Martin is an accomplished actress and model as well as "sit-down" comedienne. Her love of clothes led her to study fashion design before turning her talents to acting.

Avenues:
Catalog free.
1199 Avenida Acaso,
Suite K, Camarillo,
CA 93012;
800/848-2837.

Here

The camera shows a woman with a pale, round face and a mass of black hair sitting in a wheelchair, speaking her poems. I've shared a few Berkeley stages with Cheryl Marie Wade and she has always impressed me with the powerful way she reads her tough, intelligent poetry. This stunning performance is fierce with wit, anger, tenderness and wisdom. I'm tempted to say that every rehabilitation center should have this video, but that would imply a limit to the reach of Wade's art, an art that embraces us all. Wade is "a sock in the eye with gnarled fists," as she says, but she's also a jangling tambourine, a burst of laughter, a Billie Holiday in triumph. —MO

Here
(A Poetry Performance)
Cheryl Marie Wade. 1991;
Video, 13 1/2 mins. $25 postpaid from
CMW Out-of-Pocket Productions,
1613 5th Street, Berkeley, CA 94710-1714

OTHER GREAT RESOURCES

National Rehabilitation Information Center:
8455 Colesville Road, Suite 935, Silver Spring, MD 20910-3310; voice 800/346-6242. ABLE INFORM: modem 301/589-3563 (v.32, N-8-1); ABLE DATA: voice 800/227-0216.

National Information Center on Deafness:
Gallaudet University, 800 Florida Avenue NE, Washington, DC 20002; voice 202/651-5051, TTY 202/651-5052, fax 202/651-5054.

National Library Service for the Blind and Physically Handicapped: 1291 Taylor Street NW, Washington, DC 20542; 202/707-5100. Free cassette players, record players; books, and magazines on cassettes and records. Special cassette players work with the long-play cassettes they offer.

Environmental Health Network: Sliding scale membership, $10-$35/year. PO Box 1155, Larkspur, CA 94577; 415/541-5075. Publishes a newsletter, *The New Reactor,* focusing on issues of interest to persons with Chronic Immune Deficiency Syndrome and associated conditions: disability rights, the environment, medical treatment, and strategies for living with these conditions. Practical, political and very grassroots.

Choice Magazine Listening: Free (6 issues/year). PO Box 10, Port Washington, NY 11050; 516/883-8280. Eight hours of taped readings from such leading magazines and newspapers as the *Atlantic,* the *New Yorker,* and *Harper's.* Requires NLS cassette player.

Kurzweil Reading Edge: $5,495.
Kurzweil AdvantEdge: $1,549-$2,495. Xerox Imaging Systems, 9 Centennial Drive, Peabody, MA 01960; 800/248-6550.
Open Book Reading System: $5,395. Arkenstone Products, 1390 Borregas Avenue, Sunnyvale, CA 94089; 800/444-4443. Machines and software that turn print into synthesized speech. Some people prefer the Kurzweil products, others like Arkenstone. Technology and prices are changing fast; contact both companies before buying anything.

The Med Group: Catalog free. 3223 S. Loop 289, Suite 600, Lubbock, TX 77923; 800/825-5633. Free catalog of wheelchairs, beds, lifts and so forth, with stuff from the leading manufacturers.

Anne Morris Enterprises: Catalog free. 890 Fams Court, East Meadow, NY 11554; 516/292-9232. An unusual variety of products for blind people.

Past Due: Anne Finger. 1990, Seal Press. The author, disabled by polio, writes with precision, grace and humor of her decision to have a baby.

Differences in Common: Marilyn Trainer. 1991, Woodbine House. Raising Ben, a boy with Down Syndrome. An inspiring book.

World Institute on Disability: 510 16th Street, Suite 100, Oakland, CA 94612-1500; 510/763-4100. Researches disability history, writes laws, runs BBSs, kicks ass.

The Disability Rag: $17.50/year (6 issues). PO Box 145, Louisville, KY 40201; 502/459-5343. The best source of news on disability. *The Rag* is still nasty after all these years.

Apple Computer Disability Services:
800/776-2333. Free information on disability-related products for Apple computers.

IBM Independence Series: 800/426-4832. Ditto from Big Blue.

New Mobility: $18/year (6 issues). PO Box 4162, Boulder, CO 80306; 303/449-5412.

American Printing House for the Blind

This organization produces books and other products for blind and visually impaired people. They sell a wide variety of products, but are especially well known for teaching aids, devices, and materials.

The APH catalogs list everything from large print, recorded and Braille textbooks and reference books (including dictionaries and an atlas) to gadgets for producing raised-line drawings, tac- *tile maps, graph paper, tape player/ recorders designed to play the 4-track tapes produced by such sources as the NLS and RFB, and aids to help teach blind children mathematical and spatial concepts and Braille. APH is an invaluable resource for learning.*
—Carla Campbell

American Printing House for the Blind
Catalogs free. PO Box 6085, Louisville, KY 40206; 800/223-1839, 502/895-2405

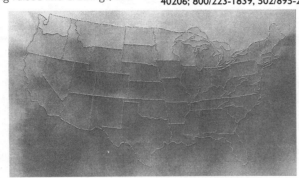

Trace Center Resourcebook

This encyclopedic volume lists everything a wheelchair user could ever need except wheelchairs. One-page product descriptions offer prices and ordering info. Appendices list organizations, magazines, BBSs and videos.
—MO

Trace Center Resourcebook
Peter Borden, Sarah Fatherly, Kelly Ford, & Greg Vanderheiden, Editors.
$40 postpaid from Trace Research and Development Center, 500 Highland Avenue, Madison, WI 53705; 608/262-6966

Product Name: **Illustrated Menu**
Vendor: **Attainment Company**
Cost: **$12.00. Illustrated Menu is a picture menu to help the user with food and beverage selection. The product has over 200 pictures of various foods and beverages as well as important key phrases (such as "Where is the rest room?") and a tip finder. The Illustrated Menu contains several pages to flip through and all are laminated so that they can be written on.**

Product Name:
F73216-0136 Page Turner and Cuff
Vendor: **Maddak, Inc.**
Cost: **$9.90**

Page Turner and Cuff consists of a lightweight cuff attached to a wooden dowel that has a rubber friction tip. The cuff fits on the user's hand by means of a D-ring and Velcro closure.

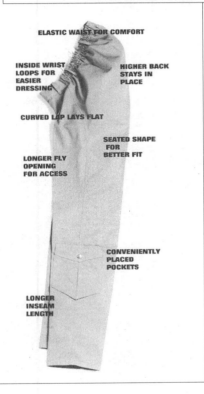

ELASTIC WAIST FOR COMFORT

INSIDE WRIST LOOPS FOR EASIER DRESSING

HIGHER BACK STAYS IN PLACE

CURVED LAP LAYS FLAT

SEATED SHAPE FOR BETTER FIT

LONGER FLY OPENING FOR ACCESS

CONVENIENTLY PLACED POCKETS

LONGER INSEAM LENGTH

Tri Visual Services

If you want only one resource for blind and visually impaired computer users, this is it. The Tri Visual Services (TVS) resource guide, thorough and excellently organized, lists hardware, software, and other computer-related products and services: everything from Braille printers to funding sources for computer access equipment; publishers of books, manuals and periodicals available in Braille, on tape or on computer disk; and even online services and forums. With detailed access info, it is updated every year.

As if that weren't enough, the folks at TVS are amazingly friendly, helpful and well-informed.
—CC

Tri Visual Services
Braille or large print editions, published annually. $15 postpaid. PO Box 221310, Sacramento, CA 95822; 916/447-7324

Computer Resources for People with Disabilities: Alliance for Technology Access. 1994, Hunter House Inc.; 510/865-5282.
— Mark O'Brien, Carla Campbell, and Susan Nordmark

LS&S Products for the Visually Impaired

You can tell time easily even in dim light; these watches and clocks feature huge numbers. Others tell you the time — in your choice of android English or Spanish. There's software for enlarging the print on screen and on paper; printers that perform in Braille; scanners that read aloud. Lighten up a bit with a noisy soccerball, a howling Frisbee-ish flying saucer, and playing cards with enormous symbols. There's even a good-quality Braille compass! Some of this unusual stuff is useful for folks with normal vision. You can try anything but the software for thirty days without penalty. Appropriately, the catalog is printed in big type, and is also available on refundable cassette. —J. Baldwin

LS&S Group
Print catalog free;
Cassette catalog $3 (refundable).
PO Box 673, Northbrook, IL 60065;
800/468-4789 (in IL: 708/498-9777)

inLARGE 2.0
Software Magnification For Macintosh

Gives visually impaired full access to all mainstream software without additional equipment. **Magnifies everything on the screen as user types or moves the mouse.** Features: System 7 compatibility; choice of screen motion options; compatible with full range of Macintosh technology; scanning mode; control from panel interface and keyboard; 2 to 16X magnification; reverse video; large, customizable crosshair indicator of cursor location; independent control of horizontal and vertical magnification; "magnifying glass" defines portion of screen for magnification and allows "blank out" of unmagnified portion. Requires: Macintosh Plus or better with 1 MB of RAM, Running System 6.05 or later, 100K of floppy disk or hard disk space.
Model 262-IL20 . . . . $195.00

Mouth: Lucy Gwin, Editor. Sliding scale $2-$32/year (6 issues). 61 Brighton Street, Rochester, NY 14607; 716/473-6764. Angry, funny focus on "the people with letters after their names" who control and destroy the lives of disabled people.

THIS ONE KNEES IN THE GROIN ANYONE WHO SPEAKS IN A LOUD VOICE WITH WORDS OF ONE SYLLABLE

Between Heaven and Earth

This book acquaints Westerners with enough Chinese medicine to understand and develop the relationship between their mental, physical and emotional states.

Short on Taoism (from which all Chinese medicine springs) and long and lucid on what the medicine is and how it works, the book articulately demonstrates that the interconnection of mankind, nature and the cosmos is at the very heart and soul of Chinese medicine. *Between Heaven and Earth* demystifies the foreignness for the Westerner by presenting graphs, tables, and charts that are easy to comprehend.

The information ranges from basic conceptual definitions to complex methods of diagnosis. This is an excellent resource guide for the layperson; for the health practitioner, it is as invaluable as *Gray's Anatomy*.
—Cindy Cosgrove

•
Since everything is connected by the circle, health is understood broadly, defining the whole being within the social and natural order. What is good for nature is good for humanity, what is good for one is good for all, what is good for the mind is good for the body, and so on. To harm a part is to harm the whole. What is bad for the heart is bad for the body, what damages one person damages all people, what injures the earth injures me. Conversely, to restore and preserve the health of one body and mind is to foster the well-being of the whole, the earth and all life upon it.

Between Heaven and Earth
(A Guide to Chinese Medicine)
Harriet Beinfield & Efrem Korngold.
Ballantine Books, 1991; 432 pp.
ISBN 0-345-35943-7
$20 ($22 postpaid). Random House/Order Dept., 400 Hahn Road, Westminster, MD 21157; 800/733-3000

FIRE: Heart
WATER: Kidney   METAL: Lung

For the Fire type, the key relationships are between the Heart and Lung (Fire restrains Metal) and between the Heart and Kidney (Water inhibits Fire).

Before we are born our parents endow us with Essence Qi, which following birth is fortified by Air Qi from the Lungs and Food Qi from the Spleen. Both inherited and acquired Qi is collected within the reservoir of the Kidney to be dispensed as needed. To say the Kidney holds the Essence means it generates and warehouses the original material substance that forms the basis of all other tissues — it grasps the kernel from which all life springs. Kidney Essence can be likened to the genetic information encoded in DNA, the template of biological destiny, which along with basic structural proteins forms hormones and enzymes that direct cellular metabolism.

How to Find an Acupuncturist

Look in the Yellow Pages under "acupuncturist" or "herbalist." The National Commission for the Certification of Acupuncturists will send you a list of nationally certified acupuncturists practicing in your state. The request must be made in writing, with a check for $3 for each state; a reference catalog listing acupuncturists in every state is available for $22. —Sharon Hennessey

National Commission for the Certification of Acupuncturists: 1424 16th Street, NW Suite 501, Washington, DC 20036; 202/232-1404.

All acupuncturists in this catalog have met minimal educational requirements, passed an exam administered by the National Commission, and were awarded a diploma in acupuncture.

The NCCA certifies acupuncturists through the American Association of Acupuncture and Oriental Medicine. They will give a telephone referral in an emergency; otherwise, there is a $5.00 charge for a three-state listing.

American Association of Acupuncture and Oriental Medicine: 433 Front Street, Catasauqua, PA 18032; 610/433-2448.

Certification by the NCCA is not a license, and many states have specific licensing requirements. California, for example, administers its own licensing exam, and its requirements are far more stringent than those of the NCCA, with more hours of theoretical preparation and clinical experience as prerequisites to sit for their exam. A list of those acupuncturists can be acquired from the state licensing agency. In California, the state licensing agency will supply a list of state licensed acupuncturists for $10.

Acupuncture Committee: 1420 Howe Avenue, Suite 14, Sacramento, CA 95825-3233, 916/263-2680.

Alternative Medicine

This six-pound whopper, the result of four years' work by 350 physicians and practitioners, covers forty-three alternative therapies, including diet and nutrition, acupuncture, chiropractic, homeopathy, colon therapy, flower remedies — even alternative veterinary care. It describes their history, philosophical basis, and typical regimens, adds contacts and recommended reading, then cross-references 200 health conditions (from colds and headaches to cancer and heart disease) with their treatments. The book eschews jargon and true-believer enthusiasm for straightforward presentation, frequent cautions and repeated caveats to use the book and its treatments in conjunction with treatment by a physician. For readers exploring their own options or physicians looking to understand and evaluate the claims of alternative therapies, this is the place to start. —Michael K. Stone

•
Types of Neural Therapy

Direct techniques: The direct or "local" technique in neural therapy treats pain or illness with an injection of anesthetics specifically at the site of the interference field causing the problem. The injections can be made by infiltrating scar tissue, into nerve junctions, or into the area surrounding the spinal cord.

Indirect technique: If the neural therapist cannot pinpoint the exact location of the interference field, the source of pain can be tracked down by injecting related interference fields until the original blockage is found. In other cases, an indirect approach is needed when the problem area is too delicate to receive a direct injection.

IBIS (Interactive Body/Mind Information System)

IBIS is something new: an electronic database of therapies from the whole spectrum of alternative medicine.

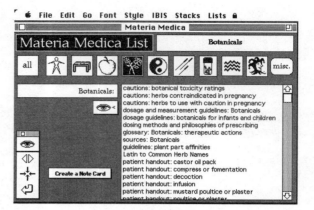

The core of IBIS is the extensive "materia medica" section, which lists treatment methods and tools from a variety of nontraditional approaches ranging from the mainstream to the weird — nutrition, herbal medicine, acupuncture, homeopathy, flower-essence treatment, and vibrational therapies. The software lists 282 medical conditions and symptoms, and provides diagnostic and therapeutic information from nine different systems of healing for each one.

As software, IBIS has its pluses and minuses. The current version is a little sluggish when moving around the database (this is particularly evident if you're using an older machine), and some of the screens are cluttered and confusing at first glance. But the information is easy to navigate once you learn the software's conventions, and it's very consistent in its use of icons and other presentation elements.

IBIS includes extensive and clever facilities for customization, too. You can annotate any entry in the database, cross-reference entries and patient records, print patient handouts and other information, and create your own indexes to this information (a necessary feature, since the database contains so much material). Features designed especially for practitioners include patient records that keep detailed track of visits, symptoms and treatments.

IBIS runs on all Macs from the Plus on, and on DOS PCs of reasonably modern vintage. CD-ROM and Windows versions are in the works, and a scaled-down "consumer version" of IBIS is also planned. — Jeanne DeVoto

IBIS (Interactive Body/Mind Information System): $895 ($903 postpaid) for DOS or Mac versions; $575 ($583 postpaid) to students. Alchemical Medical Research and Teaching Association, PO Box 14641, Portland, OR 97214; 800/627-6851.

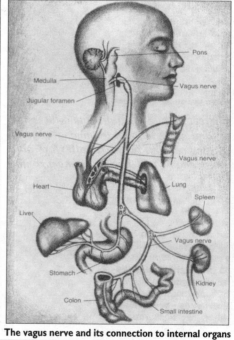

The vagus nerve and its connection to internal organs

Alternative Medicine
(The Definitive Guide)
and **Alternative Medicine Yellow Pages**
Burton Goldberg Group. 1994; 1068 pp.
ISBN 0-9636334-3-0
$79.95 ($89.90 postpaid). Future Medicine Publishing, 1640 Tiburon Blvd. #2, Tiburon, CA 94920; 800/641-4499

•
When used knowledgeably and with care, hyperthermia is a safe and effective treatment for many conditions. However, many people are sensitive to the effects of heat, such as those with anemia, heart disease, diabetes, seizure disorders, and tuberculosis, as well as women who are or may be pregnant. People with these conditions should take great care.

The New Age Herbalist

Get to know your herbs by walking in the fields — let an experienced herbalist introduce you to them, one by one. With its full-color photographs and line drawings of over 200 plants, this book is as close as you can get to a guided herb-walk without getting your shoes muddy. Want to know how to plant a formal herb garden? Which plant to use to dye your undies lavender? How to treat an earache with herbs? It's all here, and more.
—*Donna Odierna*

•

In our everyday lives we take the role of plants almost entirely for granted. If we are fortunate enough to live in the country, the changing seasons may attract our attention; in towns, we may wander to the park. But the cornflakes on our breakfast table are unlikely to remind us of the maize plant, the toast hardly suggests the blowing wheat fields. . . . In truth, we seldom have direct contact with the plants on which our comfort depends, or any experience of the labor and skill needed to make use of them. . . . Learning to use herbs in simple and practical ways can be the first time we truly begin to appreciate the value of plants.

•

Outdoor insect repellents: To prevent the evening onslaught of mosquitoes in the summer, rub a handful of fresh elder leaves on your arms, legs, and neck. This is effective for about 20 minutes, but must be renewed. . . . Oil of lavender and citron-ella . . . are both lovely scents to wear outdoors on the hair or skin, and effectively keep off mosquitoes.

•

Herbal products care for the body gently, with low chemical risk — cleavers, for example, is a safe alternative deodorant, sage a good tooth cleaner.

The New Age Herbalist
(How to Use Herbs for Healing, Nutrition, Body Care & Relaxation)
Richard Mabey & Michael McIntyre. Collier Books, 1988; 288 pp.
ISBN 0-02-063350-5
$21 postpaid. Macmillan Publishing Co., 100 Front Street, Riverside, NJ 08075-7500; 800/257-5755

Wise Woman Herbal for the Childbearing Year • Menopausal Years, the Wise Woman Way

Herbal wisdom, heart wisdom: healing in the wise-woman tradition. A different approach, a different consciousness: wisdom for women of all ages.

Childbearing Year begins with the months before pregnancy, continues on through to the post-partum period, and finishes up with a chapter on infant care. Wise-woman ways combine herbal healing, diet, and visualization. This is a detailed guide for pregnant women, women contemplating pregnancy, midwives, and other healers.

A path to be followed, an achievement, a crowning. Grandmother Growth lends a gentle, guiding hand. The wise-woman tradition is one of cycles, of acceptance, of self-love. Menopause is not a horror to be avoided at all costs and for as long as possible; it's a turn of the wheel, a step in the dance.

Menopausal Years is a valuable herbal that shows us how to celebrate this important time in our lives. —DO

•

Herbs used to encourage a pregnancy are characterized by their ability to 1) nourish and tonify the uterus, 2) nourish the entire body, 3) relax the nervous system, 4) establish and balance normal functioning of the hormonal system, and 5) balance sexual desire. —*Childbearing Year*

Pomegranate - Punica granatum   *Rose hips - Rosa rugosa*

•

Remember, the *ugly* old woman/witch is the invention of male-dominant cultures, and our own fear of death. In peaceful matrifocal cultures, the beauty of crones is legendary: old women are satin-skinned, softly wrinkled, silver-haired, and awe-inspiring in their truth and dignity.
—*Menopausal Years*

Calcium-rich herbs include nettle, sage, chickweed, red clover, comfrey leaf, raspberry leaf, and oatstraw. Enjoy a tasty infusion of any one every day. Count a big mug of infusion as 250-300 mg calcium.
—*Menopausal Years*

Wise Woman Herbal
(Childbearing Year)
Susun Weed. 1986; 204 pp.
ISBN 0-9614620-0-0
$8.95 postpaid.

Menopausal Years
(The Wise Woman Way)
Susun Weed. 1992; 228 pp.
ISBN 09614620-4-3
$9.95 postpaid.

Both from Ash Tree Publishing, PO Box 64, Woodstock, NY 12498; 914/246-8081

Medicinal Plants of the Pacific West

This book — with two of the author's previous books, Medicinal Plants of the Mountain West and Medicinal Plants of the Desert and Canyon West (Museum of New Mexico Press, 1979, 1989) — are the best resources available for the collection and use of herbs in the western half of the US. Many plants that also grow in other parts of the country are covered, to the benefit of herbalists everywhere.

The abundance of information here is presented with wit and common sense. You'll find specifics about storing herbs, making herbal preparations, and medicinal use. More than seventy-five plant monographs clearly describe

Medicinal Plants of the Pacific West
Michael Moore. 1993; 360 pp.
ISBN 1-878610-31-7
$19.95 ($22.95 postpaid).
Red Crane Books, 826 Camino de Monte Rey, Santa Fe, NM; 505/988-7070

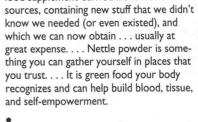

herb and habitat, with exquisite line drawings by herbalist Mimi Kamp.

We are sternly cautioned about irresponsible collecting; the author is clearly aware of the likely effects of releasing an army of Jack-the-Pickers loose on a fragile environment. —DO

•

Every year we see some new harebrained food supplement derived from weird sources, containing new stuff that we didn't know we needed (or even existed), and which we can now obtain . . . usually at great expense. . . . Nettle powder is something you can gather yourself in places that you trust. . . . It is green food your body recognizes and can help build blood, tissue, and self-empowerment.

•

Our consumer society tries to convince us that quantity is a substitute for quality. Nonsense. Learn a few good plants, collect them yourself, in the true sense of the amateur.

An Illustrated Dictionary of Chinese Medicinal Herbs

So you come home from your Chinese acupuncturist with your bag of herbs that do wonders for your ailments (really!). But you don't know what that colorful bunch of twigs and bark is. With 400 color photographs, this beautifully illustrated dictionary gives you the herbs' names, properties, and uses, as well as showing each herb and its parent plant. A great book for the curious, the botanically inclined, and the practitioner.
—*Susan Erkel Ryan*

•

IXORA *Family: Rubiaceae*
Chinese ixora

The name ixora comes from a Malabar deity. These are evergreen shrubs or small trees of the tropics. There are many attractive wild species that have yet to be brought into cultivation. Those that are in cultivation are handsome plants, as their flowers are brightly coloured and their foliage attractive. This plant is native to southern China and Peninsular Malaysia, bearing dense clusters of yellow flowers which turn orange-red with age.

Parts used:

whole plant: treats rheumatism, abscesses, bruises, relieves pain.

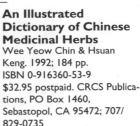

An Illustrated Dictionary of Chinese Medicinal Herbs
Wee Yeow Chin & Hsuan Keng. 1992; 184 pp.
ISBN 0-916360-53-9
$32.95 postpaid. CRCS Publications, PO Box 1460, Sebastopol, CA 95472; 707/829-0735

S E X.

The click of sudden attraction. The moan you make before you come. In the strictly Darwinian sense, the organism reduced to quivering germinal protoplasm.

Remember the old story about the groupie who for years screwed every rock star she could get her hands on? She would always say afterwards: "He was great, but he wasn't Mick Jagger!" Finally, she got to screw Mick Jagger. Her friends all asked her: "So? So?"

And she replied: "He was great, but he wasn't Mick Jagger!"

Most people live the greater part of their sexual lives in their imaginations. While sex as a reproductive strategy is common to most multicelled creatures, recreational sex is purely a human indulgence. What other animal would spread whipped cream on a lover's genitals and lick it off? What other animal employs whips and chains and ropes as a form of affection? Tumescence and its relief are not the only variations on the sexual games we humans play.

The care and feeding of an imagination is a delicate thing. Imaginations grow sluggish on a diet of misinformation. Even the details of genital anatomy are sometimes confusing or misunderstood — both by ourselves and our partners. Look at the books and resources here as a dietary supplement for a wholesome sexual appetite. This is by no means an inclusive list of all the excellent books and resources available. But it is a good place to start.

Bon appetit! —Patrizia DiLucchio

Lubricants and Body Oils

Somewhere off in the Cosmic Office for Evolutionary Planning, Hominid Division, a systems designer or an engineer forgot about lubrication. Well, maybe not forgot entirely. They just didn't specify enough of it.

The human body is like any other machine: friction wears it down. And nothing spoils good sex like friction. Friction creates unintentional pain.

Let's look at the basics. Body oils are just what they sound like: heavy, often scented or flavored lotions for external application. Lubricants, on the other hand, are meant to be used on delicate membranes as an aid to penetration.

The best lubricants are water-based, because oils break down latex — condoms, dental dams, gloves. Some lubes come mixed with Nonoxynol-9, a spermicide and detergent that can help kill HIV. The drawback is that Nonoxynol-9 tastes awful, and can sometimes inflame genital tissues. But better a funny taste in your mouth than a lifetime acquaintance with a retrovirus.

If you're thinking in terms of what's available at the local supermarket, baby oil works well externally, while K-Y Jelly is a well-known internal product. Here are some others that you may like. —Ben Trumble

OILS

Charlie Sunshine: (about $6 for 4.8 oz): A nice body oil with scents like jasmine, orange, cedar, musk, and vanilla.

Kama Sutra Love Oils: (about $12.50 for 4 oz): These essential oils are meant to be used as genital scents. Available in cherry, cinnamon, almond, and chocolate mint.

Bare Escentuals: (about $2 for 1/2 oz): These fruity sensual oils are a bit overpriced, but they come in such flavors as apricot, black cherry, and walnut.

Incredible Edible: (about $4 for 1 oz): All-natural edible massage oils using natural flavors and a base of glycerine and honey. They're rather sticky, but where else will you find flavors like tupelo honey, orange, watermelon, and kahlua 'n' cream? And they taste wonderful.

LUBRICANTS

Astroglide: (about $8.50 for 2.35 oz) Very slippery, very popular, odorless, and sweet. Resists evaporation. Probably the best lubricant currently on the market.

Embrace: (about $8 for 8 oz) Thick, odorless, and sweet.

Probe: (about $2 for 2 oz) Odorless and tasteless.

Aqua Lube with Nonoxynol-9: (about $7 for 2 oz) A good lube with a bad taste.

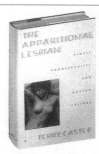

Sex in History

Who says reading about it isn't as much fun as doing it?

While it will come as no shock to readers of this book that humans have been having sex for even longer than they've been inventing history, Reay Tannahill makes for a most engaging tour guide through the theme park of human sexuality, directing our attention to those quirks of law, religious text and literature that when viewed peripherally, seem monochromatic. As always, the story behind the story is the real tale: it was only during the neolithic era — not long ago in the context of two million years of human evolution — that males took over the socially dominant role, not coincidentally the same point at which the masculine role in procreation first became understood. How ironic that shortly thereafter, sexuality acquired a set of rules — rules preserved in law, custom and attitudes, even to this day.
—PDiL

•

As far as the history of sex is concerned, the record of the early Christian church was a formidable one. Other Western societies had condemned, with varying degrees of severity, adultery (usually), contraception (rarely), abortion (sometimes), homosexuality (sometimes), infanticide (rarely), zoophilia (sometimes), masturbation (never). The Church proscribed them all.

Hovering butterflies position

Sex in History
Reay Tannahill. Scarborough House, 1982; 480 pp. ISBN 0-8128-8540-6 $16.95 ($20.70 postpaid) from National Book Network, 4720 Boston Street, Lanham MD, 20706; 800/462-6420

Other societies had ventured to suggest suitable frequencies for marital intercourse. "Three times a month," said Solon. "Every day for the unemployed," said the Jewish *Mishnah;* "twice a week for laborers, once a week for ass drivers." The Church said never, unless children were the object.

Other societies had regarded sex as pleasurable, in any position. To the Church, sexual pleasure was a sin and only the man-superior position was acceptable.

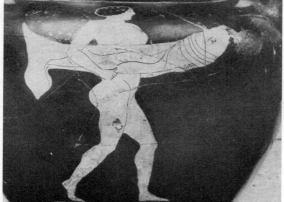

The Greeks had no doubt that a fish was a phallic object, and carried outsized images of it in Dionysiac processions.

The Apparitional Lesbian

Lesbians throughout history have been cloaked in invisibility. This pervasive cultural denial doubtless finds its source in the anxiety evoked in male-dominated civilizations by the prospect of women who do not need men — either as moral, sexual or psychological authorities, or as objects of love. Although love between women has been a motif in Western art and literature since classical times, its cultural significance has been left unexplored; lesbians are often dismissed as a modern invention of Freud and Kraft-Ebing.

In this elegantly written and meticulously researched book, Terry Castle documents the evolution of the lesbian sensibility from the mid-eighteenth century to the present. She reminds us that the very cultural and ideological blinders that prevent us from seeing lesbians in our midst are also the distorting lenses that have historically maintained Man's view of himself as superior in all ways to Woman.
—PDiL

•

In nearly all of the art of the eighteenth and nineteenth centuries, lesbianism, or its possibility, can only be represented to the degree that it is simultaneously derealized through a blanching authorial infusion of spectral metaphors. (I speak here of so-called polite or mainstream writing; the shadow discourse of pornography is of course another matter, and demands a separate analysis). One woman or the other must be a ghost, or on the one to becoming one. Passion is excited, only to be obscured, disembodied, decarnalized. The vision is inevitably waved off. Panic seems to underwrite these obsessional, spectralizing gestures: a panic over love, female pleasure, and the possibility of women breaking free — together — from

The Apparitional Lesbian
Terry Castle. 1993; 307 pp. ISBN 0-231-07652-5 $29.95 ($33.45 postpaid) from Columbia University Press/Order Dept., 136 S. Broadway, Irvington, NY 10533

their male sexual overseers. Homophobia is the order of the day, entertains itself (wryly or gothically) with phantoms, then exorcises them.

Condom Sense

The first time I had sex, as a teenager rolling around in the shadows at an outdoor party, it never occurred to me to wear a prophylactic.

This wasn't because I didn't have one. Like most boys of my generation, I'd been carrying them around in my wallet for years, the foil wrappers tattered and cracked, the latex dried and nearly caramelized. Coming of age twenty years ago, rubbers (as we almost always called them) were more a polyvinyl badge of male sexual courage, something to show off in the locker room, than a birth-control device or a measure for preventing STDs.

The best condoms in the world are made in Japan (or at least manufactured for the Japanese market). The Japanese never fell into the whole pill thing. Only recently have American prophylactics approached Asian standards.

Try the imports. It may not be quite the same as sex without a condom, but it still feels pretty good. Don't forget lubrication: a few drops of a water-based (not water-soluble) lubricant inside the condom can make all the difference in the world.

If these brands aren't available at your local pharmacy, order them from Good Vibrations (p. 201). —Ben Trumble

Trojans: By far the most common condom in America. They are everywhere, so there's no excuse not to have safe sex.

Kimono and Kimono MicroThins: These Japanese condoms will fit your penis like a second skin. The next best thing to riding bareback. Highly recommended.

Pleasure Plus (made in Taiwan): Lubricated with a spermicide.

Black Jack: The Good Vibrations logo on the little matchbook with Black Jack condom inside is commensurate with the Good Housekeeping Seal of Approval.

Gold Circle Coin: This rather expensive American microthin competes well against Asian brands.

Channel-surf or flip through the pages of any magazine and you'll discover that sex makes the car you drive faster, the beer you drink cooler, the stereo components you buy larger. But you'll never discover *how* to do it.

Never mind. You shouldn't be wasting your brain on mindless entertainment when you could be reading these books.
—PDiL

Playbooks about Sex (• for Women • for Men • for Kids)

The mirror is the best tool for self-awareness, but how often do we get the opportunity to look at our own reflection? These charming playbooks — patterned after the simple, familiar learning techniques used in elementary schools — provide a comfortable looking glass into the web of self-image, fantasy and attitudes that form sexual identity. They are designed less to teach than to help the reader discover.

The Playbook for Kids about Sex is particularly groundbreaking, because it deals less with reproduction than with the pleasures of sexuality. I remember *The Wonderful Story of How You Were Born*, the little volume my progressive parents gave me at age seven. Pages and pages detailed the evolution of the sperm and the ovum from tadpole and microdot to anatomically correct homunculus, floating in its mother's womb. But it begged the question: how did the sperm and ovum first get close enough to say hi? The very last page was a picture of a man and a woman, in heavy winter clothing, embracing. The caption read: "When a man and a woman love each other very much . . ." I think I was thirteen before I figured out how the sperm managed to make it through all those heavy layers of wool and flannel.

Children whose parents buy them **The Playbook** will know the real answer.
—PDiL

Some people masturbate with their hands or fingers. Other people like to do it other ways. Do you ever do it any of these ways?

Playbook for Women about Sex
Joani Blank. 1988; 32 pp.
ISBN 0-940208-04-0
$4.50 ($8.25 postpaid)

Playbook for Men about Sex
Joani Blank. 1981; 32 pp.
ISBN 0-9602324-8-6
$4.50 ($8.25 postpaid)

Playbook for Kids about Sex
Joani Blank. Yes Press, 1980; 56 pp.
ISBN 0-9602324-6-X
$5 ($8.75 postpaid)

All available from Down There Press, 938 Howard Street, Suite 101, San Francisco, CA 94103; 415/974-8985

The Invention of Pornography

When is pornography not pornography?

When it becomes political history.

A boisterous Italian nineteenth century lithograph featuring some inventive gymnastic routines

Debates over pornography in this country consistently involve discussion of the First Amendment. And they often raise the possibility that the freedom of speech manifested by pornography may be democracy's essential prerequisite. But pornography is a matter of cultural conditioning: freedom of speech has never been the issue per se. The real issue is who can speak, and how many at a time.

The Meese Commission itself has noted that "until the last several hundred years, almost all written, drawn, or printed material was restricted largely to a small segment of the population that undoubtedly constituted the social elite." In the library of a Tiberius, erotic scrolls sat right next to the works of great philosophers and scientists. So long as it was not available to the masses, who was to be harmed?

As the essays collected in **The Invention of Pornography** suggest, pornography is the name given a particular cultural battle zone that first became identifiable during the rise of elected governments. It was only with the proliferation of print media, and the possi-

bility that the middle class might gain access to sexually suggestive materials, that erotic images and texts became pornography. The rise of pornography as a subgenre paralleled the movements of Western modernity — the Renaissance, the Scientific Revolution, the Enlightenment, the French Revolution — that ultimately fueled the growth of democracy.

From its inception, pornography has always been about something more than sex; it was then — it remains today — about the free circulation of ideas. —PDiL

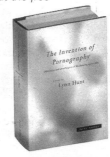

The Invention of Pornography
(Obscenity and the Origins of Modernity, 1500-1800) Lynn Hunt, Editor. The Zone Press, 1993; 411 pp. ISBN 0-942299-68-X $26.95 ($29.95 postpaid) from The MIT Press/Order Dept., 55 Hayward Street, Cambridge, MA 02142; 800/356-0343

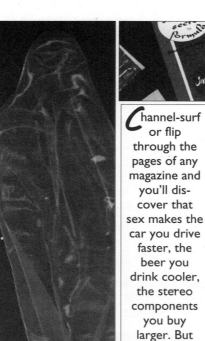

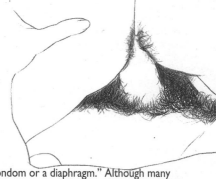

The Good Vibrations Guide to Sex

What do you think of when you think of revolutionaries? Camouflage clothing and AK-47s?

How about dildoes?

In San Francisco for the past seventeen years, a store called Good Vibrations (home of the Vibrator Museum) has been quietly staging its own revolution. The disputed territory is access to sexual information: Good Vibrations has broken new ground in the sale of sex toys, erotic aids and explicit printed materials, by providing a retail environment that feels like a pleasant, safe place to make direct eye contact — with the people who work there, with the other customers in the store, with the products themselves. Buying a vibrator here is like registering for an adult education class at an ivy-walled liberal arts college: there is nothing to be ashamed of.

The Good Vibrations Guide to Sex is one of the most complete and refreshingly open sex manuals available. Thorough and playful throughout, the book covers all the standard stuff of erotic how-to books: basic anatomy, masturbation techniques (for both sexes), erotic massage, penetration, oral sex, anal stimulation, safe sex.

The Good Vibrations Guide to Sex
Anne Semans & Cathy Winks.
Down There Press, 1994; 258 pp.
ISBN 0-939416-0
$16.95 ($20.70 postpaid). Cleis Press,
PO Box 8933, Pittsburg, PA 15221,
412/937-1555

Where this book is absolutely unique — and what makes it an invaluable addition to your library — is the attention it pays to sex toys and sexual aids. Entire sections are devoted to lubricants, dildoes, vibrators, and anal toys.

If you only buy one sex book, make it this one. And if you can visit only one place in San Francisco on your next business trip, forget the Exploratorium — go to Good Vibrations! —PDiL

●

We have one more absolute statement to make in this chapter which is critical for your health and safety: *Never use any oil whatsoever with latex products.* Oils destroy latex — this means that even the lightest weight massage oil, Albolene cream, hand lotion, baby oil or Vaseline will eat into a condom or a diaphragm and produce microscopic holes in the latex within sixty seconds of contact. When the Kinsey Institute conducted their National Sex Knowledge Test of a statistically representative body of American adults in 1989, 50% of the respondents were unaware that "Petroleum jelly, Vaseline Intensive Care, baby oil and Nivea are not good lubricants to use with a condom or a diaphragm." Although many condom manufacturers have begun labeling condoms with warnings against using them with oils, consumer education needs to happen on an even broader scale. Please take the time to read the label on any lubricant you are considering purchasing. Don't be taken in by lubes that advertise themselves as "water-soluble" — these frequently contain oils.

The Marriage Bed

How many times have we heard this lament? We had a good sex life for years; then we got married. It's repeated over and over again on talk shows and sitcoms: What went wrong? How did it go wrong?

The best part of William Womack and Fred Strauss's book is that they don't answer these questions. Instead, they focus on what married couples can do right now to make it right again. They outline a program for putting the sizzle back into strained marital sexual relationships, one that focuses on playfulness and mutual exploration: Be flexible and romantic. Be inventive and adventurous. Learn the territory. Sex isn't something you have to do at least every two weeks along with mowing the lawn. Sex is fun.

Maybe you'll end up like the eighty-year-old parents of a friend of mine: they were asked to leave their retirement community because the sounds they made when they were making love were so loud and ecstatic.

Dr. Womack wouldn't have minded! —Ben Trumble

The Marriage Bed
(Renewing Love, Friendship,
Trust and Romance)
William M. Womack & Fred F. Stauss.
1991, 191 pp. ISBN 1-879237-27-X
$11.95 postpaid from New Harbinger
Publications, 5674 Shattuck Avenue,
Oakland, CA 94609; 800/748-6273

●

Keeping a couple's love life alive and well is a lifelong challenge. Because marital and personal stresses tempt couples to put off sexual activity and pleasure, too often they'll find themselves reducing their sexual activities — in and out of the bedroom. Instead of hugging, holding, kissing and caressing at any time of the day, sexual activity becomes synonymous with intercourse. And, when their sexual activity becomes so limited, their sexual pleasure suffers. At that point, many couples discover that attempting to turn sexual emotions on and off just for bedroom activities becomes too complicated. Instead of more desire resulting from less frequent sex, the opposite happens: they aren't able to get turned on sexually when they want to.

Sensuous Magic

"This is a book for people who love each other," begins Sensuous Magic, a "guide for adventurous couples." Pat Califia, who knows what she's writing about, explains the basics of S/M lovemaking in prose that is clear, calm and leavened with humor. Califia shows people the ropes (so to speak), demonstrating how communication and awareness, sensuality and safety are inextricably linked in successful S/M (or any other sexual play).

If you like thinking about and exploring the edges of your sexuality, this book is worth the price for its glossary alone. If you think you already know everything about "the scene," grab a copy and let Califia show you some new tricks and insights for even the oldest and most experienced dogs. If you're only reading it to find out what all the shouting is about, you'll be in respectful and caring hands. And if you're just looking for titillation, you can skip to the end of each chapter for the fantasy sequences. —Elise Matthesen

●

One thing that should be made very clear is that S/M roles do not dictate who gets penetrated or who uses their mouth to get somebody else off. Ironically enough, it is the adamantly non-kinky majority who stereotype getting fucked or giving head as submissive activities. In the S/M community, the rules are much more fluid. If the Mistress's pleasure is to be orally serviced by a quick-tongued submissive on his knees, that is her prerogative. And if it pleases her to be fucked silly by seven well-hung slave boys, that is also her prerogative. The Master may train his slave girl to deep-throat him at the snap of his fingers, or he may like to tie her up and go down on her until she faints with joy, to demonstrate the fact that he owns that little button and gets to push it as much and as often as he wishes.

The only things that should govern or limit your pleasures are your own desires, the needs of your partners, and mutual consent. Anybody who tells you otherwise is simply suffering from a narrow mind. Unfortunately, such people do exist, even in sexual minorities. Don't bother to argue with them. They probably aren't getting enough, so they'll be cranky. Just smile and keep on doing what works best for you and your main squeeze.

Sensuous Magic
Pat Califia. 1993; 130 pp.
ISBN 1-56333-131-4
$12.95 ($13.95 postpaid) from
Masquerade Books, 801 Second Street,
New York, NY 10017; 800/458-3640

OTHER GREAT RESOURCES

Learning The Ropes (A Basic Guide To Safe And Fun S/M Lovemaking): Race Bannon. 1992, Daedalus Publishing. 4470-107 Sunset Blvd, Suite 375, Los Angeles, CA 90027. A dominant/submissive relationship is a carefully negotiated compact between lovers. Here's an exploration of healthy fantasy.

The Art of Auto-Fellatio (Oral Sex For One): Gary Griffin. 1993, Added Dimension Publishing. The ultimate sex for one how-to book for males; astonishing illustrations. Practice your yoga and keep the chiropractor nearby before you try this at home.

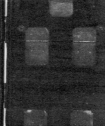

A nineteenth-century Chinese toilet box with eleven concealed miniatures. —*Erotica* (p. 198)

The Complete Guide to Safer Sex

Safe sex isn't just condoms and latex. Safe sex is an overall sexual lifestyle that emphasizes the erotic over the purely carnal. The Complete Guide offers great advice for those readers seeking to ground their lovemaking in healthy practices. Its explicit instructions will never cramp anyone's fantasies.

Let's face it, though we all hope otherwise, AIDS and HIV may very well march right along beside us into the new Millennium. Be informed. Stay healthy. With safe sex the fun doesn't have to stop. —Ben Trumble

•

If fisting is a part of your lifestyle that is important for you to continue, do not use drugs, alcohol, poppers or oil-based lubes. Use a very tender and gradual insertion of the hand and avoid excessive friction. Consistently wear a latex glove. Opera-length ones can be found in beauty supply stores. Horse condoms, which are used to collect the semen for artificial insemination when breeding race horses, can be gotten at a veterinary supply house. Never have anal intercourse before or after fisting unless a condom is used. Keep experimenting with different water-based lubes until you find the one that best works for you. While you are adjusting to using a latex glove during fisting, it is important to focus on new feelings and sensations. Do not be discouraged.

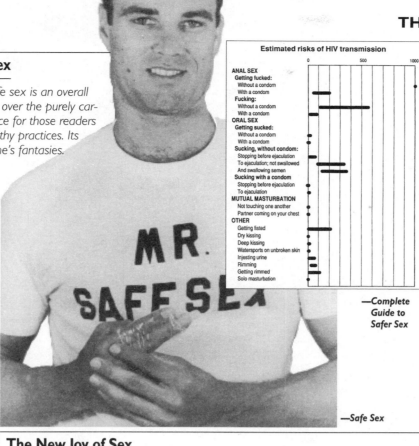

Estimated risks of HIV transmission

—Complete Guide to Safer Sex

—Safe Sex

The Complete Guide to Safer Sex
David Lourea, & et al. 1992; 200 pp. ISBN 0-942637-58-5 $6.95 ($10.45 postpaid) from Institute for Advanced Study of Human Sexuality, 1523 Franklin Street, San Francisco, CA 94109; 415/928-1133

The New Joy of Sex

Intelligent, uninhibited, and humorous, Alex Comfort's The Joy of Sex took the best of the sixties' sexual counterculture and offered it up to the middle class — ushering in the real sexual revolution. Almost twenty-five years after it first hit the bestseller lists, this latest edition remains America's favorite sexual bible.

It's still a classic. The New Joy of Sex is more than a book with a message, more than a manual, more than a collection of wonderfully erotic illustrations. The New Joy of Sex is fun, a book that forever reminds us to loosen up and leave our worries outside the bedroom. —BT

•

Skin is our chief extragenital organ — grossly underrated by most men, who tend to concentrate on the penis and clitoris; better understood by women.

She says: The smell and feel of a man's skin probably has more to do with sexual attraction (or the opposite) than any other single feature, even though you may not be conscious of it.

Skin stimulation is a major component of all sex. Not only its feel when touched, but its coolness, texture and tightness are triggers for a whole range of sexual feeling . . .

The New Joy of Sex
Alex Comfort. Pocket Books, 1991; 256 pp. ISBN 0-671-77859-5. $20 ($23 postpaid). Simon & Schuster/Order Dept., 200 Old Tappan Road, Old Tappan, NJ 07675; 800/223-2336.

Gay Sex

Less a how-to manual than a concise and comprehensive encyclopedia of sexual information for homosexually oriented men. Its format may make it difficult to read sequentially, but Jack Hart's lively style — mixing sly humor with clear facts — makes this book absolutely unbeatable for those stray moments when you're waiting for the pot to boil or the phone to ring. Entries range from discussions of intercourse, condom use and mutual masturbation to more controversial topics like pedophilia, infantilism and racial preferences. Hart is invariably clear-headed and nonjudgmental in the advice he gives. And the illustrations are terrific!
—PDiL

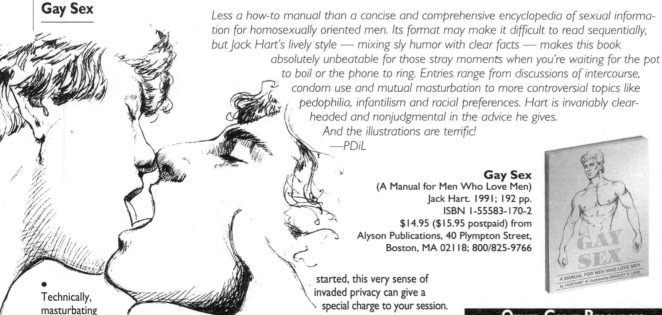

Gay Sex
(A Manual for Men Who Love Men)
Jack Hart. 1991; 192 pp.
ISBN 1-55583-170-2
$14.95 ($15.95 postpaid) from
Alyson Publications, 40 Plympton Street, Boston, MA 02118; 800/825-9766

•

Technically, masturbating with a partner is no different from doing it alone. However, most of us grew up with the message that masturbation is wrong, or that it's antisocial, or that it's okay but only if you do it in private. It's natural, given that conditioning, to feel uncomfortable the first time you jerk off in front of a partner. Happily, once you get started, this very sense of invaded privacy can give a special charge to your session.

Being masturbated by a partner is different from doing it alone. As Jeff explains, "When it's my hand and my dick, I'm completely in control. I know just what feels best, and that's nice — but for some reason, I like it better when James is jacking me off. Sex shouldn't be about being in control, it should be about giving up control. With his hand wrapped around my cock, I really let loose. That's when I get my most intense orgasms."

Anal Pleasure & Health

Anal fantasies are rarely discussed in the high-school health classes where we are given what passes for sex education. Nor is the anus apt to be a subject we'll hear much about at home, even from the most liberal of parents.

It's dirty, isn't it? It can't be safe, we might assume.

Besides, some things we just don't talk about.

In this first comprehensive, research-based work on the subject of anal health and sensuality, Jack Morin goes a long way toward dispelling fear, guilt, and misinformation about anal pleasure. Examining his subject from both a psychological and medical standpoint, Morin provides the reader with detailed explanations and sound exercises for exploring and expanding sexual boundaries. —BT

•

Some people also become concerned about orgasm in anal intercourse, feeling they have to reach a climax during anal sex. Actually, relatively few people are able to reach orgasm while receiving anal intercourse as the only source of stimulation. More men than women appear to be able to do this, probably due to the proximity of the penile bulb and prostate gland to the anus and rectum. If an orgasm for the receiver is going to be part of anal intercourse, direct simultaneous genital stimulation is usually needed. Not everyone feels a need to reach an orgasm during anal intercourse, although some believe this is expected. Similarly, the partner who is *giving* anal intercourse may feel that he is expected to ejaculate inside his partner's rectum. Some men, however, enjoy entering their partner's rectum very much, but prefer (or are only able) to ejaculate while receiving some other form of stimulation.

Anal Pleasure & Health
(A Guide for Men and Women)
Jack Morin. Yes Press, 1986; 269 pp.
ISBN 0-940208-08-3
$12.50 ($16.25 postpaid) from Down There Press, 938 Howard Street, Suite 101, San Francisco, CA 94103; 415/974-8985

OTHER GREAT RESOURCES

How To Persuade Your Lover To Use A Condom (And Why You Should): Patti Breitman, Kim Knutson & Paul Reed. Prima Publishing and Communications. Box 1260PC, Rocklin, CA 95677.

Safe Sex (The Ultimate Erotic Guide): John Preston & Glenn Swann. Plume Books. Out of print.

Sex for One

Betty Dodson is more than an accomplished painter, writer, and sex educator: she is also, undoubtedly, the single leading expert on the art of masturbation. With Dodson as your guide, masturbation is never mechanical: it's pure pleasure. Give this book to your mother, your lover, or your child off to college. Keep a copy in the bedroom, and pack another for road trips. Look at it this way: if Portnoy had had the opportunity to page through Sex for One, he wouldn't have had anything to complain about.

(Betty Dodson's video, Selfloving, is reviewed on p. 201. —Ben Trumble

Sex for One
(The Joy of Selfloving)
Betty Dodson. Harmony, 1992;
178 pp. ISBN 0-517-58832-3
$10 ($12 postpaid). Random House/
Order Dept., 400 Hahn Road,
Westminster, MD 21157; 800/733-3000

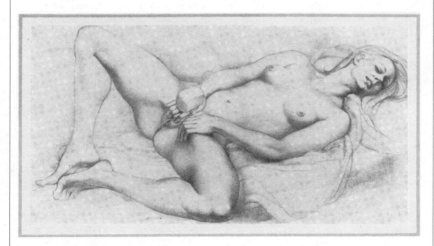

• Until my mid-thirties, my poor body had been racked with pain from hangovers, chronic muscle tension, lack of exercise, and bad nutrition — all of which interfered with erotic sensations. Mind inhibitors were guilt, fear, anger, and self-pity, which deprived me of erotic thoughts. These classical body/mind blocks impeded the flow of my sex energy, discharging it in my genitals only. I only had little orgasms that were like hiccups.

All my years of childhood and marital masturbation were about *not getting caught.* I'd trained myself to come fast while remaining silent. When I was with a lover, I avoided heavy breathing, barely moved my body, and never broke out in a sweat. In order to have "lady-like orgasms," I always held back because, basically, I was embarrassed about sex.

The Clitoral Kiss

It's a sad fact that sex guides are basically boring. The Idiot's Guide to Internal Combustion Engines that came with your '59 Volkswagen probably made for more enjoyable reading than most tomes on love-craft.

Why do they have to take themselves so seriously? This is supposed to be fun, isn't it? Not like running a marathon.

Relax.

Here's a book that's so much fun you'll quickly get over any inhibitions you may have felt when you ordered it through that place at the mall. Whether the subject is oral aerobics (to build up strength in the tongue), or any one of more than two dozen kissing, sucking, and licking games, Stubbs and Chasen never forget that sex is play, not geometry.

Hey — who ever said that you have to be serious all the time? —BT

• Introduce your mouth to her vulva with an Ice Cream Lick between the outer and inner lips as well as between the inner lips.

The Clitoral Kiss
(A Fun Guide to Oral Sex,
Oral Massage and Other Oral Delights
for Men and Women)
Kenneth Stubbs & Chyrelle Chasen. 1993;
79 pp. ISBN 0-939263-08-4
$16.95 ($19.95 postpaid). Secret Garden,
1352 Yukon Way, No. 20, Novato, CA
94947; 415/898-6430

Next, Snake Tongue the inner lips and clitoral area.

After suggesting to your lover that she hold on, suck and twirl the clitoris. Now the Clitoral Kiss followed by the tongue thrust into the vaginal orifice.

Some enjoyable additions include the Motorboat (you'll have to spread the pubic hair and labia to the sides), Gentle Breezes, and Hummin'.

The Ultimate Kiss

There's this problem sometimes with oral sex — in the naked presence of the flesh, you can get . . . tongue-tied. The spirit is willing, but the brain can't figure which pink protuberance is the start button. Do you lick it, the way a cat laps cream? Do you practice on it, scales and fingering, the slippery songs of love? And what do you do when your tongue gets tired?

This treatise takes these matters quite seriously, covering the basic mechanics: female and male anatomy, cunnilingus, fellatio. The reminiscences and interviews in the "beginning" and "advanced" techniques sections read suspiciously like letters to a men's magazine, it is true. But there is a lot of good information in this book. Plus pages and pages of intimate pix! —PDiL

The Ultimate Kiss
Jacqueline Franklin & Steven Franklin. Media Press, 1990; 128 pp. ISBN 0-917181-17-4
$12.95 ($18.45 postpaid). Play Boy Products, PO Box 809, Itasca, IL 60143-0809;
800/423-9494

• One of the most common mistakes beardless men make is to approach their partner with a slight stubble. The terribly sensitive mucous membranes that constitute the female genitalia cannot endure the abrasion of beard-stubble for more than a moment

without pain. Therefore, it is absolutely essential when providing your partner with a love kiss that you be clean-shaven. Of course, a man who wears a beard which has grown out to the point where the hair has become soft does not have this problem, but a man who is normally clean-shaven should be *freshly* shaven before offering his partner a genital kiss.

How to Get a Good Buzz

Vibrators are mechanical massage devices that can be used to enhance orgasm. Cylindrical, battery-operated vibrators can be placed over a woman's mons or a man's scrotum, leaving your other hand free to manipulate clitoris or penis shaft. Electric vibrators and smaller, coil-operated toys generate a more penetrating sonic buzz that gives a smoother, more consistent vibration. They come with a variety of attachments; you can spend endless blissful hours figuring out ways to use them all. Meltdown: minus three and counting! **Good Vibrations: The Complete Guide to Vibrators** *by Joani Blank (Down There Press. Paperback $5.50) or* **The Good Vibrations Guide to Sex** *by Anne Semans and Cathy Winks (Down There Press, reviewed on p. 194) will tell you anything else you need to know.*

Our recommendations:

Hitachi Magic Wand, *around $40. The most popular model sold by Good Vibrations, San Francisco's justly famous emporium of sexual delights. Support science (Do women or don't women . . .)! Do your own research with the G-spotter attachment! Or try the Magic Connection, an adapter for men!*

Prelude 3, *around $28. The personal choice of the editor who likes to talk big but prefers not to wake guests in adjoining hotel rooms. Standard attachments include*

penis cup, clit tickler and scalp massager.

Pink Pearl, *about $16. Battery operated, oscillating egg. May be inserted in vagina or rectum if you're lying down. Or hold it in place with a harness like the* **Leather Butterfly,** *about $24. Another battery-operated toy, the* **Rabbit Pearl** *(about $66), offers simultaneous vaginal and clitoral stimulation although users may find Bugs Bunny becoming an unwelcome addition to their erotic dreams.*

Remember: the Industrial Revolution happened to make your life easier! —PDiL

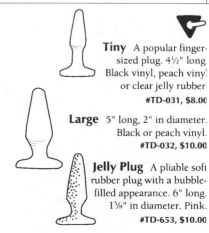

Tiny A popular finger-sized plug. 4½" long. Black vinyl, peach vinyl or clear jelly rubber
#TD-031, $8.00

Large 5" long, 2" in diameter. Black or peach vinyl.
#TD-032, $10.00

Jelly Plug A pliable soft rubber plug with a bubble-filled appearance. 6" long. 1⅝" in diameter. Pink.
#TD-653, $10.00

FORBIDDEN FRUIT grows in every garden.

In a small New York City apartment, in 1965, that garden was my mother's bookshelves. I was thirteen. Nestled in between *Ulysses* and *Naked Lunch* was a copy of *Lady Chatterly's Lover.* I chose it because I was tired of Roman mythology, and it seemed to me only sensible to keep one's clothes on while eating — after all, you might drip.

The cover was standard late-fifties pocketbook fare: buxom female in off-the-shoulder blouse leans against a tree while a man in rustic costume gazes disapprovingly into her cleavage.

I didn't know what I was looking for, exactly, but that picture seemed promising.

I took the book back into my bedroom and began to read.

Beautiful heroine. Witty, incapacitated husband. Large country house. Armies of servants, among them the taciturn gamekeeper, surly, standoffish, but wildly attractive. Descriptions of melting *loins.* (Note to self: what *are* loins?)

Heroine kneels. A tear falls on her wrist.

"You shouldn't cry," says the gamekeeper. He pets her haunches. (*Haunches?*)

He takes her by the hand and leads her to the hut. He forces her to lie down. He pulls up her skirt. His hand performs the instinctive caress of blind desire while his face is the blank, intractable mask of someone submitting to fate.

Hubba hubba!

My white cotton panties dampeneth over.

Only a few years earlier, a federal district court judge had rescued the book from literary Coventry by declaring that in between descriptions of the gamekeeper's beautiful penis and the bucolic English countryside, the novel also contained some passages of socially redeeming value.

I've never quite understood that logic.

What *isn't* socially redeeming about a beautiful penis?

The social-redemption argument continues to dog sexually explicit writing to this day, most notably in the continuing attempts to distinguish pornography from erotica as separate subgenres. Erotica, it would seem, is sex painted against a backdrop that somehow evokes *love,* while pornography is the old genital melt-down described for no other purpose than prurient pleasure. The distinction, as always, appears to be an entirely arbitrary one: Yesterday's obscenities are today's erotica. And today's smut is tomorrow's great literature. —PDiL

Erotic Literature

For as long as there has been written language, people have been using it to describe the nuances of sexual passion. The earliest known erotic writings are descriptions of the Sumerian goddess Inanna, inscribed on clay tablets in cuneiform script, and dating back roughly 3,750 years: "My vulva, the horn, the Boat of Heaven, is full of eagerness like the young moon. My untilled land lies fallow."

Anais Nin didn't have anything on the ancient Mesopotamians!

This splendid anthology spans four thousand years of sensuality, guiding its readers on a journey through the poetry, religious texts and prose of practically every civilization and culture, from ancient Greece and Rome through China, India, Arabia, and medieval Europe, to arrive full-circle at the frank sensualists of our day. Highly recommended. — PDiL

•

(From *"Figs,"* a poem by D.H. Lawrence)

The proper way to eat a fig, in society

Is to split it in four, holding it by the stump,

And open it, so that it is a glittering, rosy, moist, honied, heavy-petaled four-petaled flower.

Then you throw away the skin

Which is just like a four-petaled calex,

After you have taken off the blossom with your lips.

But the vulgar way

Is just to put your mouth to the crack, and take out the flesh in one bite.

Every fruit has its secret.

Erotic Literature
(Twenty-Four Centuries of Sensual Writing) Jane Mills, Editor. 1993; 348 pp. ISBN 0-06-270057-X
$30 ($32.75 postpaid). HarperCollins Publishers/Direct Mail, PO Box 588, Dunmore, PA 18512; 800/331-3761

The Gates of Paradise

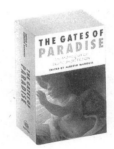

Anthologies are like candy samplers: they generally include something for everyone's taste, and are a good way to discover what you like. This collection is culled from the best more-or-less-contemporary erotica from around the world. Authors include Isabel Allende, Milan Kundera, Yukio Mishima, Doris Lessing, and more than two dozen other writers. —PDiL

•

I looked at Jesus. He was looking at me. And at my breasts. Looking right at them. Jesus was sitting there on the sun deck, looking at my breasts.

What should I do? Say excuse me and push them back into the kimono? Make a little joke of it? Look what the wind blew in, or something? Or should I say nothing? Just tuck them in as inconspicuously as possible? What do you say when a wind comes up and blows your kimono open and he sees your breasts? . . .

Jesus must have recognized my confusion, because right then he said, quite sincerely I thought, "You have nice breasts."

"Thanks," I said. I didn't know what else to say, so I asked him if he'd like more wine.
—Gloria Sawai

The Gates of Paradise
(An Anthology of Erotic Short Fiction) Alberto Manguel. C. Potter Books, 1993; 242 pp. ISBN 0-517-88050-4
$18 ($20 postpaid). Random House/Order Dept., 400 Hahn Road, Westminster, MD 21157; 800/733-3000

Magic Carpets
These can be worn underneath a single-strap dildo harness. Both have the same size pad (6½" x 2¾"); the length and diameter listed describe the dildo portion. The harness wearer slips the dildo portion of the Magic Carpet into her vagina—the ridges provide clitoral stimulation. Many women also enjoy using Magic Carpets for solo sex or with a vibrator.

TS-262 Magic Carpet 2 3" long, ¾" in diameter. **$28.00**
TS-263 Magic Carpet 3 5" long, 1¼" in diameter. **$49.00**

Whale and Dolphin
Elegant, sculptured dildos that look as good on the coffee table as they do in the boudoir.

Whale 6¼" long, 1½" in diameter. **#TS-333 $49.00**
Dolphin 5" long, 1¼" in diameter. **#TS-269 $36.50**

Dildos and Sex Toys

Dildos have been around for centuries.

As far back as the third century B.C., *Miletus — a charming resort town on the coast of Asia Minor — had established its reputation as the leading purveyor of the olisbos to the queens and noblewomen of the civilized world. These ancient dildos were made of wood or padded leather, and had to be liberally lubricated with olive oil before use.*

Most contemporary dildos are made of silicone — a resilient, nonporous material that is ideal for sex play because it retains body heat. Lubrication is still a good idea.

What do you use dildos for? Well, you insert them. In your vagina. In your anus.

(A dildo harness will hold your dildo in place for however long you want.)

Dildos come in a wide assortment of naturalistic and nonrepresentational styles, and in every color of the rainbow. Play with a dildo by yourself or with a friend; silicone is a wonderful medium for good vibrations. But be careful with teeth and long fingernails: even a small crack will progress rapidly to a tear. Why cause a rift in a significant relationship? Clean frequently; washing with mild nondetergent soap works well.

(A special subgenre of the dildo is the anal toy or butt plug. The most popular of these are diamond-shaped, designed so you can insert them inside yourself and have your hands free for other pleasures. Butt plugs may be made out of vinyl, rubber or silicone.) —PDiL

Erotica

This lovely collection of sexually in-spired art and literature covers two thousand years of human expression and is arranged not chronologically but by categories of the imagination. There are sections on voyeurism, the awakenings of first desire, dark fantasy, and taboo, among others, but the editors have deliberately chosen to exclude all depictions of violence or degradation. Perfect pillow books!
—Patrizia DiLucchio

Erotica
(An Illustrated Anthology of Sexual Art and Literature)
Charlotte Hill & William Wallace, Editors.
Vol. I: 1992; 224 pp.
ISBN 0-88184-874-3
Vol. II: 1993; 160 pp.
ISBN 0-88184-787-9
Each $16.95 ($18.95 postpaid). Carrol & Graff Publishers, 260 Fifth Avenue, New York, NY 10001; 212/889-8772

Left: Woodcut by Utamaro Utagawa (1753-1806) from *The Song of the Pillow*.
Middle: Erotic friction: an anonymous water-   color of the delights of tribadism. The Venus of Willendorf (after the place in Austria where it was discovered) was carved in the Paleolithic period around 30,000 BC. Her newly acquired name is not inappropriate. She is clearly an object of worship: an idealized woman, a celebration of female sexuality and fecundity.

The Erotic Adventures of Sleeping Beauty

Anne Rice has written about mulattos, eunuchs, witches, mummies, and, of course, the undead. But it was only in the wake of the breakaway success of **The Vampire Lestat** *that it became common knowledge that Rice, under the pen names Ann Rampling and A. N. Roquelaure, is a writer of erotica as well.*

The Claiming of Sleeping Beauty, **Beauty's Punishment**, *and* **Beauty's Release** *are written in the form of a sadomasochistic folk tale, haunting and provocative. Pleasure and pain are wed inextricably in the life of Rice's princess, and no simple kiss is enough to rouse her from her sleep.*

Anne Rice writes like few other con-temporary storytellers. —BT

•

I kissed the Princess violently, my hands greedily clutching her heavy little breasts and bouncing them and massaging them.

She went into a paroxysm of longing. Her mouth sucked at mine, her body straining forward, and I lowered my head to suck at her breasts one by one, as she cried, her hips swaying wildly. It was almost too much to wait longer.

The Sleeping Beauty Novels
(The Claiming of Sleeping Beauty; Beauty's Punishment; Beauty's Release)
A. N. Roquelaure. Plume Books, 1993;
ISBN 0-452-15298-4
$30 ($32 postpaid). Penguin USA/Consumer Sales, 120 Woodbine Street, Bergenfield, NJ 07621; 800/253-6476

Story of O

Perhaps it is significant that France is the country that has given us the two greatest writers of sadomasochistic erotica, the Marquis de Sade and Pauline Reage. (In return, of course, we have given them Jerry Lewis.) The French have a long tradition of intellec-tual openness that may have helped foster a tolerance of what, in other cul-tures, would have been labeled sexual deviance and rigorously repressed. Nevertheless, **Story of O** *shocked readers when it was first published in France in 1954, with its vivid descrip-tions of sex in which cruelty is inflicted to obtain satisfaction and release. In typical French fashion, the debate that immediately ensued centered on whether the book was mere erotica, or*

Story of O
Pauline Reage. Ballantine Books, 1981;
140 pp. ISBN 0-345-30111-0
$4.95 ($6.95 postpaid). Random House/Order Dept., 400 Hahn Road, Westminster, MD 21157; 800/733-3000

a metaphor for political and spiritual transformation.

In the best synthetic tradition of our own culture, American readers may like to think of it as profound erotica. —PDiL

The Perfumed Garden

Indiana Jones was a minor league player compared to Sir Richard Francis Burton. Just look at Burton's resumé: soldier, author, explorer, ethnolo-gist, linguist, Arabist, diplomat and student of culture. Burton the explorer searched for the source of the Nile; Burton the Arab scholar was the first modern European to make the haj to Mecca. Burton the linguist spoke forty languages. As a diplomat, he served as a British consul officer for three decades; as a transla-tor, he gave us the **Arabian Nights**.

Burton, the student of culture, shocked polite society with his frank descrip-tions of heretofore exotic sexual practices like fellatio and cunnilingus. **The Perfumed Garden** *earned him the label "pornographer."*

First published in London in the 1880s, this book is the best known of the many works of Arabic erotica. Even today it remains vibrant and exciting — unlike the perhaps more widely circulated **Kama Sutra** *of ancient India (which reads more like a contortionist's handbook than a sex manual).*

Burton was never quite satisfied with his first translation of **The Perfumed Garden**: *at the end of his life he com-pleted a second version that included previously excluded chapters of homoerotica. This later version, unhap-pily, never saw print: it was destroyed by Burton's wife Isabel (seeking to pro-tect her husband's reputation).*

The Perfumed Garden
Richard F. Burton. Park Street Press, 1992; 96 pp. ISBN 0-89281-443-8
$16.95 ($19.95 postpaid). Inner Traditions International, 1 Park Street, Rochester, VT 05767; 802/767-3174

The Park Street Press edition is the first illustrated reproduction of Burton's original translation. Buy it. Read it. Enjoy it. The Victorians did, even if they claimed they didn't. You won't be disappointed. —Ben Trumble

•

Know, oh Vizier (may God protect you!) that, when you desire to copulate, let it be when your stomach is free from food. Only then is coition healthful and good. But if your stomach is loaded, the result will be bad for both persons; you will be liable to an attack of apoplexy and gout, and the least of the ills likely to afflict you will be a stoppage of the urine or a weakness of sight. Let your stomach be free from all excess food and drink and you will have nothing to fear.

Do not unite with a woman until you have excited her with playful caresses and then the pleasure will be mutual. It is advisable therefore to amuse yourselves before you introduce your member and accomplish the act. You will excite her by kissing her cheeks, sucking her lips, and nibbling her teats. You will kiss her navel and her thighs, and lay a provoking hand upon her pubes. Bite her arms; do not neglect any part of her body; clasp her tightly till she feels your love; then sigh and twine your arms and legs round hers.

Delta of Venus

After fifty years, **Delta of Venus** *is one of the hottest books around.*

Particularly enchanting are the diary entries at the beginning of the book that document the evolution of Nin's pornographic style. "Less poetry," the anonymous patron who subsidizes Nin's forays into smut-mongering keeps telling her. At first, Nin is a dutiful hack. But ultimately, she rebels. "Sex loses all its power and magic when it becomes explicit, mechanical, overdone, when it becomes a mecha-nistic obsession," she tells him. "It becomes a bore."

And so pornography acquired a female sensibility: herotica was born! — PDiL

Delta of Venus
Anais Nin. Pocket Books, 1990; 98 pp.
ISBN 0-6717-424-93
$5.99 ($8.99 postpaid) from Simon & Schuster/Order Dept., 200 Old Tappan Road, Old Tappan, NJ 07675; 800/223-2336

The Art of Sexual Ecstasy

This wonderful book links the technology of good sex — breathing, relaxation, communication, movement, touch, and sound — with an understanding that sex begins long before we touch each other in the bedroom. It can help couples harmonize the deep differences between men and women's responses and approaches to sexuality.

The Art of Sexual Ecstasy deals with the things that precede what we usually think of as lovemaking. Foreplay loses its meaning: it's all foreplay, or none of it is. All the details matter: a clean, flower-filled space, passing a perfume bottle under the nose of your blindfolded lover, speaking your sexual joys and fears. Again, the goal is to frame sexuality differently — to make it new, playful, less embarassing, and more aware.

A step-by-step guide to what the West knows best — communication, bioenergetics, the pubococcygeus muscle — and what the East knows best — breathing, yoga, energy channels, moving orgasmic energy up the spine. The ultimate goal here is to spread orgasmic sensation to every cell of your body in a wave of bliss that lights your brain and unites the sexual and the spiritual. Write me when you get that far. There's enough here to keep you busy for years.
—Katy Butler

The Art of Sexual Ecstasy
Margo Anand. Jeremy P. Tarcher Inc., 1991;
450 pp. ISBN 0-87477-581-7
$18.95 ($21.45 postpaid). Putnam Publishing
Group/Order Dept., PO Box 506, East
Rutherford, NJ 07073; 800/631-8571

Good Sex

This book is a refreshing look at all the things that are right with American sexuality. If you like Studs Terkel, you'll feel right at home with Julia Hutton. Whether she's talking to a happily married forty-six-year-old woman with three children living in the suburbs, or a gay male graphic designer in San Francisco's Castro District, ultimately her message is the same: Love is joy. And sex is wonderful. —BT

●

"I don't think good sex is a mathematical equation: This act plus this act equals good sex. It's more a sense of well-being, physical release, and relaxation, no doubt, no worries. We have a lot of humor. Most of the giggle sessions we have are in bed, and things happen that are so hilarious. One time we attempted to lick chocolate fudge off each other, but it was really sticky so it didn't come off. It was everywhere!"

Good Sex
(Real Stories from Real People)
Julia Hutton. 1993; 222 pp.
ISBN 0-939416-57-3
$12.95 ($14.45). Cleis Press, PO Box 8933,
Pittsburg, PA 15221; 412/937-1555

Men In Love

What does it mean to be a man? And what does it mean to be a man in love? Ten years before Robert Bly, bonding, drum beats, and Iron John, feminist writer Nancy Friday, author of the justly famous My Mother/My Self, was asking just that question in her groundbreaking examination of the male psyche.

Never judgmental, Friday interviewed more than a thousand subjects for this eye-opening study. And what did she find? That the secret garden of the masculine imagination is sometimes dark and cruel — and yet emerging from that garden, most men are capable of profound acts of caring and kindness and love. Men In Love is a book for anyone who wishes to better understand lovers, husbands, brothers, fathers, sons, and especially one's self.
—Ben Trumble

●

Most of my fantasies are about my wife Sophie. Although I have many without her, I like the ones in which she stars because she's the most important person in my life. I'll start with the first and most important fantasy: I'm hiding in the closet when my wife brings a lover into the bedroom. They begin to kiss and fondle and take each other's clothes off until they are naked. He sucks on her tits and she sighs and spreads her legs wider (they are standing on a rug in front of the bed) so he can get his hand into her cunt. Then she grips his dick which is thick and long and pulls him down on top of the bed. She starts to run her tongue around the head, then slips it into her mouth. I usually come by this time, but I can make it last longer by inventing more details.

Besides my wife and you, Nancy, only one other person knows about my fantasies. He is a close friend who married my sister. I told him everything, including the idea that I would love to see him fucking Sophie. This got him very excited, and he blurted out that he'd always had fantasies that my sister was not a virgin when she married him, and that I was the one who had taken her maidenhead. To tell the truth, exchanging those ideas got us both so excited, that we were rubbing each other though our pants before we finished, and have met a few more times since then to do a few more experiments in which we combine stories about swapping wives and jerking each other off. I guess maybe I'm bisexual.

When I'm having trouble getting it up, my wife will often tell me one of her fantasies about fucking some guy, and it jumps right up. There's one guy in particular who gets me all hot and bothered when she talks about him. He works with her and really turns her on, but she's afraid to pursue it much. She was a virgin when we married, and I'm the only guy who's screwed her. I wish she would fuck another man or woman and like it. That way I could act out my favorite fantasy and get her to make it with my brother-in-law. A trio would be heaven.

Men In Love
(The Triumph of Love over Rage)
Nancy Friday. 1983, 214 pp.
ISBN 0-440-15903-2
$6.99 ($9.49 postpaid). Bantam, Doubleday,
Dell/Fulfillment Dept., 2451 S. Wolf Road,
Des Plaines, IL 60018; 800/223-6834

My Parents Never Had Sex

Normalcy can be capricious. Though almost no one thinks twice about the often very public passion of young lovers on a warm spring day, those same open displays of affection seem oddly inappropriate when the lovers in question are middle-aged or elderly. We never talk about it, but in our culture sex is for the young.

As Doris Hammond ably points out in My Parents Never Had Sex, the myths surrounding sexual aging have almost nothing to do with biological realities. We may slow down, but the fires never die. In fact, we do society a great injustice by expecting celibacy from our older members.

The good news is that attitudes are beginning to change. The bodies in the beer commercials may stay eternally twenty, but the rest of us are coming to terms with our grey hair, pot bellies, and lifelong sexuality. —BT

●

An interesting comment was offered by one of my daughters, who, when realizing I would be writing this book, told me of a conversation between her younger sister and their father. I had just been certified as a sex counselor, and the youngest daughter wondered how I could possibly know enough about sex to be a sex counselor. Her father replied, "You'd be surprised how much your mother knows!" I rather imagine that, even though my daughters can intellectualize about their mother as a "sex expert," it is just as difficult for them to imagine their father and me having sex as it is for other children to imagine the same about their parents.

My Parents Never Had Sex
(Myths & Facts of Sexual Aging)
Doris B. Hammond. 1987: 180 pp.
ISBN 0-87975-364-1
$12.95 ($15.95 postpaid). Prometheus
Books 59 John Glenn Drive, Amherst,
NY 14228-2197, 800/421-0351

Susie Bright and All Her Works

MacArthur Foundation, take note: Susie Bright is a national treasure right up there with the Grand Canyon, the battlefield at Gettysburg, the Okee-feenokee Swamp and the Smith-sonian's Nancy Reagan Memorial Dress Collection. She deserves your support!

She is more than just a writer, per-former, theorist, and editor. She is a sex crusader, and like all good educa-tors, she knows the power of positive reinforcement. When you read Susie Bright, you do not hear about all the dire consequences of erotic denial; in-stead, you discover how much fun you can have with a little lubricant and a lot of imagination. If sex is a circus, then Bright is the woman in the pink-se-quined leotard, riding the white horse at the front of the parade. —PDiL

•

Sex is also a crucial way to prepare for childbirth. Start with the premise that birth is the biggest sex act you will ever take part in, and everything will flow from that. If you are smart and take childbirth preparation classes, you may even get a teacher who knows something about the sexual side of birth.

My teacher was very subtle. She gave us an almost unreadable handout in the fourth month, an instruction sheet for an exercise called "perineal massage." I thought of my perineum, the little inch of skin running be-tween my vagina and my anus. How could rubbing something the size of a birthday candle help me in labor?

The flyer (which opened, of course, with the obligatory spiel: "Mommy and Daddy love each other very much . . .") said that Daddy should massage and finger the vagi-nal opening until he could put more and more of his fingers inside, relaxing the vagi-nal muscles through such caresses until he might be able to press a small orange or even his whole hand into Mommy's opening.

His whole hand! I called up one of my friends who has the breadth of experience as both a mother of two and a retired porn star. "Is 'perineal massage' really fist fucking?" I asked her.

"Of course," she said, laughing, "and it really helps."
—"Egg Sex," *Sexual Reality*

•

Lesbian strip shows, which emerged four years ago in San Francisco, are the most liberat-ing settings I have ever seen for women erotic performers. In case you haven't seen the lesbian Burlezk video documentary, let me explain. Every week for two years, and now sporadically, we've had a lesbian erotica show in local gay bars, which features many professional dancers who work in downtown sex clubs. These women, who are so blasé in their "straight" jobs, are as nervous as virgin brides when they perform at Burlezk.

The very secret that most of them would rather die than tell a group of dykes — "I'm a stripper" — sud-denly makes them the hottest things on the lesbian dating circuit. Rather than being viewed as confused or depraved, the lesbian strippers earn a well-de-served reputation for their guts, talent, and sexual sophistication. —*Susie Sexpert's Lesbian Sex World*

Susie Sexpert's Lesbian Sex World
Susie Bright. 1990; 155 pp.
ISBN 0-939416-35-2

Susie Bright's Sexual Reality
(A Virtual Sex World Reader)
Susie Bright. 1994; 157 pp.
ISBN 0-939416-59-X
Both $9.95 ($11.45 postpaid) from Cleis Press, PO Box 8933, Pittsburg, PA 15221; 412/937-1555

Herotica
(A Collection of Women's Erotic Fiction)
Susie Bright, editor. 1988; 150 pp.
ISBN 0-940208-11-3
$8.50 ($12.25 postpaid) from Down There Press, 938 Howard Street, Suite 101, San Francisco, CA 94103; 415/974-8985

Herotica 2
Susie Bright & Joani Blank, editors. Plume, 1992; 204 pp.
ISBN 0-452-26787-0
$11 ($13 postpaid) from Penguin USA/Consumer Sales, 120 Wood-bine Street, Bergenfield, NJ 07621; 800/253-6476

SEX ZINES

ecstasy (The Journal of Divine Eroti-cism): PO Box 862, Ojai, CA 93024. $20/year (4 issues). Is love your path to enlightenment? *ecstasy* takes a serious look at sex as a connection to the divine.

Yellow Silk (A Journal of the Erotic Arts): PO Box 6374, Albany, CA 94706. $30/year (4 issues). More than just a zine. What it is, is perhaps the most sensual magazine of literary erotica currently published in the US.

Hugh Hefner forever transformed the world of sex magazines from quasi-educational nudist promos to high-budget affairs full of sizzle and spice and steamy models with perky nipples and breasts that never quit. That's all well and good if that's what you're into. But there has always been an audience for less mainstream sex as well. Thanks to desk-top publishing, zines — little magazines once mimeographed in somebody's base-ment — have taken their place as a part of the erotic subculture. Whether your taste runs to S&M, large hairy men in leather (called bears), women on motor-cycles, or stories of rather more subdued real-life sexual experience, chances are that someone is publishing a zine that's right up your alley.

When you find a publication that you re-ally like, show your support and subscribe. On Our Backs, the now-well-known, now-glossy magazine for gay women, started out as a zine. If it wasn't for subscriptions, they might not have made the transition to support from major advertisers.
—Ben Trumble

Slippery When Wet: More! Productions, PO Box 3101, Berkeley, CA 94703. $20/year (4 issues). Billed as "bisexual, penetration-positive, nonmonogamous, and queer," this zine refuses to take itself seri-ously. Read the stories and enjoy the com-ics; stain the pages if you must, and check out the photographs by the likes of Annie Sprinkle.

frighten the horses: Heat Seeking Pub-lishing, 41 Sutter Street #1108, San Fran-cisco, CA 94104. $18/year (4 issues). This "document of the sexual revolution" is as intelligent as it is erotic. Fiction, nonfiction, news, reviews, comics, columns. All sexual orientations.

DungeonMaster and **Sandmutopia Guardian:** Desmodus, Inc., PO Box 410390, San Francisco, CA 94141-0390. $24/year (6 issues). *DungeonMaster* is hardcore S/M for gay men, while **Sand-mutopia Guardian** is aimed at a wider S/M audience. Neither is for the faint-hearted. Desmodus also publishes the gay male roleplay magazines **Drummer** and **Mach**.

Access to Cyborgasms

Interactive CD-ROM sex games appeal to the auteur in all of us. They're kind of like casting your own porn flick — you pick the stars, the scenarios, and the action. See Valerie. Make Valerie take off her negligee. See Valerie's breasts bob as she answers the door. Who will be there? You decide.

Adult titles helped to provide venture capital for the fledgling CD-ROM publishing industry, by encourag-ing the sales of players and drives. They remain something of a novelty item — they haven't come close to supplanting videos in the adult entertain-ment market. Look for them to really take off when Paramount starts leasing Captain Kirk for the ca-sual blowjob, or Disney relaxes the copyright on **Pretty Woman**.

A good source of adult CD-ROM reviews is the San Francisco-based **Future Sex** (available, alas, at far too few newsstands but easy to subscribe to: $18/year [4 issues] from 60 Federal Street, Suite 502, San Francisco, CA 94107; 415/541-7725).

Lisa Palac, former editor of **Future Sex**, has produced the first virtual audio sex experience, **Cyborgasm** ($20 [$22.75 postpaid] from Algorithm, 2325 3rd Street #339, San Francisco, CA 94107; 415/252-5595). Susie Bright, Don Bajema, and Annie Sprinkle (among others) talk dirty! —PDiL

TRANSGENDER PUBLICATIONS

IF A MAN BECOMES A WOMAN through gender reassignment, and then that woman decides that she's gay, what was she to begin with? According to experts on transgender issues, she was actually a lesbian all along. There isn't a lot available in the way of transgender resources, but here are a few current publications. —Ben Trumble

TransSisters (The Journal of Transsexual Feminism): 4004 Troost Avenue Kansas City, MO 64110. $18/year (6 issues). Transsexual women have all too often been met with hostility when they have sought to participate in feminist and/or lesbian forums. The arguments are that transsexuals have been socialized as males and are not women born women. Fortunately this is changing: a survey at the 1993 Michigan Womyn's Music Festival showed that most felt (three to one) that transsexuals were indeed legitimate participants. As you may have gathered, TransSisters was there to cover the story.

TNT (The Transsexual News Telegraph): Suite #288, 548 Castro Street, San Francisco, CA 94114. $15/year (4 issues). Published for the transgendered communities, this magazine promises that it will never contain articles about shopping or make-up.

Transformation: 13331 Garden Grove Blvd. Suite G, Garden Grove, CA 92645. $12.95/issue. This is a slick glossy for transvestites, transsexuals, and crossdressers. **Transformation** runs nothing but articles about shopping and make-up.

OTHER GREAT RESOURCES

AEGIS: American Educational Gender Information Service: PO Box 33724, Decatur, Georgia 30033. AEGIS maintains a national transgender archive, a repository for books, journals, magazines, newsletters, and films. The archive is open to the public.

X-Rated Video Tape Guide, Volumes I-III: Robert Rimmer and Patrick Riley. Prometheus Books, 59 John Glen Drive, Buffalo NY 14228. Each volume reviews over a thousand titles.

Facets Gay and Lesbian Video Guide: Facets Multimedia Inc., 1517 West Fullerton Avenue, Chicago IL 60614.

Great Pictures Mail Order: 150-50 Coolidge Avenue, Jamaica, NY 11432; 800/445-6662. For hard-to-find sex videos. If they don't have it, their search service will find it.

CATALOGS

Why leave the house? It's the nineties: we're all busy cocooning. Pass the Faith Popcorn and turn up the home shopping channel.

Even if we did want to go out to buy sex toys, where would most of us go? In most towns, the "bookstores" that deal in explicit materials and toys are dirty storefronts in battle zones where working girls ply the street corners and unshaven men in raincoats haunt the twenty-five-cent video peeps. Not exactly a romantic venue for r & r. When your feet stick to the floor and the blow-up dolls begin to remind you of Dennis Hopper's ex-girlfriends, you may wish you had shopped by mail.

Two catalogs are available through Good Vibrations (Good Vibrations Mail Order and The Sexuality Library), a catalog of toys and another of sexually explicit videos and literature. The emphasis is sex-positive and wholesome; interspersed among the product descriptions are tips for safe-sex use. Confidentiality is guaranteed; customers need never fear that their names will end up on any questionable mailing lists. All items are packaged plainly with Open Enterprises given as the return address.

The Xandria Collection somewhat more resembles the Spencer's Gift Catalog. In addition to the standard offerings of dildos and vibrators, it includes a variety of novelty items like X-rated playing cards, crotchless pantyhose and a vibro-realistic vagina (batteries not included). The catalog arrives in your mailbox in a tasteful brown-paper wrapper, looking like nothing so much as a copy of the **New Yorker**. Customer confidentiality is safeguarded. Products may be returned within a sixty-day period with a money-back guarantee.

Adam & Eve are one of the largest condom suppliers in the nation, offering a full selection of American and Japanese brands, with or without nonoxynol-9. Their toll-free number is usable 24 hours a day, seven days a week. —PDiL

Good Vibrations and **The Sexuality Library:** 938 Howard Street Suite 101, San Francisco, CA 94103; 415/974-8990.

Adam & Eve: PO Box 900, Dept. PB 132, Carrboro, NC 27510; 800/274-0333.

Xandria Collection: Lawrence Research Group, PO Box 319005, San Francisco, CA 94131; 800/242-2823.

VIDEO RESOURCES

LOW-BUDGET SEX FILMS have been around since the invention of celluloid. But throughout most of its history, erotic film has been stigmatized (unless the producers could afford to throw in subtitles) sby its association with those same lonely men who haunt adult bookstores.

Then along came video.

The introduction of consumer video, and video rentals, has transformed adult movies. The stigma of porn has given way to the commonplace of couples watching sex films in the privacy of their homes.

Tastes vary too much to include a representative sampling of entertainment. Just remember, if it turns you on, it's probably been filmed.

One particularly useful thing about sex films is their educational value. Is there something you've always fantasized about, wanted to try, but didn't know how? Seeing is learning. Sex/Ed has finally come out of the classroom to find a place in your VCR. —PDiL

Sex films range from the blatantly pornographic to cerebral sex therapists in suits and ties. Available from Good Vibrations' Sexuality Library (cited right) are the following:

The Safe Sex Sluts
—Safe Is Desire

SelfLoving. Betty Dodson Productions, PO Box 1933, Murray Hill, New York, NY 10156; 212/679-4240. $42 ($45 postpaid). This masturbation film for women comes from Betty Dodson, the best sex educator in the country. Dodson is the kindergarten teacher we all wish we'd had for show and tell. Her celebration of female sensuality is intelligent, life affirming and down to earth. Real women have real orgasms.

How to Perform Fellatio. The Sexuality Library, 938 Howard Street, Suite 101, San Francisco, CA 94103; 415/974-8990. $24.95 ($28.70 postpaid). Porn actress Karen Summer leads the cast in this one. No practical hints for deep throating, but lots of stoke and stroke action and everyone looks like they're having fun. Just remember: this one was made before safe sex had become a rule to live by.

Safe Is Desire. Fatale Video, 526 Castro Street, San Francisco, CA 94114; 800/845-4617. $33.95 ($44.95 postpaid). Safe sex does not have to be tame sex. Lots of wild and kinky action. The after-hours orgy at the Safe Sex Sluts theater will make plastic wrap one of your favorite erotic fetishes for a long time to come.

How To Female Ejaculate. Fatale Video, 526 Castro Street, San Francisco, CA 94114; 800/845-4617. $33.95 ($44.95 postpaid). Who would have expected the old vaginal-versus-clitoral-orgasm debate to resurface from the works of Freud, et al. into women's porn publisher Fanny Fatale's living room? But there it is. Erotic, but I still have my doubts. Are these women ejaculating? But there's so much of it!

The Erotic Educational Series. The Sexuality Library, 938 Howard Street, Suite 101, San Francisco, CA 94103; 415/974-8990. Set of five videos: $140 ($143.75 postpaid). This series of five films is produced in Holland and designed to make sex a lifelong pleasure. Titles include **Enjoying Sex, Erection, The Female Orgasm, Harmony,** and **The Male Orgasm.** Intelligent and explicit with high production values. For the serious student. Don't be put off by the flipcharts. Some of the best shots are of a truly aroused woman — her clitoris looks like a pearl.

WHEN I WAS A KID, I thought the whole world was Italian-American, and 85 percent of it was a blood relation. I was fortunate: the sense of kinship was pervasive in my universe, even beyond my large, extended family. We belonged to each other in the best sense of that word. We were loud and overbearing and I later found it necessary to cultivate some other ways of being, but as a kid, through my teen years, I always found solace in the experience of Family. Those people loved me, cared for me, and collectively raised me. I've always believed that my early affinity for the people in my world, a natural byproduct of this ubiquitous familiality, made it vastly easier for me to make friends and get along with others — and, more importantly, to believe that I belonged here.

In the modern world, we have all but lost this beneficial aspect of tribalism. We can't be bothered with each other, let alone each other's children. The ethos of "Don't Tread on Me" has insinuated itself into some of the most basic interpersonal relationships in our society. This allows us privacy, of course, but it also allows us to be strangers to each other in ways that hurt, and that we haven't fully accounted for.

And that has a lot to do with why there is so much spiritual hunger in America, such resurgent interest in community, such devotion to rehabilitating our inner children. If we could foster the experience of Family more effectively, we would have the natural development of a multitude of communities; we would have happy, healthy inner children growing into happy, healthy inner adults.

Most of us (in the West, anyway) know the idea of Family through the so-called nuclear family. Here we have tried to broaden the idea. In the end, what matters is not the structure of your family, but your experience of Family. We hope the tools and information you find in this domain will lead to a more rewarding, more enduring sense of Family for you and the ones you love. —Phil Catalfo

Happy is the generation where the great listen to the small,
for it follows that in such a generation,
the small will listen to the great. —Talmud

Being a parent goes right to the heart of love. Bam! After the most dramatic introduction imaginable, an emotional tsunami sweeps through the delivery room and is off with our heart.

We are left gasping for air, struggling to get above the tide and a pile of diapers. None of us make it for enough time to call ourselves our own again. But that's the point: we are *not* our own anymore. We belong to the life we have created.

Parenthood may be the most intense journey life offers. We are carried on the swiftest of currents, full of more hope than we dared imagine, as we discover what our children bring us. We've never been bigger, better or more important in anyone's eyes nor so aware of our own shortcomings. It's brutal.

A parent's art lies in recognition of the child's autonomy and respect for the person the child is becoming. Ours is not to mold, shape or coerce, but, rather, to appreciate, encourage and nurture. It takes self-control and patience. We are rewarded with rediscovery and, possibly, redemption. We get the child we deserve. Take a front seat as the life before you unfolds, and leave your ego in the mezzanine. —Nancy A. Pietrafesa

The Mosque and the City —*The Spiritual Life of Children*

time put aside?' I told her, I said, 'I'd think of Jesus, and how He said you should concentrate on what's important.' My mum looked up, and she said I was 'dead right,' and I think then I could have taken the whole afternoon off, if I'd have said I was going to say my prayers in my room!"

•

For many Christian children drawing God's face does just that — gives Him to them concretely, brings Him "around" I have never asked a Jewish or Islamic child to draw a picture of God, nor have I asked children who assert their indifference to formal religion to represent what, after all, they doubt or deny as believable. On occasion I have, however, heard both confessions and fantasies. In Jerusalem, a Jewish boy of twelve, almost thirteen, told me, after drawing a picture of Moses holding the tablets of law, of his sometime transgression: "I think of Moses a lot: he is our greatest teacher. My brother [only five] asked me what God looks like and what Moses saw when he went up the mountain: 'Did he see God?' I said, 'No, of course not: you cannot see God.' 'How can that be, if he gave Moses the tablets?' I was stymied. I said, 'These things happen.' I didn't convince him. He was all set — I could tell — to ask me a million more questions. I raised my voice and said, 'Don't ask me; ask Father, ask our rabbi.' I wanted no more questions!"

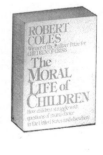

The Moral Life of Children • The Political Life of Children • The Spiritual Life of Children

Robert Coles has been listening carefully to the voice of children's souls since the late fifties . His books address subtle but important dimensions of children's emerging selves, which they are actively constructing from the environment in which they live. His keen ear and thoughtful analysis yield a comprehensive psychological and sociological portrait of the child. —NAP

•

In this conservative, traditional home, Jesus, His sayings, His stated ideals, His expressed admonitions, stimulated Anne occasionally to rebellion, to outspoken dissent. She had learned, I began to notice, that Christ's outspoken challenge to "the powers that be" worked well for her as she chafed at the everyday constraints of a well-run household: "I think of Jesus when I've got so much to do, too much. He said we should follow him, even if it means we don't do a lot of things we're supposed to do. But we get lost in all there is to get done, and we're not much thinking of Him. It's not right. I told my mum we need more time just to stop and think in this house. She said, 'Well, Annie, what would you think about, once you stopped and had all that

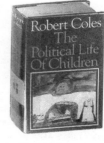

The Spiritual Life of Children
Robert Coles. 1990.; 358 pp.
ISBN 0-395-59923-7

The Moral Life of Children
Robert Coles. 1991; ISBN 0-395-59921-0

The Political Life of Children
Robert Coles. 1991; ISBN 0-395-59922-9

Each $10.95 ($13.45 postpaid) from Houghton Mifflin Co./Mail Order Dept., Wayside Road, Burlington, MA 01803; 800/225-3362

Evolution's End

Joseph Chilton Pearce wrote the classics Magical Child and Magical Child Matures, landmark works on child development and our society's pernicious effect on it. His style is dense, and when he starts talking about the structure of the brain he can run away from you. But his basic message — that the modern world is interfering with "nature's plan" for the unfolding of the human being, from infancy through childhood and adolescence — is one today's parents, and society at large, must confront. That, and his very spiritual vision of what is at stake (the "bond of power" he has written about elsewhere, the eternal imprinting from parent to child, human potential in the grandest sense) make this a book to reckon with. —PC

•

Play is the foundation of creative intelligence, but, like any intelligence, it must be developed; in keeping with nature's model-imperative, the child who is played with will learn to play. The child who is not played with will be unable to play and will be at risk on every level. One of the foundations of play is story telling. Even before they can speak, infants will listen raptly to adults speaking or telling stories. Understanding the words is almost incidental in the beginning, it's the sound of those syllables that fascinates. In his memoirs one gentleman recounted how as a toddler he loved to snuggle into his grandfather's lap and listen to him read the great philosophers, lofty words that predisposed that young mind toward higher things.

Time-honored children's tales are equally vital to the child's development. The child listens to the storyteller with total entrainment; he grows still, his jaw drops, his eyes widen, and he stares fixedly at the speaker. His vision, however, turns within where the action is, for the words of a story stimulate the creation of corresponding internal images. A little girl told me she liked radio more than television because the pictures were so much more beautiful. The radio words gave the stimulus; the beautiful pictures were her own creation. This imaging is the foundation of future symbolic and metaphoric thought, both concrete and formal operational thinking, higher mathematics, science, philosophy, everything we consider higher mentation or education.

Evolution's End
(Claiming the Potential
of Our Intelligence)
Joseph Chilton Pearce. 1992; 256 pp.
ISBN 0-06-250715-X
$12 ($14.75 postpaid) from
HarperCollins Publishers/Direct Mail,
PO Box 588, Dunmore, PA 18512
800/331-3761

•

Play develops intelligence; integrates our triune nature; prepares us for higher education, creative thought, and taking part in and upholding a social structure; helps us prepare for becoming an effective parent when that time comes. Play is the very force of society and civilization, and a breakdown in ability to play will reflect in a breakdown of society...The major damage of television has little to do with content: Its damage is neurological, and it has, indeed, damaged us, perhaps beyond repair. First, television replaced story telling in most homes, and changed the radio from a storyteller to a music box. When television is criticized, its apologists point to similar warnings made when radio burst on the scene early in this century, but radio as an endless storyteller sparked the imagination of and helped give rise to a generation whose creativity changed the face of the earth (for better or worse). Television, on the other, has now been with us far longer than radio was before television's introduction, and its programming has deteriorated at an astonishing rate for the same reasons that it damages us.

What Kind of Kid Are You Raising? Take Your Pick

Bringing Up a Moral Child (Michael Schulman & Eva Mekler. Addison-Wesley, 1985). Encourage altruism and concern for others.

Raising Ethical Children (Steven C. Reuben. Prima Publishing, 1994). Instill a sense of accountability and principled behavior.

Raising Your Spirited Child (Mary Sheedy Kurcinka. HarperCollins, 1992). Guidance for parents with vexing children.

Raising a Responsible Child (Don Dinkmeyer & Gary D. McKay. Fireside Books, Simon & Schuster, 1973). Getting your kid to remember his lunch, his jacket and his homework.

The Hurried Child

Ongoing social change has had broad and disturbing ramifications for children. They are expected to grow up quickly and sometimes alone, because overburdened parents have neither the time, patience or, often, the inclination to nurture. The emotional and psychological needs of children have been shortchanged in a world where Superkid is the norm and toddlers are expected to read. This book will sharpen your thinking on how you can still give your child a childhood. —NAP

•

Young children believe that adults are all-knowing and all-wise. When we confront them with tasks for which they are not ready — such as tests, workbooks, and homework — these children blame themselves for failure. "If this all-wise, all-knowing person tells me I should be able to do this and I can't, there must be something wrong with me." We are sending too many children to school only to learn that they are "too dumb" to be there.

•

What can we do to help children who are being pressured to grow up fast and who experience this as inordinate stress? First of all, it is important to recognize what we cannot do. We cannot change the basic thrust of American society, for which hur-

The Hurried Child
(Growing Up Too Fast Too Soon)
David Elkind. 1988; 217 pp.
ISBN 0-201-07397-8
$10.95 postpaid from Addison-Wesley
Publishing Co./Order Dept., 1 Jacob Way,
Reading, MA 01867; 800/447-2226

rying is the accepted and valued way of life. Nor can we eliminate the abiding impatience that goes along with hurrying. When hurrying reflects cultural values like being punctual, then urging children to be on time has social justification. But the *abuse of hurrying* harms children. When hurrying serves parental or institutional needs at the expense of children without imbuing them with redeeming social values, the result on the child is negative.

•

Parents who make every effort to instill a healthy sense of industry in their children

may find their efforts undermined by a school that is too bent on hurrying children into academics to acknowledge individual differences.

•

Although I have no statistics to back up such a generalization, I would venture that there is a strong tie between job dissatisfaction, on the one hand, and a disproportionate concern with offspring's success in sports, on the other. Children thus became the symbols of their parents' frustrated competitiveness in the workplace. The parent can take pride in the child's success or blame the coach for his or her failure. In any case, the parent soon vicariously invests more of a commitment in the child's athletic life than his or her own work life.

Your Baby & Child

Every new parent needs a bible, and this was mine. It held me together in the weeks and months after my first child's birth. Its reassuring tone is reinforced by an information-rich format, covering almost anything you can think of to worry about — which, as parents know, is plenty. I worried about loving my child, about how much he was eating, about whether I would spoil him. All the answers were there. More importantly, the topics covered taught me that a new parent's concerns aren't limited to questions of caring and feeding. —Nancy A. Pietrafesa

•

Wrap him warmly, hold him closely, handle him slowly, feed him when he is hungry, talk to him when he looks at you, wash him when he is actually dirty and leave him peacefully alone to come to terms with life.

•

Adjust kinds of play to your baby's moods. Like everybody else he enjoys different things when he is in different moods. When he is feeling tough and good, he enjoys rough and tumble play. It makes him triumph in his body and, gradually, in his own control and power over it. But when he is feeling tired or ill, the same games frighten and upset him. He does not feel controlled and powerful now; he feels manhandled.

When he is feeling quiet and affectionate, he revels in being cuddled and crooned to. But when he is feeling restless and energetic, the same games make him feel imprisoned.

When he is tired or hungry or miserable, no game is any good. He does not want your play, he wants bed or food or comfort.

•

Learning acceptable toilet behaviour is much more difficult for children than learning sensible eating or even sleeping habits, because the toilet behaviour that is asked of them has no obvious reward. Children who are sat in high chairs get food for which they are hungry. Children who are put to bed get rest that their bodies are demanding. But children who are put on potties just have bowel movements that they were going to have anyway. It is parents who care where the movements go. Eventually a toddler will get the reward of pleasing you and of feeling "grown up." But these are vague pleasures; behaving nicely on purpose is not your toddler's strong point.

Your Baby & Child
Penelope Leach. Alfred A. Knopf, 1983; 512 pp. ISBN 0-679-72425-7
$19.95 ($21.95 postpaid) from Random House/Order Dept., 400 Hahn Road, Westminster, MD 21157; 800/733-3000

Everything a Working Mother Needs to Know

Misapprehensions about motherhood can lead people to doubt that women with families can be effective employees. The authors give clear advice on confronting and correcting such misperceptions in the workplace. While you're raising your co-workers' consciousness, you can also learn how to break the news that you are pregnant, your legal rights with respect to your job, how to negotiate your maternity leave and benefits package, how to adjust to being at home, how to find good child care. There are also thoughtful sections on finding alternative work arrangements and on returning to the workforce after an extended absence. This book will give you the tools to balance your workload with motherhood. —NAP

•

Doubt about their performance and commitment is a real obstacle that many working mothers face upon return to work. Once a boss assumes that your commitment toward your job changes when you are a mother, that boss is likely to change his or her commitment toward you, which in turn changes your

view of your job. Thus, for many working mothers, a manager's prejudgment becomes a self-fulfilling prophecy.

•

Returning to work after a maternity leave is both terrifying and exhilarating. Your first days of balancing your job with the host of responsibilities, demands, and satisfactions that remain at home may seem overwhelming. On the other hand, after living in the irrational, unpredictable world of a newborn baby, it can be a relief to return to the familiar workday routines that you mastered successfully in the past.

Everything a Working Mother Needs to Know
Anne Weisberg & Carol A. Buckler. 1994; ISBN 0-385-42410-8
$14.95 ($17.45 postpaid) from Bantam, Doubleday, Dell/Fulfillment Dept., 2451 S. Wolf Road, Des Plaines, IL 60018; 800/223-6834

Family Mirrors

If you've ever opened your mouth to say something to your child and heard your mother's voice instead of your own, you may have felt the need to investigate your childhood further. This thoughtful book weaves personal histories and current research and advice on family life together with the author's experience. The result will enable you to make the transition from being a child in a family to being a self-aware parent in a family of your own. —NAP

•

Here lies the potentially healing power of the "second life" our children offer us, the hidden message of the ghosts in the nursery. Here is our chance to reexperience and maybe this time master our own childhood aches and uncertainties as we help our children handle and master their own.

From the desperate howls of our infants to our toddlers' fears of the monster under the bed, from our teenagers' moody withdrawals to our grown children's push and pull toward independence — if we can dig deep enough to remember these emotionally charged events in our own lives and recall how we wished our parents had responded to us, the memories can help us figure out what will work for our children now.

•

"You can drive the devil out of your garden," Miller sums up, quoting Heinrich Pestalozzi, "but you will find him again in the garden of your son."

•

Parenthood did not become difficult for me — nor truly begin — until I first heard my voice rise in anger at my sons and felt their anger coming back at me. Somewhere between sixteen and eighteen months, the blissful harmonies of infancy were suddenly interrupted by discordant sounds — unwelcome but not entirely unfamiliar. "At eighteen months, they lose their sweet natures," an all-knowing friend with two older children had warned me during the rosy blush of early motherhood. "Hers did, but mine won't," I naturally thought to myself with that overweening pride common to most of us as we watch other people's children doing those unacceptable things we are confident ours will never do — until we notice them in our own back yard.

Family Mirrors
Elizabeth Fishel. 1991; 320 pp. ISBN 0-395-44261-3
$21 ($23.50 postpaid) from Houghton Mifflin Co./Mail Order Dept., Wayside Road, Burlington, MA 01803; 800/225-3362

Solve Your Child's Sleep Problems

You don't sleep, you don't have any juice next day for parenting. Your baby doesn't sleep, you don't sleep. It's simple.

Any parent who's been there would pay serious money for effective tips on getting their little angels to stay zoned for a solid six or eight hours. Said parents will cherish this book. It's all here, including some good bedtime storybooks. —NAP/PC

•

Although ongoing sleep problems are very common in young children, they are not an inherent and necessary part of growing up (unlike *occasional* problems, which may be). You can almost always identify correctable causes of these sleep disturbances and treat them successfully. If your child is at least five or six months old, you can begin to take the steps necessary to solve his sleep problems. If you wait and do nothing, his sleep will eventually improve on its own, but it could take many months or even years. However, if you find out why your child is sleeping poorly and make the necessary changes, he should be sleeping well in a few days to two weeks.

•

Children also have sleep disturbances caused by problems in their patterns of sleeping and waking and in their daily routines. Their schedules may be too irregular, they may be regular but inappropriate in certain ways, or the time of day your child is *able* to sleep may not be the time when you *want* him or her to sleep. If your child's daily patterns are inconsistent, then her sleep at night may be broken. If she naps or eats at unusual times then she may wake too early in the morning or fall asleep too late at night. If she has become accustomed to sleeping at the "wrong" hours, then she may actually be unable to fall asleep as early or sleep as late as you wish.

Solve Your Child's Sleep Problems
Richard Ferber. Fireside Books, 1986; ISBN 0-671-62099-1
$11 postpaid from Simon & Schuster/Order Dept., 200 Old Tappan Road, Old Tappan, NJ 07675; 800/223-2336

Dr. Spock's Baby and Child Care

The first words of this book — "trust yourself" — revolutionized parental behavior for an entire generation. Our mothers read Dr. Spock like he was an Old Testament prophet. He provided direct, accessible, useful information; his book has been updated repeatedly for successive generations. The utilitarian format, with a detailed index and succinct paragraphs devoted to specific topics, lets anxious parents go straight to what they need when every second counts. Some old tools are also the best; this is one. —PC/NAP

Dr. Spock's Baby and Child Care
Benjamin Spock. NAL Dutton, 1992;
ISBN 0-671-76060-2
$6.99 ($9.99 postpaid) from
Simon & Schuster/Order Dept.,
200 Old Tappan Road, Old
Tappan, NJ 07675; 800/223-2336

Magical Child

This was the opening stanza in Joseph Chilton Pearce's ongoing jeremiad about modern society's failure to nurture the human being. It caused quite a stir in the mid-1970s, and it is no less worth reading now, especially for first-time parents. In a sense, Pearce picks up where Dr. Spock leaves off: he trusts you not only as a parent, but also as an agent of "nature's plan" for the development of your child. Some might find his viewpoint, and his way of putting it across, somewhat breathless. But we ignore his treatise at our own peril — and that of our children. —PC

•
Nature has programmed every conceivable safeguard into the biological plan. The execution of her plan is, sadly, highly problematic and subject to disaster because it can only be built in as *intent*. The success of the plan hinges directly on the infant-child's being provided with a *content* proper for that intent. A proper content is one appropriate to a particular stage of the child's development. The biological plan is wrecked when the intent of nature is met, not with appropriate content, but with the *intentions* of an anxiety-driven parent and culture. Interaction can only take place when content matches intent. Inappropriate content brings about reaction, not intellectual growth. Anxiety results when the child is forced into mismatched relating of intent and content. Interchange with the matrix and growth of personal power then breaks down, but the sequential unfolding of maturation goes right ahead. The child's ability to interact falls more and more behind and more and more energy must go into compensation. The young person's intelligence is still back there trying to make the first matrix functional. Finally, there is a breakdown in the mid-brain balance, which was designed to be smoothly synchronous.

When the capacity for abstract creativity and pure thought does not develop properly, the solution is not to try to force earlier and earlier abstract thinking, as we now try to do. Rather, we must provide for full-dimensional interaction with the living earth, without allowing abstract ideas to intercede or obscure, so that a sufficient concrete structure may be built from which abstractions *can* arise.

Our 3-billion-year heritage is truly magnificent; the promise given us is infinite in scope. But this biological plan must be nurtured, and in order to do so, we must first recognize that such a plan exists and then learn something of what that plan is about. We knew about this plan when we were around six years old and a great excitement, longing, and joyful anticipation filled us. Something else happened, of course; and even as it happened, we knew intuitively that it was all wrong. This primary knowing got covered up by anxiety conditioning, which was so deep and pervasive, so ingrained, and so continually reinforced and amplified on every hand that the deep knowing has been lost to us.

One of the more intriguing differences between the naturally delivered and nurtured child and the technologically delivered and abandoned child is in the matter of sleeping. Our newborns sleep massively, yet are easily awakened in which case they cry heavily. The reason is not hard to find. Lack of physical stimulus at birth has resulted in a failure of the reticular formation's completion. Then sensory information cannot be processed properly and sensory intake creates confusion and anxiety. The nurturings needed were also the means for reducing the high production of adrenal steroids. The combination of unrelieved birth stress and inability to assimilate and cope with sensory intake reinforce each other, they continue the flight-fight effect and adrenal overload, making the wake state intolerable.

Magical Child
Joseph Chilton Pearce.
Plume Books, 1981, 1992;
257 pp. ISBN 0-452-26789-7
$10.00 ($12.00 postpaid). Penguin USA/
Consumer Sales, 120 Woodbine Street,
Bergenfield, NJ 07621; 800/253-6476

Children: The Challenge

Rudolph Dreikurs encourages us to look at children respectfully, with understanding of their development and natural motivation. His gentle tone provides plenty of support for the parent in setting priorities, remaining consistent, and using praise as a reinforcement. Children are encouraged to be independent, and parents encouraged to replace the autocratic reward-and-punishment mentality with consistency and logical consequences for the child's behavior (and misbehavior).

Being reasonable with one's kids sometimes seems like the least achievable thing in the world; Dreikurs recognizes it for what it is — a challenge — and remains firm in your ability to meet it. —NAP

•
Never do for a child what he can do for himself. This rule is so important that it needs to be repeated many times.

•
Parental love is best demonstrated through constant encouragement toward independence. We need to start this at birth and to maintain it all through childhood. It is made manifest by our faith and confidence in the child as he is at each moment. It is an attitude which guides us through all the daily problems and situations of childhood. Our children need courage. Let us help them to develop and keep it.

•
Satisfaction comes from a sense of contribution and participation — a sense actually denied to our children in our present system of rewarding them with material things. In our mistaken efforts to win co-operation through rewards, we are actually denying our children the basic satisfactions of living.

•
The relationship between the parents sets the pattern for all the relationships within the family. If the parents are warm, friendly, and co-operative, the same relationship may possibly develop between children and parents and between the children themselves. Co-operation can become a family standard. If the parents are hostile and compete with each other for dominance, the same pattern usually develops among the children.

Children: The Challenge
Rudol Dreikurs. 1991; 335 pp.
ISBN 0-452-26655-6
$11 ($13 postpaid) from Penguin USA/
Consumer Sales, 120 Woodbine Street,
Bergenfield, NJ 07621; 800/253-6476

Parent Power

We all know kids who yell, "Jump!" and parents who answer, "How high?" It's easy for parents to find themselves in a situation where behavior is out of control. *Parent Power* offers strong support and advice for the overwhelmed parent. —NAP

•
Limits are organic. You reset them, just as you prune and cultivate a rose bush, redirecting them to fit the ever-changing situation of a living, growing being. Absolute rules are a shorthand that will net you nothing but absolute problems in the long run.

•
The most important point to remember is that, unless a child is brain-damaged or has some organic impairment, he or she will become toilet trained—that's a guarantee. The less fuss and emotion surrounding the topic, the better.

Parent Power
Bud Zukow. 1992; 235 pp.
ISBN 0-9626184-5-4
$12.95 ($14.95 postpaid) from The Bramble Company, PO Box 209, Norfolk, CT 06058;
203/542-5689

WHETHER YOU ARE FASTIDIOUS ABOUT YOUR OWN HEALTH or not, you will want only the best food and other resources for your baby's well-being. This can be a real wild-goose chase, with ever-proliferating concerns about food additives and environmental hazards. And then there's what to do when baby gets sick, as baby inevitably will. Here are the best resources we've found to help you care for your baby's temple of the spirit.

—Phil Catalfo

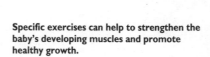

The Well Baby Book

This book is the best resource you can have, unless you're married to a pediatrician. It offers sound medical information, accurate illustrations, and patient explanations of what to do under different circumstances, including the all-important distinction between self-care and seeking trained help. Its gentle, encouraging tone may be its most important asset: the night my daughter had croup and coughed so much she couldn't catch her breath, I went from clammy panic to feeling like I could cope just by reading a couple of paragraphs. I've given away fifteen or twenty copies of this book since then; I can think of no better gift for new parents. —PC

•

Very moist air is usually of great help to a child having a croup attack. Moist air relieves the swelling in the larynx and opens up the airway. The child will begin to breathe more easily almost immediately. Children often become upset by the fact that they cannot stop coughing. Parents should encourage the child to be calm (and be calm themselves) because this will help to break the cycle of coughing. The child should be told to breathe slowly and evenly. Many children relax when they are told that moist air will stop the coughing and make the breathing easier. If there is any question of difficulty breathing, call the doctor.

Moist air can be generated quickly by running a cool mist vaporizor or humidifier in a small room, close to the child; by running a hot shower; or by running a sinkful of hot water and holding the child over it. If hot water is run in the sink, a towel or a piece of plastic can be used to create a makeshift

The Well Baby Book
Mike Samuels & Nancy Samuels. Summit Books, 1991; 402 pp. ISBN 0-671-73412-1 $16.95 ($19.95 postpaid) from Simon & Schuster/Order Dept., 200 Old Tappan Road, Old Tappan, NJ 07675; 800/223-2336

tent over the child's head. Children should *never* be held near boiling water. The chance of accidents, and their severity when they occur, is just too great. Even hot water vaporizers are no longer recommended because the steam itself can scald a child who gets too close.

The vaporizer should be allowed to run all night, even after the child is again breathing easily. In general the moisture will keep the child from having another episode. But parents should sleep where they are readily able to hear if the child coughs again or calls out. Real croup is sufficiently frightening to the parents, as well as the child, that they will want to sleep near this child, particularly if it is very young. Even older children become frightened at the difficulty they had breathing and they may want company and reassurance even after the coughing has stopped.

The vaporizer should be run in the child's room for the next several nights, and even during the day to keep the moisture content of the air high. The child should be encouraged to drink large amounts of clear, room-temperature liquids (not cold fluids or milk or orange juice) in order to liquefy the mucus and reduce the swelling of the larynx. On succeeding nights parents should check on the child to make sure the cough is loose and rattly — not tight or barklike.

OTHER GREAT RESOURCES

Healthy Homes, Healthy Kids: Joyce M. Schoemaker & Charity Y. Vitale. 1991, Island Press. Very good discussions of household environmental health issues such as lead paint, radon, pesticides, EMFs.

The Get-Well-Quick Kit: Linda Allison & Tom Ferguson, M.D. 1993, Addison-Wesley Publishing Co.

Child of Mine

This book first appeared when one of our kids was an infant, and my nutrition-conscious wife immediately latched onto it as though it were the keys to the kingdom. Which it is, in a sense: a straightforward, info-packed guide to the sometimes perplexing task of providing good nutrition to babies and children, as well as pregnant and lactating moms. For the early going, there is knowledgeable discussion of breastfeeding, introducing solid foods, caloric intake and normal growth; for later on, astute observations on eating psychology and "the feeding relationship," eating disorders, diarrhea and obesity. The author is a dietitian, a family therapist, and a mom, so she's been there and back. There may be other guides as good, but I can't imagine one better. —PC

•

Milk and Milk Products. Many women find their dislike or intolerance of milk changes during pregnancy, so give yourself a chance to like it, even if you haven't before. It is virtually impossible to get enough calcium and vitamin D from food unless you include

Child of Mine
Ellyn Satter. 1991; 463 pp. ISBN 0-923521-14-3 $14.95 ($17.95 postpaid) from Bull Publishing Co., PO Box 208, Palo Alto, CA 94302-0208; 800/676-2855

milk and dairy products. If you can't drink milk, you will probably have to take a calcium supplement. Depending on what form of calcium you use, to get the 1200 mg calcium per day you need, you will probably have to take six to twelve cal-cium pills.

Substitutes for Milk Calcium.

1 cup of milk =

1 cup buttermilk or skim milk

1 cup yogurt

1 $\frac{1}{2}$ ounces cheddar-type cheese

1 cup custard or milk pudding

1 $\frac{1}{2}$ cups ice cream

1 $\frac{1}{2}$ cups cottage cheese

$\frac{1}{4}$ cheese pizza (14 inch)

Family Guide to Natural Medicine

Reader's Digest lined up some high-octane consultants like Andrew Weil, M.D. , and homeopathy educator Dana Ullman, expanded their focus to include arcane disciplines like Ayurveda, Bach flower remedies and iridology, and produced a book that is informative and handsome. The book does not go very deeply into any one particular subject (although there is a surprisingly good section on herbal remedies, including full-color photos and illustrations of the plants), but it does provide as wide-ranging a view as you could hope to find between the covers of one book. As such, it's an outstanding introduction to a non-mechanistic health model, strong on fitness, relaxation and self-care, and an excellent tool for maintaining the health of the whole family. —PC

In China regular exercise starts early. This child is learning t'ai chi. Because the exercises are performed slowly and rhythmically, t'ai chi is suitable for people of all ages.

•

Aside from getting adequate amounts of rest and eating properly, are there active steps we can take to keep our immune systems functioning at peak efficiency? One premise of natural medicine is that we can bolster our immune systems and generally enhance our health by making a few simple changes. For instance, regular exercise

Family Guide to Natural Medicine
Alma Guiness, Editor. Reader's Digest Association, 1993; 416 pp. ISBN 0-89577-433-X $30 ($32 postpaid) from Random House/ Order Dept., 400 Hahn Road, Westminster, MD 21157; 800/733-3000

strengthens immune function, while also lowering the risk of coronary heart disease, diabetes, hypertension, osteoporosis, and obesity. In addition, there is a growing body of evidence indicating that certain foods may help our bodies fend off diseases.

People are finally recognizing that stress can take a tremendous toll on the body, leaving us prey to a range of health problems. According to practitioners of natural medicine, the effects of stress — which can include everything from migraines to heart disease — illustrate the role of the mind in health. So, too, the mind can play a role in healing. Meditation, breathing exercises, and other relaxation techniques offer natural ways of coping with stress, inexpensively and without side effects. In fact, orthodox medicine is beginning to embrace some of these techniques. And well it should, for it has been estimated that up to two-thirds of all office visits are for stress or anxiety related ailments.

Specific exercises can help to strengthen the baby's developing muscles and promote healthy growth.

The Way We Never Were • Here to Stay

The most pernicious aspect of the modern myth of the American family is that we wind up comparing ourselves to a model of family-ness that probably never existed. It's likely that families were always social groupings where great stress and strain, and even harmful behavior, were experienced. Earning a living is hard. Raising kids is hard. Making a life is hard. Sometimes we act crazy. Whose idea was it that we should all be compliant little drones, anyway?

The Way We Never Were points out that the family of yesteryear was not nearly so idyllic as we think it was, especially compared to us: alcoholism and drug abuse were more prevalent in the previous century, and pioneer-era marriages lasted less time than do today's. Here to Stay does the converse, showing that today's family is not quite so woebegone as we may think.

Both books give a renewed sense that, whatever the real nature of the challenges facing families today, we can face them. The virtues of family are, if anything, greater than ever. This pair of books can help families get a better sense of what the journey entails.
—PC

●

Our image of the self-reliant pioneer family has been bequeathed to us by the *Little House on the Prairie* books and television series, which almost every American has read or seen. What is less well known is that these stories, based on the memoirs of Laura Ingalls Wilder, were extensively revised by her daughter as an ideological attack on government programs. When Wilder's daughter, Rose Wilder Lane, failed to establish a secure income as a freelance writer in the 1930s, she returned to her family home in the Ozarks. Here, historian Linda Kerber reports, "Lane announced that she would no longer write so that she would not have to pay taxes to a New Deal government." However, "she *rewrote* the rough drafts of her mother's memoirs,... turning them into the *Little House* books in which the isolated family is pitted against the elements and makes it — or doesn't — with no help from the community."

In reality, prairie farmers and other pioneer families owed their existence to massive federal land grants, government-funded military mobilizations that dispossessed hundreds of Native American societies and confiscated half of Mexico, and state-sponsored economic investment in the new lands. Even "volunteers" expected federal pay: Much of the West's historic "antigovernment" sentiment originated in discontent when settlers did not get such pay or were refused government aid for unauthorized raids on Native American territory. It would be hard to find a Western family today or at any time in the past whose land rights, transportation options, economic existence, and even access to water were not dependent on federal funds. "Territorial experience got Westerners in the habit of federal subsidies," remarks Western historian Patricia Nelson Limerick, "and the habit persisted long after other elements of the Old West had vanished."
—The Way We Never Were

The Way We Never Were
(American Families and the Nostalgia Trap) Stephanie Coontz. Basic Books, 1992; 391 pp. ISBN 0-465-09097-4 $14 ($16.75 postpaid) from HarperCollins Publishers/Direct Mail, PO Box 588, Dunmore, PA 18512; 800/331-3761

Here to Stay
Mary Jo Bane. 1978, Basic Books.

●

In summary, demographic materials suggest that the decline of the family's role in caring for children is more myth than fact. None of the statistical data suggests that parental watchfulness over children has decreased over the span of three generations; much suggests that it has increased. The most important difference between today's children and children of their great grandparents' and grandparents' time is that there are proportionately fewer of them per family. Like children born during the 1930s, but unlike children born during the 1950s, children of the 1970s face a predominantly adult world. If the rate of population growth continues to stabilize, the society of the next decades will be older and the families smaller than in any previously found in America.

Parent-child bonds also persist despite changes in patterns of disruption and living arrangements after disruption. The proportion of children who lose a parent by death has gone steadily down over the generations. The proportion who live with a parent after a death or divorce has gone steadily up. Even in recent years when family disruptions have begun to rise again to high levels, almost no children have gone to relatives, foster homes or institutions.

The trend toward more mothers in the paid labor force has probably not materially affected parent-child bonds. Even though more mothers work outside the home and more children go to school earlier and longer, the quantity and quality of actual mother-child interaction has probably not changed much. In short, the major demographic changes affecting parents and children in the course of the century have not much altered the basic picture of children living with and being cared for by their parents. The patterns of structural change so often cited as evidence of family decline do not seem to be weakening the bonds between parents and children. *—Here to Stay*

Liberated Parents, Liberated Children • How to Talk So Kids Will Listen

When you're correcting your child's behavior, what are you communicating? The answer, in more than a few cases, may surprise or even alarm you. These two insightful books can give you the skills to communicate effectively and clearly with your children. —NAP

●

All feelings are permitted, actions are limited. We must not deny a child's perceptions. Only after a child feels right, can he think right. Only after a child feels right, can he do right.

●

Another technique that made a difference in the tenor of the household was the ability to turn a threat into a choice: "If you use that water gun in the living room once more, you'll be sorry!" now became, "The water gun is not to be used in the living room. You may play with it in the bathroom or out of doors. You decide."
-Liberated Parents

Liberated Parents, Liberated Children
(Your guide to a Happier Family) Adele Faber. 1990; 255 pp. ISBN 0-380-71134-6

How to Talk So Kids Will Listen
(And Listen So Kids Will Talk) Adele Faber & Elaine Mazlish. 1980; 242 pp. ISBN 0-380-57000-9 Each $10 ($11.50 postpaid) from Avon Books, PO Box 767, Dresden, TN 38225; 800/223-0690

LET CHILDREN MAKE CHOICES.

Are you in the mood for your grey pants or your red pants?

Would you like half a glass of juice or a whole?

We're leaving in five minutes. Do you want to go on the slide one more time or on the swing?

What would work best for you? Doing your practice before dinner or after?

These are all choices that give a child valuable practice in making decisions. It must be very hard to be an adult who is forced to make decisions about career, lifestyle, mate without having had a good deal of experience in exercising your own judgment.

Siblings Without Rivalry

I nominate fighting with a sib as the situation that drives me most crazy and makes me most on the alert for helpful books. This is the one I can praise without reservation for two reasons: it will show you, in an easy-to-understand manner, where you're going wrong in your interactions with your kids. It uses a cartoon format that juxtaposes unproductive behavior with behavior that gets results. Bingo! The point is clear. The quality of the advice is pretty dam good, too. I can't say that I apply the principles all the time, or that my kids have stopped bickering, but we've made a reasonable amount of headway toward pax familia. —NP

Siblings Without Rivalry
Adele Faber & Elaine Mazlish. 1988; 219 pp. ISBN 0-380-70527-3 $10 ($11.50 postpaid) from Avon Books, PO Box 767, Dresden, TN 38225; 800/ 223-0690

OTHER GREAT RESOURCES

Good Behavior: Stephen W. Garber, Marianne Daniels Garber & Robyn Freedman Spizman. 1987, St. Martin's Press. If you're going to a desert island with your kid and can take only one advice book, this is the one: a concise and comprehensive troubleshooting guide, offering constructive, sensible and humane approaches to behavior, from nosepicking to nosebleeding. —NAP

Don't Shoot the Dog! (How to Improve Yourself and Others Through Behavioral Training): Karen Pryor. 1985, Bantam Books. We all strive to modify the behavior of everyone around us, usually with monumental ineptitude. Learning to do it well is a service to all. —SB

Gently Lead

The author herself gently leads the reader into the never-finished process of apprehending the ineffable; the book's gift is in helping you not only to become comfortable with, but actually to embrace the Mystery. The format is as varied as the path itself — poems, meditations, essays, anecdotes — which suggests that one should not be attached to form, but engaged with heart.

Berends has worked out some of the big questions for herself, but she doesn't force them down your throat; her main mission is simply to invite you to enter deeply into an openness that makes finding things out more possible. Her faith, not just in the Divine but in the likelihood that a useful truth will reveal itself to you, is most reassuring. I can't recommend this book too highly. —PC

•

It is a little known fact that the real business of parenthood is the upbringing of the parent. Children will value what we value and rely on what we rely on. So beware. Be aware. Don't look for much technique in these pages. This is not a method. It is a catalog of surprising moments intended only to demonstrate the possibilities of God-reliant parenthood, in which it is seen that God is the parent, and both parent and child are God's children.

The little we teach our children about God is almost a side issue. In a way the less said about God, the better. And then it must not be religious, or the children will find God irrelevant. It must not be preachy, or the children will find God trivial. It must not me "should-ful" or they will resist, rebel, and reject. Let God be God's idea, occuring spontaneously and responsively to you and your children together.

Gently Lead
Polly Berends.
HarperPerennial,
1991, 192 pp.
ISBN 0-06-092266-4
$10 ($12.75 postpaid)
from HarperCollins
Publishers/Direct
Mail, PO Box 588,
Dunmore, PA 18512;
800/331-3761

UNLESS YOUR FAMILY is already firmly established in a spiritual tradition or practice, this is a tricky one, especially for boomer parents. You may have spent decades sorting out your own metaphysics, but what are you going to provide for your kids as they start sorting it out? Many parents find this one of the most elusive tasks facing them. Here are the best resources we've found in the ongoing effort to plot our family's spiritual coordinates. —PC

Something More

Like Polly Berends, the author knows that to nurture your child's sense of spirituality, you first have to cultivate it in yourself; her book is an excellent compendium of observations and exercises for doing so. Lyrically and with real heart, Jean Fitzpatrick nails all the details. Her narrative's probing questions give focus the parent-reader's philosophical inventory-taking. This articulation of significant experiences and deeply held beliefs will form the basis of any program of "spiritual nurture" you might provide your family. Fitzpatrick also provides a topnotch resource list of books, videotapes and audio recordings. First-rate.

Generation To Generation, a network founded by Fitzpatrick to help parents "share their thoughts, experiences, and challenges," publishes a newsletter and provides access to the workshops she holds at churches, synagogues and schools around the country. —PC

•

By adolescence, the child will enter what Fowler calls the "synthetic-conventional" stage of faith and base her worldview on what she knows from personal relationships. Now she understands beliefs and values as being part of what "kind of person" one is, and mirrors the spirituality she sees around her. The danger of this stage is twofold: Her "spirituality" may be a reflection of values (those of the drug culture, consumerism, satanic cults, etc.) that will ultimately fail to sustain her. Or, if she is part of an institutional church, at some point (usually after a personal disappointment) she may decide that she is no longer "part of the group" and will discard her spirituality altogether.

Most people remain at this conventional stage, according to Fowler, for a lifetime; we affiliate with a particular religion or group because that's what "people like us" are supposed to do. If we are to help our child grow beyond conventional thinking and *own* her spirituality, we need to offer her the critical tools to begin to do so. We will need to be sure, in a youth group setting or among peers, that she has access to adults who are willing really to listen as she shares her own experiences and relects on how she has come to them. In a nonjudgmental way, they can help her connect her own life with the stories and visions of generations past. Only then will her spirituality continue to deepen.

Something More
(Nurturing Your Child's Spiritual Growth)
Jean Fitzpatrick. Penguin Books, 1992; 236 pp.
ISBN 0-14-016951-2
$11 ($13 postpaid) from Penguin USA/ Consumer Sales, 120 Woodbine Street, Bergenfield, NJ 07621; 800/253-6476

Do Children Need Religion?

The author essentially answers her own question: "No." I think she may be missing something (not that I've got it all worked out), but her consideration of the question is very useful for parents who consider themselves ex-somethings — people who want to give their children a moral upbringing to their children outside of a specifically religious framework. It's well-written and provocative, and her discussions of identity, culture and tradition are especially insightful. This book is especially valuable for those who are consitutionally skittish around religion, yet engaged with moral-spiritual-philosophical issues as individuals and parents. —PC

•

Whether our children will prove any better or worse than their parents or previous generations trailing backward into history is probably a matter beyond demonstrating. But I think an argument can be made that their understanding of good and bad will be different from ours, in ways subtle and profound. Our moral obligations as children were by definition minor and personal: we were told we had responsibility for our own souls — for not lying, cheating, stealing toys from the five-and-dime. We have told our children that their moral burden is the world itself: to insure peace, to guarantee justice, to free the oppressed and redeem the bleeding earth. We should not be surprised if their moral imaginations assume a global and apocalyptic cast.

Do Children Need Religion?
Martha Fay. Pantheon Books, 1993; 237 pp.
ISBN 0-679-42054-1
$23 ($25 postpaid) from Random House/ Order Dept., 400 Hahn Road, Westminster, MD 21157; 800/733-3000

OTHER GREAT RESOURCES

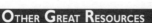

What is God?: Etan Boritzer. 1990, Firefly Books Ltd.

Kid-friendly, playfully illustrated, ecumenical and finally, warmly mystical. Good for reading to/ with kids five to ten.

Starbright (Meditations for Children): Maureen Garth. 1991, HarperSanFrancisco.

Moonbeam: Maureen Garth. 1993, HarperSanFrancisco.

With Garth's soft-touch visualization exercises, you can tuck your child's mind and soul in for the night, surrounded by images of resplendent gardens, fluffy clouds and guardian angels. Great for helping kids three to eight feel safe and start a restful sleep.

Meditation for Children : Deborah Rozman. 1989, Planetary Publications.

How to teach concentration, relaxation, meditation and yoga to children, from the "very young — prenatal to five years" up to age fifteen. A classic of its kind; the *only* book of its kind.

See "Spirituality." pp. 32–33.

Talking to Your Child About God

A very direct, straight-to-the-point, yet also thoughtful step-by-step plan for broaching the subject of God and religion. David Heller, a Boston-based psychologist, has spent a lot of time with schoolchildren, encouraging them to write letters to and draw pictures of God, so he has a firm understanding of how they come to the subject. What I like best about his approach is that it makes tolerance and respect of others' (including your kids'!) beliefs paramount. Not for the dogma-afflicted. —PC

•

Some parents do not want to express their own beliefs to their children. Often, their own parents were dogmatic and domineering, and they do not want to repeat such a pattern. Afraid to impose religious imagery on their children, they also miss out on exchanging ideas with their youngsters, and their parent-child relationship suffers as a consequence.

Other parents inundate their youngsters with religious ideas and don't allow their children to think and speak for themselves. They feel they must protect their child from incorrect or immoral ideas by teaching a set way of living. Don't be overly shy or unduly dogmatic with your child. Try to strike a balance between revealing your own beliefs and eliciting your child's ideas. If you can accomplish that, your child will learn to appreciate and respect your views as well as his or her own.

Talking to Your Child About God
(A Book for Families of All Faiths): David Heller. 1990, Bantam Books, Out of Print.

IF YOU DON'T BUY THAT STORIES ARE powerful, try making up a few, especially if you're trying to deliver some industrial-strength moral lesson. Your kids's eyes will go from glazed-over to rapt. Ask me how I know. —PC

Barefoot Books • Little Barefoot Books

There are thousands of wonderful storybooks for kids, but this new line bears special mention. Shambhala Publishers have packaged a number of immortal tales, some ancient and some from the last couple of centuries, in accessible editions that will help hook children on good stories for life.

The large-format Barefoot Books are richly (though not profusely) illustrated ancient myths from other cultures (Persia, Greece, Egypt). The pocket-sized Little Barefoot Books present modern tales in a form that begs to be taken along anywhere a child goes, for those gift moments in school or beneath a shade tree or high on a windswept hill or in the back seat of a car when losing yourself in a story means freedom. These people deserve some sort of congressional medal or something. —PC

—The Birds Who Flew Beyond Time

Barefoot Books
$15-$16 each.

Little Barefoot Books
$6 each. Both from Shambhala Publications/
Order Dept., PO Box 308, Boston, MA
02117-0308; 617/424-0228

The New Read-Aloud Handbook • Hey! Listen to This

Jim Trelease is probably the best-known storytelling evangelist in the country. His bestselling Handbook, revised several times since it first appeared in 1979, is a compelling rationale for storytelling, a step-by-step guide, a forceful critique of the social elements that erode the oral tradition (can you say "television"?), a paean to books and libraries, and a copious listing of great read-aloud books.

Hey! Listen to This goes one step fur-

ther, collecting nearly fifty terrific stories, some well-known and others not, each with brief but informed comments by Trelease. —PC

DOs

• Begin reading to children as soon as possible. The younger you start them, the better.

• Try to set aside at least one traditional time each day for a story. In my home, favorite story times are before going to bed and before leaving for school.

• Follow through with your reading. If you start a book, it is your responsibility to continue it — unless it turns out to be a bad book. Don't leave the child or class hanging for three or four days between chapters and expect their interest to be sustained.

• Occasionally read above the children's intellectual level and challenge their minds.

DON'Ts

• Don't read stories that you don't enjoy yourself. Your dislike will show in the reading, and that defeats your purpose.

• Don't continue reading a book once it is obvious that it was a poor choice. Admit the mistake and choose another. Make sure, however, that you've given the book a fair chance to get rolling; some start slower than others. (You can avoid the problem by prereading the book yourself.)

• Consider the intellectual, social and emotional level of your audience in making a read-aloud selection. Challenge them, but don't overwhelm them.

• Don't read above a child's emotional level.

• Don't be unnerved by questions during the reading, particularly from very young children. Answer their questions patiently. Don't put them off. Don't rush your answers. There is no time limit for reading a book but there is a time limit on a child's inquisitiveness. Foster that curiosity with patient answers — then resume your reading.

• Don't impose interpretations of a story upon your audience. A story can be just

Keeping Family Stories Alive

I'm in my forties, and still learning family history from my Sicilian-born grandmother. I haven't done a very comprehensive job of passing it on to my kids, but when I do tell them a story from my youth or my family's past, they eat it up. If you're the hopeful archivist of your family's lore, this book will nourish your ability to handle every aspect of the task — preparing for interviews (tips for both asker and askee), recording them (both audio and video), preserving the tapes. A most unusual, and unusually helpful, book. —PC

Keeping Family Stories Alive
Vera Rosenbluth. 1990; 175 pp.
ISBN 0-88179-026-5
$11.95 postpaid from Hartley & Marks, Inc.,
P.O. Box 147, Point Roberts, WA 98281;
206/945-2017

Awakening the Hidden Storyteller

Robin Moore is a professional storyteller: his writing, whether it's philosophical, didactic, or recounting a story, is informed by a sensibility that conveys the enchantment of full immersion in a story.

Moore provides tips on the performance side of storytelling — character voices, gestures, body language, eye contact. Where Jim Trelease is an authoritative, effective advocate, Moore is an artist, and one who can explicate his craft very ably. Each serves the same good cause well. —PC

•
VOYAGE I <u>Lighting</u> <u>the</u> <u>Flame</u>
TIME: 10 minutes
GOAL: To create a special spot in the house where the family can settle in and slip the bonds of ordinary, everyday reality; to use a candle flame as a physical and emotional centerpiece.
PREPARATION: Prepare the room and have on hand a candle, matches, and a wristwatch.

plain enjoyable, no reason necessary. But encourage conversation about the reading. Only seven minutes out of 150 instructional minutes in the school day are spent on discussions between teacher and student.

• Don't use the book as a threat — "If you don't pick up your room, no story tonight!" As soon as your child or class sees that you've turned the book into a weapon, they'll change their attitude about books from positive to negative. —The New Read-Aloud Handbook

The New Read-Aloud Handbook
Jim Trelease. 1989; 290 pp.
ISBN 0-014-046881-1
$11 ($13 postpaid) from Penguin USA/Consumer Sales, 120 Woodbine Street, Bergenfield, NJ 07621; 800/253-6476

Hey! Listen to This
Jim Trelease. 1992; 414 pp.
ISBN 0-14-014653-9
$11 ($13 postpaid) from Penguin USA/Consumer Sales, 120 Woodbine Street, Bergenfield, NJ 07621; 800/253-6476

Awakening the Hidden Storyteller
Robin Moore. 1991; 153 pp.
ISBN 0-87773-599-9
$18 ($21 postpaid) from Shambhala Publications/Order Dept., PO Box 308, Boston, MA 02117-0308; 617/424-0228

INSTRUCTIONS:
• The leader lights the candle and notes the time.
• The leader says, "Let's sit quietly and enjoy the light of our candle."
• During the ten-minute period you need not be absolutely silent, but do not talk the whole time either. Allow the family to settle into the silence and the candlelight.
• When exactly ten minutes have passed, turn on the lights. Leave the candle burning, though.
• The leader asks, "How long do you think it has been since we lit the candle?"
• Family members give their estimates.
• The leader says, "It was ten minutes."
• "The voyage is now complete."

OTHER GREAT RESOURCES

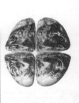

Annie Stories: A Special Kind of Storytelling. Doris Brett. Workman, 1988. Storytelling with a pragmatic purpose: assuaging fears, working through difficulties, dealing with pain, nightmares, trips to the hospital, and other tight straits of life.

Creation Stories: (IBM-compatible CD-ROM) Warner New Media, 1992. Nearly sixty creation myths from around the world. The visuals are static but quite arresting; the readings are nicely done; what is most impressive is the eclecticism of the collection.

NYONE WHO THINKS YOU have to "teach" kids to be creative obviously hasn't spent much time around kids. On the other hand, having good tools and ideas at your disposal can enable you to help your kids' creativity unfold. —Phil Catalfo

PS: Current statutes permit the use of these resources to enhance adult creativity, too.

The Creative Journal for Children • Kids Have All the Write Stuff

The best educators are not the ones who pack the most stuff into pupils' heads, but the ones who most readily stimulate in students their inborn ability to learn and to express what they know. These authors are all veteran educators, and their books are replete with techniques for catalyzing the process that has children broadcasting their ideas, feelings, dreams, fantasies, fears, visions, and incipient screenplays to an unsuspecting world.

The Creative Journal for Children, which has a bit more of a depth-psychology esthetic, covers writing and drawing and contains six dozen exercises that will provide your child with a detailed map of her creative self. *Kids Have All the Write Stuff*, which focuses on writing, contains an abundance of background discussion and advice for parents: understanding writing, enjoying writing, imagination; "whole-language learning;" and even what to do when Johnny writes on the wall. Both books are first-rate. —PC

•
Show and Tell: My Own Cartoon

HOW: Suggest that the child create his own comic strip by inventing characters, a setting, and a story and drawing the story in a series of "frames" with balloons and captions. The first time it can be done with a few frames. Later on the child can create longer stories and do them in ten or more frames.

WHY: This exercise helps children learn to visualize as they tell a story. It develops their sensitivity to dramatic development, story or plot building, and characterization.

WHEN: This exercise can be done regularly. It can be combined with any exercise in which a story is being told and is especially appropriate for young children who can't write very well or at all.
—*Creative Journal*

•
Independent, self-sustaining writers have participation and guidance from parents and other adults who regularly do some or all of the following activities:

• read aloud and write along with the kids;
• make materials readily available and accessible;
• praise a youngster's efforts at oral and written communication;
• display writing in the home or workplace;
• talk about and point out print;
• listen to a child's oral stories;
• answer questions about language;
• take dictation;
• send writing to relatives and friends;
• read to others what the child has written;
• establish regular family writing times during the day or week; and
• brainstorm and discuss possible topics and stories. —*Kids*

Kids Have All the Write Stuff
Sharon A. Edwards & Robert W. Maloy.
Penguin Books, 1992; 224 pp.
ISBN 0-14-015972-X
$10 ($12 postpaid) from Penguin USA/
Consumer Sales, 120 Woodbine Street,
Bergenfield, NJ 07621; 800/253-6476

The Creative Journal for Children
Lucia Capacchione. 1989;
144 pp. ISBN 0-87773-497-6
$17 ($20 postpaid) from Shambhala
Publications/Order Dept., PO Box 308,
Boston, MA 02117-0308; 617/424-0228

"This is a monster with 4 heads and 4 feet and 8 arms. The monster grabbed a little boy. Another little boy is waiting. I don't want to talk to this monster. He smells too much!!!"

The Listening Book

While we're on the subject, you could probably use some artistic calisthenics yourself. Here's a good place to start, especially if your creativity wants to find expression in music (but even if it doesn't). W. A. Mathieu is a pianist, composer and, let's say, musical yogi, who offers one- to two-page meditations on music, sound, and, especially, listening. "I do not seek, I find," said Picasso; Mathieu knows what he meant. Read this book and you'll be "finding" music like crazy. Be grateful if your kids don't say, "Took ya long enough!" —PC

•
I am nineteen, at a Bud Powell concert sponsored by my college jazz club. Bud Powell's plane is late, but his great bassist, Percy Heath, has arrived. The president of the club asks me if I would play the piano for a while, accompanied by Mr. Heath,

who is all accommodation. Clenching clammy hands I say yes. In public, right then and there, Percy Heath takes me on. His deep certainty becomes part of my own music. I'm riding a wave that comes from the center of the earth. Energies are compounded. My desire and his ability: resonance.

I am twenty-five, the pianist at The Second City Theater in Chicago, forming the habit of practicing every night after hours. During many months of this I learn to recognize the rush of creativity and world love that comes on around 2 A.M. Night resonance.

I am thirty-three, with lots of music behind me. A North Indian flutist teaches me how to sing a single note in tune, and the fundamental nature of this act occurs to me for the first time. I think, "Wow," and go home to try it by myself. In the privacy of my room I see how many years I've been sleeping. Learning to sing in tune is the first pink in the sky after a restless night of dreams.

•
Dance music wants to have a wedding with your body. Mystery music wants to scare you out of your mind. There is music to watch a play by, music to be romanced by, dinner music, theme music, advertising music, patriotic music, music to get lost in space by, music to fill-in-the-blank by. Pretty far down the list for most people is music to listen to.

Nothing is wrong with stories or movies or dancing or daydreaming or thinking. They all mix in their enjoyable ways with music. But none of them is the same as listening to music. If you have yet to listen to music without one of the above, a fine new experience is ahead of you.

There is a funny story going around about New Age music. A diner in a restaurant says to the waiter, "The needle is stuck on that record you're playing." The waiter replies, "No, it isn't stuck, it's New Age. It only *sounds* repetitive to the unsophis-

Kids Make Music • The Kids' Multicultural Art Book

I figure the folks at Williamson Publishing got some pixie dust stuck in their ears a long time ago, and can't stop putting out these ultrapluscool books stimulating kid artistry. Either that, or kids have taken over the company. Anyway, their books are tops. Kids Make Music has the goldurndest collection of homemade instruments, historical factoids, and you-can-play-too tricks. It also includes tips on dancing, singing, cheek popping, face drumming, and having a thematic musical party. The Kids' Multicultural Art Book shows kids how to replicate artifacts of indigenous peoples from around the world: Native American, Mexican and Central American, African, Asian. Included are a Chippewa Dream Catcher, a Japanese folding screen, Egyptian paper beads, an Aztec Sun God, and more. While kids' intrinsic yen to make stuff is being gratified, they're learning something about native culture and lore from faraway places — a Good Thing. Especially since it subtly teaches that making art is a fundamentally human act, and has been, all over the world, since the beginning. High marks. —PC

PS. : Ask for Williamson's catalog.

Bungee bass: This one could fool a professional musician — that's how good it sounds. To make it, you need one cardboard carton, open at the top, and an elastic cable or bungee. Hook the bungee on opposite sides of the carton. To play, hold the bungee up and pluck.

HOLD UP AND PLAY

ticated ear that doesn't know how to listen to it . . ."

The truth is, most of us have to learn specifically the single, pure act of listening to music. Sometimes music does come to you by itself, unexpectedly surrounding you. Startled, you wake up in a beautiful new house of sound. But for the most part, learning to listen to music takes time and patience, like training a small muscle. That is what musicians do to learn their trade — they practice listening, with ever-deepening concentration and perception.

Kids Make Music
Avery Hart & Paul Mantell.
1993; ISBN 0-913589-69-1

The Kids' Multicultural Art Book
Alexandra Terzian. 1993; 158 pp.
ISBN 0-913589-72-1

Each $12.95 ($15.95 postpaid) from
Williamson Publishing Co., PO Box 185,
Church Hill Road, Charlotte, VT 05445;
800/234-8791

5 Cut out the mask around the outer
edge. If the cut edges open, glue
them again.

6 Use the rounded end of a small
paintbrush to imprint, or mark,
designs on the foil mask as shown.
Be creative!

7 Punch a hole at the top of the mask
to hang on a wall.

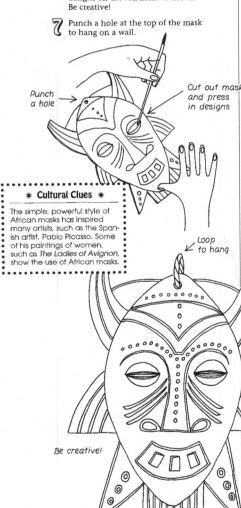

Punch
a hole

Cut out mask
and press
in designs

Loop
to hang

Be creative!

The Listening Book
W. A. Mathieu. 1991; 179 pp.
ISBN 0-87773-610-3
$13 ($16 postpaid) from Shambhala
Publications/Order Dept., PO Box 308,
Boston, MA 02117-0308; 617/424-0228

Brain: The greatest
synthesizer of them all!
Your brain works with the
rest of you to bring out the
tunes, beats, words, and
movements inside you.

Eyes: Imagine; pick up cues

Ears: Pick up sounds to play
along with

Mouth, lips, and tongue:
Sing, click, whistle, squeak,
and whoop

Voice box: Vibrates the
sound you hum or sing

Fingers: Snap and pop and
thumb

Wrist: Pulse point

Arms: Wave or sway to
the beat

Neck: Pulse point

Hands: Clap, slap, rap,
and jive

Lungs: Give power to your
sound

Heart: Best beat keeper in
the world; place where your
feelings live

Swiveling hips: Shake,
rattle, and roll; add "oomph"
to your music

Thighs: Clap like a big
bass fiddle

Legs: Dance and leap

Knees: Knockers

Feet: Stomp, pound, and
drum; happy feet for dancing

Toes: Tap out a beat

*It's amazing, but true! The
ultimate music-making
machine is you!*

—Kids Make Music

WHEN David Grisman and Jerry Garcia named their
1993 collaboration *Not For Kids Only*, they inadvertently described a whole musical genre: discs
that, although recorded with children in mind,
offer age-neutral appeal. Some artists working
this field seek a middle ground between child and adult listeners; others aim
songs primarily at kids but wrap them in sufficient musicianship to engage adult
ears and toes. Both approaches yield family-wide listening pleasure.
—Alan Reder

Not for Kids Only
*Southeastern American folk tunes make
up the bulk of this Jerry Garcia/David
Grisman collaboration. Many parents as
well as children may want to conclude
their evenings with the stately
"Shenandoah's Lullaby."*

Not for Kids Only: Jerry Garcia & David
Grisman. CD $15 ($18 postpaid); cassette
$10 ($13 postpaid). Acoustic Disc, PO
Box 4143, San Rafael, CA 94913; 800/
221-3472.

Little Dreamer
*Sweet dreams from Prudence Johnson,
whose voice you may recognize from
"A Prairie Home Companion."*

Little Dreamer: Prudence Johnson.
CD $15 ($17.50 postpaid); cassette $10
($12.50 postpaid). Red House Records,
PO Box 4044, St. Paul, MN 55104;
800/695-4687.

Shake Sugaree
*Rock-blues artist Taj Mahal talks
about and sings black roots music in the
American, African, and Caribbean traditions. A sometimes awkward production,
but musically, pure Taj.*

Shake Sugaree: Taj Mahal. CD $12.98
($16.73 postpaid); cassette $10 ($13.75
postpaid). Music for Little People, PO Box
1460, Redway, CA 95560; 800/727-2233.

Bathtub Blues
*Iowa folkie and "Prairie Home Compan-
ion" veteran Greg Brown reaches across
the age gap with all his funky, homespun
humor and insight intact.*

Bathtub Blues: Greg Brown. CD $15
($17.50 postpaid); cassette $10 ($12.50
postpaid). Red House Records, PO Box
4044, St. Paul, MN 55104; 800/695-4687.

Kid Rock • Fun Rock
*Childish old hits such as the Jackson 5's
"ABC," Traffic's "You Can All Join In," Ray
Stevens' "Ahab the Arab," and the Holly-
wood Argyles' "Alley Oop," compiled for
kid consumption.*

Kid Rock: Kid Rhino. CD $11.99 ($14.99
postpaid); cassette $7.99 ($10.99 postpaid).

Fun Rock: Kid Rhino. CD $11.99 ($14.99
postpaid); cassette $7.99 ($10.99 postpaid).

Rhino Records, 7930 Alabama Avenue,
Canoga Park, CA 91304; 800/432-0020.

Fiesta Musical
*A bilingual tour through Latin Amer-
ica and its music, narrated by Sesame
Street's Luis (Emilio Delgado) and performed by such first-rate players as Sukay.*

Fiesta Musical: Emilio Delgado, Narrator.
Cassette $9.98 ($13.73 postpaid); book &
cassette $10.98 ($14.73 postpaid); book
only $5 ($8.75 postpaid). Music for Little
People, PO Box 1460, Redway, CA 95560;
800/727-2233.

All for Freedom
*Another excursion through African-Ameri-
can musical roots, led by the vocal ensemble Sweet Honey in the Rock, with
background vocals by an elementary-
school chorus.*

All for Freedom: Sweet Honey in
the Rock. CD $12.98 ($16.73 postpaid);
cassette $10 ($13.75 postpaid). Music for
Little People, PO Box 1460, Redway, CA
95560; 800/727-2233.

Mother Goose on the Loose
*Hip-hop for the hopscotch set, by Tone
Loc and others.*

Rap: Mother Goose on the Loose:
Tone Loc, et al. CD $15.98 ($16.73 post-
paid); cassette $10.98 ($14.73 postpaid).
Music for Little People, PO Box 1460,
Redway, CA 95560; 800/727-2233.

—Jerry Garcia

Perchance to Dream • Reverie • Music for Young People

*These are the favorites of my high-
brow five year old, Ariel, and I can't
fault her taste. As inviting a musician
as I know, classical pianist Carol
Rosenberger plays from so deep inside
her repertoire that she bridges all barriers: age, culture, and musical background.* **Perchance to Dream** *collects
as lullabies twenty short piano works
by Mozart, Haydn, Bach, Beethoven,
and others. Not labeled a children's
recording,* **Reverie** *is its predecessor's
companion in spirit.*

*The Music for Young People series
includes three American Library
Award-winning story/music combos:
Stravinsky's "The Firebird," Prokofiev's
"Prince Ivan and the Frog Princess,"
and Tchaikovsky's "The Snow Queen."
They feature charming narration by
Russian ballet legend Natalia Maka-
rova and musical performances by the
Seattle Symphony ("The Firebird")
and Carol Rosenberger.* —AR

Perchance to Dream: Carol
Rosenberger. CD: $14.98 ($17.98
postpaid).

Reverie: Carol Rosenberger.
CD: $14.98 ($17.98 postpaid).

Music for Young People: CD series, 7+ titles: each $14.98 ($17.98
postpaid).

All from Delos International, 1645
North Vine Street/Ste. 340, Hollywood, CA 90028; 800/364-0645.

Pickleberry Pie

This marvelous half-hour program is heard weekly on about eighty public radio stations, and twice daily in some two hundred cities (including Mexico and Europe) via Digital Cable Radio. The show's central conceit is the Pickleberries — "tiny, bumpy, green creatures" who sound like hamsters on helium and who interview kids and guest musicians.

The Pickleberries often embody the foibles and conflicts of their young listeners, making this program a uniquely sensitive offering, but the program's core is as a showcase for the best in children's music.

The result is thoroughly delightful for three- to seven-year-olds; when my kids were younger they couldn't get

enough. The program's motto is "It's never too late to have a happy childhood"; mine is "Long live the Pickleberries!" —Phil Catalfo

Pickleberry Pie: Information from 305 Dickens Way, Santa Cruz, CA 95064; 408/427-3980, email pickle@well.sf.ca.us

Boomerang!

This monthly magazine-on-a-cassette could be described as an "All Things Considered" for kids, but ATC at its most adventurous isn't half as enjoyable as Boomerang! Where the comparison holds up is in this production's insistence that kids are interested in the whole world and everything in it — especially the big ideas that adults usually talk down to them about.

Boomerang! features a cast of kid reporters and actors (as well as one or two token adults), and has a regular but flexible format: "Turning Points" (re-enactments of pivotal incidents in the lives of such historical figures as Gandhi and Rosa Parks), "Census" (important stuff like "What's Your Favorite Pair of Socks?"), "Green Tips" (quick, hands-on suggestions for kid

eco-activism), "Natural Wonders" (portraits of wildlife), and the center-piece, "Big Ideas" (extended segments tackling serious subjects — smoking, Saddam Hussein, the First Amendment — from a kid's point of view, as delineated by a self-assured boy calling himself "the King of Complicated Stuff"). Original music and sound effects keep restless young ears focused on the substantial content.

Its young audience loves it: the producers' research shows the average subscriber listens to each issue sixteen times. —PC

Boomerang! (A Children's Audio Magazine About Big Ideas): $39.95 ($43.95 post-paid)/year (12 cassettes). PO Box 261, La Honda, CA 94020; 800/333-7858.

New York City Street Games

When I laid eyes on this, I was instantly transported to the Brooklyn sidewalks of my childhood, once again playing punchball and stickball and stoopball and skully and … This package (which includes a "Spaldeen"-like handball called Sky Bounce, a box of chalk, and two bottle caps) is an object lesson in how easy and enjoyable it can be to make a world of play out of your familiar surroundings. —PC

New York City Street Games (The Greatest Games Ever Played on Concrete)

Ray & Denis Vignola. 1993; 56 pp. ISBN 0-944661-22-X $14.95 ($18.45 postpaid) from MIG Communications, 1802 5th Street, Berkeley, CA 94710; 510/845-0953

I Declare War

This is obviously a pre-Sixties game that is not very politically correct in the post–Cold War era. But it's a great way to expend some energy.

Start by drawing a large circle with a small center circle. Then draw lines to divide the big circle into as many pieces as there are players. If you have 6 players, each player gets 1/6 of the circle as their land. Now everyone names their land after a country, a state, or a city, and decorates that land to reflect its special identity. Draw whatever you want—it's yours to defend!

1 Each player stands with one foot on his or her land.

2 The player who goes first takes the ball in hand and studies everybody's land.

3 The player with the ball says "I declare war on _____!" and names one of the lands on the board while slamming the ball down in the center of the circle.

4 All players run and scatter as the person who was named retrieves the ball, steps on the circle, and hollers "Freeze!"

5 The player with the ball may now take 10 giant steps from the circle toward any of the "frozen countries" and, with careful aim, throw the ball at one of the players.

6 If the throw hits a player, then that player becomes "it" (i.e., the person with the ball) and all others are unfrozen.

7 Unfrozen players must race back and stand on their land before the player who has the ball tags them. The last person tagged by the ball is now "it" and must declare war on a new land.

8 If the player with the ball doesn't tag anybody as they run back to their land, then that player continues to be "it." Also, if the first player who throws the ball misses the target player, then all are unfrozen and must race back to their land while the ball is retrieved by the thrower. The thrower is still "it" and must seek a new land to declare war upon.

9 The game continues until you drop or until someone throws the ball too hard at another player and a real war is about to break out. Then it's time to retreat to the candy store for peace talks.

Scoring: There is no score-keeping in this game.

Tricycle Press: PO Box 7123, Berkeley, CA 94707; 800/841-BOOK, 510/559-1600, fax 524-1052. A very appealing collection of parenting books, storybooks, and audiotapes, but the jaw-slackening posters — a rainforest series, sharks, constellations, dinosaurs — are what makes this catalog extra-special. I want 'em all!

New World Education Book Collection: Welsh Products, Inc., PO Box 845, Benicia, CA 94510. A carefully selected collection of books promoting ecological and multicultural awareness, as well as social, behavioral and learning skills.

Music for Little People: Catalog free from PO Box 1460, Redway, CA 95560;

800/727-2233. Enrapturing audio, video, musical instruments, costumes, books, and more.

Stone Soup: $23/yr (5 issues) from PO Box 83, Santa Cruz, CA 95063; 800/447-4569. A regular journal of creative work by children — not just from the US, but from all over the world.

Skipping Stones: $20/yr from PO Box 3939, Eugene, OR 97403-0939. This publication also features work by children, as well as book excerpts, news, pen pals and other material. Their aim is to encourage "cooperation, creativity and celebration of cultural and linguistic diversity" and to "explore and learn stewardship of the ecological web that sustains us."

Diddy Bop Dinosaurs and Other Music

Gary Lapow started out decades ago with the wonderful folk/agitprop group The Red Star Singers. He has recorded numerous children's albums, and each one is a joy: silly, heartfelt, progressive, hummable, and exquisitely empathetic with young listeners. —PC

Diddy Bop Dinosaurs (cassette) Gary Lapow.
Here's a Kiss Goodnight (cassette) Gary Lapow.
I Like Noodles (cassette) Gary Lapow.

Sing a Silly Song (cassette) Gary Lapow.
Each: $10.83 from Springboard Records, 2140 Shattuck Avenue, Box 2317, Berkeley, CA 94704

Diddy Bop Dinosaurs

© 1987 words and music Gary Lapow

Chorus: Doo wop diddy bop
Diddy bop dino
Sing this song and sound so fine-o
Doo wop diddy bop
Diddy bop dinosaurs

Let me tell you 'bout the diddy bop dinosaurs
They bopped and they rocked in the days of yore
They hung out on the corner
In front of the candy store
The Bronto and the Stega and Tryannosaurus
All joined together in the dino chorus
Doo wop diddy bop, diddy bop dinosaurs

Many years ago before you were born
Dinosaurs woke up early in the morning
They brushed their teeth and they combed their scales
They twiddled their toes and they tapped their tails
They turned on the dinosaur radio
Caveman Jack was their favorite show
They put on their headphones and sang along
To a doo wop, diddy bop dino song

Repeat Chorus:

Geo, Neo, Paleolithic
Dinosaurs sang so terrific
Lower than the valleys
Higher than the trees
In a doo wop, diddy bop harmony

Repeat Chorus:

Archie McPhee

If kids ruled the world, the entire mail order industry would look like this catalog: rubber chickens (deluxe, mind you), skull mugs, plastic squids (squirting or glowing, your choice), Dracula dolls, singing frogs, phosphorescent banana slugs, squirting eyeballs, Turbo Glow Luma Goo, and who could forget the Martian Popping Thing — the little hand-held squeezie guy whose eyes and ears bug out when you crush his torso.

Ain't life grand? From a kid's point of view, any four items from this catalog, bought together, make a complete protein. —Phil Catalfo

Archie McPhee (Outfitters of Popular Culture): Catalog free. PO Box 30852, Seattle, WA 98103; 206/782-2344.

6" WARTHOG (Phacochoerus aethipicus)
Warthogs are perhaps the ugliest creatures walking, and we love this high quality 6" one— even its facial warts and out-of-control canines. The warts on warthog faces actually function as protection against enemy warthog tusks and perhaps even to protect their beady warthog eyes from flying dirt when they are scuffling for underground tubers. This anatomically correct, hard plastic beast is brown and grey, excellently textured and has whitish teeth and yellow eyes. He's the best, warts and all!
9752. WARTHOG. $3.25.

CAT HEAD DISGUISE!
This fabulous feline find allows a rubbery rust-colored cat to crouch on your head. In Egypt the cat was honored as a sacred animal of the goddess Bastet, the protectress of home, mother and children. Green eyes, great detail! Wear it around to confuse and perhaps infuriate your cat. Fits most head sizes.
9794. CAT HEAD DISGUISE. $11.50 each.

Toys to Grow On

A colorful catalog of inviting toys, games, arts and crafts supplies, building blocks, play structures, and more. Loads o' fun would appear to be in the offing. —PC

Moon Shoes are out of this world. Why are kids all over the universe talking about our Moon Shoes? Because wearing them is like walking on the moon! Just strap them onto your shoes: As you walk, bounce and jump, you'll feel like you're at zero gravity! With adjustable velcro straps. One size fits kids 7 years and older; up to 120 pounds. **(7 years & up)**
#498 ♦ Moon Shoes $49.95

Slam-dunk your socks!
Who says keeping your room neat can't be fun? Our sturdy backboard and 12" hoop hooks easily over any door for shooting practice with a plus: The net is actually a laundry hamper! Super-roomy nylon net holds lots of clothes and comes with a cord to keep the bottom tied securely (just untie it to remove those dirty "2-point shots"). **(4 years & up)**

#749 ♦ Slam-Dunk Laundry Shoot $14.95

Toys to Grow On: Catalog free. PO Box 17, Long Beach, CA 90801; phone 800/542-8338, fax 310/537-5403.

Chinaberry Book Service

As far as I can tell, this is the most comprehensive collection of books, audiotapes, videotapes, and the like for kids, parents, and families — some one hundred pages of the stuff. Every item is carefully selected by the staff, and described at length in thoughtful, personal reviews. Chinaberry's high standards and commitment to family enjoyment of music and literature make them a standout; if you live in the boonies, they may also be a lifeline. Also, we're told their service is excellent. —PC

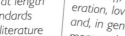

THE BOOK OF THINK
(Or How to Solve a Problem Twice Your Size)
by Marilyn Burns
illus. by Martha Weston

Did you ever have a traffic jam in your head? Did you ever say, "I can't!" Did you ever feel like some days you just won't do anything right? If the answer is YES, then this book was written for you. This book is about what to do when you're puzzles, or perplexed, or stumped, or can't get from there to here. It is about using your noggin. It is about being smart even when you're feeling dumb. (P.S. If you are a person who never has a problem, then don't read this book.) (9-14 yrs.)
3055 — Paper 125 pp $7.95

Chinaberry Book Service: Catalog free. 2780 Via Orange Way, Suite B, Spring Valley, CA 91978; 800/776-2242.

Animal Town

These folks offer a collection of books, board games, tapes, toys and other neat stuff, all of which promote cooperation, love of nature, fantasy play — and, in general, fun. Animal Town is a mom-and-pop operation (their kids were little when they started; now they're grandparents) that has kept producing its peace-loving fare from its quiet corner of Northern California since the late seventies. I was struck, when I saw their catalog again for the first time in some years, by how vital, inviting, and just plain excellent their products seemed. —PC

Animal Town Game Company: Catalog free. PO Box 485, Healdsburg, CA 95448; 800/445-8642.

Tiny People With Their Tiny Things

Children are fascinated with miniatures. To "shrink" down and be in your own tiny room is a favorite type of fantasy play. These finely made wood miniature room furnishings will provide hours of enjoyment. Youngsters can design and arrange at will. What freedom! Add your own colorful cloth for rugs and a cardbox box with handpainted "wallpaper" and you're ready to move in. Don't forget the dog! Five rooms offered, 10-15 pieces per room

#3273 Bedroom $10
#3274 Living Room $10
#3275 Children's Room $10
#3276 Kitchen $10
#3277 Bathroom $10
#3278 All Five Rooms $4[5]

HearthSong

Visiting a HearthSong store is like passing through a gnome village: millions of trinkets, whistles, candles, musicmakers, figurines, and so on, almost all made of brightly colored or oil-finished wood, cotton, wool or other natural substances. Their catalog is the next best thing. —PC

HearthSong: Catalog free. 156 N. Main Street, Sebastopol, CA 95472; 800/325-2502.

Every child loves to "dress up" and embark on make-believe adventures. Whether for Halloween, costume parties or everyday "pretend," our whimsical new **PRINCESS COSTUME SET** and **DRAGON COSTUME SET** encourage storytelling and creative play. The three piece Princess costume includes a pink satin cape (20" long) decorated with sequins and lace and fastened with a Velcro closure; a matching conical princess hat complete with flowing nylon scarves and elastic chin strap; and a magic wand (14½" long) made of clear acrylic, tipped with large quilted golden stars, and finished with lace and ric-rac accents. Our fierce but friendly Dragon set includes four colorful pieces in dragon-green felts: a shoulder tunic, two matching elastic wrist cuffs, and a marvelous hooded headpiece with a scaly tail (33" long!), fiery eyes and plenty of gleaming white teeth. Quality construction and creative design have made these costumes very popular in our retail stores. Both costume sets fit children ages 3 to 8.

#4454   Princess Costume Set $34.95
#4452   Dragon Costume Set $29.95

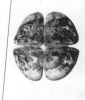

I MOVED THREE THOUSAND MILES AWAY TO BE CLOSER TO MY FAMILY.

—*Paula Poundstone*

Despite its much-lamented meltdown of recent decades, the nuclear family is still the prevailing model — or so conventional wisdom would have us believe. But even if that is true (if it ever was true: see p. 207), a great many families, and family constellations, exist outside the orbit of the putatively typical home. The differently familied, as they would surely not want to be called, need no one else's approval or consensus to thrive, but their situations can call for special resources or understanding within and without the home. The material on these pages help provide that. —Phil Catalfo

In Praise of Single Parents

More than 10 million American families are headed by one parent; this book is a love letter to them. It is also a distillation of what they've learned from what they've had to endure, and therefore wise counsel to anyone facing the same challenge.

Shoshana Alexander interviewed 150 single parents, and their disconcertingly forthright words form her book's backbone, but her own trenchant observations and gift for sifting golden insights from the river silt of experience make this book especially valuable. Not a how-to, exactly, but a how-it-is. —PC

In Praise of Single Parents
Shoshana Alexander. 1994; 256 pp.
ISBN 0-395-66991-X
$12.95 ($14.45 postpaid) from Houghton Mifflin Co./Order Dept., Wayside Road, Burlington, MA 01803; 800/225-3362

•

Buy Me Love

Absolutely nothing has been harder in raising my child alone than finding good childcare so I can work. In fact, research indicates that "the overwhelming factor in determining whether working mothers are happy is daycare." I would unconditionally amend that statement to read "good, reliable, loving, nurturing daycare." All of us carry our children to work whether we do so in a babyseat like Kirstin or in our hearts. Knowing that my son is well cared for and loved has made the entire difference in how and sometimes even *if* I have worked.

We have taken the need of children to be nurtured and tended twenty-four hours a day and coined a word that fits into the current economic thrust — "childcare." Yet there is a dilemma built into the system. Childcare is marketed as a commodity, like gas for the car, which enables me to get to work. But it's not. Childcare is a major issue of hearts and souls. I'm not looking to park my child so I can work in peace; I'm looking to buy him love.

•

For some single parents, the childrearing years do pass without the partner so many once felt they couldn't get along without. What once seemed so essential becomes "an illusion," as Marina, a mother raising her son alone, calls it. "The hardest part of becoming a single parent was realizing that my conviction that I had to have a partner in order to be happy was a fallacy. I thought I needed a man around to make me complete. Now, raising my son, I get a different sense of myself and realize that no one can make me complete from the outside."

Our children teach us a great deal about how to love and relate. If, like Sophie, we can take the time when we are focusing on them as a time to heal our wounds, we may be able to invite a partner into a functioning family unit as a welcome expansion of our love rather than as a hoped-for solution to our problems. We can use the pressure of providing our children with stability as an incentive to look carefully before we leap and to deal with our own self-destructive patterns before we choose a mirror of our deficiencies in a partner.

The Stepparent Challenge

"Yours, mine and ours" is a perfect sitcom scenario, but the problems of blended families can be significant. Questions of discipline, new sibling relationships, parental authority, and finances loom large in any marriage, but they are particularly important to a family that combines children by former marriages. This straightforward, uncluttered book will help individuals realistically assess their chances for success within a blended family. Anyone already struggling with stepchildren will find this book helpful in explaining the dynamics that can prevent a remarriage from being successful, and outlining a course of action that will strengthen the commitment of both partners. —NAP

The Stepparent Challenge
Stephen J. Williams. 1993; 125 pp.
ISBN 0-942361-72-5
$13.95 ($15.95 postpaid) from Mastermedia Limited, 17 East 89th Street, New York, NY 10128; 212/546-7649

•

The complexities of stepfamilies — even in the best of circumstances — is a real chal-

Second Chances

The wound of divorce is a deep one, and the tales of the families who shared their lives and thoughts with this researcher over a period of ten years makes excellent, sobering reading. A complex portrait emerges, from the crippling, often lifelong psychological effects of divorce to the successful remarriages and personal growth of some survivors. Because divorce entails both a breakup of what writer Pat Conroy called "a small civilization" and the subsequent search for a better life, it is a process that affects all family members and many friends. Anyone whose life has been touched by divorce, or who has contemplated ending a long-term relationship and wondered about its effect on children, will want to read this book. —NAP

Second Chances
(Men, Women, and Children a Decade After Divorce)
Judith S. Wallerstein & Sandra Blakeslee. Ticknor & Fields, 1990; 368 pp.
ISBN 0-89919-949-6
$10.95 ($12 postpaid) from Houghton Mifflin Co./Order Dept., Wayside Road, Burlington, MA 01803; 800/225-3362

•

The experience of leaving home is different for boys in intact families. Over the years, the young man detaches gradually from his parents, moving back and forth from being a little boy to being an adult and back again, sometimes in any one day. His primary emotional investment fluctuates from home to school, from friends to parents, from past to future. With time he establishes an independent stance, a more detached relationship with parents. This is part of normal adolescent development; it is in part what makes adolescence so maddening and incomprehensible to parents, unless they can think back on their own adolescence for help in understanding.

In a divorced family, adolescence is more complex and can be more painful. There is less opportunity to detach gradually from a relationship with a single parent, which is likely to be both more central and more encompassing than in intact families. Nor is it easy to be the son of a woman who is alone. The rising sexuality of the adolescent boy is very frightening to him, and he wants to get away from his mother; without his father present, he feels unprotected from his own impulses and fantasies.

•

People want to believe that divorce will relieve all their stresses — back we go to square one and begin our lives anew. But divorce does not wipe the slate clean. Some second chances come with three small children, a low-paying job, and the ghosts of the failed marriage. Some come with a sense of having been torn away from one's children and not knowing how to reestablish a home. Some second chances begin with loneliness and a feeling of being unloved and unlovable. Some bring on acute problems that turn into chronic problems. A second chance at age forty-five is not equivalent to a second chance at age thirty-two.

Other second chances bring new hope that better solutions are possible. Some come with a sense of courage that stems from having ended a demeaning relationship. Some allow people to pursue a more meaningful relationship with another person. Our second chances are not created equal.

See also
Coming Apart (p. 179).

lenge to the newly married couple. Add in difficulties with finances, former spouses, juvenile personalities, and developmental disorders, and the challenge escalates. Add to the map the types of extremely intricate and potentially difficult situations described in this chapter, and your road ahead may seem truly unmaneuverable.

Remember though, you *do* have options, and there is always help. These problems do not need to be, and probably cannot be, solved without professional help, so take advantage of the excellent counseling and intervention programs available in most cities nationwide. Work hard and aggressively to solve any underlying problems and then to strengthen the marriage itself. No mat-

ter how impossible the obstacles may seem, there is always hope.

•

Just when you thought it was safe to enjoy the marriage, one of the children may reappear at your doorstep. Natural parents aren't likely to turn their own children away. You may end up with a grown person living with you for an indeterminate time. What's more, he or she may bring home a package: his or her own children, girlfriends, boyfriends, a spouse, or who knows what other friend or relative. Think about the marital stress that can endure as you deal with these possibilities.

Down Is Up for Aaron Eagle

Each time I've seen a child with Down Syndrome, my heart has shuddered with gratitude that my own were "normal." I pitied their mothers as burdened women. And when I picked this book up, I thought I would learn more about the sorrow of living with Down Syndrome. Instead, I learned more about love: this book is anything but sad. Vicki Noble gave birth to Aaron Eagle, a boy born with a severe chromosomal abnormality, and learned to see his presence as a gift. The story of her journey to understanding the gift of her son is an enriching one — truly a tribute to the power and substance of love. —Nancy Pietrafesa

●

I have no choice but to think of being with Aaron Eagle as a spiritual practice, and clearly it is as effective as any other at help-

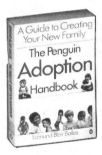

Down Is Up for Aaron Eagle
(A Mother's Spiritual Journey with Down Syndrome)
Vicki Noble. HarperSanFrancisco, 1993; 224 pp. ISBN 0-06-250737-0
$17 ($19.75 postpaid) from HarperCollins Publishers/Direct Mail, PO Box 588, Dunmore, PA 18512; 800/331-3761

ing with my personal evolution. Sitting on a pillow and staring at a blank wall, I could not cultivate any more patience and compassion than that which naturally comes to me when my heart is open to this little boy as he takes his sweet time getting where he's intended to go.

Aaron Eagle reading his favorite book, *Pinocchio.*

●

There are no straight lines, and Aaron Eagle is here to prove it.

●

I worked very hard to get in touch with my emotions about Aaron and to be truthful about my feelings in relation to him and his condition. I struggled to stay awake in the face of the confusion of holding the enormous paradoxical reality that parents of a handicapped child have to contend with. On the one hand, there was our beautiful new baby boy, responding and interacting with us in his admittedly limited ways, but responding nonetheless. And we loved him and adored him, fiercely. Wasn't he truly beautiful, or were we making that up? Did he look funny to other people, and were they kind enough not to mention it? We lost perspective and couldn't tell at times. Then there was the cultural reality of the label describing him: a person with Down syndrome, retarded, disabled.

The Lesbian and Gay Parenting Handbook

To the perplexity of the family-values crowd, many gay couples start families and, yes, raise children to adulthood.

The Lesbian and Gay Parenting Handbook
April Martin. HarperPerennial, 1993; 395 pp. ISBN 0-06-096929-6
$15 ($17.75 postpaid) from HarperCollins Publishers/Direct Mail, PO Box 588, Dunmore, PA 18512; 800/331-3761

This is an excellent resource to help them meet the unique challenges they face. The author is very knowledgeable, but her special wisdom comes in the tone of her presentation. Countless personal stories help us see that no one group has a monopoly on the longing to be a parent, or on the special love that consumes a parent's heart.

Along the way, there is a comprehensive menu of information and advice about conception, pregnancy, surrogacy, adoption, family finances, gay fathers, legal issues, particular psycho-emotional and social obstacles ("Your daddy's a faggot!" "Yeah"), childrearing, and more. —PC

Raising Black Children

Racism divides America and it divides her children. Black parents have what the authors call "mixed feelings" about passing on the manners and mores of a culture that does not value individuals equally.

Raising Black Children addresses concerns common to all parents ("How can I best use words to help my baby learn?") and those particular to black parents and others playing a role in the development of black children ("Shouldn't black children be taught to be angry in order to fight racism?"). The question-and-answer format covers a range of educational, social and emotional issues.

This thoughtful book tackles the difficult questions of race and raising children to consciousness with real wisdom. Its value is by no means limited to black families. —NAP

●

Your ongoing interest and support will give your youngster a positive sense of himself as a person. This makes it possible for him to achieve many of his goals and to view

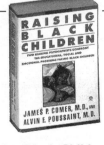

Raising Black Children
(Questions and Answers for Parents and Teachers)
James Comer. Plume Books, 1992; 436 pp. ISBN 0-452-26839-7
$12 ($14 postpaid) from Penguin USA/ Consumer Sales, 120 Woodbine Street, Bergenfield, NJ 07621; 800/253-6476

himself as competent and worthwhile. Talk about, have him read about, and expose him to African-American culture and black achievement within the total culture. "Shoot down" negative and racist attitudes about blacks, and offer logical explanations for problems within the black community. Most important, help him understand that white racist attitudes and behavior are the problems of white racists, and are no measure of his value and worth as a person. Continue this guidance and support as long as your son is in your care.

Making Sense of Adoption

"Where did I come from?" is always a sticky question, but for adopted children and their parents, the answer can be especially complicated. Parents in this circumstance have special concerns: how much information to give their children and when to give it; what information to share with others and when to share it. This book addresses the ways in which adoptive children develop and anticipates the type of information children will seek as they grow older. It provides guidelines and suggestions for families that parents will find sensitive and realistic. —NAP

●

Children in middle childhood are likely to want to know who their birthparents are. Children who have contact with their birthparents shouldn't be misled about their identities. For example, grandparents who adopt their daughter's child should make it clear that the biologic relationships in the family are. Without this honesty, the child is likely to grow up knowing that there's a family secret and may hear the truth in an undesirable way.

●

The sense of being connected to previous generations is not something that can be taken for granted in a family not genetically related. The preschool years are a good time to encourage contact between children and their extended family so adoptees feel membership in their family extends beyond their parents and siblings.

Making Sense of Adoption
Lois R. Melina. HarperPerennial, 1989; 256 pp. ISBN 0-06-096319-0
$12 ($14.75 postpaid) from HarperCollins Publishers/Direct Mail, PO Box 588, Dunmore, PA 18512; 800/331-3761

The Penguin Adoption Handbook

Prospective parents are vulnerable people. Adoptive parents are especially so, often coming to adoption after exhausting biological means. This book provides reassurance to families seeking to adopt. It is a detailed guide to the maze of national and international strategies that have developed in the last decade. Traditional and nontraditional families will find the analysis of various sources (agencies, private parties, etc.), the state-by-state variations in adoptive law, and additional resources up-to-date and comprehensive. There is also a broad measure of emotional support in this book. Bolles straightforwardly addresses the moral, ethical and emotional issues that parents may experience during the search for the child and after the child's placement. —NAP

●

Every so often a legal battle over adoption gets into the news. The cases are rare, but when they do arise, they get heavy publicity. Their combination of human interest and callous bureaucracy gives them a universal newsworthiness. As a result of the publicity, anybody with a memory stretching back over ten or more years may have the impression that there are a number of hard-fought adoptions. Of course, the one million routine adoptions during the same period have gone unnoticed.

The Penguin Adoption Handbook
Edmund Bolles. Penguin Books, 1984; 1993; 269 pp. ISBN 0-14-046947-8
$12 ($14 postpaid) from Penguin USA/ Consumer Sales, 120 Woodbine Street, Bergenfield, NJ 07621; 800/253-6476

Safeguarding Your Teenager from the Dragons of Life

Once children get past a certain size, it's often hard to realize they need protection. They do, of course, and this book is very successful at drawing our attention to the ongoing and heightened emotional and parental needs of teenagers. Parents often unwittingly withdraw at a time when they should be establishing themselves as "emotional anchors" for their teens. This book provides encouragement and guidance for establishing the strong familial bonds that protect children as they navigate their teenage years. There's good information here on emotional development and assessing and improving your communication style. In the end it is more philosophy than how-to, but its message is a thoughtful and important one.
—Nancy Pietrafesa

Safeguarding Your Teenager from the Dragons of Life
Bettie Youngs. 1993; 292 pp.
ISBN 1-55874-264-6
$11.95 ($16.20 postpaid) from Health Communications Inc., 3201 SW 15th Street, Deerfield Beach, FL 33442; 800/851-9100

●
Children learn by what they see. Your adolescent acquires a good many of her attitudes by what she sees at home. Perhaps this is a good time for you to re-examine your own relationship and to analyze the ups and downs, the good times and the struggles. Your adolescent has a natural curiosity

about love and love relationships. She is busy forming an ideal of what she wants a relationship to be. Be aware of the messages she receives from you when she observes your own relationship.

●
Your adolescent needs to understand that he is responsible for his actions, not you.

●
Adolescence is a time of exploration and discovery through experimentation. Teens need time to flex their newly discovered "muscles." Be patient. Learning these skills won't happen overnight. Remember, trial and error is the path to learning. Also remember that at each age you are dealing with a changing person, one who has not yet formed a stable sense of self.

Why Can't Anyone Hear Me?

The confusion and distress of adolescence are not limited to teenagers. Parents often find they share their children's emotions during this period of development. They are invited to share this book, which addresses the parent/adolescent relationship.

The fictional story of a teenager named Jamie acts as a kind of case study to stimulate discussion on various aspects of teenage life. It's a good device; by observing a third party, parents and teens can readily see the other's point of view.

This book, like many, emphasizes the importance of communication skills, but it is one of the few that places responsibility for communication squarely on the shoulders of both teenager and parent. Both of you will learn something from this book. —NAP

●
The kind of environment where happiness and pain can be shared, and yet where one's need for privacy will also be respected, is indeed a supportive and healthy place to be. If some family or families can in part bridge the gap that distances them from each other through experiencing this book, then everything involved in producing it has been worthwhile.

●
Establishing a supportive environment that will allow for nonjudgmental relating is essential to the adolescent/parent relationship.

●
Firmness is required on the part of the parent, but so is love. By keeping love alive and continuing to work on improving the relationship, the odds are good that the situation will improve.

●
Having mutual respect for one another makes it much easier to deal with relationships during this time. Mutual respect involves allowing for and valuing each other's opinions and attitudes. When respect, like love, is freely given and accepted, it becomes a valuable part of the relationship. When it is demanded and not returned, it is often lost.

Why Can't Anyone Hear Me?
(A Guide for Surviving Adolescence)
Monte Elchoness. 1989; 197 pp.
ISBN 0-936781-06-8
$10.95 ($12 postpaid) from Monroe Press, 362 Maryville Ave, Ventura, CA 93003; 805/642-3064

Leave Me Alone!

As a normal part of their development, teenagers are experimenters, trying on roles and behavior to accomplish the developmental tasks of their youth. Sound choices enable teenagers to enter adulthood with optimism and self-respect. Experimentation that gets out of hand can lead to serious ramifications.

This book addresses chemical dependency in teenagers and the psychiatric problems that accompany it, enabling parents to understand the dynamics of dependency. The supportive tone encourages parents to overcome guilt and sense of responsibility to become effective advocates and resources for their child's recovery. This is a clear, jargon-free guide to responding wisely to and getting help for your teenager and yourself. —NAP

●
When there are decisions affecting the whole family, consider allowing your children to problem-solve with you and your spouse even if the final decision must be yours. Your children will then feel they are a responsible part of the family.

●
As scary as it may be, the truth has a wonderful way of bringing peace within us and healing. If caught in the early stages of the chemical dependency progression, your teen has a better chance for recovery.

●
Which disorder came first is not the issue. Leave the chicken-and-egg philosophizing to others and get about the business of helping you and your teenager get well.

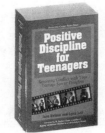

Leave Me Alone!
(Helping Your Troubled Teenager)
Belinda Mooney. 1992; 176 pp.
ISBN 0-8306-2537-2
$9.95 postpaid from TAB Books Inc./Retail Order Dept., 13311 Monterey Avenue, Blue Ridge Summit, PA 17294; 800/822-8138

Positive Discipline for Teenagers

Having a teenager in the house ensures that conflict will be in the air. Most people feel the world and their household are better off without conflict, but the authors make a strong case for the importance of conflict in adolescent development. **Positive Discipline for Teenagers** *is a guide to exercising parental authority in a manner that enables teenagers to develop self-discipline and a sense of responsibility. It is a good guide to finding the happy medium between excessive control and permissiveness, and it will help parents recognize conflict as a fundamental part of the parent/child relationship.* —NAP

●
Remember that the perceptions teens have and the decisions they make about their experiences color their pictures of themselves and help explain some of their behavior. It's also helpful to remember that

their reality may be different from yours. In addition, keep in mind that teenagers have not yet become adults — their current values, which many parents find disturbing, are not necessarily those they will hold as grown-ups.

●
We often see our teens' behavior in terms of a power struggle or revenge when in reality it has nothing to do with us. Understanding their private logic can help us quit taking everything personally.

●
Parents with long-range goals do not want to retard natural individuation (even when it looks like rebellion) for some other very important reasons. When teenage development is thwarted, teens may take extreme measures — such as suicide, drug abuse, dropping out, or running away — to ease the frustration or pain of not being able to do something that is natural and necessary to their development.

Positive Discipline for Teenagers
(formerly **I'm On Your Side**)
Jane Nelsen & Lynn Lott. 1994; 340 pp.
ISBN 1-55958-441-6
$14.95 ($18.95 postpaid) from Prima Publishing & Communications, PO Box 1260, Rocklin, CA 95677; 916/324-5718

●
Once we get our personal issues out of the way, including the feeling that our teens are trying to hurt us, we can stop feeling guilty about our kids' problems. We can also be available to help our kids if they need us, instead of interfering to save face for ourselves.

Getting Your Kids to Say "No" in the 90's When You Said "Yes" in the 60's

Hooboy, has this guy got us pegged. A pediatrician, practitioner of "adolescent medicine," and baby boomer himself, Victor Strasburger knows that we want our kids to exhibit none of the adventurousness — or licentiousness — that our generation was famous for. He also knows that it was ever thus. Most importantly, he knows the difference between trying to control your kids and helping them develop into self-reliant, mature, discriminating people.

Strasburger deconstructs the shibboleths of parenting adolescents and exhorts parents to act with good sense and discipline with regard to "teenage sex, drugs, TV, and rock 'n' roll" — and defines the parameters for that. Best of all, his voice is personal, opinionated, energetic — not the dry, detached tone we're used to in parenting-advice books.

Knowledgeable, forceful, humorous, engaging, and just in time for my oldest kid's teen years — what more could a parent ask? —PC

•

Here are the seven most common mistakes that parents make in the "letting go" process, consequently getting caught up in their adolescent's struggles:

1. Panicking. If I mention the word "adolescent" to parents of eight- to twelve-year-olds, often their pupils dilate, their breathing becomes labored, and their eyes start to roll back. They are scared to death of the next five to ten years, and their kids already know it.

2. Reluctance to Let Go. Letting go can be a very difficult and agonizing process, no

doubt about it. After all, you know your child's weaknesses better than anyone else, and you have spent the past twelve years playing the Great Protector (and appropriately so).

3. Failing to Parent. Just because much of your child's adolescence has already been predetermined by her childhood doesn't mean that you can fold your tent and head happily into the sunset. Your teenager still requires a lot of parental support, guidance, and discipline.

4. Failing to Respect Your Teenager's Privacy. Snooping around your teenager's bedroom, "accidentally" eavesdropping on his phone conversations, and reading her secret diary are all common parental behaviors that are fraught with hazard.

5. Depriving Teenagers of the Easy Symbols of Their Adolescence. For reasons beyond my understanding, many parents believe that if their teenager goes to school in torn jeans, or with green spiked hair, it "reflects back on them." Stuff and nonsense! You can't afford to have an identity crisis at the same time as your teenager. Be assured that if your teenager chooses to look like a slob, it reflects back on no one other than her.

Getting Your Kids to Say "No" in the 90's When You Said "Yes" in the 60's
Victor Strasburger. Fireside Books, 1993; 288 pp. ISBN 0-671-79796-4
$11 postpaid from Simon & Schuster/Order Dept., 200 Old Tappan Road, Old Tappan, NJ 07675; 800/223-2336

Consequently, it's *her* problem, not yours.

6. Succumbing to Peer Pressure Yourself. Teenagers aren't the only ones subjected to peer pressure. Adults are notoriously susceptible to it.

7. Overestimating the Peer Group's Influence and Underestimating Your Own. Particularly when things go wrong, it's easy to blame your teenager's peers.

Erections sometimes don't know when they're not wanted

"What's Happening to Me?"

From the same folks who gave us Where Did I Come From? *this book, like its sibling, uses humor to explain a touchy subject. Although puberty is and isn't a laughing matter (just ask your teenager), the writer and illustrator have deftly managed to dispel much of its awkwardness using a careful balance of frank information and incredibly funny illustrations. —LM*

What's Happening to Me?
Peter Mayle. 1975; 56 pp.
ISBN 0-8184-0312-8
$8.95 ($11.95 postpaid) from Carol Publishing Group, 120 Enterprise Avenue, Secaucus, NJ 07094; 800/447-2665

The What's Happening to My Body? Book for Girls • The What's Happening to My Body? Book for Boys

These two books offer solid, straightforward information presented in a nonjudgmental manner and covering every possible puberty concern. Girls get to hear about boy stuff and vice versa, helped along by excellent line drawings. Girls learn how to do a breast self-exam; boys, a testicular exam. Sexual myths are debunked left and right, as are old wives' tales surrounding ovulation and menstruation. I would have sold my grandmother for this kind of data in the sixth grade.

Given this society's concern for AIDS and teen pregnancies, these two books should be in the open reference stacks of every public library. —Linda Morgan

Also by Lynda Madaras: My Body, My Self *(1993, Newmarket Press). Companion workbook to* The What's Happening to My Body? Book for Girls.

My Feelings, My Self *(1993, Newmarket Press). Revised edition of Lynda Madaras's* Growing-Up Guide for Girls.

•

Slang words for the penis, scrotum and testicles

Penis

cock	peter	tool	wang
dick	rod	frankfurter	weiner
prick	dingus	thing	dong
schlong	dork	banger	pecker
wee-wee	meat	dinky	hot dog
wanger	pisser	penie	weenie

Scrotum and Testicles

balls	cujones	nuts
things	eggs	bangers
rocks	hangers	jewels
stones	cubes	seeds
sac	bag	

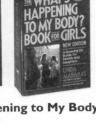

What's Happening to My Body? Book for Boys
Lynda Madaras & Dane Saavedra. Newmarket Press, 1991; 288 pp. ISBN 0-937858-99-4

What's Happening to My Body? Book for Girls
Lynda Madaras & Area Madaras. Newmarket Press, 1987; 304 pp. ISBN 0-937858-98-6

Each $9.95 ($11.95 postpaid) from Random House/Order Dept., 400 Hahn Road, Westminster, MD 21157; 800/733-3000

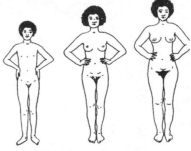

Girls in Puberty. As we go through puberty, our hips get wider. Fat tissue begins to grow around our hips, thighs and buttocks, giving our bodies a curvier shape. Our breasts begin to swell, and soft nests of hair begin to grow under our arms and around our genitals.

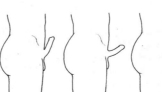

The erect penis may stick out at various angles or may stand practically straight up.

PERIOD.

First-person experiences lace this delightful book about menstruation and transform a mysterious event into something a bit more real. True to life, not all the experiences are positive — which enhances the book's credibility. Good information and fun drawings make it a helpful reference for prepubescent girls. We've come a long way from that afternoon thirty years ago when my Girl Scout troop "learned" half-truths about our maturing bodies from a fictional princess in an animated film. —Linda Morgan

PERIOD.
JoAnn Gardner-Loulan, Bonnie Lopez and Marcia Quackenbush 1991; 95 pp.
ISBN 0-912078-88-X $9.95 ($13.45 postpaid) from Volcano Press, PO Box 270, Volcano, CA 95689; 209/296-3445, fax 209/296-4515

Roxanne: "I write better poems when I'm menstruating."

OTHER GREAT RESOURCES

Sex & Sense: Gary F. Kelly. 1993, Barron's Educational Series. Wonderful detail, well-organized. Covers all sexual orientations.

AIDS-Proofing Your Kids: Loren E. Acker, Bram C. Goldwater & William H. Dyson. 1992, Beyond Words Publishing. Not a "just-say-no" book; teaches alternatives as well as how to say "no" if that's what you want to do.

Family life is hard enough under the best of circumstances. But illness, abuse, behavioral dysfunction, death — such forces forces can destroy individual family members and whole families. However, good resources are available to help people deal with crises.
—Phil Catalfo

Helping Teens Stop Violence

Some of the abstractions in this book are a bit too pat for my taste, but the exercises the authors provide for exposing unconscious assumptions and for "unlearning" sexism, racism and "adultism" are excellent.

Violence is power; when teens (like anyone else) feel a more authentic and useful kind of power is available to them, they have less need to resort to violence, whether against others or themselves. Toward that end, this book is an effective tool. —PC

•

Why do young people do poorly in school? Why do young people use drugs, or hang out on street corners, or get pregnant? A common answer to these questions is that many teens have low self-esteem, generally defined as a poor sense of one's worth or ability — a lack of confidence. Professional literature about adolescents, social service priorities, and funding trends all emphasize programs which build self-esteem.

Is the problem low self-esteem?

When I think back to my years as a teenager, I notice how much I wanted to do and how little power I had to do it. I wanted to go places I couldn't; I wanted to try to do things I wasn't supposed to. I wanted to affect and change my classes, my community, my neighborhood, and I wasn't able to. I never had the money, wheels, friends, influence, or credibility to make a difference.

There were lots of promises from adults. If you study hard, work hard, stay out of fights, stay safe, don't have sex, don't drink or smoke, don't mess up, adults promised you a life filled with power and privileges. But the promise of power 10 or 20 years in the future was not inviting or convincing. In the meantime, few adults listened to me, allowed me to participate, trusted me, or noticed me and my friends and fellow students.

Of course, when adults systematically don't notice you, listen to you, trust you, or allow you to participate in making meaningful decisions, your sense of self-worth deteriorates. When they grade you continually on your academic performance, your concept of your value can hinge on it too. If, on top of this, they belittle you, punish you arbitrarily, yell at you, put you down, beat you, or molest you, your self-esteem can plummet.

Oppression: the issue is power

Our problem as young people was not low self-esteem. Rather, we had no power over our lives. Without power to protect ourselves, we were constantly restricted, disrespected, and abused by adults. At home, at school, in stores, at work, on the sports field, on the streets — adults had the authority to decide how we should dress, how we should talk, where we could be, and who we could be with. They decided our future, through discipline, records, arrests, report cards, evaluations, allowances, and/or the lack or neglect of all of the above.

Teens face the same lack of power today. Adults make promises to them. Adolescence should be a time of promise, of open futures, of the possibility of meaningful education, fully remunerated work and healthy relationships. The reality is a broken promise: limited education, unemployment and underemployment, unplanned families, dysfunctional relationships, and an epidemic of violence.

Internalized oppression

And teens are still blamed for failure. Adults label them troublemakers, irresponsible, immature, apathetic, lazy, dishonest, underachievers, and stupid. Adults define this failure as a personal problem for each teen, a failure of self-esteem, and teens end up blaming themselves or attacking each other. Teen violence — the teen-to-teen abuse that happens in gangs, in couples, or from the school bully; the self-abuse from drugs or alcohol; unwanted pregnancy; suicide — all of these can be seen as forms of learned helplessness and hopelessness in teens. These are ways in which, because of abuse from adults, they have learned to give up on themselves.

Helping Teens Stop Violence
(A Practical Guide for Counselors, Educators, and Parents)
Allan Creighton & Paul Kivel. 1990;
152 pp. ISBN 0-89793-116-5
$11.95 ($14.45 postpaid) from Hunter House, PO Box 2914, Alameda, CA 94501; 510/865-5282

No More Secrets for Me

This simple but effective book is aimed at pre-teens and early teens, and does one thing extremely well: it models assertive behavior in stories with positive outcomes. The kids in these tales all have their privacy, feelings or bodies abused to varying degrees, and all have the gumption to stand up for themselves, either by directly confronting the person troubling them or seeking counsel and help from a neutral third party.

The entire book can be read aloud to a youngster in a few minutes, and makes an excellent launching point for an ongoing program of educating children about their right to have their physical and emotional selves respected. —PC

•

Then Marty did a weird thing. He took off his bathing suit and T-shirt and sat down naked on Greg's bunk. "First, take off your bathing suit. Then I'll show you the rest of the game," Marty said. Greg thought it sounded like a stupid idea. He shook his head no.

No More Secrets for Me
Jane Aaron. 1983;
ISBN 0-316-91491-6
$6.95 ($9.45 postpaid) from Little, Brown and Co./ Order Dept., 200 West Street, Waltham, MA 02154; 800/343-9204

National Committee for Prevention of Child Abuse

According to NCPCA, over a million children are abused each year; more than twelve hundred die. NCPCA is dedicated to preventing child abuse "in all its forms," and to that end publishes a profusion of literature about preventing child abuse, educating children, "breaking the cycle," alcoholism and child abuse, and getting help. They also have literature on child rearing, appropriate discipline, parental stress, and other critical issues that can add to the overheated atmosphere of a family under duress. —PC

National Committee for Prevention of Child Abuse: PO Box 2866, Chicago, IL 60690; 800/835-2671.

•

NCPCA's "12 Alternatives to Lashing Out at Your Kid"
The next time everyday pressures build up to the point where you feel like lashing out — STOP! And try any of these simple alternatives.
You'll feel better . . . and so will your child.

1. Take a deep breath. And another. Then remember *you* are the adult.
2. Close your eyes and imagine you're hearing what your child is about to hear.
3. Press your lips together and count to 10. Or better yet, to 20.
4. Put a child in a time-out chair. (Remember the rule: one time-out minute for each year of age.)
5. Put yourself in a time-out chair. Think about why you are angry: is it your child, or is your child simply a convenient target for your anger?
6. Phone a friend.
7. If someone can watch the children, go outside and take a walk.
8. Take a hot bath or splash cold water on your face.
9. Hug a pillow.
10. Turn on some music. Maybe even sing along.
11. Pick up a pencil and write down as many helpful words as you can think of. Save the list.
12. Write for prevention information: NCPCA, Box 2866L, Chicago, IL 60690.

Little Secrets • Silent Shame • Breaking the Cycle

Dan Gediman has produced three landmark public radio series on child sexual abuse, its survivors, and its prevention. They include searing interviews with survivors and trenchant observations by experts in the field. Illuminating, difficult, high-impact — and finally, hopeful — listening. —PC

Little Secrets
(4-hour radio series on audiocassette)
Silent Shame
(audiocassette)
Breaking the Cycle
(4-hour radio series on audiocassette)
Dan Gediman, Producer (Milestone Productions). $29.95 ($35.45 postpaid), transcripts $18.95 postpaid from The Radio Store, PO Box 5006, Madison, WI 53705; 800/747-7444

And then there is life-threatening illness (or injury), or the loss of a loved one.

We know death is the ultimate denouement of this escapade, but we are never prepared for it to intrude upon our lives, and so we go about our business as if its specter were not always there. We don't know what to do; we *cannot* know what to do, until we *must* know what to do.

Here is the best of what I've found and learned since my son Gabe became seriously ill. Happily, today Gabe is doing great. These tools helped our family get far enough to be able to say that with gusto. —Phil Catalfo

HOW TO COPE:
A ☑ LIST FOR FAMILIES

✔ **Take it as it comes.** The first days (and especially the first hours) after a diagnosis of life-threatening illness are suffused with shock and denial. You feel like an actor on the set of the wrong movie. I was physically and emotionally enervated for a day or two. Then I allowed myself to feel my own grief and fear — or I could no longer hold it back — and I reinhabited my own body, my own feelings. This was the beginning of my being able to respond.

✔ **Reach out.** Call upon your personal support network of relatives, friends, and neighbors in more mundane ways — for childcare, meals, transportation, the myriad everyday things that can seem impossible in the context of medical emergency. If you don't have such a network, start building one now: you won't earn any points for going it alone.

✔ **Pray.** I can't tell you how to do it; I can't even explain how I do it. But I can tell you to do it. I've heard parents say that they trust in God, that their child is in God's hands, that God will heal their child. I don't dispute that, but I take a more moderate view. I believe prayer has helped my son, as it has helped me and my whole family — and I see it as something to add to the complement of available tools, beginning with medical treatment. Prayer puts you in touch with reservoirs of strength and will you probably didn't know you had. And the prayers of others can create an expanded community of concern whose love will support you ineffably but tangibly.

✔ **Arm yourself with information.** There are many sources of good information about the illness you're confronting; in fact, the profusion of literature can be daunting at first. Allow yourself some time to get a sense of the literature's scope — what doesn't seem clear at first reference will probably come together the second or third time around. The American Cancer Society, the Leukemia Society, and other organizations have scores of good books and pamphlets on specific diseases, chemotherapy, emotional repercussions, medical research, and so on; much of this literature is free (and may have been given to you at your hospital). The National Cancer Institute has a toll-free number for questions, and also provides a variety of helpful literature: 800/4-CANCER. The ACS offers a range of services to patients, from transportation to information on where to get a wig; their number is 800/ACS-2345. Beyond that, any good public library will have an encyclopedia, a card catalog, and a Reader's Guide to Periodical Literature; a medical library is even better. And, of course, the person to whom you can turn first and most should be your doctor.

✔ **Keep files on the bills and insurance claims.** Accept the fact that you now have a new part-time job: dealing with the medical paper work. Review your policy thoroughly, and don't hesitate to call the insurer with questions. (In fact you should do that before a health crisis comes up.) Carefully read every piece of paper that comes in from the hospital, doctors, other providers, and insurance company.

✔ **Lobby.** You may find, once you've settled into a treatment routine and you're dealing better with the fact of the illness, that you'd like to see some change made in a service or policy. Identify and express your needs clearly, logically, respectfully, and with a reasonable, well-articulated vision of what you'd like to see. Talk with other parents to compare notes; talk with staff to raise the issue initially and see what might be possible informally. It may be necessary to write a formal letter to someone in a position of authority. It's best to control your emotions: if you initiate a discussion in a rage, the other party is likely to become defensive and not hear your complaint in any productive sense. We threw out the vitriolic language in the first draft, and took care to acknowledge the excellent care the hospital provides and our gratitude for it. —PC

OTHER FAMILY CRISIS RESOURCES

You Don't Have to Die (One Family's Guide to Surviving Cancer): Geralyn & Craig Gaes & Philip Bashe. 1992, Villard Books.

When a Friend Dies

This small, understated book has the tone of a wise and empathetic friend who appears at precisely the moment when nothing less will do. It is an eye-opener for teens who are grappling, probably for the first time, with the death of someone dear to them, someone like them, someone who was presumably immortal until that turned out not to be so. And it is an eye-opener for their parents, who are of course concerned for their offspring's emotional well-being.

When a Friend Dies is full of poignant quotes from other grieving teens, and contains short, helpful observations to help the young reader move through this grim terrain. A most compassionate book. —PC

●

"My parents are hovering over me and smothering me."

Most parents want to protect their children from hurt, and what is more hurtful than the death of a friend? You're right about feeling that they can't and shouldn't protect you from this hurt. You want to believe that you can handle it. When your parents hover, this makes you think that you *can't* handle it.

●

Sometimes it may seem easier to stay frozen and just deny that you are even bothered by what happened. Denying something will not make it go away. Denying your feelings will only keep your hurts inside so they cannot come out and be healed. If a friend dies, it has to be hard on you. Try to admit it to yourself, and talk to someone understanding.

When a Friend Dies (A Book for Teens About Grieving and Healing) Marilyn E. Gootman. 1994; 107 pp. ISBN 0-915793-66-0 $7.95 ($10.95 postpaid) from Free Spirit Publishing, Inc., 400 First Avenue N., Suite 616, Minneapolis, MN 55401; 800/735-7323

Listen. My Child Has a Lot of Living to Do

This somber anthology offers a vision of what truly foresighted care for seriously and terminally ill children, and their families, would look like. It is striking on several counts: 1) It is British; its experiences and insights are told from the perspective of the British system, which assumes (for one thing) that everyone has an unquestionable right to health care. 2) The cold touch of death pervades the book: the haunting poems of a girl who succumbed to cancer at seventeen, the fact that several authors have themselves lost children, the pieces on caring for dying children and bereavement. 3) The scope is broad, covering a range of illnesses besides cancer (cystic fibrosis, congenital heart disease, children with AIDS) and taking into account the unique roles of doctors, hospice workers, home care nurses, and family members — leading the reader to focus not on the disease itself, but on the thoroughness and coordination of the response to it.

I don't know of an equivalent book for American families and the health care professionals they rely on. If in fact there isn't one, there damn sure ought to be. —PC

●

Mercifully, malignant disease in children is not common. This does not help the general practitioner. It is most unusual for the general practitioner to make the diagnosis after seeing the child only once. Malignancy is not, nor should it be, the first thing that comes into a general practitioner's mind when he first sees a child with what might be a minor complaint. Malignant disease can present in an enormous number of ways — vague ill health, a niggling pain, a limp. I have heard many stories from parents who have taken their child to their general practitioner on several occasions when nothing seems to have been found, nor action taken. Sometimes several weeks, even months have passed before the diagnosis has been made. Sadly, when this happens the general practitioner is regarded as incompetent by the family. One hears the complaint, "If only he had made the diagnosis sooner." It is a difficult situation for the general practitioner and can put great strain on his relationship with the child and family from the start.

Listen. My Child Has a Lot of Living to Do J. D. Baum, et al., Editors. 1990; 225 pp. ISBN 0-19-261961-6 $15.95 ($18.95 postpaid) from Oxford University Press/Order Dept., 2001 Evans Road, Cary, NC 27513; 800/451-7556

Center for Media Literacy

You think you live in an over-mediafied culture? Your kid is going to live in a world of wall-to-wall media. You'd best educate her on how to deal with it. That means knowing not only how to choose among the media options but how to look at each of them critically.

This tiny nonprofit puts out trenchant material to help you do that. Their provocative quarterly newsletter, **Connect**, *is free to members; they also publish "Media Literacy Workshop Kits" that inculcate critical thinking. These are erudite without being bookish, forceful without being overbearing. The CML is fighting the good fight; it ought to be your fight. —Phil Catalfo*

Center for Media Literacy: 1962 South Shenandoah Street, Los Angeles, CA 90034; 800/226-9494; 310/559-2944.

Big World, Small Screen

The American Psychological Association formed a committee to digest all the research on the effects of television; this is their report. It is a sobering read, and a surprisingly accessible one, given the usually turgid style of academic work like this.

The bad news: too much TV-watching is definitely associated with undesirable characteristics like violent/aggressive behavior and poor reading achievement. The good news: it is probably not the sole cause. The best news: you have more influence than the TV — if you exert it. This book doesn't go into solutions much, but that's what CML and the like are for. —PC

●

McLuhan's basic notion that "the medium is the message" has had a wide appeal to scholars as well as others, but translating it into a more specific theory or verifiable hypotheses has proved to be a formidable task. Salomon conducted a series of investigations that demonstrated that children could learn specific mental skills from seeing certain filmic codes. For instance, watching slow zooms in to details of a large picture taught children visual analytic skills. A group of Israeli children who watched Sesame Street showed improved ability to take different spatial perspectives when looking at a setting. Greenfield also cited some evidence to support the hypothesis that television may promote visual spatial skills and be particularly well-suited for conveying information using motion, animation, and close-up photography. On the

whole, however, the evidence for lasting changes in cognitive processing as a result of television viewing is weak.

The hypothesis that television leads to a loss of creativity and imagination has met a similar fate; it is difficult to test and the existing evidence provides little support. In the British Columbia study, children showed reduced performance on one of two measures of creativity after television was introduced. Cross-media investigations comparing radio with television show that children generate visual images when listening, but television inspires different types of imaginative activities. It is arbitrary to decide that one type of imagining is of a higher quality than the other. Moreover, any casual observer of children is well aware that television characters and content serve as the basis for a great deal of imaginative play.

Big World, Small Screen
Aletha C. Huston, et al. 1992; 195 pp. ISBN 0-8032-7263-4 $12 ($15.50 postpaid) from University of Nebraska Press, 901 N. 17th Street, 327 Nebraska Hall, Lincoln, NE 68588-0520; 800/755-1105

OTHER GREAT RESOURCES

Mind and Media: Patricia Marks Greenfield. 1984, Harvard University Press.

Children and Television: Gordon L. Berry and Joy Keiko Asamen, Edis. 1993, SAGE Publications.

Television and the American Child: George Comstock with Haejung Paik. 1991, Academic Press (HBJ). More heavyweight reviews of the academic (i.e., research) landscape.

The National Foundation to Improve Television: 60 State Street, Suite 3400, Boston, MA 02109; 617/523-6353, fax. This single-issue group works "to reduce the amount of excessive dramatized violence shown on television." That work takes the form of lobbying sponsors, stations, networks, and the FCC.

Children's Television Resource & Education Center

C-TREC also does workshops and publishes educational materials, although not of the same depth or scope as CML. Parents may like their bite-sized "Breakouts" — capsule briefings on a given subject, e.g., helping children "survive" TV violence or video games.

From what I've seen, C-TREC tends to be a bit more alarmist in tone than is probably useful. But they have produced some very good materials, including **Getting Along — A Social Skills Curriculum** *(for K-4, available on audiotape), and some programs for television and radio. It is not always perfectly artful, but it does model intelligent, pro-social behavior for kids, and we don't get that from our disinfotainment channels yet. —PC*

●

Q. Will playing action-adventure video games make my child violent?

A. Maybe, maybe not. First let's face facts. Although there are some great educational video games coming into the market, the most popular titles are still action-adventure games in which the player must shoot, smash, blowup or vaporize his or her enemies in order to rack up the points and move to the next level of difficulty.

So far, results of a few recent video game studies look a lot like the findings from earlier TV studies: that is to say, all things being equal, playing violent video games can increase children's aggressive behavior or tolerance for aggressive behavior in others. This appears especially true for preteens. However, and it's a BIG however, whether your video-playing child will be affected by these games depends on a number of factors including: the amount of time a child spends playing these games, parents' attitudes and behavior about violence, and the child's exposure to TV, movie or real life violence.

Children's Television Resource & Education Center: 340 Townsend Street, Suite 423, San Francisco, CA 94107; 415/243-9943.

Great Videos for Kids
• The Family Video Guide

Disgusted by the "vast wasteland"? Convinced by everything else on this page that TV will burn away your kids' IQ? These books help you find stuff you'll not only let your kids watch, but want to watch with them. **Great Videos** *has a higher goo-goo quotient; let's say it's better for families with younger kids.* **The Family Video Guide** *has a surprisingly mature and tolerant range of films reviewed, and can help parents promote some pretty sophisticated social awareness with judicious viewing choices. —PC*

●

The Blackboard Jungle. Glenn Ford, Sidney Poitier, Anne Francis, Vic Morrow, Richard Kiley. 1955, B&W, 101 minutes. New teacher Ford is given a memorably rough time by teenage toughs at a New York City all-boys vocational school with a notorious discipline problem. This seminal 1950s juvenile delinquent picture shocked the nation with its grim take on urban youth crime and its disturbing implication of things to come. First "youth movie" to understand the pivotal cultural role of rock and roll, then in its infancy, by grafting "Rock Around the Clock" onto the otherwise all-jazz sound track. Poitier's breakthrough movie and the film debut of Morrow later the star of television's "Combat." Not rated. Most appreciated by ages ten and over. —*The Family Video Guide*

Great Videos for Kids
Catherine Cella. 1992; 157 pp. ISBN 0-8065-1377-2 $7.95 ($10.95 postpaid) from Carol Publishing Group, 120 Enterprise Avenue, Secaucus, NJ 07094; 800/447-2665

The Family Video Guide
Terry Catchpole & Catherine Catchpole. 1992; 188 pp. ISBN 0-913589-64-0 $12.95 ($15.45 postpaid) from Williamson Publishing Co., PO Box 185, Church Hill Road, Charlotte, VT 05445; 800/234-8791

Care Pooling

Caregiving is at the heart of family life. "Middle-aged" family members find themselves caring for the younger and older members of the family, often without relief or assistance. This book suggests an alternative to the sole-caregiver model: "care pooling," the exchange of practical help between caregivers. This boils down to asking others for help, using resources in your community that enable you to share the burden of care. It seems simple, but most people are uncomfortable asking for help. Here's direction on how to get started, what to say, and what you can expect in an exchange. Using this model, you'll find yourself more connected to your community, making some new friends, and better able to deal with some of the stress that comes with the role of sole caregiver. —Nancy Pietrafesa

•

Carepooling draws on the common ground of our collective caregiving. The details of our individual differences blur together as we learn to see that every one of us has mouths to feed, comfort to give, those we worry over, those we are learning to stand back and let go, and our own needs and wants to reconcile.

•

But making dependence inherently inferior and independence inherently superior is a defeating line of thinking when it comes to caregiving. Children, after all, have little choice but to need parents. The elderly may have few options about where they can afford to live or what care they need. Special needs children may grow up to be special needs adults, and there are many other uninvited reasons that we as adults can, at any time, become dependent on others for our care.

Being dependent to some degree is a fact of life all of our life. We never stop needing others; in fact, there is no way we can become independent or interdependent if we don't need others, learn the benefits of their help, and find self-worth in receiving.

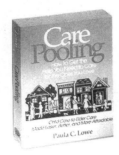

Care Pooling
(How to Get the Help You Need to Care for the Ones You Love)
Paula C. Lowe. 1993; 292 pp.
ISBN 1-881052-16-8
$14.95 ($18.45 postpaid) from Berrett-Koehler Publishers, 155 Montgomery Street, San Francisco, CA 94104; 800/929-2929

What Can I Do to Make a Difference?

The Who, What, When, Where, and How of social action. It's especially good for people who haven't had much experience in volunteering or in social action; a variety of activities, from writing a letter to organizing a boycott, should enable everyone to find his or her comfort level as an activist. We often forget to cultivate a sense of proactive citizenship in our children. This book will help you do just that. —NAP

•

The Valdez
Principles

1. Protection of the Biosphere: Minimize the release of pollutants that may cause environmental damage.
2. Sustainable Use of Natural Resources: Conserve nonrenewable natural resources through efficient use and careful planning.
3. Reduction and Disposal of Waste: Minimize the creation of waste, especially hazardous waste, and dispose of such materials in a safe, responsible manner.
4. Wise Use of Energy: Make every effort to use environmentally safe and sustainable energy sources to meet operating requirements.
5. Risk Reduction: Diminish environmental, health, and safety risks to employees and surrounding communities.
6. Marketing of Safe Products and Services: Sell products that minimize adverse environmental impact and that are safe for consumers.
7. Damage Compensation: Accept responsibility for any harm the company causes to the environment; conduct bio-remediation,

What Can I Do
to Make a Difference?
Richard Zimmerman. Plume Books, 1991; 401 pp. ISBN 0-452-26632-7
$15 ($17 postpaid) from Penguin USA/Consumer Sales, 120 Woodbine Street, Bergenfield, NJ 07621; 800/253-6476

and compensate affected parties.
8. Disclosure: Public dissemination of incidents relating to operations that harm the environment or pose health or safety hazards.
9. Environmental Directors and Managers: Appoint at least one board member who is qualified to represent environmental interests.

A Parent's Guide to Wills and Trusts

This well-written and informative guide gets us down to the facts of life — and death — related to our children and our assets. It won't enable you to do without a lawyer, but it will give you a working knowledge of what your attorney can do for you. The section on writing an ethical will — a statement of your ideals and hopes for your children — is excellent. These issues shouldn't be put off. This book will give you a good start. —NAP

•

An ethical will often tells your children the values you hold deepest, the most important lessons you've learned in life, your favorite sayings, special family expressions and the religious or secular writings you hold dearest to your heart. You might tell of mistakes you've made and, sometimes, even ask for forgiveness. This might be the time to finish unfinished business.

•

In general, setting up a living trust provides no protection against creditors. Since you can revoke the trust and maintain total control over your assets, you are considered to still own the assets while you are alive. At your death, the assets in the trust are usually subject to claims by your creditors.

It may be, however, that holding title as a joint tenant gives more creditor protection to your surviving joint tenant after you're gone. State law will determine if that's the case.

A Parent's Guide
to Wills and Trusts
Don Silver. 1992; 247 pp.
ISBN 0-944708-40-4
$11.95 ($14.95 postpaid) from Adams-Hall Publishing, PO Box 491002, Los Angeles, CA 90049; 800/888-4452

OTHER GREAT RESOURCES

Every Kid Counts: Margaret Brodkin, et al. 1993, HarperSanFrancisco.

The Kid's Guide to Social Action

Kids are a largely untapped force for social change. Elementary- and high-school-age children are aware of environmental and social problems, and care about them passionately. But few young people know what to do about creating solutions. This book showcases examples of kids who have influenced policy and solved problems in municipalities, counties, and states. It offers step-by-step advice on how to go about selecting a social problem, finding a creative solution, and putting it into action — writing letters that work, making effective phone calls, creating speeches, conducting surveys, circulating petitions, writing proposals, helping with fundraising, arranging media coverage, assisting political campaigns, lobbying. The book also offers a rich directory of resources — state house contacts, US government offices, contact groups — with addresses and telephone numbers. —HLR

Jackson kids plant eighteen 400-pound red maple trees near their school.

The Kid's Guide
to Social Action
Barbara A. Lewis. 1991; 185 pp.
ISBN 0-915793-29-6
$14.95 ($18.95 postpaid) from Free Spirit Publishing, Inc., 400 1st Avenue N., Suite 616, Minneapolis, MN 55401; 800/735-7323

MAKING TECHNOLOGY VISIBLE

THE MOST IMPORTANT PART OF ANY TECHNOLOGY, more often than not, turns out to be invisible. If you could peer through magical spectacles that would reveal the parts of aluminum cans that you normally don't see, for example, you would perceive lines of force connecting the contents of your refrigerator to global geopolitical conflicts.

When I pop open an aluminum can, it hardly ever occurs to me to think about the working conditions in the West Indies (bauxite is mined in Jamaica), or the costs of rejecting nuclear power in favor of other energy-production technologies (if the energy used to manufacture cans doesn't come from a nuclear reactor, it comes from one fossil fuel or another or from a dammed river). An aluminum can affects and is affected by the the cost-effectiveness of truck tires (which translates to miles-per-gallon-per-pound of cans) and the price of petroleum needed to transport all that ore, refined metal, and end-products around the world. Aluminum begins with someone digging the right kind of ore out of the earth, but the most expensive component of a can is the energy required to extract, process, manufacture, and transport it to your hand.

Profits and benefits from new technologies like aluminum foil and aluminum aircraft are visible, but costs and delayed or distant effects are invisible. What we need badly right now is a way for more and more people to see, understand, and decide collectively, through our discussions and our buying and voting decisions, exactly which trade-offs we are willing to make in return for technological conveniences. We need to find ways to make the invisible parts of technology more visible.

While an endless addictive quest for a "technological fix" is not the answer to the problem of building a sustainable civilization for billions of people on a planet with limited resources; neither, I believe, is it wise to reject the very technologies we are going to need in years to come. We need the best tools we can muster to manage the world of energy-consuming billions we've inherited. We can't discard our tools, despite their evident defects, because we need them for our survival.

How do we find new modes of perceiving technology, new ways to think about, design, and use tools? How can we develop more conscious means for democratic societies to make decisions about technologies? The next step beyond access to tools is access to understanding how to use them. In what directions does that step proceed? How do we start learning to look at the world of technology, and our places in it, in new ways? Before we can hope to achieve answers, we must elevate the level of discourse from an argument between tree-huggers and nuke-lovers. The world is more complicated than that. We need richer, more widespread, less simplistically polarized discourse about technology and social issues, because that is the only kind of environment where viable solutions are likely to emerge.

The following pages encompass a wide spectrum of opinion, from direct attacks upon technology to tech tricks from hardware hackers. Those who think about technology's broader consequences, and those who build virtual reality goggles in their garage, those who seek to influence public policy and those who want to roll their own technology, are included. Our eclectic gathering of critics and enthusiasts helps us look at future technologies — artificial life, artificial evolution, nanotechnology, virtual reality — and at the cultural and social impact of current tools. Think of this domain as the laboratory for a thought-experiment. Maybe one or more of you who read this will help devise solutions to the problems raised here. —HLR

Dark-tech, Bright-tech

THE MOST IMPORTANT ASPECT OF ANY TECHNOLOGY, more often than not, turns out to be how it is applied, by whom, and for what purpose. Consider lasers. They can be used for delicate eye surgery, rock dance light shows, pickups on CD players, and death rays. Corporate planners and politicians may decide what uses take precedence, but it is scientists, designers and design engineers (by whatever name) who make the deployment of a technology possible. They transform a basic technology into available products. It is unfortunate that persons with so important a mandate are so narrowly specialized and so vulnerable to compromise and corruption.

Some of the worst problems arise when a new technology is utilized for weaponry. There is some truth to the cliche that guns don't kill people, *people* kill people; but it won't do. There is a curious short-sighted state of mind that seems to dominate weapons work. For example, thousands of anti-personnel mines, permanently undetectable by any means, are buried each year in the soil of what is (temporarily) regarded as "enemy territory." Even the conquerer cannot use or reclaim the land, yet those mines are still sold. An ordinary citizen, perhaps a neighbor, got up one morning, had coffee, kissed the wife and kids, and went to the office to design those mines *on purpose* to be an ongoing, irretrievable scourge. Other good citizens made, packed and shipped the unselectively maiming devices. I wonder what those folks tell their kids they do for a living? Dark-tech tends to darken mind and spirit.

Seemingly benign technologies may have equally undesirable consequences designed into them. Automobiles were once hailed as freedom-bringing, egalitarian transport, and for their role in banishing dangerous urban diseases engendered by streets fouled with manure (horse exhaust). But car exhaust has turned out to be a leading cause of disease and environmental degradation in ways not easily foreseen a hundred years ago.

Some technologies inherently require a pact with the Devil. Auto collisions have killed and injured millions of people and animals; a price societies seem willing to pay. Some carnage is inevitable if people are to move about quickly and easily. (If cars had not been developed, millions of horses would probably be even more dangerous.) Some of the environmental damage is preventable by better car design (see pp. 117 and 342). But what's really needed is a redesign of the entire auto-based transport system, considering every aspect. Many other technological systems need similar attention if they (and perhaps we) are to continue.

Designers have not been educated or required to consider the effects of their decisions. Their clients are often investors or marketers rather than the actual users (much less Nature, who is always a client nevertheless). Until recently, designers and those who hired them had little concern for such matters as the fate of worn-out products, or the safety of the fabricating workers. Environmental problems belonged to somebody else. It is now obvious that technology-caused problems belong to all of us. People acting as designers, and their masters, must think comprehensively if technology is to be employed for the greatest good while doing little harm.

To accomplish this, Buckminster Fuller called for a new discipline — *Comprehensive Anticipatory Design Science*. It's still not formally taught. Ranging far beyond generalists who know a little bit about a lot of things, comprehensivists work to understand many specialties and the connections between them. A high standard of integrity is required. Demonstrations of comprehensive thought are scarce, but impressive. (The Rocky Mountain Institute [p. 117] is an inspiring example.) Since nobody can be entirely comprehensive, there's obviously plenty left to do. Here's some homework to get you started. —JB

Hand's End

How do nature, humanity, and technology fit together? This question is shaping up as the major challenge of the millennium. A logger, an Earth-Firster, a free-market economist, and an ethnobotanist are going to come up with very different maps of where each category begins and the other one ends.

The author's central arguments are that technology is an extension of what it is to be human, at a deep level, and that the way we see nature is powerfully influenced by our technologies. From the first hand-tools to genetic engineering, technological evolution has continually redefined our views of human nature. We see the world in a certain way that has everything to do with our tool-making penchant.

Perceiving technology, human nature and nature as existing in opposition and contradistinction has been part of the problem, Rothenberg claims: our human ability to transform the "natural" environment into an "artificial" one is something that exists within nature. We must perceive and treat technology as an extension of our humanity before we can effectively guide its use by moral decisions about the future we want to create. —HLR

●

It begins with the hand — the grasp that pulls and directs; the movements enacted then fashioned out of material. Fingers trained to guide tools to re-shape the world in our image, bridging the gap between those two infinities: human idea and tactile nature.

●

Tools change the range of humanity and the direction of human development, yet there must remain some goal outside of technology which machines should help us to reach. A common answer is mastery or control of the world, but recent events have shown that this kind of goal is not enough to prevent us from devastating the Earth in the attempt to take hold of its reins. There should be something else to strive for.

Here I will try to consider what "nature" would mean as this goal — not the irrevocable, essential forces of nature which make our evolution possible but a nature in which we struggle to fit, even after we have passed through the stage of exploitative civilization. This is not a question of looking back, but of reaching forward to imagine that we can find a home in the world after expending so much effort on its transformation.

I come to this project after several years working on the foundations of deep ecology, a philosophy of the relationship between human and natural which urges us to fit into an enveloping, moral sense of nature which is larger than any human purpose and which stands for the Earth or for life as a whole. After a time, I began to be suspicious of this approach, as it tends to narrow the meaning of nature to cover only those facets of the world which may be seen as free from human influence. My

Hand's End
(Technology and the Limits of Nature)
David Rothenberg. University of California Press, 1993; 256 pp. ISBN 0-520-08054-8
$30 ($33 postpaid) from California/Princeton Fulfillment Services, 1445 Lower Ferry Road, Ewing, NJ 08618; 800/777-4726

intuition is that nature is far more important to humanity than this — a context which we discover when we touch, use, and change it. Hence, I turned to the study of technology, the way we delineate the world according to our purposes. We are always involved in reconceiving nature, whether we know so or not. This nature is more tangible than any imagined wilderness empty of the human gaze.

Water raised up from a river by means of the energy of its own current. Wheel *T* turns lantern *P*, turning gear *B*; wheel *D* and lantern *C* cause bellows *K* to draw water up through pipe *S* into channels *N* and *R*. A blueprint from the past, technical documentation for an almost practical invention. But there is more to the image than practice. See how the building is decorated with the fantastic: legless human bodies twirled on stems; gargoyles, goblins, fish and worms — ornamentation for the mundane and the mechanical.

Machines have always been close to magic, and never far from emotion. Watch the three faces of those guiding its operation: they exhibit suspicion, anxiety, and reassurance. Natural flow is diverted through the implements of humanity. From intention to draw water away from its natural course comes the definition of the human course: bending and defining nature at one and the same time.

The Evolution of Technology

Both the tech-happy and the tech-wary will find news in this view of technology as an evolutionary system. Fascinating case studies show how society-bending inventions — even "breakthroughs" — proceed from small, incremental variations upon earlier inventions. The revolutionary Bell Labs transistor descended, with modifications, from the old-time "cat-whisker" crystal radio; Eli Whitney's "new" cotton gin had antecedents in Egypt; Watt's steam engine, often credited (or blamed) for the Industrial Revolution, was the child of a whole lineage of older working steam engines. Few things are as new as they look. Another way of saying that is: All the inventions that will push and stress our society in the near future are already alongside us in their penultimate forms.
—Kevin Kelly

●

In his utopian novel *Erewhon* (1872) and essays such as "Darwin Among the Machines" (1863) Samuel Butler whimsically explored the idea that machines developed in a fashion remarkably similar to the evolution of living beings. His ideas inspired the popular evolutionary fantasy novels of nineteenth- and twentieth-century science fiction in which rapidly evolving machines surpass and supplant humans whose own evolutionary development has stagnated. Butler's influence is also evident in modern speculative essays that predict either the coming of a new symbiotic relationship between humans and machines or the supersession of humankind by new forms of technology that are capable of self-replication, such as robots and computers.

●

The ease with which barbed wire can be made has led historian of technology D. S. L. Cardwell to suggest that it could well have been invented long before the third quarter of the nineteenth century, perhaps in ancient Greece. We might question the idea of barbed wire in

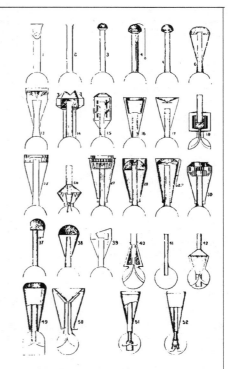

Excess of novelty: American smokestack spark arrestors (1831-57). These smokestack designs are some of the more than one thousand that were patented in the nineteenth century.

classical antiquity and move the date forward to the Renaissance when wire-drawing was first practiced on a large scale, but even that shift would not invalidate Cardwell's contention that such a simple artifact, crafted from twisted lengths of wire, could have been made much earlier than it was. The invention of barbed wire certainly did not depend on the advancement of scientific knowledge or on the perfection of some complex and precise technological process. Why then did it first appear in late nineteenth-century America? Or more specifically, what were the prevailing conditions that led three men to invent barbed wire in DeKalb, Illinois, in 1873?

The Evolution of Technology
George Basalla. 1988; 248 pp. ISBN 0-521-29681-1 $13.95 ($17.45 postpaid) from Cambridge University Press, 110 Midland Avenue, Port Chester, NY 10573; 800/872-7423 (outside NY), 800/227-0247 (NY only)

OTHER GREAT RESOURCES

Politics & Technology: John Street. 1992, Guilford Publications.

The notion that tools are neutral ignores society as cause and consequence: technology and society are interdependent. The inverse notion, that tools are not neutral, also ignores societal cause and consequence. Here's a solid background for coherent decisionmaking by an informed populace.
—John Sumser

Technics and Civilization

Lewis Mumford was an unusual man. He wasn't an engineer or a scientist, he wasn't an historian or sociologist, you can't identify him as a business-man or a literary man or an academic. He was profound, poetic, knowledge-able. He took care of the large and small things in his books.

I have read and reread his 1934 Technics and Civilization *since I first encountered it in 1957. —Steve Baer*

●

Once we have generally reached a new technical plateau we may remain on the level with very minor ups and downs for thousands of years. What are the implications of this approaching equilibrium?

First: equilibrium in the environment. This means first the restoration of the balance between man and nature. The conservation and restoration of soils, the re-growth wherever this is expedient and possible, of the forest cover to provide shelter for wild life and to maintain man's primitive background as a source of recreation, whose major importance increases in proportion to the refinement of his cultural heritage. The use of tree crops where possible as substitutes for annuals, and the reliance upon kinetic energy — sun, falling water, wind — instead of upon limited capital supplies. The conservation of minerals and metals: the larger use of scrap metals. The conservation of the environment itself as a resource, and the fitting of human needs into the pattern formed by the region as a whole: hence the progressive restoration out of such unbalanced regions as the over-urbanized metropolitan areas of London and New York. Is it necessary to point out that all this marks the approaching end of the miner's economy? Not mine and move, but stay and cultivate are the watchwords of the new order. Is it also necessary to emphasize that with respect to our use of metals, the conservative use of the existing supply will lower the importance of the mine in relation to other parts of the natural environment? *[He said this in 1934! —JB]*

●

The important thing to bear in mind is that the failure to evaluate the machine and to integrate it in society as a whole was not due simply to defects in distributing income, to errors of management, to greed and narrow-mindedness of the industrial leaders: it was also due to a weakness of the entire philosophy upon which the new techniques and inventions were grounded. The leaders and enterprisers of the period believed that they had avoided the necessity for introducing values, except those which were automatically recorded in profits and prices. They believed that the problem of justly distributing goods could be sidetracked by creating an abundance of them: that the problem of applying one's energies wisely could be canceled out simply by multiplying them: in short, that most of the difficulties that had hitherto vexed mankind had a mathematical or mechanical — that is a quantitative — solution. The belief that values could be dispensed with constituted the new system of values.

Technics and Civilization
Lewis Mumford. Harvest Books, 1963; 495 pp. ISBN 0-15-688254-X $18.95 ($22.45 postpaid). Harcourt Brace Trade Dept./Harcourt Brace & Co., 6277 Sea Harbor Drive, Orlando, FL 32887-4300; 800/543-1918

Left: Roentgen photograph of Nautilus. Nature's use of the spiral in construction.

Below: Section of modern hydroturbine: spiral form dictated by mechanical necessity.

Mechanization Takes Command

The history of the swan song of complex and ingenious handicraft: the door lock, the stove, the butcher's tools, the plow. Watch the human hand shrivel and the machine take command. Finally, I could understand how floor mats turned to spring mattresses. A comprehensive look at what European and American humans believe is necessary for comfort. —Peter Warshall

●

In the popular sense, 'streamline' is used interchangeably with the word 'modern.'

From the start, it was understood that the phrase was not to be taken literally. Today the layman, unfamiliar with aerodynamics, calls almost everything 'streamline' when he really means 'graceful lines.' We have 'streamline' radio cabinets, toasters, cigarette lighters, and even gasoline with 'streamline' action. The development of the science of aerodynamics and its application to airships and airplanes has created in the public a sense for fleeting lines, and these lines, being recognized by designers as a decorative element, have been emphasized to give the impression of speed. The automobile manufacturer, to give the sales appeal of a visual impression of the speed that the engineer has built into his machine, has used and is using 'streamlining' extensively.

Mechanization Takes Command
(A Contribution to Anonymous History) Siegfried Giedion. 1948; 743 pp. ISBN 0-393-00489-9 $16.95 postpaid from W.W. Norton & Co./ Order Dept., 800 Keystone Industrial Park, Scranton, PA 18512; 800/233-4830

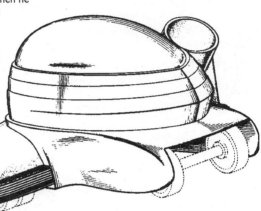

Streamlined casing for vacuum cleaner, U.S. Patent Design, 1943.

The Pentagon of Power

It's easy to O.D. on Fuller, Kahn, and other technological prophets. Lewis Mumford is a fine, careful antidote. He examines the unexamined premises that lead to excess. —SB

●

Western man not merely blighted in some degree every culture that he touched, whether 'primitive' or advanced, but he also robbed his own descendants of countless gifts of art and craftsmanship, as well as precious knowledge passed on only by word of mouth that disappeared with the dying languages of dying peoples. With this extirpation of earlier cultures went a vast loss of botanical and medical lore, representing many thousands of years of watchful observation and empirical experiment whose extraordinary discoveries — such as the American Indian's use of snakeroot (reserpine) as a tranquilizer in mental illness — modern medicine has now, all too belatedly, begun to appreciate.

●

Scientific truth achieved the status of an absolute, and the incessant pursuit and expansion of knowledge became the only recognized categorical imperative.

Now, if the history of the human race teaches any plain lessons, this is one of them: *Man cannot be trusted with absolutes.*

●

Unfortunately, if "meaning means association," as Gary Walters observes, then dissociation and non-intercourse must result in a decrease of shared meanings. Thus in time, specialized knowledge, "knowing more and more about less and less," finally turns into secret knowledge — accessible only to an inner priesthood, whose sense of power is in turn inflated by their privileged command of 'trade' or official secrets.

●

The salutary truth of the old proverb 'Haste Makes Waste' was overridden by the new principle: 'Haste and Waste Make Money.'

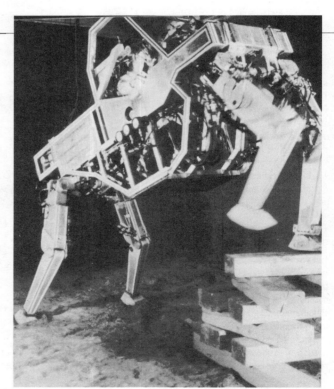

Behold the astronaut, fully equipped for duty: a scaly creature, more like an oversized ant than a primate — certainly not a naked god.

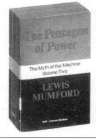

The Pentagon of Power
(The Myth of the Machine) Lewis Mumford. Harcourt Brace & Co., 1970; 496 pp. ISBN 0-15-671610-0 $12.95 ($16.45 postpaid). Harcourt Brace Trade Dept., 6277 Sea Harbor Drive, Orlando, FL 32887-4300; 800/543-1918

Architect or Bee?

A practicing engineer and Marxist social activist, Mike Cooley was one of the people behind the Lucas Workers' Plan, an effort by aerospace workers to save their jobs by proposing 150 new products for the corporation to manufacture. (Management was sublimely uninterested, and eventually managed to remove Cooley and other activists from their jobs.) His vision is of a world in which technology serves people rather than vice versa, concentrating on exchange use rather than exchange value. Cooley believes that the mass of ordinary people can and should be involved in directing the technology they live with, and he draws on many examples where this has already happened on a small scale. Though short on consideration of the externalities of manufacturing, Architect or Bee? provides an exciting hint of a future in which questioning technology has become a useful and common activity for designers and workers alike.
— Mike Gunderloy

Architect or Bee?
(The Human/Technology Relationship)
Mike Cooley. 1980;
150 pp.
ISBN 0-89608-131-1
$7 ($10 postpaid).
South End Press,
PO Box 741, Monroe, ME 04951;
800/533-8478

•

For those that do not work in the automotive industry, it is difficult to appreciate how bad the situation is becoming and to what extent workers are being paced by these computerized, high technology systems. In the section where they press out the car bodies in one car company, workers are subject to an agreement on the makeup of their rest allowance. The elements are as follows

Trips to the lavatory
1.62 minutes. It is computer precise; not 1.6 or 1.7, but 1.62!

For fatigue
1.3 minutes

Sitting down after standing too long
65 seconds

For monotony
32 seconds — and so the grotesque litany goes on.

The methods engineers located the toilets strategically close to the production line so that operators could literally flash in and flash out. What arrogance some technolo-

Autonomous Technology • The Whale and the Reactor

Autonomous Technology is very much an academic work, a survey of the philosophy of technology with special attention to the notion that somehow the things we create are no longer under our control. The more personal, more mature Whale and the Reactor surveys a variety of themes, including the political aspect of artifacts, the promise of computers, the hope of decentralization, and the shaky legacy of the appropriate-technology movement. Winner does not offer any easy solutions or put his faith in a revolution in human thinking. Instead, he suggests lines of inquiry and action which, though hard, offer some real hope of leading to change. —MG

•

The concern of science and technology with the possibilities of control have often found expression in terms which closely parallel the language of politics. This is perhaps not surprising if one recalls that both politics and technics have as their central focus the sources and exercise of power. Our thinking about technology, however, seems inextricably bound to a single conception of the manner in which power is used — the style of the despotic, one-way control of the master over the slave.

•

In most modern technological systems autonomous action is truly available to the center alone. Some have argued that peripheral parts also exercise a measure of control by selecting which information actually reaches the center. A few varieties of highly technical organization, think tanks like RAND for example, have found that attempts at central coordination are more of a hindrance than help in getting work done. Taking such paltry signs as a cue, some observers have begun to predict that a collegial decentralization is the wave of the future. But compared to the success of central command in the likes of the Apollo program or worldwide operations of ITT under Harold Geneen, the alleged counterexamples are pathetic.
—*Autonomous Technology*

•

Taken as a whole, beliefs of this kind constitute what I would call mythinformation: the almost religious conviction that a widespread adoption of computers and communications along with easy access to electronic information will automatically produce a better world for human living. It is a peculiar form of enthusiasm that characterizes social fashions of the latter decades of the twentieth century. Many people who have grown cynical or discour-aged about other aspects of social life are completely enthralled by the supposed redemptive qualities of computers and telecommunications. —*The Whale and the Reactor*

Autonomous Technology
(Technics-out-of-Control as a Theme in Political Thought)
Langdon Winner. 1977; 386 pp.
ISBN 0-262-73049-9
$13.95 ($16.95 postpaid). The MIT Press/ Order Dept., 55 Hayward Street, Cambridge, MA 02142; 800/356-0343, email mitpress-orders@mit.edu

The Whale and the Reactor
(A Search for Limits in an Age of High Technology)
Langdon Winner. University of Chicago Press, 1988; 200 pp. ISBN 0-226-90211-0
$9.95 ($12.95 postpaid) from Chicago Distribution Center, 11030 S. Langley Avenue, Chicago, IL 60628; 800/621-2736

OTHER GREAT RESOURCES

American Genesis (A Century of Invention and Technological Enthusiasm): Thomas P. Hughes. 1989, Penguin Books.

Notes on the Underground

"What are the consequences when human beings dwell in an environment that is predominantly built rather than given?" Rosalind Williams provides an uncommonly astute and provocative array of answers through the metaphor of living underground — literally and in literature. The unusual vantage point encourages self-examination; I found my own experience and ideas clarified, strengthened, and occasionally shot down. The book is a spellbinder disguised as an academic treatise. —J. Baldwin

•

What is unique about the natural environment, what can never be replaced by the technological one, is its independence of the social order.

•

Natural despoliation is not just a result of economic pressures; it is also a political action aimed at removing a source of subversion.

•

We have always lived below the surface, beneath the atmospheric ocean, in a closed, sealed, finite environment, where everything is recycled and everything is limited. Until now, we have not felt like underground dwellers because the natural system of the globe has seemed so large in comparison with any systems we might construct. That is changing. What is commonly called environmental consciousness could be described as subterranean consciousness — awareness that we are in a very real sense not on earth but inside it.

Notes on the Underground
(An Essay on Technology, Society and the Imagination)
Rosalind Williams. 1990; 265 pp.
ISBN 0-262-73098-7
$14.95 ($17.95 postpaid). The MIT Press/ Order Dept., 55 Hayward Street, Cambridge, MA 02142; 800/356-0343, email mitpress-orders@mit.edu

gist had to be able to do that to another human being! If we have strikes in the automotive industry we must not be surprised. In my view they are right to strike against conditions of this kind, yet all the time this is the kind of philosophy behind the design of much of the equipment produced for industry today.

Up to the 1940s, the draftsperson could design a component, draw it, stress it out, specify the material for it and the lubrication required. Nowadays the designer designs, the draftsperson draws, the metallurgist specifies the material, the stress analyst analyzes the structure and the tribologist specifies the lubrication. Each of these fragmented parts can be taken over by equipment such as this automatic drafting equipment.

Questioning Technology

Does our industrial techno-society have you worried? You should be, and the thirty-one writers in this anthology tell you why as they present most of the principal anti-tech arguments. We're not talking emotional airhead stuff here, either — this is the carefully thought-out view. And only the negative view; there are no balancing arguments or suggestions for correcting the problems. (Maybe no corrections are possible?) The editor says that this collection is intended to be thought-provoking. It certainly is. Your worst fears will be abundantly confirmed. Perhaps this will goad you into appropriate action. —J. Baldwin, unreconstructed technotwit

●

The vitality of democratic politics depends on people's willingness to act together — to appear before each other in person, speak their minds, deliberate, and decide what they will do. This is considerably different from the model upheld as a breakthrough for democracy: logging onto one's computer, receiving the latest information, and sending back a digitized response. No computer enthusiasm is more poignant than the faith that the personal computer, as it becomes more sophisticated, cheaper, and more simple to use, will become a potent equalizer in society. Presumably, ordinary citizens equipped with microcomputers will counter the influence of large, computer-based organizations. This notion echoes the eighteenth- and nineteenth-century revolutionary belief that placing firearms in the hands of the people would overthrow entrenched authority. But the military defeat of the Paris Commune in 1871 made clear that arming the people may not be enough. Using a personal computer makes one no more powerful vis-a-vis, say, the US National Security Agency than flying a hang glider establishes a per-

Questioning Technology
(Tool, Toy or Tyrant?)
John Zerzan & Alice Carnes, Editors. 1991; 222 pp. ISBN 0-86571-205-0
$12.95 ($15.45 postpaid). New Society Publishers, 4527 Springfield Avenue, Philadelphia, PA 19143; 800/333-9093

son as a match for the US Air Force. — Langdon Winner

●

A nightmarish vision of human workers as "materials" is conjured in the following statement by Robert Boguslaw, a leading computer systems engineer:

"We must take care to prevent . . . [a] single-sided analysis of the complex characteristics of one type of systems materials, namely human beings. What we need is an inventory of the manner in which human beings can be controlled and a description of some of the instruments that will help us achieve that control. If this provides us with sufficient handles on human materials so that we can think of them as metal parts, electrical power, or chemical reactions, then we have succeeded in placing human materials on the same footing as any other materials and can begin to proceed with our problems of system design."

As the rhythm of the workplace speeds up to match that of the computer, the resulting increase in both load and rate of work, aggravated by the reliance on symbols and abstractions that the computer demands, creates new physical and psychological pressures. — Craig Brod

Technology and Choice

*These essays from past issues of **Technology and Culture** dance around the central questions of controlling technology past and present. Individually, they furnish useful insight on how we got into our current situation. Taken as a whole, the selections exemplify the intricacies involved — a good thing to keep in mind when proposing countermeasures. —JB*

●

We can now ask to what extent popular beliefs about technology and housework are true. First, there is the popular assumption that technology has made housework easier. Certainly market services have eased some elements of work, and convenience foods may also have reduced fatigue. As for utilities, we can only surmise that, while they did reduce fatigue, their secondary effects created more and new forms of housework. None of the technologies increased general pleasantness of housework, made tasks interesting, or improved the sense of self-worth of the housewife.

Second, the popular belief that technology

Technology and Choice
Marcel C. LaFollette & Jeffrey K. Stine. University of Chicago Press, 1991; 341 pp. ISBN 0-226-46777-5
$16.95 ($19.95 postpaid). Chicago Distribution Center, 11030 S. Langley Avenue, Chicago, IL 60628; 800/621-2736

makes housework less expensive is not well supported. The impact of utilities on cost cannot be measured, while appliances and convenience foods are more expensive. Only market services appear to be potentially cheaper than work in the home, but this is contingent on placing an economic value on the homemaker's labor.

Third is the time factor, for which popular belief would lead us to expect a decrease. However, we find that if time is saved by some technological means, the saving is offset by concomitant activities and by maintaining the new technological systems. In the past, the most significant factors contributing to saving time in meal preparation were nontechnological, such as smaller families and the increased labor-force participation of women. Now, real savings can be realized primarily by removal of this activity from the home.

Finally, popular belief has it that technology has made for less housework and thus for a redistribution of household labor among household members. However, the evidence (as opposed to anecdotes) indicates that household specialization of labor probably has not changed over time and may actually have become more burdensome to women.

Who Owns Information?

The old and fundamental social contracts about privacy, property, ownership, and censorship have been rendered obsolete by fiber-optic cables and microprocessors. Tricks that used to be physically difficult to do, like reproducing an image, altering it, and sending it to millions of locations around the world, can be accomplished today in a few keystrokes. Technologies formerly restricted to governments and large corporations, such as the information-processing tools to maintain dossiers on millions of people, are now available to small businesses. Battles are beginning to break out over who owns your telephone number, whether your boss can snoop on your email, and dozens of other social issues that result from the collision of real lives and new technologies.

Anne Wells Branscomb tackles all these issues, and asks all the questions technophiles have been reluctant to confront. Most importantly for nonspecialist readers, Branscomb takes neither a legalistic or technical ap-

Who Owns Information?
(From Privacy to Public Access)
Anne Wells Branscomb. Basic Books, 1994; 320 pp. ISBN 0-465-09175-X
$25 ($27.75 postpaid). HarperCollins Publishers/Direct Mail, PO Box 588, Dunmore, PA 18512; 800/331-3761

proach. She brings each issue to life via case histories that show how the technicalities play out in daily affairs.

Right now, what we know and say about the future of our rights and responsibilities in cyberspace is a significant factor in shaping social policies. Read this book. Talk with your friends about the issues it raises. Getting the answers is not as important as raising the questions. —HLR

●

Recent advances in computers have made possible "point-of-sale" data collection systems similar to one used at Dahl's Foods Inc., in a prosperous Des Moines, Iowa, suburb. Each checkout counter holds a color computer screen and an electronic gadget to read the "frequent-shopper" cards the customers carry. Buried inside each plastic card is a computer chip that records every item purchased, along with the buyer's name, address, age, social security number, employer, income, debts, children, pets, and other personal information. Those frequent-shopper cards are tools in a technological revolution changing the marketplace in a way that should stir fears that personal privacy is being invaded on a scale more massive than ever before. Shoppers use the cards voluntarily, receiving in exchange special offers directed to their personal preferences, but are unaware of the additional use to which the store puts their cards. . . .

Citicorp . . . is building a National House-

See also Computerization and Controversy (p. 22).

OTHER GREAT RESOURCES

Ethics in an Age of Technology: Ian G. Barbour. 1992, Harper San Francisco.

War in the Age of Intelligent Machines: Manuel DeLanda. 1991, Zone Books.

hold Purchase Data Base covering 40 million households — nearly half the homes in the United States — with information to be gathered from 12,000 retail stores, and is eager to sell what its databases contain. Gerald Saltzgaber, chief executive of Citicorp's Point-of-Sale Information Services, disclosed with pride: "Imagine how Coke would like to know the households that drink Pepsi by name and address and then be able to track them. This is targeted marketing based on absolute knowledge of what the household actually purchases."

Disappearing through the Skylight

*Everything we used to know as "the real world" is disappearing. That is the thesis of **Disappearing through the Skylight**, a cross-disciplinary examination of something more fundamental than future shock.*

The author focuses on changes in nature, history, language, art, and human evolution that have taken place since the beginning of the twentieth century.

"Because the changes have been fundamental, the concepts — and even the vocabularies and images in which the concepts tend to be framed — no longer seem to objectify a real world. It is as though progress were making the real world invisible.

"This book is about the ways culture has changed in the past centuries, changing the identities of all those born into it. Its metaphor for the effect of change on culture is 'disappearance.'"

Our relationship with machines might already have altered our conceptions of ourselves: "Is the idea of what it is to be human disappearing, along with so many other ideas, through the modern skylights?" — HLR [Suggested by Shel Kaphan]

Disappearing through the Skylight
(Culture & Technology in the 20th Century)
O. B. Hardison Jr.
Penguin Books, 1990; 416 pp.
$12.95 ($14.95 postpaid). Penguin USA/Consumer Sales, 120 Woodbine Street, Bergenfield, NJ 07621; 800/253-6476

● Because of its close alliance with technology, architecture objectifies the forms of modern culture with great clarity. Since the turn of the century, a global architectural style reflecting the state of the art at the moment of design has begun to replace local and traditional styles. Thus a suspension bridge has the same form whether over a gorge in the Himalayas or the mouth of San Francisco Bay. A Hilton Hotel offers essentially the same accommodations whether in Tokyo or Denver, and the visible similarities are objective manifestations of invisible similarities in, for example, administrative structures and accounting and financial policies. By the same token, a McDonald's hamburger is the same in New York and Rome, and a Pepsi-Cola produces the same bubbles in Vladivostok and Grand Rapids. In all of these cases, the effect of change has been the disappearance of regional and parochial identities and the emergence of a global consciousness.

Technology and Culture

This is where people interested in technology and its effects on various cultures do battle. The tone is generally academic — not surprising in the quarterly publication of the august and slightly arcane Society for the History of Technology. Papers attend the history, development and philosophy of technology from megaview to angels-on-a-pinhead detail. Some dry bones here and there, but some offerings are from intrepid critics — a few with metaphorical grease on their hands — attempting to untangle the vexing questions that most investigators ignore, dismiss, politicize, or get wrong. Gems are to be found here. Among them you'll encounter the frontier, which is what we came for. Good reading for techno-twits, -crats, and -phobes. —J. Baldwin

● World War I caused the first energy crisis in Finland. The importation of coal slumped radically, and the supply of lamp oil (paraffin) gradually dried up. The scarcity of foodstuffs, combined with price regulation and rationing, precipitated the rise of a black market. Rumors about exhausted supplies of food and other necessities increased anxiety in the country. People were afraid that the supply of candles and matches would be depleted. The shortage of fuels and wartime inflation turned electricity into an unbeatable source of light. It did not vanish from the legal market like many other necessities because of hoarding and speculation; electricity could be generated continuously by means of indigenous energy sources (hydropower, firewood, and wood wastes). Owing to price regulation, electricity rates were not affected by the soaring inflation. As a result, in the areas that were wired, electricity became the cheapest and most reliable source of light . . . . In the so-called electrification frenzy (*sahko-istysvimma*), people neglected to consider technological expertise and economic profitability. The lack of equipment made the situation still worse. Distribution networks were sometimes built so hastily that barbed wire was used for overhead lines and bottlenecks for insulators.

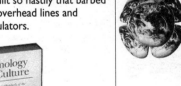

Technology and Culture
Robert C. Post, Editor.
$27.50/year (4 issues; includes membership in the Society for the History of Technology). University of Chicago Press/Journals Division, PO Box 37005, Chicago, IL 60637; 312/702-7600

Great Mambo Chicken and the Transhuman Condition

*The core beliefs of several different technology cults — immortality via cryonics, space colonies, biospheres, Dyson spheres, nanotechnology, artificial life, downloading minds into computers — were gleefully seeded by Catalogs and **CoEv**s of years past. There are people behind all of these notions: people who want to freeze their heads in liquid nitrogen and store their brains until future scientists figure out how to reconstitute them, people who are worried about the fate of the galaxy because they plan to live that long.*

Ed Regis plays the role of an anthropologist on an ethnographic expedition to the subcircles of American culture where cryogenic re-animation, galactic-scale engineering, and homebrewed space travel are commonplace subjects of conversation. Regis doesn't make fun of the people

Great Mambo Chicken and the Transhuman Condition
(Science Slightly Over the Edge)
Ed Regis. 1990; 308 pp. ISBN 0-201-56751-2
$8.95 ($12.95 postpaid). Addison-Wesley Publishing Co./Order Dept., 1 Jacob Way, Reading, MA 01867; 800/447-2226

he describes, but he does show how the grandiosity of their ideas — dismantling the outer planets to capture enough of the sun's energy to fuel a population of trillions, for example — reflects that immensely confident view of our own capacities that has distinguished the human race. We're bigger than amoebae, smaller than planets, our ancestors were swinging in the trees very recently, we're good with tools, and we've already started tinkering with the forces that light the stars. Regis evokes humor, awe, and continued reflection on the sheer chutzpah of Homo sapiens in this informal but well-informed joyride through the territory of the high-tech high-hubrists. —HLR [Suggested by Gregory Daurer]

● For Freeman Dyson, the main reason why you had to enclose the solar system was to make room for a growing population. "Malthusian pressures," Dyson had said, "will ultimately drive an intelligent species to adopt some such efficient exploitation of its available resources. One should expect that, within a few thousand years of its entering the stage of industrial development, any intelligent species should be found occupying an artificial biosphere which completely surrounds its parent star."

And for Dave Criswell, too, the essence of life was constant growth and proliferation. "Once you get growth started," he said, "it's not obvious what can stop it." Which, to Criswell, was just as it should be. The universe, after all, was just *dead matter*, and the more of it that got converted into life and mind the better.

Others, such as Frank Tipler, were even more explicit about the need for life to keep expanding out into the universe until the cosmos had been completely subdued. "If life is to survive at all, at just the bare subsistence level," he said, "it must necessarily engulf the entire universe at some point in the future. It does not have the option of remaining in a limited region. Mere survival dictates expansion."

●

Well, all that fine theoretical talk about omnipotent assemblers performing miracles of creation (*complete control over the structure of matter*), the talk about people putting themselves in computers and then installing those computers in bush robots (*in just fifty years*) , all that talk was well and good — except that a skeptical type might be permitted a brief moment of wondering what had been accomplished so far.

What progress had been made? How much of those grandiose plans had actually been accomplished? There had to be some anchor for this in the real world, otherwise all that top-notch hubristic adventuring, as adventuring, as admirable as it might have been in own right, all of it could be dismissed as . . . mere *theory*.

The fact was that the required Show 'n' tell for the hubristic intellectual voyagers actually took place. It began on Monday morning, September 21, 1987 — that's when it started, the world's first conference on artificial life. How fitting it was, too, that the conference was held at the Los Alamos National Laboratory, a place that, for obvious historical reasons, was pretty much given over to *results*. You could talk all you wanted, at the lab, about what type of explosive might be best suited for this or that sort of bomb, but then you had to go out to the canyon, or to the proving ground, or over to the Nevada test site, and put your invention to actual trial. Hopefully, it would blow up.

IVAN ILLICH ONCE commented rather impolitely, "If you insist on working with the poor, if this is your vocation, then at least work among the poor who can tell you to go to hell." He suggests that you work nearer home. When relatively rich North Americans work abroad, they often do more harm than good, especially by exporting our values — often the worst ones — into an area where they have no natural enemies to keep them in balance. I agree; my own overseas efforts have produced no significant lasting benefits to anyone. (Except me: "doing time" is a great way to learn.) A contribution of my airfare would probably have been more effective. Nonetheless, there are more and more examples of projects where a spirited, humble application of expertise has done some good; people are learning how to help in an effective way at last. The most successful projects seem to be those that deeply involve local people. —J. Baldwin

Appropriate Technology Sourcebook and Microfiche Library

More than one thousand of the proven-best-worldwide AT books are sorted out, indexed, and given succinct reviews in this most useful book. Even more remarkable is that the book also serves as the annotated index to a matching portable microfiche library containing the entire contents of every one of those books, illustrations and all. That's more than 140,000 pages! The library fits into one sturdy tacklebox. A choice of 'fiche readers is available, including 240-volt and 12-volt (as in vehicle battery or solar panel) models. The price of the whole set is an amazing bargain at less than 5 percent of the cost of the actual books (not to mention the cost of shipping and storing them abroad). It's the best single idea I've seen in my twenty-five years of AT action. If you work in developing countries, you need one of these sets. Hatched and executed by Ken Darrow of VIA (Volunteers in Asia). —JB

•

A Series of Articles on the Use of Bamboo in Building Construction, MF 25-658, collected by Dr. Jules J. A. Janssen, 1982, 177 pages, £4.50 from ITDG.

This welcome collection assembles a variety of practical bamboo articles in one place. Preservation techniques are followed by sections on the use of bamboo in housing, bridges, water supply, and concrete reinforcement. One article explains how to calculate the strength of bamboos for construction purposes.

•

The Rower Pump, MF 14-368, reports and brochures, 1984 and later, available from Mirpur Agricultural Workshop and Training School (MAWTS), Mirpur Section 12, Pallabi, Dacca-16, Bangladesh; or Mennonite Central Committee, 111, Block "A" Mohammadpur, Dacca, Bangladesh.

Thousands of low-cost direct action handpumps made of pvc pipe are being used in Bangladesh for low-lift irrigation of small plots. The Rower pump can be easily made in developing countries, and the farmer can do his/her own simple repairs. The pump pays for itself in one crop.

The extremely low cost of the hand-pump (approximately US$15) and pvc tubewell installation (approximately US$30-45) and the large economic return from small plot irrigation together make this technology an excellent investment for farmers in areas where the water table is shallow (15 feet or less). The Rower pump is probably one of the most important agricultural tools invented in the last 20 years.

Readers seeking information on the Rower pump can write to the manufacturer (MAWTS) for a brochure with technical

Appropriate Technology Sourcebook
Ken Darrow & Mike Saxenian.
1993; 800 pp. ISBN 0-917704-18-5
$23.95 ($27.45 postpaid)
Microfiche Reference Library: $895
(includes Sourcebook & 1993 Update);
1993 Update: $200 (includes Sourcebook);
Fiche reader: $250-$375-$625.
Postage & handling vary by destination.
All from Volunteers in Asia/Appropriate Technology Project, PO Box 4543, Stanford, CA 94305; 800/648-8043.

details. Some of the same material is reproduced in Handpumps Testing and Development: Progress Report on Field and Laboratory Testing. The results of an extensive laboratory test are described in Laboratory Testing of Handpumps for Developing Countries: Final Technical Report. The relevant pages from both of these books are reproduced in the A.T. Microfiche Library as MF 14-368.

VITA

For twenty-five years, Volunteers in Technical Assistance has been a reliable source of expert advice and an experienced stack of publications. You don't join VITA as you would the Peace Corps (for instance), but you can make your special knowledge available through them. Their record of action is inspiring; see for yourself in VITA News. —JB

VITA News
Vicky Tsiliopoulos, Editor.
$15/year (4 issues). 1600 Wilson Boulevard, Suite 500, Arlington, VA 22209; 703/276-1800.

TRANET

Networking and information exchange are increasingly the name of the game, and TRANET (from Transnational Network for Appropriate/Alternative Technologies) has been doing them more comprehensively than anyone else for nearly 20 years. Their lively bimonthly newsletter has brief reviews of useful books, lots of news from the front, a members' bulletin board, and reader commentary — much of it uncomplimentary to the establishment. That last characteristic gives it a noticeably Seventies character, but the level of information exchange is very much of today. The TRANET crew is often the first to spread the news globally among people taking control of their own lives. I read every issue. —JB

TRANET: Membership $30/year (includes bimonthly newsletter). PO Box 567, Rangeley, ME 04970.

ITDG

The Intermediate Technology Development Group of North America, Inc. is a child of the original British ITDG founded by the late E. F. Schumacher of **Small Is Beautiful** *fame (p. 26). ITDG has designed and executed some of the very best AT projects yet seen domestically and worldwide. They publish and distribute many of the most useful AT books and other literature. They're too multifaceted to present here in all their glory. If you'd like to work with them, give them a call. Their publications catalog offers entry into what has become a major world movement marked by increasing cooperation and information exchange. It's also a fine source for English language versions of international publications.*

ITDG produces a fine magazine, too — appropriately called **Appropriate Technology Journal.** *—JB*

•

Unacceptable biogas. The other aspect of the growth in information available to us all through data bases is that it is not usually cross indexed according to the social context or 'genetic code' that produced it. We have all heard of the plans available for all sorts and conditions of bio-gas digesters, all keenly studied by organizations throughout the world, and all seeming to reflect a keen interest in a usable and sustainable technology suited to the Third World's mix of resources. And yet the only places where there is widespread use of this technology are China and India.

There is something in the social context of biogas technology which makes it seem in-

appropriate and unacceptable in many places where, on the face of it, it would seem very relevant. In most of these places the reason seems to me very simple — the people for whom it is being considered don't like handling shit (and who's to blame them?). Rare, however, is the technical manual which says that one of the parameters to be considered for using digesters is a willingness to handle shit: mostly it's all talk about recycling oil-drums, gas pressures, ranges of temperature, etc., etc.

And finally, so much information that becomes available is not involved with looking at the actual world of the poor and assessing the value of practices and knowledge which have kept such people going for a long time, but in thirsting for new knowledge which, on the face of it, looking at the situation of the Third World today, has not been of great help. So often the solution to a problem of the poor is much more likely to be found among slightly less poor people in a culturally similar environment in some other part of the world who have faced the same problem and have found a working solution to it. If only new ideas, which are often preceded by a literature search, could be preceded by a culture search, and preferably one which is organized along ecological parameters, since the lives of the poor are bound by the natural products around them.
—*Appropriate Technology Journal*

Intermediate Technology Development Group: Catalog free. 777 United Nations Plaza, Suite 3C, New York, NY 10017; 212/953-6920.

Appropriate Technology Journal: $27/year (4 issues). 103-105 Southampton Row, London, WC1 4HH, UK.

The Fail-Safe Society

NIMBY — Not In My Back Yard — is the name for a democratic, grassroots, and often vexing social movement. As a society, people in America don't seem to be attacking technological progress; at least they seldom do it effectively. As neighborhoods, people seem able to halt the construction of everything from nuclear plants to hospices. Many believe that local opposition to scientific or technological enterprises is leading to a kind of social paralysis. As a society, we need major airports, hazardous-waste disposal sites, medical research centers, AIDS halfway houses.

Charles Piller started out as a writer with attitudes like those I had as a reader: that NIMBY is another symptom of the tragedy of the commons, and one of the forces that is leading to social breakdown; that uninformed opposition to technology has the potential for causing more misery than a well-managed technological facility. When he began to study the spectrum of community opposition, Piller changed his mind. He has changed mine, too. —HLR

•

Conventional wisdom, as promoted by those who introduce, manage, or profit from science and technology, holds that Nimbyism is the product of selfish ignorance about risk and that Nimby groups should be stamped out before they irreparably harm our ability to extend society's technical reach and advance our standard of living. When I began this book, in a basic way, I agreed with this view. I saw Nimbyism as

Nothing to Fear

The simplest technology is dangerous in some way. So is living naked on a tropical isle. How to rationally assess and manage the risks of life is the subject of this often-provocative collection of papers. Profits-firsters, Earth-Firsters, and everyone in between will find plenty here to deplore, celebrate, and deny hopefully. All will be made uncomfortable as their deepest beliefs are questioned. Sometimes creepy, but always essential. That's about all you could ask from a book. It's the best I've seen on the subject. —JB

•

The United States Public Health Service also played a central role in establishing the popular imagery associated with germ theories of disease. As the uniformed avant-garde in America's fight against contagion, the Public Health Service, a branch of the military, created a literal association between the uniformed officer and the eradication of disease. In its role as hygienic gatekeeper at Ellis Island, the service further reinforced the connection between disease and immigration, and, ultimately, between immigration and crime.

•

If some agencies are willing, whether by law or by policy, to spend more per life saved than other agencies, then our risk budget is misallocated. We are spending more money to save fewer lives than we could if we were less selectively cautious. Worse still, if we tried generally to achieve absolute safety or zero risk, we would probably achieve net negative effects by diverting resources away from pursuing other goods (like education or material comfort) that inadvertently improve our health and safety.

•

Built into the flood insurance program is a significant section — 1362 — that involves relocation of families from persistent flood hazard areas. This, and the various provisions calling for mapping and rezoning hazardous areas, made the National Flood Insurance Program the nation's first land use control law.

•

At an earthquake preparedness meeting in Little Rock, Arkansas, in 1983, the emergency managers of the State of Kentucky and of Memphis agreed that any immediate attempt to get support for earthquake hazard zoning and retrofitting of seismic risk buildings would receive little political support; they worried that if such an effort were begun at that time, the whole cause of earthquake preparedness in the Mississippi Valley would be actually set back. But they agreed that they could start raising a new generation of voters who would be knowledgeable about earthquake risks and who would eventually pressure their representatives to do what needs to be done.

Nothing to Fear
(Risks and Hazards in American Society)
Andrew Kirby, Editor. 1990; 301 pp.
ISBN 0-8165-1185-3
$35 ($37 postpaid) from University of Arizona Press, 1230 N. Park Avenue #102, Tucson, AZ 85719; 602/621-1441

•

Unlike disaster research and natural hazard research — both of which inform the work of public bodies, but are mainly carried on by academics — risk analysis practices are being systematically adopted by bureaucratic organizations. Several factors have combined to encourage its use as a procedure in public decision-making. Inquiries into spectacular disasters have turned up evidence of inadequate consideration of risks in existing technological systems: a recent report on the space shuttle Challenger concluded that the U.S. space program places too much reliance on subjective judgments and too little on formal risk assessment methods.

Normal Accidents

Your worst fears confirmed: accidents in complex technological systems are inevitable and unpreventable, and must, like a little dishonesty, be considered a normal fact of life. The author makes a worrisomely good case for this view, though his credibility is superficially tarnished by poor science editing and careless proofreading. Put aside those annoyances, and you'll find ample proof that dangerous technologies are not entirely controllable, even if the folks in charge are models of social and environmental responsibility. Horrendous examples are detailed, but they aren't nearly so disturbing as the dishonesty that accompanies disasters. Ass-covering prevarications are expected. The less-expected intellectual dishonesty short-circuits the learning process that can prevent the same sort of thing from happening again even when profits and prestige are not at stake. The question is whether certain technologies should be permitted at all if the consequences of failure are drastic. The answer is no, of course, but the author offers few solutions. We'd better get to work. —JB

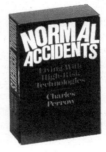

Normal Accidents
Charles Perrow. Basic Books, 1985; 400 pp. ISBN 0-465-05142-1
$18.50 ($20.50 postpaid) from Harper-Collins Publishers/Direct Mail, PO Box 588, Dunmore, PA 18512; 800/331-3761

OTHER GREAT RESOURCES

Acceptable Risks: Jonathan Kwitny. 1992, Poseidon Press, Simon & Schuster. Acceptable to one may be onerous to another. How to decide what is best for all is given a sharp look.

Acceptable Evidence (Science and Values in Risk Management): Deborah G. Mayo, Rachelle D. Hollander & Kristin Shrader-Frechette. 1991, Oxford University Press. An unusually comprehensive and clear look at the relationship between "objective" scientific evidence and values-&-beliefs in deciding how to assess risk.

Readings in Risk: Theodore S. Glickman & Michael Gough, Editors. 1990, Resources for the Future c/o Johns Hopkins University Press.

The Fail-Safe Society
Charles Piller. University of California Press, 1991; 240 pp. ISBN 0-520-08202-8
$12 ($15 postpaid) from California/Princeton Fulfillment Services, 1445 Lower Ferry Road, Ewing, NJ 08618; 800/777-4726

a vexing problem to be solved. In individual cases, of course, a Nimby response is certainly understandable or justifiable — even noble. But as a trend, I reasoned, Nimbyism is poison for a society that aspires to democratic processes and social cooperation. I saw this as the central question of the book: How can Nimbyism be eliminated without sacrificing legitimate aspirations for local control and personal safety?

•

I grew to recognize that by labeling Nimbyism as the problem I had obscured more central issues. It is not risk per se, but how hazards have been generated and distributed that has led to the Nimby era. In a society that boasts a strong democratic identity, the demand for local participation in technological decision making is hardly surprising, even if the degree of outrage over inept technological choices has startled scientists and technology's managers. (Ironically, democratic aspirations derive partly from the scientific culture itself, with its commitment to open communication and diverse participation in the definition of natural laws.)

Averting Catastrophe

Considering the variety of technological threats to which we are subjected — nuclear power, gene-splicing, synthetic pesticides, ozone depletion and the greenhouse effect, to name a few — it is sometimes surprising that anything is still alive on the planet at all. Morone and Woodhouse analyze this situation and tease out a series of heuristic strategies which are already in use to help protect us from new technologies, and which go beyond the simple trial and error most political theorists see operating in society. For example, as DNA experimentation got underway, there was a deliberate attempt to protect against possible hazards through containment, to estimate the risks conservatively, and to reduce the uncertainty by directing the research toward just what these risks were. Although they see our relative safety as no accident, the authors go on to argue for their more systematic and conscious application as we move into increasingly risky realms of technological action. One remaining serious problem is that the ensemble of available strategies is at its weakest when confronted with problems featuring high uncertainty and long lag times for effects to be known — such as our current problems with the ozone layer. —Mike Gunderloy

•

How does the objective nature of a technology relate to the widely accepted view that public perceptions and fears are what really guide technology debates and shape policy? We believe that the nature of a social problem limits what constitutes a legitimate debate. The nature of the problem in the nuclear power debate is such that there is no way to establish definitively the magnitude of the risks. Advocates of nuclear power can insist that the probabilities of accidents are very low, that the major causes of accidents have been anticipated, and that the worst case would not really be that bad, but none of these arguments can be fully verfied. Regulators are left with no conclusive basis for deciding between these claims and opposite claims. Lacking a basis for resolving the facts of the matter, factors like public perceptions and general attitudes become important. The position one takes on the conflicting estimates of the risks depends on whether one trusts the government institutions, whether one fears high technology and so on.

Averting Catastrophe
(Strategies for Regulating Risky Technologies)
Joseph G. Morone & Edward J. Woodhouse.
University of California Press, 1986; 215 pp. ISBN 0-520-05754-6
$11.95 ($14.95 postpaid) from California/Princeton Fulfillment Services, 1445 Lower Ferry Road, Ewing, NJ 08618; 800/777-4726

DESIGNERS and people acting as designers manage the application of technology. Every product and procedure has been intentionally or inadvertently designed by somebody to be the way it is. Designers attempt to influence the future with work that they hope will bring about the desired result. They often fail.

Look around you. Of the thousands of buildings erected every day, is even one both delightful and energy- and materials-efficient? Can you name a dozen objects that are well designed? Your lonely candidates represent a minority. They are probably weapons or other implements that would be unusable or unacceptably dangerous if ineptly designed. Their life cycle is unlikely to be environmentally and socially benign.

Designers and their masters often leave nature out of the design process, ignorantly assuming that nature has no vote. But nature always votes. These days, her vote is often No. People other than the designer's clients are often left out of the process, too. They are usually people of color with little money or political clout. They may vote their displeasure by performing acts of "senseless violence."

We can do better — by designing in a way that wreaks minimal harm to people and environment. Here are some ideas and tools that should help. —J. Baldwin

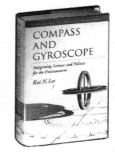

Compass and Gyroscope
(Integrating Science and Politics for the Environment)
Kai N. Lee. 1993;
ISBN 1-55963-197-X
$24.95 ($29.20 postpaid) from Island Press, Box 7, Covelo, CA 95428; 800/828-1302

Compass and Gyroscope

Scientific investigation — learning — acts as the compass needed to guide humanity onto a sustainable path. The political negotiations become the gyroscope, providing the stability necessary for the learning to be applied in time (if possible). How is such an integration (the author calls it "civic science") to be accomplished? Here's a wonderfully sharp analysis of what is so glibly called "sustainability," and of equally glib proposals for its attainment. The usual whining and easily said philosophizing are replaced by tough arguments and suggested actions based on wisdom gained in the environmental battles being waged in the Pacific Northwest. The writing is remarkably clear. This is the most useful book I've seen on how to do better. —JB

•

Sustainable development is not a goal, not a condition likely to be attained on earth as we know it. Rather, it is more like freedom or justice, a direction in which we strive.

•

The process of building a model is a way of working out a shared view of what is being managed and how the managing should be done. Often that process is conducted by a diverse group of people drawn from different institutions, some of them organizations with conflicting interests, such as Indian tribes and electric utilities. When this happens, model building becomes a way of negotiating.

Ecosystem models are always wrong, in the sense that reality conforms to their numerical projections only very rarely. Models are indispensable because without them human misunderstanding persists, unaware of its errors.

Green Products by Design
Office of Technology Assessment. 1992; 128 pp.
Stock No. 052-003-01303-7
$6.50 postpaid. Superintendent of Documents/New Orders, PO Box 371954, Pittsburgh, PA 15250-7954; 202/783-3238

Design Methods
John Chris Jones. 1992; 461 pp.
ISBN 0-442-01182-2
$39.95 postpaid from Van Nostrand Reinhold/Order Dept., 7625 Empire Drive, Florence, KY 41042; 800/842-3636

Redefining Designing
C. Thomas Mitchell. 1993; 162 pp. ISBN 0-442-00987-9
$34.95 postpaid. Van Nostrand Reinhold/Order Dept., 7625 Empire Drive, Florence, KY 41042; 800/842-3636

Green Products by Design

Designers manage the interface between technology and everything else. They are in a unique position to influence what the cumulative effects of each design decision will be, and thus how a technology will affect the environment. This U.S. government-sponsored paper (from the Bush administration yet!) recommends that designers regard environmental attributes as design objectives rather than as constraints, as is usually the case. The first chapters discuss the effects of design decisions on the environment, the middle chapters address green design strategies, and the last, inevitably, bring up the matter of proposed government regulations and the standards therefor. It's a taste of things to come — subject, of course, to the usual delaying tactics by old-mode thinkers. It isn't going to be easy. —JB

•

Perhaps the ultimate extension of the manufacturer take-back concept is the "rent model," in which manufacturers retain ownership of products and simply rent them to customers. This gives manufacturers incentives to design products to maximize product utilization, rather than simply sales.

This idea was implemented in the telephone industry for many years. Before divestiture, AT&T leased virtually all telephones and thus was able to readily collect them. AT&T designed its phones with a 30 year design lifetime, and collected almost every broken or used telephone. The phones were either refurbished or reprocessed for materials recovery. However, with the end of AT&T's regulated monopoly and the creation of a competitive market, the number of telephone manufacturers dramatically increased. Consumers were given a wide variety of product choices. The number of phones purchased by consumers, as opposed to leased from the Bell System, grew rapidly. Accordingly, the proportion of telephones that were thrown away rather than fed back to the Bell System also increased, with a corresponding drop in the number of units available for reuse or recycling. It is estimated that approximately 20 to 25 million phones are now disposed of each year.

Design Methods

The author discusses thirty-five major design strategies in this unsurpassed twenty-three-year-old book. This second edition features some adjustments and additions, but it remains the same difficult, rewarding read and is still ahead of the game. **Design Methods** *is especially strong on collaborative design involving complex requirements. —JB*

•

The stating of objectives is undoubtedly one of the most important and difficult parts of designing. Hall (1962) points out that anyone who says 'I have just determined the best objectives for this project' is simply mistaken. It is impossible to prove that objectives are correct before a system has had its intended, and unintended, effects upon the situation as-a-whole. This is because the future value of an action depends upon human opinions which cannot be foretold because they are only partially governed by the action itself; they are largely governed by the responses of persons concerned.

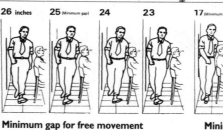

26 inches	25 (Minimum gap)	24	23	17 (Minimum gap)	16	15	14

Minimum gap for free movement   Minimum gap for restricted movement

—Design Methods

Redefining Designing

To consumers and designers alike, the word design mostly refers to how something looks — its styling. Style without thoughtfully developed function tends to produce products that are effete, annoying to use, and occasionally dangerous. Such designs are almost always wasteful of money and resources, yet they may be what sells best — for a while. Mr. Mitchell argues that the problem lies with the design process itself. Contributions from such innovators as Brian Eno, Christo, and Christopher Alexander buttress his arguments.

Mitchell has a good time blasting such bushwah as deconstructionist architecture, but he devotes most of the book to developing a new way of looking at design. He's honest enough to show the work of others; you'll find good discussions of recent work on "transparency" and "softechnica" among other concepts. Highly recommended. —JB

•

One of the most successful environment-behavior techniques is the awkwardly named Post-Occupancy Evaluation, an elaborate survey technique conducted after a building has been used to determine how well the building suits the purposes for which it was intended. Post-occupancy evaluations can usefully identify problems with buildings, but designers require methods that will help them *anticipate* the effects the designs will have. Evaluative techniques such as this are really just cases of the use of common sense and twenty/twenty hindsight; they do not change the nature of the design process itself.

•

Alexander emphasizes that his team's book constitutes *a* pattern language, not the only one possible. He views each pattern in the book as a hypothesis, though he feels more confident that some patterns represent underlying, invariant relationships between form and activities than do others. In different cultures and in application to new building tasks new patterns may have to be developed. Moreover, Alexander believes that each of us carry our own pattern language within us that, while largely shared with our culture, is personal and independent. It was these implicit pattern languages that were the source for building and craftwork before geometrical design criteria began to predominate with the onset of industrialization. According to Alexander it is now necessary to rediscover and make explicit pattern languages as a means of reacquainting people — designers and non-designers alike — with what he terms "the timeless way of building."

Living by Design

Prestigious, old-mode designers often act as teachers and shapers of public taste, thus perpetuating poor practices. Sim Van der Ryn is way ahead of most of his peers: he's been teaching nature-based architecture for thirty years or so. In this book he avoids the common (and arrogant) format that merely feeds readers currently acceptable design recipes. Instead, he concentrates on principles and how to think about ecological design. He organizes the principles as steps that, if followed thoughtfully, should ensure that your work will at least be ecologically benign and possibly even beneficial and beautiful. (Structural integrity and aesthetics are, of course, up to you — espousing design principles never guarantees excellence.) Though focused mostly on architecture, the attitudes and principles can be applied to any design endeavor. The presentation is convincing and mercifully free of ecojargon, making it especially useful for designers who need to catch up. —JB

Living by Design
(Ecological Design and the Making of Sustainable Places)
Sim Van der Ryn & Stuart Cowan.
Will be published in April, 1995 by Island Press, Box 7, Covelo, CA 95428; 800/828-1302

•

The oak chair I am sitting in has a history of its own. It was made from oak harvested hundreds of miles away. The oak was harvested in a logging operation that entailed a network of fellers, roads and trucks. From there, the oak was milled and sent to a factory for assembly into a chair. At the factory, resins, adhesives and varnishes were applied as the chair took form. Finally, the chair was packaged, shipped, warehoused, shipped, retailed, and brought home. In several decades, it will probably grow quite rickety, at which time its owner can repair it, junk it, or salvage it in some way. In a deep sense, the chair embodies the land, water, labor, tools, energy and materials used in its production and distribution. As we understand the stream of processes required to manufacture the chair, we grow closer to assessing its ecological impact.

Made strictly for cars, Barsotti's Automotive Service shop (1924) in San Francisco employed steel trusses to make its 3,000-square-foot space column-free so cars could maneuver easily. Years later, a florist, an aerobics studio, and then a clothing retailer found the space easily converted to their special needs. The building was too humble for anyone to worry about whether they were violating its historical or aesthetic integrity.

How Buildings Learn
(What Happens After They're Built)
Stewart Brand. Viking, 1994; 229 pp.
ISBN 0-670-83515-3
$30 ($32 postpaid).
Penguin USA/Consumer Sales, 120 Woodbine Street, Bergenfield, NJ 07621; 800/253-6476

How Buildings Learn

Few architects and builders have recognized that adaptability over time is a critical aspect of design, and that occupants inevitably modify their buildings in various ways, inside and out. In this sharp analysis of the process of change, Stewart Brand illuminates an ancient mystery: What design features — intentional or accidental — permit the graceful evolution that makes some buildings wonderful to look at and be in? Why do we intuitively like such buildings? Can we deliberately design buildings to be adaptable? The book is a great ride past examples of good and bad, with plenty of astutely chosen photographs lending an irrefutable air to the argument. The principles revealed can be applied to any design effort making a gesture toward "permanence." —JB

The Creative Problem Solver's Toolbox

Does this book live up to its pretentious title? Yes, it does, better than any other basic design book I've encountered, though the author's lessons-with-exercises style of delivering the goods may not appeal to everyone. He has written the early chapters for people who have never thought about problem solving. He discusses more complex and powerful tactics as the book progresses.

All concepts are illustrated with examples. The detailed table of contents describes each chapter, enabling experienced readers to easily find advice on a specific topic without wading through stuff they already know — a problem solved right there. I regard the book as good enough to be a textbook for my design students (and a good reminder for me). —JB

•

To discover flaws and weaknesses in your creative solutions, imagine specific cases that are exaggerated in ways that reveal disadvantages. Then, further refine your creative idea by eliminating these disadvantages.

In choosing how to exaggerate, keep in mind that an exaggeration can be an exaggerated sameness, not just an exaggerated difference.

•

Criticism is inevitable whether it's justified or not, so expect your creative solutions to be criticized.

History is filled with examples of innovations that have initially been heavily criticized and later became very much appreciated. Consider these examples:

Outrage was a common initial response to translating the Bible into languages that people could read.

Fannie Farmer's Boston Cooking School Cook Book was initially controversial because the recipes used quantities such as one cup instead of one handful.

The list could go on and on, but you get the point. Typically, criticism of your idea will persist until your creative idea has demonstrated its value.

The Creative Problem Solver's Toolbox
(A Complete Course in the Art of Creating Solutions to Problems of Any Kind)
Richard Fobes. 1993; 345 pp.
ISBN 0-9632221-0-4
$17.75 postpaid from Solutions Through Innovation, PO Box 1327, Corvallis, OR 97339-1327; 800/247-6553

The Bell Notes

In 1947, Arthur M. Young invented the first helicopter licensed for public use. In the process, he made some startling discoveries about how his mind worked while creating. He kept notes, which you may find as deeply useful (and occasionally as shocking) as I have. —JB
[Suggested by Robert Cumberford]

•

See how the force of the idea is made static by "explaining" it. Explanation isolates it and makes it a target instead of an influence. If I can contribute anything, it is the recognition of the working of this subtle, simple law: that which is unexpressed is dynamic, active.

•

There exists to this moment no conclusive test or combination of tests to show either the comparative high speed or the difference in speed. To get such tests requires a very strong will, which is lacking in the "organization" — hence the result never occurs. To supply this will oneself discourages its growth in others. Hence I am torn between wanting to get the answer and wanting others to want. Perhaps the answer is that we can never know where we stand.

The Bell Notes
(A Journey from Physics to Metaphysics)
Arthur M. Young. 1979; 205 pp.
ISBN 0-9609850-4-2
$10.95 ($12.45 postpaid) from Robert Briggs, Associates, 400 Second Street # 108, Lake Oswego, OR 97034; 800/447-7814

When asked, "Of what use is your latest invention?" Benjamin Franklin replied, "Of what use is a newborn baby?"

That's a Great Idea!

This book is still my favorite beginner's get-you-started goad and guide when the urge to cash in on your ideas becomes impossible to ignore. Believe me, the path to success is riddled with booby-traps, and you are all too likely to be the booby. Not snooty, this guide realistically includes schlock products. You know, the awful ones you wish your kids didn't want. —JB

•

Reducing your idea to a model or working prototype is critical. It proves that the concept is workable and helps you make improvements in function or design that you might never have known were necessary. It is far better and cheaper to find out about glitches and miscalculations while making one sample of the product than after you have geared up to make several thousand of them.

•

Having a prototype will also aid in market research and in defining your target group of consumers. It is much easier and more reliable to determine people's reactions to a product when you can show them an actual sample, rather than just describing it to them. You can find out their opinions of specific features and why they would or would not buy it.

•

Be wary of positive responses to the question, "Would you buy it?" They may only be indications of curiosity or attempts to spare your feelings. Therefore, also ask questions such as: What benefit does it provide? What need does it fill? What do you like or dislike about it? Does it solve a problem? Answers to these questions more reliably predict consumer interest and willingness to buy.

Conversely, negative responses to the would-you-buy question *are* reliable. Therefore, market research is most reliable for predicting failures, not successes. It can help you avoid disasters, but it will not guarantee winners.

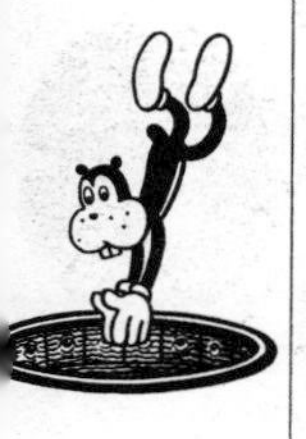

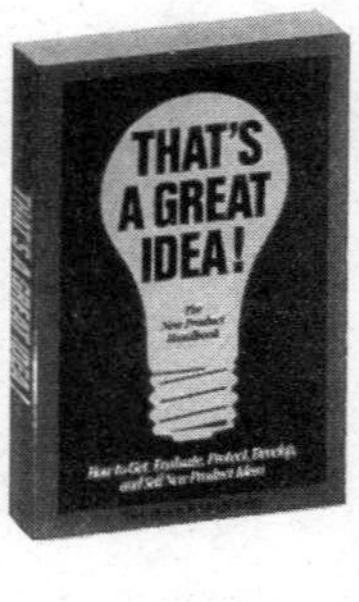

That's a Great Idea!
(The New Product Handbook)
Tony Husch & Linda Foust.
1986; 256 pp. ISBN 0-89815-218-6
$9.95 ($13.45 postpaid). Ten Speed Press, PO Box 7123, Berkeley, CA 94707; 800/841-2665

Box Beam Sourcebook

I consider the Box Beam system to be an important addition to the capabilities of prototyping folk. The system's easy changeability allows and encourages knowledge-building iterations of a design as it progresses toward perfection. The Box Beam seems obvious, but — as with all modular systems — tricky, subtle details must dance compatibly for the system to work. Box Beams are reusable.

***The Box Beam Sourcebook** tells all, clearly and well, illuminated by lots of pictures. The authors also offer a selection of compatible hardware, a video, and much more. It's one of the best prototyping schemes I've seen. —JB*

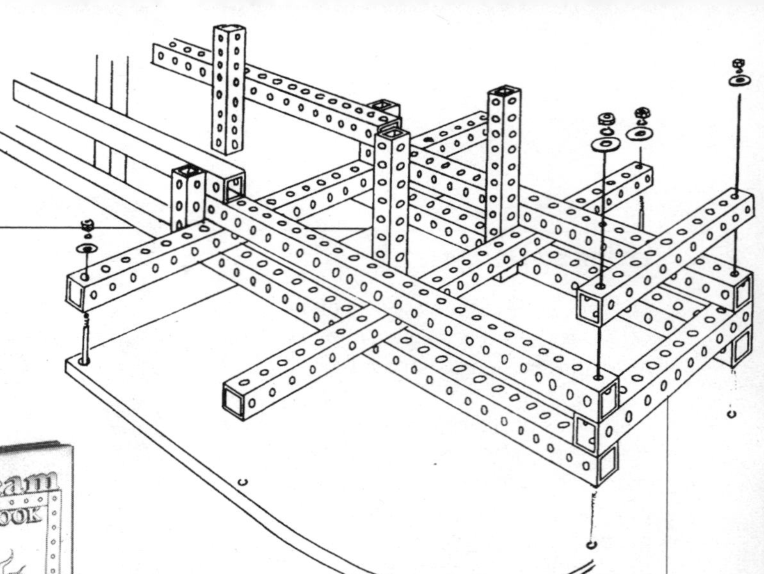

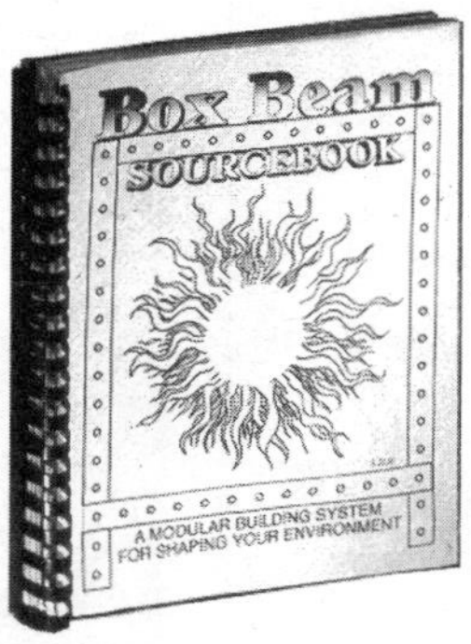

Box Beam Sourcebook
(A Modular Building System for Shaping Your Environment)
Phil Jergenson with Richard Jergenson. 1994; 100 pp.
$20 ($22 postpaid). Suntools, PO Box 1029, Willits, CA 95490; 707/459-2624

Patent It Yourself

Other patent-it-yourself books seem like mere abstracts compared to this detailed gem of a book. David Pressman presents every step of patent and copyright processes in order, complete with official forms to practice on. The language is free of legalese except where Pressman trains readers to sling a bit of it themselves for effect. The book is especially helpful in making tough tactical decisions, such as whether or not to patent at all. Software is available for all this, too. —JB

Patent It Yourself
David Pressman.
1992; 464 pp.
ISBN 0-87337-167-4
$36.95 ($40.95 postpaid)
Software: IBM or compatible, 4 MB RAM, Windows 3.1 or higher, VGA monitor. $229.95 ($233.95 postpaid)
Both from Nolo Press, 950 Parker Street, Berkeley, CA 94710; 800/992-6656 or 510/549-1976

Other Great Resources

Aircraft Spruce & Specialty Company: Catalog $5. Box 424, Fullerton, CA 92632; 800/824-1930. AS&S stocks an astounding array of items. Their catalog should interest to any person needing high-quality hardware and other imagination-inspiring goodies.

The Eastwood Company: Catalog free. 580 Lancaster Avenue, Box 3014, Malvern, PA 19355-0714; 800/345-1178, fax 215/644-0560. An exceptionally useful collection of materials, tools and information that can ease many tasks besides auto restoration.

The Gougeon Brothers: WEST SYSTEM product catalog free. PO Box 908, Bay City, MI 48707; 517/684-7286. These guys have worked out lightweight wood construction that's not just for boats. They sell the necessary supplies, too. More with less.

Micro-Mark: 340 Snyder Avenue, Berkeley Heights, NJ 07922-1595; 800/225-1066, fax 908/665-9383. Tiny tools for Lilliputian projects.

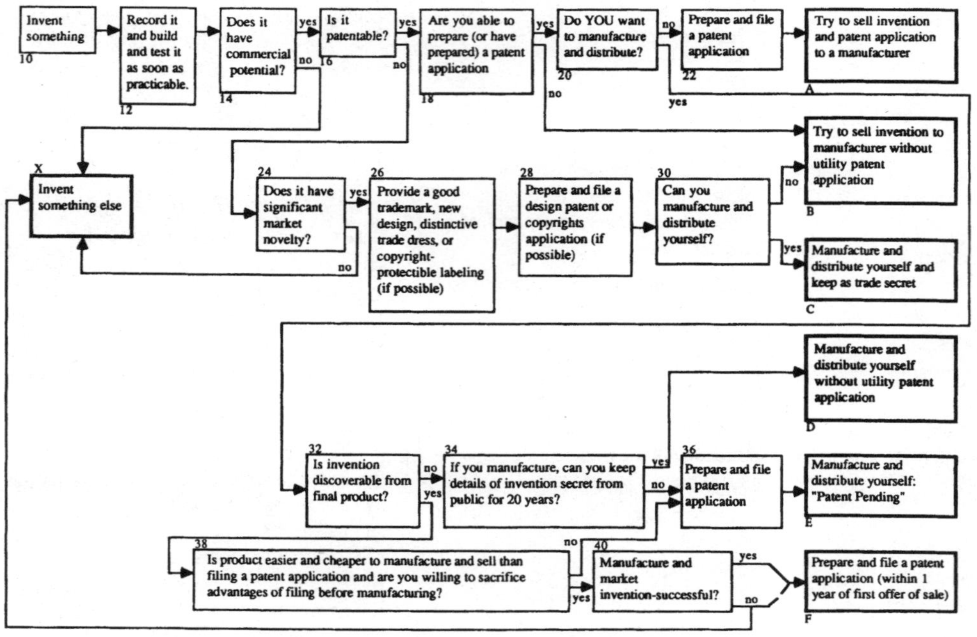

Invention Decision Chart
—Patent It Yourself

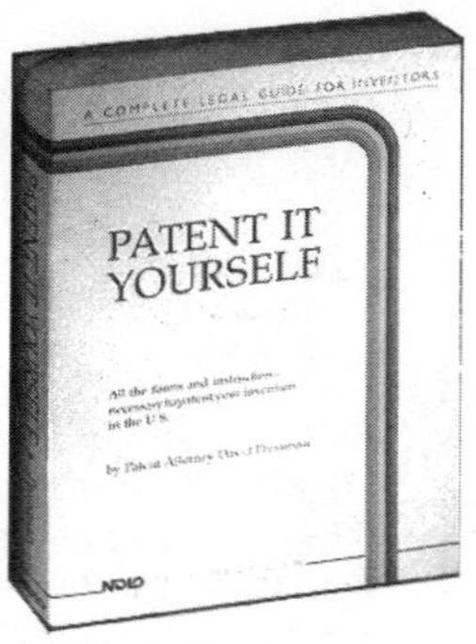

Zometool

*Cheaper and very much easier to understand than CAD (Computer Aided Design) representations, the Zometool enables you to construct and ponder drastically intricate models of Fullerenes, hypercubes and other structures in two-, three-, and the exciting five-fold symmetries that elude two-dimensional visualization. The Golden Mean is involved. Zometool's sturdy components are also useful to chemists, crystallographers, and architects. The hefty price may deter casual experimenters, but complex plastic molds don't come cheap ($250,000) and there's not a huge market for this sort of thing. On the other hand, there's nothing else like it; I'm saving up to get the big kit. The thirty-one-zone geometry was developed by (and this kit is licensed by) longtime **WER** contributor Steve Baer, otherwise famed for innovative, excellent solar equipment and acid wit. —JB*

Zometool: Whole kit (#ZT1): $675 postpaid; half kit (#ZT2): $375 postpaid. BioCrystal, Inc., PO Box 7053, Boulder, CO 80302-7053; 303/786-9888.

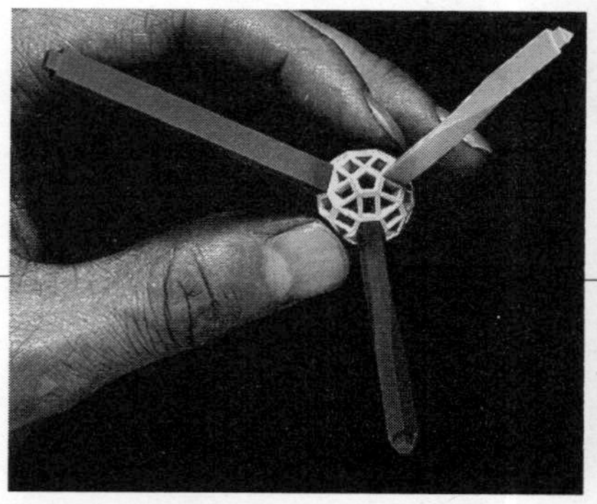

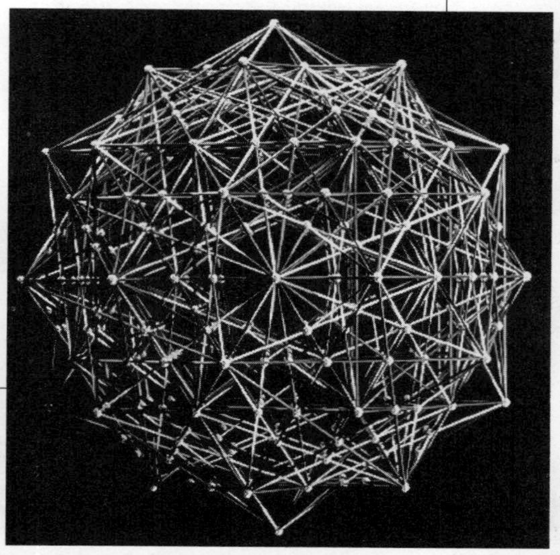

By Nature's Design

• To make a single gram of beeswax, a honeybee consumes over sixteen grams of honey and an undetermined amount of pollen. Bees construct honeycombs according to a design that minimizes the use of this metabolically expensive commodity. The wax walls of the honeycomb cells come together in threes at 120-degree angles, forming a regular array of hexagons. This pattern lets the bees minimize the amount of wax they use, while providing a rigid structure in which to store honey.

Branching of streams; branching of veins; branching of branches; closest packing; minimum surface area; fractals. The design of things natural produces patterns expressing the laws of physics, chemistry and genetics. These remarkable photographs and their guiding captions help you see beyond aesthetics into true appreciation of the beauty of this place. —J. Baldwin

• An array of soap bubbles echoes the geometry of the honeycomb. The bubbles meet in threes to form 120-degree angles, the arrangement that minimizes the stretching of the soap film.

By Nature's Design
Pat Murphy & William Neill. 1993; 120 pp. ISBN 0-8118-0329-5 $18.95 ($22.45 postpaid). Chronicle Books/ Order Dept., 275 5th Street, San Francisco, CA 94103; 800/722-6657

Life's Devices

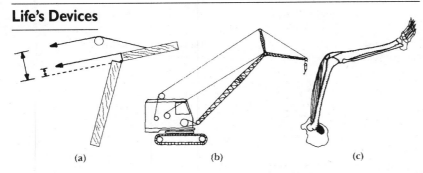

(a)   (b)   (c)

The uses of a jib. In (a) the moment arm (two-ended arrows) of a force is increased by running a cable over a pulley instead of pulling directly on the hinged member. The force is exerted in the same direction, but is much more effective when its line of action is further from the hinge. (b) An articulated crane runs the support member for its outer, hinged member over a jib for just this reason. (c) In a human leg, the tendon of the muscle that extends (straightens) the lower leg runs over an extra bone, the kneecap.

Devices? Are living things devices, like machines? Well, sort of: The natural laws that affect organisms are the same as those that affect machines and everything else.

The author of this fascinating textbook occasionally invokes comparisons with machinery, but otherwise avoids the mechanistic approach that has made so much trouble for us and our fellow beings. The discipline is called biomechanics. It's something that designers need to know about. —JB

• Curiously, softwoods (gymnosperms) reinforce with "reaction wood" especially good at resisting compression, adding it on the side subjected to increased compression, while hardwoods (angiosperms) do the opposite, adding tensile reaction wood on the side where shortening will restore a tree's natural posture.

Life's Devices
(The Physical World of Animals and Plants) Steven Vogel. Princeton University Press, 1988; 367 pp. ISBN 0-691-02418-9 $18.95 ($21.95 postpaid). California/ Princeton Fulfillment Services, 1445 Lower Ferry Road, Ewing, NJ 08618; 800/777-4726

World Game

Buckminster Fuller realized that designers would need accurate worldwide data for all manner of resources and living conditions in order to be comprehensive and anticipatory. He started World Game to develop that data and to make it available to designers and policymakers. World Game workshops are held around the world; the astounding collection of data on every country is offered in several computer-accessible forms and information densities. It's probably the most useful and complete cache available. —JB

World Game Institute: Information free. 3215 Race Street, Philadelphia, PA 19104; 215/387-0220.

The Science of Structures and Materials

J. E. Gordon is a master at explaining what makes things strong or weak, be they bridges or ostrich femurs. He delivers his explanations in a manner that tends to make them part of your intuition. Those of you that have labored through a conventional statics-and-dynamics engineering course will wonder at the way he makes it all seem so clear. Teaching at its best. —JB

The Science of Structures and Materials
J. E. Gordon & Stephen Wagley. Scientific American Library, 1988; 217 pp. ISBN 0-7167-5022-8 $32.95 ($35.95 postpaid). W. H. Freeman and Co., 4419 W. 1980 S., Salt Lake City, UT 84104; 800/488-5233

• Compression creases in wood are often a stable condition. If the wood is compressed still further, rather than extending the existing crease deeper into the wood, the additional load creates new creases. Although in force terms the stress needed to initiate a compression crease in wood is usually quite low, which is why wood is regarded as weak in compression, in energy terms the energy needed to propagate the crease is very high indeed. It is many times higher than the energy needed to propagate a tension crack, even in tough material. Thus, when we apply the ideas of modern fracture mechanics to wood in compression we find that complete and catastrophic failure is unlikely, which is one of the reasons why wood is such a safe material.

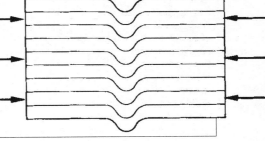

On Growth and Form

A paradigm classic. Everyone dealing with growth of form in any manner can use the book. We've seen worn copies on the shelves of artists, inventors, engineers, computer systems designers, biologists. —SB

• The engineer, who had been busy designing a new and powerful crane, saw in a moment that the arrangement of the bony trabeculae was nothing more nor less than a diagram of the lines of stress, or directions of tension and compression, in the loaded structure: in short, that Nature was strengthening the bone in precisely the manner and direction in which strength was required; and he is said to have cried out, "That's my crane!"

See also Natural History on page 16.

OTHER GREAT RESOURCES

Structural Biomaterials: Julian Vincent. 1990, Princeton University Press. The structure of biologicals viewed at the molecular level. You'll need college math to handle it.

On Growth and Form
Darcy W. Thompson. 1992; 1136 pp. ISBN 0-486-67135-6 $24.95 ($27.95 postpaid). Dover Publications/Order Dept., 31 E. 2nd Street, Minneola, NY 11501; 516/294-7000

A FUNNY THING HAPPENED on the way to the millennium: Technologists took Stewart Brand's observation seriously and began bestowing godlike powers upon humans. Virtual reality is an infant technology; by the morning of the millennium, you might not be able to tell the difference between a living ecosystem and its computerized world model. The Human Genome Project is going to enable us to redesign our bodies. Artificial life and artificial evolution are seeking to harness powers even greater than the secret of the DNA code. Street technologists and garage hackers are reinventing and repurposing the microchips and optical fibers they find in the debris of technological civilization. If it truly does look like our children are going to be as gods when they get their hands on these technologies, now is the time to think about the implications and side effects of the tools we are handing our descendants, while there is still a chance to influence the outcome. —HLR

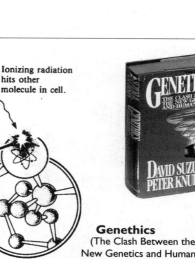

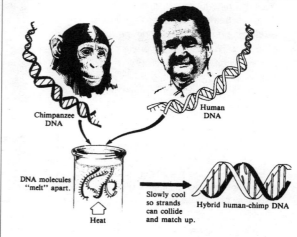

DNA damage from ionizing radiation.

Genethics
(The Clash Between the New Genetics and Human Values)
David Suzuki & Peter Knudtson.
1989; 384 pp. ISBN 0-674-34565-5
$14 ($17 postpaid). Harvard University Press/Customer Service, 79 Garden Street, Cambridge, MA 02138; 800/448-2242

The Human Genome Project

Over the next ten years, the Human Genome Project will decode and load into computer databases the entire set of genetic instructions that specifies a human being. While this will profoundly affect the treatment of genetic disorders, it also raises disturbing issues about privacy and discrimination, and stimulates darker fears about things like selective breeding and genetic weapons.

Information on the Human Genome Project is available from the National Institutes of Health, 9000 Rocksville Pike, 38A Room 605, Bethesda, MD 20892; 301/496-0844. —Mike Ashenfelder

See Risk Management, p. 229; Biotech, p. 108; Artificial Life, p. 235.

The Secret of Life

In David Suzuki's PBS series "The Secret of Life," we meet the doctors and scientists working on the front lines of genetic treatment and follow their patients' dilemmas, treatments, and outcomes. Each episode focuses on a different topic, such as cancer treatment or treating children for genetic diseases. Sprinkled throughout are first-rate animation sequences illustrating what is going on biochemically. The combination of enthusiastic descriptions by the scientists, dynamic animation, and plain good storytelling draws you right into the action like a mystery adventure. The tapes are a bit pricey for consumers but perfect for schools and libraries. A compelling introduction to genetics. —Mike Ashenfelder

The Secret of Life: David Suzuki. Eight titles; $89.95/tape, $649/ set (postpaid: add 5%). Films for the Humanities and Sciences, 12 Perrine Road, PO Box 2053, Princeton, NJ 08543-2053; 800/257-5126, fax 609/275-3767.

Geneticists convert a cancer-causing virus into a gene-delivery vehicle by snipping out and replacing its deadly gene with a new therapeutic gene and using the virus to deliberately infect the patient's cells. The virus lands on a host cell (top) and injects the bioengineered gene, which splices into the genes of its host (bottom) and transmits the new genetic instructions.

Genethics

Biologist David Suzuki has a flair for conveying complex information through vivid metaphors, good storytelling, and (in his videos) cool animation. His Genethics — co-written with Peter Knudtson— is an essential introduction to the new genetics, outlining the benefits and ethical dilemmas that will accompany the success of the Human Genome Project. The first third of this book is about how everything fits together, from DNA base pairs to chromosomes to the genetically expressed human being. The remainder of the book addresses the effect of the new genetics on society and the environment, through examples of cases as well as future scenarios. Suzuki attempts to offer concrete moral

Human-chimpanzee DNA hybridization experiment.

solutions. We need to take ethics and morality into account in order to make informed decisions, because this knowledge gives us the power to alter and redesign human beings. —Mike Ashenfelder

• Another diabolical scheme might be to enhance the ability of certain pathogens to home in on highly specific target groups of host organisms. A particularly nightmarish scenario — one that was actually proposed by a scientist writing in the American military journal *Military Review* in 1970 — would be to transform microbes into so-called ethnic weapons, agents of biological warfare that might exploit subtle hereditary differences between human populations.

The idea would be to modify a pathogen so that it would be more likely to infect members of a particular racial or ethnic group while leaving others relatively unscathed. In this way, the military might be able to deploy an offensive biological weapon that, in a sense, embodied its own defense. That is, hereditary membership in the "right" group would provide one with a measure of built-in protection against illness because of the agent's engineered host preference.

Online Resources

Gopher: *gopher genome.wi.mit.edu*
Ftp: *ftp genome.wi.mit.edu*
Usenet newsgroup: *bionet.molbio.genbank*
WorldWide Web: 1) *telnet ukanaix.cc.ukans.edu* 2) login: WWW 3) Enter terminal type: (carriage return) 4) Scroll to Information by subject, select, and scroll to Bio Sciences.
Email: The National Center for Biotechnology Information: *info@ncbi.nlm.nih.gov*

Perilous Knowledge

Despite the complex and potentially dry subject matter, this readable book goes down like a drink of cool water. In plain English, physicist/writer Tom Wilkie recounts the history of the Human Genome Project, explains the process, reports on where it is now and where it's going, and stirs up some big moral and social questions. —Mike Ashenfelder

•
I do not own my own genes; I was 'given' them by my parents and I have passed them on (or, at least, half of them) to my children. My immediate family have a legitimate interest in knowing my genetic constitution, so I cannot claim it as my private property. But the most important question to be posed in the short term by the Human Genome Project, a question which society has not even begun to answer, is who else has the right to know what is written in my genes and who can constrain how I act on that knowledge?

Perilous Knowledge
(The Human Genome Project and Its Implications)
Tom Wilkie. University of California Press, 1993; 195 pp. ISBN 0-520-08553-1 $20 ($23 postpaid) from California/Princeton Fulfillment Services, 1445 Lower Ferry Road, Ewing, NJ 08618; 800/777-4726

OTHER GREAT RESOURCES

Exons, Introns, and Talking Genes (The Science Behind the Human Genome Project): Christopher Wills. 1991, Basic Books. Focuses on the HGP's scientific and historic aspects.

Engines of Creation

The Last Technological Revolution is upon us: "nanotechnology" — the science of building molecules to order. What this might mean for good or bad is enthusiastically examined in this lively book. There is some gee-whizzing; how could there not be when the potentials include cell repair, disease reduction, and life extension? Ebullience is balanced by a serious discussion of the potential for horrifying weaponry, and the social disorder that could result from thoughtless incorporation of nanotechnology into an unprepared populace. The book is remarkably wide-visioned and comprehensively based: most unusual for this sort of thing. Future-reading at its best. —J. Baldwin

•

To visualize an advanced cell repair machine, imagine it — and a cell — enlarged until atoms are the size of small marbles. On this scale, the repair machine's smallest tools have tips about the size of your fingertips; a medium-sized protein, like hemoglobin, is the size of a typewriter; and a ribosome is the size of a washing machine. A single repair device contains a simple computer the size of a small truck, along with many sensors of protein size, several manipulators of ribosome size, and provisions for memory and motive power. A total volume ten meters across, the size of

Engines of Creation
Eric Drexler. Anchor Books, 1987; 240 pp. ISBN 0-385-19973-2, $10.95 ($13.45 postpaid) from Bantam, Doubleday, Dell/Fulfillment Dept., 2451 S. Wolf Road, Des Plaines, IL 60018; 800/223-6834

a three-story house, holds all these parts and more. With parts the size of marbles packing this volume, the repair machine can do complex things.

But this repair device does not work alone. It, like its many siblings, is connected to a larger computer by means of mechanical data links the diameter of your arm. On this scale, a cubic-micron computer with a large memory fills a volume thirty stories high and as wide as a football field. The repair devices pass it information, and it passes back general instructions. Objects so large and complex are still small enough: on this scale, the cell itself is a kilometer across, holding one thousand times the volume of a cubic-micron computer, or a million times the volume of a single repair device. Cells are spacious.

Artificial Life

If there is an a-life bible, Artificial Life is it. In his scrupulous editing of the proceedings of the historic First Artificial Life Conference in Los Alamos in September 1987, Chris Langton has implicitly sketched the horizons of this diverse field of study. Langton's opening essay is a virtual manifesto of the subject, underlining the principles by which a-lifers do their research: regard life as a pattern rather than a function of specific materials, organize from the bottom up, allow behavior to emerge instead of programming it in. At the end of the book is a deep, invaluable bibliography. —Steven Levy

•

The claim is the following: The "artificial" in Artificial Life refers to the component parts, not the emergent processes. If the component parts are implemented

Artificial Life
Christopher G. Langton, Editor. 1989; 655 pp. ISBN 0-201-09356-1 $36.75 (40.75 postpaid). Addison-Wesley Publishing Co./Order Dept., 1 Jacob Way, Reading, MA 01867; 800/447-2226

FIGURE 2 Breeding from a random starting pattern (a), random lines (b), lines of mathematical families (c), mirror algorithms (d), letting genes determine the presence or absence of mirrors in various planes of symmetry (e), and "archetypal" body form generated by *Blind Watchmaker's* artificial embryology (f).

correctly, the processes they support are *genuine* — every bit as genuine as the natural processes they imitate.

Artificial Life Lab

Experiment with alien life-forms in 3D and color! Watch amazing cyber-creatures evolve, solve problems, and reproduce before your very eyes! This book comes with a Windows-based program, "Boppers," and 3D glasses. It has dozens of pre-programmed genomes that mimic a broad range of living things along with hundreds of ways to evolve them to make millions of different ecologies. Change genetic codes to create your own living programs in cyber-worlds that you design. Then measure your creation's fitness and survival skills. Lab coat and test tubes optional. —William Mook

•

Boppers, included with this book, takes its name from the futuristic robots introduced in my science fiction novels, *Software* and *Wetware.* In *Software,* some robots are sent to the Moon where they build factories to make robot parts. They compete with each other for the right to use the parts (natural selection), and they get together in pairs

Artificial Life Lab
Rudy Rucker. 1993; 250 pp. ISBN 1-878739-48-4 $34.95 ($39.95 postpaid) from Waite Group Press, 200 Tamal Plaza, Corte Madera, CA 94925; 800/368-9369, fax 415/924-2576

(sex) to build new robots onto which parts of the parents' programs are placed (self-reproduction). Soon they rebel against human rule, and begin calling themselves *boppers.* Some of them travel to earth to eat some human brains — just to get the information out of the tissues, you understand.

Artificial Life II

I really didn't understand the scope of what computational biologists were doing with Darwinian software and supercomputers until I saw this video of the Second Artificial Life Conference. There's something about the way this stuff looks that hits you in the nucleus of every cell in your body.

It's one thing to read about pattern-games on computer screens, and another thing to watch these simple things begin interacting, and to see how higher levels of order seem to emerge from nowhere right before your eyes.

"Panspermia" is definitely the razzle-dazzle piece, at once inspiring and disturbing. The name comes from the theory that life is propagated throughout the universe by some kind of spore that can escape gravity, survive deep space, and land, as spores sometimes do, on fertile ground. If the essence of life is a pattern that works just as well in silicon as meat, then the idea of building such a spore is irresistible. This computer-generated video was created at Thinking Machines Corporation, using

Artificial Life II
Video. Christopher G. Langton, Editor. 1992; 120m video, ISBN 0-201-55492-5. $49.50 postpaid. Addison-Wesley Publishing Co./Order Dept., 1 Jacob Way, Reading, MA 01867; 800/447-2226.

Four moments from "Panspermia."

their Connection Machine multiprocessor supercomputer. The images are created by the very processes that the story they tell seeks to describe. The graphics were created from "seeds" that did not specify a blueprint for creating an image, but a set of simple "growth" rules. —HLR

See p. 21, Complexity and Chaos; p. 238, Artificial Evolution; p. 357, Media Magic.

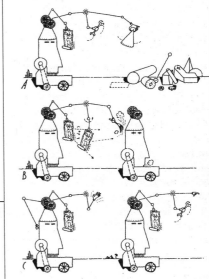

OTHER GREAT RESOURCES

Artificial Life: $45/year (4 issues) from the MIT Press, Cambridge, MA 02142; 617/253-2889; email: *journals-orders@mit.edu*

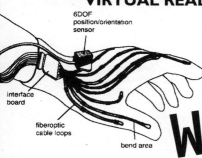

6DOF
position/orientation
sensor

interface
board

fiberoptic
cable loops

bend area

Welcome to the Virtual World

Flight Helmet head-mounted display.

This illustration shows the fiber-optic loops that measure the amount of bend or flex of a body joint like a knuckle or a wrist. The 6DOF sensor keeps track of the position and orientation of the hand in virtual space.

INFORMATION PLUGS US into the world of computerized productivity, but the open space of books balances our computer logic with the graces of intuition. —Michael Heim

Books: teachers, companions, entertainers — misleaders? Sometimes. When a trendy, complex topic such as virtual reality engages many authors, some inevitably spread confused or erroneous information. Which of the growing stack of "virtual reality" books offer the truth, are worth the trees, and aren't simply attempts to cash in on the hype?

The standouts treat VR not only as a computer-human interface but as a problem-solving tool, communications medium, and art form. They don't confound VR with multimedia and cyberstuff. They offer unique perspectives based on firsthand experiences with VR and the people behind it.

Start with *The Media Lab* by Stewart Brand (see.p. 256), the 1987 book that was the first (I believe) to mention "virtual reality."

Then turn to Howard Rheingold's groundbreaking *Virtual Reality*. The 1991 bestseller delves into the work and credos of VR leaders and legends around the world. Their eagerness to document their achievements, and to correct the mass-media hype, unlocked many doors for Rheingold. As he tracks the development of VR, he dips into the history of computer graphics, developmental psychology, theater, the Internet, and other deep, diverse subjects.

Myron Krueger's 1991 *Artificial Reality II* is required reading, although VR fanatics prefer the out-of-print 1983 *Artificial Reality*. Krueger focuses primarily on his work with computer-controlled, responsive audiovisual environments; he coined the phrase "artificial reality" in 1975 to describe them. *AR II* traces his development of this "culture-defining idea" and poses the human/computer-interface question as a problem in aesthetics. Enriched with illustrations and photos, Krueger's is a very personal and opinionated account that is fun to read.

In *Virtual Reality: Through The New Looking Glass*, VR industry technoids Kevin Teixeira and Ken Pimental present fundamental information on how "virtual worlds" are created, produced and experienced. This paperback is thorough, easy to understand, and liberally spiced with diagrams, photos, and drawings. It

includes a comprehensive product resource guide. The authors clearly describe how VR technologies work, who benefits from using them, and the challenges that concern virtual worldbuilders and tool developers.

Michael Heim's *Metaphysics of Virtual Reality* tells skeptics why they should appreciate VR and cautions VR zealots to cool their jets. Heim is an Tao-savvy philosophy teacher whose first virtual journey sent his philosophical seismograph into seizure. The resulting warmhearted, coolheaded essay collection views computing from an ontological perspective, pondering the erotic allure and the philosophical problems of cyberspace.

New technology changes faster than publishers can update the books about it. Two periodicals — an industry newsletter and an academic research report — will keep you up to date.

CyberEdge Journal covers international VR territory in the snappy, analytical style that epitomizes good newsletters. This bimonthly, 24-page newsletter details new applications, products, and events, and runs conference and lab reports, book reviews and opinion pieces.

Presence is the place where VR's most respected researchers report the results of their inquiries. The quarterly journal digs into the design of interactive environments that support sensory immersion via electronic and electromechanical devices. It explores human cognitive and sensory motor systems, telerobotics, and simulation software. To balance this technoid slant, the impact of "transformed presence" on philosophy, aesthetics, and culture comes under examination. *Presence* also treats VR as a source of humor; one issue ran a techno-paper called "A Nose Gesture Interface Device: Extending Virtual Realities." —Linda Jacobson

I didn't know the rules of "molecular docking" — a tool for helping chemists find molecules shaped like the keys to specific proteins — the way a chemist knows them, but I could *feel* them, through my hand and the force-reflective feedback mechanism built into the ARM, the Argonne remote manipulator. The metal grip felt like the handlebar of a gargantuan, well-lubricated Harley.

We can't stop VR, even if that is what we

discover is the best thing to do. But we might be able to guide it, if we start thinking about it now. —*Virtual Reality*

In 1972 I submitted a proposal for a two-way installation titled VIDEOPLACE. . . . The piece consist[ed] of two environments, each containing a rear-screen video projection of a composite image of two participants. A single participant would enter each of the separate environments, and each screen would display both people's video images. If their images chanced to touch, sound would be generated. Thus, two strangers would be placed in a situation where their normal embarrassment about touching would be conflicting with their desire to explore this unexpected way of interacting.

All our traditional art forms have one thing in common: They assume a passive audience. Passivity was appropriate when most humans toiled physically. After centuries of effort, however, we have all but eliminated the necessity for physical exertion. Ironically, since our bodies require a certain amount of exercise for health, we face a new problem — how to make our lives more active. Sports fulfill this need for some people, but there is a place for new forms of art and entertainment that involve our bodies rather than deny them. —*Artificial Reality II*

•

Keep in mind that current VR systems only have a vague understanding of real physical properties. Dropping a virtual glass onto a virtual floor of a kitchen doesn't cause it to shatter or make a sound unless the world designer specifically programmed it to do so.

Virtual prototyping promises to turn the engineer back into an artisan. He will be able to work with the design as if it were a malleable yet solid object, be able to move and handle the product as if he were crafting it in a workshop, and then produce it himself without leaving his office. —*Virtual Reality: Through The New Looking Glass*

•

Our love affair with computers, computer graphics, and computer networks runs deeper than aesthetic fascination and deeper than the play of the senses. We are searching for a home for the mind and the heart. Our fascination with computers is more erotic than sensuous, more spiritual than utilitarian.

The final point of a virtual world is to dissolve the constraints of the anchored world so that we can lift anchor — not to drift aimlessly without point, but to explore anchorage in ever-new places and, perhaps, find our way back to experience the most primitive and powerful alternative embedded in the question posed by Leibnitz — Why is there anything at all rather than nothing? —*The Metaphysics of Virtual Reality*

Virtual Reality
(The Revolutionary Technology of Computer-Generated Artificial Worlds and How It Promises to Transform Society) Howard Rheingold. Touchstone Books, 1991; 416 pp. ISBN 0-671-77897-8 $12 ($15 postpaid). Simon & Schuster/ Order Dept., 200 Old Tappan Road, Old Tappan, NJ 07675; 800/223-2336

The Media Lab
(Inventing the Future at MIT) Stewart Brand. Penguin Books, 1987; 304 pp. ISBN 0-14-009701-5 $14.95 ($16.95 postpaid). Penguin USA/ Consumer Sales, 120 Woodbine Street, Bergenfield, NJ 07621; 800/253-6476

Artificial Reality II
Myron W. Krueger. 1991; 286 pp. ISBN 0-201-52260-8 $29.25 ($33.25 postpaid). Addison-Wesley Publishing Co./Order Dept., 1 Jacob Way, Reading, MA 01867; 800/447-2226

Virtual Reality
(Through the New Looking Glass) Ken Pimentel & Kevin Teixeira. intel/ Windcrest, 1993; 301 pp. ISBN 0-8306-4064-9 $32.95 postpaid. TAB Books Inc./Retail Order Dept., 13311 Monterey Avenue, Blue Ridge Summit, PA 17294; 800/822-8138

The Metaphysics of Virtual Reality
Michael Heim. 1993; 175 pp. ISBN 0-19-508178-1 $21 ($23 postpaid). Oxford University Press/Order Dept., 2001 Evans Road, Cary, NC 27513; 800/451-7556

CyberEdge Journal: $129/year (6 issues). 1 Gate Six Road, Suite G, Sausalito, CA 94965; 415/331-3343.

Presence: Thomas B. Sheridan, Editor. $50/year (4 issues). MIT Press Journals/ Circulation Dept., 55 Hayward Street, Cambridge, MA 02142; 617/253-2889; Fax: 617/258-6779.

OTHER GREAT RESOURCES

Virtual Reality Technology: Grigore Burdea & Philippe Coiffet. 1994, John Wiley & Sons.

Virtual Reality (Applications and Explorations): Alan Wexelblat, Editor. 1993, Academic Press.

Virtual Reality and the Exploration of Cyberspace: Francis Hamit. 1993, Sams Prentice Hall Computer Publishing.

Virtual Reality Creations: Dave Stampe, Bernie Roehl & John Eagen. 1993, Waite Group Press.

CyberArts (Exploring Art & Technology): Linda Jacobson, Editor. 1992, Miller Freeman Publications.

The Art of Human-Computer Interface Design: Brenda Laurel. 1990, Addison-Wesley.

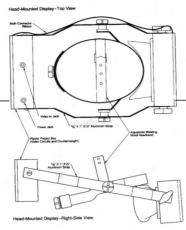

Head-Mounted Display–Top View

Head-Mounted Display–Right-Side View

Garage Virtual Reality

Three years ago, you couldn't get away with spending less than $100,000 for a VR system. Linda Jacobson's book is about the underground networks of inventors out there who pried Mattell's PowerGlove apart and turned a toy into the input device for cheap VR systems. The military and the infotainment industries won't be alone in the VR field for long. Just as a teenage Steve Wozniak started the personal-computer revolution, some kid who's messing with VR today is going to have an enormous impact on the future.

If we are going to make intelligent decisions about technologies of the future, we need to understand the full implications, beneficial and otherwise, of today's technologies. I suspect that the technological revolutions of the future aren't all going to come from the big research labs. If you want a glimpse of tomorrow, pay attention to those kids who are prying open electronic toys in garage laboratories: as Linda Jacobson points out, garage technology is an old and spectacularly successful American tradition.

And for those of you who are teenage VR hackers, this thick compendium of cheap VR lore is the motherlode: everything you need to know. It comes with an IBM-compatible, Macintosh, or Amiga version of Virtual Reality Studio1 — a 3D graphics toolkit. — HLR

Garage Virtual Reality
(The Affordable Way to Explore Cyberspace)
Linda Jacobson. 1993; 439 pp.
ISBN 0-672-30389-2
$29.95 ($32.95 postpaid). Prentice Hall Press/Order Processing Center, PO Box 11071, Des Moines, IA 50336-1071; 800/947-7700, fax 514/284-2607

Front Display–Exploded View

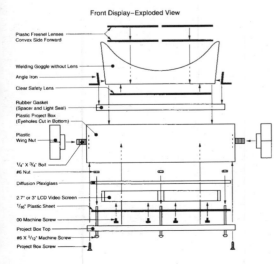

•

Some of the information in the following list was derived from FTP and VR data site lists that appear in the USENET newsgroup sci.virtual-worlds, posted by Bill Cockayne of Apple Computer and Toni Emerson of the Human Interface Technology Lab. Although the net addresses were accurate when this book was published, and most sites stem from stable educational and corporate institutions, keep in mind that net addresses, like normal (snail-mail) addresses, can change over time.

•

Just the FAQs
Virtual Reality FAQ
Host: ftp.u.washington.edu
Directory path: /public/virtual-worlds/theralfa
Maintained by Mark A. DeLoura (deloura@cs.unc.edu)

Power Glove FAQ (Glove-List)
Host: cogsci.uwo.ca (129.100.6.10)
Maintained by Eric Townsend (jet@well.sf.ca.us)
(This FAQ also is available directly from the glove-list file server. See the glove-list information in the section titled "Electronic Mailing Lists.")

Power Glove Serial Interface (PGSI) FAQ
Host: ftp.cso.uiuc.edu (128.174.5.59)
Directory path: /ACM/PGSI
Address: (pgsi@uiuc.edu)

Advanced Gravis UltraSound FAQ
Host: rtfm.mit.edu
Directory path: pub/usenet/news.answers maintained by Dave DeBry (ddebry@dsd.es.com)

•

Anonymous FTP Sites
General Information
Host: ftp.u.washington.edu (140.142.56.1)
Directory path: /public/virtual-worlds
Directory path:/public/hitl
Directory path: /public/virtual-worlds/virtus
Directory path: /public/VirtualReality

Probably the world's best-know VR information base, this site stores, among other goodies, sci.virtual-worlds archives, "TheRealFaq," code for VEOS (Virtual Environment Operating System), and self-running Virtus WalkThrough demos. Be sure to make your way down the directory path: /public/virtualreality/hitl/bibliographies, where the meticulously maintained VR Update (filename vru-vol1rev.txt) lists all recent VR books and articles.

Host: stein.u.washington.edu (140.142.56.1)
Directory path: /public/virtual-worlds

Home of sci.virtual-worlds, this is the place to log on to when you can't access ftp.u.washington.edu (and vice versa). Check out that FAQ!
Host: sunee.uwaterloo.ca (129.97.50.50)
Directory path: /pub
Directory path: /pub/rend386
Directory path: /pub/vr

A requisite stopover for all VR net travelers, this University of Waterloo site overflows with useful files and programs, including Dave Stampe and Bernie Roehl's notorious screen-rendered REND386 and its demos (read the text files first; they explain how to run the demo), a cool 3D wireframe object-viewer (which lets you use your mouse to pivot an object about), quasi-VR demos for 386 PCs, Jerry Isdale's "What Is VR?" article, and the

---

proverbial much, much more. Some of the demos support the Mattel Power Glove and/or LCD shutter glasses. Here are some other directory paths of interest to garage VR types.

pub/amiga (files related to the Commodore Amiga)
pub/glove (files and programs related to Power Glove)
pub/netgame (files related to networked games and VR)
pub/polyblit (Dave Stampe's speedy polygon code for 386 PCs)
pub/raytracers (raytracing graphics packages)
pub/sound (C source for playing sound files on a PC)
pub/vgif (GIF viewer)
Host: sunsite.unc.edu (152.2.22.81)
Directory path: /pub/academic/computer-science/virtual-reality

•

Based at the University of North Carolina, which houses one of the world's leading VR research labs, this site contains academic papers, VR demos, articles, a partial mirror of sci.virtual-worlds and the glove-list, 3D images and software, DOS VR programs, Power Glove software and information, REND386, and other fun stuff.

Host: avalon.chinalake.navy.mil (129.131.31.11).
Directory path: /pub
Mirrored on ftp.kpc.com (144.52.120.9)
Directory path: /pub/mirror/avalon

This is a massive data bank for 3D graphic objects archived in various formats, including utilities to convert between formats and documents that explain file formats.

Host: wuarchive.wustl.edu

This Seattle-based site mirrors the sci.virtual-worlds archives. It also contains Power Glove information and a wealth of graphics archives, including source code, in the directory path/graphics.

Host: parcftp.xerox.com
Directory path: /PUB/MOO/PAPERS

Site of the LambdaMOO MUD (see the section titled "In the MUD"), this Xerox Palo Alto Research Center storehouse contains scads of information on multiuser dungeons/dimensions (MUDs) — also known as text-based virtual realities— and electronic communication in general.

Host: ftp.apple.com (130.43.2.3)
Directory path: /pub/vr

Direct from Apple Computer headquarters in Cupertino, California, this cyberplace contains information on Macintosh-based VR, news of CAD projects, and a regularly updated list of FTP sites. It's also the home of the Mac VR programs Gossamer and Dr.StrangeGlove.

Host: ftp.ipa.fhg.de (129.233.17.68)
Directory path: /pub/virtual-reality

Based in Germany, this site contains files describing the work of Fraunhofer Institute for Manufacturing Engineering and Automation (IPA) in Stuttgart — specifically, the Demonstration Centre for VR, founded in 1991.

Host: ftp.ncsa.uiuc.edu (141.142.20.50)
Directory path: /VR

This relatively new site stores papers and other documentation about VR systems developed at the National Center for Supercomputing Applications (no garage VR here!).

•

LCD Shutter Glasses Information and Code

Host: wench.ece.jcu.edu.au
Directory path: /pub/sega/ [320x400|hicolor]
Host: wuarchive.wustl.edu (128.252.135.4)

These sites contain documentation and code for interfacing Sega shutter glasses with IBM PCs and compatibles.

Host: vega.hut.fi
directory path: /pub/mac/finnish/seg3d

This is the place for source code and documentation for interfacing the Macintosh with Sega LCD shutter glasses. It also provides ASCII and GIF versions of the documentation.

Macintosh VR Information

Host: ftp.apple.com (130.43.2.3)
Directory path: /pub/vr
Maintained by Bill Cockayne (billc@apple.com)

Dip into this treasure chest of Macintosh VR applications, self-extracting archives (Power Glove interface diagrams, programs and compiler for Ron Menelli's 68HC11 Glove interface, a Glove rotation control demo, and lots more). The updated list of FTP sites goes by the filename vr_sites.

•

News Groups

Usenet News Groups: sci.virtual-worlds and sci.virtual-worlds.apps

This inimitable pair of news groups contains the most active, well-known VR discussions, read by more than 15,000 people around the world. They cover developments in the field of virtual worlds technologies (sci.virtual-worlds) and applications (sci.virtual-worlds-apps). Together they serve as an international forum in which regular participants contribute news, insights into technological developments, opinions on scientific and philosophical issues, and discussions of the use of virtual worlds in commercial and social settings. Co-moderators from around the world contribute to both discussions, keeping it topical and "flame-free."

Several FTP sites (listed earlier) "mirror" sci.virtual-worlds, reflecting the daily activities for those who can't directly access the newsgroup.

Excerpts of these newsgroups occasionally appear on CompuServe, GEnie, BIX, and the WELL's VR conference.

Out of Control

Philosophers and particle physicists study the first microseconds of the universe for answers to the Big Question about the past: "Why is there something instead of nothing?" Kevin Kelly addresses a possibly bigger question about the future: "Does evolution evolve?"

Kelly sees new scientific disciplines related to chaos, complexity, artificial life, and theoretical biology as interlocking pieces of a grander puzzle. He uses new discoveries in the biological and computational sciences to unlock progressively bigger questions. By the time he is finished, Kelly makes a stunning reply to Stewart Brand's challenge in the first **Whole Earth Catalog***s: "We are as gods, and might as well get good at it." In fact, Kelly told me, when I pointed that out: "I could have called the book* **Whole Systems***."* —HLR

•

The Nine Laws of God

• *Distribute being.* The spirit of a beehive, the behavior of an economy, the thinking of a supercomputer, and the life in me are distributed over a multitude of smaller units (which themselves may be distributed). When the sum of the parts can add up to more than the parts, then that extra being (that something from nothing) is distributed among the parts. Whenever we find something from nothing, we find it arising from a field of many interacting smaller pieces. All the mysteries we find most interesting — life, intelligence, evolution — are found in the soil of large distributed systems.

• *Control from the bottom up.* When everything is connected to everything in a distributed network, everything happens at once. When everything happens at once, wide and fast-moving problems simply route around any central authority. Therefore, overall governance must arise from the most humble interdependent acts done locally in parallel, and not from a central command. A mob can steer itself, and in the territory of rapid, massive, and hetero-

geneous change, only a mob can steer. To get something from nothing, control must rest at the bottom within simplicity.

• *Sow increasing returns.* Each time you use an idea, a language, or a skill, you strengthen it, reinforce it, and make it more likely to be used again.

• *Grow by chunking.* The only way to make a complex system that works is to begin with a simple system that works. Attempts to instantly install highly complex organization — such as intelligence, or a market economy — without growing it, inevitably lead to failure.

• *Maximize the fringes.* In heterogeneity is creation of the world. A uniform entity must adapt to the world by occasional monumental revolutions, one of which is sure to kill it. A diverse heterogeneous entity, on the other hand, can adapt to the world in a thousand daily mini-revolutions, staying in a state of permanent, but never fatal, churning.

• *Honor your errors.* A trick will only work for a while, until everyone else is doing it. To advance from the ordinary requires a new game, or a new territory. But the process of going outside the conventional method, game, or territory is indistinguishable from error. Even the most brilliant act of human genius, in the final analysis, is an act of trial and error.

• *Pursue no optima, but multiple goals.* Simple machines can be efficient, but complex adaptive machinery cannot be. A complicated structure has many masters and none of them can be served exclusively. Rather than striving for optimization of any function, a large system can only survive by "satisficing" (making "good enough") a multitude of functions.

• *Seek persistent disequilibrium.* Neither constancy nor relentless change will support a creation. A good creation, like good jazz, must balance the stable formula with frequent offbeat, out-of-kilter notes. Equilibrium is death. Yet unless a system stabilizes to an equilibrium point, it is no better than an explosion, and just as soon dead. A Nothing, then, is both equilibrium and disequilibrium.

• *Change changes itself.* Change can be structured. This is what large complex systems do: they coordinate change. When extremely large systems are built up out of complicated systems, then each system begins to influence and ultimately change the organizations of other systems. That is, if the rules of the game are composed from the bottom up, then it is likely that interacting forces at the bottom level will alter the rules of the game as it progresses. Over time, the rules for change get changed themselves. Evolution — as used in everyday speech — is about how an entity changed over time. Deeper evolution — as it might be formally defined — is about how the rules for changing entities over time changes over time. To get the most out of nothing, you need to have self-changing rules.

These nine principles underpin the awesome workings of prairies, flamingoes, and cedar forests, eyeballs, natural selection in geological time, and the unfolding of a baby elephant from a tiny seed of elephant sperm and egg.

These same principles of bio-logic are now being implanted in computer chips, electronic communication networks, robot modules, pharmaceutical searches, software design, and corporate management, in order that these artificial systems may overcome their own complexity.

When the *technos* is enlivened by *bios*, we get artifacts that can adapt, learn, and evolve. When our technology adapts, learns, and evolves, then we will have a neobiological civilization.

Out of Control
(The Rise of Neo-Biological Civilization)
Kevin Kelly. 1994; 521 pp.
ISBN 0-201-57793-3
$28 ($31 postpaid). Addison-Wesley
Publishing Co./Order Dept., I Jacob Way,
Reading, MA 01867; 800/447-2226

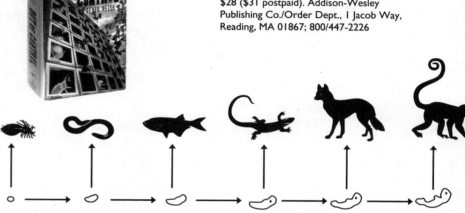

In one model of evolution, rules of thumb guide both development and evolution. Evolutionary rules of thumb work on embryos, while developmental rules work on everything else thereafter. Hereditary genes develop software routines that suggest strategies such as "try keeping the body warm if you have four legs." Plausible guesses, rather than random guesses, move an organism from one form to the next (above). If successful, a rule of thumb is stored in the genes, and reenacted for each individual during development. The same script used during evolution unfolds during individual growth (below).

—*Whole Earth Review, Fall, 1992*

The Entrapment of Form: Certain forms, such as spirals, arise in nature because they reflect the constraints of the material they are born in. On this hypothetical "landscape," down means "easier to do physically." Whatever natural selection takes an organism a step in the direction of a spiral, the form is rewarded so overwhelmingly that, whatever other tradeoffs are at hand, the organism's form gives in to the mathematical efficiency of the spiral. The form becomes a well into whose basin an organism falls. Straightness has its virtues too, and creates its own basin. An organism exploring the saddle between the two basins will sooner or later fall into the clutch of one well or the other.

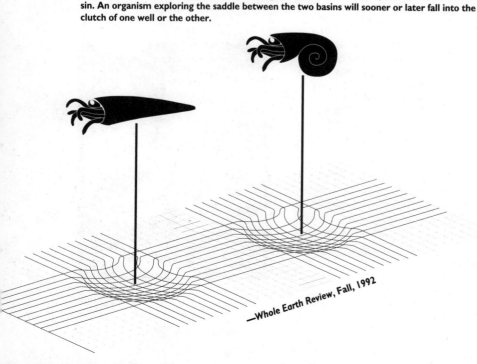

—*Whole Earth Review, Fall, 1992*

Tierra

This program's C source code creates a virtual computer and its operating system, whose architecture has been designed in such a way that the executable machine codes are evolvable. This means that the machine code can be mutated (by flipping bits at random) or recombined (by swapping segments of code between algorithms), and the resulting code remains functional enough of the time for natural (or, presumably, artificial) selection to be able to improve the code over time.

This system results in the production of synthetic organisms based on a computer metaphor of organic life in which CPU time is the "energy" resource and memory is the "material" resource. Memory is organized into informational patterns that exploit CPU time for self-replication. Mutation generates new forms, and evolution proceeds by natural selection as different

genotypes compete for CPU time and memory space.

Diverse ecological communities have emerged. These digital communities have been used to experimentally examine ecological and evolutionary processes: competitive exclusion and coexistence, host/parasite density-dependent population regulation, the effect of parasites in enhancing community diversity, evolutionary arms races, punctuated equilibrium, and the role of chance and historical factors in evolution. This evolution-in-a-bottle may prove to be a valuable tool for the study of evolution and ecology. —Tom Ray

Tierra: On DOS disk: $50 postpaid (specify 3 1/2" or 5 1/4") from Virtual Life, 25631 Jorgensen Road, Newman, CA 95360. UNIX/DOS source code and documentation (but not executables) available by anonymous ftp at: tierra.slhs.udel.edu [128.175.41.34] and life.slhs.udel.edu [128.175.41.33]

Robot Explorer

This friendly and informative newsletter covers both experimental and practical applications of robots. Features include robot professionals and hobbyists talking about their projects, reports on robot events and competition, and coverage of new theory and research. An "industry scrapbook" of new products and an event calendar complete the package. A pretty good deal at eight issues for $14.95.
—Gareth Branwyn

Robot Explorer
Raymond GA Côté, Editor.
$14.95/year (8 issues). 145 Grove Street, PO Box 458, Peterborough, NH 03458-0458; 800/GO-ROBOT

•
The concept of hordes of 'gnat' robots replacing single mobile robots has been proposed by Anita Flynn and others at the MIT

Artificial Intelligence Lab. In fact, the concept of building little machines capable of group achievement is being studied so seriously that the AI Lab is locally known as the Artificial Insect Lab.

LEGO Dacta

The plastic building blocks of your childhood have become the standard building blocks for amateur robots. LEGO Dacta, the company's educational division, offers LEGO Technic kits with applications in the sciences, mathematics, and technology.

Besides wide variations on the blocks themselves, the Technic line adds sensors, motors, switches, lights, gears, pneumatics, and computer control hardware and software. You can buy the components in kits with specific course objectives, in large building sets, or in separate parts packs. LEGO components are perfect for miniature

robotics, because they're strong, versatile, and reasonably priced (well: sort of). They can be used for designing, prototyping, or as your finished robot.
—GB

•
9609 9 Volt Technology Resource Set $199.00

1,733 pieces including new elements such as: 9 volt motor and battery box, 9 volt wire system, cam wheels, axle extenders, and a metal crane hook.

LEGO Dacta
Catalog free. 555 Taylor Road/PO Box 1600, Enfield, CT 06803-1600; 800/527-8339, fax 203/763-2466

Mobile Robots

The undisputed bible for amateur robot-makers. It covers everything from robotics theory to design, construction, operation, and trouble shooting. The detailed robot plans (for two different 'bots) included in the book grew out of work at MIT's AI Lab.

Authors Anita Flynn and Joseph Jones have done an amazing job of covering beginner- to advanced-level concepts in a lucid and easy-to-follow, but still rigorous manner. An extensive "Yellow Pages" section covers suppliers, available products, and trade journals. I couldn't be more jazzed by this volume. —GB

•
The design and construction of mobile robots is as much an art as a science. The intent of *Mobile Robots: Inspiration to Implementation* is to explain the skills involved in a manner amenable to as broad an audience as possible. Our aim is to teach you, the reader, how to build a robot. With the recent wide availability of home computers and tremendous reductions in costs for microelectronics, building mobile robots with an assortment of sensors and actuators is within the reach of nearly everyone.

•
Attention to Detail
Intermittent connections are the most frustrating to debug. The way to avoid this problem is to build your circuit neatly and carefully the first time. When soldering, do not use gobs of solder. Use heat-shrink tubing to cover exposed wires. Connectorize liberally for quick disassembly. Add strain reliefs to cable harnesses. Wire things carefully the first time. Keep in mind that a little quality goes a long way.

Mobile Robots
(Inspiration to Implementation)
Joseph L. Jones & Anita M. Flynn. 1993; 349 pp. ISBN 1-56881-011-3
$39.95 ($42.45 postpaid). AK Peters, Ltd., 289 Linden Street, Wellesley, MA 02181; 617-235-2210

The 6.270 Robot Builder's Guide

First written as course materials for an experimental LEGO Robot Design class at MIT, the **Guide** *has been reorganized to make it more useful to those teaching robotics, and to hobbyists looking to create 'bots based on LEGO technology and the Motorola 6811 microprocessor. It takes you through the assembly of the electronic components, the building of the robot, the application of various sensors, and the programming of your model, using a special C language (Interactive C, or IC), especially developed for the 6.270 robot. The* **Guide** *starts with basic electronics and soldering techniques, and builds toward a deeper (hands-on) understanding of embedded systems, sensors and actuators, microcontrol and programming.*
—GB

•
6.270 is a hands-on, learn-by-doing class in which participants design and build a robot that will play in a competition at the end of the class. From the student's perspective, the goal of the class is to design a robotic machine that will be able to navigate its way around the playing surface, and successfully interact with game objects, including the opposing machine.

The 6.270 Robot Builder's Guide
Fred Martin. 1992; 230 pp.
$15 postpaid from The MIT Media Lab/Epistemology and Learning Publications, 20 Ames Street, Room E15-315, Cambridge, MA 02139; 617/253-0330, fax 617/253-6215; email el-pubs@media.mit.edu. Also available by anonymous ftp at cherupakha.media.mit.edu [18.85.0.47]

•
Detecting collisions can only be as good as one's collision sensors. Based on the premise that such sensors are not perfect, it is a good idea to add some kind of time-based exit condition. This will prevent the all-too-frequent case of a robot that is stuck, but does not have its touch sensor depressed. Many a robot simply does not "believe" that it is stuck — its program stays stuck in some loop, taking no compensatory action.

Robot Clubs and Events

Robot clubs, competitions, and robot art/performance groups can be found throughout the US. One of the most innovative of these is Austin, Texas' Robot Group. Their skill, creativity, and sense of whimsy has created such crowd-pleasing robotic performers as a ferocious pneumatic pit bull, a robo-band called The Shrinking Robot Heads, and a number of odd flying contraptions. The group also hosts the

annual RoboFest, an increasingly popular showcase and meeting place for robot enthusiasts. For more info on the Robot Group, email: robotgroup@cs.utexas.edu. To find out about other clubs and events, check out the comp.robotics newsgroup and **Robot Explorer**. —GB

The Robot Group: PO Box 164334, Austin, TX 78716; 512/794-9105, email robot-group@cs.utexas.edu

Online Resources

Net Access to Robot Information

The Comp.Robotics Newsgroup: Information and discussion on robots, covering industrial applications, research and theory, and amateur robotics. Net access: comp.robotics

The Comp.Robotics FAQ: A massive document (70+ pages) filled with answers to FAQs, resources, contact information, and more. Indispensable. Available by anonymous ftp at rtfm.mit.edu in pub/usenet/news.answers/robotics-faq/part1 and part2

The Hobby-Bot Mailing List: Covers hobby robotics in all its forms. Subscribe: hobby-bot-request@a.cs.okstate.edu

The Mini Board Mailing List: For discussion of robot control and robot controller boards, especially the MIT Miniboard 2.0 and the 6.270 board. Send a message containing the word "help" to: listserv@oberon.com

Kevin Derricks

"Oscar" The Robot Trashcan.

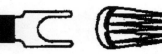

*W*e asked a diverse group of techies to share their favorite, most indispensable tools, books, catalogs, and mags with us. Here are some of their responses. —Gareth Branwyn

Cast of characters:

Dany "Xixax" Drennan *is the editor of the "tech/art/culture" zine* Inquisitor *(info: inquisitor@echonyc.com). He likes to hack microcontrollers and other homebrewed devices.*

Alberto Gaitan *is an artist and composer who works with Art Attack!, an interactive installation group. Given meager funding, they piece together most of their tech on the super-cheap.*

Sue Forslev *installs computer networks and maintains workstations.*

Bob Madderra *has been hacking robots since he was seventeen.*

Mark W. Tilden, *the "BEAM robotics guy," has built the world's first Robot Jurassic Pond; seventy robots of thirty different species interact continuously there, under solar power.*

Jay Eric Townsend *is a garage VR hacker and originator of the Internet's "glove-list," for people interesting in hacking the Mattel Power Glove.*

Bill Woodcock *builds fancy corporate computer networks by day and "chewing gum and baling wire" toasternets by night (see "Toasternet" sidebar). He builds these consummate street-tech creatures out of "borrowed, salvaged, reclaimed, recycled, dumpster-dived, and cobbled-together hardware."*

Tools:

Forslev: My two favorite tools: a pair of chopsticks and a Swiss Army knife. You can open any PC with the knife, and chopsticks are good for removing screws that fall into crevices.

Madderra: Digital Logic Probe ($18 from Radio Shack), lots of breadboards (around $10 each from Radio Shack), Linux (free software by ftp-ing from: sunsite.unc.edu)

Tilden: The Dremel MINIMITE 2-speed model 750 Cordless Rotary Tool, Lindstrom diagonal cutters, Cresta needlenose pliers — no. 3013-S (all from Jensen Tool).

Townsend: A Leatherman's tool (a combination tool with pliers, screwdrivers, and knife — around $40). Mini-Maglite flashlight. A basic digital multimeter (around $30 from Radio Shack).

Woodcock: Leviton Telecom's Test-Tone Generator and Inductive Amplifier Probe (about $100 for the pair). Other vendors make similar products, but Leviton's is the sturdiest I've seen, it's better looking than most, and they replaced mine overnight (no questions asked) after I fried the amplifier.

Books:

Drennan: Telecom Library Bookstore. Everything you could possibly want to know about telecom (except what you get from *2600* magazine). Any and all books by Forrest M. Mims III.

Gaitan: Radio Shack's electronic series. My favorites are *Understanding Electronic Control of Automation Systems* by Neil M. Schmitt and Robert F. Farwell (T. I. Learning Center) and *Understanding Digital Electronics* by Gene McWhorter (Howard W. Sams & Co.). Radio Shack has lots of books for both beginner and expert, covering subjects from simple all-purpose circuit diagrams to complete projects.

Madderra: Don Lancaster's *Incredible Secret Money Machine II* reveals (among other things) how to get trade journals and manuals for free. Also check out Lancaster's "Hardware Hacker" column in the excellent *Electronics Now.*

Tilden: Datamanuals from Texas Instruments, Motorola, and National Linear.

Townsend: Read *everything*, from crappy old TAB Books to vendors' product descriptions. Go to used bookstores, libraries, etc. There is no single source of all good info. Of course, nothing beats Usenet as a source of timely information and useful connections.

Woodcock: Harry Newton's ridiculously thorough *Newton's Telecom Dictionary* is the only place to turn when marketing droids start spouting salesspeak and engineers start in with the technojargon.

Catalogs:

Drennan: All Electronics for new and surplus parts and supplies; Fair Radio Sales Co. for commercial/army surplus.

Gaitan: The gearhead's bible: Grainger's. They have over 190 locations nationwide. The Radio Shack catalog.

Tilden: Digikey catalog.

Townsend: Radio Shack is your friend. But so are used electronic and junk shops. I buy very little through mail order. Check out your local ham-radio store: not only do hams have a wide body of experience to

---

IT'S EASY TO MAKE WIRE WRAPPING CONNECTIONS

Jensen Master Catalog

Bare Wire Sleeve

BIT

WIRE INSERTION

Step 1
WIRE ANCHORING

Step 2

Wire-wrapping provides a positive, uniform electrical connection faster and more economically than any other method. No need for soldered contacts. No skill is required to produce perfect wire-wrapped connectors of "gas tight" quality. Select the combination of bit and sleeve you need for either a Regular or Modified wrap. All bits and sleeves fit with either the manual or electric OK wire wrapping tools described on page 198. See page 200 for wire stripper.

Step 3
TERMINAL INSERTION

Step 4
FINISHED CONNECTION

What IS a Toasternet?

Toasternets are private, independent Internet-connected networks that spring up in basements, closets, wherever there's space. They are built by individuals, often using bizarre mixtures of mismatched hardware and software. Prototype high-speed routers and network hardware nestle comfortably among antiquated UNIX hosts built from ten-year-old discarded parts; alpha-test software runs on machines salvaged from junkyards and dumpsters. Macintoshes run ported PC software; PCs run one-of-a-kind operating systems. Many toasternets seem at first like hellish tangles of junk, unlikely to work at all. Fact is, the intensity of competition, the rate of propagation, and the great variety of methods and combinations have created a form of electronic Darwinism. Software, protocols, and routing algorithms are born, fan out over the net, and disappear, prey to faster, more reliable, more portable new generations. Toasternets are a hothouse for technological standards, and we all profit from the resulting hybrid vigor. —Bill Woodcock

1) FTP server drive. 2) POP mail spooler. 3) Prototype PPP router being tested. 4) Livingston Portmaster router. 5) Norris Earphone atop a stack of modems. 6) punchdown blocks. 7) HTTP server, AURP router, AFP server, PAP spooler. 8) CD drive. 9) mail, FTP, primary nameserver, shell accounts. 10) news spooling drive. 11) Powerbook serves as a mobile administration console, as well as phone book, etc. 12) news and NFS server, secondary nameserver.

Digi-Key Corporation

If there's one electronics catalog you shouldn't be without, it's this fat, juicy bi-monthly. Digi-Key's decent prices, excellent service, same-day shipping, and staggering selection of components have won the respect and repeat business of electrical engineers, repair techs, and hobbyists. The catalog gives detailed specs on most items. —GB

•

Fiber Optic Lab Manual & Lab Kit
Features: 7 Experiments • Final Design Project • Fiber Optic Glossary • Research Projects. The Fiber Optic Lab Manual is a complete 60 page technical manual on fiber optics, available alone or with the Lab Kit. It is written in an easy to understand style and fits well with any text or course on fiber optics. All the fundamentals of fiber optic systems are covered in detail. *FB100-ND (IF-LM1) Lab Manual $7.95*

Experiments include: Making a Light Pipe • Fiber Cable Transmission • Splices, Connections and Terminations • Speed of Opto-Electric Devices • Fiber Optic Transmitters • Fiber Optic Receiver Design • Making a Star Coupler. *FB101-ND (IF LMH) Kit with Lab Manual $39.95*

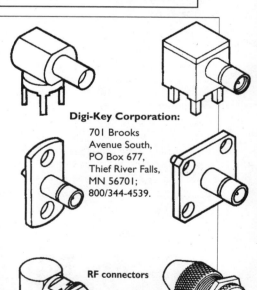

Digi-Key Corporation:
701 Brooks Avenue South, PO Box 677, Thief River Falls, MN 56701; 800/344-4539.

RF connectors

ANOTHER BACKYARD RESOURCE

American Science & Surplus: Catalog $1. 3605 Howard Street, Skokie, IL 60076; 708/982-0722. Pee Wee Herman might buy hardware here. They carry parts, tools, toys, inexplicable artifacts, from the sublime to the ridiculous. The item descriptions are great. Formerly known (and widely loved) as Jerryco.

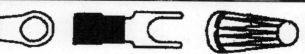
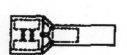

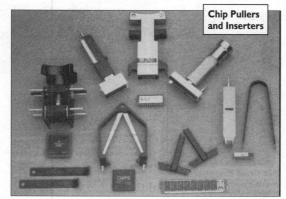

Chip Pullers and Inserters

—Jensen Master Catalog

share, but they are often expert scroungers.

Woodcock: Jensen Tools Master Catalog. Jensen has reliable next-day delivery on a huge variety of telecom, networking, and computer hardware-hacker tools. Global Engineering Documents carries EIA, TIA, ANSI, and ISO standards and specifications documents for everything from cellular telephone intercell handoff procedures to car stereos.

Magazines:

Drennan: The monthly bible for computer hackers is *Microcomputer Journal* (formerly *ComputerCraft*). All praise Jan Axelson! *The Computer Applications Journal* is bible number two. They run a companion BBS at 203/871-1988.

Townsend: Both *Midnight Engineering* and *2600* often run "how-to" articles and offer good, up-to-date information. You'll learn best by trying to build some of these projects. NOTHING that you read is going to teach you how to take things apart and put them back together; only practice will do that. ❧

Dremel Cordless Rotary Tool: #22B751. $39 ($42 postpaid). Jensen Tools Inc., below.
Diagonal Cutters: #194B880. $33.95 ($36.95 postpaid). Jensen Tools Inc., below.
Needlenose Pliers: #66B051. $13.25 ($16.25 postpaid). Jensen Tools Inc., below.
Mini Maglite: #686B002. $14.50 ($17.50 postpaid). Jensen Tools Inc., 7815 S. 46th Street, Phoenix, AZ 85044-5399; 800/426-1194, fax 800/366-9662.
Leatherman's Tool: REI, 1700 45th Street E., Sumner, WA 98390; 800/426-4840, fax 206/891-2523.
Tone & Probe Kit: #49562-TSK. About $100. Leviton Telecom, 2222 222nd Street, SE, Bothell, WA 98021-4422; 800/722-2082.
Telecom Library Bookstore Catalog: Telecom Library, 12 W. 21st Street, New York, NY 10010; 212/691-8215.
Incredible Secret Money Machine II: Don Lancaster. 1992; 157 pp. ISBN 1-882193-65-2 $18.50 ($20.50 postpaid). Synergetics Press, 3860 W. 1st Street, Box 809, Thatcher, AZ 85552; 602/428-4073.
Electronics Now: $19.97/year (12 issues). PO Box 55115, Boulder, CO 80322; 800/999-7139.
Texas Instruments: 800/336-5236.
Motorola: 800/521-6274.
Newton's Telecom Dictionary: Harry Newton. 1993; ISBN 0-936648-42-2 $24.95 ($27.45 postpaid). Telecom Library Bookstore, 12 W. 21st Street, New York, NY 10010; 212/691-8215.
All Electronics Corp.: PO Box 567, Van Nuys, CA 91408; 800/826-5432, fax 818/781-2653.
Fair Radio Sales Co.: PO Box 1105, Lima, OH 45802; 419/223-2196.
W. W. Grainger: 5760 Commerce Blvd., Rohnert Park, CA 94928; 707/584-9211.
Jensen Tools Inc.: 7815 S. 46th Street, Phoenix, AZ 85044-5399; 800/426-1194, fax 800/366-9662.
Global Engineering Documents: Catalog free. 3130 S. Harbor Blvd., Santa Ana, CA 92704; 800/854-7179.
MicroComputer Journal: $29.95/year (6 issues). MicroComputer Journal, 76 N. Broadway, Hicksville, NY 11801; 516/681-2922
Computer Applications Journal: $21/year (12 issues). 4 Park Street, Suite 20, Vernon, CT 06066; 203/875-2751, BBS 203/871-7988.
Midnight Engineering: $25/year (6 issues). 111 E. Drake Rd. #704, Fort Collins, CO 80525; 719/254-4558.
2600: $21/year (4 issues). PO Box 752, Middle Island, NY 11953; 516/751-2600, fax 516/751-2608.

Don Lancaster • Synergetics Press

One cannot talk about do-it-yourself high technology and not talk about Don Lancaster. From the early days of the PC revolution, he has cranked out reams of indispensable information and techno-wisdom on hacking digital electronics. His columns regularly appear in Midnight Engineering, Nuts and Volts, *and* Electronics Now. *He has authored thirty-two books and two videos. He maintains a free-of-charge help line. Two excellent source books offer thousands of tips and contacts related to DIY tech:* The Blatant Opportunist *(column reprints from* Midnight Engineering*) and* Resource Bin *(column reprints from* Nuts and Volts*). —GB*

• Rule #1 — Do not ever, under any circumstances, call yourself an inventor or behave like one.

Rule #2 — If you ever associate yourself with any inventor's resource, use a fake name and wear a disguise. —*The Blatant Opportunist*

• Getting onto any military surplus bidders' list has been a major rite of passage for most electronic hackers. The process is cheap and quite simple: You write or call the Defense Logistics Supply Agency and ask for their surplus sales brochure. Then you fill out a card, giving them your area and material preferences. That's all there is to it. Easy. —*Resource Bin*

The Blatant Opportunist and **Resource Bin:** Don Lancaster. Each $24.50 ($27 postpaid) from Synergetics Press: 3860 W. 1st Street, Box 809, Thatcher, AZ 85552; 602/428-4073.

Radio Shack

Radio Shack is probably responsible for the care and feeding of more hackers and weekend gearheads than any other entity. With over 6,600 stores, 73 years of experience, and a decent selection of reasonably priced electronics, the Shack is a godsend. Even though their parts area seems to be shrinking in favor of more end-consumer items, they still carry a surprising amount of essential do-it-yourself stock, with more items available through special order. Their cheap radio-controlled toys,

dialers, and other electronics are fun to hack, too! —GB

•
Getting Started in Electronics
by Forrest Mims, III. Now in its 10th printing, this book is the perfect "hands-on" introduction to electronics. It features text that's easy-to-understand and big diagrams hand-drawn by Mims, who is one of America's most popular science writers. 128 pages. 276-5003 $2.99

•
Budget Pocket Dialer
Take Touch-Tone capability wherever you go! This inexpensive manual tone dialer is

ideal for beeperless answerers plus tone-activated answering, dictation, and amateur radio autopatching. Requires 3 "AAA" batteries. *43-139* $15.99

•
Silicon Solar Cell
Harness the sun with this efficient 2 x 4 cm cell. Delivers about 0.3A at 0.55VDC in full sunlight. Use for science fair projects or get several and build a solar panel to charge batteries and operate electronic devices. *276-124* $4.19

The Radio Shack catalog must be obtained from your nearest Radio Shack.

The Underground Guide to Laser Printers • Flash Magazine

I hate to pay money for repairs I could do. So the first few times I hired a tech, I watched everything he did so that I could do it the next time. Much of what I learned is now available in The Underground Guide — *it covers the basics on cleaning, maintaining,*

changing fuser rollers, and troubleshooting image problems. There are chapters on using your printer to create T-shirt transfers, rubber stamps, laser checks, and printed circuitboards. The editors also produce Flash, *an insightful bimonthly journal for the adventurous desktop printer. —GB*

•
The paper feed cams, which pick up the paper in laser printers and copiers, are covered with textured rubber that lifts the paper and passes it through the machine. With age and use, the rubber on the cams may harden and lose its grip. Thus, the printer will miss the page pickup, causing the top of the print to appear halfway down the page. Wiping these rollers with acetone may revitalize the rubber and revive the grip. It is important not to use rubbing alcohol, because it will dry out the rubber. —*The Underground Guide*

Cleaning the transfer wires.

The Underground Guide to Laser Printers
Flash Magazine editors. 1993; 162 pp. ISBN 1-56609-045-8 $12 ($16 postpaid). Peachpit Press Inc., 2414 6th Street, Berkeley, CA 94710; 800/283-9444

Flash Magazine
Walter Vose Jeffries, Editor. $15/year (6 issues). Flash Magazine, Riddle Pond Road, West Topsham, VT 05086; fax 802/439-6463

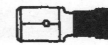

WE ARE SWIMMING in a great polluted sea of language, and we wonder why we can't write. We wonder why we don't want to read. Even worse, we cease to wonder; we just don't do it. It's as though it didn't matter any more.

As though hammers didn't matter; as though air didn't matter; as though horses and balloons had disappeared.

It's not a hardware problem; it's not a brain-wire problem. It's a writing problem. It's software, it's soft words, it's some swampish bureaucratic slide-down of mush-mouthed ass-covering prose that promotes long-term despair in humans.

It's the first feedback loop: how we read is how we think is how we write is how we think is how we read. Garbage in, garbage out — our hydroponic brains are getting overchlorinated prose. To inoculate ourselves against this particular virus, this excess of speechifying and voter-pamphlet prose and nicey-nicey high school anthologies and meaning-stripped feel-good advertising jargon and pyramidal journalism and two-handed essays ("on the other hand comma weasel. . ."), it is necessary to seek density and clarity.

Density and clarity.
Density and clarity.

OUR THUMBS GOT SMART LONG BEFORE our tongues woke up: *Homo sapiens* have been speaking to each other for far less time than our ancestors spent swinging from limb to limb together. But once we started using our mouths to sling symbols around, we intelligent apes started changing ourselves and our planet at a furious pace.

Human communication and tool-building talents have amplified each other, accelerating the pace of change for our species and the parts of the world we affect; alphabets multiplied the power of language a scant five thousand years ago, and the worldwide communications web is less than a hundred years old.

Communications media create wealth and change the balance of political power because control of communications media means control of people's thoughts and beliefs about the world. (See "Electronic Democracy," p. 288.) One side-effect of the miniaturization revolution has been the diffusion of significant communication power, formerly reserved for elites, into the hands of millions of citizens. Desktop publishing, desktop radio, desktop video, desktop computer networking now give knowledgeable individuals global reach. "Communication" encompasses far more than those activities that can be enhanced by electronic devices: comix, zines, street performance and theater, investigative reporting, graphic communication and visual thinking, writing, poetry, ritual.

If you want to publish a zine, set up a computer network, design propaganda, make your own musical instrument, start a pirate radio station, create a television program, distribute music, understand or subvert mass media, you'll need the tools, tips, and world views found on these pages. —HLR

more powerful is a word! It can restore kingdoms, restore reputations, restore kitchen cabinets.

Do this at home: Commit an act of clarity. Say the sentence that is the precise description of who you are and where you are. Now ask yourself: Would you rather be a pair of ragged claws scuttling across the floor of silent seas?

Between the question and the answer lies the act of writing, the act of reading, the act of meaning.

The reason for the passion is the fear of loss. We are pissing our language away; we are beating our verbs into formats. *Meaning held hostage!* As Monty Python asked: "What do we mean by 'mean?'" Our brains are at stake, the narrow line of clarity between the folds of gray mush inside our skulls.

This is God's video game now. At stake are our declining natural prose reserves.

In the gathering darkness of an airless stairwell, Amina Sinai is climbing towards a prophecy. Lifafa Das is comforting her because now that she has come by taxi into the narrow bottle of his mercy, he has sensed an alteration in her, a regret at her decision; he reassures her as they climb. The darkened stairwell is full of eyes,

It is as William Strunk said to E. B. White all those years ago in that Cornell classroom, before the war to end wars had quite finished failing, grasping his lapels and leaning forward: "Omit needless words! Omit needless words! Omit needless words!" Brevity is so important that it must be tripled in size; density is so important it must be expanded upon.

Do this at home: Utilizing your Millennium-approved Gaia-friendly by-gum-degradable access to paper-and-pencil technology, omit needless words everywhere. Omit them from your cereal boxes and your VCR instructions. Omit them from your conversation and your letters. Now, put them back. . . slowly, slowly. *They are precious.* They are gifts from God, these words. They are molecules of meaning, and the right sentence can cure cancer, can cure loneliness, can cure ham.

> We have lingered in the chambers of the sea
>
> By sea-girls wreathed with seaweed red and brown
>
> Till human voices wake us, and we drown.

Eliot! Why not? Old Possum has his tricks; they can be your tricks. *Concentrate on that comma!* That is where the heart turns over, in that crooked eyebrow between the pronoun and the conjunction. If a comma is that powerful, think what a word can do. No, but seriously, folks: Think what a word can do.

Think of what a word can do.

Concentrate on that paragraph. All by itself, one line, indented for extra emphasis. An indent, negative space — that nothing that draws attention to the something beside it. Think what nothing can do. How much

eyes glinting through shuttered doors at the spectacle of the climbing dark lady, eyes lapping her up like bright rough cats' tongues; and as Lifafa talks, soothingly, my mother feels her will ebbing away, What will be, will be, her strength of mind and her hold on the world seeping out of her into the dark sponge of the staircase air. Sluggishly her feet follow his, up into the upper reaches of the huge gloomy chawl, the broken-down tenement building in which Lifafa Das and his cousins have a small corner, at the very top. . . here, near the top, she sees dark light filtering down on to the heads of the queueing cripples. 'My number two cousin,' Lifafa Das says, 'is bone-setter.' She climbs past men with broken arms, women with feet twisted backwards at impossible angles, past fallen window-cleaners and splintered bricklayers, a doctor's daughter entering a world older than syringes and hospitals; until, at last, Lifafa Das says, 'Here we are, Begum,' and leads her through a room in which the bone-setter is fastening twigs and leaves to shattered limbs, wrapping cracked heads in palm-fronds, until his patients begin to resemble artificial trees, sprouting vegetation from their injuries. . . then out on to a flat expanse of cemented roof. Amina, blinking in the dark at the brightness of lanterns, makes out insane shapes on the roof: monkeys dancing; mongeese leaping; snakes swaying in baskets; and on the parapet, the silhouettes of large birds, whose bodies are as hooked and cruel as their beaks: vultures.

That's Salman Rushdie, who was a genius long before he was a famous pre-dead writer, and that paragraph is a post-graduate course in everything you need to know. "The darkened stairwell is full of eyes";

EXHIBITS A, B, C.

James Donnelly

THERE WAS WOMAN'S FEARLESS EYE,
LIT BY HER DEEP LOVE'S TRUTH;
THERE WAS MANHOOD'S BROW SERENELY HIGH,
AND THE FIERY HEART OF YOUTH.

—FELICIA D. HEMANS

there is no better way to say that, every needful word included, every texture honored, and that is seven words in a paragraph of 310 words in a book of 552 pages. That already is a miracle, the act of writing it and the act of reading it. It is the miracle of meaning.

What can you find there? That last colon: Good. The dark sponge of the staircase air: Yes, yes. You can feel your forehead moving toward the sentence fragment. Physiological changes! Hook up the electrodes, darling, I feel some prose coming on.

Those patients like trees. Imagine that you were a boy in Bombay and you had been to the magician and you had seen the leafy splints and many years later you could pour that story like water onto a page. Better yet: Imagine that you had only imagined it, and could make it real. It's the gift that keeps on giving! It's eternal life!

We tell ourselves stories in order to live. Joan Didion said that.

The narrative of Rushdie's, which is the maybe-true story of the birth of the maybe-him, is just like your narrative. It is separated from your narrative only by will and skill. Talk about Empowerment! You can create the story of your own birth and make it live in the brains of people around the world. Mythmaker! Swallower of worlds! Many-verbed keeper of clarity! It's Show Time! —Jon Carroll

Collected Poems of T. S. Eliot

T. S. Eliot is the bottleneck through which all English poetry passes, inescapable and intransigent, deeply annoying, amazing. He is like the apparition in the throne room of the Wizard of Oz, a huge head floating, serene above all ambitions, his anger woven of artifice, a voice, a presence, a wisp of steel. We pay no attention to the man behind the curtain because we cannot locate the curtain; he is too cunning for us. He moves us against our will. —Jon Carroll

Collected Poems, 1909–1962
T. S. Eliot. 1963; 221 pp.
ISBN 0-15-118978-1
$16.95 ($20.45 postpaid). Harcourt Brace Trade Dept., 6277 Sea Harbor Drive, Orlando, FL 32887-4300; 800/543-1918

•

Although I do not hope to turn again
Although I do not hope
Although I do not hope to turn

Wavering between the profit and the loss
In this brief transit where the dreams cross
The dreamcrossed twilight between birth
    and dying
(Bless me father) though I do not wish to
    wish these things
From the wide window towards the granite
    shore
The white sails still fly seaward, seaward
    flying
Unbroken wings

"Ash Wednesday"

•

How unpleasant to meet Mr. Eliot!
With his features of clerical cut,
And his brow so grim
And his mouth so prim
And his conversation, so nicely
Restricted to What Precisely
And If and Perhaps and But.
How unpleasant to meet Mr. Eliot!
With a bobtail cur
In a coat of fur
And a porpentine cat
And a wopsical hat
How unpleasant to meet Mr. Eliot!
(Whether his mouth be open or shut).

"Five-Finger Exercises"

Midnight's Children

The sad narrative of Salman Rushdie has overtaken his life and his works; he is the man under the death sentence, the human sacrifice to the ideals of the Enlightenment. It is easy to forget how profoundly uneasy Rushdie had been with the West, with materialism, with Christianity and colonialism. In Midnight's Children, he created a character who is nothing less than India herself, wired telepathically to all the other children born at the very instant when India became a nation, enfolding all contradictions, sinned against and sinning, mad as hell and forgiving all. —JRC

Midnight's Children
Salman Rushdie. Penguin Books, 1982; 448 pp. ISBN 0-14-013270-8
$11 ($13 postpaid). Penguin USA/Consumer Sales, 120 Woodbine Street, Bergenfield, NJ 07621; 800/253-6476

•

Shiva and the angel are closing closing, I hear lies being spoken in the night, anything you want to be you kin be, the greatest lie of all, cracking now, fission of Saleem, I am the bomb in Bombay, watch me explode, bones splitting breaking beneath the awful pressure of the crowd, bag of bones falling down down down, just as once in Jallianwala, but Dyer seems not to be present today, no Mercurochrome, only a broken creature spilling pieces of itself into the street, because I have been so-many too-many persons, life unlike syntax allows one more than three, and at last somewhere the striking of a clock, twelve chimes, release.

Yes, they will trample me underfoot, the numbers marching one two three, four hundred million five hundred six, reducing me to specks of voiceless dust, just as, in all good time, they will trample my son who is not my son, and his son who will not be his, and his who will not be his, until the thousand and first generation, until a thousand and one midnights have bestowed their terrible gifts and a thousand and one children have died, because it is the privilege and the curse of midnight's children to be both masters and victims of their times, to forsake privacy and be sucked into the annihilating whirlpool of the multitudes, and to be unable to live or die in peace.

The Elements of Style

Absorb and ignore. Absorb and ignore. It is necessary to forget every one of William Strunk's rules in order to write well; it is necessary to know them in order to forget them. They are the default mode of good English. When in doubt, return to the Elements. They are your landing gear; there are days when they are a lot more useful than wings. —JRC

6. Do not overwrite

Rich, ornate prose is hard to digest, generally unwholesome, and sometimes nauseating. If the sickly-sweet word, the overblown phrase are a writer's natural form of expression, as is sometimes the case, he will have to compensate for it by a show of vigor, and by writing something as meritorious as the Song of Songs, which is Solomon's.

20. Avoid foreign languages

The writer will occasionally find it convenient or necessary to borrow from other languages. Some writers, however, from sheer exuberance or a desire to show off, sprinkle their work liberally with foreign expressions, with no regard for the reader's comfort. It is a bad habit. Write in English.

The Elements of Style
William Strunk, Jr. & E. B. White. 1979; 86 pp. ISBN 0-02-418200-1
$5.95 postpaid. Macmillan Publishing Co., 100 Front Street, Riverside, NJ 08075-7500; 800/257-5755

THE USA HAS RICH COMMUNITIES of dream and tragedy, refugees from all continents, neighborhoods renewing archaic traditions and inventing futuristic responses to history. Despite arts budget cuts over the past two decades, there's never been so much good poetry available. Lack of money won't prevent someone from setting up a reading series in a cafe or bar or museum. Xerox machines, desktop publishing, old hand presses and linotype machines purchased at bargain prices — the shallowest pocket can and does publish and distribute the most fortifying and durable work. And beneath all those crazily postmodern facades, the archaic powers of language persist. Love song or political protest, disjunct collagist analysis or electronically amplified rant — you can find it in nearly every sizable city or bookstore in the country. Here are a few places to go for the news. —Andrew Schelling

Handbook of Poetic Forms

An alphabetical dictionary of the forms of poetry prevalent in contemporary USA verse writing. Haiku, insult poem, ghazal, found poem, rap, senryu — you can't get a quicker, smarter course in what poetry's been up to for millennia.

Copy, steal, invent, make and break forms. Gather friends to work on collaborative exercises . This book will teach you more than most workshops, for a hell of a lot less money. —AS

●

In the Western world, poets usually envision themselves writing alone (in a room or perhaps on a mountain top), yet for over a thousand years Japanese poets have collaborated in writing the *renga*, a poem written by two or more poets together.

There are many ways to collaborate in poetry:

• Writing alternate lines of a poem, with or without looking at what the other person has written.

The Handbook of Poetic Forms
Ron Padgett. 1987; ISBN 0-915925-23-4 Listener's guide and 5 audiocassettes $13.95 ($15.45 postpaid) from Teachers & Writers Collaborative, 5 Union Sq. W., New York, NY 10003-3306; 212/691-6590

• Writing a long work as a whole class or group of people, each contributing to a single subject, such as dreams, memories, or bee stings.

• Writing one poem or a series of poems through the mail, each poet "answering" the other in agreed-upon form.

• Intermingling your own poetic lines with those of a poet you admire.

Technicians of the Sacred

They came to
Tamoanchan,
The Place of Origins,
& built a temple.
As they were feasting
at the end
of 5 counts of time,
the sacred tree
broke open—
this was the omen
that told them
to leave that place.

Aacatl told a representative of the 8 tribes
that they would have to continue their journey
along separate paths;
in sorrow the representative agreed.

Before leaving,
the Mexica
did penance
before Huitzilopochtli,
& prayed
for guidance.

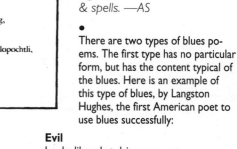

Technicians of the Sacred
(A Range of Poetries from Africa, America, Asia, Europe and Oceania)
Jerome Rothenberg, Editor. University of California Press, 1985; 636 pp. ISBN 0-520-04912-8
$17 ($20 postpaid) from California/ Princeton Fulfillment Services, 1445 Lower Ferry Road, Ewing, NJ 08618; 800/777-4726

What has the "language-making animal" been up to for the past 40,000 years? Renewed without interruption since Paleolithic times, elegant arts of speech and song have woven themselves across every inhabited reach of our planet. This book celebrates poet, bard, epic songster; Anglo-Saxon scop, African griot, Tungus shaman — all the "technicians" of sacred song. Equally present in these pages are daily events brought into speech — lullaby, fertility chant, hunting song, work song, funeral poems, spells of love and war, curses, and whispered initiatory teachings. What are the hidden lairs of thought, where the shape of mind changes when the throat opens? This anthology offers a range you can't match elsewhere. Fur, feather, sinew and bone are basic — but so are vowel and consonant, the hissing of breath, names & visions & spells. —AS

●

There are two types of blues poems. The first type has no particular form, but has the content typical of the blues. Here is an example of this type of blues, by Langston Hughes, the first American poet to use blues successfully:

Evil
Looks like what drives me crazy
Don't have no effect on you—
But I'm gonna keep on at it
Till it drives you crazy, too.

The second type of blues poem is one that has blues content and the structure of the old blues songs. Here's an example, again by Hughes:

Morning After
I was so sick last night I
Didn't hardly know my mind.
So sick last night I
Didn't hardly know my mind.
I drunk some bad licker that
Almost made me blind.

Sulfur

A gathering of the tribes — that was the motto of Caterpillar, Clayton Eshleman's historic journal of poesy, art, translation and political outrage through the sixties and seventies. Sulfur is its re-invention for the eighties and nineties. This thing has edge, ferocity, risk, and plenty of work that's shaping the future. At the back is a section given over to notes, reviews, controversies, correspondence — savviest place I know to get the real news. —AS

Sulfur
(A Literary Bi-Annual of the Whole Art)
Clayton Eshleman, Editor.
$14/year (2 issues) from English Dept., Eastern Michigan University, Ypsilanti, MI 48197

I know the last few years I heard you and saw you dressed up all purple and shit, it did scare me. All that loud ass rock and roll I wasnt in to most of it, but look brother I heard *Tutu* and *Human Nature* and *D Train*. I heard you one night behind the Apollo for Q, and you was bashin like the you we knew, when you used to stand coiled like a blue note and play everything the world meant, and be in charge of the shit too. I'll always remember you like that Miles, and yr million children will too. With that messed up poppa stoppa voice, i know you looken up right now and say (growl) So What? —Amiri Baraka

6. Protect
the house
(THE GATE WAS
OPEN AND THEY
COULDN'T FIND IT)
(Gen. 19.11, after Y. de la Reina)

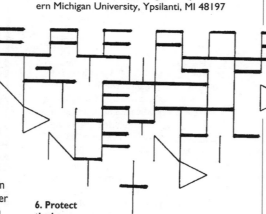

(Thanks to Hacsi Horvath)

The Jack Kerouac School of Disembodied Poetics: Naropa Institute, 2130 Arapahoe Avenue, Boulder, CO 80302. Less a writing school than a caravansary, a formation of nomad tents with whispered traditions of insight and language coming live out of the air. You can get a BA or MFA, or just pull in for the Summer Writing Program, which invites forty to fifty guest faculty each year.

New College of California Poetics Programs: 50 Fell Street, San Francisco, CA 94102; 415/626-1694. BA & MA Poetics Programs

The Postmoderns (The New American Poetry Revised): Donald Allen & George F. Buttrick, Editors. 1982. Grove Press. The classic document of the great midcentury shift in American poesis.

The Poetics of the New American Poetry: Donald Allen & Warren Tallman, Editors. 1973, Grove Press. Out of print but widely available in used bookstores. Any clear understanding of the present state of American writing will probably be grounded in knowledge of these essays by the important poets of this century.

Women in Praise of the Sacred (43 Centuries of Spiritual Poetry by Women): Jane Hirshfield, Editor. 1994, HarperCollins Publishers. Deep, beautiful poems by more than seventy women, written over the past four millennia.

The Prepublishing Handbook

Smart idea. This nifty little book takes you through the practical realities of small publishing: the many hats you must wear, the financial realities, the time commitment. It asks the question should you publish a book?

This is the one to start with if you've considered putting your time and hard-earned money into a book venture, but are not sure what's involved. Introduction by Dan Poynter of Self-Publishing Manual fame. —Cliff Martin

●

Wholesalers and distributors who sell to bookstores generally buy from publishers on consignment; that is, you don't get paid until they get paid — for the books *they* have sold. Distributors often have catalogs, costly to produce; sometimes they also have sales representatives. They have to sell to their buyers at a discount, and consequently they order from the publisher at a deeper discount. They handle the collection and fulfillment of orders. For their services they may demand discounts of up to 60 percent of the list price of the book. On your $12.95 book, you may do well to get $5.18.

●

In evaluating the situation for yourself, how many hats can you wear? We will look at the primary hats. Do you really have the time to devote to the promotion of your product? If you thought writing a book was time-consuming, keep in mind that was the easy part. Can you, or do you want to, wear all the various hats that are in the publisher's office? Do you have the means (that is, will the book do well enough) to pay someone else for the services that you are unable or unwilling to do? *Treasure your time — it is one*

of your major resources, and try to be as efficient at doing these things as you can.

. . . the independent publisher, if able to do most of the various tasks personally, can successfully publish a book that a larger publisher cannot. The smaller publisher is not paying all the overhead of salaries, workers' compensation, insurance and office space. Furthermore, the smaller publisher can shop, just as the larger publisher can, for cost-efficient work.

THE GROWTH OF SMALL AND self-publishing in the last five years has been phenomenal. This year's Books In Print added a staggering 5,500 new publishers to its list. A hasty conclusion is that the lightning-fast hardware and "quick & easy" desktop software make for small-publishing success. Not so. As a publishing consultant of twenty-five years, I see the same mistake made over and over again: a weak marketing plan. "Niche marketing" is right on the money. Identify a specific audience and *have a precise plan to reach it.*

Bookstores are not the best places to sell books: shipping, billing, customer service, and collecting money are a headache for the small publisher. Libraries order mostly from reviews. The best markets are the "special sales" markets: mail order catalogs, corporate or "premium" sales, specialty outlets (sporting goods, cookware, auto parts, etc.), and sales to individuals by mail.

The mini-library that surrounds this box will help to get you on the right track. —Cliff Martin

The Prepublishing Handbook
(What You Should Know Before You Publish Your First Book)
Patricia J. Bell. 1993; 117 pp. ISBN 0-9618227-2-4 $12 ($13.50 postpaid) from Cat's-Paw Press, 9561 Woodridge Circle, Eden Prairie, MN 55347

Book Publishing Resource Guide

Dreams do come true! When I first started out in the book business about twenty years ago, I wished there was a single reference book that had everything in one place; I was fed up with switching from media guide to association lists to mail order directories. This book tempts me to overdo the superlatives. It is as important to a small publisher as having a telephone! —CM

●

The newspaper section features 682 newspapers in the United States and Canada. Because many newspaper book reviewers tend to focus primarily on fiction, biographies, current events, and some general nonfiction, we also list the editors of the other major sections, such as business, arts and entertainment, sports, lifestyle, travel, and more.

●

Zondervan Family Bookstores
Don Kooima, Audio & Book Buyer
Greg Frey, Bibles/Reference Bks
Paula Elenbaas, Buyer, Children's Books

Book Publishing Resource Guide
Marie Kiefer. Open Horizons Publishing Co., 1993; 378 pp. ISBN 0-912411-38-4 $25 ($28 postpaid) from Ad-Lib Publications, PO Box 1102, Fairfield, IA 52556; 800/669-0773

Glenn Williams, Music Buyer
Corporate Headquarters
5300 Patterson Avenue SE
Grand Rapids, MI 49533
616-698-6900; Fax: 616-698-7300
130 Stores

The Complete Guide to Self-Publishing

I raved about this book in Whole Earth's Signal (Harmony Books, 1988). The new revised edition is even better — updated information on new technologies and electronic rights, information for Canadian publishers, expanded information on distribution methods and discount stores, and many small-press case studies.

Well researched, readable, easy to use, up to date, and full of real-life experience. An essential resource for anyone even considering self-publishing —CM

●

Because the author knows the subject so well, he or she is usually too close to it; objectivity is lost. A professional editor can help detect passages that are unclear or poorly organized.

Short of hiring a pro, which is best, enlist the help of several literate friends or associates to go over your work. It's a good idea to give them some instructions. Ask that they underline any misspelled or questionable words, circle unclear passages, and note rough transitions with a question mark. Also encourage them to jot any suggestions in the margin.

The Complete Guide to Self-Publishing
Tom & Marilyn Ross. Writer's Digest Books, 1994; 432 pp. ISBN 0-89879-646-6 $18.99 ($21.99 postpaid) from Communications Creativity, PO Box 909, Buena Vista, CO 81211; 800/331-8355

●

Always follow up on prime review copies. This can be done by letter or telephone. Some editors of major publications reportedly are so busy that phone calls from publishers are annoying. We haven't found this to be typical. If approached in a sincere and businesslike manner, most reviewers are quite congenial.

●

Apply the 80/20 rule. This says you'll get 80 percent of your results from twenty percent of your efforts or customers. In essence, it means determine what's working and keep that priority uppermost in your actions. Don't waste time on marginal paybacks. Spend 80 percent of your time pursuing the most profitable 20 percent.

Small Publishing Associations

Networking brings many rewards. These groups have newsletters, meetings, co-op programs, local chapters and other hands-on benefits.

International Association of Book Trade Consultants: Box 50123, Eugene, OR 97405; 503/342-6901. For referral to a publishing expert by subject or geographic area.

National Association of Independent Publishers: PO Box 430, Highland City, FL 33846-0430; 803/648-4420. Has local chapters, and the bi-monthly **Publisher's Report**.

COSMEP (The International Association of Independent Publishers): PO Box 420703, San Francisco, CA 94142; 415/922-9490. The oldest small-press group. Newsletter, annual conference, co-op exhibits.

Publishers Marketing Association: 2401 Pacific Coast Highway, Suite 102, Hermosa Beach CA 90254; 310/372-2732. Newsletter, co-op marketing and exhibit programs, meetings.

Muticultural Publishers Exchange: PO Box 9869, Madison, WI 53715. Newsletter.

Audio Publishers Association: PO Box 1957, 340 Woodhouse Avenue, Wallingford, CT 06492; 203/949-1927. For books-on-tape publishers. Newsletter.

OTHER GREAT RESOURCES

Business and Legal Forms for Authors and Self-Publishers: Tad Crawford. 1990, Allworth Press. Useful and unique. Includes traditional (publishing contract, agent contract), and unconventional (non-disclosure contract, audio rights).

Tips & Ideas on Self-Publishing: Bernard Klein. 1993, Campion Publishing Co. This latest self-publishing tome is strong on marketing and publicity, especially advertising and direct mail.

The Self-Publishing Manual: Dan Poynter. 1993, Para Publishing. Buy this if you want a quick overview of self-publishing.

Desktop Publishing (Dollars & Sense): Scott Anderson. 1992, Blue Heron Publishing, Inc. A "nuts & bolts" guide to small publishing from the desktop.

Papers For Printing: Mark Beach & Ken Russon. 1991, Coast to Coast books. How to select paper, control costs, meet deadlines. Contains forty-four paper samples.

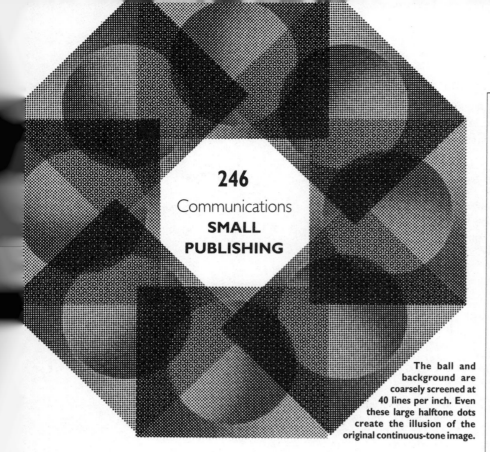

The ball and background are coarsely screened at 40 lines per inch. Even these large halftone dots create the illusion of the original continuous-tone image.

Is There A Book Inside You?

This is the natural precursor to Dan Poynter's **The Self-Publishing Manual***. It's a down-to-earth "how-to" and a kick in the pants to get you going. Even if you're not planning to write, it's a great insight into the publishing process.*

Contents include picking a subject, formulating a plan, scheduling and time management, working with co-authors, editors and partners, considering your publishing options, and a sensible listing of other resources. —CM

•

What To Look For In a Partner

Compatibility You must not only get along and work easily with your temporary partner, you must like each other. You will be working very closely in this temporary marriage; you are handing over a segment of your life to this person.

Make sure the chemistry is right. Does your writer grasp your aims and goals quickly? You should be able to work together so that the result is greater than the sum of the individual contributions. Your partner may do some things better than you — that is what a good partnership is all about. Is there mutual trust? Some people are very protective about what they commit to paper and editing their work can cause unnecessary strain in the working relationship. Be sure to cover this topic thoroughly in the interview before agreeing to hire the writer.

Is There a Book Inside You?
(A Step-by-Step Plan for Writing Your Book)
Dan Poynter & Mindy Bingham. 1992;
236 pp. ISBN 0-915516-68-3
$14.95 ($16.95 postpaid) from Para Publishing, PO Box 4243, Santa Barbara, CA 93103-0232; 805/968-7277

1001 Ways To Market Your Books

Marketing is 75 percent of the success factor in small publishing. **1001 Ways** *covers virtually every possibility for selling books: the traditional (bookstores, libraries, schools, mailorder) and the "fringe" (but highly lucrative) markets (corporate and "premium" sales, specialty retail shops, fund-raisers, government sales).*

John's marketing background truly comes through in this impressive book. He lists promotional methods (e.g., radio/TV interviews, billboards, remnant ad space), and gives detailed, clear instructions on how to do a professional job.

This book is responsible for a lot of independently published bestsellers. It eliminates most of the trial and error in selling books. I can't recommend it highly enough! —Cliff Martin

•

How to Get Reviews: Rule #1

Send out review copies. Send out lots of them. Send out more than you think you should. Hit every major newspaper and magazine which you think might be at all interested in the subject of your book. In most cases this means sending out somewhere between 300 and 500 review copies.

Don't be stingy about sending out review copies. For every hundred copies you send out, you'll get perhaps ten reviews. And those ten reviews will bring you anywhere from twenty to one hundred direct sales and many more indirect sales. Even at a conservative estimate, you'll receive 200 orders for every 100 copies you send out. That's cheap advertising.

•

16:02 Tips on Selling Subsidiary Rights

To make subsidiary rights sales, you must be well-organized, persistent, and attentive to details. When I published *Mail Order Selling Made Easier*, I actively promoted rights sales. As a result, I sold U.K. rights to McGraw-Hill, book club rights to Newbridge's Executive Program and Fortune Book Club, serial rights to *Income Plus*, and reprint rights for a new trade paperback and casebound edition to John Wiley & Sons (who, in turn, published the updated edition as *The Complete Direct Marketing Sourcebook*). Total income from rights sales amounted to more than $12,000. And Wiley sold book club rights for their edition to Fortune Book Club again!

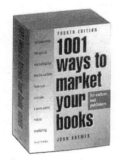

1001 Ways to Market Your Books
John Kremer. 1993; 544 pp.
ISBN 0-912411-42-2
$19.95 ($23.45 postpaid) from Open Horizons Publishing Co., PO Box 205, Fairfield, IA 52556; 800/796-6130

OTHER GREAT REFERENCES

The Writer's Book of Checklists: Scott Edelstein. 1991, Writer's Digest Books. This little book helps me to remember things like the preferred format for submitting a nonfiction book, typical fees for different types of articles, the number of words per eight-by-eleven inch page, a list of cover letter contents, types of fiction, and proofing marks.

Publishing Newsletters: Howard P. Hudson. 1988, Charles Scribner's, Sons.

Editing Your Newsletter: Mark Beach. 1988, Coast to Coast Books.

Directory of Printers

Every type of printer is covered here: books, catalogs, calendars, maps, posters, you name it. Small publishers and others can save a bundle by using the easy comparative charts and listings showing printers' specialties and capabilities.

Invaluable information on how to work with printers and get estimates, scheduling tips, contracts, using foreign printers and more. The new edition also covers pre-press companies (like binderies). —CM

•

20 Points to Consider When Selecting a Printer

• Experience — How long have they been printing books? How long have they been in business? What kinds of books and other printed items are they accustomed to producing?

• Reputation — Do they have a reputation for doing quality work and delivering on schedule? Do you know anyone who has used them before? Can they provide references?

Directory of Printers
Marie Kiefer. Open Horizons Publishing Co., 1994; 352 pp. ISBN 0-912411-43-0
$14.95 ($19.45 postpaid) from Ad-Lib Publications, PO Box 1102, Fairfield, IA 52556; 800/669-0773

Getting It Printed

I find the printing world baffling and overwhelming in its complexity; so many paper types and inks and an extensive technical jargon. This book, now revised to include all the latest electronic developments, is a relief. It explains how the printing process works, how to communicate with printers, and meet budget and time deadlines. It also includes a glossary of industry terms, ready-to-use forms, and lists of associations and industry publications. A unique book. —CM

Getting It Printed
Mark Beach. North Light Books, 1993; 208 pp. ISBN 0-89134-510-8
$29.95 ($32.95 postpaid) from F & W Publications, 1507 Dana Avenue, Cincinnati, OH 45207; 800/289-0963

Looking Good in Print

People do judge a book by its cover! Second only to a great marketing plan, the design of a book and its cover and your company's general aesthetic appeal are key elements in acceptability and sales.

Looking Good in Print *gives a sense of the purpose of different types of printed material, and how to approach them. Letterhead, brochures, book covers, ads, etc., all have a different function, and should therefore be designed differently.*

The book is long on example and short on preaching. Its biggest selling point is the amount of hours it will save you having to explain things to a graphic artist or printer. —CM

•

BOOKS

Increasingly, entire books are being submitted to publishers fully designed and formatted.

Desktop publishing gives authors control of the graphic as well as the textual content of their books.

Desktop publishing offers another advantage. Because production costs are reduced, publishers can afford to produce more books and in a timely manner.

Book design requires constant attention to page-to-page consistency and flow.

•

Be careful when setting isolated words in boldface type in the middle of a block of text. The bold type can draw more attention to a word than it warrants and create a "checkerboard" look to the page.

Looking Good in Print
Roger C. Parker. 1993; 423 pp.
ISBN 1-56604-047-7
$24.95 ($29.45 postpaid) from Ventana Press, PO Box 2468, Chapel Hill, NC 27515; 919/942-0220

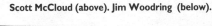

THUS, WHEN YOU LOOK AT A PHOTO OR REALISTIC DRAWING OF A FACE-- -YOU SEE IT AS THE FACE OF *ANOTHER*.

BUT WHEN YOU ENTER THE WORLD OF THE *CARTOON*-- --YOU SEE *YOURSELF*.

I BELIEVE THIS IS THE *PRIMARY CAUSE* OF OUR CHILDHOOD FASCINATION WITH CARTOONS, THOUGH OTHER FACTORS SUCH AS *UNIVERSAL IDENTIFICATION, SIMPLICITY* AND THE *CHILDLIKE FEATURES* OF MANY CARTOON CHARACTERS ALSO PLAY A PART.

THE CARTOON IS A *VACUUM* INTO WHICH OUR *IDENTITY* AND *AWARENESS* ARE *PULLED*...

...AN *EMPTY SHELL* THAT WE INHABIT WHICH *ENABLES* US TO TRAVEL IN *ANOTHER REALM.* WE DON'T JUST *OBSERVE* THE CARTOON, WE *BECOME* IT!

THAT'S WHY I DECIDED TO *DRAW* MYSELF IN SUCH A SIMPLE *STYLE.*

WOULD YOU HAVE *LISTENED* TO ME IF I LOOKED LIKE *THIS*??

Understanding Comics

If I were king, this extraordinary book would be made available to every kid in high-school art class. As an exposition of the elements of communication and an example of how to elegantly stuff fifty pounds of information into a ten-pound sack, it should be primary reading for anybody who wants to present information in its most potently concentrated form — that is, through images.

There's a brilliant discussion of comic art, as per the title. But the discussion approaches an understanding of much more than "comics": understanding graphic design. Understanding language. Understanding perception, semiotics . . . and time. (Well: maybe "practical understanding" is more accurate.)

Understanding Comics presents itself in a loose, rather conservative comics format: the exposition is embedded in the example. The fireworks aren't in the art but in the stripdown and inspection of its constituents — abstraction, artifice, and idiom. Scott McCloud leads the tour at top speed. His work is so compact and gleefully idea-heavy that at times you can only bounce helplessly in his wake. (MWEC art director Kathleen O'Neill fell off her chair while reading this book. She got right up and finished it.) —James Donnelly [Suggested by Josh Gordon]

Understanding Comics
(The Invisible Art)
Scott McCloud. 1993; 215 pp.
ISBN 1-56862-019-5
$19.95 ($24.95 postpaid) from Kitchen Sink Press, 320 Riverside Drive, Northampton, MA 01060; 800/365-7465

Scott McCloud (above). Jim Woodring (below).

IN A MEDIUM WHERE TIME AND SPACE *MERGE*-- --THE STORYTELLER HAS SOME UNUSUAL TOOLS AT HIS/HER DISPOSAL-- --SUCH AS THE *POLYPTYCH,* WHERE A MOVING FIGURE OR FIGURES-- --IS IMPOSED OVER A *CONTINUOUS BACKGROUND.*

The Book of JIM

Bobbing on the coppery waters in his little boat, Jim feels the line go taut; sees the float vanish. After a flailing struggle he reels in JIM: hooked by one galosh, wall-eyed and bellowing in panic, pockets alive with glistening mudlizards, limbs enwreathed with hairy ropes of night terror.

Jim Woodring, bane of the Jungians, here presents a Best Of the first four JIM comicbooks. The stories are composed with the pacing, tension, and eloquence of a wholly mature, if overtly peculiar, artist. The draftsmanship is beautiful — inadequate hackneyed word — with a unique organ-twanging resonance (did I live in this desolate granary: why do I know these broken gaudy toys?)

The Book of JIM is a guestroom-nightstand amenity that will make that old .38 seem fatuous; an heirloom that will really make the kids think twice.
—James Donnelly

The Book of JIM
Jim Woodring. 1993; 120 pp.
ISBN 1-56097-091-X
$14.95 ($17.95 postpaid) from Fantagraphics Books, 7563 Lake City Way NE, Seattle, WA 98115; 800/657-1100

Access to Comix

Within the universe of "sequential art" there are separate galaxies of collectible comics, underground comix, graphic novels, Japanese manga, erotica and pornography, and Pulitzer-prize winners like Spiegelman's *Maus*. With not all that much money and these three catalogs, you can go a long way toward exploring the territory Scott McCloud portrays so grandly in *Understanding Comics*. — HLR

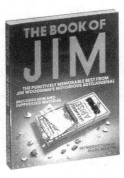
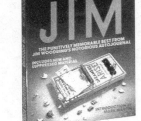

Fantagraphics Books: Catalog free. 7563 Lake City Way NE, Seattle, WA 98115; 800/657-1100. Jay Kinney, our in-the-family comix guru, sez Fantagraphics "publishes the majority of the best alternative comix these days." Yummy full-color illos inside the catalog. Extraordinary silkscreen prints of great comix art, a few select trading cards and T-shirts.

Last Gasp of San Francisco: $2 for quarterly comics catalog, $3 for annual heavy-duty catalog. 777 Florida Street, San Francisco, CA 94110; 415/824-6636, fax 415/824-1836. The last of the original San Francisco underground publishers is still going strong. Comix, grafix, body modification info, tattoo books, alternative and deviant fiction and nonfiction. The "Heavy-Duty Catalog" says of itself (and I agree): "A fine source for ancient, postmodern & beatnik literature, mature and adult comix, rock music books, tattoo, piercing, and fetish material, t-shirts, drug information . . ."

Kitchen Sink Press: Catalog free. 320 Riverside Drive, Northhampton, MA 01060; 800/365-7465. Kitchen Sink is the original publisher of *Understanding Comics*. This catalog is a work of sequential art in itself, with a four-color cover and sixty pages of black-and-white illustrations of comic book covers. Classic reprints, graphic novels, all-ages comics, adult comics, collectors cards, full-color Xenozoic Tales satin jackets, R. Crumb collectible puppets, Nancy and Sluggo power ties.

— short for *fanzine,* which itself is a combination of *fan* (short for *fanatic*) and *magazine* — is a very-small-circulation publication, produced for love rather than money. The producers are voices in the cultural-political wilderness, ranting to audiences of tens or (maybe) hundreds. More than 10,000 zines are available today, each one published from motives as varied as their contents and outlook.

Thanks to the increasingly affordable technology of self-publishing, paper-based zines have grown in variety and quality — necessarily so, since the paper medium must compete with electronically produced and distributed zines (ezines) for the increasingly valuable currency of readers' attention. Access to the Net is not universal, while zines are accessible to anyone who can see. (Braille zines are surely being published, but we aren't aware of any.) Given the number of collage, rubber-stamp and other nonverbal zines, even the illiterate can join the fun. On the other hand, an ezine can be distributed to hundreds of readers, and put on the Net where millions can peruse it, in less time than it takes for the average zine publisher to stuff a dozen envelopes, numb the tongue with stamps and trudge down to the mailbox.

A ZINE doesn't have to be, or look, cheap. *Answer Me!* is of very high quality (and free of typos!). The absence of advertising and the range of subject matter define it as a zine: serial killers, notorious suicides, pedophiles, Mexican deformity magazines, guns, Vietnamese gangs in Orange County, Iceberg Slim, David Duke, the Geto Boys, Anton LeVay, Reverend Al Sharpton — all the things that make the North American Free Trade Zone such an entertaining place to live. At the other end of the quality spectrum are the punk and personal zines that are handwritten and apparently copied on a liquor-store xerox. But in the realm of zines, what matters most is content — and sincerity and originality are far more important than those nebulous concepts called Truth and Facts.

There's a zine for everybody . . . almost. If you have an obscure interest, or an atypical take on a not-so-obscure interest, get a copy of *Factsheet Five* (or two, or even a subscription) and start looking. Somebody is probably publishing a zine about what you want to read. If not, then start your own — if you've got the key to the Unified Field Theory, or think you know all there is to know about Burt Lancaster movies, or want to communicate with other players of out-of-print German board games.

It is almost criminally simple to produce and distribute zines and ezines. Don't rush out and buy the most bleeding-edge desktop-publishing "solution" on the market. Those of you blessed with a McTemp job probably have access to computers, printers, photocopiers, glue sticks, and highly ironic graphics (i.e., trade magazines). Go to lunch at 11:30; return at 12:15; take advantage of the lightly populated office to learn PageMaker. I got started in self-publishing with a typewriter retrieved from one dumpster and paper retrieved from another. The only crucial stylistic concern is that what you put on the paper will be legible after it is reproduced (or, for ezines, that your text format can be retrieved and understood by your target audience).

The paper-zine process is simple: type it (or write it if your handwriting is up to the task), print it (if typed into a computer), lay out the text with appropriate graphics, photocopy it, send a copy to *Factsheet Five* and to other zines that review zines or those with whom you might be interested in trading publications, wait for the orders to come in, and fulfill them.

The ezine process is similar (and I presume you are conversant with the esoteric hoodoo I'm about to spill; otherwise, skip this paragraph and/or make use of the computer resources elsewhere in this section): type it; export or import the text into the desired format (e.g., vanilla ASCII text or sophisticated hypertext formats for better graphics); upload the documents to your local Internet provider; send the files to popular sites for ftp retrieval (e.g., ftp.eff.org, etext.archive.umich.edu, quartz.rutgers.edu), www, WAIS or gopher retrieval; post the ezine to the Usenet news groups alt.etext and alt.zines; set up a mailing list for email distribution. Then inform John Labovitz (johnl@ora.com) of your ezine's existence and how it can be obtained. John keeps the list of ezines available over the Internet, and his list is distributed worldwide. John also publishes the ultimate travel zine, *Crash.*

IF YOU WANT to sample the vastness and variety of zine culture, you'll need a copy of *Factsheet Five,* a fat roll of stamps, plenty of envelopes, a form letter that doesn't look like a form letter (or one that is blatantly honest about being a form letter) with your mailing address prominently and clearly displayed, patience, and a stack of $1 bills. Most zine publishers don't have bank accounts in the name of the zine. The two or five dollars you send to someone will barely cover costs. Many zine publishers are a bit flaky, or they may have sold all of their issues by the time you send in your request. Patience: you might have to wait months for a response. If you chronically order zines dealing with extremist politics, drug relegalization, taboo sexual practices, or other subjects you might prefer not to broach in polite company, I strongly recommend investing in a PO box or third-party mail service. You may not want to know the publishers of some zines, nor to have the morality police checking up on you. Once you start sending out letters with dollar bills, your mail receptacle will soon be overflowing with strange and wonderful information.

We at *Factsheet Five* don't see all the zines that are published. We do see most of them. The zines you get are likely to have other zines listed in them; these will lead you to still more zines. Zines have been published since Benjamin Franklin's *Poor Richard's Almanac;* they are delicious and fascinating to some people, nausea- or fear-inducing to others. The same tired old disinfotainment that the Sony-Time-Warner-CBS-RCA-MCA-USIA conglomerate spoon-feeds us won't tell you how JFK's driver killed him with a shellfish-toxin bullet to prevent his spilling the beans about the alien presence on Earth, or review the new avant-garde punk bands in Osaka, or publish comics about what it's like to be gay in Nebraska. We're overloaded with information, and the best defense is to produce some of our own.

—Jerod Pore

Murder No. 15

QUISITO ...modus informata extr...

titclamps · Holy

moby dicks and torsos: ... that all there is ... gay art?

file under "queer"

summer 1992

endarchy buzz

Factsheet Five

This is it: the zine of zines. All you might wish to know about the current state of zinedom is in here. Each issue reviews over 1,000 zines, along with records, books, and other artifacts of marginal media. The First Amendment lives and breathes within these pages. —HLR

● You are now holding in your hands the biggest issue of Factsheet Five I've ever made. There are 1,320 reviews in this issue, running a full 128 pages. Almost half of the reviews (600 of 'em) are for zines that have never been listed before in Factsheet Five. The largest growth is in the Comix, Grrrlz, Punk, Politics, Music, and Recordings sections. No wonder there are so many zines devoted to reviewing records. I've just been getting swamped with music sent in for review.

Not all news is good in zineland. Mike Diana was convicted on three counts of obscenity for publishing his comic zine, Boiled Angel, down

in Pinellas County, Florida. He only spent four days in jail, but his probation is so severe that it seriously restricts his life and ability to continue his art.

At least two other publishers recently had their personal property seized by the men in blue, in response to the sexual content of their zines. I wouldn't say this indicates a current "war on zines" but I do see this as an extension of the "war on sex" that has been raging for many years.

FACTSHEET 5

Factsheet Five
R. Seth Friedman, Publisher.
$20/year (6 issues) from Factsheet Five, PO
Box 170099, San Francisco, CA 94117-0099

OTHER GREAT RESOURCES

Asylum for Shut-Ins: $2.50/sample, $9/4-issue subscription. Mike Kole, PO Box 46581, Bedford, OH 44146. A quarterly guide to strange groups publishing rants and tracts.

Bypass: sample $3 (use IRCs if outside the EU). 21 Cave St., Oxford, OX4 1BA, England. The first issue of this British version of Factsheet Five.

Saprophile

1 $1.50

Misery and VomiT

WOMAN'S BOSS FIRES HER HUSBAND'S WARDROBE

A South Deerfield woman woke up Tuesday morning and found her boss going through her husband's closet.

"Thank God this hideous thing is finally starting to wear out," the boss said as he tore the pocket flaps off a green print sportjacket she had never seen before. He continued to ransack the closet, tearing sleeves off jackets and ripping belt loops off pants.

"My boss stood there with his hands on his hips and said, 'He's got that one good suit that fits him beautifully. Can't you make him understand that's all he needs?'" the woman told reporters.

"I had just that day determined to stop nagging my husband," the woman said. "I'll never know how my boss got into the bedroom, though." —*DreamWorldNews*

...ST DIGEST

MYSTERY SCIENCE THEATER 3000

...e 1?!

...THER ...

BOOKS ON DEAN ...

● Frank Sinatra was spotted yesterday chug-a-lugging gasoline straight from a measuring cup at an Esso station.

Esso, a long-defunct predecessor of mega-polluter Exxon, has been resurrected by Sinatra.

"It's the only brand of gasoline I could ever drink," confessed the lounge singer. "Sammy Davis Junior liked it too, God bless him." —*DreamWorldNews*

JACK RUBI... SLIPPERS I.O...

● "How many a man worsens his own condition by living in squalor amongst consumption-tainted sputum that he himself has spit upon his own floor?"

Ceaseless optimism for both cure and prevention was another firm belief of the Association. "Why cannot we throw trouble off our shoulders by vigorously shaking the right and left shoulder, even though it may appear that we are doing the enormous applesauce dance? At least we can have some fun during our stay on this roly-poly ball, the planet Earth." So asked the Mount MacGregor Sanatorium inhouse magazine; The Mount MacGregor Optimist. The American TB San flourished throughout the '20s, '30s, and '40s patterned after the Saranac Lake model which in 1937 even had a pictorial spread in LIFE magazine. Isabel Smith, a patient who appeared in one of the photos, found herself the object of adoring fan mail for years afterward. —*Saprophile*

#9*

YOU NEED IT

...ORIES the slipstream journal

● Most urinalysis are carefully monitored. Thus it became necessary to be sneaky (as well as careful.) A vial or container of simple table salt or vinegar can be hidden in one's pants or underwear. Once in the restroom (over the toilet or in the stall) empty the salt or vinegar into the sample bottle, do your 'thang' & then flush the container down the toilet. Don't forget to give the sample bottle a coupla swirls to mix the contents (vinegar mixes easier but salt is less conspicuous 'cause it has no smell). Despite what natural or chemical substance the person has been using the test will come back "negative" because the contents won't register as urine. HA! —*Iron Feather Journal*

ROULEZ
No Shortcuts on the Highway to the Truth

...N = COOL

...= 52

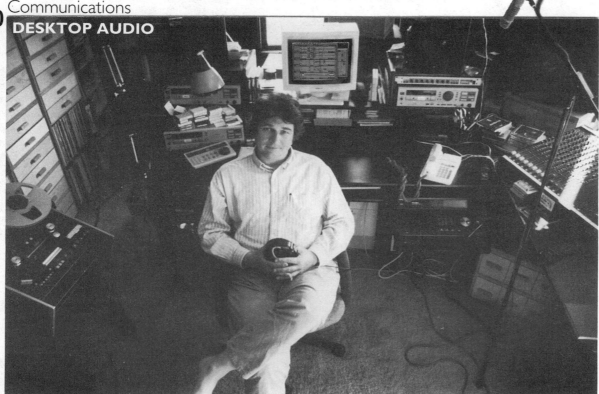

David Gans in his home studio.

I produce radio for a living, and a part of that gig that spills over into after-hours creative projects is an edit-intensive sound sculpture/collage technique I call Kaleidophonics. For example, I gathered together eight different recorded performances of the R&B song "Hard to Handle," sliced them into chunks varying in length from a beat to a chorus or two, then glued them together into a highly amusing and illuminating composite.

This art form made a huge leap with the advent of desktop digital audio. Butt-splices and quick crossfades are the hammer and ripsaw of audio editing; hard-disk editing gives you amazingly fine-grain control of everything, fulfilling the promise of the "personal computer" handsomely by eliminating huge amounts of tedium, greatly improving control of the result, and vastly expanding the creative possibilities.

One of the great benefits of this technology is random access. You can put your entire production up in the window and spot check it, listening to every transition one more time before you print to DAT. Level adjustments, tweaking fades, all that stuff — without having to listen to it all the way through every time and without waiting for tape to shuttle back and forth. It's made me more

productive and more creative and has made the product much, much more consistent.

And you can fix small errors very easily. In a recent production session in which the announcer had misread a piece of information, we did not have to rerecord the whole segment: instead, we found the correct phrase elsewhere in the voice-over and pasted it in. Took less than a minute.

The old way:

If you're analog, you prepare the elements of the program ahead of time and then lay them painstakingly into one or more tracks of a half-inch eight-track running at 15ips with dbx Type I noise reduction (if you have a music segment longer than half an hour, you run the master reel at 7.5 ips). You do as much pre-production as you can in order to keep the mixdown as simple as possible. Careful planning minimizes the opportunity to blow it. After each piece is laid into the master you go back and listen to it to make sure it's where it belongs in time, and if you missed it by a noticeable interval you ask yourself if it's bad enough to re-do. Is it off by enough to warrant spending half an hour redoing it?

And then you mix it down, following a carefully timed script and

making sure you make those crossfades smooth and the punchouts timely. If you mess it up, you start over.

With Sonic Solutions, you can design crossfades up to a hundred seconds long, controlling the length and shape of either side independently or with perfect symmetry, depending on whether you're looking for something imperceptible or "morphing" one sound into something different for musical, dramatic or comedic effect. In my business, editing live concert performances that sometimes come from imperfect source tapes, digital audio means I can experiment with various ways to cover an edit rather than choosing just one of many promising pairs of edit points, as it was in the quarter-inch days, and hoping for the best. If you got that edit wrong enough you had to go back and make a new dub of the — Jesus, you didn't cut the master, did you?

Because this editing system never touches the sound file — you work on an Edit Decision List (EDL) that shows a picture of the audio signal on each channel of each sound file —

you can try as many different edits as you want (have time for) and audition them side-by-side, and you can back away from unsuccessful experiments with the "undo edit" command. You can dump all your versions onto a DAT (or play them into new sound files) and then edit the best parts together into a perfect composite.

The pictorial representation of the audio program can be viewed and manipulated down to the individual sound wave and cut into meaningful segments that can be selected, copied, pasted and deleted, Macintosh style. You arrange these pictures in horizontal windows, up to several dozen separate audio tracks directed to two or more virtual mixer channels. If you want to, you can MIDI-connect to "real" faders and/or control the mix with an automated virtual console program.

The learning curve is steep but the rewards are considerable. Like most things Macintosh and UNIX, exploration is rewarded. You read the manual and figure out how to do what you need to do, and then a few weeks later you read the manual again and you're ready to comprehend a new section of the system, which sharpens and expands your mental maps and leads you to more efficiency and more possibilities.

The Macintosh seems to be the platform of choice for desktop audio, but systems are available for DOS and Windows as well as for higher-end workstations. I use Sonic Solutions. It is on the expensive side and a pleasure to work with. Digital audio is only going to get cheaper and more powerful in the future, and so (we hope) will CD printers (somewhere around $5,000 and declining, but the cost of writeable CD blanks is a startling $20-plus each). Soon we will be hearing CD audio zines, homegrown musical productions, personalized collections of commercial music — and who knows, maybe political and religious campaigns will promulgate their programs on homegrown audio media.
—David Gans

Sonic Solutions

The top of the line in digital-audio editing systems, with combinations of hardware and software that run from the high four figures to the high five. The NoNoise™ system is used to rehabilitate noisy old recordings from Edison cylinders to film and television soundtracks, as well as analog recordings (which were state of the art as recently as ten years ago). Sonic requires a fairly high-end Macintosh and proprietary disk drives, and there are no second sources for enhancements, but the system is amazingly versatile, greatly expandable, and — with the new SonicNet system — you can ship audio from system to system for maximum efficiency in large-scale production environments. —DG

Sonic Solutions: Information from 891 Francisco Boulevard, San Rafael, CA 94901-5506; 415/485-4800.

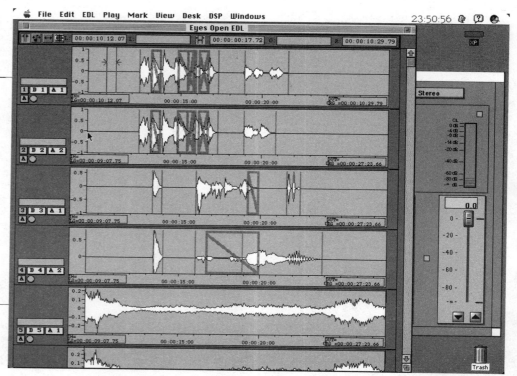

ProTools and the Digidesign Family of Products

Digidesign markets to both professional and casual users of digital-audio technology, making it easy for Macintosh users to get started with sharp digital tools at value prices. Many music, multimedia, and radio producers employ the low-end digital products listed here for independent work in the "project studio" (spare bedroom); they're also showing up in bigger shops where multiple workstations are needed for routine editing chores but fancy features aren't required on every machine.

For marketing reasons, the affordable gear and the pricier stuff do not mix and match — but as time goes by, professional features tend to migrate down to the cheaper sets.

Audiomedia II is a circuit board card the user installs inside the Mac. It's got D/A and A/D converters, digital-signal processing (DSP) power, and two channels of audio inputs and outputs. This card comes bundled with an excellent editing software package, Sound Designer II, the same environment used to edit CDs and network radio productions on the no-compromise ProTools workstation (see below). It has a practical playlist-style format for manipulating mono or stereo tracks and a strong palette of DSP features: graphic and parametric EQ, pitch and time shift, compression, sample rate conversion. SDII files are in a standard format that can be shared easily with other Digidesign products and with MIDI packages (such as Studiovision). The digital in/out is a major improvement over the original product: digital files of the highest quality may now be loaded in from any digital device equipped with better A/D converters, and then manipulated as a file without any sacrifice in audio quality. Audiomedia II will accept some of the new plug-in modules from third-party vendors, but it doesn't have the horsepower or connectivity to work with the more advanced products coming out. For the digital beginner who already has a Mac, Audiomedia II is a wise choice at $1,295.

To mix multiple tracks, the natural choice is DECK II from OSC. The original DECK was a toy, but DECK II is a remarkably powerful and easy-to-use workspace that bears a striking resemblance to the costlier ProTools. That's no accident, as the core software features were designed by the same team. With Audiomedia II, DECK II, and a high-quality DAT, a producer can make some serious recordings for distribution on CD, CD-ROM, video games, radio, or audiobooks. At $399, DECK II is the radical alternative to the high-priced spread.

Because it is a software-only business, OSC has adapted its products to run on the Apple Macintosh Quadra AV without the need for a DSP card such as Audiomedia II. The AV plus DECK is now the hot choice for anyone who needs digital and a more powerful Mac. The bonus is that AVs open the door to QuickTime video, voice recognition, and other multimedia opportunities. The downside is that for now Sound Designer II will not work on the Quadra AV alone.

SoundTools II, the fully professional two-track recording and editing system (of which Audiomedia II is a low-end copy), consists of a two-track DSP card, the two-track Sound Designer II editing and DSP software, and the Digidesign Audio Interface, a fully professional set of digital converters with four channels of balanced XLR inputs and outputs and two channels of professional AES/EBU digital in/out.

Again, DECK II is a logical choice to supplement this rig, which will likely exceed most everyone's standard of quality for years to come. SoundTools II is $3,495 and is upgradable to ProTools.

The recent addition of Session 8 to the lineup means that musicians can have an all-in-one package with eight tracks of hardware and software, including optional outboard faders and mic/line preamps. For the artist who wants to keep the technology simple, Session 8 for the Mac and IBM-compatible PC ($3,995) or Session 8 XL for the IBM compatible-PC ($5,995), offer very good quality and lots of tracks. The XL version uses the same Pro Audio Interface found on ProTools and Sound Designer II.

ProTools is Digidesign's premium hardware/software package, designed for hard, constant use. Its strongest features can be found elsewhere in the family of products (lots of tracks, speed, Pro Audio Interface) but only in ProTools are all the expansion doors wide open. This system will accept all of the drop-in software modules, expands up to thirty two tracks, and most importantly is at the center of a new open platform called the TDM Bus. This is a virtual patchbay within the computer; producers can combine hardware and software elements a la carte in one flexible, expandable, "virtual" environment. The basic four-channel ProTools system is $4,995. But plug in the Lexicon nuVerb or state-of-the-art Apogee A/D converters, and you've reached the top of the stairway to studio heaven. Plug-in some more cards, some samplers, a DSP Farm (a card of assignable raw DSP processing power), and video-synch interfaces, and ProTools can become the fully customized studio of one's wildest dreams. —Gregg McVicar

Digidesign's Open Systems approach allows the user to hot-rod the stock features by adding hardware and plug-in software modules from other vendors. This expanding family of software modules includes DINR (Digidesign Intelligent Noise Reduction) for cleaning up noisy tracks; Q10, a precision equalization environment from Australia; and Jupiter Systems' MDT, a multiband dynamics processor that brings forth a wide palette of compression, expansion, "tube" companion, and other elaborate spectral effects with the click of a mouse. The beauty of these products is that they require no additional rack space or patching; just drop the icon into the system folder. The downside is that they're not available to create that special mood during live rehearsal or tracking: they're strictly after the fact. For high-end users, this will change with the Digidesign TDM Bus and the DSP Farm, which will make possible "virtual" patches between third-party software and hardware elements through banks of digital-signal processors. This is not cheap, but it enables desktop producers to build systems of phenomenal power and flexibility for a fraction of what it cost to do the same thing a few years ago. You couldn't even do some of this stuff a few years ago.

On the hardware side, the TDM Bus can be expanded with onboard and outboard cards, such as the nuVerb or premium D/A converters from Apogee and others. There are also MIDI sampler cards (SampleCell), mass-storage devices, video synch boxes, and special controllers for video and the new Alesis ADAT multitrack digital tape recorder. —GMc

Digidesign digital audio products: Suggested list prices: ProTools $4995 (4-track); SoundTools II $3495; AudioMedia II $1295; DINR noise reduction software $995; Session 8: Macintosh $3995, IBM compatibles $3995, XL for IBM compatibles $5995. Information from Digidesign, 1360 Willow Road, Menlo Park, CA 94025; 415/688-0600, 800/333-2137.

Deck II: Suggested list price $399. Information from OSC, 480 Potrero Avenue, San Francisco, CA 94110; 415/252-0460.

TDM plug-in hardware and software: Information from Apogee Electronics, 3435 Ocean Park Boulevard #211, Santa Monica, CA 90405; 310/314-1700.

Multiband Dyamics Tool: Suggested list price $399. Information from Jupiter Systems, PO Box 697, Applegate, CA 95703; 800/446-2356.

nuVerb: Suggested list price $1799. Information from Lexicon, 100 Beaver Street, Waltham, MA 02154; 617/736-0300.

Understanding Media Powers

The power to influence people's perceptions and beliefs is more politically effective now than naked military might. Affordable minicams and desktop video are making available to citizens media-powers that had previously been the exclusive property of elites.

Access to the means of production and the channels of distribution is not sufficient, however, if you don't know what you're doing.

Understanding how communication media affect minds and populations is a prerequisite to do-it-yourself. Before you can seize the media, you have to know how electronic simulations manipulate human emotions, and how the mass mesmerism business works. —HLR

Manufacturing Consent

The essential text for anyone seeking to understand how the consensus of a corporate-political elite structures the overall fabric and content of our news media. The authors demonstrate how the mass media respond to those who hold the reins, serving the public-relations interests of incumbent politicians and well-placed war-mongerers. Manufacturing Consent *demonstrates the techniques media professionals employ to reframe issues and events (Russian invasion of Afghanistan, the Iran-Contra hearings) in order to direct public opinion and, ultimately, the policies of our elected officials.* —Douglas Rushkoff

•

One of our central themes in this book is that the observable pattern of indignant campaigns and suppressions, of shading and emphasis, and of selection of context, premises, and general agenda, is highly functional for established power and responsive to the needs of the government and major power groups. A constant focus on victims of communism helps convince the public of enemy evil and sets the stage for intervention, subversion, support for terrorist states, an endless arms race, and military conflict — all in a noble cause. At the same time, the devotion of our leaders and media to this narrow set of victims raises public self-esteem and patriotism, as it demonstrates the essential humanity of country and people.

Manufacturing Consent
(The Political Economy of the Mass Media)
Edward S. Herman & Noam Chomsky.
1988; ISBN 0-679-72034-0
$17 ($19 postpaid). Random House/Order Dept., 400 Hahn Road, Westminster, MD 21157; 800/733-3000

The Society of the Spectacle

In May 1968, when French students were building barricades and issuing revolutionary broadsides, a remarkably prescient manifesto leapfrogged far over the industrial-era Marxism of student radicals. Guy Debord foresaw a day when movie actors would become presidents and advertising agencies would dominate politics. Debord claimed that modern communication media and power politics had created a whole new kind of world, a "society of the spectacle," in which the forces of capitalism and the powers of electronic communications combine, in the guise of entertainment, to enslave us in a form of fascism. The neo-Marxist prose is a bit thick, and the geopolitics are outdated. But this is the original source document of the hyperrealists such as Baudrillard, the political critics of media such as Chomsky, and the media activists such as the Immediasts. —HLR

•

For one to whom the real world becomes real images, mere images are transformed into real beings — tangible figments which are the efficient motor of trancelike behavior. Since the spectacle's job is to cause a world that is no longer directly perceptible to be *seen* via different specialized mediations, it is inevitable that it should elevate the human sense of sight to the special place once occupied by touch; the most abstract of the senses, and the most easily deceived, sight is naturally the most readily adaptable to present-day society's generalized abstraction. This is not to say, however, that the spectacle itself is perceptible to the naked eye — even if that eye is assisted by the ear. The spectacle is by definition immune from human activity, inaccessible to any projected review or correction. It is the opposite of dialogue. Wherever representation takes on an independent existence, the spectacle reestablishes its rule.

Society of the Spectacle
Guy Debord. Zone Books, 1994;
154 pp. ISBN 0-942299-80-9
$18.95 ($21.95 postpaid). The MIT Press/Order Dept., 55 Hayward Street, Cambridge, MA 02142; 800/356-0343

Technologies of Freedom

This is my choice for the single most important book for understanding the interplay of media, the First Amendment, and government in a democracy. Pool outlines the ways in which different communications have been treated differently by government over the years, and warns of the hazards of narrowly interpreting the First Amendment to apply only to traditional print media. Communications technologies play a critical role in empowering individuals in a democracy, and Pool spells out what is necessary to keep freedom of speech and publication alive in the 21st century. —Mike Godwin

•

A process called "convergence of modes" is blurring the lines between media, even between point-to-point communications, such as the post, telephone, and telegraph, and mass communications, such as the press, radio, and television. A single physical means — be it wires, cables, or airwaves — may carry services that in the past were provided in separate ways. . . .

Technology-driven convergence of modes is reinforced by the economic process of cross-ownership. The growth of conglomerates which participate in many businesses at once means that newspapers, magazine publishers, and book publishers increasingly own or are owned by companies that also operate in other fields. Both convergence and cross-ownership blur the boundaries which once existed between companies publishing in the print domain that is protected by the First Amendment and companies involved in businesses that are regulated by government. Today, the same company may find itself operating in both fields. The dikes that in the past held government back from exerting control on the print media are thus broken down.

The key technological change, at the root of the social changes, is that communication, other than conversation face to face, is becoming overwhelmingly electronic.

•

Not only is electronic communication growing faster than traditional media of publishing, but also the convergence of modes of delivery is bringing the press, journals, and books into the electronic world. One question raised by these changes is whether some social features are inherent in the electronic character of the emerging media. Is television the model of the future? Are electromagnetic pulses simply an alternative conduit to deliver whatever is wanted, or are there aspects of electronic technology that make it different from print—more centralized or more decentralized, more banal or more profound, more private or more government dependent?

The electronic transformation of the media occurs not in a vacuum but in a specific historical and legal context. Freedom for publishing has been one of America's proudest traditions. But just what is it that the courts have protected, and how does this differ from how the courts acted later when the media through which ideas flowed came to be the telegraph, telephone, television, or computers? What images did policy makers have of how each of these media works; how far were their images valid; and what happened to their images when the facts changed?

In each of the three parts of the American communications system—print, common carriers, and broadcasting—the law has rested on a perception of technology that is sometimes accurate, often inaccurate, and which changes slowly as technology changes fast. Each new advance in the technology of communications disturbs a status quo. It meets resistance from those whose dominance it threatens, but if useful, it begins to be adopted. Initially, because it is new and a full scientific mastery of the options is not yet at hand, the invention comes into use in a rather clumsy form. Technical laymen, such as judges, perceive the new technology in that early, clumsy form, which then becomes their image of its nature, possibilities, and use. This perception is an incubus on later understanding.

Simulations

French philosopher and social theorist Jean Baudrillard calls our expanding mediaspace a "simulacre" — a simulacrum, a simulation — and believes that this artificially created illusion has warped reality itself. Baudrillard warns that our increased participation in the simulacre removes us from real experience, and stymies our ability to accurately access our social and political condition. Essential reading for any student of contemporary media. —Douglas Rushkoff

•

We are in danger of a total dissolution of TV into life, the dissolution of life into TV. . . . We must think of the media as if they were in outer orbit, a sort of genetic code which controls the mutation of the real into the hyperreal, just as the other, micromolecular code controls the passage of the signal from a representative sphere of meaning to the genetic sphere of the programmed signal.

Simulations
Jean Baudrillard. Semiotext(e).
1983; 159 pp. ISBN 0-936756-02-0
$6 ($8 postpaid). Autonomedia, PO Box 568, Williamsburg Station, Brooklyn, NY 11211; 718/387-6471

Technologies of Freedom
(On Free Speech in an Electronic Age)
Ithiel de Sola Pool. Belknap Press, 1983;
299 pp. ISBN 0-674-87233-9
$13.95 ($16.95 postpaid). Harvard University Press/Customer Service, 79 Garden Street, Cambridge, MA 02138; 800/448-2242

Extra!

Jeff Cohen, a former ACLU lawyer, decided it was time to quit grumbling about media bias and do something instead. He and a few friends created Fairness and Accuracy in Reporting (FAIR), an organization that not only scrutinizes the information we're given as "news," but also responds when gross errors are detected.

The FAIR journal *Extra!* slices through the baloney in commendable fashion.

Extra!
Martin A. Lee, Editor.
$30/year (6 issues). PO Box 911,
Pearl River, NY 10965; 800/847-3993

With quotes, pictures, and excerpts, it shows exactly how the mass media presented a story, then offers its own scrupulously documented commentary. Insights and conclusions are left to the reader. —Dick Fugett

•

The principal media obsession during the summit week was Gorbachev's public relations acumen, as though the Kremlin had somehow cracked a prized American code. . . . A frontpage *New York Times* (12-10-87) headline chimed: "Soviet Visitor is Turning on His Charm."

Curiously, a later *Times* edition changed the headline to "Soviet Visitor Mixes Charm With Venom." The byline changed as well, from Joel Brinkley to Andrew Rosenthal. But the text changed only slightly, with the addition of several paragraphs describing Gorbachev's meeting the news executives. *Extra!* contacted the *Times* writers for an explanation. When asked about the venom, Rosenthal said that Gorbachev took a hardline position at the meeting. "You might think this is a cop-out," he added, "but the headlines are written by editors not reporters. . . I didn't use the word 'venom' in my story."

Media Literacy Bookshelf

Understanding Media (The Extensions of Man): Marshall McLuhan. 1966; 320 pp. ISBN 0-451-62496-3. $4.95 ($6.95 postpaid). Penguin USA/Consumer Sales, 120 Woodbine Street, Bergenfield, NJ 07621; 800/253-6476. Start with the Master. He perceived the emergence of the world-brain, understood how our electric symbol-manipulating machinery has altered human perceptions, and foresaw how that alteration would trigger the millennial change in civilization we are experiencing now.

The New Citizen: $15/year (4 issues). Citizens for Media Literacy, 34 Wall Street, Suite 407, Asheville, NC 28801; 704/255-0182, fax 704/254-2286, email cml@unca.edu For those who are concerned about the impact of communications media on democracy, education, family, and community; full of resources for understanding how media work and for promoting media literacy.

The Age of Propaganda (The Everyday Use and Abuse of Persuasion): Anthony Pratkanis & Eliot Aronson. 1991; 320 pp., ISBN 0-7167-2211-9. $12.95 ($15.95 postpaid) W.H. Freeman and Co., 4419 W. 1980 S., Salt Lake City, UT 84104; 800/488-5233. You want to get serious about resisting thought-control? Step One is to understand how it works. The authors show us how propaganda manipulates emotions, how propagandists trick us into persuading ourselves.

Media Events (The Live Broadcasting of History): Daniel Dayan & Elihu Katz. 1992; 306 pp. ISBN 0-674-55956-8. $15.95 ($18.95 postpaid). Harvard University Press/Customer Service, 79 Garden Street, Cambridge, MA 02138; 800/448-2242. Anthropologists look at large-scale media phenomena, from Presidential funerals to Olympic dramas and Academy Awards spectaculars, as the bonding rituals of a global mythology emerging in mediaspace. —HLR

MediaCulture Review

The Institute for Alternative Journalism starts with the assumption that the mediaspace is where our issues and ideas live, breathe, and spawn. *MediaCulture Review* is the Institute's broad-based collection of articles about the strange love-hate relationship between America and its ever-expanding media. —Douglas Rushkoff

MediaCulture Review
$24/year (6 issues). Institute For Alternative Journalism, 2025 Eye Street NW #1118, Washington, DC 10006; 202/887-0022

•

"I used to watch TV talk shows casually, at random. A little Crossfire here, a little Larry King Live there, ending the day with the first half of Late Night With David Letterman. However, routine went the way of all flesh when it became apparent that 1992 was shaping up as what media types dub a "watershed" year. . . . the most important election year since 1960. . . . the biggest economic crisis since the Great Depression. . . a crisis of national self-esteem. So many issues coming to the fore, so many scandals, outrages, disasters, neuroses, controversies, trials and tribulations, one after the other, chewed up and spit out and piled high like old tires in a junk yard."
—Juan Rodriguez, excerpted from *The East Bay Express,* 10/2/92.

Adbusters Quarterly

This is surely the only magazine in the world which takes as its central theme the cataclysmic environmental consequences of advertising. Now over $100 billion per year in the US alone, consumer advertising has little function but to encourage people to buy more stuff and to universalize material values. One could make the case that advertising is the root cause, or at least the driving mechanism, for the horrific and increasing assault on the world's resources. *Adbusters* makes that case, and does so with impressive scope, detail and joie de vivre.

Adbusters also produces guides to "media wrenching," as well as sharply hilarious media strategies designed to work in tandem with video, and print materials to help free people from media and commodity addiction. If you can raise the money to place these spots on the air, or the print ads in magazines, *Adbusters* will provide them to you free. —Jerry Mander

Ten years ago, we didn't bother much about the chemicals in our food, or the toxins generated by industry because we believed they were "well within acceptable limits." We were dead wrong about that, and today we may be repeating the same mistake with mental pollution, nonchalantly absorbing massive daily doses of it without a second thought. If we continue to ignore the problem, we may soon find ourselves dealing not only with an irretrievably damaged natural environment, but also with a seriously impaired public mind.

There is an ominous resonance between these two forms of pollution. The holes growing in the ozone layer seem to reflect the great voids growing in our minds. It's frightening to realize how our polluted mental environment both diverts attention from and weakens the resolve required to tackle global crises. Distracted, apathetic citizens make for poor environmental stewards.

Adbusters Quarterly
$40/year (4 issues, airmail only to US). Adbusters Media Foundation, 1243 West 7th Ave., Vancouver, BC V6H 1B7, Canada; 604/736-9401, fax 604/737-6021

(Left) Originally this was a 1950s comic strip, but through the ages the woman and her dialog have been mutated by various artists. At points, the words have pleaded to get out of Vietnam and, later, El Salvador. This is the 1993 version.

Seizing the Media

The Immediast Underground advocates media literacy, media critique, media subversion, media liberation. "Revolution is the overthrow of government; our aim is to overthrow the media." Their weapons are humor, knowledge, deconstruction, and a focus on the real sources of power in the information age. —HLR

•

We each see how extended exposure to television and mass media dulls people with a sense of numbness and nausea. At every turn a monologue of coercion penetrates our senses and rapes our attention. Wherever we look, wherever we listen, wherever we go: the pornography of billboards, bus-side placards, subway cards, glaring storefront signs and displays, the glut of junk mail, stupid fly-by beach planes and blimps, coupons, obnoxious bumper stickers and breast pins, embarrassing service uniforms, plastic banners and ribbons, absurd parades, streetcorner handouts, windshield wiper flyers, matchbook ads, business cards, screaming radios, the daily papers, every nanosecond of television, the package wrapped around everything we buy — from the label in our underwear to the robot computer that calls us in our homes — only the upper atmosphere and the ocean floor offer any sanctuary from America's ecology of coercion.

Despite bountiful resources, corporate profits and state security continued to prevail over public needs... until...

Seizing the Media
(Version 1.2)
Immediast Underground.
$4.00 postpaid from Open Magazine Pamphlet Series, PO Box 2726, Westfield, NJ 07091; 908/789-9608

Media Virus!

Have young, media-savvy, profoundly subversive culture jammers already seized the media and turned it to secretly anti-authoritarian ends? Is this book a history, a utopian fantasy, or a primer? Douglas Rushkoff introduces us to the creators of the "Simpsons," "PeeWee's Playhouse," "Ren & Stimpy," "Liquid TV," "Beavis and Butthead," and we begin to get his point about media viruses, electronically propagated meaning bombs that disguise themselves until they reach their destinations in unsuspecting minds. We meet the Immediast Underground, Paper Tiger TV, and other merry memesters who have taken the media revolution to the streets and neurons of the worldbrain. —HLR

•

This mainstream media subversion is accomplished through careful and clever packaging. Commercial television activism means hiding subversive agendas in palatable candy shells. Most of us do not suspect that children's programs like *Pee Wee's Playhouse* or *Ren & Stimpy* promote gay lifestyles, or that *The Simpsons* and *Liquid TV* express a psychedelic worldview.

Children's television and MTV, in fact, are the easiest places to launch countercultural missiles. The more harmless or inane the forum, the more unsuspecting the audience.

The messages in our media come to us packaged as Trojan Horses. They enter our homes in one form, but behave in a very different way than we expect once they are inside.

Media Virus
(Hidden Agendas in Popular Culture)
Douglas Rushkoff. Ballantine Books, $21.95 ($23.95 postpaid) from Random House/Order Dept., 400 Hahn Road, Westminster, MD 21157; 800/733-3000

Culture Jamming

This broadside, polemic, how-to manual, and call to arms is the manifesto of a worldwide uprising of cultural guerrillas who go beyond media criticism to direct action. Billboards are altered, journalists are spoofed, zines proliferate, joke religions are founded. Intellectually grounded in political and social media criticism from Bagdikian to Baudrillard, culture jamming takes its action orientation from the Yippies and samizdat culture. Do a few self-proclaimed revolutionaries with paintbrushes, pirate radios, and media pranks stand a chance against the forces of the global media? Maybe. Culture jammers are injecting some powerful memes into the worldmind; there's no telling what will evolve from their pranks. Most hopefully, these revolutionaries seem to be having fun with what they are doing — a sign they are onto something of real value. —HLR

•

Meanwhile, the question remains: How to box with shadows? In other words, what shape does an engaged politics assume in an empire of signs?

The answer lies, perhaps, in the "semiological guerrilla warfare" imagined by Umberto Eco. "[T]he receiver of the message seems to have a residual freedom: the freedom to read it in a different way . . . I am proposing an action to urge the audience to control the message and its multiple possibilities of interpretation," he writes. "[O]ne medium can be employed to communicate a series of opinions on another medium . . . The universe of Technological Communication would then be patrolled by groups of communication guerrillas, who would restore a critical dimension to passive reception."

Eco assumes, a priori, the radical politics of visual literacy, an idea eloquently argued by Stuart Ewen, a critic of consumer culture. "We live at a time when the image has become the predominant mode of public address, eclipsing all other forms in the structuring of meaning," asserts Ewen. "Yet little in our education prepares us to make sense of the rhetoric, historical development or social implications of the images within our lives." In a society of heat, light and electronic poltergeists — an eerie otherworld of "illimitable vastness, brilliant light, and the gloss and smoothness of material things" — the desperate project of reconstructing meaning, or at least reclaiming that notion from marketing departments and P.R. firms, requires visually-literate ghostbusters.

Culture jammers answer to that name. "Jamming" is CB slang for the illegal practice of interrupting radio broadcasts or conversations between fellow hams with lip farts, obscenities, and other equally jejune hijinx. Culture jamming, by contrast, is directed against an ever more intrusive, instrumental technoculture whose operant mode is the manufacture of consent through the manipulation of symbols.

The term "cultural jamming" was first used by the collage band Negativeland to describe billboard alteration and other forms of media sabotage. On Jamcon '84 (SST), a mock-serious bandmember observes, "As

awareness of how the media environment we occupy affects and directs our inner life grows, some resist . . . The skillfully reworked billboard . . . directs the public viewer to a consideration of the original corporate strategy. The studio for the cultural jammer is the world at large."

Part artistic terrorists, part vernacular critics, culture jammers, like Eco's "communications guerrillas," introduce noise into the signal as it passes from transmitter to receiver, encouraging idiosyncratic, unintended interpretations. Intruding on the intruders, they invest ads, newscasts, and other media artifacts with subversive meanings; simultaneously, they decrypt them, rendering their seductions impotent. Jammers offer irrefutable evidence that Rightwingers have no copyright on war waged with incantations and simulations. And, like Ewen's cultural cryptographers, they refuse the role of passive shoppers, renewing the notion of a public discourse.

Finally, and just as importantly, culture jammers are Groucho Marxists, ever mindful of the fun to be had in the joyful demolition of oppressive ideologies.

•

It is no small irony — or tragedy — that semiotics, which seeks to make explicit the implicit meanings in the sign language of society, has become pop culture shorthand for an academic parlor trick useful in divining the hidden significance in *Casablanca*, *Disneyland*, or our never-ending obsession with Marilyn Monroe. In paranoid pop psych (Vance Packard's *The Hidden Persuaders*, Wilson Bryan Key's *Subliminal Seduction*), semiotics offers titillating decryptions of naughty advertising. "This preoccupation with subliminal advertising," writes Ewen, "is part of the legendary life of post-World War II American capitalism: the word 'SEX' written on the surface of Ritz crackers, copulating bodies or death images concealed in ice cubes, and so forth." Increasingly, advertising assumes this popular mythology: a recent print ad depicted a rocks glass filled with icecubes, the words "Absolut vodka" faintly discernible on their craggy, shadowed surfaces. The tagline: "Absolut Subliminal."

All of which makes semiotics seem trivial, effete, although it is an inherently political project; Barthes "set out . . . to examine the normally hidden set of rules, codes, and conventions through which meanings particular to specific social groups (i.e., those in power) are rendered universal and 'given' for the whole of society." Marshall Blonsky has called semiotics "a defense against information sickness, the 'too-muchness' of the world," fulfilling Marshall McLuhan's prophecy that "just as we now try to control atom-bomb fallout, so we will one day try to control media fallout." As used by culture jammers, it is an essential tool in the all-important undertaking of making sense of the world, its networks of power, the encoded messages that flicker ceaselessly along its communication channels.

Culture Jamming
(Hacking, Slashing, and Sniping In the Empire of Signs)
Mark Dery.
$4.00 postpaid from Open Magazine Pamphlet Series, PO Box 2726, Westfield, NJ 07091; 908/789-9608

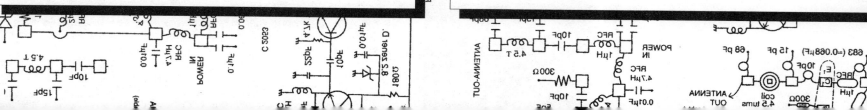

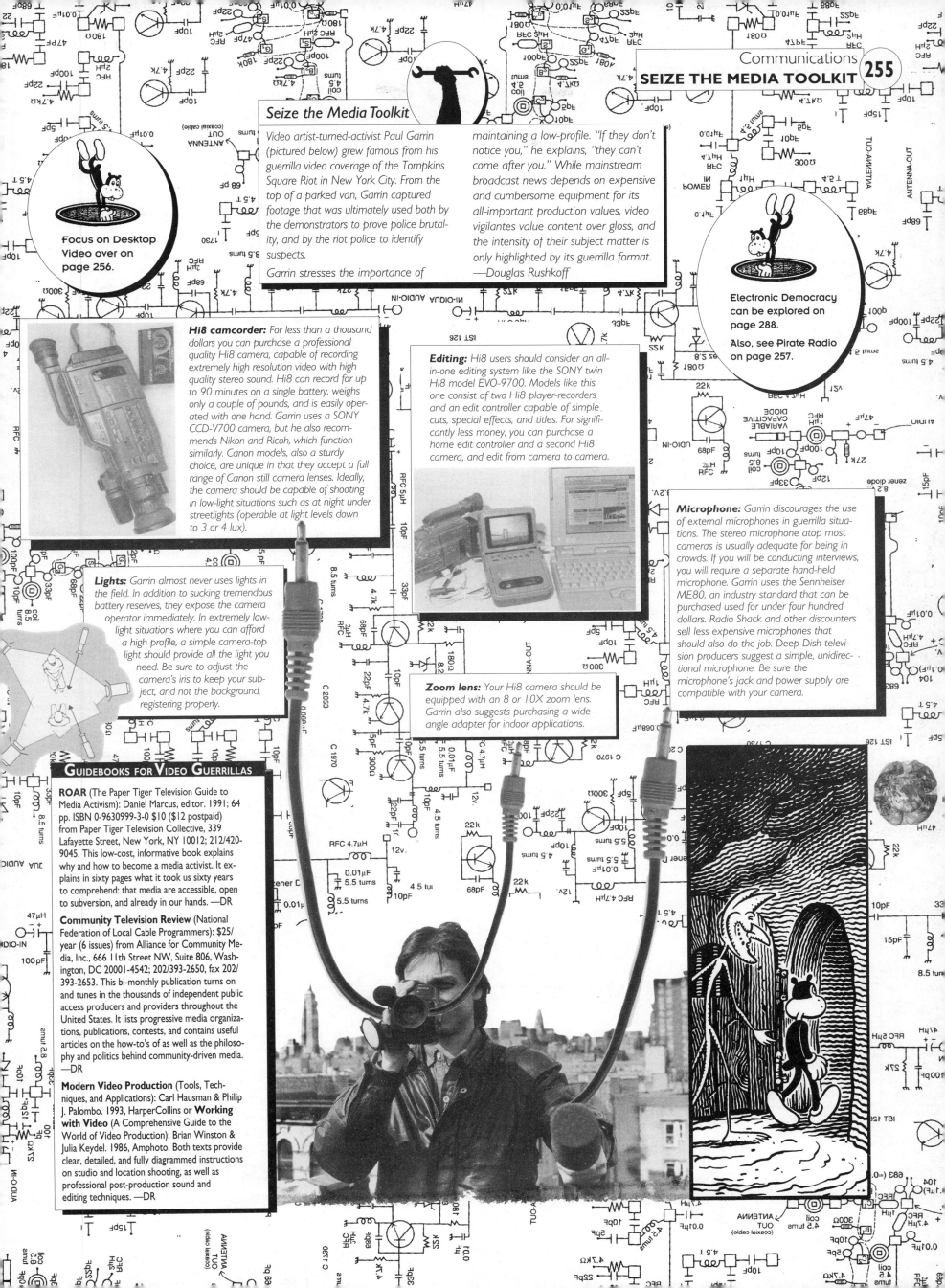

Seize the Media Toolkit

Video artist-turned-activist Paul Garrin (pictured below) grew famous from his guerrilla video coverage of the Tompkins Square Riot in New York City. From the top of a parked van, Garrin captured footage that ultimately used both by the demonstrators to prove police brutality, and by the riot police to identify suspects.

Garrin stresses the importance of maintaining a low-profile. "If they don't notice you," he explains, "they can't come after you." While mainstream broadcast news depends on expensive and cumbersome equipment for its all-important production values, video vigilantes value content over gloss, and the intensity of their subject matter is only highlighted by its guerrilla format.
—Douglas Rushkoff

Focus on Desktop Video over on page 256.

Electronic Democracy can be explored on page 288.

Also, see Pirate Radio on page 257.

Hi8 camcorder: *For less than a thousand dollars you can purchase a professional quality Hi8 camera, capable of recording extremely high resolution video with high quality stereo sound. Hi8 can record for up to 90 minutes on a single battery, weighs only a couple of pounds, and is easily operated with one hand. Garrin uses a SONY CCD-V700 camera, but he also recommends Nikon and Ricoh, which function similarly. Canon models, also a sturdy choice, are unique in that they accept a full range of Canon still camera lenses. Ideally, the camera should be capable of shooting in low-light situations such as at night under streetlights (operable at light levels down to 3 or 4 lux).*

Editing: *Hi8 users should consider an all-in-one editing system like the SONY twin Hi8 model EVO-9700. Models like this one consist of two Hi8 player-recorders and an edit controller capable of simple cuts, special effects, and titles. For significantly less money, you can purchase a home edit controller and a second Hi8 camera, and edit from camera to camera.*

Microphone: *Garrin discourages the use of external microphones in guerrilla situations. The stereo microphone atop most cameras is usually adequate for being in crowds. If you will be conducting interviews, you will require a separate hand-held microphone. Garrin uses the Sennheiser ME80, an industry standard that can be purchased used for under four hundred dollars. Radio Shack and other discounters sell less expensive microphones that should also do the job. Deep Dish television producers suggest a simple, unidirectional microphone. Be sure the microphone's jack and power supply are compatible with your camera.*

Lights: *Garrin almost never uses lights in the field. In addition to sucking tremendous battery reserves, they expose the camera operator immediately. In extremely low-light situations where you can afford a high profile, a simple camera-top light should provide all the light you need. Be sure to adjust the camera's iris to keep your subject, and not the background, registering properly.*

Zoom lens: *Your Hi8 camera should be equipped with an 8 or 10X zoom lens. Garrin also suggests purchasing a wide-angle adapter for indoor applications.*

GUIDEBOOKS FOR VIDEO GUERRILLAS

ROAR (The Paper Tiger Television Guide to Media Activism): Daniel Marcus, editor. 1991; 64 pp. ISBN 0-9630999-3-0 $10 ($12 postpaid) from Paper Tiger Television Collective, 339 Lafayette Street, New York, NY 10012; 212/420-9045. This low-cost, informative book explains why and how to become a media activist. It explains in sixty pages what it took us sixty years to comprehend: that media are accessible, open to subversion, and already in our hands. —DR

Community Television Review (National Federation of Local Cable Programmers): $25/year (6 issues) from Alliance for Community Media, Inc., 666 11th Street NW, Suite 806, Washington, DC 20001-4542; 202/393-2650, fax 202/393-2653. This bi-monthly publication turns on and tunes in the thousands of independent public access producers and providers throughout the United States. It lists progressive media organizations, publications, contests, and contains useful articles on the how-to's of as well as the philosophy and politics behind community-driven media. —DR

Modern Video Production (Tools, Techniques, and Applications): Carl Hausman & Philip J. Palombo. 1993, HarperCollins or **Working with Video** (A Comprehensive Guide to the World of Video Production): Brian Winston & Julia Keydel. 1986, Amphoto. Both texts provide clear, detailed, and fully diagrammed instructions on studio and location shooting, as well as professional post-production sound and editing techniques. —DR

Video production, from Hollywood epics to inexpensive consumer gear, is in the throes of its biggest change in forty-five years: moving from analog to digital. This change promises cheaper, more durable equipment; sharper, non-flickering images; lossless editing and duplication; and dazzling special effects. Digital video may cut production costs by 80 percent. It may result in the obsolescence of thousands of craftspersons and slash the incomes of those who survive. It may create millions of new production "studios," each contained on a single desktop.

For my money the best introduction to the communications revolution is still Stewart Brand's 1987 book *The Media Lab: Inventing the Future at MIT* (see p. 236). In non-technical language Brand previewed then what is now taking place: the convergence of the separate industries of print, broadcast and telephony into a single digital medium.

In the digital world, a doubling of speed or capacity and a halving of price every two years is the norm. In the past few years the power of computers to transform still and moving images has rocketed past the capabilities of traditional analog tools.

Here's a case in point. In 1990 Apple Computer created an electronic "newspaper" with digital-video newsclips. It required $50,000 in special hardware — Betacam VTRs, optical disk recorders, single-frame animation boards — to create digital videos no larger than a big postage stamp. A year later, a stock $4,000 Macintosh could do as well. In early 1994, the PowerPC Macintoshes ($1600-$4500) are able to make full-screen videos sixteen times larger than a postage stamp and four times as fast. New generations of computers will bring similar power to Windows users later in 1994.

Suddenly, digital video is ready for prime time. In fact, 1995 will see the first consumer digital VCRs and camcorders. They will be around $3,000 at first, but prices will fall sharply and both features and quality will improve. Until recently digital editing equipment was so costly that only professional post-production houses could afford it. But computer prices always plummet. Today such technology is within reach of hobbyists.

"Digital video" encompasses a range of technologies. It can be as simple as using inexpensive software like Abbate's Video Toolkit ($279-$299). The toolkit connects any Macintosh to VCRs and camcorders to log videotapes and to control traditional analog video editing.

For a few hundred dollars more, a video digitizing board (such as SuperMac's Video Spigot for the Macintosh [$299 and up]) can be added to existing Macintoshes and Windows machines to make digital movies on the computer. The Spigot is often bundled with Adobe's Premiere software, an excellent editing program that mixes video and sound tracks and adds special effects.

Every popular computer platform has or is developing digital-video tools. Commodore Amiga owners exult over the device that really started digital video, the NewTek Video Toaster, $1500 of hardware and software that transforms an Amiga into a useful video editing tool. Toaster users even have their own magazine, *Video Toaster User*.

Now for the bad news: the field changes too fast for books — including this catalog. Even the magazines, with their three-to-six month lead times, have a difficult time keeping current. Among the magazines, Craig LeGrow's feisty *Morph's Outpost on the Digital Frontier* seems to me the most inventive. *Digital Video World* and *New Media Magazine* are also important. By the end of 1994 there'll be another dozen new magazines, all claiming to have the best information. How can you know which of them offer real value and which are advertiser-besotted impostors? Go online.

In the online world you are in direct communication with the people who create and use these tools. My main source is The WELL's Muchomedia and Interactive Video conferences (see p. 262), where the professionals and the demanding hobbyists teach each other and share experiences. Other online sources include CompuServe's multimedia forum and the comp.multimedia newsgroup on Usenet (see p. 264).

—Roger Karraker

E Q U I P M E N T	**M A G A Z I N E S**
Apple Computer PowerPC: 800/732-3131 ext. 150, in Canada 800/665-2775 ext. 910.	**Video Toaster User:** Jim Plant, Editor. $36/year (12 issues) from AVID Publications, 273 N. Mathilda Avenue, Sunnyvale, CA 94086; 800/322-2843.
Video Toolkit: Abbate, 83 Main Street, Norfolk, MA 02056; 508/987-2337.	**Morph's Outpost on the Digital Frontier:** Craig LeGrow, Editor. $34.95/year (12 issues). PO Box 578, Orinda, CA 94563; 800/GO MORPH.
Video Spigot: SuperMac Technology, Inc., 215 Moffitt Park Drive, Sunnyvale, CA 94089; 800/334-3005, fax 800/541-7680.	**Digital Video Magazine:** Lou Wallace, Editor. $19.97/year (12 issues). PO Box 594, Mt. Morris, IL 61054; 800/998-0806.
Adobe Premiere: Adobe Systems, Inc., 1585 Charleston Road, Mountain View, CA 94039; 800/833-6687.	**New Media Magazine:** $36/year (12 issues). PO Box 1771, Riverton, NJ 08077; 609/786-4430.
Video Toaster: NewTek, 215 E. 8th Street, Topeka, KS 66603; 800/847-6111.	

See also "Seize the Media Toolkit," p. 255.

PowerPC

Power Macintosh 7100/66

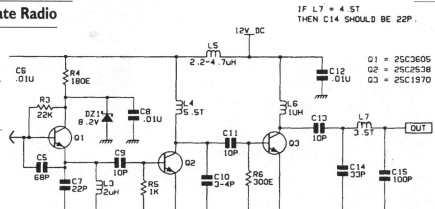

RADIO

has been a tool of freedom fighters and resistance movements since World War II. Sometimes knowing how to wire up a clandestine transmitter is more important to political resistance than access to armaments.

Clandestine radio continues this tradition. Pirate radio goes beyond the strictly political motivation of clandestine radio into the realm of pranks, performance art, and, sometimes, vandalism. Small radio stations with a broadcasting radius of a city block or less are now available for $40 in kit form.

Many American citizens believe that the private ownership of firearms keeps the government honest. These days, some citizens believe that the private ownership of radio transmitters might one day prove to be important for the same reason. —HLR

Resources for Radio Guerrillas

Usenet: alt.radio.pirate (See p. 264 for information on access to Usenet.)

An automated mail server maintained by the American Radio Relay League, which is not itself a pirate radio association, includes information useful to pirate and clandestine-radio enthusiasts. Email messages to info@arrl.org with the message: help. You will receive email instructing you on the use of the service. (See p. 265 for access to Internet.)

*A twenty-four-page booklet, the **Pirate's Guide to FM Stereo**, includes plans and instructions for modifying the Ramsey PA-1 for FM broadcast band operation. $5 for US orders, $8 overseas from mycal, PO Box 750381, Petaluma, CA 94975-0381; email mycal@netacsys.com*

The Pirate Radio Directory

A listener's guide to pirate stations, from ACID (devoted to psychedelia) to WYMN (feminist advocacy and female C&W performers). Like zines, pirate stations pop up and disappear; the directory publishes annual updates. Also a source of books and catalogs related to clandestine and pirate radio. —HLR

The Complete Manual of Pirate Radio

A cynic once said that freedom of the press belongs to those who are rich enough to own one. The author of this booklet, who goes by the nomme d'air of Zeke Teflon, feels the same way about freedom of broadcast and the transmitters required for the operation. His refreshingly anarchist attitude is that the air belongs to everyone, and he gives us a formula for reclaiming it from the media conglomerates.

The fact that most of Zeke's schemes are illegal and could land you in the pokey must be kept in mind, but that very risk adds to Zeke's zest for the venture. He gives us an overview of the possibilities — AM, FM, short wave, availability of used equipment, antenna needs, the pros and cons of fixed, remote and mobile operations, plus cost estimates, which are surprisingly low. A few hundred dollars could launch a small outfit. —Dick Fugett

•

Piracy is illegal. If you're busted, the government can seize your equipment, drag you through the courts, fine you thousands of dollars, and, theoretically, throw you in jail, although I've never heard of that happening to anyone. So, it makes sense to take every precaution to avoid The Knock (on your door from the FCC).

1-Watt FM Transmitter

The ideal way to maximize a station's listenership is to broadcast 24 hours a day, on a set frequency, with high power and a permanently mounted antenna. Attempting such operations as a pirate, however, would be suicidal.

At the other extreme, you could go straight on the air with a very low power (under 100mw) transmitter, which would be legal under FCC rules and regulations. If you would be satisfied with a broadcasting radius of a couple blocks, that would be the route to go. In fact, in cities such as San Francisco and New York, such an approach makes a lot of sense.

The Complete Manual of Pirate Radio
Zeke Teflon. 1993; 47 pp.
ISBN 0-9613289-9-1 $5 ($7 postpaid).
See Sharp Press, PO Box 1731,
Tucson, AZ 85702-1731

A*C*E

The Association of Clandestine Radio Enthusiasts (A*C*E) is for people interested in pirate and clandestine broadcasting.

"Clandestine" in this context means unlicensed stations trying to undermine the political order in a target area. Most are covertly sponsored by governments, or overtly identified with insurgent groups. Radio Venceremos, which served as the "official voice of the Farabundo Marti National Liberation Front," is a well-known example in Central America. A less well-known example, closer to home, is "La Voz de Alpha 66," an anti-Castro station based in or near Miami that broadcasts three nights a week in Spanish to Cuba. A*C*E's monthly newsletter

publishes reports about such stations, though the primary focus is on "pirates."

Pirates aren't trying to overthrow a government; they generally just want to offer an alternative to what licensed stations carry. In Western Europe, where broadcasting has traditionally been monopolized by national governments, pirates went on the air to provide local, ethnic, and commercial programming. Their popularity proved the need for such programming and in many cases led to liberalization of broadcasting controls.

A*C*E continues to be the best way to track this sort of activity. Membership gets you their monthly newsletter, with loggings, reports of busts, inter-

views with pirates, technical tips, etc. Also included are extensive listings of recent "numbers" broadcasts — mysterious coded messages believed to be instructions beamed to spies. Some people make a hobby of trying to figure out the codes or locating the transmitters. Most of this work goes on behind the scenes, but the listings in A*C*E will at least help you find the broadcasts. —Robert Horvitz

Association of Clandestine Radio Enthusiasts: Membership $18/year includes 12 issues of *A*C*E Bulletin*; sample copy $2. PO Box 11201, Shawnee Mission, KS 66207; A*C*E/ANARC (Association of North American Radio Clubs) BBS 913/345-1978.

•

According to correspondance from the station, anyone who listens to the station will then emit a fresh pine scent and will have the power to reduce car salesmen to dust.

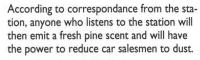

The Pirate Radio Directory
George Zeller & Andrew Yoder.
1994; 72 pp. ISBN 0-936653-57-4
$12.95 ($14.95 postpaid) from
Tiare Publications, PO Box 493,
Lake Geneva, WI 53147;
800/420-0579

While covering a major expedition in Antarctica, NPR Science Correspondent Ira Flatow took time out to do a feature on the only natives of this vast and frozen continent. Many features are byproducts of "hard news," but anything that rouses your curiosity can be the starting point for a feature story. —*Telling the Story*

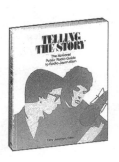

Sightseeing with the Mind's Eye

Thanks to a hardy band of independent producers, and particularly to a public radio system that has evolved (despite near financial ruin and constant political upheaval) over the past two decades, there is an impressive array of programs devoted to ideas, art, indigenous and adventurous music, and other tantalizing expressions of the human spirit. What follows are some of the best, and most underappreciated, news-and-views radio programs available today. —*Phil Catalfo*

New Dimensions Radio: *Membership $35/year includes quarterly magazine. PO Box 410510, San Francisco, CA 94141-0510; 415/563-8899. Since it began in 1973, New Dimensions Radio has broadcast some 1,200 probing conversations between host Michael Toms and the leading thinkers and visionaries of the past two decades: Joseph Campbell, R. Buckminster Fuller, Robert Bly, Ram Dass, Patricia Sun, Arnold Mindell, Matthew Fox, Bernie Siegel, and hundreds more. The resulting archive is — as the producers claim affectionately (and not inaccurately) — the "Library of Congress of the emerging culture." The weekly series "New Dimensions" is aired in some 180 markets; programs are also available on cassette.*

AudioCraft • Telling the Story

These days, it's getting easier and easier to get started in video; several hundred bucks and anyone can be a filmmaker or documentary producer. With that obvious attraction, I think people with stories to tell are picking up cameras and overlooking the audio arts. I think that's a mistake. Radio (and prerecorded cassettes) still provide a vivid, inexpensive, direct medium for fiction, fact prose and poetry. Cameras are more obtrusive and more cumbersome than microphones, and the difference between special effects for video and radio is the difference between a gaggle of wizards from LucasFilm slaving at computers, or your doing something like playing the sound of your old lawnmower backwards. Also, no other medium matches radio's penetration. No one can watch a documentary while driving to work, biking, or taking a shower, but they can listen to one. There's an old cliché in radio that goes, "The only difference between radio and TV is that on radio the pictures are better." These two books can help bring your audio pictures into focus.

AudioCraft is an entry-level primer on the nuts and bolts of radio production. It starts out with the most basic basics, such as the difference between mono and stereo, and eventually covers such topics as reverb and producing live concerts. Author Randy Thom spent years in public radio (before going off to become one of those LucasFilm wizards, picking up an Oscar for his sound work on **The Right Stuff***). He's gathered together straightforward explanations of what all those*

gadgets in the control room do. AudioCraft is widely used as a textbook at schools and community stations. It's an excellent place to start.

Much of what is best about radio, particularly radio journalism, happens at National Public Radio. Several years back, some of NPR's top reporters, producers, editors and engineers collaborated on **Telling the Story***, a book and accompanying set of audiocassettes that explain how NPR does what it does. The book and cassettes can be purchased, and used, separately, but there's synergistic effect to using them both. For example, you can read about the principles of tape editing, then listen as NPR's top editor takes a rambling, disjointed interview and makes it interesting. Or hear the individual components of an "All Things Considered" feature, and then go into the studio and listen to it being put together.* **Telling the Story** *also covers areas of journalism that fall outside the realm of* **AudioCraft***, such as reporting styles, writing for the ear, and copyright and libel law.*
—*Chris Spurgeon*

•

Many artists in a variety of fields, visual as well as aural, have said that music is the most powerfully emotive of all the arts. Remember that any sound placed in an appropriate context can be musical in the most basic sense, and inherit that magical power. —*AudioCraft*

I ask myself: can I bring all the people I interviewed for this story into this studio and read this script and play this tape right in front of them without shame, and when

I finish, can I look them in the eye (all of them) and defend everything I have just said?

If I can, I go in and record.

•

Before leaving on an assignment, have a few interviews set up. Work the phone hard before you leave, and even harder after you get there. Ask everyone you interview who else you should talk to. If the story is controversial, ask them who their most worthy opponents are and then go do those interviews. Talk to officials and professionals and shop clerks and parking lot attendants. Know what you must cover and cover those subjects with a variety of interviews. It is better to have too many than too few choices back at your editing station, better to be in a position to use only your very best interviews in the finished piece. But remember, if you just go out to fill in the blanks of a story you have already done in your mind, you won't have the story — not the real story. *—Telling the Story.*

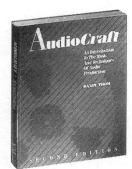

AudioCraft
(An Introduction to the Tools and Techniques of Audio Production)
Randy Thom. 1989; 200 pp.
ISBN 0-941209-02-4
$30 ($32 postpaid) from National Federation of Community Broadcasters, 666 11th Street NW, Suite 805, Washington, DC 20001; 202/393-2355

Soundprint: *4000 Brandywine Street NW, Suite 620, Washington, DC 20016; 202/885-1285. The most wide-ranging documentary series in radio today, and the premier outlet for some of the most talented producers in the country (and abroad: BBC productions are also featured). Topics range from Jay Allison and Christina Egloff's audio verité visit with street gangs in East Los Angeles to Larry Massett's visit to Mount Shasta during the Harmonic Convergence. Now in its fourth year, "Soundprint" is heard on 130 stations nationwide. Cassettes of non-BBC productions are available for $10 each.*

National Public Radio: *635 Massachusetts Ave NW, Washington, DC 20001-3753; 202/414-2000. Three excellent series provide a much-needed multicultural perspective to our news-and-information menu: "Crossroads," a weekly half-hour newsmagazine featuring original stories, indepth reports, and profiles, as well as commentaries by storytellers, poets, writers, and essayists of various ethnic backgrounds; "Horizons," an award-winning weekly half-hour documentary series "exploring the diversity of American culture"; and "National Native News," daily five-minute newscasts devoted exclusively to Native American issues.*

Pacifica Radio Archive: *PO Box 8092, Universal City, CA 91608; 800/735-0230. More than forty years ago, Pacifica Radio's KPFA-FM, in Berkeley, CA, pioneered "listener-sponsored radio." Now Pacifica also has stations in New York, Washington, Houston, and Los Angeles, and is a leading force in the nationwide legion of "community radio" stations. For many years they have archived the best of the thousands of programs produced by Pacifica and other community stations, made them available for broadcast by other stations, and in recent years have also sold them on cassette to listeners. As one might expect from Pacifica and left-leaning community stations, the twenty thousand-program archive is particularly strong in politics, ecology, religion, minority and women's issues, and the arts. Ask for their introductory catalog.*

American Public Radio: *100 N. 6th Street, Suite 900A, Minneapolis, MN 55403; 612/338-5000. The "other" public radio network. Write them and ask for a list of member stations and programs.*

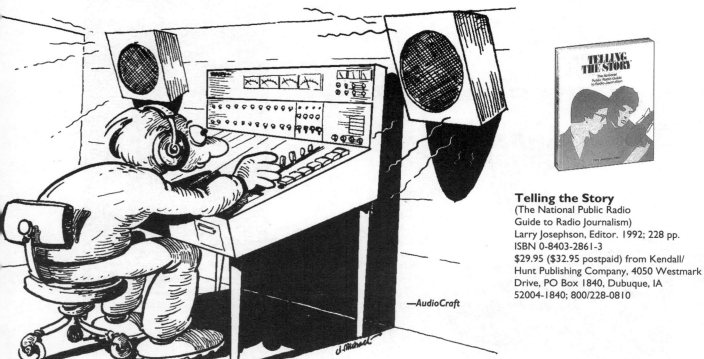

—*AudioCraft*

Telling the Story
(The National Public Radio Guide to Radio Journalism)
Larry Josephson, Editor. 1992; 228 pp.
ISBN 0-8403-2861-3
$29.95 ($32.95 postpaid) from Kendall/Hunt Publishing Company, 4050 Westmark Drive, PO Box 1840, Dubuque, IA 52004-1840; 800/228-0810

WORLD BAND

Coal Miner listening to the radio, 1938.
—from *The Radio Papers*, MHO & MHO Works

Shortwave radio broadcasting, now known as "World Band Radio," is alive and crackling away, even in the digital 90s.

No alternative yet proposed (satellite radio, personal wireless computer gizmo) offers the same combination of a cheap, portable receiver and program content that crosses borders unfiltered by any government or corporate gatekeeper.

Perhaps what you can hear is limited by who can afford a transmitter. But for the students of Tiananmen Square, desperate for independent news, what they heard crowding around their shortwave portables was heady stuff.

The same with my pal Dave McHugh, a *Detroit Free Press* reporter, when he went on vacation to Russia in the summer of '91 — and stumbled into the coup attempt against Gorbachev. I had talked him into buying a nice shortwave portable for language practice a few years earlier; now he found himself edgily pulling

out that radio at the top of the hour for the BBC World Service bulletin — all the local stations were weirdly oblique about events. ("The Beeb" actually had scooped all the other news organizations on the story. Their own radio monitoring service had picked up the coup leaders' dawn broadcast. And while Gorbachev was under house arrest, *he* found out what was going on by listening to the BBC and other shortwave services.) After the dust settled, Dave was rather emphatic about the value of a good shortwave set: "I don't leave home without it."

Volumes have been written about which shortwave radio to buy. The new "digital" models (i.e., the frequency is shown on a digital display) are vastly more convenient than older types with big "sliderule" tuning scales. For example, most stations broadcast on two or three or more frequencies simultaneously; with a modern set you can jump directly between them to see which one sounds the clearest, without a

lot of knob-twiddling. This type starts at about $150, and unless money is very short, it's probably worth it. All the brands of radio where you punch in the frequency with a calculator-style keypad are fine — just avoid the newer crop of radios with preset buttons 1-5 and no other keypad. But not even the fanciest radio turns crackly low-fi shortwave signals into CD-quality sound. —Ross W. Orr

Sony ICF-SW100 Receiver

When Sony released the SW1-S receiver in 1987, shortwave aficionados and travelers raved about the first truly usable receiver in a box no larger than a pack of cigarettes. Sony has done it again. The brand new ICF-SW100 receiver retains the best features of the older unit and adds refinements such as synchronous detection and SSB. The ICF-SW100's clamshell design allows its miniature control keyboard to lie flat on any surface while its hinged top displays a multifunction LCD screen. The top also houses a built-in speaker. Sound is tinny but acceptable; the earphones deliver very good audio, even amazingly good FM stereo.

The screen can display station frequency (five-digit), station identification (six-character), current time, and city identification for 24 worldwide locations. Frequency range is AM 150kHz-29,999kHz; FM stereo 76-108MHz. Tuning is possible in various increments: 100 Hz, (for SSB), 1 kHz and 5 kHz.

Tuning can be achieved by keying in the numeric station frequency, by selecting the most usable programmed frequency from a station page, or by scanning from a starting frequency or waveband.

Most popular frequencies for BBC and VOA are already programmed in. A synchronous detection circuit provides decent separation between stations operating on adjacent frequencies. And, most unusual in a set this size, the SSB mode will let you eavesdrop on ham radio and other utilities. Two AA batteries should power the set for fifteen to twenty hours. A universal power supply is also provided. —Philippe Devaux

Sony ICF-SW100 Receiver: Average price in Europe: about $350; Expected price in US: about $300-$320. For dealer nearest you call 800/222-7669.

World Band Listening

Equipment has all the sex appeal, but if you want to hear a lot of stations, you have to know where to tune, and when — not a trivial task with some eight hundred possible frequencies and dozens of broadcast languages. Stations change frequencies hourly and seasonally to get the strongest "skip" off the ionized upper atmosphere. (Higher frequencies work better in daylight and lower ones in darkness.) So to find that English program from Sweden, it's no good tuning around blindly. You need information.

Passport to World Band Radio: Lawrence Magne, Editor. 1993; 432 pp. ISBN 0-914941-30-5. $17.95 ($19.95 postpaid) from International Broadcasting Services, Ltd., PO Box 300, 285 Cherry Lane, Penns Park, PA 18943; phone 215/794-8252, fax 215/794-3396. This volume comes out every October. In a breezy style, it emphasizes orientation of the newcomer to shortwave listening. Extensive equipment reviews, including thumbnail reviews of most current receivers. Main-schedule listening is by frequency, so this is the book to use to answer that eternal question, "what

the hell is this station?" Supplemental schedules are listed by country, English programs by hour. Gets progressively more out of date in the months following publication.

•

Kuwait — Arabic

Radio Kuwait
9750, 9840, 11990, 15345, 15495, 15505, 21675 kHz

Lebanon — Arabic

King of Hope
6280 kHz

Voice of Lebanon
6550 kHZ

Libya — Arabic

Radio Jamahiriya
15235, 15415, 15435 kHz

Lithuania — Lithuanian

Lithuanian Radio
9710 kHz

Radio Vilnius
7150, 9710, 12040 kHz

—*Passport to World Band Radio*

World Radio TV Handbook: Andrew G. Sennitt, Editor. Billboard Books, 1993; 596 pp. ISBN 0-8230-5925-1. $19.95 ($21.95 postpaid) from Watson-Guptill Publications, 1695 Oak Street, Lakewood, NJ 08701; 908/363-4511. This volume comes out every January. A denser reference book, this covers much of the world's local radio and TV broadcasting, too. Reviews of new equipment (they also publish a separate WRTH Equipment Buyers Guide), and some semi-scholarly features. The main listing is by country — so this is the easier book for finding out "when can I hear Swiss Radio in Italian?" Grows dated just as quickly as Passport, but because the publication dates of the two books are staggered, you can stay fairly current by buying each book shortly after it comes out. —Ross Orr

eMAIL

To: The Reader
From: Cliff Figallo
Subject: Getting Started

Tens of millions of people now use computer-mediated telecommunications as routine parts of their professional and private lives. They correspond, find and distribute information, work collaboratively, and engage in social activities from home, office or more remote locations. Today's ballooning population of computer telecom users is still the vanguard of what may someday be a worldwide information distribution and communications network, as globally accessible to as many people as the telephone is now — or more so.

SEND

The Online User's Encyclopedia • Modem USA

The *Encyclopedia* blows away the fog surrounding telecommunications, subject by subject: modems, computer security, civic and community networking, global networks, the Internet, using bulletin boards, electronic mail, finding people, mailing lists, file transfer, online libraries, USENET, Talk, IRC, MUDs, Z39.50, WAIS, Worldwide Web, Gopher, TCO/IP, connecting a BBS to the Internet, UUCP, BITNET, FidoNet, Point software, PCBoard networks, message readers, saving money on your phone bill, file transfers, file conversion, compression primer, K12Net, electronic home-control, and memories and visions of the future from pioneers of the network world.

The strongest chapters reflect the author's experience setting up BBSs and interconnecting disparate systems, and his familiarity with all the software developments in the world of the Internet and dial-up BBSs. —Steve Cisler

Once your system is assembled and working, you're ready to tap into the ocean of resources available via modems and phone lines. These include the major commercial online systems — CompuServe, America Online, Prodigy, Genie — but are far from limited to them. Many smaller systems can be used for free or at low cost, and address almost every subject imaginable; new ones appear constantly. And then there's the Internet (see pp. 264–268).

The second edition of Modem USA *categorizes its recommended systems according to the recommendations of its first edition's readers. Listings under each category are then ordered by location, giving most listings a short and helpful description. —CF*

•
Community computing systems differ from traditional bulletin boards in several ways. They are typically designed around the metaphor of a city, rather than the con-

Modems Made Easy • Telecommunications

Both books do a good job of familiarizing you with modems, telecommunications software, the process of logging in and using online systems, and the selection of modems, software and systems. Modems Made Easy *favors software and instructions aimed at the IBM PC/clone user;* Telecommunications *is specific to the Mac. Both take you to a higher level of technical proficiency than most regular online users currently possess. The configuration possibilities for communicating with the diverse systems and modems on the Net can be quite complex. Likewise, modern telecommunications software can be so packed with features that the choices can be daunting. These books will help. —CF*

•
When you press the *Enter* key to send the dialing command and phone number to your modem, the modem will take the phone line off-hook (just as you take the phone off the hook when you lift the handset), wait for a dial tone, dial the phone number, and wait for another modem to answer. The amount of time the modem waits for an answer is determined by the modem's S7 status register (see Chapter 6). You will hear the following through the

ventional BBS division into message and file areas. This allows areas of the system to be devoted to local governments, K12 programs, small businesses, community activities, and entertainment. Community systems also offer access to such resources as databases or online libraries, and support public access terminals — in public libraries, cafes, schools, even post offices. The diversity of uses and access points encourages public participation.

US Environmental Protection Agency
Office of Solid Waste & Emergency Response
Technology Innovation Office
The CleanUp Information BBS
Silver Spring, MD
301 589 83 66 (1200-9600 bos)

The "CLU-IN" BBS is for hazardous waste professionals and others to use for finding current events information about innovative technologies, consulting with one another online, and accessing databases.
—*Modem USA*

The Online User's Encyclopedia
Bernard Aboba. 1993; 832 pp.
ISBN 0-201-62214-9
$34.95 ($39.95 postpaid). Addison-Wesley Publishing Co./Order Dept., 1 Jacob Way, Reading, MA 01867; 800/447-2226

Modem USA
Lynne Motley. 1994; 401 pp.
ISBN 0-9631233-6-X
$24.95 ($28.95 postpaid). Allium Press, PO Box 5752-55, Takoma Park, MD 20913-5752

modem's speaker (if you turned the speaker on with the AT Mq command):

• A click as the modem takes the line off-hook.

• A dial tone, just like the one you hear when you lift the handset of a telephone.

• Very rapid tones (as from a touch-tone) phone or pulse/rotary clicks as the number is dialed.

• One or more rings as the call goes through and the modem waits for something to answer.

• Another click as the modem on the other end answers.

• High-pitched squeals as the two modems begin their handshaking routine, adjusting to each other's speeds and the line conditions, establishing communication protocols, and so on. —*Modems Made Easy*

Modems Made Easy
David Hakala. 1993; 324 pp.
ISBN 0-07-881962-8
$16.95 ($20.95 postpaid). McGraw-Hill Publishing Co., 13311 Monterey Avenue, Blue Ridge Summit, PA 17214; 800/722-4726

Telecommunications
Stephen Taylor. MIS Press, 1992; 375 pp. ISBN 1-55828-209-2
$19.95 ($22.95 postpaid). Henry Holt and Co., PO Box 30135, Salt Lake City, UT 84130; 800/488-5233

Baud rate:	300 Baud
	450 Baud
	1,200 Baud
	2,400 Baud
Parity:	4,800 Baud
	9,600 Baud
Databits:	19,200 Baud
	38,400 Baud
Stopbits:	57,600 Baud
Duplex:	FULL

•
The illustration above shows the pulled-down menu from White Knight's baud rate (data rate) setting. No, you won't find very many 57,600 modems in computer stores, but you will find 14,400 modems that promise effective speeds of 57,600 when they're able to perform 4:1 compression on the data (4 X 14,400 = 57,600).
—*Telecommunications*

Basic Telecom Toolkit

The telephone jack is the universally accessible entry point to public electronic networks. To make this connection, you will need a personal computer, telecommunications software, and a modem.

Good used computers can be bought cheap, and will serve for 95 percent of what you'll find of use on the Net. In the Macintosh world, the Classic is powerful and modern enough to meet your basic needs. In the IBM PC/clone (DOS/Windows) world, a 386-generation computer will give you all the capabilities you need. Get at least 40 megabytes of hard disk.

Modems translate between digital (the computer) and analog (the telephone). Modems allow you to dial out and communicate with commercial online systems and BBSs; they also al-

low others (or you) to dial in computer from other locations. Through modems at either end, you can remotely control and use one computer from another computer; this can be a handy way to telecommute to the office.

All communications software programs allow you to specify how you want them to work and with whom you want to connect. Basic programs are available for free or as inexpensive "shareware" through the networks themselves. Telecom software is computer-specific: Macintosh software will not run on DOS/Windows computers, and vice versa. —CF

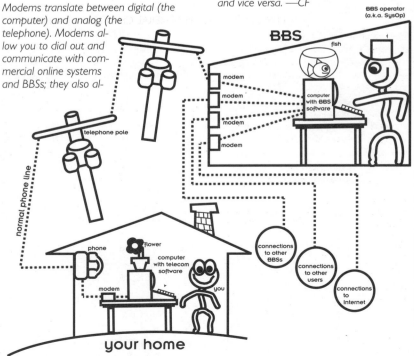

You need a computer (an inexpensive one will do), a modem, a telephone line, telecommunications software, and the telephone number of a BBS or computer network service. Then you will need an "account," free or paid, on the service.

eMAIL

To: The Reader
From: Cliff Figallo
Subject: BBS stuff

In their simplest form, computer bulletin-board systems serve the same function as a corkboard — people "post" messages for others to read. Only, instead of cork, the messages appear on the computer screens of those who log into the systems.

The first BBS was created in 1978 so owners of early, incompatible personal computers could share information through a common dial-up host computer. As of summer, 1993, *Boardwatch* magazine estimated that there were "over 53,000 dialup systems operating in North America — the vast majority run by individuals from their homes or small offices." Over thirteen-and-a-half million people were using BBSs; ten thousand a day were making their first call to one of those systems.

BBSs are the true grass roots of the electronically networked world. A BBS can serve many thousands of users (one claims over 50,000 subscribers), providing access to huge libraries of information and software, electronic mail facilities, and — increasingly — gateways to more extensive networks. Because it only requires one personal computer, one modem, one software program, and one phone line to set up, the BBS is the cheapest way to become an online information center, organizer, or entrepreneur.

Many BBSs serve special interest groups — you can join discussions of programming languages, environmental regulations, computer games, lifestyle choices, specific pets, energy statistics, and thousands of other topics. Activists from the entire political spectrum, hobbyists, and professional marketers are among the thousands of BBS sysops (system operators) who run their own independent systems.

Whatever your interests, you are likely to find helpful information and helpful allies out there. But if not, creating your own special-interest forum is an attainable goal. In their simplest form, BBSs can serve local geographical communities, requiring no long-distance toll calls or other surcharged access.

User interfaces (what the caller sees on his or her screen) range from pure text (which requires you to know a list of commands) to full-color screens controlled by a "point-and-click" menu and a mouse.

BBSs rely on the most basic technologies of phone lines, computers and modems. They do not require enhanced phone services or depend on Internet registration or regulations or special cable connections. A BBS can be set up anywhere there is phone service; via relay systems, it can be networked and accessed around the world. Regardless of where the "information highway" leads, BBSs seem to have a solid future.

SEND

Boardwatch

Jack Rickard's magazine is the one-stop shopping place for anyone interested in running their own BBS or searching for the right BBS to fit their interests. Rickard's blunt, straight-ahead style is pure American boot-strap-entrepreneurial, and he doesn't try to avoid stepping on toes. He has recruited good writers; *Boardwatch* does a creditable job of staying up to date with a fast-evolving field, offering equipment/software reviews and discussions of new technology, the Internet, access to government, Macintosh BBSs (a minority group in BBS-land), graphic-image technology, and online legal issues.

Boardwatch also features a comprehensive list of BBSs, with connection information, and the latest modem discounts available to BBS system owners (these prices are often below 50 percent of retail). —CF

Boardwatch
Jack Rickard, Editor.
$36/year (12 issues). 8500 W. Bowles Ave., Suite 210, Littleton, CO 80123; 800/933-6038

Ideas link people together across barriers of time and space

BBS Networks

Software can work in conjunction with scheduled phone connections to relay information and electronic mail between BBSs. The resulting networks are capable of connecting geographically remote users. Higher and higher modem speeds allow information to leap across these networks of BBSs almost as if the users were connected in "real time."

FidoNet, a public network of BBSs, connects thirty-plus countries around the world. It primarily performs message-handling for private "Netmail"

and for the open "party-line" messages called "EchoMail." —CF

Free Electronic Networks

You don't have to join the Internet, or pay CompuServe or America OnLine, to get into computer networking. Hundreds of thousands of people participate via free BBSs (such as many Fido and QWK BBSs) that are networked with the fee-based systems. This book tells you how to use these systems, and includes an extensive directory of free BBSs, indexed both by topic and by geographical region. —CF

•

How to Echo
You type 3 for that GENERAL CHATTER area. You wonder what those asterisks mean.

The messages in General Chatter number from 6051 to 8325. Tell the clerk which number you'd like to read from:

Does this mean there are over 2000 messages there for the reading? Yes, it does. Many newcomers will find it hard to overcome the temptation to take them all. There may not be enough time available for the megabytes of messages you'll want to read at first. Resist the temptation to pig out on information at this point. This is when it's strongest.

Type in 8225, which tells the mail door to send you a modest 100 messages from GENERAL CHATTER.

Tell the clerk if you'd like to read (A)ll mail in GENERAL CHATTER or just mail addressed to you (P)ersonally:

Type A for all. There may be a time when you want to limit the mail to those postings that are addressed with your name in the TO: field, but not just now.

Free Electronic Networks
William Shefski. 1993; ISBN 1-55958-415-7
$19.95 ($22.95 postpaid). Prima Publishing & Communications, PO Box 1260, Rocklin, CA 95677; 916/324-5718

The BBS Construction Kit

The title says it all. If you want to start your own BBS on a PC-clone machine with minimal pain, the *Kit* has all the ingredients. And the price can make the experience worth it, even if you later decide you'd rather run under a different BBS program. GAP BBS software is included; installation will familiarize you with the fundamentals of BBS setup and operation.

The book is clearly written, with sections on pre-BBS decisionmaking, choosing hardware and modems, legal issues facing the sysop, giving your BBS its "look," and the many operational responsibilities you'll face as sysop. —CF

•

With RIP graphics, you can create a mouse-driven interface for your BBS that looks and operates something like a Windows application. The quality of graphics is obviously much higher, too, giving your BBS a slicker, more professional look. There are several RIP drawing packages available.

RIP is very much like ANSI except that it is far more complex and powerful. It relies on a specific format for its code that is based on standard IBM characters. Unlike ANSI, RIP codes can be sent over 7-bit communication links. See the end of this chapter for notes on RIP codes and programming.

The BBS Construction Kit
David Wolfe. 1994; 373 pp.
ISBN 0-471-00797-8
$27.95 postpaid. John Wiley & Sons, Inc., 1 Wiley Dr., Somerset, NJ 08873; 800/225-5945

ETTING ONLINE IS ABOUT MAKING CONNECTIONS, both electronically and socially. Because you can reach a huge population regardless of geography or time, you are sure to have access to people with common interests. Electronic networks can help you find others with similar interests, taste, skills and background, or who have information you are seeking. Therein are the makings of community.

The human tropism toward community is strong and very adaptable, tending to use the tools available, as other organisms adapt to their particular environments. But humans are toolmakers, and new and improved means of communicating and delivering information appear constantly on the nets.

Commercial and noncommercial online systems, including the Internet-based group communications tools, all have their particular strengths and weaknesses when it comes to supporting community building and maintenance. Smaller and less commercialized systems have led the way in establishing community as a reason for joining online systems and in creating new software and applications to satisfy community-based needs.

All of the resources we recommend here include pointers to online systems that support community. They all contain reviews and contact information for systems from the smallest BBS to the largest commercial online behemoth. You are likely to find something that fits your definition of community on many of them. —Cliff Figallo

The Virtual Community

Howard Rheingold immersed himself in The WELL for years and explored other online hangouts. He has written a participant's-eye view of how people use networks as social and collaborative living spaces. His tour of cyberspace includes historical background, visits with key creators and participants in Japan and England, descriptions of social innovations taking place through networked "multi-user simulated environments," thorough coverage of online activism, and an overview of the challenges that lie before us in lawmaking and regulation of the information matrix. It's a must-read book for anyone interested in the societal implications of widespread network use. —CF

The Virtual Community
Howard Rheingold. 1993; 288 pp.
ISBN 0-201-60870-7
$22.95 postpaid. Addison-Wesley Publishing Co./Order Dept., 1 Jacob Way, Reading, MA 01867; 800/447-2226

●

Parents, libertarians, Deadheads, radio producers, writers, homeowners, and sports fans all have particular places to hang out in the WELL. But in the News conference, the WELL's town square, there is a deliberately general topic, Experts on the WELL, that continues to be a paradigm of one of the ways people can spin banter into an unstructured repository of valuable unclassifiable expertise.

The premise of Experts on the WELL is simple. If you have a problem or a question concerning any topic, from plumbing to astrophysics, you pose it. Then you wait seven minutes or a week. Sometimes nothing happens, and sometimes you get exactly what you want. In many instances, the answer already exists elsewhere in the WELL, and the topic serves as a kind of community librarian service that points the query toward the right part of the WELL's collection of information. And in some instances, the information requested exists in someone's head, and that person takes the time to type it.

People in virtual communities use words on screens to exchange pleasantries and argue, engage in intellectual discourse, conduct commerce, exchange knowledge, share emotional support, make plans, brainstorm, gossip, feud, fall in love, find friends and lose them, play games, flirt, create a little high art and a lot of idle talk. People in virtual communities do just about everything people do in real life, but we leave our bodies behind. You can't kiss anybody and nobody can punch you in the nose, but a lot can happen within those boundaries. To the millions who have been drawn into it, the richness and vitality of computer-linked cultures is attractive, even addictive.

There is no such thing as a single, monolithic, online subculture; it's more like an ecosystem of subcultures, some frivolous, others serious. The cutting edge of scientific discourse is migrating to virtual communities, where you can read the electronic pre-pre-printed reports of molecular biologists and cognitive scientists. At the same time, activists and educational reformers are using the same medium as a political tool. You can use virtual communities to find a date, sell a lawnmower, publish a novel, conduct a meeting.

Online Resources

WHERE TO FIND ONLINE COMMUNITY

The WELL

Central to the WELL's early growth, deliberate community-building remains an important part of its development. Like an intellectual flea market, ideas and opinions are the currency of exchange on the WELL, and the process and medium through which the exchange takes place are constantly under examination by the citizens there. The WELL has full Internet connectivity. Voice: 415/332-4335; 2400 bps: 415/332-6106; 9600bps (or greater): 415/332-8410; telnet: well.com. $15/month, $2/hour.

ECHO

Taking the regional-community cue from the WELL, Stacy Horn started ECHO (East Coast HangOut) to build a New York City-flavored virtual community. ECHO has grown slowly but steadily and is now connected to the Internet. Charge for access to the women's conferences is discounted. Compared to almost every other online system, ECHO has the largest proportion of female subscribers (40 percent) Voice: 212/255-3839; telnet: echonyc.com. $19.50/month (first month free), $1/hour after first 30 hours.

IGC Networks

The Institute for Global Communications supports PeaceNet, EcoNet, ConflictNet and LaborNet. The IGC Networks make up the world's only computer communications system dedicated solely to environmental preservation, peace, and human rights. IGC also supports a program through the Association for Progressive Communications that works to bring network connectivity to poor and technologically disadvantaged parts of the world and to activist organizations worldwide. Voice: 415/442-0220; internet: support@igc.org. $15 sign-up fee, $10/month, $5/hour off-peak and $7/hour peak.

Women's Wire

The first online system to focus primarily on women's issues and information came into being this year. Since women are significantly underrepresented in the online world (estimates range from 10 percent to 16 percent of total accounts), Women's Wire aims to attract and train more female network users by bringing women's organizations and publications to its system and maintaining a database of information on women's health, history, employment, and politics. Women's Wire offers a graphical user interface called First Class for Macintosh or PC Windows users. Voice: 415/615-8989; 1200 and up bps: 415/474-7239. $15/month, $2.50-$7.50/hour after first 2 hours.

Usenet

Usenet is the largest many-to-many conversation in the world. Discussions of more than 6000 different topics circulate in over 80 different countries. The population of users of Usenet as a whole numbers in the millions, and some newsgroups are read by tens of thousands of people every day. This anarchic and wildly varied collection of serious, frivolous, useful, absurd, heated, humorous, enlightening, and disgusting conversations is too vast to be a community, but there are hundreds of communities to be found in different newsgroups. Most people access Usenet via the Internet, but Usenet newsgroups are also carried by FidoNet and other BBS networks.

Large Commercial Systems

Community exists in the largest and busiest of cities, and so it is in the electronic world. CompuServe (800/848-8990) and Prodigy (800/776-3449) both claim to have over one million subscribers. America OnLine (800/827-6364) is gaining on them and, while Delphi (800/695-4005) and GEnie (800/638-8369) are lagging, their populations are still in six digits.

Spend some time just exploring and observing. Use keyword searching tools to find your areas of interest. Use email to contact people you'd like to get to know better based upon what you've seen of them online. Pay attention to established customs and traditions. Gradually find your way to a group and an area where you can join in discussion of topics that fit your interest. —CF

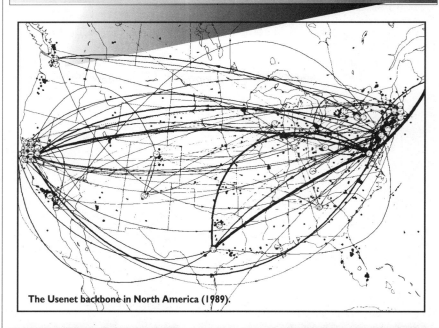

The Usenet backbone in North America (1989).

OTHER GREAT BOOKS ABOUT LARGE ONLINE SYSTEMS

How to Connect: Chris Shipley. 1993, Ziff-Davis Press. Online culture, historical information, computer viruses, and telecom basics.

Modems for Dummies: Tina Rathbone. 1993, IDG Books. Good chapters on Prodigy, CompuServe, America OnLine and GEnie.

Dvorak's Guide to PC Telecommunications: John Dvorak & Nick Anis. 1993, Osborne McGraw-Hill. Includes a PC-compatible disk with the Telix telecom program and other software; discount coupons for online subscriptions, software and modems.

THE INTERNET *IS* THE BEST-KNOWN AND MOST CAPABLE part of the worldwide mesh of computer networks. It is not BITNET, FidoNet, or UUCP. BITNET (Because It's Time NETwork) is a network built by universities in the early 1980s because they couldn't access the defense- and computer science-motivated ARPANET. Because it's no longer that time, BITNET-linked universities are joining the Internet, and BITNET is the only component of the Net that is shrinking.

UUCP and FidoNet are examples of highly decentralized networks that operate over regular telephone lines. They're store-and-forward networks, meaning that electronic mail and other traffic is stored on participating computers for transfer every hour (UUCP) or evening (FidoNet). These networks don't support real-time interactivity, but because the hardware is cheap (personal computers, small UNIX workstations), the medium is plain old telephone service, and system administration is easy, UUCP and FidoNet are important paths for getting connectivity into rural or developing areas.

Since these store-and-forward networks are part of the Net, electronic mail and global discussions (Usenet, a.k.a. network news) can float between them, the Internet, and national online systems like CompuServe, America OnLine, Prodigy, Delphi, GEnie, and MCIMail. Of these commercial services, only Delphi is fully on the Internet. America OnLine began to offer limited Internet services in early 1994, and CompuServe has committed to providing them by the end of '94.

"On the Internet" is one of the most mis-used phrases you'll come across when shopping for online access. If you're considering a service that's notably cheaper than others, make certain that it offers more than just email and Usenet. To be truly on the Internet, a computer has to speak a language, or set of protocols, called TCP/IP (Transmission Control Protocol/Internet Protocol). TCP/IP supports the kind of real-time connections that allow you sit at a computer in Texas, and browse a library catalog in Tasmania, rummage through directories of documents, images, and sound snippets in Finland, access menus of kindergarten-through-twelfth-grade resources in upstate New York, look up someone's email address in Europe, or practice your Spanish with people from Mexico, Venezuela, Spain, Israel, and Australia.

On the following pages we survey the tools you'll need to perform these tasks. The Internet doesn't reach everywhere. Even if it does go to your region, it may only support government, military, commercial, or educational organizations. But as long as you can get an account on a system that's in the Net — America OnLine in a rural area, a FidoNet bulletin-board system in the former Soviet Union — you'll have access to global electronic mail. Many of the Internet services described here are available in a limited way through electronic mail. You don't have to be on the Internet to participate in its riches.

Why online? Mark McCahill, leader of the University of Minnesota's Internet gopher team, gave a simple description of the motivation behind enhancements to the gopher suite: "Why are we doing this? Because it's *cool*." If you're already online, you probably recognize that much of what people are making available online, and much of why you enjoy being online, can thus be summed up. If you're not online, this rationale might not satisfy you.

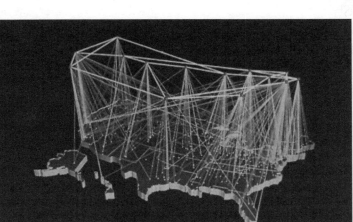

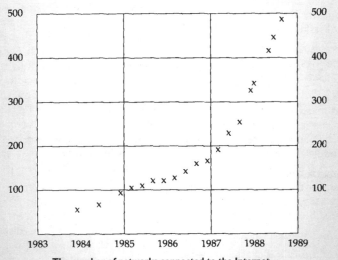

The Internet backbone in North America (1994) — in a typical month, US traffic volume can reach 100 billion bytes.

The number of networks connected to the Internet.

Online tools can be divided into two classes: those that support communication between people and those that support access to information. Electronic mail is, deceptively, the simplest. At its most basic, email allows one person to send a message to another. But, in the Net, this simple act transcends barriers of time, geography, bureaucracy, and economics. More sophisticated tools — mailing lists, centralized conferencing systems (The WELL, PeaceNet/EcoNet, Echo), decentralized conferencing systems (Usenet), and Internet Relay Chat — let many people participate in global discussions on thousands of subjects. Resource discovery tools allow you to connect to libraries, databases, and other repositories of information on an equally vast variety of topics. In practice, the tools complement each other, with communication tools spreading the word on available resources, and resources providing authorship information so that like-minded people can meet, collaborate, and develop trust and community.

What's ahead? Well, there's that Information Superhighway. Many of its promised services — 500 channels to the home plus interactive shopping — run counter to the culture and capacity of today's Internet. While the Internet is the only existing technological infrastructure that has any resemblance to the promised Infobahn, it's not at all clear that the Datapike will spring from an Internet foundation.

The privatization and commercialization of the Internet is already fairly far along, and most Internauts don't think that it's necessarily a bad thing. With the government getting out of the networking business, advances in capability, standards, and reliability can be expected to be driven more by market forces than academic grantsmanship. The explosive growth in businesses establishing presences in the Net is also not a bad thing. Consumers are more than happy to have access to customer service and sales representatives, product information and pictures, software upgrades, and the like. They just don't want it flooding, unsolicited, into their emailboxes. The least discussed, but most important aspect of what's ahead is quality assurance. The democratic nature of the Net, where eminent scientists and isolated crackpots can publish side by side, leads to wide variations in the quality of available information. Thankfully, most online communities are fairly self-policing. But information repositories continue to start strong, only to fade from a lack of organizational support or a change of jobs for a key person. Authenticating that a resource is the definitive, unedited version is next to impossible. And while some communities have taken to the Net and flourished — biologists, computer scientists, meteorologists, political activists — others are only now beginning to share their stories.

The battle for access is being won in North America, and with care, will extend globally. Working to guarantee that people find life-enhancing information once they're online is the next phase in the evolution of the Net. —Eric Theise

THE FOLLOWING MAY BE the shortest, most intense survey of network services and how-to guide in print. The `different typeface` indicates commands (etc.) that you would type in.

UNIFORM RESOURCE LOCATORS

The Internet's success comes largely from the do-it-yourself ethic embraced by its users. Interesting resources all over the world are accessible using the tools discussed here. The emerging scheme for cataloging Internet resources, Uniform Resource Locators, is designed to provide the minimum information needed to access a resource. They're readable by machines and humans, though machines have an easier time of it. If you learn to read URLs, you can find any Internet resource you need.

A URL has three parts: the tool used to access the resource, a separator, and the path to the resource. If you're using Mosaic, Cello, lynx, or another browser, you can simply key in the URL to read or obtain the file or program you seek.

ELECTRONIC MAIL AND MAILING LISTS

Electronic mail is the lifeblood of the global networks. Any email package should allow you to send a new message, respond to or forward a received message, send a copy to someone else, append the text of your .signature file, and organize your mail into separate files depending on the sender or other criterion. If you're using a terminal dial-up account on a UNIX computer, you'll have access to the `mail` program. Use this as a last resort! Check to see if the `pine` or `elm` packages — both distributed for free — are available on your system. These give you menu access to your messages, and pine comes bundled with a simple, full-screen editor called `pico`. If these aren't already on your system, ask your system administrator to pick them up from these URLs and install them:

`ftp://ftp.cac.washington.edu/pine`

`ftp://ftp.uu.net/networking/mail/elm`

If you're using SLIP/PPP or a dedicated connection, or if your dial-up provider runs a POP (post-office protocol) server, you'll be able to use a package like Eudora or POPmail. These let you manage your messages on your desktop, giving you access to familiar tools and reducing your connect time.

You'll want to know how to find someone's email address. Call them and ask. If you must search, and you're on the Internet, the easiest way is to use gopher (see below) to find out if their organization runs a phone-book server. You can also use email to query a database of people

For good books about how to use the Internet, see p. 267.

who've contributed to Usenet discussions. To find me:

`mail-server@rtfm.mit.edu`

with the message:

`send Usenet-addresses/ Theise`

Tools like netfind and `finger` are other options.

You'll also want to know about the thousands of subject-oriented mailing lists on the Net. They come in many flavors: wide-open, moderated, or limited to one-way missives from the list's owner. These are almost always free. There are two common ways to subscribe; the first involves sending an email message to an automatic list manager (these will have `listserv`, `majordomo`, `listproc`, or `almanac` in the address. To join the new-lists list, a distribution list announcing new mailing lists, I'd send email to:

`listserv@vm1.nodak.edu`

with the message

`subscribe new-lists Eric Theise`

The list manager sends me a confirmation, a mission statement, and instructions about how to unsubscribe from the list. Save these!

If I want to send a message to the hundreds or thousands of other subscribers, say, an inquiry about an unusual subject, I'd send it to:

`new-lists@vm1.nodak.edu`

Note that the list's address and the list manager's address are on the same computer in North Dakota. Subscribe/unsubscribe instructions go to:

`listserv@vm1.nodak.edu`

communications to:

`new-lists@vm1.nodak.edu`

Other lists are managed by humans, not software. For example, to join the com-priv list, dedicated to discussing the commercialization and privatization of the Internet, I'd send email to:

`com-priv-request@psi.com`

I'd include the line:

`subscribe com-priv Eric Theise`

at the top, on the off-chance that it's being read by an automatic list manager, but I'd also include a pleasant request to be added to the list. Communications go to:

`com-priv@psi.com`

instructions to:

`com-priv-request@psi.com`

In addition to the new-lists list, there are two compendia of mailing lists. The oldest is a gargantuan file maintained sporadically by SRI. It's available as:

`ftp://crvax.sri.com/netinfo/interest-groups`

Stephanie da Silva posts a different compendium to Usenet every two weeks.

USENET NEWSGROUPS

Usenet is a system for carrying discussions. Each of its thousands of subject-oriented newsgroups carries a variety of current discussions, called threads. Newsgroup names get more specific from left to right, e.g., `comp.os.ms-windows.apps.financial`. Newsgroups in the `comp`, `news`, `misc`, `rec`, `soc`, `sci`, and `talk` hierarchies are distributed globally, and are created only after a formal discussion and vote by Usenet participants. Your provider may offer the Clarinet `clari` groups, a fee-based service that carries newswires. You may see regional newsgroups, such as `ba` (Bay Area) or `chi` (Chicago). And then there are the `alt` groups. Their creation is the least formal — at best, requiring little discussion; at worst, requiring a few keystrokes from an overprivileged undergraduate — and their distribution is spottier. Every computer that participates in Usenet keeps one copy of every current message, or article, and deletes (or "expires") the article after a period of time specified by the system administrator — typically between three days and two weeks.

You'll use a newsreader to participate in Usenet. Newsreaders let you read articles, start your own threads, and respond to existing discussions publicly, via a follow-up post, or privately, via email to the article's author. You can save articles of interest, and use built-in tools to convert gibberish into executable programs (e.g., `comp.binaries.amiga`) or viewable images (e.g., `alt.binaries.pictures.fuzzy.animals`). Use the newsreader named `tin` if it's available through your dial-up account. `nn` is acceptable, `rn` isn't. If you're using SLIP/PPP or a dedicated line, you might click on icons marked Nuntius or Newswatcher (Macintosh) or Trumpet Newsreader (Windows).

Usenet patriarch Gene Spafford described the system as being "like a herd of performing elephants with diarrhea — massive, difficult to redirect, awe-inspiring, entertaining, and a source of mind-boggling amounts of excrement when you least expect it." Accurate. But Usenet features some of the wittiest and most knowledgeable people on the planet. Many newsgroups publish their own Frequently Asked Questions (FAQs), covering the group as well as its topic; hundreds of FAQs can be found in news.answers, on subjects such as angst, body art, car parts, dog breeds, genetic algorithms, Macintosh screensavers, urban legends, or woodworking. FAQs on using the networks, including da

Silva's mailing list compendia, can be found in:

`news.announce.newusers`

TALK, IRC; MUDs, MUSEs, MOOs, AND MUCKs

All of the communication tools discussed thus far are asynchronous: people make comments, and the comments sit in mailboxes or news spools until others respond. Other tools allow synchronous, or real-time, communication. `talk` is a split-screen application that allows two people on the Internet to type to each other. `irc` (Internet Relay Chat) is a global service, divided into hundreds of subject-oriented channels, that allows dozens of people to converse, one line at a time. Public irc channels are not for the faint of heart, but the ability to create private or secret channels does allow for low-cost, global conference calls. The `/help` command puts you into the irc help facility, but what you really want is Nicholas Pioch's excellent "IRCprimer":

`ftp://cs.bu.edu/pub/unix/irc/docs`

Multi-User Dimensions and Multi-User Simulated Environments are text-based virtual realities. People can and do chat with each other, but they also use simple programming languages to create interactive objects having engaging properties. Some MUDs and MUSEs are oriented toward learning, others are adventure or role-playing games. Scott Goehring maintains "The Totally Unofficial List of Internet Muds":

`ftp://caisr2.caisr.cwru.edu/pub/mud`

TELNET

Sharing of computer resources — powerful CPUs, advanced software — was the original motivation behind the `telnet` command. Today it is used to access global Internet services, including library catalogs, commercial conferencing systems and databases, and hundreds of esoteric experiments.

The most common use of telnet involves only the Internet address. To connect to Registration Services at the Internet Network Information Center (`telnet://rs.internic.net`), a dial-up terminal user would type

`telnet rs.internic.net`

Other Internet services require you to specify a port number, a userid, or a userid and password. For example, the bilingual subway locator (`telnet://metro.jussieu.fr:10000`) runs on the nonstandard port 10000. You'd type:

`telnet metro.jussieu.fr 10000`

If you get stuck while telnetting to another computer, you can close your connection by typing `Ctrl ]`, then quit at the telnet> prompt.

FTP AND ARCHIE

The file transfer protocol — `ftp` — was developed to support the transfer of datafiles from one computer to another. Regular ftp requires that you have accounts and passwords on both systems. But you'll most likely use anonymous ftp. Thousands of Internet computers allow you to login as `anonymous` (or `ftp`), specifying your email address as a password. These computers (file servers) allow software, documents, images, and sound files to be picked up by anyone with access to the Internet.

To use ftp you must be familiar with directory navigation. The `pwd`, `cd`, and `dir` commands allow you to see where you are, change it, and get a listing of what's available. File suffixes clue you in as to whether a file should be transferred in ASCII (`.txt`, `.ps`) or binary (`.Z`, `.zip`, `.sea`, `.sit`) mode; to transfer a non-text file, type `binary` before the `get` or `mget` (multiple get) commands.

If you're lucky enough to be using a Macintosh that's truly on the Internet, you should install Fetch, an elegant point-and-click replacement for ftp.

`ftp://ftp.dartmouth.edu/pub/mac`

If you're not on the Internet, but have email, you can use `ftpmail`. To receive instructions on how to use ftp mail, check with your system administrator about limits on the size of incoming mail, then send the message `help` to:

`ftpmail@decwrl.dec.com`

Not long ago, the only way you'd know that resources were available via anonymous ftp was to read about them on Usenet or mailing lists. Some sites had reputations for carrying certain types of files, but until Alan Emtage, Bill Heelan, and Peter Deutsch turned a hobby into an service, there was no way to determine where a particular file was archived.

`archie`, a nickname derived from "archive," scoots around the Internet building a database from directory listings at thousands of anonymous ftp sites. Using telnet to connect to an archie server and using its `find` command, you can search for the location of a file or directory name if you know part of the name. You'll be given a listing of Internet sites and directory paths to what's found. For example, if I was looking for Pretty Good Privacy encryption tools, I'd telnet:

`archie.rutgers.edu` login `archie`, and `find pgp`.

I'd get a vast listing, a fragment of which says:

`Host ftp.uga.edu (128.192.1.9)`
`Last updated 08:03 13 May 1994`
`Location: /pub/msdos/mir-ror/windows3`
`FILE -r—r—r— 456860 bytes 06:40`

`7 Apr 1994 winpgp10.zip`

I'd quit archie, ftp `ftp.uga.edu`, and login `anonymous` with password `verve@cyberwerks.com` (my email address). I'd charge directories (`cd /pub/msdos/mir-ror/windows3`), switch to binary mode, and get `winpgp10.zip`; the file transfers to my current directory on cyberwerks.com.

If you're not on the Internet, but have email, you can use an email interface to archie. Send the message `help` to:

`archie@archie.rutgers.edu`

WIDE-AREA INFORMATION SERVERS

WAIS is unique among Internet services. It gives you access to hundreds of indexed collections of text files spread across the Internet. Some of these collections are archived discussions from Usenet or mailing lists (alt.gopher, BGRASS-L, and soc.culture.thai-1994). Others are collections of abstracts (impeccable offerings from Australian National University or Indiana University Biology) or documents (e.g., White House Papers), or single, massive texts, such as the Bible, Quran, or CIA World Factbook.

There are several WAIS clients that you can telnet to, logging in as wais; the one at wais.com is the best known. (`telnet://wais@wais.com`) When WAIS starts up, you'll see a list of hundreds of indexed sources, arranged alphabetically. A `?` gives you a screenful of information about how to navigate. Browse to see what's there; if you're interested in a particular source, the `v` command will reveal a description of its contents.

To search, tag the source under your cursor by hitting the space bar. An asterisk will appear to the left of the entry. You can tag as many sources as you like. Type `w`, followed by the keywords you're searching for. When WAIS returns the results of its search, it attaches a score to each item based on the frequency and mix of the words in each document. To deliver the item under the cursor to your screen, hit the space bar again.

Other commands to note are `m`, which emails retrieved documents to any address you specify, and `o`, which lets you tweak WAIS options — especially the variable `maxhits` that, by default, limits the number of retrieved items to 40.

GOPHER AND VERONICA

In the early 1990s, a team at the University of Minnesota was charged with the task of developing an easy interface to networked computers across their campus. The result of their work — `gopher`, named after the school mascot and its go-fer capabilities — shielded users from the complicated business of telnet, ftp, finger, and WAIS. Since clients were easy to use, servers were easy

What will happen to me when I start using this stuff? See p. 290.

to maintain, and the whole menu-based gopher distribution was available via anonymous ftp (`ftp://boombox.micro.umn.edu/pub/gopher`), gopher spread like wildfire across the Internet.

If you're on a UNIX system, you start by typing `gopher`. On a SLIP/PPP or direct-connected Mac, you'd click on TurboGopher. Typically, this puts you at the mother of all gophers. You can explore U of MN resources while you're there, but your Internet adventures begin when you select "Other Gophers and Information Servers." You can investigate thousands of gophers, segregated by continent, around the globe.

Gopher is capable of delivering files to your screen, mailbox, home directory, or printer. It's smart enough to guess whether they should be transferred as ASCII or binary. It'll route you to institutional phone books so you can search for email and snailmail addresses, and it's capable of performing a variety of search functions. And it will do virtually all of these things in response to your cursor and `<return>` keys. Type `?` for help.

If there's a specific gopher you want to connect to — say, the Online Career Center — you'd type:

`gopher garnet.msen.com 9062`

Although it took years for someone to create the archie search tool for ftpspace, it took only a few months for Steve Foster to develop one for gopherspace. `veronica` — Very Easy Rodent-Oriented Net-wide Index to Computerized Archives — harvests every menu from every gopher into a single database that is distributed to sites around the world. Look for menus marked "Search titles in gopherspace using veronica." They'll connect you with a veronica FAQ, a guide to composing queries, and access to veronica servers.

If you're not on the Internet, but have access to email, you can use an email interface to gopher. Send the message `help` to:

`gophermail@calvin.edu`

The gopher/veronica combination is the Internet service you should try first, because it's so easy. You'll continue to use it because of its power, speed, and the low load it puts on the Internet.

THE WORLD-WIDE WEB

The idea of global hypertext has been around for decades. The World-Wide Web is making it happen over the Internet. Thanks to the initiative of Tim Berners-Lee and CERN, a Swiss particle physics lab, WWW traffic on the Internet is growing at an unprecedented rate.

There are several World-Wide Web browsers. The National Center for Supercomputer Applications' Mosaic is far and away the most popular, but there are others. Mosaic (Macintosh, Windows, X Window) and Cello (Windows) require a SLIP/PPP or direct Internet connection. The University of Kansas' lynx browser works with text-only portions of the Web, and is presently the only option for users of dial-up terminals.

`ftp://ftp.ncsa.uiuc.edu/Web`

`ftp://ftp2.cc.ukans.edu/pub/lynx`

WWW documents contain embedded links — URLs — to other resources. Under Mosaic, these appear as blue, underlined text; under lynx, as reverse-video text. Choosing them — a mouse click or press of the `<return>` key — requests whatever's linked: another document, a still or moving image, sound, or any of the Internet services we've covered, from telnet to gopher, located anywhere on the Internet. To open a specific URL using lynx, choose the `G)o` option; under Mosaic or Cello, pull down the `Open URL` menu item.

Before you get too excited about Mosaic, remember that image and sound files can be huge. If you're connecting over a phone line using SLIP/PPP, the experience can be like sipping jello through a straw. Mosaic looks good at T1 speed, which is commonplace at CERN and NCSA. From home, even at 28,800 bps, those hourly SLIP/PPP charges add up, with most of your connect time spent waiting for images to transfer.

The Web is, for better or worse, people's information space of choice as we move into the second half of the 1990s. But using it comfortably requires high bandwidth connections that are currently beyond most home users. —Eric S. Theise

ACCESS TO THE INTERNET

Where do you live? What do you do for a living? These are the big questions when it comes to hooking into the Internet and other networks. San Francisco area computer professionals, for example, have an abundance of options. But if you work for a struggling nonprofit, or live in a rural area or developing country, the cost of getting connected to anything may be an insurmountable barrier.

This is changing. In North America, commercial providers like Netcom, Delphi, and Performance Systems International offer Internet connectivity to individuals in hundreds of medium-to-large cities. The community networking movement aims to provide free or low-cost access to network services on a regional basis. And the efforts of proselytes in academia and activist organizations around the world (The Internet Society, Association for Progressive Communications) are bringing connectivity to previously unthinkable areas through strategic alliances with strange bedfellows.

There are four general classes of access:

Terminal. If you're affiliated with a business, government agency, university, community college, or forward-thinking K-12 school, you may have access to the Internet, BITNET, or UUCP via terminals located in your computer lab, library, or office. The terminals — a minimal combination of keyboard and monitor without disk drives or on-board smarts — are wired directly to your computer center or management information systems department. You may need to request an account, or you may automatically get one with your job or through a class you've enrolled in. Ask around.

Terminals are adequate for electronic mail, Usenet news, and the full range of text-based services. They're inadequate for graphics or for transferring information between a personal computer and the central computer. Getting a printout often requires a hike down the hall or across campus.

Dialup terminal. You'll probably access network services by connecting over a telephone line using your personal computer, modem, and telecommunications software. This is an elegant solution for people who already have access to a computer since the additional outlay can be as little as $20 for a 2400 bps modem. Minimal terminal software will be included with the modem, and is a standard accessory under Windows. Increased capabilities come with faster modems (under $150 for 14,000 bps with fax) and better telecom software.

Dialup terminal access lets you connect to bulletin boards (FidoNet, RIME, OneNet) and conferencing

systems (America OnLine, CompuServe, New York's Echo, DC's MetaNet, PeaceNet/EcoNet, Prodigy, The WELL). You may choose to subscribe to an email provider only (MCIMail), public Internet (Netcom has set the price at $17.50 for dozens of local providers across the US), or UUCP services (UUNET). You should also be able to dial in using a school or work account.

SLIP/PPP. To make full use of the Internet your computer needs to be on the Internet, speaking its protocols, occupying an address. As a dialup terminal, your computer isn't on the Internet, though your provider may be. When you use network services, the bits and bytes underlying those transactions shuffle around your provider's computer, not yours. To move them to your computer requires up- or downloading. A new generation of Internet tools is emerging. They're closer to what you expect to see on your desktop, incorporating ideas from Macintosh and Windows environments. For now, most of them work only if your desktop is on the Internet.

SLIP (Serial Line Internet Protocol) and PPP (Point-to-Point Protocol) are functionally equivalent methods for attaching your computer to the Internet over a regular telephone line. Although the real cost of providing this service is as cheap as providing dialup terminal access, the benefits are significantly greater. And so the charges are higher. Providers that charge a flat monthly rate for terminal access charge hourly connect fees ($1-$3) for SLIP/PPP, although we're beginning to see flat monthly rates ($30). Expect fluctuation in SLIP/PPP pricing in the near future.

Dedicated Network. Even if the latest modem standard, V.FAST, becomes widespread, dialup and SLIP/PPP connections will be limited to a transfer rate of 28,800 bps. While this is overkill for text-based applications, it's still not enough for comfortably accessing image and sound files, or for organizations supporting multiple users on multiple computers. ISDN, and 56Kbps and T1 (1.5 Mbps) leased digital lines are three of the options for organizations requiring higher bandwidth connections. Even in areas where connectivity is bountiful, these typically cost hundreds or thousands of dollars per month, in addition to specialized hardware and high installation fees. Prices are coming down — some services couldn't be purchased at all a few years ago — but dedicated network connections remain beyond the means of most individuals and small businesses. University students are often fortunate to have this level of connectivity on well-networked campuses. —Eric Theise

Nobody planned the Internet. It just grew.

—James Donnelly

Internet Books and Kits

The Internet is more like a jungle than a freeway: nobody planned it, it just grew. Getting the big picture means considerable stretching of your sense of the possible; learning how to navigate the Net seems hopelessly bewildering at first, and now, because people have been hungry for information, the market for Internet books has become a jungle, too. There are a million new Internet users every month, and a dozen new titles. There's going to be a shakeout soon, when the overflowing aisles of the Internet section in today's technical bookstores will shrink to a shelf or two. The books that survive will have to be those whose authors update annually, because a beginner's guide to last year's Internet is often frustratingly behind the times.

I bet that the first break-away bestseller of Internet bookdom, Ed Krol's **The Whole Internet User's Guide and Catalog**, will be among the evergreens. Already in its second edition, the book pays homage to the Whole Earth style of text-graphic collage. Krol introduces the reader to the Internet and its resources with a light touch, and the resource guide is rich material for new Internauts with the itch to explore. The book's publisher, O'Reilly Associates, was catapulted from a small successful publisher of highly technical books to a slightly larger, very successful publisher of the first Internet bestseller. When O'Reilly went online to the World Wide Web with their multimedia Internet magazine, **Global Network Explorer**, they began providing Internet access to updated editions.

The richness of the Net is in its resources of people, information, and now pictures and sounds and even software, so the key to every netguide is in its contents. With the condensed set of instructions on page 264 of this catalog and a good resource book, you can be your own tour guide. The way to learn the Net is to surf it yourself. An excellent resource guide, rich, deep, over eight hundred pages thick and well presented, is **The Internet Complete**

Reference by Harley Hahn and Rick Stout; an earlier effort by the same authors, **The Internet Yellow Pages**, created a whole new genre of Internet guides.

To explore the Net, you need more than a book. You need special software and an account with an Internet provider, such as the ones listed on p. 267. An emerging trend is "Internet In A Box," which is actually the name of a product in production but not yet published by O'Reilly Associates. A similar product from another well-known publisher, Ventana, is **Internet Membership Kit**, which provides Windows and Macintosh versions of useful mail, file-transfer, and Internet interface software, an excellent Mac **Internet Tour Guide** or PC **Internet Tour Guide** book, a copy of **The Internet Yellow Pages**, and a membership in an Internet service (CERFnet). The kit approach offers easier access for the vast majority of the population, which doesn't want to learn special technical gobbledygook in order to get their minds around intellectual resources and human discourse. —HLR

The Whole Internet User's Guide & Catalog: Ed Krol. 1992; 400 pp. ISBN 1-56592-025-2. $24.95 ($27.95 postpaid). O'Reilly & Associates, 103A Morris Street, Sebastopol, CA 95472; 800/998-9938, fax 707/829-0104.

Internet: The Complete Reference: Harley Hahn. 1993; ISBN 0-07-88190-6. $29.95 ($33.95 postpaid).

The Internet Yellow Pages: Harley Hahn & Rick Stout. 1994; 447 pp. ISBN 0-07-882023-5. $27.95 ($31.95 postpaid).

Both from Osborne McGraw-Hill, 2600 10th Street, Berkeley, CA 94710; 800/722-4726.

The Internet Membership Kit: $69.95 ($74.45 postpaid). Macintosh & Windows versions available. 9600 baud or faster modem recommended. Ventana Press, PO Box 2468, Chapel Hill, NC 27515; 919/942-0220.

Online Resources

FAQ: International E-mail Accessibility
Olivier M. J. Crepin-Leblond
Updated every two weeks, this online document provides a thumbnail of every country's networking capabilities. Wondering if it's possible to send e-mail to Senegal? Look here first. To get a copy, send the e-mail message "send usenet/news.answers/mail/country-codes" to mail-server@rtfm.mit.edu

The Public Dialup Internet Access List (PDIAL) Peter Kaminski
This frequently-updated online document is the closest thing we have to a definitive list of providers around the world offering dialup terminal access to the Internet. To get a copy, send the e-mail message "send pdial" to info-deliserver@netcom.com

Internet Access Provider List: Dedicated Lines (DLIST) Susan Estrada
Newer than PDIAL, this online document lists providers offering dedicated lines to the Internet. To get a copy, send any e-mail message to dlist@ora.com

BITNET Node List
An online list of organizations having addresses on BITNET. Useful if you're searching for connectivity. To get a copy, send the e-mail message "get bitnet sites" to listserv@pucc.princeton.edu

FidoNet Node List
Updated every two weeks, this is an exhaustive list of all FidoNet BBSs in the world. The list only goes to FidoNet system operators, but a WAIS-searchable version is on the Internet as fido-nodelist.src (telnet://wais@wais.com). FidoNet News is posted to the USENET newsgroup, comp.org.fidonet, and other FidoNet information is archived at gopher://gopher.fidonet.org

NIXPUB Bux Technical Services
Far from comprehensive, the NIXPUB (public UNIX) list is still useful for discovering inexpensive UUCP sites around the world. To get a copy, send the e-mail message "get PUB nixpub.long" to mail-server@bts.com

INTERNET ACCESS: NORTH AMERICA

United States

Alabama
Huntsville: Nuance Network Services:
205/533-4296.

Alaska
Anchorage, Barrow, Fairbanks, Homer,
Juneau, Keni, Ketchikan, Kodiak, Kotzebue,
Nome, Palmer, Sitka, Valdez: University
of Alaska Southeast, Tundra Services:
907/465-6453.

Arizona
Glendale, Scottsdale, and Tempe:
CR Laboratories Dialup Internet Access.*
Phoenix: CR Laboratories Dialup Internet
Access*; Evergreen Communications*;
Internet Direct, Inc.*
Tucson: Data Basix: 602/721-1988;
Evergreen Communications*; Internet
Direct, Inc.*

California
Berkeley and East Bay: CR Laboratories
Dialup Internet Access*; DIAL n' CERF*;
HoloNet: 510/704-0160; Netcom
Online Communication Services*.
Los Angeles: CR Laboratories Dialup
Internet Access*; DIAL n' CERF*;
KAIWAN Public Access Internet Online
Services: 714/638-2139; Netcom Online
Communication Services*.
Orange County: DIAL n' CERF*; Express
Access: 800/969-9090, 301/220-2020;
KAIWAN Public Access Internet Online
Services: 714/638-2139; Netcom Online
Communication Services*.
Pasadena: DIAL n' CERF*; Netcom Online
Communication Services*.
Sacramento: Netcom Online
Communication Services*.
San Diego: CTS Network Services: 619/
637-3637; The Cyberspace Station data:
619/634-1376; DIAL n' CERF*; E & S Sys-
tems Public Access Nix: 619/278-4641;
Netcom Online Communication Services*.
San Francisco Peninsula and North Bay:
a2i communications: 408/293-8078;
CR Laboratories Dialup Internet Access*;
DIAL n' CERF*; Institute for Global
Communications (PeaceNet, EcoNet,
ConflictNet, LaborNet, HomeoNet): 415/
442-0220; Netcom Online Communica-
tion Services*; The Portal System: 408/
973-9111; The Whole Earth 'Lectronic
Link (The WELL): 415/332-4335.
San Jose and South Bay: a2i communica-
tions: 408/293-8078; Netcom Online
Communication Services*; The Portal
System: 408/973-9111.
Santa Rosa: CR Laboratories Dialup
Internet Access*.

Colorado
Alamosa, Durango, Fort Collins, Frisco,
Glenwood Springs/Aspen, Grand Junction,
Greeley, Gunnison, Pueblo, Telluride:
Colorado SuperNet, Inc.: 303/273-3471.
Boulder/Denver: Colorado SuperNet, Inc.:
303/273-3471; Community News Service:
719/592-1240; Netcom Online Communi-
cation Services*; Nyx, the Spirit of the
Night data: 303/871-3324.
Colorado Springs: Community News
Service: 719/592-1240; Old Colorado City
Communications: 719/632-4848,
719/593-7575 or 719/636-2040.

Connecticut
Bridgeport, New Haven, and Storrs: John
von Neumann Computer Network*.

District of Columbia
DC metropolitan area: CAPCON Library
Network: 202/331-5771; Clark Internet
Services, Inc.: 800/735-2258 then 410/
730-9764; Express Access: 800/969-
9090, 301/220-2020; Merit Network, Inc.:
313/764-9430; The Meta Network:
703/243-6622; Netcom Online
Communication Services*.

Delaware
Wilmington: Systems Solutions:
302/378-1386, 800/331-1386.

Florida
South Florida: CyberGate, Inc.:
305/428-GATE.

Georgia
Atlanta metropolitan area: CR Laboratories
Dialup Internet Access*; Netcom Online
Communication Services*.

Illinois
Champaign-Urbana: Prairienet Freenet:
217/244-1962.
Chicago metropolitan area: InterAccess:
800/967-1580; MCSNet: 312/248-UNIX;
Netcom Online Communication Services*;
XNet Information Systems 708/983-6064.

Louisiana
New Orleans: NeoSoft's Sugar Land Unix:
713/438-4964.

Maryland
Baltimore: CAPCON Library Network:
202/331-5771; Clark Internet Services,
Inc.: 800/735-2258 then 410/730-9764;
Express Access: 800/969-9090,
301/220-2020.

Massachusetts
Boston: NEARnet 617/873-8730; Netcom
Online Communication Services*; North
Shore Access: 617/593-3110; NovaLink:
800/274-2814; The World:
617/739-0202.
Worcester, Cambridge, Marlboro:
NovaLink 800/274-2814.
MA: Anomaly - Rhode Island's Gateway To
The Internet: 401/273-4669; NEARnet:
617/873-8730; North Shore Access: 617/
593-3110.

Michigan
Eastern Michigan: Merit Network, Inc.:
313/764-9430; MSen: 313/998-4562.
Western Michigan: Merit Network, Inc.:
313/764-9430.

New Hampshire
Nashua, NH: NEARnet: 617/873-8730.
Many NH communities: MV Communica-
tions, Inc.: 603/429-2223.

New Jersey
New Brunswick: Express Access:
800/969-9090, 301/220-2020.
Newark and Princeton: John von Neumann
Computer Network*.

New York
Garden City: John von Neumann Computer
Network*.
New York City metropolitan area: Echo
Communications: 212/255-3839;
Maestro: 212/240-9600; MindVOX:
212/989-2418; Netcom Online Communi-
cation Services*; PANIX Public Access
Unix: 212/877-4854, 212/691-1526;
The Pipeline: 212/267-3636.

North Carolina
Greensboro: Concert-Connect:
919/248-1999.
Asheville, Charlotte, Chapel Hill, Durham,
Greensville, Raleigh, Research Triangle
Park, Winston-Salem: Concert-Connect:
919/248-1999; Vnet Internet Access, Inc.:
704/374-0779.

Ohio
Cincinnati: OARnet*.
Cleveland: APK - Public Access UNI* Site:
216/481-9428; OARnet*.
Columbus: OARnet*.
Dayton: Freelance Systems Programming:
513/254-7246; OARnet*.

Oregon
Portland, Beaverton, Hillsboro, Forest
Grove, Gresham, Tigard, Lake Oswego,
Oregon City, Tualatin, Wilsonville: Netcom
Online Communication Services; RainDrop
Laboratories: info@agora.rain.com;
Teleport: 503/223-4245.

Pennsylvania
Harrisburg: PREPnet*.
Philadelphia: John von Neumann Computer
Network; PREPnet*.
Pittsburgh: PREPnet; Telerama Public
Access Internet: 412/481-3505.

Rhode Island
Providence/Seekonk Zone: Anomaly -
Rhode Island's Gateway To The Internet:
401/273-4669; John von Neumann
Computer Network*.
East Greenwich and northern RI: The IDS
World Network: 401/884-7856.

Texas
Austin: RealTime Communications (wixer):
512/451-0046.
Dallas/Ft. Worth metropolitan area:
Netcom Online Communication Services*;
Texas Metronet: 214/705-2900, 817/
543-8756.
Houston metropolitan area: The Black
Box: 713/480-2684; NeoSoft's Sugar
Land Unix: 713/438-4964; South Coast
Computing Services, Inc.: 713/661-3301.

Virginia
Norfolk, Virginia Beach, Portsmouth,
Chesapeake, Newport News, Hampton,
Williamsburg: Wyvern Technologies, Inc.:
804/622-4289.

Washington
Everett: Eskimo North: 206/367-7457;
Olympic Peninsula/Eastern Jefferson
County: Olympus - The Olympic
Peninsula's Gateway To The Internet:
206/385-0464.
Seattle: Eskimo North: 206/367-7457;
GLAIDS NET (Homosexual Network):
206/323-7483; Halcyon: 206/955-1050;
Netcom Online Communication Services*;
Northwest Nexus, Inc.: 206/455-3505.

Canada

Alberta
Calgary: UUNET Canada, Inc*.
Edmonton: PUCnet Computer
Connections: 403/448-1901.

British Columbia
Vancouver: Wimsey Information Services,
Inc.: 604/421-4741;
UUNET Canada, Inc*.

Ontario
Hamilton, Kitchener/Waterloo, London,
Ottawa, Toronto: HookUp Communication
Corporation: 519/747-4110; UUNET
Canada, Inc.*; UUnorth: 416/225-8649.

Quebec
Montreal, Laval, South Shore, West Island:
Communications Accessibles Montreal:
514/931-0749; UUNET Canada, Inc*.
—Eric Theise

---

* FREQUENTLY CITED RESOURCES

CR Laboratories Dialup Internet Access:
415/381-2800.
DIAL n' CERF: 800/876-2373 or 619/455-3900.
Evergreen Communications: 602/955-8315.
Internet Direct, Inc.: 602/274-0100.

John von Neumann Computer Network:
800/35-TIGER or 609/897-7300.
Netcom Online Communications Services:
800/501-8649 or 408/554-8649.
OARnet: 614/292-8100.
PREPnet: 412/268-7870.
UUNET Canada, Inc.: 416/368-6621.

OTHER ON-RAMPS AND CONSTRUCTION ZONES

Delphi • America Online • Compuserve
In addition to other services offered, Delphi
(800/695-4005) provides full Internet access;
America OnLine (800/827-6364) and
CompuServe (800/848-8990) offer limited
but rapidly increasing access to the Internet.
Call for updated information. —HLR

OTHER GREAT BOOKS THAT CAN HELP

Connecting to the Internet: Susan
Estrada. 1993, O'Reilly & Associates, 103A
Morris Street, Sebastopol, CA 95472;
800/998-9938, fax 707/829-0104.

This is the place to start unraveling the mysteries of bandwidth. Good discussions of the
differences between dialup and dedicated
lines, plus worksheets and checklists to help
you match your needs to a provider's offerings. Appendices include PDIAL and DLIST
(see Online Resources).

O'Reilly and Associates publishes deep books
on narrow subjects. Always worth studying,
but not always the first thing to reach for
when putting out a fire. (That's what Usenet
is for!) Visit O'Reilly online at gopher://
gopher.ora.com

The Matrix (Computer Networks and
Conferencing Systems Worldwide): John S.
Quarterman. 1990, Prentice Hall Press.

Matrix News: Online $25/year, paper $30/
year (12 issues). Matrix Information and Directory Services, 1106 Clayton Lane, Suite
500W, Austin, TX 78723; 512/451-7602,
fax 512/452-0128; email mids@tic.com

While much of The Matrix is now out of date,
it still provides a sound framework for thinking about the functionality, uses, technical
protocols, and administration of the world's
interconnected networks. Great index, rich
with references. Matrix News, edited by John
Quarterman, offers monthly news on cross-
network issues.

The Internet Connection (System Con-
nectivity and Configuration): John S.
Quarterman & Smoot Carl Mitchell. 1994,
Addison-Wesley Publishing Co.

Limiting yourself to one book on putting your
computer(s) on the Internet full-time? This is
the one. But don't be surprised if you find
yourself needing an O'Reilly book or three.

I F YOU'RE TIRED of walking into the local video store and finding yourself at the mercy of this week's over-hyped, over-budget, steroid-laden Hollywood entertainment product, you're in luck. A number of mail order outfits offer independent, fringe, foreign, and forgotten movies on video and laserdisc. Most of these companies sell their vids (prices average around $20 a tape), but a few — such as Facets — have weekly rental rates. Most of these mail order houses specialize in one or two areas of video: horror, art films, lesbian sex, tattooing and piercing, archival music from the fifties and sixties, Japanimation, sexploitation, and scientific visualizations. —Richard Kadrey

Stand and Be Proud-Voice Of The City: Over 25 choirs from South Central L.A. and the Hollywood Bowl Orchestra gathered to record this anthem to the rebuilding of L.A., written by David Cassidy and wife Sue Shifrin. —Spectrum Music Video

Absolute Beta: Catalog free; membership $9.95 from PO Box 130, Remington, VA 22734; 800/937-2382. A video club with hundreds of classic and recent releases in Sony's Beta format. Membership gets you bimonthly updates, a newsletter, video search service, and discounts. Sample catalog free; full catalog available with membership.

AnimEigo: Catalog free from PO Box 989, Wilmington, NC 28402; 910/251-1850, fax 910/763-2376. Huge selection of quality Japanimation, including the Bubblegum Crisis series.

Beta Library: Catalog free (with SASE) from PO Box 836224, Promenade Station, Richardson, TX 75083-6224; 214/233-4552. Beta-format videos: artsy films such as Antonioni's *Zabriskie Point* to goofy Al Yankovic music videos. New-customer specials give you discounts toward future tapes with each tape you buy.

Discount Video Tapes: Catalog free from 833 "A" N. Hollywood Way, PO Box 7122, Burbank, CA 91510; 818/843-3366, fax 818/843-3821. The sample catalog has more than four hundred titles; the full catalog, two thousand. You can also rent tapes.

Facets Multimedia, Inc.: Catalog $9.95 from 1517 W. Fullerton Avenue, Chicago, IL 60614; 312/281-9075 or 800/331-6197. Some of the best independent, foreign, art and instructional films available. Their huge catalog is like an encyclopedia of nontraditional video styles and subjects. Highlights include Larry Jordan's eccentric animation (such as *Sophie's Place*) and James Broughton's very personal and erotic short films. All of Facets' titles are for sale or rent.

Fatale Video: Catalog free (with SASE) from 526 Castro Street, San Francisco, CA 94114; 415/861-4723 or 800/845-4617. Producers of erotic videos by and for lesbians. Recommended tapes are *Suburban Dykes* and *Bathroom Sluts*, the latter a hot example of amateur lesbian sex videos.

Flash Publications: Catalog free from PO Box 410052, San Francisco, CA 94141; 415/267-7651. Charles Gatewood's documentaries look at extreme subcultures: tattooists, piercers and fetishists of all kinds. And his travel vids are like none you've seen: *Forbidden Photos, Weird San Francisco, Weird New Orleans, Weird Amsterdam . . .*

Mystic Fire Video: Catalog free from PO Box 2249, Livonia, MI 48150; 800/292-9001. A fabulous range of titles covering the old and the new, feature films and documentaries: Joseph Campbell's Power of Myth series, Derek Jarman's films, William Burroughs and Lydia Lunch performances, the Indonesian documentary *Ring of Fire*, and Kenneth Anger's short films.

Satan's Bed: (1965) When the local smack pusher chooses to give up his life long career for the love of a beautiful woman, the neighborhood junkies decide to cancel his wedding plans. The infamous creative team Michael & Roberta Findlay had a hand in this warped wonder. Rest assured you'll get your money's worth of rape, sadism, & murder. Stars the little known acting talent of artist, musician & famous Beatle 5th wheel, Yoko Ono. —Something Weird Video

Manga Mania: Catalog free from Central Park Media, PO Box 461, New York NY 10023; 800/626-4277. Probably the biggest selection of Japanimation titles available. They also specialize in adult-oriented (i.e., grittier and much more violent) versions of popular Japanese titles (such as The Guyver series), and distribute the notorious science fiction-fantasy-over-the-top sex-and-violence-fest, *Urotsukidoji: Legend of the Overfiend*.

Rhino Home Video: Catalog free from 10635 Santa Monica Boulevard, Los Angeles, CA 90025; 800/357-4466. Vintage music videos, kidvids (check out Frank Capra's science edutainment cartoon, *Hemo the Magnificent*), old TV, offbeat horror, and great fifties and sixties exploitation titles, some in double-feature packages like the Saturday Night Sleazies series.

The Right Stuf: Catalog free from PO Box 71309, Des Moines, IA 50325-1309; 800/338-6827, fax 515/279-7434. Japanese animation from Japanese TV. Titles include *Astroboy, Gigantor, The Eighth Man*. They also carry T-shirts, posters and books.

Sinister Cinema: Catalog free from PO Box 4369, Medford, OR 97501-0168; 503/773-6860. Horror, suspense, science fiction and serials, all for about $17 a tape!

Something Weird Video: Catalog $3 from Dept F.U.N., PO Box 33664, Seattle, WA 98133; 206/361-3759. Comprehensive catalog of softcore sexploitation films from the thirties through the early seventies, including Betty Page bondage flicks. They also carry B horror.

Spectrum Music Video: Catalog $4 (refundable with first purchase) from PO Box 1128, Norristown, PA 19404; 800/846-8742. My favorite music video catalog. Their videos include rock, jazz, easy listening, country, New Age, gospel and more. Exhaustive.

Video Search of Miami: Catalog free from PO Box 16-1917, Miami, FL 33116; 305/279-9973. An excellent source for Hong Kong, Japanese and Italian action videos, as well as rarities from Euro-trash directors like Jess Franco. They also have a great selection of out-of-circulation U.S. videos (such as *Forbidden Zone* and Rock Hudson's oddest and best flick, *Seconds*). Caveat emptor: these are gray-market items, so video quality varies greatly. Some titles are pristine, while others look as though they were recorded by a spy satellite off a drive-in movie screen. Gambling, though, is part of the fun.

Whole Toon Access: Catalog $2 from 1907 3rd Avenue, Seattle, WA 98101; 206/441-4130. Cartoons! Intense Japanese adventure toons, Flintstones, Ren & Stimpy, Disney, and more. Toys and some laserdiscs, too.

George of the Jungle: (1967) 4 episodes: Shep the elephant; mad scientist & Super Chicken; the Ira K. Dismal Swamp Buggy Race; Juju the rain god. —The Whole Toon Catalog

Wanna make your own? See Desktop Video (page 256)

Devil Girl from Mars: (1954) Hazel Court, Hugh McDermott. Not the kind of girl you want to get involved with. She's got a killer robot, a giant spaceship, and is taking men back to Mars for breeding purposes. Rich, rich camp. —Sinister Cinema.

Fried Shoes, Cooked Diamonds; A joyous reunion of the Beat poets at the Jack Kerouac School of Disembodied Poetics at Naropa Institute in Boulder, Colorado. With a very personal narration by Allen Ginsberg, the film shows the ease of interchange between the poets, who read to each other, discuss their thoughts and partake in an anti-nuclear demonstration at Rocky Flats. —Mystic Fire Video

Beware
Multimedia
HYPE

In the broadest context, multimedia refers to anything that involves more than one medium: slide shows to collages. In these pages we use a more restricted definition: software-based text, still pictures, audio, and video that can be composed and played right now on a personal computer equipped with a CD-ROM drive.

A word of warning: for a satisfying experience, multimedia applications require a computer equipped with a fast CPU (processor), a color monitor, a CD-ROM drive, plenty of RAM, a big internal hard drive and a pair of external speakers. In the Windows environment, multimedia applications also require a special audio attachment. Although Macintoshes come with built-in audio capabilities, we have not yet arrived at the plug-and-play era, as software tidbits still need to be installed.

However, if you do have access to a multimedia-ready machine, and a lot of patience, some excellent material is available if you know where to get it. The following reviews focus not on the technology but on the aesthetic possibilities of multimedia. Keep in mind that these products do not provide the high-adrenaline interactivity associated with video games; instead, they enable users to experience multiple points of view and to explore webs of interrelated audio-visual information at their own pace — a process more contemplative, and slightly less participatory, than the hype would lead you to believe. —Abbe Don

OTHER GREAT RESOURCES

Expanded Book Toolkit: (See access this page.) Voyager makes the tool used to create Expanded Books available to anyone interested in creating their own hypertext publication. Ideal for universities, businesses, or for writing your own Great American Electronic Novel.

Explora: Interplay Productions, 17922 Fitch Avenue, Irvine, CA 92714; 800/969-4263. Take a walk through Peter Gabriel's world that includes a tour of his recording studio, the Womad Festival (see p. 274), and playful videos of world music available on the Real World label.

MYST: Brøderbund Software/Customer Service, PO Box 6125, Novato, CA 94948-6125; 800/521-6263. A tale of betrayal set in a 3D virtual world. You must explore to find out who betrayed whom and why through the ages. Warning: it's not as simple and straightforward as it looks, but exploration and puzzle cracking are worth the effort.

The Voyager Company

This electronic publisher is committed to commercially risky but culturally valuable books, movies and experimental art that have explicit social and political content. By distributing these works as laserdiscs, Expanded Books, or CD-ROMs, Voyager not only keeps the titles alive and available, but also provides an opportunity for the artists and authors to annotate their works and to provide a rare look behind-the-scenes at how the works were created.

If you don't own a laserdisc player, Voyager's The Criterion Collection catalog may entice you to purchase one. This eclectic mix of black-and-white classics, foreign classics, "director approved" transfers of contemporary films (such as **Brazil** and **Bram Stoker's Dracula**) offers the technical advantages of wide-screen transfers, where scenes are not cropped to fit television screens, as well as such extra goodies as production sketches, interviews with the directors, outtakes, and explanations of special effects. It's the best of film school right in your own home.

Voyager sells its Expanded Books and CD-Roms through its Where Minds Meet catalog. Expanded Books come on computer diskette and are designed for large desktop monitors and PowerBook screens. For example, in The Complete Annotated Alice readers can follow characters and themes with a search command or annotate their favorite sections. I still prefer to read fiction books sitting under a tree in Golden Gate Park but find the Expanded Books reading style very appropriate for nonfiction.

Voyager is the best place to look for highbrow CD-ROMs. While many of these titles are CD-ROM versions of work previously published in other media, Voyager is also releasing works that will make their publishing debut as CD-ROMs.

See Media Magic on page 357.

Voyager CD-ROM Gems

The early Voyager list was heavily Mac-centric, but they are committed to providing more Windows-compatible products over the next eighteen months. Here are my favorites. —AD

The two pictures on this page are screengrabs from The Complete Maus CD-ROM.

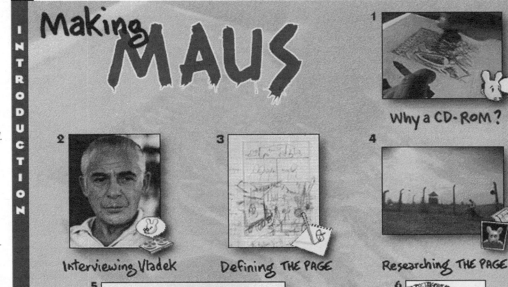

Making **MAUS**

2 Interviewing Vladek   3 Defining THE PAGE   1 ... 4 Why a CD-ROM?   Researching THE PAGE   5 Refining THE PAGE   6 Complaining about the screen

The Complete Maus: The original **Maus** was Art Spiegelman's extraordinary rendering of his father's experiences in Auschwitz, cast in comic book form. Odd as it sounds, portraying Jews as mice and Nazis as cats in the sequential art form of a comic book works stunningly well. Though the CD-ROM is no substitute for the original **Maus** comic book, it adds a dimension by allowing Spiegelman to walk us through the thirteen-year development of the project, revealing original sketches; most importantly, the complete text and drawings from the book are linked to audio interviews with Vladek, Art's father. It's one thing to read the rendering of Vladek's story, and quite another goose-pimply eerie experience to hear the voice of the very man to whom these awful events occurred.

The Residents Freak Show: The Residents are a San Francisco-based cult band. Nobody knows the musician/performance artists' identities — they are most commonly seen with eyeballs covering their heads, garbed in tuxedos and top hats. A truly weird but thoroughly professional media-

edge sensibility. In collaboration with 3D animator Jim Ludtke, The Residents have created here an odd little world, literally a carnival freak show, superbly rendered — an alternate reality that beckons you to explore. Embedded in it are the legitimate documentary history of freak shows, a marketplace for Residents fan gear, the complete archive of The Residents' documented performance art, and the freaks themselves — fictional characters whose individual trailers are worlds unto themselves. This work of art was conceived and executed specifically for interactive CD-ROM.

Salt of the Earth: The original black-and-white film about a miner's strike, produced by blacklisted Hollywood filmmakers shortly after a real-life miner's strike in Silver City, New Mexico in 1951. Labor politics, race relations between gringos and Mexican-Americans, and gender roles in the labor movement are some of its themes. In a key scene, a court issues an injunction forbidding striking miners to stay on the picket line, so the wives of the miners cleverly find a loophole in the injunction and take their husbands' places. The men reluctantly stay home to take care of the kids and keep house as the strike continues! **Salt of the Earth** includes the story of how the film was made, which parallels the story line of the film: when the studios and the House Committee on Un-American Activities got wind of the subject matter of the film, it became difficult to finish it. Also included is the short **The Hollywood Ten**, and critical, historical, and biographical essays.

Abbe Don archives four generations on CD-ROM.

Family Media and Kodak Photo CD

As a child, I spent many weekends listening to my great-grandmother tell stories while she taught me to make traditional Jewish foods. As an adult, I have used those family storytelling experiences as a context for creating interactive media. I recently began putting my family photographs onto Photo CD, a special CD format developed by Kodak for storing negatives or slides. Photo CDs run on many different types of CD-ROM players with Photo CD capability. I can take a Photo CD from my Macintosh, play it on my father's Windows machine, then head to my grandmother's house and play it on a Kodak Photo CD Player attached to her television. And images from Photo CD expand the possibilities for storytelling and multimedia playfulness.

You don't have to be an expert to begin the process. You can put up to 100 images on one Photo CD. Obtain slides or negatives of your favorite family pictures. (Horizontal images match the aspect ratio of the computer and television screens; vertical pictures will appear sideways unless you pay extra to have them rotated.)

Many local Kodak photo finishers can put your negatives or slides on Photo CD. Service bureaus that specialize in Photo CD and related services often have lower prices (I use Palmer Photographic in Sacramento, CA: 916/441-3305). The cost ranges from 90 cents to $2 per image, depending on how many images are in your order and the scan quality you choose. "Consumer quality" is more than adequate, unless you plan to do extensive, high-resolution printing.

You now have a reliable archival medium. Whether the pictures are on a computer screen or television, they often act as catalysts for reminiscing and passing on stories when the family gathers to view them.

The following ideas, based on Macintosh software, suggest some possibilities for a foray into digital media creation.

Digital Greeting Cards: An advantage of digital images is that you can easily cut, copy, paste, and rearrange images without damaging the originals. Each Photo CD includes an application called Slide Show Viewer. You can view each image from the CD sequentially, at a size of 160 x 120 pixels. From Slide Show Viewer, you can open a picture with applications such as Adobe Photoshop. Once the image is open, you can resize it, change the colors, add text, or collage it with other pictures. Make a collage of family photographs, add a greeting, and save the file onto a floppy disk. Take it to a service bureau and print your annual holiday greeting card on photographic paper.

Digital Family Album: Using a paint program, create a template for a digital family album that can be viewed on screen or printed. You can tell a story through artful sequencing of the images. Play with the placement of pictures to juxtapose each sibling at various rites of passage, such as first steps, graduation or wedding.

Collecting Oral Stories: Sit with your favorite family storyteller and look at the pictures on screen. Use the built-in microphone with audio-capture software (the audio palette that comes with HyperCard, or the capture feature in Adobe Premiere). Kid Pix and Adobe Premiere let you make slide shows with accompanying audio stories and save them to your hard drive as QuickTime movies. As you view the slide show, prompt reticent family members to share their versions of the stories.

Interactive Family Stories: Kodak has developed another format called Photo CD Portfolio Disc. With it, you can assemble your family history, complete with pictures, stories, and music, onto a cross-platform CD package. Kodak's Create-It software, a separate application, is designed to simplify the authoring process for end-users, though it has a clumsy interface and still requires familiarity with the structuring of interactive presentations. After assembling your media and linking them in Create-It, take all your media files and the Create-It scripts to a local Sir Speedy Service Bureau to have the Photo CD Portfolio disc made. Some Sir Speedy franchises also offer production assistance and handholding, but the prices for this added service fluctuate wildly. Watch for prices to drop and for more flexible tools to emerge. —Abbe Don

Kodak Photo CD: Kodak Information Center, 343 State Street, Rochester, NY 14650; 800/242-2424, International 716/724-1021, fax 716/781-5986.

Sir Speedy: Call 800/854-8297 for the shop nearest you.

KidPix II: $39.95 ($43.95 postpaid). Brøderbund Software/Customer Service, PO Box 6125, Novato, CA 94948-6125; 800/521-6263.

Create-It Photo CD Presentation Software: Requires System 7 or higher, 8-bit or 24-bit color monitor, 8 MB RAM recommended, Kodak Photo CD-compatible CD-ROM XA drive. $219. Eastman Kodak Company, 343 State Street, Rochester, NY 14650; 800/866-5533.

Adobe PhotoShop 2.5: Suggested retail price $895; CD-ROM edition $995.
Adobe Premier 3.0: Suggested retail price $795.
Both from Adobe Systems Inc., 1585 Charleston Road, PO Box 7900, Mountain View, CA 94039; 800/833-6687.

Demystifying Multimedia

This comprehensive book lives up to its title by focusing on the design and development process, rather than on specific technologies. Illustrated case studies and interviews with seasoned producers serve as mini-apprenticeships, sharing insights that might otherwise take years to learn through trial and error.

Pay close attention to the Design and Prototype chapter, regardless of the scale of your project — people too often assume "there is too little time and money to spend on prototyping and move too quickly to production before they've adequately thought out their needs." Check out the Roles section for a sense of how your current skills apply to multimedia. The Projects chapter succinctly describes the elements of common multimedia formats.

The book's structural elements — pithy margin notes and quotes, cross-referencing, navigation bars, and iconic summaries — are themselves a case study in interactive design. —AD

•

The greater the level of interactivity, that is, the greater the audience involvement and control, the greater the effort required to design and produce a multimedia product. The level of interactivity also gauges complexity when estimating project duration and cost. Levels of interactivity include passive, interactive or adaptive.

Passive multimedia are presented in a linear manner like a slide show or videotape.

Interactive multimedia allow users to control the action and chart a personal course through the content.

Adaptive multimedia are at the highest level of interactivity. They allow users to enter their own content and control how it is used. This content can be original text, illustrations, sound, video, commentary on content already in the project, or a new sequence or arrangement of the existing content.

•

Shaping the design for a multimedia project begins with an outpouring of ideas and creative exploration of possibilities. The real strength of development is in collaboration, and begins with brainstorming. Brainstorming is a dynamic process of generating ideas without judgment or constraint. The purpose of brainstorming is to open the spigot of creativity for everyone involved in the project: managers, artists, production staff, potential users, clients (if there are any). A good brainstorming session results in a collection of ideas and solutions that become the basis for designs and their prototypes.

•

Design and Prototype Tips
• It is much easier to make changes in the prototype stage than in the production stage.

• A design on paper is not enough. Most multimedia products require a working prototype or model for everyone to understand.

• Don't spend a large amount of money until you know exactly what you are going to build.

• Don't get so attached to an idea or technique that you lose sight of the project's purpose.

• Allow team members creative autonomy but figure out ways for them to work together.

• User test early and often.

Demystifyng Multimedia
(A Guide for Multimedia Developers from Apple Computer, Inc.)
Ken Fromm & Nathan Shedroff, Editors. 1993; 284 pp.
$30 ($33 postpaid); order #T1115LLA. APDA/Apple Computer, Inc., PO Box 319, Buffalo, NY 14207; 800/282-2732 (international calls: 716/871-6555), fax 716/871-6511

Below are handy icons representing some of the topics covered in the book.

Topics with specific relevance to animators.

Topics with specific relevance to video professionals.

Topics with specific relevance to information designers, interface designers, or programmers.

Topics with specific relevance to interactive education..

Topics with specific relevance to writers, editors, and researchers.

OTHER GREAT RESOURCES

I Photograph To Remember/Fotografio Para Recordar: Pedro Meyer. Macintosh or Windows versions. The Voyager Company (see p. 269). An intimate portrait of photographer Pedro Meyer's parents as they confront their own mortality.

A Celebration of American Family Folklore: Steven J. Zeitlin, Amy J. Kotkin & Holly Cutting Baker. 1982, 1992, Yellow Moon Press. A wonderful collection of American family folklore, with an excellent section on collecting your own.

Guide to Genealogy Software: Donna Przecha & Joan Lowrey. 1993, Genealogical Publishing Company. The most comprehensive review of genealogy software available for Macintosh, Windows and DOS, including shareware and commercial programs as well as an overview of discussion groups around the net.

Do-It-Yourself CDs, Tapes (and LPs)

In 1987, after years of shopping around demo tapes to big labels looking for record deals, we decided to venture into record production. Someone told us about a place in Dallas, Texas — A+R Music — that did small-run vinyl-pressing and cassette-duping, dirt cheap.

A+R proved to be inexpensive, friendly, and reliable. Our 500 records and 500 cassettes looked and sounded good enough to get airplay and to find their way into local music stores. Since we caught the "indy" music bug, my wife —jazz singer Pam Bricker — has released eight music and audio-art projects, on tape, vinyl, and CD, and we have helped countless other musicians with their recordings. Besides A+R, we've used Disc Makers in Philadelphia and Nimbus in Charlottesville, VA.

A+R Music is still selling services, via a multitude of sales broadsides — no slick color catalog or "how-to" flow charts. They keep it simple, cheap, and basement-grade. A+R is the perfect place to go for vanity recordings, spoken art, quick-and-dirty recordings to shop to labels or to get airplay, punk rock, and local choir recordings. They do CDs and tape, and they still press vinyl.

Disc Makers is like an indy-music fast-food restaurant. They offer attractively priced CD/tape combination deals, with varying turnaround time, tape quality, and art amenities (two-color, full-color). In addition to recordings, they produce album art, promotional materials, and company logos. While we've been happy with our Disc Makers projects, we have heard some hard-luck stories. The bottom line seems to be that Disc Makers is the place to go if you need it fast, with professional-looking artwork, and you're not too picky about cassette quality (no one has complained about their CD quality).

Disc Makers' catalog has lots of cover design ideas and useful general information on the duplicating process. They also have three free booklets available: "Guide to Master Tape Preparation," "Guide to Independent Music Publicity," and "Directory of Independent Music Distributors."

Online Resources

Check out these Usenet newsgroups:

alt.cd-rom, comp.multimedia, comp.publish.cdrom.hardware, comp.publish.cdrom.software, comp.publish.cdrom.multimedia

There is also an informative FAQ available by anonymous ftp from: ftp.cdrom.com: /pub/cdrom/faq

---

Nimbus Manufacturing represents the "high end" of the CD duplicators. They are known for quality and for their long-standing eminence in the industry. Their prices are higher than either A+R's or Disc Makers' and they charge separately for graphic services. Their catalog comes with acetate overlays that can help you in designing package and label art. Nimbus also offers CD-ROM duplication. Their CD-ROM Replication Guide comes with a nifty clear CD-ROM disc that makes a useful design aid and serves as an attractive coaster! —Gareth Branwyn

•

Special Radio & Promo Packages
(Under 10 minutes/side)

100 12" Records - $575.00
500 12" Records - $950.00

Includes: Reference Acetate • Mastering • Stampers • Pure Vinyl Pressing • Label Typeset • Label Proof • One Color Printed Label • White Die-Cut Jacket with Shrink Wrap. —A&R

•

Our Best Seller! 500 Full-Color CDs plus 500 Chrome Cassettes for only $3,490 with four-page CD folder. —Disc Makers

•

Other Helpful Hints
• When using halftone images, for best results stay within the 20% to 80% dot range.

• For computer-generated film we recommend using 2400 or higher dpi for screens, blends or graduations, as well as 4-color process work. This will help to avoid banding, or moiré patterns.

• If you intend to overprint colors, remember that some light colors change when printed over a dark background. For the best results use a light background color, with a darker foreground color. —Nimbus

A + R Record & Tape Mfg: Product information: 902 Industrial Boulevard, Dallas, TX 75207; 800/527-DISC, fax 214/741-7310.

Disc Makers: Free catalogs and booklets: 1328 N. 4th Street, Philadelphia, PA 19122; 800/468-9353, fax 215/236-7763.

Nimbus Manufacturing: Free CD-Audio and CD-ROM catalogs: SR Guildford Farm, Ruckersville, VA 22968; 800/782-0778.

CD-ROM Replication

CD technology has become cheap enough that individuals can use the medium to store or distribute all kinds of digital data. You can send your project to a replication house for multiple copies, get a "one-off" done at a CD-R (compact disk-recordable) service bureau, or buy a CD-R deck and roll your own.

The One-Off CD Shop is a growing little franchise of CD-ROM service bureaus. They offer CD-R one-offs, mass replication, and consulting services. They are also authorized retailers of Philips, Sony, and Yamaha CD-recorders.

Disc Manufacturing, Inc. produces excellent, free technical publications. They include "Compact Disc Terminology," "A Glossary of CD And CD-ROM Terms," and "An Overview To Multimedia CD-ROM Production." Disc Manufacturing also offers full replication services. —GB

•

When a CD has data (CD-ROM) and audio (CD-DA) tracks, it is referred to as a Mixed Mode disc.

The most common type of Mixed Mode disc is one where the 1st track on the disc is Yellow Book, CD-ROM Mode 1, and the Red Book, normal audio tracks. —"Compact Disc Terminology"

•

Frame rates for computer generated animations are lower than video. A rate of 10-15fps is generally accepted as high quality. For computer generated graphics, an animation program is frequently used to move painted objects from one part of the screen to another. A simple way of creating motion is Slide-show motion. Slide-show motion is the rapid display of images to the monitor. Storing long sequences of motion in Slide-show fashion requires a lot of storage space and produces slow play back speeds. —"An Overview to Multimedia CD-ROM Production"

One-Off CD Shops: call 800/387-1633 for information.

Disc Manufacturing, Inc.: Free technical papers. 1409 Faulk Road, Suite 103, Wilmington, DE 19803; 800/433-DISC.

The CD-Recordable Bible

For those who are just getting started in CD-R, this very useful primer covers basic terms, standards and procedures, how to select a CD-R system, and how to create discs. It also includes a series of articles, reprinted from CD-ROM Professional magazine, that evaluate available software and hardware. —GB

•

The CD-R platform includes the following items:

• Personal computer • Compact disc recorder • Authoring software (optional) • Premastering/ mastering software • Blank media

•

Disadvantages: Few and Tolerable
Reading from a CD-ROM is considerably slower than a hard disk, as much as ten times slower, but how many 600MB hard drives can you get for $20 apiece?

•

Regardless of the technical capabilities of the hardware, it's the premastering/mastering software that links the computer to the CD recorder. Functionality and ease-of-use depend heavily upon this link.

The CD-Recordable Bible
(An Essential Guide for Any Business)
Ash Pahwa. Eight Bit Books, 1994; 185 pp.
ISBN 0-910965-11-0
$24.95 ($27.95 postpaid). Online, Inc., 462 Danbury Road, Wilton, CT 06897; 800/248-8466

Learn Media Literacy on page 220.

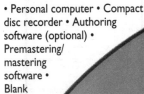

Experimental Musical Instruments

Bicycle seat violins? Machine gun violas? A combination baseball bat/cane/cello? These hybrids all appear in a single issue of Experimental Musical Instruments. This quarterly ("for the design, construction, and enjoyment of unusual sound sources") relates the theory and practice of such instruments. Ranging from the prosaic to the wild and woolly, they are depicted in abundant diagrams and lively photos. You'll also find announcements of events, reviews of experimental-instrument recordings, and pointers to articles of interest in other periodicals.

This long-lived magazine has expanded over the years, to forty pages in 1994. It is easily the most comprehensive resource available.
—Richie Unterberger

Experimental Musical Instruments
$24/year (4 issues).
PO Box 784,
Nicasio, CA 94946

The Seaweed Horn is made from bull kelp, dried and finished. Six bells of different lengths provide a broader range of pitches. In truth, this thing is more successful as an exercise in silliness than as a concert instrument. But natural horns, saxophones and oboes of the same seaweed can be amazingly effective musically, not to mention beautiful, and they provide one of the most economical means for producing conical-bore instruments short of setting up a brasswinds factory. The horn was made and is played here by Bart Hopkin, editor of *Experimental Musical Instruments*.

Homespun Tapes

Founded in 1967, Homespun was the first American company to give music lessons via audiotape. They're going stronger than ever, though instructional videos now make up the bulk of their stock. Homespun's specialty is teaching styles — folk, bluegrass, rock, and jazz — combining a relaxed, just-between-friends attitude with slowed-down demonstrations and detailed explanations.

It is far easier to learn from tapes than from books: you can listen, watch, rewind the tape, repeat passages, and practice the music until you have it down cold.

Though they teach mainly stringed instruments, Homespun also sells tapes on drums, piano, accordion, harmonica, and voice. If you've always wanted to learn to play music, it's

never too late to start; if you already know how, it's never too late to learn a new style. —Mike Ashenfelder

●

Doc's Guitar, Fingerpicking And Flatpicking
taught by Doc Watson

America's favorite country guitarist teaches more than a dozen of his most requested fingerpicking and flatpicking tunes. Split-screen images and close-ups allow students to take an intimate look at Doc's technique, while simultaneously watching his picking and fretting hands.

Homespun Tapes: Catalog free. Box 694, Woodstock, NY 12498; 800/338-2737, fax 914/246-5282.

(Right) The Ship is assembled from various metal materials and objects, to create something like but unlike an electric guitar. There are about twenty-five strings, many of which are actually coil springs. They produce reverb-like drones, metallic clangs and grinding sounds, along with more familiar-sounding guitar-like lines.

JAZZ PIANO STANDARDS
taught by **Andy LaVerne**
CAT.#VD-LAV-JS01
LEVEL 3/4
90-MIN. VIDEO $49.95
INCLUDES MUSIC
———
A top jazz pianist uses six beautiful standards to illustrate chord changes, voicings, reharmonization, melodic invention and other essential tools that will broaden a student's jazz vocabulary and technique. The Yamaha Disklavier is used to record and play back—at half speed—Andy's unique piano stylings. Songs: *Just Friends, My Romance, How Deep Is The Ocean, Night And Day, Body And Soul* and *Like Someone In Love.*

ANDY LAVERNE'S GUIDE TO MODERN JAZZ PIANO
For Solo Or Group Playing
taught by **Andy LaVerne**
with special guests John Abercrombie, Steve LaSpina and Jeff Hirshfield
CAT.#VD-LAV-JP04
LEVEL 2
90-MIN. VIDEO $49.95
INCLUDES CHORDS + MUSIC
———
Andy LaVerne delves into the intricacies of jazz improvisation, chord voicings, rhythm comping and other techniques which can be used both in a solo or a band situation.

DR. JOHN TEACHES NEW ORLEANS PIANO
taught by
Mac (Dr. John) Rebennack
Complete two-tape series
Special price $79.95
Cat.#VD-DRJ-NO03
———
These two videos are full of powerful playing, slowed-down instruction and the unmistakable sound of Dr. John!

Video One:
CAT.#VD-DRJ-NO01
LEVEL 3/4
60-MIN. VIDEO $49.95
INCLUDES MUSIC
———
Styles of Professor Longhair, Pine Top Smith, Fats Domino, James Booker and others.

Video Two:
CAT.#VD-DRJ-NO02
LEVEL 3/4
60-MIN. VIDEO $49.95
INCLUDES MUSIC
———
Styles of Huey "Piano" Smith, Tuts Washington, Allen Toussaint and Mac (Dr. John) Rebennack himself.

Instrument Catalogs

Don't limit yourself to learning what you can find at the local music store; there's more than one, indeed more than a million, ways to play a tune. A world of sounds, shapes, and tones awaits you via these specialty mail-order houses. —RU

Anyone Can Whistle: Catalog free. PO Box 4407, Kingston, NY 12401, 800/435-8863. Unusual instruments and musical collectibles from all over the world — handmade Native American drums, Indonesian cat bells, cactus rainsticks.

Safari Maracas from Anyone Can Whistle.

Lark in the Morning: Catalog free. PO Box 1176, Mendocino, CA 95460; phone 707/964-5569, fax 707/964-1979. Lark's 96-page catalog contains the widest selection of hard-to-find musical instruments, music, and instructional materials that I've ever seen. Nifty illustrations and descriptions of items like hog-nosed plucked psaltery, singing bowls, and French court musettes make for entertaining reading, whether you want to invest or not.

Didgeridoos

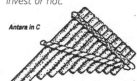

The Aboriginal Didgeridoo has been re-discovered and is used in contemporary settings for consciousness alteration by practitioners of shamanism, music therapists, and adventurers in consciousness. The Didgeridoo or Yidaki, as it is called in the Yolno language, is the traditional instrument played by the indigenous tribal people of Australia. The "People," as they call themselves, are one of the oldest intact cultures surviving on this planet tracing their known origins back 40,000 years. The Didgeridoo is actually created by termites who eat away the inner-cores of the "Stringybark" trees, leaving behind the hollowed-out trunks. By tapping on the fallen trees, the aborigines selectively determine their suitability and hollowness, cut off both ends of the chosen stick, and clean it out, thereby producing a Didgeridoo. Add a little bees-wax for a mouthpiece, and there you have the oldest wind instrument in the world, used for thousands of years to accompany singing, dancing and to alter the state of consciousness of both player and audience. Traditionally aboriginal children are given the Didgeridoo and encouraged to take it out into the Bush for nature be the teacher. After a few hours the Didgeridoo will teach you how to play it. Medium DIO002 $225.00, Large DIO003 $285.00, Ceremonial DIO004 .... $350.00

Elderly Instruments: Catalog free. PO Box 14210, Lansing, MI 48901; phone 517/372-7890, fax 517/372-5155. Eighty pages of string and wind instruments, handmade acoustic guitars, nose flutes, slide whistles. Elderly also offers catalogs of instructional tapes and videos, electric instruments, and roots music recordings.

Antara in C

ANDEAN PIPES

Andean panpipes — also called the antara — are traditionally arranged in a straight row and tuned either to a pentatonic or diatonic (do-re-mi) scale. We're delighted to carry these panpipes made by Edmond Badoux, one of the founding members of the popular South American group SUKAY and now half of the fabulous duo CHASKINAKUY. All are handmade of durable bamboo and tuned to concert pitch.

ANTARA IN G - (*Rondador Pequeno*) Single row, pentatonic, 9 tubes, D E G A B D E G A (keys of G-Em).
ANTG $31.95

ANTARA IN C - Same as above but with 11 tubes in pentatonic tuning, G A C D E G A C D E G (keys of C/Am).
ANTC $44.95

DIATONIC ANTARA IN C - Same as ANTC but with 15 tubes, tuned G A B C D E F G A B C D E F G.
ANTDC $60.95

Mix Bookshelf

"Comprehensive" is a fine word to apply to this catalog of videos, cassettes, and booksbooksbooks about every aspect of sound and recording, and quite a few aspects of music. It's not a discount house, but Mix Bookshelf's impressive depth and concise, informative product summaries make it an invaluable resource to anyone wanting to know anything about recording, digital audio, live sound, MIDI, multimedia, music business, or playing most instruments found in popular music.

Bookshelf often taps the staffs of its siblings, Mix and Electronic Musician magazines, to produce books on topics of special popular interest, like George Petersen's recent Modular Digital Multitracks. —Larry the O

●

The Compact Disc Handbook, 2nd Ed. Ken Pohlmann

Newly updated and expanded edition of the definitive guide to CD technology by the acknowledged authority on the topic. Includes coverage of new formats, including CD-I, CD-ROM, DVI and MiniDisc, explains emerging technologies such as low-bit conversion and noise shaping, discusses weakness and shortcomings in the format, and exposes frauds like disc stabilizers. Features full chapters on CD-player design and the disc mastering/manufacturing process, plus an extensive glossary and index. 1992, 349 pp., $34.95

Getting the Most out of Home Recording, Level 1 with Julian Colbeck

New entry-level video focuses exclusively on cassette multitracks and the fundamentals of demo recording. Clearly explains what all the knobs, buttons and jacks are for, demonstrating with multitrack decks from four different manufacturers, so you'll understand the common features they each share. Focuses on special considerations for recording guitar and vocals. Hard to find; imported from the U.K. 1992, 70 min. VHS, $39.95

Mix Bookshelf:
Catalog free. 6400 Hollis Street, Suite 12, Emeryville, CA 94608; 800/233-9604, fax 510/653-3609.

PRINCIPLES OF DIGITAL AUDIO, 2nd Ed., *Ken Pohlmann* • This best-seller is a recommended technical introduction to digital concepts and technology. Clearly and thoroughly explains the fundamentals like sampling, coding and error correction. Describes real-life implementations, including DAT, optical storage, the various CD formats, and workstations. ©1989, 474 pp. (P) **1481C) $29.95**

THE COMPACT DISC HANDBOOK, 2nd Ed., *Ken Pohlmann* • Newly updated and expanded edition of the definitive guide to CD technology, by the acknowledged authority on the topic. Includes coverage of new formats including CD-I, CD-ROM, DVI and MiniDisc, explains emerging technologies such as low-bit conversion and noise shaping, discusses weakness and shortcomings in the format, and exposes frauds like disc stabilizers. Features full chapters on CD-player design and the disc mastering/manufacturing process, plus an extensive glossary and index. ©1992, 349 pp. (P) **1475D) $34.95**

RDAT, *John Watkinson* • Fully describes the operating theory and applications of Digital Audio Tape, with complete info on A/D conversion, digital recording, error correction, tape transports and using R-DAT as a computer data recorder. Clear explanations, ample illustrations, an absolute minimum of math, plus information on time code and SCMS. ©1991, 244 pp. (H) **1488D) $69.95**

Cassette Mythos

The several dozen essays in Cassette Mythos present reflections by some prolific and prominent musicians who use cassettes as their primary medium, as well as a few by reviewers, distributors, and fans (who naturally are sometimes cassette artists as well). They cover many angles of the genre: its history, its advantages and disadvantages, home-studio production advice, how cassettes have changed the production and consumption of music in Java (one of the most interesting pieces), and the role of the Walkman in modern society.

There are contributions by Sue Ann Harkey, Chris Cutler, Annea Lockwood, and John Oswald, though essays by more obscure figures are equally interesting. They all share a love for the personal expression of recording whatever music you want in whatever way you please. —Richie Unterberger

●

Lately I have been thinking about giving up making records, and just doing cassettes. I don't know if I will ever do this, because I love records too. However, they come with the stain of shit, the vibe of the music industry that still dominates what gets released and distributed. Even though the number of do-it-yourself LPs has increased tenfold since I started out in Canada, all one has to do is check out what cassettes are available and the conclusion is obvious — records are only telling a small part of the story, and the safest part in many cases. "This is for a record — let's make it sound really slick." "I like that but I don't want to put it on the record." "This is my first LP, I really have to impress people." "I'll do something like this later, but for now I have to do such-and-such to get a record…"

Cassette Mythos
Robin James, Editor. 1992; 192 pp. ISBN 0-936756-69-1 $14 postpaid from Autonomedia, PO Box 568, Williamsburgh Station, Brooklyn, NY 11211; 718/387-6471

All of these are common attitudes amongst record producers, no matter what they are planning to transfer from $1/2$-track to vinyl. But cassettes . . . the most common point of view is: "Who gives a shit? If you don't like it, dub over it." And after more than a decade documenting my music that's the most exciting thing I've heard.

●

The River Archive — I started it back in about 1966-67 recording a series of Welsh and Scottish rivers/streams/springs. Why? Well, I'm a New Zealander, and rivers are a major part of New Zealand life, especially if, like my family, you do a lot of climbing, etc. Very powerful, New Zealand rivers. Also, I'd been reading about the use of riverine environments for healing in Chaldes, in a book by John Michel (English writer), just when I myself was thinking a lot about sound as energy-form, its various effects on the body, etc. So the Archive was both an absurd project (since it intends to include all the world's rivers) and a practical project — a way of studying water sounds and their physiological effects.

I've not counted how many rivers the Archive now has, contributed by friends and acquaintances, as well as my own collecting.

MIDI for the Professional

MIDI is the scheme used to connect modern electronic musical instruments and their brethren into coordinated networks. There are good introductory books on MIDI, and it's covered in several widely available periodicals. But once you get out of the starting gate, there isn't much, short of the actual specification documents themselves, from which to glean intermediate to advanced information. "Actually, I know of no good lit. on electronic music, and I've been stuck in it for at least a dozen years," sighed Wendy (née Walter) Carlos twenty-three years ago in the Last Whole Earth Catalog (1971). I have often felt that way about MIDI literature.

MIDI for the Professional fills this gap. Starting with an overview of the specification and its history, MIDI moves through a thorough, generic discussion of related instruments and tools; this is followed by nine chapters of accessible real-world applications and a chapter on MIDI's future. It's the best organized and most concise (yet rigorous) treatment I have seen of the subject. —Larry the O

MIDI for the Professional
Paul Lehrman & Tim Tully. 1993; 239 pp. $19.95 ($22.70 postpaid) from Music Sales Corp., 5 Bellvale Road, Chester, NY 10918; 800/438-6873

●

Step-time Entry
A sequencer's ability to play at different tempos makes it possible to record difficult passages at a slow tempo, then play them back much faster. Step-time entry allows even more accurate recording by letting you first specify the duration of notes, and then play them at any speed or rhythm. Most step-time functions allow a wide range of durations, including complex rhythms, like filling two beats with three notes, filling five beats with seven notes, filling three beats with nineteen notes, and so on. A new duration can be selected as you enter each note, so that you can program any conceivable musical line.

photo: Steve Neilig

WOMAD

Best known as a wildly eclectic music and dance festival, World of Music Arts and Dance was founded in 1981 in the UK. Primarily Western audiences at over forty festivals have been introduced to such performers as Salif Keita and Hugh Masekela through WOMAD, along with a host of lesser-known acts sharing billing with familiar faces like the Pogues and Sinead O'Connor. In keeping with founder Peter Gabriel's bent for the latest technology, recent WOMAD festivals have featured Future Zone, a tent chock with CD-ROM gadgetry. Attendees can dabble in interactive musical and video effects, creating their own version of a music video to take away. WOMAD also works in conjunction with Gabriel's Real World Records, which records many of the festival artists live and in the studio, and serves as a music publishing company for festival performers.

Officially an educational charity since 1983, WOMAD's broad mission is to both entertain and inform. To this end, performers give participatory workshops in subjects such as dance, drumming, voice, and even mask-making, both at the festivals and in schools. WOMAD also publishes a series of multimedia resources, currently used in British schools but also available outside the UK, called "Exploring the Music of the World."
—Dana Mayer

WOMAD: Millside, Mill Lane, Box, Wiltshire, SN14 9PN, UK; phone 44-225-744-044, fax 44-225-743-481.

The Jazz And Blues Lover's Guide to the U.S.

I'm not much of a traveler (I'd rather stay home and listen to records) so the best compliment I can make to Christiane Bird's music book-cum-travel guide is that it makes me want to go and check out the places she's uncovered. By combining a historian's approach with current information about record stores, radio stations, and night clubs, Bird (working with many local informants) has written what amounts to a sociology of jazz and blues.

Bird brings an infectious enthusiasm to her subject, coupled with a realist's attitude to cover charges and sight lines. If you want to know how to find W. C. Handy's grave or Thelonious Monk's former apartment in New York, this book is for you. Now if you'll excuse me, I've got a plane to catch.
—Stuart Kremsky

•
Probably the best-known blues club in Chicago, B.L.U.E.S. is small and dark, paneled with old black wood and strewn with Christmas-tree lights. All of the greats — Sunnyland Slim, Koko Taylor, Big Walter Horton, James Cotton, Pinewood Perkins — have played on its tiny, rickety stage, which is only a few feet away from the audience … Especially wonderful are Sunday nights, when blues godfather Sunnyland Slim, now in his eighties, is hunched over his piano, pounding the keys and smiling out at the crowd through deep-set eyes.

•
Helena, Arkansas
Located across the Mississippi from Clarksdale, Helena was a thriving wide-open port town during the '30's and '40's. The main street, Cherry, which paralleled the levee, had dozens of white saloons, while Elm Street, running just behind, had dozens of black. Bluesmen from all over — Johnny Shines, Robert Johnson, Howlin' Wolf, Sunnyland Slim, and Roosevelt Sykes (born in Helena) — congregated here by the dozens, knowing they could get work. Roosevelt Sykes wrote a song called "West Helena Blues," and Memphis Minnie sang about "Reachin' Pete," an unpopular policeman who patrolled Cherry Street.

"Most everywhere you'd go back then, you'd step into them blues," says one longtime Helena resident.

Today, Helena is a sad little place with no steady live blues joints. Cherry is still the main street — and it's lined with some wonderful pre-World War I buildings that the town is trying to restore — but the heart has gone out of it.

Helena sponsors one of the best blues festivals around, the King Biscuit Blues Festival, held every October (see "Major Festivals," page 359) in honor of Sonny Boy Williamson. Williamson was the town's most famous resident, and even though most of Helena's citizenry were or are oblivious to the blues, those who knew him still talk about him with amazement.

The Jazz and Blues Lover's Guide to the U. S.
Christiane Bird. 1994; 385 pp.
ISBN 0-201-62648-9
$14.95 ($16.45 postpaid) from Addison-Wesley Publishing Co./Order Dept., 1 Jacob Way, Reading, MA 01867; 800/447-2226

DOCKERY FARMS
EST. 1895 BY
WILL DOCKERY 1865-1936
JOE RICE DOCKERY
1906-1982

Dockery's Plantation, once home to Charlie Patton, may be the actual place where the blues were born.

A call of horns announces the arrival of Tulshi Rinpoche (Tibet).

Voices of Forgotten Worlds

In this sumptuous set (a book with two CDs), twenty-eight brief, "sonically illustrated" essays are complemented by color photos and observations by musicologists and tribal people. *Voices* is an inspired reminder that until very recently music was not a vehicle to individual stardom but a communal activity — an intrinsic part of ritual, celebration, and storytelling — a function it still serves in the world's imperiled traditional cultures.
—Richie Unterberger

•
In 99% of the world, the overtones naturally present in a human voice are ignored. But in Tuva, an isolated land wedged between Siberia and Mongolia, overtones are treasured; they are seen as an expression of one's feelings about nature. Overtones are nurtured, not lost through lack of use.

For the rest of us, bringing out the overtones in our own voices is next to impossible, something like trying to learn an obscure foreign language with few native speakers available to help us get it right. Nevertheless, we can hear the overtones in a Tuvan's voice.

"San Sventa N'Ahual San Lorenzo" or "Song For Our Lord San Lorenzo" is used during the Fiesta of Mother Guadelupe, patron saint in the town of Nabenchuac. In this ceremony, musicians lead a long procession of religious officials in full regalia. Women follow, carrying flowers for the saint as fireworks explore in the background. (The noise of the fireworks is believed to attract the rain god.) As the procession reaches the plaza, the bell of the town church punctuates the sounds of the amay, a reed flute and tambor, a colonial military drum.

•
Uighur people all can sing, and most play some kind of folk instrument. Every family has at least one "dutar" (lute). Uighurs cannot have a party without singing and dancing.

Voices of Forgotten Worlds
(Traditional Music of Indigenous People)
Larry Blumenfeld, Editor.
ISBN 1-55961-221-5
Book & 2 CDs. $34.95 ($38.95 postpaid) from Ellipsis Arts, 20 Lumber Road, Roslyn, NY 11576; 800/788-6670

Option

This magazine was created in the mid-eighties to preserve and nurture what its predecessor, the inimitable OP, had begun: a forum for critiquing obscure music of every genre. In addition to reviewing mostly independently produced albums, Option loudly championed the homemade cassette (CDs were virtually unknown at the time). In 1985, this was referred to (without apology, embarrassment, or irony) as "alternative music." Option was the zine to be read (or to be reviewed in) if you were interested or involved in the musical underground.

*Option still focuses on new and unusual music, and many of its subjects have gone on to grace the covers of bigger publications. No longer concerned with the homemade-cassette format, and now getting plenty of major-label ad money, Option has managed to avoid becoming pretentious, clubby, or trendy. It continues to uncover musical gems from all over the world (on both major and indy labels) with intelligent articles, reviews, and newsbits on topics like CD reissues, copyright protection, and industry shenanigans. Don't worry about the occasional celebrity cover band. Inside you'll still find artists as varied as Don Cherry, Butch Hancock, Baba Maal, and Beat Happening — the musical world at your fingertips.
—Lorry Fleming*

Option
Mark Kemp, Editor.
$15.95/year (6 issues). 522-B Cloverfield Boulevard, Santa Monica, CA 90404; 310/449-0120

•

You can almost see the dollar signs twinkle in their eyes when they talk about "expanding markets" and "international distribution networks." Listening to them, I felt like I'd dropped in on a big-bucks, sci-fi version of the do-it-yourself days of punk. But I learned not to mention the punk comparison to these new rave entrepreneurs. It only made them laugh. To these people, punk was not a break from the old ways at all, just the last dying gasp of the '60s.

The government has also been cracking down on music and dancing, yet for some inexplicable reason they allow Happy Land to stay open for two hours twice a week.

One evening we go there. It is almost completely empty …

It's only 40 minutes before the club has to close. The night looks likes it's going to be a dud. Suddenly, one after the other, young African men come streaming in. All Southerners … they have walked five and a half hours across the desert to get there. They fill the place up and start to do some serious damage on the dance floor. None sit around and just talk. They are there to dance. The music becomes harder to hear, drowned out by a frenzy of whooping and shouting and pounding of feet. The European expatriates get up to try to leave, but they have to pass the dance floor to get to the exit and it's too crazy. So they retreat. For 30 minutes the crowd goes off the wall. Then the police arrive, the music stops, and everyone quickly leaves the club.

The Beat

The Beat
$12/year (6 issues). Bongo Productions, PO Box 65856, Los Angeles, CA 90065

*Reggae may have retreated slightly from the pop consciousness, but the pulsating rhythms of Jamaica continue to rock the island's dancehalls and influence other continents. Founded as Reggae Beat, this bimonthly recognized that the international audience's hunger for new rhythms, which Marley did so much to ignite, has spread to new vistas. It now covers reggae, African, Caribbean, and world beat with opinionated zeal. In addition to dozens of reviews of US and import releases, and columns by the likes of Roger Steffens and Gene Scaramuzzo, on-the-spot reports from budding music scenes (like a recent diary of a search for the roots of soukous in the heart of the Congo) unearth the soul of their communities as well as their sounds.
—RU*

•

"Dancehall artists need to know their responsibility," warns Rebel prophetically. "They need to realize the power of words. They need to realize how influential music is … how music can give strength and how it can weaken dem too. They are like the watchmen of the city and they are supposed to sound the trumpet and if they don't … the guilt will be on their shoulders."

Living Blues

*No other publication tells the stories of America's most powerful and influential indigenous music as well as Living Blues. Attention is paid both to the blues' immense legacy and to living (and emerging) musicians. The archival level of detail in some of the historical pieces may be too minute for some general readers, but the writing and presentation manage to be scholarly and accessible at the same time.
—Richie Unterberger*

•

How did you come to meet Bo Diddley?

I passed a restaurant, and there was two guys with guitars and a washtub with a piece of wood and a string to make a bass, and so I walked in and they were sittin' there eating hamburgers or something and I asked him where was they going to play. And he said, "We're going up to the Midway Theater, there's a talent show." So I told him I played harmonica … after the show we came out of the theater and Bo Diddley told me, said, "We play on the streetcorners every weekend. Why don't you come on by and play with us."

About ten o'clock that morning we walked up on 47th, which was right near the 708 club, where Muddy Waters played. Robert Nighthawk was playing there at the time: Muddy Waters, Elmore James. And we started playin' in front of the 708 club. And a crowd of people gathered around and they started throwin' money to us, you know. I was playing the harmonica and Bo Diddley would let me sing one … We played there for maybe ten or fifteen minutes, then we go up the street, few more blocks and draw another crowd and we go all up and down 47th, 43rd, and we wind up on the West Side at about nine or ten o'clock that night.

Living Blues
David Nelson, Editor.
$18/year (6 issues). Center for the Study of Southern Culture, University of Mississippi, University, MS 38677-9836

Folk Roots • Dirty Linen

The audience for traditional folk and acoustic music never died. But in the mid-eighties one could be forgiven for thinking that international roots music had disappeared. Emerging at around that time, from England and America, Folk Roots and Dirty Linen have filled the gap and more. Each has done its part to revitalize folk, with devoted, enthusiastic coverage not only of traditional folk music but of the exploding African and world music scene, as well as of the folk rogues who bring rock'n'roll sensibility to traditional music.

Folk Roots, the UK's premiere roots-music magazine, and Dirty Linen share roughly similar types of material (features, interviews, reviews, discographies, events and release listings). Dirty Linen, the less glossy and less comprehensive, also offers tour information via several online services. With their different slants and specialties, these publications complement one another well. —RU

Folk Roots
Ian Anderson, Editor.
£45/year; 12 issues (please pay in £ Sterling). Southern Rag Ltd., PO Box 337, London N4 1TW, UK; phone 44-081-340-9651, fax 44-081-348-5626

Dirty Linen
Paul Hartman, Editor.
$20/year (6 issues). PO Box 66600, Baltimore, MD 21239; phone 410/583-7973, fax 410/337-6735

The older arena audience enjoying the Yunnan Ensemble from China. —*Folk Roots*

OTHER MUSICAL RESOURCES

Grass Roots International Folk Resource Directory: Leslie Berman & Heather Wood. 1993, Publishers Book & Audio.

Thousands of listings of folk clubs, concert venues, festivals, stores, radio programs, and other folk music resources from around the world.

The Virgin Directory of World Music: Philip Sweeney. 1992, Henry Holt and Co.

MUSIC BY MAIL

Want to find a Swiss CD of experimental Moroccan dub/hip-hop, a German boxed set of vintage Johnny Cash, a cassette of Indonesian gamelan music, and the new independent CD by that great band you saw for the first time last week? Such eclectic shopping lists are becoming the norm as our society grows increasingly multicultural, and our ears become more receptive to sounds from around the world. Until the distant day (which may never arrive) when we can download whatever we want from a central database containing all the music ever recorded, you'd be hard-pressed to find all of the above records at the best store in the world — or maybe even the best fifty stores.

For the motivated and curious, though, a network of mail-order sources for recordings is already in place. What follows is just a partial list of outlets (and one magazine). Taken together, they offer an enormous selection that the electronic shopping malls of tomorrow will have a tough time matching.
—Richie Unterberger

Compact Disc Connection: 1030 E. El Camino #322, Sunnyvale, CA 94087; 408/985-7905, fax 408/985-0464, modem 408/985-8982. An online service that distributes over 80,000 CD titles in all genres. Customers can browse, select, and pay for albums via modem, and even access several thousand *All Music Guide* reviews as they peruse titles. Access via telnet from the Internet, and via modems from over 75 US cities.

Midnight Records: PO Box 390, New York, NY 10113-390; 212/675-2768. The world's largest mail-order vendor of independent and reissued rock'n'roll CDs and LPs. Especially strong on fifties and sixties rock and new alternative rock.

Roundup Records: PO Box 154, Cambridge, MA 02140; 617/661-6308, fax 617/868-8769. Free catalog. Thousands of vintage and contemporary roots rock, blues, R&B, reggae, jazz, and world music CDs, LPs, and cassettes.

Original Music: 418 Lasher Road, Tivoli, NY 12583; 914/756-2767, fax 914/756-2027. World music of all genres.

RRRecords: 151 Paige Street, Lowell, MA 01852; 508/454-8002. Free catalog. Covers the most extreme and harshest end of electronic, avant-garde, and experimental music.

North Country: The Cadence Building, Redwood, NY 13679; 315/287-2852. Distributes hundreds of independent labels — principally jazz, but other progressive/experimental music as well. Affiliated with the excellent progressive jazz magazine *Cadence*.

Roots'n'Rhythm: 6921 Stockton Avenue, El Cerrito, CA 94530; 510/525-1494. The mail-order catalog arm of the Down Home Music store. Extensive selection of blues, R&B, folk, Celtic, world, early rock'n'roll, country, and early jazz music.

Round World By Mail: 591 Guerrero Street, San Francisco, CA 94110; 415/255-7384. Specializes in African, Arabic, Latin and Caribbean music, including imports, both contemporary and traditional.

Wayside Music: PO Box 8427, Silver Spring, MD 20907-8427; 301/589-6047. Offers the most extensive selection of avant-garde/experimental/progressive rock music by mail.

Goldmine: $35/year (24 issues) 700 E. State Street, Iola, WI 54990; 715/445-2214. The Bible of the record-collecting community, this magazine includes reams of tiny-print ads for mail-order companies and individuals selling private collections. Lengthy features and reviews of vintage rock and other music.

The Trouser Press Record Guide

The Trouser Press Record Guide
Ira A. Robbins, Editor. 1991; 800 pp. ISBN 0-02-036361-3
$20 postpaid from Macmillan Publishing Co., 100 Front Street, Riverside, NJ 08075-7500; 800/257-5755

Formerly a guide to new wave records, the **Trouser Press Record Guide** *now bills itself as "The Ultimate Guide To Alternative Music." It's the most comprehensive reference to music that can trace its roots to the mid-1970s birth of punk and new wave. The 750-page fourth edition reviews discs by "alternative" rock groups around the world. This book gives more weight to independent releases and imports than the more mainstream (though also worthy)* **Rolling Stone Album Guide;** *entries for each artist are prefaced by lengthy discographies*

noting year of release, label (and country for non-UK imports), side projects of group members, and whether the record has been issued on compact disc.

Editor Ira Robbins (who edited the now-defunct Anglophile/new wave magazine **Trouser Press**) and several dozen contributors give concise descriptions of 2,500 artists and nearly 10,000 discs. At times one wishes that the evaluations were more critical; on the whole they are too generous, with a love of power-pop that can border on weakness. The **Guide** is nonetheless the best source of information on a movement that continues to influence rock and pop. —RU

•

DRAGONS
Parfums de la Révolution (Fr. Blitzkrieg) 1982

A piece of punk exotica: three underground musicians from mainland China recorded in secret by a visiting Frenchman. (Done, thankfully, before the brief 1985 tour there by Wham!) Using only vocals, electric guitar, rudimentary drums and Chinese violin, the trio attempts "Anarchy In The UK" and "Get Off My Cloud" with truly bizarre results; the remaining seven tracks are originals in a more traditional Oriental vein. A fascinating transliteration of rock from a country not generally considered in terms of modern music.

All Music Guide

It's like a **World Almanac** *of recorded music — full of nifty facts and labels, with a unique assortment of time-capsule histories of musical genres. Based on a database of over 100,000 records, tapes and CDs, it gives concise, punchy overviews of the best recorded music in twenty-three categories.*

Strong points are its completeness and thoroughness in rarely documented categories (women's music, gay music, rap), and obscure but important sub-genres like Hawaiian and marching-band music. Some of the 23,000 items reviewed are currently unavailable, or not on CD yet — there is no compromise here on what's good.

I can't imagine a serious music lover, record store, radio station, or library without a copy. And twenty bucks is a steal. **All Music Guide** *is an ongoing project that is not limited to the book format. It has been issued as a CD-ROM, and its database is accessible via online services.* —Cliff Martin

All Music Guide
Michael Erlewine & Scott Bultman, Editors. 1992; 1176 pp. ISBN 0-87930-264-X
$19.95 ($25 postpaid) from Miller Freeman Publications/Order Dept., 6600 Silacci Way, Gilroy, CA 95020; 800/848-5594

The Penguin Guide to Jazz

Given the prolific recording careers of many jazz musicians, it has always been somewhat intimidating for the newcomer to deduce what's good and what's not — a problem that has become more acute with the flood of CD reissues. Suppose, for example, you have just heard Miles Davis' classic "Kind Of Blue" and (naturally) enjoyed it. Where do you go from there? Directly to this book.

A few caveats are in order, mostly stemming from the fact that this was written for a British audience. Reference to prominent UK musicians who

The Penguin Guide to Jazz
(on CD, LP and Cassette)
Richard Cook & Brian Morton. Penguin Books, 1993; 1312 pp. ISBN 0-14-015364-0
$22.50 ($24.50 postpaid) from Penguin USA/Consumer Sales, 120 Woodbine Street, Bergenfield, NJ 07621; 800/253-6476

are practically unknown over here will have many American readers scratching their heads. More serious are the differences in availability, since this is one of the factors that goes into their ratings. It would have benefited from some editing, but Cook and Morton's generous attitude and obvious knowledge of worldwide jazz trends make the **Guide** tremendous fun to dip into and argue with. And it will pay for itself if it keeps you from buying a few clunkers. —Stuart Kremsky

•

Anthony Braxton (reeds)
★★★★ *Seven Compositions (Trio) 1989* [hat Art CD 6025; CD] Braxton; Adelhard Roidinger (bass); Tony Oxley (drums).

Anthony Braxton records are a little like No.12 buses. There's always another one along in a moment. He is, perhaps, the most extensively documented contemporary improviser — remarkably so, given the dauntingly cerebral character of at least some of his output. There is a further problem: is Braxton's music jazz at all, since a large proportion of his work, solos and all, is — gasp! — scored? The 1989

trio settles the second of these at least. Whatever the prevailing definition of jazz (and as the man said, if you have to ask...), this music conforms majestically: rhythmic, virtuosic, powerfully emotive, constantly reinventing itself. Tony Oxley, a veteran of the British free jazz movement of the 1960s, plays superbly and is beautifully recorded. Braxton runs through his usual gamut of horns... and sounds assured and confident. There's even a standard, a powerful "All The Things You Are." If you've room for only one Braxton... look no further; no question at all as to the validity of this particular release.

Thinking with a Pencil

Good title, wonderful book — an inviting, pragmatic introduction to the full range of image representation. Henning Nelms makes it look easy, and like great fun.
—Stewart Brand

This great example of a book-as-tool has proved its fitness by staying in print for more than three decades. Every page is a demonstration in using illustrations as thinking tools. You have to think visually to communicate visually. —HLR

Distinguishing several positions of the same object by dotted lines. Also note use of a dotted line to indicate the path of the ball.

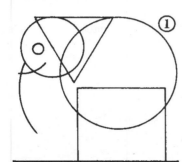

How construction works. Once a framework of geometrical shapes has been constructed, a child can complete the drawing — if he has a source to follow.

●
Practical drawings are mental tools. Once you have learned to make them, you will find that they are as useful in solving problems as saws and hammers are useful in carpentry.

Omitting the useless is as important as including the essential. Aristotle stated a fundamental truth when he said that everything which does not add will detract.

Thinking with a Pencil
Henning Nelms. 1986; 347 pp.
ISBN 0-89815-052-3
$14.95 ($17.95 postpaid) from
Ten Speed Press, PO Box 7123,
Berkeley, CA 94707;
800/841-2665

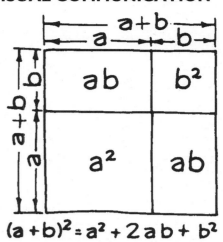

$$(a+b)^2 = a^2 + 2ab + b^2$$

Abstract Ideas. Concrete objects, such as rat mazes, are easy to visualize because we can imagine them as they would appear. But how can we visualize abstract ideas that no one can see?

Daniel Smith Inc.

Daniel Smith, Inc.
Catalog $4. 4150 1st Avenue S.,
Seattle, WA 98124; 800/426-6740

Here is an immense selection of absolutely first-rate supplies for the fine artist, as well as a wonderfully prompt and efficient mail-order house. Their goods are discounted (generally 20 to 30 percent off retail), and are interestingly and informatively presented in a photo-illustrated yearly catalog (supplemented by intermittent special-sale catalogs). In terms of care and knowledgability, no other art supplier I have found comes close. —Garta Hodge

Isabey Series 6234 Squirrel Mop. Unlike many mops these are handcupped using the true end of the hair for the tip. The watercolorist looking for a sky or wash brush will find this a good choice.

Perspective

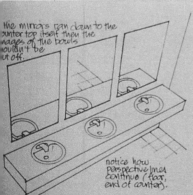

Why draw perspectives when CAD software will do it for you? Because all you'll get is "computery-looking buildings," says architect/artist Malcolm Wells, as he gently nudges and inspires us to better things. Nothing computery here, not even a font. It's as good a drawing lesson as you're likely to find anywhere. —J. Baldwin

Perspective
Malcolm Wells. 1993; 96 pp.
ISBN 0-9621878-7-9
$12 postpaid from Malcolm Wells,
673 Satucket Road, Brewster, MA 02631

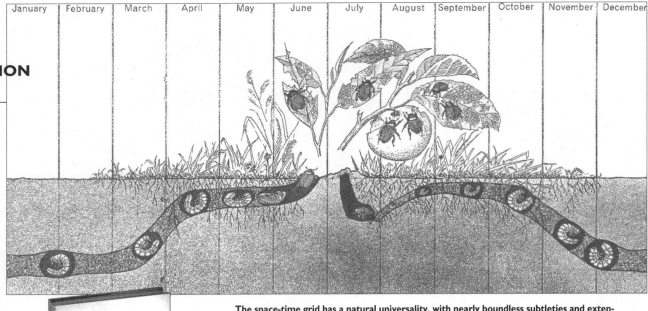

Envisioning Information

Buy this book. Keep it with the few others that you plan to pass on to the next generation. It is a passionate, elegant revelation of how to render the three dimensions of experience into the two dimensions of paper or screen. As in his previous classic, **The Visual Display of Quantitative Information** *(below), Tufte is promoting a new standard of visual literacy. This latest book (immaculately printed in 23 colors) is a lyrical primer of design strategies for reading and creating messages in "flatland." No other book has been so highly recommended to us by so many varieties of professionals — architects, teachers, technicians, hackers, and artists. —Kevin Kelly*

The space-time grid has a natural universality, with nearly boundless subtleties and extensions. Organized like the graphical timetable, this unusual arrangement above simultaneously describes two dimensions, space *and* time, on the horizontal while maintaining a vertical spatial dimension. A complete year-long life cycle of *Popillia japonica Newman* (the Japanese beetle) is shown, transparently, in a smooth escape from flatland brought about by doubling up variables along the horizontal.

Envisioning Information
Edward R. Tufte. 1990; 128 pp.
ISBN 0 -9613921-1-8
$48 postpaid from Graphics Press,
PO Box 430, Cheshire, CT 06410;
203/272-9187. 800/822-2454

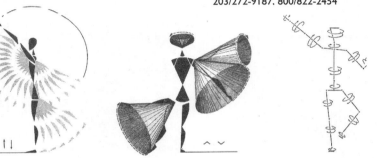

Multiplied consecutive images eerily trace out motion, in these original diagrams from an earnestly scientific system of movement notation. The proliferating cones and plates perhaps help to envision the range of three-space action, although the substance might be forgotten amid witticisms provoked by the eccentric drawings.

The Visual Display of Quantitative Information

Turn to any page in this finely printed volume; you'll be treated to another ingenious chart that is at once simple, communicative, and beautiful. Flamboyant graphs, particularly those dressing up inadequate data, are bad craft: "If the statistics are boring, then you've got the wrong numbers." Tufte gives memorable, handsome examples of information presented with integrity and clarity. The whole book is a good example. It's the one you'll consult before you pick up graph paper. —KK

● Just as a good editor of prose ruthlessly prunes out unnecessary words, so a designer of statistical graphics should prune out ink that fails to present fresh data-information. Although nothing can replace a good graphical idea applied to an interesting set of numbers, editing and revision are as essential to sound graphical design work as they are to writing. T. S. Eliot emphasized the "capital importance of criticism in the work of creation itself. Probably, indeed, the larger part of the labour of an author in composing his work is critical labour; the labour of sifting, combining, constructing, expunging, correcting, testing: this frightful toil is as much critical as creative."

The Visual Display of Quantitative Information
Edward R. Tufte. 1983; 197 pp.
ISBN 0-9613921-0-X
$40 postpaid from Graphics Press,
PO Box 430, Cheshire, CT 06410;
203/272-9187, 800/822-2454

Fear

⟹ **Rage**

...wherein the data points are themselves
data. Here the effect of two variables
interacting is portrayed by the faces on
the plotting field.

see also
p. 245, comix

OTHER **R**ESOURCES

1983, University of Wisconsin Press. A monumental work, essential in its theory. A visual feast, full of transparent layers of beautifully defined content. Ultimately desirable. No wonder it's out of print.

Editing by Design: Jan V. White, RR Bowker 1982. Outstanding book on design — using the image of the page to carry a message with clarity.

When the entire globe is to be represented in a single image, the choice of projection is of fundamental importance.

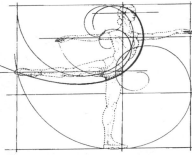

The Secret Art of the Performer

A true how-to book on practical magic. Education, friendship, courtship, parenting, politics, art, commerce, warfare all depend upon a strong element of performance.

This book is an intense combination of astonishing and useful lore about how performers perform, everywhere in the world, illustrated by a profusion of equally astonishing and useful photographs and drawings. Mudras, minuets, masks, ritual, biomechanics, dramaturgy, rhythm, staging, improvization, semiotics, footwork, make-up, choreography, mythology and other phenomena are examined in **The Secret Art**. *The different aspects of the full spectrum of human performance are addressed with attention to the spiritual, communicative, social, and aesthetic meanings of each variety of performative behavior. It is a vibrant example of what anthropologist Clifford Geertz means by "thick description." —HLR*

**A Dictionary of
Theatre Anthropology**
(The Secret Art of the Performer)
Eugenio Barba & Nicola Savarese.
1991; 272 pp. ISBN 0-415-05308-0
$29.95 ($32.45 postpaid) from Routledge,
Chapman and Hall/Order Dept.,
29 W. 35th Street, New York, NY
10001-2291; 212/244-6412

Street Theatre

*Bim Mason, founder of the Mummer and Dada Theatre Company and a teacher at Britain's national circus school, discourses with loving zeal upon all aspects of outdoor theatre: processions, site-specific works, guerilla performances, strolling performances, busking, and much much more. Insightful analyses of dozens of performers and groups (primarily European) evince the wonderful possibilities of working in the open air.
—Adam G. Gertsacov*

•

Another piece involves a number of very normal people in out-of-date clothes, brown macs, suits, and trilby hats. They carry placards saying 'Down with Bicycles' and 'Pedal Power? No Thanks!'. They march down the street like a mini-protest, forming a line at suitable locations such as a bicycle repair shop. Coming across a line of parked bicycles they 'sabotage' them by laying them on their side. Sometimes they will avoid and sneer at bicycle-owners, other times they will confront them, pulling at their pannier straps, or laying lines of drawing pins in their path. Occasionally they take more extreme and ludicrous measures

•

Among the ten qualities of the dancer in Indian tradition, there is one quality which has to do with knowing how to see, how to direct the eyes in space. It is a sign that the dancer is reacting to something precise. At times, a performer's training exercises appear to be extraordinarily well-executed, but the actions have no power because the way of using the eyes is not precisely directed. On the other hand, the body may

Drawing of an arabesque for a false window in the Isfahan mosque (Iran).

by lying down in front of them. A cyclist who pedals away may be chased by these placard-wielding objectors. Although there is a confrontation it is gentle, never verbal and as far as possible spread amongst a whole group rather than focused on a few individuals. What they seem to be trying to achieve is to make fun of self-righteous reactionary forces but also to provoke the spectators into expressing their opposition to these characters, safe in the knowledge that it is only a game.

**Street Theatre and
Other Outdoor Performance**
Bim Mason. 1992; 176 pp.
ISBN 0-415-07050-3
$18.95 ($21.45 postpaid) from Routledge,
Chapman and Hall/Order Dept., 29 W.
35th Street, New York, NY 10001-2291;
212/244-6412

be relaxed, but if the eyes are active – that is, if they see in order to observe – then the performer's body is brought to life. In this sense, the eyes are like the performer's second spinal column. All the Oriental traditions codify eye movements and the directions the eyes must follow. This has to do not only with what the spectator sees, but also the performer herself, the way she populates the empty space with lines of force, with stimuli to which she must react.

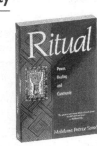

Schematic analysis of an arabesque, one of the basic positions in classical ballet.

Ritual: Power, Healing, and Community

Ritual is where performance converges with community and conjures spirit. The author was raised in a small African village, holds degrees from the Sorbonne and Brandeis, and shows that he knows something serious about the essence of ritual, from both academic and ground-truth perspectives. —HLR

•

In the ritual, one has to have participants who are invisible and can actually produce a result that is unexpected. And because we take the risk or the initiative of putting a request to the spirits to intervene in our affairs, their coming turns our activity (ceremony) into a ritual. It still means that we as individuals play a central role in making a ritual happen. The gods themselves will not enact the ritual without us. What actually makes ritual a requirement is far beyond what the world, as it is, can handle. In the surface world our ability to make things happen is very limited. This limitation is a reflection of the incompleteness of a world without the spirit realm. So Spirit is our channel through which every gap in life can be filled. But the spirit realm will not take care of these gaps without our conscious participation. Thus our collaboration makes us central to the actual happening of a ritual.

•

A functioning community does not need to peer at its members to make sure that they comply with the law. A functioning community is one that is its own protection. And one cannot form a community whose goal is to tear the rest of the society apart. A community that wants to "correct" the current sense of community is not going to survive.

An Actor Prepares

*The Source Text. Stanislavski's studies of the techniques of the best actors of his day are the basis of all subsequent teachings. His dedications and worship of nature are an inspiration.
—Peter Coyote*

•

Never lose yourself on the stage. Always act in your own person, as an artist. You can never get away from yourself. The moment you lose yourself on the stage marks the departure from truly living your part and the beginning of exaggerated false acting. Therefore, no matter how much you act, how many parts you take, you should never allow yourself any exception to the rule of using your own feelings. To break that rule is the equivalent of killing the person you are portraying, because you deprive him of a palpitating, human soul, which is the real source of life for a part.

An Actor Prepares
Constantin Stanislavski. 1989; 320 pp.
ISBN 0-87830-983-7 $14.95 ($17.45 postpaid) from Routledge, Chapman and Hall/
Order Dept., 29 W. 35th Street,
New York, NY 10001-2291; 212/244-6412

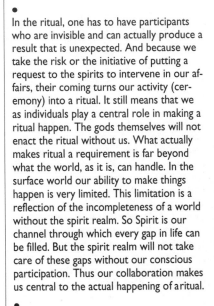

**Ritual: Power, Healing,
and Community**
Malidoma Patrice Somé.
Swan Raven & Company, 1993; 127 pp.
ISBN 0-9632310-2-2
$12.95 ($16.95 postpaid) from
Atrium Pub.,11270 Clayton Creek Road,
Lower Lake, CA 95457; 800/275-2606

THE SKY'S NO LIMIT

In 1945, a budding science writer named Arthur C. Clarke first envisioned placing a satellite in orbit 22,300 miles directly above the equator, where it would appear stationary to receivers on the ground. Today dozens of communications satellites orbit the "Clarke Belt," and more than 4.3 million parabolic dishes are installed in the backyards of America alone. The launch of DBS (direct broadcast) satellites in 1994 made it possible to bring down 150 channels on one eighteen-inch antenna, at a total hardware cost less than $800.

So what's on those "birds" that you can't already receive on your local cable or that old rabbit-ears antenna? Well, how about the latest news from China, Portugal or Peru. Or twenty-four-hour coverage of NASA flights. Or computer advice. Take your choice of Mac TV, The Computer Network channel or New Media Computer News.

Of course these nuggets are nearly lost in the barrage of thousands of hours of movies and the same old TV dreck: sitcoms, dog racing, religious shows and endless shopping networks (hawking everything from hunting knives to fine art). Pay channels are proliferating to serve the new "mini mass markets": a golf network, at least one channel devoted solely to talk shows, another with quilting lessons, more religion networks and, of course, hard-core pornography channels (which have mostly moved to Canadian satellites to avoid lawsuits).

Some special-interest groups are well served: Radio Talking Book Network offers an audio channel with sight description of PBS and nature programs, and the In Touch Service provides readings for the sight impaired. The Americana TV channel features bluegrass musicians, folk programs and storytelling. And special audio channels transmit radio stations in almost every format. —Kim Spencer

The Hidden Signals on Satellite TV

This book helps you modify a home receiver to decipher the myriad data communications hidden on TV satellites: teletext services, stock market reports and commodity news, digital radio channels, private corporate communications and more. Such eavesdropping may, or may not, be legal. —KS

•

Satellite capacity is huge. We talk glibly about a transponder being 36 Megahertz wide, little realizing that takes up everything from sound waves to well up into the lower portion of the VHF spectrum. Do you have any idea how many 10 MHz-wide AM (as in broadcast radio) signals could be shoved into that much spectrum if somebody tried? Well, the answer is 3,600 . . . And that's for one transponder. SATCOM and WESTAR have 24 transponders and if one such satellite was utilized for AM radio, we would have 86,400 "clear channel" continent-wide, AM broadcasting channels to play with.

•

Sure, you know all about TV and the wonderful world of R-rated films, unending sports, non-stop religion, or Ted Turner's attempt to rewrite the news coverage business with dawn-to-dawn reporting. But you probably don't know where to tune in the current Kenai Flight Service Weather Forecasts from Anchorage, or National Public Radio, or several dozen Holidex (Holiday Inns of America) toll-free reservation line circuits, or a major computer company's inter-office, 24-hour a day satellite relayed executive "tie-line". . .

The Hidden Signals on Satellite TV
Thomas P. Harrington. 1992; 238 pp.
ISBN 0-916661-04-0
$19.95 ($22.95 postpaid) from Universal Electronics, Inc., 4555 Groves Road, Suite 13, Columbus, OH 43232; 800/241-8171, fax 614/866-1201

Steve Newman's Satellite TV Picks

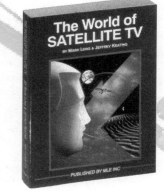

Steve Newman is a meteorologist who publishes "Earthweek: A Diary of the Planet." Syndicated in 120 newspapers worldwide, "Earthweek" reports on global weather, and natural and man-made environmental events. At his small ranch in Northern California, Steve's five dishes receive weather data and monitor news reports from around the planet. Here are some of his favorite satellite TV and radio programs:

• Up-to-the-minute news from all over the globe: BBC Breakfast News (at 3:00 am Eastern); RTVP from Lisbon, Portugal; Dubai TV News; Reuters closed-circuit news feeds from all continents.

• International TV programs: Latin American news and game shows on the SUR network; TV5, a channel devoted to French TV programs; the SCOLA language-education channel showing programs from more than thirty-five national TV networks.

• Country dancing on TNN (The Nashville Network).

• Television network programming: If he misses a favorite show, Steve can catch it later that evening on the transmission from Anchorage, Alaska.

• Music and information on audio subcarriers: The front page of tomorrow's New York Times is read each night at 11:00 pm Eastern on WQXR radio; five hours of live Grand Ole Opry Friday and Saturday nights at 7:30 Eastern, on an extra audio channel of TNN; Jazz stations KJAZ (Alameda, CA), KLON (Long Beach, CA), CBC-FM (Toronto).

Also: Ingenious: More than twenty of the world's wire services and information databanks — including Agence France Press, Tass (Russia), Xinhau (China), Kyodo (Japan) — downlinked via satellite dish to a standard PC. Also available on many cable systems. —KS

Satellite TV Week • ONSAT

These weekly guides list all the satellite TV programs viewable in the Western Hemisphere, and indicate whether they are scrambled or transmitted in the clear. —KS

Satellite TV Week
$52/year (52 issues) from Fortuna Communications/Satellite TV Week, 140 S. Fortuna Blvd., Fortuna, CA 95540-0308; 800/345-8876

ONSAT
$49.95/year (52 issues) from Triple D Publications, PO Box 2347, Shelby, NC 28151-9976; 704/482-9673

The World of Satellite TV

A readable handbook useful to both experienced dish owners and newcomers. —KS

•

In December of 1985 . . . an American satellite (ATS-6) was leased to India for an experimental project that transmitted television programming into satellite earth stations located in remote villages across the subcontinent. English amateur radio enthusiast and BBC technician Steve Birkill learned of the project and set out to build his own receiver and antenna for these transmissions...From well outside the satellite's footprint, with a five foot antenna made from screen, he proved that individuals with limited resources could still bring satellite television into their own homes.

•

Single Channel Per Carrier (SCPC) is an audio transmission system that commonly is used to transmit a variety of audio program services via satellite. Selected transponders on Galaxy, Satcom K, Anik E and Morelos satellites collectively relay more than 150 channels of audio programming around the clock. These SCPC services offer a wide selection of program possibilities ranging from news broadcasts, talk radio and commodities reports, to religious broadcasts and a wide spectrum of music formats. . . . dish owners in rural farming communities can tune in to the weather, agricultural and farming services that can keep them up to date with the latest farming developments.

The World of Satellite TV
Mark Long & Jeffrey Keating. 1992; 302 pp.
ISBN 0-929548-07-8
$24.95 ($27.95 postpaid)
Available volumes: The Americas. 1992, ISBN 0-929548-07-8; Europe, Africa and the Middle East. 1993, ISBN 0-929548-10-8; Asia and the Pacific Rim. 1992, ISBN 0-929548-08-6. Each $24.95 ($27.95 postpaid) from MLE Incorporated, PO Box 159, Winter Beach, FL 32971; 305/767-4687, fax 407/589-9411

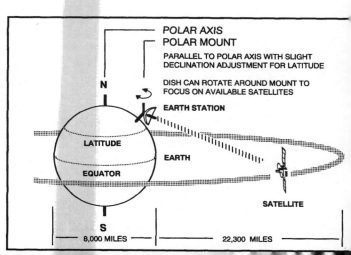

POLAR AXIS
POLAR MOUNT
PARALLEL TO POLAR AXIS WITH SLIGHT DECLINATION ADJUSTMENT FOR LATITUDE

DISH CAN ROTATE AROUND MOUNT TO FOCUS ON AVAILABLE SATELLITES

EARTH STATION

LATITUDE

EARTH

EQUATOR

SATELLITE

8,000 MILES   22,300 MILES

he free and often irresponsible press is not always pleasant to behold; however, politically protected journalism, messy as it is, is sometimes the only forum where justice can be done and questions of governance can be settled. If you know how to do it, journalism can be a powerful tool for exposing corruption and focusing public attention on injustice, incompetence, and malfeasance. — HLR

Competitor Intelligence

A comprehensive guide to sources and methods of gathering intelligence when the target is a business. Designed to help corporations forecast and X-ray their competition, this manual would be just as helpful to environmental groups investigating polluters, unions estimating employer profits, or peace activists studying military contractors. Countless lists of references and information contacts, with addresses and phone numbers. Tips on creative investigative techniques (nothing illegal). Illuminating discussion of how economic activity produces information that flows, pools, leaks and decays. More tools and ideas than you can shake a corporate structure at.
—Robert Horvitz

•
Public data does not necessarily mean published data. There are other sources [of intelligence] that are also publicly available, yet are not found in published form. They include telephone interviews, counting the number of parking spaces in a parking lot, and attending a trade show. All the intelligence you discover about your competitor through these nonpublished sources is still valid intelligence and is very much in the public arena.

Competitor Intelligence
(How to Get It, How to Use It)
Leonard M. Fuld. 1985; 479 pp.
ISBN 0-471-80967-5
$49.95 postpaid. John Wiley & Sons, Inc.,
1 Wiley Dr., Somerset, NJ 08875;
800/225-5945

Center for Investigative Reporting

So you suspect wrongdoing and want to investigate and do a story. Who do you call first? Maybe you should start with the Center for Investigative Reporting. A loose association of freelance journalists, CIR keeps in touch with information sources — public interest groups, concerned officials, news media — that could have the lead you're looking for.
—Sarah Vandershaf

Center for Investigative Reporting
Muckraker Journal $20/year (4 issues). 568 Howard Street, 5th Floor, San Francisco, CA 94105; 415/543-1200.

Rich Sigberman

The intelligence-gathering pyramid —**Competitor Intelligence**

CREATIVE SOURCES (STEP 3)
- Classified Ads
- Environmental Impact Statements
- UCC Filings • FCC
- Corrugated Boxes
- Trade Shows • Buyers Guides
- Visual Sightings • R&D Sources
- Yellow Pages • City Directories
- How to Create Intelligence Sources • How to Build a Financial Report

THE BASIC SOURCES (STEP 2)
- Investment Manuals • Industry Directories • Financial Periodicals
- Getting Government Documents • Statistical Sources • Management Biographies
- Special Magazine Issues • Current Industrial Reports • Wall Street Transcript
- SEC Filings • Data Bases • Credit Services
- State Corporate Filings • State Industry Directories • Foreign Sources

THE TECHNIQUE (STEP 1)
- Doing Your Homework • Designing Questionnaires • Know Thy Industry Before Your Target Company
- Milking Articles
- Checklists • Friendly vs. Unfriendly Sources
- Using Industry Groups • Debriefing

THE FOUNDATION
- Understanding Intelligence • Creative and Basic Sources • Intelligence-Gathering Traits
- Assembling a Research Team • Key Intelligence Factors • Developing a Business Library

The Reporter's Handbook

Most good reporting starts when a reporter smells that something's wrong. But you don't have to be a professional reporter to follow your nose. Anyone can help stop a local abuse by tracking down the facts, but it often means an extended hunt down a trail of paper and interviews. This manual for following that trail is an encyclopedic directory in itself, listing dozens of documents, agencies, and reports that you might never hear about any other way. Put together by a group of experienced investigative journalists, it's one of the few college textbooks that's fun to read.
—Art Kleiner

•
You're methodically researching your project on the ridiculously expensive monorail the county wants to build at the new zoo when your editor starts flailing his arms and hollering at you. The police desk has an update on a bust at a disco last night. It turns out they found in the back room 10 bales of marijuana, 20 kilos of cocaine and 100,000 Quaaludes. A Colombian citizen was among those arrested.

The cops are cooperating with the Drug Enforcement Administration, not with you. They're giving out nothing beyond the arrest sheets.

There are a hundred unanswered questions. Who owns the disco? What else does this person own — land, buildings, cars, boats, airplanes? What's the disco owner's economic background? Has the owner ever been accused of a crime? Does the owner use corporations to hide behind? Is there a limited partnership involved? Who are its investors? How much did they invest? Who's in business with this person?

Public records will answer every one of those questions for you in a few hours.

The Reporter's Handbook
John Ullman & Jan Colbert, Editors. St. Martin's Press, 1990; 442 pp.
ISBN 0-312-00435-4
$22.95 ($26.95 postpaid) from Publishers Book & Audio, PO Box 070059, Staten Island, NY 10307; 800/288-2131

Counter Spy Shop

If you've ever watched a spy movie and wondered whether all those odd little gadgets the actors were using were real, this catalog is the place to find out. Counter Spy Shop is a company that keeps a low profile. They deal in surveillance and countersurveillance equipment, essentials in the Lifestyles of the Rich and Paranoid. Their clients range from private individuals to multinational corporations to embassies that want to keep tabs on their rivals, and, even more important, prevent their rivals from keeping tabs on them. If you think you're being watched, or are just in the market for a terrorist-proof limo, a tear gas pen, a voice scrambler, or a new night vision scope, you need look no further. —Richard Kadrey

Counter Spy Shop: $25 complete catalog and video. 444 Madison Ave., New York, NY 10022; 212/688-8500.

Dialog Information Services

In addition to participating in electronic communities, sometimes you need to get your hands on canned information: access to stored articles in magazines, newsletters, and reports. By far the most accessible and complete service available is Dialog Information Services. It's been an indispensable research tool for me since the mid-1980s, and I'd sooner stop all my magazine subscriptions than live without it. I particularly like the "ASAP" data banks, in which you can search back through magazine articles by key word, and print out the full text of the articles on your screen. Dialog takes some getting used to; its commands are arcane and confusing. But their excellent manuals make a difference. I recommend learning the commands, rather than trying to use a "front-end" or "graphic interface" program; as with all bibliographic data bank services, the trick is learning to gather what you need quickly, so your pay-by-the-minute costs stay low.
—Art Kleiner

Dialog Information Services: 3460 Hillview Avenue, Palo Alto, CA 94394; 800/334-2564.

The Sourcebook of Public Record Providers

Understanding public records is an essential survival skill for investigative journalists. An entire industry has grown up around providing public information. Knowing which database to search, or which public information provider to query, can be crucial to an investigation; this book can help you narrow the search sharply and quickly. —HLR

The Sourcebook of Public Record Providers
Carl R. Ernst, Editor. 1994; 281 pp.
ISBN 1-879792-13-3
$29 ($32 postpaid) from BRB Publications, 4653 S. Lakeshore, Suite 3, Tempe, AZ 85282; 800/929-3764, fax 800/929-4981

Consider the Elvis stamp.

We the citizens of a great democracy were recently encouraged to express our preference of images for a 29¢ postage stamp. For you recent immigrants, the question was: Shall the image on the stamp be that of Elvis Presley in his prime, in rubicund close-up as he bawls "Teddy Bear" into the microphone? Or that of Elvis in his twilight — a pasty, blubbery, drug-addled dotard spraying the Vegas multitudes with "Hunk a hunk a burning love"?

That my preference for Elvis-at-trail's-end over the callow, saccharine Baby Elvis turned out to be a minority opinion is not the issue here. I want to call you folks's attention to the interesting aspects of the Elvis commotion — all of which took place on its periphery, not at its brainless, bankrupt center.

1. This is the sort of thing our vote is held to be good for. We are let to vote, emphatically enjoined to vote, told we are bad citizens not to vote, but the bulk of our choices are Elvis-caliber; to get even a peashooter's shot at changing anything more pertinent to our actual situations takes patience, acuity, and a high tolerance for hogwash.

2. This is the sort of misdirection used by cheesy carnie magicians to swindle the rubes. We look for Elvises up the prestidigitator's sleeves as he smoothly lets our trousers drop to our ankles.

3. The mainstream media eagerly support such connivances. They beat each other in the face for the opportunity to sell us the Elvis Choice and similar worthless notions. But they are after all in the business of selling advertising, not information, and it misses the point to blame them for inundating us with slurry.

4. We are mostly consensual in the process of being led astray. This is because we tend to be suckers. Remembering not to believe without examination is an exhausting job. In the unceasing surf of misinformation, disinformation, sugar syrup, viciousness, venality, happy horseshit, arterial blood, denial, race hatred, simple answers, military solutions, anti-intellectualism, and lockstep clodhopping Dodo Fascism, remembering not to believe without examination almost certainly qualifies you as a crank. So we consent, then forget that we might have done otherwise.

> The best lack all conviction, while the worst
> Are full of passionate intensity.

I interpret Yeats's observation to mean: the smarter people are, the more habitually they see the complexity of a situation and the multiple sides of an issue. And so they are immobilized while the brutes and murderous fools forge ahead to run the show, not being troubled by doubt or empathy or the absence of the long view.

Impeded by fairness, swamped by false choices, we still have a choice that we can give ourselves: we can keep trying to improve the way we are ruled. We can strive not to let matters get worse; not to let our society slide further into isolation, mutual fear, heartless cruelty. "Our society" sounds like a great big thing, and it has that alienating sour flatulent sound of a phrase that the hacks have chewed, but what it is, is just us. In this very small boat.

Our best hope is to work for change at the bottom of the pile: locally, personally, in human scale. When they work hard enough, and hold on long enough, people win at this game. These pages supply the proof. The resources in this section offer the example and advice of people — *just us* — who have successfully sought change to the system. They are tools for making choices and making a difference.

Government at the top is, by its nature, isolated from its constituents. And in view of its nature, we are better off down here on the street, operating in our most natural, efficient configuration — as a rabble — but an informed, focused rabble, assembled through consensus: the stranger the bedfellows, the livelier the action. "Come, let us reason together." That means us, such as we are.
—James Donnelly

Making Things Happen

Aw God it's so tedious! Such endless thankless work! Oh spare me this mile-high heap of unstuffed envelopes, this truckload of bright posters — and these my fellow volunteers and likeminded makers of common cause!

Volunteering for political efforts can bring tears of frustration to your eyes. Similar tears may be seen in the eyes of those efforts' "volunteer coordinators." In this top-notch book, Joan Wolfe shows how a volunteer staff can function effectively and bring lasting satisfaction to its members. In the course of doing so, she imparts a whole other book's worth of general and specific ways to make a formidably agile and foresighted organization.

Wolfe's style is casual and readable, but she doesn't waste a word; Making Things Happen *is dense with broadly applicable information.* —JD

•

Volunteers are not nearly as effective as they could be for the time and effort they expend. Members of clubs and other organizations do countless jobs they aren't trained for: working with others and leading them (which is a lot different from working with people who are paid to co-operate), introducing speakers, conducting meetings, raising money, publicizing events.

Too often, volunteers play by ear. We repeat each other's mistakes. We need advice. We live in an age in which we can't afford the wasted time, frustrations, and misunderstandings that are too often a part of organization life. More than ever, members must make their time productive and personally worthwhile.

That is what this book is all about — helping you become more effective in your efforts, making your voluntary organization successful. This book tells you how to publicize events, how to run meetings, how to treat speakers. It offers ideas for keeping hard-working members and for tapping the talents of introverted ones. It tells you how to affect decisions in the public realm. And it tells you how to manage your own competing priorities so that volunteerism doesn't become an intolerable burden.

•

Petitions are another way to get your organization's point across. You need to understand their appropriate use. One kind of petition is a legal tool to force an issue onto a ballot. The other is a device to demonstrate the strength of public opinion.

Although decision-makers are seldom influenced by public opinion petitions, no matter how many are sent, such documents can be extremely useful. They call people's attention to the cause, and perhaps even more important, they generate a list of supporters and their addresses. It pays to keep petition signers informed and to enlist their help at crucial times.

Written materials that inform decision-makers, elicit support, and tell citizens how they can help are necessary to most campaigns. Choose the format that best fits your needs — a question-and-answer sheet, a brochure, a straightforward information flyer, or any combination of these.

•

Provide [supporters] with specific information about meeting dates, times, and loca-

Making Things Happen
(How to Be an Effective Volunteer)
Joan Wolfe. 1991; 226 pp.
ISBN 1-55963-126-0
$15.95 ($20.20 postpaid) from Island Press, Box 7, Covelo, CA 95428; 800/828-1302

tions, and explain what you want them to do when they get there. If you want them to write letters, give them the names and addresses of people they should contact. When you spell things out, you are much more likely to get the response you want.

If you are asking supporters throughout your state to write their legislators, include a complete list of their names, the general location of their legislative districts (not just the district number; most people don't know what district they are in), and addresses to write to. Your local or state League of Women Voters or your local library are usually good sources for this kind of information.

•

Once organizations begin to communicate, they discover many ways to help one another. In our community, the local TB and Emphysema Society offered space, computer, and mail-sorting services upon learning the needs of a fledgling group concerned with air pollution. Several agencies and groups provided leadership training courses for volunteers. Groups learned that more than fifty people in the community were paid to help volunteers, yet their services were unknown to most of the community, and many of them overlapped. The public library kept a speakers' file for use by program chairpersons. Few people knew about it; the file was seldom used, and the library had trouble keeping it current. The Chamber of Commerce had a list of volunteer groups in the community — an invaluable aid to other groups — but again, it was underused and incomplete. The groups also learned that a number of organizations would provide free space for meetings.

OTHER GREAT RESOURCES

How to Save Your Neighborhood, City, or Town (the Sierra Club Guide to Community Organizing): Maritza Pick. Sierra Club Books, 1993.

Praying for Sheetrock: Melissa F. Green. 1991, Fawcett Columbine Books. Unlikely success in extreme circumstances. Preachy yet edifying.

Saving the Neighborhood

Slingshot ammo for battles against Goliath developers. Slow-growth advocate Peggy Robin understands all sides of the development issues and the many variations of politics, conflicts, and negotiations. She describes each possible step in the process — from community organizing to the Planning Commission hearings — and offers options and winning strategies culled from case studies. —Mike Ashenfelder

●

Even if your city's planning/zoning employees are patient and willing to explain the system, however, you may want to seek information first from the office of your local *elected* official. If development has ever been an issue before in your district, you will undoubtedly find your representative and/or the staff people well-versed about the system's rules and procedures. As you are a constituent and a voter, you should find your questions more courteously received and more speedily answered than if you brought them directly to the civil servants of the agency involved. You might also find it a plus to have this additional contact with the staff or the politician who serves your electoral district. Later, when you come back seeking support for your neighborhood's position, you'll be a familiar name, and your concern about the development will have been noted early on.

●

Now you've figured out who besides yourself is interested in the problem; you've perhaps even talked to the developer or to city officials to find out how fast the plans are moving and how much time you have to react. Whether the development is going fast or slow, you should take the same next step: You must call a meeting.

It will — unfortunately — be the first of many meetings you can expect to attend if you're going to be a player in this field. But with a little forethought and a few easily learned management tips, you will be able to hold the length and the number of your meetings to a bare minimum. Some groups exhaust themselves meeting endlessly and pointlessly into the night, and that's a fate you'll want to work hard to avoid!

Each meeting should have a stated purpose, a written but *brief* agenda, a designated person to run it (not necessarily given the formal title of "chairman" but at least understood to be in charge of the flow of discussion), a set time limit (say, two hours) and, by the end of the meeting, a common understanding of what each participant is supposed to do next.

If you start out your first meeting under these terms, you'll find all subsequent meetings that much easier to handle. But start off with sloppy meeting procedures — no person in charge, everybody talking at once, no agenda, no time limit — and you'll waste hours, days, weeks of your life re-explaining things, arguing, trying to figure out who was supposed to do what — and generally going in circles.

●

When is the best time

Saving the Neighborhood
(You Can Fight Developers and Win!)
Peggy Robin. 1990; 428 pp.
ISBN 0-933149-33-6
$16.95 ($20.95 postpaid) from Preservation Press, 1785 Massachusetts Avenue NW, Washington, DC 20036; 800/766-6847

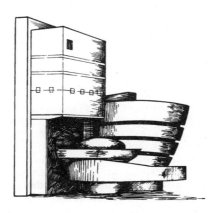

In the case of the Guggenheim, a spiral, bowl-shaped building, the new addition was to rise like a tall block behind it, causing at least one architecture critic to scoff that it looked like the tank to a giant toilet bowl. A redesign has since been commissioned.

of day for acts of civil disobedience? The morning rush hour has many advantages. It will be easy to draw a crowd of spectators. You can call for cars to honk their support as they drive by. Print journalists will have time to go into the office and write up the story before the deadline for the next day's early edition. Camera crews will be able to have the film in to the editing room, ready to show on the 6 o'clock news, with maybe a smaller snippet repeated at the 11 o'clock as well.

What day of the week? Find out if there is any day that your daily paper likes to focus on in different sections of the metropolitan area — for example, on Thursdays the *Washington Post* runs a special section with various neighborhood reports. When calling for coverage, I spoke to reporters who work specifically for that section, and worked out the timing of the civil disobedience around their assignment schedules. . . .

Whether few or many, the people need to be well-briefed and to come prepared. They should wear comfortable shoes (preferably ones without laces, which in some

jails are confiscated during detention) and clothing that they don't mind getting dirty (bulldozers can kick up a lot of dust). What not to wear: jewelry and belts (since these will almost certainly be taken away before you are put in a cell). In case bail is required, bring about $100 in cash, and have the phone number of a lawyer to call in case there is some complication about your release before trial. It's a good idea to eat a big breakfast. You might not arrive at the lock-up in time for lunch, or if you do, you might take one look at it and decide not to touch it. And clear your calendar for the whole day; even if you're arrested at 8 a.m., you still might not be out until late in the afternoon.

I f you want to get a lot of people together to do something, first you have to get a lot of people together. That's called "community." Please refer to the Community section (pp. 121–145) for prerequisite material on the principles of organizing, decisionmaking stratagems, and tools for creating consensus. —James Donnelly

Organizing: A Guide for Grassroots Leaders

I have acquired* serious doubts about the effectiveness of voting as a process of social change — if voting changed anything, it would be illegal. But I do believe that the way to overcome the abuse built into the global economic system is through democratic participation of workers in all levels of industrial decisionmaking, and that the most direct route to that social condition is through the building of grassroots organizations of all kinds. All power to the people.

Si Kahn's book is an operating and maintenance manual for the small engines of modern society — small groups of humans organized around specific issues and trying to change things collectively. In this process, some assembly is required, and Mr. Kahn's handbook guides the reader from the pile of parts on the workbench to the chugging little powerplants in clear and simple language, with a minimum of mumbo jumbo and a good supply of troubleshooting hints.

This revised edition is best used as a field guide to organizing techniques rather than a front-to-back primer in community involvement. If you think you want to try your hand at getting folks together around some issue, read the Afterword — it contains a good moral pattern for any prospective organizer of human beings. —JD Smith

* . . . having been one of those northern, liberal, Student Nonviolent Coordinating Committee, outside agitators who invaded the Sovereign State of Mississippi in the summer of 1964. And also having been a member of a Trotskyist wish tank.

●

Involving people's organizations in electoral politics isn't easy. There are dangers. There can be a tendency to put too much value on politics, to put a lot of the organization's resources into getting people elected and

much less into building and maintaining the organization.

Many people's organizations find the coalition style of electoral politics difficult. In an electoral campaign there are usually two parties and two candidates. Other institutions and interest groups in the community split between these two camps. A people's organization may find itself in an electoral coalition with many groups that it finds difficult to deal with.

●

Let's say your neighborhood organization endorses a candidate for the city council on the basis of the commitments that candidate has made to the organization. If the election returns show that the people in your neighborhood split their vote evenly, then politicians will not take your group's endorsement seriously the next time.

This means that electoral politics in a people's organization must be handled carefully. If a decision to endorse a candidate is made by the leaders of the organization but the members do not share in that decision, then it's very likely that those members will not back the candidate the organization endorsed. Before becoming involved in this type of electoral politics an organization has to make a careful evaluation to see whether it can actually deliver votes to the candidates it endorses.

Organizing
(A Guide for Grassroots Leaders)
Si Kahn. 1991; 343 pp. ISBN 0-87101-197-2
$25.95 ($28.95 postpaid) from NASW Press, PO Box 431, Annapolis Junction, MD 20701; 800/227-3590

The Activist's Almanac

Your favorite excuse for not making the world a better place might be that you just don't know where to start. Here is the place. The Activist's Almanac describes 105 prominent national advocacy organizations, telling you their history, how to get in touch with them, and how to help their causes. It supplies the essential details you need to support the idealistic struggle of your choice.

Unlike most guides to nonprofits and advocacy groups, for example, the Almanac supplies complete information about the tax status of each group it mentions. It explains the different IRS categories of PACs, foundations or lobbying organizations. (If you are in a position to donate money, you need to know such details.) Other particulars that set this book apart include concise profiles of groups' founders, why they started their organizations, and the organizations' mission statements. You'll also find a list of the issues, bills, and campaigns a given group is currently working on.
—Caius van Nouhuys

•

Becoming a citizen activist is as simple as picking up a pen, or sitting down at a word processor. Writing letters to legislators or the local newspaper is a useful place to begin. Notices of current key bills are available to anyone who joins a legislative alert network. You can lobby legislators by telephone to their Washington or home offices, or make an appointment to visit when they are back in the district. Join or help organize a local group of a national organization. Learn how to raise money, put out a newsletter, take part in direct action. Have fun, and learn from experience. Keep in mind what David Cohen, dean of public interest lobbyists, concludes: "The challenge is to blend the visionary with the mundane."

•

Sierra Club: 730 Polk Street, San Francisco, CA 94109 (415) 776-2211

Founded: 1892; *Members:* 580,000; *Local Groups:* 382; *Budget:* $40 million *Staff:* 250 *Tax Status:* 501(c)(4): Sierra Club; 501(c)(3): Sierra Club Foundation; *PAC:* Sierra Club Political Committee

Purpose: "To explore, enjoy and protect the wild places of the Earth."

Background: In 1892 two professors at the University of California at Berkeley helped John Muir launch a club modeled after the eastern Appalachian Mountain Club. With 182 charter members, the Sierra Club's of-

The Activist's Almanac
(The Concerned Citizen's Guide to the Leading Advocacy Organizations in America)
David Walls. Fireside Books, 1993; 432 pp. ISBN 0-671-74634-0
$18 postpaid from Simon & Schuster/Order Dept., 200 Old Tappan Road, Old Tappan, NJ 07675; 800/223-2336

ficers elected Muir president, an office he held until his death in 1914. Among the Club's first goals were establishing national parks, including Glacier and Mount Rainier, convincing the California legislature to give Yosemite Valley to the federal government, and saving California's coastal redwoods. Muir escorted President Teddy Roosevelt through Yosemite in 1903. Two years later the California legislature ceded Yosemite Valley and Mariposa Grove to the federal government, marking the Sierra Club's first lobbying victory, and the establishment of the country's second national park, after Yellowstone in 1872.

The Workbook

One of the most significant developments in social-change movements in the last decade has been the common perception among peace, environmental, and social-issue activists that their causes are inextricably linked. The Workbook has covered this broad, interrelated range of concerns as they have taken shape. Each issue features a long research article and related further-reading reviews, and a core section of reviews by the specialty editors of nutrition, Third World issues, the environment, women, work, and more. The Workbook's reviews include special reports from research institutes and universities that you probably wouldn't hear about anywhere else — with ordering information. Highly recommended. —Jeanne Carstensen

The Workbook
Kathy Cone, Editor.
$12/year (4 issues) from Southwest Research and Information Center, PO Box 4524, Albuquerque, NM 87106

•

Everyone, it seems, is talking about a war on the Western range these days. *U.S. News and World Report* has called it a "burgeoning ecological range war"; *Newsweek* has dubbed it "The War for the West," warning of a "storm on the range."

Although this "war" may not be as violent as the rhetoric suggests, it's just as dramatic. Ranchers, who have grazed cattle on federal lands for more than a century, are coming under increasing fire from environmental groups, who say that cattle are wreaking havoc on the West's fragile environment, and from federal land managers charged with protecting the public's natural resources.

The pressure from the government has come in the form of increased regulation and monitoring of cattle grazing. From environmentalists, it has come in the form of such battle cries as "Livestock-Free by '93" and increased pressure on Congress to sharply curtail federal lands grazing by raising fees and strengthening regulatory efforts. The issues involved are by now widely familiar—both national and regional media coverage has been heavy.

The question that is perhaps pivotal to the dispute, however, has been the subject of far less scrutiny. Whether a grazing permit to the federal lands constitutes a private property right, or is merely a privilege meted out by the government, has more often than not been the sticking point between ranchers and environmentalists. It is precisely this question that has spawned a whole legal strategy by ranching interests attempting to establish once and for all that their permits to graze are in fact protected rights under the Constitution.

Pat Oliphant and all his works

He is the Best (if not the Only Good) Pat in Politics. A few minutes' rooting in one of his collections of syndicated cartoons is good for a deep frisson of outrage and invigoration in roughly equal measure. See the depredations of yesteryear! Marvel that we're (mostly) all still here! —JD

April 21, 1988

Nothing Basically Wrong
Pat Oliphant. 1988; 176 pp.
ISBN 0-8362-1833-7
$8.95 ($10.95 postpaid)

What Those People Need Is a Puppy!
Pat Oliphant. 1989; 176 pp.
ISBN 0-8362-1857-4
$8.95 ($10.95 postpaid)

Both from Andrews & McMeel, PO Box 419150, Kansas City, MO 64141; 800/826-4216

Resource Manual for a Living Revolution

The how-to book for planning actions and maintaining organizations, while paying scrupulous, compassionate attention to the group's dynamics and each member's equal development. —Stephanie Mills

It's dense (even leaden) and very, very earnest: not pleasurable reading. Full of the real stuff, though. —JD

•

Holding a Press Conference

1. Figure out the two or three most important points you want to make and find ways of repeating them no matter what the question.

2. Hold the press conference at a time when reporters can come and meet their deadlines. Morning seems to be best.

3. It is often good to hold the conference at a significant location, e.g., at the mayor's office if you are refuting a statement by the mayor.

4. Be sure you are in a place where cameras are allowed and people can move in and out easily. Check availability of electric outlets for lighting equipment.

5. Send an announcement of the press conference to a contact person as well as someone on the city desk.

6. When announcing an action, don't pretend to have more people than you do. You are trying to build a good long-term relationship with press contacts.

Resource Manual for a Living Revolution
Virginia Coover, et al. 1985; 330 pp.
ISBN 0-86571-056-2
$14.95 ($17.45 postpaid) from New Society Publishers, 4527 Springfield Avenue, Philadelphia, PA 19143; 800/333-9093

7. Keep clearly in mind how you are going to end the conference. You might keep one good piece of information until the end and find a way to close with it.

The Tide

*If you're given to complaining about the government's wrongheaded and foolish behavior, but you never actually get around to letting your elected representatives know how you feel about anything, **The Tide** could be the tool you've been waiting for. We got a subscription last year as a Christmas present, and while it hasn't completely eliminated our urge to procrastinate, it makes writing to Congress almost irresistibly easy.*

Each month the newsletter focuses on one important piece of legislation before Congress — "Anticrime Measures"; "Guns: Rights & Restrictions"; "Bosnia-Herzegovina" — and presents a compact, easy-to-follow, nonpartisan examination of the issues, including some historical background and an explanation of the positions on both, or all, sides. Each issue also includes brief House and Senate "vote descriptions" and a listing of how your representatives voted on each measure.

*But the best part of a subscription to **The Tide** is that with each newsletter you receive a set of postcards pre-addressed to the president, and to your particular members of Congress. You can choose postcards that are blank and ready for your own forceful and well-reasoned message, or preprinted with what the publishers consider the typical Democrat's or Republican's position on that month's featured legislation. You can change your preference as often as you like. We opted for the blank cards, and I must say that when we write our opinions down and mail them off to Washington, we feel a small*

You got to watch 'em like a hawk. I'm not sure it is possible to present information that is both truly nonpartisan and comprehensible. When people make the statement that their message is free of bias, immediately examine what they have chosen to write the message about. We have to watch *ourselves* like hawks. —JD

self-righteous glow of participatory democracy. Maybe that's a good place to start. —Cecily Donnelly

•

Season's Greetings

Next year, Congress will have historic debates on reforming our health care and social welfare systems, and 468 of the 535 positions in Congress will be up for election. Without citizen input these decisions will be made as they have been in the past — *out of touch* with average citizens and *in the pocket* of big money and special interests. Do your part. I do my best each month to make staying informed and sending your message to Washington as easy as possible. Even just signing and mailing the postcards is tremendously important. An increase in a congressperson's volume of mail tells her that more citizens are watching her votes in Congress and she better be sure she's voting their wishes.

Your Tool For Changing Congress

The Tide
Scott D. Silverman, Editor.
$26/year (12 issues). 8205 Santa Monica Boulevard #1-292, Los Angeles, CA 90046; 213/654-3453, fax 213/656-5373

Macrocosm USA

The first half of this multipurpose reference work consists of brief reprints from many small-circulation, low-budget, low-visibility publications. Some of these essays tend toward well-trodden left/green paths — familiar, at least, if you live in Northern California, the Concern Capital of America. They are nevertheless worthwhile, some are really swell, and to have seen them all before you would have to know where to find some pretty obscure organizations and periodicals.

*Which knowledge, really, is **Macrocosm**'s principal use: the second half is a densely cross-indexed directory of progressive endeavors — organizations, periodicals, computer media, publishers, businesses, and reference resources. The directory's index to subjects alone runs to thirteen pages; all told, there are about 5,000 entries. This book has serious potential as a tool for the making of connections, and of coalitions.* —JD

•

Bringing Politics Home
by Sam Smith / The Progressive Review

In the book *Systemantics*, John Gall argues that "systems tend to oppose their proper functions." The ideal proper function of the American system is life, liberty, and the pursuit of happiness. Yet as it gropes its way into the 21st century, the system in reality increasingly endangers human life, denies personal liberty, and represses individual happiness.

Unfortunately, complex systems that are failing have little capacity to save themselves, in part because the solutions come from the same source as the problem.

Complex systems usually try to save themselves by doing the same thing they have been doing badly all along — only harder. This is because the salvation of the system is considered far more important than the solution of any problems that might be

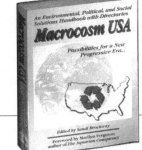

Macrocosm USA
(Possibilities for a New Progressive Era . . .)
Sandi Brockway, Editor. Macrocosm USA, 1992; 421 pp. ISBN 0-9632315-5-3 $24.95 ($27.45 postpaid). UAP Books, Box 457, Hinesburg, VT 05461; 800/356-9315

causing the system to fail. Solutions that bring into question the effectiveness of the system itself are not tolerated.

We have seen some classic examples of this phenomenon in recent times. The Vietnam War quickly became a battle to justify the decision to enter it. In the Alaskan oil spill, we found ourselves relying upon the world's most powerful government and the world's largest corporation to repair the damage caused by *their* policies.

The question we should be asking is not what the system should be doing but whether the existing system can do anything except to make matters worse.

Soapbox Software

Grassroots lobbying without stamps or typewriters! Concerned citizens can link their MCI accounts (or printers) to this federal database, identify key employees and elected officials, and quickly generate mass correspondence with the aid of the writing guide and forms ("As a voter and constituent represented by you . . ."). The finished product can be printed out or transmitted electronically by MCI's fax, mail, or overnight delivery, personalized with your custom letterhead and cursive signature.

This software is perfect for those donated, "tax-deductible" computers of yesteryear, standard issue for most community-based organizations: it runs on 286 (or better) IBM compatibles and its RAM and disk space requirements are minuscule. (You need a modem to receive the quarterly updates)

At $129 for a one-year subscription, why not donate a kit to your school district? —Anita Susan Brenner

Federal SoapBox
IBM compatible, 80286, DOS 3.0 or higher, 640K RAM, 7MB on hard disk. Includes program, database and 1-year subscription (3 updates). $129 ($135 postpaid). SoapBox Software, 10 Golden Gate Drive, San Rafael, CA 94901; 800/989-7627

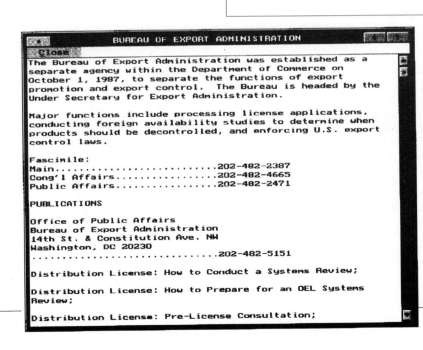

```
╔══════════════════════════════════════════════╗
║         BUREAU OF EXPORT ADMINISTRATION       ║
╠══════════════════════════════════════════════╣
║ Close                                         ║
║ The Bureau of Export Administration was established as a
║ separate agency within the Department of Commerce on
║ October 1, 1987, to separate the functions of export
║ promotion and export control.  The Bureau is headed by the
║ Under Secretary for Export Administration.
║
║ Major functions include processing license applications,
║ conducting foreign availability studies to determine when
║ products should be decontrolled, and enforcing U.S. export
║ control laws.
║
║ Fascimile:
║ Main......................202-482-2387
║ Cong'l Affairs...........202-482-4665
║ Public Affairs...........202-482-2471
║
║ PUBLICATIONS
║
║ Office of Public Affairs
║ Bureau of Export Administration
║ 14th St. & Constitution Ave. NW
║ Washington, DC 20230
║ ....................................202-482-5151
║
║ Distribution License: How to Conduct a Systems Review;
║
║ Distribution License: How to Prepare for an OEL Systems
║ Review;
║
║ Distribution License: Pre-License Consultation;
╚══════════════════════════════════════════════╝
```

Where the Money Is

Prospecting the deep pockets of America's rich is a full-time occupation for nonprofits, politicians, and universities. And because over 80 percent of all charity comes from individuals, there's a big market in books and magazines that tell you how to find essentials on the wealthiest. This is a guide to the guides, recently updated with a chapter on how to dig up addresses and stats online.

If you are not yet a pro, you will either be amazed or appalled at the sheer number of these fundraising guides amassed, by the author during her years as the District of Columbia Public Library's head librarian. She includes elite lists, like Who's Who and the Social Register, as well as the many guides by those who scour resources like newspapers, annual reports, and (more than likely) garbage cans.

The bibliography alone is worth the book's price; then, be ready to do the digging that's required, if you don't have the connections. —Peggy Lauer

•

When citizens speak of "the best Congress money can buy," it is a concern for the politician as well as the voter. Many have recently spoken out against the fund raising which is necessary to stay in office. Thomas F. Eagleton (D-Missouri), when he retired from the Senate in 1986, said he was tired of "being on the phone, talking to fat cats that I don't even know. Imploring them to send me X dollars, because somebody gave me a list of names and said these are rich people who might give you something. That's the way it has become around here." And he was the incumbent.

•

Because the incumbent has a definite advantage, it is often more difficult to raise money for first-time women candidates.

Now, a political network for Democratic women is available. EMILY's List (an acronym for "Early Money Is Like Yeast" — it makes the dough rise) identifies and supports viable candidates for key federal and statewide office. Since 1988 EMILY's List has been the largest financial resource for women's candidates in the country. In the 1990 elections, its members contributed $1.5 million to 14 pro-choice Democratic women candidates. The network also publishes a very useful booklet, *Thinking of Running for Congress: A Guide for Democratic Women.*

•

Once a researcher gets hooked on online, it is impossible to retreat to manual searching for some types of searches. The case for such expenditure of funds is something which must be determined at each institution, but online is becoming recognized as very useful in both large and small fundraising offices. An office which needs this information in a prompt manner and

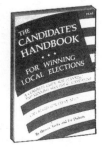

Where the Money Is
(A Fund Raiser's Guide to the Rich)
Helen J. Bergan. 1992; 257 pp.
ISBN 0-9615277-6-5
$29.95 ($31.95 postpaid) from BioGuide Press, PO Box 16072, Alexandria, VA 22302; 703/820-9045

has a computer cannot ignore the potential of online. Offices which have used online from the beginning are amazed as more and more useful databases are offered each year. Some of these will b e discussed later in this chapter.

You can make use of these marvelous new technologies even if you do not have a computer in your office, or a modem, or if you do not wish to do the search yourself. You may be able to get the information you need at a public or academic library if online searching is offered for patrons.

Get the Facts on Anyone

Welcome to the world of "backgrounding," the systematic methodology of researching the minutiae of individuals and entities.

Not since Bibliography One have I seen such a thorough and comprehensive overview of research tools, sources and techniques. This concise, well-organized manual is oriented toward the amateur backgrounder, emphasizing investigative endeavors that are legal and without potential ethical compromise.

Backgrounding relies heavily on cooperation from agencies and databases with the pertinent information. **Get the Facts** *describes the various styles of inquiry that may be most effective for specific situations. There is considerable information on accessing computer databases, whether those of periodicals or of government agencies. Specialized database vendors and other commercial providers are also detailed.*

The appendices and bibliography are particularly useful as further sources of information and accumulated research. —Jeff L. Thompson

•

Candidates for local, state, and federal office must file nominating petitions in order to enter a major party primary or get on the ballot as an independent or minor-party candidate in the general election. Depending on which office the candidate is running for, thousands of signatures (with addresses) may be required. Party or cult leaders, themselves aloof from the work of petitioning, may sign to help fill up a sheet, thus revealing the address of their secret bunker. You might browse through the nominating petitions at the Board of Elections to see how many addresses of known cult members you can find — this could give you a unique picture of their communal living arrangements.

Most of the other signatures will be useless to an investigator, since the signers will have no real connection to the party or

candidate — they may have thought they were signing for George Bush. The chief importance of the petitions is that each sheet must be signed at the bottom by the person who gathered the signatures — the petition "witness." Examining the witness signatures enables you to compile a list of those party supporters who are sufficiently committed that they will scurry around the street or ring doorbells to collect signatures. If the local Populist Party turned in 200 petition sheets signed by a total of fourteen petition gatherers (say, for the Populist candidate for Congress), you may have gained thereby a list of virtually the entire active membership in your area.

Get the Facts on Anyone
(How You Can Use Public Sources to Check the Background of Any Person or Organization)
Dennis King. Prentice Hall Press, 1992; 208 pp. ISBN 0-13-351859-0
$15 ($19 postpaid). Loompanics Unlimited, PO Box 1197, Port Townsend, WA 98368

•

If your target is a celebrity or an elected public official, newspapers and periodicals are the obvious place to start your search. But newspapers, especially local dailies, can also provide a wealth of easily accessible data about tens of millions of noncelebrities, from stockbrokers to muggers and from debutantes to shopping bag ladies. The back issues of America's newspapers and periodical — and the knowledge and working files of the vast number of journalists working for these publications and for wire services — are a potential intelligence resource to rival the combined assets of the CIA and KGB.

The Candidate's Handbook . . .
• Winning Local and State Elections

These very different books work well as a pair. **The Candidate's Handbook** *presumes total inexperience on the part of candidate and supporters; its advice is rock-bottom basic and tends to suppose that the campaign budget is minuscule. It is roughly produced (self-published) and variously pithy and sketchy — the chapters look almost like outlines. The last quarter or so is devoted to checklists, or shorthand recapitulations of critical points: excellent (photocopyable) cribsheets to keep the harried candidate and her amateur staff on target.*

Winning Elections *addresses the campaign with more of everything: experience, people, and money. Where one book has you gumming donuts with prospective constituents at the Deere dealership, the other dives right into voting behavior, demographics, and "percent-of-effort targeting." It is much longer, heavier on theory, and more detailed. At that, the political-consultant authors cover a lot of territory and some of the coverage necessarily hits only the high spots.* —JD

•

If there are only a few main thoroughfares leading into and out of the community, signs and posters along roadways can be very effective. Conversely, if there are too

many main roads, the cost per sign and poster coverage becomes prohibitive.

Residents of some communities have an intense dislike of campaign signs. Thus, even though they might be seen by a lot of voters, they could have a negative effect on your campaign.

The same might be true of bumper stickers and lawn signs.

Probably the most cost-effective advertising is door-to-door delivery by volunteers of a good campaign brochure. All you pay is the cost of printing; then deliver only to homes of registered voters.
—*The Candidate's Handbook*

•

Most targeting is usually done by breaking votes down along party lines, especially in a general election. You can also measure voting behavior along ideological lines if candidates can be clearly identified as progressive or conservative in the races that you choose for comparison. If initiative and referendum ballot issues play an important political role in your state, consider them in choosing comparison races. If the major theme of your campaign is very similar to a "yes" vote on a recent ballot measure, an analysis of the returns from that vote may provide valuable information. In this case, count the votes supporting the ballot measure in the same manner as you would count votes for a candidate similar to yourself in a comparison race.
—*Winning Local and State Elections*

The Candidate's Handbook
For Winning Local Elections
Harvey Yorke & Liz Doherty. 1992;
110 pp. ISBN 0-9607598-0-8
$5 ($6.05 postpaid) from Jane Yorke, 495 Rowland Boulevard, Novato, CA 94947

Winning Local
and State Elections
Ann Beaudry & Bob Schaeffer. Free Press, 1986; 208pp. ISBN 0-02-902490-0
$27.95 postpaid. Macmillan Publishing Co., 100 Front Street, Riverside, NJ 08075-7500; 800/257-5755

Ralph Nader Presents A Citizens' Guide to Lobbying

This classic manual is blunt about how to get your way in civic legislation. In the era of special interests, here are the survival skills used by any side of an issue. Not all of them are nice.
—Kevin Kelly

●

A time-honored tactic of some legislators and opposition lobbyists is to confuse the issue with smokescreens. They may try to intimidate you as a citizen lobbyist, with technical or professional jargon or with citations of their vast experience in the area. The implication usually is that you are not qualified to be seeking this legislation or making your arguments. Often the first question by legislators who are attorneys is: "Have you studied law?" If you have not, make sure you can say truthfully that you have had an attorney work with you on it, and that if the legislator has any technical questions about the bill, you can get an answer. Do not hang your head over not being able to cite any professional expertise. Remind legislators, if necessary, that citizens have a right to participate in the legislative process and that you are representing nonexpert citizens.

●

Seizing opportunities. Lobbyists who come to know legislators well can vary their lobbying approaches depending on individual quirks and inside information.

A CCAG lobbyist had learned that a senator was particularly angry at the governor for opposing one of his bills. When a crucial vote on an important anti-environmental bill came up, our lobbyist casually informed the senator that the governor really wanted the bill to go through. The senator's eyes lit up and a smile appeared on his face. The senator, not known for any environmental concern, cast the deciding vote against the governor and for the state's environmental interests.

●

Some committees are simply careless — not bothering to eliminate incompatible bills, send misdirected ones to the proper committee, check into overlaps with other committees, or reconcile new legislation with laws already on the books. You may sometimes have to do a legislator's job by performing these tasks. Remember that legislators' lack of information provides a major opening for all lobbyists. Always look for opportunities to supply information, even at the last minute and even to the most indifferent legislators.

●

Keep contributors informed. Most contributors, if they are enthusiastic about your group, will become very interested in your activities. They want you to tell them why their contribution was a good investment. Keep your contributors up to date on your activities. Even a simple mimeographed one-page newsletter listing recent and upcoming events lets contributors know that their money is *doing* something, and it makes them more likely to contribute in the future.

●

Your story should include a positive *call for action.* We dislike, and we think the press and the public dislike, an approach that consists always and only of attacking without ever advancing some positive action. In every story, we attempt to suggest some remedy for the problem we are pointing out. There are times, of course, when you just have to challenge without proposing any solutions.

Ralph Nader Presents A Citizen's Guide to Lobbying
Marc Caplan. Dembner Books, 1983; 208 pp. ISBN 0-934878-27-7
$6.95 postpaid from Essential Information, PO Box 19405, Washington, DC 20036

The Muckraker's Manual

Although the pseudonymous author touts this handy pocket manual as a handbook for investigative reporters, there isn't much in it that a journalist wouldn't learn in her first ten days on the job or at a brief internship at the Center for Investigative Reporting. The methods, processes, and ethics of journalism are so different from those of citizen activism that separate investigative curricula are necessary. This book is a good primer for exposing your adversary's chicanery.

*Citizen investigators will gather some valuable hints about documentation, source development, interviewing, infiltration, and editing. If, when they have finished this book, you stll feel a trifle short of investigative skills, look for **The Reporter's Handbook** or the classic **Investigative Reporting and Editing**.*
—Mark Dowie

●

Lobbying reports can also be gems, even though laws requiring lobbyists to register are not very well enforced and are full of loopholes. . . . If you find a lobbyist you are interested in, then to get the full report that tells how much money the lobbyist supposedly spent, you'll have to try the government directly. This can be very difficult if you don't live near the District of Columbia. Lobbying reports filed with the U.S. Senate, for example, are not copied for journalists. (In a pinch, your own congressman may be willing to get the information for you if you don't want to hire a researcher in the capital.)

●

In the mid-70s an anonymous document was circulated in far right political circles that accused a lot of people of, among other things, being homosexuals. It was an intriguing bit of black propaganda. The document, which came to be known as the "DeGuello" manuscript, had been mailed (no return address) to key leaders in the far right. (I later estimated the total number of people who got original copies to be about 100.) "DeGuello" caused quite a stir and hundreds of copies were xeroxed and passed around. There were enough facts in "DeGuello" to make some of the accusations sound convincing, and just about every right wing leader was accused of something. The effects of "DeGuello" were to foment distrust in the right with the obvious intent of disrupting its effectiveness. For about one or two years "DeGuello" succeeded in achiving this goal.

The puzzle about "DeGuello" was: Who was the author? . . .

Whoever it was knew a whole lot about the right wing — not only the names and addresses of 100 or more leaders, but a lot of facts about their lives.

It was the best example of black propaganda I've ever seen, and I'd love to meet the authors.

The Muckraker's Manual
(Handbook for Investigative Reporters)
M. Harry. 1984; 148 pp.
ISBN 0-915179-03-2
$12.95 ($16.95 postpaid) from Loompanics Unlimited, PO Box 1197, Port Townsend, WA 98368

OTHER GREAT RESOURCES

Campaigns & Elections (The Magazine for Political Professionals): $29.95/year (7 issues). 1835 K Street NW #403, Washington, DC 20006; 202/331-3222.

Lobbying on a Shoestring: Judith C. Meredith. 1989, Greenwood Press. Out of print. Hard-won strategic insights and basic lessons on political power.

Earthworks Press: 1400 Shattuck Avenue, Box 25, Berkeley, CA 94709; 510/652-8533. Earthworks published two exemplary voters' references for the 1992 federal elections — *The Women's 1992 Voting Guide* and *Vote for the Earth*. They're both out of print. I sure hope we'll see the 1996 editions: *The Women's Guide*, in particular, was a goldmine of resources.

An Electoral Process

(Heard in Challis, Idaho, 1992)

"I ran for office once, and sorta won, but it turned out to be kind of an embarrassing deal.

"It was over on the Big Wood River about twenty years ago. I decided to run for supervisor on the Soil Conservation District. About that time my friend Mike Walker decided to do the same damn thing.

"The only reason there was an election in the first place was that part of the Soil Conservation District operation was funded by county tax money, and Idaho law stated that if you were going to be spending the taxpayers' money, then you were by God going to be elected by the taxpayers. Otherwise the District folks could've just come around to my door and asked me if I wanted to sit in on a couple of meetings and tell them what I thought. But Hell no, we had to have an election.

"So Mike's and my names were added to the general ballot one fall, kind of down in one corner of the paper, looking like the 'For Official Use' part of a government form. In the first election, there were all of two votes cast in the race for supervisor, Mike's vote and mine, and we voted for each other . . . dead tie, new election.

"Printing up a special ballot and advertising the runoff election cost the county a couple of thousand bucks. When the second election was over there were four votes cast, and we were still tied, two to two. Nobody but farmers care about agricultural issues, and they are too busy to vote in the daytime. I don't know who cast the other two votes, but I know I voted for Mike again, and figured he must have voted for me.

"Next thing you know we got hauled up in front of the county commissioners and they asked us if there wasn't some way we could settle our dispute without costing the county any more money.

"Dispute mind you. Since there was probably no way Mike or I were going to change our votes, it just wouldn't have looked good to vote for yourself, I suggested that we draw straws or cut cards or flip a coin.

"Of course, Mike won the toss and I got stuck with serving one term on the Soil Conservation District, which was kind of fun, all in all. People should forget about the federal government and pay attention to things at home. A lot goes on in those grassroots organizations. I did get awful tired of explaining to folks how it was that I ended up being an elected official. I damn sure wasn't going to go through it twice." —JD Smith

"A popular government without popular information, or the means of acquiring it, is but a prologue to a farce or a tragedy, or perhaps both. Knowledge will forever govern ignorance, and a people who mean to be their own governors must arm themselves with the power which knowledge gives." —James Madison

Skillfully used, new communication media can amplify the power of grassroots groups to gather critical information, organize political action, sway public opinion and guide policymaking. You can learn about the tools themselves, from modems to BBS software, in Communications (pp. 242-281). On the following pages, you can learn how to use these communications devices as political tools.

Most processes for guiding public policy or influencing electoral politics involve communication: meeting people, developing ideas and arguments, persuading people to adopt your views, enlisting support, negotiating compromises, organizing actions. Each of these spheres of action can be enhanced through the use of computer-mediated communications. Here are a few examples:

Matt Wuerker

When the Colorado Springs, Colorado city council proposed a law that would effectively prohibit telecommuting, Dave Hughes, a retired West Point instructor and combat veteran of Korea and Vietnam, made his first foray into electronic democracy.

"I was the only person to stand up in front of the planning commission and testify against the ordinance; the planners tabled the matter for thirty days. I brought the text of the ordinance home with me and put it on my computer bulletin board system," Hughes recalls. Hughes sent letters to two local papers, inviting people to dial into his BBS and read the ordinance. At the next city council meeting, more than 175 citizens showed up to protest the ordinance. It was defeated. Hughes points out that "ordinarily, the effort needed to get involved with local politics is enormous. But the economy of effort that computers provided made it possible for me to mobilize opinion and action."

Ask Jim Warren what a computer database has to do with electoral politics, and he'll look at you like you just asked him why an aquarium needs water. A computer programmer and one of the original advocates of "computers for people," Warren volunteered to help a candidate in a local Congressional race because he was outraged at the tactics of an incumbent. When Warren volunteered his services to the challenger, he realized that the political organization could gain a bonanza because he knew how to use publicly accessible computer data. Knowing exactly where your candidate's supporters are located, how they responded to recent communications from your campaign office, and how to contact them in geographic order, is information with high value on election day. (See "How to Use GIS in Electoral Campaigns," p. 293.)

Environmental activists (see Ecoactivism, p.109) have demonstrated that it is possible to build global networks even if you don't have the financial resources of a multinational corporation. Earthtrust is a worldwide nonprofit organization dedicated to resolving transnational environmental problems that are not addressed by local environmental movements. Earthtrust's director, Don White, has organized a global network on a shoestring, equipping volunteers in remote areas with inexpensive computers, modems, and electronic mail accounts. The well-planned use of electronic mail enables him to knit together a geographically dispersed organization highly effectively. "Our organization has accomplished goals over the last two years that rival the achievements of organizations with twenty times Earthtrust's annual budget," he claims.

Nonprofits and NGOs (nongovernmental organizations) do the people-feeding, prisoner-liberating, house-building, wilderness-saving, humanitarian and environmental work that falls between the cracks of government and for-profit organizations. The Red Cross, CARE, Amnesty International, Rainforest Action Network, Greenpeace, the Sierra Club, and a proliferation of increasingly international NGOs are forming what Howard Frederick of Econet/Peacenet calls "Global Civil Society." Traditionally, such organizations are overworked and underfunded. Even though they might gain power and save money by computerizing, the staff of many such organizations don't know where to start. Now, first wave technology-knowledgeable activists are providing expertise and training to others.

A nonprofit itself, CompuMentor matches volunteer technical advisers with nonprofits; mentors help organizations choose and purchase the right equipment at minimal price, then set up databases, publish newsletters, organize electronic mailing lists. The Association of Progressive Communications (APC) brings affordable electronic mail and conferencing to hundreds of NGOs and nonprofits worldwide; APC's Econet, Peacenet, and Conflictnet furnish activists with all the benefits of worldwide networking.

Others who are working to improve the quality of civic life have been experimenting with an application of many-to-many communications known as civic networking.

COMPASS, funded by the Oregon Lottery, offers statewide access to BBSs, electronic mail, computer conferencing, and the Internet. School House, an item in the COMPASS main menu, is "a place for K-12 teachers, students, and parents to meet." Other menu options are government information, state university libraries, health and wellness information, community calendars, "teleports" to other locations in the Internet, and a "Public Square."

Since 1988, Montana's Big Sky Telegraph has linked one-room schoolhouses with Internet tutors and connected nonprofit organizations such as the Women's Resource Center with sources of information and support. Rural schools, public libraries, rural economic development offices, organizations for employing the disabled, rural hospitals, were connected using inexpensive telecommunication technology that was in turn plugged into the vast network of networks known as the Internet.

It's happening in Hawaii and the Heartland; in Taos, New Mexico; Blacksburg, Virginia; and Bloomsberg, Pennsylvania. There is LatinoNet, PeaceNet, and EcoNet. NativeNet and INDIANnet connect not only cities and states, but tribes.

Net technology makes possible a more democratic medium of expression than did previous communication technologies. A BBS-like public conversation is open to anyone who wants to join the discussion; it is not a "few-to-many" medium like television, talk radio, newspapers or magazines, but a "many-to-many" medium that gives large numbers of people access to large numbers of people. The power to persuade and educate — to influence people's beliefs and perceptions — is radically decentralized when people can communicate in this way: control is spread throughout the network.

In Bucharest and Moscow, crucial recent battles were not fought over armories: instead, television broadcast stations were the battlegrounds — because mass-communication nerve centers are strategic chokepoints in the flow of words, images, and ideas. The power to transmit information, in old-style mass media, is concentrated in a small number of locations and institutions. Networks are radically different: technically, any node on a high-capacity computer communications network can send, as well as receive, words, sounds, images, computer software, video, to any other node. Plugged into an ordinary telephone, a personal computer becomes a printing press, a broadcasting station, a town hall meeting.

Conferencing systems structure discussions according to topic, making it easier for people to find others who share their interests, and to request and offer specific information about problems. A person concerned about ecology can go to an ecology discussion area and browse the list of discussions, selecting from topics devoted to local water resources or national air quality. With information organized this way, networks of people can serve as informal support systems for each other; a conferencing system that includes a broad base of members with a wide variety of expertise is a "living database" in which everyone can serve as a librarian and consultant for everyone else. (see Virtual Communities, p. 262.)

Geographic Information Systems (see p. 14) combine maps and computer databases, creating another tool for political activists. Again, the falling price of computing power makes a tool that was once practical only for elite use now available to citizens; for instance, GIS can be used to track the use or misuse of natural resources, or to detect illegal redlining in cities.

No tool in itself can be an answer to a human problem. Clear goals based on some variety of moral groundedness, provide the all-important context: do you know what you want to build or destroy when you pick up a tool? Can you use the means at hand to enhance the welfare of your community? Much depends on how — and why — we use the tools that are now becoming available. —HLR

Arthur Asa Berger

Media Technology and the Vote

Another sourcebook on politics and communication technology that grew out of a colloquium organized by the Annenberg Washington Program. Non-partisan, wide-ranging, and full of juicy footnotes and bibliographies. More issues than answers, suggestions for research that needs to be done, and lots of case histories by political-campaign professionals about the ways new technologies are changing the electoral process. —HLR

•
We have a package that can take a map of any scale and overlay data onto it — take an existing database and throw it into the map. The geographic analysis that we can do will help with (1) finding out where particular points are in a political campaign's database, (2) overlaying this database onto actual maps and seeing what it means; and (3) comparing the geographic relationships among different sets of data. Thus, we can facilitate redistricting because the computer can now draw experimental boundaries and tell us what those boundaries mean. We can then shift the boundaries as desired.

Come election day, getting out the vote is what counts. If you have access to personal computers and learn how to use simple database programs, you can gain an advantage: maintaining and sorting databases for direct mail and walking-order lists is the perfect kind of task for an inexpensive computer. Computers, used this way, have long been powerful weapons for the wealthy and knowledgeable political parties. Now, personal computers and grassroots political campaign tactics can work together. Here's one effective way: Seek volunteers who own personal computers and have skills in database management. Professional campaign support companies often charge naive campaigners big

Users can quickly modify a boundary on the screen and ask, "How does this affect the density of a certain age group, party affiliation or ethnic group?" Then, they can shift the boundaries again and repeat the calculations. The significance of tables of figures also can be easily grasped when they are displayed geographically.

MapInfo can work with multiple layers of data. On a street map of a city we can display points representing the location of voters, and in addition, show boundaries. We can display up to 50 layers of data and independently turn any of them on or off. We can also zoom in or out of any neighborhood to the whole country. In this way one can see the "nitty-gritty" — where each voter lives, his or her party affiliation, race, sex or age — or zoom back and see the summary of that data for a county.

New Communication Technologies in Politics

This collection of papers asserts that, to be effective, local political campaigns must adopt the technologies of direct mail, computer conferencing, and market-polling software. Case studies analyze the successes and problems of campaigns that did so. —Kevin Kelly
[Suggested by Robert Horvitz]

•
Without the computer, the success of grass roots lobbying would not be possible. Where we once compiled lists manually from paper directories, we now purchase brokered lists on computer tape and merge them, letting the computer determine the "strength" of a name based on the frequency of its appearance. At the same time, duplicate names are eliminated.

Eventually, more and more voter registration lists will be available on computer tape, and will give us even greater targeting capability.

Instead of manually entering ID numbers to identify a potential participant, a bar code will be entered with a wand band, much like that currently used at the grocery checkout counter. Such a procedure will virtually eliminate the already minuscule .005 percent current error rate.

Other changes are ahead. Computers have made paperless phone banks possible: phone list, book, tally sheet and message will all be on a video terminal. The computer dials the phone, so the worker will not waste any time with disconnects or misdialed calls. Today 60 percent of our telephone efforts are wasted on that kind of erroneous call — despite the impressive percentage of volunteers per contact we achieve.

In the next two decades, there will be new levels of addressability. Eventually, two-way cable like the experimental QUBE program in Ohio will spread throughout the country. By videotext, direct-satellite broadcast, or

bucks for list processing. You can save those costs and leverage your power by using personal computers. CompuMentor (415/512-7784) is the first of a new breed of nonprofit organizations whose role is to match nonprofit organizations, including political organizations, with technology-savvy mentors who want to donate their services to a cause they support. With one computer and one person who knows how to use it, take these steps:

• *Get the list of registered voters on magnetic tape or floppy diskettes,* from your local registrar of voters. It should cost very little; incumbents controlling such fees want them as low as you do.

• *Get the walking-order address sequences* for streets in your district, again in machine-readable form, again at very low cost — from your main post office.

• *Convert that data* into a form that your personal computers can handle. If you can't do it yourself, look for "media conversion services" in local computer publications. Check around; prices vary widely.

• *Put the data and other public records into a personal computer database.* Then it's a relatively simple task to merge your databases and turn them into a walking-order list of voters, or

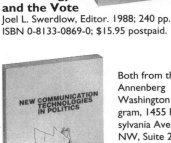

Media Technology and the Vote
Joel L. Swerdlow, Editor. 1988; 240 pp.
ISBN 0-8133-0869-0; $15.95 postpaid.

Both from the Annenberg Washington Program, 1455 Pennsylvania Avenue NW, Suite 200, Washington, DC 20004; 202/393-7100

New Communications Technologies in Politics
Robert G. Meadow, Editor. 1985; 145 pp. ISBN 0-933441-00-2; $15 postpaid.

cable, you will be able to go to a cable channel and broadcast a message directly into the home.

As our process and methods get more sophisticated, the issue of privacy could become more significant. the public must eventually decide what information we — both commercial and political communications consultants — have a right to know, and what information will remain "behind closed doors."

a zip-sorted list needed for bulk-mailing.

COMMUNITY POWER VIA FAXMODEM

More and more people can now receive messages by fax. Many who have personal computers also have faxes. Coupled with a faxmodem, the personal computer can be used as a powerful tool for organizing quick community action — often needed, as self-serving bureaucrats and arrogant elected officials seek to ram through policies before the people can defend themselves. Weekly community newspapers can be too slow and/or unwilling to provocatively publicize politicians' plans.

In the past year, my rural and mountain neighbors and I have begun organizing an increasingly broad and effective fax-plus-leaflets network. With a faxmodem plugged into the telephone port on my computer, it's easy to draft a notice and fax it to (computer maintained) lists of others who are interested in these issues, without ever having to touch hardcopy, or to feed it, over and over, through a manual fax.

Many of those who receive these fax alerts have low-cost copiers at home. Many have agreed to make copies of the notices when they arrive, and pass them along to neighbors or post them on local bulletin boards.

With the increasing availability of computers and faxmodems, the power to influence elections is there for the taking. But that power isn't going to come to you automatically. You have to believe strongly enough in an issue or a candidate to go out and exercise that power yourself.
—Jim Warren and Howard Rheingold

OTHER GREAT RESOURCES

Public Opinion Polling: Celinda C. Lake & Pat Callbeck Harper. 1987, Island Press.

The Electronic Commonwealth: Abramson, Arterton and Orren. 1988, Basic Books, Inc.

La Plaza de Taos TeleCommunity Foundation in New Mexico is designing a community network with a new interface. Pictured is the start-up screen with a photograph of the historic plaza surrounded by icons representing the kinds of local and national information available to users.

A HUNDRED YEARS AGO, Americans were discussing the benefits of electricity and arguing about who should build and run the electrical power networks. Would the cities be served and the rural areas ignored? Should the cities own their own power system or should private companies? In Europe many of the benefits of electricity were seen as a social good; in America these were seen as a business. Political policy as well as market conditions determined who had access to the new technology.

The debates about the so-called information superhighway in some ways parallel the discussions held a century ago. While some of the decisions are going to be made at the national, state, or corporate level, local residents are realizing they have a great deal to say and do about how the national information infrastructure will look in their town, county, region, or Indian reservation. Many different groups are working on this challenging problem, some since the 1970s but most since 1990 or later. This movement is called community networking or civic networking. There is no single national organization, no books available as this Catalog goes to press, no journals, and no annual tradeshow. Nevertheless, a great deal of activity is taking place online and in schools and community centers and libraries as these civic networks take hold.

These networks have provided healthcare and employment information, community discussion of local issues, citizen grassroots organizing around local issues, timely information about local services (libraries, city halls, zoning regulations, city council proceedings, etc.) to community residents. These community networks have been organized by grassroots groups of computer enthusiasts, community workers, teachers, librarians, and businesspeople, but some are for-profit ventures; these may become services provided by large companies running local systems. No matter what your interest or talent, you can help start or even help operate a community network. You can help support these networks even as a user.

The formation of these networks is akin to an electronic barn raising. Different elements of the community gather to work toward a common goal, and one of the first benefits is that people who may have never met before begin to discuss important issues concerning information and its dissemination, as well as how they communicate with the government and with each other. The local information for the networks comes from many sources: the city, nonprofit social organizations and hobbyists, the school district, university, political parties, the library, and religious groups. Some community networks exclude business activity from their information mix, but others see it as an ingredient crucial to the success of the system. Because of the growing interest in access to the Internet, most community networks allow the user to reach at the very least a limited set of destinations on the Internet and to exchange email with people worldwide.

Some systems serve as information refineries. Boulder Community Network in Colorado ferrets out information from local sources such as the United Way, the city, the library, the school district, the newspaper, and local businesses to help them arrange the information in the correct electronic formats, mount it on the file server, and pump it to other networks or BBSs. These same systems are engaged in training and providing support to the local community (computer and network training, consulting on how they can use telecommunications to further their mission, interagency communication), so each network has a large amount of personal contact.

Most community networks consist of a single computer connected to

Sources of Information about Community Networking

Organizations

National Public Telecomputing Network: 34555 Chagrin Blvd., Moreland Hill, OH 44022; phone and fax: 216/247-3328, Internet: info@nptn.org Assists organizing groups that want to start a Free-Net in their town or community. Many of their materials are on the anonymous ftp site at: nptn.org (cd into: /pub/info.nptn).

Online Resources

Art McGee's List of Community/ Rural Electronic Mailing Lists

Art McGee maintains a list of electronic mailing lists that is now too long to include on this page. If you have email access, this list of lists will connect you with all the community and rural networking enthusiasts you have time to meet.

The latest version of this list is available via anonymous FTP from ftp.netcom.com in directory: pub/amcgee/community If you only have access to email, then you can use FTPmail to do the same thing. Send a help message to: ftp-request@netcom.com You can also access this list by sending email to or fingering: amcgee@grex.cyberspace.org This last address is not for correspondence, please.

International Association of Community TeleService Centers: 44 avenue de la Marne, Batiment "B", F-06100 Nice, France; phone: 33-93-81-91-84, fax: 33-93-81-50-75, Internet: lars.engvall@sp1.y-net.fr This organization studies existing centers and helps in the creation of new ones in both developing and industrialized nations.

Center for Civic Networking: PO Box 65272, Washington, DC 20037; 202/ 362-3831, Internet: rciville@civicnet.org CCN provides technical assistance on a consulting and a partnering basis in the planning of civic networking projects. They work on both the state and federal level to bring about policy changes that will help community networks to flourish.

Community Technology Development Center: 8260 Willow Oaks Corporate Drive, Suite 700, Fairfax, VA 22031; Internet: info@commtech.org Conducts and distributes research on community networking technologies and systems, and assists groups with the organization and deployment of community networks and network-based information services.

The Morino Institute: 768 Walker Road, Suite 289, Great Falls, VA 22066; phone: 703/759-0477, fax: 703/759-9548, Internet: info@morino.com Provides fellowships, education programs and facilitation of pilot and research projects to help individuals and communities work toward social change through the potential of electronic communications.

Books

Several works are in the planning stage, but only these volumes could be listed at press time.

Community Networks (Building a New Participatory Medium): Douglas Schuler. 1995, Addison-Wesley. For ordering information, contact 1 Jacob Way, Reading, MA 01867, 800/447-2226. Schuler wrote the definitive article on community networks in the January 1994 issue of the **Communications of the ACM**. His book will expand on the article's themes.

Emerging Communities (Integrating Networked Information into Library Services): Ann Bishop, Editor. 1994; 304 pp. ISBN 0-685-64821-4. $30 ($33 postpaid). University of Illinois at Urbana-Champaign, Graduate School of Library & Information Science/Publications Office, University of Illinois, 501 E. Daniel Street, Champaign, IL 61820; 217/333-1359. Contains a large section of papers on community networks. The papers may also be found online on ftp.cni.org in the CNI/documents/illinois.dpc/text folder.

Electronic Sources

Boulder Community Network runs a World Wide Web server. The address is http://www.cs.colorado.edu/homes/bcn/public_html/Home.html

Peter Scott of the University of Saskatchewan maintains pointers to other networks on his home page: http://www.usask.ca/~scottp/free.html

The WELL gopher — gopher.well.sf.ca.us (port 70) — contains a large sub-directory of information on community networks, including papers, discussions, and organizing information.

There are numerous community systems, but some are so busy handling local callers that they may be hard to reach by modem or the Internet. Here are some representative systems to try:

Big Sky Telegraph: Western Montana College. 710 S. Atlantic Ave., Dillon, MT 59725; modem (1200 baud): 406/683-7680, Internet: 192.231.192.1

Columbia Online Information Network (COIN): University of Missouri Campus Computing. 200 Hinkel Building, Columbia, MO 61211; modem: 314/884-7000, Internet: bigcat.missouri.edu

Victoria Free-Net: Vancouver Island Advanced Technology Centre, Suite 203-1110, Government St., Victoria, BC V8W 1Y2 Canada; modem: 604/595-2300, Internet: freenet.victoria.bc.ca

Wellington Citynet: Wellington City Council. PO Box 2199, Wellington, New Zealand; modem: 64-4-801-3060, Internet: 192.54.130.34

See the Community Domain beginning on page 121

one or more phone lines via modems. The power of the computer varies with the size of the system and the applications offered. As the networks grow, the systems must expand, and if a community system is very popular, there can be severe problems in supplying enough phone lines or public access sites to meet the demand.

The most popular model for many community networks is the Free-Net. The first Free-Net was born in Cleveland, growing out of an Apple II electronic bulletin board system for medical school faculty at Case Western Reserve University. It has expanded into a Unix-based multi-line Internet host serving local callers with modems and distant users who use the telnet protocol to connect remotely. The National Public Telecomputing Network (see Sources of Information about Community Networking) helps new Free-Nets get start-up information and find the right software for urban or rural sites. It also supplies a variety of services for organizing committees and already functioning systems.

Many communities have very limited communications infrastructures, and a low percentage of residents who own computers. In Scandinavia in the mid-1980s groups began setting up tele-service centers or tele-cottages to provide basic computer and telecommunications services to local residents through telephone. A townsperson visiting one of these centers has a choice of using telephone, fax, computer network, satellite receiver, or in some cases, video production equipment. More than one hundred centers now exist in Scandinavia, and many other countries are emulating the model. Successful tele-service centers could be precursors to community networks in states like Kentucky, where two centers are being planned for Pike County and Elizabethtown.

Because the printed information on community networks is so scarce in mid-1994, you may have to rely on electronic sources. What follows are organizations that maintain an electronic presence with archives, electronic-mail help, and more advanced systems such as gopher and World Wide Web. You can also use the plain old telephone to reach many of these groups. —Steve Cisler

Connect with the Virtual Community on page 262.

Boulder Community Network in Colorado uses World Wide Web software to serve information to public access sites, homes, schools, and businesses. Pictured is a Mosaic client interface to the Web that works on the Macintosh, X-window, and Microsoft Windows computers to present a mix of text, images, and sound. One click moves the browser to another screen of pictures and text.

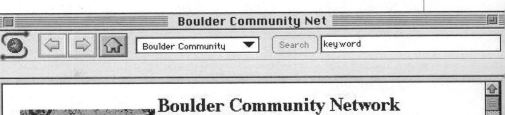

Boulder Community Network

Welcome to the Boulder Community Network (BCN) prototype!

BCN Information Centers

- **About BCN**
- **Business Center**
- **Community Center**
- **Education Center**
- **Government Center**
- **Health Center**
- **Library**
- **Media Center**
- **Transportation Center**
- **Visitor Center**
- **Informacion en Espanol... (Information in Spanish)**

Online Resources

These groups mainly focus on electronic rights and broad issues that will affect local systems.

The Electronic Frontier

Computer Professionals for Social Responsibility: PO Box 717, Palo Alto, CA 94301; phone:415/322-3778, fax: 415/322-3798, Internet: cpsr@csli.stanford.edu *A public interest alliance of computer scientists and others interested in the effects of computer technology on society. CPSR works to influence decisions regarding the development and use of computers because those decisions have far-reaching consequences and reflect basic values and priorities.*

Electronic Frontier Foundation: 1001 G Street NW, Suite 950 E., Washington, DC 20001; phone: 202/ 347-5400, fax: 202/393- 5509, Internet: ask@eff.org — *"The Electronic Frontier Foundation (EFF) was founded in July of 1990 to ensure that the principles embodied in the Constitution and the Bill of Rights are protected as new communications technologies emerge.*

"Since its inception, EFF has worked to shape our nation's communications infrastructure and the policies that govern it in order to maintain and enhance First Amendment, privacy and other democratic values. We believe that our overriding public goal must be the creation of Electronic Democracy."

Society for Electronic Access: PO Box 7081, New York, NY 10116- 7081; 212/592- 3801, Internet: sea@sea.org—*"The purpose of SEA is to help make our corner of the digital world a civilized place to live, work and visit. We believe that the world of computers and the communications links that bind their users together ('cyberspace') should be open to everyone." SEA runs discussion groups and maintains a gopher archive: SEAgopher.eff.org*

The wheel diagram with axes: Distributed, Communications, Local resources, Fee, Graphic Interface, Multi-lingual, Centralized, Information, Internet Access, Free, Text Interface, English Only.

Local designers make choices about how their community network will function with the Community Network Wheel, which shows some of the choices facing each group (e.g., will it be free, or will you charge a fee; will you emphasize access to information or citizen-to-citizen communication). Community network planners can begin to develop a profile of the system they want to build by placing marks on each axis of the wheel.

CITIZEN ON-LINE ACCESS TO GOVERNMENT INFORMATION

"ACH HOUSE SHALL KEEP A JOURNAL of its proceedings, and from time to time publish the same, excepting such parts as may in their judgment require secrecy; and the yeas and nays of the members of either house on any questions shall, at the desire of one-fifth of those present, be entered on the journal." —Article 1, Section 5 of the U.S. Constitution

Most state constitutions and local government charters have a similar provision. However, actually accessing the journal can be a challenge. In theory, you can ask your elected representative to supply you with the text of bills and votes on them. This process assumes: 1) you know what to ask for; 2) you have time to wait for it.

Several states and many cities now have computer dial-in services. Most are BBSs. The legislature of the state of California is now on the Internet. So is the town of Colorado Springs. The U.S. Congress is lagging, although they have laid the foundations. If your congressional representatives are not on this list, ask them why. —Michael Marotta

Congressional Representatives Online

Sam Coppersmith, Arizona: samaz01@hr.house.gov

Jay Dickey, Arkansas: jdickey@hr.house.gov

George Miller, California: georgem@hr.house.gov

Pete Stark, California: petemail@hr.house.gov

Sam Gejdenson, Connecticut: bozrah@hr.house.gov

Newt Gingrich, Georgia: georgia6@hr.house.gov

Dennis Hastert, Illinois: dhastert@hr.house.gov

Dave Camp, Michigan: davecamp@hr.house.gov

John Conyers, Jr., Michigan: jconyers@hr.house.gov

Vernon Ehlers, Michigan: congehlr@hr.house.gov

Charlie Rose, North Carolina: crose@hr.house.gov

Mel Watt, North Carolina: melmail@hr.house.gov

Martin Hoke, Ohio: hokemail@hr.house.gov

Elizabeth Furse, Oregon: furseor1@hr.house.gov

Karen Shepherd, Utah: shepherd@hr.house.gov

Maria Cantwell, Washington: cantwell@hr.house.gov

So far only two House committees are accessible by email:

Committee on Natural Resources: natres@hr.house.gov

Committee on Science, Space, and Technology: housesst@hr.house.gov

You can encourage Congress via: comments@hr.house.gov

There are also private sellers of this information. StateNet and LegiTech of California track the federal legislature and provide online access. Unlike public sellers, these organizations are customer-driven to remain competitive. During the 1993 battle to bring California online, StateNet and LegiTech both lined up on the side of open access.

StateNet: 1900 14th Street, Sacramento, California 95814-9830.

LegiTech: 1029 J Street, Suite 450, Sacramento, California 95814.

The new kid on the block is the Washington Post's LEGI-SLATE (800/733-1131). LEGI-SLATE sells an impressive array of information for "$1900 to $50,000 or more, depending on what services you need." Databases include bill text and tracking, the Congressional Record, committee and subcommittee reports, the U.S. Code, and the Congressional Quarterly.

Mail to the Chief

Now you can send email to: president@whitehouse.gov and vice.president@whitehouse.gov

The Entrenched Bureaucracy

Of course, the 500-plus people in the House and Senate, the prexy and veep, are but a small fraction of the REAL government. Insulated from commercial demands and protected by civil service, many offices have let their techies run loose with this democracy stuff. Here are a few of the active dial-ups:

Coast Guard: Global Positioning System BBS: 9600 baud: 703/866-3894; 2400 baud: 703/866-3890.

Environmental Protection Agency: Research and Development BBS: 2400 baud: 513/569-7610.

Environmental Protection Agency: Office of Wetlands, Oceans, and Watersheds: 2400 baud: 301/589-0205.

Federal Aviation Administration: FAA Safety Exchange: 2400 baud: 800/426-3814.

Federal Communications Commission: Public Access Link: 1200 baud: 301/725-1072.

Library of Congress: Automated Library Information Xchange: 2400 baud: 202/707-4888.

NASA Marshall Space Flight Center: NASA Spacelink: 2400 baud: 205/895-0028.

National Institute of Standards and Technology: Data Management Institute: 1200 baud: 301/948-2048.

National Institute of Standards and Technology: North American ISDN Users Forum: 2400 baud: 301/869-7281.

Office of Personnel Management: Washington Area Service Center BBS: 2400 baud: 202/606-1113.

Office of Personnel Management/Detroit: Midwest Federal Jobs: 2400 baud: 313/226-4423.

Small Business Administration: 2400 baud: 202/205-6269.

Justice for Some

The U.S. Supreme Court has made its records available through several outlets. The Rotunda News Service run by Hannah Information Systems of Ohio carries them, as does the Cleveland Freenet. However, it seems that West Publishing owns a fair bit of the cumulative judicial records in the United States. Ralph Nader's Taxpayer Assets Project (TAP) runs a "Crown Jewels Campaign" to get these documents back into the public domain where they belong.

The campaign is a grassroots effort to open up access to JURIS, as well the SEC's EDGAR system, the House of Representatives LEGIS system, the CIA Foreign Broadcast Information Service (FBIS), the Patent and Trademark Automated Patent System (APS), and others. The Crown Jewels Campaign is a joint effort between Essential Information and TAP. TAP information policy notes, including all Crown Jewels Campaign memorandums, are disseminated through tap-info, a low-volume list (not a discussion group).

Taxpayer Assets Project: PO Box 19367, Washington, DC 20036; phone 202/387-8030 fax 202/234-5176.

internet: tap@essential.org

tap-info postings are archived at cspr.org

ftp: *ftp.cspr.org*
gopher: *gopher.cpsr.org*
wais: wais.cspr.org

Send subscription requests to: tap-info-request@essential.org

The State of the States

Most states now have electronic access. Even so, only Wisconsin, Hawaii, and California provide free access to the general public. In most states, access is expensive: $100 per year in libertarian New Hampshire and in Alaska and up to $10,000 per year in authoritarian New York. And these are the prices charged by the government. Private providers tend to charge more and deliver more. For instance, in Michigan, the state's own Legislative Service Bureau sells access for about $100 per year but its databases do not include the actual text of bills. Their competitor, Hannah Information Systems, does provide this. Hannah also provides a slew of databases that the state does not.

The annual State Legislative Sourcebook (about $150) is a complete overview of government at the state level that includes all providers of legislative reporting, public and private.

Government Research Service: 701 Jackson Avenue, Topeka, Kansas 66603.

Get a listing of public and private legislative systems in each state from the National Conference of State Legislatures: 1560 Broadway, Suite 700, Denver, Colorado 80820 303/830-2200.

OTHER GREAT RESOURCES

The InfoCalifornia pilot kiosk located in the main library of California State University in Sacramento gives access to information on government services.

Making Government Work: Electronic Delivery of Federal Services: U.S. Congress, Office of Technology Assessment, OTA-TCT-578, 1993. Online citizen access to government information far beyond the realm of legislative records is not just good for the health of democratic institutions — it has high potential for economic benefits as well, to both citizens and government. This definitive study shows why and how to implement this foundational building block of electronic democracy.

How to Use GIS in Electoral Politics

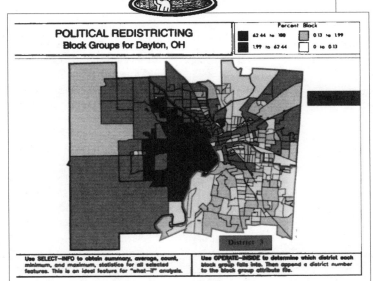

See also GIS, p. 14 and Ecoactivism, p. 109.

BILL CLINTON'S 1992 CAMPAIGN strategy focused on states where large numbers of "Reagan Democrats" had split their tickets in past elections, sending a Republican to the White House and Democrats to Congress and to state and local offices. Enhanced by geographic information systems, this geographic targeting was successful in thirty of thirty-one such states.

During the heat of a political campaign, enormous amounts of data have to be quickly assimilated to develop responsive strategy, especially when a race is tight or contentious. "The challenge was to find a way to analyze the information we received from a variety of sources each day," noted Clinton technology strategist Janet Handal. Handal and her co-workers used AtlasPro and AtlasGIS software products from Strategic Mapping, Inc. (SMI), Santa Clara, California.

The late Paul Tully, former political director of the Democratic National Committee, was an early evangelist for the use of mapping technology. When he unexpectedly died during the campaign, Handal took over as Clinton's chief mapmaker.

During the campaign, strategists pored over maps showing media market information, past voting patterns, and the latest polling data. They used maps to chart trends, to decide where to send their candidates and to recruit volunteers. The ability to quickly display a variety of information was key to being responsive.

GIS was used at the highest levels of the campaign to determine the number of TV ads to buy in a specific market. Area of dominant influence (ADI) boundaries used to identify TV markets generally don't follow nicely segmented political boundaries. However, it's these political boundaries that are used to summarize voting statistics. Without GIS, there's no way to quickly and effectively put these two kinds of data together. According to SMI's Sarah Lathrop, who provided technical support to the campaign, Handal developed hybrid ADI/political-jurisdiction boundaries that allowed her to do just that.

Eric Hawkins, deputy director of the National Committee for an Effective Congress, a Democratic political-action committee, believes that GIS allowed the Clinton campaign to make targeted TV buys while the Bush campaign wasted money on a buckshot approach.

Rick Bloomingdale is the campaign's national deputy political director responsible for securing union endorsements and enlisting volunteers from organized labor. He knew there were heavy concentrations of steel workers around Gary, Indiana, but couldn't tell from AFL-CIO data that many steel workers were located across a broad belt of southern Missouri and Illinois.

"Just looking at this information in tabular form for the separate states, we wouldn't have made the connection," Bloomingdale explained. "When we displayed the data on a map, it was instantly apparent there were people we wanted to reach in regions no database could have identified. Looking at the information visually brought it to life." That last phrase should sound familiar to anyone who's been involved in GIS for any length of time.

While the Clinton campaign is the first national campaign to make extensive use of this technology, GIS and politics are not strangers. A Reagan campaign consultant made limited use of the technology as far back as 1980. For example, in Boston, Dual Independent Map Encoding files and demographics were used to categorize the voters by zip code. A campaign letter was then customized with specific paragraphs focusing on the likely concerns of a particular voting group.

Both Republican and Democratic congressional committees used GIS to support redistricting efforts that followed the 1990 census, as did many states (figure 1). In fact, it was probably the Republicans' use of GIS during

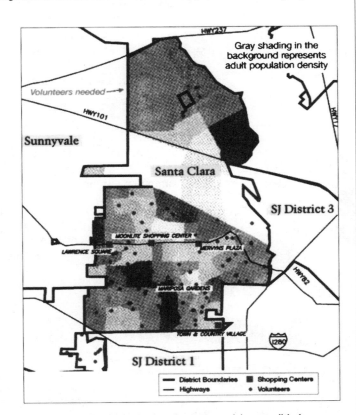

POLITICAL REDISTRICTING
Block Groups for Dayton, OH

Percent Black

District 3

Use SELECT–INFO to obtain summary, average, count, minimum, and maximum, statistics for all selected features. This is an ideal feature for "what–if" analysis. Use OPERATE–INSIDE to determine which district each block group falls into. Then append a district number to the block group attribute file.

Figure 1. Both the Democratic and Republican parties used GIS during redistricting that followed the 1990 census, to locate key data such as block groups.

Gray shading in the background represents adult population density

HWY237
Volunteers needed →
HWY101
Sunnyvale
Santa Clara
SJ District 3
MOONLITE SHOPPING CENTER
LAWRENCE SQUARE
SERVING PLAZA
MARIPOSA GARDENS
TOWN & COUNTRY VILLAGE
I280
SJ District 1
HWY82

— District Boundaries ■ Shopping Centers
— Highways ● Volunteers

Figure 2. Recruiting volunteers is an important task in any political campaign. Mapping the location of possible volunteers and their proximity to potential rally sites is easily accomplished using GIS.

redistricting that allowed them to do as well as they did at the state level in the last election.

According to at least one software vendor, the Perot campaign in 1992 also analyzed the possibility of using GIS. The software application they considered using focused on recruiting and effectively using volunteers (figure 2). —Nora Sherwood Bryan

Abridged from an article titled "GIS Helps Produce Clinton's Victory." Reprinted with permission from Business Geographics, March/April 1993. Copyright GIS World, Inc., 155 E. Boardwalk Drive, Suite 250, Fort Collins, CO 80525.

GIS and Ecoactivism

Politics is about advocacy and persuasion — convincing people to support your legislation or candidate. And seeing is still believing: if you can *show* people what you are talking about, you can amplify your influence. Because GIS uses maps and map overlays to help people visualize geographic databases, it can be used as a dramatic means of persuasion. Environmental activism is one political battle where GIS systems are becoming increasingly important.

Eric and Steve Beckwitt of the Sierran Biodiversity Institute succeeded in influencing the U.S. Congress to preserve some of the remaining old-growth forests by using GIS to demonstrate how little is left, and how important it is. The Institute's six billion-byte database includes ancient and modern maps of remaining forests, watershed information, survey information, geological data, species data, and other information relevant to the endangered region. Their multimedia show before the House of Representatives demonstrated the importance, fragility, and extent of endangered biodiversity in the Sierran region.

Urban political advocates and activists can make use of GIS to detect and demonstrate redlining — illegal and racist financial discrimination. Historic preservationists and urban ecologists will also find GIS useful for local political planning and advocacy as the price of the hardware and software becomes more affordable. —HLR

Electoral politics is a zero-sum game with precisely defined rules. If you want to get involved, you must know the official campaign rules — you can get them from your county clerk or secretary of state. Amateurs often torpedo their own efforts by failing to meet legal reporting requirements, or through some other fundamental misapprehension of the rules.

The most important campaign lore appears in no official rulebook. Campaign managers who survive to become veterans do so through their facility for learning, and deploying, strategies that include those briefly summarized here. —HLR

EFFECTIVE Citizen ACTION

by Jim Warren

How I Learned What I Learned

IN THE ANTI-WAR SIXTIES, I was General Secretary of the (California) Midpeninsula Free University during its greatest growth and activity. In the early eighties, I took on San Mateo County, California, for abusing and exploiting its unincorporated rural minority. This prompted a grand jury investigation, which supported my complaints. The planning director was forced to resign, and a citizens' appeals board was created.

I was later elected a county-wide trustee of the three-campus community college district. This was a highly politicized position in a county with a population of 600,000, where it has been said that the Number One avocation is politics. Thereafter, disgusted by the ongoing abuse of the mountain and rural residents who were supposed to be represented by a county supervisor — "Atherton Anna" Eshoo — I ran against her when no one else would. I knew I didn't have a chance of winning, but I simply wasn't going to let her arrogance go unchallenged.

As soon as I filed, all sorts of political pros came out of the woodwork, offering advice as to what really works — versus what naive citizens *think* should work. A lot of it was simple advice, gained from direct experience, and proven in numerous municipal, county, and statewide elections.

If you recognize these realities, your potential political clout is much greater than that of those who are unaware of them or who refuse to accept them. If you apply this information, it will enhance your ability to cause change, with reduced wheelspin and campaign fatigue.

All of this advice requires work, time and effort to implement. Most of it can be used by rich and poor alike. Computer power can make a major contribution to your efforts (see p. 289), but it is not absolutely required.

Political Action:

Most professional campaign managers agree that the following are effective campaign tools — listed in approximate order of effectiveness, starting with the most effective.

1. Face-to-face contact
by candidate or supporter, door to door and in public places. If you have volunteers with good people skills, don't waste their valuable talent by assigning them to stuff envelopes in a back room. Send them out to meet people. Equip them with some brief comments, a well-designed brochure and a walking-order list of registered voters (I'll say more about these later).

2. "Dear Friend" notes and cards,
distributed by candidates' or issues' supporters to people who know the writer. The best advertising for anything is still word-of-mouth recommendations from someone you know, even though it may be the most casual of aquaintances. ("This guy, Charlie somebody, told me a Yugo was much better than a Honda, and . . . ")

Send out lots of "Dear Friend" cards or notes. They can be very brief — little more than "I support X and hope you will, too." Include your signature. Aggressively "designed" typeset notes are the

Getting Started

- **Start Early.** If you want to run a successful political campaign, you have to start many months before the beginning of the campaign season. Wait until people are thinking of politics and you've waited too long.

- **Do It Right.** If your interest is a candidate or initiative with a campaign already in progress, you can volunteer to work with their organization or start your own. Either way, follow the campaigning regulations or expect major public embarrassment.

  Trivial example: It's useful to send "Dear Friend" cards (see above) and other publications. They are more effective with a personal name and address than with a "Com-

mittee to Elect" address. But any artifact funded by, or even coordinated with, an official campaign organization must have that organization clearly identified in it.

The rules are extensive and explicit. Visit the local election officer at your county clerk's office; say you want to run for office or to form a campaign committee or create an initiative. Unless the folks you speak to are real political hacks, they will be very helpful and will provide you with instructions. Nonetheless, you had better assume that everything you say will be repeated to any interested incumbents, often within minutes. It depends on how cozy the clerk is with those incumbents.

It is easy to misinterpret the requirements of the various

campaign laws and regulations. The instant you miss a reporting date or misreport information, your opponents — if they know what they are doing — will accuse you of VIOLATING the Fair Political Practices Act and LYING in your political reports. And the newspapers will print the accusations.

- **Open a Bank Account.** Open a separate bank account in the name of "The Committee for _____" or in the name of "X for Dog Catcher." Don't let campaign money flow through your own account. Ask people to make checks out to the special account. Some will be drawn to you, personally; just endorse them over to the special account.

What Works, What Doesn't

least effective. Most "dear friends" do not typeset their notes to one another.

3. Candidate statements included with ballot materials.
There is a word limit to these optional statements; they are written by the candidates (that is, they have broad latitude in, uh, "accuracy"), and their printing costs are shared among those candidates who choose to have such statements distributed as part of the official ballot materials.

These are the statements that most voters read, and they are given the greatest credence by voters — in spite of the fact that they are candidates' "un-refereed" propaganda. This is something an outside activist can't do, except possibly in the "for" and "against" statements for a ballot initiative. It's something over which outsiders have no control, but I include it in this list because of its importance. If your candidate is thinking of not including a ballot-packet statement, find another candidate.

4. Directly distributed materials —
letters, brochures, leaflets. These are usually distributed by direct mail, but they can also be distributed by hand, door to door. If you want to influence an issue or a candidates' campaign, you can do a lot without opening an office and a bank account. Simply write and distribute your own note, letter, leaflet, newsletter or tabloid.

Cover your neighborhood ("My family and I live nearby and feel this is so important that we have hand-delivered this to you . . . "). Distribute your publication to your business clients, if you dare.

In warm months, hand them to drivers at stoplights and bank drive-up queues. If it is a sufficiently sincere and effectively written item, you might risk putting it on automobile windshields (the risk is that recipients' irritation with the leaflet will act against your cause). I used to paper Silicon Valley with "windshield editions" of the Silicon Gulch Gazette and received no complaints, to my absolute amazement.

5. Television advertising
can be powerful, but only for creating emotional bias — for and against. And it isn't within reach of average-income folks. Enough said?

6. Radio advertising
runs a distant sixth, and is often considered almost useless except for costly drive-time ads. Paid radio advertising is not feasible for citizen activists. Call-ins to talk shows, however, can be really valuable.

7. Signs and posters
are unanimously considered to be almost completely useless except for encouraging the candidate's volunteer campaign workers — who want to see them and want to display them. Ditto for lapel buttons. Junk! If you do put up political posters, it is far wiser to pay a political poster company to do it than to waste limited volunteer resource time.

Designing Effective Flyers and Direct Distribution Pieces

- Something with an individual's return address, or from a group of named individuals, is a lot more effective than something from "the campaign to elect . . ." (but follow campaigning regulations).

- The biggest problem with handouts and direct mail is getting the residents to open the envelope. So eliminate the envelope. Print on a 14-inch piece of paper; fold it twice. Don't staple it. Use paper stock heavy enough to meet postal requirements for a self-mailer.

- Increase circulation of flyers by printing the reminder "please post and circulate" near the top of the document.

- Turn the labeling, bundling and sorting over to a professional mailing house. Do not waste volunteers' time on bulk mailings.

- Create brochures that espouse your cause in the form of a small set of key points that can be read at a glance (for example: "Eshoo Opposed Affordable Housing: 'There's not a problem; don't fix it!'"). Another example that *WER* might use: "The articles in most magazines satisfy advertisers. The articles in *WER* satisfy readers." By the time somebody reads the headlines to determine whether or not they are interested in your document, they've read the statements you want them to read.

After each main point, *briefly* justify it or detail it, for those who give it more serious — or suspicious — consideration.

- Don't commit the most common sin of amateur desktop publishers. Keep it typographically simple. Don't use too many typefaces, too much boldface or italics or underline, too many fancy borders or illustrations.

- Make sure that everything you say is accurate. Nobody trusts political advertising. Make sure nobody can catch you in a lie. Give the reader information about how to verify your statements.

Negative Campaigning Can Be Done with Integrity

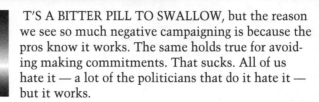

T'S A BITTER PILL TO SWALLOW, but the reason we see so much negative campaigning is because the pros know it works. The same holds true for avoiding making commitments. That sucks. All of us hate it — a lot of the politicians that do it hate it — but it works.

One of my supporters, a successful pro of twenty years' experience, once told me, "Look, you have to realize that when you take positions on ten issues and somebody likes nine of them but opposes the tenth, they will vote against you because they've found something to dislike." That's why professional politicians simply don't make any commitments about anything except God, mother, and apple pie. Then the only thing remaining for them to say is to criticize their opponents.

Negative campaigning can be legitimate. Back to County Supervisor Atherton Anna Eshoo. She spends most of her time running for office, any office. When she ran for U.S. Representative, after years of screwing the county residents she was supposed to represent, I publicized her record — and believe me, it was negative, but legitimate, campaigning.

Just before the election, I made up a flyer. It was a 14-inch sheet of heavy-stock paper, had nothing but type on it — no pictures, no graphics, no color, no stars and stripes. It was folded and folded again into approximately letter size. The return address said "Jim Warren and Neighbors." The area to the left of the address label said: "We're from all political parties and we're totally *fed up!* We're paying for this from our own, personal pockets. No party politics, no PACs, no outside special interests, no 'business contributions' — and no more patience!" That probably overcame the biggest single problem of direct-mail promotions — getting people to glance beyond the return address.

After the address fold, there was a series of boldface headlines, each followed by a brief explanatory paragraph. One headline said, "Eshoo Opposed Housing for Single Parents and Small Families." Another said, "Eshoo Overran County's Budget Limits," followed by "Budget Balancing? Eshoo Didn't Do It!"

Another said "Eshoo Dodged Ocean Dumping Problems," and still another said, "Eshoo Opposed Coastal Preservation Initiative." Each following paragraph detailed the headline's justification and how anyone could verify it.

At the end — very important — I listed the names and addresses of those supporting the flyer. No politicos; just fed-up neighbors.

It was a negative campaign, but it was completely justified. Eshoo had been campaigning as pro-environment, pro-housing, a single mother, and fiscally responsible. We simply publicized her actual public record that exposed the hypocrisy, and gave the means for verifying her statements and votes.

Her opponent won — by a tiny margin.

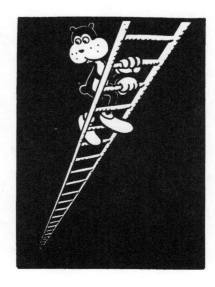

Ultra Left < Communist < Socialist < Liberal < Moderate >Conservative > Ultra Conservative > Radical Right

THE FRENCH ARISTOCRATS and lawyers who assembled in the Estates General of 1789 — with the nobility on the King's right and the bourgeois "third estate" gathered on his left — would probably have been struck speechless if they had been informed that, two hundred years later, the world would still be trying to fit its understanding of politics onto the left/right template formed by that seating arrangement. Real life rarely falls into such neat dichotomies, and real politics is no exception. However, despite this drawback, no alternative conceptual grid has arisen to replace the old left/right model. Thus, most groups and ideologies on the political landscape still locate themselves somewhere to the left or right of each other.

The following brief survey is one possible approach to the political spectrum. I've chosen to spotlight magazines instead of political groups because over the years I've found that magazines provide the most direct routes to grasping the world views of the different ideological camps they represent. Unlike an organized group or party, a magazine will rarely come knocking on your door trying to recruit you into some sort of membership, yet at the same time the tone and unspoken assumptions of its writers, reviewers, and letters to the editor often leap off the page and provide many unexpected insights. Magazines leave you free to draw your own conclusions.

Since each magazine chosen here represents a different ideological camp, I recommend regularly dipping into publications from across the spectrum. It is particularly valuable to read publications that reflexively make your skin crawl, as an exercise in preventing mental calcification. Dehumanizing one's opponents is a time-honored political device practiced by nearly everyone. Cross-spectrum reading can help you extricate yourself from such a tendency.

The most common model of the left/right continuum has generally located moderate upholders of the status quo in the center. As one travels further out from the center on both the left and the right, dissatisfaction with the present set-up increases and increasingly radical solutions proliferate. In this fashion, the far left and far right tend to mirror each other psychologically. This helps account for the phenomenon of disillusioned communists flipping over and becoming hard-bitten conservatives. A typical ideological chart from left to right would read like the one at the top of this page.

This is approximately the model I have employed in the following reviews, though it has numerous flaws, not the least being its illusion of linearity. The left generally upholds economic intervention by the government, yet the ideological tendency usually considered farthest to the left is anarchism — which advocates the abolition of government. Similarly, in this scheme, the right is usually seen as upholding limited government intervention, yet fascism is usually considered on the extreme right despite its support of an active corporatist state.

For the sake of simplicity, let's start our survey in the center and work our way out. —Jay Kinney

• Moderate

Moderate or Centrist is the category that nearly everyone falls within but hardly anyone wants to claim. It tends to be marked by an earnest support for our democratic

—The New Republic

institutions, a tendency to try and accommodate the claims of those farther to the left and right, and a reluctance to rock the boat. Pragmatism rules. Though his rhetoric tends to tilt further left, President Clinton's actual behavior is classically centrist.

Similarly, The **New Republic** has long had a reputation as a liberal "weekly journal of opinion" but its editorial positions in recent years have been largely moderate (or "neo-liberal"). **TNR** is the quintessential "beltway" magazine, edited in Washington, and one of the liveliest political/cultural publications around. It is also among the most influential magazines in powerful East Coast circles, a fact that garners sneers from the envious on both left and right.

The New Republic: Andrew Sullivan, Editor. $34.99/year (48 issues). PO Box 602, Mount Morris, Il 61054; 800/827-1289.

• Liberal/Socialist

Meanwhile, the one-two punch of the Reagan/Bush years and the collapse of Soviet communism has sent everyone left of center into an extended identity crisis. Formerly inclusive ideologies such as mainstream liberalism and democratic socialism, which once saw themselves as defending the interests of justice and opportunity for the vast majority of working people, have evolved into unstable coalitions of radicalized minorities (women, people of color, gays, the disabled, the elderly, et al.), competing for recognition and entitlements. Amid this turmoil, the old boundaries between liberalism and socialism have collapsed into a general defense of the welfare state, public-sector growth, and rights legislation: not exactly an inspiring vision with which to rally widespread support. Since a good portion of the left in the sixties and seventies included the brightest students in college, much of their political activity has relocated to the pages of abstruse academic journals as they've pursued professorships and tenure.

In These Times (which started out in Chicago in the mid-seventies as "the independent socialist newspaper" and has since become "the alternative newsmagazine") and **The Nation** (featuring the cream of the left/liberal intelligentsia) speak for this political stratum in alert and readable fashion, while remaining generally nonsectarian. Both feature good reporting and serious writing tackling the challenges facing the left. **Socialist Review** is arguably the best of the more scholarly journals, perhaps because it comes from a non-academic urban editorial collective rather than from some university department. Titled **Socialist Revolution** once upon a time, **SR** has faithfully mirrored the shifts on the left over the years. It is currently a lively and unpredictable forum for socialist debate.

In These Times: James Weinstein, Editor. $34.95/year (26 issues). 1912 Debs Avenue, Mount Morris, IL 61054; 800/827-0270.

The Nation: Victor Navasky, Editor. $35.95/year (47 issues). PO Box 10791, Des Moines, IA 50340-0791; 800/333-8536.

Socialist Review: David Trend, Editor. $21/year (4 issues). Socialist Review/Duke University Press Journals Fulfillment, 90660 College Station, Durham, NC 27708-0660; 919/687-3600.

• Communist

Fifteen years ago, this next category was arguably the most active on the left, with hoards of Maoists, Trotskyists, Third World national-liberation support groups, and other Leninist varieties busily contending with each other and trying to build The Party. Communists looked with disdain at

—In These Times

socialists, who were less revolutionary than they, and held high the banner of the dictatorship of the proletariat. While a few lonely remnants of those heady days are still around, it is a measure of the changes that have occurred that none really warrants mention here. The major hard-left weekly paper, **The Guardian**, went belly up in 1992. The Soviet-aligned CPUSA, which had struggled on through glasnost, split in the wake of Yeltsin's actions in 1993. And after Tiananmen Square, no one looks to China for inspiration anymore. Former communists remain peppered throughout the left, particularly in antiracist, antirightist organizations, but these days they tend to hang their dusty Mao caps in the closet. Will the last Marxist-Leninist to abandon the revolution please turn out the lights?

• Anarchist/ Anti-Authoritarian

The last decade has seen both ups and downs for the Anarchists, our farthest left camp. The association of a visceral anarchy with the Punk movement swelled the ranks of anarchist circles for much of the eighties, but hitching one's wagon to the wild horses of youth is implicitly not a long-term strategy, as the proponents of a radical youth culture discovered in the sixties. Various attempts to fashion national organizations of anarchists or national anarchist newspapers have sputtered, although there are a good couple of dozen (primarily local) anarcho-zines and magazines around — certainly a stronger showing than the communists.

One notable success has been the growth of **Anarchy** ("A Journal of Desire Armed") from a scrappy tabloid into a solid and attractive desktop-published quarterly. A potpourri of analytical pieces, columns, numerous reader letters, and exhaustive listings of other anarchist publications keep things vital.

Anarchy: Jason McQuinn, Editor. $12/year (4 issues). C. A. L. Press, PO Box 1446, Columbia, MO 65205-1446.

• Neoconservative

If we return to the center and wander toward the right, we soon come to the neoconservatives. Mostly former East Coast liberals who switched camps in reaction to the excesses of the sixties New Left, the neoconservatives rose to greatest prominence during the Reagan years. Neocons were vociferous anticommunists (and were big on pushing their version of "democratic capitalism" around the globe), but domestically they often kept their old liberal reflexes in accepting the welfare state and cultural pluralism — positions which have since raised the hackles of the more conservative.

*Irving Kristol is often considered the "godfather" of the neocons; he has his hand in publishing several conservative policy journals. One of them, **The National Interest**, is generally engaging and outspoken. However, the neocon flagship has to be **Commentary**. A sixties bastion of liberalism, **Commentary** shifted to the right in the seventies and continues to speak for the neocon perspective.*

The National Interest: Owen Harris, Editor. $21/year (4 issues). PO Box 3000, Denville, NJ 07834.

Commentary: Neal Kozodoy, Editor. $39/year (12 issues). 165 E. 56th Street, New York, NY 10022; 800/829-6270, x195.

• Conservative

*Though one might assume that mainstream conservatism has always been with us, it is actually a creation of the fifties. It was preceded by what is now called the Old Right, whose proponents were largely isolationist and intensely skeptical of "big government" and "big business" alike. In 1955, following a stint in the CIA and time spent defending Joseph McCarthy in print, William F. Buckley, Jr. launched **The National Review**, a self-consciously conservative weekly which proceeded to rally conservatives into a movement whose early high point was Goldwater's 1964 Republican presidential nomination. Buckley and his colleagues worked hard at distancing respectable conservatism from radical, re-*

—*The National Review*

actionary, populist, and overtly bigoted elements, while at the same time sanctioning the buildup of the military-industrial-national security complex as a necessary defense against the overarching threat of world communism.

*The National Review remains the foremost proponent of establishment conservatism, although in recent years it has had to share the field with R. Emmett Tyrell, Jr.'s **American Spectator**, a less genteel mix of neo- and mainstream conservative writing. The American Spectator forged a sassy*

*and sarcastic journalistic style during the seventies, when it was published on a shoestring in the wilds of Indiana. However, its move to Washington, DC during the Reagan years gained it both prestige and better funding, rendering what had been underdog irony into self-satisfied smirks. Booted from its new top-dog position by Clinton's victory, **The American Spectator** has been out for blood ever since; this has resulted in some hair-raising investigative reporting. Perhaps that makes it the best present representative of mainstream conservatism in the nineties.*

National Review: John O'Sullivan, Editor. $57/year (25 issues). PO Box 668, Mount Morris, IL 61054-0668; 815/734-1232.

The American Spectator: R. Emmett Tyrell, Jr., Editor. $35/year (12 issues). PO Box 657, Mount Morris, IL 61054.

• Paleoconservative

The implosion of the Eastern Bloc and the much-touted end of the Cold War affected not only the North American left but the right as well. With the Evil Empire in eclipse, anticommunism began to lose its power to unify the conservative movement. The gaze of the right was turning inward, toward the domestic scene, when suddenly Bush crossed swords with Iraq and a new war loomed. Despite the yellow ribbons and CNN fireworks, a certain minority of conservatives strongly opposed the war as a foreign entanglement that hardly served American interests. The American right split, and Patrick Buchanan charged into the Republican primaries as a challenge to Bush from the right. Thus emerged the so-called Paleoconservatives, self-conscious throwbacks to the Old Right.

*In short order the paleocons (spearheaded by Buchanan, **Washington Times** columnist Sam Francis, and the Rockford Institute in rural Illinois) realigned with the most conservative of the libertarians (like Murray Rothbard). They soon found themselves embroiled in protracted battle with the neocons, who accused Buchanan and cohorts of anti-Semitism, nativism, and worse. The paleos flung back charges of*

elitism, financial manipulation, and betrayal of conservative principles. Perot's candidacy gained, in part, from echoes of this conflict reverberating on down to the grassroots; it is possible that political shifts on the American landscape may evolve out of this ideological conflict.

Chronicles, the monthly "magazine of American culture" published by the paleo Rockford Institute, is both exuberantly non-

PC and intellectually formidable, a dynamo of pent-up ire against the status quo of both right and left. The New American is the biweekly news magazine of the John Birch Society, which was drummed out of mainstream conservatism in the sixties by the Buckley camp, only to pop up again in bitter proto-paleo opposition to Bush and the Iraq war.

Chronicles: Thomas Fleming, Editor. $28/year (12 issues). PO Box 800, Mount Morris, IL 61054; 800/877-5459.

New American: Gary Benoit, Editor. $39/year (25 issues). PO Box 8040, Appleton, WI 54913; 414/749-3783.

• Libertarian

There was a time in the late seventies when it looked like the Libertarian Party might challenge the two-party Republicrat monopoly. This movement for personal freedom, private property, free markets, and minimal government was gaining momentum, publicity, and enthusiasts in a truly impressive manner. But it turned out that much of the funding for the numerous libertarian journals, think tanks, and political activities came from a few millionaires

—*Reason*

whose favor could be withdrawn as easily as it was bestowed.

*The surviving libertarians may be the stronger for having to stand on their own feet, but their ranks are diminished. Some have abandoned the LP for the Republican Party, others have gone off to counsel with the paleocons, and some have stuck it out on the fringe. **Reason** magazine ("Free Minds & Free Markets"), a slick Southern California monthly, makes the best case for practical libertarianism. Well-written and -researched articles delve into the specifics of economics and politics, offering alternatives and critiques. **Liberty**, a scrappier bimonthly from the Pacific Northwest, is the best forum for libertarian debate and opinion.*

Reason: Virginia I. Postrel, Editor. $19.95/year (11 issues). PO Box 526, Mount Morris, IL 61054-7868; 815/734-1102.

Liberty: R. W. Bradford, Editor. $19.50/year (6 issues). PO Box 1167, Port Townsend, WA 98368.

• General Resources

The preceding survey is subjective and incomplete, of course. I've left out groups and publications that veer too far off the left/right continuum, and the overt peddlers of hate or sectarian vehemence. For a better view of the extremes, as well as some common-sense analysis of civil-liber-

*ties issues and political dialogue, I suggest **Nazis, Communists, Klansmen and Others on the Fringe**, by John George and Laird Wilcox — two noteworthy researchers of the left/right spectrum.*

Wilcox also publishes directories of both the left and right, providing addresses and classifications for thousands of political organizations and publications.

Nazis, Communists, Klansmen and Others on the Fringe (Political Extremism in America): John George & Laird Wilcox. 1991; 320 pp. ISBN 0-87975-680-2 $39.95 ($43.90 postpaid). Prometheus Books/Warehouse & Fulfillment Center, 59 John Glenn Drive, Amherst, NY 14228-2197; 800/421-0351.

Guide to the American Left, 1993 (93 pp.; ISBN 0-933592-70-1), **Guide to the American Right, 1993** (75 pp.; ISBN 0-933592-69-8): Each $19.95 postpaid. Laird Wilcox Editorial Research Service, PO Box 2047, Olathe, KS 66051; 913/829-0609.

The circulation figures of all of the magazines listed above are fairly minuscule. Perhaps the most influential political opinion mongers are the syndicated columnists of the dailies' op-ed pages. Two weekly tabloids, almost identical in design and intent,

*reprint almost all of the liberal and conservative pundits' output respectively and serve them up with generous helpings of editorial cartoons from left and right. If, like me, you have a low tolerance for pundit cant, **Liberal Opinion** and **Conservative Chronicle** will likely drive you up the wall. But for quick and dirty access to the current teapot tempests, these publications are unbeatable.*

Liberal Opinion: $42/year (weekly). PO Box 468, Vinton, IA 52349; 800/338-9335.

Conservative Chronicle: $39/year (weekly). PO Box 11297, Des Moines, IA 50340; 800/888-3039.

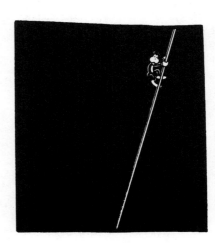

The Oxford Companion to the Supreme Court

You need not be a lawyer to be fascinated by this stunningly comprehensive reference work. The contributors' list (a resource in its own right) includes professors of law and related disciplines, attorneys, judges, and a sprinkling of journalists: this probably explains the breadth of the book's appeal.

*Hundreds of alphabetical entries are cross-indexed by case name and by topic. These include summaries of leading decisions, profiles of all justices, and essays on trends and issues before our High Court. The **Companion**'s detail and esoterica will pique the veteran courtwatcher, who will devour sections on the architecture of the Supreme Court Building, the historical antecedents to the Court, and the traditional quill pens. Yet the basics are included for the willing novice. This compendium would be a thoughtful graduation present, considerably more useful than Black's Law Dictionary. A word of caution: do not loan this interesting book to your lawyer. She might not return it! —Anita Susan Brenner*

*Long essays on subjects such as Contraception and Speech and the Press put a range of Court opinions into context, explain the troubling issues that resurface from case to case, or trace the development of Court doctrines and practices. My personal favorite is Bryan Garner's entry on the changing literary style of Supreme Court opinions. The **Companion** is a must for people who want to understand what the Supreme Court does and what its decisions mean. —Mike Godwin*

●

Furman v. Georgia, 408 U.S. 238 (1072), argued 17 Jan. 1972, decided 29 June 1972 per curiam by vote of 5 to 4; Stewart, White, Douglas, Brennan, and Marshall each concurred separately; Burger, Blackmun, Powell, and Rehnquist dissented jointly and separately. The Supreme Court, for the first time, struck down the death penalty under the *cruel and unusual punishment clause of the *Eighth Amendment. A jury in Georgia had convicted Furman for murder, and juries in Georgia and Texas had convicted two other petitioners for rape. All three juries imposed the death penalty without any specific guides or limits on their discretion. The Supreme Court in *McGautha v. California* (1971) had previously held that such guidelines were unnecessary. All three petitioners were African-American. Three justices for the majority found that jury discretion produced a random pattern among those receiving the death penalty and that this randomness was cruel and unusual. Two justices found capital punishment a per se violation of the Constitution. . . .

The dissenters argued that the courts should not challenge legislative judgments about the desirability and effectiveness of punishments. They also pointed to opinion polls showing general public support for the penalty.

●

*Webster v. Reproductive Health Services (1989) eliminated the trimester framework and represented a significant retreat from abortion rights. In upholding a Missouri law that declared that life began at conception,

The Oxford Companion to the Supreme Court
Kermit L. Hall, Editor. 1992;
1032 pp. ISBN 0-19-505835-6
$49.95 ($54.95 postpaid). Oxford University Press/Order Dept., 2001 Evans Road, Cary, NC 27513; 800/451-7556

forbade the use of any public funds and facilities for abortions, and required viability testing in abortions after twenty weeks, the Court sustained restrictions similar to those it had invalidated in *Akron* and *Thornburgh*. *Webster* stopped short of overturning *Roe v. Wade* outright — but only by one vote. Justice O'Connor, who supported the restrictions on the choice of abortion, refused to join the other four members of the majority in an outright reversal. Chief Justice Rehnquist's charge that "the dissent accuses us . . . of cowardice," Justice Scalia's sarcastic prediction that "the outcome of today's case will doubtless be heralded as a triumph of judicial statesmanship," and Justice Blackmun's "fear for the integrity of, and public esteem for, this Court" typify the reaction to *Webster* within and outside the judiciary. The courts have never been detached from politics, but in *Webster*, the Court politicized itself to an unprecedented degree; no opinion, and no public reaction, made any distinction between result and doctrine. Students of the Supreme Court's role in American politics might conclude that this episode illustrates the dangers of the Court's attempting to resolve political disputes. But we might just as plausibly conclude that the real lesson of *Webster* is the danger of any efforts by elected officials to remove constitutional rights once courts have recognized them.

●

On 19 January 1970, Nixon nominated Carswell for the Supreme Court vacancy created by the resignation of Abe *Fortas . . . .

The Carswell nomination was attacked on both political and professional grounds. He was criticized for racial remarks in a 1948 campaign speech, for his courtroom treatment of African-Americans, and for helping a municipal golf course evade desegregation while he was U.S. attorney. Prominent lawyers and law professors criticized his judicial record, noting that his reversal rate as district judge was among the highest in his circuit. Republican senator Roman Hruska of Nebraska, who was floor manager for the nomination, did not help Carswell with his comment, cited in the *Congressional Record*, that even the mediocre are "entitled to a little representation."

The Fourth Estate and the Constitution

This skeptical history describes the Revolutionary courts' discriminatory interpretation of common law where it applied to Loyalist printers. Close scrutiny of the Constitution's framers, and analysis of the contentious process by which the First Amendment was drafted, reveal the pragmatic, very political foundation for what is now an American principle — freedom of the press.

The author examines key issues in the media's emergence as our Fourth Estate: excessive damages in libel cases, prior restraints, access to sources and information, the media as a monopoly (antitrust). Powe also outlines some judicial models that suggest both descriptive and prescriptive accuracy.*

Weighing the ideal of a fair press against the imperative of a free press, Powe concludes with Justice Robert Jackson's statement that "the very purpose of a Bill of Rights was to place certain subjects beyond the reach of majorities," noting that freedom of the press is — theoretically, at least — not for the Fourth Estate's benefit, but for that of the public at large. —Anita Susan Brenner

** The English estates of governance are the Lords Spiritual, Lords Temporal, and Commons. "Fourth estate" describes any politically influential entity other than these. But it is generally understood to refer to the press. I mean the Media. —JD*

●

When it really counted, the Supreme Court guaranteed that the press could perform its various roles in our democracy. But, apart from Justice Douglas, and with the exception of some overblown dicta from other justices, the Court never saw the right-to-know model as a viable First Amendment doctrine. Whether out of distrust of the press, distrust of its own abilities, or faithfulness to a simpler constitutional ideal, the Court never embraced either side of the right to know. In rejecting that theory, however, it never endangered the essential autonomy of a free press.

●

The First Amendment, after all, does not refer to press "responsibility" even in the limited sense of the "abuse" clause found in most state constitutions. Nor can we look to the Bill of Rights generally, or to the press of the late eighteenth century, or even to evolving traditions, to import fairness into the First Amendment. Some parts of the Bill of Rights, such as the "fair trial" provisions, promote fairness; others, such as the right against self-incrimination, do not. The First Amendment, to the extent that the framers would have thought about it in that way, is a provision that would not promote fairness. The framers knew a partisan and scurrilous press, not a fair one. Two hundred subsequent years may have toned the press down, but even since the advent of so-called objective journalism it is still debatable whether fairness has become a journalistic norm.

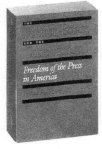

The Fourth Estate and the Constitution
(Freedom of the Press in America)
Lucas A. Powe, Jr. University of California Press, 1991; 350 pp. ISBN 0-520-08038-6
$14 ($17 postpaid) from California/ Princeton Fulfillment Services, 1445 Lower Ferry Road, Ewing, NJ 08618; 800/777-4726

Nolo Press

I owe Nolo Press a bit of a debt of honor. Back in my late teens, their books helped me out of a bad marriage.

Nolo's legal self-help books can disentangle the legal complexities attending life's conflicts and tragedies, large and small. They are also quite strong on sub-legal advice for all kinds of vexations: living together, the landlord/tenant relationship (as viewed from both vantage points), planning for one's demise, and the nightmare of divorce and child support. Written in plain English, they carefully guide the reader through Byzantine legal processes in a very accessible and comprehensible manner. Their catalog/news-

NEW PRODUCTS & NEW EDITIONS

Nolo's Pocket Guide to California Law

$10.95 / CLAW • Attorney Lisa Guerin & Nolo Press Editors • California 2nd Edition • ISBN 0-87337-244-1

The only plain English guide to the laws that affect Californians everyday. Get quick, clear answers to questions about child support, custody, consumer rights, employee rights, government benefits, divorce, bankruptcy, adoption, wills and much more.

Nolo's Pocket Guide to California Law on Disk

Available April 1994
Windows $24.95 $17.47 / CLWIN
Macintosh $24.95 $17.47 / CLM

Special Sale! 30% off   Offer expires June 1, 1994

Nolo's Pocket Guide to California Law is also available on disk. With this new format, you have plain English summaries of California law just a few key strokes away. You can rapidly search through California law by topic and subtopics, or by using the key-word index. The program tracks and saves searches, and allows you to save text to a file for later use.

Nolo's Pocket Guide to Family Law

$14.95 / FLD • Attorneys Robin Leonard and Stephen Elias • National 3rd Edition • ISBN 0-87337-217-4

Here's a clear, easy-to-read resource for anyone who has a question or problem involving family law—marriage, divorce, adoption, custody, surrogacy, living together and more.

Nolo's Pocket Guide to Consumer Rights

$12.95 / CAG • Barbara Kaufman • California 2nd Edition • ISBN 0-87337-218-2

Nolo's Pocket Guide to Consumer Rights provides practical solutions to hundreds of consumer problems. Get clear, concise answers to your everyday consumer questions and learn how to assert your rights when things go wrong. Learn what to do when you have a problem with: airlines, insurance companies, dry cleaners, credit cards, travel agents, misleading ads, junk mail, contractors, lawyers, movers, defective merchandise, warranties, and much more.

May It Please the Court

Important hunks of law are here, significant cases and sharp arguments and strange excursions into the internal contradictions of the American Constitution, that sturdy document of unexpected perfection: Roe, Gideon, the Heart of Atlanta Motel. Most astonishing on the six cassettes that originally made up this set were the voices of the participants, the florid, courtly drawls of the Southern prosecutors, the sharp bark of impatient justices, the odd emphases and asides revealing the deep stresses within the court. It was the sound of a sincere striving for perfection by imperfect humans — a very rare thing.

You can't get the tapes any more (try your library). The book is the voices stilled, on the one hand, and given a lower more lasting resonance on the other. —Jon Carroll

•

Narrator: Dr. Solomon Grayzel, a Jewish scholar, told the lower court that parts of the New Testament were "offensive to Jewish tradition." Verses about Jesus as Messiah could be "psychologically harmful" to Jewish and other non-Christian students. Sawyer stressed this testimony.

Sawyer: The New Testament, the concept of Christ, a man who historically lived, as being the Son of God, is, as Dr. Grayzel testified, to Judaism a blasphemy. This was in fact Christ's crime. It is a blasphemy. You can't gloss this over by saying there's some minor differences. He pointed out that there's ridicule of the Jewish hierarchy throughout the New Testament. He pointed out, and think of it, gentlemen, the scene of the trial of Jesus before Pilate, where the multitude cries out not for Barrabas but for Jesus, and Pilate washes his hands. And the version exculpates the

May It Please the Court
(Transcripts of 23 Live Recordings of Landmark Cases as Argued Before the Supreme Court)
Peter Irons & Stephanie Guitton, editors,
The New Press. 1993; 375 pp.
ISBN 1-56584-046-1
$30 postpaid from W.W. Norton, 800 Keystone Industrial Park, Scranton, PA 18512; 800/233-4830

Romans for the death of Christ. And then the Jews say, and they're so described, they say, his blood be upon us and our children. And Dr. Grayzel said that sentence has been responsible for more anti-Semitism than any single sentence in history, and I can't doubt it.

•

Narrator: Justice Thurgood Marshall debated "probable cause" with Reuben Payne.

Marshall: When did he get probable cause to arrest?

Payne: He received probable cause for arrest when he turned Terry around and ran his hands over the outside of his clothing and, feeling a gun in the upper left breast pocket, and indicating emphatically at that time that, "What I felt was a gun, a weapon."

Marshall: Well, he didn't have it, as counsel for petitioner says, he didn't have it when he laid hands on him and turned him around?

Payne: I would agree with — he did not have probable cause to arrest. (Marshall: Right) I would agree that he would have probable cause to frisk, or to lay hands on him, at this point.

Marshall: Why?

Payne: Because of the nature of the circumstances and protection of his own life.

Narrator: Marshall shifted his questions.

Marshall: Mr. Payne, in this case this arresting officer testified, did he not, that he had never seen anybody "case a joint"?

Payne: That is correct; he did so testify.

Marshall: He also testified that he had been on that same area for some thirty years, doing the following things: checking for pickpockets and shoplifters?

Payne: That is correct.

Marshall: So where did he get his expertise about somebody's about to commit a robbery?

Payne: I think that he would get his expertise by virtue of the fact that he had been a member of the police department for forty years, and by being a member of the police department for forty years, I am quite sure that, even if by osmosis, some knowledge would have to come to him of the various degrees of crime.

Marshall: Now we're getting intuition by osmosis? (laughter)

American Broadcasting and the First Amendment

In the old days, in England, printers had to have a license from the King in order to do business. This system of licensing made it extremely difficult for the English press to play any role as a critic of government actions or government officials.

*We learned enough from the English experience of press licensing to establish press freedom under the First Amendment. But there has long been a curious exception to First Amendment protections of speech and press — the licensing of broadcasting. Lucas A. Powe tells the story of broadcast licensing in the US, giving special attention to the questionable legal arguments used to justify regulation. It's hard to read his book without reaching the conclusion that the Federal Communications Commission's ability to regulate content on the airwaves should be abolished altogether.
—Mike Godwin*

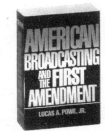

American Broadcasting and the First Amendment
Lucas A. Powe, Jr. University of California Press, 1987; 295 pp. ISBN 0-520-06467-4
$13 ($16 postpaid) from California/Princeton Fulfillment Services, 1445 Lower Ferry Road, Ewing, NJ 08618; 800/777-4726

•

The Commission was telling licensees to ban countercultural music or risk losing a license. And the court, part and parcel of the generation looking aghast at a culture in revolution, refused to see what could not have been clearer. The Commission's lawyers deserve credit for bailing it out, but only a willful neglect of the factual setting by the D.C. Circuit allowed the lawyers' version to prevail.

Amazingly, if the Commission thought its double-barreled actions on indecency and drug lyrics would clear the air and make radio safe for middle America again, it was in for a huge surprise. Between June 1972 and June 1973 the complaints to the Commission concerning "obscenity-indecency-profanity" took a fifteenfold jump, outstripping by over ten thousand the complaints received on all other topics during the period. A new radio format had hit the air, and it was a winner....

"Topless radio," a live talk show, featured telephone conversations with a male host in which the caller, typically female, would disclose intimate personal and sexual details over the air. It arrived first, as always, in California, but spread like wildfire.

Legal Breakdown

My lawyer pal maintains that many of the intricacies of law are there for good reason, and that the price to be paid for proceeding in ignorance of the system can be terribly steep. But Legal Breakdown is worth a look, as a knowledgeable philippic against our convoluted system and as a manifesto for legal reform. —JD [with the reluctant help of Anita Susan Brenner]

Legal Breakdown
(Forty Ways to Fix Our Legal System)
Stephen Elias et al. 1990; 88 pp.
ISBN 0-87337-136-4
$8.95 ($12.95 postpaid). Nolo Press, 950 Parker Street, Berkeley, CA 94710; 800/992-6656 or 510/549-1976

---

paper, *Nolo News*, is excellent and also free. —Carmen Hermosillo

Most of Nolo's efforts tend to clarify legal procedures that are neither very complex nor very likely to meet with professional opposition. Knowledgeable and goodhearted law professionals stress that when the other side has unleashed the dogs of war, it is folly not to retain a good lawyer. But Nolo publications give access to some of the fundaments of the law, and — even better — they may enable you to resolve a situation without recourse to litigation. —James Donnelly

•

Even when a claim is handled by the books, the worker often ends up with the short end of the stick. One woman submitted a compelling story of how her teenage daughter was severely injured while working a fast-food restaurant. Although her daughter received fine, free medical care, the amount of her permanent disability compensation was based on her hourly wages at the time of the accident — a paltry $4.35 an hour. The award included nothing for her pain and suffering and nothing for her permanent disfigurement.

What can be done to improve the workers' comp system? Here are some suggestions submitted by readers:

1. Increase benefit levels for injured workers and pay for the increase by reducing insurance companies' profit margins.

2. State workers' comp offices should assign one person to each case, to assist the injured worker and monitor the case.

3. Every injured worker should be sent to a doctor agreed to by the worker and insurance carrier within a month after the injury if the injury may be chronic or permanent. This would not only prevent further injury but help weed out fraud in the system.

4. Insurance companies should make frequent, unannounced visits to the employer's place of business to make sure that working conditions meet applicable laws and that the employees' work habits are safe.

5. Streamline the system so that bills for medical treatment and physical therapy are paid on time, and workers aren't on the hook for paying these bills. —*Nolo News*

Nolo Press: 950 Parker Street, Berkeley, CA 94710; 800/992-6656 or 510/549-1976.

On Human Rights: The Oxford Amnesty Lectures 1993

This is an excellent collection of difficult questions about human rights. The essays are diverse in their approaches and styles, and their subjects range from the cruelty of children on playgrounds to the consequences of choices made by governments.

The most thought-provoking of these is Agnes Heller's discussion of justice and the heinous crime. Can such crimes be punished? Is it really possible to administer justice in the face of evil? Evil, Heller says, is different from mere badness and weakness, and her arguments are convincing.

In the most beautiful essay here, Jean-François Lyotard contributes a moving meditation on the forms and meanings of the act of silencing someone. He examines that act from playground ostracism to government censorship of minority opinions. It led me to think hard about the meaning of the silent wars that individuals sometimes wage in personal relationships.

There is also a piece by feminist Catharine A. MacKinnon. It is an emotional and touching statement of her

beliefs that morality and respect for others can be legislated.

This little book is full of ideas that seem important to me.
—Carmen Hermosillo

•

After the demise of totalitarianism, it is not difficult to distinguish between the originally evil and those who became evil through secondary infection. The former originate the evil maxims, stick to their principles to the last, their consciences unruffled, and ascribe the defeat or failure of their principles to the weakness of their followers. The followers, by contrast, can get confused, rewrite their pasts, forget the evil they have committed and remember only the evils they have suffered; they can slough off their totalitarian self. This is how evil could seem banal to Hannah Arendt. But evil is not banal, even if evil persons become banal after the demise of their power base. The soul is not healed just because the epidemic has passed. The pathetically banal soul does not even feel guilty; he or she feels only the remorse of having bet on the wrong horse.
—Agnes Heller

•

Evil is not an accumulated or excessive moral badness distinguished from all other

categories of badness by quantity. Evil is *qualitatively* different from the morally bad. This qualitative difference has become explicit in modern times. . . . The knowledge of moral evil emerges through reflection. Where these is no freedom to choose principles of action, there can be badness but not evil. Moral evil requires a fairly sophisticated and consistent system of self-justification. —AH

•

The human speaker is always afraid that a "keep quiet" will debar his words. He complains of the precariousness of his membership in the speech community. Even the good silence of the writer, the monk, or the pupil contains an element of suffering. Any banishment is a harm inflicted on those who undergo it, but this harm necessarily changes to a wrong when the victim is excluded from the speech community. For the wrong is the harm to which the victim cannot testify, since he cannot be heard. And this is precisely the case of those to whom the right of speech is refused.
—Jean-François Lyotard

•

The abjection suffered in the camps horri-

On Human Rights
(The Oxford Amnesty Lectures 1993)
Stephen Shute & Susan Hurley. Basic Books, 1993; 262 pp. ISBN 0-465-05223-1
$25 ($27.75 postpaid) from HarperCollins Publishers/Direct Mail, PO Box 588, Dunmore, PA 18512; 800/331-3761

bly illustrates the threat of exclusion which weighs on all interlocution. On the school playground, the child to whom the others say "We're not playing with you" experiences this unspeakable suffering. He suffers a wrong equivalent, on its own scale, to a crime against humanity. . . .

In his analysis of the sublime effect, Edmund Burke termed *horror* the state of mind of a person whose participation in speech is threatened. —JFL

The Big House • Surviving in Prison

Both authors come off as trying hard to be honest. Both books are oppressive (the one written for prospective cons is less so) and filled with contempt (the one written for administrators and guards is more so) for the big Other.

*You could accuse the author of **The Big House** of a total lack of pity for his fellow man. I believe his response would be that the inmates he is talking about are not his fellow men. **Surviving In Prison** is an anecdotal primer on doing time: quick sketches of administration and power structure and a certain amount of padding — reproductions of hearing requests, etc. —JD*

•

Road camps, when an inmate can get assigned to them, are a quick way out of most prison systems, but the inmates who are there are subjected to lengthy work hours and a minimum of extra programming. They are set up as work camps and are run as such. . . . Inmates dig ditches, clear irrigation trenches, and generally furnish labor that the highway department doesn't want to be bothered with because the task is too time consuming or dirty. An inmate serving a long prison sentence would not find a road camp or even a medium security facility very comfortable. The staffs at these institutions are low grade personalities that are used to handling inmates with very little self-respect. Consequently, the staff there will treat the inmates accordingly. A man with a substantial number of years to do would quickly get burned out with the petty rules and attitudes of the administration, and would either escape, or ultimately hurt one of the employees and wind up catching more time for it.
—*Surviving In Prison*

•

Long-term effects of drugs help keep the

The Big House
(How American Prisons Work)
Tony Lesce. 1991; 184 pp.
ISBN 1-55950-075-1
$19.95 ($23.95 postpaid)

Surviving in Prison
Harold S. Long. 1990; 122 pp.
ISBN 1-55950-044-1
$14.95 ($18.95 postpaid)

both from Loompanics Unlimited, PO Box 1197, Port Townsend, WA 98368

prisoner incapacitated. There are effects on the central nervous system, including a Parkinson-like disorder called "tardive diskinesia." Neurological side-effects of psycho-active drugs have even affected prison slang. The "Stelazine shuffle" and "Thorazine shuffle" describe the peculiar gait of people under the influence of these drugs. The benefits of physical incapacitation, as well as psychic dulling, combine to help make those under long-term dosage docile and manageable, especially as some effects are permanent. —*The Big House*

Drugs and Rights

Starting with the question "Do adults have a moral right to consume recreational drugs?" (yes), Douglas Husak goes on to define the terms so flexibly used, and so widely taken for granted, in popular debate. Exactly what is a drug? (What makes marijuana a drug and alcohol a beverage?) What right does the State have to interfere with personal autonomy? (What constitutes being a danger to oneself or others?)

I recommend this book to judges and lawyers as well as to lay readers. An interesting fact not mentioned here is that some controlled substances are now known to occur naturally in the human nervous system. Both N,N-dimethyltryptamine (DMT) and morphine are present in detectable quantities in normal people. The legal and biochemical implications of these findings remain to be seen.

A federal judge recently wondered whether, in years to come, he and his fellow jurists will have to assert the Nuremberg Defense — "I was only following orders" — to justify the number of people they are sentencing to prison for decades, or for life. Good question. —Steven K. Gill

•

A federal district court judge, Robert Sweet, shocked his colleagues by calling for the decriminalization of all illicit drugs. After reciting some of the cost-benefit advantages of decriminalization, he continued: "Cocaine gives a sense of exhilaration, heroin a glow, a warmth, and marijuana a sense of relaxation and ease. What then is wrong?"

Nonetheless, my attempt to confine the context of discussion to the recreational use of drugs is not entirely unproblematic. Weil has challenged the viability of distinctions between the several purposes for which drugs apparently are consumed. He

claims that "the desire to alter consciousness periodically is an innate, normal drive analogous to hunger or the sexual drive." The "omnipresence of the phenomenon" of drug use in various societies throughout human history has led him to conclude that "we are dealing . . . with a biological characteristic of the species." Behavior that satisfies a biological need cannot be understood as a purely recreational form of activity, comparable to scuba diving or mountain climbing.

More recently, a variation of this basic theme has been developed by Ronald Siegel. Studies of animal behavior persuade him that "we must expand the definition of self-medication to include drug use for purposes of intoxication." Siegel believes that even the most dangerous of intoxicants really function as medicines. He contends that the distinction between medical and nonmedical drug use should be dissolved in favor of conceptualizing drugs as "adaptogens," defined as "substance[s] that help people to adjust to changes in their physical or physiological environments." Thus Siegel denies a principled distinction between the use of "esterene, to alleviate the pain and depression of arthritis," and the use of "heroin, to fight the gloom and despair of consciousness."

Drugs and Rights
Douglas N. Husak. 1992; 312 pp.
ISBN 0-521-42727-4
$17.95 ($19.95 postpaid) from Cambridge University Press, 110 Midland Avenue, Port Chester, NY 10573; 800/872-7423 (outside N.Y.) 800/227-0247 (N.Y. only)

Girls Lean Back Everywhere: The Law of Obscenity and the Assault on Genius

The willingness of governing bodies to shut people up is so common as to seem a generic characteristic of government. But the US has seen an increasing understanding by the government of the role of free speech in our society, and an increasing tolerance of frank and graphic presentations of sexual material. How did we get here?

Girls Lean Back attempts to compile in a single volume the recent history of censorship in America. Starting with the Comstock laws (which classified information about contraception as "obscene"), Edward de Grazia traces the battles between writers and artists on the one side and would-be censors on the other over the last century. De Grazia, a professor of law, includes countless interviews and statements by the principals involved. There are notable discussions of the treatment of Joyce's Ulysses, *Nabokov's* Lolita, *Miller's* Tropic of Cancer, *and Lenny Bruce's famous nightclub act, and chapters dealing with the Holly Hughes/NEA contretemps and with the 2 Live Crew prosecutions.*

The title comes from a statement by a publisher of Ulysses — *she was defending Joyce's decision to describe a woman on a swing who allows the character Leo Bloom to look up her dress.* —Mike Godwin

•

Robin West, a professor of law at the University of Maryland, has distinguished between "good" and "bad" pornography for women, based upon the premise that, whatever else it might be, "pornography is an aid to sexual pleasure." West considers that pornography cannot be said to be victimless in the light of testimony by women who said they suffered serious injury either in the making of violent pornography or from violent sexual acts by men who claimed to have been incited by viewing pornography; for West this is bad pornography. But, she points out, the anti-porn feminists and the Meese commission investigators both refused to describe the good pornography that has brought positive sexual experiences to women, and is also good for feminists because it impeaches conservative patriarchal morality with its profound denial that virtue and sexuality are compatible in women.

•

LOIS SHEINFELD [Professor, New York University School of Journalism]: On the evening of July 10 [1984], a 23-year-old Minneapolis woman doused herself with

Girls Lean Back Everywhere: The Law of Obscenity and the Assault on Genius
Edward De Grazia. Vintage Books, 1992; 814 pp. ISBN 0-679-74341-3
$17 ($19 postpaid) from Random House/ Order Dept., 400 Hahn Road, Westminster, MD 21157; 800/733-3000

gasoline and set herself aflame to protest pornography. She was taken to the hospital in critical condition. Three days later, the Minneapolis City Council passed a package of antipornography legislation. The legislation included a censorship ordinance condemning pornography on the theory that it violated the civil rights of women. That ordinance was the product of an intensive campaign mounted by two feminists, Catharine MacKinnon . . . and Andrea Dworkin. . . . Last year, MacKinnon and Dworkin drafted a similar ordinance and persuaded the City Council to adopt it . . . following highly emotional legislative hearings. . . . Mayor Donald M. Fraser vetoed the ordinance.

NAT HENTOFF: Perhaps the most bizarre turn in the tumultous history of "the new censorship" was a letter sent to the President of the Minneapolis City Council . . . — "in dissent and dismay" at Fraser's veto — by the justly celebrated First Amendment gladiator Professor Laurence Tribe of Harvard Law School. In the letter, Tribe chastised the mayor for "hiding behind the First Amendment" by not letting the courts decide, instead of unilaterally killing the bill by veto. The Dworkin-MacKinnon legislation, said Tribe, "is not obviously unconstitutional" and its supposed invalidity "follows surely from no clear precedent." Tribe added that while he is uncertain as to how a judicial test will come out, he feels the MacKinnon-Dworkin creation "may eventually be found to be the first sensible approach to an area which has vexed some of the best legal minds for decades." If Laurence Tribe's mind can turn to mush on this matter, can anyone be sure of what the Supreme Court will say?

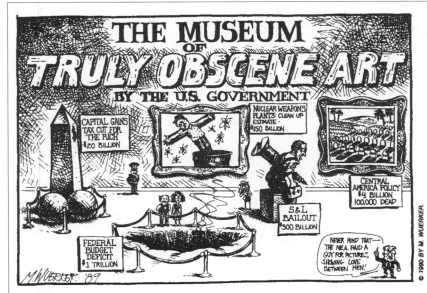

50 Ways to Fight Censorship
Dave Marsh. 1991; 128 pp.
ISBN 1-56025-011-9
$5.95 ($8.95 postpaid) from Thunder's Mouth Press, 632 Broadway, 7th Floor, New York, NY 10012; 212/780-0380

50 Ways to Fight Censorship

The author is a writer on rock music, late of Rolling Stone, *and his outrage over music censorship comes through on every page. If this useful little book has a flaw, it could be that its anger blinds it to its opponents' point of view. You'll find very little sympathy for the family-values crowd here, and it even takes a poke at (then Senator) Al Gore. But mostly, it swings back and forth between describing common-sense political action and relating anecdotes of stupid censorship in action.*

In terms of concrete, hold-the-line vigilance against book-burners, the recommended tactics seem comprehensive. I especially liked the author's advice for acquainting children with the issue: there's a list of six things kids (presumably starting with anybody old enough to read) can do, including recruiting their parents, getting involved with the American Library Association's Banned Book Week, and contacting the Student Press Law Center for help in fighting censorship by school officials.

On the other hand, I was a little disappointed to find no discussion of — philosophical? — tactics. The author apparently assumes that you've thought through the issues; *he doesn't mention the individual fight against repression, the personal struggle against self-censorship, and the potential paradox in which the prevention of censorship becomes censorship itself.* 50 Ways *is an angry book, and anger isn't a particularly philosophical emotion.* —Joseph McConnell

•

Speaking out is the primary duty of every freedom fighter — or good citizen, if you want to put it that way. It's the job that we all have to do, separately and collectively, where we see injustice and where injustice has been going on for so long it's become invisible. Silence is a form of censorship, and when important issues are at stake, silence is a form of death.

•

In 1982, in Calhoun County, Alabama, it started with Doris Day's autobiography. A minister's daughter brought the book home to write a report about it; the minister objected to some of its language. And by the time he and a self-appointed committee of 50 other parents and ministers were done, they'd decided that the county library ought to ban not just Day's book, but Anthony Burgess' *A Clockwork Orange* and everything by John Steinbeck.

•

On the Origin of Species — Charles R. Darwin. Banned from Trinity College in Cambridge, England (1859). Banned in Yugoslavia (1935), and in Greece (1937).

The teaching of evolution was prohibited in Tennessee from 1925–67.

One Hundred Years of Solitude — Gabriel Garcia Marquez. Purged from the book list used at the Wasco, CA Union High School (1986) because the book, by the winner of the 1982 Nobel Prize for Literature, was "garbage being passed off as literature."

Our Bodies, Ourselves — Boston Women's Health Book Collective. Challenged at the William Chrisman High School in Independence, MO (1984) because the book is "filthy." The controversial feminist health manual was on a bookshelf in a classroom and was the personal property of the teacher.

OTHER GREAT RESOURCES

The Rise and Fall of California's Radical Prison Movement:
Eric Cummins. 1993, Stanford University Press.

Pelican Bay Information Project:
2489 Mission Street, #28, San Francisco, CA 94110.

Broken Ground: John Keeble. 1987, HarperPerennial. Out of Print.

Interfaith Prisoners of Conscience:
2120 Lincoln Street, Evanston, IL 60201.

New Society Publishers: 4527 Springfield Avenue, Philadelphia, PA 19143; 800/333-9093.

Loompanics Unlimited

The Loompanics people label themselves "the lunatic fringe of the libertarian movement." Their catalog's self-description — "The Best Book Catalog in the World" — is entirely too modest. Even self-sequestered I, living out where the spotted owls are gagging on their own publicity, have heard Loompanics called "a pan-ideological resource," "a latter-day compendium of secret decoder rings," "the skinhead ghost shirt," and "jerkoff material for sociopaths."

There is something viral and iconoclastic (and a bit snotnosed) about an enterprise that sells ten volumes dealing with the picking of locks, **The Poisoner's Handbook**, a video called "The Art of the Bullwhip," three Tim Leary titles, an entire shitload of books about the home manufacture of weapons and explosives, **The Structure of Scientific Revolutions**, **How to Buy Land Cheap**, and a few versions

of the **Whole Earth Catalog** — which, as we all know, is the best book catalog in the world.

You ought to invest the five bucks in these folks' product, even if you are interested not a bit in the manufacture of eight kinds of invisible ink, don't believe in the neuroendocrine theory of aging, and foresee no need to learn physical interrogation techniques. Merely laying this catalog on your (fresh-ground French-roast) coffee table will peel the peace stickers off your guitar case. —JD Smith

●

Part-Time Diplomacy For Fun, Profit & Prestige by James Basil-Hart

Have you ever dreamed of becoming a world-class diplomat? James Basil-Hart has. So he contacted several countries in Eastern Europe and before long they were issuing him credentials.

Part-Time Diplomacy tells you exactly how to acquire genuine diplomatic credentials

without having to purchase them. Basil-Hart didn't have riches or influential friends. But he did have persistence and the desire to be a diplomat. In this exciting new book, he shows how you can get diplomatic credentials without spending a lot of money and without ever leaving home. . . .

Chapters include:
• How Diplomacy Developed
• Benefits of Diplomatic Status
• What Diplomats Do
• Diplomatic Protocol and Traditions
• Private Diplomacy and Public Policy
• Why Countries Need You
• Picking Your Country
• Planning Your Campaign
• Making Your Proposal
• The Public Relations Campaign
• Your Diplomatic Duties
• Pitfalls of Part-Time Diplomacy

$14.95 (order number 61134)

●

None of the Above is a classic book presenting the case against voting in elections. Well worth reading! Here are some selected quotes:

Loompanics Unlimited
Catalog $5 postpaid from Loompanics Unlimited, PO Box 1197, Port Townsend, WA 98368

"Non-voting is now viewed as a political force which has the potential to alter the entire political system." Chapter 1

". . . you can hardly expect a politician to give up power, any more than you can expect a baboon to give up bananas." Chapter 14

$4.95 (order number 94094)

Loompanics' Greatest Hits

There are times when the agreements about reality need to be renegotiated, and those times are (as the old Chinese curse suggests) likely to be interesting. It would, I think, surprise no one if it turned out that we are living during one of those moments of renegotiation.

With writing that encompasses the relatively low-key Revisionist View of the Declaration of Independence and the more or less unbelievably weird Interview with a Holocaust Revisionist, this singular anthology speaks to the failure of consumer culture and documents a yearning for authentic conversation about the circumstances and choices of our daily lives. Especially when considered along with its parent catalog, it questions our assumptions

and our received ideas, beginning with our notions of morality.

Here you will find the suggestion that ballpoint pens may ultimately have more exchange value than gold coins; the fundamental assumption that identity may be a flexible rather than a fixed construct; the notion of the money order as a weapon in the battle for personal financial privacy; and speculation that "obsolete" low-energy technologies may be invaluable for future individual survival.

This isn't starry-eyed futurism. Read it; discuss it with friends. No one will be bored, and your grandchildren may thank you someday.
—Carmen Hermosillo

●

Loompanics: Then you find that the little guy can't get satisfaction by working strictly within the system?

Victor Santoro: Of course not! The big guys don't work within the system. Just look at the headlines that have appeared recently. Who made a hundred million on Wall Street by using illegal "insider" information? Who lined his pockets by selling arms to Iran? This is only the crud that's come to the surface. The system is a set of rules and laws designed to keep the little guys in line. The big guys ignore them.

Another point is that anyone who tries to play it honestly will get very frustrated. The machinery of the system is so large and cumbersome because it's designed so that the little guy can't easily use it. This is a point I brought out in the

Loompanics' Greatest Hits
(Articles and Features from The Best Book Catalog in the World)
Michael Hoy, Editor. 1990; 308 pp. ISBN 1-55950-031-X
$16.95 ($20.95 postpaid) from Loompanics Unlimited, PO Box 1197, Port Townsend, WA 98368

Harassment books. If you get fired unfairly, just try to get satisfaction by working through the system. It's not set up to help you, and the sooner you realize that, the better off you'll be. You'll have a more realistic outlook, and you'll realize that the proper way to get satisfaction is to wait a couple of years and trash the boss who did it to you.

Harassment was a series of guidebooks to direct action. It's necessary to use harassment techniques because the system fails. We see the same in the political scene. In fact, we hear the expression, "Write to your congressman," as a sarcastic reference. Writing to a congressman doesn't do any good.

Loompanics: The methods outlined in your book seem rather mild. Is this intentional?

Santoro: Because to do a good job on a candidate, it's better to destroy him by ridicule than by physical harm.

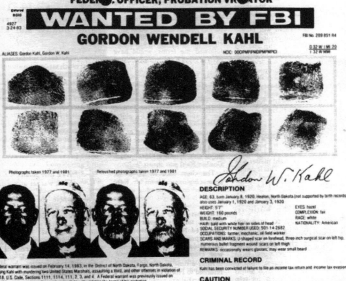

"Give a mugger the slip and you may sleep contentedly; but give the taxman the slip and watch out, for they are willing to hunt you down even if it costs them more than they could possibly get out of you."

"The judge constructed a diabolical life sentence for Kahl: die a spiritual death by submission or face a rerun of the whole farce over and over again until his death."

Sneak over to Privacy on page 134.

Loompanics' Golden Records

Excerpts from the far shores of Loompanics Land! Alienated history, disgraceful commentary, paranoiac social visions, and the most horrible story I've read — even relatively speaking — about sex with the dead. LGR has no place in the Political Tools section, except perhaps as an odiously bitter tonic or Bullworker to toughen up your sense of what is allowable.—Jas.D

●

A real Hey Martha! is a story that grabs you by the brain stem and yanks you into the paper. If you're standing in line at the supermarket, you will buy the paper because this story is too unbelievable to not be absolutely true. A story that hooks something in your darkest fears. Or maybe something that promises you an edge over reality.

"Grossed-Out Surgeon Vomits Inside Patient" was our all-time best. Every copy sold out. No one could resist it. How disgusting! How possible! How horrible that nobody thought to prevent such a thing! Hey Martha! Look at this!

"Scientists Discover Secret Day of the Week" was another. Imagine, a three-day weekend,

Citizen Soldier

When I was discharged in 1971, fresh from Vietnam, few people cared to listen to the tales of immorality, injustice, racism, graft, and oppression I had experienced in the military. Citizen Solider is a GI and veterans' rights group whose periodical, On Guard, *is dedicated to "bringing a message of peace and non-intervention to American GIs." The Tailhook cover-up, rampant sexual harassment/rape, eyewitness accounts of war crimes perpetrated by the US in Iraq, conscientious objectors being jailed and silenced, racism at all levels, were some of last year's factually written, well-documented stories.*

I would like to see a Citizen Soldier representative have the opportunity to speak with every prospective high-school ROTC candidate. —Les Caulfield

Citizen Soldier also publishes excellent single-subject pamphlets and distributes books on the military. —JD [Suggested by C. Kuriakose]

●

Raw data obtained from a Freedom of Information request to the Michigan Department of Public Health has suggested an extraordinary rate of childhood leukemia in the first born children of Vietnam veterans. A group of 49,220 veterans who served "in country" during the Vietnam war reported 1,545 cases of childhood leukemia in first born children.

This was 30 times the rate of childhood

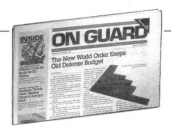

Citizen Soldier
Tod Ensign & Tricia Critchfield, Editors. $10 donation/year from Citizen Soldier, 175 5th Avenue, Suite 808, New York, NY 10010; 212/777-3470

leukemia reported in a control group of Vietnam era veterans who did not serve in country. When ABDC discussed this data with the Michigan Health Department, they pointed out that the cases were self-reported and had not yet been confirmed through medical records. ABDC will follow up on the continued analysis of this study. —On Guard

●

Does the military have to keep its promises of job training, assignment, etc?

Maybe. If your enlistment contract contains a written promise to train you in a specific school or field, you may be eligible for discharge if the military breaks its promise. However, there are a lot of "ifs." For one thing, each enlistment contract contains the following language: "Laws and regulations that govern military personnel may change without notice . . . REGARDLESS of the provisions of this enlistment document." For example, if a military school decides to admit no more students (or to raise its minimum scores for graduation) this may negatively affect your chances. —*The Military Enlistment Contract and You [brochure]*

Stand Up to the IRS

There's a CP-2000 notice from the IRS in your stack of mail. They say you owe them $1,000 and change. Are they correct? Shit, you can't even read the notice; looks like Greek.

Or maybe you've received a letter informing you of an audit and requesting your presence in the local IRS office within ten days. What do you do?

Not everyone has a competent tax accountant standing by to assist them. But here's a hands-on guide to help taxpayers defend themselves against the tentacular bureaucracy we know as the Internal Revenue Service. It uses plain English to tell how to respond to, and (hopefully) extricate yourself from, any number of common situations that can occur when dealing with the IRS. Whether you're defending yourself in tax court, appealing an audit, filing back tax returns, avoiding liens and levies, or just responding to the assertion that you didn't report $500 in savings-account interest, this book will arm you with information and diminish the intimidation to a manageable level. —Andrew Stern

●

Tax law is so voluminous and complex, most IRS auditors don't know it well either. Moreover, the training and experience level of IRS personnel is declining while the law is getting more difficult to understand. This means that auditors of individual (non-business) tax returns normally stick to basic audit issues. A taxpayer with very high income or an intricate tax issue, however, may be assigned an auditor with more experience. But if you are well prepared and understand the audit process, you come out okay (experiencing the minimal damage) most of the time.

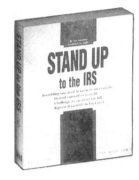

Stand Up to the IRS
Frederick W. Daily. 1992; 250 pp. ISBN 0-87337-162-3
$19.95 ($23.95 postpaid) from Nolo Press, 950 Parker Street, Berkeley, CA 94710; 800/992-6656 or 510/549-1976

---

every weekend! And doesn't it just make sense that the government would slap regulations on it the very first thing? Now the only people allowed to use that day are specially licensed researchers. And they're saying maybe we should leave the extra day alone and leave it as nature intended it. —*A Day in the Life of a Tabloid Editor*

Loompanics' Golden Records
(Articles and Features from The Best Book Catalog in the World)
Michael Hoy, Editor. 1993; 200 pp. ISBN 1-55950-092-1
$14.95 ($18.95 postpaid) from Loompanics Unlimited, PO Box 1197, Port Townsend, WA 98368

War Tax Resistance

About half of your income tax goes to support the military, past and present. Over half of the national debt is attributable to the military. For moral reasons or just plain outrage at expensive toilet seats and bombers that don't fly, both liberal and conservative have cause to decry the spending of such huge sums on killing when there are so many more pressing needs.

What can you do about this matter? Can you refuse to support the military by paying only half your taxes? If you do that, what will happen next? Are there ways to avoid paying for the military and still stay out of trouble? (Yes.) This book, in its fourth edition since 1981, presents the tax resistance arguments, the rules of the game, your options for personal action, and the probable results. Maddening, tantalizing, and realistic. —J. Baldwin

●

In 1972 the FBI called [Presbyterian minister Maurice] McCrackin to talk about the money they said he owed. He told them it would be a waste of their time because he wouldn't discuss it. A few days later a subpoena from the Justice Department was served ordering him to come in and pay the fine, but saying nothing about unpaid taxes. He didn't appear and never heard from them again.

Criminal Court and Jail
It is very rare that the IRS will use the courts and the threat of jail to force payment or punish a war tax resister. A classified IRS directive handed down on July 15, 1980, told its agents not to pursue felony prosecution of tax refusers for fraud or failure to file unless underpayments average *at least $2,500 a year for three years straight.*

War Tax Resistance
(A Guide to Withholding Your Support From the Military)
Ed Hedemann. 1992; 131 pp. ISBN 0-86571-245-X
$14.95 ($17.45 postpaid) from New Society Publishers, 4527 Springfield Avenue, Philadelphia, PA 19143; 800/333-9093

OTHER GREAT RESOURCES

Fellowship: Richard Deats, Editor. $15/year (6 issues) from Fellowship of Reconciliation, Box 271, 523 N. Broadway, Nyack, NY 10960; 914/358-4601, fax 914/358-4924. I know of no better magazine on nonviolence and nonviolent change.

Covert Action Quarterly: Terry Allen & Phillip Smith, Editors. $22/year (4 issues) from Covert Action Publications, 1500 Massachusetts Avenue NW, #732, Washington, DC 20005.

Peacework: $15/year (11 issues) from American Friends Service Committee , 2161 Mass. Avenue, Cambridge, MA 02140.

Boycott Quarterly: Zachary D. Lyons, Editor. $20/year (4 issues) from Center for Economic Democracy, PO Box 64, Olympia, WA 98507.

Kick It Over: $9 US/year (4 issues) from Kick It Over Collective, PO Box 5811, Station A, Toronto, Ontario, Canada M5W 1P2.

> **"A statesman is a dead politician,
> and Lord knows we need more statesmen."**
> —Berke Breathed

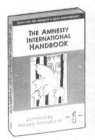

The Oxford Companion to Politics of the World

Oh boy! From Abdel Nasser, Gamel to Zionism, stopping at Brain Drain, Kyrgyzstan, Secularization, Thatcherism, and Vanuatu. A whopping big encyclopedia of countries, isms, politicians living and dead, treaties, organizations, and events, the Companion is exactly what you need to win arguments and influence people.

Like a schoolboy looking up the dirty words in a new dictionary, I immediately went looking for my favorites; I found a crisp and evenhanded article on Anarchism by Robert Paul Wolff (cross-referenced to Citizenship — a nice touch) sharing a two-page spread with Amnesty International. The piece on Mexico (Robert Kaufman) is a dry recitation of economics that almost completely ignores racial issues. "Gang of Four" is not a separate article, nor is it indexed, nor is Jiang Qing given a biographic piece — although she does appear in the index. The article on Ireland is brief and cross-referenced to Corporatism, Decolonization, Nationalism, and Religion and Politics, but not to the extensive piece on Terrorism; of all the Irish terrorist groups, only the PIRA is mentioned.

More than five hundred experts contributed, so you'll find your favorite dirty political words covered (well, maybe not — "revisionism" doesn't seem to be) in a more or less satisfying manner, depending on the individual writer's point of view. This is largely a book of definition, not of methods; coup d'etat is defined, but you won't find any instructions on how to start one. If you do much political reading, though, you probably ought to have it on hand. —Joseph McConnell

●

As a politician, Allende always exhibited a Marxist orientation, but he excelled as a practitioner rather than an ideologist or intellectual. He achieved fame in 1970 as the first Marxist ever freely elected president. Then a violent military coup d'etat on 11 September 1973 cut short his six-year term. The resultant death of Allende and Chile's socialist experiment have stirred controversy ever since.

●

The central theme of all strains of anarchist doctrine is the illegitimacy of the state. The central theme of all nonanarchist political philosophy is the legitimacy of the state — the right of the state to rule. Anarchism thus stands as the permanent Other in the discourse of political philosophy. As such, it is reviled, condemned, ignored, but always present as a challenge to established political authority.

●

Within every age, culture, nation, and people in the world, women have loved women and men have loved men. Social contexts and constructs may differ, as have interpretations and assumptions. Lifestyles have differed, and the question of identity has had varied responses. But (some) women emotionally and physically love women and (some) men emotionally and physically love men. They always have and they always will.

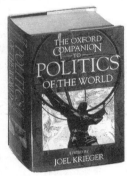

The Oxford Companion to Politics of the World
Joel Krieger. 1993; 1056 pp. ISBN 0-19-505934-4
$49.95 ($54.95 postpaid). Oxford University Press/Order Dept., 2001 Evans Road, Cary, NC 27513; 800/451-7556

Amnesty International

It's always a shock to learn that God is not interested in your pain. The best you can hope for is the help of other people.

Torture is difficult to find out about and nearly impossible to check. So far the only deterrent is public opinion. That requires a respected international investigative organization; Amnesty International delivers.

You can participate in Amnesty International through donations, letterwriting campaigns, and the purchase of their publications. —SB

●

United Kingdom

The Courts continued to review cases of alleged miscarriages of justice in England and Northern Ireland. Allegations of ill-treatment continued. Six people were killed in suspicious circumstances in Northern Ireland by security forces. Evidence of collusion between Loyalist paramilitary organizations and security forces in Northern Ireland was revealed in the courts and the media. Armed groups arbitrarily and deliberately killed civilians in Northern Ireland and England.

In Northern Ireland, violent conflict intensified as Republican groups and security forces clashed, and both Republican and Loyalist armed groups carried out torture and killings. Republican armed groups, notably the Irish Republican Army (IRA), which are predominantly Catholic, seek a British withdrawal from Northern Ireland. This aim is opposed by Loyalist armed groups from the Protestant community, notably the Ulster Volunteer Force (UVF) and the Ulster Defense Association (UDA) which acts under the name of the Ulster Freedom Fighters (UFF). In August the government outlawed the UDA following a wave of sectarian killings.

In June the Court of Appeal quashed the conviction of Judith Ward, who had been sentenced to life imprisonment for a 1974 IRA bombing in England on confession and scientific evidence which was later discredited. The court criticized members of the police, the prosecution, and psychiatric and scientific experts for failing to disclose key evidence during the original trial. —1993 Report on Human Rights Around the World.

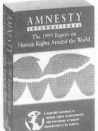

1993 Report on Human Rights Around the World
1993; 354 pp. ISBN 0-89793-140-8
$16.95 ($18.95 postpaid). 322 8th Avenue, New York, NY 10001

The Amnesty International Handbook
1991; 145 pp. ISBN 0-89793-081-9
$9.95 ($12.45 postpaid). Hunter House, PO Box 2914, Alameda, CA 94501; 510/865-5282

Amnesty International: Membership $25/year. 322 8th Avenue, New York, NY 10001; 212/807-8400.

Worldwatch Institute

This is the single best resource for understanding the problems that face our planet. Worldwatch Institute examines the kinds of economic and environmental issues that politicians by their nature have a tough time grappling with, and it suggests solutions in an evenhanded and unhysterical way. Five or six papers on various subjects are issued yearly; these become an annual book, *State of the World*. —Richard Nilsen

As far as most of us know, paper is made of natural, renewable materials, and is easily biodegradable. Yet for all its virtues, paper has turned out to be a major environmental offender.

Worldwatch Library: Includes current paperback edition of *State of the World* plus all Worldwatch Papers released during the calendar year. Membership $25/year US, $40/year international. Worldwatch Institute, 1776 Massachusetts Avenue NW, Washington, DC 20036-1904.

●

Cleaning Up After the Arms Race

Russian officials are eager not just to destroy their chemical arsenal but to derive valuable materials to offset at least some of the high costs of disarmament. One widely reported proposal is to extract arsenic from lewisite weapon stocks and to transform it into gallium arsenide used to make semiconductors. Up to 2,000 tons of arsenic could be extracted and sold for perhaps $9 billion. Another suggestion is to turn phosphorus derived from nerve gas into phosphate fertilizer. Other plans would convert mustard gas into compounds that accelerate the vulcanization of rubber, and transform nerve gas into antiseptics and fire retardants. —State of the World 1994

See Saving Biomes, p. 63, and Eco/Activism, p. 109

OTHER GREAT RESOURCES

Strategic Atlas (A Comparative Geopolitics of the World's Powers): Gérard Chaliand & Jean-Pierre Rageau. 1983, 1992, HarperPerennial. Strategic to whom? Everybody. A geopolitical history of the twentieth-century world, complete with unexpected Moëbius roots and tendrils.

How to Start Your Own Country: Erwin Strauss. 1984, Loompanics Unlimited. This is a serious, carefully researched little book about people who have done it. Sadly, most of them seem to be dreary nutcases. Everybody into the pool!

On the borders of China and several Southeast Asian countries, the profusion of minorities, their overlapping, and the fact that they are geographically exclusive, makes the geopolitical situation particularly fluid. Political guerrillas that are more or less manipulated by one power or another China, USA, etc. and bands of irregulars engaging in the opium trade continue to find rear bases or sanctuaries in these areas. —Strategic Atlas

Ethnic Groups
Vietnamese
Chinese
Thai
Khmer
Tibeto-Burman
Karenes
Miao-yao
Railways

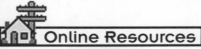

POINT — The Quarterly
PO Box 38
Sausalito, CA 94966-9932

Your
Source
for
Products
from the Millennium
Whole Earth Catalog

Our work,
our investments,
and our use of money

are probably the most tangible evidence of the contribution our lives have made. Many of us want our work to produce prosperity, in the word's best sense: we want to leave ourselves, other people, and the world better off than if our work had never taken place.

Why is it so difficult to find or create such work? Because it requires nurturing some elusive capabilities in ourselves. Chances are, these capabilities vary from person to person, but they might include learning to judge the worth of people and things; to be thrifty (taking the expense of our time and effort seriously); to work collectively; and to understand and finesse the outside forces that help or hinder us. A sense of humor and perspective help, too.

Here are the tools for building these skills in the domain of "making a living."
—Art Kleiner

The Seven Laws of Money
Michael Phillips. 1993; 196 pp.
ISBN 0-87773-949-8
$6 ($9 postpaid). Shambhala Publications/Order Dept., PO Box 308, Boston, MA 02117-0308; 617/424-0228

The Seven Laws of Money

"Do the right things and the money will follow." As a board member of the foundation that publishes this **Catalog**, Michael Phillips wrote that gem in the early seventies. Money is a symptom, a measurement, a dream, or a nightmare. It's never a cause or THE problem. Far too often, lack of imagination is excused as lack of money. Read or reread Phillips for refreshment and reminder.
—John Sumser

Two versions exist. The original contained the basic laws and commentary by Michael, with examples and meditations by Salli Rasberry, poet Jug'n'Candle, and other contributors. It was a great counter-culture artifact that, as Stewart Brand wrote, "made a lot of people cheeky enough to try stuff, and helped them get away with it." Shambhala recently released a new shirt-pocket-size version, spare and crisp with only Michael's text. I like to give the little ones as gifts, and reread the full version myself.
— Art Kleiner

The Seven Laws of Money
Michael Phillips, Stewart Brand, Salli Rasberry, & Dick Raymond. 1974; 194 pp.
ISBN 0-394-70686-2, $9 ($11 postpaid). Random House/Order Dept., 400 Hahn Road, Westminster, MD 21157; 800/733-3000

Money and the Meaning of Life

Like most people, I've always thought money was a device invented by the secular world for purely secular reasons, and that money was somehow evil or dirty, inhibiting people from examining their true nature. Philosopher Jacob Needleman painstakingly and eloquently explains that this is not so — that money holds the potential (if properly understood) to act as an instrument of self-knowledge and exploration. Needleman addresses money issues as mind-boggling as they are timeless. Are there things that money can and cannot buy? What is the morality of personal gain?

This book is packed with "aha" experiences for the reader.
— Cindy Cosgrove

We particularly recommend this book for wealthy young heirs, trying to learn to cope with the isolation, guilt, and mistrust that they might inherit along with the money. —Art Kleiner

•

To be obsessed with money is certainly to be in hell. But there is another kind of hell, which we must now acknowledge. We live in that hell when we refuse to participate in the realities of life, when dreams and fantasies, spiritual or otherwise, take the place of a real inner search.

•

In Medieval monasteries, the material and economic needs of man were not considered evil; they were considered *secondary*. The tragic misunderstanding arises when that which is secondary gets taken as evil. To give the lower nature its proper place in human life requires a fine and dynamic attention; to treat the lower nature as evil, on the contrary, invites a kind of violence toward an essential aspect of human nature. And this, in its turn, invites the reaction we have witnessed especially strongly in modern times, in which the unattended lower nature finally asserts itself like an unattended fire raging out of control.

•

If you want to take the true measure of someone, observe how he handles sex, time, and money.

Money and the Meaning of Life
Jacob Needleman. Doubleday, 1991; 321 pp. ISBN 0-385-26241-8
$21 ($23.50 postpaid) from Bantam, Doubleday, Dell/Fulfillment Dept., 2451 S. Wolf Road, Des Plaines, IL 60018; 800/223-6834

OTHER GREAT RESOURCES: YOUR MONEY & YOUR LIFE

Do What You Love, the Money Will Follow (Discovering Your Right Livelihood): Marsha Sinetar. 1989, Dell Publishing Co. This long, effective talking-to by a psychologist should be useful for people who can't quite bring themselves to believe the truth of the First Law of Money.

True Wealth: Paul Hwoschinsky. 1990, Ten Speed Press. Step-by-step exercises for developing a sense of your own worth and prospects. You articulate your values and goals, your assets (financial and non-), the risks you're taking, your advisors and financial environment, and finally your possibilities for wealth. A tad New-Age-y, but good. [Suggested by Claude Whitmyer]

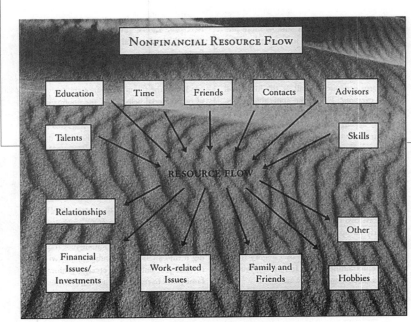

NONFINANCIAL RESOURCE FLOW

Education · Time · Friends · Contacts · Advisors

Talents · Skills

RESOURCE FLOW

Relationships · Other

Financial Issues/ Investments · Work-related Issues · Family and Friends · Hobbies

—*True Wealth*

SIMPLE LIVING

OTHER GREAT RESOURCES

Dwelling Portably: $1.00/ issue. PO Box 190-nxh, Philomath, OR 97370. A simple-format compendium of simple-living tips that really work.

Freedom Road: Harold Hough. 1991, Loompanics Unlimited. How to escape rent and build a low-cost, high-quality life by moving into a recreational vehicle full-time.

The Beggar's Handbook: M. T. Pockets. 1989, Loompanics Unlimited. For the down-and-out: creative (sometimes semi-dishonest) techniques for panhandling money in public places, without demeaning yourself or your marks too much.

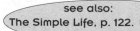
see also:
The Simple Life, p. 122.

Your Money or Your Life

This is a step-by-step guide to financial independence — to finding the freedom to live without being a wage slave. It's inspiring and well-written, but only a small fraction of its value comes from reading, it must be practiced. Each of its steps — assembling the history of your life's earning, gauging your net worth, keeping track of every cent moving into or out of your life, and judging every bit of spending by asking, "Will this really help my life's purpose?" — is a tiny move toward greater awareness of money as a tool for achieving what you want.

If you make it to the final stage, you've reduced your expenses enough so that your independent income is greater. Now you begin to accumulate capital — money or time that you can invest where you choose. That's the goal, not just of the book, but of capitalism, in its worthiest incarnation.

Despite the Rasputin-like reputation of the book's authors in some circles and the austerity they preach (they live on only $6,000 a year, and give away most of the money they earn), *Your*

Money or Your Life is remarkably, and blessedly, free of guru-ishness. Many of us will find that it's not easy to follow. Practicing the steps in this book requires letting go of the presumption that, no matter how much debt we accumulate or time we waste, we are special enough that we won't have to pay the costs. If all of us followed the book's steps, most of the cruelty and status-mongering associated with making a living might disappear.

Joe Dominguez and Vicki Robin have also produced an audiocassette set, and their foundation still offers the training courses from which the book derived. —Art Kleiner [Suggested by Mark Brady]

●

Money is something we choose to trade our life energy for. Our life energy is our allotment of time here on earth, the hours of precious life available to us. When we go to our jobs we are trading our life energy for money. . . . This definition of money gives us significant information. Our life energy is more *real* in our actual experience than money. You could even say money *equals* our life energy. So, while money has no in-

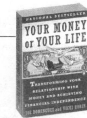

Your Money or Your Life
(Transforming Your Relationship with Money and Achieving Financial Independence)
Joe Dominguez & Vicki Robin. Penguin Books, 1992; 350 pp. ISBN 0-14-016715-3
$11 ($13 postpaid) from Penguin USA/Consumer Sales, 120 Woodbine Street, Bergenfield, NJ 07621; 800/253-6476

trinsic reality, our life energy does — at least to us. It's tangible, and it's finite. Life energy is all we have. It is precious because it is limited and irretrievable and because our choices about how we use it express the meaning and purpose of our time here on earth.

●

Discernment is sorting out the true from the chaff. Just in the process of writing down every cent that comes into or goes out of your life, you will begin to discern which expenses are fitting and fulfilling, and which are unnecessary, extravagant, or even downright embarrassing.

The Tightwad Gazette • Cheap Tricks

Two books full of tips for saving a little money here and there, often while reducing environmental pressures. Much of this is the stuff older folks learned from the Great Depression, writ modern. *The Tightwad Gazette* (compiled from the down-home, skinny little newsletter Amy Dacyczyn has published since 1990) is a browser's bible, full of tips. Here's how to make your own aluminum-free baking powder; uses for recycled milk jugs; how to darn socks. The silliness line is drawn at splitting double-strength toilet paper, the pragmatic editor noting that "you have better things to do with your life." *Cheap Tricks* is one man's penny-pinching manifesto, naming names and presenting suggested resources, complete with address and phone. In both, there's the usual stuff about saving two cents each time you wash the dishes, but most of the suggestions are things you might actually consider doing without making yourself feel excreted upon by the Fates. Both are right on the money, so to speak. —J. Baldwin

●

Dear Amy,

In 25 years of driving over 30,000 miles a year, I haven't spent a cent to own the cars.

When I first started in business, I called the local commercial credit office to inquire about repossessed cars. They had dozens, and I bought two for a total of $500 . . . sold one for $600, and that began my odyssey of not spending money for cars.

When I tired of that car (remember, I got that car and $100 to start) I ran an ad to sell my "Classic 1959 Plymouth" and sold it for $400. I used that $400 to buy a 1962 Volvo, drove it two years, ran another

"classic" ad and sold it for $600. I bought another Volvo for $500 . . . and I've repeated the process about 15 times.

Part of the formula involves negotiating. I might look at 10 cars (all private sales, no dealers) before I find one I like that can be bought right. I pull out money in $100 bills, explain that I'm on my way to look at another car, but if I could buy theirs for *X* (usually half of what they are asking) I can give them cash now.

Sometimes I have to drive away and look at more cars, but 15 times they have accepted my offer.

I prefer Volvos, as they last, hold value, and give great service. I do my own maintenance, using a Chilton's guide or the manual for that model car. I change the oil every 3,000 miles, keep them clean, had several Maaco $100 paint jobs, and always have whitewall tires.

Bill Niland
Topsfield, Massachusetts
—Tightwad Gazette

●

Jarred baby foods are convenient for occasional use but expensive for everyday use. It's easy and much more economical to mash or puree foods you've prepared for the rest of the family (use a fork, blender, or food processor). It's also easy to puree larger quantities of food and freeze the excess in ice-cube trays. Once frozen, pop the cubes into a freezer bag. Later, you can place a cube in a dish, defrost it, and serve. —Cheap Tricks

Cheap Tricks
(100s of Ways You Can Save 1000s of Dollars!)
Andy Dappen. 1992; 405 pp.
ISBN 0-9632577-0-6
$13.95 ($15 postpaid) from Brier Books, PO Box 180, Mountlake Terrace, Seattle, WA 98043; 800/356-9315

THE EXPENSIVE BOX LUNCH
(Do not try this in your own home.)

Tom's peanut butter cheese crackers (25¢)

Doritos snack size (29¢ for eight chips including broken pieces)

Del Monte fruit cup (43¢ for 4½ ounces)

Sunkist Fun Fruits Dinosaurs (33¢, or 4¢ per dinosaur)

Mott's apple-grape juice pack (33¢)

TOTAL: $1.63

—Tightwad Gazette

The Tightwad Gazette
(Promoting Thrift As a Viable Alternative Lifestyle)
Amy Dacyczyn. Villard Books, 1993; 307 pp.
ISBN 0-679-74388-X
$9.99 ($11.99 postpaid) from Random House/Order Dept., 400 Hahn Road, Westminster, MD 21157; 800/733-3000

The Tightwad Gazette: Amy Dacyczyn, Editor. $12/year (12 issues). RR1, Box 3570, Leeds, ME 04263.

A plain uncompromised 5-ounce potato, purchased in a 1-pound sack costs about 7¢. The chart below indicates what this potato would cost after the convenience-food industry repackages it into the potato products we've researched. —Tightwad Gazette

Product	Cost
Bulk Potato	2.5¢
Store Brand Mashed	6¢
Sack Potato	6.7¢
Betty Crocker Mashed	8¢
Crinkle Cut Fries	11¢
Taters	13¢
Alphabet Fries	15¢
Store Brand Fries	18¢
Betty Crocker Au Gratin	19¢
Store Brand Chips	20¢
Tom's Chips	27¢
Durkee Potato Sticks	30¢
Ruffles Chips	32¢

Consumer Reports

Before making any big purchase, check here — if only to see how long you can expect the new car, blender, TV, or stereo to last. No advertising sullies *Consumer Reports'* pages; consequently, no bias affects their tests and analyses of consumer goods and services. The Consumers' Union (as they call themselves) are best at gathering information that's outright impossible to gather yourself, such as the opinions of 250,000 auto owners.

They sum up the year's work in their annual **Buying Guide**, printed in pocket size so you can take it shopping with you. Or, if you need their ratings for just one purchase a year, you can search by topic or brand name in their own full-text file on Dialog Information Service (see page 281). However it's packaged, the information here is without peer.
—J. Baldwin and Art Kleiner

Nearly one in 10 camcorders our readers purchased since 1988 has been repaired. That's considerable, considering that the median usage of those camcorders was about 6 hours a year. And they're not cheap to fix: about $125, on average. Note that a brand's repair index includes models other than those we tested, and the data is historical in nature. Still, choosing a brand that has been reliable in the past should better your odds of getting a brand that will be reliable.

Consumer Reports
Irwin Landau, Editor. $22/year (12 issues) from Consumer Reports Books/Subscriptions, PO Box 53017, Boulder, CO 80321-3017; 513/860-1178

Everyone's Money Book

Every middle-class (or aspiring middle-class) household needs a basic household finance encyclopedia, to introduce and decrypt the lore of smart shopping, investing, banking, and retirement planning. This is the best recent guide we've seen. I particularly like this book's definitions of terms (from "adjustable-rate loans" to "zero-coupon bonds") and its long lists of resources. The extensive annotated bibliographies might entice you so much to read about money that you'll have no time to make any. —AK

•
Two kinds of discount brokers exist: *full service* and *deep discount*. The three largest full-service discounters — Charles Schwab in San Francisco, Fidelity Investments in Boston and Quick & Reilly in New York City — offer almost every service that you can get from a national full-service firm like Merrill Lynch — except advice from the firms' analysts. . . . Deep-discount firms charge even less but offer fewer services. Some of these firms — such as Jack White

Everyone's Money Book
Jordan E. Goodman & Sonny Bloch. 1993; 825 pp. ISBN 0-7931-0721-0 $24.95 ($28.95 postpaid) from Dearborn Financial Publishing, 520 N. Dearborn, Chicago, IL 60610; 800/829-7934

in San Diego, Brown & Company in Boston, Waterhouse Securities in New York City and about 175 others — may execute a trade for as much as 90 percent less than what Merrill Lynch or Paine Webber charges or 50 percent less than what Schwab or Fidelity charges.

See p. 122 for blending cheap living with community spirit.

OTHER GREAT RESOURCES FOR SMART SHOPPING

Great Buys by Mail, or Phone: Sue Goldstein. 1993, Penguin Books. Those who live simply will usually do better shopping by mail order — particularly if you average in the cost of your driving. Long-standing shopping maven Sue Goldstein (*The Underground Shopper*) makes mail order recommendations here.

The Wholesale-by-Mail Catalog, 1994: Lowell Miller and Prudence McCullough. 1993, HarperReference. Another guide to worthy mail order.

The Kid's Catalog Collection: Jane Smolik. 1990, Globe Pequot Press. Nicely detailed lists of mail order sources of toys, books, party supplies, sporting goods, and more.

Shopping for a Better World: 1992, Council on Economic Priorities. Pocket-sized charts rating supermarket wares — such as frozen dinners, shaving cream, pet food — according to how socially responsible, open to women and minorities, forthcoming with information, and charitable the parent company has been.

Managing Your Money • Quicken

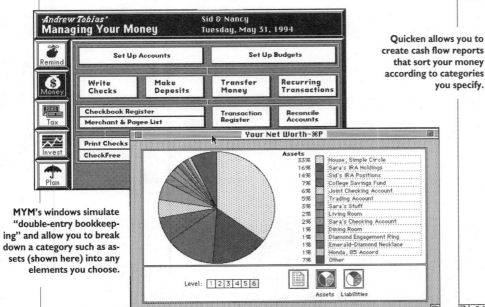

MYM's windows simulate "double-entry bookkeeping" and allow you to break down a category such as assets (shown here) into any elements you choose.

Quicken allows you to create cash flow reports that sort your money according to categories you specify.

No other computer program is so useful, so well-designed, so humorous, so easy, so exploitative of what a computer does best, as Managing Your Money. Most of us can keep up with the checkbook, but investments, tax stuff, loans, and insurance seem to inhabit worlds of their own, from which come a steady supply of bad surprises. This program eliminates all that. For the first time, I not only know what's going on, I relish my monthly session with the program, when the actuals take on the imagineds (the budget), and I come out ahead or behind in the computer game of life. —SB

As someone who used to hate to balance my checkbook, the thought of using a program to keep my finances organized took some getting used to. Then I discovered Quicken. It is hard to find a more popular program; almost everyone loves it.

Quicken does much more than just keep track of your personal income

and expenses. It can generate reports (great at tax time) summarizing your expenses and net worth. It can write checks as you enter them in your records, pay bills electronically, and help you transfer money between your different accounts. Quicken lets you be compulsive or loose about how you enter your checking and credit card information. You can specify tax categories for all checks and payments when you enter them, or do it at the end of the year, or skip it altogether — then go back later, be more specific, and generate new reports.
— Paul Hoffman

Which to choose? Both are low-priced (thanks to competition with each other), capable, and friendly. Both automatically print checks on forms you order from their companies. Quicken is easier to set up and grasp; Managing Your Money, with text by financial author Andrew Tobias (**The Only Investment Guide You'll Ever Need**), offers

more of an education. Quicken has more sophisticated electronic bill paying and credit card tracking; MYM has much more sophisticated features for budgeting, financial planning, and running a one-person business.

If you're financially illiterate, start your education not by reading, but by using one of these software packages.
— Art Kleiner

Managing Your Money
Macintosh: System 6.0.2 or higher, 2 MB RAM, 3 MB hard disk space; IBM compatible: DOS 3.0 or higher, 512K RAM, hard disk. $39.95 ($46.45 postpaid) from MECA Software, PO Box 912, Fairfield, CT 06430; 800/820-7458

Quicken
Macintosh System 6.0 or higher, 2 MB RAM, 2 MB hard disk space; IBM compatible: DOS 3.0 or higher, 640K RAM, hard disk. $69.95 postpaid from Intuit, Inc./Order Processing, PO Box 3014, Menlo Park, CA 94026; 800/756-1855

What Color Is Your Parachute?

In a field positively viscous with lame books, this perennially bestselling guide to job-seeking has no competition. It's updated annually (that's impressive), it is cheery (for a reader who could probably use some cheer) and its sound, detailed advice for an all-important task is conveyed with skill.
—SB

When To Negotiate Salary

Your Bargaining Position

Best Time

We must have you.

We got you.

Too Early

Too Late

We love you.

We like you.

Who are you?

Time

•

Jobs in the U.S. last an average of 4.2 years — and probably a similar length in other countries.

That's why surveys reveal that the number of times you will have to go job-hunting during your lifetime will likely be around eight. Eight! Therefore, the time you spend on mastering your job-hunt or career-change *now* will stand you in good stead for the rest of your life.

On the other hand, if you do it haphazardly now, you are just going to have to master it all over again, next time.

•

A job-hunter presented herself for a job-interview as public relations officer for a major-league baseball team. That evening, she wrote and mailed a thank-you note. She was eventually hired for the job, and when she asked why, they told her that they had decided to hire her because, out of thirty-five applicants, she was the only one who had written a thank-you note.

That's why every expert on interviewing will tell you two things: (1) thank-you notes are *crucial*, because they may be the one factor that gets you the job; and (2) most job-hunters ignore this advice. Indeed, it is safe to say that it is the most overlooked step in the entire job-hunting process.

•

See More Employers Each Week

In the U.S., and likely in other countries as well, job-hunters only visit six employers a month, on average; that's one reason nine million job-hunters still can't find work. As a job-hunter, you may need to see seventy employers or more, before you are through. You should determine to see at least two employers a day, one in the morning, one in the afternoon, every weekday, at a minimum, for as many months as your job-hunt may last.

It is amazing how often people do get their dreams, whether in stages or directly. The more you don't *cut* the dream down, because of what you *think* you know about *the real world*, the more likely you are to find what you are looking for.

See also resources for finding jobs around the world, pages 336-337.

What Color Is Your Parachute?
Richard N. Bolles. 1993; 461 pp.
ISBN 0-89815-568-1
$14.95 ($18.45 postpaid) from Ten Speed Press, PO Box 7123, Berkeley, CA 94707; 800/841-2665

The American Almanac of Jobs and Salaries

A friend, looking over my shoulder at this book, said, "I still haven't figured out why, for the same amount of effort, I can charge $40, someone else can charge $4, and someone else can charge $400,000." It all depends, I guess, on what you can convince someone you're worth. There is so much potential for abuse when you negotiate a salary or fee, you need to know the market value of your work. The Almanac is a heroic summary of careers, what prospects they offer, how to find a job, and what you might expect to earn. (Also see the books on negotiating skills, p. 139.)
—Art Kleiner
[Suggested by Bruce E. Coughran]

THE IVY LEAGUE

University	Professor	Associate	Assistant	Instructor
Brown University	$70,500	$48,200	$40,300	$ NA
Cornell University	74,900	52,000	46,000	NA
Columbia University	82,000	54,500	42,000	38,500
Dartmouth College	73,300	49,700	41,400	NA
Harvard University	92,200	52,000	47,800	46,600
University of Pennsylvania	80,400	57,300	48,600	NA
Princeton University	88,200	52,300	41,300	34,700
Yale University	86,100	50,700	40,600	36,900

AVERAGE BASE STARTING SALARIES FOR STATE POLICE AGENCIES, 1990	
Position	**Average Salary**
Entry-level Officer	$22,780
Sergeant	30,100
Director or Equivalent	56,900

SOURCE: U.S. Department of Justice, *Sourcebook of Criminal Justice Statistics, 1990, 1991.*

The American Almanac of Jobs and Salaries
John W. Wright. 1993; 637 pp.
ISBN 0-380-77219-1
$17 ($18.50 postpaid) from Avon Books, PO Box 767, Dresden, TN 38225; 800/223-0690

OTHER GREAT JOB RESOURCES

How to Get the Job You Want After Forty: Maxwell J. Harper & Arthur R. Pell. 1988, Pilot Books.

This handbook is succinct, upbeat (without being chirpy), experienced, and all too relevant in the era of downsizing.

The One Hundred Best Companies to Work for in America: Robert Levering & Milton Moskowitz. 1994, Plume Books.

"Gee, I'd like to work there." This all-new edition, full of descriptions of terrific workplaces, is based on visits to hundreds of companies. Useful for job hunting, for improving your current job, and (as Michael Phillips suggests) for learning more about all the varieties of good management.

Temp (How to Survive and Thrive in the World of Temporary Employment): Deborahann Smith. 1994, Shambhala Publications.

Wonderfully strategic handbook for getting

temporary jobs through an agency, and thriving thereby.

Country Careers (Successful Ways to Live and Work in the Country): Jerry Germer. 1993, John Wiley & Sons, Inc.

SALARY?

Read this before you quit your city job, and absolutely before you buy that bus ticket or hire that moving company. It's encouraging, but realistic.

The Caretaker Gazette: $18/year (6 issues). 221 Wychwood Road, Westfield, NJ 07090; 908/654-6600.

Sort of a "job zine" of (very complete) ads placed by owners of land, needing someone to live there and look after the place.

The New Complete Guide to Environmental Careers: Bill Sharp. 1993, Island Press.

By far the most complete, most engaging, and most true-to-life of the many books we've seen on getting yourself a "green job."

Skillful Means

Many books preach about the importance of right livelihood; this book tells you how to put the concept into practice. It describes, for example, some genuinely useful ways to get your mind straight while working at a job you hate, and how to turn that job into something meaningful while you're trying to figure out what to do next.
—Claude Whitmyer

•

By attempting to control the outcome of events in our lives, we establish certain limitations for our own behavior, as well as that of others. We find we must guard

against being honest, for revealing our innermost feelings would expose our self-centered motivation. We calculate our interactions with others, maintaining artificial relationships designed to protect our self-image.

We may not even notice that by doing this we are narrowing channels of communication and inhibiting personal freedom. On the surface we may appear self-confident, but at heart there is confusion, in both our thoughts and our actions. By encouraging artificial responses in our relationships, we have lost touch with our most precious possession, our open and responsive human nature.

Skillful Means
Tarthang Tulku. 1991; ISBN 0-89800-231-1
$12.95 ($15.45 postpaid) from Dharma Publishing, 2910 San Pablo Avenue, Berkeley, CA 94702; 800/873-4276

Working Knowledge

Meet Willie, all-purpose mechanic, proprietor of a modest repair garage in upper New York State. He fixes Saabs, farm machinery, and just about anything else you might need fixed. He's a member of a fast-disappearing breed.

This loving portrait is also a sharp look at how our work ethic is changing as employment becomes increasingly disconnected from the social fabric of our lives. I've never seen this melancholy matter addressed so well or truly. There is no trace of glib romance; the stark realities of a difficult but rewarding way of life are shown just as they are, with humor, dignity and grace. —J. Baldwin

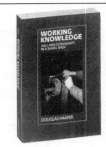

Working Knowledge
(Skill and Community in a Small Shop)
Douglas A. Harper. University of California Press, 1992; 224 pp. ISBN 0-520-07970-1
$16 ($19 postpaid) from California/ Princeton Fulfillment Services, 1445 Lower Ferry Road, Ewing, NJ 08618; 800/777-4726

•

"They say you've got to have a computer to check whether a car's in tune or not, but that doesn't always work. Look at Ray Dean there — the trouble he's had with his new Chevy. It's taken him nine months to find out one little problem that was in his carburetor. I told him that to start with. 'It's under warranty — they've got to take care of it,' he says. He kept running right back to Chevrolet there in Canton. The computer light in his car kept coming on, but they couldn't find the problem."

"How did you know what it was?"

"The sound of the engine. The way it was running. I could have fixed it in five minutes."

Which Side Are You On?

My favorite guide to the labor movement, this is an intensely personal memoir by a yuppie-turned-labor lawyer, who worked first with the mine workers of West Virginia, then with the steel workers of Chicago, and then with dissident teamsters across America. Geoghegan is a street poet in lawyer's clothing, crawling (as he puts it) at the bottom of the upper class, wrestling with the question of what people are worth, and how to help them earn it. —Art Kleiner

•

In one afternoon of work, the U.S. Congress could fix not only the problems of American labor but the entire cultural crisis of the West, by passing a law that requires an outside neutral agency to count the ballots in local-union elections. Well, perhaps there should be a few more provisions:

Require a rank-and-file vote for all officers.

Give all bona fide candidates a copy of the membership list.

Provide "public funding" from the union treasury for all the candidates.

I guess it is madness, delusion on my part, to think that simply changing the law would

Which Side Are You On?
(Trying to Be for Labor When It's Flat on Its Back)
Thomas Geoghegan. Plume Books, 1991; 287 pp. ISBN 0-452-26891-5
$11 ($13 postpaid) from Penguin USA/Consumer Sales, 120 Woodbine Street, Bergenfield, NJ 07621; 800/253-6476

make so much difference. The cultural crisis of the West would continue unabated. But I'm a lawyer, so what can you expect? I think everything can be fixed by a law. A writer of any depth, like an Orwell or Camus, wouldn't be so shallow or mechanistic, or tell their readers to write to Congress. But then anyone with depth, anyone serious, wouldn't have thrown away his life dealing with the Department of Labor.

It's true that there is a law already that requires union democracy, the Landrum-Griffin Act. But the Act is something of joke.

When Workers Decide • Putting Democracy to Work

Two good sources on workplace democracy — in which workers buy, own, take over, or collectively build up their workplaces together. **When Workers Decide** *is an anthology of real stories about employee stock ownership plans, cooperatives, community banks, and community-labor alliances. It gives you a feel for the range of possible alternatives to a remote, hierarchical boss. It also demonstrates the types of tough questions that come up — like whether or not to pay everyone equally.* **Putting Democracy to Work** *is pure how-to, full of legal and financial checklists and lots of resources for help and information. Also see "Economic Cooperation," page 141. —Art Kleiner*

•

What is an employee-owned company?

In an employee-owned company all of the employees (management, clerical, and shop floor) together own a majority of the stock of the company.

If a company is employee owned, do the employees control it?

Not necessarily. Employee-owners need at least two things to ensure democratic control of their company: *voting rights* — the board of directors is elected by the employees on a one-person, one-vote basis; and *participation* — all employees receive the information with which to understand the progress of the company and have the opportunity to participate in day-to-day decisions. —*When Workers Decide*

•

Over the years, the Basques have used job rotation plans not only to insure high worker-member morale, but, as well, to curb seasonal slumps, or economic downturns faced by particular cooperatives. Most Basque worker-members learn several jobs either to perform in their own or in another firm within the group. Thus, when employment demands rise due to seasonal sales growth, or economic upturns, work needs can be filled without resort to boom or bust hiring policies. —*Putting Democracy to Work*

When Workers Decide
(Workplace Democracy Takes Root in North America)
Len Krimerman & Frank Lindenfeld, Editors. 1992; 308 pp. ISBN 0-86571-201-8
$16.95 ($19.45 postpaid) from New Society Publishers, 4527 Springfield Avenue, Philadelphia, PA 19143; 800/333-9093

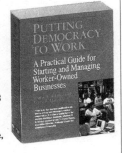

Putting Democracy to Work
(A Practical Guide for Starting and Managing Worker-Owned Businesses)
Frank T. Adams & Gary B. Hansen. Berrett-Koehler/ Hulogosi Communications, 1992; 324 pp.
ISBN 1-881052-09-5
$19.95 ($23.45 postpaid) from Berrett-Koehler Publishers, 155 Montgomery Street, San Francisco, CA 94104; 800/929-2929

Your Rights in the Workplace • Sexual Harassment on the Job

It's surprising how few rights workers actually have. **Your Rights in the Workplace** *tells you what you can do if you're being treated unfairly, and even has a chapter on how to pick a lawyer. — Jim Britell and Martha Weaver-Britell*

A subsequent Nolo Press book, **Sexual Harassment on the Job,** *covers this issue in full detail. It's aimed at women (far too many of whom are still tormented by men at work), but it's also useful for men who wonder where to stop. —AK*

•

The mere fact that you have to work hard at finding a new job usually isn't sufficient evidence to suggest blacklisting. But a strong signal might be a series of situations in which potential new employers seem to be on the verge of hiring you, then suddenly lose all interest. This indicates that, when a prospective employer checks your references just before hiring you, the blacklister is tipped off to where you've applied for work and is able to ding you.

You can hire a lawyer or a private detective to investigate whether or not you're being blacklisted. But it's easier and cheaper to conduct your own investigation by establishing an imaginary business and using that business to inquire about your own employment record with former employers. —*Your Rights in the Workplace*

•

Arthur asks Clara for a dinner date in polite language. She says no — and she makes it clear that she is not open to dating him. He persists in coming by her desk every workday for the next month and asks her if she's changed her mind and will go out with him, and each time she firmly tells him no. Arthur's request has crossed over the line from polite to harassing. —*Sexual Harassment on the Job*

 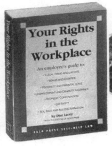

Your Rights in the Workplace
Barbara Kate Repa. 1993; 352 pp.
ISBN 0-87337-200-X
$15.95 ($19.95 postpaid)

Sexual Harassment on the Job
Bill Petrocelli & Barbara Kate Repa. 1992; 200 pp. ISBN 0-87337-177-1
$14.95 ($18.95 postpaid)

Both from Nolo Press, 950 Parker Street, Berkeley, CA 94710; 800/992-6656 or 510/549-1976

A Few Simple Rules About Investments
(For People Who Have Never Invested Before)

by
Paul
Hoffman

Paul Hoffman studied personal financial investment planning for many years until, disenchanted with the bureaucratic rules and deceit in the trade, he began devoting himself to writing about finance instead. —Art Kleiner

Investing is surprisingly difficult for many people. They agonize over the huge array of vehicles they see advertised, the moral ethics of their investments, and so on. The morass of conflicting advice available doesn't help. However, for most of us, investment choices can be very simple. Following a few simple rules can make a huge difference in getting us into a less worried frame of mind, and can produce just as great a return as if you followed the most "expert" advice.

• Buy investments with your eyes open: don't just have them sold to you. Advertising placed by large brokerages and mutual funds is often blatantly misleading, emphasizing only positive (and often irrelevant) features, and influencing the editorial recommendations of magazines that carry it. Most stockbrokers and investment counselors are salespeople: they don't make any money unless they sell their products to you. They tend to try to sell you the investments on which they will make the highest commission.

There are dozens of better sources of information, completely free of advertising. Most of them are newsletters, available by subscription. Start with *The Hulbert Guide to Financial Newsletters,* by Mark Hulbert (Dearborn Financial Publishing, 520 North Dearborn Street, Chicago IL 60610). Hulbert rates each newsletter according to whether or not their advice would have made money for you. He routinely angers the newsletter publishers because he reports honestly about them. Look not just at the newsletters' performance over time, but at which ones, based on Hulbert's descriptions and excerpts, feel trustworthy and understandable to you.

• Spend one hour of research for every $1000 you invest. Few people would consider buying a $5000 used car without spending a few hours looking at the car, or searching for comparable prices. Yet many people will buy $5000 worth of a mutual fund with little more than the two minutes it took to read the ad. This is one of the best ways to lose money.

Conduct two kinds of research: first, study the general features of the investment category (bonds, mutual funds or whatever the category may be). A good, well-written, constantly updated overview is the *Dun and Bradstreet Guide to Your Investments* (1993; Nancy Dunnan, Harper Perennial). Pay close attention to the risks, the short- and long-term returns, and the variety of options available to you.

Second, learn about the investment itself: what kind of company is selling it, how it has performed over time, and how its business is evolving.

• Analyze your short-term (under one year), medium-term (one- to five-year), and long-term investments separately. You will need different kinds of money for different times down the road, and you should invest accordingly. For instance, most people like to keep a small amount of money available for short-term emergencies, like the loss of a car or an emergency trip to visit a relative. That money should not be taken from your long-term pool, which would be earmarked for retirement. Similarly, if your analysis shows you that 90 percent of your investments are short-term, it is probably prudent to ask yourself what you want for your life ten or twenty years down the line, and how you think you might get it.

• Assume the worst for your post-employment years and invest accordingly today. If you want to live comfortably, you should probably assume that Social Security will generate less than half, and maybe only 20 percent, of what you will want to live on. This means you need to start saving a lot now, investing that money in reasonably conservative securities. The positive side of this situation is that saving for retirement starts you thinking more seriously about saving for shorter-term goals as well.

• Understand risk. To be told an investment is "low-risk" is meaningless, unless you think about which types of risk are of concern. There are many kinds of risk important to small investors, but all of them are understandable. They include:
—Risk of losing the entire investment (such as gambling at the racetrack).
—Risk of losing 25% of the investment (such as in a stock market plunge).
—Risk of not making as much on an investment as you could on a very safe investment.
—Risk that the investment will be down when you must sell it (the value of the investment may swing wildly).

Your choice of risk depends on how long you intend to keep the investment, and your tolerance for financial danger in your life.

• Invest with consciousness, not worry. It is futile to try to predict the future — either of an investment, or of your own life. But you can spend time looking at what truly matters to you, and develop your judgment accordingly. Then you can keep yourself financially happier, both in the present and the future.

Dear Whole Earth: Hey, I hope you guys are reviewing books about the stock market. Yep, those ugly words: "stock market." Too many people these days are making a ton of money in business "doing good," or want to invest their money "from the heart," but don't know enough about the markets to protect their investments. One of these days there is going to be a crash, and all that hard-earned "good money" will wind up in the pocket of some Wall Street fat cat who isn't as good as you are, but who happens to have better information. Get the picture?

New Age bliss doesn't always make and keep money. Get down and dirty. Read these books. —Richard Kent

How to Make Money in Stocks
William J. O'Neil. 1991; 224 pp. ISBN 0-07-047893-7 $9.95 ($13.45 postpaid) from McGraw-Hill Publishing Co., 13311 Monterey Avenue, Blue Ridge Summit, PA 17214; 800/722-4726. More in-depth technical analysis, market action and tape reading. Good examples of charts and how to interpret them.

Reminiscences of a Stock Operator
Edwin LeFevre. 1992; 308 pp. ISBN 0-934380-21-X $19.95 postpaid from Traders Press, PO Box 6206, Greenville, SC 29606; 800/927-8222. A thinly disguised biography of the famous speculator Jesse Livermore. The principles he followed in the 1920s and '30s are the same that exist today. Great traders all recommend this book.

The New Market Wizards
Jack D. Schwager. HarperBusiness, 1992; 493 pp. ISBN 0-88730-667-5 $13 ($15.75 postpaid) from HarperCollins Publishers/Direct Mail, PO Box 588, Dunmore, PA 18512; 800/331-3761. Great trader stories from people who trade billions, who are powerful enough to move the markets themselves. Killer tales of rags to riches to rags again. Wonderful insights into how the markets work, and the winners and losers. If you are thinking about getting into it full-time, you've got to read this.

One Up on Wall Street
Peter Lynch & John Rothchild. Penguin Books, 1990; 320 pp. ISBN 0-14-012792-5 $12.50 ($14.50 postpaid) from Penguin USA/Consumer Sales, 120 Woodbine Street, Bergenfield, NJ 07621; 800/253-6476. A good place to start. Information is all around you. Study your butt off and beat the less-than-nimble mutual funds.

Investing from the Heart

When the concept of socially responsible investing (SRI) — in which investors put their money where it is doing some social good — first became a noticeable phenomenon a few years ago, the Wall Street good-old-boy network put out the wisdom that SRI offered less return on the dollar than standard, go-for-the-jugular investments. But SRI has grown to where it offers returns no worse than standard investing, and in many cases much better. Socially responsible companies tend to be better-run, to employ more productive workers, to have closer ties to their communities, and to be far less vulnerable to wasteful litigation. This book shows ordinary folk that they can play the SRI game, for their own good as well as society's, and provides a course in the game itself. —Phil Catalfo

•

Part of what makes investing in defense industries an ethical mixed bag are the good things that some companies do. Some of the biggest defense contractors also grade high in the kinds of activities that the SRI community applauds. Nuclear Free America ranks AT&T as one of the leading nuclear weapons contractors in the country (although AT&T disputes the figures). The same company has been acknowledged in recent years by *Black Enterprise* magazine as one of the best places for blacks to work and by *Working Mother* magazine as one of the best places for women to work. AT&T, at its industry's forefront with its pledge to halve its use of ozone-eating chlorofluorocarbons by 1991 and eliminate them in 1994, also won the Council on Economic Priorities' environmental award in 1990.

•

You have no control over how your bank invests your deposits, and—with rare exceptions—banks do not consider socially responsible criteria when they make their investment decisions. Nor will you be able to track the contents of your bank's investment portfolio, which can change daily. Nevertheless, some banking institutions are better from an ethical standpoint than oth-

Investing from the Heart
(The Guide to Socially Responsible Investments and Money Management) Jack A. Brill & Alan Reder. Crown Publishing Group, 1992, 1993; 434 pp. ISBN 0-517-88069-5 $12 ($14 postpaid) from Random House/Order Dept., 400 Hahn Road, Westminster, MD 21157; 800/733-3000

ers. We have already mentioned the financial advantage of purchasing your CD at a credit union. In addition, credit unions are usually the best place to shop for your CD from an ethical standpoint. Credit unions steer clear of the complications of corporate and international involvements, because their money flow is pretty much person to person. Deposits are loaned out to members; because credit unions are non-profit institutions organized specifically to serve the banking needs of their members; members are also distributed the institution's excess profits. If you are not eligible for membership in one of your local credit unions by virtue of your work or government employment or whatever, find out if a relative who belongs can add you as a family member.

•

One of the biggest reasons so many investors choose mutual funds is that mutual funds are largely self-managing. Why track a fund's performance when the fund's professional managers are paid to do just that—by you, as a matter of fact, through the load and management fee?

The fact is, you do not need to track a fund's performance nearly as closely as you would a portfolio of stocks. But you should check in once in a while—annually, at least. A fund's managers can change, grow old, or lose their touch as easily as any corporation, and if that shows up as a downward trend in the fund's performance, you will probably want to get out—loss or no loss.

You Can Go Bankrupt Without Going Broke • The Credit Repair Kit

*Some of us don't have to worry about investments; we're too busy keeping our heads above water. Bankruptcy is like a long hangover after a binge: painful and demoralizing, but you know that it, too, will pass. Recently, I helped someone navigate through an impossible financial jam. He ended with a bankruptcy settlement that did not curb his life very much. Others are not so fortunate. **You Can Go Broke Without Going Bankrupt** spells out the factors that make a difference and describes pitfalls and options (including an approach designed especially for farmers who would otherwise lose their land). If you've got serious debts, I recommend looking here before things get more dire. It may save you a great deal of grief later.*

***The Credit Repair Kit** contains plain, simple remedies for when — thanks to no fault of your own — you get turned down for loans or get a bad credit reputation. Includes some advice specifically for women and people going through divorce. Not applicable for those swamped with debt; see* **Your Money or Your Life** (p. 306) *instead. —Art Kleiner*

•

Many people make the mistake of increasing their debts when they never intend to repay them. This is a dangerous action which restricts the ability of these people, if discovered, to make a fresh start after their bankruptcy. Filing bankruptcy and admitting you cannot repay your debts is a difficulty you don't want to exacerbate by adding fraud to the equation.

•

If you are one of the countless women who work prior to marriage and have a positive credit history in your own name, it is important to preserve that good history after you marry. Therefore, do not cancel your credit accounts, and continue to maintain at least one bank account — checking or savings — in your own name. There is no reason to merge your accounts and your money with your husband's, and it is far easier to maintain an already positive credit

You Can Go Bankrupt Without Going Broke
Lawrence R. Reich & James P. Duffy. Pharos Books, 1992; 224 pp. ISBN 0-88687-629-X $12.95 ($14.70 postpaid) from The World Almanac, One International Blvd., Mahwah, NJ 07495-0017; 201/529-6900

The Credit Repair Kit
John Ventura. 1993; 215 pp. ISBN 0-7931-0518-8 $19.95 ($23.95 postpaid) from Dearborn Financial Publishing, 520 N. Dearborn, Chicago, IL 60610; 800/829-7934

identity that is separate from a spouse's than it is to lose that identity and have to reestablish it later. Furthermore, as indicated earlier, having your own credit when married can greatly benefit your family during difficult financial times.

"LOVE YA, MOM. LOVE YA, DAD"

Helping Your Aging Parents Plan for the Day They'll Need You

by James M. Boswell

S UPPOSE THAT YOU ARE AN ADULT CHILD, with aging parents who live thousands of miles away. You talk by phone frequently, but always avoid the difficult topics of aging and paying for retirement. One day, you get a phone call from a neighbor. "Your Mom [or Dad] needs help. How soon can you get here? Who can pay the bills while she's ill?" The words you always said in phone calls — "love ya, Mom, love ya, Dad" — won't be enough today. You drop everything and fly back, only to find

> *Many of us face a looming crisis: sudden, devastating financial need by our parents, for which they and we are unprepared. Jim Boswell has seen the resulting grief and mishap many times. This article, based on his thirty years' experience helping people liquidate their parents' estate, is condensed from a book he is currently self-publishing — also called* **Love Ya, Mom. Love Ya, Dad.** *—Art Kleiner*

yourself engulfed by a crisis, with none of the support networks and services that you have cultivated. Worse still, because of illness or resentment, your parents can't easily tell you what they want. (In another era, you might have spent many hours on the porch, discussing the future with them.) The end result: you set up a long, degenerating existence for

them in a nursing home, paid for by hastily selling off their possessions, with both parent and child eventually confiding (but not to each other) that death would have been preferable.

These suggestions and resources can help you avoid that scenario.

• Early on, begin to ask your parents about their financial affairs: "Mom, Dad, do you have enough money to live in the style you want, both in the short and long term?" If the answer is "probably not," then selling their personal and real property will probably become a vehicle for financing their final years with dignity. This may be a difficult, embarrassing conversation for both of you, but it is necessary to avoid tragedy later.

For the details of estate planning, the best overall resource guide is *How to Settle an Estate* by C. K. Plotnick, Esq. and S. R. Leimberg (Consumer Reports, 1991). Or see *True Wealth* (p. 305). A great tool for helping your aging parents record and understand their assets is an IBM-compatible program called Getting It All Together (published by WWDB Radio; 800/833-WWDB). NOLO Press publishes a similar program, called NOLO's Personal RecordKeeper, for IBMs and Macs.

• Your parents should choose a manager of their affairs — both an executor of their wills, and someone trusted enough to be granted power of attorney while they are alive. This person needs the right to buy services in their name, sell their property, pay their debts, and use the money in their bank accounts if they become incapacitated. If you take on this role yourself, take the power of attorney document to a title insurance company and ask them to guarantee its legality. Otherwise, it may not be valid for real estate transactions.

If your parents want to set up a trust to transfer property and valuables to their children while they're alive, you should peruse *Plan Your Estate*

with A Living Trust by Denis Clifford (Nolo Press, 1992). You can find sample power-of-attorney forms in *Who Will Handle Your Finances If You Can't?* by Denis Clifford and Mary Randolph (Nolo Press, 1992); however, I emphatically recommend that you have your POA document overseen by a lawyer from your parents' home state.

• Beware the temptation to take part of your inheritance long before your parents pass away. When Mom and Dad run out of money, the children who have borrowed money or taken assets often conveniently forget this debt to their parents. You can avoid this by calculating, with your parents, their financial needs, and making sure enough property or money is set aside.

• Even once you've decided to sell your parents' property, it won't be easy for them to let go of special antiques and collectibles. To make this process bearable, remind each other that "nothing is forever." Your family may need to have a special ceremony to honor the items being liquidated, including recording the stories and memories represented in the material things. Make it a celebration, not an early funeral.

• In conducting the sale, avoid antique dealers; their purpose is to buy

cheap and sell high. Real estate brokers can involve you in a lengthy selling process. Your best bet is to hire a licensed real estate and personal property auctioneer (a member of the National Auctioneers Association and Certified Auctioneers Institute). As commissioned agents, auctioneers derive their fee from a percentage of sales. The more they make for their client, the more they make for themselves. They can appraise the value of the property (without conflict of interest), and tell you how to maintain it to get a good resale price. Choose local auctioneers; they have a vested interest in doing a superb job in their own hometown.

The author in his role as one of the resources he describes: a locally based auctioneer.

Guerrilla Financing

Some businesses — particularly manufacturing and technology start-ups — may require more capital than the average genius has sitting around in his or her garage. The "guerrilla" strategy for raising that money involves finding angels — wealthy, hands-on individual investors, generally in your own locale, who become your partner. (Come to think of it, that's how Steve Jobs originally financed Apple). This method is best used in conjunction with, not instead of, the "simple-living" strategy of starting with too little money, not too much. Bruce Blechman and Jay Conrad Levinson also offer an overview of other methods, including dealing with professional venture capitalists. —AK

•

Receivable financing is getting money from either a factor or receivable lender as you ship and bill or invoice your customers. You get your cash when you ship your orders without having to wait for your customers to pay. In some types of receivable financing, you get paid without even taking the risk

Guerrilla Financing
(Alternative Techniques to Finance Any Small Business)
Jay C. Levinson & Bruce Blechman. 1992; 352 pp. ISBN 0-395-52264-1
$10.95 ($13.45 postpaid) from Houghton Mifflin Co./Mail Order Dept., Wayside Road, Burlington, MA 01803; 800/225-3362

that your customer might never pay your bill!

The great aspect of receivable financing is that the faster your business grows and the more you ship, the more you will get in receivable financing. Receivable financing automatically adjusts to your rate of growth because it depends on your invoices to trigger the financing.

OTHER GREAT RESOURCES

How to Write a Business Plan: Mike McKeever. 1992, Nolo Press.

The best guide for small businesses. It discusses the options thoroughly and makes it easy for you to translate your personal goals into either an argument for someone else to invest in your future, or into the discovery that you're not ready.

The Grass Roots Fund Raising Book: Joan Flanagan. 1982, Contemporary Books and **The Grassroots Fundraising Journal:** $25/year (6 issues). Berkeley, CA 94701.

The preeminent resource book for nonprofit groups, activists, community organizations, and artists who need to develop financial sources of support.

The Corporate Finance Sourcebook:
1993, National Register Publishing.

Fifteen hundred pages-worth of listings of venture capitalists, financiers, lenders, and banks. Expensive, but available at some libraries. Good complement to Guerrilla Financing. [Suggested by Larry MacDonald]

Starting on a Shoestring

I've known for a long time that starting a business with little or no money is not only possible — it happens all the time. I started two businesses that way, and many of my tax clients are small businesses whose start-up capital is practically zero.

This book spells out how it's done better than any other I've seen, and it is just as useful for people who have a lot of money to start with. Business success really has little to do with how much money you do or don't have; it has more to do with common sense. —Bernard Kameroff

•

Balancing investment between "fixed assets" (furniture, fixtures, and equipment) and "working assets" (inventory and working capital) requires special consideration with the shoestring enterprise. The successful start-ups throw as much money as possible into the working assets and as little as possible into fixed assets.

There are two reasons for this strategy: First, it's the working assets that create the lifeblood for the shoestring venture — sales and cash flow. The second reason is that the carrying costs on expensive fixtures are a fixed cost the struggling shoestring venture can well do without.

I have seen many start-ups, particularly in the retail trades, with the fanciest fixtures in town and reciprocally the least amount of inventory in town. The lesson is that customers buy inventory not fixtures.

•

The shoestring enterprise rarely fails because it starts out with too much debt. It fails because the entrepreneur couldn't cultivate the creditors and put them on hold until the venture gained a financial foothold.

•

What the business can logically justify as an investment and what you will invest are two different numbers. The goal is to prune investment to the smallest possible amount. Cutting investment not only cuts losses but provides a better return on what you do

The Simple-Living Business Strategy

by Michael Phillips

IN THE EARLY 1970s, I became an advisor to hundreds of small businesses in the San Francisco area. When we counted up the numbers after ten years, my friends and I found that nineteen out of twenty of these businesses were still in operation five years after they had started. This contrasted sharply with the American norm (as true now as it was then), in which three-quarters of new small businesses fail after three years. The proprietors we advised had only one secret in common: they understood and practiced the values of simple living.

Simple living is an approach to life. It embodies austerity (few possessions, well cared for) as well as sensuality, flexibility, tolerance, and the avoidance of rigid ideologies. Those that practice it understand that business involves not just the exchange of goods and services for money, but also the exchange of information, caring, personal attention, repair, recourse, fun, visions, wisdom, and social values. "Simple living" businesses embody a sense of caring — about the welfare of suppliers, workers, customers, neighbors, the community, and friends. These businesses try not to be demeaning, degrading, destructive, rude or careless. Instead, they try to be honest, imaginative, educational, optimistic, far-sighted, and subtle. For example, many of these businesses have gained the long-standing trust of suppliers, customers, and creditors by making their books available to all.

Simple-living precepts nearly always outperform conventional business wisdom. For example, many financial experts state that small businesses fail because they are undercapitalized. Nonsense! Too much capital is often a more serious problem — it makes people lethargic. They become like Fred, a man who opened a natural-foods restaurant in a low-rent neighborhood with a large vegetarian population. Fred spent hundreds of thousands of borrowed dollars renovating his building to emulate an elegant restaurant in a ritzy resort town twenty miles away. As a result, his higher-priced food and "slick" atmosphere put people off. It took him two years of running an empty restaurant before he found a way to attract customers — he converted it into a singles' bar and grill.

By contrast, people who start their businesses without much cash (knowing that they will have to cut back their personal income if the business doesn't thrive) usually have high personal labor and emotional stakes invested in what they do. They respond immediately to suggestions about small changes that would help them reach customers. They develop the ability to innovate, the knowledge of how to cut overhead when they need to, and a network of mutually supportive people around them — all vital resources for any enterprise.

invest. In many of my own ventures I'll target the optimum investment at perhaps $10,000 - 15,000 and then see how I can accomplish the start-up goal with absolutely no money of my own.

Starting on a Shoestring
(Building a Business Without a Bankroll)
Arnold S. Goldstein. 1991; 284 pp.
ISBN 0-471-52455-7
$14.95 postpaid from John Wiley & Sons, Inc., 1 Wiley Dr., Somerset, NJ 08873; 800/225-5945

Running a One-Person Business

The number of people with their own single-person business, based at home or in a small office, has continued to grow exponentially. Since I joined the ranks in 1986, I've looked for guidance in each of the many books on the subject to come through Whole Earth. This is the first that I enthusiastically recommend.

I particularly like the double-barreled dose of practical concern. On one hand, all the financial nuts and bolts are covered. On the other, there is a useful discussion of the emotional and personal factors that make working on your own so exalting and so frustrating. —Art Kleiner

•

Bookkeeping is the most important part of any business. The first business system to put in place is your books. Most people focus on marketing first, but this is a dangerous strategy. Why? Because almost anything you do to promote business will work. And the better you are at promotion the more

business you can get. But without smoothly functioning financial and organizational systems in place, the increase in volume can swamp you and put you out of business overnight. The worst possible response would be to provide lower-grade services or products because you are unable to keep up with the demand. So focus on your financial and organizational systems first.

•

In many thriving one-person businesses the only bookkeeping is a checkbook and a file folder with receipts. In our experience, businesses with such casual bookkeeping practices are usually unable to grow to an efficient size or respond effectively to changes in market demand. They also operate without the elegance and perfection that is readily achievable in a one-person business.

Running a One-Person Business
Claude Whitmeyer, Salli Rasberry & Michael Phillips. 1988; 224 pp. ISBN 0-89815-237-2
$12 ($15.50 postpaid). Ten Speed Press, PO Box 7123, Berkeley, CA 94707; 800/841-2665

Home Office Computing

The most meaningful magazine for self-employed people who need information on technology and techniques. It covers telephones, answering machines, fax machines, computers, and small office equipment. And you'll learn how to manage your office, keep books and track clients, gather and use marketing information, and stay out of trouble with the IRS. Some of the product reviews are shallow, but in general the advice is solid and relatively untainted by advertising. —Claude Whitmyer

•

In my experience teaching seminars, I've found that many people hesitate to use the following technique because it frightens them: You need to create a notebook filled with laminated letters of recommendation from your clients. These testimonials, from real people, on real letterhead, are worth their weight in gold. Prospects know that you can't buy a glowing testimonial for any amount of money, and they're inclined to trust someone who has the ability to show them one positive letter after another.

Home Office Computing
Bernadette Grey, Editor.
$19.97/year (12 issues). PO Box 2511, Boulder, CO 80302; 800/288-7812

OTHER GREAT RESOURCES

The Complete Book of Small Business Legal Forms: Daniel Sitarz. 1991, Nova Publishing. If this book were on your shelf, you wouldn't have to go to the stationery store to get (for instance) a copy of a contract for sale of real estate or a simple receipt. —Barbara Blosser

Office and Computer Supplies

Office-supply companies are hotly competitive, and salesfolks are hungry. We always look for an edge. All of these companies meet our standards for customer service, accuracy of order placement, available stock on hand, flexibility of shipping and delivery, and return policies.

Quill is at the top of the list. They have excellent house brands and the largest overall selection. The quality of Office Depot's customer service department, and the knowledgeable service of their phone reps, are exemplary (their walk-in stores aren't nearly as efficient).

MicroWarehouse/MacWarehouse generally has the lowest prices for software. We use Inmac for cables, cases, and computer accessories, and usually check Mac Connection because their catalog is so friendly. Macintosh users take heed: if you don't specify your platform, mail-order houses will send you the MS-DOS catalog by default.

We wish these companies were more environmentally conscious. They overpackage items (placing a single order of Post-It Notes in a grocery-bag-sized envelope), and they seem to send a huge new catalog every laundry day. The best of the bunch is **Mac Connection** — their shipments are packed in starch-based (dissolvable) pellets.
—J.R. Viera and Carlos Winborn, Whole Earth front office

•
Targus Leather PowerBook Case
The look, luxury and protection of real leather at a remarkable price. Full grain cowhide with turned edges. PowerBook section 15" x 11" x 2.5" with padded adjustable divider to accommodate accessories.
—MacWarehouse

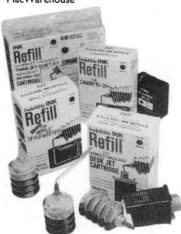

Supplies from Quill: 100% recycled self-stick notes, HP inkjet printer refill kits, and removable Post-it tape flags.

Small Business Accounting Programs

When you take on employees and have to handle payroll, you have outgrown personal finance bookkeeping programs. The next step for many small businesses is either Quick Books or One Write Plus. Quick Books allows you to change figures after the fact, giving greater flexibility, while One Write Plus is a "true double-accounting package" — once entered, items are preserved forever. This makes a difference if you have many employees and want to keep an audit trail.

If yours is a specialty business, and you belong to a trade association, see if there is a "vertical package" covering every financial and managerial task for your type of business. Even if it costs a couple of thousand dollars, it can often pay for itself by saving you the headache of reinventing an accounting system tailored to your business.

The best full-scale small business accounting and management package is Solomon. It's sold in modules for general ledger, accounts receivable, inventory, and payroll, all integrated together. You would need a program on this level when your business

reached, say, more than 100 transactions per month; for smaller businesses, Small-Time Operator may be sufficient.
—CW

Quick Books: IBM or compatible, DOS 3.0 or higher, 640K RAM, 3.5 MB on hard drive. $159.95 postpaid. Intuit, Inc./Order Processing, PO Box 3014, Menlo Park, CA 94026; 800/756-1855.

One-Write Plus: IBM or compatible, DOS 3.1 or higher, 640K RAM, 10 MB harddrive. $69.95 ($76.95 postpaid). NEBS Software, 50 Main Street, Graton, MA 01471; 800/388-4344.

Solomon: ODS modules $795 each, WIndows modules $1,295 each. Solomon Software, PO Box 414, Findley, OH, 45840; 800/879-2767 ext 783.

Small-Time Operator: The Software: Bernard Kamoroff, Steve Steinke & Emil Krause. And Books, 1992; 184 pp. ISBN 0-89708-205-2
Includes templates on disk: IBM or compatible (3 1/2" or 5 1/4") or Macintosh. Will work with most current spreadsheet software. $29.95 ($31.95 postpaid) Bell Springs Publishing, PO Box 640, Bell Springs Road, Laytonville, CA 95454; 707/984-6746

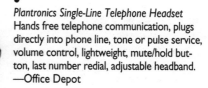

See also: How to Be an Importer and Pay for Your World Travel (p. 324).

•
Plantronics Single-Line Telephone Headset
Hands free telephone communication, plugs directly into phone line, tone or pulse service, volume control, lightweight, mute/hold button, last number redial, adjustable headband.
—Office Depot

Mac Connection: Catalog free. 14 Mill Street, Marlow, NH 03456; 800/800-0002.

Inmac: Catalog free. 2300 Valley View Lane, Irving, TX 75062; 800/547-5444.

Quill Office Products: Catalog free. PO Box 50-050, Ontario, CA 91761 or PO Box 94170, Palatine, IL 60094; 708/-634-8000, fax 708/634-5708.

Office Depot: Catalog free. 2200 Old Germantown Road, Delray Beach, FL 33445; 800/685-8800, fax 800/685-5010.

MacWarehouse/MicroWarehouse: Catalogs free. (MacWarehouse) 800/255-6227 (MicroWarehouse) 800/367-7080. Both: 1720 Oak Street Lakewood, NJ 08701.

Books about Specific Businesses

How to Start and Operate a Mail-Order Business: Julian L. Simon. 1993; 536 pp. ISBN 0-07-057565-7. $39.95 postpaid. McGraw-Hill Publishing Co., 13311 Monterey Avenue, Blue Ridge Summit, PA 17214; 800/722-4726. "The wisest investment a mail-order hopeful could make," author Kevin Kelly once wrote; he was one of many who started a successful mail-order business using this book as his text.

Starting a Small Restaurant: Daniel Miller. 1983; 224 pp. ISBN 0-916782-37-9. $9.95 postpaid. Harvard Common Press, 535 Albany Street, Boston, MA 02118; 617/423-5803. "A tough hands-on guide," says Michael Phillips, "for people who think their own cooking is great and that they should do it in their own restaurant."

So . . . You Want to Be an Innkeeper: Mary E. Davies et al. 1990; 224 pp. ISBN 0-87701-721-2. $12.95 ($16.45 postpaid). Chronicle Books/Order Dept., 275 5th Street, San Francisco, CA 94103; 800/722-6657. The best we've seen on this subject, a boon for the proprietors of small hotels and bed-and-breakfasts, and for their guests.

Weaving Profits: (How to Make Money Selling Your Handwovens): James Dillehay, Jr. 1992; 200 pp. ISBN 0-9629923-9-9. $19.95 postpaid. Warm Snow Publishers, Box 75, Torreon, NM 87061. Everything you need to know is here, and it's applicable to any craft.

—Landlording

Business Mastery (A Business Planning Guide. . .): Cherie M. Sohnen-Moe. 1991; 256 pp. ISBN 0-9621265-3-5. $19.95 postpaid. Sohnen-Moe Associates, 3906 W. Ina Road #200-348, Tucson, AZ 85741; 602/743-3936. Ostensibly for any type of business, this is really a guide for massage therapists, chiropractors, and other healing-arts professionals.

Landlording: Leigh Robinson. 1992; 414 pp. ISBN 0-932956-16-5. $21.95 postpaid. ExPress Publishing, PO Box 1639, El Cerrito, CA 94530; 510/236-5496. As Michael Phillips points out, this crisp, thorough manual is based on experience in Berkeley, California — "a tough area."

Shadow Merchants (Successful Retailing Without a Storefront): Jordan Cooper. 1993; 143 pp. ISBN 1-5595-105-7. $12.95 ($16.95 postpaid). Loompanics Unlimited, PO Box 1197, Port Townsend, WA 98368. How to make a living selling second-hand (or first-hand) goods, at flea markets or on street corners. —AK

The Legal Guide for Starting and Running a Small Business

Your small business legal questions will be answered in this volume. And if they're not, the author has included referrals to other specific texts for further detail. Very useful for the beginner. —Barbara Blosser

•

Keep in mind that if you put assets into a nonprofit corporation, you give up any ownership or proprietary interest in those assets. They must be irrevocably dedicated to the specified nonprofit purposes. If you want to get out of the business, you can't just sell it and pocket the cash. The nonprofit corporation goes on; if it ends, any remaining assets must go to another nonprofit.

•

How will partners be compensated? The first issue is how you'll divide profits once a year or at the end of some other fixed period. You should also determine if any partners can receive a monthly draw against their share of the profits—that is, be paid a portion of profits sooner than other partners. This might be appropriate if one partner is coming into the partnership with less savings than the others and is counting on partnership income for living expenses.

You'll also need to decide if any partners will receive a salary for work done in the business in addition to their share of profits. If equal partners will all work a roughly equal number of hours, there's no need to pay salaries; an equal division of profits with or without a draw should be adequate. But if one partner will work more hours than the others, paying that partner a salary may be sensible. Or you could give the harder working partner a larger share of the profits. If salaries are paid, they're a normal business expense and don't come out of profits.

The Legal Guide for Starting and Running a Small Business
Fred S. Steingold. 1992; 400 pp.
ISBN 0-87337-174-7
$22.95 ($26.95 postpaid). Nolo Press, 950 Parker Street, Berkeley, CA 94710; 800/992-6656, 510/549-1976

Small-Time Operator

Here's most of the financial recordkeeping information you need for a small business, plus a year's worth of ledger forms with excellent instructions on how to use them, plus good advice on key issues (such as when the IRS is likely to consider someone your employee).

The author lives the advice in the book. You can order a copy directly from him in Laytonville. He will package and ship it to you after he feeds the chickens and tends the garden. —Michael Phillips

The computer edition (e.g. see page 314) includes templates that run on any basic spreadsheet program. —Art Kleiner

Small-Time Operator
Bernard Kamoroff. 1993; 216 pp.
ISBN 0-917510-10-0
$14.95 ($16.95 postpaid); Bell Springs Publishing, PO Box 604, Bell Springs Road, Laytonville, CA 95454; 707/984-6746.

Growing a Business

Paul Hawken's central theme is that businesses are extensions of people, and that "successful" ones, like successful people, are valued by what they are, not by what they do — certainly not by how much money they have in the bank. If you are a good company, you'll be like a good person: helpful, interesting, honest, rewarded, and probably unstoppable. —Kevin Kelly

*Paul is no longer the proprietor of Smith & Hawken Tools, whose innovative business practices gave this book its foundation. (His more recent work, **The Ecology of Commerce**, is reviewed on p. 68.) But the precepts offered here — such as those about confronting conventional wisdom, building a sense of partnership with employees, and anticipating the detailed shifts of key business indicators — will always be current. —AK*

•

The only rational way to structure a company is in such a way that you would work well within it. In other words, you should create a company you would want to be the employee of, not merely the boss of. If you don't do that, you have instituted a double standard which will pervade the company and cause trouble. This is a major belief of mine, and it bears repeating.

The theory behind the "double standard" structure includes such assumptions as: you started the company, they didn't; you deserve everything you can get; you took the risk, you get the reward; if your workers were as smart and as enterprising as you, they would have their own company and wouldn't have to complain or be envious of your position; a living wage is sufficient, why pay more?

This standard is usually enforced in unsubtle ways, including dress, company cars, separate bathroom, deluxe office for you but cubbies for the clerks, and a host of other signals that tell your employees to keep their distance, know their place, respect your position and status. Most companies are organized this way—worldwide. The Japanese come closest to breaking this mold, but much of their camaraderie is superficial and depends on powerful cultural boundaries which cannot be transgressed by any worker without fear of censure.

Growing a Business
Paul Hawken. Fireside Books, 1987; 251 pp.
ISBN 0-671-67164-2
$11 postpaid. Simon & Schuster/Order Dept., 200 Old Tappan Road, Old Tappan, NJ 07675; 800/223-2336

The Soul of a Business

This book articulates the values, faith, joy, and dilemmas inherent in being a business person with a sense of greater purpose than merely making money. The author is perhaps the only corporate leader in America who took time out to go to divinity school. His principles have led him (and his wife/co-founder, and his employees) into some brilliantly innovative decisions. For instance, he chose not to sell his company to a big-bucks conglomerate, and to market only regionally instead of nationally. Tom Chappell describes these decisions in detail — including his reasoning, his doubts, and the step-by-step building of solid relationships among the people who had to carry them out. Among other things, the book is a valuable treatise on how to manage people; or, rather, how to find exaltation in leading a large group of them toward a common end.
—Art Kleiner

•

Our creative successes have been all about *intuition*. We have had a feel for what people think is good and what will meet that standard. Relying on our intuition and identification with our consumers gives us a very special relationship with the customer, a kind of intimacy. As in any special rela-

The Free and Responsible Corporation
(A social perspective to private incentive)

Co-Workers
Customers
Suppliers
Professional Growth
Opportunity
Quality
Be Clear
Innovation
Pay Promptly
Itself
Owners
Internal Health — Company — Build Value Dividends
Comply
Use It–Enjoy It
Draw from It
Give Back to It
Sustain and Protect
Government
Environment
Community

Responsibility in Relationships
Respect in Relationships
Balanced Responsiveness

Freedom in Service
Fulfilling Worklife

tionship, when you feel a bond with the other person, you want to imagine what it's like to be in their shoes. You want to feel their situation.

That's what Kate and I were doing with our children's brand. We knew why we had a passion for the idea — a natural fruit flavor made for a child's palate, no blue dyes, starbursts, or supersweet saccharin, no preservatives, none of the junk — even if we couldn't justify the integrity of the product by the numbers. We held our ground, Kate went ahead and developed a children's toothpaste, we shipped it, and it was an instant hit. Incredibly, 90 percent of our store accounts added Tom's Outrageous Orange and Silly Strawberry to their shelves, next to our adult toothpaste brands.

•

For years, receptionists lasted about as long as Murphy Brown's secretaries. And who

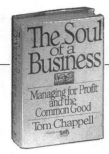

The Soul of a Business
(Managing For Profit and the Common Good)
Tom Chappell. Bantam Books, 1993; 272 pp. ISBN 0-553-47229-1 $21.95 ($24.45 postpaid). Bantam, Doubleday, Dell/Fulfillment Dept., 2451 S. Wolf Road, Des Plaines, IL 60018; 800/223-6834

could blame them? Answering the phone eight hours a day, and saying, "Hello, Tom's of Maine," is a brainless bore, as good a definition of existential hell as anyone could ever come up with. Finally, we said, no more full-time receptionists. The innovative alternative: Two full-time employees who work as secretaries also rotate daily for stints as receptionist. Incoming calls can be automatically routed to their phones. Answering the phone now is seen as "a break" from their other tasks.

The creative result: a revolving-door job gets continuity. Two employees get a break. The personnel budget saves the salary of one job position.

•

The problem: How could Tom's maintain productivity with a competent production team and not start a second shift, which would ruin the family life of those late-night workers? The ingenious solution worked out by chief financial officer Chet, who also heads up the

operational side of Tom's, and the manufacturing department: ten-hour days. Actually, the line workers put in only forty hours a week, but in four days. Crews choose different four-day stints, covering the entire week, often picking up a three-day weekend.

The creative result: manufacturing is boosted to fifty hours a week with a steady, experienced, happy crew, thus increasing overall productivity. The plan also preserved Tom's policy against working odd hours and weekends, which we all know wreaks havoc with normal family life.

Our Wildest Dreams

Excellence in business comes from operating from your strengths. Success in business means operating according to principles congruent with your psyche. This book lays out the relationship between these principles and the traits that are commonly attributed to women.

It's refreshing to see such qualities framed in a positive manner. Women who are rearing children will find that their familiar, underacknowledged skills apply in this widely valued context.
—Colleen Sumser

•

The right stuff required to launch a space shuttle, win a war, or head a traditional company may indeed be different from the "stuff" required to create the kinds of company so many women seem to envision. But if the goal is different, it is not necessarily lesser or easier. Those people intent on building companies that combine good work with good lives, demonstrate qualities rare enough and demanding enough to warrant a right stuff medal. Some of those qualities include:

1. Ease in relationships and a drive for connection
2. A head, heart and hands policy
3. Appreciation of complexity and process
4. Desire for balance and self-awareness
5. A sense of artistry, imagination and playfulness

Our Wildest Dreams
(Women Entrepreneurs Making Money, Having Fun, Doing Good)
Joline Godfrey. HarperBusiness, 1992; 246 pp. ISBN 0-88730-633-0 $11 ($13.75 postpaid). HarperCollins Publishers/Direct Mail, PO Box 588, Dunmore, PA 18512; 800/331-3761

6. An integrated vision of business and ethics
7. Courage

•

Women have been out of control for much of their lives — out of control of their rights, their financial well-being, their physical safety, and their access to opportunity. Women are rarely in a position to mandate anything, whether in politics, business, or often even in the home. In spite of that, women get things done. And they have learned to create, to influence, and to be powerful anyway. To be out of control is nothing to fear, it is an old friend, a familiar adversary that has caused us to develop other skills — skills that appear to work very well for business, thank you.

Body and Soul

Anita Roddick (founder of The Body Shop) gets a lot of publicity as a do-gooder, but she is also a fashion-business innovator. If you are running (or contemplating running) an enterprise that has to do with clothing, cosmetics, or anything fashionable — or if you are running a business that is socially responsible — I suspect you'll get a lot of inspiration, and a respect for purposeful outrageousness, out of her autobiography. A fashion business, like a theater, is uniquely focused on serving its audience.
—AK [Suggested by Claude Whitmyer]

•

The cheapest containers I could find were the plastic bottles used by hospitals to collect urine samples, but I could not afford to buy enough. I thought I would get round the problem by offering to refill empty containers or to fill customers' own bottles. In this way we started recycling and reusing materials long before it became ecologically fashionable, but again it was born out of economic necessity rather than a concern for the environment.

•

You have got to have energy to work with us and you have got to have a sense of curiosity, but what I particularly like is to find people who are bright enough to want more, who can see that there are ways of getting more within the company, who can learn and grow and be somebody, who take all the information and education we give them and run with it and challenge the management.

This happy franchisee started out as a shop staffer.

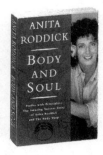

Body and Soul
Anita Roddick. Crown Publishing Group, 1991; 256 pp. ISBN 0-517-88134-9 $14 ($16 postpaid). Random House/Order Dept., 400 Hahn Road, Westminster, MD 21157; 800/733-3000

Post-Capitalist Society • The Effective Executive

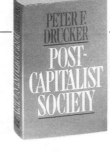

Drucker is to management what Fuller was to design and Bateson was to ecological thought: a major thinker who uses the command of one discipline to illuminate the whole range of human social relationships.

His 1992 **Post-Capitalist Society** *is a compelling vision of the current state of our wicked, beneficent, world-spanning free-market economy, and where it is likely to go in our lifetimes.*
—Michael Gruber

Many of Drucker's books are classics. Thirty years ago, **The Effective Executive** *set forth the principles that make people in a huge organization or a nonprofit or a commune accomplish what they want to accomplish. That book still serves as a primer for people entering the world of work; and if your organization or business has a lot of people who don't follow Drucker's precepts, you may be in serious trouble.*
—Art Kleiner

•

If we have learned one thing, it is that government cannot manage the economic "weather." Government cannot effectively prevent or overcome short-term economic fluctuations such as a recession. No one before 1929 expected government to be able to manage the economic weather. Since then, every government in every country has promised to be able to deliver on such a promise. Political leaders will have to learn to tell their constituents: "No one knows how to manage the economy short term any more than the physician knows how to cure the common cold. We'd better keep our hands off it." A corollary to this, however, is that the govern-ment does need to regain the ability to avoid major depressions. . . . The one effective way to counteract a depression—that is, a prolonged period of structural change—is through investment in the infrastructure; and after prolonged boom periods, the infrastructure (roads, bridges, harbors, public buildings, public lands) is always in bad repair. For governments to be able to finance such investments requires that they operate with a balanced budget during good times—and during recessions as well. They will then have the ability to raise money, especially through borrowing, when there is need to do so. In other words, governments have to learn again to keep deficits as the weapon of last resort.

•

The "super-rich" of the old capitalism were the nineteenth-century steel barons. The "super-rich" of the post-World War II boom are the computer makers, software makers, producers of television shows, and Ross Perot, the builder of a business installing and running information systems. Such great fortunes as were made in retailing — those of Sam Walton of Wal-Mart in the United States, Masatoshi Ito of Ito-Yokado in Japan, or the Sainsbury brothers in the United Kingdom — were made by reorganizing this old business around information.

In fact, whichever traditional industries managed to grow during the past forty years did so because they restructured themselves around knowledge and information. The integrated steel mill is becoming obsolete; even in low-wage countries, as we have seen, it cannot compete against the minimill. But a minimill is simply a steelmaker organized around information rather than around heat.

It is no longer possible to make huge profits on doing and moving things. It is no longer even possible to make huge profits by controlling money.
—Post-Capitalist Society

•

Individual self-development in large measure depends on a focus on contributions.

The man who asks of himself, "What is the most important contribution I can make to the performance of this organization," asks in effect, "What self-development do I need? What knowledge and skill do I have to acquire to make the contribution I should be making? What strengths to I have to put to work? What standards do I have to set myself?" —*The Effective Executive*

Post-Capitalist Society
Peter F. Drucker. HarperBusiness, 1993; 232 pp. ISBN 0-88730-661-6
$13 ($15.75 postpaid).

The Effective Executive
Peter F. Drucker. HarperBusiness, 1966; 1993; 178 pp. ISBN 0-88730-612-8
$12 ($14.75 postpaid).

Both from HarperCollins Publishers/Direct Mail, PO Box 588, Dunmore, PA 18512; 800/331-3761

—Marketing Without Advertising

this year, he received a postcard from the same florist, reminding him (1) that his mother's birthday was coming up, (2) that he had sent spider lilies and freesias last year for a certain price, and (3) a phone call to the specified number would put another beautiful bouquet on his mother's doorstep on her birthday this year.

This small, independent florist is working hard to improve her share of her customers' business. —*The One to One Future*

Guerrilla P.R.

From the jungles of the mainstream entertainment industry comes a startlingly unassuming, straightforward book (by Hollywood standards) on how to promote your business, yourself, or your cause. —AK

•

If you see an editorial that in some way relates to your project, consider contacting the station to respond. Editorial replies provide an opportunity to have your face and name broadcast across the city and further solidify your expert standing. To make this happen, contact the news department at the station and ask for the editorial director. Tell him or her you represent citizens with an opposing view and you'd like to reply. Send information on yourself and your project, such as your press kit.

If they give you the green light, you'll be informed of the parameters. You'll probably have sixty seconds to make your point. When writing your reply, think in bursts of quick three-sentence paragraphs, with your opening comments being the most potent. Begin by summarizing the station's view and stating why they're dead wrong. Detail a handful of reasons, again expressed in short easy-to-understand phrases. Close by urging a different direction, chiding the station for taking its position. That's it! You're a politician now!

Guerrilla P.R.
Michael Levine. HarperBusiness, 1993; 229 pp. ISBN 0-88730-664-0
$10 ($12.75 postpaid). HarperCollins Publishers/Direct Mail, PO Box 588, Dunmore, PA 18512; 800/331-3761

Millennial Advertising Schemes

The traditional industrial-age approach to getting customers — a big budget, foaming-at-the-mouth advertising, direct mail, and high-pressure wholesaling — doesn't work so well. (It never did for small business.) More and more books are appearing that reposition "selling" and "marketing" in terms of building better relationships with individual customers — respectful relationships, in which both sides respond to each other. Here are the three we like best.

Marketing Without Advertising *has the small, local, creative business person in mind. Your marketing task is not persuading customers, but educating them — and living up to the honesty and creativity that the role of educator demands.*

Guerrilla Marketing *offers creative, inexpensive promotion ideas — signs, telephone canvassing, trade shows, newspaper publicity, and so on. Jay Levinson's techniques are a bit opportunistic for my taste (as you might expect from a man whose four follow-up sequels include* **Guerrilla Marketing Attack** *and* **Guerrilla Marketing Weapons**), *but they do get attention.*

The One to One Future *offers a glimpse of how marketing will evolve in the next thirty years — away from mass consumerism, toward individual relationships with customers in which even the largest companies learn and respond fluidly. (Computers will keep track of the information, and coordinate the varied, individualized provision of products and services.) If you use electronic networks or have begun to think about targeting your customers with the help of a computer, you will find this book immensely valuable. —AK*

•

It is an excellent practice for businesses to print maps in the Yellow Pages as well as on any flyers or brochures. If you are hard to find, or if you draw customers from out of town, it behooves you to do this.
—*Marketing Without Advertising*

•

Because 61 percent of Americans read magazines from the back to the front, your economical classified ad will have a decent shot at being read.

As you may have heard, it doesn't cost an arm and a leg to run a classified ad. And you'll usually be offered a frequency discount. That means that if your five-line classified ad costs you $20 to run one time, it will only cost, say $18 per insertion if you run it three times, and only $15 per insertion if you run it five times. The more frequently you run it, the lower your cost per insertion.
—*Guerrilla Marketing*

•

Last year a friend of ours on the East Coast called a local, independent florist in a small midwestern city where his mother lived, to have flowers sent to her on her birthday. Three weeks before her birthday

Marketing Without Advertising (Creative Strategies for Small Business Success). Michael Phillips & Salli Rasberry. 1986; 200 pp.
ISBN 0-87337-019-8 $14 ($18 postpaid). Nolo Press, 950 Parker Street, Berkeley, CA 94710; 800/992-6656, 510/549-1976

Guerrilla Marketing (Secrets for Making Big Profits from Your Small Business). Jay Conrad Levinson. 1993; 327 pp. ISBN 0-395-64496-8 $11.95 ($14.45 postpaid). Houghton Mifflin Co./Mail Order Dept., Wayside Road, Burlington, MA 01803; 800/225-3362

The One to One Future (Building Relationships One Customer at a Time). Don Peppers & Martha Rogers. Doubleday Currency, 1993; 443 pp.
ISBN 0-385-42528-7 $22 ($24.50 postpaid). Bantam, Doubleday, Dell/Fulfillment Dept., 2451 S. Wolf Road, Des Plaines, IL 60018; 800/223-6834

HAT OLD DINOSAUR, THE CORPORATION, **is at a pivotal point of DEVOLUTION right now.**

Beneath the obvious signs (layoffs and downsizing), you can detect the rapid evaporation of most assumptions of the industrial era — such as the principle of economies of scale. Managers are discovering that the mental and hierarchical boundaries that once gave them strength are now straitjacketing them. The bankruptcy of making money at the expense of all other concerns is now evident. The effects of all this have not quite rippled out to the rest of our communities, but they will — often in unexpected ways; note, for instance, Hardin Tibbs's description of industrial ecology on p. 321.

How best to navigate the changes to come? Three strategies, I think, will help, whether you are employed in a large organization, just joining one, aspiring to join one, leading one — or opposing one.

 Be clear about your personal goals for the long run, and your aspirations for your organization.

Learn to produce good immediate performance, according to your standards — to preserve your credibility.

Pay attention to elements in your peripheral vision — people, ideas, strategies, and events that don't fit the prevailing wisdom.

Finally, cultivate the art of practicing all three of these strategies simultaneously.
—Art Kleiner

Everybody's Business • Hoover's Handbooks

As Mike Phillips points out, "Corporations have consistent behavioral qualities that resemble human personality. It is common to find a company which was notorious for bad labor relations fifty years ago and now is an environmental scofflaw. Likewise, corporations that were pioneers in high-quality products sixty years ago are now the first to have consumer representatives on their boards of directors." What we need, then, is a field guide to corporations whose products we use, whose stock we might buy, for which we might work, and near which we might live.

Everybody's Business provides incisive two- or three-page descriptions of American corporations, with lots of pictures and anecdotes and a strong sense of the companies' social and historical context.

The investor-oriented Hoover's Handbooks have more companies, more financial data, brief profiles crammed with gossip, and annual updates — a key advantage. They are entertainingly unstodgy. I particularly like the handbook of emerging companies, covering small entrepreneurial firms. Hoover's also produces regional guides to businesses in Texas, the San Francisco Bay area, Los Angeles, Chicago, and New York (valuable grist for jobseekers); CD-ROM versions of their listings; and online data banks on CompuServe, America Online and elsewhere (see p. 262). —AK

Outstanding corporate citizen — Social Conscience

Great place to work — Workplace

Lack of discernible social consciousness — Social Conscience

Woeful place to work — Workplace

●
More than 8 million Americans have worked for McDonald's at one time or another. McDonald's is the first employer of 1 out of every 15 Americans. They spend $1 billion a year on heart-tugging advertising, making McDonald's the single most advertised brand in the world.

McDonald's has only one business, and they manage it with machinelike precision. They worry as much about keeping the bathrooms clean as they do about the texture of the french fries and the thickness of the milk shakes. This is a franchise business — McDonald's owns only one-quarter of the restaurants — and getting a franchise is not easy.

Hamburgers are still the mainstay, but the average McDonald's today has a 33-item menu that includes chicken (they're the world's second largest retailer of chicken after Kentucky Fried Chicken), salads, decaf coffee and sausages — and in 1990 they were experimenting with a new pizza cooked in 5-1/2 minutes.

●
The Old-fashioned Full-line Department Stores The 1980s were open hunting season on the old, gracious, wide-aisled department stores as they came under siege from raiders of various nationalities and with various motives. They also had to defend their turf against invasions by new specialty stores honing in on a particular area: The Limited in trendy women's wear, the Gap in casual wear, Circuit City in consumer electronics, Crate & Barrel in home accessories. It was a turbulent period. Among the department stores changing hands were Marshall Field, Saks Fifth Avenue, Lord & Taylor, Foley's, I. Magnin, Bloomingdale's and Filene's. Among the stores closing their doors were B. Altman, Gimbel's, Liberty and Bonwit Teller. Peter J. Solomon, a New York investment banker who follows the retail industry, summed it up this way: "Department stores are at the end of their life cycle and have to be reinvented. People are more sophisticated. They don't want to go out and wander around department stores anymore. Department stores are no longer the dominant form of retailing, although, when good, they still have a tremendous amount of capital, muscle and drawing ability." —*Everybody's Business*

●
Going once. Going twice. Gone. Selling at the highest price is the business of Sotheby's Holdings, the world's premier auction house. . . . The Bloomfield Hills, Michigan-based company is not just for the rich and famous, however. The average lot size is less than $9,000. Sotheby's makes money before the auction by loaning money to the seller prior to the artwork's sale. The company makes money at the

Everybody's Business
Milton Moskowitz. 1990; ISBN 0-385-41629-6 $22.50 ($25 postpaid). Bantam, Doubleday, Dell/Fulfillment Dept., 2451 S. Wolf Road, Des Plaines, IL 60018; 800/223-6834

Hoover's Handbook of American Business
Gary Hoover, Alta Campbell & Patrick J. Spain. 1993; 1288 pp. ISBN 1-878753-21-5 $24.95 ($28.45 postpaid)

Hoover's Handbook of World Business
Alan Chai, Alta Campbell & Patrick J. Spain. 1994; 752 pp. ISBN 1-878753-43-6 $21.95 ($25.45 postpaid).

Hoover's Handbook of Emerging Companies
Patrick Spain, Alta Campbell & Alan Chai, Editors. 1993; 432 pp. ISBN 1-878753-17-7. $21.95 ($25.45 postpaid).

The Texas Five Hundred
Reference Press Staff, Editors. 1994; 297 pp. ISBN 1-878753-39-8. $14.95 ($18.45 postpaid).

The Bay Area Five Hundred
Reference Press Staff, Editors. 1994; ISBN 1-878753-52-5. $24.95 ($28.45 postpaid).

All from The Reference Press, Inc., 6448 Highway 290 East, Suite E-104, Austin, TX 78723; 800/486-8666, fax 512/454-9401

auction by charging commissions to both the buyer and the seller of the property.
—*Hoover's Handbook of American Business 1994*

●
Around 1630 Masatomo Sumitomo, a Buddhist priest from the Kyoto area, opened a medicine shop/bookstore following the dissolution of his sect. His descendants have preserved his writings on business ethics and consider him the spiritual founder of the Sumitomo group. The technological founder of the group was Riemon Soga, Sumitomo's brother-in-law, who researched and duplicated a Western copper-smelting technique, enabling him to build a prosperous copper company. After Soga died in 1636, his son, Tomomochi, married Sumitomo's daughter and became the head of the Sumitomo family. —*Hoover's Handbook of World Business 1993*

MAGAZINES FOR UNDERSTANDING THE CORPORATE WORLD

Multinational Monitor: $25/year (10 issues). PO Box 19405, Washington, DC 20036. This Ralph Nader-associated newsletter spells out the dangerous and malicious practices of large international corporations. It's one of the most compelling sources of information for watchdogs, activists, and business managers.

Business Ethics: $59/year (6 issues). PO Box, 14748, Dayton, OH 45413; 612/962-4700. Utopian workplaces, management ethics, corporate social responsibility, ethical investing, business environmentalism, anti-war advertising, and other life on the edge between business and social reform.

Harvard Business Review: $75/year (6 issues). PO Box 52623, Boulder, CO 80322; 800/274-3214. One-third vanity press for academics, one-third practical case histories of corporate achievement, and one-third groundbreaking insights into governance, systemic understanding, management, and the economy.

Fast Company: $29.95/year (6 issues). 1100 Massachusetts Ave., Cambridge, MA 02138; 800/505-FAST. Created by two former **HBR** editors, it's more outspoken, wider-ranging, and more eye-catching than **HBR**. It looks likely to become a credible resource for judging the value of management fads and fancies. —AK

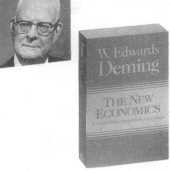

Out of the Crisis • The New Economics

Dr. W. Edwards Deming is a folk-mythic figure in mainstream business circles. Ignored in the US for thirty years after World War II, Deming taught Japanese industrialists some principles for making quality products — and helped spark that country's economic boom. His portrait in Toyota headquarters is larger than that of the company's founder. His personality was also mythic: abrasive, willing to yell at CEOs in public meetings, but also humble and responsive enough to be revered for his courtesy in Japan.

The statistical diagnostic techniques Deming taught distinguish "common causes" (everyday ups and downs) from "special causes" (unusual shocks to the system), thus showing how to improve systems overall. Deming used these techniques to argue that all "extrinsic" motivations — grades in school, bonuses, rankings, commissions, exhortations to work harder, objectives — do more harm than good. Corporations, he asserted, should learn to judge their purpose according to the standards of their customers, instead of their high-status experts. If Deming's ideas ever catch on, life will be like a Frank Capra movie — and his deepest appeal comes from making it seem that such idealism is not just possible, but necessary.

Partly because his concepts go against many managers' feelings about power, authority, and human nature, there are no fully "Demingite" companies — not even in Japan. Nonetheless, his influence is immense and, despite the hype that "Total Quality" gets, genuinely beneficial. (Compare a new Ford or GM car to one from the early 1980s.) Nor is "Demingism" just for corporations; in my one-person business, I now realize that the effectiveness of subcontractors I hire depends far less on their own capabilities than on how well I prepare for them.

Like learning about Zen, learning about Deming can be frustrating at first. His first book, **Out of the Crisis***, is 500 pages of terse, semi-explained, oracular anecdotes, aphorisms, and nuts-and-bolts charts.*

OTHER GREAT RESOURCES

Team Handbook: Peter Scholtes. 1988, Joiner Associates. For teams learning the tools and skills of taking charge of their own shop floor or office processes.

Service America: Karl Albrecht & Ron Zemke. 1990, Warner Books. For managers of service businesses or service-oriented departments (like technical support).

Quality or Else: Lloyd Dobins & Clare Crawford-Mason. 1993, Houghton Mifflin. The definitive biographical scorecard to the intellectual and managerial pioneers (of eight countries) who created the quality movement.

Everyday Heroes of the Quality Movement: Perry Gluckman & Diana R. Roome. 1993, Dorset House. Six fables about people in typical corporate roles, struggling with the unfamiliar ways of thinking that a quality-building effort typically summons forth. —AK, *with suggestions from Suzanne Thomson and Charlotte Roberts of Innovation Associates, Framingham, MA*

Shortly before he died in 1993, Deming completed a shorter overview, **The New Economics***, based on the four-day seminars he gave for thousands of middle managers. It's not really an introduction to his work (see instead the* **Team Handbook***, this page); rather, it's an introduction to his kindly, abrupt, and unusually compelling mind.* —Art Kleiner

•

Railway cars, as they pass by, are loaded with hot iron ore pellets. Pellets piled too high in a car may fall off and be lost as the train goes around a curve. Loss of half a metric ton of pellets in this way from a car was not unusual.

The plate at **A** smooths out the mountains and valleys in the top surface of the pellets as the loaded cars move by it. The result is improved uniformity and greater tonnage

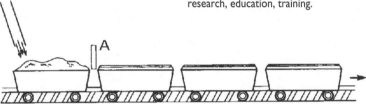

per car. Why had not the engineers thought of this before? They supposed that the loader, if she tried hard enough, could shrink the variation. Their thoughts had not before turned to the possibility that the system could be changed.

•

Pursuit of the quarterly dividend and short-term profit defeat constancy of purpose. Whence cometh the scramble for the quarterly dividend? What is the driving force that leads to the last-minute rush into a good showing on the quarterly dividend? Anyone can boost the dividend at the end of the quarter, regardless of quality: mark it shipped, and show it all as accounts receivable. Defer till next quarter, so far as possible, orders for material and equipment. Cut down on research, education, training.

•

As we shall see, apparent differences between people arise almost entirely from action of the system they work in, not from the people themselves. A man not promoted is unable to understand why his performance is lower than someone else's. No wonder; his rating was the result of a

lottery. Unfortunately, he takes his rating seriously. —*Out of the Crisis*

•

The manager of a company prescribed strict rules for absence of three days to attend a funeral and family affairs for the death of a near relative. He defined with care a near relative. An employee might even be required to produce a death certificate. Saturday and Sunday and a holiday are counted in the three days. Result: every employee took all three days at every bereavement. Then came somehow a change of heart. Let the employee make arrangements with his supervisor for absence. Result: days off for bereavement dropped to half.

•

Posted in the work rooms of a hotel: *This division has worked 7 days without an accident.* (Day after day, the sign stayed the same, 7 days.) —*The New Economics*

Out of the Crisis
W. Edwards Deming. 1986; 507 pp.
ISBN 0-911379-01-0
$60 ($63.50 postpaid).

The New Economics
(for Industry, Government, Education)
W. Edwards Deming. 240 pp.
ISBN 0-911379-05-3
$40 ($43.50 postpaid).

Both from Massachusetts Institute of Technology, Center for Advanced Engineering Study, 77 Massachusetts Avenue Room 9-234, Cambridge, MA 02139; 617/253-7444, fax 617/253-8310

Productive Workplaces

People have been trying to understand the relationship between workers and work, managers and companies, people and institutions, since the earliest days of the industrial revolution (cf. "scientific management" pioneer Frederick Taylor). The scrutiny picked up steam after World War II, with management theory innovators Kurt Lewin, Eric Trist, and Douglas McGregor. Here is the history of that venerable tradition of study, told by a creative management innovator. Marvin Weisbord began to explore the theories of work when he had to figure out how to run his own company; he describes his own experiences using them.

Among other things, this book is a terrific introduction to the team-based "sociotechnical" concept for organizing large endeavors (corporate or nonprofit) as if they were effective democracies. —Art Kleiner [*Suggested by Jeffrey Kaplan*]

•

Lewin's major contribution to management was his way of thinking: every change requires a new participative experiment. That is *the* central tenet behind the concept of a learning organization. It's also the hardest principle to master if you have been trained, in the Taylor tradition, as an "expert."

•

Using knowledge from Lewin, Bion, and the Norwegian field projects, Fred Emery drew up a list of six intrinsic factors that make work satisfying:

1. Variety and challenge
2. Elbow room for decision making
3. Feedback and learning
4. Mutual support and respect
5. Wholeness and meaning
6. Room to grow — a bright future

The first three must be optimal — not too much, which adds stress and anxiety, nor too little, which produces stultifying tedium. The second trio are open-ended. No one can have too much respect, growing room, or "wholeness" — meaning a view of both the origin and the customer's use of your work.

Productive Workplaces
(Organizing and Managing for Dignity, Meaning, and Community)
Marvin R. Weisbord. 1987, 1991; 433 pp.
ISBN 1-55542-370-1
$19.95 ($23.45 postpaid). Jossey-Bass Publishers, 350 Sansome Street, San Francisco, CA 94104; 415/433-1767

EFFECTIVE ORGANIZATIONS

OLD PARADIGM [EARLY 20TH CENTURY]	NEW PARADIGM [LATE 20TH CENTURY]
• TECHNOLOGY FIRST	• SOCIAL/TECHNICAL SYSTEMS OPTIMIZED TOGETHER
• PEOPLE AS MACHINE EXTENSION	• PEOPLE COMPLEMENT MACHINE
• PEOPLE AS SPARE PARTS	• PEOPLE AS SCARCE RESOURCE
• NARROW TASKS, SIMPLE SKILLS	• MULTIPLE, BROAD SKILLS
• EXTERNAL CONTROL: PROCEDURES BOOK	• SELF-CONTROL: TEAMS AND DEPARTMENTS
• MANY LEVELS, AUTOCRATIC STYLE	• FLAT ORGANIZATION PARTICIPATIVE STYLE
• COMPETITIVE	• COOPERATIVE
• ORGANIZATION'S PURPOSES ONLY	• INDIVIDUAL AND SOCIAL PURPOSES INCLUDED
• ALIENATION: "IT'S ONLY A JOB"	• COMMITMENT: "IT'S MY JOB"
• LOW RISK-TAKING	• INNOVATION

The Fifth Discipline • The Fifth Discipline Fieldbook

The literature of organizational change abounds with rehashings of elderly formulas. Self-renewal, quality circles, Total Quality Management, Management by Objectives, process redesign, projectized teams: all struggle with the perpetual problem of keeping work organizations flexible and adaptive. They miss the central insight of The Fifth Discipline: visible problems are symptoms of a systemic disorder.

Many smart people in the field have avoided or missed this simple but critical conclusion. Local action is easier to plan and execute without assuming the responsibility for global thought. Symptoms are easier to identify than disease.

Peter Senge can see and describe systemic disorder with clarity. He provides a solid beginning for a wholistic working description of the organization. His book describes a vision of health ("the learning organization") and models a method for diagnosing and mending organizational problems. It should be a part of every leader's toolkit.

In The Fifth Discipline Fieldbook, Senge and his associates (including Art Kleiner, editor of this section) have assembled the basic concepts of organizational change in a compact package. It is a fast introduction and a useful concordance. —John Sumser

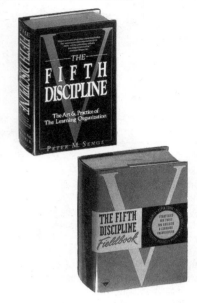

The Fifth Discipline
(Mastering the Five Practices
of the Learning Organization)
Peter M. Senge. Doubleday & Co., 1990;
424 pp. ISBN 0-385-26094-6
$27.50 ($31 postpaid).

The Fifth Discipline Fieldbook
(Strategies and Tools for
Building a Learning Organization)
Peter M. Senge, et al. Doubleday & Co.,
1994; 574 pp. ISBN 0-385-47256-0
$29.95 ($33.45 postpaid).
Both books $57.45 ($61.45 postpaid). Resources Connection, PO Box 10699,
Rochester, NY 14610; 800/295-0957

•

Find and cultivate "zoysia plugs." Zoysia is a grass, originally indigenous to Asia, which people sometimes use to start lawns. You water and fertilize plugs of grass scattered far apart. Eventually they find each other and meld into a carpet covering the whole lawn. In organizations, "zoysia plugs" are people who share your passion. They are also informal leaders who know how to "make things happen." Find them, wherever they may be, and support them however you can. Eventually, when they reach a level of critical mass, you may feel the atmosphere of the entire enterprise shift. —The Fifth Discipline Fieldbook

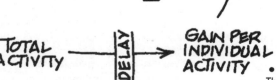

The tragedy of the commons.
—The Fifth Discipline

The Tragedy of the Commons:

Description: Individuals use a commonly available but limited resource solely on the basis of individual need. At first they are rewarded for using it; eventually, they get diminishing returns, which causes them to intensify their efforts. Eventually, the resource is either significantly depleted, eroded, or entirely used up.

Early Warning Symptom: "There used to be plenty for everyone. Now things are getting tough. If I'm going to get any profit out of it this year, I'm going to have to work harder."

Management Principle: Manage the "commons," either through educating everyone and creating forms of self-regulation and peer pressure, or through an official regulating mechanism, ideally designed by participants. —The Fifth Discipline

The Age of Unreason • The Seven Cultures of Capitalism

Two breadth-expanders from British philosophers of work, both focused on "discontinuities" — breaks between the familiar and the world to come. The Age of Unreason, Charles Handy's most powerful book, presents a tour of how large organizations might evolve during the next fifty years (flexible, disloyal, decentralized, and dependent on part-time intelligent subcontractors).

In The Seven Cultures of Capitalism, Charles Hampden-Turner (along with Dutch consultant Alfons Trompenaars) looks at the differences between business attitudes in individualistic America, harmony-seeking Japan, long-range Germany, egalitarian Sweden, the decentralized Netherlands, special-interest-driven Britain, and status-conscious France. All of these forms create wealth; any business, large or small, could learn from all of them.

Both of these books feel "pointless" at first, but that's their strength. They open up possibilities for how organizations, and societies, might be formed. —Art Kleiner

•

Organizations have got to get used to the idea that not everyone wants to work for them all the time even if the jobs are available. The ways of the core cannot be and should not be the ways of the flexible labor force, for while some may hanker after full-time lifetime jobs, many will not.

•

One of the older faculty members said [to the new business school president], gently, "Bill, in this kind of institution you cannot *tell* us to do anything; you can only *ask* us and try to persuade us to agree."

"Well then," Bill said, "let me ask you what you think we should do to put some sense into this place."

"No, Bill," the elder replied, "that's what we hired *you* for, to come up with those sort of ideas. But they will only work if we agree with them. If we don't, then you will have to persuade us or come up with some better ideas. This is, you see, an organization of consent, not of command." —The Age of Unreason

•

American scholarship dominates the field [of business administration] because it has been largely Americans who believe that any universal code of management is possible. Japan and Germany do not lack business schools because they do not know how to manage well; rather, they lack such schools because they do not believe that anything, from the running of a funeral parlor to the production of low-frequency transducers, can be covered by a coherent set of universally valid laws. It is by no means self-evident that such laws are discoverable or, even, that they exist.

•

An unusual feature of German business culture is the very large number of small and medium-sized private companies, still run by founders and their families and with an extraordinary record of sophistication and export orientation. These are among the *Mittlelstande,* the medium-sized companies at the heart of the economy, which dominate the machine-tool industry and produce 75 percent of the chemical industry's output. What is unusual about these companies is their preference for small, lucrative niches, for example, dough-kneading machines, and their disinterest in growing any larger, that is, beyond the size where people no longer have access to the private spaces of co-workers.
—The Seven Cultures of Capitalism

**The Seven Cultures
of Capitalism**
Charles T. Hampden-Turner and Alfonse
Trompenaars. Currency Books, 1993;
403 pp. ISBN 0-385-42101-X
$27.50 ($30 postpaid). Bantam, Doubleday,
Dell/Fulfillment Dept., 2451 S. Wolf Road,
Des Plaines, IL 60018; 800/223-6834

The Age of Unreason
Charles Handy. 1989; 278 pp.
ISBN 0-87584-301-8
$12.95 ($15.95 postpaid). Harvard Business School Press/Operations Dept., Soldier's Field, Boston, MA 02163; 617/495-6700

Kalundborg's "Industrial Symbiosis"

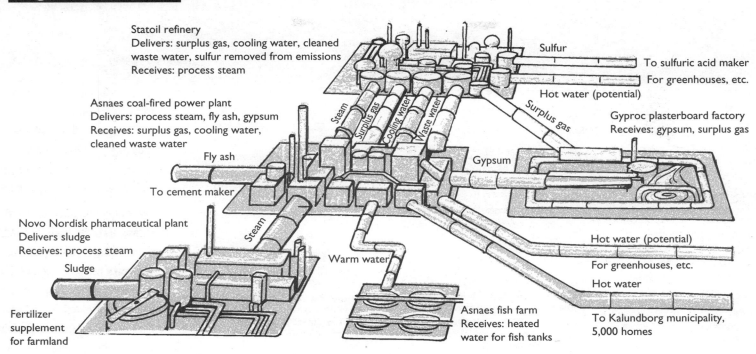

Statoil refinery
Delivers: surplus gas, cooling water, cleaned waste water, sulfur removed from emissions
Receives: process steam

Sulfur

To sulfuric acid maker
For greenhouses, etc.

Hot water (potential)

Asnaes coal-fired power plant
Delivers: process steam, fly ash, gypsum
Receives: surplus gas, cooling water, cleaned waste water

Gyproc plasterboard factory
Receives: gypsum, surplus gas

Fly ash

Gypsum

To cement maker

Novo Nordisk pharmaceutical plant
Delivers sludge
Receives: process steam

Hot water (potential)
For greenhouses, etc.

Hot water

Sludge

Warm water

Asnaes fish farm
Receives: heated water for fish tanks

To Kalundborg municipality, 5,000 homes

Fertilizer supplement for farmland

First at Arthur D. Little, and then as a senior consultant with Global Business Network (a unique organization that explores and plans for client companies' possible alternative futures), Hardin Tibbs has refined a vision of how to reframe industrial society. New projects and prototypes are emerging around the world; we expect that all industrial areas will operate this way in fifty years, and hopefully much sooner.
—Art Kleiner

A considerably expanded and much more detailed exposition of Industrial Ecology is available from Global Business Network.

Industrial Ecology
(An Environmental Agenda for Industry): Hardin Tibbs. 1993; 28 pp. $3 ($4.31 postpaid) GBN, PO Box 8395, Emeryville, CA 94662; 510/547-6822, fax 510/547-8510

INDUSTRIAL ECOLOGY is a technical and management approach to reshaping large-scale manufacturing and energy infrastructures as an ecologically integrated system. Instead of trying to conquer nature, the manufacturing community cooperates with it. Human-made "industrial ecosystems" (encompassing factories, chemical refineries, and power plants) are designed to interface with the natural ecosystem — from local water and soil ecologies to the global ecosystem. In fact, industry adopts the pattern of organization of the natural environment, and uses that model for solving environmental problems. If we can recreate the industrial world this way, it will provide a built-in insurance against future environmental surprises, because their essential causes will have been designed out.

Many characteristic features of a natural ecosystem are emulated in the industrial ecology approach:

• There is no such thing as waste in the system as a whole. Nutrients for one type of organism are derived from the death and decay of another.

• Concentrated toxins are not stored or transported in bulk, but are synthesized and used only as needed at the point of use.

• Materials and energy are continually circulated and transformed in extremely elegant ways. The system runs entirely on ambient solar energy; over time it actually shows a net gain of stored energy (in the form of fossil fuel), instead of depleted energy.

• The system permits independent activity by individual organisms (and species), yet cooperatively meshes the activities of all species. Cooperation and competition are interlinked — held in balance.

Building an industrial ecosystem means more than simply recycling materials and products

in a region. It involves creating an extensive "food web" between companies and industries to optimize the use of materials and embedded energy.

The example that demonstrates this concept best, to date, is this network of companies in the town of Kalundborg, Denmark (see above).

These companies have created a permanent waste-exchange system in the industrial district of their medium-size city. The byproduct of one industry becomes another's raw material. For example, Statoil, an oil company, removes sulfur from its natural gas, to make it cleaner-burning. The sulfur is sold to the Kemira chemical company's sulfuric-acid plant. The cooperative network (which evolved primarily as a result of business decisions, not government regulation) involves not just the refinery and sulfuric-acid plant, but an electric power-generating plant, a biotechnology production plant, a plasterboard factory, cement producers, local agriculture and horticulture, and district heating in the town of Kalundborg. Among the wastes that are traded, some by direct pipeline, are water at various levels of heat and purity, sulfur, natural gas, industrial gypsum, and fly ash.

A critical component of industrial ecology is an acceleration of dematerialization — a technologically driven decline in the amount of material and energy used to produce industrial goods. This is environmentally favorable, since it decouples economic growth from growth in materials use — a fundamental issue in the "growth versus environment" debate. Value is added by emphasizing information, or embedded knowledge, in place of product mass. This is how Japanese electronics manufacturers, who set themselves a deliberate goal of rapidly miniaturizing their products, were able to enhance the features of those products in the process.

—Hardin Tibbs

OTHER GREAT RESOURCES: CORPORATE ENVIRONMENTALISM

Pollution Prevention Review: Jean Stephenson, Editor. $132/year (4 issues). PPR/ Executive Enterprises Publications, 22 W. 21st Street, New York, NY 10010-6904; 800/332-8804. Best nitty-gritty journal for large companies (and their industrial suppliers) putting waste reduction techniques into practice.

In Business: Ruth Benedict, Editor. $18/year (12 issues). Magna Publications, 2718 Dryden Drive, Madison, WI 53704; 608/249-2455, fax 608/249-0355. Once a general small-business magazine, **IB** has evolved into the premier publication for environmentally oriented enterprise. (Suggested by Claude Whitmyer)

The E Factor (Joel Makower. 1993, Random House) and **The Green Business Letter:** Joel Makower, Editor. $127/year (12 issues). Tilden Press Inc., 1526 Connecticut Ave. NW, Washington, DC 20036; 800/955-GREEN (202/332-1700 in DC). Who's doing what, in corporate environmentalism, and why? Veteran business/ environmental journalist Makower reveals all thoroughly and insightfully.

EcoManagement: Ernest Callenbach, Fritjof Capra & Lenore Goldman, Rüdiger Lutz & Sandra Marburg. 1993, Berrett-Koehler Publishers. The first step in any act of corporate environmentalism is an audit. Here's how to plan and conduct an audit in detail.

Fifty Simple Things Businesses Can Do to Save the Earth: Earthworks Group Staff, Editors. 1991, Earthworks. From the people who brought you **Fifty Simple Things You Can Do to Save the Earth**. (Suggested by Tom White)

While our oPporTuniTiEs to reap the benefits of **Cultural exchange** have **mULTIpliEd** exponentially, so have the RISKS of SPOILING more **eco**systems and impinging on the economic, religious, and ethical values of traditional societies. Travelers need to cultivate an increased awareness and responsibility, not just of what they can gain from other people and places, but of what they're bringing with them and leaving behind.

Traveling remains the most invigorating natural high around. While money will get you anywhere, any way, you learn the most by traveling independently and on the ground. With the tools we present here, we hope to help travelers both experience and enrich other people and places, with an open mind and an open heart.
—Richie Unterberger

Lonely Planet

In 1973, Maureen and Tony Wheeler published their first Lonely Planet book, **Across Asia On The Cheap**, after traveling from England to Australia on a shoestring budget. Twenty years later, Lonely Planet has the largest catalog of international, independent, budget travel books of any publisher. Ask travelers who stray even slightly from the beaten track what their bible of choice is; chances are that they will name Lonely Planet guides.

LP offers guidebooks and phrasebooks for such underguided destinations as Iceland, the Arab gulf states, and Laos. Specialized guides cover cities, bushwalking and trekking, and traveling with children.

With the most thorough coverage of the Third World by far, Lonely Planet was instrumental in developing a network of adventurous and responsible independent Third World travelers. Their guidebooks not only include maps and information on sights, transportation, and accommodations; they also detail local customs, food, and neighborhoods, and give readers essential historical and cultural background. Without preaching, they urge readers to be aware of the environmental and social impact of their visit.

Updated every other year, the guidebooks incorporate information from hundreds of letters a week LP receives from readers. LP also offers a free quarterly newsletter of travelers' tips and anecdotes. —RU

•

We saw none of Delhi's sights, as we were attending a wedding. Indian weddings last longer than some English marriages, the wedding in question extending over a week. There was a series of parties enlivened by a vigorous and turbaned band whose traditional village songs contained Western interpolations. 'Bee-bop-a-looba' surfaced at one point, and another song, sung in Hindi. Sometimes the songs seemed to be in English. I thought I heard 'I'm a pon-y-y, you are poorly-y-y, I am bony-y-y, I'm a phony-y-y.' There was a touch of the cha-cha-cha about this one.

For the ceremony itself you were required to remove your shoes and cover your head. Not having been alerted to this in advance, I sported a big toe through a hole in one of my socks and wore on my head a handkerchief dotted with specially black bogeys caused by Delhi's pollution. —Oliver Black, UK

Lonely Planet Travel Newsletter
Free (4 issues/year). Lonely Planet, Embarcadero West, 155 Filbert Street, Suite 251, Oakland, CA 94607-2538; 800/275-8555. Internet: lonely@crl.com
Compuserve: 71165, 507
America OnLine: Inlyplanet

•

Mozambique is a wonderful country to visit. The people are very welcoming and patient. Prices are still at war-scarcity levels and lodging has risen even higher due to heavy demand from UN aid workers and returning refugees. Beira is hopping with UN soldiers from all over the world, and tourists are still rare enough to be welcomed into peoples' homes. It is no longer necessary to pay for food or lodgings in foreign currency, except for the most expensive hotels. Electricity and running water are still problematical. —Hilary McQuie, USA

OTHER GREAT RESOURCES

Americans Traveling Abroad (What You Should Know Before You Go): Gladson I. Nwanna. 1994; ISBN 0-9623820-4-3. $39.99 ($43.99 postpaid). World Travel Institute Press, PO Box 32674, Baltimore, MD 21208-8674; 800/247-6553.

Moon Publications

Although not as extensive as Lonely Planet, either in its range of titles or the depth of its coverage, Moon Publications offers several dozen international guidebooks that are also geared toward the inquisitive, independent traveler. Especially strong on the South Pacific, Hawaii, and Central America, they offer specialized guides to the Yucatan, Micronesia, and outback Australia, that are rarely afforded book-length coverage. They also have guides to thirteen US states and a few Canadian provinces that are extremely detailed and useful. All of their publications give considerable coverage of regional history and culture.

Moon also offers a free, quarterly "alternative travel" newsletter, **Travel Matters**, that features full-length articles about off-the-track destinations, reviews of other travel books, and miscellaneous news and tips; travelers will find it both useful and entertaining. Their catalog offers a wide range of independent travel guides from many publishers.

Lonely Planet and Moon aren't just guidebooks: through the resources listed, motivated readers could find out almost everything there is to know about international independent travel, from traveling healthy to trekking in Nepal. —RU

Travel Matters
Free (4 issues/year) from Moon Publications, Inc., PO Box 3040, Chico, CA 95927; phone 800/345-5473, fax 916/345-6751

•

Cuba, unlike other Latin American countries, does not present extremes of ostentatious wealth and bitter poverty. Except for government officials carefully hidden away in a few Havana neighborhoods, everyone lives at the same level: down, but not destitute. Third World travelers with no experience of pre-1959 Cuba may actually find the current standard of living not bad.

Many of the services the Cuban people complain about — the train system is the most common target — are not appreciably worse than elsewhere in Latin America. The problem most often is not quality, but quantity. Everything is in short supply, from bread to electricity, bus seats to cooking oil. Always be prepared to queue. Patience and a sense of humor are vital if you wish to return home with your sanity intact.
—Travel Matters

Falling Off the Map

Pico Iyer writes about lands that are rarely visited, from the perspective of a curious and independent visitor — not a sociological observer or a painter of pretty landscapes. His **Video Night In Kathmandu** took readers into the clash of traditional and modern values in 1980s Asia. **Falling Off the Map** is a more recent, more diverse collection of essays.

Iyer travels on his own through little-visited countries — Iceland, Bhutan, North Korea, and Paraguay. Undeterred by inconveniences (dumpy rooms, lack of basic facilities, contradictory and chaotic governmentalities), Iyer probes beyond the (sometimes nonexistent) tourist brochures in search of the country's true nature. He doesn't always succeed, but he relates his attempts with humor and irony.

Some travelers are more interested in having their cultural assumptions challenged than stimulating their senses. This book reflects the mixture of curiosity and empathy essential to that frame of mind. —RU

•

I made my way into the heart of the capital. The place was like nothing I had ever seen before. It was not just that none of the traffic lights was working, or even that straw-haired Mennonites in sky-blue-and-white clothes — like apparitions from some seventeenth-century Dutch landscape painting

Falling Off the Map
(Some Lonely Places of the World)
Pico Iyer. Alfred A. Knopf Inc., 1993; 190 pp. ISBN 0-679-42264-1
$20 ($22 postpaid) from Random House/Order Dept., 400 Hahn Road, Westminster, MD 21157; 800/733-3000

— were sauntering hand-in-hand across the street. It was not even the fact that every store that was not called "Alemán" seemed to have its sign in Korean hangul script. It was simply that Paraguay seemed indifferent — or impervious, at least — to life as it is lived around the planet.

•

In a country where crookedness is above ground and official ("Legalize Crime" might almost be the national motto: "Just Say Yes!"), people have more lucrative ways to redistribute income than by taking advantage of visitors. One could, in fact, make a Wildean case, after seeing Paraguay, for saying that if crime were made legal (as it is here), petty crime — pickpocketing and mugging and assault — would be all but eliminated. The only things I was robbed of in Paraguay were my malign preconceptions: I never looked over my shoulder here, or thought twice about taking a walk, or left my valuables in the hotel, as I would have to do in fun-loving, free-and-easy, murderous Rio. At night, there was a policeman — or a prostitute — on every street corner, keeping the peace in a kind of way.

DIFFERENCES BETWEEN 'HEAT EXHAUSTION' AND 'HEATSTROKE'

HEAT EXHAUSTION
- sweaty, pale, cool skin
- large pupils
- no fever
- weakness

HEATSTROKE
- red, dry, hot skin
- high fever
- the person is very ill or unconscious

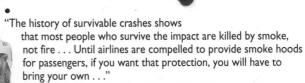

Staying Healthy in Asia, Africa and Latin America

Read this excellent travel reference before the bon-voyage party, then pack it along with the first-aid kit.

In addition to providing the obligatory "stay away from scorpions" advice, this book is a gold mine of critical information. For instance, drug safety standards differ across borders; the author identifies potentially dangerous drugs that may be found in over-the-counter cold remedies in developing countries. Elsewhere, he warns that health facilities in some countries routinely immunize many people using the same needle, and thus advises certain travelers to pack several sterile needles for the immunizations sometimes required after arrival.

Descriptions of health problems include risk, transmission, prevention, symptoms, and treatment. Every conceivable situation seems to be addressed — malaria, sea snakes, step-by-step instructions for suturing a wound.
—Linda Morgan

Staying Healthy in Asia, Africa, and Latin America
Dirk Schroeder. 1993; 185 pp. ISBN 1-56691-011-0 $10.95 ($14.45 postpaid) from Moon Publications, Inc., PO Box 3040, Chico, CA 95927; phone 800/345-5473, fax 916/345-6751

●

In many developing countries, blood is not adequately screened for the Human Immunodeficiency Virus (HIV) that causes AIDS. In case of an accident or emergency, international travelers may be at risk of contracting HIV through blood transfusions. Though the likelihood of the need for a blood transfusion process overseas is very low for most travelers, it is wise for those who will be living in a country for extended periods of time to anticipate this need in advance.

Because this is a relatively new problem, the solutions to it are not straightforward. The current WHO principles and guidelines are as follows:

1. Unexpected, emergency blood transfusion is rarely required; there is a tendency for medical personnel to perform unnecessary blood transfusions in many areas.

2. Alternatives to blood, including colloid and crystalloid plasma expanders, are strongly recommended.

3. Emergency evacuation from areas with questionable supplies is highly recommended if necessary and possible.

The option of donating one's own blood for storage is not recommmended for most travelers, but should be considered for long-term residents in areas where blood supply is known to be infected.

●

It is very important to continue taking malaria pills for 6 weeks after you return home (or after you leave the malarious area). This is necessary because most strains of malaria cycle between the bloodstream and the liver, yet the primary antimalarial drugs (chloroquine, mefloquine, Fansider, and doxycycline) only prevent multiplication of the malaria parasites while the parasites are in the bloodstream. Continuing to take malaria pills for several weeks after possible exposure ensures that all of the parasites have cycled through the blood, and been killed off.

Magellan's

A rousing catalog of supplies for the international traveler. The inevitable yupware is nicely balanced by a selection of truly useful items. Much of this stuff is difficult to find in ordinary stores, much less collected for your easy perusal and temptation. Warning: if you buy one of each of their worthwhile items, you'll weigh so much you won't be able to walk without a Crafty Native Porter (though your wallet will have negative buoyancy). —J. Baldwin [Suggested by Mike Sutherland]

●

The PentaPure® Water Jug dispenses two gallons of purified water at a time! You just fill the jug with contaminated water from any lake, stream or tap, anywhere in the world. Then open the spigot at the base and dispense microbiologically pure drinking water that has flowed through the replaceable purification cartridge. It's gravity activated — no pumping required.

PentaPure® Water Jug #FH567 $36.85

●

"It was a dark and stormy night. I needed both hands for the job I faced. Luckily, I had my 'Lite Fantastic' to hold the beam from my Mini-Maglite exactly where I needed it, for the full hour and a half. It never complained a bit." Discover this clever accessory for your AA mini-flashlight yourself. Just snap in your own flashlight and bend its durable Acetal "beads" into any shape at all to focus the light you need exactly where you need it. You can even loop it around your neck or over the head of your bed for a reading light! A big hit in our 1993 catalog. (2 oz.)

"Lite Fantastic" Holder #SP615L $9.85

"The history of survivable crashes shows that most people who survive the impact are killed by smoke, not fire . . . Until airlines are compelled to provide smoke hoods for passengers, if you want that protection, you will have to bring your own . . ."
—*Collision Course: The Truth About Airline Safety,* Ralph Nader and Wesley J. Smith.

We introduced the Israeli-made Durham Escape Hood in our Summer '93 Newsletter. It was an instant hit.

Magellan's: Catalog free. Box 5485, Santa Barbara, CA 93150-5485; phone 800/962-4943, fax 805/568-5406.

Travelers' Tales: Thailand

Any seasoned traveler knows that the best advice and experiences don't come from guidebooks. It's in those conversations at the cafe down the road, and in the fleabag hostel or overnight train berth, that the real insider information is exchanged.

The Travelers' Tales series aims to convey the excitement of voyaging through exotic territory with a vivacity that guidebooks can only hint at. Their first anthology assembles stories from Jeff Greenwald, Joe Cummings, and other travelers with absorbing tales to tell. Roaming the congested rivers of Bangkok and rural cycling paths, the authors of **Thailand** *describe the fascination and fear of discovering a new land and ideas. Other Travelers' Tales are of Mexico, India, France, and Japan. —Richie Unterberger*

●

It is no mystery why riverine Bangkok is more interesting and pleasant than the rest of the city. The contrast between the river and the interior became most apparent during a combination bus-and-boat excursion to the ruins of Ayutthaya. First we drove north along Thailand's ugly version of the New Jersey Turnpike. Billboards and plumes of black smoke marred the views, such as they were. The roadside towns were slapdash affairs, concrete egg boxes facing ditches black with waste water. There were prosperity and energy here but no beauty, and enough garbage to justify Claude Levi-Strauss's observation, "The first thing we see as we travel round the world is our own filth, thrown into the face of mankind."

But in Ayutthaya everything changed. The ancient ruins covered acres of moldering palaces and shattered temples, lines of decapitated pillars, and bell pagodas stripped of ornamentation and losing their brickwork but still showing graceful lines. The grounds of the Victory temple were a functioning monastery where monks lived in airy wood houses raised on stilts. The porches were decorated with flowering plants chosen for their lucky qualities. Signs tacked on trees carried Buddhist teachings, such as "The wise tame themselves" and "Contentment is the greatest wealth."

In this, as in other Thai temples, it was easy to find contentment. The compound was shady and silent except for tinkling prayer bells and songbirds the monks kept in cages. But just outside, our bus idled away in a parking lot made hot and noisy by tour drivers running their air conditioners so that they could stay cool while their passengers were off marveling at this oasis of beauty and calm.

●

The best massage in Bangkok has nothing to do with a lissome naked Thai beauty lathering you to distraction using every inch of her skin and the only soap pad nature has endowed her with.

Rather, it takes place with no privacy, in daylight, and both of you keep all your clothes on. Though not as profound a religious experience as is the famous "body-body," this dry alternative occurs under the incurious gaze of hundreds of Buddhist monks.

It is available daily, 7:30 to 5:00, in one of the largest temples in Bangkok: the Wat Po (Temple of Enlightenment). A Thai temple is characteristically a series of courtyards littered with gingerbread pagodas and chanting shaved-headed novitiates. The Wat Po also has tables of fake Rolex watches, at ten bucks each, plus the Reclining Buddha, the biggest in Thailand: nearly half a golden football field of him, counting the mother-of-pearl feet, smiling as if he has just received the finest Thai massage. On a recent morning I paid my respects, then went on to the next courtyard to do likewise.

Travelers' Tales: Thailand
James O'Reilly & Larry Habegger. 1994; 405 pp. ISBN 1-56592-900-4 $15.95 ($19.70 postpaid) from O'Reilly & Associates, 103A Morris Street, Sebastopol, CA 95472; 800/998-9938, fax 707/829-0104

The Insider's Guide to Air Courier Bargains

This entertaining guide lays out the unromantic details of shepherding stuff — usually boring business documents — to exotic places. You give up your checked-baggage allotment (that being where the "goods" travel) in exchange for a cheap airline ticket. It's an excellent way to see the world on a shoestring budget, as long as you've got time on your hands and can follow directions to the nth degree.

The first half deals with procedures: how to get the trip you want; how to negotiate the cheapest ticket; the importance of maintaining a professional image (dress conservatively and don't get drunk on the flight); tricks for packing light (since you're usually limited to one carry-on). The rest is an extensive directory of air courier companies and booking agencies.
—Linda Morgan

•

When you arrive at your destination, you will be met by another representative of the air courier company. You may have been instructed to hold up the envelope containing the manifests as you leave the customs area to identify you to the person meeting your flight. Sometimes you will be given a phone number to call when you have cleared through customs. (Usually you will breeze through customs by following the "Nothing To Declare" signs.)

Once you have made contact with the receiving courier company, you will be asked to wait — in the customs area of the terminal or in a building elsewhere on the air-

**The Insider's Guide
to Air Courier Bargains**
(How to Travel World-Wide
for Next to Nothing)
Kelly Monaghan. Intrepid Traveler,
1994; 234 pp. ISBN 0-9627892-6-7
$14.95 ($17.45 postpaid) from Upper
Access Books, Box 457, Hinesburg, VT
05461; 800/356-9315

port grounds — while the courier company representative walks the paperwork and the checked baggage through the customs process. Once that's done, you'll be free to leave.

In my experience, this has been a hassle-free experience. I have, however, seen other couriers who were not so lucky. While I was leaving after a five-minute wait at the courier shed in London, a courier from an earlier flight was fuming that he'd been kept waiting for hours with no explanation about the cause of the delay. On other trips to London, I haven't even been required to go to the customs shed; the rep simply asked where they could get in touch with me if they had to and let me go.

How to Be an Importer and Pay for Your World Travel

This practical and inspirational text for the novice importer resonates with the voice of experience. It is laced with examples of the mistakes and triumphs the authors have encountered in their own business.

While this book is true to its title, frequently emphasizing importing as a way to subsidize vacation travel, its information seems to favor the serious "career" importer — someone doing seasonal and volume buying. But a casual traveler interested only in personal shopping can glean valuable advice here, too. For example, much attention is given to US and foreign customs policies, bargaining with merchants in other cultures, packing and shipping abroad, and currency exchange, all at a level of detail not found in most travel guides.

Over a third of the book is devoted to an appendix that covers all manner of industry-crucial data. This includes an explanation of the international trade system GSP (Generalized System of Preferences), a comparison chart of American and European sizes, and a hefty glossary of foreign trade terms and abbreviations. —LM

OTHER GREAT RESOURCES

Airhitch: 3790 Broadway, Suite 100, New York, NY 10025; 212/864-2000. Hooks up flexible flyers willing to travel within a certain five-day period to cheap flights to Europe.
Jet Smart: Diana Fairchild. 1992, Flyana Rhyme, Inc. Over 200 tips for jet lag prevention and remedies.

**How to Be an Importer
and Pay for Your World Travel**
Mary Green & Stanley Gillmar. 1993;
215 pp. ISBN 0-89815-501-0
$8.95 ($12.45 postpaid) from Ten Speed
Press, PO Box 7123, Berkeley, CA 94707;
800/841-2665

SYMBOLS FOR MONETARY UNITS

	Chinese*	Arabic	Hebrew	Greek (Upper Case)	Greek (Lower Case)	Sanskrit
1	一	١	א	A	$\bar{a}$	१
2	二	٢	ב	B	$\bar{\beta}$	२
3	三	٣	ג	Γ	$\bar{\gamma}$	३
4	四	٤	ד	Δ	$\bar{\delta}$	४
5	五	٥	ה	E	$\bar{\epsilon}$	५
6	六	٦	ו	F	$\bar{\varsigma}$	६
7	七	٧	ז	Z	$\bar{\zeta}$	७
8	八	٨	ח	H	$\bar{\eta}$	८
9	九	٩	ט	Θ	$\bar{\theta}$	९
10	十	١٠	י	I	$\bar{\iota}$	१०

*Japanese and Thai symbols are not included here due to their similarity to the Chinese.

•

Keep your eye on what you really want. It is a usual tactic for a seller to try to confuse you and divert you by showing you other alternatives at different prices. These alternatives are designed usually to convince you that the price he is proposing for the object at issue is certainly reasonable or that if you want to spend less there are these other items which are almost as good, and these others that are better for more.

The psychology is probably that you will get into a pattern of thinking of the proposed prices as the reasonable range rather than the actual lower expected price. It also gives the seller a means of sizing you up as a negotiator. How strongly you keep coming back to the one you originally selected gives the seller a gauge of how much you want that piece and the reasons. He uses this in establishing his later counter-offers.

There is one other aspect to the merchant's game of running you through the alternatives. Sometimes a seller has a particularly fine piece which you have examined carefully before you made your first proposal. The seller may have other such pieces which are similar, but not quite as good. After confusing you with many better and lesser alternatives, if the seller suspects your choice of that original piece was not as informed as was first thought, he may finally show you not the piece you first looked at, but its lesser cousin. You'll get it back to the hotel and find a crack or a repair that you don't remember seeing in the shop.

Green Tortoise Adventure Travel

Have you ever yearned for a comfy mattress on a long Greyhound ride? Or cursed silently as the driver stops at yet another Howard Johnson's? The most extensive low-budget bus service in the United States, Green Tortoise is the independent and adventurous traveler's alternative to Greyhound. Besides offering lower prices on routes between most major cities on the west coast, it also offers lengthier excursions through Alaska and Central America, trips to attractions such as the Grand Canyon and Mardi Gras, and coast-to-coast voyages.

The Tortoise solution to those stiff upright seats? Get rid of the damn things! Long, level bunks allow passengers to sleep in reasonable comfort. Compensation for the slower pace includes vegetarian cookouts and stops at hot springs.

Green Tortoise also operates hostels in San Francisco and Seattle.
—Richie Unterberger

•

There is nothing else like a Green Tortoise trip. Possibly 99% of our passengers have a great time, and many return to travel with us again. They are the kind of people who make friends easily, because they like themselves and have respect for all lifestyles, they have a wide range of tastes, know how to help themselves and others, and love to share and preserve the beauty of nature . . . and when something does go wrong, they don't get in a funk about it.

However, we occasionally encounter a traveler who does not get it. They somehow believe they have stumbled upon a low cost variation of other trips costing much, much more. They want such things as; an exact itinerary, guaranteed arrival times, "to go shopping," "proper potty stops," showers every day, even a private berth

with privacy curtains, no nudity, no parties, and on and on. Things that we cannot control, and do not offer. This has happened most on our longer adventures, such as Alaska and Central America, but has even happened on our shortest trips.

There are no age limits on our trips, either young or old, but our trips are not for people who are unable to carry their own luggage for several blocks, crawl around on the bus, help with cookouts, maybe even set up a tent in the rain . . . be nice, etc. Parents wishing to bring children on any trip other than Yosemite or North/South must be interviewed before we can accept their reservations. The Green Tortoise reserves the right to refuse service to any person at any time.

Green Tortoise Adventure Travel:
494 Broadway, San Francisco, CA 94133;
415/956-7500.

A Journey of One's Own

This book is not just for women, and it's not just for those who travel alone. It is for those who want to truly experience cultures other than their own. Packed with the odd bits of wisdom that one collects on the road, it prepares the unseasoned adventurer for the myriad dilemmas of the less-traveled road.

The topics are familiar: planning, packing, bargain tickets, health tips, border techniques, money strategies. Thalia Zepatos' book is unusual for the depth and honesty of her counsel. Intertwined with her sage advice are detailed and charged memories — Zepatos' and those of seven other intrepid women travelers. These tales of specific travels point to larger truths, without smarm or hype.

Women travelers willing to shed their own cultures in order to immerse themselves in another will find this book invaluable. Any reader will find pleasure here. And *Journey* just could set a few armchair travelers scurrying for their passports.
—Suzanne Stefanac

A Journey of One's Own
Thalia Zepatos. 1992; 342 pp.
ISBN 0-933377-20-7
$14.95 ($16.95 postpaid) from Eighth Mountain Press, 624 SE 29th Avenue, Portland, OR 97214; 503/233-3936

•

I laughed briefly at this turn of events, until he jerked the gun at my insolence. I wore neither the long braid, not the sari or knee-length tunic over trousers of the other women on the train. My close-cropped hair, baggy pants, and collarless white cotton Indian man's shirt were chosen for comfort, ease of travel, and to help me avoid harassment. I stood and rocked unsteadily among the jumbled feet and discarded sandals of my travel-mates in the narrow space between the two facing benches. Momentarily turning my back to the old fellow, I pulled the baggy shirt taut under both arms and showed the women the outline of my chest. They roared in laughter and approval, and pushed the old man and his gun away.

Able to Travel

To the disabled traveler, boarding a plane or using one's hotel bathroom frequently presents a major obstacle. Many such concerns are addressed in these success stories and misadventures, recounted by travelers with disabilities. Helpful and inspirational to the targeted audience, it is a humbling read for the able-bodied.

The colorful tales are grouped by country and followed by notes on transportation, lodging, and other information specific to that area. The "Practicalities" section offers invaluable advice regarding access, red tape, and health/comfort, including information for travelers with hidden disabilities such as diabetes or the need to dialyze. —Linda Morgan

•

A pencil and paper is not always ideal for bush use, and Sten was a slow writer, so it had to be a series of hand signals to identify the various animals. The most graphic was undoubtedly the scratching of the armpit to represent the baboon! In fact, Sten was quite an expert, as he had done all this before.

Some of his (safari) clients did not speak English (or his native Swedish), so hand signals became the common language when out on the hunt where quietness is absolutely necessary. Although I was armed with nothing heavier than a selection of cameras, the same rules apply: game must be stalked silently for a good shot.

A deaf person moving through the bush is presented with another problem. It is easy to presume that because you hear yourself making little or no noise, you are moving quietly. Not so! You may well only feel the

Able to Travel
Alison Walsh, Jodi Abbott & Margaret L. Smith. Rough Guides, 1994; 603 pp. ISBN 1-85828-110-5
$19.95 ($21.95 postpaid). Penguin USA/Consumer Sales, 120 Woodbine Street, Bergenfield, NJ 07621; 800/253-6476

dry twig snap, or your boot scuff on a rock, or the numerous thorns raking across your clothing, but the noise will be clearly audible to the nearby animal life.

OTHER GREAT RESOURCES

Easy Access to National Parks: Wendy Roth & Michael Tompane. 1992, Sierra Club Books.

Women Travel (Adventures, Advice, and Experience): Natania Jansz & Miranda Davies. 1990, Prentice Hall Press.

Travel with Children: Maureen Wheeler. 1990, Lonely Planet Publications.

Kidding Around Series

Armed with information from any book in this excellent series the eight- to twelve-year-old set will surely claim their rightful voice in planning and executing the family vacation. The information is much the same as that in a grown-up guidebook, but rendered in Kidspeak. The authors speak to the reader as a decisionmaker, not a tag-along visitor. Colorful illustrations have mass appeal, especially to younger siblings. And kids who live by sound bites will enjoy the factoids and odd bits of history in the margins. The hand-drawn maps are simplified from regular street maps; they could prove more helpful to adults than the fancier models.
—Linda Morgan

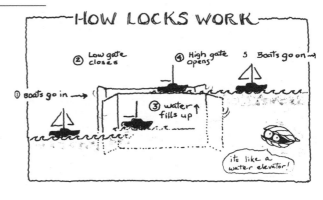

Are You Two . . . Together?

This funny, sensitive book is for same-sex traveling companions, gay or straight. For each of fourteen European capitals and resorts (including Amsterdam, London, Bavaria, Copenhagen, Paris, Berlin, and Capri), a section gives general hints, gay attitudes, suggestions on where to eat and sleep (and where not to), how to find out about current events from local sources, historical trivia, and recommended reading. You'll find honest, humorous, trenchant observations on every page. —Marguerita I. Castanera

•

On January 15, 1990 — Martin Luther King, Jr.'s birthday, as fate would have it — two gay men were refused a double room at a hotel in Gerona, an old cathedral town not far from Barcelona. Instead of slinking off miserably to the boudoir equivalent to the back of the bus, they call in FAGC, the Catalan gay liberation organization. In an inspired protest, FAGC installed an ornate, hand-carved, king-sized bed in the street outside the hotel, where two men cuddled and frolicked between the sheets for the assembled crowds of onlookers, reporters and photographers.

Are You Two ... Together?
Lindsy Van Gelder. 1991;
ISBN 0-394-58454-6
$18 ($20 postpaid) from Random House/Order Dept., 400 Hahn Road, Westminster, MD 21157; 800/733-3000

•

A sunken V-shaped wall of highly polished black granite designed by 21-year-old student Maya Lin and dedicated in 1982, it is inscribed with the names of all 58,000 Americans killed or missing in the Vietnam War, arranged in order of date of casualty and grouped by year. At first you may think, "So what? It's just a wall." Wait. Vietnam was a very recent war. Your father may have fought in it, or certainly your parents knew someone who did. And the people who knew those whose names are written here come every day and night to bring flowers, letters, and American flags to their dear ones. Some who visit are in uniform themselves. Some cry. Others stand silently, remembering, or ask a Park employee to make a rubbing of a special name to take away with them. After just a few minutes of watching this continuous, quiet drama you begin to get a vivid sense of the human cost of war: the pain, the loss, the bewilderment.
—Kidding Around Washington, DC

Kidding Around Series
Atlanta, Boston, Chicago, Hawaiian Islands, Los Angeles, New York City, Philadelphia, San Diego, San Francisco, Santa Fe, Seattle, Washington DC: $9.95 each ($13.70 postpaid); National Parks of the Southwest, Spain: $12.95 each ($16.70 postpaid). All from John Muir Publications, PO Box 613, Santa Fe, NM 87504; 800/888-7504

Asia Through the Back Door

Like its sister Europe Through the Back Door, *this offers thorough advice on all facets of independent travel throughout Asia, emphasizing people, culture, and experience rather than sights and comforts. Rick Steeves and Bob Effertz address the essentials — health, customs, language, transportation on a modest budget — with zest and humor. The fourth edition covers thirty "back-door" destinations (Indian beaches, Cameroon Highlands jungle walks). A "Nitty Gritty" supplement includes unclassifiable information on ten of the most visited Asian countries.* —Richie Unterberger

•

Imagine a couple of hundred James Dean imitations, their long, wavy black hair slicked back into ducktails, cigarettes rolled up inside T-shirt sleeves.

Imagine several dozen more Sandra Dee look-alikes, ebony ponytails replacing blond, plaid skirts lifted high above bobby sox and tennis shoes.

Imagine these young boppers rockin' and reelin' in colorful, choreographed harmony to everything from Danny and the Juniors to rap and reggae.

This isn't a Broadway stage setting. It's a typical Sunday afternoon in Tokyo's Harajuku district.

"I want to bring the '50s back to life," seventeen-year-old Susumu told me in all seriousness as he dropped a pair of dark glasses over his eyes and lit up a Winston. "That was such a wonderful time."

Susumu, of course, remembers the 1950s well. His "to be" parents were just entering elementary school. But he's seen all the films — *Rebel Without a Cause, Beach Blanket Bingo, American Graffiti.* He's listened to all the music, Elvis and Buddy Holly and Leslie Gore. He bought a life-sized poster of James Dean at a shop in Shinjuku. And now, "Don't you think I look like James Dean?"

Asia Through the Back Door
Rick Steeves & Bob Effertz. 1993; 380 pp. ISBN 1-56261-109-7
$16.95 ($20.70 postpaid) from John Muir Publications, PO Box 613, Santa Fe, NM 87504; 800/888-7504

China Travel Survival Kit

China remains one of the most challenging destinations for the international traveler. Even the hardiest visitors still face high linguistic and cultural barriers.

Lonely Planet's Travel Survival Kit, *the most exhaustive guide to the vast nation, offers detailed practical information on the remote provinces as well as the large cities, with nearly 200 maps and a wealth of cultural and historical background.* —RU

•

If you want to meet English-speaking Chinese then go to the "English corners" which have developed in many large Chinese cities. Usually held on a Sunday morning in a convenient park, Chinese who speak or are learning English gather to practise the language. Also seek out the "English Salons" — evening get-togethers at which the Chinese practise English, listen to lectures or hold debates in English. Don't expect to remain a member of the audience for very long; you may soon find yourself giving the evening lecture and struggling to answer hard questions about the outside world.

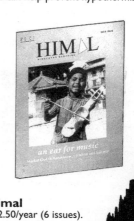

Terracotta soldier from the tomb of Qin Shihuang.

China — A Travel Survival Kit
Joe Cummings & Robert Storey. 1991; 882 pp. ISBN 0-86442-123-0
$25.95 ($27.95 postpaid) from Lonely Planet Publications/Embarcadero West, 155 Filbert Street, Suite 251, Oakland, CA 94607-2538; 800/275-8555

Himal

Produced in Nepal, this bimonthly magazine acts as a medium for the exchange of information and ideas in the Himalayan region. Political analyses, articles on the environment, coverage of the arts, news briefs, and book reviews give context to the area (Nepal, Bhutan, and Tibet) that most guidebooks can't. Travelers and trekkers are advised to seek this out. —RU

•

Every season, porters from the lower hill areas like Trisuli and Tanahu die in the high lekhs because of a combination of exposure, altitude sickness, and exhaustion. Many low hill villagers with little or no experience of high mountain travel moonlight as porters when the fields have been planted and there is free time on the farm. They rarely know what they are up against, particularly when the weather takes a turn for the worse.

The safety of their porters is primarily the responsibililty of the trekking agency, and some are better than others. The Western trekkers can also help keep portering safe by asking some pointed questions before selecting an agency. One of the most important is, does the agency provide porters with proper gear for crossing high passes? This can help prevent hypothermia.

Sulawesi: Island Crossroads of Indonesia

Perhaps less oriented toward the independent traveler than the Lonely Planet or Moon series, and not as exhaustive in their details of practicalities (though they offer plenty). But Passport covers the vast, and vastly diverse, regions of Indonesia more thoroughly than any other line of guidebooks. The guides (to Sulawesi, New Guinea, Spice Islands, Borneo, Sumatra, and underwater Indonesia, as well as Bali and Java) offer cultural and historical background essays, excellent color photos, and an unusually clean layout. They are a pleasure to read and to use. —RU

•

From the caves you must return to the highway and hail a passing bemo to continue on to Bantimurung. You cannot miss the entrance to the park: the road leads beneath the legs of a concrete monkey standing 6 meters (20 ft) high. This area, with its spectacular waterfalls, cliff and chasms, and its butterflies and birds, has always attracted visitors. In 1856-57 the British naturalist Alfred Russel Wallace spent "some of the most pleasurable moments of [his] life" here, catching many rare

Sulawesi
(Island Crossroads of Indonesia)
Toby Alice Volkman & Ian Caldwell, Editors. Passport Books, 1990; 241 pp. ISBN 0-8442-9906-5
$15.95 (postpaid) from NTC Publishing, 4255 W. Touhy Avenue, Lincolnwood, IL 60646; 800/323-4900

specimens of insects, birds and butterflies, including the *Papilio androcles,* one of the largest and rarest swallow-tailed butterflies. Wallace wrote, "Such gorges, chasms and precipies as here abound, I have nowhere seen in the Archipelago. . . ." His detailed descriptions have attracted numbers of archaeologists, prehistorians, and lepidopterists, including Vladimir Nabokov, who wrote a scientific article on the butterflies he discovered here.

Other Great Resources

India: A Travel Survival Kit: Geoff Crowther, Hugh Finlay & Bryn Thomas. 1993.

Trekking in the Nepal Himalaya: Stan Armington. 1994.

Trekking in the Indian Himalaya: Garry Weare. 1991.

All from Lonely Planet (above).

Today Bantimurung has been proclaimed a protected area, as many species of its wildlife are threatened by overenthusiastic collectors. Nevertheless, visitors will find themselves beseiged by children with boxes of brilliantly-colored butterflies. The best time to see the butterflies in the living state is when the sun comes out after a rain, as they flutter over the water and around the vegetation nearby.

Himal
$22.50/year (6 issues). Barbara Bella & Associates/Subscriptions, PO Box 470758, San Francisco, CA 94147; 800/203-8600

The Japan Experience

Each issue of this sixteen-page quarterly magazine is crammed with news, tips, and columns of interest to Japanophiles and to anyone expecting to spend some time living or working in Japan.

A year's worth of issues covered Japanese software and PC networks, Japanese-American marriage, and tips on travel lodging and learning the language. My favorite feature, "Japanorama," collects odd and insightful tidbits of news from the country that you're unlikely to find on any of the wire services. Regular martial-arts features pay equal attention to the spiritual and the physical aspects of the discipline. A calendar of events and directory of classes and services is rapidly growing into a nationwide listing. Even the ads (for other English-language magazines on Japan, Japanese-language computer services, calendars, business cards) are useful references for expert and novice alike. —RU

• The traditional male-oriented image of Japanese society may be changing. That is the opinion of Shiro Sugiyama, who runs an obstetrics and gynecology clinic in Tokyo, and claims an 80% success rate in helping

couples choose the sex of their baby. "Ten years ago," he says, "many couples who came to see me wanted to have boy babies. But recently, more and more want girls."

A nationwide survey by the Health and Welfare Ministry shows a clear shift in preference from boys to girls. Of couples wanting only one child, 75.7% wanted a girl. Of couples wanting two children, most wanted one boy and one girl, but those wanting two girls outnumbered those wanting two boys by about a 4-to-1 ratio. By contrast, in most Asian countries, boys are almost universally preferred.

Why the shift in preferences? Shigesato Takahashi, director of the Ministry's population dynamics division, says, "Generally speaking, parents think that girls will take better care of them later in life than boys." Another factor, according to sociologists, is the belief that Japanese women lead easier lives than men, who are under great pressure from an early age to dedicate themselves to their work.

• JWP is a freeware Japanese word processing program for PCs running Windows. If you have Windows on your machine, this is

the best program of the ones we distribute. It's quite easy to use, since it basically works like any other Windows program, with the usual menus, icons, etc. It has all the basic features such as cut and paste, search and replace, paragraph and page margins, and page headers and footers. It comes with three fonts, including the high-resolution 48 X 48-dot font for high quality images.

The Japan Experience
$7/year (4 issues) from Metal Magic Productions, PO Box 871895, Dallas, TX 75287; 214/394-0541

Japan Solo

The most outstanding features of this guide for independent travelers are the nearly 200 detailed regional and city maps, with walking tours of some of the country's most scenic parks and interesting neighborhoods. You'll also learn how to navigate bus and train systems, using tear-out conversation cards to facilitate basic "how do I get from here to there?".

Stick to the reliably excellent Lonely Planet and Moon Japan guides for budget travel information and background history — the listings here are perfunctory in comparison. —RU

Tokyo's transportation system.

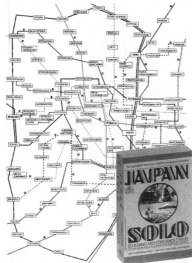

Japan Solo
Eiji Kanno & Constance O'Keefe. 1988; 392 pp. ISBN 0-446-38821-1 $14.95 ($17.95 postpaid) from Little, Brown & Co./Order Dept., 200 West Street, Waltham, MA 02154; 800/343-9204

Power Japanese • Kanji Moments

Unless you were born to it, learning to speak Japanese is about as easy as attaining enlightenment. Aside from grammar, syntax, and pronunciation, many of the sentiments that underlie ordinary Japanese conversations don't exist in the West. And to read a Japanese newspaper, you must understand two separate alphabet-like syllabaries, as well as thousands of ideographs that represent entire words.

Power Japanese interactive software teaches you basic orthography, grammar, and pronunciation, using digitized recordings of native speakers — just like a standard cassette-and-workbook language course. But the program adds animated graphics, interactive drills, and exercises; never needs rewinding; and feels more like a game than training. Ten or fifteen minutes a day with Power Japanese takes you through the Hiragana and Katakana syllabaries as well as basic grammar in a matter of weeks. You can review lessons as often as you want, and jump freely around the hypertext interface.

Kanji Moments carries on where Power Japanese leaves off, training you to read, write, and pronounce several hundred Kanji ideographs, while imparting more grammar and vocabulary. BayWare intends to release six volumes of the software, covering a total of 2,000 characters — a good working vocabulary for the gaijin executive or Zen aspirant. —Scott Spanbauer

Power Japanese
Windows 3.1 or later, PC or compatible, 4 MB RAM and CD Drive (or 16 MB hard disk space for floppy disk version), with VGA display adapter, and MPC compatible sound card. $199 ($205 postpaid).

Kanji Moments
Windows 3.1 or later, IBM AT, PS/2 or compatible with 3MB RAM and 8 MB hard disk space, VGA or SVGA monitor, and MPC or compatible sound card. $89 ($95 postpaid).

Both from BayWare, Inc., 1660 S. Amphlett Boulevard, Suite 128, San Mateo, CA 94402; 800/538-8867

Below: Power Japanese

Mangajin

This is an outstanding periodical for anyone trying to learn Japanese — or anyone interested in contemporary Japanese culture. It contains fully translated and glossed manga plus feature articles and book reviews. —Frederick Lee

Mangajin
$35/year (10 issues) from Mangajin, PO Box 10443, Atlanta, GA 30319; 404/590-0091

Japan Inside Out

Perhaps the most massive guidebook to any country anywhere, with nearly 1,500 densely packed pages. It's more useful for those planning to live in or for students of that country than those just planning to visit. Japan Inside Out is clumsily written and edited, but it's doubtful that any other single volume has as much travel information: hundreds of maps and listings of festivals augment the more usual information on accommodations and sights. —RU

Japan Inside Out
Jay Gluck, Sumi Gluck & Garet Gluck. 1992; 1344 pp. ISBN 4-89360-035-4 $19 ($22.50 postpaid) from Weatherhill, Inc., 41 Monroe Turnpike, Trumbull, CT 06611; 800/437-7840

Mystical
Ayers
Rock

Outback Australia Handbook

A guide to one of the most sparsely populated and geologically fascinating regions on earth. Outback Australia Handbook covers the region's parks, historical reserves, and wilderness areas while providing an historical context for the understanding of Aboriginal history, culture, and mythology. Several dozen detailed maps aid bushwalkers and adventurers. There are also chapters on such cities as Perth and Adelaide that are useful as both launching points and respites.
—Richie Unterberger

•
If you want to climb The Rock, you are supposed to be in excellent physical condition (a real chuckle once you check out some of the climbers). Also be aware that the higher slopes are often hit by gale-force winds (climbers have died while trying to retrieve a Foster's visor). Check with the park rangers for necessary equipment. Another option is the three- to four-hour walk around the base, fringed with caves, waterholes, and a variety of desert vegetation.

The Olgas (Kata Tjuta, or "Many Heads," to the Aborigines) lie about 27 km to the west and are also part of the protected Uluru National Park. These huge rocks, just as old and once much larger than Ayers Rock, are a jumble of more rounded monoliths, separated by gorges, valleys, and chasms. Many visitors enjoy exploring the Olgas more than the Rock because they have more hidden areas to discover, are a bit less intimidating, *and* less touristed.

Outback Australia Handbook
Marael Johnson. 1992; ISBN 0-918373-79-4
$15.95 ($19.45 postpaid) from Moon Publications, Inc., PO Box 3040, Chico, CA 95927; 800/345-5473, fax 916/345-6751

Adventuring in Australia

Besides the Outback, Australia is abundant with natural beauty and interest: the Great Barrier Reef, tropical rainforests, a diverse wildlife population. The Sierra Club's Adventuring in Australia is devoted to such outdoor activities as backpacking, scuba diving, and river rafting. Written from an engagingly personal perspective, it's the most wide-ranging reference for enjoying the country's natural resources.
—RU

•
The best way to see the reef is to don a mask and join the fishes. The usually good to excellent water visibility and the fact most of the reef life can be found in the first 10 meters under the surface make snorkeling ideal throughout the reef. The only prerequisites are the ability to swim and reasonable judgment.

Snorkeling and diving increase the quality of your reef experience a hundredfold over glass-bottom boats and subs. The snorkeler becomes part of the underwater world, and fish are less apt to go into hiding, which often happens when a glass-bottom boat or submarine maneuvers overhead.

For the less aquatically inclined visitor, there are glass-bottom boats, motorized floating observatories called submarines or semisubmersibles, and underwater observatories.

•
My trip to the Cradle Mountain Lodge ranks at the top of the most memorable wildlife experiences of my life. I was driving at night on the final stretch of the dirt road and was slowed to 5 kilometers per hour by the abundance of wildlife hopping, scurrying, and dive-bombing past my car. Rufous wallabies stood huddling in the center of the road, while quolls scurried across the roadway, one holding a small rodent in its mouth. Bennett's wallabies bounded every which way. The numbers were astounding. My real excitement came when a Tasmanian devil, the largest living (assuming the Tasmanian tiger is extinct) marsupial predator, ran across the road in a slow, rocking-horse gait. Minutes later two more devils, chewing on a wallaby carcass, were caught in my headlights.

I made it to the lodge around midnight and was greeted by owners Simon and Anne Currant. When I explained I'd seen a Tasmanian devil and a number of other creatures, Simon grinned. "So, you like devils." We walked to the back porch and there were about five devils eating table scraps left out for them.

Adventuring in Australia
Eric Hoffman. 1990; 482 pp.
ISBN 0-87156-742-3
$14.95 ($17.95 postpaid) from Sierra Club Store Orders, 730 Polk Street, San Francisco, CA 94109; 800/935-1056

Camel trekking, Western Australia

Hawaii, Naturally

In welcome contrast to gaudy brochures extolling opportunities for golf and cocktails in Crass Entertainment Hawaii, this book guides us to what's left of Incredible Natural Wonder Hawaii. All the parks are there in detail, including the ones overrun by tourists (of which you are one — the author realistically recognizes that Cliche Hawaii certainly exists). But along with access to the obvious are the less well-known places, even some favored mostly by locals. Hawaiian environmental organizations and their activities are listed. The whereabouts of botanical gardens, campgrounds, and even health-food stores are revealed. The enticing descriptions of hiking trails alone are enough to invite mad "stuff-it" phone calls to mainland bosses. Ironically, the book is so tempting, it will likely draw even more tourists, however eco-righteous, to the islands. Sigh. —J. Baldwin

•
Shirakawa Motel: Billing itself as "The Southernmost Motel in the U.S.," the Shirakawa is well known for its quaint setting, clean rooms, and budget prices. It is located in Kau district, near the road to South Point. The kindly Japanese woman who owns and runs the place cares for her guests like she does for her flower garden. The motel is situated on the makai side of Mamalahoa Highway (Hwy 11), about a mile west of Naalehu. Contact them at: Shirakawa Motel, P. O. Box 467, Naalehu, Hawaii 96772. 808/929-7462.

•
Nechung Drayang Ling — Wood Valley Temple: In the early 1900s Japanese sugar workers in Kapapala/Wood Valley Camp built a Buddhist temple that was subsequently abandoned in the 1950s, when workers moved to nearby Pahala. In 1973 the temple was restored as the residence of Nechung Rinpoche, the Tibetan lama of Nechung Dorje Drayang Ling Monastery. He attracted a devoted following in Hawaii. A second temple was moved from Pahala to Wood Valley to serve as a retreat center for the growing Buddhist community. In 1980 the Dalai Lama visited and dedicated the center. The facilities now serve individual travelers, community and church groups, workshop organizers, and others who seek a quiet atmosphere. Dormitory rooms and private quarters can accommodate a maximum of 27 persons. The rates are quite reasonable (around $15/night), the atmosphere is certainly peaceful, and there are numerous opportunities for involvement in retreat activities (meditation, yoga, workshops, Hawaiian dance and crafts, etc.). To reach the temple/hostel, proceed north on the Wood Valley Camp/Kapapala road, located off Mamalahoa Highway (Hwy 11) in Pahala, Kau district. The temple is marked by signboards at the end of the Kapapala Road. Contact: Nechung Drayang Ling, P. O. Box 250, Pahala, Hawaii 96777. 808/928-8539.

Hawaii, Naturally
David Zurick. 1990; 206 pp.
ISBN 0-89997-108-3
$12.95 postpaid from Wilderness Press/Order Dept., 2440 Bancroft Way, Berkeley, CA 94704; 800/443-7227

OTHER GREAT RESOURCES

Hawaii Trails: Kathy Morey. 1992. Wilderness Press.
Bushwalking in Australia: John Chapman and Monica Chapman. 1992. Lonely Planet.
Hidden Hawaii: Ray Riegert. 1993. Ulysses Press.
Paddling Hawaii: Audrey Sutherland. 1988. The Mountaineers.
Maui Trails: Kathy Morey. 1991. Wilderness Press.

Africa on a Shoestring

There's no question that this voluminous guidebook to fifty-four countries offers the most comprehensive information on Africa.

Each country has its own chapter that includes extensive history, background, and important facts for visitors. You can find out how to get around by car, bike, bus, or thumb; listings of places to eat and sleep include campgrounds and four-star hotels. Suggested diversions include main attractions like the old walled medina in Fez and jungle hikes to see gorillas in Rwanda. The book's 350 maps cover countries, cities, and towns.
—Marguerita I. Castanera

•

There are taxis in most cities in Egypt. The most common and cheapest are the black-and-white taxis in Cairo and the black-and-orange ones in Alexandria. Almost all of them have meters but most of the meters don't work, so you have to pay what you think is right and be prepared to argue and bargain.

When you reach your destination, get out of the cab and then pay. If you think the driver is trying to cheat you, then just mention the police, and the taxi driver will probably accept your price to avoid any hassle. Don't be intimidated by the driver's yelling; it's usually just an act to get you to cough up more money. If he agrees with you about seeing the police, then the fare you offered is probably too low.

•

There can be few cities in the world with a history as rich as Cairo's. Where else could you see 4500-year-old pyramids (some of the world's largest constructions) and the Sphinx, Roman ruins, Byzantine Coptic churches, exquisitely carved and brilliantly conceived mosques and fortresses from the days when Cairo was the cultural centre of the Islamic world, traditional lateen-sailed boats on the river, a camel market and even catacombs? All this plus a vibrant modern political and social culture which is second to none.

Here is the essence of Islamic culture and Africa's largest city. The only one which comes close to it in size is Johannesburg, though the comparison would probably not be appreciated.

There's an endless variety of things to see and do — noisy, bustling bazaars packed into narrow winding streets, and those 1001 aromas (delicious, evocative and occasionally repulsive) which characterise so much of the East.

Africa on a Shoestring
Geoff Crowther. 1992; 1363 pp.
ISBN 0-86442-127-3
$27.95 ($29.45 postpaid) from Lonely Planet Publications/Embarcadero West, 155 Filbert Street/Ste. 251, Oakland, CA 94607-2538; 800/275-8555

Adventuring In East Africa

Travelers who love nature, animals, and the outdoors will get the most use from this Sierra Club guidebook to East Africa's wildlife reserves and national parks.

Allen Bechky provides essential background reading, useful tips, and the best animal-watching opportunities in Kenya, Tanzania, Eastern Zaire, Rwanda, and Uganda. He includes safari etiquette and information on shopping, health care, and safety.

Thorough descriptions of each park address conservation issues, accommodations, access and fees. There is also a brief glossary of basic Swahili and a list of safari tour operators.
—MIC

•

English is the only language you need for comfortable travel in East Africa and southern Africa. French is essential in West Africa. One or the other will be spoken by all educated people in these regions, and will be widely understood by many others. . . .

It is virtually impossible to prepare yourself to speak even a fraction of the tribal dialects that you could encounter in a single country. It is useful to learn the polite forms of address and expression in the local language of whatever region you will concentrate your visit: it always brightens faces when a foreigner is able to respond to greetings. Phrasebooks in local languages are generally available in capital cities. The only African language dictionaries and phrasebooks available in the United States are for Swahili. Swahili is widely spoken only in East Africa and Zaire, where it enjoys official status among the dozens of local languages.

In postindependence Africa, government officials spread the view that tourists took pictures of Africans only to mock them as curiosities, "just like the animals in the game parks." Officials took a particularly dim view of photos of bare-breasted or spear-toting natives. They were anxious to project a modern image for their countries, not to be seen as "primitives." In some places it became illegal to take pictures of colorful tribespeople. Generally, the word was put out that Africans shouldn't allow themselves to be photographed. That view mellowed with the increasing influx of tourists. Once it became clear that tourists were willing to pay for pictures, photo privileges became an economic resource. Now it's standard to pay people if you wish to take their picture. Many visitors take umbrage at having payment demanded for photos, but you can hardly blame the Africans for asking. They know that foreigners are all wealthy by their standards and can easily afford a small payment. They also know that pictures are potentially valuable — that they can be sold to magazines for a great deal of money, none of which they will see. They have no way of knowing which shots will end up in a private photo album and which on the cover of *National Geographic*. It really is not unreasonable to pay them a modeling fee.

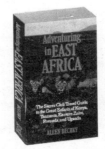

Adventuring in East Africa
Allen Bechky. 1990; 446 pp.
ISBN 0-87156-747-4
$14.95 ($17.95 postpaid) from Sierra Club Store Orders, 730 Polk Street, San Francisco, CA 94109; 800/935-1056

Zimbabwe and Botswana: The Rough Guide

Zimbabwe and Botswana have wonderful game parks and safaris, majestic scenery, a thriving and innovative popular music scene, and rich cultures that have only recently established independence from long periods of colonial domination. This book is packed with information about such interesting features and historical tidbits as Matopos rock paintings, the Mwari religious cult, the controversial hunting of Chobe elephants, and the political imbroglio of the marriage between Botswana heir Sir Seretse Khama and a white Englishwoman.

You get a nice feel for the natural and cultural forces that have shaped these lands and societies. Rough Guides are also available to Kenya, Morocco, Tunisia, and Egypt. —RU

•

So prolific is the output of Africa's largest artists' community that acres of land around Tengenenge seem to have been planted with sculptural works — primitive, crude, representational or grotesque, and in overwhelming quantities. Sculptures perch on walls, window-sills and above the doors of derelict buildings; others stand on wooden plinths driven into the ground or lie tossed aside in the grass. You can walk around the village looking at the carvings and chat to sculptors chipping away at new works. Almost everything is for sale and if you're looking for a quality bargain by an unknown, this is definitely the place.

•

The most interesting of all the zimbabwes, Naletale stands at the top of a natural granite dome. As you gaze onto the wooded valley, it's difficult to imagine a better prospect, with trees growing between the long-deserted walls and *daga* hut fragments. The site is small in size — you could do a circuit of the whole place in fifteen minutes — but it's easy to while away half a day wandering about.

From close up the walls don't look terribly special but step back from the northwest section, the best preserved, and take in the patterning. Better still, lie down, prop your head on one of the pillow-sized rocks scattered about, and just gaze. The tapestried wall is, without doubt, the pinnacle of the Zimbabwe-Khami masonry tradition, the only one standing that includes all five types of patterning: chevron, chequer, herringbone, cord and ironstone. The outer wall, originally topped by small towers with monoliths, enclosed a large raised platform which was surrounded by a number of courtyards and other smaller platforms. When Donald Randall McIver, the first professional archaeologist to investigate Great Zimbabwe, dug here, he found elephant tusks embedded in the remains of one of the huts.

•

One of the eeriest features of the Makgadikgadi Pans are the fossil-like extrusions of rock — "islands" in a sea of grey sand. Most notable, and magical, is Kubu Island, a mound of lumpy rocks, pushing 10m above the Pan floor in the southwest corner of Sua Pan. It doesn't sound like much, but in a landscape as flat as a billiard table, it gives you a fantastic view of the surrounding brineland. On the outcrop are the grotesque red-tinged baobabs that inspired Michael Main to write, in his book *Kalahari: Life's Variety in Dune and Delta:*

Gnarled, usually leafless, their dwarfed and twisted forms suggest the agony of ages spent on salted waters beneath a remorseless sun. Some, seen in silhouette against the stark, grey pan, suggest a visit to another world, unutterably remote and lonely.

Zimbabwe and Botswana
(The Rough Guide)
Barbara McCrea & Tony Pinchuck.
The Rough Guides, 1993; 423 pp.
ISBN 1-85828-041-9
$16.95 ($18.95 postpaid) from Penguin USA/Consumer Sales, 120 Woodbine Street, Bergenfield, NJ 07621; 800/253-6476

South America on a Shoestring

This enormous volume will take the independent, budget-conscious traveler to turtles in the Galapagos, the Carnaval in Rio, the liveliest disco in Peru, and the spectacular glaciers in Patagonia.

Lively descriptions of hundreds of hotels and restaurants (with a wide range of prices) are included. Every city offers a huge variety of day excursions, to spots both hot and little-known. On a Shoestring offers Spanish, Portuguese, Quechua, and Aymara basic phrase guides, solid background information, and 233 maps.
—Marguerita I. Castanera

South America on a Shoestring
(Travel Survival Kit)
Wayne Bernhardson. 1994; 1161 pp.
ISBN 0-86442-199-0
$24.95 ($26.45 postpaid). Lonely Planet Publications, 155 Filbert Street, Suite 251, Oakland, CA 94607-2538; 800/275-8555

●

The Hotel Miramar (214-756), Calle 10C No 1C-59, is an exceptional place. Not only does it offer the cheapest accommodation in town, but it also has a better range of tourist facilities and information than you'll find in virtually any other budget hotel in Colombia. No wonder it has become the archetypal gringo hotel, where you're likely to meet the majority of foreign backpackers passing through town. It's obviously not a Hilton, but has acceptable rooms with fans (some with private bath) for about US $1.50 per person. If the rooms are full, the manager can give you a hammock or a mattress (either for US $1), or find somewhere for you. If you have your own hammock, you can string it up for a nominal charge.

●

If you cannot stay with your vehicle every minute, you can expect that something will be stolen from it. Stealing from vehicles being shipped is big business. If you ship the vehicle with all your possessions in it, take every precaution, and even then, don't be surprised if thieves get your stuff. Remove everything removable (hubcaps, wipers, mirrors, etc.) and take everything visible out of the interior. Camper vans are a special target — seal off the living area from the driving compartment, double-lock the living area, cover the windows so no one can see inside, and double-lock your possessions again inside the cabinets.

South America's National Parks

South America's National Parks
William C. Leitch. 1990; 286 pp.
ISBN 0-89886-248-5
$16.95 ($18.95 postpaid). The Mountaineers Books, 1101 SW Klickitat Way, Seattle, WA 98134; 800/553-4453

●

If you intend to visit several parks within one country, you would be wise to begin your tour with a visit to park service headquarters in that country's capital city. Such visits are by no means necessary or expected, but they are considered to be courteous, and are more customary practice in South America than elsewhere. A visit not only indicates good manners, but helps to indicate to park staff the level of interest shown by foreign tourists in certain parks. There are also practical reasons for courtesy calls. Park staff may be able to suggest which parks will most likely satisfy your interests. You may be given printed information and maps that have not yet been distributed to individual park offices. In some instances, it is customary to provide visitors with letters of introduction to park directors. These letters are again matters of courtesy, but they may help to ensure that you can make use of overnight accommodations, enter protected areas, and so on. For a few parks or reserves, you must obtain authorization from park service headquarters prior to your visit.

●

About 80 miles (129 kilometers) from Paramaribo [Suriname], on the Brownsberg Plateau, Brownsberg Nature Park lies smack in the middle of the rain forest at elevations

The Apple (Maça), a bizarre rock formation in the *planalto* section of Itatiaia National Park, Brazil.

Saints be praised: we have at last a guide to South America's national parks. Before, you had to spend much frustrating effort to find out even a fraction of what has been gathered here. Maps, descriptions, photos (some in color), access, climate, and tips that take you right to specific trails — everything you need but the plane tickets and a bit of local inquiry when you get there (some useful hints on that subject are given, too). In a word, Bait. —J. Baldwin

The New Key to Costa Rica • The New Key to Belize

The New Keys are among the best-written and -researched guides available. **The New Key to Costa Rica** *has long been the premier guide; its new companion leads the way for travelers to explore this tiny, immensely popular nation.*

The first half of each guide focuses on history, ecology, planning your trip, and advice for once you've arrived. The latter part provides region-by-region descriptions of selected restaurants and hotels, from jungle lodges to thatched cabanas overlooking the ocean. This is where you'll find suggested things to see and do (the authors must love being outdoors!).

Tourism has already changed Costa Rica and Belize profoundly. A "green rating" scale in both books rates tourist facilities on their commitment to local ecology and culture.
—Marguerita I. Castanera

●

Ask anyone who's spent a night in the jungle and they will tell you: The most ferocious animal is not a jaguar but a mosquito. Mosquitoes fiercely protect their territory in this region of the world, known aptly as "The Mosquito Coast." The little buzzers are thickest in rainforests, swamp areas and along coastal bush. The best defenses are long sleeves and pants, and plenty of good insect repellent.

What works for you may not work for someone else. People who wish to avoid DEET, the active chemical in most commercial mosquito repellents, may want to investigate some other methods. Herb shops and health food stores in the U.S. sell good-smelling potions that are more or less protective lotions made from oils and herbal essences. Some people swear by daily doses of Vitamin B-6 or garlic, others by tobacco smoke. The new electronic mosquito repellent devices, which emit a sound pitched at the high edge of human hearing, got high marks from a visitor to Guatemala's dense Peten jungle. Many Belizeans, following an ancient Maya custom, burn abandoned termite nests to chase away mosquitoes. After trying dozens of different brands, pills and treatments, I found that only the strongest repellent (such as Deep Woods OFF!) keeps me bugless. For areas of moderate infestation, the pleasant smelling lotion Skintastic (also made by OFF!) does the trick. —Belize

●

When crossing the street in downtown San Jose, always look over your shoulder at cars coming from behind you. In practice, the pedestrian does not have the right of way. Drivers love to whip around corners whether or not people are trying to cross.

When a traffic light for oncoming cars changes from green to yellow or red, do not take it to mean that cars will stop. Look at the cars, not the light. When you see that the cars have stopped, run across real quick. This habit is easily developed because another characteristic of San Jose is that traffic lights are hung so that pedestrians cannot see them. —Costa Rica

The New Key to Costa Rica
Beatrice Blake & Anne Becher. 1992; 289 pp. ISBN 0-915233-76-2
$13.95 postpaid.

The New Key to Belize
Stacy Ritz. 1994; 205 pp.
ISBN 0-915233-93-2
$13.95 postpaid. Both from Ulysses Press, PO Box 3440, Berkeley, CA 94703; 510/601-8301

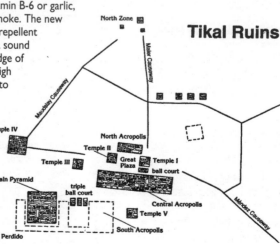

Tikal Ruins

that range from 700 to 1,400 feet. Facilities are comfortable, and simply strolling around camp is a modest jungle experience, but the real attraction of Brownsberg is its network of forest trails.

The park has by far the finest rain forest trails in South America. They are expertly laid out, well marked, and superbly maintained. Though only about 7 miles (11 kilometers) of trails weave through the park's 21,000 acres, they are designed to enable visitors to visit several sections of the park on long or short day hikes, and return to camp for a shower before dinner and darkness.

Mural, St Croix. —*The Caribbean*

Undiscovered Islands of the Caribbean

*"Undiscovered" is relative, of course. Few of these forty-plus tiny nations and protectorates are sufficiently developed to interest group-tour promoters. This guide covers the gamut of possibilities, from an island humming in the prosperity of a conch and lobster export industry to one with only 100 inhabitants and no airport.
—Linda Morgan*

●

I discovered one of Barbuda's most interesting social phenomena during a walk through Codrington at dusk. As [a resident] later explained, every morning the village residents open their gates and let their small herds of goats roam and graze freely around the island. Around such public buildings as the school and government house, the goats mow the wild grass into neat, closely cropped lawns. As sunset approaches, the goats migrate back to town in herds one hundred or more strong. Once they reach the streets of Codrington, they break off into smaller groups and walk confidently through the neighborhood to find their own yard.

●

A few miles south of Ambergris is less-visited and less-expensive Caye Caulker. The island is so narrow that you can see the water on the other side as you approach one of the little docks that the locals call "bridges." The caye is virtually all beach, and the inhabited portion is so small that one can easily walk its length and breadth within an hour. It is a barefoot island; all the road and paths are sand, free of rocks and broken glass. After a day or two, one gets to know many of the 450 friendly islanders and the visitors who come from all parts of the world.

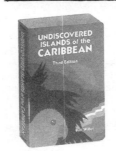

Undiscovered Islands of the Caribbean
Burl Willes. 1992; 264 pp. ISBN 1-56261-068-6
$14.95 ($18.70 postpaid) from John Muir Publications, PO Box 613, Santa Fe, NM 87504; 800/888-7504

Latin America by Bike

To its credit, this guide acknowledges that bicycling affects all parts of travel — accommodations, food, security, maps, even buses (as you'll find when you try to load that bike on local vehicles to traverse routes that can't be navigated on two wheels). Walter Sienko has distilled the practicalities and unpredictabilities of bicycle travel into a roadworthy manual for touring, maintenance, and safety. When you need that spare part in Peru, or a map that shows you the unpaved roads and roadless hills of Colombia, you'll be glad it's in your satchel. —RU

●

Two routes head southward through Patagonia. The main one, Ruta 3, follows the coast and carries almost all the traffic. On certain stretches, only one lane of the road remains paved, allowing traffic the benefit of traveling on pavement and yielding to gravel when encountering head-on traffic. Apart from the coastal road, other routes are unimproved gravel. The infamous Ruta 40, skirting the western foothills, is a rough challenge. Adding to the highway's difficulty are the toils of wind and isolation. Despite that, Route 40 conveniently connects Tierra del Fuego with the Lake District and western South America. Everyone who travels this route has stories about it. Good or bad, the difficulty of this rocky, sandy highway and its harsh beauty are unforgettable.

Latin America by Bike
Walter Sienko. 1993; 256 pp.
ISBN 0-89886-365-1
$14.95 ($16.95 postpaid). The Mountaineers Books, 1101 SW Klickitat Way, Seattle, WA 98134; 800/553-4453

●

Bicycles and bicycle shops are best viewed as a joke. Expect nothing for bicycles in Peru. I was in shops that only sold water bottles — no tires, tubes, or patches — just water bottles. With the country's restrictive import laws, a 26-inch tire is a unique find. In the mountains, market stalls devoted to selling bike parts sit beside hub-cap dealers and banana vendors. These vendors, displaying chains, wheels, hubs, spokes, and bearings in neat organized rows, have parts compatible only with the cargo bikes used in towns as taxis. . . .

The best chances for finding parts and tools are at independent organizations. Surprisingly, Peru has several bicycle racing clubs. You can ask at these clubs for information and help. For example, in Trujillo, Hugo at the Demarco Cafe enjoys helping visiting cyclists and has a guest book for all the foreign bicyclists who have pedaled through town.

The People's Guide to Mexico

*The author has traveled Mexico by foot, car, bus, truck, burro, kayak, and dugout canoe. His love and admiration for Mexico and its people come through from the very first page of this ninth edition. It is amazingly dense with information, advice, and humor, supported by clever illustrations and thorough appendices.
—Marguerita I. Castanera*

The People's Guide to Mexico
Carl Franz. 1992; 588 pp.
ISBN 1-56261-098-8
$18.95 ($22.70 postpaid). John Muir Publications, PO Box 613, Santa Fe, NM 87504; 800/888-7504

●

I rate Mexican bus and train rides high on my "must-do" list, along with such experiences as sleeping in a hammock, haggling for avocados in the market and drinking sweet, cinnamon-laced *cafe de olla* from an earthenware mug. In the Yucatan, like all of Mexico, buses and trains are literally "moving experiences."

For travelers who've heard too many stories of stomach-clenching bus trips through dizzying mountain ranges, the Yucatan's flat terrain and straight highways offer an excellent opportunity to ease into public transportation. Whether you're traveling on a budget or with a deck of credit cards, public transportation is a direct introduction to the "real" Mexico. The fact that bus and train rides are federally subsidized and ridiculously inexpensive is frosting on the cake. If you want to meet the locals on a one-to-one basis, practice your halting Spanish, enjoy Mexican food, fine humor and hospitality, just buy a ticket for the next train or bus.

●

Tourists who find themselves being hassled for such minor things as traffic violations, drunkenness or disputes with taxi drivers should remain calm. Don't shout, "By Gawd, I'm an American citizen and you can't do this . . . blah . . . blah . . . !" or you'll find yourself facing strong resentment. In almost every case the police will prefer to settle the matter quietly, on the spot, rather than have you drag in tourist bureau officials or lawyers. Be reasonable; if you're in the right but expected to pay a small "consideration," do and forget about it.

The Adventure Guide to Jamaica • to the Dominican Republic • to the Virgin Islands

Adventure Guide to Jamaica
Steve Cohen. 1992; 275 pp.
ISBN 1-55650-499-3
$17.95 ($20.45 postpaid).

Adventure Guide to the Dominican Republic
Harry S. Pariser. 1993; 233 pp.
ISBN 1-55650-537-X
$13.95 ($16.45 postpaid).

Adventure Guide to the Virgin Islands
Harry S. Pariser. 1993; 224 pp.
ISBN 1-55650-597-3
$14.95 ($17.45 postpaid).
All from Hunter Publishing, Inc., 300 Raritan Center Parkway, Edison, NJ 08818; 201/225-1900

Each has its own style and format, but their common goal is to lead travelers to unusual, unforgettable vacations. Jamaica leans heavily toward outdoor activity. You may find the information on dining and accommodations a little brief; however, the author seems well informed on where to find authentic crafts, reggae, "ganja," and Rastafarians.

The Virgin Islands and Dominican Republic guides provide ample history, background, practical advice, and activities. Both take budget into consideration when suggesting hotels and restaurants. —Marguerita I. Castanera

●

There are literally thousands of street artists in Jamaica, mass producing souvenirs or junk found in Kingston's crafts market, to the real things you can buy from Peggy Laura or I-Rise. The museums and best galleries hold classics. The streets hold the breath of today, as fresh as the morning and as fleeting as the mist. Grab it while you can. —*Jamaica*

Europe Through the Back Door

This twelfth edition investigates Europe's under-visited, under-appreciated places: idyllic hamlets in the Swiss alps, a tiny Danish island, the urban blight of Belfast.

This organization also provides the European traveler an array of services: mini-guidebooks, organized tours to unusual sights, inexpensive backpacks and moneybelts, and a public television series about some of Europe's more interesting destinations. Details on Back Door publications and services are included in their free quarterly catalog/newsletter, which occasionally features interesting articles and letters. —Richie Unterberger

•

Moneybelt $8

Absolutely required no matter where you're traveling! An ultra-light, sturdy, under-the-pants, one-size-fits-all (well, up to

Europe Through the Back Door
109 4th Avenue N., PO Box 2009, Edmonds, WA 98020; 206/771-8303, fax 206/771-0833. BBS 206/771-1902

46 inches), nylon pouch, our svelte moneybelt is just the right size to carry your valuables comfortably. It comes in neutral beige with a nylon zipper, an empty (sorry) plastic wallet insert, and full technical instructions. Made to ETBD's exacting specifications, this moneybelt is your only guarantee against theft — when you wear it, feeling a street urchin's hand in your pocket will become just another interesting cultural experience.

Let's Go: Europe

Still the bible of choice for budget and student travelers. This series, providing staggeringly detailed coverage of the sights, hostels, and eateries, now has expanded information on Eastern Europe and the former Soviet Union.

More specialized guidebooks cover off-the-beaten-track highlights that this book misses. Let's Go publishes more comprehensive volumes for several European countries (not to mention their guides to North America, Mexico, and Israel). This massive (900+ page) tome is still the most thorough single resource to pack if you're going the Eurailpass route and want to carry as little weight as possible. —RU

OTHER GREAT RESOURCES

The Scientific Traveler: Charles Tranford and Jacqueline Reynolds. 1992. John Wiley & Sons, Inc. A guide to scientific historical sites in Europe.

Budget Europe Travel Service: 2257 Meade Court, PO Box 8401, Ann Arbor, MI 48107; 313/668-0529. Tips, information, and products for the low-budget traveler.

•

Dingle Peninsula, County Kerry's northernmost, has one of Ireland's few surviving Gaelic-speaking communities. Skip over Tralee, at the Peninsula's base, and head straight for Dingle, chock full o' traditional music, craft shops, and small restaurants, before the growing tourist flood drowns all the charm. The ex-hippie owner of Rainbow Hostel (tel. 510 44), 1/2-mile west of town on Strand Rd., his son, and a team of students maintain this small, friendly setup. (IR£5; private rooms IR£15). Good, inexpensive food can be had at Eiri na Greine, Green St., opposite the church, behind Dick Mack's pub. Though fewer than 1500 people live in Dingle, the town has 52 pubs — drink up.

No matter how tight you think your schedule is, you will inevitably be waylaid by glorious Slea Head and its inviting, though clandestine, strand. Dunquin youth hostel (HI) (tel. (066) 561 21) looks out into the sea. (Lockout 10:15 am-5 pm. £4.50. Sheets 60 p.) Northeast of Dunquin lies Ballydavid and Brandon Creek, the exact spot from which St. Brenda, patron saint of Kerry, is said to have set sail for the "Heavenly Isles" (almost certainly America). In Ballydavid proper, follow the signs to the Tigh TB

Let's Go: Europe
Let's Go, Inc., 1994; 886 pp.
ISBN 0-312-09846-4
$18.99 ($21.99 postpaid) from Publishers Book & Audio, PO Box 070059, Staten Island, NY 10307; 800/288-2131

The Rough Guide Series

Produced in Britain and now easily available through US publishers, these guides aren't updated as regularly as some others. But here you'll learn the hidden histories of back alleys, the shifty politics behind those gentrified neighborhoods, and the histories of the minority cultures so rarely highlighted at the tourist office. Unabashedly personal and witty, Rough Guides resist hype, steering you away from the overcrowded Mona Lisa to the relatively undiscovered Da Vinci that lies just to the right, and to the neighborhoods where the locals go to drink their java, not the visitors.

Rough guides are available for most European countries, some territory in other continents, and other European cities. Each book has an appendix with political history, essays, and a bibliography of resources for those who want to learn more. —RU

•

The old working-class district of Prenzlauer Berg radiates out from the city centre in a network of tenement-lined cobbled streets, and is rapidly usurping Kreuzberg's role as home of the Berlin *Szene*. But then, even in GDR days it was a uniquely vibrant and exciting corner of East Berlin, home to large numbers of artists and young people seeking alternative lifestyles who chose to live here on the edge of established East German society (literally as well as figuratively — the western boundary of Prenzlauer Berg was marked by the Berlin Wall). Given the all-embracing nature of the state, this was not as easy as in "alternative" West Berlin, as in the GDR even minor acts of nonconformism, or actions that wouldn't have been regarded as out of the ordinary at all in the west, like organising an unofficial art exhibition or concert, could result in a run-in with the police or attract the unwelcome attentions of the *Stasi*. It was no coincidence that during the Honecker years more cars here flew white ribbons from their radio aerials, signalling that the owners had applied to emigrate to the west, than anywhere else in the city.

Hostel (tel. 553 00; no lockout or curfew; kitchen; IR£5). From Dingle town to the northern side of the peninsula, the 1000-ft.-high Conor Pass, a winding cliffside road too narrow for buses to traverse, crosses the mountains and affords ripping views of the bays and valleys.

Since 1989 various new bars and galleries have opened, mainly in the streets around Kollwitzplatz, thriving partly because the area's original inhabitants have been joined by an influx of people (often students) drawn from the west by cheap accommodation and squatting opportunities — squatting was already established in GDR days, and now some are looking to re-establish the squat-based counterculture that thrived in the west a decade ago, though with many buildings being reclaimed by their original owners, the best days for breaking into the squat scene are probably already over. Most of the new bars aren't dramatically different from those of western Berlin, but they have a sense of freshness, and are less jaded and established than Kreuzberg and Schöneberg haunts. —*Berlin*

The Rough Guide Series
Information from Penguin USA/Consumer Sales, 120 Woodbine Street, Bergenfield, NJ 07621; 800/253-6476

Undiscovered Islands of the Mediterranean

The "Undiscovered" in the title is sort of a reverse Columbianism; of course the islands are already occupied — some for millennia — but they are unknown to the tourist hordes, especially North Americans. Some of the destinations are unfashionable enough (like Île du Levant, off the Côte d'Azur) to share an island with a military base. Many are just now recovering from decades of economic depression and abandonment. From France to Turkey, these islands combine the special appeal of isolation in a warm blue sea, with a history reaching to the roots of Western civilization.

In competent guidebook fashion, we are pointed to walking trails and given ferry directions. Recommendations for lodging and dining are also offered. The authors' gift to the reader is the transparency of their prose style, a graceful informality perfectly suited to the islands' ambiance. Illustrated with photos and spare, charming maps. Rapture of the deep strikes again! —Don Ryan

•

Even in late September, the midday heat and intense light discourage exploration; dawn is the perfect time to watch the island come to life. First to appear are the farmers who bring their produce to stores that have pastel-tinted walls faded by decades of sunlight. A black goat grazes against the remains of a mottled green wall that glistens from the rays of the early morning sun. Old women appear from behind ornately carved doors to wash their

Eastern Europe on the Loose

At 634 pages, On The Loose is the most thorough and up-to-date guide to the cities, villages, and countrysides of Hungary, Bulgaria, Poland, Romania, Slovakia, and the Czech Republic. It will help to untangle the particulars of finding accommodations and transportation in countries that are still adjusting to private enterprise, and help you find the mineral baths of Bulgaria, the forests of Transylvania, and the salt mines outside Krakow. Berkeley guides are also available to other regions of Europe, as well as a few destinations on other continents.
—Richie Unterberger

●

Even if you sign some sort of contract with a flat's legal tenant, realize that it will probably be worth no more than the paper it's printed on. If you deal with a real-estate agency you may get a solid arrangement, but you'll pay heavily for it. Among the foreign residents of Prague, horror stories of being evicted from a flat with only a day's or even a few hours' notice are so common that they are traded with gusto over beers in the pubs — almost everybody who has stayed longer than a few months has such a story. On the whole, your options are to find a tolerant and dependable Czech person to let you live undisturbed in their place (and they do exist), pay the

price for a real-estate middleman, or keep possessions at a minimum and accept the transience most foreigners in Prague learn to live with.

●

A front-runner for the most surreal sight in Slovakia, the Museum Muderného Umenia (Museum of Modern Art) must be seen to be believed. But to see it, you'll have to travel to Medzilaborce in the far reaches of northern Slovakia, 50 kilometers northeast of Presov and 10 kilometers from the Polish border. Set in this cow town where horse-drawn carts still have run of the streets, the gleaming white museum, with two 7-foot Campbell's soup cans forming the entryway, looks as if it were accidentally dropped from the sky. The entire museum is dedicated to the work of Andy Warhol, whose parents emigrated from the nearby village of Mikova to Chicago in the early part of the century; this tenuous connection inspired the recent establishment of the museum. The collection has grown from one small lithograph of a cow (appropriate) to over two dozen works. Chances are high that

Eastern Europe on the Loose
Alison Huml & Chelsea Mauldin. Berkeley Guides, 1994; 634 pp. ISBN 0-679-02595-2 $17.50 ($19.50 postpaid) from Random House/Order Dept., 400 Hahn Road, Westminster, MD 21157; 800/733-3000

you will have the museum all to yourself, and it is an eerie experience to wander the large, empty space and study Warhol's pop-culture sensibility taken so far out of context. A number of family artifacts are also on display, such as Andy's baptismal gown, personal letters, and paintings by Warhol's brother and nephew. The museum contains a cinema which appropriately dispenses pop-culture imperialism with showings of the latest Hollywood movies.

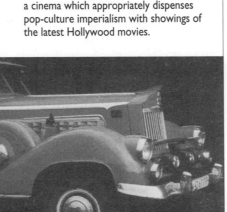

—The Georgian Republic

Moscow-St. Petersburg Handbook

Already in its second edition, this is the most up-to-date resource for exploring Russia's two largest cities, as well as the Golden Ring — the towns and villages between the two metropoli. Written by filmmaker Masha Nordbye, who has worked and traveled throughout Russia for nearly twenty years, it includes introductions to Russian music, festivals, history, language, and food, as well as detailed listings of sights, accommodations, and amenities. —RU

●

If you're really adventurous, you can rent a car and drive it yourself. You can visit many more towns in just one day, especially from Moscow, without having to overnight anywhere. Just make sure you find out where the gas stations are located along the way — they're not so easy to find, and they don't always have gasoline. All these op-

tions must be paid for in foreign currency.

If you have some Russian friends with a car, have them drive you around the area for a day. Or find a Russian who has a car who will be willing to take you around for the day. Many Russians with private cars (or taxis) are looking to pick up some extra cash, especially on the weekends. Bargain for a price — add a little tip as a further incentive and you'll be on your way. Zagorsk is less than an hour's ride from Moscow. If you go with other Russians, most likely they've been there a few times and can show you around.

Moscow-St. Petersburg Handbook
(Including the Golden Ring)
Masha Nordbye. 1993; 259 pp.
ISBN 0-918373-91-3
$13.95 ($17.45 postpaid) from Moon Publications, Inc., PO Box 3040, Chico, CA 95927; 800/345-5473, fax 916/345-6751

Practice at the Moscow Circus.

steps with buckets of water, a tradition performed for centuries. Next, the cat population begins to stir, then to amble down toward the waterfront for the arrival of the fishermen with the daily catch. Birds flutter through the empty windows of a now-abandoned Greek church. Inside are water-damaged frescoes and exposed brick columns that are hauntingly beautiful. Around 8:00 a.m., small, happy groups of children walk down the quiet streets to their elementary school behind the yacht harbor. Their black jackets, shorts, and newly pressed white shirts are spotless. Some of the youngsters have put an elegant finishing touch to their uniform, a starched white handkerchief in the tiny jacket pocket. The waterfront cafés fill up for morning tea, and then with the arrival of the fishing boats, the cats are fed and the midday meal is delivered in handmade baskets to the restaurants and hotels. The day is in full swing in Çunda; life moves with gusto and much pleasure on this now shimmering Turkish island.

Undiscovered Islands of the Mediterranean
Linda Lacione Moyer & Burt Willes. 1990; 220 pp. ISBN 0-945465-53-X $14.95 ($18.70 postpaid) from John Muir Publications, PO Box 613, Santa Fe, NM 87504; 800/888-7504

People to People

The guides in this series have more charm and personality than most travel tools. Each is essentially an index of a country's residents who want to meet Americans, show you around their town, and (sometimes) have you stay in their house. I can't think of a better way to get to know a place than hanging out with a local.

Featuring about one thousand individuals, of all ages and professions, the books are organized by city with a brief description of each person's interests, languages, address, phone number, and occupation.
—Marguerita I. Castanera

●

From a student in Lithuania:

Now I sit by the table and think: what to tell you about myself, how to make a beginning. . . . I live with my mother and sister. My town is near the sea, which is a part of my life. All natural phenomena whisper to you: "you are living, that's your state in life." I play the piano and sing. There are also a great many things mysteriously interesting and tempting: philosophy, religion, architecture . . . Association with my friends helps me to live. I'm ready to reply to anyone. Keep happy till the next time.
—Baltic Republics

People to People Series:
Jim Haynes, Editor. 1992, 1993
• Baltic Republics
• Czech-Slovakia, Hungary, Bulgaria
• Poland
• Romania
$10.95 ($13.95 postpaid) each from Zephyr Press, 13 Robinson Street, Somerville, MA 02145; 617/628-9726, fax 617/776-8246

OTHER GREAT RESOURCES

Alternative Moscow: The Institute For Social Inventions, 20 Heber Road, London NW2 6AA, UK, 081/208-2853.

Jewish Heritage Travel: Ruth Ellen Gruber. 1992. John Wiley & Sons, Inc. A guide to Jewish-oriented sights and the remaining Jewish communities in Central and Eastern Europe.

The Georgian Republic: Roger Rosen. 1992. Passport Books. One of the few detailed guides to an individual state in the former Soviet Union.

Moon Handbooks to US States

While they publish an outstanding selection of international guides, Moon's greatest achievements may be the individual state books they offer those looking for alternatives to AAA guides.

Those trusty road manuals tell you how to get from here to there well enough, but Moon's more interested in the hot springs, saloons, and ghost towns in between. Oriented toward independent and modestly budgeted travelers, the series so far focuses on the western US. Moon not only digs up little-discovered attractions, but also offers thumbnail sketches of the culture and state politics of regions that rarely make national headlines.
—Richie Unterberger

•

When gambling was legalized in 1931, Elko started up its casino industry in the venerable Commercial Hotel. Newton Crumley, who'd owned hotels in Tonopah and Goldfield, and a saloon in Jarbridge, had bought the Commercial six years earlier. The Crumleys followed the lead of Raymond and Harold Smith of Reno by making the new gambling accessible and acceptable to the masses. But the Crumleys went an important step further and began to book big-name acts to do the floor show in the

Nevada has the country's loneliest roads

lounge. A rousing success, this began the tradition of headliners and floor shows in casinos.

This booming town has a brash, modern, frontier energy all its own. It's easy to slip into Elko's strong stream of hustle and bustle, which seems to keep pace with the cars and trucks on the superhighway, the freight and passenger trains chugging right through town, and the planes landing at and taking off from the airport. Yet Elko also has a warm, homespun vitality to it. Coming into Elko after a long drive from any direction is like stepping up to a blazing campfire on a cold desert night. And you seem to return to Elko again and again, after playing around for awhile up in the Rubies or up around Jarbridge, or just passing through on your comings and goings. So get to know Elko. Within and around it is everything you could need or want from a major Nevada town.

Nevada is full of travelers' oases such as this one.

Moon Handbooks
AK/Yukon, AZ, Baja, Big Island (HI), BC, Catalina Island, CO, HI, ID, Kauai, Maui, MT, NV, NM, Northern CA, Oahu, OR, TX, UT, WA, WY, Yucatan: $11.95-$14.95. Catalog free. PO Box 3040, Chico, CA 95927; 800/345-5473, fax 916/345-6751

Roadfood

Covering every state in the union, Jane and Michel Stern take us to the tastiest and most colorful of those neighborhood establishments and highway cafes that you'll never find in the guidebooks. Before you dread that overnight stop in Cincinnati, read the Ohio chapter. (Bet you didn't know it was the chili capital of America).

Written with respect for good food and a sincere, often hilarious appreciation of local character and ambience, this book is an entertaining document of Americana in its own right. —RU

•

We had checked into a motel on the strip leading into Bowling Green; and having no other hot leads, found ourselves at Kaufman's for dinner. The original Kaufman's was (and still is) downtown on Main Street. The new branch, on the strip, is what was once Howard Johnson's. "The best food in town!" our motel clerk assured us. We were dubious. It looked so ordinary. Before going, we telephoned Kaufman's to investigate, quizzing them to find out if their mashed potatoes are handmade or instant. When they said they peeled and mashed spuds every day, we were on our way.

Roadfood
Jane Stern & Michael Stern.
1992; ISBN 0-06-096599-1
$15 ($17.75 postpaid) from HarperCollins Publishers/Direct Mail, PO Box 588, Dunmore, PA 18512; 800/331-3761

Inside the ex-HoJo's, what used to be the soda fountain is now a bar. The place is rather disheveled; the help is mostly young people, as in the average nobody-cares franchise … so you think. But you are wrong. The lad who brings the crock of cheddar cheese and crackers hors d'oeuvre takes an oath that the mashed potatoes are real. "Nothing we do here is phony," he assures you. And by golly, he is right.

Everything isn't necessarily wonderful. In this relatively *Roadfood*less region, however, we are grateful for apple sauce that is real, chunky, homemade — yes, homemade. And real home-baked dinner rolls even if, at the end of a busy weekend, they have the dried consistency of yesterday's.

A Foreign Visitor's Survival Guide to America

This book is a no-nonsense primer to American customs, practicalities, and mores. Covering housing, financing, food, health, etiquette, and difficult situations, it's useful not only for visitors and those planning to live in the US, but also for Americans hosting and working with foreigners. —RU

A typical American table setting

•

Two issues that can cause friction even between people of the same culture are money and privacy. It is important to realize that your agreement to pay your share of the rent has to be discharged in money. As an immigrant, your assets are often in kind, not cash, but this does not help your roommate pay the landlord or the landlord pay his or her property taxes. Another common misconception held by newcomers with socialist backgrounds is that the one with greater assets at the time should pay what is due or be willing to extend credit until the other has enough money to pay. This expectation will rarely be met in the United States.

A Foreign Visitor's Survival Guide to America
Shauna Singh Baldwin & Marilyn M. Levine. 1992; 211 pp. ISBN 1-56261-059-7
$12.95 ($16.70 postpaid) from John Muir Publications, PO Box 613, Santa Fe, NM 87504; 800/888-7504

Hidden Guidebooks

This series takes you to little-traveled trails and homey diners as well as famed attractions, and reminds you of how much sparsely inhabited or uninhabited territory we still have. —RU

•

Just down the road from Billy the Kid's grave, Fort Sumner State Monument (505-355-2573) marks the site of the army outpost for which the town was named. By the time Billy the Kid came to town, the fort had been converted to a ranch headquarters, and it was here that Garrett killed him. Just a few years earlier, the fort was the scene of larger and more infamous events. Colonel Kit Carson, after forcing the entire Navajo tribe to walk 300 miles from their homeland to this place, ordered them to build Fort Sumner as a concentration camp. More than 11,000 Indians lived in captivity here for six years, and 3,000 of them died of starvation and disease. Finally the government concluded that keeping the Navajo at Fort Sumner was too expensive and that their homeland was without value to the white man. Then the surviving Navajo people were allowed to walk back home. Today, no trace remains of the original fort. Low adobe walls mark the location of the main fort buildings. The most moving part of the monument is a simple shrine of stones brought from all over the Navajo Reservation and left here by Native Americans in memory of those who lived and died here.

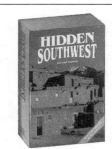

Hidden Guidebooks
New England, Boston & Cape Cod, FL, Florida Keys, Rockies, Pacific Northwest, San Francisco & Northern California, Southern California, Coast of California, Southwest, HI, Mexico: each $14.95 postpaid from Ulysses Press, PO Box 3440, Berkeley, CA 94703; 510/601-8301

The Route 66 Traveler's Guide

For the first half of this century, Route 66 was an enduring symbol of American mobility. It was the first interstate link between the heartland and the West Coast, starting in Chicago and ending in Los Angeles.

Route 66 no longer exists in its original form. But with Tom Snyder's guide, and its forty-two reproductions of 1930s AAA maps, you can get off the superhighway and investigate the meandering blue ribbons that are all that remain of Old 66.
—Richie Unterberger

•

As you drive through town, consider how all this might look now if Flagstaff had become the movie capital of the world. Because it almost did. A few years before Route 66 began service, a talented and extremely ambitious young man was steaming west on the Atchison, Topeka & Santa Fe. Folded in his coat pocket was a new screenplay, and in his mind's eye he could see every detail of how it would be made — in the real West, with real cowboys and Indians, under open skies. Fed up with Long Island studios where no one knew a cactus from a tin can, the young man was certain from his readings of Zane Grey that Flagstaff was the perfect destination. The film he would make there would be grand, sweeping, magnificent — an *epic*.

It would also be wet, if he tried to make it in Flagstaff, where great, sodden flakes of snow were plopping softly into streams of icy mush along the platform as the train pulled in. For young Cecil B. DeMille, though, one look was not enough. He never even left his Pullman, but went right on to Los Angeles, where he made the world's first feature-length film, *Squaw Man*, using regular drugstore cowboys. But the incident must have left its mark on him, for through the monumental, biblical films DeMille later made, there always ran a theme of uncontrollable natural forces. And water, lots and lots of water.

The Route 66 Traveler's Guide
Tom Snyder. St Martin's Press, 1990; 136 pp. ISBN 0-312-04587-5 $9.95 ($12.95 postpaid) from Publishers Book & Audio, PO Box 070059, Staten Island, NY 10307; 800/288-2131

The original participants in the Greensboro lunch counter sit-ins re-enact the scene at a thirtieth anniversary observance.

Historic Black Landmarks

African-American history hasn't just been written out of school textbooks; it's often been written out of guidebooks as well. Historic Black Landmarks *goes a long way toward addressing that imbalance, detailing hundreds of black history museums, homes of famous African-Americans, and parks and neighborhoods that played key roles in black history and culture. The real value of this book is not so much as a guide to sites, but as a springboard for George Cantor's informed and fascinating retellings of little-known incidents and people that shaped black America.* —RU

•

Effigy Cemetery,
Mount Nebo Baptist Church

The making of masks is a cultural motif that runs throughout African art. Placing an effigy mask of the deceased on the burial place has two purposes. It is a way of remaining in the presence of one's ancestors. It is also meant to mislead evil spirits, who might interfere with the passing of the dead into the afterlife, into thinking that the mask was really the living soul of the deceased.

It's rare to find effigy cemeteries in this country, but one of the best-preserved is near this southern Alabama town. The iron masks were cast by a local artisan, Isaac Nettles, and placed on the gravestones in the Mount Nebo Baptist Church cemetery.

•

Mobile
Africa Town

The African slave trade was officially ended by an act of Congress in 1807. But for over half a century more, illegal slave ships slipped into hidden landing places throughout the South to unload smuggled human cargo. The last such ship on record was the *Clothilde*, build by Timothy Meaher of Mobile in 1859. It returned from its first voyage later that year with a cargo of kidnapped inhabitants of the Guinea coast. Alerted to its arrival, federal boats were on patrol in Mississippi Sound. But Capt. William Fowler managed to slip past them into the Mobile River, unloaded his cargo, and burned his ship. With federal authorities all around the area, Meaher and Foster found it impossible to dispose of the intended slaves, and eventually turned them loose.

Many of the freed familes banded together to form a community nearby in an area known as Plateau. Their descendants still inhabit the vicinity, four miles north of downtown Mobile, in the shadow of the port city's most industrialized area. The last of the original *Clothilde* passengers, Cudjoe Lewis, died in 1935. A memorial to him, put up by his descendants, now stands at the heart of the Africa Town community, the Union Baptist Church, on Bay Bridge Road. Lewis lived next door to the church until his death and was noted for his prodigious memory; although illiterate, he could quote entire Bible chapters by heart.

Historic Black Landmarks
George Cantor. 1991; 372 pp. ISBN 0-8103-9408-1 $17.95 ($19.70 postpaid) from Visible Ink Press/Attn: Virginia Rigish, PO Box 71701, Chicago, IL 60694; 313/961-2242

Indian America

Irish/Choctaw author Eagle/Walking Turtle provides a cultural context for basic information on more than three hundred US tribes. Details of ceremonies and crafts at each site are supplemented by a large appendix with a glossary and a list of Native American events.

Of the several worthy guidebooks to Native America, I've found this to be the most user-friendly. The introductory chapters are illuminating essays. —RU

•

Mikasuki

Location: The tribal complex is 25 miles west of Miami on the Tamiami Trail, which is Highway 41.

Public Ceremony or Powwow Dates: Call for the dates of the Green Corn Ceremonies and stomp dances. The Arts Festival featuring dancing, arts, and crafts is held the week after Christmas.

Art Forms: The Miccosukee museum shows traditional Miccosukee life in exhibits, films, photos and paintings. There is a reconstructed village with open-sided Miccosukee "chickees," the old fashioned houses of the tribe. Here you can find traditional colorful Miccosukee clothing, dugout canoes, and arts and crafts demonstrations and sales.

Indian America
Eagle/Walking Turtle. 1993; 460 pp. ISBN 1-56261-110-0 $18.95 ($22.70 postpaid) from John Muir Publications, PO Box 613, Santa Fe, NM 87504; 800/888-7504

Visitor Information: Don't miss the alligator wrestling. Across the street from the village is the Miccosukee restaurant serving Miccosukee and regular fare. Adjacent to the restaurant are the Miccosukee airboat rides, which fly you through the Everglades. Your guides will be happy to take you to a small tree-covered island to show you a real old-time Miccosukee camp that is still in use.

The Mikasuki are a former Seminole division. They spoke the Hitchiti dialect and were partly emigrants from the Swaokli towns on the lower Chattahoochee River, Alabama. At this time, they had 300 houses, which were burned by General Jackson. There were then several villages near the lake, known also as Mikasuki towns, which were occupied almost wholly by blacks. In the Seminole Wars of 1835-1842, the people of this town became famous for their courage and audacity.

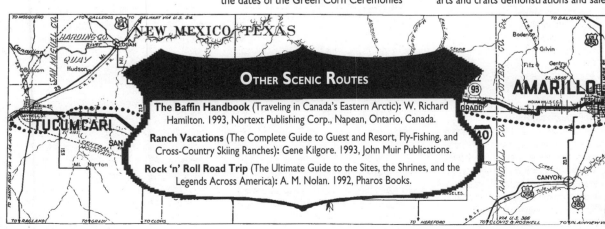

OTHER SCENIC ROUTES

The Baffin Handbook (Traveling in Canada's Eastern Arctic): W. Richard Hamilton. 1993, Nortext Publishing Corp., Napean, Ontario, Canada.

Ranch Vacations (The Complete Guide to Guest and Resort, Fly-Fishing, and Cross-Country Skiing Ranches): Gene Kilgore. 1993, John Muir Publications.

Rock 'n' Roll Road Trip (The Ultimate Guide to the Sites, the Shrines, and the Legends Across America): A. M. Nolan. 1992, Pharos Books.

Harvesting olives in Crete.

Transitions Abroad

This bimonthly magazine for "learning, living, and working overseas" aims to "provide active travelers of all ages with practical, usable information on economical, purposeful international travel opportunities — travel that involves learning by living, studying, working, or vacationing alongside the people of the host country." Each issue is packed with information that's useful for anyone looking for an international experience of greater depth than the typical vacation. Transitions Abroad also publishes an annual international resource guide and an educational travel directory, as well as a few dozen specialized guides such as Spanish Language Schools In Central America, Teaching Overseas, *and* Responsible Travel In Asia.
—Richie Unterberger

•

With unemployment in France at 25 percent for recent university graduates, more and more people are performing underground. The Paris metro often resembles an international circus, with mimes, musicians, and puppeteers vying for the public's attention.

Transit authorities issue free licenses to buskers, allowing them to stand at certain spots and entertain the passerby. The only stipulation: Do not beg or play too close to the tender ears of metro personnel. It's against the law to perform on the trains, but many do. Most buskers spend their days riding back and forth, adroitly staying one station ahead of the metro police.

Diane began busking when her husband was finishing a graduate degree and they ran out of money to pay the rent. The couple has made up to $50 to $75 an hour. Through connections made underground, Diane and her husband found work as entertainers for

a catering company. They also recently recorded a demo after performing unawares for the owner of a Parisian studio on one of the trains.

Diane has never been fined by the metro police. In fact, some of the controllers have even contributed money in appreciation of her act. The transit system itself provides its own brand of entertainment: Since 1977, it has sponsored concerts, plays, and even chess tournaments at certain stations as part of a public service program aimed at humanizing the metro.

Servas

U.S. Servas Committee: Membership $55/year. 11 John Street, Room 407, New York, NY 10038; 212/267-0252.

If you're sincerely interested in meeting local people as you travel the world, or if you'd like to host foreign visitors, an international organization exists that facilitates short stays in people's homes in over ninety countries.

Called Servas, its primary goal is to promote world peace by bringing people of diverse cultures, races and backgrounds together in homes throughout the world. A visitor typically stays for two days, although one may be invited to stay longer.

While the rules vary from country to country, in the US one can join Servas (Esperanto for "we serve") in order to stay in other people's homes without being required to host visitors. The annual membership fee for travelers is $55, with a refundable deposit of $25 for lists of hosts; there is no fee for children under eighteen traveling with a parent. Servas requests that hosts contribute $25 per year.

While there is no charge for lodging, the organization is interested in travelers looking for more than just a free place to stay. (Travelers should not depend on having continuous access to hosts.) What is important, says

Transitions Abroad

Transitions Abroad
(The Guide to Learning, Living, and Working Overseas)
$18/year (6 issues) from Transitions Abroad Publishing/Dept. TRA, Box 3000, Denville, NJ 07834; 800/562-1973

Harvesting olives in Crete.

Work Your Way Around The World

The most thorough regularly published guide to work opportunities abroad; it is strongest on Europe, but also covers North America, Australia, Asia, Africa, and Latin America. After a general overview of work strategies and the professions (hotels, couriers, English teachers) most commonly available to travelers and nonresidents, it details specific organizations, employers, work permits, and available resources in dozens of countries. Frequent anecdotes by worker/travelers in such occupations as grape picker and ski instructor add a human dimension to the overwhelming number of options presented here. Griffith has also written a similarly exhaustive book devoted solely to Teaching English Abroad. —RU

•

Most English teachers in Czechoslovakia agree that the situation in state schools is generally better than in private schools. Recruitment of untrained teachers for state schools takes place through the Students for Czechoslovakia section of the Academic Information Agency (AIA) in both the Czech and Slovak capitals. This is how the American Natalia de Cuba found her job after falling in love with Prague on a European motorcycling trip and deciding to stay:

OTHER GREAT WORK/STUDY/HOMESTAY RESOURCES

The International Directory of Voluntary Work: David Woodworth. 1993; Peterson's Guides.

International Workcamp Directory: $10/year (membership, directory and newsletter). Volunteers for Peace, Tiffany Road, Belmont, VT 05730.

Pasporto Servo. A free service which connects Esperanto speakers with hosts in 72 countries. Esperanto League for North America. PO Box 1129, El Cerrito CA 94530; 800/828-5944.

American International Homestays, Inc.: PO Box 7178, Boulder, CO 80306; 800/876-2048. Organizes moderately priced homestays for American travelers in the former Soviet Union and Eastern Europe.

Servas's Jenny V. Batterson, is that the visits become meaningful through involvement in the household. Servas strives to foster "understanding between people . . . through the person-to-person sharing of ideas, questions, interests and concerns."

Membership requires an interview and references. The United States Servas Committee approves about 2,000 travelers and a similar number of hosts annually.

Servas was founded in Denmark in 1948 by an American conscientious objector and a group of his friends, to enable young people to "learn the ways of peace." Servas is affiliated with the United Nations as a nongovernmental organization.
—Arthur P. Glickman

The Vacation Home Exchange and Hospitality Guide

This guide lists various kinds of home exchanges, mostly international. There are also chapters on hospitality exchanges (i.e., reciprocal visits vs. strict exchanges), as well as bed-and-breakfast exchanges and extended homestays. The descriptions of the programs are basic, evaluated according to their strengths and weaknesses; plenty are listed, with fees and (when available) percentages of American/foreign users. —RU

•

Friends in France does not accept hosts who are interested merely in renting out a room or in a bed-and-breakfast operation. Only those hosts who have a genuine desire to know their guests and offer them hospitality are enlisted. All facilities are visited on an average of once a year and most have a wonderful track record according to the directors.

The homestays offer a variety of flexibility. Meals are optional, as is the amount of time spent with the host family. Hosted tours and driving services are often available. Linens and fresh towels are provided, but you will be expected to straighten your own quarters and take care of laundry. Children are welcome and if you wish to practice

The Vacation Home Exchange and Hospitality Guide
John Kimbrough. 1991; ISBN 0-9628199-0-5
$14.95 ($16.95 postpaid) from Kimco Communications, 4242 West Dayton Fresno, CA 93722; 209/275-0893

your French, host families will refrain from speaking English.

The host homes do not want to be used as bed-and-breakfast stops by transients nor as boarding houses by permanent guests. As a result a minimum stay of 3 nights and a maximum stay of two weeks in any one family is imposed. Many clients choose to visit more than one family, and some guests have visited as many as eight families on a trip. Whatever you wish, the club will be happy to work with you.

Birmingham, UK
(fast food restaurant)

Ana Maria Guernes Circuit

Toronto (waitress)

Germany
(au pair on
American base)

**Work Your Way
Around the World**
Susan Griffith. 1993; 432 pp.
ISBN 1-85458-074-4
$17.95 ($23.70 postpaid) from
Peterson's Guides, PO Box 2123,
Princeton, NJ 08543;

Texas
(nanny
for a month)

Athens
(offered
summer job in
travel agency)

Mexico
(leaves home
after university
July 1990)

Israel (kibbutz)

Burgos, Spain
(voluntary grape-picker, October 1992)

I went to the AIA and had a job and accommodation for two in a Teacher's House (Dum Ucitelu) the next day. No one looked at my qualifications. I began with a 2-month contract in a commerce high school as a substitute for a teacher with health problems. We were lucky enough to have one set of Cambridge books which we carted around from class to class. After the contract finished I was offered and accepted conversation lessons after school. I was paid only 30 crowns an hour, but maintained my accommodation. Through the AIA there are often short-term contracts (but no summer work).

What You Can Do for Your Country

A hard-boiled, absorbing history of the Peace Corps from its inception as a Kennedy campaign promise through its inroads into Eastern Europe during the waning days of the Bush administration. Schwarz looks unflinchingly at what it has and hasn't accomplished in developing countries, and its possible political motives as a PR instrument for the US. The Peace Corps has at times undercut its mission by sending poorly prepared or unneeded volunteers. It's also been speculated that volunteers have been used as pawns to further several administrations' (usually anti-socialist) interests, as when missions were dramatically increased to Honduras in the mid-eighties.

The most riveting voices are heard when several dozen volunteers of the past thirty years, all ages and backgrounds, recollect their stints in their own words. Some joined out of altruism; some joined to evade the draft; some joined for no clear reason. Their efforts to improve conditions within the Peace Corps itself were often met with indifference and, occasionally, disciplinary action. Their experiences are both inspiring and cautionary tales that should be of interest to prospective Peace Corps volunteers. —RU

●

I looked at my life in this community center and realized that this was it for two years: Collecting dues for cake decorating classes. The notion that any kind of social change can occur through the efforts of naive, well-intentioned American college kids is

**What You Can
Do for Your Country**
Karen Schwarz, Editor. Anchor Books,
1993; 320 pp. ISBN 0-385-46898-9
$12.95 ($15.45 postpaid) from Bantam,
Doubleday, Dell/Fulfillment Dept., 2451
S. Wolf Road, Des Plaines, IL 60018;
800/223-6834

totally ludicrous. I came to the conclusion that the volunteers' purpose was to do public relations for Uncle Sam.
—Margot Jones (Ecuador, 1965-67)

One of the directors told me that they would not send anybody to Katowice, the most polluted city in Poland. But two of the oldest volunteers have been assigned there. A lot of people said, "This is how the Peace Corps is — everybody hates the training and hates the bureaucracy, but they love the country and the people. When they go off to their site, the Peace Corps disappears and they have a great time." I think that that is just not right. If I had begun thinking clearly earlier, I probably would not be in the Peace Corps right now. But I felt too involved in the country and the people I'd met and too committed to helping, to make going back to the U.S. an option. —Jennifer Olsen (Poland, 1990-92)

Alternatives to the Peace Corps

This directory contains dozens of thorough listings of voluntary service organizations, technical service programs, work brigades, and study tours in the Third World. This information is prefaced by issues to consider before enlisting in the Peace Corps, the different needs of study/volunteer/work programs, and answers to the most commonly asked questions about humanitarian work/travel programs in developing regions. The text is supplemented by a good bibliography and list of other resources.

It's a fine starting point for those considering the many options available in these fields. —RU

●

Peace Brigades International
Box 381233
Cambridge, MA 02238
Tel: 617/491-4226

Peace Brigades International's (PBI) Central America Project sends nonviolent/nonpartisan teams to Guatemala to monitor human rights violations. International volunteers accompany threatened individuals, give workshops in peace education (mediation, human rights, conflict resolution, etc.), and upon their return, conduct public education programs through speaking tours. Volunteers should be 25 years or older, fluent in Spanish, and able to make a commitment to work a minimum of seven months. Volunteers must also undergo training in nonviolence before being accepted. Volunteers pay transportation and health insurance; other costs are paid by PBI.

Alternatives to the Peace Corps
(A Directory of Third World &
U. S. Volunteer Opportunities)
Anette Olson, Editor. 1994; 88 pp.
ISBN 0-935028-62-5
$6.95 ($8.95 postpaid) from Institute for
Food and Development Policy, 398 60th
Street, Oakland, CA 94618; 800/888-3314

Work, Study, Travel Abroad

While less personal than Work Your Way Around The World, Work Study Travel Abroad has a wider and more education-oriented scope, covering university exchange/study programs and basic travel info. Arranged by country are thousands of descriptive listings of overseas learning institutions and programs for North American students. The book also details overseas organizations that offer work opportunities. While this is their flagship book (updated every two years), the Council on International Educational Exchange publishes more specialized guides such as Smart Vacations: The Traveler's Guide to Learning Vacations Abroad and Going Places: The High-School Student's Guide To Study, Travel, and Adventure Abroad. They are also affiliated with the budget travel agency Council Travel, which can be contacted directly at 205 E. 42nd St., New York, NY 10017. —RU

●

World Learning/School for International Training. *College Semester Abroad*. Hanoi, Hue, Da Nang, Nha Trang, and Ho Chi Minh City. Fall and spring semesters. Intensive language, seminar on Vietnamese life and culture, field-study methods seminar, homestays, independent-study project, and

Work, Study, Travel Abroad
(The Whole World Handbook, 12th Ed.)
Council on International Educational
Exchange. 1994; 606 pp.
ISBN 0-312-10578-9
$13.95 ($16.95 postpaid) from Publishers
Book & Audio, PO Box 070059,
Staten Island, NY 10307; 800/288-2131

excursions. Sophomores to seniors with 2.5 GPA. Apply by May 7 for fall; October 7 for spring. Contact: College Semester Abroad Admissions at (800) 336-1616.

REST-STOP PUG WASHING
James Donnelly

Online Resources

Travel information has a short shelf life. Online information sources are a conduit for current intelligence on changing conditions and for the advice of experienced travelers.

The following online services can be accessed from IBM-compatible and Macintosh personal computers equipped with modem and telecommunications software (the latter is provided in the services' sign-up kits).

The Internet *(p. 263) offers a dizzying variety of message-exchange forums, and travelogs from nearly every country on the planet.*

Global Network Navigator Travel Resource Center. *This free Internet-based service is devoted exclusively to travel information, with 100+ travel newsgroups, a currency converter, weather forecasts, and maps. Phone 800/338-6887 (voice) or email info@gnn.com .*

America OnLine *(p. 267; 800/827-6364) has a voluminous travel forum and reservation services.*

CompuServe *(p. 267; 800/848-8990) boasts a wide range of reservation services and travel information databases, but its diminutive travel forum may disappoint. "Basic services" include government travel information and restaurant guides.*

The WELL *(p. 262; signups 415/332-6106) and **GEnie** (p. 267; signups 800/638-8369). Strong travel forums.*

CABB *(the State Department's Consular Affairs Bulletin Board) provides a free, well-organized and -maintained database of traveler advisories. 202/647-9225.*

Worldwide Brochures. *Users can order from 10,000 free maps, travel guides, and brochures through this BBS. $12/year; no online charges. 1227 Kenneth St., Detroit Lakes, MN 56501. 800/8526752 (voice); BBS #: 218/847-3027.* —Rodney Paul

See pp. 260, 262, and 263 for plenty more online arcana.

Quick time movie

InterOptica CD-ROM: Macintosh, DOS, or MPC versions available. $13.90 – $49.90. InterOptica titles can be found under the Apple StarCore heading in Tiger Software's free CD-ROM catalog.
Tiger Software: PO Box 569005, Miami, FL 33256-9005; 800/666-2562. Complete title list available from Take Two, 575 Broadway, New York, NY 10012.

Slide show

Desktop Travel Publications

No travel book can keep up with changing political climates or airfares, or great cafes. Homemade, desktop-published travel newsletters keep abreast of changing travel conditions and attractions; their personal reflections, observations, and anecdotes can be equally valuable. —RU

*The pamphlet-size, bimonthly **Globe** features absorbing tales of worldwide independent travel, as well as related letters, book reviews, and classifieds. A typical issue might have travelogues from South America, Cuba, Malawi, Czechoslovakia, and the Arctic Wilderness.*

Globetrotters Club: Membership $18/year (includes 6 issues of *Globe*). Globetrotters Club, BCM Roving, London, WC1N 3XX, UK.

Using a computerized recumbent bicycle he calls the Winnebiko, Steven K. Roberts wanders North America, publishing the quarterly **Nomadness Report** *as a forum for his (and his pals') travel writing and technological innovations.*

Nomadness Report: $15/year (4 issues). Nomadic Research Labs, PO Box 2185, El Segundo, CA 90245.

As a backpacker and as a business traveler, Arnie Weissman has visited over eighty countries. His most valuable reports cover little-trod countries such as North Korea.

Weissmann Travel Reports: PO Box 49279, Austin, TX 78765; 512/320-8700.

Let's look at the idea of an electronic Yellow Pages that's sensitive to your current position. You're driving in a metropolitan area with a database that combines your regional map with businesses that have provided their geocoded addresses (i.e., their latitude and longitude coordinates). You're interested in Thai restaurants within 5 minutes of your current position. The map highlights the possible locations; clicking on any of them pops up the Yellow Pages entry, with their phone numbers and hours. Second, imagine that you are driving home during rush hour. Your car has a radio data receiver that collects information about road conditions. Your display shows an animated interpretation of this data, showing the relative movement of traffic with trouble spots highlighted. Since this data is received in real time, you can be up to the minute with traffic conditions, long before your local radio station gets around to broadcasting the latest conditions. A simple extension of this idea could include weather conditions and detour information. —*The Nomadness Report*

●

[North] Korean pop music sounds quite innocuous — like background music at an ice skating rink. But, as with everything else, the lyrics tend to be politically correct. Among two songs classified as "light music" are The Two Comrades Were Criticized and We'll Live Happily With Mother. . . .

The carpeting has been removed from the Volvos, Mercedes and other touring cars and replaced with rather ugly linoleum. "Easier to clean," our driver told us. The "justswept" appearance of the city streets carries over to rural areas as well. We even saw a school child remove a leaf off an otherwise pristine country road. —*Weissman Travel Report*

InterOptica

CD-ROM travel guides combine text, digital video, still pictures, maps, and sounds of faraway places. Even with the limitations of digitized video, it's fascinating to actually see that Inca ruin or Asian market. You can click on keywords in the text to see (for example) architectural arcana of Chartres Cathedral. Supported by commentary from noted travel authors, these guides inform and entertain with an immediacy that even the best guidebook can't match. —Richie Unterberger

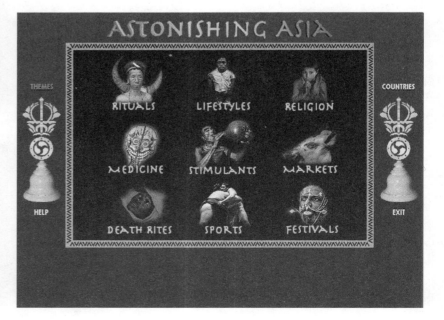

Earthwatch

Would you like to participate in a real scientific expedition? Join one of the many sponsored by this group. You have to pay them instead of them paying you, but you'll learn a lot, and you'll actually be doing something useful with your time and (tax-deductible) money. You get to choose from a wide range of expeditions, here and abroad, undertaking projects in rainforest ecology, archaeology, geology, marine sciences, life sciences, and social sciences. You're going to work hard, though most schedules include time off for local explorations. I've heard few complaints. Fellowships may be available. You must be 16-85, and in appropriate health. Tempting! —J. Baldwin

●

Island Rain Forest (Ilha do Cardoso, Brasil) *Field Conditions:* Teams, working in shifts day and night, will search for caiman nests; observe the animals' behavior; record the local habitat; map streams, swamps, and other topographic features; photograph animals and their habitats; and enter data in computers. They will also set traps for other reptiles and amphibians, collect any animals that are caught (snakes will be handled only by staff members), and help set up a photographic index of the island's species.

Summer volunteers in the Albion Mountains gently transport a study subject.

Teams will stay in research station houses and dormitories, which have some electricity, running water, and flush toilets. Meals will be prepared by station staff. Because

the island is so close to shore and major cities, there will also be occasional access to restaurants. Music makes up a regular part of the Brazilian culture and the life of

Earthwatch: Membership $25/year (includes 6 issues of *Earthwatch Magazine*). 680 Mount Auburn Street, PO Box 403, Watertown, MA 02272; 800/776-0188.

the camp as well. Both Moulton and Magnussen play instruments, as do most of the Brazilian staff members; volunteers are encouraged to join in. Related interests: photography, mapping, computers, biology, drawing.

The New Internationalist

Travelers leave their marks not only on a region's ecology, but on its culture as well. The New Internationalist celebrates travel, but it also looks at issues that tourist bureaus would rather sweep under the rug: children stolen from their mothers in Honduras for adoption in the US, the "sex-tourism" industry in Asia, "sewer children" in Colombia, deforestation in Nepal. Contributors include local activists, environmental experts, travel writers. It's an inspiration for traveling with a social conscience. —Richie Unterberger

●

"The trouble is, the Indians have become mercenary, changing their traditional dances for the tourists' benefit," says Marcos Chavez, Paraguayan vice-consul in Sao Paulo. "The trouble with the Indians is that they don't do any work, they don't produce any wealth, they bring backwardness," says Bartolome Quinonez, former director of Paraguay's international airline LAP. These declarations come from two of the people most responsible for promoting the tourist trade of a country unique in South America for institutionalizing its indigenous heritage. The Paraguayan currency is the Guarani; Guarani is taught in schools and, alongside Spanish, constitutes the second national language.

Their statements expose an essential ambiguity. The fact is that South American governments exhort visitors to discover their countries' picturesque Indian villages and unspoilt villages, while doing everything in their power to dispossess their indigenous peoples and destroy their forests. Themselves thoroughly colonized by Northern values, and with an instinctive belief that "if the gringos are prepared to pay to see it, it must be good," South America's urban elites pay lip service to the need to preserve the "purity" of the noble savage's culture to the point where many of them actually start to believe it. Their traditional

attitude to Indians as an irritating obstacle to "development," however, remains essentially unchanged.

Vice-consul Chavez insists that there is an "enormous potential market" for tourism based on "getting close to indigenous culture" in his country. The official tourist board's brochure Paraguay, land of sunshine is careful to include a picture of a smiling Indian girl. It describes the monumental Jesuit mission ruins in southern Paraguay as "witnesses of the civilizing, spiritual and cultural legacy of Paraguay from the nineteenth century." This version of the country's history is based not on "getting close to indigenous culture," but on forcing the Indians to "get close" to European culture.

●

The brochure is silent on the continuing presence of this legacy in the Chaco scrublands of western Paraguay. The Chaco is "a vast plain crossed by numerous non-navigable rivers . . . the habitat of an abundant fauna." The accompanying photograph shows a flock of jaboru storks; there is no

The New Internationalist
$42/year (12 issues). PO Box 1143, Lewiston, NY 14092; 416/946-0406, fax 416/946-0410

mention of the indigenous Chamococo and Maskoi people who still die from unfamiliar diseases, shock and despair in the "catechism camps" to which they have been brought for "civilizing" by the Florida-based New Tribes Mission.

●

Just months before Hurricane Iniki we scored a victory when a large tour-boat industry on the north shore of Kauai was shut down after years of opposition to its environmental and cultural effects. The State has begun to identify beaches and shore areas that are exceeding capacity and where conflicts between residentsd and visitors continue to escalate.

In the last ten years Hawaii has gone through a spurt of speculative development in which mega-resorts have been built by the dozen on each major island. They were based in part on the fantasies of the Hawaii Visitors Bureau, which projected a doubling of the number of visitors to Hawaii from six to eleven million by the year 2000. These projections were made by political bureaucrats indifferent to the impact of tourism and consumed with greed. While the hotels go up, community infrastructure such as sewage, roads, housing and schools are already 10 to 15 years behind current community needs.

But in the aftermath of the Gulf War demand has collapsed. On Kauai almost every hotel has had ownership transfers or filed for bankruptcy.

After a hurricane as destructive as Iniki you realize how quickly we can get in touch with deeper community values. Pacific cultures are based on a high level of environmental awareness. The relationship of people to land and of people to sea is spiritual and religious. When tourism takes away the land, the fishing grounds or the right to gather food or medicine the Hawaiian loses a primary means of livelihood and — more important — meaning in life.

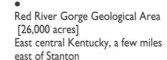

Going off the Beaten Path

This original and eclectic travel guide takes you to places oriented to environmental and social change — wilderness areas, urban community gardens, a museum of giant political puppets, protest sites, composting sites, national historic sites, vegetarian restaurants, bioregional councils.

Its listings include the Bread and Puppet Museum in Vermont, an old barn that houses life-size puppets, masks, paintings, and graphics used in international political performances by the Bread and Puppet Theatre. An old school bus houses a ten-cent museum store; they bake fresh sourdough rye bread in outdoor Quebec-style clay ovens.

Another destination is the Fruitlands Museum in Massachusetts, once the site of an attempt at utopian community. The despotic overseer Bronson Alcott (Louisa May Alcott's father) didn't like physical labor himself, and eventually left the women and children to harvest the crops and finally go hungry. The house is now a museum of the Transcendentalist movement, with mementos of Thoreau, Emerson, Alcott, and others.

Buy Going Off the Beaten Path *to learn about the excitement people are (and were) up to around the country.*
—Lisa Winer

•
Red River Gorge Geological Area
[26,000 acres]
East central Kentucky, a few miles east of Stanton

The Red River area in Daniel Boone National Forest contains eighty natural arches, the second largest group of arches in the nation. The arches and rock shelters under the cliffs occur where sandstone has resisted the erosion that has caused weaker, lower layers of rock to disappear. The terrain is a mixture of low creek bottoms and high, dry ridges covered with pines and hardwoods. Rock outcrops afford spectacular views. Wendell Berry, poet, essayist, farmer, and Kentucky native, devoted a book, *The Unforseen Wilderness* (Univ. of Kentucky Press, 1971), to the gorge, "a country of overtowering edges." Canoeing, which Berry describes, is one of the recreational opportunities offered by the area. Another is rock climbing.

The plant population is complex and rich, with 555 species in 100 families. Protected microenvironments in the narrow valleys have allowed the establishment and protection of some southern species. The successive advances and retreats of glaciers caused northern species to migrate to the area. The rare White-Haired goldenrod is endemic, as is the Canadian yew, which is outside its normal range.

In 1985 13,300 acres in the east of the geological area were designated as the Clifty Wilderness Area.

For information contact the supervisor of Daniel Boone National Forest, 100 Vaught Road, Winchester, Kentucky 40391 (606/745-3100).

Going off the Beaten Path
Mary Davis. 1991;
466 pp. ISBN 1-879360-01-2
$15.95 ($18.95 postpaid) from the Noble Press, Inc., 213 W. Institute Place, Suite 508, Chicago, IL 60610; 800/486-7737

A volunteer banding the small, swallowlike American Kestrel in California.
—*Environmental Vacations*

OTHER GREAT RESOURCES

Rainforests: James L. Castner. 1990, Feline Press. This is the first reference book designed specifically for people who wish to visit a rainforest, whether to do research or simply to enjoy the beauty and biological diversity.

Eco Journeys: Stephen Foehr. 1993, Noble Press. This book covers both raw adventure and "safe thrills" — including trips for people with special needs — worldwide.

University Research Expeditions Program Director Jean Colvin with two Rendille men of northern Kenya.
—*Environmental Vacations*

The Monk and the Monkeys

My daughter was living on the sixteenth floor of an apartment building, a block off the strip at Waikiki. I had scraped ice off an old station wagon in Idaho and flown for ten hours to keep her company, while her mother looked into a rumor that a tiny bird was gagging into extinction on the fumes of the equipment that serviced the observatories atop the mountains on the Big Island.

One Sunday morning Delta announced that she and I and her pal Max were going to the Honolulu zoo. When she phoned to invite Max, his father asked to speak with me. He explained that he was providing a halfway house for Tibetans fleeing Chinese oppression, and asked if one of the monks could accompany us. You bet.

After being lost for an hour in a catacomb of streets with only vowels in their names, Delta and I, in her mother's car, finally stumbled across Max's house. There, waiting on the steps, were little bright-eyed Max and a featherweight guy wearing grape-colored robes, black hightop Keds, and a chrome Timex with a metal expansion band.

On the way to the zoo, Max explained that he couldn't say the monk's name, that the monk didn't speak English, had been in America only three weeks, slept sitting up, smoked too many cigarettes, and was a professional wristwatch repairman.

The kids ditched us at the entrance to the zoo. We made quite a couple, the happy face in a Crown Royal bag and the overheated drugstore cowboy in lace-up logger boots, wandering down the paths, smoking Camel stubbies, pointing at the animals and giggling at each other's name for the critters. We had a lot to talk about, but couldn't. The Tibetan word for giraffe sounds like "chewing gum."

At the cat cages, he was shuffling along, looking back over his shoulder at a yawning lion, so when he turned forward he came eye to eye with a standing Bengal tiger. The monk immediately crouched into the overheated self-defense posture. From somewhere down in that pile of purple curtains came a throbbing yowl that was so low in pitch I froze up for a few seconds, before I realized that this fellow had grown up where tigers run wild, and that he didn't care for them. I stepped between them and broke the spell. The monk looked at me, looked at the tiger, nodded his head, then fired up the smile again.

On a concrete island a middle-aged chimpanzee was playing games with the humans, throwing a knotted gunnysack over the moat to the crowd. When it was tossed back to him, he tucked it behind a chunk of driftwood, performed a cheerleading routine, then reached behind the log and threw the cloth ball back into the audience. During the third act of this performance, when the tourists were packed around the ditch, popping flashbulbs, the monk grabbed me by the arm and led me up on a knoll, away from the show, just as the star finished his arm-flapping, foot-stomping segment, reached behind the driftwood, filled his hand, and sprayed ten thousand dollars' worth of camera equipment with chimpanzee shit.

The kids were waiting at the lunch counter. We bought popcorn and Pepsi, and sat on a warm concrete bench in the shade, munching and slurping, while the pigeons swarmed around us. I fed the birds by broadcasting popcorn by the handful and watching the neck-bobbing scramble. The monk carefully chose one kernel, held it between his thumb and forefinger, zeroed in on one pigeon, fed that individual the piece of popcorn, then switched birds.

When we finished snacking, the kids ran off to see the seals, and the monk, using universal sign language, made it clear that he had to use the restroom. I pointed to the appropriate door, then stretched out on the bench, and fell asleep.

The kids woke me, wondering where the monk had gone. I checked the men's room, then the tiger cage, no monk, then began asking the visitors if they had seen a hairless guy in purple anywhere. A young couple from South Dakota said they had seen something like that down by the telephones.

When we found him, the monk was sitting cross-legged on the grass, staring at a pay phone in a plastic clamshell. Max claimed he was asleep. I kneeled beside him and gently tapped the face of his Timex. He snapped from his reality into ours, smiled, and followed us to the parking lot. On the way back to Max's, over the noise of the kids discussing whether an elephant could beat up a killer whale, I thought I heard the monk humming a few bars of "Love Me Tender."
—JD Smith

Researcher studies langurs on the slopes of Mount Abu, Gujerat, India.
—*Environmental Vacations*

Ecotours and Nature Getaways

Each chapter of this diverse book focuses on a different part of the world and includes general-interest nature tours; birding, botany and wildflower tours; safaris; whale-watching expeditions; photography trips; cruises; rafting and canoe trips; and research and service trips. The section introductions provide background geared to environmental interests.

A concluding chapter presents an annotated list of the operators whose trips are described in the previous eight chapters. A portion of the book's proceeds go to the Wildlife Conservation Society and the World Wildlife Fund. —Perry Garfinkel

•

Bear in mind that seeing animals in the wild is quite different from what is portrayed on television nature programs. In order to capture all that fascinating activity on camera, filmmakers spend months in the field in blinds or canopy shelters waiting for something to happen. If you take an afternoon hike through a tropical rain forest, you're not going to come face-to-face with a Tapir.

Ecotours and Nature Getaways
Carole Berglie & Alice M. Geffen, Clarkson Potter, 1993; 322 pp. ISBN 0-517-88068-7 $15.00 ($17.00 postpaid) from Random House/Order Dept., 400 Hahn Road, Westminster, MD 21157; 800/733-3000

Remember that most animals are active primarily at dawn and dusk. If you want to see birds or mammals, you have to be up early and in the refuge or forest when activity is at its peak. Second, you must be quiet. Animals can hear you stomping through the woods, crushing leaves and breaking branches. Most especially, they can hear you talking, and they'll move away without your ever knowing they were there. You'll probably have more luck if you just find a promising spot and stay there. In tropical forests, it is important to wear dark clothes; bright colors will frighten away birds.

Hammock house and sleeping quarters at Placer Trésor. (Near Roura, French Guiana)
—*Rainforests*

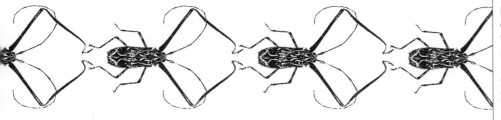

The Nature Conservancy

In addition to doing highly effective environmental work, The Nature Conservancy offers trips for folks who wish to see what needs to be, or is being, conserved. They offer inspiring field trips and tours to a variety of locations in the States and Latin America. Conservancy members and local guides lead the trips, making sure that the proper sensitivities and attitudes are celebrated. Many find that it is a special pleasure to travel and learn in a group with similar concerns. You'll be helping out a bit, too; part of your fee contributes to Nature Conservancy's efforts. —J. Baldwin

•

Ecuador and Galapagos Islands, Aug. 1, Sept. 5. Visit the environmental education center and the montane forest of Pasachoa Reserve. Contrast this with the jungle world of Cuyabeno Reserve, an unspoiled tropical rainforest in the Amazon basin. Extend your adventure to the Galapagos Islands. Enjoy land tortoises, magnificent frigate birds, and perhaps a waved albatross in this tremendous archipelago. $2598. Galapagos extension. $1398.

Each trip is hosted by a Conservancy representative and includes visits or lectures by local conservation experts, as well as the services of a trained in-country naturalist.

Nature Conservancy International
$25/year (membership, 6 issues of national magazine, and state newsletters). 1815 N. Lynn Street, Arlington, VA 22209; 703/841-5300

A murre chick relaxing after being banded on St. George Island, Alaska.
—*Environmental Vacations*

Green Travel Sourcebook

Eighty organizations and programs the authors selected "according to how firmly committed they are to ecological and societal responsibilities, how unique and unusual their programs and challenges are, and how vital and useful the services they perform." These programs may be among the most conscientious in the burgeoning green/ecotravel industry.

The book's most valuable tip: when you travel with a group that holds non-profit status, such as the World Wildlife Fund, you may declare the travel expense as a tax-deductible contribution — a ploy I thought only us travel writers knew we could get away with. —Perry Garfinkel

•

The dollars we spend can help support a region's economic or political system. Does that mean that by going to certain countries, we are also supporting the status quo? Should we boycott a repressive regime to express solidarity with the people of that country? Or does our avoidance of their homeland also mean that there will be fewer jobs, less money to feed their children, and a greater restriction on the freedom of information about the world outside their borders?

Economic sanctions do tend to work, when and if they are directed toward a clear-cut

purpose, uniformly enforced. A good case in point is South Africa, which has had to change over the past decade in order to appear more appealing to the rest of the world. On the other hand, the isolation that such sanctions create can be a fertile breeding ground for further repression and injustice, especially since there are no outside witnesses to report it.

Green Travel Sourcebook
Daniel Grotta & Sally W. Grotta. 1992; ISBN 0-471-53911-2 $14.95 postpaid from John Wiley & Sons, Inc., 1 Wiley Dr., Somerset, NJ 08873; 800/225-5945

OTHER GREAT RESOURCES

The Buzzworm Magazine Guide to Ecotravel: 1993, Buzzworm Books. Details on one hundred ecotravel adventures throughout the world.

Environmental Vacations: Stephanie Ocko. 1992, John Muir Publications. Subtitled "Volunteer Projects to Save the Planet," this book helps you find out how to "map a coral reef, count marine mammals, build housing, or immunize the local population."

Squirrel-squashing, land-eating, people-mauling, omnipolluting cars are taking over the planet! Let's get rid of 'em this very day! Starting with yours, though — I happen to need mine. It takes me, family, friends, and stuff from where we are to where we need to go, on the route and schedule of our choice, with privacy and reasonable protection from weather and thug. Except for taxis, no public transportation even approaches such convenience. History shows that for the past century or so, most people in most societies have been willing to pay the private auto's price, if not its cost. The true societal and environmental costs of auto use are becoming obvious, and the bill is past due. But what can be done in a society deliberately built to *require* cars?

First and most important: reduce the need for driving. Since 1980, the total number of cars, the number of cars per capita, and the annual miles driven per car have all risen at a much faster rate than the rise in population. That's why smog persists despite a 90 percent improvement in individual auto emissions.

Most of the increase in driving is forced by poor land use planning and zoning laws, not by people driving around just for the hell of it.

Change for the better is largely a matter of imagination, resolve, and politics. Malls combine with individual homes (however charming and bucolic) to make traffic congestion *inevitable*; the average car is used six times a day. Discourage fripperous motoring, especially by fuel-hungry poseur pickups and never-used-off-road 4x4 models. Vote against sprawlmaking, auto-insistent policies and politicians. Drive less.

At the same time, the cars themselves can be made cleaner, safer, lighter, and more easily recycled. According to a respected analysis by Amory Lovins, it is possible right now, using existing technology, to produce a roomy four-passenger "supercar" that is sporty, much safer than present models, and that can

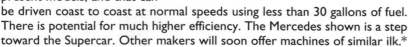

In a commendable burst of leadership, Mercedes has announced that they will definitely produce a car much like this four-seater Vision A93 concept vehicle before the decade is done. Smaller and lighter than a VW bug, but as roomy inside as a big car (with rear seats folded, several mountain bikes can be carried upright), this clever machine averages 62 miles per gallon of diesel. Electric and gasoline versions are also planned, and a hybrid fuel-electric model is a possibility. Typical Mercedes competence and crash safety are claimed. "About $20,000."

be driven coast to coast at normal speeds using less than 30 gallons of fuel. There is potential for much higher efficiency. The Mercedes shown is a step toward the Supercar. Other makers will soon offer machines of similar ilk.*

Assuming you actually need a car, what kind should it be? Cheapest is an oldie in good shape. Miles-per-dollar is more important than miles-per-gallon. Size doesn't matter much since fuel costs are only 16 percent of total auto expenditures. Your conscience need not be completely besmirched — older models are more polluting to run, but driving one till it drops avoids the resource depletion and pollution of making a new one.

If a new one is what you need, and a small one will do, the Honda Civic hatchback is hard to beat. It's not the top mileage champ, but in the USA it's probably the best small car overall. For most uses, I recommend the popular DX model over the super-efficient VX, which requires unfamiliar driving technique to squeeze just a few more miles from each gallon when conditions are ideal. If the Civic is too small, then your choice widens to the point where no firm suggestion can be made. Competent models are available to fill most any requirement except simplicity.

Note that the best-selling vehicle in the world is the full-size Ford F-series pickup. Studies have shown that most pickups are used as image-enhancing *cars*, not as load-carriers. Their popular 4x4 Sport-Utility cousins, 95 percent of whom will never be used off pavement, share similar environmental despicability. (Ironically and dishonestly, their advertising often shows them as a means of enjoying nature rather than as a principal despoiler.) If you really need 4x4 traction, there are less aggressive choices such as a Subaru wagon. Insist on antilock brakes and dual airbags (and *side* airbags, when they become available) on any vehicle. Sun-reflecting white is the color of choice; you won't run the fuel-hungry air conditioner as much, and may not need AC at all.

What about electrics and other ecocars? At this writing, you cannot buy an electric vehicle that can perform all the tasks customarily asked of a family car. Kits that convert gasoline vehicles to electric are compromises at best, and are unlikely to have been crash tested. (I've seen homebuilts that are

just plain dangerous.) A few purpose-built electrics meet government safety standards, but most don't. In any case, the tiny ones are eminently squashable. (Eco-righteousness is not armor.) All have problems involving lack of interior room, little supporting infrastructure (such as experienced mechanics), drastically reduced cold-weather range (especially with heater and headlights in use), sluggy performance, and expensive battery replacement. So far, improving this situation has proved to be an elusive goal, though there is no shortage of electric-vehicle hype.

What about alternative fuels? You can buy a Ford Taurus that runs well on alcohol-gasoline mixtures, but in this country, most alcohol comes from natural gas or corn. Traditional corn-raising techniques result in unacceptable soil depletion — already a disaster in progress. It is possible to convert a car to run directly on compressed natural gas (CNG), eliminating the need to convert gas to alcohol, but adding a bulky CNG tank to the car. (United Parcel Service is trying out some CNG trucks with the tank shoehorned into normally wasted space.) CNG vehicles need a special refueling facility; a delivery service can install one at the mother terminal. I'd guess that CNG will be the interim alternative fuel for fleet use until hydrogen inevitably takes its place as the next century's preferred vehicle fuel.

That's frustrating news for someone who wants an ecocar right now. But if you can wait for another three or four years, and all goes as planned and rumored, there will be interesting choices for the first time. While waiting, you might work on ways to reshape your life so you won't need the thing.
—J. Baldwin

* Amory's startling "Supercars" paper is available from the Rocky Mountain Institute (p. 117).

Urban Transit

Ah. Nothing is so edifying as a bit of heresy. The author even advocates the use of private cars instead of mass transit! (Under appropriate circumstances, of course.) His willingness to be politically incorrect both to the eco-chic and to officialdom adds to his credibility — important if his bristly ideas are to be taken seriously by a public that has been misinformed for years by emotional anti-auto ranting.

*The book's main point is that years of government management of public transport systems and policy has resulted in drastic inefficiency that would be best reduced by privatization. For example, legalizing jitneys would give a system with the flexible schedule and routing necessary to serve areas with low population density — service that almost always bankrupts the usual municipal transit authority. Vehicles can be added or subtracted as conditions change, regulated automatically by market demand. An expensive, interruption-prone mass transport system is thus made obsolete. Where this has been tried, it works fine despite noisy bureaucratic predictions of dis-*aster. *(Note: Since **Urban Transit** was written, computer technology has made an efficiently dispatched jitney service even more feasible.)*

Professor Lave makes his points neatly and answers his critics with logic, example and humor; the book is surprisingly easy to read. Citizens' groups and city managers need to read this: the answers here could be implemented right now. —J. Baldwin

•

The most transit-dependent city in the United States, New York, now allows private firms to operate express bus services. These firms not only provide a higher quality of service than the city-operated vehicles, but do so at a profit, and without government subsidy.

•

Artifically *low fares* resulted from two goals: first, to lure commuters out of their cars — which did not work because rising incomes made commuters more sensitive to transit quality than to transit cost; second, to provide low cost transportation for the poor — though it would have been far less costly to subsidize them directly, rather than erecting a low-fare structure used by rich and poor alike.

Life on the Road

I lived in an Airstream trailer (the "Silver Turd") for thirteen years. It was a high-tech and mobile, cozy, dematerialized manner of living. You can get used to it — I've seen estimates claiming that six million Americans live on the road in RVs. I'd guess that most of them are there by choice. If you think this seems high, I invite you to visit Quartzite, AZ (pop. 3,500) in February: up to a quarter-million RVs simultaneously disgorge their inhabitants into an outrageous rock-&-gem fleamarket. It looks like an invasion by enthusiastic Martians.

As always, problems come along with adventure and the freedom to move on. How do you bank? What about medical services, taxes, vehicle licensing, phone and mail? Living on the road can cost a lot less than an apartment or permanent home, but how do you

do it? Where do you park? What are the tricks of the trade?

These books attend the romance and the fears, the joys and the aggravation. They're written from many years of experience. My own experience tells me that this is good advice. —JB

The Silver Turd provides temporary quarters once again — this time on Cape Cod.

Living Aboard Your RV
Janet Groene & Gordon Groene.
Ragged Mountain Press, 1986;
250 pp. ISBN 0-87742-340-7
$15.95 postpaid from McGraw-Hill
Publishing Co., 13311 Monteray Avenue,
Blue Ridge Summit, PA 17214; 800/262-4729

Automap Road Atlas • Automap Pro

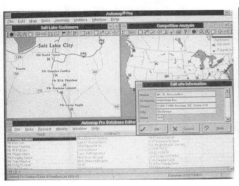 

If you are organizing a carpool or jitney service, rolling your own just-in-time delivery service, planning an automobile trip across the country or across the state, or if you do a lot of

*automobile travel and address-finding in your occupation, the **Automap Road Atlas** is an incredible resource. Street maps of 200 US cities and hundreds of intercity and interstate highways are combined with databases for route planning (including sightseeing options). **Automap Pro** ($250 to $350; Windows only) allows you to customize your sites and databases. Plug in a Global Positioning System unit (around $650; call Trimble Navigation, 408/481-8000) to a portable computer, and you can even use satellite position-location technology to help you find your way from here to there. —HLR*

Automap Road Atlas
$29.95 to $59.95
Available in DOS, Windows, CD-ROM for Windows, and Mac versions. Information $5.50 from Automap, Inc., 1309 114th Avenue SE, Suite 110, Bellevue, WA 98004; phone 800/440-6277, fax 206/455-3667

The Joy of Carpooling

Think of this brief but practiced pamphlet as a box of Car Pool Helper. Add people, a bit of determination, and things should go well. Good stuff. —JB

•
If the cost of a taxi alarms you, remember the money you are saving by carpooling, and the relative infrequency of emergencies which would require a cab ride. Check with your employer to see if they have a commuter program which pays for a guaranteed

•
It is important to remember that transit did not lose passengers because of deficits; it lost passengers because it did not provide the kind of service they desired.

•
Transit need not be limited to buses and rail cars. The largest source of public transit rides in the United States is the ordinary taxi cab. Taxis not only carry more total passengers than standard buses or trains, they even carry more poor passengers.

Urban Transit
Charles A. Lave. 1985;
372 pp. ISBN 0-88410-970-4
$12.95 ($14.95 postpaid) from Pacific Research Institute for Public Policy, 177 Post Street, Suite 500, San Francisco, CA 94108; 415/989-0833

The Car Buyer's Art • Used Cars • Leased Cars

These books are an education in counter-car-dealer tactics and strategy. I have personally used all three to save much money for myself and for friends — I figure that following this advice has paid me about $1,000 an hour as an actor. Best result so far is the $4,200 my wife and I haggled off the sticker on a new Camry for her dad. Highly recommended tools for easing essentially dirty work. —JB

•
"But how can you expect to buy a cream puff from a new car dealer at below wholesale price? They'd never go for that."

"Sure they would," Andy answered, "because they stole the equity from the previous owner."

"Stole?" the Writer asked.

"Sure. Say a car is worth $7000 wholesale. Its owner wants to trade it in on a new car, and they give him only $5000. They have, in effect, stolen $2000 from him."

Joan continued the thought. "Then what we do is buy that car from the dealer at about $6000. We got it below the wholesale price of $7000 and the dealer makes $1000 profit." —*Used Cars*

•
Turnover in the car selling profession is high. Because of this, a young salesman is very likely to be a new salesman, which is exactly what you want. Here's why. Being new in the business, he will lack the hardened "take 'em to the cleaners at all cost"

ride home by taxi in case of emergency.

•
A good carpool for a five-day workweek consists of four partners. Each of you drives the carpool one day, and one day a week each of you drives alone. That way, each of you has a car at your disposal two days a week.

The Joy of Carpooling: $5 postpaid from Susan Shankle, 3182 Campus Drive #364, San Mateo, CA 94403; 415/574-2301

attitude of the more experienced veteran. Along the same lines, his persuasive skills will probably not be fully developed. And finally, remember, he is keenly aware that in order to remain employed, he must sell cars. In order to accomplish this and gain an initial foothold in the profession, there's a good chance he'll work his heart out for you and settle for a sale "on the books" even if the commission is small.
—*The Car Buyer's Art*

The Car Buyer's Art
Darrell Parrish. 1985; 183 pp.
ISBN 0-9612322-7-7; $6.95 postpaid

Used Cars
Darrell Parrish. 1991; 204 pp.
ISBN 0-9612322-3-4; $5.95 postpaid

Leased Cars
Darrell Parrish. 1992; 260 pp.
ISBN 0-9612322-4-2; $6.95 postpaid

All from Book Express, PO Box 1249, Bellflower, CA 90706; 310/867-3732

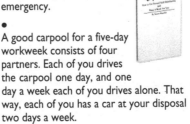

Bikes get better —
again.

A bicycle-and-rider moves more efficiently than any other vehicle or animal, including birds and fish! Though not entirely pollution-free (most things aren't, including you) the bicycle's remarkable efficiency and affordability make it the best choice for personal transportation where conditions permit. Mountain bike technology has made all but the cheapest safer and easier to ride and maintain. If you haven't ridden a late model of respectable quality (more than about $450, less than 27 lbs.) you might be pleasantly surprised. Several hundred dollars more will bring you a truly satisfying machine that meets your personal needs with few compromises. That sounds like a lot of money for a bike, but it's less per day than busfare. You might also consider the 58 cents-per-mile consumed by the average car. There's a lively debate raging as to whether bicycles need suspension (they do) and which designs are best (not clear yet). It won't be long before bikes without suspension will seem quaint. Suspended bikes are definitely not all the same. I recommend reading road tests, inspecting for small engineering details (such as pivot bushings necessary for long wear), and riding every model in your price range. I have rarely seen such a paroxysm of ingenuity and claim-whooping by inventors and hucksters, but a few of the new machines are real jewels. The best transform eyeball-rattling torture rides into pleasant jaunts. As the price of suspended bicycles drops, widespread use will reduce the need for expensively paved bike paths. Using a bike for errands and commuting is becoming more reasonable than ever before. —J. Baldwin

One of the most advanced steeds available, the radical Crosstrac is specifically designed for suspension rather than being a traditional bike with added springing. Its long-travel (4") suspension bestows amazingly secure roadholding and posh comfort on rough pavement, gravel or dirt.

Bicycling Science

For twenty years this book has been the best place to learn the engineering principles of bicycle design. The information is solidly backed by extensive lab and field testing, yet is presented in a jargon-free, easily understood manner. All aspects of the bicycle are covered, including the rider and bike/rider relationship (ergonomics). If you're considering the construction of a bike or human-powered vehicle, or are just curious about your mount, this is lesson one. —JB

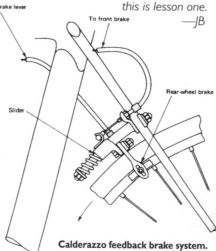

To handbrake lever

To front brake

Slider

Rear-wheel brake

Calderazzo feedback brake system. After operating handbrake, rear brake is carried forward on slider against spring, actuating front brake simultaneously. If bicycle starts to pitch forward, rear wheel is no longer rotated by road surface, and front brake is released.

Bicycling Science (2nd Edition) Frank R. Whitt & David G. Wilson. $21.50 ($24.50 postpaid) from The MIT Press/Order Dept., 55 Hayward Street, Cambridge, MA 02142; 800/356-0343

Bike-Pro Buyer's Guide

It took me nearly two hundred hours of reading, interviewing, weighing and measuring, and yakking up a dozen patient bike shops, to specify a state-of-the-art suspension mountain bike for myself. Had this guide been available, I could have chosen and ordered everything but the custom stuff in an evening. Many of the best available mountain bike and road racing components are measured, weighed to one-fourth of a gram, chattily described, and photographed. Charts permit easy comparisons. Basics are discussed; unworthy models are dissed. This is the sort of information-honing that improves the breed and inspires excellence. Would that other fields besides bicycles had such a resource! —JB

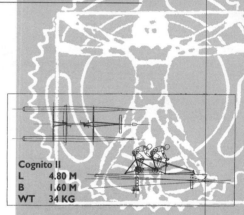

• For the bearings, both cups have stainless steel precision sealed bearing cartridges pressed into them. They are well shielded from moisture and should provide years of life if not the permanent solution to anyone's headset problems. They come in three stack height sizes. Standard European 43.5 mm (Campagnolo height), a Short Stack Japanese 34.0 mm, and a BMX size that is also used for Yeti framesets. The 1" Short Stack headset weighs 109 grams. All Chris King headsets are available in Blue, Black, Silver or 3DV (Violet/Lavender).

07-89-300 (Color-B-BK-S-L) Short-1" $89.99
07-89-3 (Size 18-14/B-BK-S-L) Short 1 1/8"-1 1/4" $109.99
07-89-500 (Color-B-BK-S-L) Standard $89.99
07-89-500 (Color-B-BK-S-L) Yeti/BMX-1" $89.99

Bike-Pro Buyer's Guide: Information from 442 Steele Lane, Santa Rosa, CA 95403-3149; 800/Bike-Pro.

The International Human Powered Vehicle Association

*People-as-engines is what IHPVA is about. **HPV News** reports from the front lines, and **Human Power** is their technical journal. Both seethe with innovation, controversy, and the hot-blooded spirit of pioneers searching for more efficient transportation. It's hard to resist joining the fun. —JB*

• On August 1, 1993, the third "Dream Ship Design Contest" was held in Tokyo with over 30,000 spectators. The contest included a 200-meter standing-start human-power speed race.

The author's team won the race with a new record time of 30.21 seconds by a two-man fully submerged hydrofoil named "COGITO-II."

Cognito II
L   4.80 M
B   1.60 M
WT   34 KG

Human Power David Gordon Wilson, Editor $20/year (4 issues, membership and newsletter) from PO Box 51225, Indianapolis, IN 46251; 317/876-9478

OTHER GREAT RESOURCES

The Third Hand: Catalog free. PO Box 212, Mt. Shasta, CA 96067. This is THE place to get everything you need for serious bike-building, maintenance and repair. Good tools, catalog, and folks.

Velo News: $33.97/year (18 issues). PO Box 53397, Boulder, CO 80322; 800/888-6087. Just that, and lots of it.

Bike Friday: Information free from Green Gear Cycling, 4065 W. 11th Avenue #14, Eugene, OR 97402; 800 777-0258. Would you believe a respectable, high-quality bike that ships in a standard Samsonite two-suiter? No dinky folder, it looks a bit odd but rides just fine.

Terry Precision Bicycles for Women, Inc.: 1704 Wayneport Road, Macedon, NY 14502; 800/289-8379. Georgena Terry makes bikes, including mountain, specially proportioned and equipped to fit women of just about any size and shape. I've noticed that Terry owners smile a lot. Um, I ride a Terry saddle; no macho hardpan for me!

Effective Cycling: John Forster. 1993, MIT Press. Most everything you need to know under one cover.

Slime. A terminally oogy material the self-seals punctures up to a claimed eighth-inch or so. About $3.95/4oz. at local bike shops.

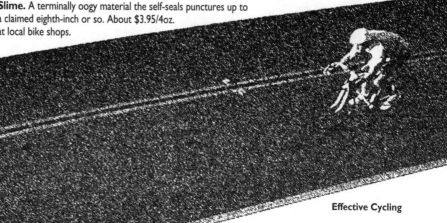

Effective Cycling

Long Haul Cargo Bicycle

Pedal-powered mini-pickup trucks are an old idea. Many two- and three-wheeled models are available around the world, but most examples are awkward, unsafe, difficult to ride, too heavy, and consequently very hard on their human "motors." Indeed, studies show that human powerplants so burdened tend to have short, unhappy lives; many literally die of broken hearts. Some cities in the Far East have banned them.

Bike transportation expert Jan VanderTuin has come up with a pedaled hauler that all but eliminates the problems afflicting its ilk, assuming the boss doesn't counter with a new, equally heart-breaking schedule. It's a slim two-wheeler that doesn't hang out dangerously into auto traffic. I've ridden this thing — at first with wobbly trepidation, but only a minute or two later with unexpected agility and even hubris in dense pedestrian traffic. (OK, I'll admit to scattering a few craven peasants.) The Long Haul is remarkably easy to ride, whether empty or loaded to its 200-lb. capacity. I tested it with an understandably nervous and squirmy youth as cargo, and still had no problems deftly avoiding potential plaintiffs. Junior High-size kids can ride it with casual impunity; it's actually rather fun. In any venue of modest vertical contour, this well-designed machine makes a lot of sense. Available built to specifications, and priced (fairly) accordingly.
—J. "choo-choo" Baldwin

Long Haul Cargo Bicycle: $995-$1395. Information from Human-Powered Machines, PO Box, 1005, Eugene, OR 97400; 503/343-5568.

Burley Lite Trailers

This trailer hitches low to the axle, adding weight in a stop so you don't go over-the-bars so easily. Handling is surprisingly obedient and free of evil tendencies. Cargo or kids can be hauled covered or in the open. Yes, you can turn the bike either way, despite the asymmetric hitch. It's no surprise the Burley Lite is so popular.
—JB

Burley Lite Tourist Bicycle Trailer: $235

Burley Lite Bicycle Trailer: Child-carrying model $250

Burley d'Lite Bicycle Trailer: Foldable child carrier

Check your local bike shop. Nearest dealer information from Burley Design Cooperative, 4080 Stewart Road, Eugene, OR 97402; 503/687-1644.

Dahon

Dahon Bicycles
$180 – $380.
Information free from 2949 Whipple Road, Union City, CA 94587; 800/442-3511

Why buy a little bitty bike that makes you look like a circus bear act? Answer: theft resistance: bring it inside with you. Easy storage: keep it in the trunk of your car or in the closet. Take it with you on the bus or train. Eliminate the shuttle problem: stow it in your river raft, then ride it back to get the car. You'd be surprised how much use a folder gets. This one isn't the best or lightest folding bike ever to hit the market, but its wide distribution has made it the only commonly available such bike. It does the job pretty well, exhibiting acceptable road behavior,

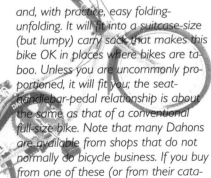

and, with practice, easy folding-unfolding. It will fit into a suitcase-size (but lumpy) carry sack that makes this bike OK in places where bikes are taboo. Unless you are uncommonly proportioned, it will fit you; the seat-handlebar-pedal relationship is about the same as that of a conventional full-size bike. Note that many Dahons are available from shops that do not normally do bicycle business. If you buy from one of these (or from their catalogs), you may have to tune or even reassemble the bike after purchase. Bottom line: Useful. —JB

Mountain Bike Action • Road Bike Action

The irreverent, hard-ridin' writers of these two magazines are famous for subjective judgments, controversy, and speaking with tongues only slightly forked by threats from advertisers. They're not afraid to call gems gems and junk junk. Less into image, more into useful information, frontiers and fun than rival mags. —JB

Mountain Bike Action • Road Bike Action
$19.98/year (12 issues). PO Box 957, Valencia, CA 91380-9057; 800/767-0345

Bike Two'sday Tandem (24 Speed, touring and sport). —Bike Friday

Adventure Cycling

Born in 1973 as Bikecentennial, this non-profit recreational cycling organization has become a sponsor of organized bike tours, a lobbying force, and the best source of bicycle touring maps. It's the maps that are special; drawn with the biker in mind, they indicate the best routes through both country and urban tangle. —JB

Adventure Cycling: $22/year (membership), catalog $1 (free with membership), PO Box 8308, Missoula, MT 59807; 800/721-1776.

Rails-To-Trails Conservancy

What's the best use for abandoned railroad rights-of-way? As a cyclist, I say make 'em into bike trails. (Locomotives and bicycle riders have about the same idea of what constitutes a reasonable gradient). The long, thin corridors are rarely useful for parkland, highways, or real estate, but the red tape involved in using them for anything besides trains tends to paralyze innovators. The Rails-To-Trails Conservancy knows how to deal with the deadly details that must be handled before bikers and hikers can puff where the engines once did. RTC publishes success stories, a legal manual (essential!) and the comprehensive *Converting Rails-To-Trails: A Citizen's Manual.* If you have an old rail line near you, better get to work on it now: I learned the hard way that when they take out the bridges and tunnels, trail conversions are much less likely to happen. —JB

Rails-To-Trails Conservancy: $18/year (membership and newsletter).
RTC Legal Manual: $42.50 (members 32.50).
Converting Rails to Trails (A Citizens Manual): $17 (members $12).
All from Rails-To-Trails Conservancy, 1400 Sixteenth Street NW, Suite 300, Washington, DC 20036; 202/797-5400.

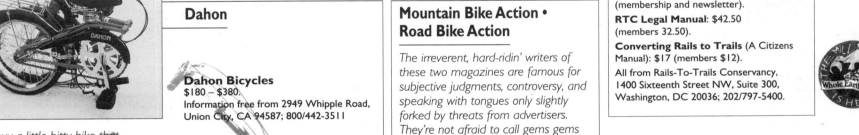

You're the motor — one-eighth of a horsepower is average — of these simple, silent, agile craft. Assuming no ugly surprises from the weather, you can adjust the level of danger from near zero when wafting across a glassy lake at sunset, to near suicidal in furious, fangy rapids. New designs and materials have made just messing about in boats more satisfying than ever. —J. Baldwin

This "intentional miss" assures you that Bermuda will be east of you. —*One-Day Celestial Navigation*

Northwest River Supplies

They mark the end of five-gallon-bucket water fights, but self-bailing whitewater rafts take a lot of the unnecessary danger out of river-running. (Nothing like losing control of a swamped raft weighing tons!) More adventurous river rats might like the advanced-design catamaran rafts that have remarkable capabilities in the rough stuff. The inflatables are accompanied by a few kayaks and a good assortment of the other equipage needed for serious big water. It's all enticing enough to provoke uncontrollable deployment of your VISA. —JB

Northwest River Supplies: 2009 S. Main Street, Moscow, ID 83843-8948; 800/635-5202.

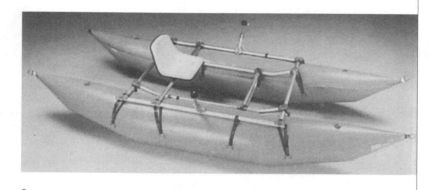

Wildcat The wildcat surfs, does enders, and is primarily a solo playboat. The 6' waterline, curved tubes and stiff fabric give you maximum maneuverability and increased surfing capabilities. Extremely lightweight, the wildcat is sensitive to your "body english," and portages are easier on those Class VI runs. Made in Idaho. *Size:* 12'6''L x 6'4''W. *Weight:* 54 lbs (without frame)

1171 AIRE Wildcat
$1250.00

The Boundary Waters Catalog

The Minnesota II - our favorite Boundary Waters canoe
The more we use this canoe, the better we like it. And now our customers are asking for it so often that it has become our primary rental model and last year's best seller. Why such popularity for a canoe that was never even advertised? Because the people who tried it loved it, and word of mouth is still the best advertising. The MNII has the fastest, most efficient hull design that can carry a big load and remain stable in wind and waves. The bow is flared for dryness, yet narrow enough for small bow paddlers to easily reach the water. At 18 1/2' there is plenty of room for gear, kids, pets, or whatever you like to take canoeing. And, of course, there's the best hi-tech feature of all - it only weighs 42 pounds.

Depth at bow 20" · Depth at stern 16"
Depth at center 12.5" · Gunwale width 33.5"

Fiberglass x-rib	68 lbs.	$975
Fiberglass PVC core	52 lbs.	$1225
Kevlar PVC core	43 lbs.	$1750

A few hundred years of boating around in the Boundary Waters country shared by Canada and Minnesota have made canoeing a highly developed art. This catalog abounds in appropriate canoes and equipment, augmented by a fine library to put you in the proper mood. The Fall & Holiday edition of the catalog features items you'll need when the place freezes up. Nice folks, too. —JB

The Boundary Waters Catalog: 32861 Arbor Vine Drive, Union City, CA 94587; 800/223-6565.

Great River Outfitters

These folks have been around long enough (fifteen years) to know what's good. Their offerings include many of the most popular canoes, river kayaks and sea kayaks, plus all the other stuff you need to get on the water. Books, too. Yum. —JB

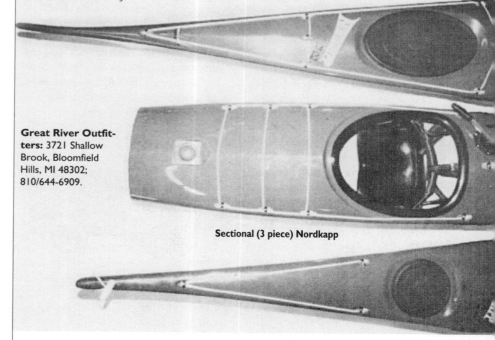

Great River Outfitters: 3721 Shallow Brook, Bloomfield Hills, MI 48302; 810/644-6909.

Sectional (3 piece) Nordkapp

Simon & Schuster's Pocket Guide to Wilderness Medicine

The black widow spider, showing the characteristic hourglass marking.

In this pocket guide, physician and sports medicine columnist Paul Gill covers the essential info to have with you when you trek beyond easy reach of medical facilities. Written clearly and with an appropriate dose of reassuring humor, it's worth making some extra space in your backpack to minimize the risks of leaving civilization.
—Richie Unterberger

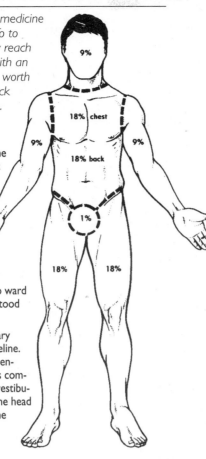

• The size of the burn is expressed in terms of the percentage of body surface burned. The easiest way to do this is to use the "rule of nines." The head is considered to be 9 percent, the front and back of the torso each 18 percent, each upper extremity 9 percent, each lower extremity 18 percent, and the genitals 1 percent of the body surface area.

• There is a sea chest full of tricks you can use to ward off motion sickness. Here are a few that have stood the test of time:

• Keep your eye on the horizon or any stationary object, such as a lighthouse, island, or the shoreline. This gives your brain a fixed point to focus on, enabling it to "tune out" most of the other signals coming in from the body position sensors and the vestibular system. Sit in a semireclined position with the head motionless and the eyes straight ahead. Bart, the would-be salmon fisherman, made the cardinal error of lying down in the cabin. He had no fixed points of reference in there, and his seasickness worsened.

• Sit in the center of the boat. There is much less movement there. If you are in an airplane, sit over the wing. In a car, sit in the front seat, or get out of the car and lie on the ground with your eyes open.

• Eat stewed tomatoes and saltines before you set out on the water. Or a cola drink, or whatever you have heard works. If you believe it's going to help, it probably will. I can think of no scientific reason why a full stomach should help, but the placebo effect can be very powerful in this malady in which anxiety and stress play such large roles. Most medical authorities recommend a liquid diet starting a few hours before the trip, with no solids at all until you are back on terra firma. Do what seems to work for you.

Simon & Schuster's Pocket Guide to Wilderness Medicine
Paul G. Gill, Jr. Fireside,
1991; 204 pp. ISBN 0-671-70615-2
$9.95 postpaid. Simon & Schuster/Order Dept., 200 Old Tappan Road, Old Tappan, NJ 07675; 800/223-2336

Water Filters

Are you familiar with the term "explosive defecation"? These days, you may well find out if you slurp from that sparkling mountain stream without purifying it first. There are many brands and types of filters available. Here are the basics: All do a creditable job of removing dirt, bacteria such as typhus and cholera, trip-spoiling Giardia cysts, and the especially nasty cryptosporidium. Some filters have carbon elements that will remove pesticides and bad tastes, but I've seen test results that show contaminated carbon filters acting as Petri dishes after a while, making things worse. Some filters must be cleaned with fresh water (in short supply when they clog); others need none. Some have virus-killing capability (an iodine source). Some work slowly, making them annoying for group use. A few require strong hands for pumping; others don't require pumping at all. Prices range from about $25 to $250. REI (p. 349) has a nice selection, with good descriptions.

For suitcase tripping, I carry a Water Tech Purifier that looks like a smallish drinking cup with a lid. An inner cup has a bacteria/virus filter in its bottom (Dirty water must be run through a disposable coffee filter first). Set the inner cup on top of the outer one and add the suspicious water. The lower cup is soon full — one hundred gallons if you're thirsty and have the time to do it swig by swig. It's ideal for world travelers (astronauts use it). Clean, sturdy, and compact, requiring no odd rituals, it should be standard travel equipment right alongside your toothbrush.
—J. Baldwin

Water Tech Water Purifier: $20 to $40. Magellan's, Box 5485, Santa Barbara, CA 93150-5485; 800/962-4943, fax 805/568-5406.

Wilderness Cuisine

Recipes for blood oranges and capers with spring-mix baby lettuces, sunflower-caraway cabbage salad, and sherried mushroom bisque — for the campfire? And I thought it was a major triumph when we had eggplant casserole. Carole Latimer provides 130 recipes and covers kitchen equipment, packing food and keeping it fresh, home-drying food, and tailoring menus to trips of varying lengths and types. Includes plenty of options for veggies, too. —RU

Dilled Baby Lima Salad
Makes 4 servings

This bean salad is great for a lunch in camp on a rest day, or as a side dish accompanying grilled meat. For the dressing, use a fragrant, cold-pressed peanut oil.

2 cups cooked dehydrated lima beans
Dressing:
1/4 cup safflower oil
1/4 cup peanut oil
1 TB fresh dill or 1/2 tsp dried dillweed
1/3 cup Marukan seasoned gourmet rice vinegar

At Home: Package the dehydrated beans in ziploc bag. Combine the dressing ingredients and put in a nalgene bottle.

In Camp: 1. Rehydrate beans with just barely enough water to cover. Be careful not to add too much water. 2. When beans are rehydrated, drain off excess water and add dressing. If possible, marinate for 2-4 hours before eating.

Wilderness Cuisine
Carole Latimer. 1991;
239 pp. ISBN 0-89997-114-8
$14.95 postpaid. Wilderness Press/Order Dept., 2440 Bancroft Way, Berkeley, CA 94704; 800/443-7227

• If you cook at 8000' or higher, you'll notice that everything takes longer to cook. Water boils at a lower temperature when atmospheric pressure is lower. Water doesn't have to reach the sea-level boiling point of 212 degrees before it begins to bubble; water boils at 196.9 at 8000' and at 194 degrees at 10,000'. At 14,000', water boils at only 187.3 degrees.

How do these facts affect specific foods? Commercial dry pasta, for example, requires very hot boiling water to cook well. I've had good luck cooking thinner pastas (angel hair, vermicelli) up to 10,000' by using furiously boiling water and a high water-to-pasta ratio, and cooking it longer. But somewhere around 11,000' — I'm not sure just where the failure line is — the water boils furiously and the pasta slowly but surely turns into a glutinous mass. I can remember cooking up a pot of something like wallpaper paste at an 11,000' camp near Mt. Lyell in Yosemite.

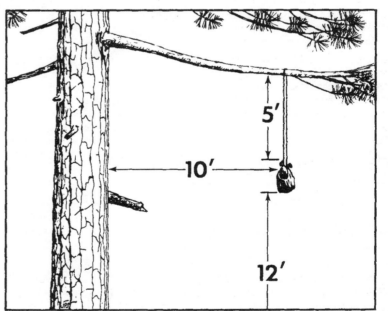

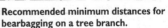

Recommended minimum distances for bearbagging on a tree branch.

OTHER GREAT RESOURCES
The Outward Bound Wilderness First-Aid Handbook: Jeff Isaac & Peter Goth. 1991, Lyons & Burford Publishers.

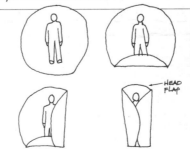

The human burrito. This wrap method of insulating allows quick and easy access to the hypothermia patient, as well as protection.

Flyfishing: First Cast to First Fish!

It isn't always easy for the aspiring fly-fisher to get started. The equipment and techniques — not to mention where to start, what fish to pursue in a given location, and the whole mystique surrounding the sport — can be daunting. And most of the literature on the subject has historically been addressed to an experienced audience.

This new reference book has nine "how-to" chapters, covering the selection and assembly of equipment, basic and specialized casting techniques, "reading" the water and locating fish, techniques for wet and dry flies, streamers and nymphs, and for fishing streams, lakes or salt water, tying knots, strike detection, and playing and landing your catch. **Flyfishing** *is profusely illustrated, packed with photographs, and eminently readable.* —Tom Valtin

•

The point of seeing the fly can't be overemphasized, the reason being that you'll be selecting a target area to drop your offering so as to have it drift, drag-free, into the fish's sight window. In order to do this you need to know where your fly is. Has it landed where anticipated? Is it getting a good drift, acting as a natural would? Is there drag? When should I mend the line to avoid the drag and extend the float? Was that a rise to my bug or to a natural near it? And, of course, most importantly, when to react to a strike and set fast the hook.

There are several ways to know where your fly is located. For one, know how much line you're casting and where to expect it to land. A larger fly or one with upright wings will be easier to see if not inappropriate to conditions. A parachute or slack line cast can make it easier to spot your fly fluttering down onto the water. Learn to lock into your fly's silhouette as it

Flyfishing
(First Cast to First Fish!)
Joseph F. Petralia. 1994;
246 pp. ISBN 0-9605890-8-2
$14.95 postpaid. Sierra Outdoor Products
Co., PO Box 2497, San Francisco, CA 94126

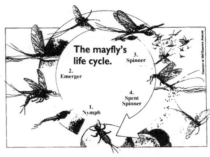

The mayfly's life cycle.
3. Spinner
2. Emerger
4. Spent Spinner
1. Nymph

will help you distinguish it from the background. If glare or reflection off the water is making it difficult to follow your fly's drift, moving your position by a couple of feet can help. A hat with a wide brim or visor and polarized sunglasses also help in this regard.

Wilderness Basics

Neophytes can be forgiven for feeling intimidated when they browse the magazine rack at the local sporting-goods store, full of bronzed mountain climbers and hardy whitewater rafters. All you want to know, essentially, is how to find your way back to the campsite, cross streams safely, and keep your kids out of the clutches of the bears.

Wilderness Basics covers these essentials without losing beginners' confidence or intermediates' interest. More in-depth sources are cited at the end of each chapter. —Richie Unterberger

Locating your position by map alone.

White clothing helps keep desert hikers cooler.

Wilderness Basics
(The Complete Handbook for Hikers & Backpackers)
San Diego Chapter/Sierra Club.
1993; 224 pp. ISBN 0-89886-348-1
$14.95 ($17.95 postpaid).
The Mountaineers Books, 1101 SW Klickitat Way, Seattle, WA 98134;
800/553-4453

Adventuring with Children

Taking kids camping or sailing is more interesting than piling them in the car and cruising the interstate for two weeks. But the problems of keeping them from getting bored, sick, or bellicose, remain — even as those of safety and preparation become more challenging.

The authors, experienced worldwide travelers with twins in tow, know the importance of treating kids like people and adjusting to their social and biological needs. They give tips on camping, hiking, bicycling, sailing, and canoeing, and address practical concerns that are relevant to any form of family travel. They also list sources for children's outdoors equipment. —Richie Unterberger

•

If we were to recommend taking just two pieces of baby equipment on any adventure, they would be a backpack for carrying the child and a harness for confining it. A harness is lightweight, inexpensive, easy to use and adaptable to any form of adventure travel. It allows a baby the freedom to roam without the risk of straying too far. On a boat, at the beach or in a campground it can be clipped to something nearby so the baby can explore without constant parental vigilance.

Some mothers, when I suggest this, voice a dislike of having their crawling baby get dirty, something that wouldn't happen in a playpen. First of all, most campsites aren't on dirt — grass is much more likely. Nor is sand much

Adventuring with Children
Nan Jeffrey & Kevin Jeffrey. 1992;
327 pp. ISBN 0-935701-89-3
$14.95 ($19.45 postpaid). Foghorn Press, 555 De Haro Street #220, San Francisco, CA 94107; 800/364-4676

of a problem, as that can be brushed off at the end of your time at the beach. If dirt does seem to be in evidence, dress your baby in the same pair of overalls or whatever when playing at the campsite. This means only one outfit will get dirty instead of his whole wardrobe in a couple of days.

Land Navigation

We've reviewed many "Where are we?" books over the years, but this one is easily the clearest and easiest to use. All those little symbols you see on maps are discussed, and after 25 years of trail experience I finally found out what those yellow markers you see along trails are for. The author even gets into navigation with an altimeter! And there's a good chapter on finding your way by the stars — even in the Southern Hemisphere, in case you end up in New Zealand. It'll be a long time before someone does this subject better. —JB

•

Draw lines from the peak that just miss the edges of the swamp. Then measure with your compass the bearings along these lines toward the peak. Say you get 60° and 110°.

You can approach the peak from any direction and be certain to avoid the swamp as long as the peak bears less than 60° or more than 110° from you. You can see from this drawing that you'd pass North of the swamp when the bearing is more than 110°.

Land Navigation Handbook
W. S. Kals. Sierra Club Books, 1983;
230 pp. ISBN 0-87156-331-2
$12 ($15 postpaid). Sierra Club Store Orders, 730 Polk Street, San Francisco, CA 94109; 800/935-1056

OTHER GREAT RESOURCES

America's Secret Recreation Areas: Michael Hodgson. 1993, Foghorn Press. Forgotten wildlands of the BLM.

Fly Rod & Reel: $11.97/year (6 issues). PO Box 10141, Des Moines, IA 50347-0141; 800/888-6890.

The Great American Wilderness (Touring America's National Parks): Larry Ludmer. 1993, Hunter Publishing, Inc.

REI Mountaineering Axe. Ideal for general mountaineering. Aluminum alloy shaft tests to UIAA tensile strength standards (880 lbs.) Chromoly steel head; positive-clearance pick. 1 lb. 9 oz. $68

REI

The typical REI outlet carries an impressive array of backpacks, sleeping bags, footwear, tents, field gear, cookware, fuel, first aid, sunglasses, binoculars, watches, climbing equipment, cycling gear, paddling and rafting gear (including rafts), luggage, outdoor clothing (for adults and children), topo maps, books, magazines, and camp food. Many offer bicycle maintenance and repairs, ski mounting, camping/ backpacking/climbing/ski equipment rentals, and on-premises repair of stoves, lanterns, tents, and other gear. Some of the larger examples offer indoor climbing walls, photo developing, ski-school programs, fishing licenses, lectures (and clinics and slide shows) on topics like adventure travel, recreational resources, environmental concerns, and (true!) espresso carts.

The nation's largest consumer co-op, REI also puts out one of the most comprehensive catalogs around — maybe the most extensive in its field. —TV

Sherlock Walking Staff. Take this along on your scrambles, hikes, and fishing trips. Doubles as a field monopod, too — walnut handled knob removes to reveal 35 mm camera mount. Comfortable foam grip. Push-button shaft adjusts from 40" to 56". Steel end point with removable rubber tip. Packed length: 32". 1 lb. $50

Outdoor Research Advanced Bivy Sack. This is the answer for backpackers and climbers who want the light weight and no-frills shelter of a bivy sack, but also want extra ventilation and room. Set it up to enjoy starry skies and bug-free slumber, or batten down the hatches to sleep dry through that unexpected storm. Top is waterproof, breathable Gore-Tex®/nylon; bottom is nylon taffeta with waterproof Hydroseal® coating. Taped seams. Peak ht: 18"; 90" long; 2 lbs. $200

REI GeoDome.

A great choice for anyone looking for a spacious, strong tent. Backpackers and alpinists like the GeoDome's performance in the mountains, while family campers appreciate the roominess of our 4- and 6-person GeoDomes. Fly features dual side poles for enhanced strength that stands up to high winds and heavy snow. Netted roof vent on 4- and 6-person tents allows stargazing and adds extra ventilation. Mesh pole sleeves ensure improved ventilation between tent body and fly.

2-person. $275; 4-person. $325; 6-person. $375

REI (Recreational Equipment Inc.): Catalog free. 1700 45th Street East, Sumner, WA 98390; 800/426-4840, fax 206/891-2523.

Cutlery Shoppe

The Shoppe sells most of the best makes and models of factory-made knives, at exceptionally low prices. Their 55-page color catalog has big photos to aid mail-order decision. Brands and prices* include Victorinox (the full-dress SwissChamp is $54 here, around $90 elsewhere), Gerber (Parabellum $50, not $90), Buck (BuckLock $39, not $70), BK&T (Campanion $70, not $100), Blackjack, Tekna, SOG,

A Merlin $44
B Endura $39.20   Endura in pocket.
C Delica $34.40

Ek, Aitor, Boker, and others. The Cutlery Shoppe also has good sharpening tools, kitchen implements, related useful stuff, and really nice service.

An excellent (and now much-copied) design is Spyderco's Clipit line — serrated folders that clip to the top of your pocket and open easily with just one hand. Lansky makes a superior sharpening kit, and Spyderco's Tri-Angle is the best of the touch-up-the-edge rigs. —SB

* *I mention prices here to show the sort of spread you can expect from Cutlery Shoppe. You should not necessarily expect them to be current when you read this.*

Cutlery Shoppe: Catalog free. 5461 Kendall Street, Boise, ID 83706; 800/231-1272.

Nomadics Tipi Makers

Besides made-to-order canvas tipis of various sizes, Nomadics' catalog offers liners, door covers, ropes, rain caps, hand-painted designs, and rugs. The catalog is good reading in its own right, offering helpful tips and explanations for their tipi construction and designs. Nomadics claims to be "the world's largest makers of Native American Indian tipis," producing more than 11,000 over the last 25 years. —RU

• The Marine Treatment is a trade term indicating that the fabric has a mold-resistant, a mildew-resistant, and a fungi-resistant treatment. It also has an ultra-violet inhibitor and it has been pre-shrunk to 2%.

By resisting mold and mildew, the marine treatment retards rotting that might result from recurring exposure to rain and snow. This treatment also makes the canvas water-repellent. It is not desirable that the canvas be waterproof. Waterproofed canvas does not "breathe." The tipi fabric must breathe in the same way that leather boots, wool shirts, or down sleeping bags do. If the tipi fabric is waterproofed, condensation can accumulate on the inside of the tipi cover or within the fiber of the cotton threads themselves and may promote mold and mildew growth.

The three most common trade names for marine treatment are Sunforger, Permasol and Terrasol. All three names indicate the same marine finish, they are simply from three different finishing companies.

Nomadics Tipi Makers: Catalog $2. 17671 Snow Creek Road, Bend, OR 97701; 503/389-3980.

Fourteen-foot ceremonial tipi.

Inside our 18 ft. tipi.

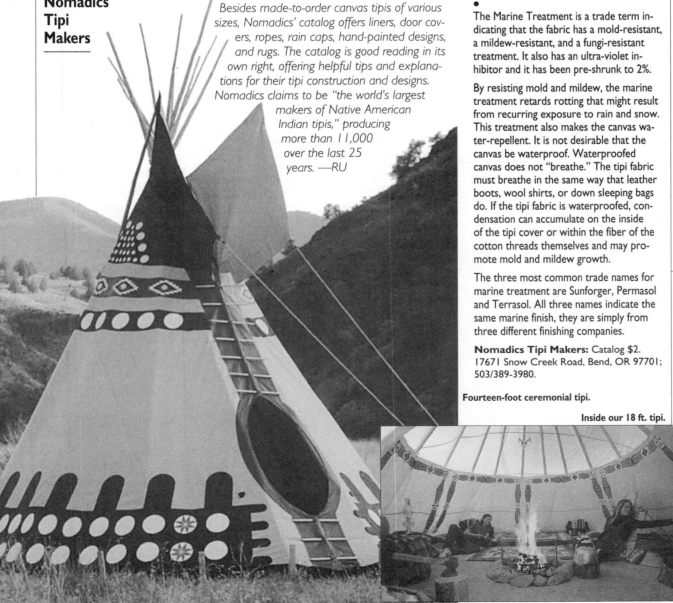

Outside

This 200-page monthly covers land, sea, and air sports and outings from the perspectives of beginners and professionals. Travel, ecology, and land management articles will interest even the housebound. Tons of product reviews, columns, resource references, and events listings are presented with a balance of lively writing and expertise. —Richie Unterberger

•
A first attempt at boardsailing is about like balancing on a bongo board while repacking a parachute in a high wind, with maybe an enraged orangutan on your back, determined to drown you. No, it's more like you're standing on a kind of greased ball; you simultaneously hold an unwieldy lever inserted into the wind, which if you manage it correctly will make the ball go scooting out from under. Splunk.

Ah, yes, the lever *is* the wind: the mast, anchored to the board by a U-joint that allows it to flop with spineless irresolution in any direction. Operation of the sail is simple. Lean it toward the rear of the board to steer into the wind. Lean it toward the front of the board to steer away from the wind. Lean it away from or closer to your body for balance. Increase or decrease its angle to the wind for a throttle. Do this in gentle, subtle increments, except when wind and water and desperately unsure balance force you to do it in lurching recoveries. Splutch.

Careful readers will notice that this means using two hands to do three things at once — in at least six different directions, although in practice the number of directions is infinite. Then there are the two feet, with which you not only maintain balance, but also help steer and trot around the mast to reverse direction. Helicopter pilots come to mind, muttering about rubbing the belly while patting the head. Four appendages working simultaneously, differently, appropriately, pursuing control. Master the sail while you are mastering the board. A mixed medium. See juggling on a unicycle, above.

Outside Magazine. Mark Bryant, Editor. $14.95/year (12 issues) from PO Box 51733, Boulder, CO 90321-1733; 800/678-1131

Great Expeditions

Neither strictly an ecotourism magazine nor strictly an outdoor-excursion magazine, Great Expeditions' focus ranges from travelogs of solo adventures to rundowns of organized whitewater rafting trips. It leads you toward nature-oriented journeys that are as challenging as you want (or don't want) them to be. No continent is off-limits; respect for the regions' ecosystems and cultures is always urged. —RU

•
It took two laborious days to coax my Hercules one-speed bike the 4,000 feet up (1200 m), but when I was finally above the populated coast, I realized it was worth it. Kerala's interior was Eden.

Hidden amidst tea plantations which carpet nearly every slope of the Western Ghats is an eclectic assemblage of pristine parks and wildlife sanctuaries. Secluded preserves — with challenging names like Periyar, Eravikulam and Parambikulam — provide safe haven to abundant wildlife and blessed solitude for those fleeing the crowded coast. Periyar National Park was my first stop.

Women in saris and men in their finest sarong-like dhotis travel across India to enjoy day cruises on pristine Lake Periyar, centerpiece of the park which bears its name. Boasting nearly 1,000 elephants in 300 sq. miles (800 sq. km), Periyar offers unparalleled pachyderm watching. Only a rare boatload returns without sightings to gleefully recount. Witnessing a herd of elephants ford Lake Periyar is truly captivating. Like grey icebergs floating with wrinkled snorkels, the uncommonly graceful swimmers leave hardly a wake. If there is an infant among them, the adults watch with uncompromising vigilance to insure junior's safe passage.

Few people venture beyond Lake Periyar into the park's interior. Indian tourists seem singularly averse to exploring their national parks, but even if they didn't, administrators discourage independent wandering. The park is a wilderness area managed exclusively for the benefit of the resident flora and fauna. So unless you possess a letter of introduction from Gilbert Grosvenor (or can forge one) or have a background in wildlife biology (or can fake it), perseverance and patience is your only recourse. Coercion, as I discovered in Periyar, is a tactic doomed to failure.

Great Expeditions
Margaret J. Newbold, Editor. $18/year (4 issues) from PO Box 18036, Raleigh, NC 27619; 800/743-3639

The author's bicycle at 5500 feet. Kerala.

Afoot & Afloat Series

Leisurely hikes and boat rides are restorative to the soul. This series sets an admirable standard for nature guides. Its five volumes address the practicalities of trails and waterways, the beauty of birds and mountains, and cultural and ecological background on the region. —Richie Unterberger

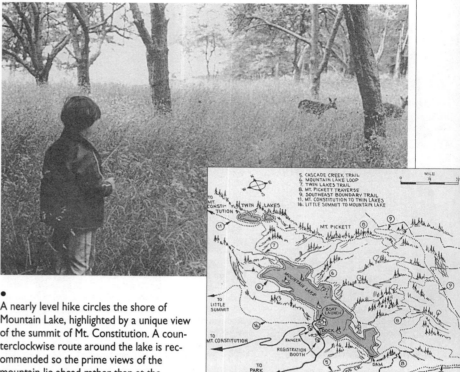

•
A nearly level hike circles the shore of Mountain Lake, highlighted by a unique view of the summit of Mt. Constitution. A counterclockwise route around the lake is recommended so the prime views of the mountain lie ahead rather than at the hiker's back.

The long summit ridge of Mt. Constitution rises above the lake. Little Summit can be seen on the left and the stone observation tower of the main summit far on the right. Below the summit precipitous 1,000-foot cliffs show their dramatic profile.

Look for bald and golden eagles, hawks, and osprey soaring the updrafts near the mountain. Four pairs of osprey are believed to nest in the vicinity, although others summer here. The same factors of population, pollution, and pesticides that threaten bald eagles have severely reduced the osprey population. In addition, bald eagles frequently steal fish they have caught and generally harass them, at times causing them to leave. Ospreys, which resemble small white-breasted eagles, favor the heights of Mt. Constitution, with its remote nesting sites and fish-filled lakes.

Afoot & Afloat Series
Marge & Ted Mueller. 1988, 1990
•The San Juan Islands
•North Puget Sound
•South Puget Sound
•Middle Puget Sound & Hood Canal
$12.95 ($15.95 postpaid) each from The Mountaineers Books, 1101 SW Klickitat Way, Seattle, WA 98134; 800/553-4453

OTHER GREAT RESOURCES

Great American Learning Adventures: Harriet Webster. 1994, HarperPerennial. A guide to over 200 educational vacations in the United States, with emphasis on outdoors activities and crafts.

World Cruising Routes: Jimmy Cornell. 1992, International Marine Publishing. Guide to nearly 400 cruising routes around the world, geared to small-boat sailors.

Covers the top destinations and guide services for dozens of activities — ballooning, arctic trips, skydiving, ocean kayaking. Each section reviews and rates outfitters, schools, tour operators, books, magazines, videos, and organizations. A lot of these excursions ain't cheap, and not all have room for novices, but outdoor sport and travel enthusiasts of all levels will find a gold mine of information.
—*RU*

•

If you want the most exotic ski holiday available anywhere, consider Wintergreen Adventures' Siberian Arctic tour — a traverse of the Chukotka Peninsula using skis and reindeer sleighs. After arriving in Northern Siberia, tour members will be helicoptered to a remote village basecamp, where they will stay in the homes of native Chutkotkans, nomadic reindeer herders. These people still maintain their traditional culture, herding caribou, and driving sleighs made of antler and driftwood. Next, the group will take "vizdahotes," heated halftracks, to the jumping-off point for the ski crossing. The guide will be Paul Schurke, leader of the 1989 Bering Bridge dogsled expedition, and co-leader of the 1986 North Pole dogsled expedition.

With clothing loaded in backpacks and gear stowed on reindeer sleighs, the group will make a 100-mile passage on skis from the Chukotkan interior plateau to the Arctic Ocean. The snow conditions are excellent, and Chukchi sled-drivers can provide lifts for tired skiers. Along the way the group may camp with Chukchi families in their yurangis, fur-lined yurts. At journey's end, the skiers will be treated to a traditional Eskimo celebration. The 12-day trip runs in late April, a time of long days and moderate weather. Cost will be about $3,500 with airfare from Alaska. Contact Wintergreen Adventures, 1101 Ring Rock Road, Ely, MI 55731, Phone/FAX: (218) 365-6602.

The Ultimate Adventure Sourcebook
Paul McMenamin, Editor. Turner Publishing, 1992; 432 pp. ISBN 1-878685-18-X $29.95 ($32.45 postpaid) from Andrews & McMeel, PO Box 419242, Kansas City, MO 64141; 800/826-4216

California Thrill Sports

It might be easier to take the plunge in the Golden State than most other places, but the author's tips and info are inspirational to thrillseekers the world over. This novice-friendly guide covers bungee jumping, parasailing, ballooning, whitewater rafting, kayaking, skydiving, rock climbing, paragliding, and hang gliding, and — unlike some volumes of this sort — doesn't make you feel like a fool for being scared the first time. Each chapter lists related books, magazines, schools, and organizations. Down-to-earth quotes from experts in various sports give this guide a human tone that offers both reassurance and encouragement. —*RU*

•

"I heard you have to learn how to use grappling hooks and drive big spikes into granite if you want to climb vertical rock walls."

You're thinking of that scene in *The Dirty Dozen* where Charles Bronson has trouble getting a grappling hook onto that chateau full of helpless German officers, aren't you? Or maybe you're thinking of aid climbers who bolt whole campsites onto vertical rock during multi-day big wall ascents.

The truth is: Free climbing is more like vertical gymnastics or vertical dance than anything else. It really has nothing to do with technical expertise in the use of hammers and spikes. Other than the simple rope/harness/anchor system which protects you from an accidental fall, the only mechanics involved in free climbing are the human mechanics of leverage, balance and precise application of muscular force.

Free climbing is a whole body/soul experience, not a whole hardware store experience.

California Thrill Sports
Erik Fair. 1992; 351 pp. ISBN 0-935701-32-X $14.95 ($19.45 postpaid) from Foghorn Press, 555 De Haro Street #220, San Francisco, CA 94107; 800-FOGHORN

The Encyclopedia of Recreational Diving

Many professional dive shops and instructors point to the Encyclopedia as the best all-around source of information on scuba diving. Published by the Professional Association of American Diving Instructors (PADI), this fully illustrated volume is an indispensable tool for experts and beginners alike and the most comprehensive compendium of information on the sport currently available.

Both PADI and NAUI (National Association of Underwater Instructors) dive centers can be found across the country, and offer scuba training and certification programs, equipment sales and rentals, dive boat and underwater tour information, travel reservations, instruction in underwater photography and video, swimming and "aquacise" classes, and more.

Authorized PADI or NAUI dive centers are generally the best places to get both information and dive gear.
—*Tom Valtin*

The Encyclopedia of Recreational Diving
Al Hornsby & Karl Shreeves, Editors. 1993; 565 pp. ISBN 1-878663-02-X Sold at PADI dive centers. Suggested price $31. List of dive centers available from PADI International, 1251 E. Dyer Rd., #100, Santa Ana, CA 92705-5605; 800/729-7234

•

No diving instrument is infallible. Dive computers are subject to battery failure and damage through improper handling.

Some dive computers put themselves through an initial self-test when first activated. This should alert divers immediately to malfunctioning circuitry. The nature of computers is also such that a computer that malfunctioned during a dive would most likely display nonsensical information, rather than a deceptive reading.

Most computers use long-life lithium batteries and warn when these batteries need replacment.

If a diver has maintained a record of the depths and times of his previous dives, and if these dives would not have required decompression stops if using conventional dive tables, then the diver may continue diving with conventional instruments and tables should his computer's battery fail. Otherwise he should remain out of the water for at least 12 hours.

O NCE, WHILE I WAS CLIMBING the flanks of the southern Sierra Nevada, I unexpectedly came upon one of the premier hang-gliding launch sites in North America.

Walt's Leap hangs almost a mile above the floor of Owens Valley, an edge-of-the-world sort of spot. One after another, as I watched, the "pilots" steadied their craft, took a few running steps, and soared out into the sky ... for miles. One pilot was particularly choosy about his takeoff, waiting for the wind to be just right. When finally he stepped into the void, he didn't float into the valley as the others had done; he spiraled nearly straight up, riding the thermals blowing up out of the valley. I watched for fifteen minutes until he was just a speck — and still rising. Word has it that someone once flew more than 200 miles from Walt's Leap, touching down two states away!

Those who would be eagles can learn how to fly through the United States Hang Gliding Association (USHGA), a self-supporting, nonprofit organization based in Colorado Springs, Colorado. Currently numbering about 11,000 members, the association is a clearinghouse for information on what they call "the purest form of flight." A $54 annual membership makes you part of the USHGA's Pilot Rating System and includes a subscription to *Hang Gliding* magazine. You also get voting privileges in local and regional elections, eligibility for awards, affiliation with the National Aeronautical Association and the Federation Aeronautique International, and even $1,000,000 (per occurrence) liability insurance; this has opened many flying sites to hang gliding.

The association is nationally subdivided into twelve regions — primarily for the purpose of electing locally savvy regional directors, but also in consideration of local hang gliding patterns, climatic and topographical conditions, and population density. The USHGA handbook outlines the organization's history and provides information on programs, events, and awards, as well as regulatory, policy, and technical data. *Hang Gliding* is a great resource for instruction and technique, glider design, competitions, locations, and related literature.

If your interest runs to paragliding — a cross between hang gliding and parachuting — the USHGA is still the umbrella organization. Paragliders look like parachutes, but they are designed for soaring. A paraglider is an inflatable fabric canopy whose twelve to twenty-four cells are connected by a stiff front rib. Suspension lines connect the canopy with a seat harness, which the pilot uses along with a steering line to control direction, speed, and lift.

Most paragliders weigh less than twenty pounds, and some are designed to fold up and fit in a backpack, enabling pilots to take flight from remote areas not accessible to hang gliders. The current men's distance record is 88 miles; the woman's record is 63 miles. At the extreme of paraglider design are propeller-driving "paramotors." These are still in their infancy; lighter, cheaper engines are hitting the market each year. —Tom Valtin

Hang Gliding • Paragliding

About 9,000 of the USHGA's members are primarily hang gliders, the other 2,000 primarily paragliders. The latter group receives **Paragliding**, *not* **Hang Gliding**; *otherwise, membership privileges are the same.* —TV

•

As a basic rule of thumb you should plan on spending an absolute minimum of $700 for a reasonably good used beginning glider, but $1,000 to $1,500 is more realistic when it comes to a quality used wing. Again, buy new if possible.

Don't buy a glider with lots of rust on the hardware. If the glider you're looking at has rusted bolts it's not been taken care of very well. You should do a thorough inspection of the glider and its hardware. If you find rust on any of the bolts and/or other hardware you should also thoroughly inspect the aluminum tubes for corrosion (inside and out). Corrosion on aluminum has a different look than corrosion on steel. On aluminum, corrosion will look like a white powder that is adhered to the corroded part. Usually this will be found on the inside of aluminum tubes and under sleeves. Look very closely at the end of all sleeves and around bushings and rivets. If you discover any significant amount of corrosion, move on to the next glider.

Don't buy a glider with dented or bent frame parts unless there is a professional willing and able to fix the glider with the appropriate parts. It is nearly impossible to find parts for many gliders on the used market. If a leading edge or crossbar is damaged it may be necessary to remove the opposite, undamaged part and duplicate it with raw materials. This is extremely labor intensive, and by the time your "new" glider is ready to fly you may have more money in it than you had planned on. The answer to this problem is to stick with a late model made by a manufacturer that is currently in business. —*Hang Gliding*

•

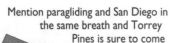

Mention paragliding and San Diego in the same breath and Torrey Pines is sure to come

United States Hang Gliding Association
Membership $49/year, includes: 12 issues of Hang Gliding magazine or 6 issues of Paragliding—The Magazine, liability insurance, ratings, etc. From USHGA, PO Box 8300, Colorado Springs, CO 80933; 719/632-8300, fax 719/632-6417

to mind. Some out-of-towners have heard about Little Black and Horse Canyon. One of the best kept secrets (oops!) in San Diego is Blossom Valley. . . .

Just like everywhere else in Southern California, the launch area is dirt and rocks. It faces west and there's enough room to have maybe two gliders laid out. Since it's at one end of the valley, the launch isn't too wind direction sensitive, as long as it's blowing onshore. The main ridge is about

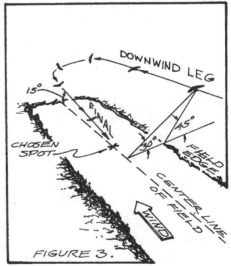

FIGURE 3.

one quarter mile long. Directly below launch is the "finger." This is a little raised area with a road on top that's easy to land on. If you get below launch and start getting low, chances are this is where you'll be landing. If this happens, pack your glider up and head for the road where one of your friends will pick you up. The worst thing you can do is to fly straight out and land in some farmer's field in the valley. Don't jeopardize the site by being a bonehead. —*Paragliding*

See Stormtrack (p. 83).

Climbing • Summit

Once the province of a few daredevil extremists, the sport of climbing — the scaling of sheer, exposed faces of rock, snow and ice — has achieved rapid growth in a very short time. Widely circulated periodicals devoted to the sport have emerged only recently. The best of these differ mainly in emphasis and style.

A typical issue of **Climbing** *contains half-a-dozen feature articles — adventure travel, profiles, history, fiction — and roughly two dozen departments: fitness and training, reviews of books and equipment, medical information, events, competition results and classifieds.*

Summit*'s major departure from* **Climbing** *is in its attention to adventure travel and mountaineering history, at the expense of practical topics like equipment and technique. It is more literary and esoteric, and less service-oriented. The two publications complement each other nicely. —Tom Valtin*

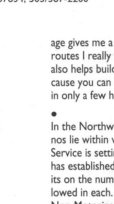

Climbing Magazine
Michael Kennedy, Editor.
$28/year (8 issues) from
Climbing Magazine, 1101
Village Road, Carbondale,
CO 81623; 303/963-9449

Summit Magazine
John Harlin III, Editor.
$24.95/year (6 issues) from
Summit Publications, PO Box
3000, Dept. SUM, Denville,
NJ 07834; 503/387-2200

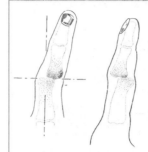

Dislocations of the fingers which occur most commonly at the second joint, may be corrected quite easily immediately after the dislocation by pulling on the injured digit. The injured finger can then be splinted effectively by taping it to an adjacent uninjured finger. — *Medicine for Mountaineering*

Mountaineering: The Freedom Of The Hills

Now in its fifth edition, **Mountaineering** *has been the standard text on climbing and mountaineering for decades. The new edition contains expanded chapters on equipment, technique, glacier travel and safety, brand-new sections on rock climbing and winter expeditions, and 350 new illustrations.*

Founded in 1906, The Mountaineers is a nonprofit club that sponsors classes and activities like hiking, mountain climbing, ski-touring and snowshoeing. The club's conservation division supports environmental causes through educational activities, legislation, and informational programs. —TV

Mountaineering
(The Freedom of the Hills)
Don Graydon, Editor. 1992; 447 pp.
ISBN 0-89886-309-0
$22.95 ($24.95 postpaid) from The
Mountaineers Books, 1101 SW
Klickitat Way, Seattle, WA 98134;
800/553-4453

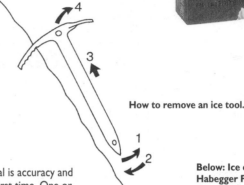

How to remove an ice tool.

Below: Ice climbing on Habegger Falls, Bishop Creek in California's Sierra Nevada.

age gives me a mental base to approach the routes I really want to on-sight. Bouldering also helps build knowledge in a hurry because you can attempt hundreds of moves in only a few hours. —*Climbing*

•

In the Northwest, where numerous volcanos lie within wilderness areas, the Forest Service is setting strict limits on access. It has established three distinct zones and limits on the number of human encounters allowed in each. They are: 1) "Semi-Primitive Non-Motorized," with ten or fewer encounters allowed a day; 2) "Primitive," with six or fewer encounters; and 3) "Pristine," with a maximum of one encounter per day.

Many of the Northwest's summits — and their crowded, well-established routes — are now zoned Primitive or Pristine. When the Forest Service starts enforcing these rules, this year in some areas, unwary climbers will be in for a surprise; they might not be allowed in. Critics counter that limiting access on the main routes will simply disperse climbers to more remote areas, which may be more detrimental to the overall ecosystem. In an effort to resolve both the access and degradation aspects, Jim Angell of the Access Fund has suggested a new zone to add to the plan, called the "Corridor of Concentrated Use." This zone would allow continued heavy use on selected popular routes, while still giving the Forest Service the authority to limit traffic elsewhere.

However, the Forest Service doesn't seem interested in the idea. Early on, the agency convened a citizens' task force to address recreational use of wilderness areas in the Northwest. According to Angell, the Forest Service staffers kept pushing the social encounters question even though the task force members repeatedly said that it was a non-issue. "I don't know why the Forest Service is making an issue out of social encounters," Angell said, "unless it's to get revenge against the people who got the Wilderness Act passed." —*Summit*

With any ice tool, the goal is accuracy and a solid placement —the first time. One or two swings saved at the bottom of a pitch mean that much more energy at the top. It takes a lot of practice to learn pinpoint placement. But with a combination of proper technique and equipment, you should be able to place a tool easily and precisely, keep it secure for as long as it's needed, and extract it with less effort than you took to place it.

Study the ice for a good placement. A slight depression above and slightly to the side is likely to be good. Ice is more compact and holds the pick better in depressions than in bulges, which shatter or break off under the impact of an ice tool. Try to make placements in opaque ice, less brittle than clear ice because it has more air trapped inside. Minimize the number of placements by planting the axe as high as possible and by moving upward as far as you can with each placement.

Different climbers will have different experiences, though they may be using identical tools on the same climb, because of differences in ability and climbing background. The more experienced climber, for instance, may climb confidently with only a small bite of the pick into the ice, while another climber might not feel comfortable without slamming the tool deep. On most tools, only the first few teeth provide any useful bite in the ice, and the upward angle of the pick in the ice provides most of the holding power. (On an ice tool, small teeth often perform better than large teeth.) Keep your tools sharp.

Rests, such as the knee-lock pictured here, are not as common on plastic as real rock. —Climbing

•

Every style of rock speaks its own language, and every climbing area has its own dialect. Good climbers learn to speak granite, quartzite, and sandstone, and can then quickly assimilate new dialects as they encounter them. A climber who only understands cranking off tiny granite edges will flail at Red Rocks until he builds a mental dictionary of the unique language of soft sandstone. Consider a climber looking at the edge of a hold from below. On steep granite, the hold will probably be reasonably sharp, and it makes sense to grab it in a crimp grip. But on the water-washed slabs of Whitehorse Ledge in New Hampshire, the hold will probably be rounded and he will need to grab it with an open hand for maximum friction.

The best trick to adapting to a new rock type is building a mental model of its character. Just as listening to French tapes may help you shop in Paris, spending time analyzing the rock at a new area will improve your success rate and climbing experience. I like to spend my first day in a new area climbing as many routes as I can - the mile-

Mi mejor Amiga Es Any.
Y me gustaba jugar alas muñecas.
Siempre Ibamos Ala escuela juntas.

[My best friend is Any.
And I liked to play dolls
with her. We always went
to school together.]

Ena Patricia

Smart Schools, Smart Kids

*Citing overwhelming evidence of massive national failures in basic education, Ed Fiske sounds the alarm to abandon the assembly-line-inspired school system of the past one hundred years. Educational institutions, he argues, need to develop students capable of incorporating new information, not just digesting old knowledge, and for this task the old educational blueprint won't work. Some schools (even entire state school systems, as in Kentucky) are making bold moves in this direction. Fiske's descriptions of these innovations present the components needed to build "smart" schools.
—Betty Rappaport*

•

The renewal of public education in this country requires nothing less than a frontal assault on every aspect of schooling — the way we run districts, organize classrooms, use time, measure achievement, assign students, relegate schools to their surroundings and hold people accountable. Trying to get more learning out of the current system is like trying to get the Pony Express to compete with the telegraph by breeding faster ponies.

•

The factory-model school succeeded because no one ever asked it to educate large numbers of students to a high school level. No one ever asked it to teach most American students to *think*.

•

Carroll's "Copernican change" involves the school schedule. "Instead of having students change locations, subjects, and activities seven to nine times each day, we ask them to concentrate on one or two subjects at a time, each taught in an extended 'macro-class'," he explains. Eighty students — about half of the ninth grade class —

take two hundred-minute classes each day for sixty days, then switch to two new classes. David Dolber, a social studies teacher, told *Education Week* that the change permits more coherent teaching and learning. "In a hundred-minute span, I can talk about Martin Luther, about the Counter-Reformation, and about the Thirty Years' War, as well as the themes running through the three events," he says. By contrast, he would spend a day on each topic in the traditional program and be unable to discuss the common themes because the lessons were too disjointed.

Smart Schools, Smart Kids
(Why Do Some Schools Work?)
Edward B. Fiske. Touchstone Books, 1991; 305 pp. ISBN 0-671-79212-1
$11 postpaid. Simon & Schuster/Order Dept., 200 Old Tappan Road, Old Tappan, NJ 07675; 800/223-2336

•

Teachers should help students to see that human beings, including the students themselves, are learning all the time; and that all our live experiences, and the people with whom we live, play, and work have an emotional and intellectual impact on us. Teachers must also help students recognize the value of the knowledge they already possess and that not all knowledge is gained through books and formal schooling.

Parents and communities need to be seen as equal contributors of understanding and knowledge to the educative process. Power relations that presently exist in the school structure must be opened up so that parents can become participants in their children's learning by contributing their oral or written words, ideas, and experiences as part of the text of schooling.

Building Communities of Learners

Faced with students from a variety of languages, cultures and family backgrounds, how do teachers begin to teach literacy while simultaneously preserving and valuing this diversity? Sudia Paloma McCaleb finds a way to solve the dilemma through a process called participatory research. She encourages parents to relate their childhood experiences with school, learning, and teachers. In doing so, two important outcomes develop: Meaningful themes emerge and become the topics for family (parent-child) stories. Parents begin to see that their lives and experiences possess relevance and value. Marginalized families may also develop stronger literacy skills. —BR

Ena Patricia's contribution to the book was a description of her best friend, Amy.

Building Communities of Learners
(A Collaboration Among Teachers, Students, Families, and Communities)
Sudia Paloma McCaleb. St. Martin's Press, 1994; 210 pp. ISBN 0-312-09163-X
$17.95 ($21.95 postpaid). Publishers Book & Audio, PO Box 070059, Staten Island, NY 10307; 800/288-2131

Mi papá me dijo que no caminara debajo de los árboles de papaya porque allí viven los alacranes y ellas pueden caer en mi cabeza.

Village children were warned not to play under the trees because the *alacranes* (scorpions) like to sleep there. They could jump down on your head and bite you hard.

The Having of Wonderful Ideas

Can you unlock the secrets of the universe by studying a grain of sand? If we consider learning as a process that goes beyond acquisition of specific information, Eleanor Duckworth's essays come close to convincing us that it's possible. In keeping with Piaget's constructivist philosophy, she concerns herself with the pathways to gaining knowledge, focusing our attention on the hypotheses students continually make and test as they work with materials, events, and ideas. Through her observations, particularly of the moon-journal assignment for her college education class, we gain an understanding of how the most basic of materials — a grain of sand, for example — can set the stage for learning or "the having of wonderful ideas." —BR

The Having of Wonderful Ideas
(and Other Essays on Teaching and Learning) Eleanor Duckworth. 1987; 151 pp. ISBN 0-8077-2876-4
$15.95 ($18.95 postpaid). Teachers College Press, PO Box 20, Williston, VT 05495; 800/488-2665

•

[From a student journal]
October 10: The Morning Moon

7:00 A.M.

6:00 A.M. What! The moon is where it was at 7:30 P.M. last time I saw it. It's early morning. What time did it rise? Why? Is there a connection between its waning and its rising time?

October 11-16: The Moon Turns Around (or seems to)

During this five-day period, I am intent upon systematically measuring the angle of the moon in the sky. I am also checking whether or not I can see it well into the morning. I record the moon on the 11th day as shaped like this. (above) Then, between the 13th and 15th I lose it, don't see it at all.

6:15 P.M.

One evening coming out of Longfellow Hall, 6:15 P.M., I see it right up Appian Way toward the Charles. As if that's not astonishing enough, I notice and record (thank goodness) that the *direction of the horns has changed*. I commented on it in my diary, but had thought little more of it until right now.

•

David Hawkins has said of curriculum development, "You don't want to cover a subject; you want to uncover it." That, it seems to me, is what schools should be about. They can help to uncover parts of the world that children would not otherwise know how to tackle. Wonderful ideas are built on other wonderful ideas. In Piaget's terms, you must reach out to the world with your own intellectual tools and grasp it, assimilate it yourself. All kinds of things are hidden from us — even though they surround us — unless we know how to reach out for them. Schools and teachers can provide materials and questions in ways that suggest things to be done with them; and children, in the doing, cannot help being inventive.

OTHER GREAT RESOURCES

Teaching Stories: Judy Logan. 1993, Minnesota Inclusiveness Program. Elders' lives as bridges between the world of adolescents and adults.

Wally's Stories (Conversations in the Kindergarten): Vivian Gussin Paley. 1991, Harvard University Press.

White Teacher: Vivian Gussin Paley. 1979, Harvard University Press.

Schools That Work

George H. Wood describes actual elementary and high-school classrooms that are places of joy, purpose, caring and collaboration. They differ from conventional classrooms in several important ways: young people are given greater responsibility for planning the curriculum and setting class rules; learning is pursued through thematic projects and out in the world, rather than in textbooks and workbooks; there is less fragmentation by rigid scheduling and the "tyranny of the clock."

Wood is primarily concerned with educating for a truly democratic society. He offers these examples of innovative classrooms to support his critique of the competitive, test-driven, narrowly economic purpose that public education serves in the US today.
—Ron Miller

Schools That Work
(America's Most Innovative
Public Education Programs)
George H. Wood. Plume Books, 1992;
290 pp. ISBN 0-452-26959-8
$11 ($13 postpaid). Penguin USA/
Consumer Sales, 120 Woodbine Street,
Bergenfield, NJ 07621; 800/253-6476

•

What does democratic life require of us? What of those things can we effect in schools? Fundamentally, democracy requires citizens who participate broadly in informed public decision-making with an eye toward the common good. Citizens must thus be literate, able not only to master the rudiments of reading, writing, and computing, but able to use these tools as ways of understanding the world and making their voices heard in it.

•

Marcia [Burchby]: "We have to respect the child's work as his or her work. It may not be perfect, and it may not even be like anything we have seen before. But it is that child's and we should respect it as that."

This respect for the child as a learner, as a collaborator, shows up again on the sheet of poster board that displays the class rules. At first glance, a list that begins with "No Smoking" and proceeds to "No Throwing Books at the Lights" seems a bit unusual for a first-grade room. "Well, they made all the rules themselves as a group," I'm informed. "It's their space as much as mine. Besides, we all agree that the rules boil down to taking care of each other and our stuff."

•

There is a temptation among school reformers to fantasize about the future of

schooling. Painting rosy pictures of the schools of the future, they seldom talk about the hard work of getting from here to there. It's as if they only need to wish it for it to come true. But people involved in the day-to-day work of educating and raising children know that such fantasies just aren't possible. They know that schools are very much driven by tradition, that they often respond slowly if at all to calls for change, and that grandiose, one-size-fits-all reforms seldom have an impact on the daily lives of kids in schools. Joette Weber put it this way: "You know, I hear about all the things the state legislature is supposedly doing to make schools better. But when it gets right down to it, when I close my door, it's just me and my little guys. All that stuff doesn't have much effect. It doesn't help me at all. I haven't noticed one bit of positive difference from all the noise and money spent by those guys." This refrain sounds strangely familiar from state to state.

What is possible in restructuring schools is change on a more local scale. The basic building block of the school system in the United States is the local school. If genuine, democratic school reform is to occur, it must begin at this most fundamental level, proceeding school by school, district by district.

Of course, this is the most frustrating way to think about school reform. We all long for the grand stroke that will turn schools around and suddenly solve all our problems. But as quickly as that stroke could be carried out, it could be undone. Lasting change will take a deep commitment to the daily work of making schools the component of democratic life that they were intended to be.

How to Get Your Child a Private School Education in a Public School

This book has become my Bible in dealing with schools and my children's attitudes towards them.

The authors (who are educators and parents) firmly believe that it is unnecessary to spend megabucks on private schooling. Their advice on checking out the teacher, deciding if a school is right for your child, and coping with the minutiae — morning madness, to painless papers, recess success — is pragmatic and thought-provoking. Lots of good ideas and common sense here! —Nancy Rhine

•

Choosing a school based on reputation is better than not choosing at all. Some parents don't choose because they think they don't have a choice. Private school is not

How to Get Your Child a Private School Education in a Public School
Martin Nemko. 1989; 191 pp.
ISBN 0-89815-277-1 $8.95 ($12.45 postpaid). Ten Speed Press, PO Box 7123, Berkeley, CA 94707; 800/841-2665

an option for them, and they believe their child can only attend the local public school. This is often untrue. For years, parents-in-the-know have been getting their children into public schools other than their local one.

Why Do These Kids Love School?

"You mean you haven't seen this before?" said my wife when I brought this videocassette home to get her opinion. Like many other citizens, Judy cares enough about our daughter's public school to work as a volunteer classroom helper and community fundraiser. She informed me that the video is a respected classic among people

who believe schools can become exciting learning environments. If you are a teacher, a parent, a school administrator of the kind who builds arks when everyone else is predicting rain, this documentary is irrefutable and inspiring evidence that committed communities can work wonders.
—HLR

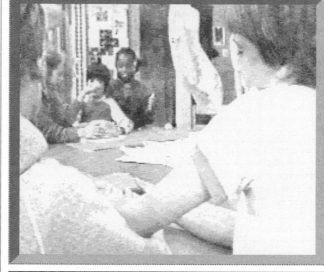

Why Do These Kids Love School?:
Dorothy Fadiman, 1990; 60m. VHS video. $95 ($100 postpaid). Pyramid Film & Video, PO Box 1048, Santa Monica, CA 90406; 800/421-2304.

Building Support Networks for Schools

Pat Wagner has been facilitating connections between people for over a decade, through the Denver-based Office for Open Networks. Her networking wisdom embraces everything from characteristics of successful network builders to specific network-building tools. Although the book is not about electronic networking, its strategies and ideas would help any group construct an interactive idea/information/ project exchange in their community. Wagner even includes the design for a network workshop you can run yourself (complete with pages to be copied for handouts).

This is a valuable tool for any teacher, administrator, or community member interested in developing resource networks. —Lisa Kimball

•

Network versus Archive
Many kinds of human behavior and organizations satisfy some of the criteria of successful network building. However, the differences are crucial and warrant attention. On the spectrum of information man-

agement, network building is at one end and archive building is at the other.

A network is based on the relationships among people in the web, while an archive relies on documents. In this context, documents include any recorded information, from books and papers to computer databases and artwork. The more time spent collecting, cataloging, and retrieving information, the less time can be spent focusing on people.

Building Support Networks for Schools
Pat Wagner. 1991; 206 pp.
ISBN 0-87436-615-1
$35 postpaid from ABC-CLIO, Inc., PO Box 1911, Santa Barbara, CA 93116-1911; 800/422-2546

YOUNG ARTISTS

The Whole Language Catalog

Metaphorically, "whole language" describes an educational ethos that, like language, develops in a social context, imparts meaning, and symbolizes experience. Fragmentation between person and process, individual and society, thinking and learning violate its principles.

This metaphor runs throughout **The Whole Language Catalog***, a powerhouse of a book that lives up to its educational principles. There are entries from all types of participants in the educational process, including classroom teachers, administrators, parents and children.*

Features include parent perspectives on working to improve education; children's "marvelous inventions" as they work with oral and written language; teacher reflections on changes in their

thinking and classroom practice; stories of adults becoming literate; articles about early leaders in the progressive education movement; descriptions of successful classroom demonstrations; profiles of exceptional teachers; and fundamental concepts of whole language.

Good education equips one with tools that work in present and future contexts for the individual and society. The Whole Language Catalog *provides tools for that purpose.*
—Betty Rapoport

•

In defining themselves as *mediators* whole language teachers understand that less can be more. They realize that helping a learner solve a problem is better than giving him or her an algorithm or a solution.

I wonder if creative thinkers like Andy invented the way *ecnalubmA* is presented on emergency

vehicles or the way signs are written on streets for drivers to read as they approach intersections. Regardless, what is important is that Andy is not writing backward because he has a perceptual or cognitive deficit. In fact, the opposite is true. Andy is using his developing perceptual and cognitive strategies to make sense of the graphic information of the world and to work out concepts of directionality.

The Whole Language Catalog
Kenneth S. Goodman, Lois B. Bird, et al., Eds. 1991; 446 pp. ISBN 0-07-020102-1
$34.95 ($38.20 postpaid) from American School Publishers, 1221 Farmers Lane, Suite C, Santa Rosa, CA 95405; 800/882-2502

The Holistic Curriculum

The first coherent and systematic description of holistic education, John P. Miller's The Holistic Curriculum *remains the most useful and concise introduction to the field.*

Miller explores the roots of holistic thinking in various religious and philosophical traditions, and shows how an emphasis on connectedness, interdependence, context, and meaning in all aspects of life can have dramatic consequences for educational theory and practice. Citing Waldorf education, confluent education, and invitational education (among other models) he describes how holistic education cultivates imagination, intuition, mindfulness, self-awareness, and social responsibility. —Ron Miller

•

The focus of holistic education is on relationships — the relationship between linear thinking and intuition, the relationship between mind and body, the relationship between various domains of knowledge, the relationship between the individual and community, and the relationship between self and Self.

•

By exploring psychophysical re-education, movement, dance, mindfulness, and eurythmy we can help the student connect mind and body. By connecting mind and body we facilitate human wholeness.

Robert Assagioli, the founder of psychosynthesis, articulated the concept of the Higher or Transpersonal Self. Below is a diagram of Assagioli's conception of consciousness:
1. "Lower" unconscious
2. Middle unconscious
3. Superconscious
4. Field of consciousness
5. Personal self, or "I"
6. Transpersonal Self
7. Collective unconscious

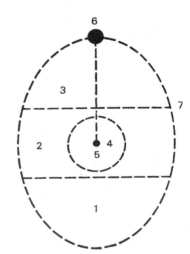

The Holistic Curriculum
John P. Miller. Ontario Institute for Studies in Education, 1988; 140 pp.
ISBN 0-7744-0320-9
$24.50 ($27 postpaid) from Scholarly Book Services, Inc., 77 Mowat Avenue, Suite 403, Toronto, Ontario M6K 3E3 Canada; 416/533-5490

Leap Into Learning

This book argues that using creative dramatics and dance games in the teaching of language arts, social studies, and mathematics can energize classrooms and help students learn. Kristen Bissinger and Nancy Renfro have created an incredible number of activities for kindergartners through seventh graders, giving instructors a great deal of choice.

The authors have been ingenious in devising ways of getting students physically and intellectually involved in the learning process.
—Arthur Asa Berger

•

By guiding children through a creative learning adventure, one in which they have input and take an active part, we are able to provoke thinking — and motivate interest and research.

In a study of Christopher Columbus, for example, we might provoke thinking and motivate research through enacting the answers to questions such as: "What were the prevailing beliefs about the ocean and the world in Columbus' time?" "What hardships were faced in soliciting funds to finance such an adventure?" or "How did Columbus and his crew feel when they sighted land?" By putting themselves in the shoes of the great explorer and his crew, the students are given an opportunity to assimilate far more than dates, loca-

tions and names of the ships used in the voyage.

The classroom material presented in this book is beautifully suited for all types of students, whether they learn auditorially, visually, or kinesthetically; whether they are accelerated learners or those who learn more slowly.

Leap Into Learning!
(Teaching Curriculum Through Creative Dramatics and Dance)
Kristen Bissinger & Nancy Renfro. 1990; 201 pp. ISBN 0-93-1044-18-9
$20.95 ($26.70 postpaid) from Renfro Studios, PO Box 164226, Austin, TX 78716; 800/933-5512

Partner Sculpting
Objective: To explore body shapes, physical contact and trust.

SCIENCE TOYS

Scientific tools, used as toys, are the world's most powerful mind-amplifiers and universe-openers for bright, curious kids of all ages. —HLR

Learning
SCIENCE TOYS 357

Explorabook

This truly is a museum in a book — or at least some tasty bites from one of the best museums around, San Francisco's Exploratorium.

Among the things built right into this spiral-bound book are a full-page Fresnel lens, two packs of agar (for growing cultures of bacteria), a one-way mirror, and a diffraction grating. There's even a fairly powerful magnet in a wand that comes attached to the binding. All these items are used in the more than fifty activities described and wittily explored within.

My seven-year-old son Nate spent a whole weekend with this book when

he first got his hands on it. He especially liked the optical illusions — an Exploratorium specialty — and the opportunity to grow a culture of his own mouth bacteria.

One thing I've always liked about the Exploratorium is its conviction that nothing is learned until it is self-taught — and the more hands-on the learning, the better. It's fitting that they have created one of the most hands-on books around. —Keith Jordan

•

How to Use the Explorabook
First of all, please do not simply read this book. If you own the Explorabook for more than a few hours, and do not bend or smear any of its pages, nor tear open the agar

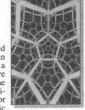

The Explorabook
(A Kids' Science Museum in a Book)
John Cassidy & the Exploratorium Staff.
1991; ISBN 1-878257-14-5
$17.95 ($21.95 postpaid) from Klutz Press,
2121 Staunton Court, Palo Alto, CA 94306;
415/857-0888

packets, nor attempt to lose the attached magnet, then you are probably not using it correctly. It is a tool. Please treat it that way.

Experiment Number
Bacteria Safaris

You can do this one with a shallow dish filled with a half-cup of agar gel.

1. Go find a roll of Scotch tape. Now prowl around the house looking for something where millions of bacteria or fungi might be hiding. Remember, this is not hard. The dog dish, a door knob, punch bowl, shaving brush, your silverware, the toilet seat, practically anything will do.

2. When you've chosen something, stick a piece of tape to it. Pull the tape up and stick it back down once or twice. Then take it and hurry back to your already prepared agar bowl.

3. Lift off the plastic wrap, press the sticky side of the tape down onto the gel surface, remove it, and immediately re-cover the gel.

4. Put your dish on a cool shelf somewhere out of the sun. Results will be about a week in coming.

LOOK FOR THESE HABITATS!

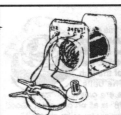

Actinomycete, common soil-borne bacteria
Penicillium

Experiment Number 1 Results
Check this dish to see what your hunting luck was like. The more fuzzy spots you have on your gel—the more bacteria or fungi you picked up.

Penicillium with bacteria ringing it

Aureobasidium

OTHER GREAT RESOURCES

There Are No Electrons (Electronics for Earthlings): Kenn Amdahl. 1991, Clearwater Publishing Co. The easiest and clearest course in basic electronics imaginable.

The Thousand-Yard Model or, The Earth as a Peppercorn: Guy Ottewell. 1989, Astronomical Workshop. A walk of the solar system. Guy Ottewell publishes a bunch of neat astronomical teaching activity books.

Powers of Ten (About the Relative Size of Things in the Universe): Philip Morrison & Phylis Morrison. 1991, Scientific American Library, W.H. Freeman & Company. The original galactic-

to-subatomic graphic zoom, along with other mind-boggling images and text about the scale of the universe.

Thinking Physics is Gedanken Physics: 1989, Lewis Carroll Epstein. For sample pages send an SASE to Insight Press, 614 Vermont Street, San Francisco, CA 94107. The imagination is the grandest laboratory, and thought experiments are both tools and toys for physics education.

Relativity Visualized: 1988, Lewis Carroll Epstein. For sample pages send an SASE to Insight Press, 614 Vermont Street, San Francisco, CA 94107. Relativity understood relatively easily.

Catalogs of Rheingoldian Science Tools and Toys

American Science & Surplus:
Catalog free. 3605 Howard Street, Skokie, IL 60076; 708/982-0870, fax 800/ 934-0722. They live up to the claim on the cover: "incredible stuff, unbelievable prices." Mini-air compressor ($25) and airbrush ($17.50), "gruesome medical instruments" (3 for $2.95), pencil butane torches ($7.95).

BUILD YOUR OWN CRYSTAL RADIO
A good basic kit with everything you need to build a very simple crystal radio. This is not hi-tech hi-fi. Geared for ages eight and up, it is a complete kit with wonderfully straight forward instructions which walk the experimenter through winding the coil, hooking up tuning needle, crystal diode, and earphone, and experimenting to find useful antennas. Then on to a little explanation of theory and development of a circuit diagram. Excellent education, recreation and discovery device all at the same time. A simple kit with hours of fun in it.
88028   Crystal Radio Kit $10.00/each

TransTech: *Catalog free from Creative Learning Systems, 16510 Via Esprillo, San Diego, CA 92127; 800/458-2880. Technology education at its finest: kits, books, videos, tools, toys, from ecology to robotics.*

The LASY Control Display/ Off-Line Programmable Module can be plugged into the LASY Control Interface, and 32 commands can be programmed into the combined units. The total unit will then run as a standalone unit—without being connected to a computer...**$134.99**

Media Magic: *Catalog $1.00. PO Box 598 WE Nicasio, CA 94946; .Unbelievably cool. I could spend $500 on beautiful scientific visualization videos, books on chaos, A-life lab kits, mathematics videos, physics software. Disclaimer: they carry my book on virtual reality (they carry every book I've ever heard of, and more, on virtual reality, artificial life, chaos, fractals, cyberculture). The catalog itself, unlike its richer utilitarian cousins, is itself a work of art. Prices are reasonable. A great place to do some gift shopping for a science-minded friend, blow some minds with a theoretical topology animation video, encourage a kid to get interested in science, mathematics, or computers.*

NOT KNOT
By The Geometry Center, University of Minnesota
$40   #v75

Not Knot is a guided tour into computer animated hyperbolic space. The video leads the viewer from an exhibit of knots to the inside of the complement of a specific link - the Borromean Rings. Viewers are shown everything from the deceptively simple to the bewildering and complexly beautiful. The video graphically details the geometry of the knot compliment, or the area around the knot which changes into hyperbolic space, and takes viewers through the experience of 'flying through' this hyperbolic space. It goes well beyond Euclidean geometry, showing the dynamics of curved space, as studied in modern cosmology. The video is accompanied by a 48-page booklet detailing all of the concepts and graphics shown in the video. *20 minutes, 1991.*

THE MILLENNIUM
Whole Earth Catalog
IS HERE

M. C. ESCHER
Symmetry and Space
By Michele Emmer
$40   #v49

This video is dedicated to the symmetry aspects of the graphic work of the Dutch artist M. C. Escher. It is a video full of special effects and animations, whose idea is to give new dimension and movement to the work of a great artist. Bruno Ernst, a close friend of Escher, provides anecdotes on the life of Escher in Italy. Crystallographer C. Macgillavry, who co-wrote a book on symmetry with Escher, explains the structure of some of Escher's periodic drawings. The most attractive parts of the movie are the animations and deformations of the works of Escher, each based on an original Escher print. Originally filmed in the 80's, this program is now available for the first time on videotape. *27 minutes, 1993.*

Edmund Scientific Company: *Catalog free. 101 E. Gloucester Pike, Barrington, NJ 08007; 609/ 547-8880. The classic source for optics, lasers, gizmos, micropositioners, solar cells, immersible telescopes and thousands of other items. A two-hundred page, full-color catalog that is both a serious science hacker's resource and a cheap science toyland.*

S-CARGO ROBOT: Robot is controlled by a condenser microphone and a printed circuit board. A handheld activator or your own hand clap will activate the robot's pre-programmed movements.

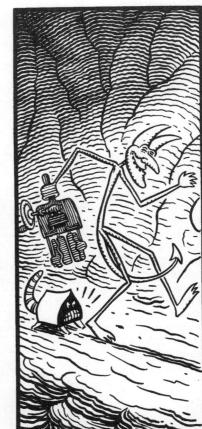

The Teenage Liberation Handbook

Griff: *My three boys (12, 14, 16) could hardly handle it when I showed them the title of this book. "Dumb." "No way." "Weird." But they kept thumbing through it and sat transfixed whenever I read a few passages out loud. I could see the seeds of doubt beginning to sprout in their psyches, struggling against nagging self-doubt ("What if I just goof off all day?") and future dread ("What about college? How will I ever get a good job?"). When they finally sat down to read Part I: Making the Decision, they all decided — within three days — to drop out of school (or more correctly, "rise out").*

Collin (age 16): *I had a closed mind about homeschooling. I felt it was odd, and I wasn't interested in doing anything odd. But I quickly changed my mind after reading the first section of this book. First of all, I liked it that the author was talking to me. Second, I kept saying to myself, "This lady knows what she's talking about because this is exactly what is happening to me at my school." Teachers and the school system do many things to take away your freedom and hinder your interest in learning. The ones that stood out for me were mainly the small amount of time that is given to each subject: just as you are getting interested, they cut you short, and then you have to go on to something you really hate. And they don't let you choose the things you want to learn, in most situations. You have to pretty much learn their stuff at their pace. So this book has really helped me out. If I have any questions or just want to go over an important topic, Grace is right there on my bookshelf with the answers.*

Griff: *It's primarily a practical handbook, bursting with clever strategies, valuable resources and wise guidance on how to design an interest-driven self-education. It was the sole inspiration for our family to take on an endeavor we thought was out of the question. If you've ever considered the idea of homeschooling, no matter how remotely, read this book.*
—Griff and Collin Wigley

Homeschooling parents of teenagers are rarely *teachers*, in the school sense of the word, and this book never suggests that you forsake your own career or interests in order to learn calculus (etc.) fast enough to "teach" it. Healthy kids can teach themselves what they need to know, through books, various people, thinking,

and other means. (A freshly unschooled person may at first be a lousy learner; like cigarettes, school-style passivity may be a slow habit to kick.) . . .

If you have helped with or supervised your children's homework, or stayed in close touch with their teachers, homeschooling need not drain your energy any more than that.

•

Maybe you believe you aren't ready for freedom?

On some level, no one ever is; it's not a matter of age. People of all ages make mistakes with their freedom — becoming involved with destructive friends, choosing college majors they're not deeply interested in, buying houses with rotten foundations, clearcutting forests, breaking good marriages for dumb reasons. . . . Sure, teenagers make mistakes. So do adults, and it seems to me adults have a harder time admitting and fixing theirs. . . . The only alternative to making mistakes is for someone to make all your decisions for you, in which case you will make their mistakes instead of your own. Obviously, that's not a life of integrity. Might as well start living, rather than merely obeying, before the age of eighteen.

•

Schools play a nasty trick on all of us. They make "learning" so unpleasant and frightening that they scare many people away from countless pleasures: evenings browsing in libraries, taking an edible plants walk at the nature center, maybe even working trigonometry problems for the hard beauty and challenge of it. . . . By calling school "learning," schools make learning sound like an excruciatingly boring way to waste a nice afternoon. That's low.

Check out Kid Creativity on Page 210.

Turn to page 357 for Science Toys.

The Teenage Liberation Handbook
(How to Quit School and Get a Real Life and Education)
Grace Llewellyn. 1991; 401 pp.
ISBN 0-9629591-0-3
$14.95 ($16.95 postpaid) from Lowry House Publishers, PO Box 1014, Eugene, OR 97440-1014

OTHER GREAT RESOURCES

Real Lives: Grace Llewellyn, Editor. 1993, Lowry House Publishers. Eleven teenagers who took the advice of *The Teenage Liberation Handbook*, dropped out, and educated themselves; their eloquence speaks their success.

Dumbing Us Down: (The Hidden Curriculum of Compulsory Schooling): John Taylor Gatto. 1991, New Society Publishers. Gatto, an award-winning career schoolteacher, speaks the hard truth about schools as the last place you want to put a bright and curious child.

Geography unclass: Kyla and friend Cedar Dunn make big plans. —Real Lives

Homeschooling for Excellence

This book has something for everybody: it's the ideal book for beginning homeschoolers who need reassurance that homeschooling really works, and who need some guidelines on how to make it work.

It's great for families with older homeschoolers who are thinking about applying to colleges or preparing for careers. It appeals to the "loner" homeschoolers who don't join organizations, use prepared curricula, or follow anyone else's philosophy: the Colfaxes are independent and exquisitely opinionated folks who made their own way, every step of the way. Above all, it's the perfect gift for skeptical grandparents who will be reassured to read about students with fairly unstructured learning programs who were admitted to Harvard with full scholarships, graduated with honors, and went on to become successful, interesting adults. The authors mention many resources and the book includes beautiful photographs of the Colfax children growing up on the homestead in Boonville, California.
—Elizabeth Churchill Hamill

•

Toys are not always given proper credit for the part they play in the social, intellectual, and physical development of the child. Perhaps this is because we realize that their contribution is often less than positive . . . .

Of course there are some perennial classics which do not merit such an indictment — honest toys such as Tinkertoys, Legos, Lincoln Logs, and, more recently, Fischer Techniks — and which stimulate the imagination and help develop motor skills. . . . parents may find Sally Goldberg's *Teaching with Toys and Growing with Games* (University of Michigan Press, 1985) valuable for children up to three years of age, and for three- to six-year-olds, respectively.

Homeschooling for Excellence
David Colfax & Micki Colfax. Warner Books, 1988; 142 pp. ISBN 0-446-38986-2
$10.99 Postpaid. PO Box 353, Philo, CA 95466

The Home School Source Book

This book lives up to its title. It tries to be a Whole Earth Catalog for homeschoolers, and does a darn good job. Two hundred and sixty-five pages packed full of resources, reviews, and rants. —HLR

• **Fine Arts on Video**
Art & Artists, concerts, opera, literature, ballet, and many other special interest video tapes; many produced in cooperation with the National Gallery and the Metropolitan Museum of Art. Colorful Catalog. HOME VISION, 5547 N. Ravenswood Ave., Chicago, IL 60640.

The Home School Source Book
Donn Reed. 1991; 265 pp.
ISBN 0-919761-24-0 $15 ($16 postpaid) from Brook Farm Books, PO Box 246W, Bridgewater, ME 04735

Growing Without Schooling

We've reviewed this perennially, because it's the perennially great periodical, review, and resource guide for homeschoolers. Still excellent. —HLR

• **Leaving School in 9th Grade**

Irv Lofberg of Wisconsin writes:
I clearly remember, in seventh grade, accidentally enjoying myself while writing a history essay. In the school I attended it was an absolute taboo to enjoy oneself while learning. I knew it was customary to groan when the class was assigned to read an entire chapter for class, but occasionally I would get lost in the words and be truly fascinated by the subject. Of course, I thought there was something grotesquely wrong with me. Enjoy learning? This was the greatest sin.

I also remember an assignment we had in eighth grade, which was to write a diary by a member of the Lewis and Clark expedition. Students would go to the podium to read, but would leave much of their wonderful detail out in fear of being labeled a "geek" or a "brain" (creativity was another taboo). My diary was long and very detailed. I felt ashamed reading my work, especially when I heard groans from my peers because I was taking too long. I sat down, wishing I hadn't read it.

I found myself struggling to express myself in school, but also fearing to do so in the horror of being pushed out by my peers. The only peace I found in school was through writing. But this was also taken away when the writing was picked apart and graded. It stifled my creativity rather than helped it to bloom, because I learned

how to write for the teacher instead of for myself. In group assignments it was worse. Most of the students said "I don't care" and closed their minds. Obviously, I was only learning how to suppress and mold myself to fit appropriately into the system. My mental and physical health were fading fast. I had to find a way out.

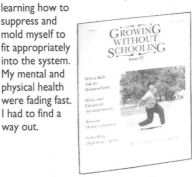

Growing Without Schooling
Susannah Sheffer, Editor.
$12/year (6 issues). 2269 Massachusetts Avenue, Cambridge, MA 02140; 617/864-3100

Child's Work: Nancy Wallace. Holt Associates, 2269 Massachusetts Ave., Cambridge, MA 02140. Nancy Wallace's homeschooled kids are, from her descriptions, extraordinarily gifted, which might be why it worked to allow them to do what they wanted to do rather than what society expected them to do. Her thesis is radical — that children's work of joyful learning and unbounded exploratory play is as important as adult work, and that, for the most part, kids should be left to find their own way.

Home Education Magazine: $18/year (6 issues). PO Box 1083, Tonasket, WA 98855; 509/486-1351. David and Micki Colfax (*Homeschooling for Excellence,* opposite page) recommend this. Substantial, well-produced; even the ads are resources.

Home School Supply House

The catalog I've ordered from for the past five or six years. They have the Saxon Math books, lots of great literature in inexpensive paperbacks, an excellent series of high school science textbooks.
—Elizabeth Churchill Hamill

• **The Art of Styling Sentences**
by Waddell, Esch, & Walder
20 different fundamental sentence patterns are explained and sentence examples diagrammed and analyzed. Students are thus encouraged to broaden their writing style by adapting the sentence patterns to their own ideas and needs. Supplementary chapters discuss combining different sentence patterns, as well as using similes, metaphors, allusions and analogies to enhance meaning and writing style as well. (9th-12th grade)

Home School Supply House
Catalog free. PO Box 7, Fountain Green, UT 84632; 800/772-3129

• **Indian, Soldier & Settler**
A rare & wonderful book, offering the true stories of a Sioux warrior, a bugler in the American infantry, & a girl who was captured by Cheyenne. As their stories unfold, a balanced historical interpretation of the struggles involved reveals how the Native people lost their land, freedom, and way of life.

Saxon Math Books

The best we've seen for working independently. The kids almost never have questions about things they don't understand.
—Elizabeth Churchill Hamill

Saxon Math Books
Catalog free. 1320 W. Lindsey, Norman, OK 73069; 800/289-7019

Aikido and the New Warrior

Is it possible to defend one-self from attack and still practice nonviolence? A man named Ueshiba created (he would have said "discovered") an impressive answer to this question — a set of practices known as Aikido.

In Aikido, the automatic response is to blend with the attacker's moves, to move into a position that shows you the world from the attacker's point of view, before redirecting your attacker's physical energy in a way that minimizes harm to everybody. In Aikido, you learn to instruct those who attack you, and thus take responsibility for the attacker's well-being as well as your own.

Yes, when you get good at Aikido, you can protect yourself better. But you protect yourself better not because you know secret pressure points or have developed callused hands, but because you have trained yourself to pay attention to the way the universe

works. Everybody who studies Aikido for any time realizes that it is a way of being in the world, with the world, with yourself, and with other people.

You can't learn Aikido by reading about it, but you can learn about it, especially if you read the right authors. Richard Strozzi Heckler, editor of this volume, knows what he's talking about. —HLR

•

Through blending with a confrontative situation one learns to resolve the confrontation without being a loser, on the one hand, or hurting someone, on the other. The principle reveals itself through countless Aikido techniques and enables these youth to replace their conditioned reflexes with a more responsible and appropriate response.

As they learn Aikido, the fundamental thing that begins to happen to these young people is that their ability to feel and sense is awakened. When they allow themselves to feel, they are often terrified by the rush of sensations, streamings, and emotions that come with feeling. But as they learn to be with feelings from a centered and grounded place, they find a new sense of power and ease. They embody power instead of imitating it. To feel and experience life rather than pretend or fantasize about it is a fundamental principle of Aikido. It is a first step in throwing off the dictator within. This path of self-dis-

Aikido and the New Warrior
Richard Strozzi Heckler, Editor. 1985; 230 pp. ISBN 0-938190-51-2 $12.95 ($15.45 postpaid) from North Atlantic Books, PO Box 12327, Berkeley, CA 94712; 510/559-8277

covery emphasizes the importance of executing each technique with the proper spirit or energy. The kids quickly learn that Aikido is not necessarily a collection of techniques to perform on someone, but a presence of being that can both be practiced in the Aikido classes and lived in daily life. This presence is an attitude that includes a priority of self-responsibility — perceiving conflict and pressure as actual opportunities in which to grow and discover oneself, blending with situations as an alternative to fighting or running, and trusting their own feeling and intuitive direction.

China's Living Treasures

The martial arts are deeply rooted in China, and have as much to do with medicine, meditation, and physical fitness as with self-defense. For thousands of years, these exercises have been passed on in a direct line from master to initiate. The "living treasures" of this videotape series are old masters in China, performing for the video camera.

You still have to find a sifu (teacher) to learn the arts, but several of these

China's Living Treasures
26-volume video series. Each volume $49.95 ($54.95 postpaid). Information from One Hand Video, PO Box 185, Mamaroneck, NY 10543-0185

tapes offer excellent instruction in simple, ancient, beautifully flowing daily exercises. Get your exercise, stimulate your internal organs, and experience a moment of grace — a welcome break from traditional exercise videos. —HLR

Master Yu Hua Long. —Vol. 7

Master Zhang Xve Xin (left). Master George Xu (right). —Vol. 15

•

Volume Fifteen

Chan Ssu Chin Silk Reeling Cocoon Training Featuring Master Zhang Xue Xin

Master Zhang at sixty-five has studied the martial arts since he was nine . . . and has studied with the most famous Chen style teachers still living in China.

On this tape Master Zhang demonstrates the Chan Ssu Chin exercises. "Chan Ssu" means silk reeling cocoon, and "Chin" means internal flowing energy. The name comes from the way that the practitioner attempts to move his internal energy. The silk spirals as it is removed

and the cocoon rotates. The silk represents the way energy flows through the body, and the cocoon represents your waist as it rotates on its axis. These exercises originated in the Chen system, which is the original Tai Chi Chuan. This relaxing, non-impact, exercise routine has universal benefit, however, for anyone interested in loosening the eighteen moveable joints of the body. People of all ages regardless of martial art backgrounds can experience the positive effects of this practice. Follow the exercises with Master Zhang as he demonstrates the twenty-five movements beginning with the head and ending with the feet.

OTHER GREAT RESOURCES

The Code of the Warrior: Rick Fields. 1991, HarperCollins. A history of the world through the eyes of warriors, and a spiritual exploration of warriorship.

In Search of the Warrior Spirit: Teaching Awareness Disciplines to the Green Berets: Richard Strozzi Heckler. 1992, North Atlantic Books. A student of peace and his warrior students struggle with the higher meaning of warriorship. This is a book about whole systems.

The Way of the Peaceful Warrior: Dan Millman. 1980, H. J. Kramer. What warriors have to teach peacemakers.

Tao of Jeet Kune Do: Bruce Lee, 1991, Ohara Publications. A detailed, articulate and concise guide to the art and science of fighting.

Self-Defense for Kids

I live in an otherwise lovely suburban neighborhood where the bogeyman actually did carry little girls away and do horrible things to them. First, a soccer coach was convicted of molesting at least eight girls, ages six to eight. Then, a year later, a twelve year old, Polly Klaas, was snatched from her bedroom thirty miles from here and murdered. What do you say to your little girl when her worst fantasies are in the daily headlines?

I took my daughter to a psychotherapist. The therapist said "the girl is frightened." My daughter pointed out that everybody knew that the things that frightened her were real: "It's on the television news every night." So I took her to a local Taekwondo (a Korean form of karate) class. We were fortunate to find the right teacher on our first try.

In two years, her teacher tells me, Mamie will be strong enough and skilled enough to take down a grown man against his will, if she has to. But dealing with her fear turned out to be only a small part of the benefits: the art of self-defense is a physical challenge that can be breathtakingly graceful; my daughter and many of the other little girls in my daughter's class take to Taekwondo the way other peers take to ballet, with all the same poise and precision. Beyond getting rid of the fear is learning self-respect, and the ability to look other people in the eye. There is discipline and self-discipline, but no cruelty, and much respect.

It isn't for everybody, but I highly recommend martial-arts training for all children who are willing to try, provided that the teacher is strict enough (there is no such thing as a chaotically supervised martial-arts class for kids), caring enough (you can tell by watching a sensei work with children whether the children love and respect their teacher), patient enough (give high marks to a sensei who makes a special effort with the most awkward beginners), and respectful enough of his students as people (walk out if a sensei ever humiliates a child). Sit through a couple of classes. You don't want a drill sergeant. You want somebody who can teach your children how to deal with the scariest parts of their lives. I've seen children as young as six thrive with the right teacher.

All martial-arts classes should welcome observers; if they don't, you wouldn't want to be a student there, anyway. —HLR

Protecting Children from Danger

If you want to give your children the best chance of surviving into the next millennium, teach them how to deal with fires and other emergencies, firearms and armed people, kidnappers and sexual predators. Teach them the self-reliance, self-respect, and street skills they are going to need when you can't be around to protect them.

My daughter, my wife and I, and a dozen other families, spent most of a day with one of the authors of this book in a workshop that was enjoyable and warm despite the grim subject matter. Bob Bishop and Matt Thomas teach common sense, self-reliance, and specific techniques for dealing with dangerous situations, which are rehearsed over and over again. This book is essential for parents and teachers. —HLR

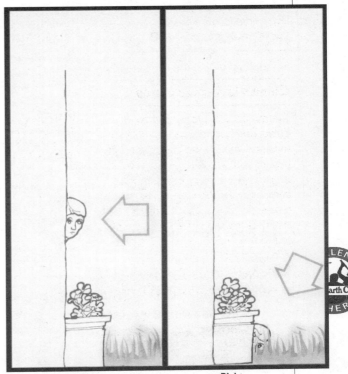

Protecting Children From Danger
(Building Self-Reliance and Emergency Skills without Fear)
Bob Bishop & Matt Thomas. 1993; 185 pp. ISBN 1-55643-159-7
$12.95 ($15.45 postpaid) from North Atlantic Books, PO Box 12327, Berkeley, CA 94712; 510/559-8277

•
Self-esteem is the basis for anyone's behavior during a crisis. How have we prepared our children? At one extreme, if we perceive them as completely inadequate in the face of danger, and they in turn mirror this attitude, then except for natural defense mechanisms, they are left tragically unprepared for danger or crisis. At the other extreme, they might feel unrealistically confident. However, given the opportunity to develop courage and experience success, they will expect to succeed. Changing our children's self-expectations in daily life is crucial to preparing them for emergencies.

Overprotection actually decreases children's self-esteem and forces them to withdraw from their own natural defense mechanisms. The more over-protective we are, the more they retreat into our shadows. The more we see them in our shadows, the more over-protective we become. This downward spiral ultimately limits growth and fosters resentment. Anyone with a teenager knows this spiral well.

•
If none of this works, and the child is under the control of the assailant, it is absolutely essential for the child not to give up, but to recognize that this is only a temporary setback. We call this *waiting for the opening.* And when the opening comes, the child needs to use surprise, distraction, and physical lever-

age simultaneously to escape. For example, if an abductor has the child in a car and pulls up to a stop light, the child can open the car door, scream, kick the abductor, and then quickly jump out. For such a strategy to work, the child must know how different types of car doors and locks work. This is something that parents can do with their children. *Whenever you're in a different car, make sure that your child understands the locking mechanism and how to get the door open quickly.*

Wrong · Right

Observation from hiding places.

Mi Zeng Wei, granddaughter of Internal Arts Master Wen-Mei Yu.

MIND GYMNASTICS FOR KIDS

WE'VE been through three years of software testing at our house, and it is clear that if it isn't fun, the software's other virtues don't count. The first big test is whether Mamie will try a program more than once. When she prefers playing with the program to an opportunity to watch television, the software passes the next hurdle. If she's still using the software a year later, it's worth recommending. Mamie reviewed Kid Pix in 1991, when she was six and a half; she still uses it, although she's added Dabbler to her art tool file. If your favorite small person is old enough to have the dexterity to control a computer mouse, a computer color paintbox can provide instant fascination — and a real sense of mastery that is hard to find in other fine motor activities at age six. Mamie used Mavis Beacon to teach herself to type at age eight and a half. She reviewed Travelrama CD-ROM in 1994, when she was nine.

All of the software here is fun. Most of it also gives the young user a means of expressing his or her own creativity: drawing tools, typing tools, writing tools, logical puzzles. A computer is no substitute for a sunny day in spring, or the feel and smell of clay or old-fashioned crayons, but the right kind of software can be as useful and enchanting as a magical brush or a kid-size writing machine. These are the tools our children will be using in the next century, and the technology inside these boxes threatens to grow fearsomely powerful over the coming decades; if the generation that is going to come of age in the first decades of the twenty-first century is going to start messing with these machines now, they might as well start out by trying to create something beautiful. —HLR

Kid Pix

I like Kid Pix even better than the grown-up drawing programs because it has lots of noises and it's fun to experiment with all the different goodies. It's more fun to play with than Nintendo because I can make up my own stuff. I can explore the menus and always find new things to play with. The stamp pad is neat. I can make my own stamps. If I hold down the shift key, I can make things bigger. My dad showed me how to put my own voice in the drawings, too, so I can make up picture stories that talk and sound like me. There are different pens and pencils and erasers. I like the eraser that goes BOOM and the eraser that shows you a secret picture. And sometimes I make my own coloring book by printing my drawings and

Kid Pix 2: Macintosh: System 6, 1MB RAM (mono), 2MB (color); System 7, 2MB (mono), 4MB (color). Windows: 386 or later, 2MB RAM, 3 1/2" high-density disks. $39.95 ($43.95 postpaid). Brøderbund Software/Customer Service, PO Box 6125, Novato, CA 94948-6125; 800/521-6263.

coloring them with crayons.
—Mamie (age nine)

(Note from Mamie's dad: We all love this software. It's a very well-designed product; it even has a Small Kids Module that makes it impossible for a very young explorer to do naughty things to your own files. Mamie plays with it for hours, and sometimes I sit down and doodle with it and record a secret message when Mamie is asleep. In the morning, she sees a new drawing on the screen and plays the sounds.
—HLR)

The Writing Center

This is really neat writing software. You can choose what kind of font you want. You can even have a secret language or make the letters bigger or smaller. There are two hundred pictures you can use and you can change their size, too. If you use the spell checker, it will show you the words you

The Writing Center: Macintosh: 1MB RAM; System 7, 2MB RAM. $89.95 ($92.95 postpaid). The Learning Company, 6493 Kaiser Drive, Fremont, CA 94555; 800/852-2255.

misspelled and you can change it. This is much easier than an adult writing program. I've used it for letters, reports, and for writing this review.
—Mamie

Mavis Beacon Teaches Typing

Even little kids can learn how to type. Typing makes it a lot easier to write books and articles and letters and to play games and to use computers and to write homework for school. Mavis Beacon Teaches Typing helped me learn how to type without looking at the keyboard. The program shows a keyboard up on the screen and which finger to move. When you get better, you go to the next level where you don't have a keyboard on the screen, so you have to just do it by feel. If you

Mavis Beacon Teaches Typing: Information from Software Toolworks; 415/883-5157

miss a word it puts a little X under it and you can go on to the next word. When you get better, there are races and speed limits and different games you can play. And the more you play the games, the better you learn to type! In one week, I learned how to touch type. I practiced for about a half an hour every day. Now I'm in the fourth grade and I can type all my homework. —Mamie Rheingold

The Even More Incredible Machine

I love to see how things work and solve problems. The Even More Incredible Machine makes me think and tinker until I can make each machine and move to the next level. Each level gives you a list of parts like pulleys, gears, bouncing balls, springs, windmills, wires, pipes, faucets, batteries, motors, that you can drag around and fit together like an animated puzzle.

When you find a way to fit the parts together so the whole thing works, you can pop a balloon or fire a cannonball or turn on a light. Then you get to go to a new level. The levels seem never ending, and that feels better than doing the same game over and over. Once you get really good at it, you can make up your own puzzles.
— Mamie

The Even More Incredible Machine: Macintosh System 6.0.7 or later, 4MB RAM for color. DOS 386X or later, 640K memory, VGA. Windows 3.1, 386X or later, 20 MHz, 2MB RAM for 26-color, 4MB RAM for 256-color. $34.95 ($38.95 postpaid). Sierra Online, PO Box 53250, Bellvue, WA 98015-3250; 800/326-6654.

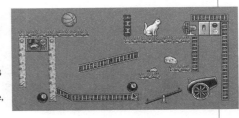

Dabbler

This program lets your artistic ability go wild! You can use virtual pens, paintbrushes, spray paints, crayons, and they really look like they do in real life. If you want to change the tool or color you just open the drawer above it and click on a new one. Dabbler is not for technical drawing but it is terrific for anyone who wants to dabble or doodle.
—Shannon Hottinger (age eleven)

Dabbler: Macintosh System 6.05 or later (32-bit Quickdraw), 13" monitor or larger, 4MB RAM. $99 ($106 postpaid). Fractal Design, PO Box 2380, Aptos, CA 95001; 800/647-7443.

OTHER GREAT CREATIVITY TOOLS FOR KIDS

Print Shop Deluxe: Brøderbund. Kids love to make specialized birthday cards, posters and banners for school, and with a little writing and drawing, they can put together their own newspapers. Print Shop Deluxe, with its templates, image banks, and whimsical fonts, makes creative page design fun.

EasyBook: Chickadee Software, HCR62, Box 449, Center Harbor, NH 03226. Just as Kid Pix is a small-person-sized computer illustration tool, and The Writing Center is a kid-scale word processing program, EasyBook is a simple, fun page layout and design tool. The software includes its own painting and word processing tools that enable kids to write, illustrate, design, lay out, and print their own books.

The Oregon Trail

One hot item! This game teaches you how to use maps, and many survival techniques. It is about you and four other people traveling across the country. Your goal is to get across the country safely before the winter. You may go through many lifelike experiences such as sickness, snakebites, and even death. You make many hard decisions such as how to cross a river, how much food each person gets and many more! We think this computer game is good for anybody five or older.
—Caitlin Gibb and Bridget Sumser (both age eleven)

The Oregon Trail: Macintosh: System 6.0.7 or later, System 7 recommended; 2MB RAM for color display, 4MB for System 7. $49.95 ($53.95 postpaid). Macintosh CD-ROM: $69.95 ($73.95 postpaid). DOS 3.3: 386SX or later, 2MB RAM; CGA/EGA: $49.95 ($53.95 postpaid). Deluxe VGA: $59.95 ($63.95 postpaid). Windows 3.1: 386 or later, 256 color video, 4MB RAM. $59.95 ($63.95 postpaid). Windows CD-ROM: $69.95 ($73.95 postpaid). MECC, 6160 Summit Drive Minneapolis, MN 55430; 800/685-6322.

Travelrama USA

I am a nine-year-old girl in the fourth grade. This game is great for fourth graders because we are learning geography. Travelrama is a CD-ROM game that uses geography, map skills, planning, and math. The object of the game is to collect five specific postcards and return to the starting place without running out of miles. If you're playing alone you start with 3000 miles and if you're playing against an

Travelrama: Information is available from Apple Computer at 800/538-9696.

opponent you start with 500. To get postcards, you have to know state capitals, which you can get from the map. Travelrama is as addictive as Nintendo except in this game you know all about the state capitals after you play long enough.
—Mamie

SimCity 2000

Wow! I am an eleven-year-old mayor and designer of a town! As the mayor, I make many decisions such as how high or low taxes should be, where to put houses, how to make a healthier town and keep your citizens happy, where to put industrial areas so people can work. Then you see what happens to your city after you make your decisions. I really like this game

SimCity 2000: Macintosh: LC or later, 8-bit color monitor, 4 MB RAM, System 7 or later, mouse. DOS 3.3: 386, Extended or Super VGA, 4 MB RAM, mouse. $54.95 ($59.95 postpaid). Maxis, 2 Theatre Square, Suite 230, Orinda, CA 94563; 800/336-2947.

because you get to make a place that you would want to grow up in and feel safe. —Bridget

Reader Rabbit's Ready for Letters

Kids play at activities that help them develop reading skills while exploring in and around Reader Rabbit's house. Activities include shape recognition, memory skills, relativity skills, letter recognition, and word identification. Easy interface allows kids to control the program right away with little help from adults. Well crafted, fun, absorbing, and effective. —Mike Ashenfelder

Reader Rabbit's Ready for Letters: Macintosh: 2 MB RAM, System 7.X or later 3 MB RAM, 256 color graphics card and HD required. IBM: 640K RAM, VGA; Windows or DOS 3.3 or later. $59.95 ($62.95 postpaid). The Learning Company, 6493 Kaiser Drive, Fremont, CA 94555; 800/852-2255.

Redshift

This CD-ROM game is marvelous. You don't have to be an astronomy expert to enjoy it. Redshift is based on a high level of scientific accuracy, which allows you to experience dramatically realistic views of space. You can see color pictures of distant galaxies, the solar system, the earth. There's an astronomy dictionary with hypertext links, and a movie recorder that helps

Redshift: Macintosh: System 7 or later, 4 MB RAM, CD-ROM drive. Windows 3.1: 4 MB RAM, CD-ROM drive, MSCDEX 2.0 or later, Super VGA. $64.95 ($69.95 postpaid). Maxis, 2 Theatre Sq. Suite 230, Orinda, CA 94563; 800/336-2947.

you make your own journeys through space. What a great way to see a variety of astronomical phenomena and events! —Bridget Sumser

The Backyard • The Playroom • The Treehouse

The Backyard is a freewheeling exploration program in which preschool-age kids can poke around a yard full of responsive objects and — while playing — learn about nature, spatial relationships, symbols, music, and much more. The Backyard has the same high-quality graphics, sound, and instructional design as Brøderbund's other two similar discovery-based programs, The Playroom and The Treehouse, though it doesn't focus as much on kid's math and literacy as learning about the world around them.

The interface is pleasant, fun, and simple: just point and click the mouse and almost everything on screen reacts. Paint the fence boards different colors and play the fence like a xylophone. Paste faces on a scarecrow and learn the names of emotional facial expressions. Follow pictorial maps to find the sandbox treasure, or create your own maps. Water the garden and grow vegetables. Get a close look at the external anatomy of animals by piecing together animal cookies. Develop counting strategies and deductive reasoning in the knothole game. In the habitat sticker book, place animals in their natural habitats and see how they respond.

Kids control this world, though it has many surprises. If the program sits idle for a while, something spontaneously happens: a flower grows, the wind chimes jingle, or the on-screen playmate sighs, stretches, or tosses a ball. For parents, the program guidebook also suggests related non-computer activities that correspond with what's going on on screen. This is cafeteria-style learning, where kids choose different learning activities according to their individual levels. And there's a lot to grow into: my co-reviewer, four-year-old Kate Sumser, who's an expert with The Backyard, is still learning left, right, up, down, side, and similar basic concepts. Nuggets of such knowledge are buried in The Backyard, waiting for her to discover them. —MA

The Backyard Fence: You paint it the color that you want to do. You press blue, paint the fence, it turns blue. You press the fence, it makes noise. You can do it to any one you want.

The Animal Habitat Sticker Book: Press the aminal that goes in the right place where it needs to be. You press the aminals, any one you want. The Emerald Boa, put in a tree. Press it, it's moving its head. Now press the other aminal that you want to do to, that seal. "Leopard Seal," the book said [digitized voice]. You put it on the ice or the snow. It's in the water, it's moving its head. Pick the other aminal, Killer Whale. The book said, "That's the aminal that's where it's cold." You put it where there is ice and snow.

The Animal Crackers: They're crackers aminals. The body felled off, we put them back together again. You press that, the aminal thing; you put it on the Killer Whale. That's the mouth, you put it right there. Now do the fins, you put it on the back. It turned into a Killer Whale.

[Summary] I like it a lot because it has a lot of things that you can do.
—Kate Sumser (age four)

The Backyard, The Treehouse, The Playroom: Macintosh: System 6: 1MB RAM (mono), 2MB (color); System 7: 2MB (mono), 4MB (color). DOS and Windows: 386 or higher, VGA, 640K RAM, 3 1/2" disks only.

Each $38.95 postpaid from Brøderbund Software/Customer Service, PO Box 6125, Novato, CA 94948-6125; 800/521-6263.

High/Scope Buyer's Guide to Children's Software

In their annual report, the nonprofit High/Scope Educational Research Foundation evaluates more than five hundred software programs for kids ages three to seven. Through an exhaustive process of observation and testing — described in detail in the appendices — they look for programs that are easy to use, interactive, childproof, strong in content, designed to aid learning, easily child-controlled, and worth the price. An invaluable book for teachers and parents to consult before reaching for their wallets. —Mike Ashenfelder

High/Scope Buyer's Guide to Children's Software 1993
Warren Buckleitner. 1993; 280 pp. ISBN 0-929816-53-6
$19.95 ($23.70 postpaid) from High/Scope Press, 600 North River Street, Ypsilanti, MI 48198; 313/485-8000

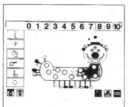

Millie's Math House

Early math skills

◆◆◆◆◆◆◆◆ 97 FINAL RATING
◆◆◆◆◆◆◆◆ 93 User Friendliness
◆◆◆◆◆◆◆◆ 100 Educational Value
◆◆◆◆◆◆◆◆ 98 Instructional Design

Edmark Corporation
1992
$49.85
Ages 2-6
Mac* (4.3MB), IBM
NB/1,3,4,5,8 SE/1,3,4
SP/4,7,8 CL/2 CP/4

Child sees Millie, a talking cow, along with items representing six well-designed math and logic activities. Child can build a mouse house by matching shapes to a diagram, create simple sequences by sight or sound, count jellybeans used by a cookie machine, find sets (up to 10) shown on a cash register, match shoes to feet according to size, and decorate a bug. Design allows child to control the amount of structure in each activity. Management features enable adults to keep individual records and control the presentation.

Sunburst

As the plummeting prices of multimedia hardware (CD-ROM and videodisc) bring sophisticated capabilities to more schools, the difficulty becomes sorting through all the offerings in the burgeoning software marketplace to find the one gem worth the price. Sunburst has a reputation for presenting the best of the high-end multimedia products. Their forty-seven-page catalog includes plenty of color screenshots, descriptions of programs, classroom activities, and lists of awards, to help educators select science, ecology, math, and language arts software for kindergarten through high school classes. —HLR

Sunburst Communications Catalog
Catalog free. 101 Castleton Street, PO Box 100, Pleasantville, NY 10570; 800/321-7511, fax 914/747-4109.

●
The Voyage of the Mimi Videodisc Collection
Designed by: Bank Street College of Education

This videodisc collection offers you the thirteen dramatic episodes and expeditions on an exciting new technology — plus a whole lot more!

Each episode/expedition is followed by a new section in which a variety of extension topics are introduced. For example, students will learn all the parts of a boat, explore the art of scrimshaw, and examine whale artwork.

The videodisc also includes special, behind-the-scenes information that will give students insight into how The Voyage of the Mimi was made, and make them more aware of the film medium as well.

Use the videodisc collection with the Explore and Discover software to get a truly interactive MIMI experience.

VIDEODISC UPGRADE
Now you can upgrade your Voyage of the Mimi videotapes to the videodisc collection. Simply return your videotape collection with your order.

Videodiscs are closed-captioned in English and Spanish. Spanish telecaptions require a 2-channel telecaption converter.

7 videodiscs, CAV format, videodisc guide, overview guide.
636402-HA The Voyage of the Mimi Videodisc Collection $950
640002-HA Videodisc Upgrade $300

The Learning Company

This relatively small educational software house consistently dominates the awards for good design. Years ago I met the people who started this company, and from the looks of their recent products, The Learning Company continues to uphold its founders' high standards. Two of the most consistently praised programs, Reader Rabbit and The Writing Center (see pp. 362-363), are products of theirs. They will send you a parents' guide to children's educational software along with their catalog. Their products are compatible with Windows, DOS, and Macintosh. —HLR

The Learning Company
Catalog free. 6493 Kaiser Drive, Fremont, CA 94555; 800/852-2255.

●
Reader Rabbit's Ready for Letters
Ages 2-5, Pre-K-1

Get children ready for reading!

Enchanting and challenging activities help children explore patterns, colors, shapes, and sizes; identify letters by sight and sound; and learn simple word meanings. Digitized speech in the Macintosh version helps pre-reader learn.

22050 IBM $59.95
13050 Macintosh $59.95

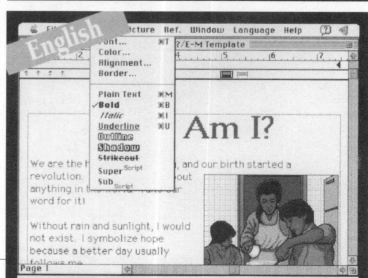

The Bilingual Writing Center

"A child, as well as an adult, needs plenty of what in German is called *Spielraum*. Now, *Spielraum* is not primarily 'a room to play in.' While the word also means that, its primary meaning is 'free scope, plenty of room' — to move not only one's elbows but also one's mind, to experiment with things and ideas at one's leisure, or, to put it colloquially, to toy with ideas . . ."
—Bruno Bettelheim, "The Importance of Play,"
The Atlantic Monthly

P lay is where cognition and culture meet. It's a mental can opener for liberating new ideas. But in the West, ever since John Calvin linked work and salvation, "just playing around" has been seen as quasi-sinful. That taboo is changing. More people are recognizing what a few visionaries have been saying for some time: play might be our most important thinking tool — particularly when we are learning to think in new ways.

In some places, play is literally the fundamental act of the cosmos: The authors of the Hindu Vedas had a word — *lila* — that means "the universe is what happens when God wants to play." Play might be related to the origins and maintenance of culture as well as cognition. It can be used to organize thoughts and societies. Johan Huizinga, the rector of Leyden University in Holland, published a book in 1938 called *Homo Ludens* ("man, the player"). Huizinga challenged the prevailing anthropological wisdom of that era (and this one), that our ancestors' use of tools was the primary reason for the origins of culture. It was play, not tool use, Huizinga claimed, that propelled Homo Sapiens to the top of the food chain.

Huizinga had been trying to understand why medieval Christendom continued to maintain archaic cultural elements such as codes of honor, heraldry, and chivalric orders. Huizinga discovered that these were vestiges of primitive initiation rites — sacred play. People took part in them because they were fun or deeply engaging, and because, in Huizinga's view, play was a vehicle for creating culture.

Only recently have psychologists become interested in studying the role of play in early development and adult life. Some psychologists, notably Jean Piaget, discovered that play can be a way of organizing our models of the world and models of ourselves, of testing hypotheses about the meaning of our perceptions.

Play is like a computer simulation that we run inside our heads: "What if I pile these blocks up as high as I can?" "What does it feel like to smoosh together everything in the spice drawer?" "This isn't a cardboard box. It's a castle." I sensed that something important was happening when my daughter, at around eighteen months, lifted a rattle to the mouth of her teddy bear and started to feed him a "bottle." She was learning to use one object to symbolize another. She was learning to schematize information in a qualitatively new way — by using her memories of previous experiences to create a representation of a new kind of experience. She was playing with her mind.

A tendency to play around with ideas, to play "let's pretend," to imagine outcomes, is an important skill for humans of all ages. Are you the kind of worker, communicator, decision maker, designer, artist, businessperson, or engineer who builds a detailed plan for each creation, then follows it, step by step? Or do you just start pottering around with ideas or materials until some kind of order begins to emerge? If you are the latter kind of worker, you've probably suffered the jibes of your more analytically minded colleagues; if you are any good at "thinking by the seat of your pants," you also know that you are capable of putting together concoctions on the fly that the careful preplanners will probably never achieve in years of deliberate effort. Take heart, bricoleurs, for anthropologist Claude Levi-Strauss has given us a word to use with pride.

Levi-Strauss used the term *bricolage* as a model for the way all humans (primitive or civilized) build scientific theories by pottering around with natural objects in various combinations. A bricoleur plays with concepts and objects in order to learn

There is
Fun Stuff
on
pages
212-213.

about them. The word was picked up by the computer scientist and educational expert Seymour Papert. In his book *Mindstorms*, Papert points out how the terms can extend to an entire way of thinking:

"The process reminds one of tinkering; learning consists of building up a set of materials and tools that one can handle and manipulate. Perhaps most central of all, it is a process of working with what you've got. We're all familiar with this process on the conscious level, for example, when we attack a problem empirically, trying out all the things that we have ever known to have worked on similar problems before. But here I suggest that working with what you've got is a shorthand for deeper, even unconscious learning processes . . . Here I am suggesting that in the most fundamental sense, we, as learners, are all bricoleurs. . . ."

And I am suggesting that improvisatory bricolage and a finely developed sense of play are essential skills for the next millennium. —HLR

PLAY RESOURCES

Homo Ludens: Johan Huizinga. 1955, Beacon Press. Anthropologists and others are beginning to pick up Johan Huizinga's theories, which were too radical for their time, the 1950s.

The Piaget Primer: Ed Labinowicz. 1980, Addison-Wesley. Earlier in this century, Jean Piaget spent years watching young children play. This sourcebook, full of exercises and illustrations along with the explanations, practices what it preaches: modern educational theory and practice, centered on Piagetian notions of systematic play.

Mindstorms: Seymour Papert. 1993, Basic Books. Although much of the book is about Logo, the computer language for children that failed to revolutionize education ten years ago when the first edition of this book was published, Seymour Papert's ideas about how kids learn by scientifically playing with the world extend Piaget's notions into a more modern context.

THE MILLENNIUM IS HERE
Whole Earth Catalog

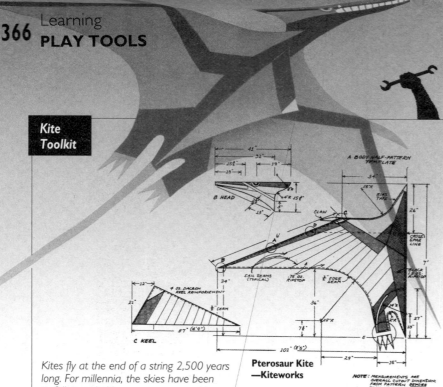

Kite Toolkit

**Pterosaur Kite
—Kiteworks**

NOTE: MEASUREMENTS ARE OVERALL CUTOUT DIMENSIONS FROM PATTERN BEFORE SEALING THE EDGES!

Kites fly at the end of a string 2,500 years long. For millennia, the skies have been joyfully invaded by gossamer assemblages beginning with leaves or woven reeds. Today, nylon and fiberglass soar in the latest of this art form's great flourishes. Kite-flying and -making can provide a lifetime's lessons in craft, beauty, and attentiveness. It has put me in touch with a worldwide community of the similarly enraptured.

The Art of the Japanese Kite inspires through example. Tal Streeter's clear prose profiles Japan's last traditional kitemakers. For a general history, plus plans for many historic and contemporary kites (both Eastern and Western), see Pelham's classic *Penguin Book of Kites*. More detailed instructions in kitebuilding techniques are found in *Kiteworks*; even Buckminster Fuller gets pulled in for his applicable innovations.

Two- or four-lined kites ("stunters") propel much of the current kite renaissance. David Gomberg's *Stunt Kites* is a fine introduction to the sport, though lean on graphics. For abundant color photos of all species of kite, as well as information on clubs and organized flies, subscribe to the oldest and finest mag, *KiteLines*.

For mail-order kiteware, I recommend Into the Wind. The owners and staff test every available kite that seems worthy, and only carry what they deem wonderful. They also sell string, winders, nightlights, a small but well-chosen selection of books, and everything a kitemaker could need for materials.

An active discussion of kites and a terrific collection of FAQs may be found on the Internet's kite newsgroup <alt.rec.kites>. For more traditional networking, join your local or national kite club: breeding grounds for dreamers seeking to improve upon Daedalus' design. —Winslow Colwell

The Art of the Japanese Kite:
Tal Streeter. 1980; 184 pp.
ISBN 0-8348-0157-4. $23.95 (27.45 postpaid); Weatherhill, Inc., 41 Monroe Turnpike, Trumbull,, CT 06611; 800/437-7840.

The Penguin Book of Kites:
David Pelham. Penguin Books, 1976; 224 pp. ISBN 0-14-004117-6. $12.95 ($14.95 postpaid). Penguin USA/Consumer Sales, 120 Woodbine Street, Bergenfield, NJ 07621; 800/253-6476.

Kiteworks (Explorations in Kite Building and Flying): Eden Maxwell. 1991; 288 pp. ISBN 0-8069-6713-7. $16.95 ($18.70 postpaid). Sterling Publishing Co., 387 Park Avenue S., New York, NY 10016 800/367-9692.

Into The Wind: 1408 Pearl Street, Boulder, CO 80302; 800/541-0314

Stunt Kites! (A Complete Flight Manual of Maneuverable Kites. Revised fifth edition): David Gomberg. 1994; 90 pp.
ISBN 1-884496-02-4. $11 at kite stores.

American Kitefliers Association: $20 per year (includes 6 issues of Kiting Magazine) 1559 Rockville Pike, Rockville MD, 20852-1651, 800/AKA-2550.

Kites & Kids

Kitemaking opens kids' minds. That is how a part-time teacher with no formal training in education, like myself, can hold the attention of young children while discussing ancient China, meteorology, Expressionism, and Bernoulli's principle. "History" may be dull, but learning about the Asians of Confucius' era who made the first kite is learning about unmet friends of the past. And knowing how weather works can help you get your newly made kite aloft.

Kites are a terrific learning tool for kids, but be warned: there are few kitemaking projects appropriate for children under nine. The simple sled kite is nearly success-guaranteed. A reprint with instructions for one or a hundred are available through the

folks at *KiteLines* for $1 postpaid. Classroom veteran Margaret Gregor's *Kites for Everyone* includes the sled, along with more complex projects.

For the youngest ones, elder-made paper kites are wonderful surfaces to color. And their eyes will do the same smiling squint-thing as they see it take off and rise wild blue yonder-ward. —WC

KiteLines: Valerie Govig, Editor. $14/year (4 issues). Aeolus Press/KiteLines, PO Box466, Randallstown, MD 21133-0466; 410/922-1212, fax 410/922-4262.

Kites for Everyone: Margaret Gregor. 1984; 104 pp. ISBN 0-9613680-0-4. $13 at kite stores.

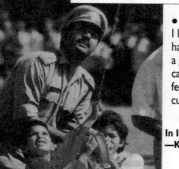

I learned that there's considerably more subtlety to Indian kites than I had been told! First, the kites vary immensely in quality and flyability, and a good Indian fighter kite can be flown well in winds up to 15 mph and can lift a whole line of candlelit paper lanterns into the night sky. The differences between ordinary and high quality *manja* — glass- coated cutting line — are also immense.

In India, everyone is a kiteflier.
—KiteLines

Juggling for the Complete Klutz

Picture this: goofy Catalog staff heathens bumbling wearily around in a blathering haze . . . and they're juggling! These klutzes learned how to juggle all kinds of inanimate (and animate) objects by reading this book. Don't buy it unless you want your life to turn into a bizarre circus . . . because it works.
—Todd Tibbetts

• Edibles
For a beginning juggler, the produce department of any grocery store can take on a wonderful new dimension. My own favorite is the bananas. They're difficult to get the hang of at first, but even a little practice pays off quickly. If you don't try to flip them end for end, you'll find it easier.

Juggling for the Complete Klutz
John Cassidy & B. C. Rimbeaux. Third Edition 1988; 82 pp. ISBN 0-932592-00-7
$9.95 ($13.45 postpaid). Klutz Press, 2121 Staunton Court, Palo Alto, CA 94306; 415/857-0888

Tensegritoy

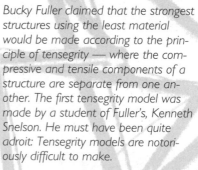

Bucky Fuller claimed that the strongest structures using the least material would be made according to the principle of tensegrity — where the compressive and tensile components of a structure are separate from one another. The first tensegrity model was made by a student of Fuller's, Kenneth Snelson. He must have been quite adroit: Tensegrity models are notoriously difficult to make.

The clever Tensegritoy kit allows even the undextrous to make models of several geometrical forms. The parts are nicely made from painted wood and elastic, and the directions are illustrated in minute detail. The resulting models are aesthetically nifty and instructive. —J. Baldwin

Tensegritoy: $30 ($36.50 postpaid). Buckminster Fuller Institute, 2040 Alameda Padre Serra, Suite 224, Santa Barbara, CA 93103; 805/962-0022, fax 805/962-4440.

Boomerangs

You 'rang? Boomeranging is both cosmic (catching your own toss is not unlike old Ouroboros eating his own tail) and great fun. My first successes (fifteen minutes with good instruction) produced a giddy feeling I couldn't wait to repeat. Finesse and awareness of your microclimate count for more than strength or the size of your boomerang budget.

The learning curve (circle?) is aided by the right 'rang. The tough plastic numbers designed by world-class thrower and kid-class teacher Eric (Turning Point) Darnell are your ticket. The Tri-Fly is a 3-blader that can be thrown right or left handed. The Pro-Fly is a right-hand 'rang with the traditional shape. Both are forgiving of less-than-perfect throws and have instructions molded right in. Range is thirty to forty-five yards.

The Air Dancer is a serious foam 'rang, also ambidextrous,

for throwers without access to wide-open spaces. It cuts a smaller arc (10 yards or so), and being soft it's also friendlier to parked cars and unwary craniums.
—WC

Turning Point: Norwich, VT 05055. Tri-Fly $6, Pro-Fly ($7), and Air Dancer ($10) Shipping: $2 for first boomerang, $1 each additional.

Boomerangers keep up with things in *Many Happy Returns*, the newsletter that comes with membership in the U.S. Boomerang Association. —JB

Many Happy Returns:
$10/year (4 issues, membership included) from U.S. Boomerang Association,
P.O. Box 182,
Delaware, OH
43015.

OSTRICHES HAVE A SECRET WORLD, HERETOFORE UNSUSPECTED by MANKIND.

James Donnelly

Altered States of Consciousness

This acknowledged classic presents the best overview of "altered" states. It begins with a definition of "normal" consciousness as the state in which an individual "spends the major part of his waking hours," and the altered state as "one in which he clearly feels a qualitative shift in his pattern of mental functioning." Since the first (1969) edition, academic explorations of ASC have grown in number and sophistication; however, Tart found all the original articles still timely at republication in 1990. The articles are seminal works on dreams, meditation, hypnosis, and psychedelics, all must-reads for students of this field.
— Jon Lebkowskyl

•

The concept of sensory translation offers an intriguing explanation for the ubiquitous use of light as a metaphor for mystic experience. It may not be just a metaphor. "Illumination" may be derived from an actual sensory experience occurring when in the

Altered States of Consciousness
Charles T. Tart. HarperSanFrancisco, 1990;
691 pp. ISBN 0-06-250857-1
$16.95 ($19.70 postpaid). HarperCollins
Publishers/Direct Mail, PO Box 588,
Dunmore, PA 18512; 800/331-3761

cognitive act of unification, a liberation of energy takes place, or when a resolution of unconscious conflict occurs, permitting the experience of "peace," "presence," and the like. Liberated energy experienced as light may be the core sensory experience of mysticism.

•

The imagery of descent to represent falling asleep is an example of a phenomenon described by Federn (1952). The experience of loss of self or loss of "body-ego" seems to evoke imagery which expresses the descent into nothingness. At the same time, opposite images of hardness and verticality represent the struggle to stay awake, that is, to maintain "body-ego." The appearance of "marble" in the imagery might also perhaps be understood as an example of the appearance of breast imagery during the hypnagogic period, as described by Isakower.

Conversations with Neil's Brain

*"Mind'" may or may not live in "brain." There's certainly a clear link between the two. It's worthwhile to plug into neurobiology, to understand brain function from a purely scientific perspective and apply that understanding to your study of consciousness. Calvin and Ojemann explain the neurobiological perspective through fictional conversations with a candidate for brain surgery. Their earlier book **Inside the Brain** used the same device, but was less focused on the cerebral cortex. — jonl*

•

You don't gain access to established memories very well during sleep, and you usually can't establish new memories either. Actually, it's a bit of a puzzle why you ever form permanent memories of dreams, given how poor the recall usually is. But there's a way around that, at least if you awaken before the five minutes are up. If you recall a dream before it fades, when your circuits for memorizing new things are working once again, then you can memorize the *recall* rather than the original happening.

If you make a habit of reviewing your fading dreams upon awakening, you can memorize quite a collection of nonsense. Keeping a dream diary can thus clutter up you head with a lot of things that didn't really happen — and we have enough trouble as it is, just keeping straight those things that really happened from all those things that we merely imagined or planned.

Conversations with Neil's Brain
(Searching for the
Narrator of Consciousness)
William H. Calvin & George A. Ojemann.
1994; ISBN 0-201-63217-9
$23 ($26 postpaid). Addison-Wesley
Publishing Co./Order Dept., 1 Jacob Way,
Reading, MA 01867; 800/447-2226

DON'T THINK OF A HORSE

Brain tuners (or mind machines) use rhythmic light and sound to alter brainwave activity. Through a process called entrainment, they "tune" the brain to brainwave frequencies associated with the states of consciousness associated with meditative and trance states.

The Daydreamer is a low-tech machine similar to a tall scuba mask with two circular holes over the eyes. When you blow into a hole at mouth level, a rotor spins, alternately blocking each eyehole. If you do this with eyes closed while facing a bright light, the flashing effect can alter your consciousness.

The Esprit is a compact electronic unit with goggles and headphones. The goggles contain lights that flash, and the headphones carry subtle sounds, according to six preprogrammed sequences producing alpha, theta, and beta states.

The Synergizer, a high-end programmable PC-driven mind machine, comprises a card that plugs into a PC and state-of-the-art goggles and headphone. —jonl

The Daydreamer: $16.95 postpaid.
Esprit ESP-1, by Synetic Systems:
$132 postpaid.
Synergizer, by Synetic Systems:
$475 postpaid.
All from FringeWare,
Inc., PO Box 49921,
Austin, TX 78765;
512/477-1366,
fax 512/477-
8465.

Brain/Mind Bulletin

Easily the handiest way to stay current with news and gossip on the soft-psychology frontier. Despite success and a burgeoning of the subject matter, editor Marilyn Ferguson has admirably kept the bulletin's format to a terse, packed four pages. — Stewart Brand

•

A startling new finding: Not only do the brain hemispheres switch dominance every 90 to 120 minutes throughout the day, but the sides of the body switch regularly in their dominance of sympathetic tone.

Researchers sampled nervous-system transmitters by taking blood from both arms every 7.5 minutes for periods of three to six hours. They found that the catecholamines — dopamine, norepinephrine, epinephrine (adrenaline) — were more concentrated on one side or the other every two to three hours.

Brain/Mind (Bulletin of Breakthroughs):
Marilyn Ferguson, Editor. $35/year (17 issues).
Interface Press, PO Box 42211, Los Angeles, CA 90042.

ANOTHER GREAT RESOURCE: YER OWN BRAIN!

IBVA (Psychic Lab, Inc.): $1,295 postpaid. FringeWare, Inc., PO Box 49921, Austin, TX 78765; 512/477-1366, fax 512/477-8465: The Interactive Brain Wave Analyzer system allows realtime 3D graphical display of brain-waves on a Macintosh computer. A very cool way to do biofeedback.

THE MILLENNIUM IS HERE
Whole Earth Catalog

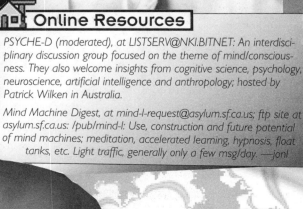

Online Resources

PSYCHE-D (moderated), at LISTSERV@NKI.BITNET: An interdisciplinary discussion group focused on the theme of mind/consciousness. They also welcome insights from cognitive science, psychology, neuroscience, artificial intelligence and anthropology; hosted by Patrick Wilken in Australia.

Mind Machine Digest, at mind-l-request@asylum.sf.ca.us; ftp site at asylum.sf.ca.us: /pub/mind-l: Use, construction and future potential of mind machines; meditation, accelerated learning, hypnosis, float tanks, etc. Light traffic, generally only a few msg/day. —jonl

—IBVA

Mindfulness in Plain English

"You could attain Enlightenment right now, if you are ready." So ends the next-to-last chapter of this valuable and practical manual. The author explains, as the title promises, how to attain mindfulness through practicing insight meditation. As a meditation student I found this book quite helpful, even though my practice is a different style from the one taught here. The author credits his teachings to Theravadan Buddhism, but religion and philosophy keep to the sidelines in this presentation.

Mindfulness is the purpose of meditation, and concentration is the tool. Unimportant to mindfulness is the content of the mind. To whatever states of mind we encounter, meditation applies bare mindfulness, without grasping and without aversion. Therein lies the difficulty. There are inevitable distractions to concentration and many barriers to meditation practice. Mindfulness in Plain English teaches how to overcome these difficulties gently, firmly, and sensibly, modeling how the meditator should treat them.

Through developing meditation practice, the meditator achieves discipline of mind and patience. Exploring with these tools the richness of our human existence leads to wisdom. Failing this, all states of mind lead ultimately nowhere. —George Hasty

Mindfulness in Plain English
Henepola Gunaratana. 1991; 191 pp.
ISBN 0-86171-064-9
$10 ($14 postpaid) from Wisdom Publications, 361 Newbury Street, Boston, MA 02115; 800/272-4050

•

Somewhere in this process, you will come face to face with the sudden and shocking realization that you are completely crazy. Your mind is a shrieking, gibbering madhouse on wheels barreling pell-mell down the hill, utterly out of control and hopeless. No problem. You are not crazier than you were yesterday. It has always been this way, and you just never noticed. You are also no crazier than everybody else around you. The only real difference is that you have confronted the situation: they have not. So they still feel relatively comfortable. That does not mean that they are better off. Ignorance may be bliss, but it does not lead to Liberation. So don't let this realization unsettle you. It is a milestone actually, a sign of real progress. The very fact that you have looked at the problem straight in the eye means that you are on your way up and out of it.

See also pp. 32 to 35: "The metaphysical side of meditation is mysticism."

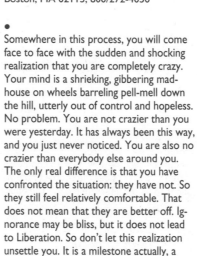

"In the beginner's mind there are many possibilities, but in the expert's there are few." This book and its teachings are deceptively simple, but then simplicity is the essence of Soto Zen, which was Shunryu Suzuki-Roshi's practice. Just sit, just breathe, just be empty. I've carried this book for twenty years, and these simple instructions are still difficult to master.

When we talk about 'states of mind,' we often discuss diverse practices and supporting technologies as though the key to the mastery of those states were some complex thing, but perhaps it's as simple as this instruction: "To take this posture is to have the right state of mind. There is no need to obtain some special state of mind."

By all means try every path, but don't overlook the simplest and most difficult: just sitting quietly, doing nothing, counting breath. **Zen Mind, Beginner's Mind** is a different book every time I read it. Behind the simplicity, it is dense with Zen wisdom that flashes like lightning as you read and reread. —jonL

Zen Mind, Beginner's Mind

Zen Mind, Beginner's Mind
Shunryu Suzuki. 1970; 132 pp.
ISBN 0-8348-0079-9
$7.95 ($11.45 postpaid) from Weatherhill, Inc., 41 Monroe Turnpike, Trumbull, CT 06611; 800/437-7840

•

But it is when you sit in zazen that you will have the most pure, genuine experience of the empty state of mind. Actually, emptiness of mind is not even a state of mind, but the original essence of mind which Buddha and the Sixth Patriarch experienced. "Essence of mind," "original mind," "original face," "Buddha nature," "emptiness"— all these words mean the absolute calmness of your mind.

Flow

Flow is the deeply happy and satisfied state of mind associated with peak performance. Having studied such states for two decades, Mihaly Csikszentmihalyi explores the psychology of flow ("the state in which people are so involved in an activity that nothing else seems to matter") and offers help in achieving, controlling, and maintaining that state. —Lisa Winer

•

Contrary to what we usually believe, moments like these, the best moments in our lives, are not the passive, receptive, relaxing times — although such experiences can also be enjoyable, if we have worked hard to attain them. The best moments usually occur when a person's body or mind is stretched to its limits in a voluntary effort to accomplish something difficult and worthwhile. Optimal experience is thus something that we *make* happen. For a child, it could be placing with trembling fingers the last block on a tower she has built, higher than any she has built so far; for a swimmer, it could be trying to beat his own record; for a violinist, mastering an intricate musical passage. For each person there are thousands of opportunities, challenges to expand ourselves.

Flow
(The Psychology of Optimal Experience)
M. Csikszentmihalyi. HarperPerennial, 1991; 320 pp. ISBN 0-06-092043-2
$13 ($15.75 postpaid) from HarperCollins Publishers/Direct Mail, PO Box 588, Dunmore, PA 18512; 800/331-3761

Yoga Journal

Yoga synchronizes mind and body and provides the conditioning needed for postural flexibility, which can enhance meditation and trance experience. The bimonthly Yoga Journal covers the field of mind/body holism with refreshing clarity. —Jon Lebkowsky

Yoga Journal
Rick Fields, Editor.
$18/year (6 issues).
PO Box 469018, Escondido, CA 92046-9952; 800/359-9642

Inner organs: turn with outer muscles following

Lungs: expand into shoulders and arms

Knee: presses gently against arm

Base of the rib cage: draws inward

Shambhala

Chogyam Trungpa was a Tibetan Buddhist meditation master. However, the vision he presents in these teachings is secular, rather than religious. Trungpa shows the possibility of warriorship and enlightened society in this human existence. He gives an overview of the full path of warriorship, a path that begins with the practice of meditation and a glimpse of basic goodness in our world. Sitting meditation — simply following the breath, labeling whatever thoughts or emotions come up as "thinking," not pushing them away or chasing after them — is the means to synchronizing mind and body.

Shambhala
Chogyam Trungpa. 1984; 201 pp.
ISBN 0-87773-264-7 $13 ($16 postpaid) from Shambhala Publications/Order Dept., PO Box 308, Boston, MA 02117-0308; 617/424-0228

From the viewpoint of this book, states of mind become incidental to the discipline and joy of the warrior's journey. *"You are willing to be awake in whatever situation may present itself to you, and you feel that you can take command of your life altogether, because you are not on the side of either success or failure."* This is a rich book; to one who follows the path of warriorship that it describes, its text is ever-changing and fresh. Much remains obscure until the student's experience has ripened. That should not put off the beginner, who may find here inspiration to step forward. —GH

Where the Spirits Ride the Wind

*Medallion on jug no. 2, gold treasure
of Nagyszentmiklos, Hungary;
10th-11th century A.D.*

Trance, like any subjective state, is hard to study and categorize scientifically, but Felicitas Goodman has succeeded by approaching the subject experientially and opening to her intuition about visionary trance experiences. Her work links successful staging of trance states to particular postures combined with rhythmic stimulation (such as a drum or rattle). She also connects visionary trance experiences and mythic archetypes, implying that the interior trance dimension touches an objective reality that we all share. —Jon Lebkowsky

•

The greatest mystery of all, however, is the agreement in visionary content. Where we do have evidence in local traditions, it is clear that cross-culturally the postures elicit almost identical experiences, as in the case of the posture of the Bear Spirit or the Chiltan Spirits. This flies in the face of one of the most cherished tenets of anthropology, namely, that the individual cultural system shapes the content of the experience. It is supposed to supersede all else, even structuring visual illusions, as Segall et al. have shown in their research on the influence of culture on visual perception. There are those who would argue that the reason for the agreement is that the source of the visions is the body itself: We all have the same nervous system; therefore, everything else being equal, that is, the posture and the religious trance, we of course have the same visions. It seems to me that those holding this view contend, taking a simile from technology, that the source of the radio program is the set. As should be clear by now, I take a contrary position and consider the source of the visions to be the alternate reality. The body is tuned by the posture in the trance in such a manner that we are enabled to experience, to perceive a certain part or aspect of the other dimension.

Where the Spirits Ride the Wind
(Trance Journeys and Other Ecstatic Experiences)
Felicitas D. Goodman. 1990; 258 pp. ISBN 0-253-20566-2
$12.95 ($15.95 postpaid) from Indiana University Press, 601 N. Morton Street, Bloomington, IN 47405; 800/842-6796

Drumming at the Edge of Magic

An inquiry into the origins of drumming and the consciousness-altering nature of percussion. —Jonathan E.

•

A large part of music's power and pleasure, says Blacking, comes from its ability to reconnect the player and the listener with the deeper rhythms they're unconscious of. It accomplishes this by taking us out of the clock-ticking world of ordinary time and into a special world of time that Blacking called virtual time.

But how does a drum alter consciousness? That was the question I'd started with and now I thought I could see an answer shimmering beneath the data. My first thought had been that there was something unique in the sound. Andrew Neher had seemed right in his theory that percussive noise played loudly over time eventually overwhelmed the hearing apparatus and this played a large part in inducing trance. The shamanic ritual, held in a small, enclosed space, seemed designed to enhance these percussive effects. In addition, the loudness of the drums would also activate the adrenals, flooding the body with adrenaline.

Drumming at the Edge of Magic
(A Journey into the Spirit of Percussion)
Mickey Hart & Jay Stevens. HarperSanFrancisco, 1990; 240 pp. ISBN 0-06-250374-X
$19.95 ($22.70 postpaid) from HarperCollins Publishers/Direct Mail, PO Box 588, Dunmore, PA 18512; 800/331-3761

Planet Drum

When Mickey Hart appeared on a network TV show with a monk from the Gyuto Choir, the host asked what the drummer of the Grateful Dead and a Tibetan chanter have in common. "We're both in the transportation business," Hart replied. This book and music provide the opportunity to find out what he meant. —HLR

•

Divine Horsemen

In the terminology of Voudoun, it is said that the loa "mounts" a person, or that the person is "mounted" by the loa. The metaphor is drawn from a horse and his rider and the actions and events which result are the expression of the will of the rider. Since the conscious self of the possessed person is, meanwhile, absent, he cannot and does not remember the events; he is not responsible, either for good or for bad; and he cannot, as a person, himself benefit from that possession. The function and purpose of such divine manifestation is the reassurance and instruction of the community.

The drummer, apparently impervious to the embattled anguish of the person, persists relentlessly; until, suddenly, the violence ceases, the head of the person lifts, and one recognizes the strangely abstracted eyes of a being who seems to see beyond whatever he looks at, as if into or from another world. The loa, which the song had been invoking, has arrived. —Maya Deren

Planet Drum
(A Celebration of Percussion and Rhythm)
Mickey Hart, Fredric Lieberman & D. A. Sonneborn. HarperSanFrancisco, 1991; 224 pp. ISBN 0-06-250397-9
$24.95 ($27.70 postpaid) from HarperCollins Publishers/Direct Mail, PO Box 588, Dunmore, PA 18512; 800/331-3761

*Dholak and tin box.
(India ca. 1980)*

From trance to plants:
see Plant Powers, p. 107.

Hearing Solar Winds

The technique of overtone singing (especially as practiced in Mongolia and Tibet) coaxes the harmonics out of their timbral hiding places in the human voice to produce eerie flute-like tones, or growling bassoons in the subharmonic series. One who hears this phenomenon for the first time can scarcely believe it: a single human voice is singing chords.

David Hykes was the first of a wave of musical explorers who brought this technique to Western music in the 1970s. Hearing Solar Winds, recorded in 1983, remains a classic of contemporary music.

I remember being seized by this music and strapped onto an implacable cosmic roller coaster moving in slow motion, and not without its moments of darkness and horror, until I was finally precipitated into zero G, a vast space of luminous darkness and total serenity. This music aspires to something far beyond overtone singing for its own sake. There is no doubt about the power of this recording to alter consciousness, as testified by its ubiquitous presence at diverse human potential workshops. Many listeners report profound healing experiences from Hearing Solar Winds. Yet unlike most "New Age" music, with which it is usually grouped in record stores, it has a compositional depth and an uncompromisingly radical exploratory quality. —Joseph Rowe

Hearing Solar Winds
(The Harmonic Choir, David Hykes, Director)
Cassette: Ocora 4558607, $12.98 ($16.48 postpaid); CD: Ocora 558607, $18 ($21.50 postpaid) from Harmonia Mundi, 2037 Granville Avenue, Los Angeles, CA 90025-6103; 310/478-1311 ext. 119, fax 310/996-1389

OTHER GREAT RESOURCES

Mongolie: Maison des Cultures du Monde (distributed by Auvidis), 101 Bvd. Raspail, 75006 Paris, France.

The Gyuto Monks: Windham Hill Records.

Sufi Music of Turkey: Kudsi Erguner & Süleyman Erguner. CMP Records, PO Box 1129, 5166 Kreuzau, Germany.

PIHKAL

The book of choice for both amateur and professional psychonauts. Its first half is a human-to-human love story, while the second half is a human-to-chemical romance. The latter — which consists of notes on the effects of the chemicals that are cataloged within — reads like a party-favor wish list for the psychedelic underground: synthesis, dosage, duration, extensions, and commentary for everything from AEM-a-Ethyl-3-4,5-trimethoxy-PEA to 4-T-TRIS 3,5-Diethoxy-4-ethylthio-PEA.

Personal accounts of the states of mind associated with the chemicals in question are clearly, concisely written. The entry for DOI — 2,5-Dimethoxy-4-Iodoamphetamine — begins (with 0.6 mg): "There was a nice spacey light-headedness for a few hours, and time seemed to move quite slowly. Then a generic sadness came over me, as I reminisced about earlier days (recalling pleasures now gone) and wondered if I would be allowed to be here on the Farm when I am old and not important. . . ."

With its encyclopedic listing of 179 states of mind, PIHKAL is a valuable reference tool for exploring specific emotional responses and thought processes.

The human story documents the life and love of the Shulgins, humanizing the research aspect of the book. The authors, who wrote this book to fill the information gap on phenethylamines, plan to release a second volume documenting the other side of the psychedelic coin — tryptamines.
—Joseph Matheny

PIHKAL
(A Chemical Love Story)
Alexander Shulgin & Ann Shulgin. 1991; 978 pp. ISBN 0-9630096-7-2
$18.95 ($21.95 postpaid). Transform Press, PO Box 13675, Berkeley, CA 94701; 501/934-4930

●

Each of us, at some point in his life, will feel himself a stranger in the strange land of his own existence, needing answers to questions which have arisen from deep within his soul and will not go away.

Both the questions and the answers have the same source: oneself.

This source, this part of ourselves, has been called by many names throughout human history, the most recent being "the unconscious." Freudians distrust it and Jungians are enraptured by it. It is the part inside you that keeps watch when your conscious mind has drifted, that gives you the sense of what to do in a crisis, when there is no time available for logical reasoning and decision-making. It is the place wherein are to be found demons and angels and everything in between.

This is one of the reasons I hold the psychedelic drugs to be treasures. They can provide access to the parts of us which have answers. They can, but again, they need not and probably will not, unless this is the purpose for which they are being used.

It is up to you to use these tools well, and in the right way. A psychedelic drug might be compared to television. It can be very revealing, very in-

structive, and — with thoughtful care in the selection of channels — the means by which extraordinary insights can be achieved. But to many people, psychedelic drugs are simply another form of entertainment; nothing profound is looked for, thus — usually — nothing profound is experienced.

The potential of the psychedelic drugs to provide access to the interior universe, is, I believe, their most valuable property.

From Chocolate to Morphine

It's weird living in a culture that has decided to be so confused about drugs. On the one hand, we're a "drug culture," massively enamored of alcohol, caffeine, and various over-the-counter remedies, of whose physical effects we are largely ignorant. On the other hand, we restrict (or prohibit altogether) access to particular drugs, some of which are arguably no more harmful than those that are perfectly legal. All this without taking much time to study the effects of all these drugs, singly or in combination.

From Chocolate to Morphine is a comprehensive guide to psychoactive drugs based on the authors' belief "that education based on truthful information is the only solution to the drug problem." The original 1983 edition was met with the usual denial response: some folks wanted to ban it from school and public libraries. In fact, if you're interested in fixing drug problems — your own, someone else's, perhaps society's — you should have a copy of this book in your home library. And make sure that your public library has a few, as well. — jonl

Brad Hamann

Psychedelic Illuminations

Despite the turn to stimulants and downers in the seventies, and the War on Drugs in the eighties, the psychedelic scene has ambled along, though driven far underground. It was almost buried until rave culture emerged in the nineties, with the same splashes of intense color and trance-inducing sound that characterized sixties psychedelia. The same, that is, but with stronger technology and weaker LSD. A friend who hadn't tripped in years told me that he was amazed by the numbers of hits of acid his associates were taking at once 'til he decided to trip again himself, and found how weak were the individual doses.

One sign of the public resurgence of

A Huichol yarn painting, showing the sacred deer, spirits, and three peyote plants.

●

Finally, remember that wanting to change your consciousness is not a symptom of mental illness or an unhealthy need to escape from reality. It is normal to want to vary your conscious experience. Drugs are just one way of doing it, though, and if you come to rely on them before you are grown up, you may not be able to appreciate a whole range of nondrug experiences that are more subtle but more rewarding over time. There is no question that drugs can get you high, but they are difficult to master and will fail if you take them too often.

Psychedelic Illuminations
$27.50/year (4 issues). PO Box 3186, Fullerton, CA 92634; 714/733-1252

psychedelia is the popularity of magazines like Psychedelic Illuminations. This little zine has everything: political updates, rave coverage, pieces on Terence McKenna and the Shulgins, a column by Robert Anton Wilson, Native American ecstatic religions, etc. By the way, you don't have to be using psychedelics to appreciate the insights here. —Jon Lebkowsky

●

We (the editor/publishers) are dedicated to the pursuit of truth and the support of those who pursue truth. We neither advocate nor discourage the use of illegal drugs as this is an individual decision. Our aim is to provide a forum for ideas and information so that those who choose to alter their own body and brain-states may be as well-informed as possible.

From Chocolate to Morphine
(Everything You Need to Know about Mind-Altering Drugs)
Andrew Weil & Winifred Rosen. 1993; 256 pp. ISBN 0-395-66079-3
$13.45 ($15.95 postpaid). Houghton Mifflin Co./Mail Order Dept., Wayside Road, Burlington, MA 01803; 800/225-3362

ANOTHER GREAT RESOURCE

True Hallucinations: Terence McKenna. 1993, HarperSanFrancisco. The bard of the psychedelic millennium spins a fantastic yarn, raises profound questions about the nature of mind and reality, and reminds us that near-naked shamans in Amazon jungles know far more about the uncharted interior of mindspace than all of the psychedelic-averse orthodoxy of western psychology. —HLR

See.
Plant
Powers
p. 107

Obviously, however all ideas expressed are not necessarily shared and belong first to those who first express them. We also gratefully affirm the fundamental natural law of freedom to self-medicate, and right of individual access to spiritual ritual and rite of passage. Our shared evolutionary imperative demands that individuals take responsibility for their own freedom — internal and external, lest we all slide a little deeper into ignorance, indifference, and tyranny. When the uses and properties of various plants are described, the information should be regarded and respected in the context of historical traditions and present-day experience.

•

Ultimately, we must face the question of how willing we are to accept the reality of other dimensions — not the lip service paid to heaven and hell by the monotheistic religions, but the possibility of immediate personal perception of other realms of experience. Materialistic cultures are focused on the world, hence anything questioning materialism is perceived as a threat to their social reality construction and hence, their stability. Drug induced altered states of consciousness are labeled as illusions in our culture, hence dangerous, hence something to forbid at all costs. (Murderers have received lesser prison sentences than some people arrested with psychedelics in their possession.) This is group invalidation of individual experience, and might have some claim to validity if it weren't for the fact that the credibility of our culturally-endorsed belief-system is now being eroded past the point of acceptance by rational minds.

Creative Dreaming

A compelling, lucid history of dreamwork throughout the centuries and around the world, Creative Dreaming introduces several different approaches to self-analysis, touches on the highest aspects of dreamwork — lucid dreaming and other methods for altering dreams as they happen — and offers practical advice on keeping dream diaries and developing dream control. —HLR

•

The best time to begin developing skill in dream recall is during an unpressured time in the morning when you awaken naturally (it will be from a REM period). If you have trouble recalling your dreams plan a time when you can spontaneously awaken and be unhurried.

When you awaken from a dream, lie still and allow the dream images to flow back into your mind. If no images come, let yourself run through the important people in your life; visualizing them may trigger association to your recent dream.

When dream recall is complete in one body position, move gently into other sleeping positions to see whether you have additional dream recall in these positions. Always move gently into any recording position.

DREAMWORK consists of remembering your dreams and seeking to understand them. There's nothing esoteric or psychologically dangerous about it. It's simply a matter of taking a look at what's right in front of your mind's eye, and using what you see to improve your life. We all know how to turn on televisions, ride elevators and open pop-top cans, but nobody teaches us how to dream. The situation is changing rapidly, however, because the most important "secret" of dreamwork is becoming more and more widely known: anyone who has tried to remember dreams and understand their meaning has discovered that the ability to obtain valuable knowledge is not a gift or talent but a *skill*, like tying your shoelaces, reading a book, or driving a car.

Your basic tools for dreamwork are a pad of paper and a pen with a small flashlight taped to it, or a tape recorder, to record dream impressions, images, plots, and keywords in the middle of the night; a larger sketchbook or notebook to expand, amplify, and interpret those midnight jottings; and some knowledge of what to do with your dreams once you've learned to recall and record them. Fortunately, the secrets of the ages are now out in paperback. — HLR

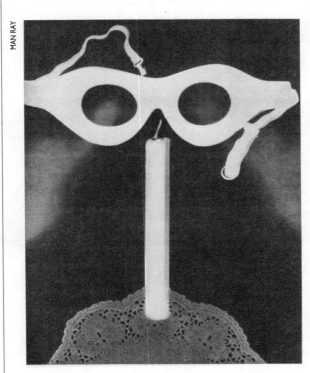

MAN RAY

Record your dreams whenever they come to you, immediately, later in the day, or several days later.

Creative Dreaming
Patricia Garfield. Ballantine Books, 1985; 256 pp. ISBN 0-345-33144-3 $4.95 ($6.95 postpaid). Random House/Order Dept., 400 Hahn Road, Westminster, MD 21157; 800/733-3000

Dreamgropers' Toolkit

You're walking down the street where you live, heading toward home at sunset. Your house is over there on the left at the end of the block, with the sun going down behind it. But something's wrong with this scene — the sun can't be going down there, because it's due East!

Hm. Could this be a dream?

If you're lucky, such a moment can trigger a full awakening of your mind within the dream, while the body remains fast asleep. If the body really continues sleeping, and the mind really wakes up, then it's a lucid dream. Typically, at this moment of realization, everything leaps into vivid full-color 3D hallucinatory reality — a reality of your own creation — or is it?

Stephen LaBerge, the foremost scientific researcher of lucid dreams, founded the Lucidity Institute, where the DreamLight was developed. Had you been using the Dreamlight in the above scenario, you might been pushed toward lucidity by seeing the sun flashing on and off — a typical translation of the flashing lights in the comfortable mask you are wearing in physical reality. These lights are cues that the Dreamlight's computer has detected significant REM, evidenced that you are in the midst of a dream. The package is light, small, extremely well designed, and far more reliable than its competitors.

The Lucidity Institute tends to be biased toward scientific approaches to lucid dreaming, and there is little questioning of the extent of the dreamer's "control" over events in lucid dreams, or of the positive value of lucid dreams in all contexts. A deeper psychological approach and discussion of other viewpoints is available in archived issues of Lucidity Letter (or simply Lucidity), a superb but now defunct publication whose back issues contain original material on lucid dreaming unavailable anywhere else. The Monroe Institute also provides a different perspective, considering "out-of-body" experiences a separate category from lucid dreams. —Joseph Rowe

Lucid Dreaming: Stephen LaBerge. Ballantine Books, 1986; 304 pp. ISBN 0-345-33355-1 $4.95 ($6.95 postpaid) from Random House/Order Dept., 400 Hahn Road, Westminster, MD 21157; 800/733-3000.

Lucidity Institute: Membership $35/year (includes newsletter). 2555 Park Boulevard, Suite 2, Palo Alto, CA 94306, 800/465-8243.

Monroe Institute: PO Box 505, Lovingston, VA 22949; 800/541-2488.

OTHER DREAM DATES

Dreams and Spiritual Growth (A Christian Approach to Dreamwork): Louis M. Savary, Patricia H. Berne & Strephon K. Williams. 1984, Paulist Press. A resource for anyone who is interested in the spiritual aspects of dreamwork.

Symbols of Transformation in Dreams: Jean Clift & Wallace Clift. 1986, Crossroad Publishing Co. A clear, short, non-technical account of Jungian ideas about dream symbols as harbingers of psychological and spiritual transformation.

THE MILLENNIUM IS HERE — Whole Earth Catalog

NEWS FLASH: Everybody dies. While less technically advanced societies are comfortable with the notion that birth and death are both points on the continuum through which all life cycles, our culture — despite its preoccupation with violence — continues to hide death from view. It's hard to be an educated consumer in the face of cultural denial. But what can you do? Preparing for death requires the same degree of foresight as preparing for an earthquake.

Five areas must be considered when confronting life's final stage. First, the legal issues (you knew there'd be a lawyer in there somewhere!): wills, power of attorney, guardianship of minor children, death certificates. Probate is its own specialized field of the law with its own courts. Then come the financial issues: estate planning, life insurance, casualty insurance, funeral insurance, death benefits. Then the medical decisions, involving living wills/ advance directives, choosing a physician, choosing a hospital, organ donation, and the hotly debated option of assisted suicide. The immediate needs of the dying individual must rank high on any list, as well. The home, a hospital or a hospice nursing home: where is the best place to die? Finally, there are the survivors. Grieving isn't easy and when faced with choosing between a memorial or a funeral, cremation or burial, there's precious little time to say goodbye.

The books cited here offer some useful guidelines. —Patrizia DiLucchio

Mourning & Mitzvah

Grief is the heart seceding from the consciousness. Grief is the drop-kick into the void. Grief is the most isolating of human emotional expressions — and yet, the commonality of human pain is the lesson behind all great religions. While conventional mourning rituals may appear anachronistic to many, throughout history they have permitted individuals the space and time to see their losses through to resolution. Mourning & Mitzvah uses a creative interpretation of ancient Jewish practices to help its readers make just this transition. Some readers may find themselves reluctant to entrust their pain to what they believe to be a proscriptive religious ritual. They shouldn't be. Though Judaism is not as value-neutral in this culture as, say, Native American tradition or Buddhist tradition, don't be deterred.

Unriddling the issues of mourning and separation is difficult to do without collective support. The focused exercises and guided meditations described in this book make it a splendid resource for readers of any philosophical persuasion. —PDiL

•
In bereavement groups, there are two signs that tell me that healing is occurring. When participants, who have idealized the person who has died, begin to remember some of his or her less attractive qualities, recalling peccadillos or faults, I know that they are moving beyond idealization and into a phase that will take them beyond mourning. Or, in relationships that have left many negative feelings in their wake, I know that the mourner is moving toward healing when he or she begins to recount some of the good qualities of the person who has died.

Mourning & Mitzvah
Anne Brener, 1993; 248 pp.
ISBN 1-879045-23-0
$19.95 ($22.95 postpaid) from Jewish Lights Publishing, PO Box 237, Woodstock, VT 05091; 800/962-4544

המקום ינחם אתכם
בתוך שאר אבלי ציון בירושלים

Nolo's Simple Will Book
• WillMaker
• Legal Form Kit: Wills

"Kill all the lawyers!" Shakespeare wrote. Well, maybe that's a bit extreme; besides, according to Nolo Press, you don't need a lawyer for a simple will when you have this book. It contains all the forms and explanations you'll need to write a will, choose an executor for your estate, set up simple trusts for your heirs, or name a guardian for your minor children in every state except Louisiana.

Nolo's WillMaker software is available on 3.5" disks for Mac or IBM PC. Now there's no excuse to be without a will. Whether you choose the book, the disks, or the forms alone (Nolo Legal Form Kit: For Wills), give your loved ones the protection that comes from a planned estate. —PDiL

Nolo's Simple Will Book
Denis Clifford. 1989; 256 pp.
ISBN 0-87337-108-9
$17.95 ($21.95 postpaid)

WillMaker 5.0:
DOS 3.0 or higher,
512K RAM; Windows
3.1, 2 MB RAM;
Macintosh System
6.0.4 or higher,
1 MB RAM. $48.95 ($52.95 postpaid).

**Nolo's
Law Form
Kit: Wills**
1992; ISBN 0-
87337-181-X
$14.95 ($18.95
postpaid)

All from
Nolo Press:
950 Parker
St., Berkeley,
CA 94710;
800/992-6656,
510/549-1976.

There's more about Nolo Press on p. 298.

Dealing Creatively with Death • Caring for Your Own Dead

A simple, comprehensive reference source for death information, Dealing Creatively with Death has sold more than 250,000 copies. Its chapters deal with every nuance of dying, from the philosophy and practice of hospice care to the ins and outs of organ donation. Its appendices (which take up a full third of the book) contain directories of state hospice organizations, funeral and memorial societies, and grief support groups, as well as a detailed bibliography, a sample living will, and simple ceremonies with which to commemorate your dead. Highly recommended for all fans of Jessica Mitford's The American Way of Death.

For those few areas of information that Dealing Creatively with Death doesn't cover, read Caring For Your Own Dead, a guide to assuming personal responsibility for death arrangements, with a state-by-state listing of pertinent laws, regulations, and services. This book is especially useful for information about cremation. —PDiL

•
Living Will Declaration
Following is the Living Will Declaration which the Society for the Right to Die recommends when no state form is provided:

To My Family, Doctors, and All Those Concerned with My Care

I, _____, being of sound mind, make this statement as a directive to be followed if I become unable to participate in decisions regarding my medical care.

If I should be in an incurable or irreversible mental or physical condition with no reasonable expectation of recovery, I direct my attending physician to withhold or withdraw treatment that merely prolongs my dying. I further direct the treatment to be limited to measures to keep me comfortable and to relieve my pain.

These directions express my legal right to refuse treatment. Therefore, I expect my family, doctors, and everyone concerned with my care to regard themselves as legally and morally bound to act in accord with my wishes, and in doing so to be free of any legal liability for having followed my directions.

I especially do not want: [*enumerate*]

Other instructions/comments: [*list them*]

Proxy Designation Clause: Should I become unable to communicate my instructions as stated above, I designate the following person to act in my behalf:
[*Give name and address*]

Signed: _____ Date: _____
Witness: _____ Witness: _____

Caring for Your Own Dead
(A Final Act of Love)
Lisa Carlson. Upper Access Publishers, 1987; 343 pp. ISBN 0-942679-01-6
$12.95 ($15.45 postpaid) from UAP Books, P.O. Box 457, Hinesburg, VT 05461; 800/356-9315

Dealing Creatively with Death
(A Manual of Death Education
& Simple Burial)
Ernest Morgan & Jenifer Morgan.
Barclay House Books, 1990; 167 pp.
ISBN 0-935016-79-1
$11 ($13 postpaid) from Zinn Communications, 35-19 215th Place, Bayside, NY 11361; 718/225-5178

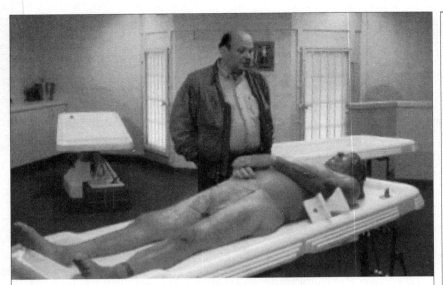

The author (left) and "Max"—San Francisco School of Mortuary Science.

Death

*If dying and the afterlife were respectively a train ride and Disneyland, then Seattle broadcaster Greg Palmer would serve as a near-perfect conductor cum Mickey Mouse. Originally conceived as a PBS television series, **Death** — the book — addresses questions both frivolous and profound.*

*Did you ever consider that MGM's **Wizard of Oz** could pass for an account of a near-death experience? Is it possible that slasher films are good for our psyche? If death ever truly took a holiday (probably in a cryonics chamber) you can bet that author Greg Palmer would be there to write about it. —Ben Trumble*

•

As the product of a relatively normal American childhood, death was certainly a stranger to me for a long time. I knew it existed as I knew Africa existed. I just didn't think I'd ever go there. According to experts who like to ask kids such questions, children are aware of the basic existence of death very early, even as young as age three. In those early years, however,

death seems to have more to do with fear of abandonment than fear of personal involvement. If one morning the family goldfish is doing an extremely slow backstroke on the surface of the tank, does that mean the next morning we'll find Mommy belly up to the ceiling of her bedroom, just because we fed her too much the night before? And if so, who's going to take me to get my new sneakers?

Death
(The Trip of a Lifetime)
Greg Palmer. HarperSanFrancisco,
1993; 294 pp. ISBN 0-06-250802-4
$23 ($25.75 postpaid) from HarperCollins
Publishers/Direct Mail, PO Box 588,
Dunmore, PA 18512; 800/331-3761

Perhaps the world's only 75-horsepower coffin, at Benjamin Sowah's Fantasy Coffins, Accra, Ghana. The wooden Yamaha was commissioned by a fisherman who was the first in his village to own the real thing and didn't want anybody to forget that.

See also: Birth (pp. 186-187), Spirituality (pp. 32-35), and Composting (p. 167).

Closer to the Light

The big question: What happens after death? Melvin Morse offers intriguing insights by applying quantitative methods to the near-death experiences of a sample group of children; the reader can presume they have been spared the cultural and religious programming that colors the perceptions of their adult counterparts. Morse set up a control group of 121 children who, while critically ill, were not near death to see if the classic near-death experience could be attributed to the use of narcotic analgesics, hypoxia, acid-base disturbances, or high serum carbon dioxide levels. His conclusion: the out-of-body perceptions described by individuals whom death has touched are a natural psychological process associated with dying.

Read this book and draw your own conclusions.

Is God quite as popular an extra in the crowd scenes that populate the dying moments of, say, Southeast Asian children? Do adoptees see their biological mothers waiting at the end of that great shining tunnel of light? The sophisticated reader may be left with some unanswered questions. But therein lies death's mystery. —PDiL

•

Mark first mentioned his near-death experience when he was three years old. Then, following a Christmas pageant, he said that God didn't look like the man in the play they had just seen. When his father asked him what he meant, Mark told him what had happened during that frantic night two years earlier:

"I saw nurses and doctors standing over me, trying to wake me up. I flew out of the room and [went to the waiting room where I] saw Grandpa and Grandma crying and holding each other. I think they thought I was going to die."

He then reported seeing a long, dark tunnel and crawling up it . . . At the end of that tunnel, he found a "bright place" and "ran through the fields with God." He was very animated when he described this run with God. He said that "one can double-jump in heaven" . . . Mark remembered this experience vividly until the age of five, when doctors removed the trachea tube they had inserted to remedy a problem known as tracheomalacia, or floppy windpipe. Then the memory of the experience began to fade.

Closer to the Light
(Learning From the Near-Death Experiences of Children)
Melvin Morse. Ivy Books,
1990; 236 pp. ISBN 0-8041-0832-3
$5.99 ($7.99 postpaid) from Random House/Order Dept., 400 Hahn Road, Westminster, MD 21157; 800/733-3000

Death (The Comic)

*The slickest wordspinner in comics, Neil Gaiman (writer of **Sandman**), offers us up a new twist, a revisionist Grim Reaper — a cross between Nico and a young Louise Brooks — a beauty called Death. Death doesn't waste much time worrying about her job, and she doesn't make deals. If you want a hot look at what's fresh in alternative fiction, go with **Death**. She'll be ready when you are. —BT*

Death (The Comic)
Neil Gaiman.
$23.40/year (12 issues). DC Comics,
PO Box 0528, Baldwin, NY 11510

OTHER GREAT RESOURCES

Who Dies? Stephen Levine. A compassionate and powerful primer on dying and living with awareness. One of the books most recommended by readers in the history of Whole Earth. 1989, Anchor Press, Doubleday & Co.

How We Die: Sherwin B. Nuland. A longtime physician looks death in the face, sparing none of the clinical details. 1994, Alfred A. Knopf.

On Death & Dying: Elisabeth Kübler-Ross. Still the classic for understanding dying from the perspective of the dying person. 1969, 1993, Macmillan.

The Tibetan Book of Living and Dying: Sogyal Rinpoche. A practical, liberating guide to awareness in both states. 1992, Harper San Francisco.

THE MILLENNIUM IS HERE
Whole Earth Catalog

Digger in his own version of virtual reality.

Art Kleiner evaluates
capitalist tools.

C

Barbara Blosser tests a new
method of seed dispersal.

The somber and saturnine
Caius van Nouhuys.

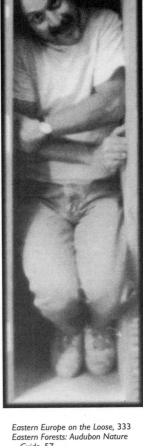

We have to find David Burnor a bigger office.

Todd Tibbetts

Don Ryan makes another fruitless attempt to melt butter in his mouth.

Bridget Sumser

Jim Woodring contemplates his escape.

Jon McIntire: thinking all the time.

Todd Tibbetts

"Good morning. I'm John Sumser, and this is my tongue, Billy."

James Donnelly: artist, poet, biker trash.

Hacsi Horvath, ambassador from the planet Bolinas.

G

Who shot JR?

JD Smith, instilling a healthy skepticism in Young Smith.

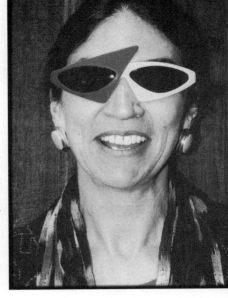

Todd Tibbetts

Karen Van Epen obscures her Husky-blue orbs.

Todd Tibbetts

Howard Rheingold gestures hypnotically.

I

K

J

Standard J. Baldwin features include extra-large hands, head, heart.

Gaetano Kazuo Maida

Mike Stone — the only time he sat down in 1994.

Carlos Winborn, the happy buccaneer
of Gate Five Road.

Mike Ashenfelder practices
auto-brain-surgery.

Kathleen O'Neill demon-
strates the Art Gang Walk.

The Peach & Philcat show (Nancy Pietrafesa and Phil Catalfo).

Lisa Winer, meditating on a punctuation mark.

Patrizia DiLucchio: "Sort of a slatternly Sophia Loren type."

Peter "I laugh at deadlines" Warshall.

S

Richie Unterberger, having a thought.

Todd Tibbetts

Richard Nilsen prevents topsoil loss.

T

Todd Tibbetts

Ruth Kissane: muscle control personified.

Michael Westfort

Todd Tibbetts, a good kid gone bad.

Dr. Tom Ferguson, the self-health man.

Todd Tibbetts

Hardscrabble pixel farmer Winslow Colwell scans the pitiless sky for signs of rain.

M W E C

Editor-in-Chief	**Howard Rheingold**
Managing Editor	**Ruth Kissane** (first phase)
	Michael K. Stone
Senior Editors	**J. Baldwin,**
	James Donnelly
Land Use Editor	**Richard Nilsen**
Art Director	**Kathleen O'Neill**
Designers	**Winslow Colwell,**
	Todd Tibbetts
Copy Editor	**Lisa Winer**
Photographer/Scanner	**Don Ryan**
Researcher/Indexer	**David Burnor**
Librarian	**Caius van Nouhuys**
Editorial Assistant	**Mike Ashenfelder**
Stories	**JD Smith**
"Frank's Real Pa"	**Jim Woodring**
Ways and Means	**Digger,**
	Jon McIntire
Office Support	**Barbara Blosser,**
	Hacsi Horvath,
	J.R. Viera,
	Karen Van Epen,
	Carlos Winborn

POINT FOUNDATION

Founder	**Stewart Brand**
Executive Director	**John Sumser**
Board of Directors	**Chris Desser** (Emeritus)
	Jerry George
	Peggy Lauer
	Gaetano Maida
	John Sumser
	Beau Takahara
Further INstitute Director	**Colleen Sumser**
Livestock	**Tesla, Shadow,**
	Jake, Magritte,
	Chunky, Wired
Literary Agent	**John Brockman**

DOMAIN EDITORS

Howard Rheingold	Whole Systems, Taming Technology, Communications, Learning
Peter Warshall	Biodiversity, Sustainability
Stephanie Mills	Community
J. Baldwin	Household, Taming Technology
Tom Ferguson	Health
Patrizia DiLucchio	Sex
Phil Catalfo, Nancy Pietrafesa	Family
James Donnelly	Political Tools
Art Kleiner	Livelihood
Richie Unterberger	Nomadics

ONE HUNDRED CHARACTERS*

Seemingly long, long ago, in a fundraising frenzy, we promised the donors of $500 or more that we'd print a few of their words in this Catalog.

All of those whose wisdom and/or humor and/or uplift appear here gave not $500 but $1,000. Imagine!

Dear Folks: We absolutely could not have done it without you.

PROHIBITION KILLS! Free drug users, help abusers . . . decriminalize & watch drug lords weep! —T. Green

I encourage us to spend as much time in nature as possible so we will know its value and our connectedness with all that is. —Allan Hogle

Our earth is precious. Compassion for all living things is the key to the richest treasure. —Norman and Denise Alm

* More or less.

Watch out! Searching for the tooth . . . may lead to a root awakening. —Bernie Bildman, D.D.S.

In every moment the only choice we make is love or fear. Be still and observe your choice. —David and Kay Hines

Let's develop the mind-expanding (even reality-altering) tools, to help the mind evolve. —Bob Wallace

Thanks, WEC, for 20+ years of great ideas, information and insights. —Joe Colombe, Cary, NC

PCT: Millennial scientific psychology! CSG, 73 Ridge Pl. CR510, Durango, CO 81301 <g-czolp@uiuc.edu>

I'm 87 years old and I guess I'm still listed as a maniacal contributor. The best of all possible futures to you. —Kit Tremaine

Useful tools and books, easily available by mail — thanks for the good guidance. —Norman Pease

USA NE FOREST DIES NOW . bugs +adapt man toxin/birds . USE NO POISON . Unjudge good/bad beings . Aid your loves/ignore the rest. —Best, Alex Funk

It doesn't matter what happens, it's how you handle it. —Jim A. Sanders

It's less than 200 million seconds to the millennium, so the *MWEC* is coming out just in time for me. —Eric Haines

The gift must always move. —in memory of Geoffrey Calvert

What's the point in allowing Anger to dictate Action when Anger itself alone can accomplish nothing? —Bob Dunn

"Anxiety is the enemy of intelligence." Demonstrate intelligence: tend your own anxiety. —Mark Brady

How different do you think 12:01am on 1/1/2000 will really be from 11:59pm on 12/31/1999? —Michael Nathan, Winchester, MA

Remember, this isn't a rehearsal. —Iwan Williams

Special thanks to Mitch Kapor, Mountain Girl, and two extraordinary anonymae, who helped to keep the wolves from the door while the Catalysts rode to the rescue.

FINANCIAL STATEMENT

Editorial	$ 247,562.00
Design	72,435.00
Proofreading	39,879.00
Photography	6,754.00
Library	43,278.00
Support	61,984.00
Phones	4,765.00
Postage	17,856.00
Supplies	27,436.00
Contributors	67,500.00
Overhead (rent, utes)	87,645.00
Equipment	152,750.00
Total	**$ 829,844.00**
Publisher's Advance	$ 425,000.00
Agent's Commission	(63,750.00)
Catalog Costs	($ 829,844.00)
Net Investment	**($ 468,594.00)**

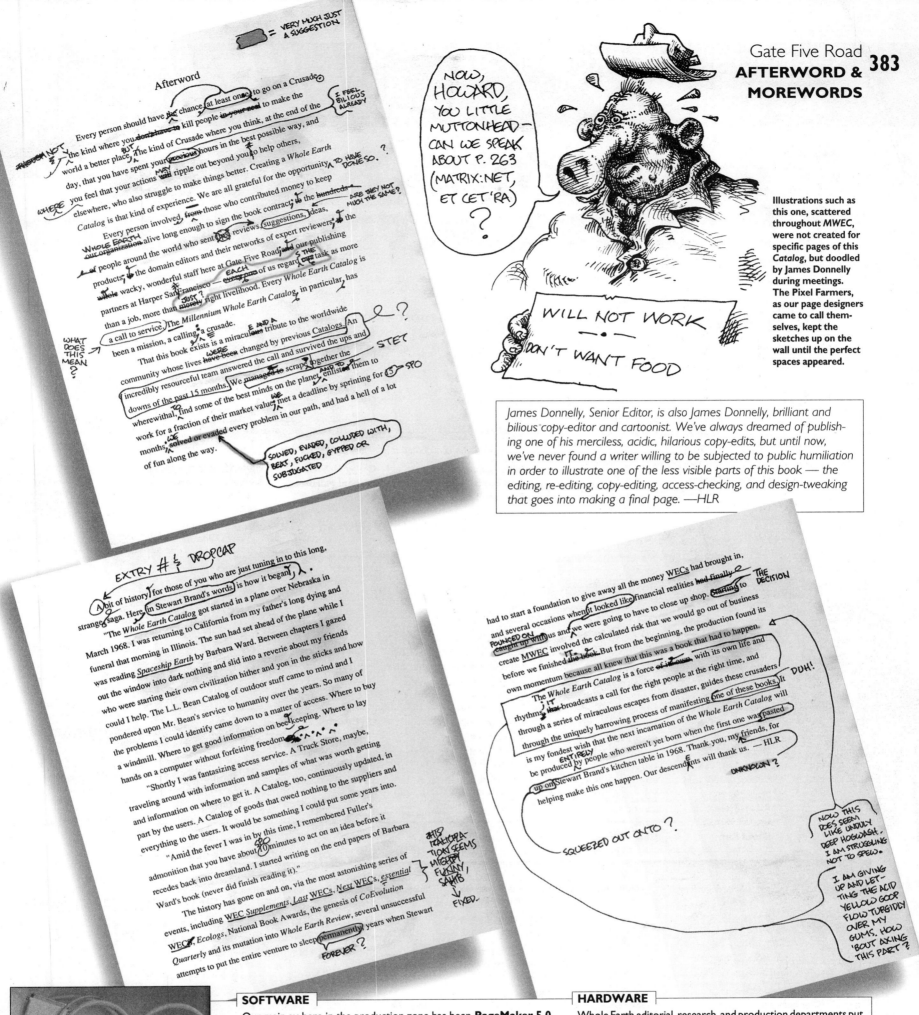

Illustrations such as this one, scattered throughout *MWEC*, were not created for specific pages of this *Catalog*, but doodled by James Donnelly during meetings. The Pixel Farmers, as our page designers came to call themselves, kept the sketches up on the wall until the perfect spaces appeared.

James Donnelly, Senior Editor, is also James Donnelly, brilliant and bilious copy-editor and cartoonist. We've always dreamed of publishing one of his merciless, acidic, hilarious copy-edits, but until now, we've never found a writer willing to be subjected to public humiliation in order to illustrate one of the less visible parts of this book — the editing, re-editing, copy-editing, access-checking, and design-tweaking that goes into making a final page. —HLR

How We Made This Book

MWEC is the first *Whole Earth Catalog* to be produced entirely on that overworked metaphor, the digital desktop (locally known as the Pixel Farm). Everything within these covers was typed or scanned into our Macintosh computers and wrangled into the form before you. The process has involved lots of blood, sweat, and bytes. As well as the following tools.

SOFTWARE

Our main ax here in the production zone has been **PageMaker 5.0**, page layout software by Aldus. Big thanks to them for their excellent product and support (especially Donna Sandstrom!). Photographs and illustrations were scanned using **Ofoto 2.0**, then corrected/cropped/manipulated in **PhotoShop 2.5.1**. We created line art and backgrounds in **Illustrator 5.0** and **TypeStyler 1.5**. The marginal morpho-movie was perpetrated with, appropriately enough, **Morph 2.0**.

Upstream from the art department, we processed words as if they were salmon in **Microsoft WORD 5.0**. Researchers David and Caius used **Filemaker Pro** to track the thousands of addresses, phone numbers, and internet addresses that make this catalog so useful. Howard did the initial outlining in **MORE 3.0**. We all used **Z-Term 0.9**, **Eudora 2.0**, and **Mosaic** to retrieve reviews and data online.

Helpful utilities: **Retrospect Remote** for archival backup, **Apple Fileshare 4.0** and **Timbuktu Remote** for network management, and **Now Boomerang** and **Now Menus** to optimize **Apple System 7.1**.

HARDWARE

Whole Earth editorial, research, and production departments put high mileage on **Apple Macintosh Quadra 610s, 650s,** and **800s, Performa 520s, Power-books, Mac IIs,** and a **Mac SE**. We used **Apple ADB mice, Kensington trackballs,** and screens by **Radius, SuperMac,** and **Apple**. Proof printing was done on two **Apple Laserwriter II NTXs** and an 11x17" **QMS 860** laserprinter. To store and archive the entire 1.45 gigabyte project, we used hard drives from **Seagate** and **Apple**, a **PLI** 88mg Syquest drive, and a DAT drive by **Micronet Technology**. For scanning, we put **AppleScanners** and an **HP ScanJet** through an endurance contest. We took slides to **MarinStat** (Mill Valley, CA) for scanning. Modems by **Global Village, U.S. Robotics,** and **Meridian** got us connected. The Whole Earth computers are on an EtherNet local-area network installed by LanMinds of Berkeley, using a **Shiva FastPath** and a **Farralon Star Controller**. And we couldn't of done it without the amazing flying **Woosh**. Wheee!!!

—Winslow Colwell

WHAT'S YOUR BUDGET FOR ENLIGHTENMENT?

NOTHING: WE PAY YOU

It's no secret: you are our most valuable tool.

And we'll pay to borrow you for a while. The reviews in this *Catalog* need constant updating. We know you are an expert at something. While we're trying to find the best new tool, it's already in your hand. And you'll hear about what's better long before we do. We'll pay for every published review. Sending what you know is how we become more excellent and useful.

Here are our guidelines for new ideas:

- The perfect recommendation is a polished gem of 75 to 100 words. It is packed with meaning. It celebrates its subject.

- Keep it simple.

- If the subject is a book, choose two or three excerpts that sparkle with the essence of the work. Excerpts total 200-300 words. Fewer? Fine. Pictures? Excellent.

- Type the review and excerpts on a 3.5" Macintosh disk, one review per disk, send the book, disk and a printout to Ruth Kissane, Managing Editor, *Whole Earth Review*, 27 Gate Five Road, Sausalito, CA 94965. Or email to ruth@well.com.

Don't Hold Out On Us!

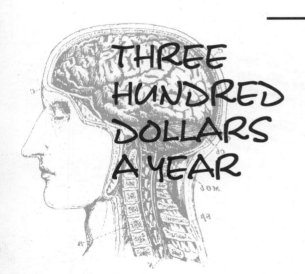

THREE HUNDRED DOLLARS A YEAR

The Dalai Lama guest-edited *Vogue*.

**It was a very good idea.
We decided to make it into a magazine.**

So we contacted the most interesting people in the world, and made each of them this offer:

*We always hear about you, but never from you.
You don't write books, because you have real work to do.
We are very good at our work; producing magazines.
So keep doing your work, and let us work with you.
You'll be our editor for three months.
At the end of that time, we'll turn your words into a readable
and beautiful publication.
And the next time someone interrupts your work,
just hand them the magazine.*

POINT
THE QUARTERLY

It is called *POINT — The Quarterly*. It is a personal letter from the brightest minds in the world. We believe great things will happen if these people write to each other, and to you.
Send in the bind-in card to subscribe, or to receive a list of the 1995 Editors of *POINT - The Quarterly*.

6¢ A DAY

Don't buy a new paradigm 'til you've taken it out for a test drive.

Whole Earth Review lets you do that all year long. We are the ongoing voice of the *Catalog*. Each issue offers a toolkit of new ideas and new ways of looking at things.

Whole Earth Review consistently makes the headlines — two years down the road. Electronic mail, alternative medicine, even personal computers made their first appearances in our pages. May we offer you next year's hot topics?

Think of us as a guidebook to the new world order, the information superhighway, and your plumbing.

You can charge it at 6 cents a day, or the money-saving $20/year plan.

WHOLE EARTH
REVIEW

ALWAYS FREE

Now we must grow serious, because we're talking about our parents.

Point Foundation is the umbrella organization responsible for all of the *Catalogs*, *Quarterlies*, and *Reviews*, since '68. If we are the vision, they were the visionaries. Point's job is to accelerate the expansion of human effectiveness.

Point works much like a mother eagle. She founded and nurtured the WELL (Whole Earth 'Lectronic Link) in 1984. When it was world-famous, self-sufficient, and too big for the nest in 1993, she chased it out on its own.

Which leaves time and money for new frontiers. Like Whole Earth Radio, coming soon to an NPR station in your neighborhood. Like Kidzlab, where we give power tools to children. Power tools like reviewing, writing, advertising, and creating video games as well as playing them.

We'd love to tell you more about Point Foundation. Please send us a self-addressed envelope for more information.